ALSO BY EDMUND MORRIS

—

The Rise of Theodore Roosevelt

Dutch: A Memoir of Ronald Reagan

Theodore Rex

Beethoven: The Universal Composer

Colonel Roosevelt

COLONEL ROOSEVELT

Edmund Morris

RANDOM HOUSE

NEW YORK

Copyright © 2010 by Edmund Morris

Published in the United States by Random House,
an imprint of The Random House Publishing Group,
a division of Random House, Inc., New York.

RANDOM HOUSE and colophon are registered
trademarks of Random House, Inc.

LIBRARY OF CONGRESS CATALOGING-IN-PUBLICATION DATA
Morris, Edmund.
Colonel Roosevelt / Edmund Morris.
p. cm.
Continues: Theodore Rex.
Includes bibliographical references and index.
ISBN 978-0-375-50487-7
eBook ISBN 978-0-679-60415-0
1. Roosevelt, Theodore, 1858–1919.   2. Presidents—United States—
Biography.   3. United States—Politics and government—1909–1913.
4. United States—Politics and government—1913–1921.
I. Morris, Edmund. Theodore Rex.   II. Title.
E757.M8825 2010   973.91'1092—dc22   2010005890
[B]

Printed in the United States of America on acid-free paper

www.atrandom.com

246897531

FIRST EDITION

Frontispiece photograph: Theodore Roosevelt by George Moffett, 1914

Book design by Barbara M. Bachman

To
Robert Loomis

IT HAS BEEN OBSERVED IN ALL AGES, that the advantages of nature or of fortune have contributed very little to the promotion of happiness; and that those whom the splendour of their rank, or the extent of their capacity, have placed upon the summits of human life, have not often given any just occasion to envy in those who look to them from a lower station; whether it be that apparent superiority incites great designs, and great designs are naturally liable to fatal miscarriages; or that the general lot of mankind is misery, and the misfortunes of those, whose eminence drew upon them an universal attention, have been more carefully recorded, because they were more generally observed, and have in reality been only more conspicuous than those of others, not more frequent, or more severe.

—*Samuel Johnson*, THE LIVES OF THE POETS (1781)

CONTENTS

AUTHOR'S NOTE

For compatibility with quotations, and stylistic empathy with the period 1909–1919, most place-names and usages remain unmodernized in this book. Hence, *British East Africa* for what is now Kenya, *Christiania* for Oslo, *Near East* for the Middle East, *Mesopotamia* for Iraq. *Turkey* is synonymous with the Ottoman Empire, and *England* with the United Kingdom.

Racial, personal, and sexual attitudes of the time have not been moderated. Hence, in the African prologue, such words as *savage, boy,* and *native* (the last regarded as respectful now, but tending toward disparagement then). And in the chapters proper, *crippled*, *Miss* or *Mrs.* Married or unmarried, women were hardly ever referred to by surname only. The word *race,* when quoted, usually connotes a national rather than ethnic identity. Although some "hyphenated" minorities achieved recognition during World War I, the phrase *African-American* did not challenge *Negro* as a universal term. The world was divided into the *Occident* and the *Orient,* and each hemisphere had its *Indians.* God was masculine; countries, ships, and cyclonic disturbances feminine. *United States* and *politics* were still sometimes employed as plural nouns.

A few archaic capitalizations, such as *Government* and *Nation,* have been dropped. Other spellings that have changed only slightly since 1919 are updated without comment: *Czar* becomes Tsar, *Servia,* Serbia, and *Moslem,* Muslim. Punctuation marks are altered for clarity only in transcripts of oral remarks.

Colonel Roosevelt

The Roosevelt Africa Expedition, 1909–1910

SITTING ABOVE THE COWCATCHER, on an observation bench rigged for him by British East Africa Railway officials, he feels the thrust of the locomotive pushing him upland from Mombasa, over the edge of the parched Taru plateau. He has the delightful illusion of being transported into the Pleistocene Age.

His own continent recedes to time out of mind. Is it only seven weeks since he was President of the United States? His pocket diary indicates the date is 22 April 1909—not that the calendar matters much in this land of perpetual summer, with equal days and nights. Nor will many of its natives be able to read, let alone recognize the name THEODORE ROOSEVELT, prominently stenciled on a gun case riding behind him in the freight car. They are more likely to be impressed by what the case contains: a "Royal" grade .500/.450 double-barrel Holland & Holland Nitro Express, the most magnificent rifle ever made. (It contrasts with a portable library of about six dozen pocket-size books, ranging from the Apocrypha to the *Pensées* of Pascal, all bound in pigskin and shelved in a custom-made aluminum valise.)

He gazes through eager pince-nez at the prehistoric landscape opening ahead. Waves of bleached grass billow in all directions. Baobab trees, pale gray and oddly elephantine, writhe amid anthills the color of dried blood. Black men and women, naked as the stick figures in cave paintings, stare expressionlessly as he bears down upon them. He will have to get used to that opaque scrutiny wherever he treks in Africa. It is a look that neither absorbs nor reflects, the stone face of savagery.

Less disconcerting, but just as foreign, are the birds that flap and flash around the locomotive's progress: tiny, iridescent sunbirds, green bee-eaters, yellow weavers and rollers, a black-and-white hornbill rising so late from the track he could catch it in his hands. Much as he loves all feathered things, the zoologist in him is distracted by horizon-filling herds of wildebeest, kongoni, waterbuck, impala, and other antelope. Errant zebras have to be tooted off the rails. Long-tailed monkeys curlicue from tree to tree. A dozen giraffes canter alongside in convoy, their tinkertoy awkwardness transformed into undulant motion.

Polish his lenses as he may, he cannot see the Tsavo reserve, "this great fragment of the long-buried past of our race," through twentieth-century eyes. The word *race,* with its possessive pronoun, comes easily to him, connoting not color but culture. Even when culture is at its most primitive, as here, something in him thrills at the prospect of soon being where there is no culture at all.

⌒

EITHER THESE FLORA and fauna are reluctantly giving way to him, as an armed intruder from the future, or he is, in a sense, regressing into them, finding again the Dark Continent he embraced as a child, in a copy of David Livingstone's *Missionary Travels and Researches in South Africa*. Before he could read that book, let alone manage its weight, he had dragged it around his father's Manhattan townhouse, begging adults to "tell" him the pictures: elephants spiked with assegais; surging, snap-jawed hippos; a lion mauling a white man.

From then on, the rule of tooth and claw in nature seemed as supreme as his own success at becoming "one of the governing class."

At puberty he had set out to prove that it was possible for the frailest of small boys, nearly dead at three from asthma and nervous diarrhea, to punish bone and muscle till both grew strong. If an overstrained heart fluttered in protest, it must be ignored.

"Doctor," he had said on leaving college, "I'm going to do all the things you tell me not to do. If I've got to live the sort of life you have described, I don't care how short it is." Privately, he allowed for sixty years.

At first, paradoxically, he had had to struggle free of privilege. His eminence, at twenty-two, as the head of one of New York City's "Four Hundred" best families disqualified him for politics, in the opinion of the rough professionals who dominated the state Republican party. Hustling for votes was not the business of a young gentleman with a *magna cum laude* Harvard degree.

So he had fought—if not with tooth and claw, then with whatever weapons, blunt or subtle, cleared his path—north to Albany as assemblyman from the "Silk Stocking" district, west to Dakota Territory as ranchman and deputy sheriff, south to Washington as civil service commissioner, back to New York City as police commissioner, south again to Washington as assistant secretary of the navy. In the process he won wide admiration for political skills so great as to render him unstoppable in his quest for power. If he was not alone in plotting the Spanish-American War, he did more than anyone else in the McKinley administration to bring it about. Then, as colonel of his own volunteer regiment, "Roosevelt's Rough Riders," and *generalissimo* of its faithful press corps, he transformed himself into a military hero. Fresh out of uniform at forty, he became governor of New York, and at forty-two, vice president under the reelected William McKinley. In September 1901, an assassin's bullet made him President of the United States.

Not surprisingly, given his physical and rhetorical combativeness, many Americans greeted his accession to the presidency in 1901 with dread. Those of nonconfrontational temper shuddered at his "despotic" reorganization of the army, and demands for a navy big enough to dominate the Western Hemisphere. Their fears seemed realized when he used warships to safeguard the Panamanian Revolution of 1903, securing for the United States the right to build an isthmian canal—and, not incidentally, the ability to move its battle fleet quickly from ocean to ocean. At the same time, they had been amazed at his promptness in granting independence to Cuba in 1902, his willingness to accept less than total victory in exchange for a cease-fire in the Philippines insurrection, and his discreet mediation of the Russo-Japanese peace settlement in 1905—not to mention intervention in the Morocco crisis of 1906, which for a while seemed likely to plunge Europe into war.

His Nobel Peace Prize, the first won by an American, was in recognition of these last two achievements. Had the prize committee been aware of how successfully—and secretly—he had worked to contain the *Weltpolitik* of Kaiser Wilhelm II, the most dangerous autocrat on the international scene, it might have made its award sooner.

Nevertheless, he has never been quite able to resolve whether action is not preferable to negotiation, and might the superior of right. Even the most scholarly of his books, *The Naval War of 1812* and the four-volume *Winning of the West,* are muscular in their bellicose expansionism. Read in sequence, his biographies of Thomas Hart Benton, Gouverneur Morris, and Oliver Cromwell amount to a serial portrait of himself as a prophet of Manifest Destiny, a cultured revolutionary, an autocrat reconciling inimical forces. For bloodlust—strangely combined with tenderness toward the creatures he shoots—few memoirs match his Western trilogy, *Hunting Trips of a Ranchman, Ranch Life and the Hunting Trail,* and *The Wilderness Hunter.*

Sexual lust is a subject he deems unfit for print. He is as delicate about the most intimate of acts as a Dutch Reformed dominie. That does not stop him from condemning birth control as "race suicide"—using the word *race,* now, in the loose sense of *nationality.* An advanced society must reproduce more and more, to swell its economic power and keep its "fighting edge." He rejoices in having sired six children and betrays an obvious, if unconscious, desire to castrate men "who think that life ought to consist of a perpetual shrinking from effort, danger and pain." Such are the intellectual elitists "whose cult is nonvirility," and other "mollycoddles" unwilling to play a masterful role in making the world. *Masterful* remains one of his favorite adjectives. This British railroad, for example: this "embodiment of the eager, masterful, materialistic civilization of today," pushing through the Pleistocene!

⤜⤏

THE ICE CAP OF KILIMANJARO floats like a bubble, the blue of its lower slopes dissolving into the blue of heat haze. Somewhere in that southern swim, parallel with the line of the railway, runs the uneasy border between British and German East Africa. He has no plans to cross it. Having spent much of his presidency perfecting Anglo-American relations, and much of his life visiting and corresponding with well-placed English friends, he is almost an honorary British citizen. "I am the only American in public life whom the Europeans really understand," he says. "I am a gentleman and follow the code of a gentleman."

Right now he is the guest of His Majesty's Colonial Office, as an honored collector of specimens for the National Museum in Washington, D.C. King Edward VII has sent him an official telegram of welcome to the Protectorate. Fifty-six eminent English peers, parliamentarians, naturalists, and men of letters are the donors of his Holland & Holland rifle. Given a high state of alarm in Parliament over Germany's current arms buildup (the Reichstag has announced the construction of three new dreadnought battleships), it would be undiplomatic of him to quit one empire for another, even if a record rhinoceros beckons.

Packed among his safari gear is the typescript of a speech he has been asked to make at Berlin University next spring. In it, he praises the Wilhelmine Reich for its "lusty youth"—a compliment he feels unable to bestow on France or Britain, in similar addresses written for delivery at the Sorbonne and Oxford. He has taken pains to make all three speeches sound as academic as possible, not wanting to exacerbate the rivalries of Europe's main powers. Like it or not, he will still be listened to as an American foreign policy spokesman.

So much for his fantasy of fading from popular memory in Darkest Africa. His safari has generated worldwide interest. British East African authorities have extended him special privileges: this train, for instance, comes courtesy of the acting governor. For as long as he roams the Protectorate, he must pay reciprocal respects to every district commissioner who flies a Union Jack over a hut of mud and wattle.

The East African phase of the expedition will end sometime in early December. If personal funds permit, he will then lead a smaller safari through Uganda to the headwaters of the Nile. In the new year, he will cruise down the great river to Egypt, stopping at leisure to hunt northern big game, not reconnecting with civilization until his wife meets him at Khartoum. That should be about eleven months from now. He wants to show her Aswān and Luxor and Karnak, where as a boy he first felt himself regressing in time. (She has somehow always figured in his recall: at twelve, the mere sight of a photo-

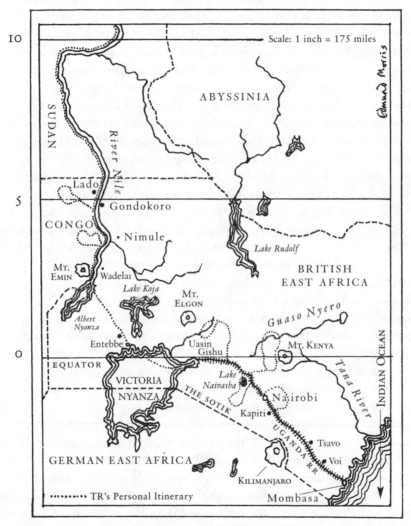

Roosevelt's safari route through British East Africa, 1909–1910.

graph of little Edith Kermit Carow was enough to stir up in him "homesickness and longings for the past which will come again never, alack never.") From Alexandria, they plan to sail to Italy and revisit the scenes of their honeymoon. After that, his northern speech engagements beckon. He does not expect to return to the United States until the early summer of 1910.

❧

"JAMBO BWANA KING YA AMERIK!"

The shout comes from more than three hundred porters, gunbearers, horse boys, tent men, and *askari* guards. They stand in two lines outside the little station of Kapiti Plains, five and a half thousand feet above sea level. Pitched behind them are sixty-four tents, and the half-distributed paraphernalia of the largest safari yet mounted in equatorial Africa. Were it not sponsored by the Smithsonian Museum and financed in large part by Andrew Carnegie, it could almost be a British military foray, with its crates of guns, ammunition, and rocket flares, its show of blue blouses and puttees, its sun helmets shading a few authoritative white faces. But four tons of salt, scalpel kits, powdered borax, and enough cotton batting to unspool back to Mombasa betray the safari's field purpose. And instead of the Union Jack, a large Stars and Stripes floats over the field-green headquarters of the "King of America."

His original plan, conceived while fending off Republican attempts to nominate him for a third term in 1908, was for a private hunting trip in the environs of Mount Kenya. "If I am where they can't get at me, and where I cannot hear what is going on, I cannot be supposed to wish to interfere with the methods of my successor." But as his preparatory reading extended from J. H. Patterson's *The Man-Eaters of Tsavo* to Lord Cromer's *Modern Egypt,* and anti-hunting advocates protested his bloody intentions, he let scientific and political considerations reshape a more public-minded itinerary. The Smithsonian Museum is avid for male and female specimens of all the big-game species he can shoot, plus a complete series of smaller East African mammals. He is also expected to collect flora. The Colonial Office wants him to advertise its new railway, and attract settlers along the line to Victoria Nyanza. The British foreign secretary hopes he will cast a sympathetic American eye on Anglo-Egyptian problems in Khartoum and Cairo.

He has, besides, his own image to worry about. Having made almost a religion of conservation in the White House, and laid the groundwork for a world conference on the subject, he can ill afford to be seen again, as he was in youth, as an indiscriminate killer of big game. In fact, he has always hunted for constructive reasons: as a boy, to fill the glass cases of his "Roosevelt Museum of Natural History," and teach himself the minutest details of anatomy and coloration; in youth, to fight his way out of invalidism, choosing always to make the chase as difficult as possible; and in early middle age, to promulgate, as founder-president of the Boone & Crockett Club, the paradox that hunters are practical conservationists, needing to preserve what they pursue— not only birds and animals and fish, but the wilderness too.

Hence this highly professional expedition organizing itself at Kapiti. It does so under the orders of his official guide and manager, R. J. Cuninghame, a bearded, bowlegged Scot and slayer of many elephants. Burned nearly black by wanderings extending from South Africa to the Arctic Circle, Cuninghame affects a Viking look that does not quite conceal the cultured poise of a Cambridge man. Leslie Tarlton, representing a Nairobi safari agency, is assistant manager, a tense little Australian and virtuoso sharpshooter. Three American naturalists represent the scientific side of the expedition. Edgar A. Mearns, a retired army surgeon, began his zoological career by collecting "a most interesting series of skulls" on active duty in the Philippines. He is also a botanist. Edmund Heller is a field taxidermist from Stanford University, and J. Alden Loring a mammalogist from New York. Seventh and last in the ranks of command is the official photographer, Kermit Roosevelt, a willowy nineteen-year-old on leave from Harvard. Kermit is *Bwana Mdogo* ("Little Master") to the safari porters.

As for *Bwana Mkubwa Sana* ("Very Great Master"), he congratulates himself on putting together a team of the kind of sinewy, well-bred, not overly scrupulous men he has always admired. His son may not qualify. Kermit is handy with a Kodak, and also with a mandolin; he is a reader and lover of languages, sure to profit from exposure to Africa's tapestry of cultures. But the boy needs, or seems to need, toughening, having a broody, mother-fixated quality that sets him apart from the rest of the family.

How Edith Roosevelt feels about consigning them both to a year in the wilderness is another matter. She accepts that her husband craves danger, perhaps in compensation for his own inclination to bury himself in books. He has proved to be practically indestructible. So has Ted, their grown son. Archie, halfway through Groton, is if possible even flintier. Quentin, the youngest and brightest, is currently a fiend hidden in the cloud of late puberty, yet promises to emerge from it a natural leader and risk taker.

Kermit is made of more fragile material. He, his brothers, and his sisters, Alice and Ethel, worship their father as a sort of sun-god emanating power and love. Edith trusts that in Africa, the aura will be protective.

❧

BY NOW SHE SHOULD have answered or destroyed most of the fifteen thousand farewell letters that had poured into Sagamore Hill before he left. He has retained just one, hand-delivered the day he sailed, along with a gold expanding ruler—just the thing a man needs on safari. The ruler is engraved THEODORE ROOSEVELT FROM WILLIAM HOWARD TAFT: *Goodbye—Good luck— and a safe return,* and the letter, on heavy White House stationery, reads:

> My dear Theodore: If I followed my impulse, I should still say "My dear Mr. President." I cannot overcome the habit. When I am addressed as "Mr. President," I turn to see whether you are not at my elbow. . . .

I write to you to say "farewell," and to wish you as great pleasure and as much usefulness as possible in the trip you are about to undertake. I have had my qualms about the result, but in thinking it over they disappear. You will undertake no foolhardy enterprise, I know. . . .

I want you to know that I do nothing in the Executive Office with-

"KERMIT IS MADE OF MORE FRAGILE MATERIAL."

Kermit Roosevelt in 1909.

out considering what you would do under the same circumstances and without having in a sense a mental talk with you over the pros and cons of the situation. I have not the facility for educating the public as you had through talks with correspondents, and so I fear that a large part of the public will feel as if I had fallen away from your ideals; but you know me better and will understand that I am still working away on the same old plan.

Taft cannot find it easy to succeed the most confident executive in modern memory. "Mr. President," in contrast, is happy to sacrifice supreme power—and along with it, a third term virtually guaranteed by the Republican Party and the American electorate. He waves aside token respect. "I am no hanger-on to the shreds of departing greatness."

That said, there is one title he cherishes, and asks everybody to use from now on: "Colonel Roosevelt." He feels that it is both valid, reflecting his rank in the Reserve Army of the United States, and merited through bravery in battle. He was, after all, briefly and gloriously commander of a regiment of volunteer cavalrymen in '98. If war ever comes again and finds him fit to serve, he intends to reactivate his brevet at once.

He is already "Roosevelt, (Col.) Theodore" in *The New York Times Index*. Reporters do not intend to drop him as a subject, even as he retreats into the wilds of Africa. For more than a quarter of a century they have pursued him, drawn by his "Teddy-bear" caricaturability, perpetual motion, heroic glamour, machine-gun quotes, and ricochet denials. Most attractive of all is his disaster potential—the likelihood that one day he will spend the last cent of his legendary luck, and be destroyed by either violence from outside, or hubris within.

This potential seems especially fraught now that he has elected to test his fifty-year-old body, and faulty vision, in some of the world's riskiest hunting grounds. Aware of it himself, he has announced that his safari will be closed to all press coverage, save for occasional statistical bulletins that he may issue through cable facilities in Nairobi. Any attempt to follow in his footsteps will be "an outrage and an indecency." He does not want every missed shot headlined—or, worse still, captured on camera by the increasingly annoying phenomenon of news photographers.

And should he survive, he wishes to tell his own story. A lucrative publishing contract with Charles Scribner's Sons calls upon him to write an account of his safari, in articles that will appear monthly in *Scribner's Magazine*. After the safari is complete, the series will be edited for republication in book form. His payment for the articles is to be $50,000, and the book will earn him a 20 percent royalty. This is the most money he has ever negotiated as a writer. He could have gotten twice as much from *Collier's Weekly*, but feels that periodical is too slick. A touch *bon marché*, as Edith would say.

HE RIDES OUT to hunt with Kermit, while Cuninghame, Tarlton, and the naturalists continue their preparations. Two local ranchers act as guides. The sortie amounts to a rehearsal for the big safari soon to begin, with gunbearers, grooms, and porters trailing in a precedence as formal as any line he had led as President.

Kapiti's dry *veldt,* a word he recognizes as a particle of his own Dutch sur-name, does not compare in fecundity with the well-watered Athi preserve he passed through on the train. After two years of drought, it is largely depopu-lated of game. But the Intertropical Convergence Zone seems finally about to drift north across the equator, ahead of them as they ride. When it does, this plain will turn green, and masses of game arrive to graze. At present, ticks alone seem to thrive, attaching themselves like miniature grape clusters to the legs of the ponies. He is grateful for his leather-patch trousers, buttoned tight from knee to boot. A stiff sun helmet, *de rigueur* for all white travelers in the tropics, uncomfortably covers his large head. He yearns for his beloved slouch hat, but defers to the notion that solar rays are lethal in these latitudes.

He strains to adjust his one good eye to the veldt's visibility, particularly il-lusive when the sun is overhead, and makes out the delicate prancings of two species of buck. He aims his custom-sighted Springfield .30 at a Grant's gazelle, but undershoots and misses. Focusing on a small Thomson's at 225 yards, he breaks its back with a bullet that goes only slightly too high. It is his first African kill, and he looks forward to venison for dinner.

What he really wants to shoot this afternoon, to set the right collecting tone, is "two good specimens, bull and cow, of the wildebeest." It is the scien-tist in him, not the hunter, who first responds to a glimpse of brindled gnu moving blue-black and white across the plain, like shadows of the advancing storm clouds. He sees no evidence in that chiaroscuro of the fashionable the-ory of "protective coloration," one of his pet biological peeves. How protec-tive is a white throat mane, in angled light? How inconspicuous are zebra, to a lion? He notes, for his book, that Africa's large game animals "are always walking and standing in conspicuous places, and never seek to hide or take advantage of cover." Only the smaller quadrupeds, "like the duiker and stein-buck . . . endeavor to escape the sight of their foes by lying absolutely still."

Wildebeest, duiker, steinbuck—he is already picking up the Cape Dutch nomenclature that Afrikaans settlers have brought to British East Africa. Their language reminds him of the nursery songs his grandmother used to croon to him, in earliest memory:

> *Trippa, troppa, tronjes,*
> *De varken's in de boonjes.*

Reminiscent, too, is the Paleolithic profile of a wildebeest, as he closes on it in a sudden squall of rain. His first big trophy was an American buffalo, hunted in similar conditions twenty-three years ago. Then, the rain was so dense on his spectacles, he could not be sure what was bison, and what mere beading water. This shape shrinks at four hundred yards to something more slender than massive. Nevertheless, it is a good-sized bull. He wounds it into a run. Kermit, galloping with teenage abandon over rotten ground for more than six miles, administers the *coup de grâce*.

By "veldt law," credit goes to the man who shot first.

AFTER A WEEK OF hunting around Kapiti, he feels confident enough to stalk lion with dogs. They do not have to sniff far. The hair rises on their backs as they follow catspaw prints down a dry donga, and his horse boy hisses, "*Simba.*"

He follows the line of the pointing black finger. Just four yards away, something yellow moves in a patch of tall grass. He fires at once with his .405 Winchester. With nothing but color to aim at, he does not know if the movement will materialize into a lion. Kermit fires too. Presently two half-grown cubs emerge, both wounded. They have to be finished off.

Disappointed as the day wanes without result, he allows one of his party to reconnoiter another ravine. More prints show in the sand, much larger this time, and at once he and Kermit are off their horses, alert to crashing, grunting noises in the brush ahead.

> Right in front of me, thirty yards off, there appeared, from behind the bushes which had first screened him from my eyes, the tawny, galloping form of a big maneless lion. Crack! the Winchester spoke; and as the soft-nosed bullet ploughed forward through his flank the lion swerved so that I missed him with the second shot; but my third bullet went through the spine and forward into his chest. Down he came . . . his hind quarters dragging, his head up, his jaws open and lips drawn up in a prodigious snarl, as he endeavored to turn to face us. His back was broken. . . . His head sank, and he died.

There is no time to exult over the carcass, because he sees a second lion escaping. He runs it down and fires. The lion rolls over, one foreleg in the air, then takes two more bullets before dying at his feet.

Three days later he kills a much bigger lion, plus another half-grown cub and a lioness. All are destined for the Smithsonian. He hopes that his trophy quota, set by Protectorate authorities, will eventually allow him to shoot a *simba* for himself. It is dark before the lioness is borne back to camp, swinging between two poles. A nearly full moon illumines the porters as they lope into view, intoning a deep, rhythmic song. He tries to notate it phonetically: *Zouzou-boulé ma ja guntai.* They cluster around him as he stands by the fire, then begin to dance. Their chanting rises to a climax. He adds a descant of his own, obscurely derived from Irish folksong: "Whack-fal-lal for Lanning's Ball."

The firelight glows on the body of his prey, and on the white and ebony of his jostling celebrants. Around them, the plain lies pale under the moon.

LIKE A PYTHON TOO enormous to shift all its coils at once, the safari begins to move while still based at Kapiti Station. By early May it is in full motion, carrying its own weight, hunting as it goes, sending out flickering forays in search of choice specimens.

As leader, he does his share of collecting and cataloging. *Dendromus nigrifons, Arvicanthis abyssinicus nairobae, Myoscalops kapiti heller, Thamnomys loringi, Pelomys roosevelti. . . .* Latin classifications come easily to him; he has been inscribing zoological labels since boyhood. He assists Heller and Loring in writing life histories, enjoying the precision of scientific description. Before politics, this was what he wanted to be: a naturalist in the field. *Coarse bristly hair,* he writes of the meadow mouse named in his honor. *The dorsal coloration is golden yellow overlaid by long hairs with an olive iridescence; the under parts are silky white.*

But his main literary labor, at night in camp after dinner, is to process pocket-diary jottings and fresh memory into serial installments for *Scribner's Magazine.* By 12 May he has completed his first article, "A Railroad Through the Pleistocene." Eight days later he finishes another, describing his wildebeest hunt and visit to a Boer ranch, not failing to quote *Trippa, troppa, tronjes.* With a storyteller's instinct for pacing, he reserves his lion kills for installment three, betting that readers who stay with him that long will stay to the end—unless his own end intervenes. "During the last decades in Africa," he reports, "hundreds of white hunters, and thousands of native hunters, have been killed or wounded by lions, buffaloes, elephants, and rhinos." A unique

"A PRECEDENCE AS FORMAL AS ANY LINE HE HAD LED AS PRESIDENT."
Roosevelt's safari gets under way, May 1910.

feature of his book is that it is being written on the march. The possibility of foreclosure adds an agreeable note of suspense to the narrative.

He writes it as he talks—superabundantly, always interestingly, with clarity and total recall. Elegance of style is not his concern. He sometimes repeats himself, relying on his sharp ear to protect him from cliché, not always with success. He is aware of the page-filling benefits of purple passages, and scatters dying sunsets and brilliant tropic moons with a fine hand.

Beyond these indulgences, the power of his prose comes from its realism. He is an honest writer, incapable of boasting, or even the discreet omissions tolerated by nonfiction editors. If he kills any animal clumsily, wasting bullets, he tells how, in detail. The same truthfulness keeps him from false modesty— the "my poor self" affectation of so many German and English memoirists. Being brave, he admits to acts of bravery; swelling with new experiences, he does not hide the breadth of his knowledge. As a result, his indelible pencil gouges the capital letter *I* with a frequency tending to blunt the point.

Pressing down is necessary, because he writes with two sheets of carbon stuffed into his manuscript pad. One copy of each article is sealed in a blue canvas envelope and dispatched to Nairobi by runner, thence to be sent down the railroad to Mombasa and shipped via two oceans to New York. To insure against loss, a duplicate goes by the next sea mail, and he retains the third copy for himself.

As he falls into the cross-rhythms of riding and shooting, collecting and writing, he becomes in effect a hunter of Africa itself, seeking to capture it whole—alive or dead—and process it into food for mind and body. His pursuit is not for the squeamish. Each new animal fixed in his sights poses a different combination of danger and documentary interest, whether in the number of bullets it absorbs, or the sounds it makes as it dies, or the inches it registers on his tape measure, or the browsing habits he deduces from the contents of its stomach. A bull rhino, shot through lungs and heart, bears down with such momentum that it skids to death just thirteen paces away, plowing a long furrow with its horn. A lion, nine feet long and copiously maned, comes on even faster, only to be hit in the chest, "as if the place had been plotted with dividers . . . smashing the lungs and the big blood vessels of the heart." Two swamp buffalo bulls, black and glistening in the early morning light, fall to his biggest rifle, and two giant eland, heavy and dewlapped as prize steers, to his smallest. A lioness yields not only herself, but two unborn cubs. Three giraffes topple over in a single morning, followed by a whole family of rhinos, the bull needing nine bullets to finish off, the cow performing a "curious death waltz," and the calf dropping with "a screaming whistle, almost like that of a small steam-engine." His kills become repetitive. Yet another rhino, then another, and another, and another; two more lions and a lioness, somersaulting left and right in her final agony; more buffalo, more eland, more giraffes.

In a sudden translocation to a world of water, he finds himself in a row-boat with Kermit, gliding among purple and pink water lilies. Delicate jacana birds race across the pads, treading so lightly the flowers barely dip. His ornithologist's eye and ear rejoice at a wealth of other bird life: tiny kingfishers coruscating in the sun like sapphires, white-throated cormorants, spur-winged plover clamoring overhead, little rills threading the papyrus, grebes diving, herons spearing, and baldpate coots resembling the kind he collected as a teenager, except, he notes, for "a pair of horns or papillae at the hinder end of the bare frontal space."

But he is looking for hippos. The prodigious beasts prove surprisingly fast and difficult to kill in the water. He hits one, this first day on Lake Naivasha, and another the next; but they submerge at once, and decline to float up dead. On the third day, just as he feels an attack of malaria coming on, he encounters a big bull wading. He fires shakily, breaking its shoulder, whereupon it flounders at him with open jaws. He fires again and again, trying to control his tremor, and finally shoots right down its throat. The tusks clash like a sprung bear trap. At point-blank range, the hippo swerves a little, and he drills it through the brain.

Then, curling up on the floor of the boat, he succumbs to his fever.

⌒

HE KNOWS THIS IS NOT African malaria, but the Cuban variety that has plagued him since Rough Rider days. Always the sudden convulsions, the cracking headache, then zero at the bone. And always, since he believes illness is weakness (like grief or fear or self-doubt), he fights it off until it fells him. Fortunately, attacks never last long. He is well enough after five days to go out looking for more hippos. This time he leaves Kermit behind, and orders two "boys" to row him alone across the lake.

Although he assures himself that he has spilled no more blood, so far, than is necessary to satisfy the Smithsonian and feed his safari, he is aware that his hunter's luck has been extraordinary. It is the talk of the sundowner set in Nairobi. In just three months, he and Kermit have bagged multiple specimens of most of the major African species. Thanks to herculean skinning and salting by Heller and Mearns, he can congratulate himself on having shipped, via the railway to Mombasa, "a collection of large animals such as has never been obtained for any other museum in the world on a single trip."

The trouble with such luck is that it is bound to be perceived by critics of big-game hunting as indiscriminate slaughter. Local "bush telegraph" exaggerates the number of his kills, not to mention his profligacy with bullets. He is sensitive of being caricatured as anything other than the serious leader of a scientific expedition, and begins to regret his press ban. Perhaps he should do more than send the occasional scrawled trophy tally to the little pool of reporters in Nairobi. It is not the kind of "copy" they want.

Whenever he veers near the capital, he can feel their avid interest pulling at him, like magnetic current. The fact is, he is magnetized himself. Despite his pose of privacy, he remains irredeemably a public figure, obsessed with his own image, half wanting to confide in those he holds at bay. He misses the worshipful cadre of young scribes who took virtual dictation from him in Washington. That "Newspaper Cabinet" is now disbanded, and Taft's self-deprecating envoi ("I have not the facility for educating the public as you had") suggests that the White House is going to be a poor source of news for the next four years. American editors will have to look farther afield for good material. No story could be more surefire than that of Colonel Roosevelt daily risking death in Africa!

Hence the presence, this day in Naivasha, of F. Warrington Dawson, a young United Press correspondent who has pursued him all the way to Kapiti. Dawson—Southern, French-educated, the author of two successful novels— is obviously eager to serve him. They might discuss how in camp tonight. That hippo "bull" of five days ago turned out, embarrassingly, to be an old cow. The misidentification was excusable, for she was barren, and had developed male characteristics. But it is exactly the sort of thing he does not wish broadcast, as some kind of joke.

⁂

IF ONLY TO IMPRESS DAWSON, he wants to get a big bull, and get it cleanly—not an easy task with low-profile quarry.

The lake lies almost still. For an hour of stealthy progress, he cannot be sure what are mere strips of mud, wetly gleaming, and what the possible heads of hippos. At last he distinguishes a dozen flat foreheads. He fires at seventy yards, and they all sink without trace. He thinks he may have hit one of them. Still standing, he orders his rowers to advance. He catches their sudden fear, then the boat shudders over some vast upheaval, knocking him off his feet. The water roils as back after huge back rises in rage. Repeatedly, he fires his .30-caliber Springfield at the closest heads (one with a lily-pad eye patch that reminds him, in the midst of panic, of "a discomfited prize-fighter"). The other hippos plunge for cover.

Calm returns to the lake. He waits for it to give up its dead. After an hour, to his surprise and shame, four carcasses surface. One of them is the bull he wanted, but the rest are cows, unneeded as trophies, undeniable as kills. He persuades himself that they will be a food bonanza for his porters, and for the natives of Naivasha.

Darkness falls as he supervises the laborious business of belaying, mooring, and towing tons of meat. The night grows stormy. Long swells roll through the reeds. He does not get back to camp until three the next morning. Before dawn, he awakes with an attack of acute despair. Alarmed at his haggard look, servants go to fetch Dawson. *"Bwana Mkubwa* kill *mingi kiboko!"* Many hippos.

"Warrington," he says when the reporter appears, "the most awful thing has happened."

He need not worry. Dawson is so touched to be confided in ("I don't know what to do. . . . We shall have to let the papers know") that the story goes out as an attack by, rather than on, the herd of hippos. It is released by a young man who can now style himself secretary to the former President of the United States. In his diary for 23 July, Dawson proudly notes, "Wrote letters for the Colonel."

⊷

THE LETTERS, DICTATED with much snapping of teeth, pacing back and forth, and smacks of right fist into left palm, are in response to the first overseas mail the safari has received in nearly two months. Senator Henry Cabot Lodge and other politically obsessed correspondents report that President Taft is proving an inept executive, and that Republican insurgents now pose a serious threat to the unity of the Republican Party. But the immediacy of such bulletins fades in proportion to the distance they have come, and the leisurely pace of African "runners."

There is, in any case, little that a former Party head can do, other than express polite concern. Lodge must understand that he has divorced himself from affairs of state. "Remember that I never see newspapers. . . . I am now eating and drinking nothing but my African expedition."

He admits to Dawson that he would rather not hear anything about the Taft administration. Insofar as he will discuss his own future, he talks of returning to Oyster Bay for a quiet life of writing books and articles. He says he would like to become "a closer father" to his two youngest sons, whom he feels he may have neglected during his years as President.

However, he does dictate one startling remark that Dawson fails to recognize as news. It occurs in a message of sympathy to Henry White, whom President Taft has dismissed as American ambassador to France: "He said without any qualification that he intended to keep you. It was, of course, not a promise *any more than my statement that I would not run again for President was a promise.*"

⊷

HE IS NEARER DEATH, around midday on the nineteenth of August, than he was on Kettle Hill in Cuba, or when he battled for breath as an asthmatic child. An elephant bears down upon him in dense jungle, creepers snapping like packthread in its rush. There are no bullets left in his Holland & Holland rifle: both barrels were needed to dispatch another elephant, only moments before. He dodges behind a tree, ejecting the empty cartridges and jamming in two fresh ones. R. J. Cuninghame fires twice, with the hair-trigger reaction of a professional. The elephant stops in its tracks, wheels, and vanishes, trumpeting shrilly. A copious trail of blood marks its departure.

Hunters' etiquette requires that it be followed. But the contrary duty of a collector is to begin, at once, the task of skinning the specimen already killed, a big bull carrying a hundred and thirty pounds of ivory. Several days' work lies ahead, in humid weather (they are on the lush piedmont of Mount Kenya). He watches fascinated as the safari team—porters, gunbearers, and 'Ndorobo guides alike—throw themselves bodily into the work of flaying and cutting up his quarry.

> Soon they were all splashed with blood from head to foot. One of the trackers took off his blanket and squatted stark naked inside the carcase, the better to use his knife. Each laborer rewarded himself by cutting off strips of meat for his private store, and hung them in red festoons from the branches round about. There was no let-up in the work until it was stopped by darkness.
>
> Our tents were pitched in a small open glade a hundred yards from the dead elephant. The night was clear, the stars shone brightly, and in the west the young moon hung just above the line of tall tree-tops. Fires were speedily kindled and the men sat around them, feasting and singing in a strange minor tone until late in the night. The flickering light left them at one moment in black obscurity, and the next brought into bold relief their sinewy crouching figures, their dark faces, gleaming eyes, and flashing teeth. . . . I toasted slices of elephant's heart on a pronged stick before the fire, and found it delicious; for I was hungry, and the night was cold.

BLOOD, NAKEDNESS, FLESHY festoons, music, moon, and fire, his mouth full of cardiac meat: after four months, he has arrived at the heart of darkness. He is at one with the mightiest of animals, its life juices mingling with his own, at one with all nature, with the primeval past. No longer a mere time traveler in the Pleistocene, he has become a virtual denizen of it. The pages of his safari diary, covered with sketches of every animal he has slain (usually shown in motion, extremities tapering off into blankness), uncannily recall Paleolithic art. Yet a part of him is repelled by much of what he observes: baboons tearing open newborn lambs to get at the milk inside them, a hyena suffocated by the very guts it burrows into, flies walking around the eyes of children. "Life is hard and cruel for all the lower creatures, and for man also in what the sentimentalists call a 'state of nature,' " he writes. "The savage of today shows us what the fancied age of gold of our ancestors was really like; it was an age when hunger, cold, violence, and iron cruelty were the ordinary accompaniments of life."

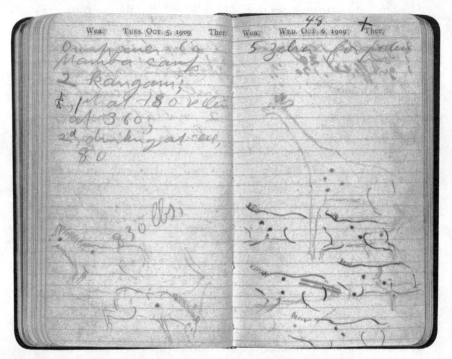

"THE PAGES OF HIS SAFARI DIARY UNCANNILY RECALL PALEOLITHIC ART."
Roosevelt records his kills on 5 and 6 October 1909.

The intense physicality of Africa so stimulates him intellectually that he has already read most of his Pigskin Library—some covers stained with blood, oil, ashes, and sweat till they look like saddle leather. He balks only at three or four of Shakespeare's plays. The aphorisms of Omar Khayyám, Sir Walter Scott, Ferdinand Gregorovius, and Lewis Carroll are as apt to flavor his campfire conversation as ornithological data. He seems to register everything he reads, just as he mentally photographs everything he sees—the new moon reflected among water lilies, a clutch of hartebeest droppings, a mirage's "wavering mockery," ostriches "mincing along with their usual air of foolish stateliness." His ear for sounds is just as acute, and he notes them down with extreme precision: the "batrachian" croaks of hyraxes, the "bubbling squeals" blown through the nostrils of a submerging hippo, the *pack* of a bullet hitting rhino hide, the "bird-like chirp" of a cheetah.

One sound falls with especial sweetness on his ear: Kermit playing "Rolling Down to Rio" on the mandolin. He is proud of his son, who despite a weedy physique has managed to emulate all his own hunting feats—even shooting an elephant. The boy has taken surprisingly well to the African wilderness—so much so, he would seem born for life in an alien environment. He has a linguistic gift, and has added a fairly fluent command of Swahili to the French, Latin, and Greek he learned at Groton. Socially, Kermit tries to be friendly, but is inhibited by a lackluster personality. He is happiest when hunting, and remains cool in the face of danger.

Possibly the image of another narrow-chested Harvard undergraduate, thirty years ago, amazing the backwoodsmen of Maine with equal feats of courage and endurance hovers in a father's memory. Nothing dull about *that* youth! Even then, people seemed to be irradiated in contact with him. His peculiar glow, which he gives off as naturally as a firefly, has not transmitted to any of his children—unless Alice's fitful sparks of conversational brilliance, and signs that Quentin is developing an exceptional charm, can be regarded as genetic.

He has grown used, over the years, to being surrounded by crowds wearing the strange fixed smile, half-awed, half-predatory, that is celebrity's reflection. On the rare occasions he visits Nairobi to pick up supplies and mail, the smile greets him as if he were still President, as if he were not a private hunter in one of the remotest colonies in the world. He has to laugh when he returns to the trail, and finds himself surrounded by a "thoroughly African circle of deeply interested spectators." Wildebeest and kongoni form the perimeter; a rhino peers shortsightedly with small pig's eyes, less than half a mile away; four topi advance for a closer look; a buck topi and a zebra follow suit; and high overhead, vultures wheel. So long the center of other circles, social, intellectual, and political, he is now, apparently, a focal point of the Sotik plateau.

Quitting the safari entirely for a week, with only Kermit and a few Kikuyu servants for company, he camps in the cold highlands of the Guaso Nyero. Freak rains fall almost every night. Snug in his tent and stoutly clad by Abercrombie & Fitch, he is concerned at the way his half-naked men cower under bushes, instead of building some sort of roof for themselves. He has to drive them to chop and plait leafy boughs.

It is plain to him that the pagan tribes of British East Africa are in a state of development far behind that of the Pawnee and other aboriginal peoples. It would be useless to offer them any kind of independence: "The 'just consent of the governed,' in their case, if taken literally, would mean idleness, famine, and endless internecine warfare." He declines, however, to treat them as irredeemable, in the manner that comes so naturally to their colonial masters. They have as much civilized potential as his own ancestors did, back in the days when bison roamed the forests of Europe. He shocks the complacency of a dinner in his honor, at the Railway Institute in Nairobi, by saying, "In making this a white man's country, remember that not only the laws of righteousness, but your own real and ultimate self-interest demand that the black man be treated with justice, that he be safeguarded in his rights and not pressed downward. Brutality and injustice are especially hateful when exercised on the helpless."

⊷

AS HIS FIFTY-FIRST BIRTHDAY approaches on 27 October, he begins to pine for Edith. A mighty hunter, with much killing yet to do, should not give way to "homesickness" (the word he applies to all private desires), but he finds himself counting the months and days until they meet in Khartoum. A chance reference to the Song of Solomon, in the midst of a letter he addresses to an editorial friend, makes him segue into a rhapsody on domestic bliss: "I think that the love of the really happy husband and wife—*not* purged of passion, but with passion heated to a white heat of intensity and purity and tenderness and consideration, and with many another feeling added thereto—is the loftiest and most ennobling influence that comes into the life of any man or woman, even loftier and more ennobling than the wise and tender love for children."

In November, on the seventeenth, another anniversary looms: that of his engagement to Edith. He writes to her from his camp beside the River 'Nzoi:

> Oh, sweetest of all sweet girls, last night I dreamed that I was with you, that our separation was but a dream; and when I waked up it was almost too hard to bear. Well, one must pay for everything; you have made the real happiness of my life; and so it is natural and right that I should constantly [be] more and more lonely without you. . . . Do you remember when you were such a pretty engaged girl, and said to your lover "no Theodore, that I cannot allow"? Darling, I love you so. In a very little over four months I shall see you, now. When you get this three fourths of the time will have gone. How very happy we have been these twenty-three years!

He signs it "Your own lover."

Moving on to Londiani on the last day of the month, he disbands the main body of his safari. He has already spent almost all of the $75,000 Andrew Carnegie and a few other American sponsors have lavished upon the expedition. It has collected all it needs in British East Africa—indeed, more than it is officially entitled to: almost 4,000 mammals large and small, plus 3,379 birds, 1,500 reptiles, frogs, and toads, and 250 fish. In addition there are uncounted numbers of crabs, beetles, millipedes, and other invertebrates, and several thousand plants.

From now on, he and Kermit will hunt in Uganda Protectorate and the Sudan with a much smaller retinue of porters and horse boys. Heller, Loring, and Dr. Mearns insist on staying with him. They are insatiable for more spec-

" 'OH, SWEETEST OF ALL SWEET GIRLS.' "
Edith Kermit Roosevelt in 1909.

imens, and airily confident that the safari will stay in business for another three very expensive months. This worries him. He is generous by nature, but also improvident, with little understanding of the real value of money. He has insisted on paying his and Kermit's own way so far, not dipping into sponsor funds. Edith is bound to remind him, if the funds run out, that he has two more sons to put through Harvard—with Quentin unlikely to graduate until the spring of 1919. He is by no means financially secure. His entire presidential salary went toward entertaining, and his Nobel Peace Prize award, totaling almost $40,000, has been placed at the disposal of Congress, as something he feels he has no right to keep. Nor is he likely ever again to negotiate a publishing contract as big as his current one.

He is therefore relieved to hear that Carnegie will be sending him a check for $20,000 for the naturalists, along with a promise of further cash if needed. "I am now entirely easy as to the expense of the scientific Smithsonian part of the trip," he writes, emphasizing that he and Kermit will continue to finance themselves. He does not want to become personally indebted to anyone. His experience as a professional politician has been that donors always look for repayment in the coin of their choice. What Carnegie craves is influence over affairs of state. Already there have been indications that the steelmaker, an ardent pacifist, wants to draft him into the international arms control movement—a cause he has never much cared for.

Revisiting Nairobi in mid-December, he sends off another plump envelope to his publisher. He is pleased to hear from Robert Bridges, the editor of *Scribner's Magazine,* that the first installment of his safari story has been a runaway publishing success. "The very large edition of the October number (much the largest we have ever printed) is completely exhausted." Subsequent print runs are to be even larger. With eleven installments already mailed, he has only two more to write, and can look forward to publication of his complete African book in less than a year.

In Nairobi's little bookstore, he amplifies the Pigskin Library with Darwin's *Voyage of the Beagle,* nine volumes of Julian Huxley's *Essays in Popular Science,* and every classic he can lay his hands on: Cervantes, Goethe, Molière, Pascal, Montaigne, Saint-Simon. Then, on 18 December, he takes the Uganda Railway to Lake Victoria, and sails in a small steamer for Entebbe. As he does so, he crosses the equator and reenters his home hemisphere.

CHRISTMAS DAY FINDS him marching northwest toward Lake Albert, parallel with the Victoria Nile. It is elephant country, and he cannot resist downing another leviathan—his eighth—and guzzling the "excellent soup" made from its trunk. He is in superb health, having (perhaps with the aid of Cuban fever) deflected all local diseases. If the rheumatism he began to complain of in his last years as President still troubles him, he has stopped mentioning it. His stride is tireless, unusually long for a small-boned man five feet nine inches tall. He can run, carrying a heavy gun, for one and a half miles in 102°F heat. He eats enormously, but his constant activity burns up fat. He looks better than at any time in his adult life: tanned, hard-muscled, sun bleach gilding the slight gray in his hair. Even his monocular eyesight seems improved. He is the first in his party to spot a distant herd of buffalo, "their dark forms picked out by highlights on the curve of their horns." His hearing remains phenomenal, and he is intrigued to find that his sense of smell has become animal-like, alerting him to the nearness of invisible prey.

He has, in short, reached his peak as a hunter, exuberantly altered from the pale, overweight statesman of ten months ago. Africa's way of reducing every problem of existence to dire alternatives—shoot or starve, kill or be killed, shelter or suffer, procreate or count for nothing—has clarified his thinking, purged him of politics and its constant search for compromise. Yet on the seventh day of the new year, as he enters the valley of the White Nile at Butiaba, he begins to accept that his retreat into the Pleistocene is over. A reverse journey is under way: he feels himself "passing through stratum after stratum of savagery and semicivilization . . . each stage representing some thousands of years of advance upon the preceding."

The advance is as slow as he can make it. It proceeds amphibiously, with most of his porters trekking inland from Kobe to Nimule, while the white command meanders downriver in a flotilla of five small boats. He orders a three-week halt just south of the third parallel, and in a hunting orgy with Kermit, kills nine white rhinos.

✒

A MONTH LATER, he reaches Gondokoro in the southern Sudan. By now, after a final chase after giant eland, he feels that he has advanced at least as far as the seventh century. A letter from Henry Cabot Lodge jerks him further forward. It warns that a phalanx of foreign correspondents will waylay him at Khartoum, 750 miles north. "There is a constantly growing thought of you and your return to the Presidency. . . . They will all try to get you to say things. I think it is of the first importance that you should say absolutely nothing about American politics before you get home."

He insists in reply that all he wants to do is finish his book, tour Europe with Edith, Kermit, and Ethel, and then come home as a private citizen. "At present it does not seem to me that it would be wise, from any side, for me to be a candidate. But that can wait."

✒

THREE MEMBERS OF THE KHARTOUM press contingent, however, cannot. On 11 March they emerge from the Nile's dawn mist in a commandeered steamboat, waving sun helmets and the Stars and Stripes. Encouraged by his return of salute, they introduce themselves as representatives of the *Chicago Tribune,* New York *World,* and United Press. He invites them to dinner aboard his new ship, the *Dal,* a luxury sternwheeler made available by the Governor-General of the Sudan. But when they row over that evening, they find the table laid on its forward barge, full of malodorous hides. The message is clear: he still considers himself a traveling hunter.

They listen frustrated as he tells story after safari story, his face silhouetted against a papyrus fire in the swamp of Ar Rank. Eventually he gives them a statement—of sorts—for publication: "We [*sic*] have nothing to say and will have nothing to say on American or foreign policy questions. . . . I will give no interviews and anything purporting to be an interview with me can be accepted as false as soon as it appears."

Courteously, the next morning, he orders the newsmen back downriver, and spends the next two days writing in his stateroom. Every time he goes on deck for a breather, he recognizes more and more of the Nile birds he pursued and stuffed as a boy, thirty-seven years before on his father's rented dahabeah: cow herons, hoopoos, bee-eaters, black-and-white chats, plover, kingfishers, desert larks, and trumpet bullfinches. At night, he sits under the stars and listens to other, unseen species calling to one another in strange voices. He watches crocodiles and hippos slide through the black water and thinks up a phrase to describe the luminosity they shed from their backs: "whirls and wakes of feeble light." His narrative has caught up with him: he is writing now almost in real time.

All that remains is to list the game he has shot on safari: 9 lions, 8 elephants, 6 buffalo, 13 rhino, 7 giraffes, 7 hippos, 2 ostriches, 3 pythons, 1 crocodile, 5 wildebeest, 20 zebras, 177 antelope of various species, from eland to dik-dik, 6 monkeys, and 32 other animals and birds: 296 "items" in all. Kermit has bagged 216—a total almost as impressive as the young man's ability to match Heller and Mearns drink for drink.

"Kermit and I kept about a dozen trophies for ourselves," Roosevelt writes in a final defensive paragraph. "We were in hunting-grounds practically as good as any that ever existed; but we did not kill a tenth, nor a hundredth, part of what we might have killed had we been willing."

Shortly before noon on 14 March, Khartoum's palms and minarets emerge from a red dust haze downriver. The *Dal* swings into the mouth of the Blue Nile and bears down on the private dock of the governor-general's palace, where at last he sees, in his own half-regretful image, "the twentieth century superimposed upon the seventh."

PART ONE

1910–1913

*The epigraphs at the head of every
chapter are taken from the poems of
Edwin Arlington Robinson (1869–1935),
whom Theodore Roosevelt rescued from
poverty and obscurity in 1905. He went on
to win three Pulitzer Prizes.*

CHAPTER 1

Loss of Imperial Will

Equipped with unobscured intent
He smiles with lions at the gate,
Acknowledging the compliment
Like one familiar with his fate.

THE KISS THAT THEODORE ROOSEVELT longed for did not materialize when he stepped ashore in Khartoum on 14 March 1910. Instead, he had to return the salute of Sir Rudolf Anton Karl von Slatin Pasha, G.C.V.O., K.C.M.G., C.B., inspector-general of the Sudan, and pass an honor guard of _askaris_ into the palace garden, where the elite of Anglo-Sudanese society awaited him amid the silver paraphernalia of afternoon tea. He was informed that Edith's train from Cairo was delayed, and that she and Ethel would not arrive for another couple of hours. In the meantime, Slatin would not hear of the Colonel checking in to a hotel. A suite for his party had been readied in the palace, and a private yacht was standing by for sightseeing during his stay.

What Roosevelt wanted to see, more than anything but Edith's face, was Omdurman. The battlefield, where General Kitchener's Twenty-first Lancers had staged the last great cavalry charge of the nineteenth century, lay only ten miles away. Kitchener had been on his mind in recent days, if only because HMS _Dal,_ the boat that had brought him north from Gondokoro, had been the triumphant commander's flagship. On its boards, twelve years before, Kitchener had proclaimed British control over the entire Nile Valley, from Uganda to the Mediterranean.

The success of that dominion—or condominium, as the Foreign Office called it, as a sop to Sudanese, Egyptian, and Turkish sensibilities—was palpable in Khartoum's tranquil, orange-blossom-scented air. Rebuilt by Kitchener from the ruins of a thirteen-year Muslim interregnum, the city was laid out like the Union Jack, its crossbars lined with stone villas and its triangles filled with seven thousand trees. Once the most violent flashpoint on the African continent, it now lazily breathed *pax Britannica*. In the sunburned, aristocratic faces of his hosts, in their perfect manners and air of unstudied authority, Roosevelt recognized the attributes he had always admired in the English ruling class, along with "intelligence, ability, and a very lofty sense of duty."

"THE ELITE OF ANGLO-SUDANESE SOCIETY AWAITED HIM."

Roosevelt arrives in Khartoum, 14 March 1910.

Yet he was aware of the constant menace of Arab nationalism, obscure yet encircling, like the mirages wavering on the desert horizon. The haze that hung over the city seemed, to his vivid historical imagination, to be red with the blood of General Gordon, murdered in this very palace by Mahdist dervishes.

KHARTOUM'S NORTH STATION was cordoned off when he met the Cairo express at 5:30 P.M. He climbed into his wife's private car the moment it came to a halt, and remained inside for a long time. Finally the two of them emerged arm in arm, with Kermit and Ethel close behind. All four Roosevelts were laughing.

Edith's smile transformed her normally stiff public face, exposing perfect teeth and lighting up the blue of her eyes. At forty-eight, she was no longer slender, but had just enough height to carry off the consequences of never having had to cook for herself, and her wrists and ankles and sharp profile were as elegant as ever. She had suffered during her year-long separation from

Theodore, more from worry about him on safari than distress about herself: books and music and children had always been her solace.

That evening, Roosevelt changed into a tuxedo and replaced the wire spectacles he had worn on safari with beribboned pince-nez. Transformed thus, he looked dapper for the first time in nearly a year, and worthy of the place card that confronted him at Slatin Pasha's table: THE HONORABLE COLONEL ROOSEVELT.

So far he had managed to keep at bay the reporters that Henry Cabot Lodge had warned him about. They were clamoring for statements on a hot local news item—the murder, by a Nationalist student, of Egypt's Coptic prime minister, Boutros Ghali Pasha. Roosevelt had heard about this incident before arriving in Khartoum.

He was not unwilling to speak about it, but preferred to wait until he made a scheduled address on the issue of condominium at Cairo University in two weeks' time. As for commenting on American issues, he needed first to go through a fat sack of telegrams and letters from home. John Callan O'Laughlin of the *Chicago Tribune* had collared the sack and was offering to serve as his traveling stenographer, as F. Warrington Dawson had in British East Africa. Roosevelt was fond of O'Laughlin, an experienced foreign policy man, and admired his sass. (It had been "Cal" who, scattering piastres like couscous, chartered the steamboat that met the *Dal* at Ar Rank.) However, another contender for secretarial honors was at hand: Lawrence F. Abbott, president of *The Outlook*. Roosevelt felt that, as an employee of that magazine himself (he was listed in its masthead as "Contributing Editor"), he could not turn Abbott down. His work for *Scribner's Magazine* was done, and he must look to *The Outlook* for income—and, not incidentally, space to promulgate his political views.

So O'Laughlin was consoled with a promise of special access, the press corps invited to accompany the Omdurman excursion, and Abbott granted a close-up position from which to observe, and record, the Colonel's return to public life.

⬥

EDITH KERMIT ROOSEVELT was a woman of impeccable *sang-froid*—a phrase that came naturally to her, as did other Gallicisms deriving from her Huguenot ancestry. About the only scrutiny that shook her public composure was that of the camera lens. As mistress of the White House, she had managed to avoid it almost entirely. But now, to her consternation, she found a battery of photographers waiting at Omdurman. Worse still, they continued clicking as camels kneeled to carry the Roosevelt party to the battlefield.

In the event, she withstood the swaying journey better than her husband, enjoying herself as Slatin Pasha pointed out the plain on which Arab bodies had piled up in masses under the fire of Kitchener's artillery. Roosevelt chafed, not having been in a saddle of any kind for more than a year. But Slatin was impressed by his knowledge of every detail of the battle.

They dismounted by the dry watercourse where four hundred cavalrymen, trailed by vultures, had collided with Arab troops in a charge as suicidal as that of Pickett at Gettysburg. It had occurred only two months after Roosevelt's own charge up the Heights of San Juan in 1898. "All men who have any power of joy in battle," he had written then, "know what it is like when the wolf rises in the heart."

Slatin certainly knew, having fought for British control of the Sudan no fewer than thirty-eight times, endured eleven years of Arab imprisonment, and been forced to watch the presentation of Gordon's head to Mahdi Muhammad Ahmad.

Roosevelt stood on the crest of Jebel Surgham, from which Winston Churchill had looked down on wave after wave of black-clad Arabs, firing bullets into the air and waving banners imprinted with verses from the Koran. Now he saw only empty sand, and the shabby sprawl of Omdurman Fort, and the Mahdi's tomb rising like a ruined beehive. His soul revolted against all he had read about "the blight of the Mahdist tyranny, with its accompaniments of unspeakable horror." Those sons of the Prophet had tortured and killed two-thirds of their own number—mostly blacks in the southern Sudan—in a fanatic interpretation of *jihad*. If that was what today's Egyptian Nationalists looked for, as they smuggled in bombs through Alexandria and called for the murder of every foreign official in the condominium, then it was plainly the duty of the British government to stand for humanity against barbarism.

Omdurman fascinated Roosevelt so much that he was loath to leave. By the time the camelcade got back to the riverbank it was already dark, and a quarter moon had risen. Khartoum's stately buildings glowed white across the Nile.

☙

CAL O'LAUGHLIN AND ABBOTT were generous in sharing all the domestic news the Colonel had missed, or failed to register, in nearly a year. The contents of his mail sack amplified every story they had to tell, from betrayal of the Roosevelt legacy on the part of Taft administration officials to what looked like significant stirrings of strength in the Democratic Party, long dormant as a national political force.

One long, anguished letter, from his protégé Gifford Pinchot, was especially disturbing. It confirmed a rumor Roosevelt had heard some weeks before (courtesy of the naked messenger from Gondokoro) and refused to believe. Taft had dismissed Pinchot as chief forester of the United States.

It was understandable that the President might find such a passionate reformer difficult to deal with. But of all men, Pinchot was the one most identified with Roosevelt's conservation record, and by extension, with all the progressive reforms they had worked on together after 1905—reforms that Taft was supposed to have perpetuated.

"We have fallen back down the hill you have led us up," Pinchot wrote, "and there is a general belief that the special interests are once more in substantial control of both Congress and the Administration." He portrayed a well-meaning but weak president, co-opted by "reactionaries" careless of natural resources. Wetlands and woodlands Roosevelt had withdrawn from commercial exploitation had been given back to profiteers. The National Conservation Commission was muzzled. Pinchot's longed-for World Conservation Conference had never happened. His main villain was his boss, Interior Secretary Richard A. Ballinger, whom he had publicly accused of trading away protected waterpower sites in Alaska, and allowing illegal coal claims in a forest that had been Theodore Roosevelt's final presidential gift to the American people. Taft, consequently, had had no choice in dismissing Pinchot from office.

Other letters made clear that "the Ballinger-Pinchot Controversy" had become a flashpoint of American political anger, as recriminatory on both sides as the Coal Strike of 1902. Except now, the sides were not free-market adversaries, but the left and right of a Grand Old Party that Roosevelt thought he had left unified.

Taft had endorsed an equally divisive overhaul of the nation's revenue system, already infamous as "the Payne-Aldrich tariff." Touted as a downward revise of protectionist duties on products ranging from apricots to wool, and debated in the Senate with extraordinary acrimony, it had somehow become law, to the continuing enrichment of America's corporate elite.

"Honored Sir: Please get back to the job in Washington, 1912, *for the sake of the poor,*" one plaintive note read.

Captain Archibald Willingham Butt, the gossipy military aide who now served Taft as he had once served Roosevelt, reported that the President had been cast down by a stroke suffered by Mrs. Taft, the previous spring. "I flatter myself that I have done something in the way of keeping him from lapsing into a semi-comatose state by riding with him and playing golf. . . ."

Roosevelt paid no attention to several appeals for him to run for mayor of New York, or senator in the New York state legislature—stopgap positions, obviously, from which he would be expected to launch another run for the presidency in 1912. "My political career is ended," he told Lawrence Abbott. "No man in American public life has ever reached the crest of the wave as I appear to have done without the wave's breaking and engulfing him."

⟨∾⟩

THE LATE EVENING of 17 March found the Colonel, his party, and press pool clattering north by train toward Wadi Halfa. He was not sorry to leave Khartoum, where an excess of formal engagements, climaxing in a thousand-plate dinner, had tried his patience after nearly a year in the wilderness.

At least, one delicate encounter, with a group of "native" army officers whom Slatin suspected of anti-British sentiments, had gone well. Roosevelt had reminded them of their sworn duty to the Crown, without saying anything controversial about Arab nationalism, and they had been polite enough to cheer him.

There was no question in his mind that all the North African lands west of Suez were better off as imperial protectorates. He admired what the French had done in Algeria, and hoped they would do the same for Morocco. Likewise, he thought that the British should continue to govern Egypt—if only to protect it from the Turks and that self-proclaimed "friend of three hundred million Muslims," Kaiser Wilhelm II. His own country was constitutionally unfit for empire, yet he approved of its missionary work in the Nile Valley and in Lebanon. He had not hesitated, as President, to send gunboats into the Mediterranean whenever American interests seemed threatened, and he had followed up with the Great White Fleet in 1908, signaling that the United States would henceforth be a strategic presence in the Near East.

On the morning of the eighteenth, desert sands disclosed themselves, undulating unbroken to the horizon. Phantom lakes shimmered, running like mercury with the progress of the train. This Nubian landscape was the last depopulated country Roosevelt would see. For several months, he was told, a series of imperial or royal capitals had been bidding for the privilege of entertaining him. So many invitations were already on hand that Lawrence Abbott warned he would need another secretary, if not two, when he got to Europe. "Darkest" Africa had polished his public image to a dazzle of celebrity.

The appearances he had long promised to make at the universities of the Sorbonne, Berlin, and Oxford were now but stops on an ever-expanding grand tour of Europe. In Rome, both the Pope and the King of Italy insisted on receiving him. So did the Emperor of Austria-Hungary, who expected him to visit both Vienna and Budapest. Next in line were the President of France, the Queen of Holland, and the monarchs of Belgium, Denmark, Sweden, and Norway, where the Nobel Prize committee wished him to make an address on world peace. Kaiser Wilhelm II wanted to show him the German army, and King Edward VII the British. Not only *têtes couronnées,* but aristocrats, intellectuals, industrialists, press lords, and politicians of every persuasion clamored for a few moments of the Colonel's time. Even the Calvinist Academy of Geneva was threatening hospitality.

Roosevelt's reaction was a half-humorous, half-resigned willingness to do what diplomacy required—as long as his schedule permitted, and he was treated as a private American citizen. He prepared himself for the coming ordeal in typical fashion. Around sunset, Abbott became concerned by his absence from the family car.

> I searched the train for him and finally discovered him in one of the white enameled lavatories with its door half open. . . . He was busily engaged in reading, while he braced himself in the angle of the two walls against the swaying motion of the train, oblivious to time and surroundings. The book in which he was absorbed was Lecky's *History of Rationalism in Europe.* He had chosen this peculiar reading room both because the white enamel reflected a brilliant light and he was pretty sure of uninterrupted quiet.

ROOSEVELT WAS NOT new to the scholarship of William Edward Lecky (1838–1903). In his youth, he had found the great historian too Old World, too Olympian. Now he was mesmerized by an intellect that encompassed, and gave universal dimensions to, the odyssey he had embarked on. Lecky showed how Europe had passed, age by age, from heathenism through paganism, early Christianity, Islamic infiltration, totalitarian Catholicism, Reformation, and Renaissance—arriving finally at an Enlightenment based on scientific discovery, materialistic philosophy, and the secularization of government. Roosevelt's present passage out of the Pleistocene into lands still medieval-Muslim in atmosphere duplicated this vast arc of human progress.

Right now, he had to deal diplomatically with two clerical provocations that suggested that rationalism still had a way to go before the twentieth century could consider itself emancipated from the intolerances that Lecky chronicled. The head of an American missionary school in Asyūt wrote to say that if he did not come to visit, Presbyterians everywhere would be "very seriously" offended. The Vatican advised that Pope Pius X would grant him an audience on the fifth of April, providing that he did not embarrass His Holiness by associating with any Methodists in Rome.

Roosevelt was prepared to stop by the mission. But he could not permit Vatican officials to tell him whom he might see or not see, as a private traveler en route through the Eternal City. To him, no faith was superior to another, and none to the dignity of individual will. "Moi-même, je suis libre-penseur," he confided to a French diplomat.*

He had done his Sunday school bit as a teenager, teaching children the

---

* "I myself am a free thinker."

rudiments of Christianity, more out of duty than conviction. Throughout adulthood he had been a regular worshipper, gradually switching from the Dutch Reformed Church of his forefathers to Edith's Episcopalian Church—though without her piety. He had no capacity for devotion, unless his love of nature qualified as that. He scoffed at theories that could not be proved, sentimentalities that put a false face on reality, and extremes of religious belief, whether morbid or mystical. As President, he had tried to remove the phrase "In God We Trust" from the national coinage. When consoling bereaved people, he would awkwardly invoke "unseen and unknown powers." Aside from a few clichés of Protestant rhetoric, the gospel he preached had always been political and pragmatic. He was inspired less by the Passion of Christ than by the Golden Rule—that appeal to reason amounting, in his mind, to a worldly rather than heavenly law.

Much as Roosevelt admired the contributions of medieval Islam to the development of European civilization, he had no patience with the interfaith squabble now going on in Egypt between Muslims and Coptic Christians. Their inability to tolerate each other proved the necessity of condominium with the British, who at least had advanced far enough into the modern age to know there were more important things than dogma.

Public works, for example. His dinner guest this evening was Sir William Garstin, the builder of the Aswān Dam. And what had the defeat of the Sudanese caliphate been, if not a triumphant demonstration of the superiority of British railway engineering?

❧

TRANSFERRING OVERNIGHT at Wadi Halfa to the Nile steamer *Ibis,* the Roosevelts cruised downriver to Shellal, where they were welcomed to Egypt by condominium officials. They toured the tomb of Rameses II and Sir William's great waterworks at Aswān before proceeding to Luxor. There, on 21 March, a colder greeting awaited them, in the form of a Nationalist warning that if the Colonel condemned the assassination of Boutros Pasha during his Cairo address, he would suffer the same fate. Roosevelt at once began work on a speech in direct defiance of this threat.

Three days later at Giza, Cleveland H. Dodge, a wealthy friend of Taft's, was amused to see the Colonel, arms folded, contemplating the Sphinx.

"Theodore, what are you thinking about?" Roosevelt seemed startled by the question.

One thing he had in common with the Sphinx at the moment was inscrutability—at least on the subject of American politics. *The New York Times* was reporting that he had "summoned" Gifford Pinchot to meet with him somewhere in Europe, for a briefing on the Taft administration's anti-progressive policies. Apparently the former chief forester was already halfway across the Atlantic.

Roosevelt remained mute on Pinchot, but swung into action on other matters as soon as he had settled into Shepheard's Hotel in Cairo. He dictated a telegram to the American minister in Rome: "It would be a real pleasure for me to be presented to the Holy Father, for whom I entertain a high respect both personally and as the head of a great Church . . . [but I] must decline to make any stipulations or to submit to any conditions which in any way limit my freedom of conduct."

Next, he embarked on a series of local excursions, in order to weigh up Egypt's current security situation. Remembering the squalor he had seen in Cairo as a boy, he marveled at the "material and moral" improvements brought about by twenty-eight years of British rule. Yet he was dismayed at the quality of the current army regime, some of whose officers reminded him of the worst caricatures in Kipling. Arrogant in their Englishness, obsessed with tennis and polo, they seemed unmindful of what the assassination of Boutros Ghali portended. Egyptian Nationalists had made plain that the former prime minister had been murdered for being a proponent of condominium, and for supporting long-term extension of Great Britain's Suez Canal rights.

Roosevelt detected an uncertainty of purpose behind the hauteur of British officials in Cairo. He knew that Herbert Asquith's Liberal government at home was plagued by anti-imperialists who felt that Egypt should be returned to self-government. But he saw no local elite, Coptic or Muslim, capable of holding the country's teeming multitudes together—or even apart, since various sects seemed intent on slaughtering one another. Native Christians had democratic ideals, but were hugely outnumbered. Nationalist leaders, with their red fezzes and European clothes, struck him as "quite hopeless as material on which to build," given only "to loud talk in the cafés and prone to emotional street parades."

The real danger to condominium, in Roosevelt's opinion, throbbed among "the mass of practically unchanged bigoted Muslims to whom the movement meant driving out the foreigner, plundering and slaying the local Christian, and a return to all the violence and corruption which festered under the old-style Muslim rule, whether Asiatic or African." This threatened the world balance of power, for Germany, with its East African protectorate, clearly coveted British control of the Nile.

Sir Eldon Gorst, the new British consul general in Cairo, entreated him to stay off the subject of political assassination in his forthcoming speech at Cairo University. Roosevelt reacted as he had to the Pope's attempt to strong-arm him. He said that if he could not address "the one really vital question which was filling the minds of everyone," he would rather not speak at all. Gorst backed down.

Islamic fundamentalists resented the establishment of the university, only two years earlier, as a school for their accommodationist brethren. So on 26 March, Roosevelt made a goodwill visit to Al-Azhar Mosque, the world's oldest religious academy. He found nine thousand students, all male, squatting on classroom floors and chanting in Arabic. To the amazement of the library staff, he asked to see a scroll of the fourteenth-century *Travels of Ibn Battuta,* and proceeded, with the aid of a translator, to locate and recite passages he had read in French, many years before. This so pleased his hosts that he left the mosque with a copy of the Koran under his arm. It was the first ever presented by Al-Azhar to an infidel.

Interest on all sides was therefore intense two days later, when Roosevelt rose to address the general assembly of Cairo University. Small and struggling, with only apathetic support from local authorities, the institution typified, for him, Great Britain's loss of imperial will. He tried not to show his contempt for the khaki-clad soldiers around him on the platform, so querulous about native feelings, and the Nationalist Muslims whose tarbooshes dotted his audience.

At first he was tactfully equivocal. "Those responsible for the management of this University should set before themselves a very high ideal," he said. "Not merely should it stand for the uplifting of all Mohammedan peoples and of all Christians and peoples of other religions who live in Mohammedan lands, but it should also carry its teaching and practice to such perfection as in the end to make it a factor in instructing the Occident."

Swinging into the preaching mode that came naturally to him, he counseled the university professors headed for study in Great Britain to embrace, rather than resist, the best findings of Western Enlightenment. He emphasized that a full education "is attained only by a process, not by an act," and compared it to the political gradualism inevitable in any backward nation's attempt to modernize itself. "The training of a nation to fit itself successfully to fulfill the duties of self-government is a matter, not of a decade or two, but of generations." He quoted an Arab proverb: "*Allah ma el saberin, izza sabaru,* God is with the patient, if they know how to wait."

The tarboosh-wearers found this so patronizing that they broke into derisive laughter. But the soldiers applauded, and Roosevelt ploughed on toward the reference Sir Eldon was bracing for:

> All good men, all the men of every nation whose respect is worth having, have been inexpressibly shocked by the recent assassination of Boutros Pasha. It was an even greater calamity for Egypt than it was a wrong to the individual himself. The type of man who turns out an as-

sassin . . . stands on a pinnacle of evil infamy; and those who apologize for or condone his act, those who by word or deed, directly or indirectly, encourage such an act in advance, or defend it afterward, occupy the same bad eminence.

Englishmen used to pomposities, and Levantines to elaborate circumlocutions, were aghast at Roosevelt's readiness to call a spade a spade. What Lawrence Abbott described as an "electrical" thrill ran around the hall. But there were loud cheers when Roosevelt ended with a call for mutual respect between Islam and Christianity.

Next day, comments on the speech in native newspapers expressed widespread resentment of Roosevelt as a stooge for the British. He was accused of not really caring whether Arabs were oppressed or not. "How," asked the *Shaab*, "could a man who so denies liberty and individual rights have been chosen president of a free people?" Hundreds of furious students marched on Shepheard's Hotel and shouted, "Give us a constitution!" at his terrace windows. The Colonel was engaged elsewhere, but got back to the hotel in time to see the demonstration breaking up.

When he embarked with his family from Alexandria the following afternoon, the dockside jostled with both Copts and Muslims. He was pursued across the water with roars of "Long live Roosevelt!" and "Down with Roosevelt!"

CHAPTER 2

The Most Famous Man
in the World

As long as Fame's imperious music rings
Will poets mock it with crowned words august;
And haggard men will clamber to be kings
As long as Glory weighs itself in dust.

ON 2 APRIL the Colonel arrived in Naples, and found that his celebrity in Africa was nothing compared to that awaiting him in Europe. Municipal, ecclesiastical, and military uniforms glowed and glittered. Evidently he was to be treated everywhere as if he were still a head of state. He fobbed off several dozen reporters with advance copies of his Sorbonne, Berlin, and Oxford speeches, to hold until delivery, and that night sought refuge at the opera. But his entry precipitated a ten-minute ovation. He saw less of Giordani's *Andrea Chénier* than of constant visitors to his box, begging to be introduced.

Moving on to Rome the following day, Roosevelt managed to clear from his calendar any appointments with Catholic clerics. Cardinal Merry del Val, the Vatican secretary of state, would not back down on the see-no-Methodists condition of a papal audience, while Reverend Ezra Tipple, an American preacher given to calling Pius X "the whore of Babylon," publicly boasted that the Colonel would at least see *him*. The comic-strip aspects of this squaring off of two clerics with bibulous names delighted Roosevelt, and gave him the chance to outmaneuver both. He acknowledged the Pope's right to decline audiences "for any reason that seems good to him," while claiming the same right for himself. And he canceled an embassy reception that Methodists would have attended, on the grounds of Tipple's discourtesy toward the Holy Father.

His own tolerance—religious, social, and political—embraced, with humor and an easy response to all cultural challenges, the schedule of engagements that now crowded upon him. He rejoiced in the fact that both the mayor of Rome and the Prime Minister of Italy were Jews—"in the Eternal City, in the realm of the Popes, the home of the Ghetto . . . !"—and treated King Victor Emmanuel III as a fellow scholar, equally well informed on the Savoyard preference of Roman over Lombard law. Flattered, the king held a dinner for him in the Palazzo del Quirinale that had all the trappings of a state function. Roosevelt was unfazed at having to sit between Queen Helene, a Montenegrin, and her niece, the Princess Royal of Serbia. Conversing in rough but rapid French, he revealed his command of Balkan history and a lively interest in Slav literature, citing in particular some translations of Romanian folk songs by Carmen Sylva. They were enchanted, and teased him about having a daughter nicknamed "Princess Alice."

❧

BEFORE THE ROOSEVELTS PROCEEDED with their European tour, they snatched a brief family vacation at Porto Maurizio, on the Italian Riviera. Edith's unmarried younger sister, Emily Carow, lived there. She called her home Villa Magna Quies—"house of great quiet"—but its peace was disturbed on 11 April by the arrival of Gifford Pinchot.

Lanky, passionate, and sad-eyed, the former chief forester had a litany of sins against progressive Republicanism to blame on President Taft. He specifically cited sixteen. In his monomaniacal hostility toward all who would not believe as he did, Pinchot was not unlike Reverend Tipple—except that for him, God was in nature, and man's duty was to serve the Almighty with practical works: environmental, economic, and social. Physically hard and cold, he had spent his life trying to make himself more so, sleeping on the floor with a woodblock pillow—outdoors, if possible—and getting his valet to douse him every morning with buckets of ice water.

Roosevelt admired the hardness, if not the narrowness that came with it. Pinchot, born to Main Line wealth, had never had to live on equal terms with the "plain people" he invoked so patronizingly. Unmarried at forty-four, he had fathered no children, lost no electoral campaigns, faced no bullets in battle. Roosevelt, in contrast, had—and in those respects alone was the bigger man. Which probably explained Pinchot's increasing devotion, now that neither of them held power.

They spent most of that day and evening together. Pinchot got the attention he craved ("One of the best & most satisfactory talks with T.R. I ever had"), while Roosevelt pored over a sheaf of disturbing letters from other progressive Republicans. All warned that some of his most cherished reforms were doomed, unless something was done soon to check the alliance developing between the administration and reactionaries in Congress.

He was more impressed by the letters than by their carrier. Perhaps Taft had been right to fire so uncompromising a person. "Gifford is a dear, but he is a fanatic."

∽

FOUR DAYS LATER, Roosevelt and Kermit, traveling stag while Edith and Ethel proceeded independently to Paris, arrived in Vienna. A familiar, courtly

" 'GIFFORD IS A DEAR, BUT HE IS A FANATIC.' "

Gifford Pinchot, former chief forester of the United States.

figure awaited them at their hotel: Henry White, whom Taft had so brusquely removed as American ambassador to France. Roosevelt was overjoyed to see him. He had written ahead to ask if White, schooled in the nuances of Old World diplomacy, would consider being at his side in Berlin and London.

Vienna was a plus. As somebody who had dealt personally with many of the monarchs he was to see during the next month and a half, White would be a useful adviser—particularly on how to handle Wilhelm II, that constant imponderable on the international scene. Roosevelt could look after himself in republican France. He wanted to avoid the danger of becoming an emissary between the four most truculent powers in Europe. No matter how often he protested that he was "merely a private citizen," he could not ignore the consequences of his presidency, his Nobel Peace Prize, his international circle of acquaintance, and (perhaps most persuasive of all) the publicity glow he generated in motion, like that of the great comet currently approaching Venus.

After a reunion breakfast, the two men went over to the Hofburg palace at the invitation of Emperor Franz Joseph. White sat in an anteroom while Roosevelt had the disarming experience of being hailed as the embodiment of "the present and future" by an octogenarian who admitted to being "the last representative of the old system."

Franz Joseph had held Austria and Hungary together, with difficulty, for sixty-one years. He spoke in French, out of courtesy to the Colonel's rusty German, and confessed that he was curious to see for himself how somebody so modern "felt and thought." Roosevelt had detected a similar *tempora mutantur* wistfulness in the conversation of Victor Emmanuel, who seemed resigned to socialistic trends in Italy. Both rulers evidently felt that republicanism would soon be the doom of royalty, in Europe as well as Russia.

Aware that he was gazing for the first time into the eyes of a Habsburg, he was interested, but not awed. The best that could be said of the old monarch was that he was "a gentleman"—in Roosevelt's mind, the highest of social categories. Not so the Emperor's nephew and heir apparent. Archduke Franz Ferdinand struck him as "a furious reactionary in every way, political and ecclesiastical both."

Meeting later with the Austrian Prime Minister, Richard von Bienerth, and Baron Alois von Aehrenthal, minister of foreign affairs, Roosevelt felt more at home. They were statesmen like himself, well-born *Realpolitikers,* executives of driving force. Yet he sensed a strategic insecurity in their conversation, not unlike that of condominium officials in Egypt. They clearly relied on Germany to hold their multicultural empire together. At the same time, they were worried about German disapproval of Austria-Hungary's recent annexation of Bosnia-Herzegovina (the hyphens alone betrayed the looseness of the overall structure), not to mention calls for revenge in Russia and Serbia, likely allies in any Balkan war. Germany's fear of such an imbroglio was understandable: if

Russia marched to Serbia's aid, the Reich was treaty-bound to defend Austria-Hungary.

Roosevelt repeated to Bienerth a prophecy he had heard from the Duke of Abruzzi in Rome, that two great wars were certain: one between Great Britain and Germany, and another between the United States and Japan. He said he personally doubted the latter, as long as his government kept up a strong defense, and fortified Hawaii and the Panama Canal.

For the next thirty-six hours, he had to submit to the same quasi-royal honors that had at first amused, then exasperated him in Italy. Trumpets blared, swords and rifles clashed, and crowds blocked every street and square as he moved from the sixteenth-century Spanische Hofreitschule, through the Jockey Club to a medieval country castle, and finally to Schönbrunn Palace. He tried without success to make his hosts understand that he was no longer President of the United States. The non-republican mind, it seemed, could not conceive of sovereignty as finite.

Surrounded by flunkeys, guarded wherever he went, Roosevelt was screened off from the extraordinary changes occurring at lower levels of Viennese society—changes more radical than anywhere else in Europe, and coincident with Austria-Hungary's thrust into the Balkans. He did not see the pornographic nudes of Klimt and Schiele, Kokoschka's explosive studies of *angst*-filled burghers, the rectilinear architecture of the Secessionists. He was deaf to the atonality of Schönberg and the warnings of local poets and playwrights that an apocalypse was coming.

All he knew, as he attended a dinner in his honor at Schönbrunn Palace, was that he had chosen the right country to be born in. Halfway through the banquet, he watched aghast as Franz Joseph and fellow guests performed an ablution dating back to the days of Maria Theresia. Finger bowls were brought in, each with a small glass of water, and the flower of Habsburg aristocracy proceeded to swig, rinse, and spit.

These people, Roosevelt realized, were not merely old-fashioned, but "living in a world as remote from mine as if it had been France before the revolution."

REMOTER STILL WAS that of the Magyar oligarchy in Hungary, where Serbs and Slovaks were suppressed with such discrimination that only one citizen in twenty could vote.

Roosevelt was met at the border by Count Albert Apponyi, an old patriot resentful of the "Dual Monarchy" linking royal Budapest to imperial Vienna. He noticed, as he and Kermit rode to Apponyi's castle for lunch, that each village they passed through had a separate ethnic identity: either Slav, or Magyar, or Teuton. It was Sunday morning, 22 April. Catholic and Protestant churches disgorged their separate congregations.

Multicultural himself, he flabbergasted Apponyi with a long, almost verbatim quotation from a Magyar saga, which he said he had not thought of in twenty years. Proceeding after dark to Budapest, where thousands welcomed him in heavy rain, he scrupulously alluded to Franz Joseph as their "king," not their emperor. Next morning, he made an extempore address to the mostly Magyar members of parliament. He pretended to be surprised when they reacted in ecstasy to his rapid-fire citations of Árpád, St. Stephen, Mátyás Corvin, the Golden Bull, the Battle of Mohács, the Bogomil heresy, and other episodes from Hungary's history. He was, of course, showing off, in a way that would have made Edith Roosevelt cringe, had she been there. But his audience had never heard a foreign statesman express such understanding of them.

Twenty-four hours later, after a round of visits to ambassadors and state officials, Roosevelt was accorded the greatest popular demonstration seen in Budapest since the return of Franz Liszt in 1846. His carriage had to force its way through well-wishers along the esplanade. Cheers pursued him into his hotel until he reemerged to make a speech of thanks. It was translated line by line into Magyar. Cal O'Laughlin, standing by, reported: "With every expression there was a shout which rolled over the berg across the river and came back in a thundering echo. I have seen many demonstrations, but that one by the Danube has not been surpassed in my experience."

BY THE TIME ROOSEVELT reached Paris on the twenty-first, it was apparent that he was the most famous man in the world. In their respective sovereignties, the Kaiser, King Edward VII, and the Tsar of Russia might be better known, but none had his democratic appeal, nor his press appeal across three continents. "When he appears, the windows shake for three miles around," one overawed correspondent wrote. "He has the gift, nay the genius of being sensational."

He knew enough of fame not to expect it to last. But with seven kingdoms still to visit, and reports of a massive homecoming being planned for him in New York, he had to brace himself for more and more adulation. "Like the elder Mr. Weller's Thanksgiving turkey," he joked to Robert Bacon, the American ambassador waiting to greet him at the Gare de Lyon, "I am old and tough and I will be all right for everything."

Jules Jusserand, Bacon's opposite number in Washington, was also on the platform. Roosevelt adored the spry little diplomat, a medieval scholar and veteran of his White House "Tennis Cabinet." It had been Jusserand's idea to have him address the Sorbonne. Both ambassadors had been working for some months to balance their desire to have him meet France's political elite, and his preference for the society of intellectuals. As a result, his calendar for the next week juxtaposed the names of President Armand Fallières, Prime Minister Aristide Briand, Foreign Minister Stéphen Pichon, the Radical leader Georges Clemenceau, and other public men with those of Edith Wharton, Auguste Rodin, the historians Victor Bérard and Pierre de La Gorce, and a brace of literary barons, Paul d'Estournelles de Constant and Pierre de Coubertin.

En route to the Sorbonne on Saturday, 23 April, Roosevelt stopped off to thank officers of the Académie de Sciences Morales et Politiques for electing him an associate member. He did so in French, apologizing for his abuse of the language of Voltaire. "Quand on parle français, on manie l'instrument le plus précis et le plus éclair qui existe."*

Shortly before three o'clock he entered the grand amphitheater of the university to a standing ovation. Jusserand had seen to it that he was flanked onstage by representatives of the French Institute's five academies: Arts, Letters, Sciences, Belles Lettres, and finally the Académie Française itself, represented by eleven green-robed *immortels.* Elsewhere sat ministers in court dress, army and navy officers in full uniform, nine hundred students, and an audience of two thousand ticket holders. The vice-rector of the Sorbonne announced that the greatest voice of the New World was about to speak. Turning to Roosevelt, he said, "Vous unissez le moral à la politique et le droit à la force."†

No thirteen words could have better proved the Colonel's linguistic point, made just an hour earlier. He stuck to English, with the help of an interpreter, as he proceeded to read his long oration, entitled "Citizenship in a Republic."

Acknowledging the right of the French to be proud of their old and sophisticated civilization, he made no apology for the relative rawness of his own. He boasted that the first Roosevelts in New Amsterdam had fought off hostile Indians and lived on equal terms with "traders, plowmen, woodchoppers, and fisherfolk." This somewhat rusticated his family's urban history. But he sought to emphasize that "primeval conditions must be met by primeval qualities" before a nation could think of becoming a republic. Even after it did, it was likely to exhibit "all the defects of an intense individualism" for a century or so. The "materialism" of contemporary industrial America was simply the pioneer spirit *redux.*

Politically, however, the United States and France were of mutual stature. Sister republics in a world of Empire, they represented "the most gigantic of all possible social experiments," that of perfecting democratic rule. They were not dependent on the excellence, or incompetence, of hereditary monarchs; they must rely on the quality of the average citizen.

And on his fertility too. With a directness probably not heard at the Sorbonne in a century, except in lectures on anthropology, Roosevelt declared:

---

* "When one speaks French, one handles the clearest and most precise instrument that exists."
† "You unite morality with politics, and right with might."

"The chief of blessings for any nation is that it shall leave its seed to inherit the land." France (he did not need to name her in this connection: her falling birthrate was well-known fact) had to fight "the curse of sterility." She must breed soldiers to protect her and assert her rights.

This touched on France's other neurosis: fear of conquest by a Germany expansive on land and at sea. War, he granted, was "a dreadful thing." But shrinking from it when it loomed was worse. "The question must be, 'Is right to prevail?' . . . And the answer from a strong and virile people must be, 'Yes,' whatever the cost."

Roosevelt bit off every word as was his habit, with snapping teeth and wreathing lips. Spectators in the farthest recesses of the hall could feel the force of his opinions even before the interpreter translated them. Their ears, attuned to the mercurial flow of French speech, had to adjust to his raspy, jerky delivery (accompanied by smacks of right fist into left palm) and the strange falsetto he used for extra emphasis. Nothing could be less *mielleux*. But his foreignness excused him, and won repeated applause.

The loudest came when he attacked skeptics "of lettered leisure" who, cloistered in academe, "sneered" at anyone trying to make the real world better.

It is not the critic who counts; not the man who points out how the strong man stumbles, or where the doer of deeds could have done them better. The credit belongs to the man who is actually in the arena, whose face is marred by dust and sweat and blood; who strives valiantly; who errs, and comes short again and again, because there is no effort without error and shortcoming; but who does actually strive to do the deeds; who knows the great enthusiasms, the great devotions; who spends himself in a worthy cause; who at the best knows in the end the triumph of high achievement, and who at the worst, if he fails, at least fails while daring greatly, so that his place shall never be with those cold and timid souls who know neither victory nor defeat.

IF ONLY BECAUSE ROOSEVELT clearly identified himself with the man in the arena, he had scored one of his greatest rhetorical triumphs. The *Journal des Débats* printed the speech as a special Sunday supplement, declaring that nobody who heard it could help being "attracted, seduced, disoriented, and conquered." *Le Temps* sent copies to every schoolteacher in France. Royalist as well as republican commentators praised it as a call for centralized authority over Marxist sedition. Military patriots rejoiced in the Colonel's moralization of war.

Only two chauvinistic journals, *L'Éclair* and *La Patrie,* sneered at him for uttering American banalities. That did not stop Librairie Hachette from issuing a luxury reprint of his address on Japanese vellum. A popular pocket-book edition sold five thousand copies in five days. Translations appeared in many European cities, while the original text became known to British and American readers simply as "The Man in the Arena." Roosevelt was surprised at its success, admitting to Henry Cabot Lodge that the reaction of the French was "a little difficult for me to understand."

He wanted to spend 27 April, his last day in town, sightseeing with Edith. But Jusserand informed him that the German Emperor was planning "a big review" in his honor. France would "take it amiss" if he did not recognize her, too, as a great military power. Roosevelt saw that the ambassador was upset, and agreed to watch troops stage a mimic battle at Vincennes.

Command headquarters of the French army, the castle glittered with national pride—or what was left of pride, besmirched by the conspiracism and antisemitism of *l'affaire Dreyfus*. For two and a quarter hours that morning, Roosevelt sat on horseback as cannons boomed and blank bullets rattled. The action was fought at double-quick pace, to accommodate his schedule. He could have been viewing a Pathé newsreel, yet in color and with sound. Across the vast field beyond the garrison, relays of infantry charged. Cavalry forces engaged them in rearguard action. At the end of each rush, machine guns spat fire.

❧

NEXT DAY, THE COLONEL and his entourage (now including Cal O'Laughlin as a press spokesman, and two aides, Lawrence Abbott and Frank Harper, courtesy of *The Outlook*) reentered the world of monarchy. They traveled east via Brussels, where they were received by King Albert and Queen Elizabeth of Belgium. The huge, awkward young ruler endeared himself to Roosevelt with his "excellent manners and not a touch of pretension." Queen Wilhelmina of Holland repelled him with exactly the opposite combination. He thought her "not only commonplace, but common . . . a real little Dutch middle-class *frau*."

A sobering display of German naval might greeted him when he transferred to a Danish steamer at Kiel on the morning of 2 May. He was en route to Norway, and would not properly enter the Reich for another week. Even so, the dreadnoughts and battle cruisers cramming Kiel's inner fjord presented their great guns, and rank upon rank of sailors saluted him as he cruised out of the harbor.

From where he stood on the steamer's bridge, he could glimpse the entrance to Kaiser Wilhelm Canal, crossing the Jutland peninsula. A miniature of his own project in Panama, it showed signs of ominous enlargement. Those dreadnoughts would soon have no problem moving between the Baltic and the North Sea.

Denmark opened out to port: flat, fertile, easily conquerable. King Frederick VIII was unavailable to greet the Roosevelts in Copenhagen, being out of the country on vacation. But by royal command, they were put up at the palace, and entertained by Crown Prince Christian. Roosevelt was informed that the last occupant of their suite had been the King of England, whom he might or might not be seeing later in the month.

According to news reports, Edward VII was not at all well.

They journeyed on to Christiania by night train, arriving there at noon on 4 May. Again they received a royal welcome. King Haakon VII and Queen Maud were on hand at the station, more palace accommodations provided, and the inevitable state banquet loomed.

Norway, despite its energetic attempt at pomp and circumstance, looked to Roosevelt "as funny a kingdom as was ever imagined outside of *opéra bouffe*." Crowds lining the streets cheered with a peculiar barking sound. The royal family was palpably bourgeois: "It is much as if Vermont should offhand try the experiment of having a king." However, given the inability of Europeans to think of continuity except in terms of heredity, he had to admire the way Norway had democratized its monarchy.

On the following day, he braced himself for a round of academic exercises in honor of his Nobel Peace Prize. He did so without enthusiasm, resentful of pressure from Andrew Carnegie to make a speech pleading for arms control, prior to lobbying the Kaiser. The pesky little millionaire ("Here is what I should say to His Imperial Majesty, were I in your place"), then expected to be invited to a follow-up disarmament conference in London—as a return, presumably, for financing Roosevelt's safari.

Christiania was the obvious forum for a condemnation of the Anglo-German naval race, which vied with the Balkan situation as a likely cause of Europe's next war. But what Roosevelt had seen of uneasy peace in North Africa, fractious peace in Austria-Hungary, and resentful peace in France had revived his old doubts about "the whole Hague idea of talking away conflicts that had to happen."

In addition, he had developed a case of bronchitis. It was too late, though, for him to wheeze regrets. Christiania was bedecked with flags and evergreens. Long before he arrived at the National Theater, where the Nobel Committee awaited him, all 1,800 seats were taken by eager members of the public.

Roosevelt's oration was understandably brief and hard to hear. It drew little applause. He thanked the Committee for honoring him, and said he had dedicated his prize money to a foundation, not yet active, that would help resolve major labor disputes. "For in our complex industrial civilization of today, the peace of righteousness and justice—the only kind of peace worth having—is at least as necessary in the industrial world as it is among nations."

This was not the kind of peace Carnegie, or the Committee, hoped he would salute. When he did raise the subject of the naval arms race, he said only that "something should be done as soon as possible" to check it. He gave conditional support to the idea of arbitration treaties between powers "civilized" enough to hate war, and was prepared to believe that a Third Hague Conference might improve on the First and the Second. Finally he said something unequivocal. "It would be a master stroke if those great Powers honestly bent on peace would form a League of Peace, not only to keep the peace among themselves, but to prevent, by force if necessary, its being broken by others."

The idea was arresting, if hardly new. It went back to Hugo Grotius's "Society of States" linked by one law. Even the phrase "League of Peace" had been used before, by the British statesman Sir Henry Campbell-Bannerman. But Roosevelt gave it an original twist by warning that such a body would count for nothing if it did not have punitive, as well as judicial, authority. The impotence of the permanent court of arbitration at The Hague tribunal was a case in point. World peace, in his opinion, could be effected only by a concert of mature nations exercising "international police power." He repeated the words *police* and *power,* as well as *force* and *violence,* three times each before sitting down.

Carnegie, disgusted, gave up all faith that the Colonel would serve as his personal peace envoy at Potsdam. "There's a trace of the savage," he wrote, "in that original compound."

❧

THE NEXT ROYAL PERSON to greet Roosevelt, at Stockholm's Central Station early on the morning of 7 May, was Crown Prince William. He had news that threw into disarray all the future plans and protocol Lawrence Abbott had been working on. King Edward VII had died of pneumonia during the night.

Coughing and feverish himself, Roosevelt was relieved to have an excuse to shorten his stay in Sweden. Five weeks of being the most famous man in the world had been enough for him. He was happy to cede his title to a corpse, and did not care if he never stayed in another palace with European plumbing.

He sent a telegram to Berlin, asking if the Kaiser—King Edward's nephew—might "in view of the circumstances" like to withdraw his gracious offer of accommodations in the Royal Castle. Word came back that the German court had gone into official mourning. His Majesty, however, looked forward to entertaining Colonel Roosevelt privately, and to riding with him at the military exercises in Döberitz Field. After that, Wilhelm would leave for Great Britain, to attend the royal funeral. So would almost every other head of state and government leader on the Continent. The exact date of the ceremony would not be announced for several days. Only then could Roosevelt decide what to do about his own British engagements.

Meanwhile, there hung in the sky over Europe, fading slightly in the light of dawn, the immense apparition of Halley's Comet. It had shone with peculiar radiance in the small hours just after Edward died.

⌒

THE FIRST THING Roosevelt noticed, when his train reentered Germany on Monday, 9 May 1910, was the smallness of the crowds at every railway station. Some depots offered no welcome at all. Throughout every country he had traversed so far, he had been greeted "not as a king, but as something more than a king"—to quote one reporter in his entourage. Here, people who bothered to notice him at all were at best civil.

It was not dislike that showed on their faces, so much as lack of interest. They stolidly believed that Germany was the foremost nation in Europe, and would soon eclipse Britain as the world's dominant power. To them, Theodore Roosevelt represented a republic of inferior culture, distant, disorganized, racially inchoate. Their press was free, their educational system unsurpassed, their economy explosive, their social security the envy of other states. They had the strongest army on earth, and the second strongest navy. How long could Britain—with aging, inefficient factories, acute class conflict, and twenty-one million fewer citizens—afford to keep ahead of the *Kaiserreich* in battleship construction?

Germany's fields and forests were beautifully tended, its towns clean, its roads and rails smooth, its factories new and thrumming with energy. There were no equivalents of the peasant hovels of Hungary and Belgium, the slums of Italy, the trash heaps and hideous advertising that blighted the American scene. Neat shops and markets bulged with produce. The efficient movement of traffic in the streets, obedient to every police signal, bespoke a national desire for order and discipline. This was plainly a country where everything worked.

Except, to Roosevelt's amusement, the timing and choice of terminus for his arrival in Berlin. There was a frenzied scurrying of imperial officials before he was apologetically received at Stettiner Bahnhof at 9:15 A.M. on Tuesday. They said that the Kaiser would have been present if protocol had not confined him to Potsdam. His Majesty expected the whole Roosevelt family there at noon.

Checking in first at the American Embassy, Roosevelt sprayed his bronchi and prepared to meet a ruler he felt he had gotten to know almost personally as president. The prospect was not intimidating. Wilhelm II in 1910 was no longer the most dangerous man on the international scene. Two years earlier,

"THEY STOLIDLY BELIEVED THAT GERMANY WAS THE FOREMOST NATION IN EUROPE."

The Reich around the time of Roosevelt's visit.

he had come close to abdicating, after boasting too frankly about the German naval program to a British reporter. Since then, he had been further embarrassed by a homosexual scandal involving his circle of intimates. The hushed-up details were lurid enough for Wilhelm to remain in dread of the oligarchy of generals, admirals, and professors who held real power in Germany.

Fortunately for him, those Prussians were archtraditionalists, devoted to Hohenzollern rule. They thought of him as *their* homeland king, more than they cared about him being emperor of the multipartite Reich, which had yet to celebrate its fortieth anniversary. And *he* (a fantasist of Münchausian dimensions) saw himself as Frederick the Great reincarnated, with his love of male society, his need for performance art, and his obsession with military display.

He received the Roosevelts outside Frederick's Neue Palais, wearing the white-and-gold tunic of the Garde du Corps and a brass helmet, on which rode a silver spread eagle. Removed, the helmet revealed gray hair fast turning to white. At forty-nine the Kaiser was still, with his slate-blue eyes and erectile mustache, a transfixing figure—even if some of the fixity was provoked by his too-small left arm, cramped by forceps at birth.

Were it not for that deformity, and the laughable contrast between his finery and Roosevelt's black frock coat and top hat, the two men were alike enough to be brothers. They were the same height at five feet nine, the same weight at two hundred–odd pounds, and both hyperenergetic, with punchy gestures and body-shaking laughs. Their diction was clipped (the Kaiser spoke flawless English) and their talk torrential. But whereas Roosevelt was a careful listener and responder, Wilhelm heard little. He deviated in all directions, not out of evasiveness, but instability.

"HE . . . SINCERELY BELIEVED HIMSELF TO BE A DEMI-GOD."

Wilhelm II, Emperor of Germany, ca. 1910.

They sat apart during lunch in the Jasper Room, doing duty with each other's wives. Elsewhere around the six small tables, Kermit and Ethel followed suit with diplomats and government officials, including Chancellor Theobald von Bethmann-Hollweg. When the party adjourned to the Shell Room, Wilhelm and Roosevelt began a marathon conversation. They stood face-to-face under corals and iridescent *coquilles,* taking no notice when their aides consulted pocket watches.

Reporting afterward to the British historian Sir George Otto Trevelyan, Roosevelt wrote that he found the Kaiser affable and modest, and more humorous than most Prussians—although the humor turned to pomposity when Wilhelm was quizzed on subjects that he did not understand, "such as matters artistic and scientific." Military, economic, and social affairs found them both on equal ground, as did the "fundamentals of domestic morality." But Wilhelm would not go as far as Roosevelt in applying those fundamentals to foreign policy.

> At least we agreed in a cordial dislike of shams and of pretense, and therefore in a cordial dislike of the kind of washy movement for international peace with which Carnegie's name has become so closely associated. . . .
>
> I said to the Emperor that it seemed to me that a war between England and Germany would be an unspeakable calamity. He answered eagerly that he quite agreed with me, that such a war he regarded as unthinkable; and he continued, "I was brought up in England, very largely; I feel myself partly an Englishman. Next to Germany I care more for England than for any other country." Then with intense emphasis, "I ADORE ENGLAND!"

Roosevelt asked about the possibility of a moratorium in the Anglo-German arms race. Wilhelm at once stiffened, saying there was no point in discussing it. Germany "was bound to be powerful on the ocean." However, with his immense army, he was happy to let the Royal Navy maintain a strategic edge at sea. But English politicians must stop demonizing Germans as people bent on war.

This sounded reasonable enough to Roosevelt, and confirmed his impression that neither the Kaiser nor Bethmann-Hollweg had designs across the Channel. Wilhelm seemed much more concerned about the "Yellow Peril" of Japanese expansionism. "This I was rather glad to see, because I have always felt that it would be a serious situation if Germany, the only white power as well organized as Japan, should strike hands with Japan. The thing that prevents it is Germany's desire to stand well with Russia."

❧

BY THE TIME the Colonel got back to Berlin that night, his voice was completely gone. He was diagnosed with laryngitis on top of bronchitis, and begged off a dinner in his honor. But before he could retire, a cable from the White House removed all doubts about his future itinerary:

ROOSEVELT CARE AMERICAN EMBASSY BERLIN
I SHOULD BE GLAD IF YOU WOULD ACT AS SPECIAL AMBASSADOR
TO REPRESENT THE UNITED STATES AT THE FUNERAL OF KING
EDWARD VII. I AM SURE THAT THE ENGLISH PEOPLE WILL BE
HIGHLY GRATIFIED AT YOUR PRESENCE IN THIS CAPACITY AND
THAT OUR PEOPLE WILL STRONGLY APPROVE IT. HAVE AS YET
RECEIVED NO OFFICIAL NOTICE OF THE DATE OF FUNERAL BUT
IT IS REPORTED THAT IT WILL TAKE PLACE ON THE 20TH OF
THIS MONTH. PLEASE ANSWER.

WILLIAM H. TAFT

He cabled back, "Accept," and went to bed.

MORE VOCAL WEAR and tear threatened in the morning, when a yellow imperial limousine came to transport him to Döberitz Field for the army exercises. The Kaiser awaited him, resplendent in blue and gold. Roosevelt's slouch hat and khaki riding suit looked dingy in contrast. Henry White stood discreetly by, ready to mediate if needed.

"Roosevelt, *mein Freund,* I wish to welcome you in the presence of my guards," Wilhelm said, as the three men climbed onto their horses. "I ask you to remember that you are the only private citizen who ever reviewed the troops of Germany."

Roosevelt knew this was not true. General Leonard Wood, his old colleague from Cuba days, had been accorded the same courtesy in 1902, albeit as a senior officer of the U.S. Army. Perhaps Wilhelm was emphasizing the word *private.* But there was more to bother a foreign visitor, now, than semantics. The maneuvers he witnessed for the next five hours both amazed and depressed him. Five cavalry, six infantry, and four artillery regiments engaged in a clash of arms that made the charges at Vincennes look puny in comparison. Then the whole force split into two armies, each commanded by a Hohenzollern prince, and collided again. Battle conditions prevailed, with no hint of "game" playing, even when all three thousand troops marched past at the end, goose-stepping in salute to the Kaiser.

Lifting his hat every time Wilhelm touched his helmet, Roosevelt mantained a genial façade, but was aware only of the vast difference between himself and his host. It was not simply that the Kaiser held power, while he had none, nor the obvious fact that they were king and commoner. It was that he, self-made, had an integrated point of view, whereas Wilhelm personified the classic German neurosis of the *Doppelgänger.* Born to power, but also to disability, the Kaiser had "a sort of double-barreled perspective" on everything.

One self—the imperial—surveyed the passing troops, exulting in supreme command. The other self—Wilhelm's "mental ghost"—had ridden some way off, and was observing the whole scene with a quizzical detachment. Of the two, man and ghost, the former was the more disturbing to Roosevelt. "He was actually, as far as I could discover, one of the last of those curious creatures who sincerely believed himself to be a demi-god."

"The Colonel of the Rough Riders lecturing the
Chief of the German Army."
Wilhelm II's caption to this photograph of himself and Roosevelt at Döberitz.

When Edith saw her husband alone, late in the day, she got the feeling that he had undergone an epiphany. "I'm absolutely certain now, that we're all in for it," he told her. "Facts and figures . . . aren't half so convincing as the direct scrutiny of a thing—especially such a monstrous thing as this!"

HE RECOVERED HIS CHEERFULNESS overnight, along with much of his voice. This encouraged him to address the University of Berlin in person, dispensing with the offer of a substitute reader. The proceedings in the Aula auditorium amounted to a Germanic replay of those at the Sorbonne, only now, Roosevelt was made a *Doktor* of philosophy, and spoke with an emperor smiling and nodding at his feet.

Wilhelm had never visited the university before, so the atmosphere was stiff. Five jackbooted commanders of the student army corps stood immobile on the platform, swords drawn, throughout Roosevelt's eight-thousand-word speech. He gave it in English, but in view of its length it was untranslated, and received in a heavy silence. Defining his theme as "The World Movement," he began with a hoarse preamble on the rise and fall of civilizations. Germans, he said, had developed early as "castle-builders, city-founders, road-makers." They had turned back waves of barbaric invaders from the East, and helped Christianize Danes and Magyars and Slavs. He made much of the day when "the great house of Hohenzollern rose, the house which has at last seen Germany spring into a commanding position in the very forefront of the nations of mankind."

Roosevelt had learned as president that the Kaiser needed praise as much as oxygen, so he kept invoking imperial values as he went on. But when he remarked on the longevity of some cultures, as opposed to others that died, he used one of Wilhelm's least favorite words, dropping it like acid into the balm of his previous flattery. "Those ideas and influences in our lives which we can consciously trace back at all are in the great majority of instances to be traced to the Jew, the Greek, and the Roman."

Nor was he finished:

> The case of the Jew was quite exceptional. His was a small nation, of little more consequence than the sister nations of Moab and Damascus . . . [yet] he survived, while all his fellows died. In the spiritual domain he contributed a religion which has been the most potent of all factors in its effect on the subsequent history of mankind; but none of his other contributions compare with the legacies left us by the Greek and the Roman.

The last statement, at least, was calculated to get the Kaiser's head nodding again. Roosevelt swung into his main argument, which was that the spread of Greco-Roman culture across half the globe presaged the "world movement" now known as Western civilization. He listed the main features of European history since the invention of printing, in such primer-like fashion that scholars in the audience—many of whom had spent their careers studying the complexities of each—listened with expressions ranging from surprise to bemusement. Those who could understand English did not know whether they were being patronized, or merely disregarded by this species of *genus Americanus egotisticus*. Roosevelt certainly seemed to care little for the Kaiser's racial phobias:

> Here and there, instances occur where . . . an alien people is profoundly and radically changed by the mere impact of Western civiliza-

tion. The most extraordinary instance of this, of course, is Japan; for Japan's growth and change during the last half-century has been in many ways the most striking phenomenon of all history. Intensely proud . . . intensely loyal to certain of her past traditions, she has yet with a single effort wrenched herself free from all hampering ancient ties, and with a bound has taken her place among the leading civilized nations of mankind.

So much for the Yellow Peril. Roosevelt went on to suggest that the best aspirations of all modern cultures were connected, as never before, by a web of global communications. "The bonds are sometimes those of hatred rather than love, but they are bonds nevertheless."

As at the Sorbonne, he spoke too long, and equivocated too often. So the most cautionary part of his address, a reminder that the world's new interconnectedness could just as easily bring about its destruction, lulled more than it alarmed:

Forces for good and forces for evil are everywhere evident, each acting with a hundred- or a thousand-fold the intensity with which it acted in former ages. Over the whole earth the swing of the pendulum grows more and more rapid, the mainspring coils and spreads at a rate constantly quickening, the whole world movement is of constantly accelerating velocity. . . .

The machinery is so highly geared, the tension and strain are so great, the effort and the output have alike so increased, that there is cause to dread the ruin that would come from any great accident, from any breakdown, and also the ruin that may come from the mere wearing out of the machine itself.

But it was a warm afternoon, and the auditorium was stuffy. Here and there, grayheaded professors slept.

⁓

ROOSEVELT'S BERLIN UNIVERSITY ADDRESS was even less of a success than his speech in Christiania. Local newspapers gave it scant attention. Nevertheless, he enjoyed substantive interviews over the next two days with many eminent Berliners, from Bethmann-Hollweg and Admiral Alfred von Tirpitz to the aeronaut Count Zeppelin and the wildlife photographer C. G. Schillings. The German he had learned as a teenager in Dresden came back to him, and he had no difficulty making himself understood.

Back at the embassy, he was tickled to receive a set of photographs of himself and the Kaiser conversing at Döberitz. Each print was annotated on the back by Wilhelm, with heavy Prussian humor:

The Colonel of the Rough Riders lecturing the Chief of the German Army

A piece of good advice: "Carnegie is an old Peace bore"

The German and Anglo Saxon Races combined will keep the world in order!

Just before he left for London, an emissary came to ask if he would mind returning the pictures. Clearly, someone in the imperial suite dreaded that they might be published. But Roosevelt could already see them framed in glass, front and back, on display at his home in Oyster Bay.

"Oh, no," he said. "His Majesty the Kaiser gave the photographs to me and I propose to retain them."

CHAPTER 3

Honorabilem Theodorum

—————
—————

The man Flammonde, from God knows where,
With firm address and foreign air,
With news of nations in his talk
And something royal in his walk,
With glint of iron in his eyes,
But never doubt, nor yet surprise,
Appeared, and stayed, and held his head
As one with kings accredited.

ROOSEVELT EMERGED FROM his train at London's Victoria Station early on Monday, 16 May, with a band of black crape round his silk topper and another band around his left coat sleeve. A solemn and silver-bearded gentleman bade him welcome. It was Whitelaw Reid, whom five years before he had appointed American ambassador to the Court of St. James's. Another familiar figure pushed forward, lean, long-faced, unmistakably English: his old friend Arthur Lee, M.P. Both men were wealthy, with stately homes in the country, and both were competing to introduce Roosevelt to the *ne plus ultra* of British society.

Reid had won the first round, since protocol demanded that the special ambassador stay in his official residence, Dorchester House. But Roosevelt planned to escape from that gilded prison as soon as the funeral obsequies were over. He preferred the self-effacing Lee to Reid, who, like so many former press barons, was inclined to be pompous.

For the next six or seven days, he had to behave with extreme formality. He was assigned a royal carriage, a military attaché, two British aides-de-camp, six grenadier guards, and even a bugler, to herald his comings and goings. Reid explained that he must make calls at all the noble houses and ranking embassies in London, and be at home when his calls were returned. He should be particularly solicitous toward the monarchs and ministers who had entertained him in Europe. On Thursday, he would take his place among the grandest of these grandees at a pre-funeral banquet in Buckingham Palace, and on Friday, join them in following Edward VII's cortège to Windsor Castle.

Although his special status would lapse after that, Roosevelt found himself committed to a packed schedule of interviews, reunions, lunches, teas, and dinners that would fill his every waking hour for the next three weeks. In short, he would see little of Edith and even less of his children. In view of Kermit's apparent resolve to mourn Edward in a panama hat, that was probably just as well.

First of all, homage had to be paid to the new king. Roosevelt breakfasted at the embassy, then proceeded with Reid to Marlborough House, where George V awaited them.

His Majesty turned out to be a fortyish retired naval officer, simple and unaffected in manner. He thanked Roosevelt for making a salutary speech at Cairo University, and wondered if "something of the kind, but stronger," could be said in London. Roosevelt offered to do so at a reception planned for him in the Guildhall, at the end of the month. But it would be necessary to get the approval of Sir Edward Grey, the British foreign secretary. The King gratefully kept talking for almost an hour, and introduced him to Queen Mary and other members of the royal family.

Roosevelt's laryngitis was still bad enough that he spoke with occasional gasps. For the first time in his life he obeyed a royal command, and went to Edward VII's personal throat doctor for treatment. As a result, he was hardpressed to make his appointments with other heads of state before lunch.

His "at home" sojourn that afternoon offered little respite. No sooner had he climbed Reid's marble stairway to deal with his correspondence than a footman portentously announced, "The King of Norway is below, sir."

Roosevelt threw down his pen in mock annoyance. "Confound these kings; will they never let me alone!"

⁓

HIS LAST VISITOR of the day was royalty of another sort. If Alice Roosevelt Longworth was no longer, at twenty-six, the scintillating "Princess Alice" she had been before her marriage, she had matured into a more complex, richly eccentric personality. Always exquisitely dressed, in rembrandt hats and fabrics that complemented her long-lashed, amethyst eyes, she now sported a cigarette holder, and knew just when to wave it, as she smokily discharged one of her patented sarcasms. In contrast to her sedate half sister, Alice was a born socialite, happiest under the chandeliers of the very rich. However, she also had a yen for rough, male political parlors—as her father had, in that never-mentioned period when he was married to the original Alice.

She floated into Dorchester House an hour before midnight, fresh from a transatlantic steamer, bringing a gale of Washington gossip with her. Alice's chat amounted to primary information, for she was a favorite of President Taft, and the wife of one of his closest associates, Congressman Nicholas

Longworth of Cincinnati. She clearly saw that her father's return home was going to cause a crisis of leadership in the Republican Party. At all costs he must stay aloof from politics—unless in his heart he wanted to be president again. Alice certainly wanted that in *her* heart. She had buried what she called "a voodoo" in the White House garden.

"A BORN SOCIALITE, HAPPIEST UNDER
THE CHANDELIERS OF THE VERY RICH."

Alice Roosevelt Longworth, ca. 1910.

FOR THE REST OF THE WEEK Roosevelt went about his business, while hundreds of other envoys fulfilled similar obligations. Name after titled name crowded his calendar: the Princess Royal, the Duke and Duchess of Connaught, King George of Greece, Prince and Princess Christian, the Duke of Norfolk, Princess Henry of Battenberg, the Marquess of Londonderry, the

Duchess of Argyll, Lords Lansdowne, Clarendon, and Cromer. More to his taste was an interview with Sir Edward Grey—"one of the finest fellows I ever met."

Emerging one morning from Buckingham Palace with Henry White, he was pounced on by Wilhelm II. "My dear friend, I am so glad to have arrived in time to see you. . . . I have an hour to spare, and we can have a good talk." Roosevelt glanced at his watch and said that, unfortunately, he was not quite as free. "I'll give you twenty minutes."

His bluntness was so unlike the reverence Wilhelm was used to that it beguiled rather than offended. The Kaiser settled for as long as he would stop, and was rewarded with inside information on what members of the House of Lords felt about Germany's naval program. Roosevelt was uninhibited in saying what he thought of scaremongers like Lord Londonderry: "No more brains than those of a guinea-pig." Wilhelm quoted this remark in a cable to Bethmann-Hollweg. It did not seem to cross his mind that the Colonel might be just as frank in talking about *him* to British leaders.

By late Thursday afternoon, as Roosevelt sat at tea in Dorchester House with a large company of English and American guests, he was beginning to show symptoms of explosive effervescence, as always in periods of intense activity. "I'm going to a Wake this evening," he wheezed, chortling. Heads turned in shock as he repeated, "I'm going to a Wake at Buckingham Palace!"

⊸

"I HARDLY KNOW what else to call it," he wrote afterward, in a private account of his service as a diplomat. At one protocol level, the "wake," hosted by George V, was a gathering of some seventy special ambassadors, many of them royal; at another, it amounted to a dinner in honor of Wilhelm II, the senior monarch present.

In contrast to the star-studded uniforms on display, Roosevelt wore what the State Department considered appropriate for a representative of the New World: a swallow-tailed black suit with black studs in his boiled shirt-front. Minus the studs and plus a top hat, it would do him as well at the funeral. For all the severity of his appearance and carefully solemn expression, the satirist in him saw that the next twenty-four hours were going to be rich in comedy.

He was buttonholed at once by the self-styled "Tsar" of Bulgaria, who was a pariah at the party for having recently declared his country an empire. The bearded former prince was triumphant after denying Archduke Franz Ferdinand of Austria-Hungary transit rights through his *wagon-lit* on the train they had shared from Vienna to Calais. As a result, the archduke had been forced to alight at station stops whenever he got hungry, and march furiously down the platform to the dining car.

Wilhelm II did not find this as funny as Roosevelt did. Seeing him in conversation with the Tsar, he walked up and thrust himself between them. "Roosevelt, my friend, I want to introduce you to the King of Spain. *He* is worth talking to."

That proved to be the case, although there was a chilly moment when Alfonso XIII said, "I have admired your career, and I have also admired your military career, though I am sorry that your honors should have been won at the expense of my countrymen." Evidently, memories of the Spanish-American War still rankled south of the Pyrenees. The King went on to express gratification over the Vatican incident, saying that Catholicism in Spain had begun to encroach intolerably upon civilian life, and was causing an anarchist backlash, not unlike that in the Balkans. "I assure you that much though I object to the anarchists, I do not regard them as more dangerous to my country than are the ultraclericals. Of the two, I mind the extreme right even more than I mind the extreme left."

Roosevelt had been saying the same thing, in almost identical words, for at least ten years, and was proportionately impressed.

His solemnity was further strained when Stéphen Pichon, the French minister of foreign affairs, approached him for a republican *tête-à-tête*.

> He is a queer looking creature at best, but on this particular evening anger made him look like a gargoyle. His clothes were stiff with gold lace and he wore sashes and orders. . . . He got me aside and asked me in French, as he did not speak English, what colored coat my coachman had worn that evening. I told him that I did not know; whereupon he answered that his coachman had a black coat. I nodded and said Yes, I thought mine had a black coat also. He responded with much violence that this was an outrage, a slight upon the two great republics, as all the Royalties' coachmen wore red coats, and that he would at once make a protest on behalf of us both. I told him to hold on, that he must not make any protests on my behalf, that I did not care what kind of coat my coachman wore, and would be perfectly willing to see him wear a green coat with yellow splashes—"un paletot vert avec des tauches jaunes" being my effort at idiomatic rendering of the idea, for I speak French, I am sorry to say, as if it were a non-Aryan tongue, without tense or gender, although with agglutinative vividness and fluency. My incautious incursion into levity in a foreign tongue met appropriate punishment, for I spent the next fifteen minutes in eradicating from Pichon's mind the belief that I was demanding these colors as my livery.

The Kaiser swooped again when he saw Roosevelt being accosted by the henpecked Prince Consort of Holland. The King of Denmark introduced the

King of Greece, whom he already knew. Monarch vied with monarch in getting him to tell stories of Africa, Cuba, and "the Wild West."

As the all-male evening dragged on through dinner and cordials and cigars, Roosevelt was treated to royal confidences of embarrassing intimacy. Prince Ernest of Cumberland complained that "if it were not for him"—glowering across the table at Wilhelm II—"he would be the King of Hanover." The King of Greece begged him to lend his voice to Greek claims on Crete, just as George V wanted him to do on behalf of British rule in Egypt. Even after he had said goodnight, three more kings pursued him to the palace door.

> They knew that I was not coming back to Europe, that I would never see them again, or try in any way to keep up relations with them; and so they felt free to treat [me] with an intimacy, and on a footing of equality, which would have been impossible with a European. . . . In a way, although the comparison sounds odd, these sovereigns, in their relations among themselves and with others, reminded me of the officers and wives in one of our western army posts in the old days, when they were shut up together and away from the rest of the world, were sundered by an impassable gulf from the enlisted men and the few scouts, hunters and settlers round about, and were knit together into one social whole, and nevertheless were riven asunder by bitter jealousies, rivalries, and dislikes.

FRIDAY, 20 MAY 1910, was a day so beautiful that all London seemed to want to be outdoors and see the procession scheduled to depart from Buckingham Palace at 9:30 A.M. Hours before the first drumbeat sounded, a mass of humanity blocked every approach to the parade route along the Mall to Westminster Hall. There was little noise and less movement as the crowd waited under a cloudless sky. Green Park was at its greenest. The air, washed clean by rain overnight, was sweet and warm, alive with birdsong.

Roosevelt arrived early in the palace yard, where horses and coaches were lining up, and was again accosted by a furious Stéphen Pichon. The Duke of Norfolk had decreed that because of their lack of royal uniforms, they could not ride with the mounted mourners. Instead, they were to share a dress landau. Pichon noted, in a voice shaking with rage, that it would be eighth in a sequence of twelve, behind a carriage packed with Chinese imperials of uncertain gender. Not only that, it was a closed conveyance, whereas some royal ladies up front had been assigned "glass coaches."

The landau struck Roosevelt as luxurious all the same, and he admitted afterward, in describing the funeral, that he had never heard of glass coaches "excepting in connection with Cinderella." But Pichon could not be calmed down:

He continued that "ces Chinois" were put ahead of us. To this I answered that any people dressed as gorgeously as "ces Chinois" ought to go ahead of us; but he responded that it was not a laughing matter. Then he added that "ce Perse" had been put in with us, pointing out a Persian prince of the blood royal, a deprecatory, inoffensive-looking Levantine of Parisian education, who was obviously ill at ease, but whom Pichon insisted upon regarding as somebody who wanted to be offensive. At this moment our coach drove up, and Pichon bounced into it. I suppose he had gotten in to take the right-hand rear seat, to which I was totally indifferent. . . . But Pichon was scrupulous in giving me precedence, although I have no idea whether I was entitled to it or not. He sat on the left rear seat himself, stretched his arm across the right seat and motioned me to get in so that "ce Perse" should not himself take the place of honor! Accordingly I got in, and the unfortunate Persian followed, looking about as unaggressive as a rabbit in a cage with two boa constrictors.

Band music blared as the gates of the palace opened and the Duke of Connaught rode out onto the Mall, escorting the two chief mourners, George V and Wilhelm II. Behind them came file upon file of mounted monarchs, princes, dukes, pashas, and sultans. The pace of the procession was so slow that people in the crowd were able, with the help of printed lists, to identify every strange or famous face. Eyes lingered longer on the Kaiser than on King George. He sat erect on a gray charger, helmet and jeweled orders flashing in the sun, his little left arm curving into the horse's reins in a practiced *trompe l'oeil*.

When the last royal rider, Prince Bovaradej of Siam, had meekly trailed a posse of minor-state European dukes out the gates, the coaches and carriages started to roll. Edith Roosevelt stood with Kermit and Ethel on a private balcony overlooking the park, searching for her husband's landau. They were among the few spectators to pay any attention to it when it passed. Roosevelt sat well back, with the strange reticence that sometimes overcame him on ceremonial occasions, avoiding eye contact with the crowd. There was no indicating that he was being subjected to a further Gallic tirade:

Pichon's feelings overcame him. . . . He pointed out the fact that we were following "toutes ces petites royautés," even "le roi du Portugal." I then spoke to him seriously, and said that in my judgment France and the United States were so important that it was of no earthly consequence whether their representatives went before or behind the representatives of utterly insignificant little nations like Portugal, and that I thought it was a great mistake to make a fuss about it, because it showed a lack of self-confidence. He shook his head, and said that in

Europe they regarded these things as of real importance, and that if I would not join him in a protest he would make one on his own account. I answered that I very earnestly hoped that he would not make a row at a funeral (my French failed me at this point, and I tried alternately "funéraille" and "pompe funèbre"), that it would be sure to have a bad effect.

A Franco-American accord (Persia abstaining) was reached before the landau made its first stop in Parliament Square. Pichon agreed to wait and see where he was seated later in the day, at lunch in Windsor Castle, before making his placement a *casus belli* that might prevent France's attendance at the future coronation of George V.

THE ENORMOUS PARADE, growing ever more brilliant as the sun climbed high, looked almost festive until King Edward's coffin was brought out from Westminster Hall, to a single toll of Big Ben. Cannons boomed across the river. The casket was placed on a gun carriage, which led the way up Whitehall. By now, the procession was a mile long. Moving to the implacable rhythm of funeral marches by Handel, Beethoven, and Chopin, it took over an hour to get to Marble Arch. Roosevelt remained unobtrusive, but caught the eye of Sir Arthur Conan Doyle, reporting for the *Daily Mail:* "One remembers the strong profile of the great American, set like granite as he leans back in his carriage."

Another profile, less strong but equally expressionless, was that of the heir to the thrones of Austria and Hungary. Franz Ferdinand, plumed and corseted, gave off waves of hauteur that disagreeably affected many observers. An American correspondent predicted that the archduke was "destined to make history in Southeastern Europe."

Belgium's enormous young king made a handsome figure, modestly dressed in a dark uniform that reproved the baroque costumes of the German dukes. They in turn failed to match the splendor of the Bulgarian Tsar, sweating under a white fur hat and carbuncled from groin to shoulder with decorations. The Tsar whom everybody would have preferred to see had stayed home in Russia, preoccupied with a pogrom against the Jews of Kiev. He was represented by his brother and mother.

Epaulettes pulsed like golden jellyfish and hundreds of medals swayed as the Earl Marshal, worrying about the approach of noon, tried to hurry his lead horses down the Edgware Road to Paddington. By 11:57 every dignitary expected at Windsor for the interment service was aboard the waiting royal train. It departed with no further ceremony, hauling a white-domed coffin car. Bystanders on the platform who had watched that equipage bearing away the Victorian Age, only nine years before, now saw it carry off the Edwardian.

M. PICHON'S MOOD began to improve when he was required to walk ahead of Roosevelt on the long march from Windsor Station to the castle. The midday heat was stifling, and only an occasional breeze darkened the buttercup

"EPAULETTES PULSED LIKE GOLDEN JELLYFISH."
Roosevelt (far right) marches in the funeral procession of Edward VII, 20 May 1910.

fields stretching down to the Thames. Roosevelt suffered in his black clothes. For some reason, his aides-de-camp had made him carry an overcoat. He shifted it uncomfortably from arm to arm, making no attempt to keep step with his marching companions. It was plain that the special ambassador of the United States had had enough of *pompe funèbre*.

But there was more to come. The cloister of St. George's Chapel was heavy with the scent of stacked flowers. Members of His Majesty's government sat waiting inside. To the delight of one socialistic reporter, there were no pews available for the royal mourners. They stood perspiring, awkwardly jockeying for position as the burial service got under way. Their swords and thigh boots made kneeling difficult, and getting up even more so. The liturgy was interminable, and the air in the room almost too close to breathe. Roosevelt began to look pale under what was left of his African tan.

Not until almost two o'clock did the coffin descend into the crypt. The mourners filed by to take a last look at it—Wilhelm II visibly distraught—then adjourned for lunch in the castle. Roosevelt sat at the King's table. M. Pichon sat at Queen Mary's, and seemed satisfied that the honor of France had been restored.

⌁

THAT EVENING ROOSEVELT and his best English friend, Sir Cecil Spring Rice, were entertained to dinner at Brooks's Club by Lord Haldane, the Liberal minister of war.

"Dear old Springy" was now fifty-one, and a senior ambassador in the British diplomatic corps. He was deeply versed in the affairs of Germany, Belgium, Russia, and the United States, as well as those of Turkey, Persia, and Japan. From his current posting in Stockholm, he was able to keep a close watch on German naval aggrandizement in the Baltic, and quailed at it even more than Lord Londonderry.

Roosevelt enjoyed discussing grand strategy with Spring Rice, but the presence of another guest at Haldane's table diverted his attention. David Lloyd George, the merry-faced chancellor of the exchequer, was the most revolutionary force to erupt in Parliament since the days of Reform, eighty years before. His "People's Budget," enacted just one week before King Edward's death, had plunged Britain into a governmental crisis so acute that Conservatives—Arthur Lee agitatedly among them—were predicting the collapse of its historic class system into socialism, or worse. Lloyd George was no socialist, but for years, as the Liberal Party's radical evangelist, he had looked for a means of destroying the power of the House of Lords. He had found his weapon in a budget that proposed a supertax on all unearned income and inherited estates. Prime Minister Asquith's government was now threatening a general election, in order to force through a Parliament Bill that would abolish the notion of an unelected upper house. If that happened, nearly a thousand years of landed privilege were to be swept away by the little Welshman who now sat breaking bread at Brooks's.

Fond as Roosevelt was of Tories like Lee, he found himself more drawn to Lloyd George, Haldane, and other Liberals who had come to power during his own, increasingly progressive, second term as president. (One exception was Winston Churchill, whom he considered to be a boor and a turncoat, and refused to see.) He admired the laws they had passed to benefit workers, pensioners, aspiring homeowners, and small traders. They seemed to be irresolute in formulating foreign policy, but he suspected that Sir Edward Grey supported the new king's desire for a stronger imperial presence overseas.

Five days after the funeral, he breakfasted with Sir Edward and showed him a draft of his proposed Guildhall speech. It was as provocative toward "Little Englanders" as his Cairo address had been toward Egyptian Nationalists. The foreign secretary approved every word, unconcerned that many members of the British establishment were bound to find it presumptuous.

⟨━⟩

BY THEN, ROOSEVELT had forsaken Whitelaw Reid's luxurious hospitality ("Not exactly what I am used to at home") and was staying with Edith and Alice in Arthur Lee's town house on Chesterfield Street. Kermit and Ethel were off on a tour of Scotland. He could not escape so easily. Determined visitors kept ringing Lee's doorbell: Conan Doyle, Rudyard Kipling, the hunter Frederick Courtney Selous, Kogoro Takahira, the former Japanese ambassador in Washington, even Seth Bullock, the sheriff of Deadwood County, South Dakota. They were more congenial to him than the royals he had endured for the past seven weeks. "I felt if I met another king I should bite him!"

On 26 May he went to Cambridge University to accept an honorary LL.D. and found, to his pleasure, that undergraduates seemed to be in control there. A Teddy bear greeted him, sitting with outstretched paws on the ancient cobbles. At the end of the ceremony in the Senate House, a second, monstrous Teddy was winched down from the gallery to hang over his head. He was informed that Charles Darwin had been similarly saluted with an ape, and Viscount Kitchener with an effigy of the Mahdi.

Coincidentally, he met Kitchener two days later at Chequers, Lee's Elizabethan manor in Buckinghamshire. The hero of Omdurman repelled him as a large, squinting loudmouth, "everlastingly posing as a strong man." Just back from seven years in command of the Indian Army, Kitchener was as overbearing as he was opinionated. He said that the United States had made "a great mistake" in not building a sea-level canal in Panama. Roosevelt cited the advice of engineers to the contrary.

"All I would do in such a case," Kitchener declared, "would be to say, 'I order that a sea-level canal be dug, and I wish to hear nothing more about it.'"

"If you say so. But I wonder if you remember the conversation between Glendower and Hotspur, when Glendower says, 'I can call spirits from the vasty deep,' and Hotspur answers, 'So can I, and so can any man, but will they come?'"

Lee's other guests that weekend were easier to take. The most distinguished of them was Arthur James Balfour, who had been prime minister during Roosevelt's first term as president, and was now leader of the Opposition. Balfour, like Kitchener, was a bachelor, but in all other respects the viscount's opposite: languid, cerebral, delicate as any aesthete drawn by Aubrey Beardsley. The delicacy was deceptive. For thirty-five years Balfour had trodden softly on the bodies of men who underestimated him.

He was now sixty-one, with a good chance of becoming prime minister again, if the Liberals failed in their assault on the House of Lords. At first, Roosevelt was not inclined to show him much respect. Balfour, he thought, was responsible for much of the war talk he had heard in Europe, having recently announced that there was an international consensus that Great Britain was "predestined to succumb in some great contest," with a country that sounded very like Germany. Was the Tory leader just another doomsayer like Lord Londonderry, and had British Conservatism become a negative force, recoiling from the new dynamics of the twentieth century?

Arthur Lee wanted to counteract such doubts by getting them into a strategic conversation. The problem was, Balfour was shy and needed to be warmed, like a cold honeycomb, before any sweetness began to flow.

That happened sooner than Lee expected. Balfour, the author of several works of philosophy, had admired Roosevelt for years as a fellow scholar in politics. He had been overwhelmed in 1908 to receive a two-thousand-word letter from Roosevelt in praise of his book *Decadence*. In it, the President of the United States had swallowed whole his basic premise—that a civilization could not advance unless its elite was made to comprehend technological revolutions—but had extended it into the field of biology, comparing the disappearance of South America's post-Tertiary fauna to just such a failure to adapt to what was new and strange.

"So it is, of course, with nations," Roosevelt had written.

In view of his own party's failure to adapt to the rise of the Liberal species, Balfour had begun to wonder if the torch of Western leadership should not pass out of British hands into those of this prodigal American. Who was better qualified to become the first truly global statesman of the twentieth century, pulling together North America, Britain, and the whiter parts of the British Empire into one giant power bloc?

He had gone so far as to draft a proposal, entitled "The Possibility of an Anglo-Saxon Federation," for Roosevelt and Edward VII to consider before they met. Perhaps the former president could be put at the head of such a superpower, balancing the Occident against the Orient, the Northern Hemisphere against the Southern, and, by virtue of overwhelming naval superiority, dictating universal peace.

"It would be a fitting conclusion to Roosevelt's career," Balfour wrote in a covering note to the King, "that he should go down in history as the prime author of the greatest confederation the world has ever seen."

For some reason, possibly relating to Edward's death, he had abandoned his grand design. But Arthur Lee was delighted to see the former prime minister and former president hitting it off. Their minds, in his own expression, "fizzed chemically."

The other guests at Chequers that weekend—Field Marshal Earl Roberts of Kandahar, Alfred Lyttelton M.P., and Cecil Spring Rice—shared a gloomy sense of Britain's imperial decline. Roosevelt took advantage of their presence to discuss his forthcoming speech on Egypt.

"I never heard a man talk so continuously, or eloquently about himself," Balfour's secretary J. S. Sandars wrote afterward. "Amusing too after his fashion. He said that if we allowed Egypt to slip, as it was doing, out of our control, the first consequence would be seen in India."

⁂

WHICH WAS MORE or less what Roosevelt said again at the Guildhall the following Tuesday, ignoring the stares of the Lord Mayor of London and his red-robed aldermen. They had just awarded him the freedom of the city, and had not expected a lecture in return. But he was no longer an ambassador, and felt it his duty to help King George and other defenders of the Empire.

He said he had just spent nearly a year in four British protectorates on the African continent. "You are so very busy at home that I am not sure whether you realize just how things are, in some places at least, abroad."

This allusion to the crisis in Parliament got a few nervous laughs. In venturing some advice about handling native unrest along the Nile, he said, he wished only to pass on what he had learned himself, as President, during the Philippines insurrection. "You have given Egypt the best government it has had for at least two thousand years—probably a better government than it has ever had before; for never in history has the poor man in Egypt, the tiller of the soil, the ordinary laborer, been treated with as much justice and mercy. . . . Yet recent events, and especially what has happened in connection with and following on the assassination of Boutros Pasha three months ago, have shown that, in certain vital points, you have erred; and it is for you to make good your error."

Sir Edward Grey, sitting on the dais with Balfour and Arthur Lee, whispered delightedly, "This will cause a devil of a row." Some other distinguished guests, including Conan Doyle and John Singer Sargent, applauded more out of surprise than gratification. Were they being spoken to, or scolded?

Britain's "error," Roosevelt explained, lay in doing too much, rather than too little, to appease Egyptian feelings. "Uncivilized peoples" needed education and example. Fanatics in their midst throve on softhearted concessions. The willingness of Egyptian Nationalists to engage in sedition and murder had shown that they had no real understanding of democratic process. They would make "a noxious farce" of independence, if it was granted any time soon. "Of all broken reeds," Roosevelt declared, "sentimentality is the most broken reed on which righteousness can lean."

Scattered cheers were heard as he grew more peremptory:

Such are the conditions; and where the effort made by your officials to help the Egyptians toward self-government is taken advantage of by them . . . to try to bring murderous chaos upon the land, then it becomes the primary duty of whoever is responsible for the government in Egypt to establish order, and to take whatever measures are necessary to that end. [*"Hear! Hear!"*]

. . . Now, either you have the right to be in Egypt or you have not. Either it is or it is not your duty to establish and keep order. [*"Hear! Hear!"*] If you feel that you have not the right to be in Egypt, if you do not wish to establish and to keep order there, why, then, by all means get out of Egypt. [*"Hear! Hear!"*]

"I just *love* that man," Balfour said afterward.

WHEN ROOSEVELT CAME DOWN to breakfast next morning, Lee greeted him with, "Well, the attitude of the English newspapers can best be expressed in the one word 'gasp.' "

Liberal newspapers were infuriated that a foreigner, however distinguished, should instruct His Majesty's government in condominium policy. "No summary can do justice to the vulgarity and ignorance of the oration which Mr. Roosevelt delivered at the Guildhall," the *National Review* remarked. The *Daily Chronicle* felt he had "outraged every conventional canon of official and international propriety." *The Nation* excoriated his "jackboot doctrine" of might over right, and obvious contempt for Islam. "Mr. Roosevelt talked as if the whole Egyptian people had adopted assassination as a political method," commented the *Manchester Guardian.* "This is not robust or virile thinking; it is muddled, boyish thinking."

Conservative reactions were more favorable, if stunned. The *Pall Mall Gazette*—Lee's kind of paper—said that the former president had delivered "a great and memorable speech that will be read and pondered over throughout the world." *The Times* reproved him for taking freedom of the city too far, but granted that his basic intent was "friendly." The *Daily Telegraph* praised him for his candor, and asserted that Britain had "no intention of going," either from Egypt or India. And the editor of *The Spectator* thanked him for "giving us so useful a reminder of our duty."

After a few days, two of the most acerbic columnists in the country weighed in. George Bernard Shaw praised Roosevelt's performance "in his new character of the Innocent Abroad," and suggested that if Britain was indeed qualified to govern other peoples without their consent, it should recolonize America. W. T. Stead, the editor of *Review of Reviews,* remarked apropos of the murder of Boutros Pasha, "We have caught the assassin, tried him, and sentenced him to death. What more did Mr. Roosevelt do when an assassin made him President of the United States?"

⌇

WHEN FURTHER COMPLAINTS were heard in Parliament about Roosevelt's "insult" to the intelligence of the British people, Balfour rose in his defense. "I was an auditor of that speech," he said, "and I hope I am not less sensitive than others." No foreign observer could have delivered "a kindlier, more appreciative, and more sympathetic treatment of the problem with which we have long had to deal, and of which America is now feeling the pinch."

Sir Edward Grey spoke next. "I should have thought that to everybody the friendly intention of that speech would be obvious. . . . It was, taken as a whole, the greatest compliment to the work of one country in the world ever paid by the citizen of another."

So with hyperbole on both sides of the aisle, the Little Englanders were confounded. Roosevelt spent a few relaxed days in London, gallery-hopping with Edith and lunching with a grateful King George. "He has enjoyed himself hugely," Spring Rice wrote to a friend, "and I must say, by the side of our statesmen, looks a little bit taller, bigger and stronger."

The Colonel declined to be taken too seriously. When a report went around that he had murmured, "*Ah! Tempora mutantur!*" in front of one of Frith's vast panoramas of Victorian life, he telegrammed a denial to the editor of *Punch*.

STATEMENT INCORRECT. I NEVER USE ANY LANGUAGE SO
MODERN AS LATIN WHILE LOOKING AT PICTURES. ON THE
OCCASION IN QUESTION MY QUOTATIONS WERE FROM
CUNEIFORM SCRIPT AND THE PARTICULAR SENTENCE TO
WHICH YOU REFER WAS THE PRE-NUNEVITE PHRASE HULLY-GEE.

⌇

ONE LAST PUBLIC appearance was required of him before he left the Old World for the New: his Romanes Lecture at Oxford University on Tuesday, 7 June. For once, Roosevelt was not sure of himself. He wanted to strike the right donnish tone, which did not come as naturally to him as the hortatory. His subject, "Biological Analogies in History," was one he had pondered since discovering, as a teenager, that he was equally drawn to science and the humanities. It seemed to him that these disciplines, rigorously separated in the nineteenth century, might draw closer again in the twentieth, as scientists looked for narrative explanations of the mysteries of nature, and scholars became more abstract and empirical in their weighing of evidence. Evolutionary science, in particular, had much to teach historians studying the rise and fall of civilizations.

At first, the proceedings in Oxford's Sheldonian Theatre seemed appropriately formal. Lord Curzon of Kedleston, the university chancellor, introduced him in Latin as "Honorabilem Theodorum Roosevelt," who by virtue of public achievements, merited a doctorate in civil law. As beadles escorted him onstage, Curzon's prose turned to poetry:

> *Hic vir, hic est, tibi quem promitti saepius audis,*
> *Cuius in adventum pavidi cessere cometae*
> *Et septemgemini turbant trepida ostia Nili!*

A translation of these lines was helpfully printed in the official program:

> *Behold, Vice-Chancellor, the promised wight,*
> *Before whose coming comets turned to flight,*
> *And all the startled mouths of sevenfold Nile took fright!*

Roosevelt took his place amid general laughter. It became evident that members of the Oxford faculty fancied themselves as classical wits. Perhaps they had heard about his telegram to *Punch*. Speakers compared him to Hercules in his battle against the trusts, and to Ulysses for his wanderings after a period *in Africae solitudinibus*. Henry Goudy, regius professor of civil law, archly noted that the Colonel had served two terms in the White House, and might yet extend that record to three—*numero auspicatissimo*, "most auspicious of numbers."

Curzon, draping Roosevelt in scholarly silk, hailed him as *Strenuissime, insignissime civium toto orbe terrae hodie agentum*—"Most strenuous of men, most distinguished of citizens dominating today's world scene." In a final access of humor, the chancellor praised his friendliness toward all men—*ne nigerrimum quidem*—"even the blackest of the black."

At least there was no giant Teddy bear to detract from Roosevelt's dignity when he mounted the podium and began his lecture. He said that as an eighth-generation American visiting the heart of English academia, he felt less "alien" than one of his Dutch, French, Irish, or Scottish ancestors might have, in "the spacious days of great Elizabeth." The phrase was a quotation from Tennyson. He left it unattributed, not wanting to condescend to his hosts, and swung into his main text with an eloquence that made their earlier joshing sound sophomoric:

> More than ever before in the world's history, we of today seek to penetrate the causes of the mysteries that surround not only mankind but

all life, both in the present and the past. We search, we peer, we see things dimly; here and there we get a ray of clear vision, as we look before and after. We study the tremendous procession of the ages, from the immemorial past when in "cramp elf and saurian forms" the creative forces "swathed their too-much power," down to the yesterday— a few score thousand years distant only—when the history of man became the overwhelming fact in the history of life on this planet. And studying, we see strange analogies in the phenomena of life and death, of birth, growth, and change, between those physical groups of animal life which we designate as species, forms, races, and the highly complex and composite entities which rise before our minds when we speak of nations and civilizations.

Only the continued use of blind quotations betrayed his uncertainty as an academic speaker. Echoing Balfour, he called for a scientific literature that went beyond jargon, so that tomorrow's humanists could synthesize and explain what today seemed so confusing. He conceded that patterns in natural and human history did not duplicate one another. "Yet there is a certain parallelism. There are strange analogies; it may be that there are homologies." He spoke for almost a quarter of an hour about the development of higher lifeforms, from Eocene beginnings through the arrival of *Homo erectus*. Phylogenetically, he said, the word *new* denoted only a trend deviant enough to seem original. The same was often true of obsolescence: what looked like extinction might just be transformation. Thus, the small three-toed *Neohipparion* had variously become the horse, the donkey, and the zebra.

Clearly enjoying himself, Roosevelt ranged over some of the factors, environmental, pathological, and geomorphological, that determined which species should flourish or disappear. He applied them to the evolution of societies. All the modern countries of Western Europe had arisen from earlier Teutonic and Nordic ethnic overflows, mixing like cold rivers with the warm sea of Roman civilization. He defined two types of neonate states—those growing out of barbarism, and those mutating from previous cultures—and left unsaid the implication that the difference between them was that obtaining between Germanic or Slavic nations on the one hand, and Britannic or Japanese on the other. Evolution aside, there were differing types of "death" in human societies, such as those of the Greeks and Romans who once dominated all of Asia Minor and North Africa. For nearly a thousand years they had flourished, civilizing each community they absorbed. "Then they withered like dry grass before the flame of the Arab invasion."

Roosevelt nudged his thesis into modern times by arguing, in words he would certainly not have risked at the University of Berlin, that anthropological science now clearly perceived "how artificial most great nationalities are."

At least, in the racial sense: "There is an element of unconscious and rather pathetic humor in the simplicity of half a century ago which spoke of the Aryan and the Teuton with reverential admiration, as if the words denoted, not merely something definite, but something ethnologically sacred." Nationality was not myth, but a matter of common speech and purpose, of values shared between peoples whose origins might be various.

He acknowledged "that these great artificial societies acquire such unity that in each one all the parts feel a subtle sympathy, and move or cease to move, go forward or go back, all together, in response to some stir or throbbing, very powerful, and yet not to be discerned by our senses." But whatever romance attached to nationalism had little to do with race.

Roosevelt was using the last word carefully, distinguishing it from *ethnic,* which he made clear had only cultural connotations for him, as *ethnos* had for the Ancient Greeks. Turning to a subject much more sensitive to his audience, he ventured some of the reasons why empires went into decline. One was when the sovereign authority devolved too much power to its provinces. In that case, "the centrifugal forces overcome the centripetal," and the whole flew to pieces. He cited also greed, love of luxury, declining birth-rates, and loss of the "fighting edge."

These drumskins, which he had been pounding for a quarter of a century, awoke the politician in him. The Romanes Lecture of 1910 degenerated into a stump speech, so prolonged it made his Sorbonne and Berlin orations seem epigrammatic in comparison. Toward the end—Roosevelt had been speaking for well over an hour—he did make one notable claim, that he considered himself "a very radical democrat," opposed to any long-term domination of one group over another. But it was drowned out by the thunder of his exhortations.

"It would appear that the biological analogies in history are three," a weary Oxonian remarked afterward. "Longitude, Latitude, Platitude."

⁓

AFTER A FAREWELL dinner at Dorchester House, attended by the heads of the government, judiciary, and Anglican Church, Roosevelt left London for Southampton early on Thursday, 9 June. His ship was not due to sail until the following day, but he had an unusual assignation in Hampshire, en route to the port.

For years he had dreamed of roaming the English countryside "at the time of the singing of the birds." Bird-listening was his primary delight as an ornithologist—almost his only delight in childhood, when he had been so myopic he had difficulty tracing the source of any song. Now, with his left eye blinded, he again wanted to hear, if not see, some of the British species he had studied as a boy.

Sir Edward Grey was happy to act as his guide through some melodious plot of beechen green. The foreign secretary was a passionate outdoorsman, extremely knowledgeable about avian life. He had suggested they tour the meadowlands around Highland Water, deep in the New Forest. There was a country inn nearby at Brockenhurst, where they could spend the night. Southampton lay only eight miles away. Roosevelt's wife and children could travel there separately the following morning, and meet him at the docks.

With one of the longest days of the year to spare, the two men took a preliminary hike down the valley of the Itchen. Then they drove to Stoney Cross and fortified themselves with tea. At 4:30 P.M. they disappeared into the New Forest, and were not seen again until nine o'clock that evening.

The weather was overcast and the season late for a full chorale, but Grey was able to identify twenty-three different songs of forty-one observed species. Roosevelt listened and watched with a sense of literary familiarity. He had read Marryat's *Children of the New Forest* as a boy, and many of the names his guide whispered to him—the nightingale, the skylark, the thrush, the blackbird—evoked poems he had by heart. But the beauty of their live music thrilled him. The cuckoo wrought its traditional spell, and the "ventriloqual lay" of the sedge warbler mocked him among the river reeds. If the "singing and soaring" of a skylark reminded him of Wordsworth, rather than Shelley, and its melody degenerated sometimes into chatter, he felt it deserved its place in the quotation books.

He heard nothing that quite equaled, to his ear, the chimes of the American wood thrush, the high, brilliant tessitura of the northern winter wren, or the unstoppable mockingbird that had once kept him awake one moonlit night in Tennessee. Nevertheless, "the woods and fields were still vocal with beautiful bird-music, the country was very lovely, the inn as comfortable as possible, and the bath and supper very enjoyable after our tramp; and altogether I passed no pleasanter twenty-four hours during my entire European trip."

⌐◦⌐

ROOSEVELT SAILED FROM Southampton the following afternoon on the *Kaiserin Auguste Victoria*. "Take care of him," Rudyard Kipling wrote to a friend in New York. "He is scarce and valuable."

The ship was crowded with a record number of American passengers, many of whom had shortened their vacations in order to accompany the Colonel home. Stateside, his voyage was already being called "the Return from Elba." Similar imagery was employed in France. "Never since Napoleon dawned on Europe," *Le Temps* remarked, "has such an impression been produced there as has been made by Theodore Roosevelt." Some British commentators, still smarting over the Guildhall speech, would not have been sorry to see him head for St. Helena. "He is an amiable barbarian with a veneer of European civilization," wrote S. Verdad, foreign correspondent for *The New Age*. "To give him credit for any diplomatic talent is a huge joke." But the *Westminster Review* spoke for the majority in declaring, "Mr. Roosevelt is becoming more and more the commanding figure of the English-speaking world."

All this attention—not to mention eight thousand letters received to date by his overworked secretaries—testified to a fact obvious to many, if denied by himself: that he was perceived as the once and future President of the United States. Those jokes at Oxford about him running for another term had been diplomatic. So, looking further back, had the state receptions, the military reviews, the royal confidences lavished on him since he stepped ashore in Khartoum. He would not have been *mein Freund* to the Kaiser, or George V's chosen oracle of Empire, nor even Sir Edward Grey's bird-watching buddy, if specialists in the Wilhelmstrasse and Whitehall really believed that he was headed for retirement. And the vehemence with which Muslims attacked him (a spokesman for the Young Egypt Party regretted that he not been shot dead in Cairo) bespoke a new neurosis in international relations: fear that the United States, which he had personally shaped into the great Western power, would expand its influence eastward under a third Roosevelt administration. Maybe even a fourth: he was still only fifty-one.

There was, of course, the complicating factor of William Howard Taft. One of the longest letters in the Colonel's prodigious stash of mail came from 1600 Pennsylvania Avenue. It was a litany of Taft's personal and political troubles, beginning with, "I have had a hard time" and ending with an indirect appeal for help: "It would give me a great deal of pleasure if after you get settled at Oyster Bay, you could come over to Washington and spend a few days in the White House."

⁂

HEADING FOR HOME, Roosevelt was a different person from the gregarious, Africa-bound adventurer of two springs before. He paced several hours a day on the first-class deck, a black hat shading his eyes. Fellow promenaders sensed his distraction and left him alone. He was willing to pose for the occasional "kodaker," and made himself available for a general handshaking session. Otherwise, passengers saw little of him. He spent most of his time with Edith and Alice in their respective staterooms, while Ethel roamed the ship with a little black dog, and Kermit played bridge in the smoking room. Invariably, the family ate together in the ship's exclusive "Ritz Carlton" restaurant.

They had much to talk about, and more to ponder individually, with changes looming in all their lives. Edith wanted nothing more than to have her husband back at Oyster Bay for good. Her dream was to grow old with him in

Sagamore Hill, their big house overlooking the sea, filling it with more books as it emptied of children. But she knew him well enough not to bet against some urge for action taking him away from her, sooner or later. She had seen him brood at Omdurman, noticed how he huddled with Pinchot in Porto Maurizio, heard him exalt the Man in the Arena in Paris, registered what he said the night he came back depressed and raspy-voiced from Döberitz. At Windsor, she had watched as he walked with kings, and—in Kipling's cliché— kept his bearing. At none of these times had Theodore looked like a spent force.

Alice, attuned to every political overtone humming around Washington, saw trouble looming between the President, her father, herself, and her husband. Nick was in a difficult position, since he came from a family long associated with the Tafts. Alice's dread was that, in the event of a Roosevelt-Taft split, Representative Longworth would resign from Congress and run for governor of Ohio. To ultra-sophisticated Alice, the prospect of life in Columbus was only slightly better than death.

Kermit had two more years of Harvard to brace for, with little enthusiasm. During his *annus mirabilis* with his father, he had discovered himself both as a man and a wanderer. Restless, nervous, intoxicated by danger, he had earned social respect on safari, only to discover, as he trailed Roosevelt through Europe, that people still took no notice of him. He was too grown-up now (and too fond of cards and liquor) to expect any sympathy from his mother. Ethel was his new soul mate.

And *she*—eighteen years old, the shyest, most studious member of the family—had been transformed too. Her first experience of the world outside America had filled her with a vast curiosity, which reading would no longer satisfy. For that reason alone, Ethel hoped that Roosevelt would not get back into politics. She was starved for his company, his warm physicality, and his universal knowledge. "I love Father so much that it frightens me at times."

THE COLONEL PRESERVED his sphinx-like silence about domestic politics all the way across the Atlantic. He agreed to speak only at a Sunday service for first-class passengers, and preached a lay sermon on "scribes and Pharisees, publicans and sinners." Afterward he said that he felt uncomfortable that similar worship was not provided for lower-class passengers. "Let's see if we can't carry this righteousness down to the steerage people and the stokers."

Arrangements were made on the bottom deck, to vast excitement. When Roosevelt descended, escorted by the captain, he found more than a thousand Poles crowded around a makeshift altar draped with the German and American flags. The only light in the windowless space came from candles. He asked a Polish priest to say on his behalf "how earnestly he wished the adventure into the new land would be a turning-point in their lives; wished that they might find there all their dreams had painted for them; and how earnestly he, as a citizen of the great republic, welcomed them to it." Many in the congregation began to weep as these words were translated. He stayed to hear them sing a litany and receive the priest's benediction. As he made his way out, a girl seized his hand and kissed it. Others followed by the dozen, catching at the skirts of his coat and pressing it to their lips. He proceeded to another gathering on the third-class deck, where, speaking partly in German, he extended the same good wishes.

Later in the day, musing, Roosevelt said to one of the journalists on board that he would like to see steerage done away with, so that all American immigrants "might, from the beginning of the voyage, feel that they were entering into a new life of self-respect, with privacy and cleanliness."

CHAPTER 4

A Native Oyster

The palms of Mammon have disowned
The gift of our complacency;
The bells of ages have intoned
Again their rhythmic irony;
And from the shadow, suddenly,
'Mid echoes of decrepit rage,
The seer of our necessity
Confronts a Tyrian heritage.

JOSEPH YOUNGWITZ, of 610 East Sixth Street, Manhattan, was among the smallest and least elegant of the one million New Yorkers ready to welcome Theodore Roosevelt home on 18 June 1910. His savings as a messenger boy were insufficient to gain him admission to the reception area in Battery Park. But he had $2.75 to spend on a bunch of flowers, and vowed, somehow, to get them into his hero's hand.

That task looked progressively more difficult as police formed a double cordon up Broadway and Fifth Avenue, holding back a crowd that began collecting at dawn and soon filled both sidewalks all the way north to Fifty-ninth Street. It was a warm, humid morning. Straw boaters undulated twenty deep, like water lilies amid a bobbing of froglike bowlers. Female hats were fewer, but women were in the majority on the jerry-built scaffolds, some three stories high, offering ROOSEVELT PARADE SEAT RENTALS.

At 7:30 A.M. the first of twenty-one cannon shots flashed and boomed from Fort Wadsworth, and the *Kaiserin Auguste Victoria* loomed out of the haze at the head of New York bay. She was escorted by a battleship, five destroyers, and a flotilla of smaller vessels. At once a small launch bearing representatives of the federal government put out from the presidential yacht *Dolphin,* determined to beat four cutters loaded with Mayor Gaynor's official welcoming committee, Roosevelt family and friends, local politicians, and gentlemen of the press. They raced one another to where the great liner was mooring in quarantine.

⟨D⟩

WHEN ROOSEVELT, SITTING IN his stateroom, heard the cannonade, his wife noticed a curious mix of pain and pleasure on his face. "He was smiling, but looking forward"—to what, Edith did not say.

Possibly he was struggling with feelings beyond the comprehension of anyone who had not been, for seven and a half years, President of the United States. The twenty-one guns, the great gray battleship with its men standing at quarters, the launch coming alongside to a shrill of whistles; the arrival on board of his former secretary of the navy, his former secretary of agriculture, and most familiar of all, in a gold-laced uniform, his former military aide, Archie Butt—it was difficult to think of them as anything but paraphernalia of an administration still in power.

Of course they were not: the two cabinet officers, George von Lengerke Meyer and James Wilson, simply symbolized continuity between old times and new, and Captain Butt was extracting, from the leg of his boot, some letters from President and Mrs. Taft. Yet Roosevelt could not help falling at once into the habit of treating them authoritatively—just as Archie was heard to say, when they all went on deck to see the cutters approach, "Will you kindly let the President pass?"

Edith was the first to spot another Archie, sixteen years old, blond and bone-thin, on the foremost boat, *Manhattan*. He stood with his younger brother, Quentin, and other family members, among whom could be discerned the natty figure of Theodore Roosevelt, Jr. Edith's New England reserve cracked, and she looked as though she wanted to jump overboard. "Think—for the first time in nearly two years I have them all within reach!"

Bidding farewell to his fellow passengers, Roosevelt escorted her down a gangway to the *Manhattan* at 8:20. He wore a silk topper and black frock coat. Edith presented a trim, if matronly figure in dark blue and white. Kermit, panama-topped, followed with Alice in a plaid dress and Ethel, looking almost pretty in mushroom linen, clutching her little black dog. For the next hour they were mobbed by Roosevelts of all ages and relationships, while Nicholas Longworth (impeccably dressed as always, to compensate for his bald shortness) and Henry Cabot Lodge staged a miniature conference of the House and the Senate.

Roosevelt embraced his sisters "Bamie" and Corinne, the former now deaf as well as bent by arthritis, the latter ravaged by the suicide of her youngest son at Harvard. Ted presented his petite fiancée, Eleanor Butler Alexander. The latter had won quick family approval, since she shared four *Mayflower* ancestors with Edith, and was the only child of wealthy parents.

While the Colonel continued to kiss and hug and pump hands, his distant

Democratic cousin, Franklin Delano Roosevelt, stood apart. Tall and slender, he sported a straw boater, and kept close to his own Eleanor,* an aggressively shy young woman whose chin receded as far as his own protruded. Franklin was said to have political ambitions.

Another cannonade began as Roosevelt transferred alone to the recep-

"THE NATTY FIGURE OF THEODORE ROOSEVELT, JR."

Roosevelt's eldest son at the time of his engagement to Eleanor Butler Alexander.

tion steamer *Androscoggin*. It was to ferry him ashore, after a short foray by the official flotilla up the Hudson. He crowed with delight when he saw that the battleship leading the way was the *South Carolina*. Twin-turreted fore and aft, still so new that her paint seemed polished, she was the first

---

* Niece of Theodore Roosevelt.

American dreadnought, a proud symbol of his efforts to build a world-class navy.

Roosevelt could not resist climbing out onto the *Androscoggin*'s bridge and standing there for a while, feeling himself the center of a vast marine movement churning north. Ahead to port and starboard, the warships (grimly gray now, not white as they had been in his day) guarded him. Behind came the cutters, flanked by a growing armada of private vessels and sightseeing boats. Well-wishers clustered on both New York and New Jersey piers. The air shrilled with steam whistles.

At Fourteenth Street the flotilla swiveled south. On the way back down-river, the Colonel shook the hands of the eminent New Yorkers who had arranged and paid for his homecoming. Most of them were greeted with his famous memory flashes. "My deadly rivals!" he joked at the sight of the editors of *Munsey's* and *Everybody's* magazines. And, "Hello, here's my original discoverer!" to Joseph Murray, who had put him forward as a candidate for the New York State Assembly in 1881. Even when the recognition was obviously faked, his grin and vigorous squeeze exuded friendliness.

He was, in short, already politicking, bent upon charming as many people as he could see—even the black cook making him breakfast. Yet in the midst of his effusions, Roosevelt the writer could not resist secluding himself with the latest issue of *The Outlook,* to see how a story he had dispatched from Europe looked in print.

When, at last, he stepped onto the soil of his native city, a huge shout went up from the crowd waiting in Battery Park and ran echoing up Broadway. It built into such a roar that for the first time in his life he was brought to public tears. He had to turn toward the pilothouse and polish his spectacles before proceeding.

⌖

TO THE CHAGRIN of three thousand ticket holders in the park, Mayor Gaynor's welcoming speech and Roosevelt's reply were so brief that the parade got under way at 11:30, almost an hour earlier than scheduled. Reporters were left to guess what, if anything, the Colonel had meant when he said, "I am ready and eager to do my part . . . in helping solve problems which must be solved."

During his ensuing five-mile drive uptown, standing most of the way in the mayor's open carriage, he was deluged in ticker tape and confetti, and subjected to ceaseless roars of "Teddy! Teddy!" A man with a megaphone bellowed, "Our next President!" to a crescendo of applause. The parade was almost as long as the marine file had been, with a vanguard of mounted police and bandsmen followed by Rough Riders prancing on sorrel horses. "I certainly love my boys," Roosevelt yelled at them. Thirteen carriages of dignitaries trailed his own. Then came another band, a marching mass of Spanish War veterans, two more bands, and finally more mounted police, guarding against incursions from the rear. The heat by now was tremendous, and he glistened with sweat as he waved his topper at the never-thinning crowd.

Archie Butt and William Loeb, collector of the Port of New York, rode in the carriage just behind him. Loeb had been Roosevelt's private secretary in the White House, and agreed with Butt that there was "something different" about their former boss. So, for that matter, did Lodge and Nick Longworth. Butt was best able to express their collective thoughts:

> [We] figured it out to be simply an enlarged personality. To me he had ceased to be an American, but had become a world citizen. . . . He is bigger, broader, capable of greater good or greater evil, I don't know which, than when he left; and he is in splendid health and has a long time to live.

Just above Franklin Street, a small boy broke out from the curb, screaming, "Hey, Teddy! I want to shake hands with you!" The Colonel reached down and they managed a quick clasp, then police hustled the boy away.

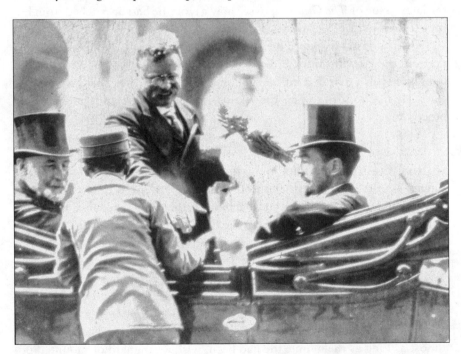

"'HEY, TEDDY! I WANT TO SHAKE HANDS WITH YOU!'"

Joseph Youngwitz presents a bouquet to his hero, 18 June 1910.

The parade thumped on up Broadway and Fifth Avenue. About an hour later, as it approached its end at Grand Army Plaza, the same urchin—who evidently knew how to ride subways—reappeared, this time waving flowers. Roosevelt took the cluster and called out, as police again swooped, "I think I have seen you before."

Joseph Youngwitz confirmed to a reporter that this was true. He had shaken hands with his hero on a presidential visit to New York "about five years ago."

━━━━━

THAT EVENING ROOSEVELT sat in a rocking chair on the veranda of Sagamore Hill, watching the sun set over Long Island Sound. The day that had begun so loudly, with cannon booms and the most sustained shouts of adulation ever to assault his ears, was ending in quiet bird music. A storm during the afternoon had rinsed the air clean. From the belt of forest at the foot of his sloping lawn came the sleepy sound of wood thrushes chanting their vespers. Overhead in a weeping elm, an oriole alternately sang and scolded. Vireos and tanagers warbled. When dark came on, he heard the flight song of an ovenbird.

As a boy he had sat here when there was no house and no trees, only a grassy hilltop sloping down to Oyster Bay and Cold Spring Harbor. He and his first wife had planned to build their summer place on it. Death parted them before the foundation stone was laid. Being a young widower had not stopped Roosevelt from completing the full three-story, seven-bedroom structure before Edith arrived in the spring of 1887, already pregnant with Ted. Here, presumably, he would welcome his first grandchild. And here, probably, he would die.

"One thing I want now is privacy," he told a *New York Times* reporter. "I want to close up like a native oyster." Only two public functions threatened: Ted's wedding in a couple of days' time, and a Harvard visit at the end of the month. Beyond them, all of July lay free. He could settle at his desk in the library, and pursue his new career as contributing editor of *The Outlook*. He had taken a vow of political silence for two months.

During the next twenty-four hours he either heard or saw forty-two species of birds. This beat by one the total that Sir Edward Grey had been able to identify in the New Forest. From the point of view of melody, there was no contest at all. When he strolled around the house, or jogged down the hill to bathe, his ears rang with the calls of thrashers in the hedgerows and herons in the salt marsh, the hot-weather song of indigo buntings and thistle finches, the bubbling music of bobolinks, the mew and squeal of catbirds, the piercing cadence of the meadowlark, the high scream of red-tail hawks.

All of them were listed in the catalog, *Notes on Some of the Birds of Oyster Bay, Long Island.* He had no need to consult that authoritative work, having written and published it himself, at age twenty.

⌒

OVER THE WEEKEND, newspaper editorials generally agreed that Theodore Roosevelt stood at the peak of his renown. To the Pittsburgh *Leader,* the welcome extended him by New Yorkers had approached "deification." The *New York Evening Post* described it as "sobering" in its implications, but praised him for not taking political advantage of the moment. "Never before in the history of America," commented the Colorado Springs *Gazette,* "has a private citizen possessed the power which Mr. Roosevelt now holds." The Philadelphia *North American* held that he could win a third term as President in 1912, even if he ran as a Democrat. Few sympathies were extended to the man he had chosen to succeed him. "Never mind, Mr. Taft," the Chicago *Daily News* jeered. "When you are an ex-President you can be a celebrity yourself."

In trekking so many thousands of miles, so far from home, Roosevelt seemed to have been away a long time. Taft's presidency felt almost over, as though the coming elections were to mark its twilight, rather than its meridian. In fact, Taft had been in the White House less than a year and a half, and was not averse to a second term. He enjoyed his job's lavish perks, if not the work that came with them. But he had learned to minimize that. By nature an administrator, he saw no reason to initiate policy. The Constitution, as he read it, provided him unlimited time off for golf, free first-class travel, and the right to doze during meetings. He liked his $75,000 salary, and dreamed of being a justice of the Supreme Court after his prolonged sabbatical in the executive branch.

There was, besides, an all-powerful lobby determined to renominate him. While most of Manhattan had been brilliant with flags on the day of the Colonel's great parade, Wall Street had remained defiantly drab. Bare poles projected from the House of Morgan, National City Bank, and the New York Stock Exchange. The austere men who ran these institutions were convinced that Roosevelt was insane: a politician so deficient in financial sense as to need medical treatment. At all costs he must be kept safely rusticated at Oyster Bay.

Roosevelt remained so close-mouthed that not even Henry Cabot Lodge, an early guest at Sagamore Hill, was able to divine his thoughts. But he had to make a quick decision which was bound to be interpreted politically: what to do about the President's offer of hospitality. The letters Archie Butt had unbooted on the *Kaiserin Auguste Victoria* repeated the invitation three times. One was a copy of the long, querulous screed Roosevelt had already received in

Britain. The second, addressing him as "My dear Theodore," had been written while he was at sea, and the third, from Helen Taft, expressed the hope that Edith, too, would come to stay in the White House.

"I do not know that I have had harder luck than most presidents," Taft's *cri de coeur* read, "but I do know that thus far I have succeeded far less than have others. I have been conscientiously trying to carry out your policies but my method of doing so has not worked smoothly." Page after page, the self-pity went on. "My year and two months [*sic*] have been heavier for me to bear because of Mrs. Taft's condition. . . . I am glad to say she has not seemed to be bothered by the storm of abuse to which I have been subjected. . . . The Garfield-Pinchot Ballinger controversy has given me a great deal of pain and suffering."

Taft even complained about being unable to lose weight.

Roosevelt had long been aware that the President lacked confidence. Uxorious and inordinately susceptible to guidance from his brothers Henry and Charles, Taft was always looking for approval. But this whining note was unbecoming for a chief executive. It did not augur well for the program of progressive reform he was supposed to have consolidated and extended. Taft took credit for "a real downward revision" of tariff rates, laws to improve labor safety and bolster postal savings, and a conservation bill giving the Department of the Interior increased powers of land withdrawal. But he wrote more convincingly about rising prices, opposition in Congress, and a hostile press. He thought there was a real possibility that the GOP would lose its House majority in the fall, and the White House in 1912.

In that case, Taft stated, Senators La Follette of Wisconsin, Cummins and Dolliver of Iowa, Bristow of Kansas, Clapp of Minnesota, Beveridge of Indiana, and Borah of Idaho—Midwestern insurgents to a man—would be responsible. "[They] have done all in their power to defeat us." Whether by "us" the President meant himself and his administration, or himself and Roosevelt as a continuum, was unclear.

He mentioned in passing that it had been his idea to send the *South Carolina* to New York "and give you a salute from her batteries."

Roosevelt sensed that he was being coerced. He replied on 20 June with a letter that began and ended affectionately, but contained one paragraph of startling coldness:

Now, my dear Mr. President, your invitation to the White House touches me greatly, and also what Mrs. Taft wrote Mrs. Roosevelt. But I don't think it well for an ex-President to go to the White House, or indeed to go to Washington, except when he cannot help it. Sometime I shall have to go to Washington to look over some of the skins and skulls of the animals we collected in Africa, but I thought it would be wisest to do it when all of political Washington had left.

Having thus relegated Taft to a level of less consequence than zoological specimens, Roosevelt went with his family to attend the wedding of Ted and Eleanor in New York.*

TWO DAYS LATER, emerging from the office of Charles Scribner's Sons, on Fifth Avenue, he was mobbed by a crowd so overexcited that mounted policemen had to ride in and free him. "They wanted to carry me on their shoulders," he told his sister Corinne. Gone was the frank adoration that had touched him during his parade. "It represented a certain hysterical quality that boded ill for my future. *That type* of crowd, feeling *that* kind of way, means that in a very short time they will be throwing rotten eggs at me."

A dinner in his honor that night at Sherry's, the most exclusive restaurant in the city, also failed to inspire him. The evening's proceedings (printed on rag paper with illustrations hand-colored by Maxfield Parrish, bound in soft calfskin, and stamped with the Roosevelt crest) seemed to warrant a major statement. But his only reference to his future was cryptic, and disappointing to many guests. "I am like Peary at the North Pole," he said, comparing himself to America's other celebrity of the moment. "There is no way for me to travel but south."

As soon as he returned home, political pilgrims began to make the three-mile trek from Oyster Bay station to Sagamore Hill. To President Taft's alarm, they were all of the progressive persuasion. Gifford Pinchot arrived with James R. Garfield, a fellow conservationist who had served Roosevelt as secretary of the interior. Joseph Medill McCormick, the idealistic owner of the *Chicago Tribune,* came with Francis J. Heney, a Californian prosecutor famous for attacking corporate fraud. Booker T. Washington, Roosevelt's former conduit to black Americans, wished to renew old ties. So did Senator Robert M. La Follette, although in this case the ties had never been strong. "Battling Bob" almost comically personified insurgency. His pompadour and soaring brow comprised fully half of his head, and a good deal of his height. "I am very much pleased with my visit to Colonel Roosevelt," he announced.

Most of the pilgrims expressed similar pleasure. They were vague as to what, exactly, Roosevelt had said to them. Outsiders could only infer he was not praising William Howard Taft.

---

* From now on, unqualified references to "Eleanor" should be understood to refer to Mrs. Theodore Roosevelt, Jr., not her later more famous namesake.

"He says he will keep silent for at least two months," the President remarked, sulking over the morning newspapers. "I don't care if he keeps silent forever."

The most far-seeing commentary on Roosevelt in retreat came, ironically, from a blind Democrat, Senator Thomas P. Gore of Oklahoma.

Colonel Roosevelt is now in the most difficult and delicate positioning of his career. Has he the power to stand this greatest draft on his talent or his tact? . . . If he is to continue to progress, he must leave behind those whom he has created in his own image. If he does not now progress, he will be left behind by that great popular procession of which he delighted to imagine himself both the leader and the creator.

I trust that the progressives will have just cause to rejoice at his return and that the stand-patters will be compelled to bewail it as a catastrophe. I hope that enlightened, rational reform will find in Roosevelt the ablest reformer, otherwise there may be more of fiction than fact in this back-from-Elba talk, for, as I remember, the return from Elba was followed by the campaign of the Hundred Days, and the campaign of the Hundred Days was followed by Waterloo and a night without a dawn.

IN HIS REPETITIONS of the words *progress* and *progressive,* as well as *Roosevelt* and *reform,* Senator Gore showed much political acuity. If he had identified the Colonel's followers more narrowly as Republican *insurgents,* he would have excluded forward-thinkers in his own party who found progressivism a realistic alternative to William Jennings Bryan's sentimental "democracy of the heart." Gore was, in effect, challenging Roosevelt to reform the Republican Party along "enlightened" lines. If its Old Guard leaders "stood pat" behind President Taft, then the "great popular procession" of progressivism might change avenues, and march behind a Democratic drummer.

Actually, the movement was not great in any statistical sense. To be *progressive* in 1910 was to belong to America's middle class—only a fifth of the general populace—and want to make bourgeois values the law of the land. To be *insurgent* was to belong to a much smaller, politically active minority, determined to write those values into Republican ideology. Roosevelt had been wary of the latter presumption since the fall of 1902, when La Follette and Albert B. Cummins, both Midwestern governors, emerged as pioneer insurgents. He happened to agree with some of their demands, such as regulation of railroad rates, but they had struck him as too parochial, uninterested in the other worlds that lay beyond their respective horizons of water and corn. He had done nothing to encourage the spread of further insurgencies through the central states during his first term, and little to welcome La Follette to Washington as a senator in 1906. Yet he had been pleased when reformers of both major parties praised his own "progressive" swing that same year. By 1908, the GOP insurgents had more or less ceded their cause to him.

Now it appeared that during his time out of the country, *insurgent* and *progressive* had become synonymous on orthodox Republican lips. Henry Cabot Lodge could barely force either obscenity through his reactionary whiskers. Roosevelt, describing himself as a "radical" at Oxford, meant, in the European sense, to convey that he was "a real—not a mock—democrat," protective of the *petite bourgeoisie* like Clemenceau, liberal like Lloyd George. To Americans, the word unfortunately connotated grass roots.

Like many well-born men with a social conscience, Roosevelt liked to think that he empathized with the poor. He was democratic, in a detached, affable way. However, his rare exposures to squalor had been either voyeuristic, as when he encouraged Jacob Riis to show him "how the other half lived," or vicarious, as when he recoiled from the "hideous human swine" in the works of Émile Zola.

Gifford Pinchot had the same kind of aristocratic fastidiousness. But most progressives looked down from a less exalted height. They felt threatened by the lower ranks of society. These were, in descending order, organized labor, represented by the AFL (trades-oriented, exclusionary, anti-immigrant), then the immense subpopulation of unskilled workers who toiled in factories and stockyards and mines, followed by poor whites, and at the dreg level, imported coolies, reservation Indians, and disenfranchised blacks.

Except for the two years he had lived with cowboys in North Dakota, and being the employer of a dozen or so servants, Roosevelt had never had to suffer any prolonged intimacy with the working class. From infancy, he had enjoyed the perquisites of money and social position. The money, through his own mismanagement, had often run short, and he was by no means wealthy even now, but he had always taken exclusivity for granted. The brownstone birthplace in Manhattan, the childhood tours of Europe, the open doors of Harvard and the Porcellian, the riverside ranch and hilltop estate, the gubernatorial mansion and the White House; Mrs. Astor's balls, Brahmin clambakes, diplomatic banquets, and most recently, royal receptions; custom clothes, first-class sleepers, private boxes, pro bono lawyers, investment managers, club privileges, a driver and a valet—he had them all. Every night except Sunday he dressed in black tie for dinner, and when he rocked on the piazza, gazing out over his estate, he saw no other roofs, heard no street noise, breathed only the freshest air.

Ensconced, he lacked some of the neuroses of progressives—economic envy and race hatred especially. His radicalism was a matter of energy rather than urgency. It wanted to spread out and embrace social (not socialistic) reformers, labor leaders who spoke decent English, churchgoing farmers, businessmen with a sense of community responsibility, and even the occasional polite, self-made Negro, such as Booker T. Washington. He had no attraction toward the Vanderbilts and the Rockefellers in their parvenu palaces. A strong sense of fairness saved him from complacency. If he was less motivated by compassion than anger at what he saw as the arrogance of capital, he chafed, nonetheless, to regulate it.

⤛⤜

DURING ROOSEVELT'S ABSENCE OVERSEAS, a book by the political philosopher Herbert Croly had become the bible of the new social movement. Entitled *The Promise of American Life,* it was Hamiltonian in its insistence on the need for a strong central government, yet Jacksonian in calling for a war on unearned privilege—and it named Theodore Roosevelt as the only leader on the American scene capable of encompassing both aims. "An individuality such as his," Croly wrote, "wrought with so much consistent purpose out of much variety of experience, brings with it an intellectual economy of its own and a sincere and useful sort of intellectual enlightenment."

A close reading of *The Promise* showed that many of its ideas derived from Roosevelt's Special Message of January 1908. More than any other utterance in his career, that bombshell had convinced Wall Street and the Old Guard that "Theodore the Sudden" was a dangerous man. The issues he raised then—automatic compensation for job-related accidents, federal scrutiny of boardroom operations, value-based regulation of railroad rates, redress against punitive injunctions, strengthened antitrust laws—were the issues his followers wanted him to fight for now. The violent language he had used— "predatory wealth," "purchased politician[s]," "combinations which are both noxious and legal"—had become commonplaces of progressive rhetoric. When insurgents called for a "moral regeneration of the business world," and insisted that their "campaign against privilege" was "fundamentally an ethical movement," they were shouting through a megaphone Roosevelt had left behind.

His own voice from those times echoed back to him:

> The opponents of the measures we champion single out now one, and now another measure for especial attack, and speak as if the movement in which we are engaged was purely economic. It has a large economic side, but it is fundamentally an ethical movement. It is not a movement to be completed in one year, or two or three years; it is a movement which must be persevered in until the spirit which lies behind it sinks deep into the heart and the conscience of the whole people.

Sooner than he had predicted, and embarrassingly coincident with his return to America, the movement had begun to achieve critical mass, converging at state and local levels. "Is this not the logical time," the *Kansas City Star* asked in a front-page editorial, "to look forward to a new party which shall include progressive Democrats and Republicans—a party dedicated to the square deal and led by Theodore Roosevelt?"

The fact that a respected GOP organ could propose such a thing, along with "Roosevelt Clubs" springing up like wheat elsewhere in the plains states, explained why Taft's Republican Congressional Campaign Committee was determined to suppress all insurgents running for state and federal offices in the fall of 1910. Roosevelt took no responsibility for the clubs. "I might be able to *guide* this movement," he told Senator Lodge, "but I should be wholly unable to *stop* it, even if I were to try."

<hr>

ON 29 JUNE, Theodore Roosevelt, A.B. *magna cum laude,* Harvard, '80, returned to Cambridge for the thirtieth anniversary of his class. He found himself walking in the commencement procession next to Governor Charles Evans Hughes of New York. For once, the bearded inellectual, whom he privately mocked as "Charles the Baptist," did not irritate him. They became so absorbed in conversation that they delayed general entry into Sanders Theatre.

Hughes wanted help. A mildly progressive Republican, he had served three and a half years in Albany at great personal cost, frustrated at every political turn by the state party machine. He was about to be relieved with a seat on the Supreme Court, courtesy of an admiring President Taft. Before resigning, he was determined to take the power of nomination to state offices away from party officials, and transfer it to the rank and file, voting in direct primaries. A bill to this effect had been blocked by standpatters throughout the regular session of the legislature. So he had convened a special session to pass it, in defiance of William Barnes, Jr., boss of the state GOP.

Hughes saw Roosevelt as the only New Yorker powerful enough to exert more influence than Barnes, and asked him if he would get behind the bill. Cannily, he emphasized that the lawmakers supporting it were all Roosevelt Republicans.

Many times, over the years, Roosevelt had compared the workings of politics to those of a kaleidoscope. Brilliant, harmonious patterns, sometimes carefully shaken into shape, sometimes forming of their own accord, could at the slightest touch fall into jagged disarray, with clashing colors and shafts of impenetrable black. Hughes's appeal had just such an effect on his current outlook. On this pleasant June day, under the elms of Harvard Yard, he was confronted with a situation of bewildering intricacy, sharp with factional danger.

He did not like Hughes, but then, neither did anybody at close range. It was impossible to warm to a man who exuded such cold correctness, and grinned with horse-toothed insincerity. However, there was no denying the

"HE WAS ABOUT TO BE RELIEVED WITH A SEAT ON THE SUPREME COURT."

Charles Evans Hughes as governor of New York State.

governor's intellectual brilliance (he was at home in Japanese, and in infinitesimal calculus), nor the acclaim he had won as an incorruptible advocate of the common good. Not to help him would be to signal approval of Barnes's bossism. Even Taft supported the New York primary bill.

By supporting it too, Roosevelt saw an opportunity to show that he was as willing to work with the President, as a Party regular, as with Hughes or any other moderate progressive. Surely the three of them, with their combined prestige, could swing the bill's passage. Hughes would go out of office in glory, and establish himself on the Supreme Court, no doubt, as a progressive interpreter of the Constitution. Taft would be seen as hospitable to reasonable reform, and the Old Guard would have to accept that progressivism was now a permanent part of the Republican agenda. Best of all, Theodore Roosevelt would go down in history as a statesman who had made one final, selfless gesture of conciliation before retiring from Party politics.

"Our governor," he announced at a luncheon for Hughes following the commencement ceremony in Sanders, "has a very persuasive way with him. I had intended to keep absolutely clear from any kind of public or political question after coming home, and I could carry my resolution out all right until I met the governor this morning, and he then explained to me that I had come back to live in New York now; that I had to help him out, and after a very brief conversation I put up my hands and agreed to help him."

⸺

AFTER COFFEE, ROOSEVELT seemed to want to retract his pledge. William N. Chadbourne, a Hughes lieutenant from New York County, said that party members who had gotten into politics because of him would be deeply disillusioned if "the old group" reasserted machine control in Albany.

The Colonel hesitated. "What shall I do?"

"You'd better send a telegram to Lloyd Griscom."

Griscom was chairman of the New York County Committee. Roosevelt sat down and scribbled the brief message that was to reinvolve him in politics. "I believe the people demand it," he wrote of the direct primary bill. "I most earnestly hope that it will be enacted into law."

⸺

EXHILARATED AS ALWAYS by the prospect of a fight, he went on to stay with Henry Cabot and Nanny Cabot Lodge at their summer home in Nahant, Massachusetts. Old mutual friends, the Winthrop Chanlers, were there too. Margaret Chanler wrote:

> He was bursting with the things he wanted to tell us. He always liked to talk from a rocking chair; so one was brought out on the piazza, and the Lodge family, including the three children . . . and Winnie and I sat around him while he rocked vigorously and told one story after another, holding us enchanted, making us laugh until we cried and ached. . . . Some of his best stories were about King Edward's funeral, or "wake" as he irreverently called it. . . .
>
> I do not think the rest of us spoke a hundred words. . . . It was a manifestation of that mysterious thing, nth-powered vitality, communicating itself to the listeners.

Lodge was doubtful about Roosevelt's New York venture, but pleased to hear that he was cooperating with the President on something.

Taft happened to be vacationing nearby on the North Shore. That made it impossible to put off their reunion any longer. So the following afternoon, with Lodge for company, Roosevelt donned a panama hat and motored up the coast to the "summer White House" in Beverly. It was a large rented cottage overlooking the surf at Burgess Point. Taft liked it more for the proximity of the Myopia golf links than for its ozone.

"I know this man better than you do," a secret service agent, James Sloan, said to Archie Butt as they stood looking out for the Colonel's automobile. "He will come to see the President today and bite his leg off tomorrow."

Sloan despised Taft. He claimed he had once heard Roosevelt say, "Jimmy, I may have to come back in four years to carry out my policies." Butt was ambivalent. He had become fond of his boss, finding him to be essentially good-natured and high-minded. When convinced of the rightness of a course of action, Taft pushed all obstacles out of his way, like an elephant rolling logs. However, again like an elephant, he had a tendency to listen to whichever trainer whispered in his ear.

He came out of the house now, as Roosevelt arrived. "Ah, Theodore, it is good to see you."

"How are you, Mr. President? This is simply bully."

"See here now, drop the 'Mr. President.' "

"Not at all. You must be Mr. President and I am Theodore. It must be that way."

They affected male exuberance, with shoulder punches reminiscent of their old friendship. But the strain between them was palpable. Taft led the way to a group of wicker chairs on the breezy side of the porch. Roosevelt said that he "needed rather than wanted" a Scotch and soda. Nobody else drank. Lodge and Butt puffed cigars.

To get a dialogue going, Taft raised the subject of Hughes's primary bill. He confirmed that he would do all he could to help its passage. Roosevelt said that as a citizen of New York, he supported it too. This lame exchange went nowhere, and a telephone message from Lloyd Griscom gave them no encouragement. The chairman advised that every member of his committee looked on the fight as "hopeless."

Taft and Roosevelt were clearly cast down. The President blustered that he would continue to issue appeals for votes.

"I wish they had both remained out of it," Lodge muttered to Butt.

The arrival on the porch of Mrs. Taft, still half mute from her stroke, put a further damp on the proceedings. Roosevelt was sensitive enough not to force her into conversation. He rambled politely until she relaxed.

"Now, Mr. President," Taft said, "tell me about cabbages and kings."

Roosevelt was willing to oblige, but protested being called by his old title.

"The force of habit is very strong in me," Taft said, with the simplicity

Summer Residence of

"TAFT LED THE WAY TO A GROUP OF WICKER CHAIRS ON THE BREEZY SIDE OF THE PORCH."
The summer White House in Beverly, Massachusetts.

that was a large part of his charm. "I can never think of you save as 'Mr. President.' "

For an hour, Roosevelt told royal stories, and was funny enough about M. Pichon and "the poor little Persian" to get everyone laughing.

When he got up to go, Lodge informed him that there were about two hundred newsmen and photographers waiting outside the gates. Roosevelt asked Taft for permission to say that their visit had been personal, and delightful. "Which is true as far as I am concerned."

"And more than true as far as I am concerned," Taft answered. "This has taken me back to some of those dear old afternoons when I was Will and you were Mr. President."

They parted with tacit acknowledgment that whatever remained of their friendship, "dearness" was no longer an option.

BEFORE LEAVING BOSTON for New York, Roosevelt paid a visit to Corey Hospital in Brookline, where Justice William Henry Moody lay bent and emaciated with rheumatoid arthritis. Only fifty-six, Moody was the last, and to some minds the most distinguished of his three appointments to the Supreme Court. Yet after four short terms, the justice had been felled by a streptococcal storm that left him unable to walk and deeply depressed.

It was a poignant reunion for both, and Roosevelt was mute about it afterward. He had looked to Moody to serve for many years as his representative

H. Taft at Beverly, Mass.   Copyright 1909
                                             Wm Mills & Son, Prov.

on the bench, whenever cases arose that tested the constitutionality of his presidential policies. Back when nobody quite knew what *progressive* meant, Moody had been his most forward-looking cabinet officer, first as secretary of the navy, then as a resolutely antitrust attorney general—along with Root and Taft, one of the administration's famous "Three Musketeers."

Now that happy trio was disbanded. Aramis was bedridden for life, Athos intellectually stifled in the Senate, and Porthos no longer the jovial giant. Bereft of their company, whither D'Artagnan?

CHAPTER 5

The New Nationalism

He'll break out some day like a keg of ale
With too much independent frenzy in it.

ROOSEVELT RETURNED HOME on the evening of 1 July to news that despite his advocacy, Hughes's direct-primary bill had been defeated by a combination of machine Republicans and Tammany Hall Democrats.

This was exactly the kind of political "trust" he had battled as a young assemblyman in Albany. But then, legislative disappointments were to be expected. Nearly three decades later, a former president and toast of foreign monarchs could ill afford such a rebuff. Senator Gore had to be laughing. Roosevelt's ancient scourge, the New York *Sun,* printed a one-line wisecrack: "And the 'Hundred Days' lasted just thirteen."

The question now was whether he should nurse the bruise William Barnes, Jr., had inflicted on him, and wait for sympathetic critics to point out that he had merely tried to help out his governor and his President. Or, seek revenge on Barnes for humbling all three of them?

Lloyd Griscom came to see him in a funk. At all costs, the triumphant boss must be stopped from bulldozing the New York Republican convention at Saratoga Springs in September. If Barnes prevailed, his machine would write the platform, nominate whom it pleased to local, state, and federal offices, and advertise to the world that the Old Guard was back in control of Party affairs. The result was bound to be a Democratic sweep in November. Griscom suggested that Roosevelt run, with White House support, for chairman of the convention. Barnes doubtless had a conservative candidate in mind, so the contest would pit the forces of moderation against those of reaction, and maybe compensate for the primary-bill debacle.

Roosevelt listened without committing himself. He was not fooled that Griscom—a Taft man—wanted to do anything other than serve the administration. But here was a chance to influence the nomination of a decent man for governor, and push for a moderately progressive state delegation to the national convention in 1912. At the very least, cooperation with Griscom would signal that Roosevelt and Taft were not drifting apart.

The trouble was that they were, and both of them knew it.

"Archie, I am very greatly distressed," Taft told Captain Butt on 6 July. "I do not see how I am going to get out of having a fight with President Roosevelt."

He was still inclined to use the last two words when preoccupied or flustered. A rumor was going around that Roosevelt wanted to prevent Interior Secretary Richard Ballinger from running for the the U.S. Senate. True or not, the rumor reminded people that the Colonel had always been close to Ballinger's enemy, Gifford Pinchot.

"I confess it wounds me very deeply," Taft said. "I hardly think the prophet of the Square Deal is playing it exactly square with me now." His wife was taunting him with the possibility that Roosevelt might beat him for renomination in 1912.

Butt asked if he believed Roosevelt really wanted to challenge him.

"I do not know. I have thought sometimes that he did, and then I don't see how he can. In his mind, however, it may be the only logical way of reaching a third term. Then, too, his tour of Europe, his reception there, and the fact that every crowned head seemed to take it for granted that he would be elected . . ."

The President spent the rest of the morning soothing his soul with golf.

Later that same day at Sagamore Hill, Roosevelt put both hands on the shoulders of two old friends, the civil-service reformers Lucius Burrie Swift and William Dudley Foulke, and said, "I could cry over Taft." He escorted them upstairs to a private room, complaining that the President had been a good lieutenant, but was unfit for higher command. Then, closing the door, he said, "I will talk to you with perfect frankness. I would not consider another nomination unless it was practically universally demanded."

It was a classic Rooseveltian recruitment ploy: the physical embrace, the melodramatic confidentiality, the denial of personal ambition. Swift and Foulke left convinced that he was already running. A trio of Kansas insurgents, Senator Joseph L. Bristow, Congressmen Victor Murdock, and Edmond H. Madison, got the same impression.

"Are you aware," Bristow asked the others as they walked back to Oyster Bay, "that we have been participants in a historic occasion where a former President definitely broke with the man he had made his successor?"

Madison expressed awe, but Murdock was skeptical. A former newspaperman, he noted the vehemence of Roosevelt's private denunciations of Taft and the coyness with which he declined to be quoted.

Actually Roosevelt was struggling, as throughout his life, between the desire for power and the ethics of responsibility. It was a struggle he had never been able wholly to resolve: indeed, its contrary tensions held him together. He wanted to destroy Taft because Taft had failed. He wanted Taft to succeed because Taft was an extension of himself. He knew he was no longer President, yet he was seen as presidential—the emperors of the Old World had made *that* clear, not to mention Taft in conversation. Although not running, he was running. Even as he maintained his vow of silence, he was shouting from the hustings.

⎯⊸⎯

"THE GREATEST SERVICE I can render to Taft," Roosevelt wrote Lodge, "the service which beyond all others will tend to secure his renomination . . . is to try and help the Republican Party to win at the polls this Fall, and that I am trying to do."

That meant resisting, on the one hand, pressure from GOP leaders to come out with a "flaming endorsement" of the President, and on the other, appeals from insurgents to proclaim himself in opposition. Either course, he felt, would cost him friends, and split the Party. The fault line ran right through his own family. Alice shared his reformist philosophy, while Nicholas Longworth was a regular, albeit moderate, Republican.

Roosevelt felt sorry for them both. If any single person symbolized the urgency of holding the Party together, it was Nick: son-in-law to the most eminent progressive in America, yet a former law student of William Howard Taft, hailing from the same district in Cincinnati, even representing Taft in Congress.

In response to a letter from Nick, saying it was essential that the President keep control of his own home state, Roosevelt wrote to say he agreed. "Of course you must stand straight by Taft. . . . He is your constituent." He urged the same spirit of cooperation on Gifford Pinchot. "I do hope you won't take any position which would make it impossible, or even merely exceedingly difficult, for you to support him if necessary." The President had started off badly, he felt, through having no real qualities of leadership. "He is evidently a man who takes color from his surroundings. He was an excellent man under me, and close to me. For eighteen months after his election he was a rather pitiful failure, because he had no real strong man on whom to lean, and yielded to the advice of his wife, his brother Charley, the different corporation lawyers who have his ear, and various similar men." With a midterm review coming his way, however, Taft must surely start considering the interests of the people. "He may and probably will turn out to be a perfectly respectable President, whose achievements will be disheartening compared with what we had expected, but who nevertheless will have done well enough for us to justify us in renominating him—for you must remember that not to renominate him would be a very serious thing, only to be justified by really strong reasons."

The Colonel was putting the case as favorably for Taft as he could. "Otherwise I could see very ugly times ahead for me, as I should certainly not be nominated unless everybody believed that the ship was sinking and thought it a good thing to have me aboard her when she went down."

⟨⁓⟩

ROOSEVELT PONDERED WHAT to say about the state of the nation when his two-month vow of silence was up. His every word would be listened to as if megaphoned. Plainly, he would have to make a major address, or Americans would ask why he was willing to orate to Europeans, but not them. A poll conducted by *World's Work* magazine showed that more than three out of every four of its readers wanted him back in the White House. Progressive Democrats were likely to defect to him in large numbers. "I have just returned from a trip across Wisconsin and Minnesota," one respondent wrote, "and in talking with men on the train [about] Roosevelt and the presidency, the answer in *every* instance was that he could not help being President again."

He was in receipt of almost two thousand speaking invitations. Most were from committees or candidates desperate for help in endangered GOP constituencies. It did him little good to protest that the prospect of a return to the hustings filled him with "unalloyed horror." So he yielded to pressure from the Republican Congressional Campaign Committee to make a sixteen-state campaign trip, beginning in late August. The foray would take him west of Ohio into the heartland of insurgency. His itinerary would advertise his progressivism, no matter what dutiful words he uttered in behalf of the Party leadership.

To his annoyance, he heard that the Committee was raising money with the specific purpose of destroying every insurgent running for election or re-election in the fall—Senator Beveridge of Indiana, for one. Even Taft had contributed funds. The more Roosevelt thought about it, the more he convinced himself that his big speech on tour—most likely at Osawatomie, Kansas— must be a restatement of his Special Message of 1908, updated and expanded to embrace the aspirations of the anticorporate middle class.

"My proper task," he wrote an insurgent editor, "is clearly to announce myself on the vital questions of the day . . . and take a position that cannot be misunderstood."

For the rest of July, he chopped wood and swam, rowed, and camped with Archie and Quentin, when his huge volume of mail allowed him. He passed what were to him the most precious minutes of any day reading with Edith— either back and forth aloud, or sitting silently together with their books, as they had when they were children. Once or twice a week he was driven into Manhattan to attend meetings at the *Outlook* offices, traveling in a new automobile, a Haynes-Apperson Model 19. He quickly learned to drive himself, and became, in Edith's word, "addicted" to it.

At either end of his commute, the political pilgrims kept coming: more and more insurgents, Old Guard "mossbacks," fund-raisers, former appointees, emissaries of the New York Republican Party. All wanted something, if only the pleasure of having a former president listen to their "advice," on the presumption that he wanted it.

Those begging him to make personal appearances were particularly bothersome. Roosevelt had long ago discovered that the more provincial the supplicants, the less able they were to understand that their particular need was not unique: that he was not yearning to travel two thousand miles on bad trains to support the reelection campaign of a county sheriff, or to address the congregation of a new chapel in a landscape with no trees. His refusal, however elaborately apologetic, was received more often in puzzlement than anger. Imaginatively challenged folks, for whom crossing a state line amounted to foreign travel, could not conceive that the gray-blue eyes inspecting them had, over the past year, similarly scrutinized Nandi warriors, Arab mullahs, Magyar landowners, French marshals, Prussian academics, and practically every monarch or minister of consequence in Europe—not to mention the maquettes in Rodin's studio, and whatever dark truths flickered in the gaze of dying lions.

⁂

ON A VISIT to the summer White House, Lloyd Griscom encountered at first hand the President's desire to evade any contretemps not occurring on the golf course or poker table. Taft indicated that he might not support Roosevelt for chairman of the New York State convention in September. His explanation was simple: a gratified Boss Barnes would deliver a pro-Taft delegation to the national convention in 1912.

Then Barnes announced on 16 August that the machine had endorsed Vice President James Schoolcraft Sherman as its candidate for chairman of the convention. The Colonel was aghast at the news. Sherman was an archconservative who, he felt, could not have been nominated without Taft's approval. But he kept to his vow of silence, which had a few more days to run.

Taft could not refrain from chortling. "Have you seen the newspapers this afternoon?" he asked Archie Butt. "They have defeated Theodore."

Butt was so angry he had to go outside and stare at the sea to calm down. "It makes me ill," he wrote his sister-in-law that night, "to see the President lessen his own character by lending himself and his great office to these petty devices to humiliate his predecessor."

A news flash from Oyster Bay next day reported that the Colonel had told friends that he might have to oppose Taft in 1912 to preserve his progressive legacy. He neither confirmed nor denied that rumor, contenting himself with an announcement that he would go to Saratoga as a delegate from Nassau County, and would run against Sherman for the chairmanship. Barnes warned that there would be dead bodies in his way. "So they want a fight, do they?" Roosevelt responded. "By George, they shall have it." With that, he left New York on his western tour.

"BARNES WARNED THAT THERE WOULD BE DEAD BODIES IN HIS WAY."

William Barnes, Jr.

ROOSEVELT WAS GLOOMY about embarking on a "Teddysee," closely watched by the press, which might well leave the Party more fragmented than it was already. He had lost his former zest for whistle-stop speeches and—though he would not admit it—much of his love for crowds. He worried that his throat, sandpapered by dusty drought conditions on Long Island, would not stand the strain of nearly three weeks of shouting at people. "Ugh! I do dread . . . having to plunge into this cauldron of politics."

The truth was, he was not well. Earlier in the month, he had visited the anthracite country of Pennsylvania, and been struck by a recurrence of the same ailment that had immobilized him during the Coal Strike of 1902: an inflammation of the left shinbone, complicated by an attack of Cuban fever. He was also regaining the weight he had lost in Africa. He vowed that after this tour, and a lecture trip he was committed to the following spring, he would never again go on the road for any length of time.

Without much hope that anyone would believe him, Roosevelt insisted that he was traveling as an independent commentator, in behalf of *The Outlook*. This did not deter representatives of other magazines and newspapers from attaching a special car to his train. "It is incredible that there should remain a single American citizen," declared the New York *Sun*, "who does not see that Theodore Roosevelt has undertaken a campaign for the presidential nomination in 1912."

Rolling north on 23 August through Albany (stronghold of William Barnes, Jr.) and Utica (hometown of Vice President Sherman), he tried at first not to talk about politics at all. His provincial audiences reacted with dismay, and he realized that they wanted him to behave like a candidate for the presidency.

"I don't care *that* for it," he said, snapping his fingers, to O. K. Davis of *The New York Times*. "I've had all the work and all the fun and all the glory of it."

Davis waited for the inevitable follow-on. "Of course, if there were a big job to be done which the people wanted me to handle, that would be a different thing."

Proceeding via Buffalo into Ohio, Roosevelt began to address current issues—conservation, corporation control, labor and welfare reform—but carefully pitched his rhetoric so as not to offend conservative opinion. He praised the administration in the blandest possible language, refraining from any direct endorsement of Taft. As Ohio gave way to Indiana and the plains states, where insurgent candidates were registering dramatic gains in primary elections and conventions, he began to sound more progressive. But he said little that the President might not have said, to please the same audiences. He wanted to give maximum impact to what he called his "credo" at Osawatomie.

FOR A FEW RECREATIONAL HOURS, in Wyoming on the twenty-eighth, he was Roosevelt the Rough Rider again, happily participating in the Frontier Days celebration outside Cheyenne. The constant thunder of hooves, the band music, and the fluttering of myriad Stars and Stripes triggered a longing within him that went deeper than politics, deeper than patriotism, to some dark core of desire unsatisfied since his "crowded hour" in Cuba. Riding across the prairie with Robert D. Carey, a local rancher, he said that it was the ambition of his life "to go to war at the head of a brigade of cavalry."

With no war immediately at hand, Carey thought little of this strange remark. He had no inkling, and Roosevelt's subconscious may not have acknowledged, any connection between their current trot and the charge of the Twenty-first Lancers at Omdurman. Yet it had been there, some five months before, that Roosevelt had committed to come to Cheyenne.

◈

ADDRESSING BOTH HOUSES of the Colorado legislature in Denver the next day, Roosevelt gave Eastern conservatives the first hint of radical oratory to come. He accused the Supreme Court of favoring big corporations and creating a judicial no-man's-land around them, into which neither state nor federal government could trespass. A notorious case in point, he said, was *Lochner v. New York*. By striking down as unconstitutional a state law against excessive workplace hours, the Court had shown itself to be "against popular rights."

The word *popular* sounded, to conservative ears, like *populist,* and the idea that the Court was capable of hostile acts in defense of liberty of contract showed how far Roosevelt had come from his Social-Darwinist youth. President Taft, who venerated appellate justice as something superior to *vox populi,* thought his remark smacked of anarchy. But Roosevelt was only warming up.

At 2:15 P.M. on the thirty-first, he climbed onto a kitchen table in a grove outside Osawatomie, Kansas, where John Brown had fought the Missouri raiders in 1856. A crowd of thirty thousand Kansans waited to hear him declaim his "credo." The prairie sun was strong, but there had been a cloudburst earlier in the day, and many stood ankle deep in mud.

Addressing himself repeatedly toward the Civil War veterans who sat in a special place on the battleground, Roosevelt roared over the calls of food vendors, "There have been two great crises in our country's history: first, when it was formed, and then, again, when it was perpetuated." The name of John Brown, he declared, would "be forever associated" with the second of these national crises. Having said that, he avoided any further tribute to the bloody old fanatic.

It was a looming third crisis he wished to discuss—one utterly modern, yet still subject to the wisdom of Abraham Lincoln. The Emancipator had advocated harnessing a universal dynamic, whose power derived from the struggle between those who produced, and those who profited. Roosevelt quoted Lincoln's famous maxim, *Labor is the superior of capital,* and joked, "If that remark was original with me, I should be even more strongly denounced as a communist agitator than I shall be anyhow."

Nevertheless, he was willing to go further in insisting that property rights must henceforth be secondary to those of the common welfare. A maturing civilization should work to destroy unmerited social status. "The essence of any struggle for healthy liberty has always been . . . to take from some one man or class of men the right to enjoy power, or wealth, or position, or immunity, which has not been earned by service to his or their fellows."

America's corporate elite, Roosevelt said, was fortifying itself with the compliance of political bosses. He revived one of his favorite catchphrases: "I stand for the square deal." Granting that even monopolistic corporations were entitled to justice, he denied them any right to influence it, or to assume that they could buy votes in Congress.

> The Constitution guarantees protections to property, and we must make that promise good. But it does not give the right of suffrage to any corporation. The true friend of property, the true conservative, is he who insists that property shall be the servant and not the master of the commonwealth; who insists that the creature of man's making shall be the servant and not the master of the man who made it. The citizens of the United States must effectively control the mighty commercial forces which they have themselves called into being.

Gifford Pinchot sat listening with collaborative satisfaction. He, James Garfield, and William Allen White, the progressive editor of the *Emporia Gazette,* had drafted significant sections of the Colonel's speech.

Roosevelt explained that there could be no check to the growth of special interests so long as channels of collusion flowed back and forth between secretive boardrooms and secretive halls of government. To that end, the people must insist on "complete and effective publicity of corporate affairs,"* and a law prohibiting "the use of corporate funds directly or indirectly for political purposes."

There should be federal regulation, and physical valuation, of the stock flotations of all industrial combinations doing an interstate business: not only railroads and steamship lines, but those dealing in meat, oil, coal, and other necessities. Executives and "especially" the board members of such corporations should be held responsible for breaches of antitrust law. Roosevelt cited one of the proudest creations of his own administration, the Federal Bureau of Corporations, and said that it and the Interstate Commerce Commission should be handed greater powers. He further advocated "the great central task" of conservation of natural resources, second only to national security on his agenda; graduated income and inheritance taxes on big fortunes; a judiciary accountable to changing social and economic conditions; comprehensive workmen's compensation acts; national laws to regulate the labor of

---

* In 1910, the word *publicity* was understood to mean exposure of something generally hidden.

children and women; higher safety and sanitary standards in the workplace; and public scrutiny of all political campaign spending, both before and after elections.

Throughout his address, the food vendors had loudly continued to advertise peanuts, popcorn, hot dogs, and pink lemonade, and a merry-go-round whistled not far away. But Kansans stood rapt as the Colonel, acknowledging that there could be such a thing as too much federal power, called for a compensatory spirit of democratic redress, as strong in the extremities of the country as at its center.

Three times, he defined this spirit as "New Nationalism." One of its principal features would be a judiciary that favored individual over property rights. "I rank dividends below human character," Roosevelt shouted, and swung into his peroration:

> If our political institutions were perfect, they would absolutely prevent the political domination of money in any part of our affairs. We need to make our political representatives more quickly and sensitively responsive to the people whose servants they are. . . . It is particularly important that all moneys received or expended for campaign purposes should be publicly accounted for, not only after election, but before election as well. . . .
>
> No matter how honest and decent we are in our private lives, if we do not have the right kind of law and the right kind of administration of the law, we cannot go forward as a nation. That is imperative; but it must be an addition to, and not a substitution for, the qualities that make us good citizens. . . . The prime problem of our nation is to get the right type of good citizenship, and, to get it, we must have progress, and our public men must be genuinely progressive.

ROOSEVELT'S "NEW NATIONALISM" speech made front-page headlines all over the country. Newspapers printed the text in full. Progressive editors reacted with understandable warmth, forgiving the Colonel for his reluctance—still—to condemn the administration outright. "The dominant note of the whole address was its humanity," remarked the *Fort Wayne Sentinel*, "its demand for the square deal, and its placing of the rights of man above the rights of property." Conservative organs of both major parties condemned him as a "neo-Populist," a "peripatetic revolutionist," and "a virtual traitor to American institutions." Criticism was particularly shrill in New York, center of the American financial industry. "The character of his addresses in the West during the last few days," remarked *The New York Times*, "has startled all thoughtful men and impressed them with the frightful danger which lies in his

political ascendancy." The *New York Commercial* described New Nationalism as "more and worse than rank socialism—it is communism at the limit."
The *Tribune* noted that Roosevelt had traveled to Osawatomie by way of the
state lunatic asylum.

Perhaps the most trenchant commentary was that of the *New York
Evening Post*, focusing on what he had not said:

> He never once mentioned the party to which he is supposed to be-
> long . . . nor referred in the remotest way to the President. . . . What
> are we to make of this? Are we to infer that Mr. Roosevelt proposes to
> found and head a new party, made up of elements from both the old
> ones? Is this speech to be taken as a bold bid for the Presidency in 1912?

Even taken at its face value, the *Post* went on, "his speech yesterday out-
strips not only the most extreme utterance that he himself ever made previously, but that of any of the most radical men of our time."

Roosevelt himself granted that he had probably gone too far at
Osawatomie—at least, voiced his "deepest convictions" on the subject of radical reform too soon. "I had no business to take the position in the fashion
that I did," he wrote Henry Cabot Lodge. "A public man is to be condemned
if he fails to make his point clear . . . and it is a blunder of some gravity to do
it." He would have difficulty, now, in pretending that he was a regular Republican. *Progressive* had been the final word he threw at his Kansas audience, before jumping down off that kitchen table to roars of applause.

He tried to sound as conciliatory as possible toward the administration in
stump speeches on the way back east, arguing that Republicans had to remain
unified in the face of the threat they faced in November. But the damage was
done. In future, nothing he said about Party policy could be interpreted as
constructive. As Taft scoffed privately, the program Roosevelt had advanced at
Osawatomie "could never be gotten through without a revolution or revisions
to the Constitution."

James Bryce, currently British ambassador to Washington and a lifelong
observer of the American scene, was reminded of Disraeli's remark "that
when a majority in the House of Commons is too large and the opposition
too weak, part of the majority becomes detached and begins to fill the function of an opposition." Republicans had simply been too strong too long, in
all three branches of government. Since the Democrats had failed to mount an
effective challenge to them, in seven successive election seasons, the GOP's
own "progressive and so-called radical section" had begun, almost without
realizing it, to think and campaign like another party. Chief among the apostates was Theodore Roosevelt. Their transformation was his transformation.
Except that, having changed so much as President, he had continued to

change during more than a year of removal from domestic politics. The "en-larged personality" immediately obvious to four intimates on his first day home, the new capability of "greater good or greater evil," was now an in-escapable challenge to the leadership of both major parties.

"A break between the President and the Colonel might not be altogether regrettable," *Harper's Weekly* remarked. "Like the removal of Mr. Pinchot last winter, it might clear the atmosphere, lessen the need for pretence and hypocrisy, and greatly simplify the task of the average Republican in making up his mind where he stands."

In no way did Roosevelt seem more radically threatening than in his moralistic attitude toward justice. If constructionists could believe their ears and eyes, he proposed to subject the Constitution itself to moral review. "When I see you," Henry Cabot Lodge wrote on 5 September, "I shall want to have a full talk in regard to this matter of court decisions, about which I admit I am very conservative. . . . The courts are charged with the duty of saying what the law is, not what it ought to be, and I think that to encourage resis-tance to the decisions of the courts tends to lead to a disregard of the law."

Roosevelt answered that his attack on the Supreme Court's pro-corporate bias had been prompted by none other than Justice William Henry Moody, whom he had met with the day after seeing Taft in June. Not only that, he had "most carefully" consulted with another constitutional expert, Professor Arthur D. Hill of Harvard. Moody believed "that the courts . . . sometimes erred in deciding against the national government," and Hill had even com-pared the Court to "an irresponsible House of Lords."

Since both consultants hailed from Massachusetts, the center of Lodge's universe, no further dissent was heard in Nahant. But the damage to Roo-sevelt's reputation as a regular Republican was a perceived fact when he got back home, hoarse and depressed, on 11 September.

To Edith, the debilitating effect campaign travel now seemed to have on him was worrying. "He comes home in the saddest frame of mind that can be imagined," she wrote Jules Jusserand, "and requires much cheering from his family." On the trail, Roosevelt was as conscientious and energetic as he had always been, stopping his train up to thirty times a day whenever he saw a crowd, large or small, waiting for a glimpse of "Teddy." He shouted or rasped or squeaked with all his old fervor, repeating the bromides that delighted them, glowing with charm, humor, and goodwill, leaving behind an image that never faded. ("His tour through the West has been one continuous ova-tion," Taft marveled, with a touch of envy.) But Edith could see that her hus-band had changed in some fundamental way. He had lost his compulsion for electoral favor. No matter how passionately he believed in the New National-ism, the statesman in him cringed at the prospect of having to go back to sell-ing it.

❧

THERE WAS ONE pleasant development, however, to cheer Roosevelt on his return: the popular and critical success of his safari book, just released by Scribners. *African Game Trails: An Account of the African Wanderings of an American Hunter-Naturalist* was selling strongly. Thanks to first serial and foreign rights, it promised to be the most profitable title he had ever published. Five hundred signed copies of the two-volume first edition, boxed and printed on Dutch handmade paper, had been followed by a one-volume trade issue, hardly less luxurious in three-quarter pigskin with uncut pages, and a subscription edition for the mass market. Lavishly illustrated, *African Game Trails* was irresistible to readers who could stomach the meticulous descriptions of bullets drilling hearts and brains. Even those who could not (Cecil Spring Rice found it sickening, "rather like the diary of a butcher") had to concede that Roosevelt was scientific in his scrutiny of every aspect of the African wilderness, and often movingly lyrical. The density of recorded details, whether ornithological, paleontological, botanical, or anthropological, was almost overwhelming. Most came not from notes, but from the author's movie-camera memory, which in advance of any system yet available in nickelodeons, registered both sight and sound.

Over and above its documentary appeal, the book exuded a kind of savage romance new to American readers. Roosevelt's authenticity of voice made the Western novels of Zane Grey and Owen Wister seem pallid: "So, with the lion-skin swinging behind two porters, a moribund puff-adder in my saddle pocket, and three rhinos threatening us in the darkness, we marched campward through the African night."

Reviewers acknowledged the occasional overripeness of his prose style, but excused it in view of the curiosity and courage with which he had traversed lands hitherto seen as hostile to foreign exploration and settlement. *The Nation* noted that what he wrote was of secondary importance to what he had done to place the African section of the Smithsonian Museum "in the front rank of zoological collections."

Roosevelt felt he had not done enough. As soon as he had extricated himself from his current political embroilment, he intended to collaborate with Edmund Heller on a volume of life histories of African game animals that would last in libraries long after the New Nationalism had become old.

❧

ROOSEVELT AND TAFT were so clearly on divergent roads by mid-September (the former calling for authority to be centered in the executive, the latter for its enshrinement in the judiciary) that Party intermediaries felt it was crucial for them to meet again, in a show of Republican unity. Lloyd Griscom arranged a lunch rendezvous at Henry White's summer house in New Haven, Connecticut, on 19 September. Roosevelt crossed Long Island Sound by motorboat. It was a stormy voyage, into which the press did not fail to read portents, but he received a pleasant reception from Taft and a small group of friends and aides.

Covers were laid for six. By prearrangement, the President and the Colonel were left alone at the end of the meal, and the dining room door was locked. "I suppose it is the New York situation you want to discuss," Taft said. He allowed that he was willing, after all, to support Roosevelt's bid for the chairmanship of the Saratoga convention, now only one week away. But the White House would not oppose any gubernatorial candidate or policy initiative that might result if he lost. Roosevelt, for his part, was unwilling to beg any further favor. When after a considerable time they emerged, it was evident that their polite estrangement continued. They parted with strained joviality, and contrary impressions as to why they met and what they each had said.

To Roosevelt's annoyance, Charles D. Norton, the President's devious young secretary, authorized a wire report stating that the Colonel had come to New Haven hat in hand. Taft, genuinely concerned about Barnes manipulating the convention, had agreed to support Roosevelt's candidacy over that of his own vice president, James S. Sherman.

Roosevelt indignantly denied Norton's wire, annoying Taft in turn. The President complained to Archie Butt that Roosevelt had been "offish" during their meeting, while lecturing him on the need to keep the GOP intact. "If you were to remove Roosevelt's skull now, you would find written on his brain '1912.'"

Yet the owner of the skull in question recoiled from the prospect of a petty political battle in Saratoga. "Twenty years ago I should not have minded it in the least," Roosevelt wrote Henry Cabot Lodge. "It would have been entirely suitable for my age and standing. But it is not the kind of fight into which an ex-President should be required to go."

❧

NOW HERE HE WAS, in his thirtieth year as a practicing Republican, positioning himself, as he had in 1880, against the lowliest type of machine politicians. He climbed aboard a train full of convention delegates heading up the Hudson Valley, and confessed to a sense of *déjà vu*. "It reminds me of the old days when I was first elected to the Assembly." He introduced Lawrence Abbott to a red-faced old ward heeler from the Twenty-first District of Manhattan. "I want you to know my friend, Joe Murray. He started me in politics. Take him into the smoking room and get him to tell you the story."

Saratoga's pink, High Victorian town hall overbore the modest resort as much as the State Capitol dominated Albany. Its chandelier-hung auditorium and thirty-foot stage looked more appropriate for plays than politics, and indeed functioned as a theater for much of the year. On the opening day of the convention, 27 September, the thespian in Roosevelt rose to the challenge of impressing a thousand fellow Republicans that he, not Sherman, was best qualified to chair the proceedings.

He did it by exuding such jovial, uninhibited charisma that all eyes were drawn to him when the list of candidates was announced. William Barnes, Jr.—pale, long-fingered, weary-looking—made the mistake of asking the smallest politician present, Abe Gruber of New York, to make a speech opposing Roosevelt's nomination. Gruber tried to make up in stridency what he lacked in height. But he came up short in both respects, and succeeded only in evoking hilarity. When he tried to portray the returned hunter as a trigger-happy revolutionary ("Looking for other fields of shooting practice, this man is now shooting at the courts"), Roosevelt rocked in his seat with laughter, slapping the thigh of a fellow delegate.

The subsequent vote, however, was a solemn affair. No previous state convention had ever been required to choose between a former president and sitting vice president. It decided in Roosevelt's favor, 567 to 445. Sherman had to escort him onstage and listen to his keynote address.

As a forum for oratory, Saratoga Town Hall did not compare with the Sorbonne or Oxford University. Roosevelt's audience that hot afternoon was unlikely to be receptive to any biological analogies in history, nor, for that matter, to much New Nationalism. He soothed it with an opening list of laws creditable to Republicans in Congress, "and to our able, upright, and distinguished President, William Howard Taft."

Except for his conspicuous avoidance of any other reference to the administration, this sounded like the endorsement Taft had been craving all summer. The word *upright* had a sycophantic ring to progressives still chafing over the Ballinger-Pinchot affair. But Roosevelt wanted to strike a moral note early. "We are against the degrading alliance which adds strength to the already powerful corrupt boss and to the already powerful corrupt head of big business," he shouted.

He was trying to galvanize the convention into a wholesale revolt against Barnes. In fact (as Democratic observers were pleasedly aware), no boss could worsen, no reform ticket could improve the GOP's appalling fortunes in New York. Not to mention other parts of the country: Taft and his tariff were simply too unpopular, and the Party too divided to inspire voter confidence. Already Maine, that most rock-ribbed of Republican states, had just elected a Democratic governor and legislature, and, for the first time in half a century, returned two Democrats to the House of Representatives.

For the moment in Saratoga, Roosevelt gave the Party an illusion of unity. He paced the stage with such jut-jawed force that O. K. Davis, in the press

box, was reminded of a caveman on the prowl. The audience sat stunned as
words flew out of him in spasms, punctuated by loud palm punches: "The rule
of the boss is the negation of democracy."

At least one delegate was able, by virtue of long friendship, to distinguish
the performer from the performance. "Theodore," said Elihu Root, putting a
hand on his shoulder, "you are still the same great, overgrown boy as ever."

By far the most distinguished man to have served him, as political patron,
legal adviser, secretary of war, and secretary of state, Root now represented
New York in the U.S. Senate. He might even have done so in the White House,
if the "overgrown boy" had not regretfully decided, in 1908, to choose a successor with fewer ties to Wall Street. It was ironic that Taft had turned out to
be a much more divisive figure. For all Root's conservatism, he was capable, at
sixty-five, of liberal attitudes—toward strategic autonomy for Latin America,
for example, or the ideal of a permanent international court of justice at The
Hague. Almost alone among orthodox Republicans, he declined to be fazed
by New Nationalism. "If it means having the federal government do the
things which it can do better than the states and which are within the limits of
its present constitutional power, I am for it. If it means more than that, I am
against it."

Root opposed, by reflex, any challenge to legal authority. He had been instrumental in persuading Taft to fire Gifford Pinchot for insubordination. He
did not admire the President, but accepted him as someone sanctioned by the
people, by the Party, and by Theodore Roosevelt. Behind that gibe at Saratoga
flashed an admonition, as from father to son: *Behave yourself.*

THE CONVENTION'S MOST important business on its second day was to
name a successor to Governor Hughes, now about to take his seat on the
Supreme Court. Roosevelt had his candidate: Henry Lewis Stimson, the unim-
peachably correct U.S. attorney for the Southern District of New York. Barnes
put forward a tame congressman, William S. Bennet. Stimson was chosen, 684
votes to 242. Roosevelt then forced the adoption of a progressive platform that
pledged to introduce the direct primary. By now, his control of the convention
was so absolute that he even got delegates to stop smoking. "It shows an utter
lack of consideration for the rest of those present," he scolded, as they meekly
crushed out their cigars.

Less than three months after his reluctant reentry into politics, he had become the architect of the Party's fall campaign. But by so personalizing a local
struggle widely seen as hopeless (Stimson was an unpromising candidate,
with all the charm of a bluefish), the Colonel was once again risking his reputation.

"I do not think we can win," Roosevelt told O. K. Davis after the convention adjourned. "However, the fight was worth the making. We have beaten the reactionary machine, and the progressives are in charge of the party organization."

Democrats assembling in Rochester for their own convention acknowledged this by nominating John A. Dix, a wealthy, boss-beholden industrialist, to oppose Stimson. They made clear that their long-term purpose was to defeat Roosevelt so badly that he would never again run for president. "We have got a bitter fight ahead of us—a fight against a marvelous man," one orator declared. "Let us take it out of him!"

⟨⟩

HOME AT SAGAMORE HILL, Roosevelt consented to an off-the-record interview with Ray Stannard Baker, one of the progressive journalists he had accused of "muckraking" back in 1906. Now he merely teased the younger man for being "a reasonable exponent of the extreme left of the Party," and said, "Ask me anything you like."

He sat relaxed in his library, still perspiring from an early morning ride, and talked exultantly about his victory at Saratoga. Sooner or later, Republican reactionaries were going to have to adjust to changing times. "Root is all right, but he needs me to direct him. Taft is the same sort of man. He needs direction."

Baker had gotten used, over the years, to Roosevelt's amazing self-confidence, but this imperious note, not unmixed with contempt for former allies, was something new.

"Are you a candidate for the presidency in 1912?"

"I will answer your question as plainly as you have asked it." Roosevelt leaned forward, as he always did for emphasis.

"I don't know."

⟨⟩

THE GROWING SUSPICION that the Colonel was running for a third term caused his old enemies on Wall Street to look with disfavor on the Saratoga ticket. Their newspaper of choice, the New York *Sun,* kept printing an editorial leitmotif, "The time to beat Roosevelt in 1912 is on November 8, 1910." Even stalwart Republicans solicited funds for Dix and other Democratic candidates. They knew they were embarrassing President Taft, but their corporate consciences were clear: the vital thing was to keep government weak, and business strong.

Roosevelt spent the next forty days trying to save the GOP inside and outside his own state. He traveled wherever he felt needed—south through Georgia and Mississippi to Hot Springs, Arkansas; west to St. Louis and back through Illinois and Indiana (where Albert J. Beveridge's Senate seat was under siege); northeast in aid of the similarly threatened Henry Cabot Lodge; up, down, and around New York State, making twelve to fifteen speeches a day, hoping to convince voters that reform and Republicanism were not incompatible. "He is trying to be both radical and conservative," Baker observed. *"It will not work."*

Occasionally Roosevelt's passion for social reform got the better of him. On 22 October he attacked Simeon E. Baldwin, the retired chief justice of Connecticut, for ruling in *Hoxie v. the New Haven Railroad* (1909) that a brakeman was not entitled to compensation for the loss of a leg in a collision of two trains. Judge Baldwin had held that the Federal Employers' Liability Act of 1906 denied liberty of labor contract within states. Because such liberty was, in the judge's view, a form of property protected by the Constitution, Congress had no power to override the personnel policies of a private railroad.

The liability law was one of the most progressive achievements of Roosevelt's presidency. He had seen it strengthened just before he went out of office, and was furious to find that a provincial judge had thrown it out of court. Railroad lobbyists were now seizing on the *Hoxie* decision as an argument in favor of deregulation, and sending copies of it to conservative candidates across the country. Baldwin himself was running for governor of Connecticut on the Democratic ticket, and suggesting that the New Nationalism was an authoritarian plan for the dismantling of states' rights. Back of it, he warned, lay the desire of a dangerous man to radicalize the Supreme Court. "So far as I am aware, ex-President Roosevelt has had no special training for undertaking such a task."

The judge was clearly spoiling for a fight, and Roosevelt was quick to oblige. As he explained to Elihu Root, "When I'm mad at a man I want to climb right up his chest." Speaking extempore in Concord, Massachusetts, to a supportive crowd, he accused Baldwin of holding that the Constitution gave industrial employees the right to sign contracts that later prevented them suing for loss of life and limb.

Baldwin, incensed at newspaper reports of the speech, denied that personal feelings had influenced his *Hoxie* decision. In an open letter addressed to Roosevelt, he insisted that he had ruled according to legal precedent— specifically, the "fellow-servant" defense hallowed by common law—and pointed out that his own campaign in Connecticut touted workmen's compensation. "I trust that your remarks at Concord were misinterpreted; if not, you certainly were misinformed. If you did, in fact, make the charge against me, or one substantially of that character, I write to request that you would retract it."

In a return open letter of his own, Roosevelt stood by the substance of what he had said. "I feel that it is in the highest degree retrogressive (or, if you prefer the term, Bourbon and reactionary), to take the view that the fellow-servant rule . . . rests . . . 'upon consideration of right and justice.' "

The exchange was an obvious first skirmish in an ideological battle whose repercussions would probably extend far beyond the current campaign. At stake was the classical, or "mechanical" jurisprudence of Baldwin and his constructionist counterparts on the Supreme Court *versus* the "sociological" jurisprudence of William H. Moody and other progressive legal thinkers. The common law itself needed to be redefined, either as the unchanging thing it had seemed to be through most of the nineteenth century, or as Justice Oliver Wendell Holmes, Jr. (another Roosevelt appointee), had famously proposed, as a codification of "the felt necessities of the time."

Nobody "felt" the changing demands of American society more viscerally than Theodore Roosevelt in the fall of 1910. Herbert Croly intellectualized them; Moody and Holmes gave them constitutional sanction; La Follette and Pinchot formulated them as dogma; writers as various as Upton Sinclair, Theodore Dreiser, and William Allen White gave them literary expression. But Roosevelt was unique in the force of his conviction that these "necessities" must be translated from desire into political reform—unique, too, in his ability to persuade voters of the possibility of such reform. He "felt" so strongly that he was prepared to temporize, pleading for Republican unity, as progressivism burgeoned into the fundamental issue of the next presidential election. "One thing always to remember in politics," he told White, "is that it takes a long time to overcome inertia, and that, when it has been overcome, it takes an equally long time to stop momentum."

Judge Baldwin, by contrast, amounted almost to a caricature of the old paternalist neurosis, on the wane everywhere except on Wall Street and in Brahmin Boston. He believed not only in states' rights over federal power, but in trusts as always trustworthy, and the rich as "stewards for the public good," not to mention flogging, castration, and other methods of social control. As such, he was clearly a candidate, not only for governor of Connecticut, but for one of the most devastating weapons in Roosevelt's arsenal: a no-holds-barred, public "posterity letter."

Nothing in their previous correspondence could have prepared Baldwin for the missive he received on 2 November: two thousand words long, specific, and packed with argument. Readers of the newspaper transcript had no need to consult *African Game Trails* for further evidence that the Colonel, in full hunting cry, was a formidable adversary.

He brushed aside Baldwin's legalistic self-defense ("My criticism of you as a reactionary was based, not upon what you may have said as a law writer, but upon what you did as a judge") and said that Section Five of the Federal Employers' Liability Act voided any contract that enabled a common carrier to exempt itself from liability for accidents due to negligence. In indemnifying the New Haven Railroad against any claim from employees mutilated on the job, Baldwin had flouted that structure and in effect decided that "the right to get killed" was a property right sanctioned by the Constitution. "Congress aimed at giving the railroad employee a substance. You construed the act as giving him a shadow by solemnly declaring that to give him substance is to take away his property in the shadow."

Shadows over substance, words rather than deeds, precedents hampering change, technical injustice precluding practical justice: Roosevelt had been attacking statutory pedantry since his days as a law student at Columbia University. Even in 1881, he had stood out among his classmates, arguing "for justice against legalism," and complaining about the "sharp practice" of corporate lawyers. As President, he insisted that courts, no less than churches, were places where plain morals had to be expounded. Judges should no more sanction an abusive policy, in the name of the Fourteenth Amendment, than priests should cite the Old Testament in favor of child sacrifice. He had gone so far as to suggest, in his eighth annual message to Congress, that the judicial branch of government was actually a branchlet of the legislative. Now out of office, he was as righteously didactic as ever:

> In this opinion of yours . . . not a line appears which can be distorted into the slightest recognition of the right to life and limb of the employee, into the slightest recognition of the grave perils of the men engaged in railway work; not a word appears in the whole opinion as to the grave importance of the question from the point of view of the thousands of railway men annually killed, and hundreds of thousands annually injured in their dangerous calling.

Roosevelt followed up on 4 November with a near-libelous attack on Baldwin in Des Moines. The judge was too busy with his own gubernatorial race to respond. "I shall waste no more words on him," he announced, "but intend, when I have leisure . . . to bring a suit."

❧

RETURNING TO NEW YORK, Roosevelt found that Stimson was boring audiences into somnolence. "Darn it, Henry, a campaign speech is a poster, not an etching." His own last speeches, delivered in Manhattan on election eve, were little more than weary croaks.

By the following evening, 8 November, it was clear that the GOP had suffered one of the worst defeats in its history. It had lost control of the House for the first time since 1894, and of the Senate too, unless a small swing group of progressives could be counted as faithful Party members. Even they were chagrined by the defection of many Eastern progressive voters to the Democrats. Beveridge crashed. Ninety-eight Republican congressmen lost their seats. More than half the states chose Democratic governors. As Maine went, so went Massachusetts, Connecticut, New York, New Jersey, Maryland, Ohio, Indiana, Kentucky, Missouri, and Oregon. The first Socialist representative in American history was elected in Milwaukee, Wisconsin.

For the Republican National Committee, the results were particularly upsetting. Despite all the money Aldrich, Crane, and others had raised to suppress insurgent candidates, conservatives prevailed in only three out of nine reform-minded states. Nick Longworth barely survived the anti-Taft turnaround in Ohio. Nationwide as at home, the voting pattern amounted to a rejection of everything Taft had stood for so far. He was shocked into a rare burst of metaphorical excess. "I should say, it was not only a landslide, but a tidal wave and a holocaust all rolled into one general cataclysm."

The President was still, however, head of the Party, with immense reserves of patronage to help him rebuild his devastated landscape. Roosevelt, in contrast, was swept into political exile with a force that had analysts doubting he would ever again figure in national affairs. He had been humiliated in his own state, where Stimson lost to Dix by a plurality of 67,410 votes. Democrats won other key offices and both houses of the legislature. Young Franklin D. Roosevelt of Hyde Park became a Democratic state senator. Only fourteen Republicans were elected to New York's thirty-seven-man Congressional delegation. Even Oyster Bay sent a Democrat to the House of Representatives.

Elsewhere, the results looked even worse for Roosevelt. Every candidate he had campaigned for had been defeated, while all those he opposed had won. Perhaps his worst humiliation was in Connecticut, where Judge Baldwin had been triumphantly elected governor. Less than five months after being welcomed home by a million New Yorkers, the Colonel was seen as human, vain, and fallible.

⟋⟍

HE SECLUDED HIMSELF from reporters at Sagamore Hill, pleading that he needed a rest. This was true: since coming down the Nile he had been almost continually onstage. He was exhausted, sick of posturing and orating. "I am glad to think that I have Father safely caged at Sagamore," Edith wrote Kermit.

Only one journalist was permitted to visit, on Sunday, 13 November. Mark Sullivan, the editor of *Collier's Weekly*, was a good friend, and could be relied on to respect Roosevelt's desire for privacy. More sympathetically than most, Sullivan understood the complex feelings of duty and desire that had reinvolved Roosevelt in politics. He had been at Harvard, observing, on that fateful day when Governor Hughes asked the returning hunter for help.

The big brick house was quiet, with double windows blocking more sound than cold, and all its children's rooms empty, except the one Ethel still occupied, keeping her parents company.

"Don't go," Roosevelt said, when Sullivan made a move to return to Oyster Bay station. "The time will come when only a few friends like you will come out to see me here."

"HE WAS EXHAUSTED, SICK OF POSTURING AND ORATING."
Roosevelt reading on the North River ferry, New York, fall 1910.

Sullivan stayed on for some time, then again tried to leave. Roosevelt clung to him.

He suggested that I should not take the train from Oyster Bay but that the two of us should walk four miles across Long Island fields to another station on the main line, at Syosset. At the station, as we parted, he made me a present of the cane he carried, as if he wished to make some enduring seal of what he regarded as probably a diminishing number of his future friends. As I looked out the window of the car and Roosevelt waved a final good-by and turned back toward Sagamore Hill, I felt sorry for the thoughts I knew would accompany him through the four miles of winter dusk.

ROOSEVELT'S MOOD WAS not as melancholy as Sullivan imagined. For a few weeks, he alternated between bravado ("The fight for progressive government has merely begun") and relief that a repugnant campaign was over ("I have never had a more unpleasant summer").

One piece of good news was that Simeon Baldwin might not, after all, sue him for libel. The governor-elect felt there was little political capital to be gained by dragging a still beloved former president into court, and suggested arbitrating their differences. Roosevelt declined to arbitrate and insisted, once again, on the primacy of national law over states' rights. Baldwin replied that in view of the Colonel's obvious sincerity, he would not proceed against him.

Gradually Roosevelt began to feel more cheerful about his disastrous decision to reenter politics. He gave thanks that there would be no more talk of him challenging the President for renomination. "It looks to me as if, ultimately, the best thing that could happen to us now would be to do what we can with Taft, face probable defeat in 1912, and then endeavor to reorganize under really capable and sanely progressive leadership."

He thought that he had behaved responsibly at Saratoga, fighting against machine politics with the approval of the administration. And he was pleased that, although his too-big personality seemed to have hurt some progressive candidates, his promulgation of the New Nationalism had helped others to win big in the West and Midwest. The swing vote that Republican insurgents now wielded in the Senate was encouraging. If Democrats had been shameless in cottoning on to the progressive cause, at least their imitation was a sincere form of flattery. One of them, Woodrow Wilson, the former president of Princeton University, had been elected governor of New Jersey on a campaign platform of corporate control, railroad taxation, humane labor policies, and primary reform that the Colonel himself could have written.

⌒

AS THE END of the year approached, Roosevelt and Taft began—half-shyly, half-warily—to reconcile. They had mutual bruises to nurse, as well as memories of an era when they had been on happier terms, forever roaring with laughter.

On 19 November, the Colonel put in a surprise appearance at the White House. He pretended not to know that Taft was away on a Caribbean cruise, and said only that he had time to kill before engagements at the Smithsonian and National Geographic Society. Munching corn bread from the kitchen and trailed by an excited group of former servants and clerks, he marched over to the West Wing to look at the new Oval Office that Taft had built over his former tennis court.

Without a trace of self-consciousness, he sat behind the President's desk and said how "natural" it felt to be there. He praised everything he saw, and remembered the names of all around him, including scullery maids. Then he was off, leaving behind a calling card for Mrs. Taft. Ike Hoover, the White

House usher, wept when describing the event to Archie Butt. "It is the only happy day we have had in two years, and not one of us would exchange it for a hundred-dollar bill."

When Taft returned to reclaim his chair, he wrote Roosevelt to say he was sorry to have missed him, and insisted that he stay at the White House next time he came to the capital. "I think you are a trump to ask me," Roosevelt replied, but was vague about future visits. A political instinct sharper than the President's warned him to keep his distance. That did not stop him lobbying Taft to appoint Edward Douglass White, a Southern Democrat and a Catholic, as Chief Justice of the United States, instead of Charles Evans Hughes, who had shown no gratitude for services rendered earlier in the year. Taft was happy to oblige, and in return asked the Colonel to review a draft of his annual message to Congress. "There is nothing for me to say," Roosevelt replied, "save in the way of agreement and commendation."

Notwithstanding their politesse on paper, a residue of personal disapproval remained. Taft used the phrase *deeply wounded* so often, in complaining about Roosevelt's post-Africa attitude, as to sound almost masochistic. It was clear to aides that the President was mentally and physically ailing. Over the summer his weight had ballooned to 330 pounds, and he kept falling asleep during the day. A doctor advised that his heart was under serious strain. He lived for play rather than duty, procrastinating endlessly—"I would give anything in the world if I had the ability to clear away work as Roosevelt did." Tabulatory games obsessed him: when his golf score was low, or his bridge and poker winnings high, he was unconscious of time passing, and the resentment of companions wanting to go home.

Roosevelt was more healthy in mind and body, although he had trouble shaking his travel fatigue. He claimed to be reconciled to life on the sidelines, and wrote Eleanor, now settled with Ted in San Francisco:

> What I now most want is just what is forced on me: to stay here in my own home with your mother-in-law, to walk and ride with her, and in the evening sit with her before the great wood fire in the north room and hear the wind shrieking outside; to chop trees and read books, and feel that I am justified in not working. I don't want to be in Africa, or on the ranch, or in the army, or in the White House; I like to think of them all, now and then, but the place I wish to be is just where I am.

CHAPTER 6

Not a Word, Gentlemen

And that's over. Here you are,
Battered by the past,
Time will have his little scar,
But the wound won't last.

SAGAMORE HILL WAS A BLEAK PLACE in January 1911, with no windbreak except leafless, lower woods to cut gusts sweeping up from the ice sheet of Oyster Bay. On still afternoons, Roosevelt could hear the *ha'-ha'-wee, ha'-ha'-wee* of long-tailed ducks lying under the lee of the shore. It was a harsh, not unmusical clangor that had enchanted him as a boy, and prompted his first attempt at autobiographical writing. But to older ears, the calls spoke of *temps perdu.* Here was yesterday's "Teedie" in his fifty-third year, trying to adjust to the fact that the American people had gotten tired of him.

So it seemed, judging from the quietness of his driveway. Cabs from the station no longer disgorged groups of politicians. The few who came offered little in the way of cheer. Lloyd Griscom visited once. Henry Stimson, a close neighbor, stopped by occasionally, but could not help bringing with him, like wisps of fog, cold reminders of defeat. Roosevelt's Harvard classmate, Congressman Charles G. Washburn—defeated too—came one day to commiserate.

"You are now enduring the supreme test," Washburn said. He looked around the house. It had the used, not to say abused look of a home that had seen many children grow up and go their various ways, while also functioning for a quarter of a century as the country headquarters of a public man. Never elegant—it was too darkly paneled, too cluttered, with horns protruding from the walls and flattened animals snarling underfoot—it had gone through its comfortable and luxurious phases and begun to be shabby. Between faded oriental rugs, the hall floorboards were pitted from the pounding of hobnail boots. Foundation cracks ran around the frieze of the hall mantel. Years of creosote deposits had darkened the cannonballs that lay like testicles at the base of two penile, brass-sleeved shell cartridges serving as andirons in the hearth. The great North Room, built for presidential receptions, now functioned mainly as a gallery for the display of mementos (Wilhelm II's indis-

"A GALLERY FOR THE DISPLAY OF MEMENTOS."

The North Room of Sagamore Hill, ca. 1911.

creetly captioned photographs prominent among them). Roosevelt's library, with its excess of ill-matched chairs, dangling pelts, and shelfloads of battered books, was cozier, warmed by a large fire. A stuffed badger lurked in one corner, and a hollowed-out elephant's foot near the desk served as a wastepaper basket. Edith's parlor was the only feminine room in the house, light-filled and vaguely French. Through her muslin-draped windows could be seen a poignant symbol of power *passé:* a stretch of veranda with the balustrade removed. On countless occasions, the President of the United States had stood on that ledge and shouted at crowds stretching down the hillside. Today it projected only over snow.

Washburn pursued his point. "You have retired from a position of great power and are now a private citizen. Can you endure the change?"

"Well, I have never been happier than in the past months since the election."

It was Roosevelt's stock reply, but Washburn accepted it. He knew his old friend to be a genuine democrat, indifferent to splendor. The huge sums Theodore had spent on redecorating the White House and entertaining Washington's *crème de la crème* had signified nothing more than respect for the dignity of the state. At home, he and Edith were unpretentious, even bourgeois in the plainest old-money style. Their breeding showed itself in manners. Washburn noticed how courteous the Colonel was to servants, and how he talked with equal animation about his gardener and the King of Italy.

More snow was falling when the congressman left. Roosevelt insisted on coming outside hatless to say goodbye.

Later, Washburn wrote in his diary: "I adhere to my original estimate of him, contrary to that held by almost anyone else— A child of nature, doing what he feels impelled to from day to day: more resources, simpler tastes, and more enthusiasm than any man I ever knew. He will be an interesting figure as long as he lives."

BECAUSE ROOSEVELT WAS, in the image of Professor Brander Matthews of Columbia University, "polygonal," visitors saw only certain facets of his personality at any given time. People less three-dimensional looked for the facet that best reflected their own views, and judged him accordingly. Washburn's impression was accurate only so far as the "child of nature" was willing to play along. Lloyd Griscom needed to believe that the Colonel was "a changed man," lonely and listless, no longer a threat to Party unity. This information found its way to the White House.

"I don't see what I could have done to make things different," Taft said to Archie Butt. "It distresses me very deeply, more deeply than anyone can know, to think of him sitting there at Oyster Bay alone and feeling himself deserted."

The President wiped away a sentimental tear. "I hope the old boy has enough philosophy left to take him through this period. . . . If he could only fight! That is what he delights in, and that is what is denied him now."

ROOSEVELT'S OSAWATOMIE SPEECH, along with three supplementary essays on morality in politics, was now published in book form as *The New Nationalism*. Many progressives read it skeptically, in view of his steady refusal to break with the President. "He thinks that compromise is the only thing,"

William Allen White complained to Mark Sullivan. Gifford and Amos Pinchot kept reproaching the Colonel for calling Taft an "upright" man at Saratoga. Roosevelt, irritated, wrote the brothers off as "ultraextremists" who came "dangerously near the mark of lunacy."

He knew that they were plotting with Congressional insurgents to form a third party if Taft was renominated. Sure enough, their names, along with White's, appeared on the stationery of a new group calling itself the National Progressive Republican League. Most of the other men listed—Beveridge, Bristow, Clapp, Cummins, Garfield, Madison, Murdock, and Senator Miles Poindexter of Washington—still professed to be Roosevelt supporters. But one name in particular, that of Robert M. La Follette, made him suspect that the League was a presidential campaign committee in disguise. Now that *he* had dropped out of contention, "Battling Bob" looked to be the white hope of Republican progressivism.

La Follette begged Roosevelt to join the League. The Colonel was reluctant to compromise himself. He still talked of holding the GOP together. Dividing it was unlikely to stop the Democrats from completing their sweep of the government in 1912. Four years out of power should convince conservative Republicans that the age of protectionism was over, and that of progressivism—*his* enlightened kind, not La Follette's bristling zealotry—an evolutionary fact. Conceivably, 1916 might see him restored to Party leadership. Not that he would admit to any desire to be President again. "There is nothing I want less."

He saw little of his New Nationalism in the Progressive League's manifesto: no proposal to regulate corporations, no plea for conservation, nothing on the deteriorating relations of capital and labor. La Follette wanted to see direct voting in primaries and senatorial elections, direct participation in sending and instructing delegates to national conventions, laws to restrict corrupt practices, and, in a mantra beloved of populists, "the initiative, the referendum, and the recall."

This last triple demand, for voter involvement in the passage and repeal of laws, was evidence to Roosevelt of the insurgents' tendency to overreach. Reforms to benefit democracy in some states, such as the judicial-recall clause proposed for the new constitution of Arizona, would not necessarily do so in all. The vituperation he had brought down on his own head, for suggesting that the Supreme Court needed to adapt itself to new industrial conditions, had shown how negatively progressivism was perceived in some quarters. But in declining to be associated with the League, he did not want to sound like yesterday's radical turned timid. "I think," he wrote La Follette, "that we wish to be careful not to seem to be dictating to good people who may not be quite as far advanced as we are." He noted that the senator's own constituents in ultra-progressive Wisconsin had not yet accepted the initiative or the referendum.

Roosevelt promised to make clear in *The Outlook* that he was in "substantial agreement" with most of the things the new group stood for. "But I hardly think that it would be of service from the public standpoint for me to go into such a league at present."

⁓

ON 21 JANUARY, the same day that the National Progressive Republican League was organized in Washington, Taft sent a major new proposal to Congress. It was for tariff reciprocity with Canada, and sought to double the number of free imports from that country, mostly agricultural, while protecting the wide range of American exports, mostly manufactured, that flowed north. Roosevelt praised it as "admirable from every standpoint" in a personal letter to the President. "Whether Canada will accept such reciprocity, I do not know," he added, "but it is greatly to your credit to make the effort."

Experience had taught him that economic considerations mattered less, in foreign negotiation, than those of national pride. The Dominion might well jib at a trade agreement that could transfer all its important bank credits to New York and Chicago—making it what Taft, with typical clumsiness, called "a virtual adjunct of the United States." But Roosevelt saw hope in the fact that Sir Wilfrid Laurier, the Canadian prime minister, favored reciprocity.

Favoring it himself, he was aware that he was once again in conflict with Henry Cabot Lodge. His old friend, just reelected to the Senate by a tiny majority of the Massachusetts legislature, had found it difficult to be polite about New Nationalism last fall. Poor Cabot was fighting a lonely battle against the initiative in behalf of Bay State fishermen.

Any protectionist west of the clambake fringe could see that Taft's proposal stood to benefit American corporate interests. Roosevelt might have been expected to oppose it for that reason, out of loyalty to the small businessmen and farmers who had always voted for him. Instead, he seemed to be siding with the administration—pandering to it, even, when he said he wanted "to see radicalism prosper under conservative leadership."

The words made no sense. However, as a born operator, it was characteristic of him to salute the only brilliant tactic of Taft's presidency so far: sponsorship of a pro-business bill that progressives would have difficulty opposing, because it granted their demand for a reduction in tariff excess. The odds were good that before the Sixty-first Congress passed out of existence in March, Taft would have a treaty to offer to Canada.

⁓

THE COLONEL'S JOB AS contributing editor of a serious, not to say sedate, weekly journal enabled him to stay in touch with current affairs and write about them. He commuted into Manhattan on Tuesdays and Fridays, usually by automobile. When the roads were icy he took the train, hanging on a strap like any other citizen, but suffering because fellow travelers would not leave him alone. In *The Outlook*'s headquarters at 287 Fourth Avenue he could at least control whom he wanted to see. Ray Stannard Baker, watching him hold court there one morning, was struck by the executive charade:

> He is a sort of president-regent—"one vested with vicarious author-ity." In some ways he possesses more power than the president, for he is essentially the real leader of the people. And yet he really has no power at all. . . . Somehow I felt, as I sat there today, that his work had passed its apex: that he could not return to his former power. There was a lack, somewhere, of his old grip on things. The movement has gone beyond him!

Roosevelt was not deceived as to his polarizing effect on public opinion. Passions aroused by last November's election still ran high in New York City. He joked to O. K. Davis that he could not leave the building without provok-ing someone. "If I go down by the side elevator, that is evidence of furtiveness. If I go down in front, that is proof of ostentation."

He worked hard for his $12,000 salary, always delivering copy on time, and soliciting articles from other progressive writers. "There is no fake in Roo-sevelt's reference," a fellow editor remarked. "His memory is prodigious. He can meet any man—any specialist on his own ground." Lyman and Lawrence Abbott, the father-son duo in charge of *The Outlook,* valued him as a pre-cious resource. They knew that glossier periodicals had offered him four, if not five times as much money as they could afford. He told them he found their moralistic brand of progressivism congenial. However spent a political force (and they were not sure that he was), Theodore Roosevelt had made *The Outlook* one of the most influential organs in the country.

In January alone, he reviewed a book on the subject of foreign disaster re-lief, wrote three articles for a new series entitled "Nationalism and Progress," and published the texts of his exchange with Governor Baldwin. These contri-butions were meant to show that he had lost none of his radical fervor, and to prevent La Follette from co-opting one of progressivism's prime issues: that of employers' liability.

ROOSEVELT WAS PLEASED to hear in February that *African Game Trails,* which had been named 1910's "Book of the Year" by the *New York Herald,* had sold 36,127 copies in all editions. Charles Scribner sent him a royalty check for $28,620, and wrote that the book was still moving off the shelves.

"It is a great sight to see a lion coming on with his mane all bristling, and his teeth showing, with one of those grunting roars," the Colonel told an audience of enraptured children on Washington's Birthday. "A great sight." Showing a fair number of teeth himself, he regaled his audience with stories, alternately frightening and funny, about his year in Africa. The children were in stitches at his descriptions of man-eater attacks on Indian employees of the Uganda Railway. "A lion came up and tried to get inside the station [at Voi] and the Hindoo inside sent an agitated telegram running, 'Lion fighting station. Help urgently necessary.' "

The more the great safari receded into memory, the more he accepted that he was living in a state of anticlimax. Whether this would prove a permanent condition, he could not tell, but he clearly had no future in active politics as long as Taft maintained a semblance of control over the Republican Party, and progressives continued to be disappointed in him. He could at least look forward to the doubtful satisfaction of becoming an elder statesman.

⌁

AROUND THIS TIME Roosevelt became disapprovingly aware of a new, legalistic peace-advocacy group. It styled itself "The American Society for Judicial Settlement of International Disputes," and its honorary president was none other than William Howard Taft.

The word *judicial* in the society's title reflected the influence of Elihu Root, who, as secretary of state in 1908, had been frustrated by the failure of the Second Hague Peace Conference to establish a strong world tribunal. Taft would have been happy to do without strength, in the sense of punitive power, altogether: his preference was for a peace movement that put its faith in arbitration. Optimistic and sentimental, he believed that all human beings were the same at heart. "If we do not have arbitration," he told the society in his inaugural address, "we shall have war."

Roosevelt scoffed at such naïveté. He had stood in the way of too many charging lions to believe for one minute that aggression was not a fact of nature. He detected no common peaceableness among human beings, let alone between nations vying for power. Men were either weak or they were strong. Only the strong could enforce "righteousness"—a word that the dictionary was vague about, but which to him had concrete meaning.

A case in point presented itself early in March, when revolutionary unrest in Mexico threatened the authoritarian government of Porfirio Díaz. Forces headed by Francisco Madero, Pascual Orozco, and Pancho Villa prepared to attack Ciudad Juárez. Taft, worrying about the security of American interests, stationed twenty thousand troops on the border. He assured Díaz that this mobilization was for exercise purposes only, and was "not intended as an act hostile to the friendly Mexican government."

Roosevelt smelled civil war, and a consequent need for *el Coloseo del*

Norte to restore order. The vague urge that had stirred him at the Cheyenne rodeo returned and clarified itself. "I most earnestly hope," he wrote the President, "that we will not have to intervene. . . . But if by any remote chance . . . there should be a serious war, a war in which Mexico was backed by Japan or some other big powers, then I would wish immediately to apply

"OPTIMISTIC AND SENTIMENTAL, HE BELIEVED THAT
ALL HUMAN BEINGS WERE THE SAME."

William Howard Taft as President of the United States.

for permission to raise a division of cavalry, such as the regiment I commanded in Cuba." He was certain that, given a free hand, he could whip up "as formidable a body of horse riflemen . . . as has ever been seen."

Anyone less passionate, pressing such a dream upon Taft, would have heard the President's slow rumble of amusement, his great sedentary body (unimaginable in military uniform!) quivering like blancmange. But Roosevelt was already mentally recruiting ten or twelve thousand rough riders. "My brigade commanders would be Howze and Boughton of the regular army, and Cecil Lyon of Texas. My nine colonels would include . . ." As he drummed out name after name, his dream shifted from the prospect that beguiled to a retrospect that filled him with bloodthirsty pride. "I ask, Sir, that [you] remember that in the war with Spain our regiment was raised, armed, equipped, mounted, dismounted, drilled, kept two weeks on transports, and put through two vigorous fights in which it lost almost a quarter of the men engaged, and over one third of the officers, a loss greater than that suffered by any but two of the twenty-four regular regiments in that same army corps; and all this within sixty days."

Coincidentally, Roosevelt happened at that moment to be heading to El Paso, just across the river from Ciudad Juárez. It was as if fate was speeding him toward the epicenter of the Mexican revolution, via the very country where he hoped to find most of his recruits.

But for the moment, his mission was peaceful. He was on the southwestern leg of a fifteen-state lecture tour. Edith was traveling with him. She wanted to see two of their sons—Archie in Mesa, Arizona, where he was registered at a health-building school, and Ted, establishing himself as a businessman in San Francisco. Cool and equable, Edith saw no prospect of her husband being ordered back into the saddle for any war.

Neither did Taft. The President politely acknowledged Roosevelt's eligibility for a command, but informed him that the administration would make no move into Mexico without the consent of Congress.

ROOSEVELT ROLLED ON through deserts and mountains stippled with spring flowers. It was, he assured Taft, "the last speaking tour I shall ever make." The campaign of 1910 had enabled him to visit much of the Midwest, Deep South, and Atlantic seaboard—exactly half the forty-six states. Now he wanted to chant a swansong across the borderland and up the Pacific Coast into the Northwest. He spoke and gripped flesh with all his old energy, but as Ray Stannard Baker had noted, he seemed to have lost his political touch. Taft was convulsed to hear that the Colonel's response, to a Texan complaining that Mexican *insurrectos* had carried off his son, had been an absentminded "Fine, fine, splendid!"

In further evidence that he was no longer front-page news, he found himself, for the first time since 1898, without a press car hitched to his train. Only local correspondents reported his appearances, and few of their stories were syndicated nationwide. Even such a story as his dedication, in Arizona on 18 March, of Roosevelt Dam—the monumental apotheosis of his reclamation policy as President—rated no higher than page sixteen of *The New York Times.*

He pressed the obligatory button, and three cascades spilled out into the

"MONUMENTAL APOTHEOSIS OF HIS RECLAMATION POLICY."
Theodore Roosevelt Dam, Arizona.

Salt River Valley. The reservoir was still only half full, but it had already submerged the dam's construction town (also named after him) and collected enough water to irrigate the Phoenix area through two years of drought. Nothing he had accomplished, he said, matched this project for grandeur—except the Panama Canal.

PRIDE IN THE LATTER achievement overcame him five days later at the University of California at Berkeley. The canal was much on local minds, for San Francisco had just been chosen as host city for a grand "Panama-Pacific" international exposition, once the western and eastern oceans were joined. That consummation no longer seemed remote: after a record one and a half million tons dug in February, the immense earthwork was more than two-thirds complete.

Speaking in the university's Greek amphitheater, Roosevelt said, "The Panama Canal I naturally take an interest in, because I started it."

He had come to Berkeley to deliver a series of lectures on morality in politics, but today was Charter Day, and the sunshine was sweet. His audience was enormous, spreading out onto the surrounding slopes, pointillistic in places with academic silk.

"If I had acted strictly according to precedent," he continued, "I should have turned the whole matter over to Congress; in which case, Congress would be ably debating it at this moment, and the canal would be fifty years in the future."

Roosevelt was referring to the controversy, early in his presidency, over whether to cut an isthmian waterway across Nicaragua or Panama. He began to talk about another controversy, concerning his role in the Panamanian Revolution of 1903. Why he raised this vexed subject, half-forgotten over the years, was a mystery. He could have been rambling, were he not reading from his own script.

The revolution, he joked, had "fortunately" occurred when Congress was in recess, enabling him to act with executive freedom. "Accordingly I took a trip to the Isthmus, started the canal, and then left Congress—not to debate the canal, but to debate me. But while the debate goes on, the canal does too; and they are welcome to debate me as long as they wish, provided that we can go on with the canal."

What his script said was not what all note-takers in the amphitheater recorded. A staff stenographer entered the words *I took a trip to the Isthmus* into the official text of Roosevelt's remarks, for publication in the next issue of the University of California *Chronicle*. Scattered reporters, however, alternately heard, or thought they heard, *I took the Isthmus, I took Panama, I took the Canal Zone*. The last phrase was what *The New York Times* chose to quote under the headline ROOSEVELT BOASTS OF CANAL, along with a free transcription of the boast itself. Accurate or not, the transcription became canon:

> If I had followed traditional, conservative methods I would have submitted a dignified state paper of probably two hundred pages to Congress, and the debates on it would be going on yet. But I took the Canal Zone and let Congress debate, and while the debate goes on, the canal does also.

Actually, lawmakers had long ceased to question Roosevelt's opportunism in 1903. What "debate" there was these days concerned the canal's strategic and commercial potential. Naval and military authorities wanted to fortify it, while American shippers lobbied for preferential tolls, or none, since its construction costs were borne by the United States. But now the syntagma *I took* (what, exactly, had he taken—a trip, a zone, a country, a historic opportunity?) echoed south of the border, and revived Colombia's anger at having been cheated of its expectations in 1903.

Philander Chase Knox, his not very supportive attorney general at the time, was now Taft's secretary of state, and remained unconvinced that Roosevelt had been fair in denying Colombia any compensation for the loss of its precious province. Knox agreed with Senator Root that the United States was pledged from the start to be "passive" in any domestic revolution in Colombia, albeit "active" in maintaining transit across the Isthmus. He also agreed, to an extent, with the Colonel's current language, but not for reasons Roosevelt would consider supportive: "The fact is we *practically* took Panama. We did not take it from Colombia, we took it from the Panaman[ian]s, and this is the only sense in which that statement is true."

Roosevelt, luxuriating in the warmth of his reception at Berkeley, and the even warmer hospitality of Ted's house in San Francisco, seemed not to care about the fuss his "boast" had caused. He had other priorities now. Eleanor was pregnant with his first grandchild. After a final few farewell speeches en route home—one, in Wisconsin, to praise Senator La Follette—he should be back at Sagamore Hill in time to see the budding of the fruit trees. *Qui plantavit curabit.*

OLD FRIENDS WERE not persuaded that this was the Colonel's last political tour. "Quiescence for him is an impossibility," James Bryce observed in early April, comparing Roosevelt to Gladstone for out-of-office fame. "He is a sort of comet . . . but much denser in substance; and not so much attracted by as attracting the members of the system which he approaches." At every whistle-stop, women stood holding up their children for him to touch. "It seems," Edith wrote Cecil Spring Rice, "as if in proportion with the hatred of Wall Street, is the love which is lavished upon him in the West."

Taft continued to woo him, in the hope that their rapprochement would strengthen the GOP through difficult days ahead. The Sixty-first Congress had just come to an end, and with it the Party's majority rule. Opposition from both progressives and Republican stalwarts had stalled Taft's pet project, reciprocity with Canada. He had called an immediate session of the new Congress to reconsider the measure. That meant dealing from now on with hostile Democrats, and the President, seeking to counter their hostility, needed allies.

He sought to please Roosevelt with a pair of cabinet appointments almost pandering in their progressiveness: Walter L. Fisher as secretary of the interior, and Henry L. Stimson as secretary of war. The former, replacing Richard Ballinger, was a Pinchot-friendly conservationist, and the latter could be counted on to deploy the Colonel in any military emergency. But Roosevelt felt that Taft was "absolutely lost" as a leader. Ballinger's resignation was symbolic in more ways than one. It cast a moral afterglow on the accusations of Gifford Pinchot, and reestablished conservation as an ideological issue of prime importance.

Rhetorically, what was more, Taft and the Democrats deserved one another. Champ Clark, the new Speaker of the House of Representatives, had just managed to insult Canadians by suggesting that reciprocity was merely a step toward the day when the Stars and Stripes would fly "up to the North Pole." Roosevelt, cooling on the issue, declined to associate himself with such jingoism.

⤛

ON CAPITOL HILL, Representative Henry T. Rainey, Democrat of Illinois, demanded "an investigation of the means by which President Roosevelt 'took' the Isthmus of Panama from the United States of Colombia." *The New York Times,* usually quick to criticize the Colonel, remarked with some sympathy that the move persecuted a man who was at present "down and out." Ambitious Democrats thinking ahead to 1912 seemed to be hoping for "some kind of scandal that will wipe the name of Theodore Roosevelt clear off the map of political possibilities in this country." The Panama Canal was "about the most popular asset of recent history, and it will be very difficult to convince the public that Mr. Roosevelt was not a great public benefactor in 'taking' the canal zone."

⤛

"NOT A WORD, GENTLEMEN," a suntanned Roosevelt told reporters when he got back to New York on 16 April. "Not a word to say."

This did not stop him from saying plenty about the political situation in private to such intimates as James Garfield and Gifford Pinchot—the latter reunited with him in mutual contempt for Taft. All three agreed that the President could be renominated only "by default" in 1912, absent a major progressive challenger. La Follette did not appear to be developing any real strength in the East. If anyone was, it was the Democratic Party's rising star, Governor Woodrow Wilson of New Jersey.

Roosevelt did not wait for Stimson to move into the War Department before making his first public break with Taft. His weapon of choice was a signed editorial in *The Outlook.* He wished to discuss national honor, and what he saw as the President's willingness to compromise it.

Since agreeing to head up the American Society for Judicial Settlement of International Disputes, Taft had fixated on the concept of a series of arbitration treaties that would subject all signatory nations to the authority of a world court, when situations arose to threaten the security of any of them. Roosevelt voiced no particular objection to Taft's prototype treaty with Great Britain, feeling that it merely cemented an Anglo-American alliance already in place. But he noted that France and Germany—whose intense mutual hostility he had so recently felt at first hand—were also on the State Department's wish list, not to mention Japan, and a number of other warlike or meddlesome powers.

Roosevelt was aware that he had espoused the spirit of arbitration himself as President, in the moderation of labor disputes and such international questions as the proper plotting of borders. When calling for "a League of Peace" in his address to the Nobel Prize Committee, however, he had stressed that such an authority should be armed. Nor had he ever countenanced the idea of the United States abrogating the right to police its own interests.

Taft proposed to do just that, telling the peace society, "Personally, I don't see any more reason why matters of national honor should not be referred to a court." The President believed that its judges, like himself, would be gentlemen who "understood" what honor meant.

This kind of fantasy was enough to provoke, in private, Roosevelt's hottest language. He restrained himself in print, addressing only the British treaty and declaring, "The United States ought never specifically to bind itself to arbitrate questions respecting its honor, independence, and integrity." But the fact that he had never before criticized Taft publicly made his demurral sound like a shout.

Its echoes were still reverberating on 6 June, when he found himself seated next to the President at a jubilee in Baltimore honoring James Cardinal Gibbons. Fellow celebrants looked for signs of rancor between them, but they managed the encounter well, laughing or pretending to laugh at private jokes. Between chuckles, Roosevelt advised Taft that he would soon testify before a Congressional committee investigating charges of White House collusion with U.S. Steel during the fiscal crisis of October–November, 1907. It was not to be confused with the committee looking into his alleged rape of Panama, but both probes were obviously part of the new majority's effort to impugn the Republican Party in advance of the next election. Taft advised him to stand on his dignity and refuse to appear. Roosevelt was determined to defend himself. They kept on grinning at each other, so much so that the Associated Press reported that the Colonel had promised to support Taft for renomination in 1912.

Roosevelt denied the report as soon as it was published. A few days later, he sent the Tafts a silver wedding-anniversary gift. The President thanked him for it on 18 June, and from then on their estrangement was total.

⟨⟨⟩⟩

SO—NARROWLY AT FIRST, then yawningly as the ideological landscape split—a double division began to run, not only between Taft and Roosevelt, but between dreamers of peace and *Realpolitiker* who believed that in time of war, treaties were not worth the parchment they were written on. In 1911, the average American voter could not remember Gettysburg, let alone feel what Henry Adams, relocated to Paris, described as "this huge big storm cloud gathering in Central Europe." Adams prophesied that the cloud would one day burst over Austria and the Balkans, then move southeast to the Levant, sweeping away the Ottoman Empire. Roosevelt had explored much of that territory himself, both as a boy and ex-President. He was not sure that Western Europe would escape the cataclysm. The heads of state and other eminences he had met, in nation after nation from Italy to Norway, had betrayed, in their various, defensive ways, a general consciousness that some breakdown of civilization was on its way. Whether it happened soon, as Balfour and Spring Rice kept predicting, or held off for a decade, as Adams hoped, it was unlikely to be deflected by arbiters droning on at The Hague.

Roosevelt believed that the United States (if Taft could be stopped from signing away its strategic independence), would succeed Great Britain as the enforcer of world peace—"never mind against which country or group of countries our efforts may have to be directed." It would do so, if necessary, with an armed hand. "We ourselves," he told a German visitor to *The Outlook,* "are becoming more and more the balance of power of the whole globe."

Like many men of martial instinct, the Colonel claimed to be peaceable. But it was plain to everybody that he loved war and thought of it as a catharsis. War purged the fat and ill humors of a sedentary society whose values had been corrupted by getting and spending. Waged for a righteous cause, it reawakened moral fervor, intensified love and loyalty, concentrated the mind on fundamental truths, strengthened the body both personal and political. It was, in short, good for man, good for man's country, and often as not, good for the vanquished too. In celebrating its terrible beauty, Roosevelt often came near the sentimentality he despised among pacifists—so much so that some of his most affectionate friends felt their gorges rise when he romanticized death in battle.

He used the strongest language to emasculate men who hated militarism, or recoiled like women from the chance to prove themselves in armed action: "aunties" and "sublimated sweetbreads," shrilly piping for peace. (The tendency of his own voice to break into the treble register was an embarrassment in that regard.) He noted with scorn that such "mollycoddles" as Governor Baldwin of Connecticut and Boss Barnes of New York supported the Judicial Settlement Society. Andrew Carnegie had established a multimillion-dollar

Endowment for International Peace, and was lobbying the President to recognize it. "I feel," Roosevelt wrote a fellow veteran of the Cuban war, "somewhat as if we were all threatened with death by drowning in an ocean of weak tea with too much milk and sugar."

⤙⤚

TAFT REMARKED THAT on occasion Theodore Roosevelt was possessed of "the spirit of the old berserkers." If so, the Colonel's savage beast was as often soothed by the bird music he heard at Oyster Bay, spring after warming spring:

> There is nothing that quite corresponds to the chorus that during May and June moves northward from the Gulf States and southern California to Maine, Minnesota, and Oregon, to Ontario and Saskatchewan; when there comes the great vernal burst of bloom and song; when the mayflower, bloodroot, wake-robin, anemone, adder's tongue, lover-wort, shadblow, dogwood, redbud, gladden the woods . . . when from the Atlantic seaboard to the Pacific, wood-thrushes, veeries, rufous-backed thrushes, robins, bluebirds, orioles, thrashers, catbirds, house-finches, song-sparrows . . . and many, many other singers thrill the gardens at sunrise; until the long days begin to shorten, and tawny lilies burn by the roadside, and the indigo-buntings trill from the tops of little trees throughout the hot afternoons.

CHAPTER 7

Showing the White Feather

===================

Time passed, and filled along with his
The place of many more;
Time came, and hardly one of us
Had credence to restore
From what appeared one day, the man
Whom we had known before.

QUENTIN ROOSEVELT BROUGHT a diminished rush and noise of boyhood back to Sagamore Hill that summer. At nearly thirteen, he had little innocence left, and seemed to have exchanged his genius for mayhem for serious study. He had flabbergasted his parents—and made the front page of *The New York Times*—by winning a scholarship at Groton.

Always precocious, he read adult books to widen an already impressive vocabulary. Since attending an air show with his mother at Reims, France, in 1909, he had loved anything that turned over, vibrated, clattered, or flew. "You don't know how pretty it was to see all the aeroplanes sailing at a time . . . the prettiest thing I ever saw." Big of brow and burly bodied, forever baring his teeth in fits of laughter, he was no longer a miniature version of his father, but stood half an inch taller.

Archie, Quentin's former knockabout buddy, was now a loping, long-limbed youth of seventeen, not unlike an Apache with his hawk features and Arizona tan. The slowest of the six Roosevelt siblings, he could spare little time for tennis matches with "Q," having to study for his Harvard entrance exams. Whether accepted or not—he was characteristically pessimistic about his chances—Archie had another year at the Evans School in Mesa to face. One of the family's secrets was that he had been expelled from Groton in 1910 for insubordination.

For Theodore and Edith, there was a temporary feel to the lingering presence of Kermit and Ethel under their roof. It was likely to be Kermit's last summer at home. After graduation next year, he would be looking for a career in business. And judging from the "motor" excursions he and his sister kept taking to visit with Hitchcocks and Bacons and Rumseys and Whitneys—the Meadowbrook set—it might be the last summer Ethel remained "a young girl entitled to think primarily of her amusements," as Roosevelt, trying to sound like a tolerant father, put it. She was about to turn twenty, and must address herself to the serious business of choosing a husband.

There were no nurses and governesses upstairs anymore. Edith had pensioned off the last of the old family servants during Theodore's absence in Africa. The Roosevelt retinue was now reduced to five white women—a cook, a waitress, and three housemaids—and five black men, including a butler and a "chauffeur" for the Haynes-Apperson. The hay and corn fields were farmed by freelance laborers, among whom could often be seen the former President of the United States, husky and sweating in white blouse and knickerbockers.

"I am really thinking more about natural history than about politics," he wrote to Arthur Lee on 27 June, boasting that he had finished "a masterly article on 'Revealing and Concealing Coloration in Birds and Mammals.' " He was being arch, but his assessment was justified when the monograph saw print. It filled 112 pages of the *Bulletin of the American Museum of Natural History*, and summed up forty years of field observation. Roosevelt followed it with a quirky essay in *The Outlook* entitled "Dante and the Bowery," arguing that literary stylists had grown too precious in eschewing contemporary imagery. There was as much epic grandeur and poignant example to be found in modern life, he suggested, as there was in Greek myth, or for that matter, thirteenth-century cosmology. He used his regular column to editorialize on intercollegiate athletics, labor unions, conservation, and class. He wrote reviews of Arthur E. Weigall's *Treasury of Ancient Egypt* and Houston Stewart Chamberlain's *The Foundations of the Nineteenth Century*, and, showing signs of intellectual restlessness, ordered a translation of *De Contemptu Mundi*. Erasmus's ambivalent attitude to monastic retreat—was it an austere giving up, or a voluptuous letting go?—spoke to his current half-happiness, half-regret at being rusticated.

Somehow, he could not bring himself to start on the "big work" he had contemplated when he left politics. Both the Century Association and Scribners were offering him large sums for a life of Lincoln. But he was chilled by their demand that he deliver it within the next six months, while his name "still had a value." Apparently, they had no more concern for literary quality than for him—in the past, one of their most valuable authors.

"As you know I am not a rich man," Roosevelt wrote to Judge John C.

Rose, a friend in Baltimore, "and if possible I want to continue earning some money until all my boys get started in life. Eight years hence Quentin will have graduated if things go as they should go." He himself would then be sixty, and able to retire. He had the income from a $60,000 trust fund, which was not

"'A YOUNG GIRL ENTITLED TO
THINK PRIMARILY OF HER AMUSEMENTS.'"
Ethel Roosevelt, ca. 1911.

enough to support four children, let alone run a large country property. Edith had some money of her own, but he did not like to touch that, in case he predeceased her. They must live off his pen, and the modest investments his cousin Emlen managed for him.

He used a favorite metaphor in dismissing the prospect of his ever returning to public service. "The kaleidoscope changes continually and the same grouping of figures is not ever repeated."

<hr />

NOT ONLY HE HAD been shaken out of the pattern, but so had almost all of the Old Guard senators he had dealt with as president. Henry Cabot Lodge and Elihu Root alone remained, in uneasy alliance with Winthrop Murray Crane of Massachusetts and Boies Penrose of Pennsylvania. Root wanted to return to private life at the expiration of his current term. Now that Republican progressives were no longer "insurgent," but established as an independent voting block, Congress was in effect divided into three parties, with the Democratic majority exuberant over its split opposition, and determined to keep it so through next year's GOP convention.

Roosevelt confessed that there were moments when "I very earnestly desire to champion a cause," but he was not unhappy to be out of politics. The feeling was tinged with something like triumph on 5 August, when he appeared in New York before the House committee investigating his role in the stock crisis of 1907. Neither then nor now had he understood much about the acquisition by U.S. Steel of the Tennessee Coal & Iron Company, and less still about the secret ways banking houses connived with one another. But he testified with such righteous vigor ("You must apply to some one else if you want an expert on Wall Street"), that Congressman Augustus Stanley, in the chair, became incoherent in trying to show that he had gone along with a monopolistic coup, vastly to the profit of the the world's biggest trust. Roosevelt insisted that his only thought at the time had been to prevent the bankruptcy of Moore & Schley, a giant brokerage firm whose collapse might have triggered a worldwide depression. "The word *panic* means fear, unreasoning fear," he said. "To stop a panic it is necessary to restore confidence."

Even *The New York Times* felt that he had acquitted himself. Congressman Stanley, the paper remarked, had failed to expose the former president as a stooge, while showing a "partisan" and "ignorant" attitude toward U.S. Steel. "It is indeed fortunate that Mr. Roosevelt dealt with the panic instead of Mr. Stanley."

<hr />

ON 6 AUGUST, the day the editorial appeared, Edith Roosevelt turned fifty. To her adoring husband, who presented her with a thermos pitcher and four vol-

umes of *Punch,* she was still the indoor and outdoor companion of child-hood—so "very young looking and pretty in her riding habit" as she trotted beside him on horseback, through the woods to Cold Spring Harbor or along the bayside road. Today the weather was too hot for horses, so he took her for an afternoon row to Lloyd Neck.

Constant in their love for each other and their six children—Edith had al-ways treated Alice as her own daughter—they were preparing themselves now for the emotional elevation of grandparenthood. News came from San Fran-cisco on the seventeenth that Eleanor had had a baby girl, Grace. Roosevelt wrote her and Ted: " 'The birth pangs make all men the debtors of all women.' " He was paraphrasing Jules Michelet's *Priests, Women and Fami-lies,* a humanistic tract that exactly expressed his view of sex, faith, and na-ture. Eleanor was invested with the same glow of fulfilled femininity that he saw shimmering around Edith, and regretfully did not see around Alice. For the first time in his life, he signed himself *Grandfather.*

ONE EFFECT OF THE new arrival upon Theodore Roosevelt, Jr., was to em-bolden him to show signs of political independence. Grimly determined, a squat knot of muscle and sinew, Ted confided to Eleanor that his ambition was to earn a lot of money quickly, then use his fortune to go into public life. In order to learn the dry basics of business—not something Harvard had pre-pared him for—he had taken a dreary job as the West Coast representative of a Connecticut carpet company. But in the day-to-day slog of salesmanship— "I do *love* work!"—he was proving to be a dynamo. He had also involved him-self in Californian progressive politics. He let his father know that if Taft and Woodrow Wilson were nominated in 1912, he might vote for the governor.

"Do remember," Roosevelt wrote back, "that to say anything in public, or to take any public stand against Taft, especially by supporting his Democratic opponent, would cause me very great embarrassment, and . . . create the im-pression that I, while nominally supporting Taft, am underhandedly doing all I can do against him."

His caution seemed unreasonable, because he was expressing more and more disapproval of the President's policies in the pages of *The Outlook.* And he was not alone among Republican commentators in doing so. The wide-spread admiration Taft had won by calling for reciprocity with Canada was dissipated. Endless wrangling over rates had dragged the special session of Congress into midsummer. A compromise act had been passed and sent to Ottawa: Sir Wilfrid Laurier had gambled his whole government on the issue, and dissolved Parliament so that all Canadians could vote on it. This was not necessarily good news. Republicans remained deeply divided over tariff reform, with conservatives alienated from conservatives, and progressives from progressives. Taft was blamed for the passions aroused.

About the only politician to profit from the battle on Capitol Hill was Robert La Follette. He seized on reciprocity, which he eloquently opposed, to announce that he would challenge the President for the nomination in 1912. No Shakespearean upstart, all arms and arrogance, could have thrown down his gauntlet in front of a less popular king. Republicans clustered uneasily behind the one or the other. With Roosevelt offstage, they lacked any leader strong enough to hold them all together.

La Follette imagined that he had the Colonel's support, after Roosevelt praised his radical record in *The Outlook*. A warm exchange of letters followed. But when La Follette sent an emissary to Sagamore Hill asking for a specific endorsement, he was turned down.

Roosevelt saw no chance of La Follette being nominated. "My present intention," he wrote Ted, "is to make a couple of speeches for Taft, but not to go actively into the campaign." He thought that Woodrow Wilson was the strongest Democratic candidate. Taft, in contrast, was "a flubdub with a streak of the second-rate and the common in him, and he has not the slightest idea of what is necessary if this country is to make social and industrial progress."

As for foreign policy, he gave the President little credit. Arbitration treaties with Britain and France were fated to shred like leaves in any gale-force storm. Right now, a second "Morocco crisis" loomed between Germany, France, and Great Britain, as dangerous as the one that had nearly precipitated war six years before. France had recently expanded its military presence in Morocco, only to see a German gunboat, the *Panther*, appear at once in the Atlantic port of Agadir. This incursion into waters not normally considered part of Germany's sphere of influence had, in turn, brought about massing of the Royal Navy in the English Channel. The British government was bound to make such a move, by virtue of its *entente cordiale* with France. But neutral observers were startled at the vigor with which David Lloyd George was insisting that "Britain should at all hazards maintain her place and her prestige amongst the great powers of the world." Yesterday's peace advocate and anti-imperialist had evidently come to share the dread of Sir Edward Grey that German naval expansionism in North Africa menaced the Suez Canal, and with it, access to India.

Britain's unwillingness to see that France, not Germany, was the prime aggressor in the affair demonstrated, for Roosevelt, the fatuity of any faith in "judicial" peacekeeping. Great powers were not interested in behaving justly, when they could misbehave to their own advantage and get away with it. They wanted to dominate one another, either singly or in combination, at the first opportunity. Germany's response to Lloyd George's bluster had been to withdraw the *Panther* and replace it with the *Berlin,* a battleship three times larger.

Roosevelt raged in a letter to Henry Cabot Lodge against the inability of the President "and all the male shrieking sisterhood of Carnegies" to see that in any serious international dispute, might made for right. "If war is to be averted, it will be only because Germany thinks that France has a first-class army and will fight hard, and that England is ready and able to render her some prompt assistance. The German war plans contemplate, as I happen to know personally, as possible courses of action, flank marches through both Belgium and Switzerland."

LIKE A PAIR OF sopranos deliberately setting out to irritate someone who disliked opera, Taft and Governor Wilson chose this moment to sing a duet in praise of pacifism. They did so in the September issue of *The Christian Herald.* "I yield to no one in my love of peace, in my hatred of war, and in my earnest desire to avoid war," the President wrote. "If I have my way and am able to secure the assent of other powers, I shall submit to the Senate arbitration treaties broader in their terms than any that body has heretofore ratified."

Wilson's statement revealed a prose stylist adept at making graceful generalities, while avoiding any personal commitment: "I consider the present agitation for international arbitration and world peace a deep-seated and permanent thing, representing the fixed and universal desire of the human heart."

Roosevelt published his own views on the subject in an editorial, "The Peace of Righteousness," in *The Outlook* on 9 September. Its tone was forceful yet restrained, as was often the case with him after he had blown off steam in private correspondence. "I sincerely believe in the principle of arbitration," he wrote, " . . . but I believe that the effort to apply it where it is not practicable cannot do good and may do serious harm. Confused thinking and a willingness to substitute words for thought, even though inspired by an entirely amiable sentimentality, do not tend toward sound action."

As an example of proxy words, he cited *justiciable,* which Secretary Knox had applied to the kind of disputes best suited to arbitration by The Hague: "It can be defined in any way that either party chooses." Was the Monroe Doctrine *justiciable,* along with the administration of the Panama Canal, U.S.-Cuba relations, West Coast immigration policies, and even Canadian reciprocity? If so, were they to be arbitrated by judges sitting in The Hague? A president willing to let foreigners decide questions affecting America's national security "was not fit to hold the exalted position to which he had been elected," Roosevelt declared.

Taft laughed the editorial off. "The fact of the matter is, Archie, the Colonel is not in favor of peace."

●

ROOSEVELT SAT ONE AFTERNOON on the piazza at Sagamore, drinking tea with the veteran journalist Henry L. Stoddard.

"This is the only spot on earth for me," he said. "I'm never satisfied away from here."

They talked about the old days of the Harrison administration. Roosevelt remembered wanting to live in the White House every time he walked past it.

Stoddard suggested there might be a call for him to live there again.

"No—I've had the title of President once—having it twice means nothing except peril to whatever reputation I achieved the first time."

He was silent a moment, then said, "Do you know the only title that appeals to me now?"

"I suppose it is 'Colonel.' "

Roosevelt admitted that he liked being called that. "But if I were asked what title I would prefer, it would not be President or Colonel; it would be Major General in the U.S. Army in active service."

●

ON 15 SEPTEMBER, the President set off on a thirteen-thousand-mile cross-country tour, which he hoped would drum up popular support for his arbitration treaties and force the Senate to ratify them without change. In response to Roosevelt's editorial, he remarked, "I don't think that it indicates that a man lacks personal courage if he does not want to fight, but prefers to submit questions of national honor to a board of arbitration."

Taft had faith in his ability to persuade people by speaking at stupefying length (the transcripts of his presidential addresses already totaled twenty volumes). He also relied on travel as a means of escape from the bad political news that kept seeping into the Oval Office, like cold air through cracked windows. But the gust that came down from Ottawa on the first day of fall was enough to chill him in Kalamazoo, Michigan. Canadians had voted against reciprocal tariffs, and elected a new government skeptical of the goodwill of the United States.

Roosevelt was relieved of the need to pay any further lip service to Taft's foreign policy. He had supported reciprocity, he wrote Arthur Lee, only because he favored closer relations with the British Empire. England was much in his thoughts, what with her quarrel with Germany over Morocco and Lloyd George's success—at last—in wresting parliamentary power from the House of Lords.

Contrite at not having finished an account of his European grand tour, long promised to Sir George Otto Trevelyan, he took up the manuscript and resumed it with enormous enjoyment. *I found I was expected to walk in with the queen on my arm and my hat in the other hand—a piece of etiquette which reminded me of nothing with which I was previously acquainted except a Jewish wedding on the East Side of New York. . . .*

By the last day of September his letter was approaching the length of a small book, at more than thirty thousand words. That afternoon, he went riding with Edith. They were galloping along the bay road when her horse swerved and threw her headfirst onto the pavement. She was knocked unconscious for thirty-six hours, and remained semicomatose for ten days, waking to terrible pain. Throughout her life, she had been prone to neuralgia, retiring to her room for days at a time. This trauma went beyond any in her experience, permanently wiping out her sense of taste and smell.

The family doctor found no concussion, and she slowly recovered. But the accident, following so soon after her fiftieth birthday and the advent of baby Grace, served as a notice to Roosevelt that they had both reached the years of physical decline. His mustache was going from gray to white, and chronic rheumatism assured him that he would never again stride out as freely as he had in Africa. He comforted her with a copy of Edith Wharton's new novel *Ethan Frome*—not that she found much to enjoy in the climactic crash scene—and in his only speaking engagement of the season, called passionately for a social policy more considerate toward the frailties of women and children. "I am not talking to you tonight about abstract things," he told a packed audience at Carnegie Hall, "but about flesh and blood and the ills of flesh and blood."

Worried as he was about his wife, he was only distractedly aware that the Agadir crisis had eased, with Germany being "compensated" for French supremacy in Morocco with a large slice of the Middle Congo and several billion tsetse flies. It sounded like the kind of arbitral accord that the President favored. Meanwhile Taft, still traveling, was trying to publicize himself as a trust-buster. He launched an attack on monopolistic combinations in Boise, Idaho, and warned that his attorney general, George W. Wickersham, would prosecute violations of the Sherman Act, "whether we be damned or not." Coming from a self-proclaimed conservative, this language sounded like a parody of Roosevelt's own radical rhetoric, or at best, an attempt to win back Westerners lost to reciprocity. The first national convention of Republican progressives responded on 16 October by endorsing Robert La Follette for the presidency in 1912.

Eleven days later, on Theodore Roosevelt's fifty-third birthday, Taft handed him an unwelcome present.

⁓

THE HEADLINES THAT MORNING on the front page of the New York *Tribune* could not have been more enraging:

GOVERNMENT SUES TO DISSOLVE
STEEL TRUST AS ILLEGAL COMBINATION
IN RESTRAINT OF TRADE

*Mentions 36 Companies as Defendants
and Names J. P. Morgan, J. D. Rockefeller
and Andrew Carnegie*

SAYS ROOSEVELT WAS DECEIVED

RECITES PURCHASE OF TENNESSEE COAL AND IRON COMPANY
AND DECLARES THAT E. H. GARY AND H. C. FRICK
MISLED THE PRESIDENT AS TO THEIR REAL PURPOSE
AT TIME OF PANIC

Other newspapers treated the story similarly, with the words *deceived* and *misled* recurring like drumbeats. Roosevelt was stunned into temporary wordlessness. It was as if everything he had told the Stanley Committee, and subsequently published, word for word, in *The Outlook,* was disbelieved by the Justice Department. With friends like Taft and Wickersham, he did not need enemies in Congress.

For two and a half years, he had tried to keep quiet about Taft. In the process he had disappointed and even lost many of his progressive colleagues, who were now, with varying degrees of enthusiasm, supporting La Follette. He debated what to do about his credibility and the fragmentation of the GOP, cracking like a salt lick under the President's elephantine missteps. Labor despised Taft; the insurgents always had; free-traders and protectionists alike blamed him for the reciprocity debacle; Democrats could not wait for 1912. Even the Republican Old Guard deplored this prosecution, which could be justified only on the most legalistic grounds.

As James Bryce noted, U.S. Steel was not technically a monopoly: it often lost out on large orders to smaller competitors. Wickersham had therefore focused on the Tennessee Coal & Iron deal as monopolistic *in intent*, enabled by Theodore Roosevelt. His petition granted that the former president had acted honestly in 1907. But to readers of newspaper headlines four years later, Roosevelt's innocence looked like naïveté—if not complicity in what the financial expert John Moody called "the best bargain [any] concern or individual ever made in the purchase of a piece of property."

Taft professed not to have known that his attorney general was going to name the Colonel. But the plan's political intent was plain. Wickersham wanted voters to know that he and the President had launched almost as many antitrust prosecutions in two years as "Teddy the trust-buster" had in seven and a half. The fact that they were both pro-business did not betray their mutual commitment to the letter of the law.

"I know you will agree with me that the only wise course for me to pursue is that of absolute silence," Roosevelt wrote the president of the Reform Club, in reply to a sympathetic letter. By that he meant only oral speech: he would have plenty to say in print. If he spoke out too forcefully to reporters, he would start hearing from Roosevelt Republicans again, and find himself pitted against both Taft and La Follette in 1912.

He told two progressive friends, William Allen White and Governor Hiram Johnson of California, that an emergency could conceivably arise which would require him to make the "sacrifice" of a presidential run. Otherwise, it was best that he remained a private citizen. "I very sincerely believe that if I should be nominated, you would find that it was a grave misfortune not only for me but for the progressive cause. . . . I ask with all the strength that is in my power . . . to do everything possible to prevent not merely my nomination, but any movement looking toward my nomination."

JOHNSON, BEING A POLITICIAN, took note of the condition and ignored the disclaimer. It was useless for Roosevelt to try to persuade such men that he meant what he said: that his fears were for progressivism rather than for himself. But if he was one day to be nominated against his will, he had to do something about his present low esteem on Wall Street. At Carnegie Hall he had spoken, he thought, "with guarded moderation" about court rulings that favored property rights over the public interest, "but every single New York newspaper was bitterly against me, and for the most part suppressed my speech, merely playing it up in the headlines as an attack on the judiciary."

He therefore worked with extreme care on an article responding to the steel suit. *How* he expressed himself did not really matter. *What* he was saying, in so many words, was that he no longer supported William Howard Taft as President of the United States.

The article, headlined "The Trusts, the People, and the Square Deal," appeared in *The Outlook* on 16 November. It proved to be not so much a cry of outrage as a sober, detailed statement of his regulatory philosophy, adapted to new conditions, and accepting that combination was a fact of American life. For all its lack of sensationalism, it quickly sold out its press run, and tens of thousands of offprint copies had to be issued to satisfy public demand. Newspapers reprinted it nationwide.

Roosevelt tersely reaffirmed his self-defense in the Tennessee Coal & Iron matter, as testimony confirmed by all the principals involved. He devoted the rest of his space to a repudiation of Taft's "chaotic" and overly judicial antitrust program. Admitting that he had invoked the Sherman Act himself against such trusts as Northern Securities, American Tobacco, and Standard Oil (and succeeded all the way to the Supreme Court), he said he had done so only when convinced of corporate mischief. Throughout his presidency he had exhorted Congress to create an independent agency that would constantly regulate, rather than sporadically punish, the doings of trusts—most of which were law-abiding, and all of which were entitled to be as big as they liked, as long as they did not monopolize their sector of the economy. "Size in itself does not signify wrong-doing."

The time had come, he wrote, for an administrative policy of "close and jealous" monitoring of business combinations. Whatever body was created to exercise this authority—perhaps a strengthened version of his own Bureau of Corporations—must have power to override states' rights and restrain unbridled competition. He acknowledged that the last word was holy to many self-styled progressives. But those who thought that the Sherman Act was good for competitive rights represented "not progress at all but a kind of sincere rural toryism." They dreamed of bringing back the primitive freedoms enjoyed by village shopkeepers and smallholding farmers before the Civil War. "The effort to restore competition as it was sixty years ago, and to trust for justice solely to this proposed restoration of competition, is just as foolish as if we should go back to the flintlocks of Washington's Continentals as a substitute for modern weapons of precision."

Roosevelt insisted that in arguing for less prosecution and more regulation, he was not advocating socialism. He merely wanted a government that was democratic, and an economy that was moral. Under federal regulation, competition would flourish without becoming "an all-sufficient factor" that justified the exploitation of workers. Plutocrats in future should be held to account on "all questions connected with the treatment of their employees, including the wages, the hours of labor, and the like." Once again he paid La Follette a compliment by noting that Wisconsin had already pioneered such a policy. There was not a hint, elsewhere in his text, of any personal animus against President Taft, or any desire to return to power.

⟨⊷⟩

FOR ALL THE article's reticence, it was regarded as an "editorial explosion" by the *Boston Globe*, and was the talk of financial and political circles for days. Steel shares on the New York Stock Exchange registered a confident surge. Roosevelt was widely seen as having regained his conservative senses, and in an ironic reversal of image, earned praise for opposing the administration's "war on business interests." Henry Clews, the oracle of the finance industry, was outspoken in his approval. *The Washington Post* said that he had mutated into "an able and highly influential advocate of constructive business policies." Joseph Pulitzer's anticorporate New York *World* did not know whether to be suspicious or admiring. In an article headed HAS THEODORE ROOSEVELT NOW BECOME MR. MORGAN'S CANDIDATE FOR PRESIDENT?, it commented:

> He presents Wall Street's resentment against Mr. Taft more forcefully and coherently than Wall Street itself has been able to do. . . . He provides the mask of radicalism which any movement to prevent Mr. Taft's renomination requires in order to be successful.
>
> Mr. Roosevelt is palpably a candidate, and his extraordinary political genius has set for itself the task of bringing about a coalition of the anti-Taft progressives in the West and the anti-Taft plutocrats of Wall Street.

As so often before, Roosevelt found himself misunderstood by partisan critics for seeing things in the round. "Most men seem to live in a space of two dimensions," he complained to Charles D. Villard, a California progressive. He had no desire to challenge Taft, and even less interest in speaking for investment bankers—about the only living species that bored him. All he asked in their behalf was a square deal. Never before had he openly advocated federal price-fixing, yet conservatives chose to think that he liked the idea of guaranteed profits. And manifestly, in his dismissal of "rural toryism," he had once again dashed the hopes of progressives that he might lead them.

Or so he thought. James Garfield's Republican club in Ohio annoyed him exceedingly by endorsing him for President in 1912. At once the Philadelphia *North American,* whose editor, E. A. Van Valkenburg, often served as a spokesman for the Colonel, printed "an authoritative statement" of his non-availability. On 27 November, Gifford Pinchot assured a dinner of the Insurgents' Club that "Bob" La Follette would be the nominee of the Republican Party in 1912.

Asked if he was acting on orders from Sagamore Hill, he said no. "Since Mr. Roosevelt eliminated himself, Senator La Follette is his logical successor."

❧

LA FOLLETTE WAS not flattered by this grudging endorsement. "I'm nobody's cloak. I'll fight to the finish!" Money from both the wealthy Pinchot brothers mollified him, but as precinct and district bosses plotted the GOP state conventions that would begin to choose delegates early in the new year, the Senator's principal weakness—a lack of support east of the Mississippi—became apparent. The *Wall Street Journal* remarked that if Taft faltered at the national convention, his support was unlikely to devolve to La Follette. A compromise candidate was sure to emerge: "someone who has personal qualifications, the voice, the power greatly to stimulate enthusiasm, the impressive presence. . . . That man's name need not be spoken to the convention, for every delegate has it in his heart."

Unauthorized Roosevelt "clubs" began to sprout in Idaho, Montana, Michigan, and Ohio. On 11 December, the Republican National Committee held its annual meeting in Washington, D.C. It split at once into progressive and conservative factions. Taft members were in control of the proceedings, but their loyalty to the President (sulky and ailing in the White House, too gouty to venture outside) was more out of reflex than conviction. Nobody could see where funds for next year's campaign were going to come from. Postmaster General Frank Hitchcock, an ornithological friend of the Colonel, made no secret of his disillusionment with the administration. The atmosphere was funereal, even doom-laden, as both sides agreed to summon their delegates to Chicago at noon on 18 June 1912.

A group of three progressive state chairmen, led by W. Franklin Knox of Michigan, telephoned Roosevelt in New York to ask if they could come to see him. He said he would prefer to be left alone. But the group was persistent, and descended on him at Sagamore Hill.

KNOX	Colonel, I never knew you to show the white feather, and you should not do so now.
TR	(*angrily*) What do you mean by that?
KNOX	Why, you are basing your refusal on the possibly bad effect another term might have on your reputation. I contend that you ought to look at this thing from the Party's interests and not your own. The Party has honored you, and it now turns to you to do a service for it. It is in distress and it needs you.
TR	By George, that would be a good argument if I were the only man available, but I am not. I agree that Taft cannot be elected, but if the Party can win, I am not the only Republican with whom it can win. I am not ungrateful for the honor I have had, but I think I have repaid in service. When I left the White House every state we had any right to expect was in the Republican column. It is not my job to put them back again.

There was no arguing with him, and the group left frustrated.

⌐⊸⌐

IN A MONTH FULL of adulation and importuning, opposite in all political respects to his dark December of 1910, Roosevelt chose to publish an extraordinary essay—what was, for him, almost a religious confession. Entitled "The

Search for Truth in a Reverent Spirit," it appeared in *The Outlook* just as his private will not to run was wavering. Nothing he had written in that piously inclined periodical compared with it in philosophical, if not theological weight, and never had he come so close to confessing his own faith. It was ignored by the political commentators who had read so much into his previous editorial on the trusts. Yet to an intellectual minority able to follow him in his self-avowed "search" toward a universal understanding beyond that of any contemporary public figure—Arthur Balfour alone excepted—it was an infinitely more important statement, indicating that whatever Theodore Roosevelt did with the rest of his life would have to have moral purpose.

The essay was a review of twelve recent scientific, religious, historical, and philosophical books, including Carlos Reyles's *La morte du cygne,* Thomas Dwight's *Thoughts of a Catholic Anatomist,* Alfred Russel Wallace's *The World of Life,* Henry M. Bernard's *Some Neglected Factors in Evolution,* Émile Boutroux's *Science et religion dans la philosophie contemporaine,* William De Witt Hyde's *From Epicurus to Christ,* and Henri Bergson's *Creative Evolution* and *Time and Free Will.* Concentrating mainly on the pessimistic materialism of Reyles, the Christian apologetics of Dwight, and the radiant, octogenarian wisdom of Wallace, Roosevelt synthesized multiple points of view into his own argument for wider recognition of "the psychical accompaniment of physical force"—by which he meant the spiritual qualities inherent in all materialistic pursuits, from science to business and politics.

Reyles's dying swan was a metaphor for Latin civilization in Europe, which the author, a wealthy Uruguayan and disciple of Nietzsche, believed to be doomed unless France, Italy, and Spain shook themselves free of political and clerical absolutism and turned to the acquisition of money and arms. As long as those countries remained at peace, they should cultivate an "ideology of force" to avoid being left behind by Northern powers, particularly Germany and the United States.

Roosevelt was revolted by the book, and not just because parts of it echoed his frequent celebrations of strenuosity. He found in it a "hard dogmatic materialism" indistinguishable from that of his new boosters on Wall Street. Modern worship of the golden calf (Reyles actually used the phrase *métaphysique de l'Or*) struck him as more pernicious than any medieval superstition. He rejected the pro-Americanism of a writer who could not distinguish between the democratic tradition of Washington and Lincoln and the anti-constitutionalism of tycoons.

Rigid materialistic standards in science, rejecting the imaginative or metaphysical eurekas that had always aided advances in knowledge, were equally retrogressive, in Roosevelt's opinion. They worked against discovery. But he was uneasy with the Catholic values that Dwight, a venerable figure at Harvard, sought to apply to "infidel science." Logically extended, they could "plunge us back into the cringing and timid ignorance of the Dark Ages." He quoted Henry Osborn Taylor's characterization of medieval man: "Subject to bursts of unrestraint, he yet showed no intelligent desire for liberty."

Dwight was effective, however, in reminding the young czars of evolutionary theory of what Roger Bacon had proclaimed in the thirteenth century: "*The first essential for advancement in knowledge is for men to be willing to say, 'We do not know.'* " There could be no advancement, Roosevelt wrote, in a scientific dogma that saw only itself, and liked what it saw:

> The establishment of the doctrine of evolution in our time offers no more justification for upsetting religious beliefs than the discovery of the facts of the solar system a few centuries ago. Any faith sufficiently robust to stand the (surely very slight) strain of admitting that the world is not flat and does move around the sun need not have any apprehensions on the score of evolution, and the materialistic scientists who gleefully hail the discovery of the principle of evolution as establishing their dreary creed might with just as much propriety rest it upon the discovery of the principle of gravitation. Science and religion, and the relations between them, are affected by one only as they are affected by the other.

He took up the ancient antithesis of *fides versus ratio* and argued that an embrace of both faith and reason was necessary for a person of "conscience" to search for truth, as something wholly practical, yet (since truth-seeking was a form of prayer) divine. An egregious preacher of "intolerant arrogance and fanatical dogmatism" was Dwight's didactic opposite, the German anatomist Ernst Haeckel. Not only were Haeckel's assumptions "unscientific" in their absolute refusal to accept mystery as part of knowledge, they were as ideological as the ecclesiastical tenets they sought to refute. Roosevelt noted that Boutroux, Bergson, and William James felt the same way about Haeckel as he did. It said something for the materialism of contemporary Germany that the man was still admired there.

For himself as a natural historian and social reformer, he most admired and identified with the great English prophet of natural selection. Wallace had followed a curious trajectory since his days of co-discovery with Darwin, becoming more mystical (and politically progressive) as his scientific expertise grew.

Meanwhile, Henry Bernard had gone further than Wallace in opening up what Roosevelt considered to be "a new biological and even sociological field of capital importance"—the theory that the principle of group development in human beings was as instinctive, and organic, as that in biological evolution. Bernard was willing to entertain the role of the soul in science. But he fell "into the great mistake of denying freedom of the will, merely because he with his finite material intelligence cannot understand it." This incomprehension led him to call illogically for the remoralization of society, and for judicial reforms that would catch up with modern psychical perceptions. Roosevelt did not boast that he had recently called for the same things himself, but he remarked that a perfect community was unattainable "if there are no such things as freedom of the will and accountability."

Not to mention love, an emotion scientists hesitated to analyze. It bonded the basic human cluster, the family, better than economic or environmental forces. Saint Augustine had correctly proclaimed that "the truths of love are as valid as the truths of reason." Another essential was plain old common sense—too common for most philosophers, but not for Bergson, who regarded it as different from, and superior to, reason. In his new masterwork, the French philosopher had, in Roosevelt's words, shown that "Reason can deal effectively only with certain categories [of knowledge]. True wisdom must necessarily refuse to allow reason to assume a sway outside its limitations; and where experience plainly proves that the intellect has reasoned wrongly, then it is the part of wisdom to accept the teachings of experience, and bid reason to be humble—just as under like conditions it would bid theology be humble."

Roosevelt felt that Dwight and other cautionaries against purely materialistic thought were performing "a real service" in warning that dogmas, no matter how provable they seemed in the laboratory or the marketplace, were often as not swept away by the currents of historical change. Today's "law" might be tomorrow's superstition. But if there was to be any steady scientific or social advance, theists and materialists alike must give way to "bolder, more self-reliant spirits . . . men whose unfettered freedom of soul and intellect yields complete fealty only to the great cause of truth, and will not be hindered by any outside control in the search to attain it."

The word *progress* sounded repeatedly in his essay as he continued to equate faith and reason as coefficients, not opposites, in improving the human lot. "In the world of politics," he wrote, "it is easy to appeal to the unreasoning reactionary, and no less easy to appeal to the unreasoning advocate of change, but difficult to get people to show for the cause of sanity and progress combined the zeal so easily aroused against sanity by one set of extremists and against progress by another set of extremists."

For a moment Roosevelt seemed tempted to veer into one of his habitual either-or mantras, but remembering that the theme he had set himself was truth-seeking in a spirit of reverence, he resumed his assault on "the narrowness of a shut-in materialism." While praising materialistic scholars for "the whole enormous incredible advance in knowledge of the physical universe and of man's physical place in that universe," he ascribed superior wisdom to James, Boutroux, and Bergson because they understood "that outside the purely physical lies the psychic, and that the realm of religion stands outside even of the purely psychic."

He argued that those who professed faith while allowing reason to persuade them that evolution was a material fact were not having philosophy both ways. They were, on the contrary, "in a position of impregnable strength," rightly holding that religion itself was evolutionary: it too had to adapt as it progressed. Roosevelt came near to articulating his own spiritual aspirations in summarizing theirs: "To them Christianity, the greatest of the religious creations which humanity has seen, rests upon what Christ himself teaches: for, as M. Boutroux phrases it, the performance of duty is faith in action, faith in its highest expression, for duty gives no other reason, and need give no other reason, for its existence than 'its own incorruptible disinterestedness.' "

In conclusion, he wrote:

> Surely we must all recognize the search for truth as an imperative duty; and we ought all of us likewise to recognize that this search for truth should be carried on, not only fearlessly, but also with reverence, with humility of spirit, and with full recognition of our own limitations both of the mind and the soul. . . . To those who deny the ethical obligation implied in such a faith we who acknowledge the obligation are aliens; and we are brothers to all those who do acknowledge it, whatever their creed or system of philosophy.

THE YEAR ENDED WITH the Colonel insisting "I am not and will not be a candidate." He declared over and over that his nomination would be a "calamity" both for him and the Republican Party. But privately he equivocated, for reasons implicit in his confessional article. All the books he had discussed concerned *progress* from one state of held beliefs to another—whether from paganism to Christianity, or clerical orthodoxy to free-market capitalism, or from rationalism to theism in science. All accepted, or tried in vain to deny, that belief itself was as transformative a force as materialism, and a necessary chastener of it. After a lifetime of rejecting spiritual speculation, in favor of praise of the body electric and the physics of military power, Theodore Roosevelt had conceded the vitality of faith—not necessarily Bible-thumping, but at least the compulsive "ethical obligation" that distinguished the unselfish citizen from the mere hoarder of gold.

His best interest would have been to announce that under no circumstances would he run, or accept a draft, for the presidency. But that prospect was beyond his present policy of noncommital. He did, however, entrust a strange message to his elder daughter, who he knew was a friend of Major Butt in the White House.

"Alice, when you get the opportunity, tell Archie from me to get out of his present job. And not to wait for the convention, but do it soon."

CHAPTER 8

Hat in the Ring

Nothing will help that man.
You see the fates have given him so much,
He must have all or perish.

ONE OF THE FOLK SAYINGS that Roosevelt liked to share with audiences was "They say that nothing is as independent as a hog on ice. If he doesn't want to stand up, he can lie down."

As 1912 dawned, he found himself faced with the hog's dilemma. He could run and slip, and this time there would be no recovery. Or he could maintain a low profile, and feel the chill of inactivity slowly spreading through his bones.

Were it not such a momentous year, politically speaking, he might keep himself warm with literary production: perhaps write his "big work," or continue pouring out editorials for *The Outlook* on any subject that interested him. (He was proud of his latest essay, on medieval scholarship, and sent a copy to Edith Wharton.) The life of a dignified elder statesman, such as Arthur Balfour had embarked on in Britain, was what Edith Roosevelt wanted for her husband. She felt that biweekly trips into town, with a busy schedule of meetings and lunches, would be worldly action enough for him. On other days, he could satisfy his intellectual hunger at home with books, and there was always the estate to take care of excess energy.

"You can put it out of your mind, Theodore," she said. "You will never be President of the United States again."

The problem was putting it out of the minds of other people. His response to the U.S. Steel suit had created the general impression, which no number of denials could dispel, that he was running. A convention of the Ohio Progressive Republican League declined to endorse Robert La Follette, and spawned the first of many state "booms" for the Colonel. Governor Chase Osborn of Michigan urged both Taft and La Follette to withdraw in Roosevelt's favor.

Some sober-minded industrialists and stockbrokers were tempted to agree, suggesting that it might be better to have the Square Dealer renominated, in his new, responsible regulatory mode, than risk the prosecutorial zeal of his rivals.

"It now looks as if Roosevelt, not Taft, would get (or rather, take) the Republican nomination," Woodrow Wilson wrote a friend. "*That* would make a campaign worth while."

To Edith's dismay, Sagamore Hill once again became a political mecca. The pilgrims Roosevelt had attracted after his return from Africa in 1910 were nothing to the *hajj* that converged on him now. In cabs and carriages and automobiles, they took advantage of the metaled road he had rashly built up the slope of Sagamore Hill. Freezing rain did not keep them away. He got even less peace in his office at *The Outlook,* which began to look like a campaign headquarters, minus the posters and spittoons.

Once more the sad, worshipful eyes of Gifford Pinchot and James Garfield burned into him, beseeching him to free them from their commitment to La Follette. They argued that only he was capable of preventing the Party split that would surely occur if Taft was nominated in June. Midwesterners loyal to "Battling Bob" lobbied Roosevelt to proclaim himself a non-candidate, loud and clear. Progressive governors, National Committeemen, publishers, and businessmen tried to make him do just the opposite. George W. Perkins, the star executive of J. P. Morgan & Co., offered him financing.

Old friends he had not seen in nearly two years paid court, drawn by a fascinated desire to observe Theodore *redux.* They included Henry White and William Allen White, about as socially different as two namesakes could be, united in their admiration for him; Cal O'Laughlin, now head of the Washington bureau of the *Chicago Tribune;* Jules Jusserand, trying to avoid detection by the press; and even Archie Butt, on an espionage mission approved by Taft.

Roosevelt was inscrutable to all. After leaving him, Jusserand asked Butt what he made of the Colonel's attitude.

"He is not a candidate, but if he can defeat the President for renomination he will do it."

"Exactly my opinion."

Taft received Butt's report pettishly. "If he is not a candidate, why is he sending for governors and delegations all the time?"

Roosevelt was not soliciting support so much as advice from professional politicians, in genuine agony of mind as to what he should do. Mail flowed in by the sackful, every correspondent wanting or urging something. "I would much prefer to wait until 1916," he told a neighbor, Regis H. Post.

That indicated he had not altogether lost his desire for power. To Representative George W. Norris of Nebraska, he wrote, "I am not a candidate and shall not be a candidate, but hitherto to all requests as to whether I would accept if nominated I have answered in the words of Abraham Lincoln that nobody had a right to ask me to cross that bridge until I came to it."

Nothing less than a draft, representing popular rather than partisan feeling, would square Roosevelt's sense of honor with his sense of duty, and make him commit himself to a campaign that was bound to be one of the most brutal in Republican history. Outside of a few electoral areas, in the Deep South and Brahmin precincts of New England, the American people loved him to a degree that Taft and La Follette had to envy. He was attractive even to the progressive Democrats currently being courted by Woodrow Wilson. The promise he seemed to personify of social justice, and a White House made lively once again, was what made his political enemies desperate to keep him away from the hustings.

The radical wing of progressivism represented by La Follette noted the Colonel's recent rightward swing and doubted that he would swing left again, once renominated by a majority of the Party. Old Guard Republicans got exactly the reverse impression. They looked at his latest article in *The Outlook* and saw, with a group shudder, that he had begun to advocate the recall of judicial decisions. What socialist mayhem would he visit upon the courts, if by some perversion of democracy he returned to the White House?

"Theodore Roosevelt is a presidential impossibility," declared Felix Agnus, publisher of the *Baltimore American*. "The sooner this fact is recognized and the more firmly it is stated, the sooner will the Republican Party get its true bearings, and the drivel of hysteria that invokes his name as a saviour of the Party and the country will be checked."

HENRY ADAMS, WALKING at dusk one night in downtown Washington, was accosted by what he at first took to be a hippopotamus. "It was the President himself wandering about with Archy [*sic*] Butt, and I joined them as far as the White House Porch. He . . . gave me a shock. He looks bigger and more tumble-to-pieces than ever, and his manner has become more slovenly than his figure; but what struck me most was the deterioration of his mind and expression. . . . He showed mental enfeeblement all over, and I wanted to offer him a bet that he wouldn't get through his term."

At the other end of Pennsylvania Avenue, a bitter Senator La Follette was blaming Roosevelt for retarding the progress of his campaign. "What can you do?" Gifford Pinchot taunted him. "You must know that he has this thing in his hands and can do whatever he likes."

La Follette's real problem—and Roosevelt's too, if he ran—was that Taft had executive control of the Party machinery. His fat hand lay heavy on levers only he could wield, sending thrills of power along the patronage grid Mark Hanna had assembled, state by state, in the 1890s. The grid terminated in about a thousand convention delegates or delegates-to-be, many already pledged to him. This advantage was furthered by the tradition that a sitting president was entitled to renomination unless he declined to serve again. It made Taft an almost unbeatable opponent through June, even if his lack of popularity made him a gift to the Democrats thereafter.

Roosevelt, in contrast, was hampered by another tradition, that of no president ever running for a third term. He had endorsed it himself, in his famous declaration after the election of 1904: *The wise custom which limits the President to two terms regards the substance and not the form. Under no circumstances will I be a candidate for or accept another nomination.*

It was a "custom" in the sense that the Constitution did not mandate it. He now began to claim that its wisdom lay in denying an extension to any president who (as he laboriously put it), "is in office and has been in office for eight years." There was nothing to prevent such a man from returning to power after taking some time off to hunt lions, or for that matter, hippopotami.

He defended his cagey public stance in a letter to Frank A. Munsey, the wealthy owner of *Munsey's Magazine* and an ardent progressive. "In making any statement it is not only necessary to consider what the man actually means and actually says . . . but also to consider what the statement will be held to mean by the great mass of people who are obliged to get their information more or less at second hand, and largely through instrumentalities like most of the New York dailies, such as the *American,* the *World,* the *Evening Post* and the *Times,* that is, through people who make their livelihood by the practice of slanderous mendacity for hire, and whose one purpose, as far as I am concerned, is to invent falsehood and to distort truth."

Roosevelt's conviction that such organs were mendacious was not paranoid. Few seemed disposed to favor him if he ran. The only major papers he could count on were the *New York Press* and Baltimore *News,* both owned by Munsey, E. A. Van Valkenburg's Philadelphia *North American,* Medill McCormick's *Chicago Tribune,* and W. R. Nelson's *Kansas City Star.* William Allen White's *Emporia Gazette* was passionately supportive but small-town in its influence, compared to the "yellow" Pulitzer and Hearst tabloids, with their millions of readers and Democratic bias.

Again citing Lincoln, Roosevelt quoted the Emancipator's policy of lying low whenever journalists were on the prowl: *What they want is a squabble and a fuss, and that they can have when we explain; and they cannot have it if we don't.* He felt that this "homely common sense" applied to his current situation. He had been accused of overweening ambition often enough in the past to know that if he gave any hint of wanting to be drafted, it would be seen by most editors as fatal insolence.

✒

ON 16 JANUARY, a "Roosevelt National Committee" was independently established in Chicago. It set up offices in the Congress Hotel. What *Current Literature* called a "Roosevelt obsession" at once spread to all parts of the country where GOP primaries were being planned. Speculation mounted in the press that the Colonel would announce his intentions in Ohio in late February.

"I fear things are going to become very bitter before long," Taft told Major Butt. "But, Archie, I am going to defeat him in the convention."

The President had no doubt that a progressive revolution was being plotted at Oyster Bay. He had heard from Henry Stimson that the Colonel was "as hard as nails" in his anger at having been named in the steel suit.

Taft seemed less affected by the prospect of a split in the Republican Party than by the lingering effect of that anger. "It is hard, very hard, Archie, to see a devoted friendship going to pieces like a rope of sand."

Major Butt noticed, as Adams had, that the President was deteriorating mentally and physically. He stayed up later and later at night, and during the day kept nodding off—so often on public occasions that Butt had to keep elbowing him in the ribs and coughing loudly in his ear.

La Follette, too, began to ail under the stress induced by Roosevelt's silence. He saw that his most influential backers, James Garfield, Medill McCormick, and Gifford and Amos Pinchot, were daily less loyal to him. It was obvious that the slightest positive signal from Oyster Bay would make them beg to be released from their pledges. The senator announced through a spokesman that "nothing but death" would keep him from pursuing the nomination, right through to the convention.

He had hoped to shine at a showdown between himself, Taft, Roosevelt, and Woodrow Wilson in early February, at the annual dinner of the Periodical Publishers Association in Philadelphia. All four were invited to appear, but the President and the Colonel, not wanting to look like co-equals, sent regrets. La Follette summoned up what strength he had left to write and rehearse the most important speech of his career. A spellbinding political orator, less preachy and ambiguous than Roosevelt, he felt confident of his power to win over the shapers of public opinion. Progressives who had already heard Wilson on the stump were less sanguine.

✒

WITHIN TWO DAYS of the opening of his national headquarters in Chicago, the pressure on Roosevelt to declare had increased to such a point that he decided to yield—but only to a petition that made clear his reluctance to run. He asked the four Republican governors who were most energetically championing him (Chase Osborn of Michigan, Robert P. Bass of New Hampshire, William E. Glasscock of West Virginia, and Walter R. Stubbs of Kansas) to send him a written appeal for his candidacy. If they would argue that they were acting on behalf of the "plain people" who had elected them, he would feel "in honor bound" to say yes.

Frank Knox was appointed his roving emissary between the governors. Big and bluff, Knox was amply equipped to handle the various egos involved. He took it upon himself to solicit more gubernatorial signatures, and added those of Herbert S. Hadley of Missouri, Chester H. Aldrich of Nebraska, and Joseph M. Carey of Wyoming. With subsequent endorsements from Hiram Johnson of California and Robert S. Vessey of South Dakota, the appeal group represented a wide swath of country—considering that the South was Democratic territory, and the major industrial states were controlled by Taft-beholden bosses.

All this coordination took time, since some of the governors were more progressive than others, and regretted having to betray La Follette's candidacy. Roosevelt complicated matters by toying with each executive separately, as if he wanted to delay the very petition he had invited.

Meanwhile, delegate-selection proceedings were under way in several states that had not yet adopted the primary system. On 23 January, Oklahoma's Fourth District Republican convention grotesquely dramatized the factionalism of a party splitting three ways.

The local committee chairman, Edward Perry, was a Roosevelt man who hoped to create a progressive stampede for the Colonel. A letter from Gifford Pinchot reminded him that, as yet, La Follette was Taft's only official challenger. Perry read the letter to the convention, but made plain that he still favored Roosevelt. This infuriated the rank and file supporting Taft. Pandemonium ensued, with Perry roaring "Slap Roosevelt in the face if you dare!" over contrary shrieks and howls. A posse of fake Rough Riders invaded the hall. For fifteen minutes they tried to storm the stage, but found it harder to take than the Heights of San Juan. Cigar-smoking Taft forces repelled them. One cavalryman got through on a miniature pony: the young son of Jack "Catch-'em-Alive" Abernathy, a friend of Roosevelt's famous for seizing wolves by the tongue. The boy shrilled "I want Teddy!" to the crowd, touching off further furor. But then the organization men suppressed him, and the convention endorsed Taft over La Follette by a vote of 118 to 32. Perry, locally known as "Dynamite Ed," showed his displeasure by going outside and detonating five hundred pounds of high explosives.

His district may have returned a slate of delegates loyal to the President, but he wanted the world to know that progressivism was a force to be reckoned with.

⌒

ROOSEVELT MAINTAINED FOR the rest of the month that he was not a candidate. "Do not for one moment think that I shall be President next year," he cautioned Joseph Bucklin Bishop, one of his most obsequious acolytes. "I write you, confidentially, that my own reading of the situation is that while there are a great many people in this country who are devoted to me, they do not form more than a substantial minority of the ten or fifteen millions of voters. . . . Unless I am greatly mistaken, the people have made up their mind that they wish some new instrument, that they do not wish me; and if I know myself, I am sincere when I tell you that this does not cause one least little particle of regret to me."

By 2 February, however, the governors were on the verge of approving the language of their group petition, and Roosevelt confirmed to Hiram Johnson that he would run. He did not want to announce until the petition had been formally delivered to him. No word of his intent leaked through to members of the Periodical Publishers Association, meeting that night in Philadelphia. But before the evening was over, they had another news story, of major proportions.

Woodrow Wilson preceded Senator La Follette to the podium and delivered a short, urbane, perfectly pitched address. Ray Stannard Baker, co-author of La Follette's campaign autobiography, was present and felt excitement building in the audience. Wilson, he scribbled in his notebook, was somebody endowed with "unlimited reserves of power."

La Follette, in contrast, behaved like a candidate not for office, but for a psychological breakdown. He was weak from a recent attack of ptomaine poisoning, starved of sleep, and possessed by the notion that Roosevelt wanted to destroy him. Before standing up, he swigged a glassful of whiskey. He began to speak at 10 P.M. and was still at it long after midnight, at times rereading whole chunks of his text without noticing, at others rambling so incoherently that Baker left the room in an agony of embarrassment. Wilson's long face expressed alarm. Of all subjects, La Follette chose to rant at the "subservience of the press to special interests," not to mention "a subtle new peril, the centralization of advertising, that will in time seek to gag you." Magazine magnates boggled as his language grew personal, then, when it degenerated into yells of abuse, went to collect their hats and coats. The senator continued to rave, in a virtually empty hall, before slumping forward onto his script.

"That was a pitiable tragedy," Roosevelt mused, after reading about it in the newspapers. He wrote a letter of sympathy when he heard an extenuating detail: La Follette had been distraught over the imminence of a life-threatening operation on his daughter. Nevertheless, most progressives agreed with Pinchot that the senator had forfeited their support.

The pressure on Roosevelt to run now became overwhelming. "Politics are hateful," a worried Edith Roosevelt wrote Kermit. "Father thinks he must enter the fight since La Follette's collapse." Unable to bear the sight of any more politicians in broad-brimmed black hats besieging Sagamore Hill, she decamped, first to New York, then to Panama and Costa Rica with Ethel. She did not want to be around to hear Theodore make his announcement.

⁓

MARY LA FOLLETTE survived, and as she recovered, so did her father. He brushed aside the advice of his aides to withdraw as a candidate, saying he would consider doing so only if they could get the Colonel to issue a declaration of insurgent principles dictated by himself. For a week, representatives of the two camps tried to broker such an agreement. But Roosevelt declined to make any statement whatever until 21 February, when he was due to address a convention drafting a new constitution for Ohio. His words there, moreover, would represent his own philosophy and nobody else's.

Meanwhile, in what was seen as an ominous portent, Roosevelt supporters bolted the Florida Republican convention when it elected a delegate slate loyal to the President. Feeling themselves to be in the majority against Taft's operatives, they chose their own delegation, and vowed to send it to Chicago in June, in an official contest for seating rights.

On the ninth, about seventy members of the Roosevelt National Committee, representing twenty-four states, met in Chicago and authorized the dispatch of the governors' petition. It was treated as a private communication that he could publish if he liked. But the governors made clear their feelings in a statement given to the press, even as Frank Knox, petition in hand, hurried to catch the fastest possible train east:

> A principle is of no avail without a man. A cause is lost without a leader. In Theodore Roosevelt we believe the principle has the man and the cause the leader. It is our opinion that this is the sentiment of the majority of the people of the United States.

Taft, seriously disturbed, told a Lincoln's Birthday gathering of Republicans in New York that there were certain "extremists" in the Party who wished to give ordinary Americans—"people necessarily indifferently informed"—a participatory role in handling great public issues best left to Congress and the courts. "Such extremists are not progressives—they are political emotionalists or neurotics," the President declared, in what was taken as a reference to Roosevelt.

Actually, he meant La Follette, who was still under neurological care. But Taft's dread of progressivism as an anarchic force, destabilizing the polity he revered—a nation governed by laws not men, answerable only to judges—was obvious, as was his likely rhetorical course if the Colonel dared to challenge him.

Roosevelt remained silent, working on his Ohio speech and urging a distraught Nicholas Longworth to remain loyal to the President. He himself could not. "If I were any longer doubtful, I would telegraph you to come and talk to me, but it would not be any use now Nick. I have got to come out."

He admitted that his chances of beating the White House organization were no better than one in three. Already, political appointees suspected of favoring him were being dismissed around the country. For that reason, he needed to mount the most formidable and well-financed campaign possible at such a late date. Fortunately, there was no shortage of progressive idealists eager to volunteer their services, either because of the magic of his name, or because they believed he would further the cause. Recruitment was proceeding so well in thirty-one states that his organization looked to be virtually complete by the time he announced his candidacy.

Elihu Root made a last-minute effort to dissuade him from accepting the draft of the governors. "It seems to me that those who ask you to make a declaration are asking you . . . to incur the considerable probability of being defeated for the nomination, or, if successful in that, of being defeated in the election, and that the consequences to your future, to your power of leadership in the interests of the causes which you have at heart, and to your position in history, would be so injurious that . . . no number of friends have any right to ask such a sacrifice."

Root wrote pessimistically, knowing that nothing was less likely to deter his old friend than warnings of personal risk. "The time has come," Roosevelt replied, "when I must speak."

He was beyond caution now, beyond the moralizing over duty and ideals that had obsessed him much of the past year. Day by day, he felt battle lust rising. And typically, when he rose in Columbus to address the Ohio constitutional convention, he said nothing about the governors' petition and espoused the most radical issue in progressive politics.

LITTLE MORE THAN two weeks before, he had assured Henry Stimson, "I do not myself believe in the recall of the judiciary." The secretary of war was still trying to live down their doomed double effort to launch a reform *coup d'état* in New York in the fall of 1910, and had been rendered nervous by Roosevelt's *Outlook* article recommending the annulment of judicial decisions that favored property rights over human rights. No proposal could be more certain to enrage the President, who regarded even questions of national honor as "justiciable." Was this to be a theme of his coming campaign? Would he also suggest the recall of judges, state and federal? And if so, were justices of the Supreme Court next on his Robespierrean agenda?

Roosevelt set a defiant tone at the outset by declaring, "I believe . . . that human rights are supreme over all other rights; that wealth should be the servant, not the master of the people." Yet for the next half hour his speech, cast in the form of an ideological lecture, was not provocative. It covered the whole range of issues with which a modern state had to deal as it adjusted itself to an age in which individualism was secondary to collectivism. Only a revitalized democracy could prevent industrial and political combinations from making property rights the basis of all law.

"Shape your constitutional action," he advised the delegates, "so that the people will be able through their legislative bodies, or . . . by direct popular vote, to provide workmen's compensation acts, to regulate the hours of labor for children and for women, to provide for their safety while at work, and to prevent overwork or work under unhygienic or unsafe conditions."

No reasonable Republican could object to granting such benefits, although there was a hint of Jacksonian threat in the phrase *by direct popular vote*. It implied more participation in policymaking than William Howard Taft (to name one Ohioan) felt ordinary Americans deserved. Roosevelt proceeded to recite the basic progressive creed, pledging himself to direct primaries, direct senatorial elections, and—when legislators quailed or failed—the initiative and referendum. As to the recall of short-term elective officers, he favored it, but only when public disillusionment was extreme.

"There remains the question of the recall of judges," Roosevelt said.

> I do not believe in adopting the recall save as a last resort. . . . But either the recall will have to be adopted or else it will have to be made much easier than it now is to get rid, not merely of a bad judge, but of a judge who, however virtuous, has grown so out of touch with social needs and facts that he is unfit longer to render good service on the bench. It is nonsense to say that impeachment meets the difficulty. . . .
>
> When a judge decides a constitutional question, when he decides what the people as a whole can and cannot do, the people should have the right to recall that decision if they think that it is wrong. We should hold the judiciary in all respect, but it is both absurd and degrading to make a fetish of a judge or of any one else.

At no point did he mention the President as the nation's ranking such fetishist. However, Roosevelt's contempt for legalistic justice, as opposed to executive action in favor of human rights, was plain. He cited a workmen's compensation suit against the Southern Buffalo Railroad, recently rejected by the

New York State Court of Appeals. The judge in that case, like Judge Baldwin in *Hoxie v. the New Haven Railroad,* had declared the federal statute unconstitutional in terms of common law. "I know of no popular vote by any state of the union," Roosevelt said, "more flagrant in its defiance of right and justice, more short-sighted in its inability to face the changed needs of our civilization."

⮸

THE REACTION TO "Roosevelt's Recall Speech" was angrier and more widespread than that following his New Nationalism address eighteen months before. The American Bar Association came out solidly against it. He was assailed from quarters as far away as Great Britain for the "sheer madness," "demagogy," "absolutism," and "despicable nature" of his prejudice against judges. It was to be expected that the New York *World* should accuse him of inciting "mob rule," and that the *Wall Street Journal* should wisecrack: "Those most enthusiastic over the recall of judicial decisions are prevented by prison rules from working for the Colonel." But even such progressives as Congressman Victor Murdock and Senator William E. Borah felt that Roosevelt had gone too far. "One statement frequently heard today," *The New York Times* reported on 22 February, "is that the Colonel's speech makes Senator La Follette look like a reactionary." The Texas Progressive Republican League voted to support William Howard Taft.

Academics reverent of anything canonical in law or political doctrine were especially vituperative. Andrew Dickson White, the former president of Cornell, called the notion of popular amendment of state constitutions "the most monstrous proposal ever presented to the American people, or any other people." James Day, chancellor of Syracuse University, declared, "Emma Goldman could not make a more violent attack on our institutions." Even clerics weighed in. The aged Episcopal bishop of Albany, who had known Roosevelt since his days as governor, called him "erratic, unsafe, and unfair."

Doubts about Roosevelt's sanity recirculated. Justice W. O. Howard of the New York Supreme Court described him as "a madman" with "the instinct of a beast." The editor of the *Journal of Abnormal Psychology* theorized that the Colonel would "go down in history as one of the most illustrious psychological examples of the distortion of conscious mental processes through the force of subconscious wishes." A Chicago lawyer offered $5,000 to any medical or charitable institution that could arrange to have Roosevelt certified. Henry Adams warned Brooks Adams, "His mind has gone to pieces. . . . He is, as Taft justly said, a neurotic, and his neurosis may end like La Follette's, in a nervous collapse or acute mania."

An appalled Henry Cabot Lodge could only say to reporters, "The Colonel and I have long since agreed to disagree on a number of points."

❧

ALMOST UNHEARD IN the general uproar over Roosevelt's speech was a casual remark he had made en route to Columbus: "My hat is in the ring. The fight is on and I am stripped to the buff." It took several days for the seventeen monosyllables to work their way into the folk consciousness. But when they did, realization spread that he had, at last, confirmed his candidacy—in yet another of the popular images he coined so effortlessly. By 25 February, when he arrived in Boston to issue his formal acceptance of the petition of the governors, The Hat in the Ring had already joined The Man in the Arena, The Strenuous Life, The Big Stick, The Square Deal, The Black Crystal, and Malefactors of Great Wealth in the American political lexicon.

❧

"I WILL ACCEPT the nomination for President if it is tendered to me, and I will adhere to this decision until the convention has expressed its preference."

As Roosevelt's letter to the governors went out on the evening wires, he relaxed in the Boston home of Robert Grant, a liberal and literary judge he had known for many years. Grant thought that the Colonel had made a self-destructive mistake, and carefully observed his looks and behavior for the record. "I never saw him in better physical shape. He is fairly stout, but his color is good. . . . He halts in his sentences occasionally; but from a layman's point of view there was nothing to suggest mental impairment, unless the combination of egotism, faith in his own doctrines, fondness for power and present hostility to Taft . . . can be termed symptomatic. . . . He was a most delightful guest."

For all the pleasure Judge Grant took in the Colonel's company—and that of William Allen White and the biographer William Roscoe Thayer as fellow dinner guests—he was not disposed to congratulate him on running for the presidency again. "Has not every one of your friends advised you against it?"

Roosevelt admitted that was true. For a long time, he said, he had been "very uncertain" about what to do. But the urgency of the progressives who looked to him for leadership had finally convinced him that he had to rescue the reform program so disastrously mismanaged by President Taft. To have ignored their appeals, to have waited until 1916 to run again, would have been "cowardice," he said—"a case of *il gran refiuto*."

Dante's phrase clearly appealed to him, and he repeated it, evoking the refusal of a thirteenth-century hermit to accept elevation to the Papacy.

"But you will agree that Taft has made a good president this year?" Grant spoke out of a sense of fairness, rather than loyalty to the administration.

Roosevelt said he thought that all Taft had done was to reduce the Republican Party to a torpor reminiscent of that of "the Bell and Everett Whigs just before the Civil War." He plunged into a discussion of patronage with White, and Grant noticed that he saw betrayal in every reasonable move Taft had made to consolidate himself as president.

"But will any of the Party leaders support you?" the judge asked.

"No. None of them; not even Lodge, I think." He said he believed his only hope of winning was to "reach the popular vote through direct primaries," in states democratic enough to hold them.

"But the situation is complex, I suppose? You would like to be President."

"You are right, it is complex. I like power; but I care nothing to be President as President. I am interested in these ideas of mine and I want to carry them through, and feel that I am the one to carry them through." He cited, by way of example, his belief that the will of the people was being "thwarted" by reactionary courts.

Grant was a bona fide member of the Harvard Republican establishment, but unlike most of his associates, saw no constitutional threat in the Colonel's Columbus speech. Thayer did, saying that anyone advising the recall of judicial decisions wished to subject American institutions to "the whims of the populace at the moment." Roosevelt, keeping his temper, pointed out that he had excluded the Supreme Court from his proposal. Nor was he advocating the removal of judges themselves. He was concerned only with judicial *decisions* at the state level, in cases where humanitarian legislation was struck down on fake constitutional grounds.

Thayer and Grant were impressed with his self-assurance. But Theodore in private was different from Theodore on the stump. They saw that his moral fervor, the way he had of charging argument with more passion than it needed, would prevent persons of colder blood from understanding that he was actually a thoughtful man.

For five hours, with White, they tried in vain to change his resolve to run. At eleven-thirty the party broke up. Thayer, who was not staying over, went out into the night, feeling saddened and apprehensive. Just before the Colonel went up to bed, Grant made the mistake of mentioning his cool treatment of Taft.

Roosevelt stopped at the foot of the stairway. "It was through me and my friends that he became President."

It was a tense moment. Both of them were aware that his announcement was even now thumping through printing presses across the country.

They continued on up the stairs. Roosevelt stretched out his arms and said, "I feel as fine as silk."

CHAPTER 9

The Tall Timber of
Darkening Events

=======

He may do more by seeing what he sees
Than others eager for iniquities;
He may, by seeing all things for the best,
Incite futurity to do the rest.

THE CONTRARY FORCES ALIGNING themselves for and against the campaign of Theodore Roosevelt to unseat his successor were on display in Cambridge, Massachusetts, on 28 February 1912. He attended a meeting of the Harvard board of overseers and was ostracized by his fellow members. They stood with their backs to him until he was joined by a sympathetic friend, Colonel Norwood P. Hallowell. Yet on emerging into the Yard, he was greeted by a crowd so boisterously affectionate that ten patrolmen were needed to get him into his car. It was clear his only hope of being nominated was to appeal to the people over the opposition of conservative Republicans.

"I am alone," Roosevelt told his old hunting companion, Dr. Alexander Lambert, back at Sagamore Hill that weekend. "You can't imagine how lonely it is for a man to be rejected by his own kind." He said that he and Hallowell were made to feel "like a pair of Airedale terriers that had walked in on a convention of tom cats."

In a cultural essay published some weeks before in *The Outlook*, he had noted that whenever a medieval man fought against prevailing orthodoxy, the tendency of society was to outlaw him. Now, after a lifetime of Party regularity, he found himself both free and shunned, loved and despised. It took some getting used to, and a considerable amount of evasion when friends as worried as William Allen White asked if he was prepared, in the likelihood of defeat, to found a new party. "We made the too obvious pretense in those days of our party loyalty," White wrote afterward, "whistling in unison through the tall timber of darkening events to support our courage."

As March loomed, Taft's organization accelerated the pace of delegate selections in states that it controlled. This portended an agonizing choice for Roosevelt Republicans, bluntly expressed by Senator Jonathan Bourne of Oregon, at a strategy session in Washington: "Gentlemen, the first thing we have got to decide is a matter of fundamental policy. If we lose, will we bolt?"

The company sat stunned. Bourne had been a founding member of the Progressive Republican League, set up more than a year before to advance the fortunes of Robert La Follette. As such, he was a courageous, even a rash man, willing to back the most radical challenger to Old Guard rule. But the question of "bolting" had never occurred to the League, which meant only to advance the cause of progressivism within the Party.

Bourne persisted with his motion. "I move that we agree, here and now, and not be too secretive about our agreement, that if we lose, we bolt."

There was silence while the politicians around the table considered their prospects. Those in Congress knew that apostasy would likely excommunicate them forever. And could progressivism, born of the Party, survive long without it? If Taft was nominated and then defeated as badly as everybody expected, it would be difficult even for GOP stalwarts to stay in office through the election of 1916. What real chance was there, at this late date, of Roosevelt recruiting enough delegates to commandeer the national convention in June?

William Allen White was in attendance. He was a bona fide progressive, but also, proudly, a member of the Republican National Committee, and hated the idea of splitting the Party. He sensed fear building in some quarters of the room. Senator Joseph Dixon of Montana had Bourne's kind of recklessness, and so did their former colleague, Albert J. Beveridge of Indiana, unseated by a Democrat in 1910. But Senators William E. Borah of Idaho, Moses E. Clapp of Minnesota, and Joseph L. Bristow of Kansas had won their seats as insurgents and enjoyed the balance of power they maintained in the upper chamber. White doubted they would willingly give that up. Representative Victor Murdock was for Roosevelt whatever happened, but understood the risks. "This rebellion," he had said earlier, "has a long, long way to go before it wins."

With Bourne's motion on the table, a debate ensued that sounded, to White, more loud than sincere. At the end, loyalty overcame expediency. A non-voting consensus was reached that the answer to the question was "yes."

⪻

REGULAR REPUBLICANS WHO had always considered the Colonel to be one of their number reacted to his candidacy with varying degrees of perplexity. The most common theory was that he had lost touch with reality. Senator

Root thought that he was motivated by vainglory. "He aims at a leadership far in the future, as a sort of Moses and Messiah for a vast progressive tide of rising humanity."

Henry Cabot Lodge wrote Roosevelt, "I never thought that any situation could arise which would have made me so miserably unhappy as I have been during the past week." He blamed himself for not realizing how long they had been at political odds. Now that Roosevelt had embraced judicial recall as a campaign theme, Lodge felt he could remain silent no longer. He had given a statement to the press. "It is at least honest although it gives no expression to the pain and unhappiness which lie behind it."

> I am opposed to the constitutional changes advocated by Colonel Roosevelt in his recent speech at Columbus. I have very strong convictions on those questions. . . . Colonel Roosevelt and I for thirty years, and wholly apart from politics, have been close and most intimate friends. I must continue to oppose the policies which he urged at Columbus, but I cannot personally oppose him who has been my lifelong friend, and for this reason I can take no part whatever in the campaign for the political nomination.

"My dear fellow," Roosevelt consoled him, "you could not do anything that would make me lose my warm personal affection for you. For a couple of years I have felt that you and I were heading opposite ways as regards internal politics."

President Taft told Archie Butt that Roosevelt was delusional if he thought he could control the forces of anarchy he had unleashed. "He will either be a hopeless failure if elected or else destroy his own reputation by becoming a socialist, being swept there by the force of circumstances just as the leaders of the French Revolution were swept on and on."

Butt listened to the President ramble, as he had listened for three years, and decided to take a vacation. Divided in his loyalty to both candidates, he had no stomach to see them heading into a contest that had all "the irresistible force of a Greek drama." With Taft's permission, he booked himself a passage to Europe.

"If the old ship goes down," he wrote his sister, "you will find my affairs in shipshape condition."

⟶

THE ENERGY OF the progressive movement, now that Roosevelt had committed to it, was explosive. By early March, the three main hubs of his campaign organization were staffed, financed, and running. The Executive Committee, chaired by Senator Dixon, operated out of New York, from a rapidly expanding "skyscraper suite" on the twenty-fourth floor of the Metropolitan Life tower. When Roosevelt visited, he could look down on the decaying town house, three blocks south, where he had been born. Generally he stayed away, preferring to hold court in his office at *The Outlook,* one block east. He told reporters he was content to leave the direction of the campaign to Dixon and Frank Knox, as vice chairman. The rest of the executive team consisted of hardened professional politicians—none harder than former congressman William L. Ward of New York, a manufacturer of nuts, bolts, and rivets, and William "Big Bill" Flinn of Pittsburgh, a power player set on dismantling Pennsylvania's reactionary Republican machine.

At the Congress Hotel in Chicago, Truman H. Newberry, Roosevelt's former navy secretary, assumed the vital role of treasurer of the National Committee. A millionaire local merchant, Alexander H. Revell, served as overall chairman, commuting to executive meetings in New York. In Washington, Frank Munsey gave space in his own press building—and a $50,000 startup budget—to the Roosevelt propaganda bureau.* Its manager was Cal O'Laughlin, who had come a long way in politics since waylaying the Colonel on the Nile. The bureau operated under the ideological control of Gifford and Amos Pinchot, James Garfield, and Medill McCormick—all of them thankful to be free of their obligations to La Follette. Another former journalist who joined the campaign was O. K. Davis of *The New York Times.* He attached himself to Senator Dixon as a pen for hire.

Branch offices opened in thirty other states, from New Hampshire west to California, and North Dakota south to Louisiana. Only the most reactionary corners of the old Confederacy, and the flintiest extremes of Republican New England, were deemed beyond the reach of new ideas. Wisconsin was ceded to La Follette, who could count on being nominated there, if nowhere else. Roosevelt's eight original gubernatorial backers chaired their respective state committees.

The case that Dixon (dark, smooth-shaven, intense, and tireless) decided to present to rank-and-file Republicans was that three years of Taft's leadership had reduced the Party to near impotence. The President had managed to turn a GOP majority of sixty in the House of Representatives into a minority of seventy, and a two-to-one overbalance of power in the Senate into virtual equipoise. His blindly supportive National Committee had lost control of a dozen states in the North and West. He was perceived as well-intentioned but weak; his obsessive traveling looked more like running away than reaching out. Whatever his support among the editors of loyal Republican periodicals, Dixon pointed out, reporters and cartoonists every-

---

*In 1912, the word *propaganda* had not yet acquired its modern, truth-bending connotation. It meant, simply, "publishable information."

where mocked him as long-winded, lazy, and obese. To Woodrow Wilson or whatever other falcon the Democrats might uncap this summer, Taft was easy meat.

Roosevelt, in contrast, was leading Taft by more than 66 percent in regional popularity polls across the country. According to the same surveys, he had more potential votes than all the other presidential contenders combined. But the goodwill of ordinary Americans counted for little at this stage of the political process. Only six states offered direct, preferential primaries: California, Nebraska, New Jersey, North Dakota, Oregon, and Wisconsin. In the remaining forty-two, delegates were selected, rather than elected, by the state parties in caucuses or conventions. And since these proceedings were controlled by bosses, or manipulated by sit-pat officeholders in favor of the *status quo,* they were democratic shams.

"You understand, my dear fellow," Roosevelt wrote Newberry, "that probably Taft will be nominated. This is not a thing we can say in public, because of course such a statement discourages men; but I am in this fight purely for a principle, win or lose."

Unfortunately, that principle was now perceived to be the recall of judicial decisions, rather than the broad "Charter of Democracy" he had tried to present at Columbus. Senator Dixon's long-term strategy was to recommunicate, through the Washington propaganda bureau, the progressive content of the rest of that speech. It would serve as a campaign platform, and—if the Colonel would only shut up about judges—recall would have faded as an issue by June.

In the short term, Dixon wanted to persuade as many caucus-convention states as possible to adopt the popular selection of delegates, while there was still time for legislative action. Seven of them—Georgia, Illinois, Maryland, Massachusetts, Ohio, Pennsylvania, and South Dakota—were seen as amenable to primaries, thanks to parallel lobbying by the progressive arm of the Democratic Party. If they fell in line, Roosevelt could count on perhaps ten large delegations pledged to him. The number of delegates admitted to the national convention was 1,078, meaning that a consensus of 540 votes would clinch the nomination. His mass appeal might yet achieve that miracle. And there was always the chance (though no gentleman would think of mentioning it) that the President, at 330 pounds plus, might take one golf swing too many.

NEITHER TAFT NOR ROOSEVELT undertook to campaign personally at first. Tradition required major candidates to remain aloof from delegate-hunting. The Colonel contented himself with press relations. One day he allowed two of the investigative journalists he had slammed as "muckrakers" during his presidency to buy him lunch at the Colony Club in New York. Ida Tarbell, who had made herself famous by exposing the monopolistic practices of the Standard Oil Company, was by no means his fan. She had not forgiven him for his epithet, which had stuck to her ever since. Ray Stannard Baker knew Roosevelt well enough to doubt that he was as pure in his progressivism as Senator La Follette—or for that matter Governor Wilson, with whom Baker was now ideologically infatuated.

Both writers, however, were captivated by the Colonel's charm. His political image was so swashbuckling and his quoted rhetoric so pugnacious that skeptics were always surprised to find how gentle he was in private. "Again he impressed me with his wonderful social command," Baker wrote afterward. There were two other women present, along with William Allen White, and Roosevelt showed himself to be "keenly sensitive to everyone in the party," bringing out all personalities. It was not possible to be shy in front of him. He disarmed by being frank about himself, not hiding the fact that he had been snubbed by the Harvard overseers, and admitting that some people considered him crazy.

Baker thought that he looked "wonderfully well," sitting relaxed in a soft dark suit and bright tie. The light through the club's big windows shone on his straw-brown hair and showed it to be thinning slightly at the crown. There was little gray in it, in contrast to streaks of white in his mustache. In his sharp voice, he talked about his career, saying that as a young man he had felt most comfortable with fellow members of the Knickerbocker aristocracy. Later he had come to admire self-made men like Mark Hanna, who made fortunes in industry and parlayed it into political power, until their amorality repelled him and he had realized that "the real democratic spirit lay deeper," in the bosoms of the plain people he had bunked with out West, and fought with in Cuba.

Baker sensed that Roosevelt's conscious adoption of their values had, over the years, become visceral. "This is his strong point—that he voices rather than creates the sentiment which he expresses. He is not a pioneer, but a reporter." As such, he did not seem to care if he won or not, as long as "the great fundamental principles" of progressivism prevailed.

The only prejudice he displayed during two hours of conversation was a refusal to accept that La Follette was as idealistic as himself. Baker had to conclude, "He is nearer the *true liberal* in spirit than any man now in public life . . . a great man—a genius in his way."

❧

MEANWHILE, ROOSEVELT'S AGENTS fought for every delegate who could be cajoled, bullied, or bribed. It was an embarrassment to him that men like Ward and Flinn, bosses themselves, were employing methods contemptuous of his pronouncement at Saratoga in 1910, "The rule of the boss is the negation of democracy." Every Pennsylvanian ward heeler looking for a new job in a new machine, every Southern Negro who yielded to the charms of Ormsby McHarg, Dixon's none-too-scrupulous representative in Dixie, shrugged at what the Colonel had to say about righteousness.

The problem was that, no matter how honest most of his campaign executives were in command of their various field operations, they had to rely on professional politicians at the state and lower levels—when such men could be found. Often as not, "Republicans for Roosevelt" were passionate amateurs who had never worked in a campaign before, and who needed to be trained and supervised. In Massachusetts, he was served by a committee of seven Harvard men, all from families dating back to the seventeenth century, all young, and all except one possessed by the notion that progressivism was a form of *noblesse oblige*. But with Senator W. Murray Crane controlling the Bay State GOP organization (for as long as Lodge recused himself), the Harvard men were as rowers without a cox: all muscle, but no coordination.

It followed that Roosevelt had to tolerate, or choose not to know about, signatures forged on nominating petitions in New York, horses traded with conservative mercenaries in Indiana, and baseball bats wielded to discipline delegates in Missouri. He contented himself with occasional letters of admonition or restraint.

His first convention victory over Taft in Oklahoma on 14 March was at least a start, albeit coerced by a progressive enthusiast standing behind the chairman with a loaded revolver. The result, achieved at the cost of one death and three casualties, was ten delegates-at-large and six district delegates. Frank Knox thought that some of the minority pledged to Taft might be unseated by appealing to the Republican National Committee in June.

All at once, the Colonel's campaign seemed to be gaining momentum. A series of separate headlines in *The New York Times* on 18 March proclaimed:

NORTH CAROLINA FOR ROOSEVELT

N.D. MAY BE ROOSEVELT'S

ROOSEVELT MAY CARRY OREGON

OHIO DRIFTING ROOSEVELT'S WAY

TEXAS ALL FOR ROOSEVELT

AGAINST ROOSEVELT IN WISCONSIN

The last news was not bad news, since La Follette was Wisconsin's favorite son. What was most significant was the trend in Ohio—Taft's home state. If Roosevelt could pull off a miracle there, the blow to the President's prestige would be severe. However, that primary was not due to be held for another two months, giving the White House plenty of time to continue its steady banking of pledges.

In the meantime, the speculative nature of the *Times*'s headlines was quickly exposed. On 19 March, North Dakota, the plains state Roosevelt most identified with as a former ranchman ("Here the romance of my life began"), gave him only 23,669 votes to La Follette's 34,123. Taft scored a humiliating 1,876, but that was a small consolation to Senator Dixon, given the fact that La Follette was supposed to have committed political suicide only six weeks before. Roosevelt urged the chairman to inflect the story as an "emphatically anti-administration" win for progressivism. He argued that even a La Follette delegation would count, in the end, as his own. But the claim sounded wishful.

He was, in fact, lagging in his race for the nomination. Infighting among his regional supporters was chronic, defectors from the La Follette organization were being shunned rather than welcomed, and would-be delegates were running against one another, rather than together for *him*. Nor had there been much evidence of "Teddy's" alleged mass popularity. As James Bryce scoffed in a report to Sir Edward Grey, "The prairies did not burst into flame as soon as his consent to become a candidate was known."

Roosevelt began to show signs of panic, snapping at a suggestion by the publisher Hermann Kohlsaat that he withdraw in Taft's favor, and admitting, "I tend to get pessimistic at times." A childhood friend, Frances "Fanny" Parsons, came to stay with him and noticed that he had lost the bubbling high spirits that had enchanted her forty years before. She tried to keep up with him on one of his frenzied marches down Cove Neck. "On that long, rapid, for me almost breathless walk through the leafless woods, I realized that he was starting out on a strange untraveled road, the end of which he could not see."

ONE THING THE COLONEL had not lost was his power over audiences.

Carnegie Hall was crammed to the door when he rose to speak there on the night after the North Dakota primary. It was his first public appearance in almost a month. Arcs of women in evening dress glittered in the first and second tiers (Edith and Ethel looking down from box 61), standees crammed even the upper levels, and the stage behind him groaned with representatives of the New York Civic Forum. Outside in the street, five thousand disappointed attendees milled around, hoping he would address them later.

Noticing William Barnes, Jr., and a henchman, Timothy L. Woodruff, in the orchestra section, Roosevelt began by remarking that if Lincoln's formula of government by the people was to be abandoned for minority rule, he knew who its chief exponents would be in New York State. "It will be Brother Barnes and Brother Woodruff."

Barnes glared at him from the parquet, but the audience rose in a standing ovation when Roosevelt continued, "I prefer to govern myself, to do my own part, rather than have the government of a particular class." For the rest of the evening he was in complete control. He rephrased, but at the same time reaffirmed, all the points he had made at Columbus, emphasizing that he was advocating the recall only of judicial decisions that took elite advantage of the Constitution. "The courts should not be allowed to reverse the political philosophy of the people." He named Taft as the nation's top reactionary in favor of oligarchy rule.

Roosevelt's sharp voice scratched every sentence into the receptivity of his listeners, and his habit of throwing sheet after sheet of manuscript to the floor seemed to mime points raised and dealt with. His peroration brought even Barnes to his feet in applause:

> The leader for the time being, whoever he may be, is but an instrument, to be used until broken and then to be cast aside; and if he is worth his salt he will care no more when he is broken than a soldier cares when he is sent where his life is forfeit in order that the victory may be won. In the long fight for righteousness the watchword for all of us is "Spend and be spent."
>
> We, here in America, hold in our hands the hope of the world, the fate of the coming years; and shame and disgrace will be ours if in our eyes the light of high resolve is dimmed, if we trail in the dust the golden hopes of men.

Afterward in one of the political clubs, Barnes was defensive. "Roosevelt, confound him, has a kind of magnetism that you cannot resist when you are in his presence!"

⁂

BARNES RECOVERED from the magnetism in time to hand the Colonel another defeat in the New York primary on 26 March. Republicans amenable to Party discipline voted two to one for Taft. Those of more independent temper appeared to have stayed home.

It turned out that hundreds of Roosevelt supporters had gone to the polls in New York County, only to be frustrated by mysterious equipment failures and closings. Others had been handed preposterously long ballots folded like concertinas, with up to three feet of blank space separating the Roosevelt ticket from its emblem. People tore off what they thought was waste paper, then found themselves unable to vote for the Colonel. The sole delegate he won in the city of his birth was an unopposed candidate in Brooklyn. Statewide, he netted seven delegates to Taft's eighty-three. Every winner of a state committee seat or district leadership was a machine man. And when, later that same evening, the Indiana and Colorado GOP conventions elected their delegates-at-large, all were instructed for Taft.

The net results were so damaging that it availed Dixon little to complain that the New York vote was "a joke." Taft now had a roster of 265 pledged delegates, with 539 needed to win. Roosevelt had 27.

He received the news of his triple defeat while traveling west aboard the Chicago Limited. Already he had concluded that his only chance of avoiding catastrophe was to forget about ex-presidential dignity and campaign in person, as strenuously and widely as possible.

"They are stealing the primary elections from us," he said. "All I ask is a square deal. . . . I cannot and will not stand by while the opinion of the people is being suppressed and their will thwarted."

If the eight thousand people who awaited him in the Chicago Auditorium that evening were voyeurs expecting a valedictory, what they got was a battle cry. Roosevelt roared against "fraud" in New York, "brutal and indecent" exclusion of his delegates in Indiana, and "outrageous" machine tactics in Denver. He called upon Illinois voters to insist on a direct primary, so they could register their personal preferences. Without saying so, he made it clear that if the RNC continued to thwart the will of progressives, he would bolt the Party and fight under a new banner.

He was back in New York at the end of the month, after a five-day swing through Indiana, Missouri, Minnesota, and Michigan. Almost immediately he was off again, on an itinerary reminiscent of his marathon tours as president. At the top of his fraying voice, he preached progressive Republicanism at municipal receptions, church socials, chautauquas, spring festivals, and rallies huge and small. He zigzagged south through West Virginia and Kentucky, then eastward via Illinois, Indiana, and Pennsylvania to New York, Massachusetts, and New Hampshire. Another flying visit home, and he was off across the Midwestern states to Iowa and Nebraska and Kansas, then down into Oklahoma, Arkansas, and North Carolina. From dawn until long after dusk, sometimes in pajamas from the back of his caboose, he harangued the citizens of Albia, Amboy, Ashland, Auburn, Aurora, Ayer, Beatrice, Blairsville, Clinton, Coatesville, Crete, Danville, Dixon, Hinton, Latrobe, Mattoon, Minonk, Mount Sterling, Nashua, Olive Hill, Osceola,

Ottumwa, Ozark, Pawnee City, Peru, Point Pleasant, Polo, Ronceverte, Salisbury, Shelbyville, St. Albans, Tecumseh, Tuscola, Urbana, Wymore, and a hundred other places, until the names blurred into Anytown and the faces became the single face of Everyman.

On 9 April, just as he was preparing to deliver a major address on judicial reform in Philadelphia, he was rewarded with the first really good news of his campaign. Republicans in Illinois had coaxed a direct primary out of the legislature, awarding him a two-to-one-plus victory over Taft. Fifty-six of the state's fifty-eight delegates were his, and a popular majority of 139,436. The dispatch hit with especial force in Washington, where most political gossips had already renominated the President.

"No one can explain it," Henry Adams marveled, "and I think no one expected it."

Six days later, Roosevelt scored an even bigger win in Pennsylvania. It coincided with the first wire report of a catastrophe beyond belief in the North Atlantic. "The *Titanic* is wrecked," Adams wrote aghast. "So is Taft; so is the Republican Party."

The President, nearly frantic as the extent of the tragedy became known, spent most of that evening in the White House telegraph office. He wanted to learn the fate of one passenger in particular: his indispensable aide, Major Archibald Willingham Butt.

Roosevelt claimed to be as bereaved as Taft when survivor testimony confirmed that Butt had helped women and children escape before going down with the ship. "Major Butt was the highest type of officer and gentleman," he said while campaigning in Lindsborg, Kansas. "I and my family all loved him sincerely."

His syntax did not escape the attention of E. W. Kemble, the great cartoonist working for *Harper's Weekly* and, by extension, for the Democratic Party. As Roosevelt continued to rack up primary wins, trumpeting each victory as a personal triumph, Kemble began a savage series of caricatures portraying him as a self-obsessed spoiler. Grinning toothily, "Theodosus the Great" crowned himself with laurels; he toted a tar-bucket of abuse and splattered it, black and dripping, across the Constitution, Supreme Court, and White House. He emboldened every capital *I* in a screed reading:

> I am the will of the
> people I am the leader
> I chose myself to be
> leader it is **MY**
> right to do so. Down with
> the courts, the bosses

and every confounded thing that opposes
ME. I AM IT
do you get me?
I will have as many terms
in office as **I**
desire. *Sabe!**
T.R.

⟨⟩

TAFT SUPPORTERS BECAME seriously alarmed when Roosevelt went on to take Nebraska and Oregon. They did what they could to discredit him. Rumors that "Teddy" was a toper—what else could explain his exuberant animation and rapid-fire speech?—spread to such an extent that he had to issue an order that no alcohol be served on his campaign train. Lyman Abbott issued a wry statement that the Colonel indeed imbibed excessively, being addicted to milk.

Roosevelt did not know whether to be amused or irritated. "Since I have been back from Africa, I have drunk an occasional glass of madeira or white wine, and at big dinners an occasional glass of champagne. That is literally all." But when hints of alcoholism began to appear in print, he looked for an open libel that would enable him to sue "for the heaviest kind of damages."

On 23 April, Taft won New Hampshire, an Old Guard fiefdom that Roosevelt had written off. One week later, the Massachusetts primary loomed. Legislators there had bowed to popular pressure and agreed to a direct vote. Roosevelt had so far won every preferential contest he entered, but the power of the Massachusetts Republican leadership made him doubt his luck this time. "I think Taft will carry the state, because ours is only a fight of minutemen under sergeants and corporals, and all the generals are against us."

Taft was nervous enough to travel to Boston on the twenty-fifth and say out loud what he thought about his opponent. No president had ever campaigned for his own renomination. "I am in this fight to perform a great public duty," he told a reporter, "—the duty of keeping Theodore Roosevelt out of the White House." At every stop en route, he played for sympathy, saying that he had never wanted to take his predecessor on. "This wrenches my soul." But he felt entitled to defend himself against the false charges of a political turncoat—"one whom in the past I have greatly admired and loved, and whose present change of attitude is the source of the saddest disappointment."

That night in the Boston Arena, Taft was greeted by a capacity audience so

*Understand!

welcoming as to disprove the notion that he was loved only by the Old Guard. His opening words promised a speech of unusual frankness: "The ordinary rules of propriety that restrict a President in his public addresses must be laid aside, and the cold, naked truth must be stated in such a way that it shall serve as a warning to the people of the United States."

Taft proceeded to attack Roosevelt in lawyerly fashion, reading for more than an hour from a typescript. As he did so, the enthusiasm around him cooled to respectful silence. Unlike La Follette, he did not lose his place or ramble. There were no Rooseveltian riffs, no high-pitched jokes, no fist-smacks, only the steady strong voice of an aggrieved man. His performance was boring, yet persuasive in its relentless accumulation of detail.

He itemized eleven specific charges the Colonel had laid against him, and in denying or correcting them, kept asking how a man could allege such things and yet pretend to stand for a square deal in politics. Disingenuously, he defended his use of White House patronage by saying that 70 percent of federal officeholders were still Roosevelt appointees. This was a false argument, because no customs clerk or farm inspector dared to risk the wrath of a sitting president. Moreover, Taft was either lying or in a state of ignorance when he insisted that "not a single" person had lost his job for political reasons. Dismissals of progressives had been going on since February.

In the manner of counsel holding up exhibits for adjudication, the President read some friendly letters that had passed between him and the Colonel during their rapprochement in the winter of 1910–1911. He cited the addresses and dates of each letter, and even the superscriptions "Personal" and "Confidential." He claimed to be Roosevelt's faithful follower, and reviewed his own, professedly liberal executive and legislative record at such length as to cramp the hand of any shorthand scribe. The crowd in the Arena became listless, but livened up as Taft, trembling and sweating, swung to a powerful conclusion:

> Mr. Roosevelt ought not to be nominated at Chicago because in such a nomination the Republican Party will violate our most useful and necessary government tradition—that no one shall be permitted to hold a third presidential term. . . . (*Loud applause*)
>
> Mr. Roosevelt would accept a nomination for a third term on what ground? Not because he wishes it for himself. He has disclaimed any such desire. He is convinced that the American people think that he is the only one to do the job (as he terms it), and for this he is prepared to sacrifice his personal comfort. (*Laughter*) He does not define exactly what the "job" is which he is to do, but we may infer from his Columbus platform it is to bring about a change of the social institutions of the country by legislation and other means. . . . I need hardly say that

such an ambitious plan could not be carried out in one short four years.[sic] . . . There is not the slightest reason why, if he secures a third term, and the limitation of the Washington, Jefferson, and Jackson tradition is broken down, he should not have as many terms as his natural life will permit. If he is necessary now to the government, why not later?

One who so lightly regards constitutional principles, and especially the independence of the judiciary, one who is naturally so impatient of legal restraints, and of due legal procedure, and who has so misunderstood what liberty regulated by law is, could not be safely entrusted with successive [sic] presidential terms. I say this sorrowfully, but I say it with the full conviction of truth. (*prolonged applause*)

After returning to his train, Taft put his head in his hands and cried.

THE COLONEL WAS in Worcester, Massachusetts, the next day, and responded in tones of outrage. It was "the grossest and most astounding hypocrisy," he said, for the President to claim that he had always been a faithful Rooseveltian. The words sent a momentary shiver through his audience, unused to such *lèse-majesté*. Then cheers and catcalls broke out. "He has not merely in thought, word, and deed been disloyal to our past friendship, but has been disloyal to every canon of ordinary decency and fair dealing. . . . Such conduct represents the very crookedest type of a crooked deal."

Roosevelt said that the President had set the tone of their rivalry early on, calling him a "neurotic" and "demagogue," and then, pathetically, pretending that it hurt to do so. "No man resorts to epithets like these if it really gives him pain," Roosevelt scoffed. No gentleman, moreover, would read out another's private correspondence without permission.

Responding to Taft's charge that he had no right to a third term in the White House, he emphasized that he was not an incumbent seeking to perpetuate himself with patronage. He was a private citizen with the rights of any other. He went on for an hour and twenty minutes, using the personal pronoun 181 times, not admitting a single mistake or error of judgment. At the end, he managed to convey a kind of contemptuous sympathy for the President as a good-natured misfit dominated by stronger men: "He means well, but he means well feebly."

Later he spoke at the Boston Arena, as Taft had twenty-four hours before. A boxing match had been held there in the interim, and the ropes were still in place. This enabled Roosevelt to make a stooping, straightening, fist-pumping entrance that touched off a seven-minute roar of applause. He had become, literally, the Man in the Arena.

"Now you have me," he shouted, after yet another statement of his recall philosophy. "Am I preaching anarchy?"

The answer was a roof-raising, "*NO!*"

As Elihu Root remarked to a friend, "He is essentially a fighter and when he gets into a fight he is completely dominated by the desire to destroy his adversary."

THE EXTRAORDINARY VEHEMENCE with which Taft and Roosevelt defended themselves in Massachusetts indicated that the nomination battle had entered its critical stage. Taft was not as far ahead as his late-April total of 432 delegates seemed to imply. All had been pledged or instructed in states where the Party still controlled its own representation. Consequently they were less reflective of the *vox populi* than Roosevelt's 208 delegates, elected for the most part in direct primaries. Massachusetts, a conservative state about to mount its own primary for the first time, offered Taft his best chance yet to demonstrate that ordinary voters were prepared to give him the benefit of the doubt.

VOTE OF BAY STATE MAY BE DECISIVE, *The New York Times* proclaimed before the election, suggesting that it might end the brief Roosevelt boom. Taft was reportedly hoping to sweep all thirty-six delegates. If so, he was disappointed. The vote, on 30 April, was indecisive. He won a small statewide majority of 3,622, but that allowed him no more delegates than Roosevelt, at eighteen each. The draw was broken by eight delegates-at-large, who pledged themselves to the Colonel.

Roosevelt, overjoyed but noting Taft's larger vote, was quick to take moral advantage of it. "In this fight," he announced, "I am standing for certain great principles. . . . Foremost of these is the right of the people to rule." He said he would order his delegates-at-large to switch their allegiance to the President.

By early May, with only four weeks of active campaigning left and 540 delegates needed to win the nomination, *The New York Times* estimated Taft's complement at 468, Roosevelt's at 232, and La Follette's at 36. Senator Cummins of Iowa had a favorite-son slate of 10. The newspaper forecast that Taft would soon capture Nevada and Arkansas, followed by the primary states of Maryland and New Jersey. These, plus a swath of far-western states—Washington, Idaho, Montana, Utah, and Wyoming—should yield him over a hundred more delegates, and eliminate his challengers well before June.

The *Times* acknowledged, however, that a large number of delegates were neither pledged nor instructed, but just "leaning" toward one candidate or the other. Its editorial tilt was clear. There was no mention of the Colonel's strong prospects in California and Minnesota, nor of his popularity in Ohio—birthplace of so many presidents (Taft included), and the most delegate-rich state of all. A primary was due to be held there on the twenty-fifth. Even if

Taft won elsewhere as the *Times* projected, failure to hold his native soil would almost certainly end his hopes of reelection.

Over the next week, Roosevelt captured Maryland, Kansas, and Minnesota. Arkansas held two state conventions, one instructing its slate for him and the other for Taft. So another brace of rival delegations was added to the swelling number that intended to contest seats at the national convention. Roosevelt's campaign team, ecstatic, calculated the President's strength at only 175 bona fide delegates. This was a gross underestimate. But when, on 14 May, Roosevelt went on to sweep California, Taft put aside affairs of state for a final desperate stand in Ohio. "If I am defeated," he wrote his brother Horace, "I hope that somebody, sometime, will recognize the agony of spirit that I have undergone."

TAFT'S TENDENCY TO whine was accompanied by a genius for political gaffes. His latest was, "I am a man of peace, and I don't want to fight. But when I do fight, I want to hit hard. Even a rat in a corner will fight."

The unfortunate metaphor stuck as his train raced from corner to corner of Ohio, and Roosevelt's followed suit. Both candidates smelled blood. Their vocabulary of personal invective got terser and uglier. Taft called the Colonel a "dangerous egotist" and "bolter." Roosevelt replied with "puzzlewit," "reactionary," and "fathead," and convulsed a crowd in Cleveland by comparing the President's brain unfavorably with that of a guinea pig. La Follette, vying for attention, weighed in with imprecations of his own, until it was difficult for Republican voters to figure out which "demagogue," "hypocrite," and "Jacobin" was calling the other a "brawler," "apostate," and "honeyfugler." Democrats rejoiced in a report that one night Roosevelt and Taft had, after a fashion, slept together, with their Pullmans parked side by side in the Steubenville depot.

Roosevelt covered eighteen thousand miles across the state, addressing about ninety rallies. Unlike the President, who traveled even farther and spoke more, he was able to leaven his insults with wit. "Mr. Taft," he said at Marion, "never discovered that I was dangerous to the people until I discovered he was useless to the people."

It did Taft little good to seethe in private at "the hypocrisy, the insincerity, the selfishness, the monumental egotism, and almost the insanity of megalomania that possess Theodore Roosevelt." He had powerful issues to level against his opponent—among them the third-term question, the reliance on anti-administration bosses, and the acceptance of enormous sums of money from trust lords, as long as they styled themselves as "progressives." (One name that agitated the President's mustache more than any other was that of George W. Perkins, of U.S. Steel and the International Harvester Company.)

Taft could not understand why his detailed, droning exposures of such liabilities failed to excite more anger against his opponent.

He went home to Cincinnati to vote on the twenty-first, only to hear that one of his own supporters had asked Roosevelt to consider the idea of backing a compromise candidate—possibly Charles Evans Hughes. The Colonel's reply was characteristic: "I will name the compromise candidate, he will be me."

⟶◠⟵

THE OHIO PRIMARY was so complete a victory for Roosevelt that it took several days for Taft's full loss to be computed. Cincinnati remained loyal to him, but that was largely because his challenger had bypassed the city, not wanting to make things awkward for Nick Longworth. Overall, Taft won only eight delegates out of forty-two. He comforted himself with the probability that the state convention would award him another eight delegates-at-large, while his campaign managers insisted that he had a national lead over Roosevelt of 555 to 377. But the fact remained that the President had lost his own state by a margin of almost forty-eight thousand votes.

Roosevelt's astonishing subsequent triumphs in the New Jersey and South Dakota primaries further eroded support for Taft. A new word was coined: "TRnadoes." The Democratic governor of New Jersey expressed concern for the fate of the nation. "Your judgment of Roosevelt is mine own," Woodrow Wilson wrote a friend. "God save us of another four years of him *now,* with his present insane distemper of egotism!"

When the nomination campaign ended on 4 June, the Colonel had amassed more popular votes than either of his opponents combined—at 1,214,969 for himself, 865,835 for Taft, and 327,357 for La Follette. Demonstrably, he was the runaway favorite of rank-and-file Republicans in the thirteen states that had granted them a direct voice. Outside of Maryland, all his victories had been landslides. He had beaten Taft two to one in California and Illinois, and three to one in South Dakota and Nebraska. Several other states controlled by the Party machine were embarrassed by upstart Roosevelt delegations vowing to fight for seats at the national convention. This made the actual, pre-ballot strengths of the three candidates difficult to assess. All that could be said with certainty was that, before the Chicago Coliseum opened its doors on 18 June, the RNC would have to decide the eligibility of every contesting delegate.

And of those decisions there could be no recall.

CHAPTER 10

Armageddon

Are we no greater than the noise we make
Along one blind atomic pilgrimage
Whereon by crass chance billeted we go
Because our brains and blood and cartilage
Will have it so?

TO DEMOCRATS PREPARING for their own convention in the spring of 1912, there was a pleasing symbolism in the rainstorm that drowned out a baby parade in New Jersey, on the last day of the Republican primary campaign in that state. A plump competitor dressed as "President Taft" had his silk hat and frock coat ruined, while "Baby Roosevelt," riding on another float, cried so loudly he had to be rescued and comforted.

Après le déluge, qui? Next morning, the New York *World* had an endorsement to offer all adult voters tired of childish squabbles in the GOP: FOR PRESIDENT—WOODROW WILSON.

Ideologically, there was less difference between Wilson and Roosevelt than between any of the Republican candidates. The governor's success in bestowing a raft of progressive reforms upon New Jersey had helped Roosevelt to his big win there. But it also bolstered Wilson's own campaign for the Democratic nomination. A further similarity was that he and Roosevelt were both running a strong second to holders of high office in their own parties. And they were both hopeful of sweeping their respective conventions, if they could shake "organization" control of the proceedings.

Champ Clark, Speaker of the House of Representatives, was the man ahead of Wilson: a garrulous, vaguely progressive, cornpone Westerner. With Democrats not scheduled to meet in Baltimore until after the Republican convention in Chicago, Wilson might yet benefit from Clark's propensity for political gaffes—as Roosevelt had already done from Taft's.

In the interim, the governor did not have to worry about getting his delegates seated. Roosevelt did. Most of *his* convention support, over and above the delegates he had won in primaries, lay in the claims of 254 "shadow" delegates to be recognized as the true representatives of their states, on grounds ranging

"'SEVEN-EIGHTHS LAWYER AND ONE-EIGHTH MAN.'"

Senator Elihu Root.

from miscarried conventions to outright fraud. Only seven of them were Taft men. As Roosevelt well knew, a fair number of his own claimants were wishful, especially those purchased with snake oil and other charms by his Southern salesman, Ormsby McHarg. Still, he had considerable strength on paper. The New York *Tribune,* a pro-administration paper, put him ahead of Taft, at 469½ potential delegates to 454. Taft's vaunted total of 583, or 43 more than necessary for a first-ballot win, presupposed winning virtually all the seating contests. *The New York Times* allotted the Colonel only 355 delegates, 85 short of the number he needed, and reported that Taft hoped to unseat a further twenty.

But all these calculations were little more than chalk on a blackboard due to be dusted, rewritten, and dusted again when the Republican National Committee began its convention eligibility hearings early in June. Only two figures could not be erased: 1,078, the legal number of seats available to delegates, and 540, the number needed to nominate.

⟶⟵

EVEN BEFORE THE RNC arrived in Chicago, it had decided to recommend Elihu Root, the Party's most rational conservative, as chairman of the convention. Roosevelt found himself in the painful position of having to oppose this choice, which boded well for Taft and ill for himself and La Follette. If Senator Root was acceptable to a majority of the delegates, he would influence the proceedings more than any other Party official. And the nature of that influence could be predicted.

"Elihu," Roosevelt used to joke, "is seven-eighths lawyer and one-eighth man." That had been in happier days, when Root served only his purpose. Now the legal construct had a new brief: to defend orthodox Republicanism at a convention under radical siege, and ensure the renomination of William Howard Taft.

Old friendship could not survive such a clash of interests. Roosevelt had to accept that Root, along with Henry Cabot Lodge and many other former political allies, must henceforth be a stranger to him. Or rather, *he* had become strange to *them*. They could not understand why he had rejected their advice not to run.

The issue of the chairmanship was forced by William Barnes, Jr., Taft's principal tactician on the Republican National Committee. On 3 June, he telegraphed all delegates elected to the convention, except those pledged to the Colonel:

I AM WIRING YOU IN BEHALF OF THE NEW YORK DELEGATION, WITH THE EXCEPTION OF A VERY FEW, TO ASK YOUR SUPPORT FOR SENATOR ROOT FOR CHAIRMAN. WE BELIEVE THIS CONTEST IS THE MOST SERIOUS ONE WHICH HAS AFFLICTED THE

REPUBLICAN PARTY, AND THAT THE ATTEMPT TO NOMINATE
MR. ROOSEVELT CAN LEAD ONLY TO DISASTER. . . . WILL YOU
PLEASE WIRE ME, NEW YORK CITY COLLECT, WHETHER WE CAN
RELY ON YOUR SUPPORT FOR SENATOR ROOT FOR CHAIRMAN?

Thus goaded, Roosevelt announced that he would instruct his delegates to
vote for Governor Francis E. McGovern of Wisconsin, a progressive sympathetic to both himself and Senator La Follette. "Root," he complained, "is
simply the representative of Barnes in this matter."

He relied on his organization in Chicago to seat as many as possible of his
contesting delegates—potentially almost a quarter of the convention. Fifty
more would make his bid for the nomination serious, and he hoped for 80 or
90. Assuming a minimum of 278 uncontested delegates from his primary victories, and another minimum of 133 non-primary pledges, his solid first-
ballot strength was 411, with 540 needed to win. He therefore had to press
another 129. There were 166 uninstructed delegates. Perhaps he could persuade enough of them to combine with his accreditees for a winning edge,
however narrow.

Unfortunately, most of the uninstructed seemed to favor Taft. And so did
a majority of the Republican National Committee.

⌖

ROOSEVELT COULD ONLY hope the Committee would be fair, rather than
blacken the GOP's already tarnished political image with a show of discrimination. Many of the delegates pledged to Taft were obviously fraudulent. To
seat a decent number of progressive challengers would make for good public
relations, and confound the RNC's pro-Roosevelt minority. That group was
dominated by William Flinn, Francis J. Heney, and Senator Borah of Idaho, an
austere, brooding maverick who had once voted for Bryan. All were formidable men, determined to shame their opposing trio of senior reactionaries:
Barnes, Boise Penrose, and W. Murray Crane.

Barnes, of course, was already the Colonel's open enemy. "Big Grizzly"
Penrose was Taft's chief supporter on Capitol Hill, infamous for reactionary
machine politics. He would be seeking revenge on Roosevelt and Flinn for recently unseating him as boss of the Pennsylvania GOP. Crane was a Yankee
paper manufacturer, as stiff and traditional as his own business cards. As for
the Committee chairman, Victor Rosewater of Nebraska, the best that could
be said of him was that he was not a professional politician. Moderate, frail,
and with luck, malleable, Rosewater might be receptive to arguments that progressivism was a social force that the Republican Party had to accommodate,
or else cede to the candidacy of Woodrow Wilson. He was a key figure, since

he would serve *ex officio* as temporary chairman of the convention until giving way to either Root or McGovern.

The rest of the Committee, apart from ten or so members friendly to Roosevelt and La Follette, consisted of about thirty-five Party regulars who served at the President's pleasure.

⁂

ROOSEVELT CHAFED AT Sagamore Hill as the hearings proceeded alphabetically, state by state. On the first day, all twenty-four of his delegates from Alabama and Arkansas were barred from the convention, and on the second, his entire slate from Georgia. In electoral terms, those states counted for nothing. Still, the Committee's bias against him seemed clear. Senator Dixon complained to reporters of "theft, cold-blooded, premeditated and deliberate."

For a while, Roosevelt tried to maintain control of his representatives by long-distance telephone. But he hated the instrument and suspected it was being tapped. A private telegraph in the attic, a relic of his time as president, was even less satisfactory. He preferred the clicking of his own teeth in face-to-face confrontations, the feel of lapels gripped in his hand.

Behind his frustration lay the embarrassing fact—harped on in many newspapers—that about a hundred of the delegates he needed to seat were no more legitimate than the machine men on Taft's list. The kind of progressives-for-hire rounded up by Ormsby McHarg would have sold themselves quite as willingly to the Socialist candidate for the presidency, had Eugene V. Debs reached them first. Roosevelt remained convinced, however, that bona fide claimants were being discriminated against. Asked by a reporter whether he intended to barnstorm the convention, he said, "If circumstances demand, of course I'll go!"

That was as good as a threat to the Republican National Committee, which proceeded to throw out all but 19 of his delegates, and seat 235 of Taft's.

⁂

TWO FACTS WERE clear in the aftermath of the Committee's action: first, that Roosevelt no longer had a credible chance of being nominated, and second (what he was prevented by blind rage from seeing) that most of the contests had been decided fairly. Perhaps thirty to thirty-five had not. But there would have been as much bias in favor of himself, had Taft been the challenging candidate, and he the Party leader. An impartial observer might conclude that neither man had enough honestly elected delegates to nominate him.

All the same, Roosevelt had reason to accuse the Committee of being out of touch with current Republican sentiment. Penrose, Crane, Rosewater, and a dozen other members were themselves ineligible to serve as delegates, having been defeated in their home primaries. Ten further members hailed from Southern states in the grip of the Democratic Party, and four from "territorial possessions" (including the District of Columbia) that could not vote in November. These eunuchs, comprising more than two-thirds of the Committee, had power *before* the convention to defeat a candidate who was overwhelmingly the people's choice.

"The Taft leaders speak as if they were regular Republicans," Roosevelt said in an icy public statement. "I do not concede that theft is a test of party regularity." He had never deluded himself that he could be elected in the fall, even if nominated in the spring. But the pugilist in him, so bruisingly evident on the stage of the Boston Arena, was now aroused beyond control. It was the phenomenon Root had seen coming: *When he gets into a fight he is completely dominated by the desire to destroy his adversary.* There was nothing for him now but to go to Chicago and beat the convention into submission—or else bolt through the ropes and precipitate a riot.

Specifically, Roosevelt intended to use his huge primary vote to persuade the Party as a whole not to ratify the exclusion of his delegates, and to accept that progressivism was a natural, desirable evolution of Republican doctrine. Root, whose gavel would probably determine the issue, sent out word that any attempt by the Colonel to rewrite convention rules would lead to "confusion and comparative anarchy."

❧

EIGHTEEN-YEAR-OLD Nicholas Roosevelt, one of the Oyster Bay cousins who had grown up as virtually a member of the Colonel's own brood, visited Sagamore Hill on Friday, 14 June. He found Roosevelt unusually silent over breakfast, and "Cousin Edith" exuding frosty disapproval of whatever was brewing in the house beside coffee. Later, without saying why, she insisted on accompanying her husband into town.

"Well, Nick," Roosevelt called out, as their automobile started down the driveway, "I guess we'll meet at a lot of Philippics soon."

This was a clear hint to the young man to pack his bags for Chicago—and maybe other cities as well. Nicholas was ardently interested in politics. Confirmation came by telephone at noon that Colonel and Mrs. Roosevelt were booked on the Lake Shore Limited, departing New York at 5:30 P.M. When Nicholas arrived at Grand Central, he found Kermit and two other cousins, George Roosevelt and Theodore Douglas Robinson, also ready to go. Word had also gone out to Ted and Eleanor (tired, now, of San Francisco, and keen to reestablish themselves in New York). They would travel to Chicago separately. So would Alice, to whom conventions were catnip. The New York party was amplified by Regis H. Post—rich, progressive, retired, a willing workhorse—two or three *Outlook* staffers, and Frank Harper, the Colonel's tiny

English secretary. And like bees attracted to the sudden popping of a lily, newsmen swarmed to ride along.

For twenty-two hours the Limited puffed west. A hot damp inversion enveloped it the following morning as it crossed from Ohio into the industrial flats of Indiana. Roosevelt laid aside his current reading—Herodotus—and labored on the text of a speech that he planned to deliver in the Chicago Auditorium on Monday night, the eve of the convention. He declined to provide reporters with an advance copy, but told Nicholas it would be "the great effort of his life."

In mid-afternoon, the train stopped at South Bend, and the ubiquitous Cal O'Laughlin climbed aboard. He had an optimistic projection to deliver. According to campaign headquarters, some of Taft's uncontested delegates were wavering. They had been recruited under pressure, and resented it. If they defected, the President would find himself four votes short of a majority on Tuesday.

This was a number easier for Taft to reduce than for Roosevelt to expand, but it caused the Colonel to bubble over with joy. He began to talk about winning rather than bolting—an act that should be considered "only in the very last extremities."

At 4 P.M. he stepped down onto the platform of Chicago's LaSalle Street station. He wore a new, tan campaign hat that said, louder than words, that the Rough Rider was back in the saddle. Its brim, fully five inches wide, failed to obscure the brilliancy of his teeth. A howling crowd broke through barriers erected by the police and surged so voraciously that Nicholas, George, and two other youths had to form a wedge around him and batter their way toward the station exit. Meanwhile, a band thumped out his old marching song, "There'll Be a Hot Time in the Old Town Tonight." Outside in Van Buren Street, the crowd was even larger and louder. Two other bands blared in Ivesian discord. A line of flag-decked automobiles stood waiting. Roosevelt hauled himself into the first, accompanied by Senator Dixon. The motorcade got under way with difficulty. As Nicholas recorded in his diary:

> People packed the windows and lined the roofs and the elevated tracks and were so thick in the streets we could hardly move in the procession. . . . Everyone was howling with delight, and cries of "Teddy!" filled the air. At the cross streets, as far as we could see to either side, or back or forward, people were wedged in like pins. Everyone cheered. Everyone screamed. Everyone was hurled along in the irresistible force of the delighted mob. Ahead rode Cousin Theodore, bowing to right and to left. . . . Even now the thought of it makes shivers run up and down my back.

It was as if Chicago sought to emulate the welcome that New York had given Roosevelt on his return from Africa. The noise reminded one reporter of a boiler factory, with all the station bands following, and trumpets sounding ragtime riffs ahead. By the time he arrived at the huge Congress Hotel, the crowd was so dense as to be dangerous. But another protective wedge was waiting for him. Five large guards handy with their fists got him inside with minimal violence, preceded by yet another band. It played "Hail, Hail, the Gang's All Here" until displaced by a large number of screaming suffragists. Roosevelt had no sooner found sanctuary in the hotel's presidential suite than the crowd, resurgent up the stairs and jamming the corridor outside his door, drove him to climb through a window onto a stone balustrade overlooking Michigan Avenue. His grin reassured the thousands below that he was not about to jump.

Far to his left and right, a flotsam of faces swirled. The smoky, coppery sky seemed to press down on the city, concentrating its heat and noise. Waving his hat for quiet, he yelled in his high voice, "Chicago is a mighty poor place in which to try and steal anything."

"And they better not try to steal anything from you!" somebody shouted.

"From us, you mean," Roosevelt replied.

This caused a roar of delight. He pointed at a banner declaring that the California delegation was solid for him, in defiance of exclusions by the Committee. "California's twenty-six votes are mine. They are mine, and they will be counted for me."

"Hurrah for Teddy!" came another shout.

He leaned over the parapet, still holding his hat in the air. "The people have spoken, and the politicians must learn to answer or understand. They will be made to understand that they are the servants of the rank and file of the plain citizens of the republic."

For several minutes, the cheering made it impossible for him to continue. Red-faced and sweating, he listed a few of the derelictions of the Committee. "It is a fight against theft," he said again, "and the thieves will not win!"

With that, he climbed back inside. The crowd in the street dispersed, but a lone band kept playing as evening came on. Hotel guests unassociated with the Republican Party enjoyed little rest that night. In the Gold and Florentine banquet rooms, tabletop orators respectively barked the merits of Taft and Roosevelt to whoever would listen. "We are in danger of monarchy," Boss Barnes bawled. "The country must be saved!" Groups of delegates roamed the corridors in long frock coats and black beaver hats, singing and shouting.

THE FERVOR OF the Colonel's supporters—much more truculent, in scattered brawls and curses, than Taft's or La Follette's—reached its peak at 8:15 P.M. on Monday in the Chicago Auditorium. The immense, five-thousand-seat hall was packed to the doors, and could have been filled four times over with the multitude outside. Two hundred and fifty policemen struggled to keep Congress Street clear.

Roosevelt got only a short burst of applause when he strode onstage, after being introduced by Senator Borah. The audience was so eager to hear what he had to say that it fell silent almost immediately. Indeed, once he began talking, attempts by barkers to generate ovations were thwarted by hisses and cries of "Shame." Addressing his listeners as "fellow Americans" rather than "fellow Republicans," Roosevelt said that the fundamental issue at hand was moral. It transcended petty politics, and even the personal fates of a president and former president.

> If the methods adopted by the National Committee are approved by the convention which is about to assemble, a great crime will have been committed. The triumph of such proceedings at the moment would mean the wreck of the Republican Party; and if such proceedings became habitual, it would mean the wreck of popular government. The actions of the Taft leaders . . . are monstrous, and they should be indignantly condemned by the moral sentiment of the whole country.

Before describing the "naked robbery" that had deprived him of "sixty to eighty" first-ballot votes, Roosevelt appealed to Senators La Follette and Cummins to release the forty-six delegates they controlled. His primary successes proved, he said, that he was the Party's overwhelming popular favorite, and the only candidate strong enough to bring about social reform. "If I had not made the progressive fight . . . there would have been no substantial opposition to the forces of reaction and political crookedness."

The last few words set him off on an overlong tirade against the Taft administration, its corporate beneficiaries, and political bosses. Reporters who had followed him over the past two years could scribble the catchphrases in advance: *treason . . . conspiracy . . . the led captains of mercenary politics . . . the great crooked financiers . . . privilege in its most sordid and dangerous form . . . corrupt alliance between crooked business and crooked politics . . . an oligarchy of the representatives of privilege.* William Jennings Bryan (attending in his new guise as a syndicated columnist) looked bored. Roosevelt was imputing guilt by association to the RNC, which became the focus of his wrath for ignoring the message of the primaries.

"It is our duty to the people of this country to insist that no action of the convention which is based on the votes of these fraudulently seated delegates binds the Republican party or imposes any obligation upon any Republican."

The last five words, full of implication of a bolt, earned Roosevelt his first standing ovation of the evening. Encouraged, he launched into an analysis of the Committee's recent rulings that was so dense with numbers and labyrinthine in its arguments of conspiracy as to annoy anyone immune to his charisma. But there were few such unbelievers present. Almost in spite of himself, he moved from the particular to the philosophical. Conservatives, he said, "are taught to believe that change means destruction. They are wrong. . . . Life means change; where there is no change, death comes."

By now the applause was thunderous. "I am never surprised at anything Theodore may say," Edith remarked to Cal O'Laughlin, her face lit up with pride.

Again and again he declared that American society wished to transform itself. "The trumpets sound the advance, and their appeal cannot be drowned by repeating the war-cries of bygone battles, the victory shouts of vanquished hosts. Here in this city—"

He seemed about to identify Chicago as the *civitas Dei*. By now he had been orating for well over an hour, and Bryan looked ready to nod off. But a magnificent peroration was coming:

> Assuredly the fight will go on whether we win or lose. . . . What happens to me is not of the slightest consequence; I am to be used, as in a doubtful battle any man is used, to his hurt or not, so long as he is useful, and then cast aside or left to die. I wish you to feel this. I mean it; and I shall need no sympathy when you are through with me, for this fight is far too great to permit us to concern ourselves about any one man's welfare. . . . The victory shall be ours, and it shall be won as we have already won so many victories, by clean and honest fighting for the loftiest of causes. We fight in honorable fashion for the good of mankind; fearless for the future; unheeding of our individual fates; with unflinching hearts and undimmed eyes; we stand at Armageddon, and we battle for the Lord.

Never before had Roosevelt used such evangelical language, or dared to present himself as a holy warrior. And never before had he heard such cheering. Intentionally or not, he invested progressivism with a divine aura. Secular Republicans were repelled by the fanaticism of his followers, and wondered which "Lord" the Colonel really had in mind to command his mythical army. A flyer circulated around Chicago, arousing much hilarity:

At Three o'Clock
Thursday Afternoon
THEODORE ROOSEVELT
Will Walk
on the
Waters of
Lake Michigan

⟳

BARBED WIRE PROTRUDED from the bunting around the rostrum of the Republican National Convention when it opened in the Coliseum on Tuesday, 18 June. Nothing could have more graphically signaled the Party leadership's desire to fortify itself against a hostile takeover. The surrounding platform, edged in red-white-and-blue, stood shoulder-high and was inaccessible from the floor. Anyone hoisting himself up onto it would get his hands and chest slashed by the wire. A stairway just wide enough to admit one man led up from the National Committee room below, and was guarded at top and bottom by security agents. Behind yawned a dry moat, twelve feet deep. A line of Chicago policemen was deployed facing the front row of seats, and others stood in a tight circle around the delegate enclosure. One of them told a reporter, "I am for Teddy and I don't care who knows it."

By the time the building opened its doors at 10:30 A.M., Henry James's description of Roosevelt as "the mere monstrous embodiment of unprecedented and resounding Noise" was fully borne out. The bands that had greeted the Colonel's arrival in town were amplified five times over by those of marching clubs escorting the various delegations. Other kinds of din, beginning with the first nervous knock of Victor Rosewater's gavel at two minutes past noon, were clearly on the agenda, and set to build in a continuous crescendo through the nomination on Friday. One of the strangest, accompanied by whistles and screams of "Toot, toot!" was the spine-stiffening hiss of sheets of sandpaper scraped together. It was meant to express the conviction among Roosevelt Republicans that an organization "steamroller" was under way, intent on flattening their spirit of revolt.

But first came a bang of flashbulbs, as the delegates sat still for a group photograph. (Conspicuously missing, anywhere in the room, was the usual overhanging portrait of the President of the United States.) The brief glare illuminated 1,078 faces, only a few managing smiles. "It's the last time the convention will look pleasant," Rosewater said.

Contrary to rumors, Roosevelt had not asked permission to attend. Edith and all his children represented him in a special box in the gallery. He remained at the Congress Hotel, looking, in Nicholas's words, "fresh as an apple and rosy and happy as a child," and monitoring the proceedings by means of a telephone line rigged through to his floor manager, Governor Herbert S. Hadley of Missouri.

Hadley, a calm, fine-featured man of forty, cut an imposing figure on the floor. Although he had been one of the signers of the petition requesting Roosevelt to run, he was no radical, and enjoyed the distinction of having been eyed as a running mate by both major candidates. He engineered the day's first surprise by taking the rostrum as soon as the official convention call had been read. "Mr. Chairman," he said to Rosewater, "I rise to a question of information."

William Barnes, Jr., jumped up in shock from his seat with the New York delegation. Simultaneously, the President's personal representative, former congressman James E. Watson of Indiana, rushed to the edge of the stage. Neither was able to stop Hadley from asking, in an easy sonorous voice, if the Committee had drawn up its temporary roll of the convention. If not, he had an alternative roll to offer. He was sure that the Committee's draft included the names of certain delegates unacceptable to Roosevelt Republicans, and he moved that they be replaced by the names on his own list, which he felt the rank and file might prefer.

Rosewater overruled Barnes and Watson, who were protesting that the convention was not yet organized, and said that in the spirit of fairness, the governor would be allowed twenty minutes to argue his point. Hadley said that a substantial minority of the National Committee believed that the recent hearings had been manipulated. As a result, seventy-two usurpers were now sitting before him, "without any honest title to their seats."

This was a focusing of Roosevelt's assertion that "sixty to eighty" names on the draft roll were fraudulent. The latest *New York Times* estimate of Taft's majority over him (contradicting O'Laughlin's projection) was one hundred, at 466 to 566. If that was correct, the substitution of 72 progressive alternates would put him only two votes short of a first-ballot win, with plenty of time to round up a bunch of waverers.

Hadley stood no real chance of persuading the convention to set aside the National Committee's roll in favor of his own. But he had cleverly cast doubt on the former before the convention had begun to develop its own will. He was also exploiting the fact, apparent to all who had mustered at Armageddon, that Roosevelt could win in November, whereas Taft could only lose. The forecast was based on the Colonel's nearly one and a quarter million primary votes, and made more exciting by his palpable proximity to the Coliseum. Four-fifths of the spectators in the gallery, and (Hadley hoped) most people on the floor, were infused with a sense of a giant, available, reconciling personality.

"We contend," Hadley said to loud cheers, "that this convention should not proceed with the transaction of any business until it either disproves the charges of fraud and dishonesty that have been made against this roll of delegates, or until it sustains those charges, and purges the roll."

Watson again complained about improper procedure. He dropped the name of Elihu Root, in a clear hint as to whom Taft expected to succeed Rosewater on the podium. Hisses, sandpaper scrapes, and cries of "liar!" "thief!" "swindler!" rose over a roar of conservative approbation. At 1:30 P.M., Root and McGovern were announced as candidates for permanent chairman.

Tension at once mounted in the room. More than any newspaper tabulation, the vote on these nominations promised to show the President's exact strength. The first speaker for Root, Job E. Hedges of New York, scored devastatingly by quoting Roosevelt's own panegyric of some years before— "Elihu Root is the ablest man I have known in our governmental service . . . the ablest man who has appeared in the public life of any country in my time." Progressives tried to mute the guffaws this aroused by shouting "Roosevelt! Roosevelt!" Hedges fended them off with mock weariness. "You need not hesitate to cheer Roosevelt in my presence. I cheered him for seven years, and I am just trying to take a day off, that is all."

The debate that followed was vituperative, degenerating to personal abuse between rival orators. Almost forgotten, as they bellowed face-to-face and policemen raced down the aisles, breaking up fistfights, was the fact that there were more than two sides in contention. McGovern hailed from Wisconsin, Robert La Follette's home state. In backing the governor for chairman, Roosevelt had counted on the senator to approve—and, in due course, release the Wisconsin and North Dakota delegations from their pledges.

A shock comparable to a sudden shower of ice therefore descended when, at the hottest point of the afternoon, a spokesman for La Follette announced that McGovern "did not represent the interests" of Wisconsin's favorite son. Evidently La Follette was still furious at Roosevelt for entering the presidential race. After this, there was little any McGovern supporter could say except, weakly, that progressives would go home guilty if they voted for Senator Root.

"Cousin Theodore could be wrecked," a dispirited Nicholas Roosevelt wrote in his notes of the session.

At 3:21 P.M. the temporary roll was called and voting proceeded, state by state and delegate by delegate, with crushing slowness. The only note of novelty in an otherwise dutiful recitation of partisan sentiments occurred when California took the floor, and for the first time in American history the clear voice of a woman registered a vote at a national convention.

Along with 23 of her progressive colleagues, Florence Collins Porter favored McGovern.

So, about three hours later, did 13 Wisconsin delegates irked by La Follette's petulance. But the final count—558 votes for Root and 501 for McGovern— indicated that Roosevelt was still 49 votes short of the majority he needed in his quest for the nomination.

Meanwhile, the ablest public man he had ever known, in a previous life, mounted the rostrum and appealed for Party unity, to rows of emptying benches.

⸺⸙⸺

WHEN ROOT GAVELED the delegates to order at 11:15 the next morning, Wednesday, 19 June, the Coliseum was so crammed that the Chicago Fire Department had to bar entry to further would-be spectators. "The unfinished business before the convention," the chairman announced, "is the motion of the gentleman of Missouri." He said that Governor Hadley and Mr. Watson had agreed that debate on the subject of substitute delegates would be limited to three hours, divided equally.

Hadley, elegant in a double-breasted, knee-length coat that he somehow carried off casually, spoke first, expanding on his remarks of the day before. He used language as strong as Roosevelt's to describe the "naked theft" of convention seats by Taft delegates, but his manner was unprovocative and his response to every objection patiently polite. The odor of partisanship, lingering over the hall from the day before, cleared, and the convention grew calm. Even Barnes listened attentively as Hadley presented a declaration, signed by the progressive minority of the National Committee, that the validity of plausible claims for seats among the delegations of eleven states "should be determined by the uncontested delegates of this convention."

Much of the respect accorded Hadley came from a general awareness that he was the Colonel's potential running mate. Taft had wanted him too, until he became one of the governors asking Roosevelt to run. (In a sure sign that the President despaired of reelection, he had chosen to retain Vice President Sherman, who was moribund with heart disease.) "I do not know if a majority of this convention agrees with me upon the proposition that Theodore Roosevelt ought to be our candidate for President of the United States," Hadley said to a round of applause. "But there can be no difference on the proposition in the mind of any intelligent man that his voice today is the greatest voice in the western world."

A series of more provocative, fist-waving speakers took up the seating debate. The noise level of the convention began to rise. Senator Lodge's son-in-law, Congressman Augustus Peabody Gardner of Massachusetts, was so exasperated by the threat of a progressive, Henry J. Allen, to unload "two hundred pounds" of documents disqualifying the Washington State delegation that he stood on a chair repeatedly bellowing, "Are you going to abide by the decision of this convention?"

"I will support the nominee on one condition," Allen replied. Pandemonium broke out, and for some minutes he could not continue. He waited for quiet. "Upon the one condition that his nomination is not accomplished by fraud and thievery."

Instantly every Roosevelt delegate in the hall, with the exception of a few from Illinois, was leaping and cheering. William Flinn emerged as a major loudmouth, hurling insults at Elihu Root. He punctuated them with jets of tobacco juice. The chairman listened with indifference, showing disapproval only when anyone tried to interrupt a reasonable argument. Root's voice was not strong, and his orders had to be amplified by aides sprinting down the aisles with megaphones. But he projected such an air of chilly rectitude, in his morning coat and gray trousers, that usually it was enough for him to step to the front of the rostrum to restore order.

His fairness extended to stopping the clock between speeches, so that prolonged ovations could expend themselves. The hours dragged on. In mid-afternoon Hadley and Watson had an emergency conference and agreed, with mutual alarm, that the proceedings were on track to a deadlock. Unless the question of the seventy-two contested delegates was resolved, it could split the GOP—no matter whose name was placed in nomination. Watson, gray-faced, took the podium and declared, "The convention is not in a fit condition, neither is it in a fit temper . . . to judge intelligently upon any one of these contests." He said that Governor Hadley was willing, on behalf of the Roosevelt forces, to allow all seating claims to be decided by the credentials committee.

That body was not yet appointed, but for the moment, Hadley was seen as the savior of the Party. Delegation by delegation, an ovation for him built up until observers in the press box stared at the sight of William Flinn and William Barnes, Jr., cheering in tandem. The demonstration was that rare phenomenon in a national convention, a spontaneous expression of emotion, and it went through several mood changes. For the first twenty minutes it was bipartisan, with the potential of whipping up into a draft of the governor as a compromise nominee. But then rhythmic cries of "Teddy, Teddy—we want Teddy!" developed in the uproar, like the drumbeat of a coming fanfare. Attention began to divert from Hadley on the floor to a pretty woman standing in a high gallery. She wore a white dress, with a bunch of pinks at her waist. Whatever mysterious force focused fourteen thousand pairs of eyes on her, she was thespian enough to revel in it. She blew kisses at the crowd, then, leaning over the balustrade, unrolled a portrait of Theodore Roosevelt. The noise became deafening. Unfazed, she began to yell, and proved to have the lungs of a Valkyrie. "*Boys—give three cheers for Teddy!*"

A golden bear materialized beneath her, in the shape of the mascot of the California delegation. She reached out and cuddled it as it rose on the top of a proffered totem, whereupon the poles of other Roosevelt delegations joined in and jiggled up and down in phallic rivalry. The woman in white vanished for a minute. When she reappeared on the floor, it seemed improbable that the Coliseum could contain more sound. She marched up the main aisle, flushed with excitement, followed by stampeding delegates in an unconscious parody of Delacroix's *Liberty Leading the People*. As William Jennings Bryan watched from the press box, perhaps remembering a far-off day when he had stimulated almost as great a riot, she was hoisted giggling onto a shelf of shoulders and carried to the rostrum. Elihu Root tolerantly let her take control of the proceedings.

She did so without the aid of the gavel or megaphones, merely waving a long-gloved arm to increase or decrease the applause inundating her. When she again brandished Roosevelt's portrait—looking rather tattered now—the cries of "We want Teddy!" broke out with renewed force. It took fifty minutes for the tumult to die down and for the woman to be coaxed, as gently as possible, back into her box.

Hadley rejoined Root and Watson onstage. His luster of an hour before had been much diminished. As Roosevelt's floor leader, he had to regret that he had agreed to let the credentials committee decide the matter of the contested delegates. If his alternative list could have been resubmitted to the whole convention, at this moment of maximum affection for the Colonel, it would almost certainly have been approved, with Roosevelt cleared for nomination, and *he* generally accepted as the likely next vice president of the United States.

Under the circumstances, the best Hadley could do was persuade Governor Charles S. Deneen of Illinois to move that none of the seventy-two men whose seats were being contested should be allowed to participate in the election of members of the still-unconstituted committee. Nor should they be allowed to approve or disapprove the committee's report, when it was issued. The morality of this was to prevent any possibly fraudulent delegate from voting on the rightness of his own case, or the cases of his seventy-one contested colleagues.

Watson countered by moving to lay Deneen's amendment on the table.

By no flicker of expression did Root, gavel in hand, reveal that he recognized that the determining moment of the convention had arrived. He ordered a roll call on Watson's motion. "That question is not debatable."

Hadley tried to debate it anyway. "I wish to ask if the individuals whose titles to seats are here challenged are to vote upon this motion."

"The chair will rule upon that question at the conclusion of the roll call."

As the roll slowly proceeded, the heat of the demonstration went out of the room, and instinctual loyalties reasserted themselves. There were minor variations on yesterday's vote—Wisconsin announced itself as "solid this time" against Taft—but at the end of the call, the President's strength had increased by nine votes, to 567 over Roosevelt's 507, with four abstentions.

It was small comfort to Hadley and Flinn that their candidate was now only thirty votes short of being nominated, since Taft could afford to lose plenty and still defeat the Colonel. And here was Root moving in for the kill. "No man can be permitted to vote on the question of his own right to a seat in the convention," he said. "But the rule does not disqualify any delegate whose name is upon the roll from voting on the contest of any other man's right, or from participating in the ordinary business of the convention so long as he holds his seat."

Otherwise, Root pointed out, any minority could assure control of a deliberative body by bringing in enough rebels, under a surprise resolution, to transform themselves into a majority. He cited as precedent the procedural manual of the House of Representatives. Adopting Hadley's motion implied that every seat in the Coliseum could be contested, "and there would be no convention at all, as nobody would be entitled to participate."

As the realization spread that Roosevelt had no hope of seating any more delegates, his dispirited supporters in the galleries streamed out of the hall, not bothering to hear who had been appointed to the various operational committees. They knew now that the White House would control all agenda concerning credentials, permanent organization, rules, and resolutions.

THAT NIGHT THE WOMAN in white, identified as Mrs. W. A. Davis of Chicago, was brought to the Congress Hotel to meet the Colonel. He emerged briefly from his conference room, where urgent discussions were under way, and acknowledged her contribution. "It was a bully piece of work," he told her, then hurried back inside.

Had he been under less nervous strain, he might have thanked her more profusely. But throughout the day Roosevelt had been resisting moves to get him to withdraw in favor of Hadley, or even La Follette or Cummins, along with blandishments to keep him from bolting. He said he would not give way to any candidate unless the temporary roll was purged. And he told some furtive Old Guard emissaries, offering him a face-saving number of delegates if he would stay in the convention, that under no circumstances could he subscribe to the renomination of William Howard Taft.

He seemed convinced that the President was personally responsible for every dubious name on the roll. Thugs every one of them, they had stuck together in vote after vote on the individual state and district slates, completing the organization of the convention and proving that crime did pay in Republican politics. Or so it seemed to Roosevelt, in his red rage against Elihu Root as a "receiver of stolen goods." There could be no debate on the subject: his old friend was his mortal enemy. Having won the chair through the machinations of Rosewater, Watson, Barnes, and other unconvicted felons, Root had shut out the legitimate delegates on Hadley's list, all of them radiant with righteousness. Convention attendees who thought they had seen a solemn, impartial statesman on the podium were therefore subject to group delusion. Roosevelt did not need to have been there, or even listen down his telephone wire: he knew what venality looked and sounded like.

Party regulars and progressive rebels crammed his suite until well after midnight, alternately preaching loyalty and revolt. "I never saw the Colonel so fagged," Henry Stoddard wrote afterward. "For hours, his fighting blood had been at fever heat." At one point, Roosevelt sent for Edith and asked, "I wonder if it would be better for Hadley to head the Party."

Her reply was unhelpful. "Theodore, remember that often one wants to do the hardest and noblest thing, but sometimes it does not follow that it is the right thing."

The last of his visitors was Senator Borah, a man so divided that the cleft on his chin, lining up with his center part and frown, seemed to separate him into halves. He dragged Roosevelt into the bathroom and said, "This far I have gone with you. I can go no further."

Borah made it clear that many progressives like himself would be loath to risk their political careers by bolting to a third party that might not last. Roosevelt emerged from the bathroom looking furious. But he was plainly wavering.

It was now nearly two o'clock in the morning, and the suite was almost empty. Would-be bolters had gone to the Florentine Room to hold a defiant rally against the GOP organization. Their cheers and oratory could be heard down the corridor. Three tired intimates remained: Stoddard, Frank Munsey, and George Perkins. They urged Roosevelt to go on with his fight.

"My fortune, my magazines and my newspapers are with you," Munsey said. Perkins pledged his own wealth.

Roosevelt's moment of decision arrived when a delegation from the Florentine Room burst in to request that he present himself. He reached for his campaign hat and turned to Borah. "You see, I can't desert my friends now."

When he arrived at the rally he found it consisted largely of progressive delegates with legitimate seats at the convention. Some of them, indeed, were appointees to the credentials committee, but had vowed not to serve, in solidarity with their banned colleagues. His reception was tumultuous.

"As far as I am concerned I am through," he said. "If you are voted down,"—he was referring to the roll call on the committee report, expected later that day—"I hope you, the real and lawful majority of the convention, will organize as such, and you will do it if you have the courage and loyalty of your convictions."

Roosevelt went on talking for several minutes, berating the callowness of the RNC and the perfidy of Senator Root, but nothing he said matched the impact of his opening statement.

After he left the room, Hiram Johnson jumped on a table and confirmed to dazed delegates what they had just heard. "Gentlemen. . . . We are prepared for the birth of a new Republican party which will nominate for president Theodore Roosevelt." Gifford Pinchot thanked God. But Nicholas Roosevelt wrote in his diary, "I am depressed. It spells death."

⤳

AS OFTEN ON the eve of some climactic battle, there ensued a period of un-easy calm in downtown Chicago, with no bands playing and traffic in the streets returning to normal. Convention officials announced a twenty-four-hour recess, purportedly because the various committees needed time to complete their work. The real reason was that Taft's managers dreaded the coming bolt and were hoping that secessionist passions would cool.

If any sightseers were on hand that Thursday to watch the Colonel take his scheduled walk on Lake Michigan, they were disappointed. The weather was hot and damp. He spent most of the afternoon out of sight, conferring with intimates. Ominously, the Illinois delegation, which had been elected in the first great success of his primary campaign, announced that it was 56 to 2 against bolting. Four other states expressed similar qualms. Roosevelt was alarmed enough to issue a statement rejecting reports that he intended to march into the Coliseum and precipitate a riot. But he confirmed that he would bolt if it suited him, no matter how many cowards chose not to follow. "There will probably be a new national convention," he said, "and we will then build up a new party."

After that he was so much at leisure that he was able to spend four hours at dinner with his family and Munsey and Perkins. Timothy Woodruff, chafing under Boss Barnes's iron control of the New York delegation, came over to report a threat from Mrs. Woodruff: "Timmy, if you don't bolt, I'm going to Reno."

"The crisis of the convention is at hand," William Jennings Bryan wrote that evening.

> It is no pleasant situation in which the ex-president finds himself, nor is it an ordinary situation. Twice chief executive of the nation, the second time elected by the largest majority that a president ever achieved; the recipient of honors in foreign lands and supreme dictator in his own party, he now finds the man whom he nominated and elected pitted against him in the most bitter contest that our country has ever seen, and he sees that opponent operating with a skill of a past master the very machinery which the tutor constructed and taught him to use.

There was no immediate resumption of hostilities when the convention opened for business at midday on Friday. But the report of the credentials committee served only to increase Taft's majority to 605. This could not have been achieved without the defection of forty or fifty Roosevelt delegates. Significantly, the day's warmest applause was for Bryan, when he lumbered in to take his seat in the press box. Old, bald, and Democratic he may have been, but at least he had once stood for a common cause. "If you don't look out," a fellow correspondent joked, "the Baltimore convention will nominate you for President."

"Young man," Bryan said with mock sternness, "do you suppose that I'm going to run for President just to pull the Republican Party out of a hole?"

At the end of the day, it was obvious that the Taft forces were still playing for time, dragging out roll calls in order to exhaust whatever energy was left in the progressive opposition. By now, in any ordinary convention, the candidates should have been nominated. Root remarked, "Evidently there are delegates here who do not wish to go home for Sunday." During the umpteenth procedural intermission, the band played "You'll Do the Same Thing Over and Over and Over Again."

THE ATMOSPHERE on Saturday, 22 June, was different and dangerous from the start. Root gaveled the convention to order early, at 10:43 A.M., and at once the fake steamroller whistles shrilled, accompanied by accelerating, chugging puffs and a mocking cry of "all aboard." The Roosevelt family box was noticeably empty, with only Alice sitting like Cassandra, sure of coming catastrophe.

She joined in, however, when a group of delegates started chanting, "We want Teddy!" and "Roosevelt, first, last and all the time!" There was no fear of her father storming the hall and imperiling what was left of his presidential dignity. He had simply sent a message expressing the "hope" that his delegates would take no part in the nomination of a tainted candidate.

Since Hadley (secretly racked with tuberculosis, and running a 103°F fever) had joined Borah in declining to bolt, the Colonel authorized Henry J. Allen of Kansas to read this message aloud. But to general frustration, there were four further hours of roll calls to endure before Root announced that the convention was ready to hear any statement the Roosevelt forces wished to make. Allen rose at 2:54 P.M. He said that all he needed was "ten minutes of quiet attention."

What he got was forty-four minutes of such bedlam that for much of the time he could not be heard. But the pertinent phrases of Roosevelt's message sounded clear, and were telegraphed simultaneously to ten thousand newspapers across the country: *The convention [is] in no proper sense any longer a Republican convention representing the real Republican Party. Therefore, I hope the men elected as Roosevelt delegates will now decline to vote on any matter before the convention.*

From then until shortly before six, when 343 of Allen's fellow progressives boycotted the adoption of the platform, mutual hatreds seethed. At last Root ordered each state that had a presidential candidate to present its nomination, in alphabetical order. Iowa, home of Albert B. Cummins, was called first. There was no response, signaling that the governor would join the progressive bolt. An even more deathly silence followed the call for New York. The progressive delegate who would have risen to name Theodore Roosevelt remained in his seat. At four minutes past the hour, Warren Harding of Ohio spoke for President Taft, and delivered an attack on the Colonel that had clearly cost him many hours with a dictionary:

> Sirs, I have heard men arrogate to themselves the title of "progressive Republicans." . . . Progression is not proclamation or palaver. It is not pretense nor play on prejudice. It is not of personal pronouns, nor perennial pronouncement. It is not the perturbation of a people passion-wrought, nor a promise proposed. Progression is—

Harding ran out of plosives at this point, to the relief of the megaphone men, and went on to other alliterations. But in conclusion, he reverted to his favorite consonant, accusing Roosevelt of "pap rather than patriotism," and elevating Taft to the "party pantheon." His speech touched off a wild demonstration. Yet there was something fatalistic about the chants and portrait-waving. Everyone knew that the RNC had decided to field a losing candidate in November, rather than gamble on one who would radicalize its traditional platform.

After a last-minute attempt to swing the convention for Robert M. La Follette had been laughed down, Root asked the states to vote. The only disturbance to a droning succession of calls came when Massachusetts was polled, and two loyal Rooseveltians declined to vote, leaving the delegation evenly split. Root at once recognized their alternates, who happened to be Taft men, and a howl of rage arose, such as had never been heard in a convention before.

At 9:28 P.M., William Howard Taft was renominated with 561 votes. One hundred and seven of Roosevelt's supporters carried out their primary instructions and voted for the Colonel. They stayed in their seats while 344 others declared themselves "present and not voting." Then, as Root wound up the Fifteenth National Republican Convention, the bolters rose and went out into the night. They headed, not for their hotel rooms, but for Orchestra Hall, where the galleries were already full and telephone and telegraph linemen were installing wires to broadcast the birth of a new party.

WILLIAM ALLEN WHITE was so intent upon reporting Taft's nomination that he did not even notice where his colleagues from Kansas were going. Three hours later, having written and filed his story, he entered the Congress

Hotel restaurant and found it filling up with late diners. One of them jovially accosted him.

"Why weren't you over to Orchestra Hall?"

White said he had been busy.

"Well, you missed the big show."

"What show?"

"Oh, we have organized the Progressive Party. Roosevelt made a ripsnorting speech, and the crowd tore the roof off and we are on our way!"

White struggled with conflicting emotions. Chagrin at being scooped was not the worst of them. He felt as he had in Boston earlier in the year, when the Colonel had talked to him and Judge Grant of *il gran rifiuto,* and they had tried to dissuade him from running. Willing as White was to join the bolt, he secretly feared that the neonate cause might smother in Roosevelt's too-lusty embrace. Better for progressivism to fight and survive as a broad-based movement for social reform, drawing strength from both parties, than for it to be identified with one man's obsessed mission.

The fight promised to be a long one—only getting under way, he thought, this year, with little chance of premature success. White admired Roosevelt so much that he could not bear to think of his hero being humiliated in November, as a certain consequence of splitting the Republican vote, just when the Democrats (already congregating for *their* convention in Baltimore) were so strong.

Here was the splitter himself, coming into the restaurant and asking in a teasing falsetto where White had been. Somebody who knew him less well would have seen only the exuberance of a man who had just worked up a crowd and been bathed in acclamation. White, however, noticed something more disturbing. Roosevelt was bent on revenge. "He was not downcast; indeed he was triumphant, full of jokes and quips as though the teakettle of his heart were humming and rattling the lid of his merry countenance. But rage was bubbling inside him."

Elsewhere in the hotel, supporters of the President were disinclined to celebrate their victory. And from the far side of the divide that had opened up between the Colonel and the victims of his wrath came the sad voice of Elihu Root: "I care more for one button on Theodore Roosevelt's waistcoat than for Taft's whole body."

CHAPTER 11

Onward, Christian Soldiers

And what is this that comes and goes,
Fades and swells and overflows,
Like music underneath and overhead?
What is it in me now that rings and roars
Like fever-laden wine?

"MY PUBLIC CAREER WILL end next election day," Roosevelt said to a visitor on the morning after Woodrow Wilson was nominated as the Democratic candidate for President.

It was 3 July 1912. For about a week he had been able to hope against hope that his decision to run as a progressive independent might return him to the White House. Although Wilson's brand of progressivism was not radical, it had so agitated the Baltimore convention as to make the proceedings in Chicago look sedate. No fewer than forty-three ballots had been required to persuade Bourbon reactionaries that the governor was the best man to win a four-way race against Taft, Roosevelt, and the Socialist Eugene V. Debs.

Roosevelt understood that, having encouraged progressives to leave the GOP, he ran the risk of many of them choosing Wilson over himself. The man looked like a winner: already there was a group that called itself the "Wilson Progressive Republican League." A large majority of the country's editors and commentators praised this new celebrity who had proved so effective a gubernatorial reformer. Wilson appealed to what Roosevelt called the "rural tory" element, opposing, for example, recall of judicial decisions, while tacitly catering to the anti-Negro prejudice that was a powerful, if unstated, aspect of progressivism. The white, corn-fed Midwestern farmers, small businessmen, professionals, and middle-class moralists who largely composed the movement's membership did not subscribe to the lynch mentality of Dixie Democrats. But neither did they think blacks were good for much more than field labor. Word had gotten out that the Colonel favored the idea of a Negro delegate to second his nomination when the new party established itself. Veteran politicians recalled him attending his first GOP convention in 1884, and pushing for the election of a black chairman. One could not imagine Wilson, born in Virginia and bred in the South, carrying democracy quite that far.

Another factor against Roosevelt's chances of success was the lack of nerve among GOP progressives in retreat from Armageddon. Four of the seven governors who had petitioned him to run in February now declined to support him. Chase Osborn of Michigan had come out as a Republican for Wilson, railing against "malcontents" seeking to destroy the two-party system. Herbert Hadley wrote that as the head of the Republican party in Missouri, he would have to be "thoroughly convinced that it had ceased to be a useful agency of good government before I abandoned it and joined in the formation of a new party." He argued that the local machinery was "in the hands of progressives" anyway. As for veterans of the Progressive Republican League, Jonathan Bourne had answered his own question ("If we lose, will we bolt?") in the negative, while Robert La Follette, who could have followed Roosevelt out and then challenged him for the leadership of the apostates, elected to stay put and support Wilson. Eight other former insurgents, including Senator Cummins, sent regrets, saying they did not want to lose all power in their states.

In short, the nascent Progressive Party (it was not yet formally organized, and must stage its own convention as soon as possible) was already fighting for life. Money it had, and plenty of political passion left over from "the big show" in Chicago, but its frailties were obvious. Chief among these was a lack of ideological unity—not only between intellectuals of the Herbert Croly stamp and petty bosses like William Flinn, but between city men and hayseeds, suffragists and social workers, temperance advocates and the Irish, muckraking journalists and self-made millionaires. Had Wilson not been nominated, Roosevelt might conceivably have managed to compress all this dissent into one hot mass of energy. Now he saw that he had no choice but to lead a quixotic campaign on his own principles.

He left his Sagamore Hill guest, E. A. Van Valkenburg, alone for a moment, and went to fetch Edith. When they returned, he asked her to say what she thought.

"She was quite radiant with trust and affection," Van Valkenburg reported, "as she expressed her faith that the path through honor to defeat was the one to take."

❧

IN CHICAGO, EDITH had given off such waves of foreboding, as she sat quietly knitting amid the tumult around her, that she reminded William Allen

White of Madame Defarge—"weaving the inevitable destiny ahead of us out of the yard and skein where it had been wound by the hand of some terrible fate." Since then, evidently, she had reconciled herself to the idea of Roosevelt's crusade—a word that was often on the lips of his family and followers these days. Protestant for the most part, and not a few of them puritanical in their ardor (Edith herself was a descendant of Jonathan Edwards, the New England divine), they saw themselves as a persecuted minority, bound to grow stronger as their numbers diminished.

Her radiance, remarked on by other visitors as well as Van Valkenburg, may indeed have been a matter of idealism. But there was also the thought that Theodore's retirement from politics, so distressingly interrupted, must surely become permanent after November.

The Roosevelt children reacted to the coming campaign with varying degrees of excitement and fear. Alice was torn, even more than in 1910, between loyalty to her father and dread that her husband would be swept out of Congress on Taft's coattails. She did not think she could stand any more of "Cincinnasty" than she already had to endure.

To the puzzlement of many of her own relatives, Alice adored everything about Nicholas Longworth except his willingness to serve the President. His baldness, his boozing, his lust for other women—she had taken them on when she married him, and found them perversely attractive. She had even come to like the kind of *echt* German chamber music he played with some of his friends (usually on first violin: behind the Midwestern swagger, a gifted musician lurked). "Darling Nick, I love him so much." But for all her floaty, expensive clothes and party chat, Alice was as political as a ward heeler. Progressivism meant little to her as a cause. It was simply a platform that her father had chosen to run on, and in any race, she was for him "first, last and always."

Representative Longworth's position was an agonizing one. He had come to share many of Roosevelt's beliefs. But his political ties to Taft were so old, and so intertwined with those of friendship between their respective clans, that bolting the Ohio Republican party was simply not an option for him. Alice—pale and coughing, existing mainly on fruit and eggs and Vichy water—suffered along with him, finding it difficult to contain her fury against the bile his mother and sister showed toward the Colonel. If Nick lost his seat in Congress, she saw little in his future but more alcohol, and more women.

Ted was an ardent progressive who had learned much by working to elect Hiram Johnson as governor of California. In Chicago he had been ubiquitous at planning sessions for the new party. Recently hired as a bond salesman for the New York banking house of Bertron, Griscom & Co., he was staying at Sagamore Hill until he and Eleanor could find a house in the city. This gave him an inside position to observe the workings of a presidential campaign.

But he soon found out that the name of Theodore Roosevelt did not help him sell many bonds on Wall Street.

Kermit had no interest in politics. His new Harvard degree and Porcellian circle of acquaintance promised him a charmed entry into the world Ted prized—clubs, banks, lunches, squash courts, smokers, balls. But Africa had left an ache in his heart for the Land of Beyond. His parents had made it clear to him, as to all their children, that they could not afford to support adult dependents. So if he wanted the career of a gentleman adventurer, he was either going to have to do it on salary, or find himself a rich wife. Kermit had already made overtures in both directions, securing a job with the Brazil Railway Company, and courting Belle Willard, daughter of the owner of a chain of Southern hotels. The girl's financial expectations were rosy, but to distress at Oyster Bay, her parents were Democrats. So far, fortunately, Belle had not given Kermit much encouragement. He was due to sail for South America in a matter of weeks, and would see if she pined for him.

Ethel would, at any rate. For the last couple of years, brother and sister had been inseparable, swapping their favorite poems, united in their disapproval of Ted's "fast" way of life. A sedate and colorless moth in contrast to butterfly Alice, Ethel was being wooed by a thirtyish surgeon, Richard Derby. His job—not an easy one at the moment—was to convince her that life away from her father was worth living. Roosevelt was touched by her devotion, and aware of the desperate shyness that made her cling to him. "How is my sweet little apostle?" he would tease, enfolding her in bear hugs. Ethel was a devout churchgoer who had been overwhelmed, in Chicago, by the fervor of his followers. "Oh Dorothy," she told a friend about the post-bolt meeting, "every person in that hall felt as if it were the Holy War—and they crusaders."

Archie had little patience with holiness, but he loved the sound of the word *war*. Through dogged self-improvement he had managed to conquer his learning disabilities and beat back ill health, much as his father had done in the summer of '76. "His frail-looking body," Roosevelt noted approvingly, "has a certain tough whipcord-like quality to it." Terse and touchy, Archie would have liked nothing better than to enlist with firearms in the "battle for the Lord"—perhaps at the side of his hero, U.S. Marshal Seth Bullock. But a remedial term at Phillips Academy in Andover awaited him in the fall, and he must cram his slow brain for that.

Quentin was still boy enough to enjoy the political activity at Sagamore Hill (daily delegations, a constant racket of typewriters and telegraphers, reporters camping out on the lawn) without any curiosity about what, exactly, was going on. In an affectionate pen portrait written that summer, his father described him as "tranquil, efficient, moon-faced and entirely merry . . . busy about affairs which mostly have to do with machinery."

ROOSEVELT SEEMED A relieved man after the catharsis of Chicago. He had lingered there long enough to transmute what was left of rage into momentum, declaring, "I'm feeling like a bull moose." Cartoonists seized upon the image with joy, and a new political animal, all teeth and antlers, pranced onto the pages of a thousand newspapers, shouldering aside the elephant and the donkey. Gifford and Amos Pinchot and other serious souls might insist that they were at work on the constitution of the Progressive Party, but to popular perception it was already the "Bull Moose Party," and "Teddy" a rambunctious critter.

For as long as he stayed home, however, recuperating after his strenuous spring, Roosevelt's behavior was tame. He made a few mild complaints about the "miserable showing" of his lost supporters. Yet Governor Osborn wrote to apologize and explain, he was forgiving, and hinted that he might have supported Wilson himself, were it not for the reactionary bosses behind the Democratic Party's promises of social reform. Senator Dixon, reappointed as his campaign manager, could only hope that the velvet on the Bull Moose's antlers would soon wear off.

"I suppose that as we grow older, we naturally lose the natural feeling of young men to take an interest in politics just for the sake of the strife," Roosevelt wrote the British novelist H. Rider Haggard. That did not make him any less keen to fight for distributive justice. His challenge over the next four months, he felt, was to convince a majority of the American people that he was not personally ambitious. "The great bulk of my wealthy and educated friends regard me as a dangerous crank. . . . But all this is of little permanent consequence. It is a fight that must be made, and it is worth making; and the event lies on the knees of the gods."

ON 7 JULY, DIXON issued a formal call for delegates of the new party to convene in Chicago in the first week of August. The publication of this letter forced Roosevelt to confront an almost insoluble political dilemma. After being nominated by the convention (a foregone conclusion), he would be expected to campaign across the country on the Progressive Party ticket. Yet what was the sense of running on such a ticket in states where a majority of "Roosevelt Republicans" were sworn to support him? He would in effect be asking these loyalists to follow him out of the GOP, and give up their local power and affiliations.

How, though, could he claim to be the leader of a new national party unless it had a full ticket in every state? Lack of local and federal candidates would fatally weaken it in regions where Taft or Wilson were strong. And his own campaign would look like a search for glory, rather than leadership of a popular upsurge.

In weighing this and other tactical problems before the convention, Roosevelt turned less to the Pinchot brothers than to a man identified with every-

THE LATEST ARRIVAL AT THE POLITICAL ZOO

DRAWN BY E. W. KEMBLE

"A NEW POLITICAL ANIMAL, ALL TEETH AND ANTLERS."

Roosevelt emerges as a third-party candidate for the presidency, summer 1912.

thing they despised: big-business, *laissez-faire,* monopolistic capital. George Walbridge Perkins—fifty years old, flush with the proceeds of a fabulous career at the House of Morgan—was a convert to the cause of progressivism.

He had surpassed Frank Munsey as the Party's biggest bankroller. To old-money liberals like the Pinchot brothers, there was something suspect about a *nouveau riche* altruist declaring that he had the welfare of the people at heart. "Roosevelt has the right idea," the historian Frederick Jackson Turner commented, "but if he keeps Mr. Perkins as his chef, he is likely to have to take his omelet with Mr. Morgan's spoon instead of the people's spoon."

Conversely, it was difficult for small-town Midwesterners such as William Allen White to believe that Perkins—so sleek, so at ease entertaining on his palatial estate overlooking the Hudson River—had started out as an office boy in Chicago. He had come by his millions through adroit corporate climbing, up through the executive ranks of insurance and banking companies to the top echelon of some of the world's greatest conglomerates, including U. S. Steel. For well over a decade this rise had coincided, not always harmoniously, with that of Theodore Roosevelt.

If anything had converted Perkins, fully and finally, to the progressive cause, it was the Colonel's famous blast against the Taft administration for finding fault with the merger of U.S. Steel and Tennessee Coal & Iron. He believed, with Roosevelt, that there should be an entente between socially responsible entrepreneurs and a powerful, yet non-prosecutorial, government.

Exquisitely undertailored, in custom clothes that favored shades of gray and white, Perkins was a slender man with a trim, soft mustache and a soft voice. He smiled often, and was in constant motion even at rest: toe-tapping, thumb-flicking, black eyes snapping. The pudgy little White envied the drape of his mohair suits, while Gifford Pinchot despaired of ever being able to make Roosevelt laugh the way Perkins did. Behind their jealousy, however, lay an honest concern. They wondered if his real cause was not Roosevelt, but regulatory policy. If he ever became Secretary of Commerce, champagne would surely foam in a thousand corporate boardrooms.

Deep down, Roosevelt preferred the society of sophisticates (Perkins was "George," White always a surname), as long as they embraced the values of the middle class. Perkins shared his own cheerful nature and freakish ability to be both fast and thorough in dispatching great quantities of work. There was no question as to who should become the chief executive officer of the Progressive Party.

Pinchot, White, and Hiram Johnson, respectively burgeoning as leaders of eastern, central, and West Coast delegations to the convention, worried less about this than about Perkins's influence on the drafting of the Party platform. He was heard to say that competition in the marketplace was a waste of energy. To White, that sounded like a trust lord talking. It would be a cruel irony if Roosevelt allowed the platform's antitrust plank to be edited by this silky-smooth, check-writing ambassador from Wall Street.

ONE OF THE REASONS the Colonel liked Perkins was that they could talk about things other than policy, unlike the "moonbeamers," as Frank Munsey called ideologues of the far left, obsessed with social and economic theory. Roosevelt himself was so bored by some of the doctrinaires who droned around him through the first week of August that he would excuse himself and sneak off somewhere with a novel, until retrieved and reprimanded by his wife.

He had plenty of patience, however, for crucial discussions, choosing eventually to run on "a straight-out progressive ticket" in most states of the union. Excepted only were those in the hopelessly reactionary South, Wisconsin as the pocket principality of Senator La Follette, and six Republican states (Maine, West Virginia, South Dakota, Kansas, Nebraska, and California), progressive enough to have voted for him already. Elsewhere, he felt the third-party ticket would give him a chance to cut into Wilson's support.

More than that, he wanted to cut into Taft's. He would show no mercy for the entire Fagin's den who had ganged up on him in Chicago. "I regard Taft as the receiver of a swindled nomination," he wrote Van Valkenburg. "I cannot consent to do anything that looks as if I was joining with him. I won't go into a friendly contest with a pickpocket as to which of us should keep *my* watch which *he* stole."

AS THE CONVENTION loomed nearer, Roosevelt had to decide a moral issue that, agonizingly for him, related to the cause of his departure from the party of Abraham Lincoln. It concerned the right of certain delegations to attend a national convention over the claims of others. Except that this time, the rivals were all for him, and all hailed from Southern states. They differed only in that some were white and some black.

Since he personified the Progressive Party, his opinion in the matter would define its larger attitude to the question of race. A firm, yet compassionate statement would, he hoped, offer voters an alternative to the Democratic Party's "lily-white" philosophy, and the Republican Party's sectional mix of tolerance and exploitation on either side of the Mason-Dixon Line.

Such a statement would help clarify his racial views, which had confused many people over the years. Was he still, to white Southerners, the "coon-flavored" President of 1901, who had wined and dined Booker T. Washington? Or was he rather the reactionary commander in chief of 1906, who had dishonorably discharged a whole Negro regiment in Brownsville, Texas, on trumped-up evidence of rioting?

In his own mind, Roosevelt was a fair man, inclined neither to patronize nor sentimentalize those darker and poorer than himself. He was proud of having fought to elevate blacks to federal office as President, and if the number was small, it was better than Taft's deliberate score of zero. He had appointed an anti-peonage judge in the South, and been the first chief executive ever to speak out against the "inhuman cruelty and barbarity" of lynching. Brownsville was the one race-related incident in his career that might be ascribed to prejudice. But even then, he had prejudged only in the sense that he had been too quick to uphold an army investigation of the case.

Without exception, black people who knew him, from Dr. Washington down to James Amos, his valet, found his goodwill to be sincere, and never more so than when they advanced themselves by their own efforts—some farther, in the relative scheme of things, than he with all his privileges. Yet stray observations over the years had revealed him to be enlightened only in contrast to those of his peers who were outspoken in their xenophobia. Associating with such friends, he was as inclined to agree as disagree, assuring the novelist Owen Wister that blacks were "altogether inferior to the whites," and the historian James Ford Rhodes that the Fifteenth Amendment had been "bad policy," and the elephant hunter Quentin Grogan that if he could eliminate every Negro in America at the touch of a button, he would "jump on it with both feet." Or so they chose to remember.

Roosevelt was struck by the extremes of advice he was now getting on the race question, from visitors and correspondents who all assumed he was their soul mate. Some wanted the Progressive Party to be exclusively white; others, segregated. He wondered if he could not persuade the former element—concentrated in the Old Confederacy—that he posed no reconstructive threat. If so, many of those who found Wilson's brand of progressivism attractive might find his more so. To break up the "solid" Democratic South, with its 126 electoral votes, would stamp his campaign as truly revolutionary.

He decided to publish an open letter on the subject, and addressed it to Julian Harris, son of the Georgian folklorist Joel Chandler Harris.

"We have made the Progressive issue a moral, not a racial issue," he wrote. "I believe that in this movement only damage will come if we either abandon our ideals on the one hand, or, on the other, fail resolutely to look facts in the face, however unpleasant these facts may be." One fact was that Southern Democrats would never be wooed if their most unifying neurosis was threatened. "Our objective must be the same everywhere, but the methods by which we strive to attain it must be adapted to the needs of the several states, or it will never be attained at all."

He noted that in a broad swath of the North, extending from Rhode Island west to Illinois, as well as in Maryland, the Progressive Party was already selecting black officials and delegates—acting "with fuller recognition of the rights of the colored man than ever the Republican party did." In the South, however, it was confronted with the phenomenon that over forty-five years, "colored" and "Republican" had become synonymous terms. That was to say, Southern Negroes had been persuaded to trade disenfranchisement for the privilege, and cash profits, of sending representatives to Northern Republican presidential conventions. Roosevelt did not have to reach back any further than last June to cite the venal, "rotten-borough" black delegates who had stood by in Chicago while the RNC "defied and betrayed the will of the mass of the plain people of the party."

In view of this ugly record, he felt that the Progressive Party would be doomed if it "prostituted" itself at the outset to Southern politicians of color.

> The machinery does not exist (and can never be created as long as pres-
> ent political conditions are continued) which can secure what a future
> of real justice will undoubtedly develop, namely, the right of political
> expression by the negro who shows that he possesses the intelligence,
> integrity and self-respect which justify such right of political expres-
> sion in his white neighbor.
>
> We face certain actual facts, sad and unpleasant facts, but facts
> which must be faced if we are to dwell in the world of realities and not
> of shams. . . . I earnestly believe that by appealing to the best white
> men in the South, the men of justice and of vision as well as of strength
> and leadership, and by frankly putting the movement in their hands at
> the outset, we shall create a situation by which the colored men of the
> South will ultimately get justice as it is not possible for them to get jus-
> tice if we are to continue and perpetuate the present conditions.

MANY OF THE Progressive delegates converging on the Chicago Coliseum on Monday, 4 August, could be excused a sense of *déjà vu,* having been there as Republicans only seven weeks before. Once again the streets reverberated with bands, straw-hatted politicos strode along arm in arm, and flags bedecked the enormous turreted building on Wabash Avenue. Again Roosevelt established himself in the Congress Hotel, at the end of the same telephone line through to the convention floor. Except now, the only suspense was over whom he would pick as his running mate.

Further differences were apparent inside the Coliseum. Barbed wire no longer spiked the rostrum. Bright red was the prevailing color, save for scores of Stars and Stripes hanging from high rafters, interspersed with mysterious bags of white cotton. From opposite ends of the hall, a giant stuffed moose head and an oil-painted Roosevelt exchanged comradely stares.

In June, the prevailing mood among delegates had been sour and fractious. Now all was unity and exaltation. The semi-religious glow that had infused the bolters then, with Hiram Johnson declaiming, "Our work is holy work," warmed into flame as the New York delegation, led by Oscar Solomon Straus, marched into the hall singing,

> *Onward, Christian soldiers, marching as to war,*
> *With the cross of Jesus going on before.*

The record size of the convention (two thousand delegates and alternates, representing every state in the Union except South Carolina) astounded political reporters aware of the difficulty of organizing a new party in less time than corn took to grow. A sense of mass belonging thrilled the delegates themselves, many of whom had suffered, back home, the obloquy of heresy. Squads seating themselves under the banners of New Hampshire and Maine were encouraged by the sight of others in Western sombreros, or the white starched suits of Mississippi and Florida. All could be excused the delusion that Progressivism (at last styled with a capital *P*) was strong everywhere in the country, unified behind the most formidable campaigner in American history. Their common accessory was a red bandanna, tied around the neck in Rough Rider style—"common" indeed to observers who associated red with the rise of the proletariat.

Yet there was nothing lumpen about these Progressives, no representation of the poor-white element seen at Democratic conventions. They were scrubbed and prosperous-looking, well dressed and well behaved, churchgoing, charitable, bourgeois to a fault. Even the cigar-chomping Boss Flinn of Pennsylvania took care to spit sideways, so as not to stain his immaculate clothes. William Allen White surveyed the crowd and saw the sort of people he wrote for in the *Emporia Gazette*. He figured that there was not a delegate on the floor making less than two thousand dollars a year, or more than ten thousand—with a few conspicuous exceptions, such as George Perkins, "spick-and-span, oiled and curled like an Assyrian bull."

White was struck by how many women he saw in the delegate rows, looking as businesslike as possible in their frilly shirtwaisters: female doctors, lawyers, teachers, and community activists. Not a few were in their early twenties—"rich young girls who had gone in for settlement work." All seemed to take it for granted that the Progressive platform would recognize universal woman suffrage.

The social pioneer Jane Addams, founder of Chicago's Hull House project and arguably the most famous woman in America, entered to reverential applause, a Bull Moose badge on her breast. She took her place in the front row of the VIP enclave, to the joy of officials who had feared she might stay away. Roosevelt's decision not to seat Southern black delegates had disturbed her, and she had pleaded in vain with the provisional Party Committee to modify it. She was also a pacifist, and thought that the Colonel was too fond of battleships. Only the overriding importance he attached to social reform persuaded Miss Addams to support him rather than Wilson. She had agreed with some reluctance to second his nomination.

The convention came to order at 1:40 P.M., with an opening prayer remarkable for the loudness of its "Amens." Then Albert J. Beveridge mounted the rostrum, a short, handsome figure dwarfed by a yellow soundboard that hung above him like an airfoil.

The former senator had to get things going with a keynote address that would compensate for the absence of the one man everybody wanted to see. Roosevelt had in fact wanted to make a brief, inspirational appearance after the first fall of the gavel. But Beveridge, a narcissist of the purest bloom, had demanded the afternoon's headlines to himself. He was then prepared to act unflamboyantly as chairman of the convention.

Roosevelt could not argue against the wisdom of giving a better speaker than himself a chance to articulate the basic tenets of Progressivism—in a voice more silvery, with gestures less punchy. Back in the days of McKinley, Beveridge had won fame as a boyish, golden-haired prophet of America's imperialistic destiny. Now he was older, darker, and less jingoistic, but still full of frustrated ambition. He had agonized for a long time about leaving the Republican Party, aware that he might never again represent Indiana in Congress. His ego, however, could not resist this new opportunity to be an oracle.

He spoke for an hour and a half, beginning with a rhythmic affirmation of the Progressive creed: "We stand for a nobler America. . . . We stand for social brotherhood as against savage individualism. We stand for an intelligent cooperation instead of a reckless competition. . . . Ours is a battle for the actual rights of man." The Party, he said, had been gestating for years, as ordinary Americans of all political persuasions grew to resent special-interest rule, "the invisible government behind our visible government." He called for the reforms that Roosevelt had itemized at Osawatomie and elsewhere—direct primaries, direct election of senators, the initiative, referendum, and recall—arguing that popular rule would alleviate bossism, social insecurity, worker abuse, and the oligarchical concentration of wealth. America was blessed in being prosperous and thinly peopled, but cursed in making a cult of selfishness. "The Progressive motto is, 'Pass prosperity around.' "

Vigorously, his fine eyes glowing, Beveridge also inveighed against child labor, neglect of the elderly, and sex discrimination. The Party, he said, demanded that women be paid as much as men. What was more, "Votes for women are theirs as a matter of natural right alone." At this, the convention exploded. Delegates of both sexes clambered onto their chairs and shouted approval. Jane Addams controled her emotions, but her face was triumphant. Even men were seen wiping away tears everyone sang "The Battle Hymn of the Republic."

"It was not a convention at all," a *New York Times* reporter wrote that night. "It was an assemblage of religious enthusiasts."

ENTHUSIASM BECAME ECSTASY the following day, when Theodore Roosevelt materialized beneath the yellow airfoil. No presidential candidate had ever before attended a national convention. For fifty-eight minutes he stood grinning as the Coliseum shook with noise.

At least ten thousand people flooded the floor in a red tide of bandannas. Hats encircled with rings rose on the ends of canes. Two black Northern delegates climbed onstage, and Roosevelt gratefully reached out for them. They huddled with him as he talked and gesticulated, his words inaudible a few feet away. Then one pounded him on the shoulder, and for a moment the trio stood hand in hand, to roars of applause and imitation moose calls.

Jane Addams mounted in her turn. As she posed beside the Colonel, the band struck up "Onward, Christian Soldiers." Roosevelt led the singing, both arms held high.

> *Like a mighty army moves the church of God,*
> *Brothers, we are treading where the saints have trod. . . .*

The hymn was not quite to Miss Addams's taste. But its tune was impossible to resist, and not all the words embarrassed her:

> *We are not divided, all one body we—*
> *One in hope and doctrine, one in charity.*

"I have been fighting for progressive principles for thirty years," she said as she descended from the platform into a sea of well-wishers. "This is the biggest day in my life."

The celebration went on and on. Eventually Roosevelt was left alone onstage, bowing to the crowd. Senator Root's mocking prophecy appeared to have been fulfilled: *He aims at a leadership far in the future, as a sort of Moses and Messiah for a vast progressive tide of a rising humanity.* His smile betrayed a hint of alarm, as if he was bewildered by the religiosity that surged around him. Vitality he had, and passion too, for earthly attainments and even abstract ethical aims, but he could not abandon himself to this communal rapture. The crowd was unlike any other he had seen before, chaotic in its variety.

Here, waving bandannas, were former Democrats like Judge Benjamin B. Lindsey of Colorado, a power in the juvenile court movement, Raymond Robins, a wealthy labor activist, Don Dickinson, postmaster general under

President Cleveland, and Bourke Cockran, the legendary orator of Tammany Hall. Senators Dixon, Poindexter, Clapp, Bristow, and Norris represented the Republican insurgency of recent years. James Garfield, the brothers Pinchot, and other "moonbeamers" were in transports at finding their long-planned third party an actuality. The sculptor Gutzon Borglum and the novelist Winston Churchill were prominent in the Connecticut and New Hampshire delegations. Ambitious young intellectuals included the lawyer Felix Frankfurter, the essayist Walter Lippmann, Judge Learned Hand of New York, and Harold L. Ickes, a Chicago municipal reformer. Academics not normally inclined to prance and sway with party bosses brandished the same signs as Boss Walter F. Brown of Ohio and "Tiny Tim" Woodruff of Brooklyn (dazzling in white flannel, as if to advertise his conversion from Republican orthodoxy). Suffragists, political scientists, social theorists, lapsed priests, and exponents of Adlerian ethical culture looked forward to hearing Roosevelt address their respective causes.

It said something for his range of acquaintance that he knew hundreds of these people by name. Many of them, in turn, knew him from his past lives. Professor Albert Bushnell Hart of Harvard remembered him as a reed-thin freshman, punching the air in a student demonstration for "Hayes and Honest Ways." Joe Murray and Isaac Hunt had witnessed his baptism in the New York Republican Party—and now his apostasy from it. Sylvane and Joe Ferris, Bill Merrifield, and George Myers, his former ranch partners and Badlands buddies, were in attendance as excited delegates half inclined to shoot out the lights. Present too was the ubiquitous Seth Bullock, who thought Armageddon was a town in Oklahoma. The veteran civil service reformers William Dudley Foulke and Lucius B. Swift could testify that Roosevelt had been their idealistic ally as far back as 1889. W. Franklin Knox led a contingent of graying Rough Riders, all prepared to follow their Colonel up another dangerous hill.

Crowns and thrones may perish, kingdoms rise and wane. . . .

The person whose support meant most to Roosevelt may have been the quietest spectator in the hall. Edith sat as before in the family box. Only now she had none of their children with her—not even Alice, whom Nick had begged to stay away. Incredibly, for a woman who flinched at public exposure, Edith stood up when the crowd yelled for her, and smiled and waved at her husband. He responded with his bandanna.

Mine eyes have seen the glory of the coming of the Lord. . . .

They were singing the "Battle Hymn" again. After the last salvo of "Hallelujahs," the tumult finally subsided. Delegates returned to their seats. Roosevelt could not begin speaking until the formal convention photograph had been taken. Everybody froze as a corona of flashbulbs popped. The explosion somehow ignited one of the dangling white cotton bags (which apparently functioned as air purifiers) and, to screams from below, a tongue of flame leaped out. Before panic could spread, a fireman crawled catlike up the nearest beam and smothered the blazing bag with his bare hands.

⁓

ROOSEVELT'S ADDRESS, ENTITLED "A Confession of Faith," lasted for two hours. "And they wished more!" he wrote Kermit afterward. Applause stopped him 145 times, most loudly when he espoused the cause of woman suffrage, and berated the "twilight zone" between federal and state judiciaries. For all the cheers it aroused, the speech was a dry statement of policy, resembling one of the giant Messages he used to inflict on Congress every December during his presidency. It amounted to a survey of the entire Progressive program, more detailed and less self-referential than the blueprint he had issued at Osawatomic in 1910. Throughout, Roosevelt used the pronoun *we* rather than *I*.

He dismissed the Republican and Democratic parties as "husks," saying they were "boss-ridden and privilege-controlled." In the new one, only the people would rule against yesterday's alliance of Wall Street lawyers and Old Guard congressmen, aided and abetted by conservative newspaper publishers. That meant a nationwide presidential primary system, popular election of senators, votes for women, full disclosure of campaign funding, and laws to prevent fraud and trickery at the polls. The triple power of the initiative, referendum, and recall would be made available to various states, on the understanding that it should be exercised with extreme caution, in situations where representative government was threatened. Caution was not elsewhere going to be a feature of the Progressive Party's attitude toward protecting what Roosevelt, in one of his few passages of eloquence, called "the crushable elements" at the base of American society.

> The dead weight of orphanage and depleted craftsmanship, of crippled workers and workers suffering from trade diseases, of casual labor, of insecure old age, and of household depletion due to industrial conditions are, like our depleted soils, our gashed mountainsides and flooded river bottoms, so many strains upon the national structure, draining the reserve strength of all industries and showing beyond all peradventure the public element and public concern in industrial health.

He declared, as he had so often done as president, "There can be no greater issue than that of conservation in this country." He promised a sheaf of new federal statutes to set minimum wage and workplace standards, compensate for job-related injuries, strengthen his own pure-food law of 1906, and institute a system of "social insurance" with medical coverage for the poor. He endorsed an income-tax amendment to the Constitution. If he was returned to the White House, new or revived federal agencies would include a department

" 'AND THEY WISHED MORE!' "

Roosevelt's two-hour address to the Progressive National Convention, 6 August 1912.

of public health, plus commissions to inquire into the rising cost of living, improve rural conditions, and regulate interstate industrial corporations. He warned that the last-named commission would have "complete power" to investigate, monitor, publicize, and if necessary prosecute irresponsible trusts.

Once or twice, quailing at the bulk of his twenty-thousand-word typescript, he suggested that sections of it should be omitted "as read." The crowd was insatiable: "Go on, go on." He tried to skip the tariff, his least favorite subject, and was reprimanded. Even so, he tore out and crumpled some later pages. It was plain that he had written them for press release, rather than to be declaimed.

At last came the line all wanted to hear, from his oration at the Chicago Auditorium. "I say in closing what in that speech I said in closing: We stand at Armageddon, and we battle for the Lord."

The response was tumultuous. If Progressivism was, as more and more critics were suggesting, a religion, it needed its mantras, and could not hear them enough. Roosevelt ducked out of the hall at 3:30 P.M., pursued by the sound of ten thousand voices singing his name, to the tune of "Maryland, My Maryland."

✑

WHEN RAYMOND ROBINS* saw him again, in his hotel parlor late that night, he was resting his tired head against the mantelpiece.

"Colonel," Robins said, "they have just voted down four planks."

In another room, a subcommittee of the Resolutions Committee, chaired by William Draper Lewis, dean of the University of Pennsylvania law department, was trying to nail down the Party's campaign platform. Lewis had been agonizing over this all-important "contract with the people" since July. A group of moonbeamers, led by Gifford and Amos Pinchot, was determined to substitute some radical planks for the more pragmatic ones favored by Perkins, Beveridge, and the Colonel himself. Their efforts had apparently succeeded.

"Each one of those planks will go back," Roosevelt angrily told Robins, "or I am not a candidate."

The result, in the small hours of Wednesday morning, was a compromise platform that mentioned neither prohibition nor race, but awarded the Colonel his battleships and retained the regulatory plank as written by himself and Perkins—more accurately, handwritten on various slips of paper, some of them dating as far back as May. It formalized in prose all the other promises Beveridge and Roosevelt had made verbally, committing the Progressive Party to a vast program of social, economic, and environmental reform. For once, Roosevelt was entitled to a superlative when he called it "much the most important public document promulgated in this country since the death of Abraham Lincoln."

A day of steady drizzle dawned. Delegates found the visitor galleries of the Coliseum largely deserted when they filed in under the giant moose head, shaking their umbrellas. Hours of report-reading by various committee chairs, as well as presentation and adoption of the platform, had to be endured before the nominating speeches could begin. Since there was only one candidate, those were unlikely to be news. Only then would the convention be informed whom the Colonel had chosen as his running mate. Most bets were on Benjamin B. Lindsey of Colorado.

In the late afternoon, William A. Prendergast, comptroller of New York City, presented Roosevelt's name to automatic cheers. His remarks cost him

---

* Convention delegate, chairman of the Illinois Progressive Central Committee.

no effort, as he had written them over two months before to deliver at the Republican convention. "There is no other man in American life," he said, "who, in public office or out of it, has by his devotion to its interests, made so complete and genereous a contribution to the cup of its achievements."

When Judge Lindsey rose to give the first seconding speech, realization spread that the diminutive Democrat was not going to be on the ticket. Jane Addams followed him to the rostrum. "I second the nomination of Theodore Roosevelt because his is one of the few men in our public life who has been responsive to the social appeal, and who has caught the significance of the modern movement," she said, in the first address ever made by a woman to a national convention.

Finally, at seven o'clock, Beveridge announced that the Colonel had chosen Governor Hiram Johnson of California to run with him.

The two men came out together (Johnson notably shorter and stockier) to a roar of acclaim that formalized their nomination. Roosevelt seemed genuinely moved. The religiosity in the hall surged to the point of delirium, but yesterday's alarm was gone from his face. He stood arm-in-arm with Johnson as fifes and drums, a trombone quartet, and a full band led the crowd of ten thousand in singing the Doxology—its meter syncopated by the popping of a minute gun in the organ loft:

> *Praise God, from whom all blessings flow;*
> *Praise Him, all creatures here below;*
> *Praise Him above, ye heavenly host,*
> *Praise Father, Son, and Holy Ghost.*

CHAPTER 12

There Was No Other Place
on His Body

O no, not now! He'll not be going now:
There'll be time yet for God knows what explosions
Before he goes.

THE PROGRESSIVE NATIONAL CONVENTION did not strike everyone as a transcendental event. "In form, two thousand delegates, more or less, gathered in the Coliseum," Senator George Sutherland of Utah told Vice President James S. Sherman. "In reality, Mr. Roosevelt met in convention at Chicago, made a confession of faith, gave his hand to the colored brother from the north and his foot to the colored brother from the south, adopted a platform, nominated himself and brother Johnson, and adjourned with the ease of a thoroughly trained thimblerigger plying his vocation among the rural visitors to the Midway plaisance."

The more measured view of *The New York Times* was that Roosevelt's statement of Progressive policy had been "the best, the ablest, the most persuasive of all his public utterances." That did not alter the chilling fact that what the Colonel wanted was "a vast system of state socialism." If returned to power, he would regulate business with a rod of iron, fixing prices and redistributing profits. He would make Washington the nation's welfare center, and emulate Lloyd George in the profligate bestowal of old-age pensions and industrial insurance. Worse still, he would subject "the whole organic law" of the United States, including its constitutional checks and balances, "to an endless series of judgments of the people, expressed at the polls." Armageddon had no real place in his mythology. "He stood at Chicago and preached socialism and revolution, contempt for law, and doctrines that lead to destruction."

Ray Stannard Baker, noting the paternalistic trend in Roosevelt's philosophy, was no longer prepared to concede that he was a "true liberal," much less a political genius. "At this very moment of his triumph in Chicago, I believe TR to be on his way downward. He has even now passed the zenith of his power—unless it be the power for evil."

And at the lowest level of American political opinion, John F. Schrank, thirty-six years old and unemployed, read in two New York newspapers that the Colonel was determined to overthrow the Constitution. Brooding over them, he was reminded of a nightmare he had had eleven years before, in which the ghost of the assassinated William McKinley pointed at Roosevelt and said, "This is my murderer, avenge my death."

⁀

"OF COURSE I DO not for a moment believe that we shall win," Roosevelt wrote Kermit after returning to Oyster Bay. "The chances are overwhelmingly in favor of Wilson, with Taft and myself nearly even, and I hope with me a little ahead. . . ."

He may have been reading a *Washington Post* article on election odds currently being offered along Wall Street. Wilson was the 2-to-1 favorite of financiers, the class that felt most threatened by the Bull Moose platform. The odds of Roosevelt beating Taft were no better than 5 to 4 and 10 to 7. Politically, the nation was so piebald, with race prejudice darkening the South, and fields of progressivism, protectionism, socialism, and anarchism splotching the rest of the map, that not even a candidate of his enormous appeal could hope to be elected on mere popularity.

Nicholas and George Roosevelt visited Sagamore Hill that August and found their cousin uninhibited by the prospect of a doomed campaign. On the contrary, he was in uproarious form. He said he did not intend to hit the speaking trail in earnest until September, and in the meantime wanted to get as much frenetic exercise as possible. His apotheosis in Chicago seemed to have rejuvenated him. The hotter the weather, the greater his oversupply of energy. "You've got to play a set of tennis! You've got to play a set of tennis!" he chanted, beating Nicholas over the head with his racquet. The young man joined him in doubles against Archie and Ethel, and whenever Roosevelt hit a winning shot, he hopped across the court on one foot, singing and chortling.

Something of his *élan vital* seemed to communicate itself to Woodrow Wilson, summering more sedately on the New Jersey shore. "He is a real, vivid person," the governor wrote in a rare moment of self-criticism. "I am a vague, conjectural personality, more made up of opinions and academic prepossessions than of human traits and red corpuscles."

Roosevelt did not know it, but he had been the focus of Wilson's direct gaze earlier in the year. A coincidence in their respective primary campaigns had scheduled them both to address rallies in Princeton. Wilson had been able to sit in the Nassau Inn and watch Roosevelt speaking outside. He had not been impressed by the Colonel's rhetoric, with its constant, shuttlecock rebound between the extremes of any issue.

Although Wilson knew that he could never match Roosevelt's energy and charm, he underestimated his own force as a campaigner. At fifty-five, he was formidably mature, intellectually imposing, by no means inhuman, and about as vague as a racehorse in sight of the pole. A few early, disastrous failures on the primary circuit had taught him how to moderate his cerebral style without descending to the crowd-pleasing platitudes that Roosevelt used almost as a form of punctuation. Wilson developed a gift of expressing complexities in the simplest language, driven home with just the right colloquialism. When he improvised a joke, it was usually a good one. Roosevelt, so funny in social life and in confidential correspondence, was overcome by moral seriousness on the stump. The face he presented to press cameras was severe. What laughs he got with improvised asides were often the result of his squeaky voice and facial grimaces.

He had not begun to see Wilson as a threat until they both emerged as avatars of progressivism in 1911. Now they were seriously opposed to each other. For the first time in more than a quarter-century, Roosevelt assessed someone who had the power to beat him.

> Wilson is a good man who has in no way shown that he possesses any special fitness for the Presidency. Until he was fifty years old, as college professor and college president he advocated with skill, intelligence and good breeding the outworn doctrines which were responsible for four fifths of the political troubles of the United States. . . . Then he ran as Governor of New Jersey, and during the last eighteen months discovered that he could get nowhere advocating the doctrines he had advocated, and instantly turned an absolute somersault so far as least half these doctrines was concerned. He still clings to the other half, and he has shown not the slightest understanding of the really great problems of our present industrial situation. . . . He is an able man, and I have no doubt could speedily acquaint himself with these problems, and would not show Taft's muddleheaded inability to try to understand them when left by himself. But he is not a nationalist, he has no real and deep-seated conviction of the things that I regard as most vital, and he is in the position where he can only win . . . by the help of the worst bosses in this country, and by perpetuating their control of their several states in return for their aid.

He is not a nationalist. In Rooseveltian parlance, that meant Wilson, the former girls' school teacher who had sat out the Spanish-American War and signed last year's peace manifesto in *The Christian Herald,* was not likely to be a strong commander in chief.

❧

"I KNOW IT, BUT I can't do it. I couldn't if I would and I wouldn't if I could."

William Howard Taft was responding to a reporter's suggestion that he should emulate some of Roosevelt's headline-grabbing tricks in order to energize his campaign for reelection. After his desperate attempts to win sympathy in the spring, only to be humiliated in the Massachusetts, Maryland, and Ohio primaries, he was resolved not to hustle for votes again. The electorate would have to judge him by his record—in token of which, he launched now into a defense of his tariff policy, detailed enough to turn two and a half newspaper columns gray. "Under the Dingley law the average percent of the imports that came in free was 44.3 percent in value of the total importations; the average percent in value of the imports which have come in free under the Payne law is 51.2 percent of the total importations. . . ."

Taft knew that he bored people, and did not much care. Archie Butt had been dismayed at the President's lack of concern for the feelings of others. He kept people waiting for as many hours as suited him, even while he napped, and never apologized. At dinner, he would help himself to two-thirds of a beef tenderloin, before allowing his guests to share the remainder. He made no effort to shorten his speeches, aware that audiences could not walk out on a President. When his faults were pointed out to him, he listened placidly, registering nothing.

At the moment he was in a particularly obstinate mood, vetoing bill after bill as Congress sweltered to the end of its long session. The breezy golf links of Beverly beckoned. Taft was happy to let the Republican National Committee handle his campaign, under the chairmanship of his former secretary, Charles D. Hilles. As for himself, "I have no part to play but that of a conservative, and that I am going to play."

❧

WHAT WITH TED, Eleanor, and "Baby Gracie" in residence for the summer, plus Archie, Quentin, and various other Roosevelts coming and going (mostly coming, it seemed to Eleanor), Sagamore Hill was once again the noisy, teeming epicenter it had been in the first decade of the century. The only relatively quiet hours, undisturbed by phone bells and shouted dialogues up and down the bare, clattering stairs, were between one and six in the morning. The Colonel played daily host to reporters and politicos, frequently introducing group to group and then escaping on horseback before his absence was detected. At other times he took refuge in the woods, felling dead trees amid a miasma of mosquitoes, or crammed his family into rowboats and headed for "picnic spots" chosen, apparently, only for their remoteness. Eleanor, to whom the notion of *al fresco* dining conjured up pleasant associations of chicken salad and lettuce sandwiches wrapped in wax paper, was disconcerted by her first experience of one of these forays:

> By the time everybody was settled there was nowhere for me but a small space between the basket of clams and the demijohn of water in the flat-bottomed boat manned by Ted and his cousin George.
>
> Under the blazing sun we rowed and rowed. There was no breeze. The Sound was as calm as glass. . . . Two hours later we landed on a beach precisely like the one we had started from except that it was farther from home. The boats were drawn up on the sand, and we settled ourselves at the water's edge, unable to go near the trees because of poison ivy. The provisions were spread out and a kettle filled to make tea. The thought of hot tea was depressing enough, but it was worse to see the roaring fire built over the clams. When they were judged ready Colonel Roosevelt selected one, opened it, sprinkled it with salt and pepper, and handed it to me. It was large, with a long black neck. I managed to get it all in my mouth, burning myself quite badly. Although gritty with sand, it was delicious at first, but that soon wore off and it became a piece of old rubber hose. . . . Finally I slipped it under a log, but not deftly enough to escape Colonel Roosevelt's eye.
>
> "You aren't as persistent as Archie," he observed. "The first time he was old enough to eat a clam on a picnic he chewed for a time, then ate three sandwiches, some cookies, and an orange. Later he asked what he should do with the poor little dead clam. It was still in his mouth!"

Because of headwinds, it took twice as long for the party to row home. After a few weeks of Rooseveltian hospitality, Eleanor found that she had lost twenty-six pounds.

One night after dinner the Colonel sat on the piazza with Ted, Archie, Nicholas, and George. Rocking in his chair, he said he was "dumbfounded" by the fervor he had aroused at the Progressive convention.

George remarked that whereas he had once been a radical among conservatives, he must now be the reverse. Roosevelt accepted the suggestion enthusiastically. "Yes, yes! That's it! I have to hold them in check all the time. I've got to restrain them."

A more agitated rocker on the porch that August was Alice, talking politics, as Edith complained to Ethel, "like molasses blobbing out of a bottle." She and Nick were spending the summer apart, their marriage on the verge of collapse. It was 1910 all over again, except that Nick's divided loyalties were even more strained, now that his father-in-law was directly challenging the President. Nick's whole instinct was to remain in the mainstream of the Republican Party. But the moment was near when he was going to have to define himself publicly in campaigning for reelection. Edith was unsympathetic. "I wish to goodness that Nick would come out flat footed and work for Taft, or do something! It is hard on everyone!"

Contrary to her private, bookish nature, Edith had become politicized by the two Chicago conventions. Madame Defarge, sternly knitting her husband's doom in June, had been unable to resist the sight of thousands of Progressives turning toward her box, on the day of his "Confession of Faith," and roaring for her to stand up and show herself. She knew as well as Theodore did that he was headed for defeat, but she was happy that *he* was happy in his new guise as a social reformer.

⌒

BY THE END OF the month, all three candidates—or four, if Eugene V. Debs was to be counted as a presidential possibility—had launched their campaigns. Wilson chose to do so at an agricultural fair in New Jersey. His belly full of fried chicken, he surveyed his audience of two thousand farmers (their children frolicking nearby on merry-go-rounds and roller coasters) and dispensed with his prepared speech on the tariff. He told them that the White House was their property. "What I modestly suggest is that you proceed to break into your own house. . . . The tenants who have been living there a long time have been making you pay the rent, instead of paying rent to you."

Taft broke his vow of presidential silence long enough to issue a reproof to voters who registered as Republicans but supported "the candidate of another party." Every curve of his massive body, now approaching its lifetime peak weight of 340 pounds, expressed disillusionment with the office Roosevelt had cajoled him into. By universal consent, his liberation was at hand. But the prospect of handing power back to his patron was not to be borne.

"As the campaign goes on and the unscrupulousness of Roosevelt develops," the President wrote his wife, "it is hard to realize that we are talking about the same man whom we knew in the presidency." The peacemaker of Portsmouth had mutated into the half-crazed leader of a religious cult. "I have not any feeling of enmity against him," Taft told her, "or any feeling of hatred. I look upon him as an historical character of a most peculiar type in whom are embodied elements of real greatness, together with certain traits that have now shown themselves in unfitting him for any trust or confidence by the people."

As he penned these words, Debs, in Terre Haute, Indiana, was warning working-class Americans that there was little to choose between the three major candidates. All of them stood for "private ownership of the sources of wealth and the means of life." The only real choice, therefore, was between Democracy—the real, socialistic kind, with wealth and opportunity equalized by law—and Plutocracy, otherwise known as the *status quo*.

Debs was sensible enough to know that his alternative was not likely to be chosen in November, if ever in the United States as presently constituted. But he was not far wrong in suggesting that Roosevelt, Wilson, and Taft were three panels of a triptych, linked and painted with the same capitalistic brush. They differed from one another only in ideological color and fineness of detail.

On the left, the Colonel and his Party offered by far the most advanced program of reform, with enough administrative and legislative proposals to keep the federal government busy for two decades. The Chicago platform was essentially a rewording, in legalistic language, of Roosevelt's "Confession of Faith," amplified with many slighter, but still significant initiatives, such as vows to revise the currency, register lobbyists, fight illiteracy, and adjust road-ways to the coming of the motor age. There were so many other proposals re-garding health care, flood control, parcel post, patent law, and foreign commerce that Wilson joked it would take "a Sabbath day's drive" just to plow through the whole Progressive agenda.

His own, centrist platform combined the kind of small-*p* progressivism he had pioneered as governor of New Jersey with the traditional emphasis Democrats put on states' rights. If Wilson sounded, at times, like a populist, it was because he felt he had to gratify the old "Commoner," William Jen-nings Bryan, who had helped bring about his nomination. He undertook to control malfeasant corporations with as much force as Roosevelt, but said he would do so by strengthening the antitrust law, not by regulation. He was for a revenue-only tariff instead of the protective one that his rivals preferred. Woman suffrage was an issue only slightly less abhorrent, to his Southern sup-porters, than Negro enfranchisement, so Wilson was content to let Mrs. J. Borden Harriman and other Northern feminists fight that fight for him. Oth-erwise, he showed as much social concern as Roosevelt, except that he sympa-thized more with credit-stressed farmers than with workers exploited in large cities.

Taft, on the Republican right, took what had become the obligatory stance among all candidates of opposition to special privilege and monopoly. He could justifiably boast of Attorney General Wickersham's strong record as a trust-buster. Like Wilson, he called for more prosecutorial powers, and like the Progressive moonbeamers restrained by George Perkins, clearer defini-tions of acts that might be criminalized as monopolistic. This was as far as the GOP platform enabled Taft to go in appealing to popular reform sentiment. The rest of the document amounted to a virtual reprint of its predecessors in 1908 and 1904, but purged of progressive values.

AT THE BEGINNING of September, Roosevelt set out from New York with a herd of small silver bull mooses in his luggage, to give away to children. He intended to barnstorm for a month, from New England to the far Northwest, continuing via California, the Rockies, and the breadbasket states deep into Dixie. By the time he got home via the mid-Atlantic seaboard, he would have covered nine thousand miles, and become the first presidential campaigner ever to encircle the country.

Ray Stannard Baker caught an early glimpse of him at a depot in Hartford, Connecticut, addressing a large crowd in the rain. "He looked, as usual, as hard as a maple knot—and seemed to be enjoying himself." But Baker, now one of Wilson's keenest supporters, thought the Colonel was beginning to show signs of demagoguery, with bizarre proposals to emulate the authoritarian agricultural policies of Germany and Denmark, and to use American schoolhouses as political forums. "He is a dangerous man who makes the people feel intensely without making them think clearly."

Even in miserable weather, Roosevelt radiated conviviality—so much so that rumors again circulated that he was on the bottle. He had been drunk at Osawatomie, befuddled at the Ohio constitutional convention, and soused at Armageddon. A citizen of Butte, Montana, assured one of the reporters on his train that the Colonel had been seen knocking back fourteen highballs in fifteen minutes.

The reporter did not file this story, but Roosevelt heard about it and asked his campaign team to watch out for a clear case of published libel.

Although there were a few stretches of Democratic territory that received him coldly, most of the crowds greeting him were large. Official welcomers climbed aboard at every minor depot, sure that he was as thrilled as they were to see the band, bemedaled veterans, and babes in arms on the platform. Their salutations became so predictable that scribes in the press car developed a convenient code for wire dispatch, "GXLC."*

Some outdoor audiences spread so far in all directions that Roosevelt had to project his remarks at them section by section. "Friends," he yelled to a mob of twenty-five thousand at the Minnesota State Fair, "this is the only time I ever wished I could face two ways at once—or even five ways at once, but I'd have to be built like a starfish to do it."

Words failed him in Spokane on 9 September, when he found himself the only man in an auditorium full of women. Washington was one of the most advanced of the suffrage states. He could not hide the fact that for most of his

* "Great Excitement! Local Committee!"

life, feminism had passed him by. "My fellow citizens," he began awkwardly, "this is the first meeting of this kind I have ever addressed."

A strange muffled noise stopped him. It was the sound of gloved hands clapping. Unsure of how to proceed, he tried, then abandoned, the preachy tone that served him well with male audiences. He praised the Progressive Party for adopting a full suffrage plank, and spoke of his new friendship with Jane Addams. Thanks largely to her, he had become a convert to the cause. "It's because I'm a natural democrat. I don't like to associate with people unless they have the same rights I have."

By now Roosevelt was talking naturally, and his listeners were sympathetic. "I was converted from a passive suffragist to an active suffragist," he said, "by seeing women who had been doing social reform work." In addition to Miss Addams, he cited as new friends Maud Nathan, the child labor activist, and Frances Kellor, an advocate for the immigrant poor and founder of the National League for the Protection of Colored Women. He rejected Democratic and Republican warnings that extension of the suffrage would lead to the breakup of the American home. On the contrary, "I believe it will tend toward . . . an increase in the sense of copartnership between the man and the woman, and make each think more of the rights of the other than of his or her own rights. . . . People say to me, 'Men are different from women.' Yes, but I have never met any differences so great as the differences between some men and other men."

—✵—

TWO NIGHTS LATER, John F. Schrank sat writing poetry in his two-dollar-a-week apartment in downtown Manhattan. It was the anniversary of the assassination of William McKinley.

When night draws near
And you hear a knock
And a voice should whisper
Your time is up. . . .

As he wrote, he felt the ghost of the dead president lay a hand on his shoulder. It did not stop his pen.

Refuse to answer
As long as you can
Then face it and be a man.

❧

ROOSEVELT'S SUCCESS WITH local audiences was achieved at the expense of the kind of newsy, national headlines his campaign organization had been hoping for. He kept repeating his trust-control, tariff, and labor policies, and when he contrasted them with those of Woodrow Wilson, his oratory became impersonal, as if he was reluctant to launch a direct attack on the governor. By the second week in September, he had fallen into a rhythm of replying to whatever points Wilson chose to raise, without coming up with new or challenging ones of his own. There was a brief tossing of Bull Moose antlers at San Francisco on the fourteenth, when he effectively portrayed Wilson as a doctrinal academic, and Taft as a political corpse, but then his speeches became bland again. Word got back to Party headquarters in New York that the Colonel had gone "stale." The campaign was losing ground. Wilson—in the midst of his own Western tour—was moving ahead in most states. Only California seemed certain to vote Progressive.

O. K. Davis, the Party's overtaxed publicity director, set to work on a briefing book that would rearm Roosevelt with anti-Wilson material. In the meantime he hoped that his other star speakers, most notably Hiram Johnson and Albert Beveridge, would arouse audiences more than the Colonel seemed to be doing.

It was left to Charles Willis Thompson of *The New York Times* to point out that Roosevelt, stale or not, had already addressed a million people. The muted reaction to many of his speeches moreover, did not denote apathy so much as "a quiet, steady, intent earnestness that does not often characterize a crowd at a political meeting."

On the date that Thompson wrote this, Sunday, 22 September, Roosevelt spent a few relaxed hours at the Emporia, Kansas, home of William Allen White. Late that afternoon White drove him down to the station in a two-seat surrey, rolling through a sea of tall grass. Several hundred well-scrubbed souls waited on the platform. It was clear they hoped for a sermon before the candidate left town. Roosevelt managed a few bromides about righteousness. Amazingly, even these words were taken as a benediction. "There was no applause," recalled a Progressive bystander. "Tears stood in some men's eyes. When the train pulled out for the East, that crowd stood and waved as long as there was a speck in sight."

❧

IN AN EFFORT to reach voters living remote from his itinerary, but within range of a phonograph, Roosevelt cut five 78 rpm shellac discs that featured short extracts from his campaign speeches. They were distributed and sold by the Victor Talking Machine Company, along with others recorded by Wilson and Taft. His sharp singsong voice sawed through needle hiss, articulating every syllable with rounded vowels and rolled *r*s ("Ow-er aim is to prro-mote prros-perr-i-ty") and decisive downward swoops at the end of each sentence.

Personally, he was tired of his own rhetoric and press images (always distressing) of himself on the stump—two years tireder than he had been during the campaign of 1910. "I am hoarse and dirty and filled with a bored loathing of myself whenever I get up to speak," he wrote Kermit. "I often think with real longing of the hot, moonlit nights on our giant eland hunt, or in the white rhino camp, with the faithful gun-boys talking or listening to the strumming of the funny little native harp. . . ."

⟢

MISSOURI. OKLAHOMA. ARKANSAS. TENNESSEE. Grinding across the dank flats of Louisiana, he braced himself for a swing through Mississippi and Alabama to Georgia, where he would try to make the most of his Bulloch ancestry. He was in Democratic territory now, and as a Republican renegade, could not hope to see many friendly black faces. Even Booker T. Washington had decided to come out for Taft.

"Theodore Roosevelt has spent some time in Africa," the *African Methodist Episcopal Church Review* noted, "but he has never spent one second inside of a black skin." If he had, he might understand the impact of his letter to Julian Harris on people long treated as a separate species—indeed, as a sub-species. His "monstrous, unpatriotic, unjust and politically immoral" attempt to "array the Northern Negro against the Southern Negro" was reminiscent of the bad old days of Reconstruction.

> Then, men said it was to be "A White Man's War;" now, he says that his cause is to be frankly "put in the hands of the best white people of the South." . . . He refuses to fight and free the Negroes from disfranchisement, peonage and degrading laws that unjustly discriminate. He would recall judges who decide favorably in business and labor controversies, but has no word of reprobation for Judge Lynch; he would recall judicial decisions, but will not include the decisions upholding Jim Crow laws; he would destroy the political bosses, while at the same time he is delivering the Negroes into political despotism. He proclaims "the right of the people to rule;" but denies them the privilege of exercising that right if the people happen to be black.

These *touchés* might have been more damaging had they not appeared in a periodical whose title seemed designed to keep readership to a minimum. Everything Roosevelt saw of Southern Progressives flocking to his banner convinced him that his "lily-white" policy was working. "It is impossible,"

Charles Thompson reported from Atlanta on 28 September, "to give any idea of the hold that the idea of 'a new white man's party' has taken on in the South." Segregationists who believed that the Negro should nevertheless be treated as a human being felt liberated from the hate policies of the Democratic Party, while old-time Populists had turned into "religious zealots, and they look on him as an apostle."

Encouraged, the Colonel went out of his way to antagonize some Democratic hecklers when he spoke that night in the Atlanta Auditorium. He practically called Woodrow Wilson a liar for misquoting a remark he had made about the "inevitable" rise of monopolistic corporations. "He has no right . . . to attribute to me words which I have never used."

Roosevelt forgot, or chose to ignore, that Wilson's professional career had begun in Georgia. He blustered on in a way that grated on the sensibilities of his listeners, used as they were to the polite formalities of Southern speech. There were ten thousand people in the hall, including two thousand standees who crowded close to the stage to get a better view of him. As heckling spread and anger grew, he sprang onto the speaker's table and bellowed, "I'll get up here so you'll all have a chance to see me." His truculence momentarily struck the crowd dumb. Afterward, he had to be hustled out a side door.

❧

HE RETURNED TO Oyster Bay on 2 October, worn out from his trip, only to find that O. K. Davis had organized another, to begin in a matter of days. It would link strategic points of the Midwest that he had missed the first time around, including lower and upper Michigan, the main cities of Minnesota, Illinois, and Wisconsin, and scores of lesser whistle-stops across the heartland of Republican insurgency. Wilson was again barnstorming that territory, attracting huge crowds, and looking more and more like the next President of the United States. Roosevelt had so far managed only to pull well ahead of Taft and Debs. His best hope was to make such a strong second-place finish as to confirm regulatory Progressivism as the political philosophy of the future.

Willard Straight, a family friend of the Roosevelts, came to visit and found Sagamore Hill a gloomy place. He got the impression that Theodore and Edith were worried about money, with two boys still boarding in expensive schools and each looking forward to four years at Harvard. Roosevelt was also harassed by yet another Senate probe—this time into charges that he had accepted improper campaign contributions in 1904. The committee's evidence, focusing on an alleged $25,000 payment from Standard Oil in exchange for immunity from antitrust prosecution, made no sense, because he had sued the company anyway. But he now had to sacrifice a day of rest and go to Washington to testify.

After he got back, a conference of Progressive leaders took place at Sag-

amore Hill. Senator Dixon presided, with George Perkins exuding new authority as chairman of the Party's Executive Committee. Hiram Johnson was
there, a small man with a loud voice, and Oscar Straus, who was running for
governor of New York, along with Frank Munsey and Walter F. Brown, the
Ohio boss.

It was essentially a godspeed session, to cheer the Colonel up and discuss
strategy and tactics for the final four weeks of the campaign. Wilson had
come up with a catchy slogan, promising Americans a "New Freedom" to restore the balance of government and individualism that had served them so
well before the age of combination. It would be a policy subject, however, to
the restraints of modern antitrust law. In that respect it amounted to a Jeffer-
sonian rewrite of Roosevelt's New Nationalism—what Wilson, in another
telling phrase, called "government by experts."

The electorate had to be persuaded that the Progressive Party was not
paternalistic, nor was it a one-man band. Johnson had a twenty-two-state
speaking tour planned, while Straus took care of the Empire State, and Brown
worked to humiliate Taft at home. In Indiana, Albert Beveridge was also running for governor, pouring out a flood of eloquent addresses that were widely
reprinted. The Party had dozens of other gubernatorial aspirants campaigning as far south as Florida and Texas, plus state, Congressional, and local candidates in all regions of the country. A loose-strung but vital network of
bosses, reformers, publishers, and legislators supported this drive for recognition. In some states, including most of New England, the network sagged
hopelessly, due to lack of leadership or funds. But on the whole, Dixon's National Committee had distinguished itself—appointing, at the outset, four
women as members-at-large. That Progressivism had in fact spread so far,
staffed so many offices, and publicized so comprehensive an ideology since
August was something of a political miracle. Whatever the movement's immediate prospects, it looked to be firmly established in 1916. Roosevelt had to
hide the fact that he dreaded being asked to lead it again.

❧

"CHILDREN, DON'T CROWD so close to the car, it might back up, and
(*falsetto*) we can't afford to lose any little Bull Mooses, you know."

The Colonel was back in his private Pullman, the *Mayflower,* traveling
west. Young Philip Roosevelt attended as his personal aide, plus Dr. Scurry
Terrell, a throat specialist, Cecil Lyon, leader of the Texan Progressives, and
Henry F. Cochems, chairman of the Party speaker's bureau. O. K. Davis and
two stenographers, Elbert E. Martin and John W. McGrath, made up the rest
of the entourage. An adjoining car carried gentlemen of the press.

Roosevelt seemed a new man after his brief stay at home, quickly absorbing an eighty-thousand-word dossier on Wilson. Lawrence Abbott, reporting

for *The Outlook,* compared him to "an electric battery of inexhaustible energy," making decisions "with a celerity of judgment which takes one's breath away." At some stops, he was so charged that he would shadow-box through the caboose before bursting out and haranguing whatever throng he found ranged across the track. On 9 October alone, he gave thirty speeches in Michigan, pointedly quoting some anti-labor remarks that Wilson had made as president of Princeton.

"I'm fur Teddy," a scrubwoman declared. Asked why, she said, "He's fur me."

When not orating, he would dictate further speeches for use down the line. The toll on his voice soon began to show. There was something manic about the way he drove himself, and the way he ate: Philip's main duty was to keep large meals coming. Since February, Roosevelt had gained so much weight that Frank Munsey, a strict dieter, felt obliged to warn him of the coronary effect of too much heavily salted roast beef and Idaho potatoes. Rumors persisted that he was a boozer. "Did you see that?" somebody said in Duluth, Minnesota, as the Colonel's retinue hustled him through a surging crowd in the lobby of his hotel. "He was so drunk they had to carry him upstairs!"

Actually, "they" were worried about physical assaults, whether affectionate, as from those who wished to tear at his clothing, or worse. The fanaticism of his followers became more apparent the deeper he penetrated the Midwest. Almost half the population of Oshkosh, Wisconsin, turned out in pouring rain to hear him. His speech—a comparison of his and Wilson's tariff policies—was received as if it were the Holy Writ. He decided to use parts of it again when he spoke in Milwaukee, in the heart of La Follette country.

But first, Chicago beckoned: a much more favorable city, with Medill McCormick's newspaper, the *Tribune,* daily propounding Progressivism. By the time Roosevelt got there on the morning of the twelfth, Dr. Terrell was seriously concerned about his roughening throat, and persuaded him to cancel three speeches the following day. That afternoon Roosevelt addressed an open-air meeting. A raw wind blew in from the lake, nearly silencing him. After dinner he had to speak again, in the enormous Coliseum, and his voice broke altogether. For the next thirty-six hours he was reduced to whispering.

He should have nursed his laryngitis through Monday, 14 October, in order to save vocal strength for his important speech in Milwaukee that evening. But he impulsively decided to make an appearance in Gary, Indiana, the home of U.S. Steel. He wanted to show that he was not ashamed of his relationship with the world's biggest trust, nor of having one of its directors, George W. Perkins, as his closest adviser—something Wilson had drawn attention to.

Roosevelt spoke there for no more than four minutes, but it was enough to fray his voice again. He returned to Chicago for lunch. During the meal, O. K.

Davis handed him a letter from a well-wisher in Detroit, enclosing a newspaper clipping and suggesting that action should be brought against its publisher.

The clipping was only two days old, and came from the Ishpeming, Michigan, *Iron Ore,* a small Republican sheet owned and published by one George A. Newett. It concerned the Colonel's moral character, and contained the direct libel he had been looking for:

> Roosevelt lies and curses in a most disgusting way; he gets drunk too, and all his intimates know it.

He read the article through, then said to Davis, "Let's go at him."

❧

LATER THAT AFTERNOON, the *Mayflower* hitched itself to another train and headed for Wisconsin. Advance word came that a "GXLC" situation portended in Milwaukee, with plans for a grand parade and public dinner before Roosevelt's speech. Dr. Terrell refused to let his patient be subjected to these strains.

Upon the train's arrival in Milwaukee at six o'clock, members of the local Progressive committee came aboard, and were told that the Colonel was "extremely tired." He would dine privately in his car, rest for an hour or so, and not use his voice until the time came for him to speak at the Auditorium. Even then, he would be able to make only a few opening remarks. The main text of his address would have to be read for him. O. K. Davis explained that Roosevelt had long speeches scheduled every night for the rest of the campaign.

The committee chairman complained so bitterly that Roosevelt took pity on him and said to Davis, "I want to be a good Indian, O. K."

From that moment he was the committee's prisoner. He was driven through a mile-long, rejoicing crowd to the Gilpatrick Hotel on Third Street. A hospitality suite awaited him upstairs. Before sitting down to dinner, he lay back in a rocking chair and napped—something Davis had never seen him do before. Shortly after eight, he folded his speech typescript into his inner right jacket pocket and walked down two flights of stairs to the lobby. Henry Cochems and a bodyguard named Alfred Girard preceded him. He was flanked on one side by Elbert Martin and Cecil Lyon, and on the other by Philip Roosevelt and Fred Leuttisch, a Party security man.

❧

OUTSIDE IN THE ILL-LIT STREET, his roofless, seven-seat automobile stood waiting. A rope cordon kept the sidewalk clear, but several hundred onlookers clustered in the street beyond. Martin opened the vehicle's near rear door, and

Roosevelt got in. He took his customary right-hand seat while his escorts fanned out to take theirs. Lyon ran round the back. As he did so, the crowd in the street moved closer, cheering. The Colonel stood up to bow, waving his hat in his right hand.

Martin stepped up from the curb to join him. At that moment, he saw the gleam of a revolver no more than seven feet away. The stenographer was a powerful man with athletic reflexes, and was flying through the air even as John Schrank fired. Roosevelt was hit in the right breast and dropped without a sound. Philip, too horrified to move, thought, "He'll never get up again."

Martin lit on Schrank and had him around the neck in a half nelson as they crashed to the ground. Almost simultaneously, Leuttisch and Girard landed on top of them in a wild scrimmage. Lyon, whipping out his own Texas-sized automatic, threatened to shoot anyone else who came near.

It was easy enough to disarm Schrank, a weedy little man who put up no resistance. Meanwhile, Roosevelt had hoisted himself up in the tonneau. He was shaken, but did not appear to be bleeding. For the moment, nobody but he realized he had stopped a bullet. Looking down, he saw that Martin was trying to break Schrank's neck.

"Don't hurt him. Bring him here," Roosevelt shouted. "I want to see him."

Martin's blind rage cleared, and while still half-throttling his prisoner, he dragged him to the side of the automobile. Roosevelt reached down and, in an oddly tender gesture, took Schrank's head in both hands, turning it upward to see if he recognized him.

What he saw was the dull-eyed, unmistakable expressionlessness of insanity, along with clothes that looked as though they had been slept in for weeks, and an enormous pair of shoes.

By now, Dr. Terrell, O. K. Davis, and John McGrath, who were late arriving on the scene, had gotten past Lyon's gun and clustered around their chief. Roosevelt continued to stare at Schrank. "What did you do it for?" he asked, sounding more puzzled than angry. "Oh, what's the use? Turn him over to the police."

Girard and another officer hustled Schrank away as the Colonel's aides, still unsure if he had been shot, fingered his heavy army overcoat for a bullet hole. They soon found it. He explored further himself, not allowing anyone, even Terrell, to look. His hand came out with blood on it.

"He pinked me, Harry," he said to Cochems.

Terrell had heard enough. He told the driver of the automobile to head at once to Milwaukee's Emergency Hospital. But Roosevelt, to the disbelief of everyone around him, insisted on proceeding to the Auditorium.

"No, Colonel," Cochems pleaded. "Let's go to the hospital."

"You get me to that speech," Roosevelt replied, with a savage rasp to his voice.

Terrell, Davis, and Philip were no more successful in their appeals. The car cruised at parade speed to the Auditorium, through streets still lined with unsuspecting spectators. When it reached its destination, Roosevelt walked unaided to a holding room behind the stage. There, at last, he let Terrell examine his wound. It was a ragged, dime-sized hole, bleeding slowly, about an inch below and to the right of his right nipple. The bullet was nowhere to be seen or palpated. The whole right side of his body had turned black.

Again he brushed aside Terrell's demand that he seek immediate medical treatment. "It's all right, Doctor," he said, inhaling deeply, "I don't get any pain from this breathing." Plastering a clean handkerchief to his chest, he pulled his shirt down and strode onstage.

⤚⟳⤙

COCHEMS PRECEDED HIM to the podium. As the Progressive Party's senior local representative, he had the task of informing the audience—ten thousand strong, with at least as many milling outside—that Roosevelt had been the victim of an assassination attempt. He spoke shakily and vaguely, afraid of causing a riot, and caused only confusion. There was a cry of "Fake! Fake!" and direct appeals to the Colonel: "Are you hurt?"

Roosevelt stepped forward and gestured for silence. "It's true," he said. "But it takes more than that to kill a bull moose." There was some nervous laughter, so he unbuttoned his vest and exposed his shirtfront. The spreading bloodstain, larger than a man's hand, caused screams of horror. Voices called, "Turn this way—turn this way!"

He obliged, then said, "I'm going to ask you to be very quiet. I'll do the best I can."

Waiting for the noise to subside, he reached into his jacket pocket for his speech. The fifty-page typescript was folded in half. He did not notice that it had been shot through until he began to read. For some reason, the sight of the double starburst perforation seemed to shock him more than the blood he had seen on his fingertips. He hesitated, temporarily wordless, then tried to make the crowd laugh again with his humorous falsetto: "You see, I was going to make quite a long speech."

His heart was racing, and the wound felt hot. He proceeded to half-read, half-improvise a rambling rationale of his trust-control and labor policies in a voice no longer husky but weak. A knifelike pain in his ribs forced him to breathe in short gasps. Two or three times, he appeared to totter. Afraid that he was dying, Philip approached the podium and begged him to stop. But Roosevelt swung his head toward him with such a steel-gray stare that the young man retreated, helpless.

After about forty-five minutes Roosevelt asked how long he had been talking. Upon being told, he said, "I'll speak for a quarter of an hour more." In fact, he continued for well over half an hour, throwing down page after page as was his habit (the drilled sheets snapped up as souvenirs) and improvising an appeal to followers of Senator La Follette to lend their support to the Progressive Party. Although his voice remained forceful, he was clearly losing strength as well as blood. Aides stationed themselves below the footlights to

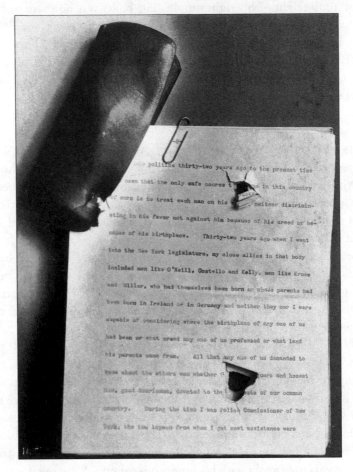

"HE DID NOT NOTICE THAT IT HAD BEEN SHOT THROUGH
UNTIL HE BEGAN TO READ."

Roosevelt's perforated speech manuscript and spectacle case.

catch him in case he fell forward, while others sitting onstage prepared to do the same behind. Toward the eighty-minute mark, Roosevelt's face was white, but he spoke on till there was no more paper in his hands. Then, turning from the tumultuous applause, he said to Dr. Terrell, "Now I am ready to go with you and do what you want."

Incredibly, members of the audience crowded around and tried to slap his back. Charles Thompson got the distinct impression that each man was intent on being the last to shake hands with Theodore Roosevelt. They were pushed away, and the Colonel, walking very slowly, was led back to his car. By ten o'clock he was in the care of doctors at Milwaukee's Emergency Hospital. Before being stripped and laid on the examination table he dictated a telegram to Edith, saying that he was in "excellent shape," and that the wound was "trivial."

He also asked that somebody contact Seth Bullock, of Deadwood, South Dakota, and be sure to mention that he had been shot with "a thirty-eight on a forty-four frame."

MEANWHILE, AT THE CITY police station, John F. Schrank was being exhaustively grilled. He was calm but badly bruised from being kicked and torn at by his attackers. If Roosevelt had not intervened to save him, he might well have been lynched. He handed over a written account of his visions of President McKinley calling for Roosevelt's death. A search of his pockets turned up another note, stating it was the duty of the United States to preserve the two-term tradition.

> Never let a third-term party emblem appear on an official ballot.
> I willing to die for my country, god has called me, to be his instrument.
> So help me god.
> Innocent Guilty
> Eine Fester Burg ist unser Gott.

A mighty fortress is our God. This is my body, this is my blood. The mock-religious aura that had glowed around Roosevelt since he first stood at Armageddon had reached its grotesque climax. News of the drama on the Auditorium stage flashed outward along telephone and telegraph wires, jolting every night editor in the country and penetrating even into the Casino Theatre in New York, where Edith Roosevelt sat watching Johann Strauss's *The Merry Countess.* She emerged from a side entrance weeping. "Take me to where I can talk to him or hear from him at once." A police escort whisked her to the Progressive National Headquarters in the Manhattan Hotel, which had an open line to Milwaukee. There, just before midnight, she heard that her husband's wound had been X-rayed and dressed. He was being transferred to Chicago's Mercy Hospital, where a team of thoracic specialists would consider whether the bullet in his chest could be safely removed.

It lay embedded against the fourth right rib, four inches from the sternum. In its upward and inward trajectory, straight toward the heart, it had had to pass through Roosevelt's dense overcoat into his suit jacket pocket, then through a hundred glazed pages of his bifolded speech into his vest pocket, which contained a steel-reinforced spectacle case three layers thick, and on through two webs of suspender belt, shirt fabric, and undershirt flannel, before eventually finding skin and bone. Even so, its final force had been enough to crack the rib.

"THE DULL-EYED, UNMISTAKABLE EXPRESSIONLESSNESS OF INSANITY."

John Schrank under arrest after attempting to kill Roosevelt, 14 October 1912.

Marveling at the freak coordination of all these impediments, a witness to the shooting noted that had Schrank's slug penetrated the pleura, the Colonel would have bled to death internally in a matter of minutes. "There was no other place on his body so thoroughly armored as the spot where the bullet struck."

❧

ROOSEVELT WAS BACK on board the *Mayflower* before midnight. His breathing hurt and his right arm was stiff, but he undressed without assistance, putting studs into a clean shirt for the morning, and shaving himself before he went to bed.

He was asleep before the train pulled out. It steamed extremely slowly, to rock him as little as possible, and glided into Chicago's Northwestern yard at

3:32 A.M. without whistling. A locomotive on an adjoining track was blowing off, but fell silent as the *Mayflower* approached and came to rest.

Even at that early hour, some four hundred persons were waiting on the platform. Among them was Dr. John B. Murphy, the nation's premier chest surgeon. He had an ambulance standing by to take the Colonel straight to Mercy Hospital, but was persuaded to let his patient sleep until it was light. At a quarter past six the ambulance drew up and Roosevelt appeared, leaning on Cecil Lyon's arm. He looked grave and pale, but when a press camera flashed and popped, he dryly remarked, "Ah, shot again."

With that he was hurried off by Murphy for more X-rays and tests.

At 10:30 the hospital issued its first bulletin, describing the extent of Roosevelt's injury, and stating a pulse rate of ninety and a temperature of 99.2°F. "No operation to remove bullet is indicated at the present time. Condition hopeful, but wound so important as to demand absolute rest for a number of days." The chief risk, since the pleura was intact, was of infection, if not poisoning, since nobody could be sure if Schrank's bullet (a floating cockroach of black ink in X-ray reproductions) had not been laced.

By 1 P.M., Room 308 of Mercy Hospital was so mobbed with personal and political visitors, oblivious of the pain it cost Roosevelt to talk, that Murphy issued another bulletin emphasizing that the wound was "serious," and that his patient needed complete quiet to recover. The surgeon was closemouthed about his decision not to probe for the bullet, but three consulting doctors concurred in a later statement that sent encouraging signals around the country:

> The records show that Colonel Roosevelt's pulse is 86; his temperature 99.2 and respiration 18; that he has less pain in breathing than he did in the forenoon; that he has practically no cough; that there has been no bloody expectoration.
>
> We find him in magnificent physical condition due to his regular physical exercise and his habitual abstinence from tobacco and liquor. As a precautionary measure he has been given tonight a prophylactic dose of antitetanic serum to guard against the development or occurrence of lockjaw. Leukocyte count 8800, lymphocytes 11.5.

Perhaps the best news for the patient was that his wife, undeterred by his repeated assurances that he had suffered worse accidents while riding, was on her way to see him and stand guard over his bed.

❧

DR. MURPHY'S POINTED reference to Roosevelt's abstemiousness spoke to one of the thousands of telegrams pouring into the LaSalle Hotel headquarters of the Progressive Party. It was from the supporter in Detroit whom O. K.

Davis had authorized to start a libel suit against George Newett, of the Ishpeming *Iron Ore*. He assumed that the Colonel still wished to proceed with the case. "I have retained Judge James H. Pound, one of the best men in Michigan, for such purposes, to represent him."

Among the other telegrams was one from William Howard Taft: "I am greatly shocked to hear of the outrageous and deplorable assault made upon you." Woodrow Wilson also wired a message of sympathy. He announced that he would suspend his campaign, bar a few unavoidable engagements, until Roosevelt was well again. "My thought is constantly of that gallant gentleman lying in the hospital at Chicago." Similar messages came in from Robert La Follette and William Jennings Bryan. A number of European crowned heads—some of whom had their own reasons to fear assassination attempts—sent get-well cablegrams. Vincent Curtis Baldwin of Chicago wrote enclosing a campaign donation of ten dollars that he said he had made selling flowers. "For I want you to be our President. If I was a man I'd help you, and work hard for you, and tell people how good you are, but I am only 10 years old."

AMONG THE MILLIONS of people wondering what effect the attack on Roosevelt would have on the election was Milwaukee's district attorney, charged with the prosecution of John F. Schrank. He informed the judge presiding at the arraignment that his prisoner would plead guilty, and asked for a postponement of trial proceedings until mid-November, so that politics would not interfere with justice. His request was approved. Senator Dixon and his committee gave public thanks for the Colonel's deliverance, but had to recognize, if only in some furtive recess of the heart, that Schrank had done the Progressive Party an enormous favor. All the hate that various political factions held for Roosevelt was subsumed in a surge of protective admiration. Mercy Hospital's bulletins indicated a slow but steady recovery, with no sepsis and no aftereffect of shock. The bullet in his ribs was apparently sterile, and he was resigned to carrying it for the rest of his days.

After a week in the hospital he was well enough to return to Sagamore Hill for his fifty-fourth birthday on 27 October. His wound was still open and his chest swollen with edema, but he decided that he needed to make another speech as soon as possible. To remain silent through the election would signal that he had been felled politically as well as physically. Voters needed to be assured that he was recovering, and reminded that Theodore Roosevelt was, surprisingly enough, the youngest of the four candidates now running. Debs was about to turn fifty-seven; Wilson would soon be fifty-six; Taft had just turned fifty-five.

He announced that he would address a mass meeting at Madison Square

Garden on the thirtieth. "I am in fine shape now," he wrote his sister Bamie, while admitting to William Flinn that he might need pharmaceutical help.

⁂

HIRAM JOHNSON was warming up the crowd of sixteen thousand at the Garden when a sound of distant cheering betokened Roosevelt's approach. It grew louder, and eventually drowned out Johnson's words. A sudden influx of newcomers filled the main entrance. For a moment or two the man they were escorting was invisible, but when he appeared on the prow of the platform, looking out over the sea of heads like a figurehead breasting foam, the uproar surged to hysterical levels. Dowagers climbed onto their chairs and screamed. Groups of men competed with one another to improvise noises even more raucous than the moose calls heard in the Chicago Coliseum in August. Heels drummed on the auditorium floor. Time and again, "Onward, Christian Soldiers" rose above the din.

As far as reporters could tell, there was nothing orchestrated about the demonstration. Roosevelt had to wait for more than forty minutes, looking at first amused, then tired, then impatient, as if his First Amendment rights were being abused. He got order at last by banging on the flag-draped speaker's table. Alert eyes noticed that he did so with his left hand. His face was ruddy, and when he began to speak, his voice easily filled the vast room. But there were no smacks of fist into palm. Occasionally he tried to raise his right arm, then winced and dropped it.

"Friends, perhaps once in a generation, perhaps not so often—" The crowd began roaring again. Roosevelt lost his temper and yelled, "Quiet, down there!" A hush ensued.

"—Perhaps not so often, there comes a chance for the people of a country to play their part wisely and fearlessly in some great battle of the age-long warfare for human rights."

This was approximately his 150th formal address of the campaign, and he had nothing new to say about Progressivism, much less about himself. As he spoke on, reporters were struck by the absence of the rancor he had often shown against Taft and Wilson on the stump. He mentioned neither by name, and seemed content to talk vaguely, yet feelingly, about the humanitarianism of his Party. "The doctrines we preach reach back to the Golden Rule and the Sermon on the Mount. They reach back to the commandments delivered at Sinai. All that we are doing is to apply those doctrines in the shape necessary to make them available for meeting the living issues of our own day."

⁂

ON TUESDAY, 5 November, a pall of privacy descended on Sagamore Hill for the first time in many months. Roosevelt was driven down to Oyster Bay at noon, and voted in the firehouse. After lunch, he and Edith went for a long walk in the woods. George Perkins arrived on the 4:05 train from New York, visited briefly, and hurried back to the station without saying anything to reporters.

At seven the Colonel dressed for dinner as usual, and dined with his wife and a cousin, Laura Roosevelt. Most of the younger family members were at the Progressive headquarters in the city, watching returns come in over the wires. Alice was in Cincinnati, miserably pessimistic, her marriage as tenuous as Nick Longworth's chances of another term in Congress.

The phone call Roosevelt was bracing for came at about eleven o'clock. Two hundred miles away, the bells of Princeton, New Jersey, began to peal, while those of Oyster Bay remained silent. Presently a servant came out of Sagamore Hill and hurried off with a telegram to Woodrow Wilson:

THE AMERICAN PEOPLE, BY A GREAT PLURALITY, HAVE
CONFERRED UPON YOU THE HIGHEST HONOR IN THEIR GIFT.
I CONGRATULATE YOU THEREON.

> THEODORE ROOSEVELT

Just before midnight the Colonel received reporters in his study. He was still in black tie. A log fire burned softly behind him.

"Like all other good citizens," he said, "I accept the result with good humor and contentment."

CHAPTER 13

A Possible Autobiography

And if he still remembers here
Poor fights he may have won or lost,—
If he be ridden with the fear
Of what some other fight may cost . . .

He may by contemplation learn
A little more than what he knew,
And even see great oaks return
To acorns out of which they grew.

BEFORE ROOSEVELT WENT to bed after hearing the election result, he dictated a letter to Kermit. It belied his sanguine words to the press. "Well, we have gone down in a smashing defeat; whether it is a Waterloo or a Bull Run, only time will tell."

He did not have to wait for a full count of the vote to see that Wilson had scored the greatest electoral victory yet accorded a presidential candidate. Forty states had gone to the governor, and only six to himself. Taft had to be content with Utah and Vermont. Debs secured none. The electoral college tally was just as disproportionate, with 435 votes for Wilson, 88 for Roosevelt, and 8 for Taft. In Congressional races, the Democratic Party was triumphant, winning control of the Senate and substantially increasing its majority in the House of Representatives.

In his still-fragile state, Roosevelt yielded to rage against Root, La Follette, and all the others who had hampered his campaign from the start. Their efforts, he told Kermit, had been backed by "95% of the press" and "the great mass of ordinary commonplace men of dull imagination who simply vote under the party symbol and whom it is almost as difficult to stir by any appeal

to the higher emotions and intelligence as it would be to stir so many cattle."
He railed at the "astounding virulence and hatred" of those who accused him
of everything from habitual drunkenness to mendacity. Even after he had been
struck down in Milwaukee, "the opposition to me was literally a mania. . . . I
now wish to take as little part as possible in political affairs and efface myself
as much as possible."

Like a female ranger living near Old Faithful, Edith Roosevelt understood
her husband's regular need to erupt. "You know him well enough," she
warned Kermit in a covering note, "to realize that he will paint the situation
in his letter to you in the blackest colors."

Gradually, Roosevelt realized that his loss was not as devastating as it at
first seemed. He had scored 4,126,020 popular votes over Taft's 3,483,922.
Wilson's winning total was only 6,286,124: William Jennings Bryan had done
better than him in *losing* four years before. Debs, by contrast, had doubled the
Socialist vote of 1908 to nearly a million. This last was a remarkable achievement, but Roosevelt's was historic. He had recruited a new party, schooled it
in his Confession of Faith, and brought it to second place in a well-fought
election. In just over ninety days, he had humbled a sitting president and deci-
sively beaten a party that had dominated national politics for forty years.
When the Progressive vote share, at just under 27.5 percent, was added to the
GOP's 23.2 percent, the Democratic total of 41.9 percent looked a lot less impressive. Technically, Wilson was a minority president.

This did not signify that Roosevelt would have inherited much of Taft's
support, had he won the GOP nomination and campaigned as a small-*p* progressive. He had always been anathema to the sort of Republicans who, on
election night in Darien, Connecticut, had stomped and burned a portrait of
him. But he might have forestalled Wilson's own nomination, so reluctantly
assented to by Democrats after forty-three ballots in Baltimore. Even if he had
not, he would have had an established party organization behind him, and a
platform that addressed itself to the changing national mood. His phenomenal personal popularity would have surged to new heights, along with his international renown. He would now probably be President-elect of the United
States, and John Schrank not in the dock for trying to kill him.

There remained the moral question that his black butler—no student of
Aristotle—was asking: whether by bolting the party that had once made him
president, had he not committed the fatal insolence? Was he now irreversibly
headed toward a pathetic, if not tragic end? Nothing in Roosevelt's strenuous
soul could entertain such an idea. He had cheated death. He had books to
write, trees to chop, sons to bring up, a daughter to marry off, and another
daughter to save from divorce (poor Nick had been defeated, and was taking
it out on Alice). Always, too, there was Edith.

ROOSEVELT ADMITTED TO feeling "a little melancholy" over the prospect of having to continue as head of the Progressive Party, when his real need was to start earning money again. His recent hospital and doctor bills, totaling between two and three thousand dollars, had cut into savings already depleted by marathon travels over the last two and a half years—not to mention the cost of entertaining hundreds of political pilgrims to Sagamore Hill. He had begun what was bound to be an expensive libel action against George Newett. And he suspected that Ethel was about to get engaged to her faithful doctor, Dick Derby. That would mean a large wedding in the spring. It could not compare in splendor to the White House nuptials of "Princess Alice" in 1906. But given the rise in prices under the Taft administration, it might run up a similar bill.

One way of making a great deal of money was to go on the lecture circuit. Demands for him to speak had become innumerable after his performance in the Milwaukee Auditorium. A novel feature of many of these invitations was the suggestion that he accompany his presentation with "moving pictures" of himself in Africa, Europe, and on the campaign trail. If there was not enough of such footage, more could easily be faked, using an impersonator and studio props.

Roosevelt was willing to address such institutions as the National Geographic Society and American Historical Association, with or without fee. He declined, however, to make an exhibition of himself on less prestigious platforms. "I could probably make a good deal of money by so doing," he wrote Kermit. "But I shrink to a degree greater than I can express from commercializing what I did as President or the reputation I have gained in public service."

He felt the same way about journalism. "I get from *The Outlook* a salary probably not more than one-eighth of what I could get by writing for the Sunday Hearst papers or the Sunday *World;* and nineteen men out of twenty would not see any difference; but there seems to me to be a very great difference." He had his dignity to consider, and in that regard, unselfconsciously compared himself to Lincoln, Milton, and Darwin. "With none of these would it be pardonable to consider the possible monetary return, whether for the presidency, for *Paradise Lost* or for *The Origin of Species.*"

There remained his perennial source of gentlemanly income: the publication of books. *African Game Trails* had been enormously profitable in its first-serial form, and a bestseller for a while, but thereafter only a modest success. The polite notes Charles Scribner attached to Roosevelt's half-yearly royalty checks did not quite mask editorial disappointment. Sales so far, in luxury and library editions, totaled fewer than forty thousand copies.

Looking back over his statements, Roosevelt could see that his other Scribner titles had lost momentum after his humiliation in the Congressional elections of 1910. Royalties earned by *Oliver Cromwell, The Rough Riders,* and *Outdoor Pastimes of an American Hunter* had fallen from $28,620 in February 1911 to $1,531 in February 1912. Oddly enough, his reemergence as the Bull Moose candidate had not arrested this slide; his latest check, for sales of all four books though 22 August, was a mere $895.

It was clear that something important had to come out of his pen during the winter, if he was going to reestablish himself as a man of letters. But what, and who would publish it? Most of the top houses in New York listed titles by him. G. P. Putnam's Sons had *The Naval War of 1812, Hunting Trips of a Ranchman, The Wilderness Hunter, The Winning of the West, American Ideals,* and *Theodore Roosevelt: Works,* a fifteen-volume set issued somewhat prematurely in 1900. The Century Company had *Ranch Life and the Hunting Trail, Hero Tales from American History, The Strenuous Life,* and *Stories of the Great West.* Houghton Mifflin had *Gouverneur Morris* and *Thomas Hart Benton;* Longmans, Green & Co., *New York: A Sketch;* and the Outlook Company, *The New Nationalism.* Bibliographically, it was an impressive list, especially when the Scribners quartet was added to it, along with overseas editions and translations. Commercially, he had to accept that all of his books except *The Rough Riders* were languishing in backlist.

Late in November he let it be known that he was thinking of publishing some autobiographical chapters in *The Outlook.* He was not sure that he would enjoy this "experiment" in self-revelation, but very sure that he wanted to be well paid if it developed into a book. Charles Scribner was upset not to be offered first serial rights, since *Scribner's Magazine* had such a wide circulation and had done so well with *African Game Trails.* But Roosevelt felt obliged to give them to *The Outlook,* which had suffered many canceled subscriptions after supporting his bolt from the Republican Party. Scribner, undeterred, scented another bestseller. It would be the first presidential autobiography since those of the two Adamses—not that *they* had been of much value. Ulysses S. Grant's famous memoir had ended with the Civil War. Roosevelt was not only a gifted writer, but his life story was as thrilling as any novel. Scribner wrote to William B. Howland, treasurer of *The Outlook,* in a state of high excitement. "This is the first time that I have ever put in a blind bid for the publication of a book." He asked if the Colonel would accept an advance of $12,000 and a royalty rate of 20 percent.

It was a generous offer, matching the record rate Scribner had paid for *African Game Trails.* He was pained when Howland replied on 3 December that Roosevelt had yielded to "another proposition [that] is distinctly better from more than one point of view."

The proposition had come from the Macmillan Company, and was better indeed, paying Roosevelt an advance of $20,000 and a royalty rate of 50 percent. In return for these amazing terms, he was required to finish his manuscript by the summer of 1913, for publication that fall. Which meant printing the first chapters in *The Outlook* early in the new year, so that the whole book could be serialized before it appeared in hardcover.

Nobody in the industry doubted that Roosevelt could, and would, deliver on time: his reputation for promptness was legendary. But before starting work on what he insisted on calling his "possible autobiography," he had some scholarly writing to do. The American Historical Association had elected him as its president, and invited him to address its year-end convention. He thought he would speak on the subject of "History as Literature," and publish his lecture as the title piece in a volume of miscellaneous essays and reviews.

His third book project for the winter was unlikely to be profitable, but would satisfy the mammologist in him. It was to be the collaborative scientific study he had long planned to write with Edmund Heller, entitled *Life-Histories of African Game Animals*. Charles Scribner was awarded full publication rights for $4,000, a not exactly glittering consolation prize.

❧

JOHN F. SCHRANK, meanwhile, was tried in Milwaukee on a charge of assault with intent to murder. He pleaded guilty, but with qualifications: "I intended to kill Theodore Roosevelt, the third termer. I did not want to kill the candidate of the Progressive Party."

A cooperative, often jocular witness, he insisted that he was neither insane nor a Socialist. He bequeathed the bullet in Roosevelt's chest to the New-York Historical Society, although some would have thought it belonged to the Colonel by right of conveyance. At times, Schrank claimed he was penniless; at others, that he had inherited Manhattan real estate from his father, a Bavarian immigrant. He had cash enough to have bought a gun and pursued the Colonel for two weeks through the Deep South and on across the Midwest—intending but failing to shoot him in at least five cities before Milwaukee. Always his phobia had been that Roosevelt, if elected, would plunge the country into a civil war.

By court order, Schrank was remanded to the custody of a "lunacy commission" of five psychiatrists. They concluded that he was a case of "*dementia praecox,* paranoid type," and unanimously recommended incarceration for life in the Wisconsin state asylum in Oshkosh. A guard escorting him there by train noticed him staring out the window at passing fields, and asked if he liked to hunt.

"Only Bull Moose," Schrank said.

❧

MUCH AS ROOSEVELT wanted to become a full-time "literary feller," as he
had proclaimed himself in his thirties, his still-evangelical followers begged
him to stay on as their leader. With four years to expand, refinance, and consolidate, the Progressive National Committee was intent on "renominating"
him for president in 1916—so much so that it had already scheduled a Party
conference in Chicago to sanction that plan.

George Perkins, seeking publicity, presided at a preliminary dinner of
"Highbrow Political Contributors" in New York. The Colonel was guest of
honor. Frank Munsey attended, along with the short-story writer Edna Ferber, the journalist Will Irwin, and Hamlin Garland, the kind of all-round man
of letters Roosevelt most enjoyed. Garland's short stories and essays were
highly regarded, and he had also written an excellent life of President Grant.

If Perkins was hoping for an evening of Progressive dialectic, he was disappointed. Garland was more interested in encouraging Roosevelt (looking fully
recovered and cheerful) to push ahead with his autobiography. He said he
knew how difficult it was for a public man to find the right intimate tone, and
passed on a recommendation from William Dean Howells, the sage of American letters: the Colonel should reminisce aloud to a stenographer.

Roosevelt was in receipt of similar advice from Lawrence Abbott of *The
Outlook,* but he let Garland think the notion intrigued him. "I'll begin it immediately, dictating the way Howells suggested."

"Don't give us too much of the political, the official," Garland said.
"Write it the way you talk to your friends."

"That's not so easy as it sounds, especially when you consider the distrac-
tions I suffer." Roosevelt's voice rose to the ironic squeak he sometimes used
when mocking himself. "Being out of politics is not precisely retirement
for me."

❧

ABBOTT'S IDEA, SHREWDER than Howells's, was to engage the Colonel in
conversations at Sagamore Hill, with Frank Harper sitting in. They should be
as informal as possible. When Roosevelt dictated, he orated. But relaxing in
front of his own fire and surrounded by his own books and mementoes, he was
a natural raconteur. He could go on for hours, with effortless sequitur and wit,
often laughing himself into paroxysms. Abbott worried, however, that he
might be inhibited by the sight of his secretary scratching away on a pad.

Fortunately Harper was so short as to be unobtrusive in any room with
large furniture. Before their first, experimental session, Abbott instructed the
young man to record everything verbatim, no matter how disjointed the sequence. They they joined Roosevelt in his study.

The Colonel began to talk about his childhood with freshness and freedom. From time to time, he remembered Harper's presence and stiffened. But as the afternoon wore on, he relaxed and Abbott went home triumphant, with a mass of material to snip and paste. After a couple of days Roosevelt had a typed draft copy for approval. He edited and punctuated it with his usual conscientiousness. The result was "Boyhood and Youth," the first chapter of what promised to be the most entertaining American memoir since Benjamin Franklin's.

> On October 27, 1858, I was born at No. 28 East Twentieth Street, New York City, in the house in which we lived during the time that my two sisters and my brother and I were small children. It was furnished in the canonical taste of the New York which George William Curtis described in the *Potiphar Papers*. The black haircloth furniture in the dining room scratched the bare legs of the children when they sat on it. The middle room was a library, with tables, chairs, and bookcases of gloomy respectability. It was without windows, and so was available only at night. The front room, the parlor, seemed to us children to be a room of much splendor, but was open for general use only on Sunday evening or on rare occasions when there were parties. . . . The ornaments of that parlor I remember now, including the gas chandelier decorated with a great variety of cut-glass prisms. These prisms struck me as possessing peculiar magnificence. One of them fell off one day, and I hastily grabbed it and stowed it away, passing several days of furtive delight in the treasure, a delight always alloyed with fear that I would be found out and convicted of grand larceny.

ROOSEVELT'S REDISCOVERY of his narrative voice was interrupted on 8 December by distant, discordant Bull Moose calls. They emanated from the Progressive conference in Chicago, where his presence was urgently requested.

Gifford and Amos Pinchot had never been able to reconcile themselves to the power George Perkins wielded as chairman of the Party's Executive Committee. Ever since the election, they had plagued Roosevelt with a proposal that the executive headquarters should be translocated from New York—Perkins's orbit—to Washington, home of the more malleable Senator Dixon. The Colonel saw a threat to his reputation. The Party was bound to self-destruct if it lost its big-city backers. Perkins would resign rather than be sidelined by the Pinchots, and Frank Munsey was wistful to rejoin the GOP. Roosevelt did not want to look like a leader unable to hold on to his best men.

Showing as much good grace as possible, he left for Chicago on a special train, and found fifteen hundred loyal Progressives waiting for him next day in the ballroom of the LaSalle Hotel. The National Committee was sufficiently convinced by his support of Perkins to vote 32 to 12 in favor of keeping the executive headquarters in New York. As a sop to the Pinchots, a branch office was established in Washington, and antitrust language reinserted in the Party platform.

Roosevelt's "renomination" two days later was more of a headline-getter than a formal nod toward 1916. He cast most of his speech of thanks in the present tense, telling the delegates that their current priority must be to fight for distributive justice at the state and federal level. He obstinately defended his philosophy of judicial recall: "The doctrine of the divine right of judges to rule the people is every bit as ignoble as the doctrine of the divine right of kings."

With that he handed the platform over to Jane Addams, and the proceedings degenerated into a dry chautauqua on questions of organization, recruitment, and finance. Charts were drawn, titles devised, plans mooted, budgets projected, lists compiled from other lists, and committees split into subcommittees. Not until the morning of 12 December was Roosevelt free to head for home and his study, with its constant fire and Frank Harper tapping away on the typewriter downstairs.

⌒

BY CHRISTMAS HE had "History As Literature" finished, as well as several essays, the first few of his African game mammal studies, and another chapter of his autobiography. He decided to discontinue interview sessions with Lawrence Abbott and write or dictate the rest of that book. To Abbott and other editors at *The Outlook,* this was a fatal decision. The Colonel could not be expected to draw himself out, lacking the stimulus of a curious—and commercially-minded—interlocutor. He was aware of their distress, but relieved to be in control of his own story. "I have had to refuse to write a whole raft of interesting and sensational things that they would have liked me to put in," he told Kermit. The result was that he became self-conscious about any revelations at all, and admitted that it gave him "a great deal of worry."

Much of his inhibition derived from that traditional mute on the autobiographical trumpet, the over-protective wife. Still headachy and frail after her near-fatal riding accident of fourteen months before, Edith did not see why hundreds of thousands of readers should be privy to the sort of personal things kept for family letters, or better still, not put on paper at all: matters of health and bereavement and money and sex. It was out of the question that he should write about *her,* let alone the dead young woman whose face and name she had so assiduously erased from his Harvard photograph album. (But a lock of honey-colored hair survived, in a secret envelope inscribed in his own hand.)

The company of Archie and Quentin over the Christmas holidays, along with Ethel, Ted, Eleanor, and little Gracie, cheered both parents up. Stuffed stockings and dense snow insulating the house added the right Dickensian touches. Edith began to look "distinctly better," Roosevelt wrote her sister. He thanked Emily for sending him two volumes of Italian short stories. "I shall read them both of course; probably the Fogazzaro first."

He was intrigued to see how fast Quentin was developing in body and mind, and described him to Kermit as a "huge, wise philosopher." Actually the boy was intelligent rather than intellectual. His instincts were tactile. Roosevelt, dictating, talked about the machinery of government; Quentin talked simply of machinery. He played the piano with ease, understanding it to be an intricate system of levers. He wrote well too, although flights of imagination seemed to engage him less than the delightful task of setting them as slugs of type, slathering them with greasy ink, and hearing them crank out during all-night sessions in the school print shop.

Ted, settled now in a Manhattan town house, with his pipe, his books, his wife and daughter, and a well-paying job, was bourgeois enough to bore a bank president—which he in fact repeatedly did, in his capacity as a bond salesman on Wall Street. Archie was what Archie would always be: faithful, dogged, inflexible.

Kermit claimed to be content in his subequatorial solitude. He was overworked and underpaid, but too proud to ask for help. Single or spliced, Edith's beloved "one with the white head and the black heart" had the mark of a loner. "I'm afraid Mother thinks I'm hopeless," he wrote Ethel, "what they call down here a *vagabondo,* which means a peculiarly useless sort of tramp." His father tried to make him feel he was still an integral member of the family. "As president of the American Historical Association, I am to deliver an address which I hope you will like. . . . I shall send it to you when it is delivered."

More excitingly to Kermit, Roosevelt mentioned that the Historical and Geographical Society of Brazil had invited him to deliver a series of lectures in Rio and São Paulo during the spring and early summer of 1913. That would be too soon for him, with his three books to finish; but both father and son felt that some sort of seed had been sown.

AT SYMPHONY HALL in Boston on Saturday, 27 December, Roosevelt had the novel experience of speaking to a capacity audience for nearly two hours without mentioning Progressivism. His listeners included not only the American Historical Association, but five other professional societies holding conventions in the city that weekend—sociologists, statisticians, economists, labor lawyers, and political scientists. He could not have asked for a forum more to his purpose, which was to offend as deeply as possible the data-drunk bores who, in his opinion, were leaching all the color and romance out of scholarship. Toward the end of the nineteenth century, American historians, modeling themselves on the German academics who wrote for one another, rather than for the general public, had forsaken the linear narrative of Prescott and Parkman and Lecky for prose that sat on the page like bagged sand.

Ironically, Roosevelt was guilty of writing this kind of history himself. His first book, *The Naval War of 1812,* had been so dense with logistics that it read like a manual in places. He had boasted at the time that the first two chapters were "so dry they would have made a dictionary seem light reading by comparison." But having proved that he could match modern historians fact for fact, he had gone on to write *The Winning of the West* in the light of his own experience of the frontier, and with all the creativity he could legitimately apply to the study of sources. And the great Parkman had praised him.

He was less concerned, now, with the passing of the amateur historian—somebody he was not sorry to see go—but with the prejudice growing in academe against any prose that did not *sound* scientific. None of the members of the American Historical Association, he suspected, believed any more that history was a branch of literature. If their attitude held, historical writing was doomed as a civilizing influence. It would degenerate into the kind of sterile jargon that only professors fed on. He proceeded to say just that, undeterred by stony stares and occasional titters among his audience.

Literature may be defined as that which has permanent interest because of both its substance and its form, aside from the mere technical value that inheres in a special treatise for specialists. For a great work of literature there is the same demand now that there has always been; and in any great work of literature the first element is imaginative power. The imaginative power demanded for a great historian is different from that demanded for a great poet; but it is no less marked. Such imaginative power is in no sense incompatible with minute accuracy. On the contrary, very accurate, very real and vivid, presentation of the past can come only from one in whom the imaginative gift is strong.

Imagination, Roosevelt argued, did not have to be invention. In nonfiction writing, it should be no more than the ability to see and feel intensely what was there to be seen and felt. "No amount of self-communion and of pondering the soul of mankind, no gorgeousness of literary imagery, can take the place of cool, serious, widely extended study." Repeatedly he declared that color—authentic color—was not an embellishment of truth: it *was* truth. Modern scientists were dazzled by their discoveries, but apologetic, not to say perverse, in failing to communicate the beauty of revelation. Modern historians should beware of going the same way.

"Do not misunderstand me," he said. "In the field of historical research an immense amount can be done by men who have no literary power whatever." As the discipline developed to keep pace with technology, so must a new type of "investigator"—as opposed to narrative historian—arise and be accepted as indispensable. Roosevelt compared the relationship of the two types to that of the stonemason and the architect. Just as religious faith had had to square itself with Darwin, so must history adjust to the immense proliferation of proven fact. "So far from ignoring science, the great historian of the future can do nothing unless he is steeped in science. . . . He must accept what we now know to be man's place in nature." As Romance died, he must illumine the usual as well as the unusual. . . . "If he possesses the highest imaginative and literary quality, he will be able to interest us in the gray tints of the general landscape no less than in the flame hues of the jutting peaks."

Except to deaf ears, Roosevelt had so far presented a plausible case. But what his friend Owen Wister called "the preacher militant" in him caused him to add that history should teach morality. It could not record the best and worst of human behavior without comment. Even as he said this, he backed down, and granted that many historical moralists, such as Thomas Carlyle, had made fools of themselves when they diverged from the abstract and started laying down principles of conduct. He fell into his old habit of equivocation, and indulged a long purple passage in praise of purple passages. This spoiled the effect of a fine admonition to the historian of the future:

> He must ever remember that while the worst offense of which he can be guilty is to write vividly and inaccurately, yet that unless he writes vividly he cannot write truthfully; for no amount of dull, painstaking detail will sum up the whole truth unless the genius is there to paint the whole truth.

Alice Hooper of Boston, sitting in for Frederick Jackson Turner of "Frontier Thesis" fame, did not know whether to be approving or critical of the Colonel's performance. "He is so self-impressed and so thoroughly sure," she wrote Turner afterward, ". . . and is so anxious to make a ten strike every time he opens his mouth that it detracts from the profoundness of his learning. . . . His personality thunders too loud! But in spite of that—what an amount of things he carries about in his head doesn't he—and admiration for his capacity must be acknowledged when all is said and done."

Whatever others present thought of Roosevelt the historiographer, they basked in his celebrity at a post-lecture reception in the Copley Plaza Hotel. So many of them crammed in to meet him that the grand ballroom had to be opened up. He spent the night in the house of his friend William Sturgis Bigelow, a Buddhist scholar, and enjoyed himself at breakfast next morning with a couple of Harvard historians receptive to his views.

"T.R. came and went," Bigelow reported to Henry Cabot Lodge in Washington. "He was apparently never better. You never said a truer thing that he has no spilt milk in his life. He was just as much interested in the next thing as if the last one had never existed."

"'UNLESS HE WRITES VIVIDLY HE CANNOT WRITE TRUTHFULLY.'"

The manuscript of Roosevelt's autobiography, 1913.

ONE CONSEQUENCE OF Roosevelt's recent escape from death was an end to his estrangement from Lodge. Since the latter's declaration of neutrality in the presidential contest, they had had little politically to do with each other. But the personal bond between them remained strong, and Lodge had reaffirmed it in an emotional telegram immediately after the shooting. With some awkwardness, they began to correspond again on the subject of Roosevelt's lecture, and on the coincidental fact that they were both engaged in writing their autobiographies.

A much frostier estrangement showed no signs of thaw on 4 January 1913, when the Colonel and President Taft were seated opposite each other at the funeral of Whitelaw Reid in New York. Appropriately bitter weather buffeted the Cathedral of St. John the Divine throughout the service, which was attended by many of the eminent Republicans who had once thought of themselves as a team: Lodge, Elihu Root, Robert Bacon, Philander Knox, Henry White, J. P. Morgan, Joseph H. Choate, Andrew Carnegie, Frank Munsey, and others. By no attempt at a smile, or even a nod of the head, did Taft acknowledge his predecessor's presence across the chancel. After the benediction, he rose quickly and marched down the stone aisle, his aides clattering after him. Eleanor, sitting with her father-in-law, asked if it was protocol for a president to walk out ahead of the coffin.

"No, dear, no," Roosevelt said. "It is not customary, but in this case Mr. Taft probably thought there should be precedence even between corpses!"

His wisecrack may have been overheard by the President's brother Henry, who was sitting close by. In a bizarre speech that night, at a GOP fund-raiser in the Waldorf-Astoria, Taft described himself as "deceased," and the dinner in his honor "a wake." He blamed Roosevelt (who was not present) for eliminating him, saying that a million Republicans had voted Democratic in order to avert the Progressive threat.

Then came a virtual wail for sympathy. "What was the political disease of which I died? I am hopeful that when historians conduct their post-mortems it may be found that my demise was due to circumstances over which I had no great control, and to a political cataclysm, which I could hardly have anticipated or avoided."

FOR THE REST OF the winter, Roosevelt was absorbed in literary work. He continued to grind out what *The Outlook* obediently advertised as "Chapters of a Possible Autobiography," as well as editorials and book reviews, and wrote his African life histories at such a rate that he had to urge Edmund Heller to keep up. In addition, he prepared "History as Literature" for publication in the April 1913 issue of *American Historical Review* and collected ten other pieces to appear with it in the essay volume he had promised Scribners. They included his three European university lectures, a paper on the ancient Irish sagas, "Dante in the Bowery," and "The Search for Truth in a Reverent Spirit," his analysis of the conflict between faith and reason.

Edith worried about the pace at which he drove himself, and the struggle he seemed to be having with his memoir. "It is very difficult to strike just the happy medium between being too reticent and not reticent enough!" he wrote her sister. "I find it difficult both as regards my life when I was a child and my political experiences." His solution in the former case was simply to omit whatever was not pleasant, and in the latter to adopt what Abbott regretfully called his "argumentative" style.

He was shy about mentioning any members of his family except the Roosevelts and Bullochs who had preceded him, expressing awe of his father ("the only man of whom I was ever really afraid"), and tolerant affection for his "entirely unreconstructed" Georgian mother, with her stories of antebellum life on Roswell Plantation and "queer goings-on in the Negro quarters." As far as any reader could tell, the woman who bore his first child had never existed. The mother of his later children was referred to only in passing as "Mrs. Roosevelt," and the children themselves were neither numbered nor named. He wrote tersely about his juvenile battles with asthma, then dismissed the subject of health altogether. Adult traumas, whether physical or psychological, went unrecorded. Autobiographically speaking, he had not squandered half his patrimony in the Badlands. He had not run for mayor of New York, let alone finished last in a three-way race. His younger brother, Elliott, had not impregnated a servant girl, the family had not paid her off, and Elliott had not died a hopeless alcoholic. Police Commissioner Theodore Roosevelt had been obstructed, rather than outwitted, by a Machiavellian colleague. Somebody else could take credit for comparing President McKinley's backbone to a chocolate éclair. And the Colonel of the Rough Riders had not lobbied for a Medal of Honor on the ground of personal heroism.

A few of these lacunae were self-serving, but most were self-aware, to be expected in the reminiscences of a former president. He knew that every word that he wrote on personal matters would be pored over. (Hundreds of newspapers, including *The New York Times,* were quoting each chapter as soon as it appeared in *The Outlook*.) His moral instinct, moreover, prevented him from recording material that did not trumpet his beliefs. Owen Wister saw clearly in characterizing him as "an optimist who saw things as they ought to be, wrestling with a realist who knew things as they were."

The optimist forged ahead with his text, cutting down on anecdotes and applying political experience to future ideals. Yet it was the realist, persuaded to reminisce by fellow editors at the magazine, who here and there set down stretches of beguiling autobiography, faithful to his own precept that vividness was a necessary part of historical truth. He wrote an elegiac chapter, "In Cowboy Land," about his years as a rancher and deputy sheriff in North Dakota:

> That land of the West has gone now, "gone, gone with lost Atlantis," gone to the isle of ghosts and of strange dead memories. It was a land of vast silent spaces, of lonely rivers, and of plains where the wild game stared at the passing horseman. . . . In the soft springtime the stars were glorious in our eyes each night before we fell asleep; and in the winter we rode through blinding blizzards, when the driven snow-dust burnt our faces. . . . We knew toil and hardship and hunger and thirst; and we saw men die violent deaths as they worked among the horses and the cattle, or fought in evil feuds with one another; but we felt the beat of hardy life in our veins, and ours was the glory of work and the joy of living.

ON TUESDAY, 4 MARCH, the present and the future simultaneously intruded themselves on literary recall. Woodrow Wilson was sworn in as President of the United States, calling upon "all honest men, all patriotic, all forward-looking men" to come to his side. "God helping me, I will not fail them, if they will but counsel and sustain me!"

Doubting, somehow, that Wilson wanted *his* advice, the Colonel went that morning to the huge new "Futurists Exhibition" at the Sixty-ninth Regiment Armory in midtown Manhattan. Since its opening two weeks before, the show, officially entitled "International Exhibition of Modern Art" and displaying well over a thousand paintings and sculptures, had drawn record crowds, setting off reactionaries against sophisticates, critic against critic, and the avant-garde against the merely curious, in a bedlam of aesthetic debate. It seemed worthy of an *Outlook* review.

Roosevelt had never written art criticism before. His references to painting, mostly in letters, were conventional and uninvolved, although Arthur Lee had managed to thrill him with the gift of some Valhallan landscapes by Pinckney Marcius-Simons, a New Yorker transplanted to Bayreuth. As for sculpture, Alice had once been convulsed by her father's admiration for a "particularly fine Diana," despite three-dimensional evidence that the figure was Apollo.

Monocular vision was part of his problem, but he also had a tin ear for music, and no sense of interior design beyond the hunter's desire to surround himself with *disjecta membra*. "Art," Roosevelt admitted, "is about the only subject of which I feel some uncertainty." That had not stopped him, as President, from being strongly supportive of the creative classes. His executive dining room had vied with Henry Adams's breakfast parlor as a meeting place for writers, artists, and intellectuals. He had put the poet Edwin Arlington Robinson, the novelist James B. Connolly, and the cartoonist Thomas Nash on the federal payroll, on the understanding that they would do as little governmental work as possible. He had sponsored a classical restoration of the White House by the architects McKim, Mead & White, teamed up with the planners of the City Beautiful movement against the yahoos of Capitol Hill, posed for John Singer Sargent, and chosen Augustus Saint-Gaudens to design the most elegant coins in modern circulation. "I'd like to be remembered in that way—a patron of art," he told Hamlin Garland.

Nevertheless, something earthy in him mistrusted what was most fine in the fine arts. He had trouble reading Jane Austen, and thought Henry James effeminate. He disliked poetry that dwelt on intuitions or sensation, preferring border ballads and Longfellow's *Saga of King Olaf* to Keats and Baudelaire. Yet his own writings demonstrated a lyrical receptivity to the sights and sounds of the natural world, plus a willingness to be surprised. He rejected nothing new until he understood it well enough to form an opinion of it— usually on moral or utilitarian grounds. Even then, he was amenable to changing his mind, if an expert could improve his perception. Unlike most of the sixty thousand traditionally minded viewers who had preceded him to the Armory, he came without prejudice. He felt that the organizers of the show were doing a public service in displaying "art forces which of late have been at work in Europe, forces which cannot be ignored."

An electricity never given off before by an art event in New York was palpable around the huge building. Double-parked automobiles crowded the streets to north, east, and south. Porters tried to control the jostle of ticket holders, and hollered through megaphones at cabs blocking the entrance. Of the two side exits, the most animated—mainly by people laughing and improvising "Cubist" jokes—was that adjoining Gallery I, notorious for its concentration of works by Matisse and other Parisian *enfants terribles*.

Roosevelt was in no hurry to bypass the American rooms, which outnumbered those of France, Britain, Ireland, and Germany almost three to one. The first area he entered, a luminous, tented space full of sculptures and decorative pieces, at once seized his attention. He was predisposed to like the lacquered oak screens of Robert Chanler, not just because the artist was the brother of one of his former Rough Riders, but because the exquisite designs that covered them fulfilled his long-held dream of a new aesthetic arising out of the paradox of American identity. Here was the work of a man like himself, a wealthy Knickerbocker who had lived in the West and served as a sheriff, yet who was at home in European salons. Chanler, too, loved nature, finding zoomorphic beauty even in the rule of tooth and claw. His Asiatic-looking black wolves, their tails flowing like serpents, bit soundlessly into the writhing bodies of white stags. Attenuated giraffes, splotched as delicately as orchids, grazed the tops of impossibly tall trees. Moonlight irradiated the needles of porcupines slinking through a forest of blue and silver. Perhaps most thrilling, to a tired man of letters planning to take his youngest sons to Arizona in July, was a representation of the Hopi Snake Dance in the "sky city" of Walpi. By transfiguring primitive movement into an ethereal choreography, Chanler was doing the reverse of what the Ballets Russes had done in Paris—where his panels were apparently admired.

Moving on through five more galleries of contemporary American art, Roosevelt saw nothing by Saint-Gaudens, Frederick MacMonnies, William Merritt Chase, and other favorites of his presidency. He did not miss them. They had had too long a reign, with their effete laurel wreaths and Grecian profiles. It was clear that the show's organizers, headed by the symbolist painter Arthur B. Davies, intended to eradicate the beaux arts style from the national memory. Even Sargent was shunned, in favor of young American artists of powerful, if not yet radical originality: George Bellows, Marsden Hartley, Edward Hopper, and dozens of women willing to portray their sex without prettification. Roosevelt was taken with Ethel Myers's plastilene group, "Fifth Avenue Gossips," whose perambulatory togetherness reminded him of the fifteenth idyll of Theocritus. He liked the social realism of John Sloan's "Sunday, Women Drying Their Hair" and George Luks's camera-quick sketches of animal activity at the Bronx Zoo. Leon Kroll's "Terminal Yards" impressed him, although it represented the kind of desecration of the Hudson Palisades that he and George Perkins had worked to curtail. From a vertiginous, snowcapped height, the artist's eagle eye looked down on railroad sidings and heaps of slag. Drifting vapor softened the ugliness and made it mysteriously poetic.

What pleased Roosevelt about the work of these "Ashcan" painters, and indeed the entire American showing as he wandered on, was the lack of "simpering, self-satisfied conventionality." All his life he had deplored the deference his countrymen tended to extend toward the art and aristocracy of the Old World. Sloan was a social realist as unsentimental as Daumier, but bigger of heart. Walt Kuhn's joyful "Morning" had the explosive energy of a Van Gogh landscape, minus the neurosis. Hartley's foreflattened "Still Life No. 1" was the work of a stateside Cézanne, its Indian rug and tapestries projecting a geometry unseen in Provence.

Davies modestly exhibited only three oil paintings. He eschewed realism in favor of a dreamlike classicism that was at once as serene yet more mysterious than the masterworks of Puvis de Chavannes. Roosevelt, like virtually every American critic or connoisseur, revered Puvis, but Davies's "Moral Law—A Line of Mountains" was perhaps the most cosmopolitan picture in the show, with its unmistakably Western chain of peaks shimmering across a prairie-like emptiness, and pale vague nudes that could have been doodled by Puvis, or traced from the walls of the Roman catacombs, floating in the foreground. Roosevelt took pleasure in it even if the title was bafflingly cryptic.

His enjoyment did not diminish when he found himself among the works of European moderns loosely cataloged as "post-impressionist." He was blind to a piece of pure abstraction by Wassily Kandinsky, but responded happily to the dreamy fantasies of Odilon Redon and the virtuoso draftsmanship of Augustus John, as well as to Whistler, Monet, Cézanne, and other acknowledged revolutionaries.

Then came the slap in the face that was Matisse. More vituperation had been directed at this painter, in reviews of the show so far, than at any other "Cubist"—a term that actually did not apply to him, but nevertheless was used as an epithet. Roosevelt gazed at his "Joaquina" and found its cartoony angularity simply absurd. Beyond loomed a kneeling nude by Wilhelm Lehmbruck. Although obviously mammalian, it was not especially human; the "lyric grace" that had made it the sensation of a recent exhibition in Cologne reminded him more of a praying mantis.

A phrase he had recently tried out on Henry Cabot Lodge, in a letter complaining about political extremists, came to mind: *lunatic fringe.* It seemed even more applicable to the French radicals who now proceeded to insult his intelligence, as if he and not they were insane: Picasso, Braque, Brancusi, Maillol. He boggled at Marcel Duchamp's *Nu descendant un escalier,* a shuttery flutter of cinematic movement propelled by the kind of arcs that American comic artists drew to telegraph punches, or baseball swings. If this was Cubism, or Futurism, or Near-Impressionism, or whatever jargon-term the theorists of modern art wanted to apply to it, he believed he had seen it before, in a Navajo rug.

At least Duchamp had had the decency not to flaunt sexual organs. Roosevelt noted no *e* on the end of *Nu* in the painting's title (helpfully lettered onto the canvas), and decided in the face of general opinion to translate it as "A Naked Man Going Down Stairs." Nakedness seemed to be a motif of the show's remaining galleries, so much so that he elected to ignore a walking nude by Robert Henri that verged on the anatomical, and a frankly lesbian study by Jules Pascin that had three girls preparing to have sex on a bed, limbs intertwined, lips caressing a proffered nipple.

As James Bryce, the outgoing British ambassador in Washington, noted, Roosevelt "wouldn't always look at a thing."

❧

HOWEVER, IN HIS SUBSEQUENT review, modestly entitled "A Layman's Views of an Art Exhibition," he declined to be as outraged as most professional critics. His tone in confessing his inability to appreciate much of what he had seen was at first almost wistful, as if to acknowledge that the new century had begun to bewilder him. But if the law of evolution was applicable to artists, those fittest to survive were not the ones who mutated most startlingly. "It is true, as the champions of the extremists say, that there can be no life without change, and that to be afraid of what is different or unfamiliar is to be afraid of life. It is no less true, however, that change may mean death and not life, and retrogression instead of development."

He thought that there was life, and much "real good" in the work of the two emergent American modernist schools, "fantastic though the developments of these new movements are." Personally, he preferred the nationalistic realism of the Ashcan artists to the violent expressionism of a Marsden Hartley. If the former group was popularist, it was at least all-American, and relatable to Progressivism, as were the new sociological novels of Theodore Dreiser, the "saleswoman" stories of Edna Ferber, and Israel Zangwill's immigrant drama *The Melting Pot,* which Roosevelt had himself endorsed as an advertisement for Western-style democracy.

What disturbed him was the Armory Show's message that the Old World was, ironically, far ahead of the New in developing a cultural response to the terrifying implications of modern science. His own written attempt at such a response, "The Search for Truth in a Reverent Spirit," could be taken as naïve, if the future—even the present!—really was as inhuman as Lehmbruck and Duchamp and Brancusi saw it. Unable to conceive of a head as a metal egg, Roosevelt abandoned reverence for humor:

> In this recent exhibition the lunatic fringe was fully in evidence, especially in the rooms devoted to the Cubists and the Futurists. . . . The Cubists are entitled to the serious attention of all who find enjoyment in the colored puzzle-pictures of the Sunday newspapers. Of course there is no reason for choosing the cube as a symbol, except that it is probably less fitted than any other mathematical expression for any but the most formal decorative art. There is no reason why people should not call themselves Cubists, or Octagonists, or Parallelopipedonists, or Knights of the Isosceles Triangle, or Brothers of the Cosine, if they so desire; as expressing anything serious and permanent, one term is as fatuous as another. Take the picture which for some reason is called "A Naked Man Going Down Stairs." There is in my bathroom a really good Navajo rug which, on any proper interpretation of Cubist theory, is a far more satisfactory and decorative picture. Now, if for some inscrutable reason, it suited somebody to call this rug a picture of, say, "A Well-Dressed Man Going Up a Ladder," the name would fit the facts just about as well. . . . From the stand-

point of terminology each name would have whatever merit inheres in a rather cheap striving after effect; and from the standpoint of decorative value, of sincerity, and of artistic merit, the Navajo rug is infinitely ahead of the picture.

❧

ROOSEVELT'S SUDDEN INTEREST in modern art, on a day when he could have stayed home and read accounts of Woodrow Wilson's inauguration, caused much editorial hilarity. A cartoon by Kemble in the *Baltimore Evening Sun* showed the new President contemplating a portrait of his toothy predecessor in the Oval Office and musing, "I wonder if that's a futurist? It can't be a cubist." The New York *World* argued that the "Square Deal" of 1903 had been a proto-Cubist conceit, doing to the Constitution what Braque and Picasso would do to color and form ten years later. As for Progressivism, there was little to distinguish it from the dizziness of Duchamp. "The 'Nude Descending a Staircase' is the perfect pictorial representation of a Roosevelt platform."

C. E. Wood, staff cartoonist for *The Independent,* drew a caricature of the Colonel explaining a Cubist construction to a fellow viewer at the Armory Show. "You don't understand this new style of painting? It's as clear as day."

The canvas's blocky shapes spelled out "1916."

❧

IT TURNED OUT that Sargent's portrait of Theodore Roosevelt was indeed the sole wall decoration to greet Wilson when he reported for work in the Oval Office on 5 March 1913. Not only that, the new desk chair ordered for him had not yet been delivered, so he found himself sitting in Roosevelt's old one, rather battered after seven and a half years of strenuous occupancy.

During the early days of his campaign, Wilson had reacted touchily when reporters suggested he should try to emulate the Colonel's dynamic speaking style. "Don't you suppose I know my own handicaps? . . . I'd do it if I could." But when formal oratory was called for, Wilson was capable of eloquence without affectation, as his inaugural address showed:

> The great government we loved has too often been made use of for private and selfish purposes, and those who used it had forgotten the people. There has been something crude and heartless and unfeeling in our haste to succeed and be great. Our thought has been, "Let every man look out for himself; let every generation look out for itself," while we reared giant machinery which made it impossible that any but those who stood at the levers of control should have a chance to look out for themselves. . . .

We have now come to the sober second thought. The scales of heedlessness have fallen from our eyes. We have made up our minds to square every purpose of our national life again with the standards we so proudly set up at the beginning and have always carried in our hearts. Our work is a work of restoration.

Washington's diplomatic corps noted that the new President had said nothing about the world outside the United States.

Roosevelt was determined not to criticize him publicly, as a matter of personal propriety as well as respect for the decision of the electorate. But his hackles were raised early by Wilson's choice of William Jennings Bryan as secretary of state. Not only was Bryan a hayseed of the purest fiber, sure to alienate the aristocrats along Embassy Row, he also quaintly believed that all foreign provocations could be talked or prayed away. That boded ill for another crisis over Mexico, where an anti-American despot named Victoriano Huerta had seized power and, apparently, condoned an armed attack on a U.S. border patrol in Arizona, the same day Wilson was inaugurated.

Republican and Progressive congressmen wishing to urge a forceful response from the new administration found themselves barred by a White House access rule that reversed more than a century of democratic tradition. Wilson's plump young secretary, Joseph P. Tumulty, announced that in future, all callers upon the President must bear invitations. This haughty policy was perhaps to be expected from a political scholar whose writings made clear that he believed in an isolated, powerful executive. Wilson felt that legislators over the years had spent too much time visiting the White House with unasked-for advice, and too little on Capitol Hill, consenting.

ON FRIDAY, 4 APRIL, there was a gathering of Rooseveltians—both Republican and Progressive—at Christ Church, Oyster Bay, to watch the Colonel give away his younger daughter in marriage to Dr. Richard Derby. Although the gathering was large, cramming the flower-filled nave beyond capacity, it was select. Conspicuous absentees included William Howard Taft (now a professor of law at Yale), and Elihu Root. George von Lengerke Meyer, who had served in Taft's cabinet as well as Roosevelt's, had needed encouragement to attend. So had Senator Lodge. They were not sure they had been forgiven for failing to stand at Armageddon. Roosevelt scoffed at their embarrassment. "I feel very strongly against Root," he told Winthrop Chanler, "because Root took part in as downright a bit of theft as ever was perpetrated by any Tammany ballot box stuffer. . . . But with Cabot and George it was wholly different. They had the absolute right to do each exactly as he did, and I never expected either of them to follow me."

Both were, in any case, Harvard men, as were Chanler, Owen Wister, and many of the other top-hatted figures attending the ceremony—not least the bridegroom. "Dusky Dick," as Alice Longworth teasingly called him (he was dark, and prone to black moods), happened also to be wealthy, with an easy expectation of twelve to fourteen thousand dollars a year over and above his

"Future generations were manifesting themselves."

The Colonel gives his younger daughter away in marriage, 4 April 1913.

professional income. This had been a further reason to approve him as an addition to the family. Roosevelt was so much a product of the Porcellian and Knickerbocker clubs that he never seemed to notice how exclusive his preferred field of acquaintance really was.

He seemed near to tears as he escorted Ethel to the altar, in contrast to his unsmiling demeanor at Alice's wedding in the White House. That had been a state function; this was private. It was, nevertheless, momentous as a rite of passage not only for the young woman at his side, glowing in ivory satin and emeralds, but for himself as a public person. Never again, probably, would he attract such a concourse, as Wister called it, of familiars. The power that he had exuded for so long was diminishing by the day while Woodrow Wilson—not to mention Cubism!—remade the world in ways not to his liking.

Had Roosevelt not decided to make his autobiography as impersonal as possible, he could have brought it to an end with an account of this ceremony, casting the congregation as a sort of *dramatis personae* of his life and times. Here was old Joseph Choate, to whom he had turned, after the death of Theodore Senior, for career advice; his classmate Bob Bacon, still the handsomest man in the world, but grizzled now and replaced as American ambassador to France; tiny, guttural Jake Riis, who had opened his eyes to "how the other half lives"; his orthographical mentor, Brander Matthews, one of the few academics he could stand; Bill Loeb, who had handed him John Hay's telegram in 1901, confirming his accession to the presidency; sleek George Cortelyou, manager of his huge electoral win in 1904; Gifford Pinchot, the architect of his conservation policies; Henry White, who had ridden with him and the Kaiser on Döbertiz Field; Lyman and Lawrence Abbott, his employers at *The Outlook*, wondering how long they could afford to showcase his political opinions; George Perkins, who intended to keep bankrolling the Progressive Party, and Frank Munsey, who did not. And here by virtue of blood was the sole Democrat present, thirty-one-year-old Franklin D. Roosevelt, recently confirmed as assistant secretary of the navy.

Dick and Ethel were married over the loud objections of little Gracie, Ted and Eleanor's daughter. Future generations were manifesting themselves.

⟡

WITH SPRING UNDER WAY and the Derbys off to Europe on honeymoon, Roosevelt reapplied himself to the literary task he was beginning to find unbearable. "I am working with heated unintelligence at my 'biography,' " he wrote Ethel. "I fairly loathe it, now."

His boredom showed as he dictated two long, dry chapters about his commissionerships in Washington and New York in the 1890s. It was difficult to interest any modern reader in the civil service and municipal problems of a quarter-century before. He tried to make them sound less dated, and fell into a presentist mode, as if he were still campaigning against Taft and Wilson. A chapter on his service with the Rough Riders in Cuba, heavily appendicized with documents testifying to his heroism at San Juan, ended with an argument for military and naval preparedness in 1913. Hindsight made him more pro-labor and better informed about the abuse of women than he had been as president. The Progressive Party platform kept intruding, like King Charles's head. He seemed to realize that his book was becoming polemical, but could not help himself. Nor could he turn, as he had in happier days, to Elihu Root for corrective sarcasm.

Lawrence Abbott tried but failed to persuade him to write more "picturesquely." It was not for lack of literary labor. Roosevelt revised some pages of typescript with such care that all four margins were crammed with interlineations. He eliminated anything that might be read as overtly boastful, assembling a sober and comprehensive account of his service as governor of New York State with the help of George Perkins, and asking Gifford Pinchot to draft a chapter entitled "The Natural Resources of the Nation." The titles of five other chapters spoke for themselves: "The Presidency: Making an Old Party Progressive," "The Big Stick and the Square Deal," "Social and Industrial Justice," "The Monroe Doctrine and the Panama Canal," and finally "The Peace of Righteousness."

Desperate to compile the most official record, he neglected his own advice to historians and wrote hundreds of colorless paragraphs unlikely to swell *The Outlook*'s subscription list. Only once, in an inserted chapter about his love of books and the outdoors, did he recapture the charmingly natural style of earlier installments. By the third week of May, he had had enough. He chose not to proceed any further than the end of his presidency, and left *African Game Trails* and *The New Nationalism* to account for what he had done since then. Simultaneously, he also finished *Life-Histories of African Game Animals,* and left on 24 April for Marquette, Michigan, on another documentary quest: to prove for all time that he was not a drunkard.

CHAPTER 14

A Vanished Elder World

Come away! come away! you can hear them calling, calling,
Calling to us to come to them, and roam no more.
Over there beyond the ridges and the land that lies between us,
There's an old song calling us to come!

THE COUNTY COURTHOUSE in Marquette, Michigan, solidly dominated a
high bluff on the south shore of Lake Superior. With its stained-glass dome
and heavy mahogany paneling, it was intended to proclaim the importance of
the little surrounding city as the manufacturing and export hub of one of the
world's richest repositories of iron ore. But its architects could not have conceived that nine years after its construction, a former President of the United
States should seek it out for justice, accompanied by a phalanx of distinguished lawyers, doctors, diplomats, editors, and reporters, not to mention a
zoologist, a trade unionist, a forester, and two secret service agents, one of
whom was detached from Woodrow Wilson's White House. In case the testimony of all these witnesses was not enough to convince a jury of his sobriety,
Roosevelt also came armed with forty depositions, signed by persons as famous as Admiral George E. Dewey and as obscure as James Amos, his own
black valet.

A jury of twelve local citizens was selected on the afternoon of Monday, 26
May, with Judge Richard C. Flannigan presiding. Attorneys for the defense,
intimidated by Roosevelt's thick-spectacled stare, challenged only one venire-
man wearing a blue Bull Moose badge. The resulting panel was about as varied as a provincial community could muster, consisting of four miners, three
teamsters, two farmers, a lumberman, a fireman, and a gum-chewing blacksmith.

When the trial proper began on Tuesday morning, George A. Newett,
owner and publisher of the Ishpeming *Iron Ore*, was escorted to a seat ten feet

away from the plaintiff. With his steel-gray hair and oddly rigid posture, he looked as industrial as any product of Marquette County, except that the rigidity related to illness. Newett was due to be operated on as soon as the jury decided his fate.

He was a commanding figure nonetheless, registering no embarrassment when the full text of his 12 October 1912 editorial was read to the court. Apart from its accusations of drinking and cursing, it characterized the Colonel as paranoiac, mendacious, cowardly, and a sore loser. But there was a telling hint of political bias: "All that Roosevelt has gained he received from the hands of the Republican Party."

Newett was a stalwart of the county and state GOP committees. Roosevelt probably did not remember appointing him postmaster of Ishpeming in 1905. Nor was he aware that Newett would have supported him in 1912 if he and not Taft had been renominated by the Party. The publisher, in other words, despised him for bolting. And if the language of the editorial was abusive, it was accurate in noting that Roosevelt himself was no slouch when it came to personal invective. "All who oppose him are wreckers of the country, liars, knaves and undesirables." Perhaps for that reason, counsel for the plaintiff, led by James H. Pound, had decided to focus on the drunkenness charge—as Roosevelt did, when he took the stand as first witness.

> I have never been drunk or in the slightest degree under the influence of liquor. . . . I do not drink either whiskey or brandy, except as I shall hereafter say, except as I drink it under the direction of a doctor; I do not drink beer. . . . I never drank liquor or porter or anything of that kind. I have never drunk a highball or cocktail in my life. I have sometimes drunk mint julep in the White House. There was a bed of mint there, and I may have drunk half a dozen mint juleps a year, and certainly no more. . . .
>
> At home, at dinner, I may partake of a glass or two glasses of white wine. At a public dinner, or a big dinner, if they have champagne I will take a glass or two glasses of champagne, but I take it publicly just as much as privately.

Asked about his medicinal use of spirits, he said that he had suffered from occasional attacks of malaria since serving in Cuba in 1898. Once, when delirious on a bear hunt as President, he had been given a shot of whiskey by Dr. Alexander Lambert. In Africa he had had two recurrences of fever and swallowed, at the direction of Dr. Edgar Mearns, "about seven tablespoons" of brandy. There had been a case of champagne among his safari effects, but he had never broken open a bottle, not even to celebrate killing lions and elephants.

According to *African Game Trails,* Mearns had treated him with whiskey, not brandy, but Roosevelt's very vagueness of recall testified to his lack of interest in alcohol. He was, manifestly to the four or five hundred reporters cramming the court, intent only on clearing his name. It was equally plain to the jurors, sitting so close to him that some of his gestures swished the air in front of their faces, why so many rumormongers had inferred over the years that Roosevelt was a toper. They stared at the red, contorting face, and listened in fascination to the unstoppable flow of speech.

∽

HAD THEY NOT BEEN compelled to retire during the first recess, they would have heard him explain why he was so ruddy. Unable to resist the lure of newspapermen, he went over to the press table and sat on it like a boy, legs dangling. "Because of my high blood pressure, I guess, I'm always a great bleeder. I get hurt and bleed so often that Mrs. Roosevelt pays no attention to it."

He proceeded to tell the kind of anecdote that Lawrence Abbott had tried in vain to have him include in his autobiography. "The other day at Oyster Bay the windmill, on a sixty-foot derrick, was squeaking. I got an oil can and climbed up to oil it, neglecting to shut off the mill. Just as I got to the top, the wind veered. The paddle swung around and took off a slice of my scalp. I started to climb down, but I'm big and clumsy and it took quite a little while. By the time I got to the house my face and shoulders were drenched with blood. Inside the door I met Mrs. Roosevelt. 'Theodore,' she said, 'I wish you'd do your bleeding in the bathroom. You're spoiling every rug in the house.' "

∽

DOCTORS LAMBERT, John B. Murphy, and Arthur D. Bevan, who had examined the Colonel during his prostration in Mercy Hospital the previous fall, proceeded to testify or depose that he was the opposite of an alcoholic patient, with sweet breath, clear urine, no enlargement of the liver, and no tremor. He had an untroubled temperament, a balanced nervous system, and "slept like a child." Their consensus was that he was a man in splendid health, with no addictive tendencies.

A qualification to these rosy opinions was expressed by Dr. Presley Rixey, who had been his physician in the White House, and had not seen him for four years. Rixey felt that Roosevelt was in only "fairly good" shape, with a noticeable gain in weight, but confirmed that he had always been abstemious. "He is about as moderate as a man could well be, and not be a teetotaler." His appetite for food was another matter. Even with his vigorous exercise schedule in Washington, "I had to resort to extraordinary means to keep him down . . . to keep down the flesh."

Roosevelt made no effort to hide his current paunch. He sat tilted back, caressing the heavy watch chain that draped over it, as witness after witness testified to the main issue of the trial. Robert Bacon, Gifford Pinchot, James R. Garfield, Truman H. Newberry, Jacob Riis, Edmund Heller, Cal O'Laughlin, O. K. Davis, Lawrence Abbott, William Loeb, and many others assured everybody in the courtroom that the Colonel's thirst for alcohol was only slightly greater than Carry Nation's.

By mid-morning Wednesday, lawyers for the defense were so desperate that they resorted to holding up the proceedings with technical objections. Judge Flannigan, seeing that they had no evidence to offer beyond rumor, called a recess and allowed them to argue that the *Iron Ore,* "a little country newspaper, having a circulation of about three thousand," should be forgiven for going only one step further than many big-city dailies in criticizing "the most talked-about man in the United States in the past year." If not, their ailing client might have to pay as much as $10,000 in damages.

James Pound said that Roosevelt was entitled to demand five times that amount. "But my client peremptorily instructed me that I was not to sue for any such sum." The Colonel had no wish to be punitive, and was not even interested in establishing malice. He merely wanted to stand on "the actual damages" to his reputation, "under the circumstances of the publication." William Belden, Newett's chief counsel, seized on this stand to claim that his client was protected by Michigan's limit on nominal damages, which meant an award of six cents. The judge warned him that an absence of expressed malice did not necessarily imply absence of real injury. "It may be six cents, it may be sixty thousand dollars."

Pound returned triumphant to the courtroom and the parade of witnesses for the plaintiff continued through Thursday. James Amos allowed that in ten years as Roosevelt's manservant, "I never yet have served him with more than one full glass of champagne." The Colonel never drank at family meals, and when sharing white wine with guests, would spritz his own glass with Apollinaris water. Cal O'Laughlin calibrated his consumption of this insipid fluid at "about an inch and a half to two inches." Philip Roosevelt stated that when Cousin Theodore was raw-throated from too much public speaking, he would dose himself with "milk punch," an infusion barely stronger than the dairy original.

Such repetitive testimony might have emptied the courtroom had it not been enlivened with details about Roosevelt's personal and family life, few of which had yet appeared (or would appear) in his serialized autobiography. The blacksmith in the jury became so engrossed he frequently stopped chewing.

By Saturday morning, George Newett had had enough, and asked to be sworn. Reading from a written statement, he described himself as somebody who had once considered Theodore Roosevelt to be "a great Republican leader," and who had contributed money and editorial support to his campaigns. "I mention these facts as indicating the impossibility of my harboring any feeling of personal malice against the plaintiff." In recent years, however, he had traveled the country and heard many authoritative-sounding stories that Roosevelt drank to excess. Newspapers on his exchange list seemed to confirm these stories, and he had come to believe them. As a loyal Republican, he had felt obliged in any case to oppose the Colonel's Bull Moose candidacy. When Roosevelt passed through Marquette the previous fall, he had gone to hear him speak, and had been angered by "what I considered a most unjust attack upon our candidate for Congress, who was one of my lifelong friends."

Newett's *mea culpa* made clear that he had libeled the plaintiff for political, rather than personal reasons. Roosevelt had indeed attacked Rep. H. Olin Young as "a tool of the steel trust," and the congressman had subsequently gone down to defeat.

The trial was won long before Newett admitted that none of the "reputable witnesses" who told him Roosevelt was a drunkard were able to provide evidence of their charges. To continue to believe them would be " an injustice" to the Colonel. Newett did not apologize for his article, but he implicitly retracted it, and he insisted that "in the publication I acted in good faith and without malice."

Throughout, Roosevelt had leaned forward listening with intense concentration, occasionally casting a flash of spectacles at the gallery. When Newett finished reading he asked to be heard. "Your honor, in view of the statement of the defendant, I ask the Court to instruct the jury that I desire only nominal damages."

—⦿—

AFTER IT WAS ALL OVER, and a nickel and a penny had been received by his lawyers, he pushed his way through a jostling crowd of congratulators. He was in a hurry to catch the 5:30 train and return home for what was left of the Memorial Day weekend. Charles Thompson of *The New York Times* managed to get close and ask, "Are you and Newett going to meet?"

Roosevelt looked back with an expression half surprised, half sardonic.

"Not if the advances are to come from *me*," he said.

—⦿—

ROOSEVELT V. NEWETT WAS a front-page news story across the United States, and received wide coverage even in Britain. Comment on the Colonel's Pyrrhic victory was generally supportive. *The New York Times* remarked that all Americans should be pleased to have seen libel rebuffed with honest truth. Satirists and cartoonists sharpened their pens. Hotels in Philadelphia reported a run on "Roosevelt punch." The *Fort Wayne News* joked that the

Colonel's major achievement had been to disillusion those millions of Americans who thought he did not drink at all.

"I am very glad I put the suit through," Roosevelt wrote Kermit, "but of course it was an unpleasant expense." Six cents would not significantly reduce his legal fees, let alone pay the travel costs of his dozens of witnesses. "The last eight months I have had three heavy expenses, the attempted assassination, Ethel's wedding, and this libel suit." His big book advance from the Macmillan Company was not due until the fall. "I shall have to make one or two speeches and write one or two articles before I start for Arizona with Archie and Quentin."

It occurred to him that Kermit was in far worse straits than himself. The young man had at last resigned from his underpaid railroad job, and was about to start work for a firm of bridge builders in the southern part of Brazil. But his new employers sounded shifty with money. Roosevelt fretted about Kermit not eating properly, in order to save enough *milreis* to marry Belle Willard. "Did you get the check for $200 which I sent you a couple of months ago? I'll send you another next month, and you will *of course* let me know if you are short of funds."

Kermit indeed had received the check, and proudly torn it up. He attached much more value to a hint that his father let drop in another letter: "Sometime I must get down to see you."

Roosevelt had in fact decided to accept an invitation from the government of Argentina to lecture in Buenos Aires sometime in November. That meant a sea journey down the South American coastline, with an opportunity to stop off and see Kermit en route. He was sure of being officially welcomed in Brazil: Hermes da Fonseca, the president of that country, wanted to take him on a hunting trip.

Secretly, Roosevelt was planning something much more ambitious. The idea of a collecting expedition linking Brazil's two great waterways, the Rio Paraguay and the Amazon, had begun to grow on him. He had long been curious about the interior of the subcontinent, working its paleontology into his theory of biological analogies in history. Now, with his political career ended (once again!), his autobiography written, and his reputation wiped free of stain, he thought he might embark on one more great adventure before he got too old. Undoubtedly it would be dangerous for a man of his age, but as he wrote in a tribute to the British explorer Robert Scott in *The Outlook,* "Great risks and hazards are warranted by the end sought to be achieved." People afraid to venture outside the pale of safety possessed "limited imaginative power."

For a variety of reasons, not all of them conscious, he wanted to feel again as free as he had in Africa, and in those ecstatic days of youth when he could ride across the prairie and never see another human being. The spread of civilization across the earth's waste spaces, which he had celebrated in *The Winning of the West,* was accelerating at such a rate that little remained of mystery in nature. Since he left the presidency, both the north and south poles had been trodden on. Automobiles and flying machines were changing the definition of distance; time and space had lost their separate identities (or so a German physicist claimed). Palpably and not altogether agreeably, modernism was asserting itself. An increasing number of "alienists" were preaching the new science of psychotherapy in the Sunday newspapers, while the eroticists of "modern art" treated sexuality and madness as subjects fit for public exhibition. In Paris, on the day Roosevelt's sips of milk punch were being itemized in Marquette, the choreography of Vaslav Nijinsky and the music of Igor Stravinsky had precipitated a riot among theatergoers.

Roosevelt no longer believed that civilization improved by expanding. On the contrary, it coarsened as it spread, and encroached on refined enclaves. He found his own sanctuary on Cove Neck in Oyster Bay invaded by a new species, the "moving-picture man of vast wealth." Somehow this mogul, J. Stuart Blackton, had managed to buy the estate next door, and gotten permission to extend a huge dock out into Cold Spring Harbor. Judging from the size of the stable he was building on a field that had once belonged to Sagamore Hill, he would soon follow up with a mansion that would rob the woods beyond of many trees.

The Colonel was not alone among the clan of fiftyish, self-styled Anglo-Saxon "gentlemen," raised on both sides of the Atlantic, who felt a sense of social claustrophobia. For such men (restless Winty Chanler was an example, and Rider Haggard and Frederick Selous and Lord Delamere), there was little left to explore north of the equator except the El Dorados of economic, political, and scientific progress. Those parts of the Southern Hemisphere that were not ice or ocean still offered, here and there, opportunities for geographical exploration to persons no longer young. Roosevelt confided a few details of his Brazilian dream to Arthur Lee, admitting, "It is rather an ambitious trip for a stout, elderly, retired politician."

If he could persuade Dr. Lambert that he was fit, and get official backing from the American Museum of Natural History, he would probably not be back home until the late spring of 1914. "I shall be glad to be out of the country for one reason, and that is the Progressive Party," he told Lee. "The temptation is for the Progressives always to lie down on me, and in the unlikely event of the party continuing to exist, it has got to learn to walk alone."

Another reason to leave home for six or seven months would be to spare himself from having to watch the Democrats pervert his political and social legacy. Here was President Wilson determined to remove all Negroes from the federal bureaucracy, and collaborating with Oscar Underwood, the House majority leader, on a tariff bill as pro-corporate as anything approved by Taft.

The pious doctrines of pacificism and prohibition had become fashionable in Washington—nowhere more so than at the State Department, where William Jennings Bryan had declared that nothing stronger than grape juice should be served at diplomatic receptions. The secretary also announced that he would continue to accept fees for delivering his famous chautauqua oration, "The Prince of Peace." Roosevelt, disgusted, took advantage of a visit of some British pacifists to Sagamore Hill to preach a sermon of his own on the text, "Thou Shalt Not Slop Over."

He was sufficiently alarmed at worsening relations with Mexico, and with Japan over the perennial problem of "yellow-peril" discrimination in California, to warn Franklin Roosevelt in the Navy Department that war with either country was not implausible. "In that case we shall be in an unpardonable position if we permit ourselves to be caught with our fleet separated."

There was little more he could say to influence administration policy without sounding meddlesome. In the fall, he intended to write a single, statesmanlike appraisal of the current political situation, and publish it in the neutral pages of *Century Magazine.* Then he would sail south and out of the public eye. He was more likely to feel liberated in the jungle, with jaguars and anacondas and peccaries, than as a beneficiary of Woodrow Wilson's New Freedom.

AS A FANTASY, Roosevelt's South American project was not new. It had been implanted in his mind five years before, by one of the intellectual eccentrics he had enjoyed entertaining in the White House. Father John Augustine Zahm, C.S.C, Ph.D., was a former professor of physics at Notre Dame University, author of *Sound and Music,* a survey of the science of acoustics going back to Pythagorean times, and—more to the President's taste—*Evolution and Dogma.* He was also the author of two travel books, *Up the Orinoco and Down the Magdalena,* and *Along the Andes and Down the Amazon.* Like David Livingstone before him, Father Zahm was a globetrotter rather than a man of God.

If it had not been for the more powerful appeal of Africa in 1909, Roosevelt might have yielded to his suggestion that they together "go up the Paraguay," then cross Brazil's central plateau and descend the Rio Tapajoz, a tributary of the Amazon. The two men had kept in touch, and Roosevelt had made a point of alluding to Zahm's evolutionary theology in his essay on faith and reason.

There was a certain inevitability to him seeing the "funny little Catholic priest" at an American Museum lunch early in June. Frank M. Chapman, the museum's director of ornithology, had gathered a group of naturalists to ascertain if any of them might like to accompany Roosevelt on his proposed expedition. Father Zahm did not quite qualify, but he was avidly anxious to participate, and had value as a multilingual scholar who knew Brazil well—or claimed to. Before the lunch was over, the Colonel and the sixty-two-year-old cleric were a team, and it remained only for Chapman to get Henry Fairfield Osborn, president of the museum, to authorize their joint venture.

Osborn and Chapman were among Roosevelt's closest scientific friends, and the expedition would cover ground unknown to collectors, so he approved them as a matter of course. Chapman suggested the names of two professionals to go along, both veterans of tropical American forests: George K. Cherrie, an ornithologist and mammalogist, and Leo E. Miller, a field naturalist skilled at specimen retrieval.

Roosevelt reviewed their dossiers and thought that Chapman had chosen well. Cherrie was one of the best naturalist-explorers in the United States. Whipcord-tough at forty-seven, with a clipped, military manner, he had spent more than half his life south of the border. The mere fact that he had sired six children, one of them born along the Orinoco within pouncing distance of jaguars, was enough to recommend him. But Cherrie had the added credentials, irresistible to Roosevelt, of having once been a gun-runner in Colombia, and a two-time jailbird for revolutionary activities in Venezuela. Readers of *The Wilderness Hunter* and *The Rough Riders* were aware that the Colonel had a weakness for men who packed pistols, impregnated their wives regularly, and showed scant reverence for the law.

Miller was currently on assignment in British Guiana. But he had youth and Chapman's word in his favor, so he was recruited sight unseen. Anthony Fiala, a forty-four-year-old former Arctic explorer who ran the sports department at Rogers, Peet & Co., became the fifth member of the expedition, in charge of equipment, supplies, and transport. Just how much gear and extra personnel would be needed depended on the final itinerary, to be mapped out by Father Zahm. Fiala soon proved his worth by ordering two light, strong, cedar-and-canvas Canadian power canoes as backups to the eight-hundred-pound steel riverboats that Zahm seemed to think suitable for jungle travel.

By the end of June, Roosevelt had a pleased sense that another great trek, and maybe another great book contract, loomed ahead in the fall. With his autobiography now in syndication, his literary essays set in type, and Edith off to Europe to visit her sister, he was free to take Archie and Quentin to Arizona. "Thank heavens! I have never had more work than during the last eighteen months."

⌖

NINETEEN YEARS OLD, graduated at last from Andover, Archie had earned the luxury of seven weeks in his adored father's company. He also loved being with "Quent." The two boys had always been close, although they were as different as Huck Finn and Tom Sawyer. Archie's special schooling in Arizona gave him at least a destinational edge on his brother. Quentin, easygoing and uncompetitive at fifteen, did not mind where anybody took him, as long as he could investigate vehicular means.

On this jaunt it was a regular train of the Santa Fe Railroad, arriving in Silver City, New Mexico, on 10 July. Two days later, they met up with Archie's other best buddy, Nicholas Roosevelt, in Williams, Arizona, and registered that night at the El Tovar Hotel overlooking the Grand Canyon.

Moonlit and mysterious, the enormous gorge filled the windows of their rooms, trivializing everything in the world that was not a million years old. One decade before—too momentary a flicker of time for the Colorado to have carved any deeper since—Roosevelt had come here and expressed his relief that the Santa Fe was not going to build another hotel at Rowe's Point. He had stood on the South Rim and, ad-libbing to those around him, made the first great conservation call of his presidency: *Leave it as it is. You cannot improve on it. The ages have been at work on it, and man can only mar it—keep it for your children, your children's children, and for all who come after you.*

Now it was a national monument, thanks to the Antiquities Act of 1906, and he was back with two of his own inheritors. Archie, that seasoned veteran of desert living, had seen the canyon before. But Quentin had not. Someday, perhaps, Roosevelt's other sons and daughters would see it too, followed by Ted's little "Graciekins," and Ethel's coming baby, and their children's children.

THE MOON WAS FULL when they began their descent into the canyon at 2 A.M. on the morning of 15 July. Roosevelt, who had been assigned to write a serial travelogue for *The Outlook,* had arranged for guides, ponies, and pack animals to cover the 330-mile itinerary ahead of them. In the course of the next six weeks, he intended to give his sons a taste of some of the lessons he had learned in pursuit, survival, and acquaintance with the primeval, beginning with a cougar hunt on the high plateau of the North Rim, and ending with a trek through the Navajo Indian Reservation to Walpi, where they would attend the annual Hopi Snake Dance.

Thirty-two hours later, having gone so deep that they lost view of both the moon and the sun, they crested Buckskin Mountain, where it was still, improbably, spring. They spent the next two weeks in Kaibab National Forest, going after cougar and camping out at temperatures close to freezing. Roosevelt apologized for being old and "slow" on the chase, but Nicholas wrote in his diary, "He still has the energy of a boy and is handicapped only by his weight." He wanted his sons to do most of the shooting, although he killed one young female to gratify Archie. After the African lion, the mountain lion did not strike him as much of a threat; he was more afraid of losing Archie in reckless chases over the edges of the canyon. The bony youth seemed to have no fear. Roosevelt had taught all his children that courage could be developed like muscle, but Archie's was uninhibited by imagination.

Lacking fresh meat, they ate a fat cougar and judged it as good as venison. Roosevelt indulged in "elderly" things like washing up dishes and sitting alone, pondering the beauty around him. He was ravished by the sound of the silver-voiced Rocky Mountain hermit thrush, by the profusion of the stars at night, and by the vastness of the canyon's views.

The first day of August found them shogging across the blindingly white and sterile wastes of the Paria Plateau east of Vermilion Cliffs. The soil was so arid, or poisoned, that it failed to grow grass even where a streamlet trickled, producing only clutches of coarse weed with tiny, flaring white flowers. Squinting into a heat haze that retreated as they advanced, disclosing nothing but more nothingness, Roosevelt was reminded of Joaquin Miller's lines *They saw the silences / Move by and beckon.* At Lees Ferry, some mule-wagons were waiting to relieve the riders of their heavy gear, and they proceeded with lightened steps southeast to Tuba Agency, deep in the dry heart of the Navajo reservation. Far off to their right, the Painted Desert glowed. They rested for a day in Tuba, then swung northeast through heavy sand toward Kayenta. It took two and a half days to get there. Harsher terrain lay ahead. Roosevelt wanted to visit Rainbow Bridge, spanning one of the most impenetrable canyons in the Plateau Province.

Kayenta was a trading post run by John Wetherill, a member of the posse of white men that had "discovered" the Bridge only four years before. He had agreed to serve as the Roosevelt party's local host and guide, and had guest rooms ready in his cedar-pole-and-rock house, surrounded by trees and lawns. It was well supplied with books and running water. Roosevelt admired Mrs. Wetherill's taste in Navajo domestic design—she had decorated the walls of her parlor with delicate *tei-bichai* figures—and found her an impressively learned woman, versed in the lore of tribal ruins. It had been she, not her husband, who had first divined the existence of a rock buttress north of Navajo Mountain, from Indians protective of it as a sacrosanct place.

On 10 August the excursion across the Utah border began, with Wetherill acting as guide and five pack horses carrying a minimum of supplies. Three days of the roughest possible riding ensued. At times the train had to pick its way along paths only six or eight inches wide, notched out of slickrock cliffs that fell hundreds of feet to stony bottoms. The boys learned to keep free of their stirrups when Wetherill pointed out the skeleton, far below, of a horse from which he had once parted company.

The immense arch eventually disclosed itself, bathed in late-afternoon sunlight while the gorge below filled up with shadow. There were pools of clear water beneath it, enticing to hot and dirty travelers. Roosevelt was soon floating on his back, amid ferns and hanging plants, looking up at the darkening sky and still darker bar holding apart the cliffs. Later, the leaping flames of a campfire threw it into relief against the stars, and whenever he awoke during the night he was conscious of its overhanging majesty.

He noted the next morning that one of Wetherill's two Indian helpers would not ride beneath the Bridge. The man was a Navajo, and took the long way around, rather than follow the rest of the party down the canyon. "His creed bade him never pass under an arch, for the arch is the sign of the rainbow, the sign of the sun's course over the earth, and to the Navajo it is sacred."

⌐○⌐

SO FAR IN ARIZONA, Roosevelt had gazed with little pity at the dark, dirt-poor sheepherders who crossed his trail, emerging like Africans from the most inhospitable crooks of the landscape. The blankets they wove might be superior to the designs of Duchamp, yet they seemed to have no desire to better themselves economically or socially. It was clear to him that until they forgot about their nomadic past, and listened to what the white man could teach them about ranching and stock-raising, they would languish in primitive poverty. He knew that a debate was dragging out in Congress over proposals to cut up and sell parts of the overpopulated Navajo reservation, for the benefit of white stockmen and railroad land grabbers. Although he held no brief for outside developers, his belief in a social "Square Deal" (first offered, ironically, to the Southwestern tribes, when he spoke at the Grand Canyon on 6 May 1903) persuaded him that aboriginals clinging to an antiquated way of life had no power to resist the facts of economics. "With Indians and white men alike it is use which should determine occupancy of the soil."

Roosevelt's attitude toward "red" Americans differed from that of most of his kind only in that he had been willing, over the years, to moderate what had once been the harshest prejudice. As a young ranchman in Dakota Territory, he had blustered, "I don't go so far as to think that the only good Indians are dead Indians, but I believe nine out of every ten are, and I shouldn't like to inquire too closely into the case of the tenth." Later, however, while researching *The Winning of the West*, he had developed a respect for Indian military heroes, and as a civil service commissioner touring reservations in the early 1890s, he had been shamed to anger at the government's infliction of the spoils system on "a group of beings who are not able to protect themselves." Some of his beloved Rough Riders had been Indians, and were therefore among the bravest of the brave.

As President, he had struggled against constant Congressional opposition to reorganize and moralize the underfunded Bureau of Indian Affairs. A passionate young musicologist, Natalie Curtis, made him see that its suppression of Indian songs and Indian art in government schools was impoverishing the national culture. He had protected Miss Curtis from official harassment when she went into the reservations with a cylinder recorder, and coaxed nervous bards to sing for her. ("Be at rest, my friend, the great chief at Washington is father of all the people in this country. . . . He has given his permission for the writing of Hopi songs.") As a result she was able to publish *The Indians' Book* (1907), a luxury anthology of two hundred native lyrics, transcribed word for word and note by note. Roosevelt had contributed a short preface to it: "These songs cast a wholly new light on the depth and dignity of Indian thought, the simple beauty and strange charm—the charm of a vanished elder world—of Indian poetry."

⌘

AFTER FIVE DAYS the excursion party returned to Kayenta. Roosevelt spent a couple more nights under Louisa Wetherill's hospitable roof before he and the boys set out for Walpi. He talked to her about the Navajo, and found that her expertise was not just to do with pots and cliff dwellings. Like Natalie Curtis, she was a scholar of the aboriginal soul. She copied out her own translation of a tribal poem for him to carry in his saddlebag across the Black Mesa:

> Dawn, beautiful dawn, the Chief,
> This day, let it be well with me as I go;
> Let it be well before me as I go;
>
> Let it be well behind me as I go;
> Let it be well beneath me as I go;
> Let it be well above me as I go;
> Let all I see be well as I go.

The poem was as moving as any in *The Indians' Book* in its acceptance of the universe as a whole, spherical, yet infinite space of many dimensions—the circle of the horizon, the bowl of the sky, the complementary curves of sun, rainbow, moon, and arch—and in its concept of existence as a journey. Roosevelt decided that when he wrote about his stay in Kayenta, he would recommend the establishment there of a cultural halfway house for aspiring young Navajos, where Mrs. Wetherill could realize her dream of bridging the nation's ancient and modern cultures.

At mid-morning on Tuesday, 19 August, the Hopi mesa rose out of the flat desert ahead, a ridge perforated with seven pueblo villages. Nicholas, Archie, and Quentin spurred their horses toward Walpi, leaving Roosevelt to plod along alone. When he rode up a sandhill below the village he was surprised to see, coming over the crest, a woman with a cup of gasoline in her hand. She was wearing clothes almost as dusty as his, and there was a black smear of axle grease on the front of her skirt. Her face was familiar, as was her voice when she called out to him, "Hail to the chief!"

It was Natalie Curtis, embarrassed to have been discovered in the act of cleaning herself up for his arrival. Roosevelt did not know that his announcement, some weeks back, that he would attend the Hopi Snake Dance festival

"SHE CALLED OUT TO HIM, 'HAIL TO THE CHIEF!'"

Natalie Curtis in Indian dress.

had become a news sensation throughout the Southwest. Walpi was thronged with white visitors, and accommodations in the town were so scarce that Miss Curtis had been forced to camp out in a peach orchard. The cup of gasoline—vaporizing even as she explained her presence—was intended to cut the grease on her skirt.

She could not help thinking, as she looked the Colonel over, that he could have used some of it as well. His khaki riding clothes were stained, and his face under a big Stetson was burned as red as the bandanna around his throat. But he was still the overwhelming presence she recalled from White House days, with a combination of drive and curiosity that had him quizzing her about the Hopi even before they moved on into town.

He told her he was writing some articles about his travels in Arizona, and wanted them to be full of information. "I am going to South America shortly, and I can stay here only a few days, so the sooner we talk the better."

Natalie was only too willing to help. He was unaware that she had come to Walpi deliberately to waylay him and plead her continuing cause, against "the tide of Anglo-Saxon iconoclasm" that was sweeping away what was left of pre-Columbian culture. Nobody in government had ever been able to answer her question, "How much longer will the American people go to Europe for inspiration and destroy the art that is at their own door?"

Roosevelt had asked much the same thing himself, in his review of the Armory Show. Much as he had admired the quasi-American art of Robert Chanler (including representations of the Arizona desert and the Snake Dance), there was something effete about it, in comparison with the vibrant reality that now confronted him.

"Tell me what I ought to see," he said to Natalie. "I always like to find students who have made a life study of certain subjects. . . . And I am glad to put forward ideas, for somehow people *do* listen to me. I have at least the faculty of making myself heard!"

They made a date to meet for an information session the following morning, before *Chu'tiva,* the Snake-Antelope ceremonials, got under way. Roosevelt then gave himself over to the local officials who were to be his hosts over the next two days. He was flattered to hear that as "a former great chief," he would receive privileges rarely accorded to white men. After lunch he climbed down a ladder festooned with eagle feathers into the *kiva,* an antechamber of the underworld where the snake priests were preparing themselves for Thursday's dance.

THE SENSE OF THE strangeness that had possessed him ever since his stay in Kayenta mounted as he stepped off the ladder and found himself in a spacious skylit room, one end of which—the end nearest his ankles—undulated with rattlesnakes. Cigar-puffing priests kept them at bay by stroking them with feather wands. He was intrigued by the sinuous movements of both man and reptile. They seemed to share a temporary accord in which, however, the threat of sudden violence lurked. He was made to sit on the floor with his back to the snakes, about eight feet away, and did not feel at all comfortable. A pot nearby imprisoned—he hoped—some dangerous-looking ribbon snakes. There were about forty rattlers along the line of the wall, some writhing in a tangle, the others free to move at will. One wriggled toward him, and he had to ask for it to be stroked away.

Meanwhile, near-naked acolytes, their coppery bodies daubed with splotches of white paint, were stitching and beading dance costumes. Their moccasins respectfully avoided a sandpainting of a coyote, framed with rainbow lines and pinned at each corner with black thunder-sticks. A priest who spoke some English informed Roosevelt that the east wall beyond it was an altar of sorts, that the prayers offered before it were for "male and female rain," and that the snakes were being courted as "brothers of men," who through their soft bellies would telegraph to the underworld gods that the Hopi craved water.

He had seen tribal ritual before—in Africa, on Döberitz Field, in the Chicago Coliseum, at Mrs. Astor's Fifth Avenue balls when he was fresh out of Harvard. But nothing as mystic as this, nothing as symbolic of "an almost inconceivably remote and savage past."

⌖

ON WEDNESDAY MORNING he closeted himself with Natalie Curtis in a schoolhouse. If he expected a lecture on Hopi mythology, he was disappointed. She was more intent on criticizing the Bureau of Indian Affairs' latest folly, the substitution of European-style houses, with rain-shedding, hot tin roofs, for the flat, cool, adobe-walled architecture that spread so naturally around him. She talked about the inability of most white men to understand either the beauty or the fitness of Indian aesthetics. She complained about Congress's failure ever to have made "a systematic study" of the whole Indian problem, ethnological, environmental, and educational. Until some great foundation like the Carnegie or the Rockefeller should finance such a study, she said, efforts to improve the lot of the tribes would be like the rain-shedding roofs—"misfits in spirit as in fact."

Roosevelt listened and memorized with a receptivity not far short of Natalie's own as a song transcriber. But he was too old, and too much of a white man himself, to admire pagan values as much as she. He went no further in his commitment to her cause than to agree that there should be "an interchange of ideas between the two races."

At dawn the following day, she went to the Colonel's quarters with a bottle of hot coffee. She had promised to take him to the crest of the ridge, so that he could see the Hopi runners coming across the plain as heralds of the great Snake Dance. But his bedroom was empty. He had already heard the call of the crier and climbed the highest butte above town in pitch darkness. By the time she found him, the "yellow line" of Pueblo cosmology was widening in the east, silhouetting Roosevelt's bulk against the sky. When the runners appeared below, they seemed aware of his importance, and leaped up the side of the escarpment as if they had not already run five miles. Painted children accompanied the winner's final, easy-breathing rush.

Roosevelt applauded, privately wishing that he could enter such a splendid athlete in the next Olympic marathon.

All thoughts of common humanity faded, however, when he returned to the *kiva* for the Washing of the Snakes. Nicholas, Archie, and Quentin were permitted to climb down the ladder with him. The ensuing drama moved beyond strangeness into the realm of dream.

About twenty Hopi took part in it, naked except for breechclouts. The number of snakes on the floor around them had increased to about a hundred, with many of the more venomous breeds now at large. Again feather wands stroked errant ones away, as the oldest priest puffed smoke and sprinkled cornmeal over a huge tureen filled with water. In deep silence, he mumbled a prayer, and the other Indians punctuated it with what sounded to Roosevelt like "a kind of selah or amen." The chant grew louder and the copper bodies began to sway, but there was little hint of any rising passion. Acolytes reached casually into the tangle of snakes and passed them, coiling and waving, to the priests around the bowl.

When each priest had a couple of fistfuls, the chant rose to a scream, the snakes were dunked in the water, and then hurled halfway across the room so violently that several thunder-sticks were knocked flat. Roosevelt boggled at their willingness to be abused. The phrase he had used in endorsing Natalie Curtis's book came to him. He was being granted a glimpse into "an elder world."

At five o'clock the climactic Snake Dance began in the village. Antelope priests and snake priests, their faces daubed, chanted and stomped in a rhythm intended to reverberate to the center of the earth. Plumed headdresses tossed and leather kirtles flapped as they circled the rock Archie had climbed. At its foot, little girls dusted the newly washed snakes with corn meal. Then the dancers broke into couples, one of each scooping up a snake and putting it in his mouth. A particularly daring priest clamped his jaws around two narrow sidewinders. The flat triangular heads were left to float free and strike at will. Roosevelt saw no bites to the face, although he judged by a definite nervousness in the dancers that such an accident was possible. Both men and snakes seemed to be moving in tandem, caught up in the universality of the dance.

> At last all the snakes . . . were thrown at the foot of the natural stone pillar, and immediately, with a yell, the dancers leaped in, seized each of them, several snakes, and rushed away, east, west, north, and south, dashing over the edge of the cliff and jumping like goats down the precipitous trails. At the foot of the cliff, or on the plain, they dropped the snakes, and then returned to purify themselves by drinking and washing from pails of dark sacred water—medicine water—brought by the women.

Roosevelt left Walpi with the boys by automobile later that evening, but not before he had set down in longhand a three-thousand-word account of the day's experiences. "If I don't write the article now I never will," he told Natalie Curtis, "because my life is too full."

He explained that in two days' time he would be taking the California Limited from Gallup, New Mexico, en route home. Then he must write four lectures for delivery in Argentina, Chile, and Brazil. The governments of the latter countries were demanding that he address their learned societies as well as the one in Buenos Aires. Inevitably, his forthcoming itinerary had had to be extended.

"I can never afford to be in arrears," Roosevelt said.

Natalie complimented him on his orderliness and dynamic drive.

"I like the strenuous life, you know," he said, smiling, "and I am going to South America now because I very much want to make that exploring trip." He figured he had about six more years of real energy left. "I am nearly fifty-five. . . . I suppose that after sixty it won't be well for me to tax my resistance in the same way."

⟶⟨⟩⟵

THE COLONEL RETURNED to Oyster Bay on 26 August to find Edith back from Europe. He was overjoyed when she agreed to accompany him on the official part of his tour, linking São Paulo and Rio to Montevideo, Buenos Aires, and Santiago. She declined to contemplate a return crossing of the Andes by ox wagon. If he was determined to see Patagonia, from whatever altitude, he could do it without her. Her plan was to sail home from Valparaiso, Chile, at the end of November, and await the birth of Ethel's baby, due early the following March. By then, she hoped, her husband's jungle adventure would be over, and they could face old age in peace. One of her favorite quotations, recalled from the story of Troilus, was, "Life is short—let us spend it together."

This appeared also to be the sentiment of the veterans of Armageddon, querulous about Roosevelt's long-term loyalty. "I am having my usual difficulties with the Progressive Party, whose members drive me nearly mad," he told Quentin. "I have to remember, in order to keep myself fairly good tempered, that even though the wild asses of the desert are mainly in our ranks, our opponents have a fairly exclusive monopoly of the swine."

He did what he could to console Party members for deserting them at the start of the new political season. On 27 September he attended the New York Progressive convention in Rochester, roundly attacked William Barnes Jr., and the state GOP, and forced the nomination of Learned Hand for chief judge of the court of appeals. He published his long-delayed commentary on the national political situation in the October issue of *The Century,* but the writing was tired: it was little more than an update of his campaign platform of the year before.

Finally he allowed 2,350 wildly applauding Progressives to give him a farewell dinner in the roof garden of the New York Theater on 3 October. He promised that before he went into the Brazilian jungle, he would impress their ideology upon the intellectual and political elite of South America. "Next spring I shall return to devote myself with whatever strength I have to working with you for the success of the Progressive Party and of the great principles for which the Progressive Party stands."

VARIOUS OTHER SERPENTS had to be stroked before Roosevelt felt free to board the SS *Vandyck*, southbound on 4 October. Lyman and Lawrence Abbott were distressed to be losing their star columnist, so he sold *The Outlook* the rights to his four South American lectures, and a like number of travel articles, for $5,000. He assuaged Charles Scribner's chagrin over his defection to Macmillan by signing a $15,000 contract for a book about his coming expedition. As with *African Game Trails,* it would be prepublished serially in *Scribner's Magazine,* then put out in hardback with a 20 percent royalty. Roosevelt kept quiet about the speaking fees he would earn in Brazil, Argentina, and Chile, but Edith privately informed Ethel that they would total "about $10,000." Even after deducting all his travel and equipment costs, he expected to clear $20,000 over the next six months.

Quentin and Archie bade their parents goodbye with adolescent equanimity, and went their separate ways to school and college. Alice was more clinging. Still childless, she had been emotionally fragile since the announcement of Ethel's pregnancy, and had to be persuaded not to sue her depressed, philandering husband for divorce. The only salvation for the Longworths, as Edith saw it, was for Nick to win back his cherished seat in Congress.

In his last literary task before leaving, the Colonel composed an introduction to the book version of his memoirs. "Naturally," he wrote, "there are chapters of my autobiography which cannot now be written."

Then for the second time in his life, he dropped below the equator.

Interlude

Germany, October–December, 1913

NEWLY COMPLETED AFTER FIFTEEN YEARS of construction, at a cost of six million marks, the pyramidal structure outside Leipzig was the largest war memorial in the world, comprising three hundred thousand tons of concrete and stone. Twelve colossal sentinels balanced their granite shields in a ring around the crown of the monument, as if to repel would-be invaders from any point in the compass.

Inevitably, they dwarfed Wilhelm II, more than 250 feet below. He bobbed in Prussian uniform down the steps from the dedication platform, his shrunken left arm clutching his sword. A crowd of sixty thousand cheered while a choir accompanied by six brass bands broke into *"Nun danket alle Gott."* The date was 19 October 1913, the centenary of the birth of the modern German state. Here, Napoleon Bonaparte had been defeated at the Battle of Leipzig, or *Volkerschlacht,* as the Kaiser preferred to call it—"the People's Battle," greatest of all European clashes of arms.

Today's ceremony also marked the twenty-fifth year of Wilhelmine rule. The significance of the occasion to all German-speakers was signaled by the attendance of a special guest, Archduke Franz Ferdinand of Austria-Hungary. Lumpen, colorless, and stiff, the heir to the Dual Monarchy was everything that the Kaiser was not. Their helmets bespoke their characters—Wilhelm's a froth of white plumes, respondent to the slightest breeze, the archduke's a stolid cylinder. The two men were, however, close friends, vacationing frequently in each other's hunting lodges, and discussing questions of offense and defense against the Slav. It was a question which of them was the more obsessive on that subject.

Their shared neurosis was nothing compared to that of Franz Ferdinand's protégé, marching a few steps behind them: General Franz Conrad von Hötzendorff, the Austro-Hungarian chief of staff. Conrad's anti-Slavism focused on Serbia, the most restive of the Balkan states crowding the Austrian border. That landlocked nation had already triggered two wars, each nominally against Turkey but strategically threatening its northern neighbor. Its aim was a southern Slav federation, a *Yugo-slavia* strong enough to resist pan-Germanism.

Now, even as Leipzig celebrated the superiority of all things Teutonic, the archduke and general had disturbing news for Wilhelm. A third Balkan war was imminent. Serbia had sent troops into Albania in an attempt to gain access to the Adriatic Sea. The Austrian government was alarmed at this development, which compromised its whole wall of security against two hostile empires—the Ottoman in the south, the Russian in the east. As a result, Vienna had sent a peremptory note to Belgrade: if Serbia did not withdraw from Albania by 26 October, it would be obliterated.

By the time this ultimatum was headlined in tomorrow's European papers (sharing space, no doubt, with the dedication of the *Volkerschlacht* monument), six days would be left. That was hardly enough time for Serbia to comply, let alone hope that nations dreading a more general war might intervene. As every half-educated burgher living west of the steppes knew, Russia was Serbia's most reflexive ally, and would not tolerate any further Austrian aggrandizement in the Balkans. The annexation of Bosnia-Herzegovina in 1908 had been provocation enough.

Wilhelm had not welcomed that particular move. But recently he had shown signs of conversion to the Austrian way of thinking. *His* particular phobia was against the Eastern Slavs: the Ukrainians, Belarusians, Russians, and even Poles who for fourteen centuries had menaced Prussia across its erasable slate of a border—the *plattland* that any tourist could see from the monument's observation deck, fading into the enormous distance. A thousand years before, Leipzig had been a Slav settlement. Those sentinels bespoke the granite determination of Teutons that it would never be so again.

"*Ich gehe mit Euch,*" the Kaiser said privately to Conrad. "I am with you. The other powers are not ready; they will attempt nothing against it. In a couple of days you would be at Belgrade."

Franz Ferdinand jealously observed the intimacy developing between Wilhelm and his general, and returned to Vienna that evening in something of a huff.

❧

LEFT ALONE TO STAND against the gray Saxon sky in the days following, after the tents and platforms and bunting had been cleared away, the Leipzig memorial became an iconic shape, inspiring to Germans, Austrians, and Reichslanders, ludicrously overwrought to citizens of other countries. French comments had been especially scathing. It was not only the largest such pile since the days of Ancient Egypt, it was something new in its *völkisch,* ethnic quality, appealing less to memory of a particular battle than to the aspirations of a people who felt that their time for dominance had come.

An eruptive bigness, as of lava rising, seethed beneath the vineyards and farms and spotless towns of the Fatherland. Since the Franco-Prussian War, the population had burgeoned to sixty-eight million, twenty-nine million more than that of France. Its notable feature was a huge new middle class, thrown up by a fabulously successful program of industrialization. To Germans, all things seemed possible in the arts and sciences. What the monument was to architecture, the symphony was to Richard Strauss. In Vienna on the night of the Leipzig celebration, that master of the modern orchestra had premiered his most gargantuan score yet, a *Festive Prelude* for 150 instruments, including eight horns, six extra trumpets, and organ. It would seem that music could not get more earth-shaking. Yet Arnold Schönberg was simultaneously opening up a new system of harmony which, like the relativism of Albert Einstein, abolished all sense of stability.

Macht alone, overwhelming political and armored might, could contain all these forces and perpetuate the Reich for who knew how many thousand years. Crown Prince Wilhelm, the Kaiser's son and heir, declared that it was the "holy duty" of his countrymen to hold themselves ready for a "conflagration" which would make the battle of 1813 seem but a first spark. "It is only by reliance on our brave sword that we shall be able to maintain that place in the sun which belongs to us, and which the world does not seem very willing to accord us."

If the prince's language sounded unduly inflammatory, it was because he sensed a Prussian militarism developing in the very *Volk* that Germany's oligarchy of princes and generals depended on to beat back, once and for all, the Eastern hordes. Although there was no denying the impressive depth and breadth of the *Kultur* that had made Germany the most powerful nation in the world, its society was paradoxically rife with socialism and "progressivism," not to mention communism and anarchism. In last year's general elections, the Social Democratic Party had won an astonishing third of the vote, and, with Catholic centrists and other anti-Prussian factions, now held the balance of power in the Reichstag.

As a reaction to that victory, the Kaiser and his court of almost exclusively Prussian generals and landowners had forced upon the parliament the greatest troop buildup in German history. The army was now increased to well over three-quarters of a million men, with seventy-two-thousand called up this month alone. Theobald von Bethmann-Hollweg, the Chancellor, argued that a record force was needed to prepare for the coming battle of "Slavdom against Germandom." The Reichstag had reluctantly granted his wish, but was looking for an issue that would transform it at last into a parliament of public opinion, rather than a tame enacter of the imperial will.

SERBIA YIELDED TO THE Austrian ultimatum. Its surly capitulation served only to accelerate Russia's long-term program of rearmament and (what made the German Chancellor ever more apprehensive) raiload building, with most lines pointing west. Aross Europe, from Königsberg to Bordeaux and from Naples to Edinburgh and Christiania, fears of a multinational war sharpened into certainty. Georges Clemenceau, France's former prime minister and its most eloquent Cassandra, had been railing since the spring against the *pangermaniste* monstrosity in Leipzig, and all it stood for. The German army bill, he wrote, made it "inevitable" that France must fight for her survival again—and soon. She was, after all, the ally of Russia. His warnings used so many words of common meaning on both sides of the Atlantic that they did not need translation. Germany was plotting a "fureur d'hégémonie dont l'explosion ébranlera tout le continent européen quelque jour." Its ultimate aim was nothing less than "une politique d'extermination."

EARLY IN NOVEMBER there was a scuffle between two army recruits on a rifle range outside Zabern, in the Reichsland.

In living French memory, Zabern had been Saverne, and the Reichsland known as Alsace-Lorraine. But the Ninety-ninth Prussian Infantry had been garrisoned in the town for twenty-five years. Restaurants served more beer than wine, and the Kaiser's portrait hung in the offices of the civil authority.

The fight on the range was broken up by Günter von Forstner, a twenty-year-old lieutenant. With members of his entire squad listening, he lectured the youths on the importance of proper behavior in a region where there was a racial difference between the conquerors and the conquered. It was especially important not to tangle with any "Wackes" downtown.

Wacke, an almost untranslatable word connoting peasant or thickheaded inferiority, had as much force locally as *nigger* in the United States. Forstner went on to say that German soldiers had, nevertheless, the right to draw arms against this subspecies if shoved or insulted. "Should you kill one of them, so be it," the lieutenant went on. "Behave right, and you'll get ten marks from me, no one will blame you."

A sergeant standing at his elbow increased the offered bounty. "And me, I'll give you three marks more."

They were indulging in what passed among Prussians as humor. But the citizens of Zabern were not amused when reports of Forstner's words were published in two town newspapers. With repetition, the lieutenant's language got stronger: "For every one of those dirty *Wackes* you cut down, I'll pay you ten marks." The story spread to Paris and Berlin.

On 7 November, a public demonstration broke out in front of Forstner's house on the main street in Zabern. Stones were thrown. Amid catcalls of "Dirty Prussian!" two toughs broke down the front door before being dispersed by police. Thereafter, Forstner was escorted everywhere by a security detail so preposterously armed that the curses thrown at him became death threats. Within twenty-four hours, officers of the entire regiment were rendered jittery by the gathering hostility. Colonel Adolf von Reuter, the garrison commander, was so provoked by shouts in the street, as he sat at dinner in the Carpe d'Or tavern, that he went out and ordered the crowd to disperse, in the tone of a man who expected to be obeyed. His pallor and flap ears succeeded only in stimulating a competition for creative insults: *"Tête de macchabée!"* *"Espèce de lapin blanchi avant l'âge!"** The fury of the crowd grew till he and his fellow diners had to retreat to the barracks, pursued by hecklers screaming, "We are not *Wackes!*"

Demonstrations followed almost daily, with cries of *"Vive la France."* Colonel Reuter warned the municipal government that if it did not keep order, he would impose martial law. He then left for an undisclosed destination, pleading ill health. Lieutenant Forstner was overheard telling recruits, "As far as I am concerned, you can shit on the French flag." This was too much for his superior officers, who disciplined him with six days' house arrest. Police contained the situation until 17 November, when Reuter returned and announced that he did so "by order of his Majesty the Emperor and King."

By now, *l'affaire Zabern* had attracted the attention of international observers, who saw it as a showdown between German and French nationalism, more fraught with strategic implications than the scare over Serbia. Reporters and photographers from as far away as Bloomington, Indiana, poured into the little town. Demonstrations against the Ninety-ninth Regiment resumed. On 28 November, a huge crowd assembled in the square outside the barracks, as if miming the attack on the Bastille. Reuter finally lost patience. He sent sixty bayoneted troopers into the mob and arrested twenty-seven Alsatians, including three members of the Zabern judiciary. The offenders, judges and all, were thrown into jail overnight, and accounts of the incident telegraphed to Berlin.

The anti-Prussian majority in the Reichstag was sufficiently alarmed to demand an explanation from Chancellor Bethmann-Hollweg and his war minister, General Erich von Falkenhayn. When Bethmann-Hollweg rose in response on 3 December, the situation in Zabern had deteriorated further. Lieutenant Forstner, freed from house arrest, was accused of molesting a fourteen-year-old girl, and, for good measure, befouling the linen of a local hostelry. Enraged by shouts of *"Bettscheisser,"*† he had slashed one Alsatian across the face.

---

* Corpse-head! You prematurely whitened rabbit!
† Bed-shitter.

The Chancellor, sounding old and weary, announced that the lieutenant was to be court-martialed. Citizens of the Reichsland would, he promised, no longer be referred to as *Wackes*. On the other hand, they had no more right to complain about ethnic discrimination "than any other branch of our people." He hedged his way through a defensive review of the situation, over roars of contempt from socialists and centrists. General Falkenhayn—every bit as bristling as his Austrian counterpart—followed with a speech praising Forstner as a young Prussian of the best military type. The majority needed no further excuse to move that Germany's entire military government be censured.

During the debate that followed, Bethmann-Hollweg tried to forestall what was in effect a vote of no confidence by offering to withdraw the ninety-ninth Regiment from Zabern. But his conciliatory gesture was ignored, and on the evening of 4 December the Reichstag demanded his resignation by a vote of 293 to 54.

⌖

TO THE AMAZEMENT of democracies around the world, the Chancellor declined to step down. He stated that he served the Kaiser, and would continue in office, with Falkenhayn at his elbow, as long as His Majesty needed him. Court-martial proceedings against Reuter and Forstner were intitiated, but their ultimate acquittals, given Prussian solidarity, were not in doubt. Socialist demonstrations of rage and shame broke out in seventeen German cities, including Leipzig and Berlin. The government's only reaction was to punish two army recruits for publicly confirming Forstner's reported insults.

By the end of 1913, *l'affaire Zabern* was yesterday's news. But the oracular Georges Clemenceau remained under no illusion as to what tomorrow's would be. In an editorial addressed to his peace-minded younger countrymen, he bade them hear (if they would not see) "the cannons on the other side of the Vosges," and warned that the noise would soon be too loud to ignore.

One day, at the fairest moment of blossoming hope, you will quit your parents, your wife, your children, everything you cherish, everything that holds your heart and fortifies it, and you will go forth, singing as you always have, yet a different song this time, with brothers (true brothers, they will be) to confront the ugly killer that mows down human lives in a veritable hurricane of steel.

PART TWO

1914–1919

CHAPTER 15

Expediçào Cíentifica Roosevelt-Rondon

'Twere better late than soon
To go away and let the sun and moon
And all the silly stars illuminate
A place for creeping things,
And all those that root and trumpet and have wings,
And herd and ruminate,
Or dive and flash and poise in rivers and seas,
Or by their loyal tails in lofty trees
Hang screeching lewd victorious derision
Of man's immortal vision.

ON THE FIRST DAY of 1914, Roosevelt got up before dawn to hunt tapir in the marsh country east of Corumbá, Brazil.

For a week he had been cruising the headwaters of the upper Paraguay in a chartered side-wheeler, the *Nioac*. It was less grand than the presidential gunboat that had brought him up the big river, courtesy of the Paraguayan navy. But it was flat-bottomed enough to steam inland along such shallow tributaries as the Rio São Lourenço, where it now lay at anchor, a few kilometers above the inflow of the Cuyabá. Neither stream was easily distinguishable at present: Brazil's rainy season had set in, and an annual flood was coursing down from the central divide, filling the vast sump of the flats to capacity.

Knowing that he had a long wet day ahead of him, Roosevelt stoked himself with hardtack, ham, sardines, and coffee. Breakfast was his favorite meal, preferably including beefsteak or buttered hominy grits, and fruit with cream. When he got the chance, he could eat twelve fried eggs in a row. Over the last couple of years, he had become portly. His paunch did not compare with the world-class embonpoint of William Howard Taft, but he lacked Taft's compensatory height. Edith was concerned enough to have persuaded him to do without lunch whenever possible. He joked to Ethel that the only result was to make him greedier at either end of the day.

This morning he ate with more purpose than pleasure. He had come north from Patagonia intent on natural history and exploration. The trouble was, wealthy Brazilians ranching along the Paraguay still thought of him as a mighty hunter. They were slowing his ascent to Mato Grosso, the central wilderness, with elaborate shooting parties in his honor. (He had managed to beg off a "Roosevelt rodeo.") The great *fazendas* of Las Palmeiras and São João, with hundreds of peons and well-stocked stables, had been placed at his disposal. He did not want to appear ungracious toward his hosts. They and their governmental colleagues in Rio de Janeiro—not to mention the similar elites of Argentina, Uruguay, and Chile—had treated him so royally, and paid him such large lecture fees, that he had to conceal his impatience to be done with "state-traveling." In any case, he felt obliged to collect, in behalf of the American Museum of Natural History, some of the large, water-loving mammals of southern Brazil, before proceeding north on his expedition proper.

He had already shot a large female jaguar, fulfilling a dream he had confessed to Father Zahm five years before. Kermit (a bridge builder no longer, having signed on as his companion and interpreter) had bagged an even larger one, male, the next day. But that was the luck of youth. The earlier cat was at any rate a good specimen—probably the last dangerous game Roosevelt would ever pursue. In his fifty-sixth year, his interest in hunting was waning. He had not found jaguar meat as good to eat as the elephant heart that so satisfied him on Mount Kenya.

All he wanted now was a tapir, and maybe a white-lipped peccary, to present to George Cherrie and Leo Miller for preservation. Then he would be free to embark on a inland journey quite different from the one he had originally planned—for that matter, the most antipodean contrast to his African safari imaginable. It was a Brazil-backed venture, focusing on geography rather than mammalogy or ornithology, called the *"Expedição Cíentifica Roosevelt-Rondon."*

❦

THE LAST NAME belonged to Colonel Cândido Mariano da Silva Rondon, a tiny man with a sun-bleached mustache, also preparing for today's hunt. Roosevelt had met up with him only twenty days before, in a Livingstone-Stanley encounter downriver. The two colonels had bonded at once, with a mutual sense that fate had brought them together. Their common language was French, which each spoke as well, or as badly, as the other.

Dr. Lauro Müller, Brazil's courtly minister for foreign affairs, was the authority behind their joint mission. It had been he who, welcoming Roosevelt to Rio last October, had persuaded him to abandon Father Zahm's idea of going down the Tapajoz and up into Venezuela. The Tapajoz was well mapped, and the dry, stony hills beyond were of little interest to anybody but collectors of cacti. Müller suggested that the American expedition might more profitably divert itself inland to Utiariti, the virtual center point of Brazil. From there, it could march eastward along the rim of the Amazonian drainage basin, to the threshold of—*quem sabe?*—thrilling discoveries.

So deep a venture into Mato Grosso, passing through dangerous Indian country, would require the services of an expert guide. Happily, Müller knew an army engineer who hailed from that region and was part Indian himself. Cândido Rondon was not only "an officer and a gentleman," but also "a hardy and competent explorer, a good field naturalist and scientific man, a student and a philosopher." For years he had been on assignment for the national telegraphic commission, laying lines across some of the remotest parts of the Brazilian interior. In the course of his duties, which included surveying, he had made many findings of geographical and cartographical interest.

One such, Müller said, was the source of a mysterious river on the high western slope of Mato Grosso. It was assumed to flow north, possibly into the Rio Madeira, a major tributary of the Amazon. If so, it might be more than a thousand kilometers long. Rondon could not guess any more than that, and had named it *Rio da Dúvida*, the River of Doubt.

Perhaps Roosevelt would like to go down this river with him, for the mutual benefit of the American Museum and the Brazilian government, which was eager to develop the resources of Amazonas. There were vast stands of rubber trees in that province, but until all its rivers were mapped, it would be difficult for prospectors to stake valid claims. Perhaps, also, Roosevelt would advertise the open spaces of Mato Grosso as ideal for European settlement, as he had those of British East Africa in *African Game Trails*. In return, the two colonels could count on the support of a team of Brazilian army officers, all trained in field specialties, and as many *camaradas*—muleteers, porters, guards, and tent-raisers—as they needed to back up their descent of the Dúvida.

Short of throwing in an unlimited supply of canned peaches, Roosevelt's favorite dessert, Müller could not have more shrewdly sabotaged the itinerary Father Zahm had worked on for so long. His scheme was that of a master politician, whom many expected to be president of Brazil one day. It made sense at many levels, promising a rich harvest of specimens and topographical information, while increasing the commercial potential of Roosevelt's book, and almost literally putting Mato Grosso on the map. (Müller dreamed of building a new capital city for Brazil there.) Strategically, too, the symbolism of a Brazilian-American expedition into Amazonas, quasi-military in character and headed by the former President of the United States, would be salutary at a time when expansionist imperialism was rampant in Europe. Brazil was a gigantic, not fully formed republic whose land borders had been defined only in the last ten years. Unless it assured itself of American protection, Müller could see a day when the Amazon basin might be co-opted as a free-passage, free-trade zone, like that of the Congo after the Treaty of Berlin.

Roosevelt had reacted to Müller's proposal with entire predictability. "I want to be the first to go down the unknown river."

The minister warned him that his personal safety could not be guaranteed in a part of the country where many explorers had died. This caution had no more effect than worried letters from Frank Chapman and Henry Fairfield Osborn, president of the American Museum.

"I have already lived and enjoyed as much of life as any nine other men I know," Roosevelt wrote Chapman. "I have had my full share, and if it is necessary for me to leave my remains in South America, I am quite ready to do so."

Caution required that he pass along Müller's warning to his six colleagues: Father Zahm, George Cherrie, Leo Miller, Anthony Fiala, Frank Harper, and Kermit. Zahm was the least thrilled. He had no interest in *terra incognita*. All he had ever done in Brazil was follow pathways that the Conquistadors had trodden before him, in reasonable safety. He liked his comforts, and preferred not to have his progress slowed by poisoned darts, *pium* flies, and other hazards of jungle travel.

Cherrie and Miller, in contrast, had reacted to the change of plan with the enthusiasm of naturalists offered a new field of study. Fiala's only concern as director of supplies was how to get five tons of baggage down a river that might be nothing but rapids. Merely transporting the stuff beyond Utiariti would be a challenge. Harper was prepared to travel where needed in his capacity as the Colonel's secretary, but he saw limited opportunities for stenography in the wilderness. Roosevelt had told all five men that they need accompany him no farther than José Bonifácio station, near the rise of the Dúvida. Anyone who then wanted to drop out could do so, return south via the Paraguay, and sail for home.

Kermit, of course, needed little encouragement. Neither love for Belle Willard, nor the melancholy that had begun to affect him in adulthood (he was now twenty-four, and inclined to seek comfort in alcohol) could compete with the thrill of another venture into another continental interior, in company with his beloved father.

⌐

AT DAYBREAK ROOSEVELT, Rondon, and Kermit stepped down from the *Nioac* onto marshy ground. It was raining heavily. Under the guidance of some *camaradas* with dogs, they headed vaguely south. They hacked their way through saturated thickets, sinking often into ponds, gasping the near-liquid air. Mosquitoes hummed on waterproof wings, insatiable for blood. But their bites were nothing to the pinching of fire ants, and potentially lethal stings from *maribundi* wasps. At length the rain gave way to a steamy sun that pulsated down without drying anything. The hunters salted their wounds with sweat, raising sores that soon festered. Palm-needle slashes were of more concern, because any flow of blood into deep water would arouse the surgical interest of piranha fish.

Rondon was used to such torments. Born on the Mato Grosso forty-eight years before, the son of a Borôro mother and a half-Portuguese, half-Guaná father, yet capable of discussing fine points of theology and mathematics, he personified Roosevelt's ideal of primitive force sheathed in civilized restraint. During their first meeting over tea, Rondon had casually described how he once lost a toe to a piranha. Roosevelt had listened with delight, memorizing every detail for publication:

He was about to bathe and had chosen a shallow pool at the edge of the river, which he carefully inspected until he was sure that none of the man-eating fish were in it: yet as soon as he put his foot in the water one of them attacked him and bit off a toe. On another occasion while wading across a narrow stream one of his party was attacked; the fish bit him on the thighs and buttocks, and when he put down his hands tore them also; he was near the bank and by a rush reached it and swung himself out of the river by means of an overhanging limb of a tree; but he was terribly injured, and it took him six months before his wounds healed and he recovered. An extraordinary incident occurred on another trip. The party were without food and very hungry. On reaching a stream they dynamited it, and waded in to seize the stunned fish as they floated on the surface. One man, Lieutenant Pyrineus, having his hands full, tried to hold one fish by putting its head into his mouth; it was a piranha and seemingly stunned, but in a moment it recovered and bit a big section out of his tongue. Such a hemorrhage followed that his life was saved with the utmost difficulty.

Rondon's fellow officers also talked of aqueous anacondas big enough to constrict a cow. While not entirely believable, these stories did not encourage a meaty *norte-americano* to wade through Brazilian waters without trepidation. But Kermit and Rondon splashed on unafraid, so Roosevelt followed suit.

Hours went by with no sign of tapir. The humid heat became insufferable.

All at once the dogs scented a jaguar. Kermit was off after them with a young man's energy, and soon disappeared. Roosevelt tried to keep up with Rondon, but at 220 pounds he was almost twice as heavy as his spry partner. He felt himself flagging when they had to swim across a *bahia* with their rifles held overhead. Afterward his sodden clothes and squelching boots dragged with a

"Primitive force sheathed in civilized restraint."
Colonel Cândido Mariano da Silva Rondon.

weight that would not lighten. By midday, he was reduced to a slow walk. He went on all afternoon, but had to face the fact that he was beginning to be old.

FOR THE NEXT FOUR DAYS Roosevelt let Rondon command the *Nioac*'s final ascent of the Paraguay to São Luís de Cáceres. He relaxed on deck with Father Zahm, talking literature under the shade of a canvas awning.

The great river was now at its maximum flood, inundating the flat country so widely that they could have been crossing a motionless lake. Palm trees—the tallest he had ever seen—protruded incongruously. Some were rubied around the crown with orchids. Restless green parakeets added and subtracted emeralds. Lower down, apparently weightless *Jesus Cristo* birds walked on the water.

Now that he saw with one eye only, he relied heavily on his hearing to identify species of avifauna—as he had in boyhood, before he got his first spectacles. The dense air was full of bird calls that he found more interesting than beautiful. If this was tropical song—the *curu-curu* of screamer storks, querulous wails of wood ibises and plover, macaws squawking *ar-rah-h ar-rah-h* and flycatchers sneezing *kis-ka-dee*—it amounted to discord compared to the choral symphony he was used to every spring at home. Howling monkeys and the amazing whistle of the locomotive cicada added to the din. There was no diminuendo at night, just an abrupt switch to the shrilling of crickets.

He rejoiced all the same in the novelty of an America so unlike his own, it could have been attached to another continent. Brazil's environment struck him as an illogical clash of extremes. The intensity of tropical coloration, whether in feathers or flowers, made no biological sense. Only a vulgarian could consider the toucan beautiful. Giant *tamanduá* anteaters lurched through papyrus groves on upside-down paws, as if crippled. The marsh fringes evaporated, in the fiery heat, at such a rate that stranded fish lay around dying. They shone silver at first, but later turned dull and began to stink. Then cloudbursts replenished the lagoons, and overfed vultures and caymans took their pick of the carrion.

One evening this liquid landscape turned gold, and reflected a sunset of such prismatic beauty that Roosevelt exclaimed, "Wonderful, wonderful!" Off to port, the Serra Amolar loomed, its dark profile etched with rose, as if it was about to erupt. The immense curve of the sky, feathered with cirrus, was duplicated in the water. Priest and ex-president sat dwarfed and humbled in their deck chairs. They were unable to move until the radiance had burned itself out, and a crescent moon replaced the gold with silver. Both of them were storing up purple prose for publication. Zahm fancied that he heard, in the sound of the Paraguay churning astern, the "cadenced voice" of the *mãe d'agua,* or water-mother, that "beauteous siren of Brazilian fable," whose mermaid-like body was enough to tempt a man to plunge into her element, and be lost forever.

As far as Kermit was concerned, the sooner Zahm took a dive the better. He thought his father's friend was vain, lazy, and manipulative, a *faux* intellectual whose remarks sounded as though they had been memorized in the library at Notre Dame. But Zahm's erudition was genuine. His quotations from Shakespeare and Dante and other poets in Italian, Spanish, and Portuguese were accurate, if excessive. He was a master of historical geography, relating every squalid village or stone fort along the river to the annals of the Conquistadors.

As such, and for as long as this placid passage up the river lasted, Zahm was an ideal travel guide. That did not persuade Kermit that he would be of any use, once the expedition proper began. Sooner rather than later, Roosevelt—who tended to like people too readily, and discount their liabilities—was going to have to realize that this sedentary old cleric was *de trop*.

⌐◦⌐

KERMIT DID NOT know it, but on passing through Corumbá (loud cries of "*Viva*"; the hot, mimosa-fragrant little city on holiday; its sole hotel proclaiming WELCOME in brilliant lights), Roosevelt had updated his last will and testament. He had no plans to die in Brazil. However, he was fatalistic enough to understand that a river named Doubt might not deliver him safely to the Amazon—assuming it flowed that far. If not, or if it proved too much for him, it could turn out to be the Styx.

On 5 January the *Nioac* reached São Luís de Cáceres, its last scheduled stop and the official point of departure for the expedition's ascent to Mato Grosso. From now on, travel would be progressively more awkward: northward in boats up the Sepotuba, a rough affluent of the upper Paraguay, then, as hills and mesas crowded in, by mule and ox wagon westward across the *sertão* grasslands of the interior. Rondon estimated it would take them about seven weeks to reach the rise of the Dúvida, nearly five hundred kilometers from Cáceres as a crow flew. No man could guess how many more weeks they would need to trace the river's full length, but they were unlikely to reach their final destination, Manáos, much before the beginning of April.

Father Zahm was sorry not to continue cruising along the less arduous itinerary he had originally planned. It had involved a minimum of marching, and a powered descent of the Tapajoz in the steel motorboats he had commissioned in Pennsylvania, with gay pennants conjoining the initials R and Z. Roosevelt had abandoned these expensive purchases after hearing that they were too heavy to be hauled across the *sertão*. Fiala's sleek Canadian canoes were light enough, but they lacked the seating and storage space for a long river trip. Rondon, accordingly, had requisitioned some extra Indian-style dugouts to be held ready near José Bonifácio.

Roosevelt spent his last evening in civilization shopping and strolling around Cáceres. It was as Cubist a composition as anything he had seen at the Armory Show, with the added charm of being unpremeditated. The white-and-blue houses with their red tile roofs and latticed windows (through which an occasional pretty face could be seen, dark or pale), had probably not changed much since colonial days. They harked back architecturally even further, through Christian and Moorish Portugal to the thick-walled quadrangles of North Africa. On doorsteps and benches under the trees of the plaza, women spread skirts of red, blue, and green. Stringed instruments tinkled in the gathering darkness.

⤨

A GASOLINE LAUNCH and two *pranchas,* or roofed cargo boats, were supposed to be available next morning to ferry the expedition up the Sepotuba. Then a message came that they were waiting at Porto Campo, a hundred kilometers north. So the *Nioac* had to be crammed to the gunwales with equipment amassed in Cáceres by Rondon's local deputy, Lieutenant João Lyra. The size of the tents the Brazilians seemed to think necessary for survival on the uplands gave Roosevelt pause. With extra *camaradas* being recruited by the hour, he saw logistical problems looming. He had learned in Africa that the bigger a safari, the slower it moved, and the faster it depleted its resources.

As things were, the *Nioac* sailed so late that it did not reach Porto Campo until just before dawn on 7 January. This was as far up the narrowing stream as its flat bottom would take it. A portion of its cargo was transferred to the *pranchas* for advance shipment upriver. It was lashed to the side of the launch, and it labored off late in the day, straining against the current. Meanwhile, the *Expedição Cíentifica Roosevelt-Rondon* established itself in a cattle pasture. Bilateral proprieties were observed. The two commanders camped side by side, behind a pair of flagpoles flying their national colors. Kermit roomed with his father, and the tents of the other principals extended in a line left and right. About a dozen *camaradas* and kitchen staff bivouacked along a second row. Every sunrise and sunset a bugle sounded and the two flags rose and fell, while all personnel stood at attention.

Despite this show of equivalence, the professional disparity between the Brazilian and American outfits was obvious. Rondon's "commission," as he called it, consisted of eleven superbly trained men. Lieutenant Lyra was an astronomer and surveyor; Captain Amílcar de Magalhães, a logistics expert; and Dr. José Cajazeira, an army physician. There was also a field detail comprising a geologist, a zoologist, an entomologist, a taxidermist, and a botanist—not to mention two general-duty officers and a cinematographer, equipped with miles of film.

Roosevelt's team of seven was, with the exception of Cherrie and Miller, amateurish. Fiala had spent four years in the Arctic, but the skills he acquired there were unlikely to be of much use in the Amazonian jungle. Kermit had some, but not much, experience of the Brazilian wilderness, and was fluent in Portuguese. Harper was out of his element and looking for an excuse to go home. Zahm contributed nothing, although his Swiss servant, Jacob Sigg, had a capable pair of hands.

The absence of the launch gave Roosevelt an opportunity to hunt for the tapir he had promised his naturalists. He soon secured a big specimen, drilling it through the brain as it swam. On 10 January, going out after peccaries, he outscored Rondon three to one. "I have gotten specimens of all the mammals I was most eager to have," he told Zahm, "and am now perfectly satisfied if I do not get a shot at another animal."

After dinner that night, he and the priest had another of their moonlight

Map of the Roosevelt-Rondon Expedition, 1914.

colloquies. Promenading like the Walrus and the Carpenter under silver-edged storm clouds, they talked, in Roosevelt's words, "of many things, from Dante, and our own plans for the future, to the deeds and the wanderings of the old-time Spanish *conquistadores* in their search for the gilded King, and of the Portuguese adventurers who then divided with them the mastery of the oceans and of the unknown continents beyond."

⟨⟩

IT TOOK ANOTHER six days for the entire expedition to be shuttled to Tapírapoan, the main telegraph station in Mato Grosso. From here, Rondon's still-raw wires ran north to Utiariti, then east to José Bonifácio, delineating the route the two colonels would now have to pursue. But first they had to organize, discipline, and mount a caravan much more cumbersome than Roosevelt's African safari.

At first sight on 16 January, Tapírapoan looked like a stock fairground, jostling with beef cattle, milch cows, oxen, and mules. Barefooted cowboys in fringed leather aprons were attempting to tame some of the pack animals, who gave no sign of having ever carried anything. The noise of bleats and brays and snapping lassos, intermixed with curses in several languages, was discordant. Flags of all the American republics flapped around the plaza. Dozens of wagons were standing by ready to load. But they remained empty while various factions of the expedition squabbled over stowage space.

It did not look as if there could be any general departure for days. Fiala and Sigg pitched in to help. Harper seized on the astonishing quantity of specimens already bagged by Cherrie and Miller—totaling about a thousand birds and 250 mammals—to volunteer to take them to New York for delivery to the American Museum. He left two days later in the launch, laden with skulls, skins, and alcohol jars. This lightened at least some of the baggage Fiala was responsible for. But a vast amount of extra equipment still crammed Tapírapoan's storerooms. The Brazilians insisted every item was necessary. They had even shipped a giant land turtle, either as potential soup or as a spare, if unreliable, bench.

Roosevelt had begun to notice a Latin need for "splendor" among Rondon and his officers, and seating seemed to be an important part of it. He was embarrassed by the gift of a silver-mounted saddle and bridle that would have looked pretentious on his best horse at Sagamore Hill, but was especially so on a mule. Courtesy required that it be accepted with appropriate *obrigado*s. But when he saw that the enormously heavy tents Lauro Müller had provided were going to displace vital provisions, he insisted half of them be left behind. He still thought the expedition was burdened with a ridiculous amount of canvas.

Rondon and Lyra, in turn, looked askance at the American food store. Both of them were small, wiry men, trained to march for months on minimal sustenance. They saw the value of a hundred tins of emergency rations that Fiala had brought from New York. Such luxuries, however, as pancake mix, malted milk, chocolate bars, two varieties of marmalade, and a spice chest full of paprika, cinnamon, chutney, and other exotic seasonings did not seem necessary for survival in the wilderness. Rondon felt it would be undiplomatic to protest, and asked his colleagues to pack and eat less, so the *norte-americanos* could "enjoy the abundance to which they were accustomed."

This was too much for the Brazilian field detail, four of whom threatened to resign. They believed themselves to be better qualified to explore and report on their own country than a gang of foreigners. Rondon was sympathetic, but had to remember the constraints placed on him by Minister Müller. He reasoned that Roosevelt was an amateur naturalist only by default. Cherrie had been on twenty-five South American expeditions, and young Miller was a born collector, alive even to the near-inaudible squeaking of bats in a rotten log. The unhappy scientists were dismissed.

On 19 January, Captain Amílcar led the bulk of hoofed and rolling stock out of Tapírapoan. His biggest wagon, hauled by six oxen, carried the two Canadian power canoes and a sloshing supply of kerosene. Sixty-four other *bois cargueiros* and about a hundred pack mules followed, many of them resentful of their burdens. A much smaller rear guard consisting of Roosevelt, Rondon, and the other exhibition principals left town two days later. They were accompanied by their servants, five hunting dogs, and enough carts and mules to keep them supplied all the way to José Bonifácio. Together, the two detachments comprised 159 men, moving 360 sacks and cases.

The plan was to reunite the expedition at, or near, the headwaters of the Dúvida, then immediately divide it again. Only a select few members were to go down the unknown river—about as many as could fit into one Canadian canoe and half a dozen support dugouts. The rest would redivide, and survey two other north-flowing streams, already partially explored. One of these was the Gi-Paraná, rising near the Dúvida. Rondon wanted Amílcar to plot its long curve into the Rio Madeira. Miller unselfishly volunteered to go on that trip, saying that Cherrie, as the senior naturalist, deserved to stay with Roosevelt. The other unmapped river, assigned to Lieutenant Alcides Lauriodó and Anthony Fiala, was the Rio Papagaio, a tributary of the Tapajoz. If the Dúvida did indeed flow into the Amazon, a general rendezvous might be possible somewhere along the great river's right bank. Otherwise they would all have to swap stories in Manáos.

It went without saying that the two colonels would have to stick together, as co-commanders, with Kermit and Lyra assisting them. The fate of Father Zahm (serenely unconcerned with anything but his own comfort) was left, for the time being, to Providence.

⌖

FIVE PACKAGES THAT Roosevelt did not have to burden his mule with were the early chapters of his book for Scribners. Each had been handwritten on the same triple-carbon pads that he had used in British East Africa, and mailed to New York from post offices along the Paraguay. The last, "Up the River of

Tapirs," had gone off in care of Frank Harper. Roosevelt intended to dispatch two more before the expedition reached José Bonifácio. The rest, describing his actual descent of the Dúvida, he might as well take home with him.

No sooner had he left Tapírapoan than he began his sixth chapter, "Through the Highland Wilderness of Western Brazil," with a sentence bound to attract the attention of armchair travelers:

> We were now in the land of the bloodsucking bats, the vampire bats that suck the blood of living creatures, clinging to or hovering against the shoulder of a horse or cow, or the hand or foot of a sleeping man, and making a wound from which the blood continues to flow long after the bat's thirst has been satiated.

He left Robert Bridges to cut the redundant second phrase, his indelible pencil eagerly moving on to other descriptions of tropical fauna. Jaguar or *jaçanã,* animal or bird, every species down to the tiniest insect was worthy of study, as were plants and flowers. Literary style mattered less, but occasionally, as in *African Game Trails,* he was capable of stretches of perfect prose:

> Next morning* at sunrise we climbed a steep slope to the edge of the Parecis plateau, at a level of about two thousand feet above the sea. We were on the Plan Alto, the high central plain of Brazil, the healthy land of dry air, of cool nights, of clear, running brooks. The sun was directly behind us when we topped the rise. Reining in, we looked back over the vast Paraguayan marshes, shimmering in the long morning lights. Then, turning again, we rode forward, casting shadows far before us. It was twenty miles to the next water. . . . The ground was sandy; it was covered with grass and with a sparse growth of stunted, twisted trees, never more than a few feet high. There were rheas—ostriches—and small pampas-deer on this plain; the coloration of the rheas made it difficult to see them at a distance, whereas the bright-red coats of the little deer, and their uplifted flags as they ran, advertised them afar off.

The command detachment proceeded across the plain. There was no need for anyone to consult a compass, thanks to the bright filaments that Rondon and his engineers had strung westward. Even if a rider went astray in search of specimens or game, he could find his way back by listening for the humming of the wires.

A daily camp rhythm soon established itself. Early every morning a bugle sounded (Roosevelt sometimes adding his own reveille, a prolonged, Sioux-

* 22 January.

like *Who-o-oo-oop-ee!*). Then Juan, Rondon's black orderly, went from tent to tent with coffee. Breakfast was served while the *camaradas* saddled up the pack animals. Each day's trek was determined by the distance between available watercourses. Every few nights there would be a line-maintenance station to sleep in, with whitewashed walls, thatched or tiled roof, and cool stone floors. Dinners in camp were served under the stars, on two rawhides spread

"*MAIS CANJA,* 'MORE SOUP.' "

Expedition members at dinner. Clockwise around the rawhide: Zahm, Rondon, Cajazeira, Kermit (cross-legged), Miller, Cherrie, three unidentified Brazilians, Roosevelt, Fiala.

on the ground. Having fasted all day, the Americans did not stint themselves of beef, venison, pork and beans, and *canja,* the rich, thick Brazilian broth of chicken and rice. (Rondon noted with amusement that Roosevelt's Portuguese vocabulary extended to just two words: *mais canja,* "more soup.")

On 24 January, Kermit noted in his diary, "We're over the divide and into the Amazon side now." The only visible evidence of this was the northerly trend of the rivers they crossed. Otherwise, the equidistance of the horizon ahead with that behind gave no sense of progress. As Father Zahm put it, in his literary way, the Plan Alto was so flat, "one felt justified in denying the earth's sphericity."

By now Kermit was openly contemptuous of Zahm, describing him in letters home as "a very commonplace little fool" and "an incessant annoyance" who seemed to think that a man of God was entitled to special privileges. Among these was freedom to beg off chores, order Jake Sigg around, and boast about how many humble souls he had saved. His laziness was so extreme that Kermit took to referring to him as "Lizzie's brother," after a languid, melon-loving *morrocoy* tortoise that Miller had trapped.

Although the priest was flattered to have been presented with a saddle almost as fine as Roosevelt's, he did not enjoy having to sit on it fourteen hours a day. A muleteer was deputized to walk beside him in case he fell off. Zahm was alarmed when boxes labeled "Roosevelt South American Expedition" began to show up in the grass, evidently bucked by some of Amílcar's resentful critters.

Relief for him was at hand at Rio Juruena station, in the form of a caterpillar-tread *caminhão* truck that belonged to the Brazilian Telegraphic Commission. It was a speedy vehicle, able to crawl at thirty miles per hour even across swamps. When Cherrie and Miller, who were unable to do much collecting on the hoof, got permission to travel ahead to Utiariti in it, Zahm jumped at the chance to ride along.

Kermit was not the only person pleased to see him go. Colonel Rondon, as a nearly full-blooded Indian and convert to the Positivist humanism of Auguste Comte, mistrusted Catholic clergymen and especially resented their "fatherly" posturing toward aboriginal people. All the way up the Paraguay, Zahm had been laying hands on the heads of uncomprehending children, blessing and baptizing. Rondon foresaw trouble ahead at Utiariti, in the heart of Nhambiquara country. The local Indians, among the most primitive in South America, were not likely to take kindly to a cassock-wearing stranger who descended on them *deus ex machina*.

Rondon's misgivings were compounded by the fact that he had himself founded Brazil's national Indian-affairs agency, the Serviço de Proteção aos Indios e de Localização de Trabalhadores Nacionais. It was no less paternalistic than the Catholic Church in seeking to pacify and assimilate interior tribes—especially the Parecís and Nhambiquaras, who lived along telegraph routes and whose labor was needed to build and maintain the lines. Yet Rondon had a deep, consanguineous concern for the dignity of all Indians. He was passionate in his Positivist belief that the descendants of the white men who had killed them in war, occupied their lands, and visited strange diseases upon them, owed them a debt that should now be repaid.

When Roosevelt first saw some Parecís Indians on the twenty-ninth, he thought they looked much the same as ordinary Brazilian *caboclos,* or backwoodsmen. They wore clothes and sandals. But that was more than could be said for their womenfolk. Some of the younger ones were content with a loincloth or less. He noted approvingly that they had many children—friendly, naked urchins who came up trustfully to be petted.

The great cascade of the Rio Papagaio heralded itself the following day with a distant roar and slowly intensifying vibration underfoot. Then mist columns appeared, swaying and breaking. Riverside trees opened out and disclosed a stupendous sheet of white-green water, thundering into an almost invisible gorge. Roosevelt was thrilled, and told Rondon so. "With the exception of Niagara, there is nothing in North America to compare with this fall at Utiariti."

He forgot, or modestly chose not to say, that he had once been compared to Niagara himself.

⌒

MUCH AS HE WOULD have liked to spend hours staring at the cataract, he had to deal with a disagreeable problem in town. Father Zahm had made himself unctuously objectionable to Utiariti's Parecís population. He was claiming "a goodly number of baptized Indians" as a result of his visit.

Kermit sneered and Roosevelt was infuriated, but Rondon felt unable to stop the priest from catechizing. The Serviço de Proteção's official policy, framed by himself, was to respect the "spiritual freedom" of Indians. That included allowing them to pledge to any creed, as long as they were not forced to do so.

When the two colonels met up with Zahm, they found him in full missionary mode. He said he wanted to spread the word of God into "Nhambiquara Land," the stretch of broken country extending from Utiariti to José Bonifácio. Rather than ride any more on a mule, he thought he would travel in a *padiola*, or sedan chair, borne by some Parecís.

"The Indian is used to carrying priests," Zahm explained. "Often in the past I've used this way of getting around."

Before Rondon could protest, Roosevelt said, "You realize, of course, that you will be abusing the principles of my good friend Colonel Rondon."

A heated three-way discussion ensued. Zahm said that Peruvian Indians considered it an honor to bear the weight of Roman Catholic clergy. Rondon replied that such servility was contrary to "the habits and character" of Brazilian tribes. His agency was working to make them full citizens of the republic. If it meant to suppress them, he added sarcastically, it would model its policies on those of the Jesuits.

Roosevelt ended the argument by summoning Zahm to his tent. He heard the priest out, then issued a formal order. "Since you can't stand to ride any more, you will return to Tapírapoan immediately, and Sigg will go with you."

Moving at once, as he had as President, to prevent any appointee from suing for wrongful dismissal, he scribbled a memo for his fellow principals to sign:

> *Every ~~American~~ member of the expedition has told me that in his opinion it is essential to the success and well being of the expedition that Father Zahm should at once leave it and return to ~~the coast civi-~~ ~~lization~~ the settled country*
>
> *Theodore Roosevelt*

Nine signatures were appended, including even Sigg's.

FEBRUARY CAME with a heavy rain that delayed Zahm's departure and cast Kermit into deep gloom. "Cat very sad," he noted in his diary, using his pet name for himself, and on the next day, "Cat most unusually sad." He was accustomed to a sense of social isolation that set him apart, even when surrounded by jocular company. But his current malaise was primarily sexual. Just before he had set off up the Paraguay with his father, Belle Willard had surprised him by accepting his written proposal of marriage. Her letter had awakened in him a vast impatience to have done with this expedition, so much less enjoyable than the great Roosevelt safari of five years before. The longer he languished in Mato Grosso, the more he feared Belle might change her mind. Her father was now President Wilson's ambassador to Spain. She was a party-loving young lady, and relocation to Madrid was sure to enlarge her already glittering field of acquaintance.

Hunting might have worked off some of Kermit's frustration, but the grasslands were lacking in game. He took what consolation he could find in reading Camões's *Os Lusíadas*, that great Portuguese epic of other yearning wanderers, filled with a bittersweet sense of loss.

The rain thinned next day, enough for Roosevelt to spend most of the afternoon contemplating the Utiariti falls. He too was restless, but only Rondon—busying himself with preparations for Lauriodó's trip down the Papagaio—knew what the reason was. Speaking as colonel to colonel, Roosevelt had confided that he was tormented by the possibility of the United States going to war with Mexico. President Wilson (whose health he had toasted on Christmas Eve, at dinner aboard the *Nioac*) had not, at last report, done anything to arrest the rapid deterioration in relations between the two countries. If hostilities broke out, Roosevelt wanted to be back in uniform and fighting for his flag, not lost to the world in a wilderness where the only armies were ropes of ants.

And where, after all, was the Rio da Dúvida? To the American team, it seemed to recede like a mirage westward, no matter how long each day's trek. At their current rate of advance, slowed by storms, recalcitrant pack animals, and Rondon's weighty marquees, they would not reach José Bonifácio for another three weeks. Meanwhile the Papagaio confronted him, running north in the direction he really wanted to go. Flecked and whitish-green, it accelerated toward its straight line of collapse. Lauriodó and Fiala would be enjoying that exhilarating momentum very soon.

Father Zahm salvaged some dignity, and saved himself and Sigg many days on muleback, by wangling two *caminhão* seats back to Tapírapoan. But the Americans were not around to bid him Godspeed. They set out for José Bonifácio on 4 February, leaving Rondon to dispatch his Papagaio crew and catch up with them later. Roosevelt began a new chapter of his book: *From this point we were to enter a still wilder region, the land of the naked Nhambiquaras.*

There followed three days of semi-progress as deluge after deluge turned the trail into a slough that eventually sucked the oxen to a halt. Browsable forage was scarce, and nine mules starved to death. The sodden plateau gave forth a myriad of bloodthirsty *pium* flies. They were about as easy to swat away as fog, and their bites left black spots that refused to fade. In order to continue writing, Roosevelt had to drape a cheesecloth over his helmet and wield his pencil with gloved fingers. "I must make good to Scribner," he kept saying.

Kermit, Cherrie, and Miller agreed with him that the expedition was bogging down in more ways than one. It must convert to mule transport only. Roosevelt hiked back to make this recommendation to Rondon, in tones that brooked no disagreement. The last Brazilian tents must be abandoned. Rain or no rain, principals would have to sleep forthwith under the lightest possible covering, and the *camaradas* left to devise their own shelters. There was no question of carrying the big Canadian canoes any farther. Rondon's requisitioned dugouts would have to do when they got to the Dúvida.

The carts were emptied and pack animals loaded only with essential equipment. Travel resumed at an improved pace (the telegraph lines undulating ahead on their numbered poles, eleven spans to the kilometer, each rise and fall counterpointed, lower down, by giant spiderwebs). After a couple of dry and bracing days the sky turned black. "It's raining mournfully, dismally, and ceaselessly; in a sort of hopeless insistent way," Kermit wrote his mother, in a letter unlikely to be mailed anytime soon.

Groups of Nhambiquaras materialized often, nude and gleaming in the downpour. They had quills jabbed through their septums and upper lips, and carried bows taller than themselves. Even the arrows were five feet long. Rondon gave them goodwill gifts while posting a constant armed guard. He said that they had killed some of his men in the early days of his pacification campaign. Generally they held aloof, but the detachment's nightly halts drew them. They were fascinated by the sight of Roosevelt at work on his manuscript, crowding so close that he had to push them gently away.

HARD RAIN. MUD SLIDING IN SHEETS. Ominous telegraph at next station. Lauriodó and Fiala overturned on a rough stretch of the Papagaio. Half their provisions swept away. Fiala nearly drowned. Rio dos Formigas. Well named: local ants small, black, carnivorous. Big blue-and-yellow macaws. Rio do Calor. Two expedition dogs stolen by Indians. Rio Juiná. *Balsa* ferry. Sand. Skeletons. Blinding sun. Most lethal part of Nhambiquara nation. Rio Primavera. Rain. Kermit plagued with boils. *Pium* flies by day. *Polvora* ("powder") flies by night, floating freely through mosquito nets. Baking heat. More rain. More rivers. Roosevelt reading Gibbon's *Decline and Fall*. Rio Festa da Bandeira. Rio Iké. Wooded country now: sparse, scrubby *chapadão*. Mules starving. Vampire bats. Bullocks streaming with blood. Rio Nicolao Bureno. Indian hunting party. Pineapple wine. Campfire. Naked dancers under the moon. Wailing pipes. Former President of United States clapping to beat of stomping feet. Fragrant jungle. No game. Rain falling *torrencialmente*. Landscape opening out. Government research farm. Melons, milk, fresh eggs. *Mais canja. Mais* nudity. Nhambiquara girls around here even pluck pubic hair. For extra allure, one maiden wears a small, live, scalp-hugging monkey. Weather clearing. Telegraph line ends in a clutch of thatched cabins. José Bonifácio station at last.

IT WAS 23 FEBRUARY 1914. The Americans had been away from home for more than three and a half months. They had taken thirty-three days just to cross the *sertão* from Tapírapoan, and their most arduous challenge still loomed. Impatient to proceed, they spent only one night in José Bonifácio before shifting to the advance camp that Amílcar had established closer to the Dúvida. It took three more days for Roosevelt and Rondon to organize the Gi-Paraná and Dúvida expeditions.

Both teams were fitted out with the barest portable minimum of provisions, ammunition, and equipment necessary to sustain them for seven weeks. Books were classified as essential cargo. Roosevelt packed the last two volumes of his Gibbon, as well as works by Sophocles and Epictetus, the *Meditations* of Marcus Aurelius, and Thomas More's *Utopia*. Kermit chose Camões and some other Portuguese works; Rondon, Thomas à Kempis's *Imitation of Christ;* Lyra, miniature editions of Goethe and Schiller in German.

The three Brazilian officers were persuaded to share one tent, and the three Americans a balloon-silk fly that kept out vertical rain, but little else.

"Crowding so close that he had to push them gently away."
TR writing, surrounded by Nhambiquaras.

Roosevelt thought it wise to stow a one-cot medical tent, "for any one who might fall sick." He finished the seventh chapter of his book for dispatch back to Cáceres, added an appendix and illustrations list, with sample photographs enclosed, and even sketched out a title page:

THROUGH THE
BRAZILIAN WILDERNESS

BY

Theodore Roosevelt

WITH ILLUSTRATIONS FROM
PHOTOGRAPHS BY KERMIT ROOSEVELT
AND OTHER MEMBERS OF THE EXPEDITION

On the morning of 27 February, Roosevelt, Kermit, Cherrie, Rondon, Lyra, and Dr. Cajazeira had a bountiful Brazilian breakfast. Then their Gi-Paraná colleagues escorted them to the spot where Rondon's telegraph engineers had thrown a rough wooden bridge across the Dúvida. Seven shovel-nosed dugouts awaited them, already loaded with stores. The vessels lay so low in the water that they needed sidefloats to hold them stable. Most of them looked strong and sound, but two were old and leaky, dragging heavily on their ropes. Someone had caulked them as best he could. Sixteen strong *canoeiros* stood ready with paddles.

The inscrutable river coursed northward into the jungle, sixty-five feet wide, swift, deep, black, and silent. Goodbyes were exchanged. Roosevelt, Cherrie, and Dr. Cajazeira took their places in the biggest canoe. It displaced one and a half tons and was manned by a bowman, steersman, and midship paddler. Rondon's and Lyra's smaller craft rode ahead, with Kermit's, the smallest of all, in vanguard position. Both were two-paddlers. The rest of the team distributed themselves among the cargo canoes, which were lashed together in pairs, or pontoons. For a moment, all twenty-two men, white, black, and bronze, were concentrated in a tight flotilla.

Leo Miller was aware of the drama of the moment. As an experienced field naturalist, he had seen many departures, but none to compare with this, involving one of the most valuable men in the world.

"THE VESSELS LAY SO LOW IN THE WATER THAT THEY NEEDED SIDE-FLOATS."
Roosevelt prepares to descend the Dúvida, 27 February 1913.

Then with a parting "Good luck!" their dugouts swung into the current and were whisked away. For several minutes we stood on the fragile structure that bridged the unexplored river and stared at the dark forest that shut our erstwhile leader and his Brazilian companions from view; and then, filled with misgivings as to whether or not we should ever see them again, we turned our thoughts to the task before us.

CHAPTER 16

Alph, the Sacred River

Between the sunlight and the shade
A man may learn till he forgets
The roaring of a world remade,
And all his ruin and regrets. . . .

And he may never dare again
Say what awaits him, or be sure
What sunlit labyrinth of pain
He may not enter and endure.

"WE WERE QUITE UNCERTAIN," Roosevelt wrote at the top of his next batch of manuscript, "whether after a week we should find ourselves in the Gi-Paraná, or after six weeks in the Madeira, or after three months we knew not where."

He noted the date, 27 February 1914, and their position at embarkation: twelve degrees one minute of latitude south, sixty degrees fifteen minutes of longitude west. One thing his travels down the Brazilian coastline, up the Paraguay, and across the *sertão* had given him was a physical sense of Brazil's size, greater than that of the contiguous United States. It amounted to a Latin re-creation of his own country, as described in *The Winning of the West:* a young republic whose borders had only recently been established, and whose indigenous tribes were not all pacified. Nine-tenths of its population lived along the Atlantic littoral, walled off from the interior by an Appalachian-like range, the Serra do Mar. Railroads were beginning to snake northwest from Rio and São Paulo (Kermit had done his bit to extend them), but much of Mato Grosso was still, as its name indicated, a "great wilderness."

Topographically, this other Brazil was an immense shield of sandstone, slightly ridged in the middle, rising to a western height of three thousand feet. One face drained southward into the vast basin of the Rio de la Plata, the other into the even vaster basin and floodplains of the Amazon. The watershed streams ran deep and abrasive, notching sharp valleys out of the sandstone until they bottomed out on crystalline granite, Brazil's bedrock. Tributaries carved what looked like flat-topped mountains but were really remnants of plateau. On the torrid northern slope of the shield, some of these high residuals kept their temperate microclimates, while the trough beneath sweltered in an almost perpetual, fetid damp, teeming with the world's greatest profusion of plant and insect life. There were so many varieties of mosquitoes in Amazonas that their contrasting whines produced harmony.

Roosevelt found himself floating down toward it now, borne on the Dúvida's seasonal swell. The momentum would have been exhilarating if Rondon and Lyra had not kept stopping to survey every curve in the river. Kermit made himself useful to them in his lead canoe, jumping out onto any promontory that commanded an equal view up and downstream. He held up a sighting rod for as long as wasps would permit, while the Brazilians worked with a telemeter and compass to calculate distances and direction. All day long the laborious process repeated itself, bend by bend, station by station. "Kermit landed nearly a hundred times," Roosevelt recorded, "and we made but nine and a third kilometers."

The jungle was lovely to look at as it drifted by on either side, unending and unchanging. It exhaled sweet scents from its densely grown, vine-wrapped depths. Visibility inland extended only a few yards. Any spaces between the trees competing for light and air were screened with pendulous, parasitic leaves that reminded him of elephant's ears. The last time he had seen *folhâs* that big, they had been attached to the real thing. At riverside, where the sun shone unrestricted, gorgeous butterflies hovered over the water. They were matched in the shade by fungi of extraordinary color and delicacy.

But Roosevelt the hunter saw little to get fat on. Butterflies greased no bread, and no explorer who valued his life would dare to cook an Amazonian mushroom. The forest canopy amounted to a separate habitat, roamed by species unlikely to descend. Bored with survey stops, he went ahead with George Cherrie and Dr. Cajazeira in the hope of finding some break in the vegetation that might yield game. A meadow presented itself as ground for the expedition's first camp. There were a few tapir trails through the trees, but none fresh enough to pursue. The river was too engorged for profitable fishing. Fiala's tinned rations would have to do until meat could be found.

Roosevelt had the tents pitched, a guard posted, and stoves crackling by the time the surveyors turned up, weary but pleased with their mapping. The sky, overcast for much of the day, cleared at sunset. Dinner was served under a brilliant powdering of stars, or *estrêlas* as Rondon called them, in one of the many Portuguese words Kermit found more mellifluous than English. Gnats, *pium* flies, and mosquitoes swarmed only moderately.

⌒

ALTHOUGH ROOSEVELT WAS taken aback by the general soundlessness of the jungle, he heard enough bird calls in the morning to help Cherrie hunt for specimens. The naturalist did the shooting. They were rewarded with a brilliant turquoise *cotinga* and a woodpecker, whose display represented every color of the rainbow except yellow.

At noon they resumed their journey downriver. The other canoes had preceded them. Roosevelt reveled again in the beauty around him. He admired the fretwork of palm fronds against the sky and the gleaming green of rain-slicked leaves, melting into gold where the sun fell. He studied the different skin tones of his half-naked paddlers as they bent their backs over the water. Julio, up front, had the olive complexion of a pure Portuguese; Luiz the steersman was black; Antonio, amidships, was a coppery Pareccís.

The Dúvida seemed charged with as much upcountry spill as its valley could hold. But just after Roosevelt's dugout caught up with the rest of the flotilla, a big affluent gushed in from the right. Rondon deduced it to be the Rio Festa da Bandeira, which the command detachment had crossed some ten days before, in Nhambiquara country. Its inflow proved that the Dúvida was a major river.

Encouragingly, 16.5 kilometers were explored that day, and 20.7 the next, despite frequent showers that dropped scrims between Kermit's rod and Lyra's *télemetro*. In such conditions they simply sat and soaked until the sun came out. Then instruments, cameras, and clothes steamed off in the slamming heat. It was March now. Signs of Indian settlement were seen: a burned field here, a vine-bridge there. But no human beings showed themselves. Cherrie shot a large dark-gray monkey, and Roosevelt enjoyed his first simian stew, which he found "very good eating."

On the fourth day the expedition was moving smoothly and surveying with increased efficiency, thanks to the high level of the river as it slid over invisible rocks and half-submerged *boritana* palms (their protruding fronds, still full of life, combing the current). After twenty kilometers the valley constricted, and the Dúvida gained pace. A roar of white water came from ahead. All canoes swung to the right bank, and the paddlers leaped out to moor them. Roosevelt accompanied a reconnaissance party forward and came upon some seriously obstructive rapids. Curls, falls, ponds, and whirlpools descended in a misty chute nearly a mile long. At one point it narrowed amazingly, forming a spout through which the water gushed with fire-hose force.

There was nothing to do but make camp and start portaging through the woods next morning at dawn. First, the stores and other baggage were moved ahead to a point where the river broadened again. This was simple, if laborious, work, with everyone shouldering as much weight as he could support. It took all day. Rain fell in sheets, but not enough to drown giant horseflies the size of bumblebees. They bit till the blood ran. Roosevelt smeared himself

" 'THE GOODWILL, THE ENDURANCE, AND THE BULL-LIKE
STRENGTH OF THE *CAMARADAS*.' "

The expedition undertakes one of its many portages.

with fly dope, which soon washed off. After dinner, it worked better, repelling at least some of the tiny *polvora* flies that swarmed about him. They waited until he was asleep and sweating, then swarmed down to prick him awake. Kermit was unsympathetic. He had the Rooseveltian propensity to boils, and was suffering from an eruption so painful that he could do little but lie on one side and read *Os Lusíadas*.

The next one and a half days were even worse, with mosquitoes, *pium* flies, and vicious little aromatic bees responding to what was clearly a general alert in the insect world. Meanwhile, fourteen men chopped a "corduroy road" along the riverbank. They corrugated it with a couple of hundred slender logs, then twined a rope around themselves and hauled the canoes over with a block and tackle. Toward the end, the carry degenerated into a series of sandstone ledges. All seven dugouts—one of which weighed 2,500 pounds—had to be winched down, their keels shaving shallower as they rasped to the foot of the slope. In the process, the biggest boat split, and the leaky one sank as soon as it was relaunched. It had to be salvaged by force. Roosevelt, aware that he was no longer capable of such exertion, wrote a tribute to "the goodwill, the endurance, and the bull-like strength of the *ca-maradas.*"

The damaged canoes were caulked and dried out enough to let the expedition continue on the afternoon of 5 March. It made another twelve kilometers, and so did its attendant swarm of aromatic bees. They had stingless cousins whom Roosevelt found even peskier. Omnipresent at every camp, these tickly creatures crawled over his extra-sensitive skin with a maddening persistence, sucking at sweat glands and trying to invade every body orifice. He got some relief when the Dúvida broadened out, and Luiz could steer a good distance from both banks.

THE NEXT RAPID took three days to bypass. Another one materialized only five kilometers below.

Roosevelt soon learned not to yield to euphoria each time smooth brown water followed white. His canoe might be gliding like a gondola, but he would see riffles and whirlpools that warned of hidden boulders. Some porphyritic outcrops were too high for any flood. They announced themselves with a distant thunder that was always depressing, because even when side channels looked runnable—the river was now a hundred meters wide—there was a risk of losing provisions from the low-riding cargo pontoons. That meant more tree felling, more portaging, and less and less progress.

On the morning of 11 March the expedition woke to find that the Dúvida had risen during the night, and shattered the two biggest canoes against some rocks. A very large dugout had to be carved to replace them. The only available tree was a yellow *tatajuba* whose wood was so dense that its chips sank in the river like bits of iron. The *camaradas* set to work on it. Rondon estimated that the job would take as long as three days. Lyra and Kermit used the interval to hunt for badly needed meat. They got a jacu bird for the principals and two monkeys for the men.

In spite of fretting that the expedition was consuming means and preying upon itself, Roosevelt took pleasure in being alone in the jungle. There were spells, all too rare, when biting insects lost track of him and he could marvel at the interrelationships, half coexistent, half predatory, of tropical flora and fauna. He drank the oily sap of milk trees, ate dark, tart honey, and luxuriated in the fragrance of white and lilac *sobralia* orchids. From time to time he was able to classify a passing flock of ant-thrushes, or put his shoe on a coral snake and watch interestedly as it spent its venom on the leather. But the green-glowing environment was for the most part bare of observable life. What sounds came from the trees at night were (to his zoological ear) either batrachian or orthopterous. They began to taper off in the small hours. Dawn, which had been deafening in the Mount Kenya forest, was often eerily silent.

Every morning he took a swim, careless of piranhas. He was usually the first man in the water. When he floated on his back, he reminded Rondon of "a great, fat fish which had come to the surface."

Immersion in no way affected Roosevelt's cheerful volubility. "I never saw a man who talked so much," Rondon marveled. "I used to love to watch him think . . . for he always gesticulated. He would be alone, not saying a word, yet his hands would be moving, and he would be waving his arms and nodding his head with the greatest determination, as though arguing with somebody else."

The best that could be said for portages was that each of them represented a further, if slight, descent into the Amazon basin. And the Dúvida's steady trend a little east of the sixtieth meridian (every sigmoid curve to the left counterbalanced by another to the right) was heartening: straight toward Manáos, exactly the destination all the principals dreamed of. This was of small consolation to the canoeiros, who had to paddle ten, sometimes twenty kilometers for every five of actual advance. So far, that amounted to less than half a degree of latitude, and a drop of not quite fifteen meters from José Bonifácio.

By midday on 14 March the yellow dugout was ready, and the expedition managed a four-hour run to its tenth camp. On the following morning, calamity struck. Kermit was leading the way as usual in his small, rather wobbly canoe, ballasted with a week's supply of tinned rations and paddled by two strong black men, João and Simplício. His hunting dog, Trig, rode along. Rondon and Lyra trailed a few lengths behind, preparing for the first survey of the day. Roosevelt came next in the new boat. The only triangulation that interested him was that of the leaves of rubber trees onshore, which he noted grew in fans of three.

A bend in the river disclosed yet another stretch of roaring water, with an island dividing it. The two lead canoes swerved and came to rest on the left bank. Rondon ordered Kermit to wait while he and Lyra walked down to see how far the rapids extended. After a while Kermit lost patience and told his men he wanted to look for a channel on the right side of the island. João, the helmsman, warned him that could be risky. The flow of water above the break looked gentle, but if they were caught in a rogue whirlpool, they might not have time to steer out of it. Kermit insisted on crossing over regardless. They reached the island with no difficulty. On their return, however, they were swept away, just as João had feared. Simplício, paddling frantically, aligned the canoe with the current before it hit the first fall.

The three men managed to stay aboard while it crashed all the way down, filling with water. Then another whirlpool engulfed them, and they were thrown out, along with Trig. The canoe spun into midstream and capsized. João swam ashore. Kermit and Simplício clambered onto the slippery keel, but seconds later, a further set of rapids dragged them under, with such force that Kermit's helmet was beaten over his face. When he at last found himself in deep water, after six hundred yards of spins and somersaults, he was at the point of drowning. A branch overhanging from the left bank saved him, although he was almost too weak to pull himself ashore. To his amazement, Trig scuttled up after him. Simplício was nowhere to be seen.

All of this had happened below the sightline of the other principals. Rondon was first to encounter a saturated Kermit coming back upriver. "Well, you have had a splendid bath, eh?"

He no longer made light of the situation when the two *canoeiros* failed to appear. Kermit said both men had swum to safety. Rondon was not reassured, and went with Lyra to the foot of the second rapid. They found João recovering, and unable to say where Simplício might be. Anguished, they searched for the rest of the day, but in vain.

It was clear to the Brazilians that Kermit could, or should, be prosecuted for manslaughter. Roosevelt's main emotion seemed to be relief at not having to communicate the loss of his son to Edith and Belle Willard. Rondon saw no point in a potentially ruinous recrimination. The expedition was too deep in the wilderness to go back, yet not so far advanced as to expect to encounter any outpost of civilization for several more weeks. There was nothing to be done but adjust to what had happened.

After a night of grief and foreboding, Rondon erected a cross by the falls inscribed,

AQUI PERECEU O INFELIZ SIMPLÍCIO

To him, it said "Here perished the unfortunate Simplício." Roosevelt thought it translated as "In these rapids died poor Simplício." Taking what comfort they could in the nuances of their languages, the two colonels set to work on another portage.

―◌―

BY NOW THE LOST canoe was either miles down the Dúvida, or more likely sunk somewhere out of sight. Kermit went in search of it and found just one floating food tin and a paddle. He swam out to reclaim them, as the expedition was critically short of necessities. It had already consumed a third of its provisions, and game was as scarce as ever (although, tantalizingly, a tapir was seen surfing the rapids, moving too fast to shoot).

The portage began in blinding rain. While it was going on, Rondon reconnoitered the right bank with his own dog, Lobo. A strange howling, not quite animal, came from the jungle. Lobo ran to investigate, and was no sooner out of sight than Rondon heard him yelping with pain. Then the grotesque duet was cut off. Rondon guessed that the howling had come from Indians trying to lure prey, probably a *coatá* monkey. He fired a cautionary shot in the air, and went forward to find Lobo dead, perforated by two long arrows.

Rondon examined one protruding point. It was of a type new to him, indicating that the local Indians were not Nhambiquaras. They had probably never seen white men before. He left beads to signal peaceful intent, and returned to the portage even sadder than he had been earlier in the day.

Later that "dark and gloomy" morning, as Roosevelt described it, misfortune struck again. The lower rapids were deemed runnable by unloaded canoes, if they were steadied from the right bank with ropes. But the big new dugout proved so heavy that it broke away and sank in the turbulence, almost drowning Luiz and taking its tackle with it.

Roosevelt and Rondon assessed the state of the expedition. In eighteen days, they had registered one death and two near drownings. They had lost four canoes, dropped only sixty-four meters below the rise of the Dúvida, and had at least five times as much river still to explore before they could hope to see the Amazon. Lobo's invisible killers must be counted as extremely dangerous. That alone precluded the carving of another canoe, which would take three or four days and use up more food. Yet the two pontoons remaining could not carry the stores that were left.

All hands not needed on the river were going to have to make way for cargo and hack along the bank. The sole exceptions were Roosevelt and Dr. Cajazeira, who were considered too old and unfit to trek far. (Rondon, at forty-eight, remained as tough and stringy as a liana vine.) Every dispensable possession had to be abandoned. The hope was that safer country lay ahead, where the expedition could regroup, cut as many new canoes as needed, and hunt for meat.

On 17 March it began its bifurcated journey downstream, leaving behind for the mystification of the Indians a detritus including tents, clothes and shoes, a box of topographical instruments, and the waterside cross.

WHAT WITH SURVEY stops and the inclination of the *camaradas* to march barefoot, or sandaled, through the fly-infested jungle (resulting in three invalids, who had to be taken aboard the canoes), the expedition proceeded more slowly than ever. Another set of rapids necessitated a four-hundred-meter portage. Roosevelt and Cajazeira had no sooner reembarked than they were drawn, like Kermit earlier, into a second fall. Their lead pontoon very nearly capsized as it crashed around some boulders hiding a serious stretch of broken water. The second pontoon came down more carefully, but now fear was added to Roosevelt's sense of mounting frustration. "Our position is really a very serious one," Cherrie wrote in his diary.

Rondon decided to issue a morale-boosting order the following morning. It was his habit to address the expedition at the start of every day, stern and rigid in military khaki, trying to impose discipline on the polyglot, often quarreling assembly. Despite his small size, he was a formidable figure, austere to the point of monkishness, never ill, never tired, taciturn and unsmiling. The men had little affection for him, yet it was he, not the American commander (genial, tolerant, regularly handing out candy) whom they respected most.

When Roosevelt and Kermit attended the general assembly, they found the Brazilians standing at attention by the river. In the background, a small but strong stream flowed in from the west. Rondon cited it as hydrological evidence that the Dúvida was not an affluent of the Gi-Paraná. No matter where the larger stream led, it had come to dominate its own basin, and therefore could no longer be called a "River of Doubt."

On behalf of Minister Lauro Müller, Rondon announced, he was renaming the Dúvida "Rio Roosevelt." Its tributary here would henceforth be known as "Rio Kermit." He then called for cheers for the two honorees, and a general cheer for the United States.

Roosevelt was taken aback by this extravagant double gesture. The renaming struck him as premature. He liked the romantic concept of a river shrouded in mystery. But he could not help being touched, and relieved that Kermit had been forgiven. He dutifully led an American cheer for Brazil, followed by another for Rondon, Lyra, and Cajazeira, and one more for the *camaradas*. Lyra asked why nobody had yet cheered Cherrie. So the naturalist got the loudest roar of all, "and the meeting," Roosevelt wrote later, "broke up in high good humor."

There was little to cheer about in the days that followed. Kermit fell sick with fever. Indians were again heard in the forest, and smelled in small dark huts that showed signs of hasty flight. Rondon was so uneasy about them that he could not sleep past two in the morning. Two more dugouts were carved out of light, red *araputanga* wood, but they hardly sped progress as the number of portages proliferated. Nor, during spells afloat, did Rondon and Lyra moderate their incessant demands upon Kermit to paddle ahead with his sighting rod.

One morning, Roosevelt lost patience and drew Rondon aside.

"First of all, Kermit was extraordinarily lucky to have escaped with his life from that accident which killed Simplício. I'm not saying that with these Indians around, he's in more danger now than other members of the expedition, just because he sits in the lead canoe. But it's not right to continue mapping the Dúvida the way we have been. We must limit ourselves to a quick survey. Leaders of a big enterprise like this should just focus on establishing the principal points."

"Personally, I can't accept that," Rondon replied.

They were speaking French, the language of diplomacy. Even as he objected, Rondon recalled that he was in the presence of a distinguished guest of the Brazilian government, and backed down.

"However, I stand ready to escort you on through this wilderness as you wish, reducing the length of the expedition to a minimum."

"Important men," Roosevelt said, "do not bother themselves with details. . . ."

Rondon deflected the pomposity. "I am not an important man, nor do I consider details bothersome. Some sort of survey of the river is essential. As far as I am concerned, the expedition will be entirely worthless without it."

After discussion, they agreed on a less laborious method of procedure. But Roosevelt made one thing clear. "*Senhor* Kermit no longer rides up front."

⌀

CLEARING SKIES AND baking heat. Rapids, rapids, rapids. Portages too numerous to count. Rare fish dinners, but still no meat. Evasive tapirs. Grilled parrots and toucans. Monkey stew. Palm cabbage. Wild pineapples. Fatty Brazil nuts. Disappearance of fifteen food tins. Three weeks of rations left. *Oxford Book of French Verse.* Mountains crowding in. Men hit with fever, dysentery. Malcontents multiply. Daily chapter-writing. How to describe the utterly worthless *camarada,* Julio de Lima? "An inborn, lazy shirk with the heart of a ferocious cur in the body of a bullock."

On 27 March, Roosevelt was standing with some other principals below an especially violent rapid. One of the pontoons came down empty, guided by two paddlers, ran into a curl, and overturned. Then the current hurled it into deep water and jammed it against some boulders. He was the first to jump into the river and try to help the paddlers save it. Cherrie and other expedition members followed. They slipped and stumbled as they hacked at the lashings of the pontoon, with waves seething round their chests. Six or seven naked, screaming men, including Kermit, clambered onto an island and threw down a rope to secure the separated canoes. Eventually both vessels were dragged free and moored. But in the struggle, Roosevelt cut his right leg on a rock.

Twelve years before, as President, he had been riding in a barouche that collided with a speeding trolley car. He had been thrown to the side of the road, unhurt except for an ugly bruise on the left shin. It had developed into an abscess serious enough to mandate two operations and several weeks in a wheelchair. The surgery, involving a syringe probe and scraping of the periosteum, had left him with a permanent feeling of fragility in that leg. During his second term, he had rapped it while riding, causing such an inflammation that the White House physician had considered another operation, to remove atrophied bone. And in the summer of 1910, there had been a recurrence of osteoperiostitis, oddly accompanied by Cuban fever.

This insult to Roosevelt's other leg caused an ache that would not go away. He began to limp and his color reddened overnight. Next morning, three black vultures sailed over the camp. Then Rondon came back from a reconnaissance trip downriver. Cherrie could tell from his expression that he had terrible news.

There was a three-kilometer gorge ahead, Rondon said, full of rapids and falls, and so precipitous (it dropped more than thirty meters) that none of the canoes could be roped through. Nor, in his opinion, could they be portaged. The forested banks were too dense and too steep. All six vessels would have to be abandoned. Every man except Roosevelt must transport as heavy a load of necessities as he could carry along the rim of the gorge until it came to an end and more canoes could be cut.

The Americans overruled him. They insisted that time and supplies were too short to permit the construction of a new flotilla. Kermit was sure he and Lyra could coax the canoes at least some of the way by water and the rest by land, winching them up one side of the gorge if necessary.

Rondon agreed to let them try. But his pessimism was contagious, worsening the expedition's morale. Each principal had to pare personal baggage down to the lightest minimum. Roosevelt kept only the helmet, clothes, and shoes he stood in, plus a change of underwear and one set of pajamas. He clung to his black manuscript box and rifle, as well as a few other essentials: "my wash-kit, a pocket medicine case, and a little bag containing my spare spectacles, gun grease, some adhesive plaster, some needles and thread, the 'fly dope,' and my purse and letter of credit, to be used at Manáos." He made a single bundle of his folding cot, blanket, and mosquito net, and crammed the veil and gantlets he needed for writing into his cartridge case.

Cherrie accompanied him on the high trek on 30 March. Roosevelt began to show signs of coronary stress. He kept sitting down and begging Cherrie to climb on ahead of him. But the naturalist was afraid to leave him unattended. Together at the crest, they looked north at a range of mountains unmarked on any map. The Dúvida (nobody had gotten used to calling it the "Roosevelt") shone here and there amid the dark trees like an arrow of light. The way it vanished into the distance filled them both with foreboding.

When they descended to the camp that Kermit had hopefully established as a "port" overlooking the gorge's worst rapids, Roosevelt had no strength left. He lay flat on the damp ground, trying to still the tumult in his chest. He could not begin to help his son with the canoes, nor Rondon in cutting a corduroy road beyond the last cataract. The most he could do, when he recovered, was wash Cherrie's shirt for him.

As if in some vast conspiracy of fate, mountains, river, and weather combined to subject the expedition to its worst punishment yet. Rain drilled down as the men started work on the skidway. Kermit and Lyra stumbled around upstream in rotting shoes, roping the dugouts down meter by meter. One boat smashed, but the other five got safely to port. Then began the Sisyphusian labor of hauling them, and the rainwater they received, up Rondon's muddy road.

By the time this operation was complete, April had begun, and all but three of the *camaradas* were broken in body or spirit. The expedition encamped halfway down the rapids. The deluge that night amounted to solid water. Its weight collapsed the only two shelters available to the principals—the little medical tent in which Roosevelt now slept alone, and the balloon-silk fly shared by his five colleagues. Wrapped in a damp blanket, he managed to get some sleep, but fears about him increased.

The following day's advance amounted to less than three meters of aneroid "drop," and subjected him to another portage. His cot was set up in a gorge even narrower than the one he had just quit.

"Worried a lot about father's heart," Kermit wrote in his diary.

THE NEXT MORNING Roosevelt had reason to believe he was in the valley of the shadow of death. The jawbone of a *Pachydermata brasiliensis* protruded from the sand. Rock walls that could have been sliced by civil engineers blocked the sky. Kermit and Lyra lost yet another canoe, reducing the flotilla once more to just two pontoons. A reconnaissance party came back with news of rapids continuing as far as the eye could see. Or the ear to hear: for four weeks now, the roar of broken water had sounded almost uninterruptedly ahead of them, like a pedal note denying any hope of final resolution.

Rondon took some men ahead to hack vines, while others, supervised by a huge black sergeant named Paixão, got the stores ready for transportation. Roosevelt was resting by the river when he noticed Julio de Lima, the pure Portuguese he had long recognized as a spoiler, drop his load, pick up a carbine, and walk off muttering. It was not unusual to see a *camarada* hunt, since everybody was half-starved. Julio alone remained fleshy and healthy-looking. He was a known food thief: Paixão had several times caught him in the act and beaten him. But his muttering today was peculiar.

Several minutes later, there was a shot outside the camp. Brazilians ran back shouting, "*Julio mato Paixão!*" Julio had killed Paixão. Roosevelt, careless of his leg, hurried to the scene of the crime with Cherrie and Dr. Cajazeira. They found the sergeant dead in a pool of blood. Julio had shot him through the heart at point-blank range. A scurry of foot marks ran into the jungle, frantically circled, then disappeared down the gorge.

Roosevelt sent for Rondon and insisted on frontier justice. "We must go after Julio, arrest him, and execute him!"

Rondon saw that he was highly excited, and tried to calm him. "That's against Brazilian law. Criminals are jailed, not put to death."

"In my country, whoever kills has to die."

"It's useless to pursue Julio," Rondon said. "A man vanishing into the forest like that. . . . You've a better chance finding a needle in a haystack. Meanwhile, he deserves his fate."

Roosevelt's concern was that Julio, having gone berserk, might return under cover of darkness and steal food or kill someone else. But when the murder weapon was found further on, he accepted that the second alternative was unlikely.

França, the cook, was confident that Paixão's ghost would seek revenge. He darkly observed that the sergeant had died falling forward. That meant the killer was doomed. "Paixão is following Julio now, and will follow him till he dies."

Roosevelt quoted this remark in his account of what had happened. The writer in him responded to the expedition's second funeral ceremony.

The murdered man lay with a handkerchief over his face. We buried him beside the place where he fell. With axes and knives the camaradas dug a shallow grave while we stood by with bared heads. Then reverently and carefully we lifted the poor body which but half an hour before had been so full of vigorous life. Colonel Rondon and I bore the head and shoulders. We laid him in the grave, and heaped a mound over him, and put a rude cross over his head. We fired a volley for a brave and loyal soldier who had died doing his duty. Then we left him forever, under the great trees beside the lonely river.

LATE THE FOLLOWING afternoon, Roosevelt felt the first, unmistakable symptoms of Cuban fever. He had to endure a hailstorm, and further heart tremors, as he limped a few hundred yards down the boulder-strewn gorge to a new camp at the foot of the rapids. His colleagues saw that he was very ill and pitched his tent in the driest spot possible, a stony slope that shed at least some rain. Roosevelt was unconscious of the tilt as he took to his cot and the malaria hit him with full force. His temperature rose to around 104°F. He became delirious, reciting some lines of Coleridge over and over again:

In Xanadu did Kubla Khan
A stately pleasure-dome decree:
Where Alph, the sacred river, ran
Through caverns measureless to man
Down to a sunless sea.

Kermit, Cajazeira, and Cherrie took turns watching over him. The doctor laced him with quinine, at first orally, and when that had no effect, by injection straight into the abdomen.

In terror, Kermit registered the details of that night. "The black rushing river with the great trees towering high above along the bank; the sodden earth underfoot; for a few moments the stars would be shining, and then the sky would cloud over and the rain would fall in torrents, shutting out sky and trees and river." If his father was the epic hero Kermit believed him to be, then nature seemed to be in a state of hysteria at the prospect of losing him.

Toward dawn the quinine brought Roosevelt's temperature down, and he summoned Cherrie and Rondon. The Brazilian was taken aback at his grim expression as he said, "The expedition cannot stop. On the other hand, I cannot proceed. You go on and leave me."

He grew agitated when he saw they would not obey him. Rondon countered with a gentle appeal to his sense of responsibility.

"Let me point out that this is called the 'Roosevelt-Rondon' expedition, so we cannot possibly split up."

A reconnaissance after breakfast brought semi-encouraging news. There were two more rapids in the offing, but beyond them was a large affluent which gave promise of smooth water further on. If Roosevelt could stand another forty-eight hot, humid hours in the sunless gorge, he would see why Rondon had named the confluence "Bôa Esperança," place of good hope. There, the expedition might at last become waterborne again.

That day's portage proved to be a long one. Roosevelt's temperature resurged. His leg showed signs of erysipelas, a hot, shiny, streptococcal inflammation of the skin. He labored past the first rapid with ineffective help from Cherrie and Lyra, both of whom had dysentery. Kermit floated him down to the next one in a canoe, but he was more dead than alive when he got to a halfway camp Rondon had pitched. Dr. Cajazeira noted with concern that although his pulse had accelerated, his blood pressure had dropped. At least he did not become delirious again overnight.

Kermit developed a fever of his own the following morning. It was 6 April, the thirty-ninth day of the expedition—or the eighty-fourth, counting back to its ascent of the Sepotuba—and almost every member was weak from malnutrition. Julio's mysterious disappearance, after the deaths of Simplício and Paixão, had depressed the *camaradas,* while the principals dreaded that Roosevelt might die too.

"Am in a blue funk, as I have been for some time, to get out of the country," Kermit wrote in his diary.

Roosevelt staggered through a second portage before the explorers reassembled at Bôa Esperança. They divided themselves between the two pontoons, with Rondon's leading, and pushed out into the broadening river. The current took them, and for the first time in weeks, they felt a momentum that they did not have to slow.

Rondon and Lyra dared not make any more survey stops for fear of enraging Roosevelt. But they hit on a way of correlating canoe speed and compass swings within imaginary rectilinear tracts superimposed on the river. They were in the midst of this absorbing geometry when a voice from the bank shouted, *"Tenente!"**

The sound of Portuguese coming out of a wilderness untrodden by white men bewildered them until they realized it was Julio's voice. Desperate, apparently, for his own life, he had seen them coming downstream and crawled along a bough overhanging the water.

Rondon was too shocked to respond. He did not want to ruin his calibrations by stopping. Roosevelt's pontoon was still some way behind. Julio would certainly hail that too. If ignored, he would try to catch up with the expedition at its next camp. Or a search party could be sent back.

After a record run of 36 kilometers, Rondon discovered another tributary of the Dúvida at almost eleven degrees of latitude. It poured in from the east over a bar of sparkling quartzite and swelled the main stream to a width of 120 meters. An abundance of *uauássú* palms soared above dense stands of rubber trees, signaling that Amazonas at last was near. Rondon named the new river the Capitão Cardoso, after a colleague who had died in the telegraph service, and pitched camp near the bar.

Here he waited for the rest of the expedition to arrive. When it did, Roosevelt's fever appeared to be on the wane, but Kermit's was worse. Julio, they said, had hailed them, but they too had not stopped. Rondon asked what they thought he should do.

Roosevelt had no doubt whatsoever. "The expedition is in a state of peril," he said. "We must devote all our resources to safeguarding the lives of present members." Julio had forfeited that membership. Nineteen half-starved men, many of them sick, were in urgent need of a return to civilization. The *camaradas* were exhausted. Some were practically naked, their clothes and underwear devoured by termites. Nobody yet knew where the Dúvida was headed. If Julio gave himself up, he would have to be fed, accommodated, and guarded night and day. It was out of the question to go back for him. "I absolutely do not consent!"

Kermit ventured to disagree. His father turned on him in rage.

"Shut up!"

Lyra murmured in Portuguese, "He thinks he is still President."

---

* Lieutenant!

Rondon, who seemed to have forgotten about letting Julio escape three days before, said that it was "the duty of a Brazilian officer, and of a man" to bring a murderer to justice.

Roosevelt's anger ebbed as quickly as it had surged. He said he would defer to Rondon's opinion. "Let the law of your country take its course."

Julio did not show up that night, despite the inviting plume of smoke sent up by the camp fire. After breakfast the next morning, two soldiers were dispatched to where he was last seen. They returned late in the day to say that they had searched a radius of many kilometers, but failed to find him.

⌒

THE *EXPEDIÇÀO CÍENTIFICA Roosevelt-Rondon* made good use of its forty-eight-hour halt. Everybody needed a break from paddling and portaging. It was pleasant to relax in an open space, reasonably insect-free, in limpid light, after so many weeks in dark forests and valleys. For once there was no rain, just abundant sun to dry out blankets, and clear pools to bathe in. Two of the *camaradas* went out with a net, and brought back a gigantic catfish, more than enough for a communal feast under the stars (among them an inverted Dipper, pointing north). A bright moon made the joining of waters gleam like tossing silver.

Roosevelt ate little. The malaria had killed his appetite. In addition, dysentery was eroding his body, leading to a gauntness that renewed Kermit's fears for him. His leg was so angry with what Cherrie called "oriental ulcers" that he was unable to get any exercise, except when forced to portage—which in turn placed a strain on his heart.

Rondon doubted there would be many more barriers to the progress of the expedition. According to his aneroid barometer, the Dúvida had fallen 202 meters since its passage under the wooden bridge near José Bonifácio. This suggested to him that the Amazon basin was bottoming out. Yet over the course of the next five days, the river continued to be as resentful of burdens on its back as Captain Amílcar's pack team had been. "We are still surrounded by hills, and the roar of rapids is in our ears!" Cherrie wrote in his diary for 8 April. Every virgin promontory, right or left, disclosed another steaming set ahead. Roosevelt had to be carried past each. Soon he was not even able to sit upright in his dugout. A platform was improvised for him to lie on—tarpaulin spread across a bed of food tins—but then the sun beat down on him intolerably, and he sweated away further body salts. His men rigged an awning that gave him some relief from the heat, if not from the humidity that steamed off the river.

He remained fully conscious, able to admire the lush beauty of palm and banana trees glistening in the forest after showers, or emerging wraithlike from the mist that hung over them every morning. Along with Kermit, obsessed with the notion of marrying Belle in May or early June, and Cherrie, longing for Vermont, he became daily more homesick for the temperate north. Maple buds would be red now around Sagamore Hill, and windflowers and bloodroot blooming. For perhaps the fortieth time, Roosevelt watched the pontoons thumping their way over wet boulders and regretted the Canadian canoes he had left behind. "How I longed," he wrote in his manuscript, "for a big Maine birchbark, such as that in which I once went down the Mattawamkeag at high water! It would have slipped down these rapids as a girl trips through a country-dance."

On 14 April the river at last allowed an advance of 32 kilometers. The explorers were so used to disappointment, they did not dare to exult. But there were no rapids the next morning, and after a smooth run of two and a half hours, somebody noticed a signpost on the left bank of the river. It read simply, "J. A."

As a boy sailing on the Nile, Roosevelt had seen the fundamentals of civilization proclaim themselves thus: the column, the tablet, the cipher. As a statesman, he had passed through the gates of many palaces. But now, having nearly died, and being threatened yet with death from blood poisoning (he had a violent abscess on his inner right thigh, and another forming on his buttock), he could look on this wooden marker as something more thrilling than Karnak or Schönbrunn.

⌒

"J. A." TURNED OUT to be Joaquim Antônio, one of the rubber-tappers who were staking claims all over Amazonas in response to the worldwide automobile boom. Had he been at home, in his clean, cool palm-thatched house, he would have been able to tell the explorers what *he* called the Dúvida, and whether he had any inkling that it originated in Mato Grosso. But he was engaged elsewhere.

They had to keep paddling for another hour until they came upon an old black fisherman, the first new human being they had seen in forty-eight days. When he got over his shock at their appearance, he said that the river they were on was known locally as the "Castanho."

Rondon did not try to make him understand that it now bore the name of the emaciated *senhor* in the big canoe. The fisherman did learn, however, that Roosevelt had once been President of the United States. It took a while for this information to register.

"But is he truly a president?"

Rondon explained that Roosevelt was now retired.

"Ah, but he who has been a king, is still majestic."

When Roosevelt heard this in translation, he thanked the fisherman, and said that no ordinary person in his own country would be capable of such eloquence.

Later in the day, the expedition reached another rubber-tapping outpost, where Rondon learned that some rough stretches of river swirled downstream. Dr. Cajazeira was afraid they might fatally delay the hospital treatment his patient needed. So far, Roosevelt had declined camp surgery, but it had become imperative to lance and drain the abscess on his thigh. No anesthetic was available. On the morning of 16 April, he submitted without complaint to the agonizing operation, in which *pium* and *boroshuda* flies greedily participated. His condition at once improved, although he continued to shed weight until his clothes drooped around him.

It took another ten days, and several more portages, before an affluent that looked even broader than the Dúvida opened out on the right bank, and a neat tent hove into view, flying the combined colors of the United States and Brazil.

Rondon knew at once who had pitched it, and what the affluent was. Early in the year he had ordered one of his junior officers in Amazonas, Lieutenant Antonio Pirineus de Sousa, to sail up the navigable river known as the *baixo,* or "lower" Aripuaná to the point that it received a river of mysterious origin, flowing north. Rondon had not been able to guarantee that the unknown river was the Dúvida, nor had he been able to predict when—if ever—he and Roosevelt might come down it. But assuming his guess was correct, he wanted Pirineus to be ready with a range of emergency supplies.

The lieutenant had been waiting for more than a month. He was consequently as relieved as Rondon was when their respective rifle salutes cracked across the water. After the joy of a champagne-sluiced reunion, Pirineus added further cheer by reporting that the Lauriodó-Fiala and Amílcar-Miller expeditions had been successful. Fiala had left for New York. Miller was in Manáos, indefatigably collecting local specimens.

It was agreed in a hydrological conference that the so-called Dúvida, Castanho, and *baixo* Aripuaná were all the same river. Broad as the inflowing *alto* Aripuaná might be, its volume was less than that of the main stream—which could now be formally "baptized" as the Rio Roosevelt.

ROOSEVELT HAD TO brace himself to stand through the long ceremony, which took place the following day, Monday, 27 April 1914. He could not sit, because of the unlanced abscess in his buttock. But at least he could look forward to immediate transportation out of the worst hell he had ever been in. There was a steamboat terminal not far away, at the little rubber town of São João, with daily departures to Manáos. Rondon had sent ahead to reserve tickets on the next service for the three *norte-americanos*. The rest of the expedition would follow after Lyra had surveyed the Aripuaná confluence for the information of Brazilian cartographers.

Helmet in hand, looking thin and spent, Roosevelt listened patiently as Rondon read an extensive summary of what they had achieved together. The subsequent ritual was anticlimactic, being a repetition of the one already conducted more than a month before. The dedicatee seemed less moved by it than by having to say goodbye to Rondon and Lyra.

"ROOSEVELT HAD TO BRACE HIMSELF TO STAND THROUGH THE LONG CEREMONY."
From right of the flag-draped marker: two camaradas, *the two colonels,*
Lt. Lyra, Cherrie, Kermit, unidentified Brazilian officer.

WHEN THE AMERICAN PARTY awoke on Wednesday morning (Roosevelt lying face downward because of the agony of his latest abscess) they found themselves cruising down the Rio Madeira aboard the SS *Cidade de Manáos.* "The throbbing of her engines seems good to us," wrote Cherrie. "She is a fast boat and is carrying us rapidly toward the Amazon."

In their sleep, they had been delivered from a river no longer mysterious, but known, every kilometer of it recorded in ink, and some paid for in blood. Roosevelt's estimate, subject to official verification, was that they had explored 1,500 kilometers, or nearly one thousand miles, of a watercourse longer than the Rhine—or in his preferred phrase, "the largest unknown river in the world." That more than fulfilled the hope he had expressed to Ethel five months before, that his expedition would represent "some small achievement of worth."

At 2:30 P.M. the Amazon manifested itself, so sluggishly that it failed to impress. It looked like a muddy lake, flooded to immobility by the rainy season just ended. Roosevelt did not have the energy to include a description of it in his latest sheaf of manuscript, entitled "Down an Unknown River." For weeks he had been unable to eat more than a few spoonfuls of solid food; now he was living on nothing but eggs and milk. Either because he was too weak to exercise his habitual circumspection about personal matters, or because his relief at having survived was so strong, he permitted himself an unusual degree of sentimentality in bringing the manuscript to an end:

> Each man to his home, and his true love! Each was longing for the homely things that were so dear to him, for the home people that were dearer still, and for the one who was dearest of all.

Roosevelt did not know it, but Rondon had discreetly timed his arrival in Manáos for the small hours of Thursday, 30 April. This was to spare him the embarrassment of having many people see him carried down the gangway in a prone position. Even so, a reception committee was on hand, and he had to endure its welcome. A luxurious private "palacette" was provided him, courtesy of the governor of Amazonas. A sack of family mail awaited. Kermit, ecstatic, stayed up the rest of the night reading letters from Belle.

"Father about the same, but much more cheerful," he noted in his diary.

Arrangements were made to ferry them the rest of the way down the Amazon on a cargo boat, along with Cherrie, Miller, and forty-eight tons of freshly harvested nuts. Such was the power of Roosevelt's name that a British Booth Line steamship, the *Aidan,* was standing by at Belém do Para, ready to take him directly to New York.

Before leaving Manáos on the first day of May, he had his rear abscess lanced. This procedure left him still unable to walk, and he was taken aboard the cargo boat on a stretcher. The subsequent river voyage took four days. He spent all of it in the captain's cabin, writing letters to his family and friends. One note was addressed to Arthur Lee in London. It showed that Roosevelt's spirit was still strong, leaping ahead to future activity:

ON THE AMAZON, MAY 4, 1912

> Dear Arthur,
> I've had a bad fever bout and two abscesses, and am still in bed, so excuse pencil.
> On June 11th I shall be in Madrid at Kermit's wedding. I shall be in London about June 15th. Will you be there then? Can I come to

Chesterfield Street? If not, can you engage me rooms at Brown's or some other old fogey hotel? And, will you see Leonard Darwin, or whoever the present head of the Royal Geographic Society is, and tell him that whereas I had to refuse to give the Society a lecture on Africa, now I can and will give them a lecture on a genuine bit of South American exploration. We have put on the map an absolutely unknown river, running through seven parallels of latitude, almost on the 60th degree of longitude, into the Madeira; no map has a hint of it, yet it is the biggest affluent of the biggest affluent of the mightiest river in the world. . . . Love to the Lady!

Yours ever
Theodore Roosevelt

HE WAS PROFOUNDLY affected, on reaching Belém, to find that Rondon had somehow contrived to beat him there. The little Brazilian wanted to make sure he got off safely.

They each needed self-control for this second farewell.

"I hope and pray that you will visit my country," Roosevelt said.

"I will do so," Rondon replied, "when I can help you be reelected President of the United States."

CHAPTER 17

A Wrong Turn Off Appel Quay

Far off one afternoon began
The sound of man destroying man.

THE FIRST PUBLISHED DESCRIPTIONS of Theodore Roosevelt returning to New York on 19 May 1914—haggard, malaria-yellow, limping on a cane, his belt hauled in six inches—were graphic enough to persuade political observers in Washington that he was now, in more ways than one, a spent force. He claimed that he had put back twenty of the fifty-five pounds he had lost on his journey into hell ("I don't look like a sick man, do I?"), but word went around that he had suffered a relapse of fever before disembarking from the *Aidan.* When a private yacht transferred him to Oyster Bay, he had needed two helpers to climb the slope of the beach below Sagamore Hill.

Consequently, the Colonel's energetic demeanor only a week later, when he marched into Woodrow Wilson's White House, took reporters by surprise. His gray suit hung slack, and his collar stood away from his neck. But the cane was gone and he was as ebullient as ever as he recognized some familiar faces—including that of Jimmy Sloan, the veteran secret service agent.

The President had heard he was coming to town to address the National Geographic Society on 26 May, and had invited him to lunch. Roosevelt was as wary of getting cozy with Wilson as with Taft, four years earlier, and had pleaded a late train journey. This enabled him to get away with a mere courtesy call.

At three o'clock he was shown into the Red Room, where his host was waiting. It was a freakishly hot afternoon, so Wilson suggested a glass of lemonade on the southern portico. For the next half hour the two men were able to take stock of each other, in a conversation that avoided politics.

⌒

THEY WERE NOT STRANGERS, having been distantly acquainted since 1896, when Roosevelt was a police commissioner of New York City and Wilson a professor of jurisprudence at Princeton. As later chance would have it, Wilson had been in Buffalo at the time of Roosevelt's emergency inauguration as President, and had visited him after the ceremony to pay his respects. Now their positions were reversed.

Roosevelt had always breezily been inclined to like Wilson, as part of his general bonhomie toward everybody until they crossed him. Wilson's attitude was ambivalent. He admired the Rough Rider's exuberant activism and envied his popularity, but had been alarmed to see him elevated to supreme power. "What is going to become of us with that mountebank in charge?" Soon, however, he had been compelled to admit that Roosevelt was "larger" than most Americans realized, "a very interesting and a very strong man."

When Wilson became president of Princeton in 1902, Roosevelt had congratulated him for exemplifying "that kind of productive scholarship which tends to statesmanship." Wilson had early on detected those same qualities in himself, along with "latent powers of oratory." But as he became more and more a candidate for office, and less and less an academic, his misgivings about Roosevelt returned. "I am told that he no sooner thinks than he talks, which is a miracle not wholly in accord with an educational theory of forming an opinion."

Roosevelt's reciprocal attitude of incurious goodwill had begun to change in 1911, when he saw Wilson's political fortunes rising in contrast to his own. It irritated him to see an academic, peace-minded intellectual—exactly the kind of "dialectician" he had always despised—achieving reform after progressive reform as governor of New Jersey, then, as his Democratic opponent in 1912, coolly poaching most of the tenets of New Nationalism and adapting them as the New Freedom. Now here was Wilson, serene after a year in the White House, taking so many steps forward and back with regard to Mexico that wags were talking of a new dance—the "Wilson Tango."

Wilson had at first pursued a paradoxical policy of refusing to recognize the assertive populist government of General Huerta, on the ground that it had seized power by bloody means. He resented having to choose between either of Huerta's more capital-friendly rivals, Venustiano Carranza and Emiliano Zapata, saying that "morality and not expediency" should be the code of American conduct abroad: "It is a very perilous thing to determine the foreign policy of a nation in terms of material interest." This distanced him from William Howard Taft's Dollar Diplomacy, but he had come to realize that other powers were profiting from his unwillingness to do business with

Huerta. So he had lifted an embargo, imposed by the Taft administration, on the shipment of arms to Carranza and Pancho Villa. Enraged, Mexican authorities had stepped up their harassment of Americans south of the border.

Just when Roosevelt was floating free of the Dúvida's last rapids, Wilson had gone before Congress to say that if such "annoyances" were to continue, they could burgeon into an outrage "of so gross and intolerable a sort as to lead directly and inevitably to armed conflict." He asked for advance approval of any military action he might deem necessary to take.

This kind of personal appeal was something new in presidential politics. Roosevelt would never have gone to the Capitol, top hat in hand, to beg legislators for any indulgence whatsoever. *His* method had been to bombard them—and the press—with written messages that amounted to draft bills, ready to be signed into law. One such had featured what was now known as the Roosevelt Corollary to the Monroe Doctrine:

> Chronic wrongdoing, or an impotence which results in a general loosening of the ties of civilized society, may in America, as elsewhere, ultimately require intervention by some civilized nation, and in the Western Hemisphere the adherence of the United States to the Monroe Doctrine may force the United States, however reluctantly, in flagrant cases of such wrongdoing or impotence, to the exercise of an international police power.

Wilson at least seemed to have come to his senses on that score. In a development straight out of the Corollary, he had acted to prevent the unloading, at the port of Vera Cruz, of a consignment of German arms ordered by Huerta. He was convinced that these weapons might be used against the United States, and had directed the seizure of the entire town. This the Marine Corps had proceeded to do, at the cost of nineteen American and two hundred Mexican lives.

Roosevelt had thrilled to the news of this *casus belli* when it reached him in Manáos. By the time he got home, however, Argentina, Brazil, and Chile had intervened as mediators, saving both Wilson and Huerta from a war that neither of them wanted.

⁘

FOR A WHILE AFTER the Vera Cruz incident, Woodrow Wilson had looked sepulchral, his normally pale skin blanched to the color of parchment. "I never went into battle, I never was under fire," he admitted to a naval audience. "But I fancy there are some things just as hard to do as to go under fire."

If any haggardness lingered as he sat making polite conversation with Roosevelt, it was due less to the burden of being commander in chief than worry about his wife, critically ailing upstairs with Bright's disease. Roosevelt, haggard himself, made a polite inquiry about her health. For the rest of the interview, he and the President were content to talk about books and his expedition (Roosevelt joking that British geographers doubted there was any such thing as the "River of Doubt").

"HIS FORTE WAS ABSTRACT, ANALYTICAL THOUGHT."

President Woodrow Wilson.

On the former subject, they had little to share. Wilson was not the sort of man to enjoy Booth Tarkington's *Penrod,* a novel for boys that Roosevelt was currently devouring. Nor, for that matter, was he likely to curl up with *Life-Histories of African Game Animals,* the Colonel's latest two-volume work of zoography. He had come to reading and writing late, after struggling with disabilities as a child, and when he did, his fields of interest had been as few as Roosevelt's were many.

During their prepresidential careers (Wilson was almost two years older), they had both written histories and biographies that showed they understood the American dynamic—its geographical push westward, and the centripetal forces that had worked against secession and defederalized the Constitution. But their respective attempts at a *magnum opus*—Roosevelt's four-volume *The Winning of the West,* and Wilson's five-volume *A History of the American People*—had nothing in common except the palpable ache of each author to be making history rather than writing it. Wilson had no gift for narrative, and absolutely no feel for the physical things Roosevelt reveled in: hunting, warfare, exploration, danger. He named no plants and heard no birds. Surprisingly, for a professor, he had been less willing than Roosevelt to scour archives and even attics for original documents. His forte was abstract, analytical thought, especially on governmental and legal issues. Questions of process and synthesis, the objective calculation of power balances (or imbalances, as in *Congressional Government,* his 1885 exposé of committee rule on Capitol Hill), and the logical resolution of conflicting ideas were the sort of cerebral challenges that delighted him. Roosevelt could no more have written Wilson's *Division and Reunion,* about the polemics of the Civil War, than the President could have published *The Rough Riders.*

Had Wilson not been so formidably sure of himself, with his calm gray gaze and air of aloof command, he might well have been intimidated by the recovering invalid opposite him. Aside from the facts that Roosevelt had served two successful terms as president, and would now be serving a third, if the Republican Party had not been so hostile to progressive reform, there was the prodigality of his worldly experience to take into account. At least a cat's quota of lives, and easy adaptation to environments as irreconcilable as Nahant, Nairobi, and the piranha pools of Brazil were embodied in the cheerful sunburned man who sat drinking the President's lemonade.

When Roosevelt rose to go, Wilson escorted him to the north door of the White House and waved goodbye as he limped back to his automobile. A crowd of several hundred spectators had collected around it. "Hurrah for Teddy!" a young man yelled. "Hurrah for our next President!"

Roosevelt, grinning, took off his panama hat and bopped the youth's head with it.

Afterward, Joseph Tumulty asked Wilson what he thought of the Colonel.

"He is a great big boy," Wilson said. "There is a sweetness about him that is very compelling. You can't resist the man. I can easily understand why his followers are so fond of him."

⊸⊷

IT WAS STILL HOT at 8:30 P.M., when Roosevelt arrived at the District of Columbia Convention Hall. The huge room was built over a street-level market, so a miasma of rotting vegetables saluted the nostrils of the four thousand people waiting to hear his lecture. Almost the entire membership of the National Geographic Society was present, in a show of solidarity against transatlantic critics who were alleging that the Colonel had explored very little, and discovered nothing new, in Brazil. An editorial in the *Daily Graphic* had compared him to Baron Münchhausen as a fantasist of improbable adventures.

He came perspiring up the stairway, and was formally escorted into the hall by a group of geographers walking backward and applauding. The ova-

" 'HURRAH FOR OUR NEXT PRESIDENT!' "
A thinner Roosevelt revisits Washington, 19 May 1914.

tion was thunderous, especially when he took the stage and flashed his white-tile grin. Veteran observers of the capital scene could not recall any former president since Ulysses S. Grant being more loudly cheered. Those more future-minded looked ahead to the possibility of Roosevelt challenging Wilson in 1916.

"I'm almost regretful to see you all here," he joked. "I have got to make a rather dry speech."

He proceeded, with the aid of a blackboard, a stereopticon screen, and three printed maps, to lecture learnedly on his expedition. "It is almost impossible for me to show you on these standard maps what I did, because the maps are so preposterously wrong. For instance, here are the headquarters of the Tapajoz de Juruena. . . ." To those in the audience who could think of Theodore Roosevelt only as a politician, the experience of seeing him, with his strangely drawn face and eroded voice, assessing bottom-flow rates at 4,500 cubic meters per second in the seventh degree of southern latitude was so bizarre that he might have been an impersonator. George Cherrie, Leo Miller, Anthony Fiala, and Father Zahm were conversely reminded that the man they had huddled with in Mato Grosso hailstorms was not, after all, their intimate, but a public figure making arch reference to them as "exhibits A, B, C, and D."

Again and again Roosevelt emphasized that he had not discovered the Dúvida, but had merely—with the professional assistance of Brazilian survey-ors—"put it on the map." He refrained from mentioning that the river now bore his name, and did not say that it had nearly killed him, except to admit that there had been times when life in camp "lacked a good deal of being undi-luted pleasure."

He was plainly exhausted afterward. But that did not prevent a *pium*-like swarm of Congressional Progressives pursuing him to the Party headquarters and talking politics until it was time for him to take the midnight sleeper back to New York.

⤙⤚

TWO WEEKS LATER, in the kind of translocation only Roosevelt could find natural, he sat at lunch with the King and Queen of Spain in the fragrant gar-den of their summer palace outside Madrid. The guests of honor were Kermit and Belle Willard, who were due to be married twice over the next two days— first by a local magistrate at a civil ceremony, then in an Episcopalian service in the private chapel of the British Embassy, so as not to profane Spain's Catholic orthodoxy. Belle's father, Joseph E. Willard, was on hand in his ca-pacity as the American ambassador, and Alice Longworth substituted for Edith Roosevelt, who at fifty-three was suffering vague female ailments, and had declined to accompany her husband overseas.

Roosevelt and Alfonso XIII already knew each other, as fellow mourners at the funeral of Edward VII four years before. Their initial meetings had been awkward. Alfonso found it hard to forget, and forgive, the defeats his soldiers had suffered in the Spanish-American War, at the hands of adversaries promi-nently including the Colonel of the Rough Riders. Now it was necessary for him to be cordial, if only because of the diplomatic importance of tomor-row's ceremony, linking the administrations of two American presidents. Roo-sevelt treated Alfonso with his usual affability, unbending him to the extent that they ended up laughing about the "wake" George V had held in Bucking-ham Palace.

Royal favor notwithstanding, the Spanish government found it necessary to surround the Colonel with heavy security during his four-day stay. Plain-clothes detectives followed him everywhere, and a detachment of police guarded his quarters at the American Embassy. He did what he could to improve his local image, holding a press conference to express love for the country of Velázquez and the Conquistadors, and saying that after what he had seen of the spread of Latin civilization in South America, he would not be surprised to see Spanish becoming the world's universal language. Socialist and republican editors were unpersuaded that he had changed since the Battle of San Juan. "We know his attitude toward Spain," *El País* remarked. "We cannot welcome him."

To Roosevelt's mild irritation, he was pestered by cable requests from American newspapers for a statement regarding his future as leader of the Progressive Party. "This trip is just a spree," he replied to *The New York Times,* "and I am not interested in politics now. I want to meet the litterateurs and geographers and see the museums."

A guest list drawn almost exclusively from the diplomatic corps, plus Edith's inscrutable absence, infused the wedding on 11 June with a sense of impersonality and dislocation. Belle was rich, brittle, snobbish, and flighty, a toothy little blonde with the sinuous neck of someone adept at casing cocktail parties. Kermit was a moth drawn to her brightness. His intent, after they had spent a brief honeymoon in Europe, was to return to Brazil and manage a market in Curytiba. He thought they might stay there for nine or ten years, if not longer. Neither the Willard nor the Roosevelt families were sure how Belle would take to social life in the Antipodes.

"I believe she will be his sweetheart almost, but not entirely, as you are mine," Roosevelt wrote Edith on the eve of his departure for London.

HE STOPPED IN PARIS to change trains, seeing nobody but the American ambassador, Myron T. Herrick. En route south the week before, he had spent two full days in the city, breakfasting with Edith Wharton, lecturing Henri Bergson and a bored Auguste Rodin on the physical characteristics of European races, and paying his respects to President Raymond Poincaré. Paris that June was, more noticeably to visiting Americans than to herself, voluptuous, shabby, chaotic, tinged with the melancholy that had settled on her like mold after the conclusion of *l'affaire Dreyfus.* Georges Clemenceau's passionate call upon his countrymen to *vouloir ou mourir,* to will or to die in response to Prussian militarism, had been answered to the extent that the French army was now as big as Germany's. But the will, palpably, was still weak. As Claude Debussy wrote an artist friend, "For forty-four years we've been playing at self-effacement."

When Roosevelt saw London again, early on Saturday, 13 June, it too had lost much of the imperial self-certainty he remembered from the spring of 1910. Now the mood was more fearful than passive, after four years of worsening social and political unrest. He had no sooner moved into Arthur Lee's Mayfair townhouse than a "suffrage bomb" went off nearby in St. George's, Hanover Square. The old church was dear to him because he had married Edith there. Sylvia Pankhurst and her followers were unlikely to know or care about that. They were merely following up on their much more shocking detonation, two days before, of a bomb right beneath the coronation chair in Westminster Abbey.

Walter Hines Page, the American ambassador to the Court of St. James's, gave the Colonel a welcoming luncheon. It was attended by Henry James, John Singer Sargent, Lord Curzon, the Spanish diplomat Alfonso Merry del Val, the agricultural reformer Sir Horace Plunkett, and other luminaries. Obscurely basking in their combined glow was Woodrow Wilson's friend Colonel Edward M. House of Texas. One of the busy little gray men who make themselves indispensable to potentates as fund-raisers, gossips, and go-betweens, House was in the midst of a private tour of European capitals. He stood close to the reception line and marveled at the sharpness of the Colonel's focus on every incoming guest.

Afterward the Lees drove him out to Chequers. They told him they were thinking of bequeathing the house to the nation as a country retreat for prime ministers. Roosevelt praised the idea in words not entirely flattering to his host, saying that an "ordinary man" could make "a definite difference in the world" by being so generous.

The company that weekend was congenial and nonpolitical, consisting of John St. Loe Strachey, owner of the *Spectator,* Sir Owen Seaman, editor of *Punch,* the literary scholar Sidney Colvin, and their wives. They gasped at his stories of murder and malaria in the jungle (a map of Brazil spread out on the floor of the Great Hall), unaware that in a country palace near Prague, Archduke Franz Ferdinand was making a much more lurid presentation to Kaiser Wilhelm II.

❧

THE HEIR TO THE DUAL Monarchy was seeking advice, as often before, on what to do about unrest in the Balkans. Serbia was increasingly resentful of Austrian repression, and was now, Franz Ferdinand believed, fomenting revolution in Bosnia-Herzegovina. He wanted to know if the Kaiser had meant what he had said in Leipzig, at the time of the dedication of the *Volkerschlacht* monument: that Germany would support any Austrian move to discipline Serbia, once and for all.

Wilhelm neither confirmed nor denied this declaration of intent. But he suggested that the archduke would be wise to "do something" about the Serbs soon. If not, Russia, currently preoccupied with modernizing her army and navy, might feel impelled to step in and defend her fellow Slavs.

WHILE ROOSEVELT MANAGED to give an impression of "abounding vitality" to the unobservant Lees, the fragility of his health was apparent when he
returned to London to address the Royal Geographical Society. Fever had left
his voice so weak that he had to ask for the lecture to be relocated to a small
hall, in spite of a tremendous demand for tickets. Over a thousand ladies
and gentlemen in evening dress showed up to hear him, and most had to be
turned away. No less a dignitary than Earl Grey, the former governor-general
of Canada, was seen climbing a wall to get into the auditorium.

Roosevelt more or less repeated the blackboard-tapping presentation he
had given in Washington. He was listened to with respect, since British geographers initially skeptical of his expedition had by now accepted the truth of
all his claims. He was beguilingly modest, hailing the Royal Society as "the
foremost geographical body in the world," again never mentioning that the
Dúvida was now named after him, and emphasizing that he had not discovered it. That honor, he said, belonged to Colonel Rondon, one of the
Brazilian pioneers who heroically, and without sufficient plaudits from the
Anglo-American world, were putting their great wilderness on the map.

The nearest he got to tweaking the nose of the Society was to brandish a
1911 British map of the territory he had explored and prove it to be almost
completely inaccurate. His manner was so mild that this merely provoked
laughter. Officials sitting on the platform with him chuckled when he went
into falsetto on punch lines, not realizing that he was using humor to disguise
the attrition of his voice.

Next morning, the same Harley Street laryngologist who had treated him
in 1910 examined his throat again and ordered him not to make any open-air
speeches for several months. Roosevelt jumped at the chance to refute a fresh
batch of stateside rumors that he intended to run for governor of New York.
"This is my answer to those who wanted me to go into a campaign," he told
an American reporter. "If anyone expected me to do so, I cannot now."

He used virtually every minute of his remaining time in London to renew
and augment his prodigious range of British acquaintance. He lunched with a
trio of humanists—Arthur Balfour, the Oxford classicist Gilbert Murray, and
John Bury, regius professor of modern history at Cambridge—and reduced
them to silence with a monologue on the interconnection of religion and philosophy. He called on Prime Minister Asquith and found him shaken after
having been physically attacked by a suffragette. It was difficult for Roosevelt
not to feel, as he paid his respects to other members of the government and
Parliament, the collective sense among British policymakers that a *dies irae*
was looming. Sir Edward Grey was furrow-eyed with overwork, haunted by a
complex of seemingly insoluble international problems: the Balkan situation,

the German-British naval arms race, sedition in Egypt and India, and the prospect of a bloodbath in Ireland, where soldiers of the King had mutinied rather than enforce Home Rule. Sir Cecil Spring Rice, back on leave from Washington, was as loud on the subject of rearmament as his predecessor James (now Viscount) Bryce was on pacifism. The Bishop of London and Sir Robert Cecil wanted the suffragettes to be placated, and the Kaiser intimidated. Prince Louis of Battenberg, First Sea Lord, one of the last remnants of Anglo-Germanism in the British royal family, was less troubled by his mixed inheritance than by the pressure put on him by the Admiralty to expend the largest naval budget in British history.

There had been a rumor, before Roosevelt's arrival in London, that the King and Queen wished to renew their acquaintance with him. But he was no longer a special ambassador, much less a possible revenant to the White House. Nothing was heard from Buckingham Palace. On Thursday, 18 June, he took the boat train to Southampton and boarded his homebound liner, the SS *Imperator*.

He was accompanied by Arthur Lee and by the valet who had looked after him during his visit. After the Colonel had bade them goodbye, Lee was surprised to see the servant in tears. "Excuse me sir, but in all my thirty years of service I have never met such a great gentleman as 'im."

∽

FIVE MINUTES AFTER being left alone on deck, Roosevelt was felled by a violent attack of malaria. He remained feverish, on and off, for the next forty-eight hours. At one point, his temperature rocketed to 105°F, higher than it had been in Brazil. Then suddenly he was better. But he found his voice was now weaker than ever, and reiterated to reporters on board that he would not be a campaigner for any office in the fall. T. R. OFF STUMP, *The Washington Post* headlined, on receiving the news by wire.

If Woodrow Wilson inferred from this that the nonpartisan politesse Roosevelt had displayed, over lemonade in late May, was going to become the keynote of his retirement, a letter from Ambassador Page made clear that the Colonel had lost none of his fighting spirit. "When Roosevelt was here," Page wrote, "he told a friend of his that he was going home [to] rip the Administration to shreds for its many sins and many kinds of inefficiencies and he mentioned the 'dead failure in Mexico.' "

Actually, Roosevelt was more bothered by what he considered to be an insult on the part of William Jennings Bryan's State Department to the most glorious achievement of his presidency. In six weeks or so, the gates of the Panama Canal would be opened to world commerce. Bryan had chosen to herald the event by signing a treaty with Colombia that expressed "sincere regret" for the conduct of the United States in 1903, when President Roosevelt had rejected the Colombian Congress's demand for a surcharge of $5 million on the transfer of its land rights in Panama, and encouraged the Panamanian Revolution. Bryan now proposed to pay Colombia a compensatory $25 million. Roosevelt angrily insisted, in an interview with James T. Du Bois, a retired diplomat aboard the *Imperator*, that the revolution was right and proper. For fifty years before, Panama had been trying to opt out of the Colombian federation, to which it bore about as much geographical relation as Cuba did to the United States. "I simply lifted my foot!"

Du Bois was still reeling when the ship got to New York late on the evening of 24 June. "If anybody thinks the ex-President is a sick man," he remarked, "I would advise him to get into a conversation with him on a subject in which he is interested for two hours and he will entirely change his mind."

BEFORE PROCEEDING TO Oyster Bay on a friend's private yacht, Roosevelt put out a two-thousand-word press release. It more than fulfilled Page's prediction that he was not going to mince his language in criticizing the administration:

> The handling of our foreign affairs by President Wilson and Secretary Bryan has been such as to make the United States a figure of fun in the international world. The proposed Colombian treaty caps the climax, and if ratified, will rightly render us an object of contemptuous derision to every great nation. I wish to call attention to exactly what was done under my administration.

He reviewed at length, in tones of righteous indignation, the slippery negotiations by which Colombia had persuaded the United States to commit to a canal across Panama rather than Nicaragua, then tried to "blackmail" Uncle Sam—first by more than doubling its own agreed-on sales price, then by threatening to confiscate the construction rights that the State Department had separately arranged to buy from a French company for $40 million.

> I would call the attention of President Wilson and Secretary Bryan to the fact that this $40,000,000 represents the exact sum which Colombia lost when the United States government of that day refused to submit to blackmail. They now only propose to pay $25,000,000 blackmail. They had better make the job thorough while they are about it and give the whole $40,000,000. Otherwise they will still leave an opening for action by some future administration of similar mushy amiability toward foreign powers that have sought to wrong us.

He went on to indict the President's Mexican policy, which he described as "a course wavering between peace and war, exquisitely designed to combine the disadvantages of both, and feebly tending first toward one and then toward the other." One of Wilson's occasional "spasms of understanding" had been to realize that allowing weapons and munitions to flow unhindered into Mexico would encourage countries supportive of Huerta, such as Germany, to gain a strategic foothold there. So Wilson, abandoning all pretense of neutrality, had resorted to sudden, irrational violence at Vera Cruz.

In doing so, he had sacrificed nineteen more American lives than Roosevelt had done in *his* Central American adventure of eleven years before. Which made it all the more grotesque that Secretary Bryan now sought to appease Bogotá for the sin of interventionism. The Colonel's belittling images—*figure of fun, mushy amiability, wavering, feebly tending, spasms of understanding*—were effectively chosen. Wilson's foreign policy had indeed been marked by vacillations and overreactions puzzling to anyone unaware that he and Bryan saw the world through evangelical spectacles. They regarded showy potentates, whether kings or corrupt power-grabbers like Huerta, with such contempt that they were ready to run guns in order to extend the reach of Christian democracy.

"We have gone down to Mexico to serve mankind if we can find a way," the President said, rhetorically including the American people in his pilgrim's progress.

◦━◦

ROOSEVELT'S HOPE WAS THAT, by making a patriotic issue of the indemnity treaty, he could encourage Republicans and Progressives in the Senate to reject it. And since he was, in spite of himself, getting involved in politics again, what to do about the partisan division that he had caused in 1912? The Progressive Party had weakened badly since then, and so had he—not only physically but in terms of separatist will. Although he could never forgive Elihu Root and the other "thieves" who (he still believed) had stolen his renomination, he remained in his heart a Republican. He longed to see Progressivism lose its capital *p*, and become once again the liberal conscience of Abraham Lincoln's party. Unfortunately, that was unlikely to happen as long as Old Guard relics like Boss Barnes of New York and Senator Penrose of Pennsylvania remained in control of the RNC.

He had just settled in at Sagamore Hill when William Draper Lewis, who was running for governor in Penrose's home state, came to remind him that he had promised to speak in Pittsburgh on the last day of the month. The event was to be a double one, kicking off not only Lewis's campaign but also a run for the U.S. Senate by Gifford Pinchot. It was to take place in Exposition Hall, so Roosevelt could not cite the doctor's order he had received in London against speaking out of doors. He felt bound, in any case, to make a few carefully scripted appearances on behalf of candidates who had once campaigned for him.

Edith was sufficiently concerned about her husband's fever attacks to demand that he submit to a complete medical examination before he did any more politicking. Dr. Alexander Lambert told him that his spleen was enlarged and that he was suffering from a "loss of vitality" ascribable to malaria. If he did not have at least four months' complete rest, his ill health might well become chronic. "You may expect to spend the rest of your days tied to a chair."

Roosevelt allowed the diagnosis, if not the warning, to be leaked to the newspapers. It worried the millions of ordinary Americans who had always regarded "Teddy" as indestructible. When he showed up at Christ Church in Oyster Bay on Sunday, 28 June, an old villager reached out in sympathy.

"Oh! I guess I'm all right," Roosevelt said, taking his hand and shaking it. "All I need is a little rest."

⟿

ARCHDUKE FRANZ FERDINAND was equally dismissive of a bullet wound he received that same day in Sarajevo, Bosnia. *"Es ist nichts,"* he said as he bled to death in his open automobile. "It is nothing."

His assassination—and that of his pregnant wife, shot in the seat beside him—was, on the contrary, everything that Gavrilo Princip could wish for: a double blow to the jugular and abdomen of the heir to the Habsburg dynasty that had abused Balkan Slavs for so long. The nineteen-year-old student, a Bosnian recruited by Serbia's Black Hand terrorist movement, could not believe his luck. He had been standing on Franzjosefstrasse, bareheaded in the early summer sunshine, depressed over the failure of a comrade, Nedeljko Čabrinović, to kill the royal couple with a grenade earlier in the day. Then he saw their open-top car take a wrong turn off Appel Quay and pass right by him. The lethal logistics that seem to operate at such moments had transformed error into opportunity. Two point-blank targets presented themselves, and Princip's gun did what it was designed to do.

⟿

BY THE TIME Roosevelt came downstairs for breakfast at 8:30 on Monday, the atrocity in the Balkans was front-page news across the United States. English-language headlines were not as large as they might be, considering their import: the words SERBIA, BOSNIA-HERZEGOVINA, and, for that matter, AUSTRIA-HUNGARY had yet to become commonplaces of American reporting. European envoys in Washington, however, were under no illusions as to the gravity of the crisis touched off by Princip's bullet.

Apparently, Franz Ferdinand had crossed the Danube into Bosnia in order to witness an exercise by two corps of the Austrian army—staged with the obvious intent of cowing local unrest. Had he any awareness that he was entering a land of long memories, he might have chosen a day other than the anniversary of the Battle of Kosovo in 1389, when a single Serb had gone behind the Turkish lines and knifed Sultan Murad I to death.

Teenage boys, Princip and Čabrinović could hardly have been aware of the full range of ironies, historical, cultural, and strategic, impinging on the archuke's visit. Franzjosefstrasse, the thoroughfare into which his driver had accidentally turned—thronged with tarboosh-wearing Muslims, bulging with Russian Orthodox domes, and bearing the name of an octogenarian Austrian Catholic—was in itself symbolic of the combustible elements that had long threatened an explosion in the Balkans. By killing Franz Ferdinand in such a place, at a moment when both Austria and Germany were spoiling for war against the East, the conspirators had acted with more lethal consequences than they knew.

Of all American public figures, Theodore Roosevelt best understood what it was like to be shot at point-blank range. For that matter, he was one of the very few who had any acquaintance with the archduke. And what he had seen of that "furious reactionary" in 1910 was not conducive to grief at his passing. But as Roosevelt traveled during the course of the day to Pittsburgh, through regions of Pennsylvania heavily populated by German speakers and Slavs, he could not fail to feel intense local excitement. Gothic and Cyrillic posters shouted alarm at every station newsstand.

AFTER A JOURNEY of twelve hours, he delivered a husky-voiced address to four thousand wildly applauding Progressives that said nothing about the international situation, except for a vague reference to the administration's "wretched foreign policy." For the most part he contented himself with a listless indictment of the New Freedom. He offered only the briefest endorsement of Dean Lewis and Gifford Pinchot, letting his presence onstage with them speak for itself. As oratory, his performance was lackluster; as politics, it was an exercise in adroit self-distancing from the party he had created. He let drop a reference to "the honest Republican rank and file" that caught the editorial attention of *The New York Times*. "It is such a speech as may be read with equal satisfaction by both parties," the paper remarked. "Without saying a word about reunion, he has made a most effective argument for it. It is as adroit a speech as even this master politician ever made." The *Times* was sure he was positioning himself for the GOP nomination in 1916. "In this speech he has struck a great blow to bring it about."

Dean Lewis was not sure that the Colonel had enough force ever to campaign again. Roosevelt struck him as a "thoroughly exhausted" man who should have stayed home. Another Pennsylvania Progressive, Thomas Robins, blamed the Rio da Dúvida for destroying his fire.

"What on earth, Colonel, has a man of your age to do with explorations, anyway?"

"Youth will be served, Tom. It was my last chance to be a boy."

⬿

ROOSEVELT WAS BACK in New York the following day, and visited a laryngologist who contradicted Dr. Lambert and said that his throat was healing admirably. This helped confirm his half-guilty conviction that he should do what he could, over the next two years, to keep progressive principles alive, if not the Party itself.

It was not a task he looked forward to. Leaving for South America nine months before, he had felt a Bunyanesque burden falling off his back. Now it weighed on him again. "I am not in good shape," he wrote Hiram Johnson. "I could handle the jungle fever all right, and the Progressive Party all right, but the combination of the two is beyond me!"

His soul shrank at the prospect of having to get back on the hustings in the fall. But he felt he must try to make the country's non-Democratic majority understand that *he* was not responsible for putting Woodrow Wilson in power. It was corrupt Old Guard bosses like William Barnes, Jr., who had split the GOP. They must be deposed before there could be any hope of a healing fusion. To that end, he would have to recuperate and rebuild his strength over the summer.

Lawrence and Lyman Abbott cited this necessity as an excuse to persuade him to resign from the editorial board of *The Outlook*. His unsuccessful campaign for the presidency in 1912 had cost them many thousands of conservative subscribers. Since progressivism had been so cleverly coopted by Wilson, they felt their magazine was suffering from its identity as the Colonel's personal mouthpiece. Letting him down as lightly as possible, they suggested that he announce his own desire to quit editing in favor of other interests, political and literary. He would still be expected to contribute about ten articles over the next year on "current social questions," but was free to sign up with another magazine. In the meantime, *The Outlook* would continue to pay his salary, as well as that of his new private secretary, John W. McGrath, and rent him an office in the city if he needed one.

Roosevelt accepted these generous terms of severance. Nevertheless, his letter of resignation, released to the press on the Fourth of July, sounded regretful: "If I had been able to be, as I expected to be, a man entirely removed from all participation in active politics, nothing would give me keener pleasure than to keep on exactly as in the past."

◦◦◦

IN BERLIN, WILHELM II confirmed to the Austro-Hungarian ambassador that Germany would support the Dual Monarchy in any act of revenge on Serbia for the murder of Archduke Franz Ferdinand. He advised quick action, so as to crush pan-Slavism, once and for all, before Russia had time to react.

Even if "a serious complication in Europe" did ensue, against his expectation, the Kaiser promised to fight on Austria's side. He said that his chancellor, Theobald von Bethmann-Hollweg, would make the promise formal. Summoned to Potsdam, Bethmann-Hollweg undertook to do so, but not without private misgivings.

"The future lies with Russia," he told an aide. "She grows and grows, and lies on us like a nightmare."

◦◦◦

WHILE WASHINGTON WAITED to see what Vienna would do, Americans went back to the business and pleasure of being American. Rep. James F. Byrnes of South Carolina presented President Wilson and Secretary Tumulty with a pair of white duck summer suits. In San Francisco, the city chamber of commerce heralded the imminent opening of the Panama Canal as "the dawn of a new era of unequaled prosperity." Members of the Buttersville, Michigan, Scandinavian Methodist Church burned their paid-off mortgage and sang "My Country, 'Tis of Thee" in alternate verses of English and Norwegian. Missouri reported that its registration of automobiles had topped thirty-eight thousand. Ty Cobb, champion slugger of the Detroit American League, was seen dining conspiratorially with the president of the Federal League. A Philadelphia market listed its latest prices for dressed poultry: "Fowls, western fancy, 18 @ 19 cents; fowls, western unattractive, 10 @ 13 cents." State hospitals in New York experimented with "lawn movies," a new therapy enhanced by Victrola music. Evelyn Nesbit Thaw announced that she would star in a full-length feature entitled *The Life of Evelyn Nesbit Thaw*. The Pacific Coast Federation for Sex Hygiene sponsored a presentation on "Sex as a Factor in High School and University Life." West Virginia went dry. Wild strawberries studded the fields around Tryonville, Pa., and Kansas wheat fields ripened northward, in a slow wave of gold.

CHAPTER 18

The Great Accident

What unrecorded overthrow
Of all the world has ever known,
Or ever been, has made itself
So plain to you, and you alone?

WHEN THE *IMPERATOR* RETURNED to New York on 15 July 1914, its register of first-class passengers included Mrs. Nicholas Longworth as well as Mr.
and Mrs. Kermit Roosevelt. Alice had stocked up in Paris with all the latest
hats and dresses, and was looking forward to wearing something spectacular
when her parents welcomed the newlyweds at Sagamore Hill that evening.

It was the first time in four years that the Roosevelts could all be together,
and it might be the last for as long again. Alice could stay only one night. Nick
(waiting at quayside for the ship to dock) urgently needed her in Cincinnati,
where he was campaigning to recapture his Congressional seat. Kermit and
Belle were booked to sail on to Brazil in just twelve days. Ethel and Dick
Derby would remain on Long Island for a while after that, with little Richard,
their son of fourteen weeks. So would Ted and Eleanor with Grace, now almost three, and Theodore Roosevelt III, just one month old. Archie, down
from Harvard, was available to drive everyone around in the family's brand-
new Buick. Quentin (fully grown now, a big boy not far off seventeen) was
getting ready for his first independent adventure, a pack-horse expedition in
Arizona.

Alice's early departure spared her one of the democratic exercises Roosevelt insisted on in his capacity as a man of the people: an open reception for
the residents of Oyster Bay. He thought they should be allowed to meet Belle.
That young lady was no more drawn to the hoi polloi than her elder sister-in-
law. But she had learned public manners in the courts of Europe, and acquitted herself gracefully as the villagers sipped tea and looked her over.

Though Belle was, as her name and accent implied, Southern-born, her plentiful teeth qualified her as an authentic Roosevelt. The sight of her laughing with Archie, Quentin, and the Colonel was enough to overexpose the fastest camera film. Kermit found it hard to smile. Otherwise, he was beginning to resemble his father. The slender graduate who had gone south in 1912 was a bulkier personage, with a broadening face and body and passé mustache. Ted and Archie, like most young men of their generation, were slick of hair and clean-shaven.

⌒

A DELEGATION OF New York Progressives tried to crash the reception, but were told that the Colonel could not see them. They had hoped to persuade him, over sandwiches, to run on their ticket for governor. Answering them obliquely on 22 July, Roosevelt announced that he would support a moderate, fusion-minded Republican, Harvey D. Hinman, for the gubernatorial nomination, in opposition to an organization man put forward by William Barnes, Jr. Readers of his statement thought that it showed more animus against Barnes than any particular regard for Hinman:

> In New York State we see at its worst the development of the system of bipartisan boss rule. . . . It is impossible to secure the economic, social, and industrial reforms to which we are pledged until this invisible government of the party bosses working through the alliance between crooked business and crooked politics is rooted out of our governmental system.
>
> In New York State the two political machines are completely dominated, the one by Mr. Barnes, the other by Mr. Murphy.* The state government is rotten throughout in almost all its departments, and this is directly due to the dominance in politics of Mr. Murphy . . . aided and abetted when necessary by Mr. Barnes and the sub-bosses of Mr. Barnes.

Barnes immediately sued him for libel and $50,000 in damages.

⌒

ON THE SAME NIGHT that Roosevelt was served with his legal papers in Oyster Bay, the foreign minister of Serbia was handed a note from Austria-Hungary. It was far harsher than the one he had received the previous October. His government was given forty-eight hours to guarantee a purge of all terrorist organizations operating on Serbian soil, ban anti-imperial propa-

---

* Charles F. Murphy, boss of Tammany Hall.

ganda, condemn its own army for Black Hand connections, and accept Austrian participation in an internal investigation of the murder of Franz Ferdinand.

The terms of this ultimatum (which had been issued at the impatient urging of Wilhelm II) were so provocative that it amounted to a declaration of war. In mid-Atlantic, Commodore Theo Kier of the *Imperator* heard the news by radio and directed his liner home to Hamburg under full steam.

Serbia rejected the ultimatum cannily, by accepting all its demands except the one for a participatory investigation. This committed Austria-Hungary to a declaration of war on the reprehensible, not to say illegal ground that it had been denied permission to infringe the rights of a sovereign nation. Germany was challenged to court the same obloquy, if it made good on its promise to support Austrian aggression.

On Saturday, 25 July, Tsar Nicholas II waited for Serbia to mobilize in its own defense. Then, reacting much more quickly than the Kaiser had expected, he ordered a partial mobilization of the Russian army. He knew that if he made it total, he would doom his own dynasty. A force consisting largely of discontented peasants was not likely to return, brutalized, from a foreign conflict and remain subservient to Romanoff rule. Nicholas had been threatened with a domestic revolution in 1905, before he allowed Theodore Roosevelt to mediate an end to the Russo-Japanese War. But no conciliatory figure was in sight now. Slav honor was Slav honor, and the Teutons had abused it enough.

When Wilhelm II heard the news from St. Petersburg, he said, more in surprise than dismay, "Then I must mobilize too."

One by one, like electrical systems activated from a central switchboard, the powers compelled to respond to a crisis in the Balkans began to generate heat. Serbia mobilized even before Austria-Hungary did. In London, Sir Edward Grey warned of a "European war *à quatre*"—a four-way conflict with Russia, Germany, and France being drawn into Austria's provincial problem. He begged his counterpart on the Wilhelmstrasse, Count Gottlieb von Jagow, to push for a mediatory conference between the first three nations and his own. Although it was plain from his tone that Britain would not stand idly by if France was menaced, Jagow's reply was evasive.

At 11:10 A.M. on 28 July, Austria declared war on Serbia. The British ambassador in Vienna reported that its citizens were "wild with joy" at the announcement. Some even got an erotic charge out of it. "All my libido is given to Austria-Hungary," Sigmund Freud wrote. Even the aged Franz Joseph approved the notion of a *Blitzkrieg* in the Balkans. He had no delicacy about shedding blood, having managed in the course of a long hunting career to kill more than fifty thousand animals.

Wilhelm II, however, felt a sudden qualm. He belatedly read the text of Serbia's reply to the ultimatum of four days before, and thought it satisfactory. "It contains the announcement *orbi et urbi** of a capitulation of the most humiliating kind, and with it every reason for war is removed." Surely, he suggested to Jagow, Vienna's few remaining grievances could be settled by negotiation. But Franz Joseph had already signed an instrument of war, and Germany had promised to support it "through thick and thin." The Kaiser's inner circle of Prussian ministers were willing to temporize only so long as it took Russia to mobilize fully, so that St. Petersburg, not Berlin, would be seen as responsible for the spread of hostilities.

France was already in a state of high alarm. Everything that Clemenceau and other Germanophobes had warned about the threat of another Franco-Prussian war seemed to be coming true. To Edith Wharton in Paris, "everything seemed strange, ominous and unreal, like the yellow glare which precedes a storm." She felt as if she had died, and woken up in a world she no longer knew.

The European republic had more than three million men under arms or on reserve, and had recently extended its period of national service from two years to three. French military commanders were confident of the impregnability of its defenses along the Rhine, but less so of Belgium's ability to withstand a German sweep westward across Flanders. That might come quickly, as a rearguard reinforcement by General Falkenhayn, before the slow Russian juggernaut began to crowd the eastern fringe of Prussia.

On 29 July the general's soul mate in Vienna, Franz Conrad von Hötzendorf, ordered Austrian cannons to start bombarding Belgrade. The first shell across the Danube landed before dawn, and the ones that followed soon became too numerous to count. Nobody knew how many million more would be fired before the last fell, and in what soil of what nation. The idea of a world war, hitherto untenable by military theorists, no longer seemed like fantasy. Conrad exulted, having called for the destruction of Serbia dozens of times in his career. At the same time, he was fatalistic about the long-term consequences. "It will be a hopeless war. . . . Nevertheless, it must be waged, since an old monarchy and a glorious army must not perish without glory."

Next morning, *The Washington Post* encapsulated the situation for Americans:

RUSSIA READY TO TAKE UP ARMS FOR SERBIA;
TSAR SENDS 1,280,000 MEN TO AUSTRIAN LINE;
FATE OF EUROPE HANGS ON COUNCIL IN BERLIN

---

* Wilhelm II reversed the words of *urbi et orbi,* a Latin phrase commonly used by the Vatican to address "the city [i.e., Rome] and the world."

"It's the Slav and the German," Walter Hines Page wrote President Wilson. "Each wants his day, and neither has got beyond the stage of tooth and claw."

Both the emperors involved—they communicated in English, calling each other "Nicky" and "Willy"—were now aghast at the drift of events. "An ignoble war has been declared to [sic] a weak country," the Tsar wired his cousin. "I beg you in the name of our old friendship to do what you can to stop your allies from going too far."

Allies, in this case, meant only Austria-Hungary. Willy was fearfully aware that Nicky had more than one ally, and formidable ones too: both Britain and France would be obliged to come to Russia's aid, should Germany enter the war. "I cannot consider Austria's action against Serbia an 'ignoble' war," he protested, pointing out that the government in Vienna had declared that its interests were honorable, not territorial. "I therefore suggest that it would be quite possible for Russia to remain a spectator of the Austro-Serbian conflict without involving Europe in the most horrible war she has ever witnessed."

Nicky could only counter-propose that the Austro-Serbian problem be referred to the Hague International Court for arbitration. In the meantime he informed Willy, at 1:20 A.M. on 30 July, that his country had moved to a state of full mobilization.

Belgium began to mobilize too. King Albert suspected that Germany was about to demand permission to march across his borders en route to Paris. Such permission could not be given without a sacrifice of Belgian sovereignty. That almost certainly meant the destruction of his country and his culture. Several great powers, including Great Britain and France, had declared Belgium "an independent and perpetually neutral state" as long ago as 1839, in the Treaty of London. But after seventy-five years of changing interests, the signatories could not necessarily be relied on, if General Falkenhayn decided to invade.

In a midnight meeting with Sir Edward Goschen, the British ambassador in Berlin, Chancellor Bethmann-Hollweg tried to send peaceable signals to London. He said that Germany regarded, or professed to regard, its military policy toward France as purely defensive. It could not allow that grudge-bearing nation to compromise the Kaiser's efforts to come to a settlement with Russia. As long as Belgium "did not take sides" in the matter, "her integrity would be respected." And if Britain, too, "remained neutral . . . in the event of a victorious war," Germany would guarantee never to change the boundaries of France.

When Goschen, remembering the Agadir crisis of 1911, asked if that extended to France's overseas possessions, Bethmann-Hollweg's tone changed. He would give no such assurance. What was more, he "could not tell to what operations Germany might be forced by the action of France."

The combined vagueness and truculence of these remarks, counterpointing the Kaiser's ambiguous diplomacy, appalled the British Foreign Office. Sir Edward Grey noted that a promise to respect territory was not a promise to respect sovereignty. The boundaries of Alsace-Lorraine had not altered since 1870, yet the flag that flew over Zabern was German. Bethmann's admission that Germany might be "forced" to negate its own guarantees amounted, in British eyes, to a check as blank as the one Wilhelm II had handed the Austrian ambassador at the beginning of July.

The last forty-eight hours of July accelerated with a momentum that Bethmann-Hollweg likened to that of a landslide. All the key figures in the crisis became terrified, with the exception of Falkenhayn and his nominal superior, General Helmuth J. L. von Moltke, the German chief of staff. Their Prussian blood pulsed to the potential of mobilizing the world's mightiest army, and deploying it east and west. The enormous dynamo was there, oiled and superbly tuned, the end product of decades of tinkering and testing. In the manner of a mechanism developed for one overriding purpose, it wanted to whir into action. Falkenhayn dreaded that the Kaiser or Bethmann-Hollweg might yet effect a negotiated settlement with Nicholas II. He raged against "those peace people at the palace" holding up German mobilization while hordes of Slavs were standing to arms. Moltke warned the Chancellor that France and Russia together would bring about "the mutual destruction of the civilized states of Europe." Since the adjective *mutual* implied only a pair of states, it was clear that Germans and Austrians felt menaced on all sides by barbarians.

"Germany does not want to be the cause of this egregious war," he wrote, "but . . . it would violate the deepest bonds of national loyalty—one of the noblest features of the German psyche . . . if it did not come to its ally's aid just when this ally's destiny is hanging in the balance."

∽

Forces for good and forces for evil are everywhere evident, each acting with a hundred- or a thousand-fold the intensity with which it acted in former ages. Over the whole earth the swing of the pendulum grows more and more rapid, the mainspring coils and spreads at a rate constantly quickening, the whole world movement is of constantly accelerating velocity.

Theodore Roosevelt's address to the University of Berlin had not gone down well in 1910, and was probably forgotten now, even by those in the audience who had managed to stay awake. The Kaiser had been one of the few who listened to every word, but his hummingbird mind never dwelt on any subject for long. If it had, he might have understood that Roosevelt—an objective American who had just toured nation after European nation—was addressing a particular warning to the German people through him: *The machinery is so highly geared, the tension and strain are so great, the effort and the output have alike so increased, that there is cause to dread the ruin that would come from any great accident, from any breakdown, and also the ruin that may come from the mere wearing out of the machine itself.*

Now, four years later, the great accident was occurring, and Wilhelm was powerless to prevent it. There was a deterministic logic to Europe's breakdown, as if that ancient seditionist, Fate, had engineered the whole thing. What empire in 1914, with the exception of the Ottoman, was more worn out than that of Austria-Hungary? Now that the heir to the Dual Monarchy had fallen, who could doubt that many more kings and emperors—maybe all of them east of Spain—would fall too, as generals and politicians became the new autocrats, and socialists and anarchists and separatists fought for post-war spoils? Even George V of England had to be afraid, with his own Irish subjects resorting to terrorism, and a general strike looming at home. France—"the French Socialist Republic" as Wilhelm contemptuously called it—had no king to kill. But it was as divided between its militaristic right and *enragés* of the left as it had been on the eve of the Revolution. Italy, nominally one of the Central Powers counterbalancing the Triple Entente, was so demoralized after its recent "Red Week" labor violence (fomented by a young socialist, Benito Mussolini) that it was likely to declare neutrality out of sheer lack of will. Russia, less centripetal than Austria or France, was more prerevolutionary than either. And the Balkans were the Balkans: forever divided between race and race, religion and religion. What Gavrilo Princip had so reflexively started would not stop.

Owen Wister had been vacationing at Triberg, in the heart of the Black Forest, when the news came from Sarajevo. He stood with other people reading the dispatch on the hotel bulletin board. Nobody spoke. The mountain air was hot and still, charged with pine fumes. An old Bavarian had said, "That is the match which will set all Europe in flames."

Now Wister was in Brussels, awaiting the conflagration. A Belgian doctor told him that Germans shared two characteristics impelling them toward war: "the mania of grandeur, complemented by the mania of persecution." It was the generalization of a frightened lowlander, certain that his country was about to be invaded, and would have been more accurate if the doctor had referred specifically to Prussians. The Zabern affair had dramatically demonstrated how great was the gulf, in Germany, between the Junker military elite and the bourgeois or working-class *Volk* empowering the Center Party, the National Liberals, the Progressives, and the Social Democrats—Europe's largest socialist group. Although the parliament of these parties, the Reichstag, was still unable to override the will of the imperial government, it had profoundly shaken it with last December's vote censuring Chancellor Bethmann-Hollweg. More recently, for the first time in history, the popular majority had refused to join in a traditional standing salute to Wilhelm II.

That insult had done much to aggravate the two manias the Belgian doctor spoke of. Even Bethmann-Hollweg, a mild and almost peaceable man by Prussian standards, was persuaded to believe, along with his ministers, that a war mobilizing the entire Reich would purify it of the toxins of socialism and communism.

He and Wilhelm hesitated, prevaricated, and panicked throughout the morning of Friday, 31 July, firing off diplomatic telegrams and summoning ambassadors. But at the same time Moltke and Falkenhayn, who cajoled the Kaiser to proclaim a state of "imminent war danger" at noon, became sure that tomorrow would be *der Tag*—"the Day" of final European reckoning. Ordinary Berliners seemed to sense the same thing. They took to the streets as the summer afternoon heated up. A belligerence as sudden as that which had gripped Vienna three days before spread outward from the imperial palace, along Unter den Linden, and down the Wilhelmstrasse, where Bethmann lived and Jagow worked. Traffic had to be rerouted from the center of the city. A crowd estimated at fifty thousand surged and sang "Heil dir im Siegerkranz," the German victory anthem:

> *Holy flame, burn and glow*
> *Unextinguishable*
> *For Fatherland!*

To foreigners listening at a distance, the words and tune could have been "God Save the King" or "My Country, 'Tis of Thee." Except that British and American crowds did not sing with this kind of bellicosity. It was not a bloodthirsty so much as an exultant sound, a roar of rapture that all Germans now had a cause worth dying for: the protection and enlargement of the Reich. Only a few patriots felt uneasy about joining in the celebration, which was duplicated in other cities. One of them, the industrialist Walter Rathenau, felt that he was witnessing a *Totentanz,* "a dance of death, the overture to a doom which I had foreseen would be dark and dreadful."

CHAPTER 19

A Hurricane of Steel

No, there is not a dawn in eastern skies
To rift the fiery night that's in your eyes;
But there, where western glooms are gathering,
The dark will end the dark, if anything:
God slays himself with every leaf that flies,
And hell is more than half of paradise.
No, there is not a dawn in eastern skies —
In eastern skies.

"THE SITUATION IN EUROPE is really dreadful," Roosevelt wrote to his youngest son on 2 August 1914. "A great tragedy impends."

Had Quentin not been in the canyonlands of Arizona, about as un-European an environment as could be imagined, he might have agreed with his father. Or more likely, yesterday's triple mobilization of Germany, Belgium, and France would have thrilled him, fascinated as he was with any kind of synchronized movement involving wheels, weight, oil, and fire. At the moment he was beyond the reach of news bulletins, and distracted by a riding accident that had badly wrenched his back. A packhorse had slipped and rolled over on him, dislodging two ribs where they joined the spine. It was not the kind of trauma a youth needed just when he was testing the limits of his new adult body.

Of all Roosevelt's children, Alice was the one most drawn to *furor teutonicus*, the German war rage that had been suppressed for so long. As a little girl, she had listened to recitations of the *Nibelungenlied* at her father's knee, and reveled in the violent parts. There was a savage streak in Alice: she approved of the strong overriding the weak. Except that she did not require, as he did, that the strong should have a moral reason to do so. She was never entirely sure what he meant by "righteousness," and why it meant so much to him.

Righteousness had killed a goodly number of Filipinos during his presidency, and discharged a regiment of black soldiers without honor or due process, and separated Panama from the Colombian federation. But if he maintained these actions had been necessary, she took his word for it.

"SHE WAS NEVER ENTIRELY SURE WHAT HE MEANT BY 'RIGHTEOUSNESS.'"
Father and daughter, thinking their separate thoughts, summer 1914.

His attitude to the developing war had so far been pessimistic yet detached. It was "a great black tornado" threatening Europe only, although Africa and Asia Minor might get sucked in. If Great Britain chose to fight, his emotions would be more engaged, insofar as he felt a solidarity with the English and their empire. (What would he be doing now, had Balfour's dream of a Roosevelt-led Anglo-Saxon federation come true?) Yet he also had his "Saxon" side, with boyhood memories of living in Dresden and bonding with a pair of scar-faced swordsmen from the University of Leipzig. Their father had been a member of the Reichstag. Their sister had taught him German poetry, which he grew to love almost as much as English. Only recently, Roosevelt had confessed in his autobiography: "From that time to this it would have been quite impossible to make me feel that the Germans really were foreigners. The affection, the *Gemütlichkeit* (a quality which cannot be exactly expressed by any single English word), the capacity for hard work and science, the pride in the new Germany . . . these manifestations of the German character and of German family life made a subconscious impression upon me which I did not in the least define at the time, but which is still very vivid forty years later."

Millions of Americans outside New England felt a similar empathy, in contrast to the hot, inscrutable loyalties of Slavic immigrants. But the ethnic complexity of the United States weighed against any national leaning one way or another. Roosevelt himself delighted in finding, or inventing, common strains of ancestry with voters ("I wish I had a little Jew in me."). Three thousand miles of seawater made the European war seem, for the moment, the Old World's problem.

⌖

ON 3 AUGUST, Germany declared war on France, for supporting Russia, and decided to override Belgium's refusal to open its roads and railways to forces of the Reich. Luxembourg, another neutral state, was already invaded and occupied. Rectors of universities from Bavaria to Schleswig-Holstein urged students to enlist in what one scholar called "the battle forced upon us for German *Kultur*."

Britain's House of Commons met that afternoon, to hear Sir Edward Grey confirm that his government would regard an invasion of Belgium as sufficient reason to declare war on Germany on behalf of France. Even the pacifists among his cabinet colleagues were agreed that a threat to the lowland countries was a threat to the English Channel—not to mention the web of support that France and Russia provided to the Empire in North Africa and the Far East.

The foreign secretary's speech was momentous, if academic, since Falkenhayn's troops were already attacking Liège. More in despair than in hope, Grey undertook to give the Germans a twenty-four-hour deadline to quit Belgian soil. "If they refuse, there will be war," he said to Paul Cambon, the French ambassador.

At the end of the day, he stood at the window of his suite in Downing Street and watched a lamplighter moving from post to post below. The same operation, presumably, was taking place on the Quai d'Orsay in Paris. Along the Wilhelmstrasse in Berlin, dark would have come an hour sooner.

Exhausted, Grey spoke to a friend who was standing with him. Afterward he could not remember what he had said, until the friend quoted his words back to him: "The lamps are going out all over Europe; we shall not see them lit again in our lifetime."

❧

THE EXTREME TENSION that gathered in Parliament on Tuesday, 4 August, communicated itself to Sagamore Hill, where Roosevelt practically danced, Navajo-style, round his library, and piped at Charles Booth, the British humanitarian: "You've got to get in! You've got to get in!"

Four Progressive intellectuals—Felix Frankfurter and the journalists Herbert Croly, Walter Lippmann, and Walter Weyl—watched half-amused, half-awed by the Colonel's vehemence. They recognized, with conflicting emotions, that if Britain did in fact enter the war, sooner or later America might be forced to "get in" too. Booth would only say that he supposed his government must make good on its threat. He was chairman of a shipping line based in Liverpool, and knew that he would be responsible for the lives of uncountable thousands of passengers if the war became general.

Roosevelt saw the issue as one of simple right and wrong. Germany was treating its neutral neighbors as dirt underfoot, on the unbelievable premise that France and Russia meant to destroy the Reich. By any definition, this was militarism gone mad: the Triple Entente had no choice but to fight. If Germany defeated France and took over her colonial possessions, the strategic and economic balance of the whole Occident would be upset. What particularly disturbed Roosevelt was the possibility of Germany being defeated and disarmed. This would be a double tragedy, because in his opinion, the United States would one day need Germany as an ally against the power that had always worried him most—Japan. Furthermore (and here his guests agreed with him), a collapsed Reich "would result in the entire western world being speedily forced into a contest with Russia."

President Wilson saw no such eventuality. "The European world is highly excited," he told reporters visiting him for comment, "but the excitement ought not to spread to the United States." He said that he would issue a proclamation of neutrality soon. Americans should have "the pride of feeling" that one great nation, at least, remained uninvolved and stood ready to help the belligerents settle their differences. "We can do it and reap a great permanent glory out of doing it, provided we all cooperate to see that nobody loses his head."

Wilson spoke with considerable self-control, not revealing that his ailing wife apparently had just days to live.

By Wednesday, *furor teutonicus* was general both east and west of the Central Powers. The front page of *The New York Times* required so many headlines to summarize all the cable dispatches from Europe that there was scarcely room for body text:

KAISER HURLS TWO ARMIES
INTO BELGIUM AFTER
DECLARING WAR.

—

LIEGE ATTACK REPULSED

—

German Guns Are Reported to
be Bombarding Both That
City and Namur.

—

BELGIANS RUSH TO ARMS

—

Parliament Acclaims King's
Appeal and Votes $40,000,000
for National Defense.

—

FRENCH BORDER CLASHES

—

Stronger German Forces Crossing
the Border Near
Mars-la-Tour and Moineville

—

RUSSIANS ATTACK MEMEL

—

The most momentous bulletin of all confirmed that since eleven the previous evening, a state of war had existed between Great Britain and Germany. Seventeen million soldiers of eight nations were now at arms. When other powers joined in, as they surely would (Italy, Japan, and the Ottoman Empire had yet to align themselves) and some of the world's biggest navies began to clash at sea, the conflict would become global. If even tiny Switzerland was mobilizing, how long could the United States delude itself that engines of foreign war would not sweep west across the Atlantic? And pass into the Pacific via the soon-to-be-opened Panama Canal, Theodore Roosevelt's gift to the battleships of all nations?

❧

ON 6 AUGUST, Ellen Wilson died. "God has stricken me," the President wrote privately, "almost more than I can bear."

In the circumstances, Roosevelt's first statement on the war attracted little attention. Issued that day from his new office at 30 East Forty-second Street in Manhattan, it was as neutral-sounding as anything Wilson had said. "Let us be thankful beyond measure that we are citizens of this Republic, and that our burdens, though they may be heavy, are far lighter than those that must be borne by the men and women who live in other and less fortunate countries." He pledged himself and his party to "work hand in hand with any public man" or combination of citizens "who in good faith and disinterestedly do all that is possible to see that the United States comes through this crisis unharmed."

If this sounded like an endorsement of the President and his administration, Roosevelt felt that as a patriotic American he could say neither more nor less. "I simply do not know the facts."

Having lost a wife to Bright's disease himself, he understood Wilson's anguish. But empathy did not stop him confiding to Arthur Lee that he had deep doubts about the administration's ability to defend the United States. Just as Europe was becoming a battleground, the President and his "prize idiot" of a secretary of state were continuing to tout the peacekeeping potential of arbitration treaties. "It is not a good thing for a country to have a professional yodeler, a human trombone like Mr. Bryan as secretary of state, nor a college president with an astute and shifty mind, a hypocritical ability to deceive plain people . . . and no real knowledge or wisdom concerning internal and international affairs as head of the nation."

Yet for the moment, Roosevelt believed that it was right for America to stay neutral. Newspapers were reporting that no rules of war had so far been broken. "The melancholy thing about this matter to me," he wrote Hugo Münsterberg, a Prussian-born professor at Harvard, "is that this conflict really was inevitable and that the several nations engaged in it are, each from its own standpoint, right under the existing conditions of civilization and international relations."

The only one he felt had a moral (as opposed to strategic or economic) reason to fight was Belgium, which had courageously vowed to defend its honor and sovereignty. He made this plain when an emissary from Wilhelm II visited him. Count Franz von Papen was military attaché to the German Embassy in Washington, and the only soldier in the diplomatic corps representing the Central Powers. Young and handsome, with a noble lineage extending back to the fifteenth century, Papen was a Westphalian gentleman of the finest sort, except that there was something unctuous about him that irritated Roosevelt.

The message he brought was more than eight months old, and consisted of nothing more than one of the Kaiser's typical protestations of esteem, updated to suit the current emergency. Papen obviously meant to take advantage of it by enlisting Roosevelt as a voice for the German cause. Bowing, he said that His Imperial Majesty had never forgotten how pleasurable it had been to entertain the Colonel four years before, "as a guest in Berlin and at the palace at Potsdam." In view of these fond memories, Wilhelm "felt assured" that he could count on Roosevelt's "sympathetic understanding of Germany's position and action."

Roosevelt bowed back. He said that he too had never forgotten the royal way the Kaiser had treated him, "nor the way in which His Majesty King Albert of Belgium received me in Brussels."

Silence fell. Papen's expression did not change. He clicked his heels, bowed again, and left the room without uttering another word.

The visit only confirmed Roosevelt's intent to support Wilson and Bryan as they pursued their policy of noninvolvement. He made his commitment clear in one of the occasional articles he now contributed to *The Outlook:* "In common with the immense majority of our fellow countrymen, I shall certainly stand by not only the public servants in control of the administration at Washington, but also all other public servants, no matter of what party, in this crisis; asking only that they with wisdom and good faith endeavor . . . to promote the cause of peace and justice throughout the world."

He commended an early offer by the President to act as a mediator in Europe, although evidence mounted daily in black headlines (swamping even, on 15 August, news of the inauguration of the Panama Canal) that the war was irreversible.

The truth was, Wilson had no diplomatic qualifications. His only exposure to the outside world—unless Bermuda counted as a foreign power—had been gained on two or three vacations in Britain, visiting universities and bicycling through the Cumberland and Scotland of his ancestors. Roosevelt had gone on four grand tours of Europe and the Middle East before he was thirty, amassing an international circle of acquaintance that now extended from emperors down to his barefoot *camaradas* in Brazil. He could converse in three languages and read in four. He had been blessed by a Pope, honored by the mullahs of Al-Azhar, and asked to mediate an international war. He had heard Casals play Bach, confronted Cubism, and watched the gyrations of snake priests and Diaghilev's dancers—not to mention the goose-steps of German troops at Döberitz. He had killed a man in battle and just four months before, on the shore of a river unknown to any cartographer, confronted death himself.

These and maybe a thousand other aspects of wisdom were embodied in the retired statesman who found few journalists, that summer, interested in his views on any subject other than Progressive politics. Ray Stannard Baker visited him at Sagamore Hill and got the impression that Roosevelt was chafing in unaccustomed obscurity. "It must indeed be a cross for him not to keep on the front page!"

⟨❧⟩

THE PRESIDENT'S TENDENCY to talk in the abstract was demonstrated in his salute to the Panama Canal as a waterway that would permit "a commerce of intelligence, of thought, and sympathy" around the world, as if such things were dry goods. On 19 August, he formally called upon Americans to be "impartial in thought as well as in action . . . neutral in fact as well as in name."

But to the handful of his countrymen who were still in Brussels, the spectacle of the German army marching into town next day was so overwhelmingly physical as to negate philosophy. Richard Harding Davis of the New York *Tribune* had seen war before—in Cuba, where he had followed Roosevelt's Rough Riders to Santiago—but he realized that the new technological century was going to make it infinitely more horrible.

Belgium's defense strategy, modeled on that of Russia against Napoleon in 1812, had been to leave the capital unprotected. By ten in the morning, all non-official citizens were off the streets and hidden behind shuttered windows. The first German to appear on the Boulevard de Waterloo was a captain on a bicycle, no more fearsome than Woodrow Wilson *en vacance*. He was followed by a pair of privates, also pedaling, their rifles casually slung. But right behind came such a gray mass of men and matériel, advancing row on row, hour after hour till sunset and beyond, that Davis was at first amazed, then numbed, then stupefied.

> Boredom gave way to wonder. The thing fascinated you, against your will, dragged you back to the sidewalk and held you there open-eyed. No longer was it regiments of men marching, but something uncanny, inhuman. . . .
>
> All through the night, like the tumult of a river when it races between the cliffs of a canyon, in my sleep I could hear the steady roar of the passing army. And when early in the morning I went to the window the chain of steel was still unbroken. . . . This was a machine, endless, tireless, with the delicate organization of a watch and the brute power of a steam roller. And for three days and three nights through Brussels it roared and rumbled, a cataract of molten lead. The infantry marched singing, with their iron-shod boots beating out the time. They sang "Fatherland, My Fatherland." Between each line of song they took three steps. At times two thousand men were singing together in absolute rhythm and beat. It was like the blows from giant pile-drivers. When the melody gave way the silence was broken only by the stamp of iron-clad boots, and then again the song rose.

Davis was conscious mainly of sound: the rumble of howitzers and siege cannons, the jingling of machine guns, chains clanking on cobbles, sharp bugle calls, the squeal of ungreased axles and grinding of steel wheels on stone. To another American reporter, Will Irwin, what was more of an onslaught on the senses was "the smell of a half-million unbathed men, the stench of a menagerie raised to the *n*th power. That smell lay for days over every town through which the Germans passed."

Neither reporter could quite express the sense each had that something entirely new and wholly frightening had been revealed to them, implicit in the gray colorlessness, the engineered sameness, the loud, crushing force of human aggression turned to science. There was not a noun for it yet, but if the young tribune of "Red Week" in Emilia-Romagna had his way, it would be coined from the Italian word *fasci*.

⟋⟍

COMPARISON OF THE developing war to a tornado, or cyclone, was so common among public figures that month that few of them noticed its precise applicability to Germany's opening military maneuver. By curving up through Flanders and then around to encircle Paris, the plan—named after its designer, Count Alfred von Schlieffen—envisaged hitting the main French defense line from behind, in a whirl timed to last just forty-two days. Russia's inadequate railroad system should delay any major offensive from beyond the Vistula for at least six weeks. France would have capitulated by then, so Germany could concentrate all its firepower in an eastern *Hunnenschlacht* that would settle the Slav problem forever.

Roosevelt had been confidentially aware of the essentials of the Schlieffen Plan since 1911. The best that could be said of the tornado in action was that it was weaker than it might have been. General Moltke, the Kaiser's chief of staff, had deflected the curve through Flanders and Luxembourg only, sparing Holland. At the same time, he was so nervous of a French reprisal in the Marne that he transferred a considerable amount of strength there. This slowed his advance in the north, where fierce resistance by the Belgians—buttressed by an expeditionary influx of seventy-five thousand British troops—cost him precious days.

"If the Franco-British armies hold their own against the Germans," Roosevelt wrote Arthur Lee, "whether they win a victory or whether the result is a draw, it is in my judgment all up with Germany." Even if Moltke succeeded in conquering France, his forces, the Colonel thought, would be too "enfeebled" afterward to mount an effective defense against Russia. Nor could they expect much help from Austria, which had its own problems in the Balkans. Germany was faced, in short, with the prospect of being reduced to "international impotence" after forty-three years of unrestricted growth.

The same prospect, mixed with panic, seemed to strike General Alexander von Kluck's commanders on the road west of Liège. Their march was hampered by sabotage and the sniping of *francs-tireurs,* freelance sharpshooters with a maddening ability to remain invisible in flat terrain. The result, on 26 August, was a German bombardment of the ancient university town of Louvain that added new dimensions to Goethe's warning, "The Prussian was born a brute and civilization will make him ferocious." Flamethrowers set fire to street after street of private houses, and people who ran from them were rounded up—the men to be bayoneted, then shot, the women and children for imprisonment in concentration camps. "Big Bertha," a cannon so huge it had to be dragged by thirty-four horses, reduced churches and dormitories to flints. One of the world's richest medieval libraries was burned to the stone. By dark, the seat of six hundred years of learning had become a huge hearth. Richard Harding Davis was there to record a modern *Gotterdämmerung:*

> It was all like a scene upon a stage, unreal, inhuman. You felt that the curtain of fire, purring and crackling and sending up hot sparks to meet the kind, calm stars, was only a painted backdrop; that the reports of rifles from the dark ruins came from blank cartridges, and that these trembling shopkeepers and peasants ringed in bayonets would not in a few minutes really die, but that they themselves and their homes would be restored to their wives and children.

DISPATCHES CONFIRMING THE destruction and evacuation of Louvain reached the United States on 28 August and caused the first wave of anti-German revulsion to spread across the country. The imperial embassy in Washington stated without apology that the Belgian city had been "punished" for "a perfidious attack" by civilians upon the soldiers of the Reich.

Woodrow Wilson remained silent.

No American soul was more tried than Theodore Roosevelt's. "I am an ex-President," he apologized to Arthur Lee, "and my public attitude must be one of entire impartiality." Criticism by him of Wilson's foreign policy would be seized on by Democrats as a campaign issue in the fall congressional elections. What had happened in Belgium enraged him, but for as long as the war did not threaten the United States in its own hemisphere, patriotism required that he address himself only to domestic issues.

That did not stop Roosevelt from doing a little private lobbying on the subject of "preparedness," a word that had begun to dominate his vocabulary. "If you have any influence with the President," he wrote a Harvard classmate close to Colonel House, "I wish you would get him to assemble the fleet and put it in first-class fighting order, and to get the army up to the highest pitch at which it can now be put. No one can tell what this war will bring forth."

If you have any influence with the President. Phrases like that, dictated through his teeth, betrayed his political impotence now that Democrats controlled the executive and legislative branches of government. All he could do about it was to help as many Progressives and moderate Republicans as possible get elected in November. Bracing himself for more of the speaking tours he had sworn to renounce, he tried to see as much as possible of his children and grandchildren.

An unexpected feature of the summer had been postponement of Kermit's departure for South America. Belle had fallen ill with a mild case of typhoid, and took her time recuperating. In the resultant flutter of home care and doctoral visits, deeply satisfying to the female Roosevelts, she and Edith had at last bonded. Ethel and Dick and little Richard also clustered around. Roosevelt wrote Emily Carow to say how much he liked having the old house full of young people. "Ted and Eleanor frequently motor over with their two babies. Gracie is the dearest small soul you ever saw and my heart is like water before her."

IN A CRESCENDO of carnage, Germany and France took out on each other the accumulated antipathy of four decades. By early September, clashing mainly in Alsace-Lorraine and the Ardennes, they had together lost more than a quarter-million men. The almost unbelievable death toll came from two new forms of firepower—the horizontal "hail" of machine guns and the vertical destruction inflicted by cannons capable of lobbing twenty shells a minute—that mocked the pretensions of cavalry regiments still prancing around with swords and lances. Airplanes patrolling the unsettled front (not yet realizing that they might effectively exchange pistol shots) looked down on skirmishes reduced, by altitude, to the comings and goings of insect colonies.

Roosevelt, working at Sagamore Hill on the preface to his new book, *Through the Brazilian Wilderness,* had seen it all before. "The fire-ants [of Mato Grosso do Sul] bend the whole body as they bite. . . . These fighting ants, including the soldiers even among the termites, are frantically eager for a success which generally means their annihilation."

Elsewhere in Brazil, and throughout his own life, he had noted the compulsion of predators to exterminate both "types and individuals." This war was too enormous for individuals to matter, or even be registered before they were blown to bits. But it was clear that certain types were marked for extinction: not just the prancing cavalry officers but generals who could not adapt to mechanized slaughter (Joseph Joffre, the French chief of staff, had already replaced more than fifty), and the emperors in whose name the individuals fought.

Perhaps the type most feared by the emperors, for as long as they clung to their crowns, was the socialist with his red flag and ominously universal hymn:

> *Masses, slaves, arise, arise,*
> *The world must shift its base,*
> *We are not nothing in men's eyes.*
> *This is the fraught finale—*
> *Together and forever*
> *The Internationale*
> *Shall be the human race!*

The government of every nation currently at war—even Serbia, even republican France—feared socialism and its derivative doctrines, communism and anarchism, as more perilous to the stability of the state than alien armies. In Germany, Chancellor Bethmann-Hollweg deluded himself if he thought that the war would ingratiate Prussians with the proletariat. France's first martyr of the war had been the Socialist leader Jean Jaurès, assassinated by a paranoid right-winger. Britain had postponed, rather than averted class war by joining in; Russia was ripe for revolution; Austria had a large Marxist minority; even "poor little Belgium," as members of the Entente had taken to calling it, was a socialist hothouse, overpopulated and harshly governed by the ruling elite.

One Western power alone, in the late summer of 1914, stood secure, able by virtue of its enormous size, constitutional freedoms, and industrial capacity to determine the outcome of the war. But that potential was, for the time being, moot. Its president was so numb with personal grief that he could concentrate only on the driest details of domestic policy: tariff tinkerings, farm loan refinance, updated definitions of antitrust practices, a federal trade commission act. When Wilson thought about foreign policy at all, he brooded over the still-unsettled situation in Mexico. He listened sympathetically to the plaints of European ambassadors, and proclaimed a national day of prayer for peace in October, when it would benefit his party in the fall elections. But he lacked the international stature—and more important, he could not summon up the moral energy—to do what Roosevelt had done in 1905, and coax the belligerents to the negotiating table. In any case, none except Belgium was ready to accept mediation. "I gather," Cecil Spring Rice wrote, "that when you intervened in the Russo-Japanese conflict you had conclusive evidence that your aid was wanted."

The war ministers, sea lords, and commanders who now largely governed Europe were persuaded by the war's extreme violence that it would be short, or, if not, long enough for a desirable number of revolutionaries to be killed.

BEFORE ROOSEVELT LEFT New York on 5 September on a campaign trip to Louisiana, he assured nervous Progressives that he would not make an issue of Wilson's pacifism. An enormous number of voters were of German ancestry and supported the Reich, while those sympathetic to Britain and her allies were not so passionate that they wanted to end American neutrality.

Returning to the hustings afflicted him with an ennui he could not conceal. "He is most pessimistic," Cal O'Laughlin noted after meeting up with him in Baltimore. "He says his usefulness in public life is at an end and that any cause he supports is foredoomed. . . . He believes the country is reactionary. . . . I encouraged him as greatly as I could, but he has the blues." Only when their conversation switched to the war did the Colonel show any animation. Neutrality, he argued, was no guarantee of security. The United States should at once train half a million men to defend itself. Germany could not be allowed to win, but neither should it be broken up in defeat. After the war, Roosevelt said, "there should be three great peoples—the Slavs, the Germans, and the English." He was negative about France, which he felt was on the way to becoming "a second class nation," due to "her failure to increase her birth rate."

He had cause to rethink these words after returning home to the news that General Joffre's troops in the Marne, aided by the tiny British Expeditionary Force, had held a line extending from the environs of Paris to Verdun. The Germans had been forced into retreat, and were now entrenching themselves beyond the Aisne. Joffre was a hero and Moltke disgraced. The slaughter had been terrible on all sides. France estimated its losses at 250,000 men, Britain at 12,733. Germany declined to release any figures at all, but the litter of gray-clad bodies on French soil gave full weight to Clemenceau's phrase *ouragan de fer,* a hurricane of steel.

Dr. Richard Derby read about Louvain, and Liège, and the Battle of the Marne, and decided to go to France to help treat the wounded. He volunteered his services as a surgeon in the American Hospital in Paris. Ethel insisted on accompanying him as a nurse. Little Richard was only five months old, but her parents were glad to look after him while she was away. She promised to return, with or without Dick, in December.

Kermit and Belle took the opportunity to book their own departure, on the same ship but to a different final destination. During his wife's illness, Kermit had negotiated a job in Buenos Aires, Argentina, better than the one he had planned to take in Brazil. It was to be assistant manager of a new branch of the National City Bank. A house and servants came with it, plus plenty of fashionable society to keep Belle happy. He would have to learn Spanish, of course, but for him that was as easy as switching to a new brand of breakfast cereal. ·

The war had wrought such havoc with ocean traffic that it was not possible to get to Buenos Aires from New York except by crossing to Liverpool and reembarking from there. Hence the double departure of the two young couples from New York on 26 September.

Edith said goodbye to them in bright, windy weather. The Colonel was off on another campaign tour, this time of the Midwest. She hated his absence and knew that he did too. Fortunately he had his voice back, and looked well again, although he complained often of rheumatism. Having encouraged him to found the Progressive Party in 1912, she could not complain about him taking, as he put it, "a violent part in the obsequies." But with him gone, Quentin back at Groton, and Archie at Harvard, Sagamore Hill was a lonely place. Edith's only company was a baby that slept fifteen hours a day. She occupied herself, as she had since childhood, with incessant reading.

As he traveled, Roosevelt pondered the text of an extraordinary letter from Sir George Otto Trevelyan:

> I have something special to tell you. In the course of the last nine or ten months I have been brought into singularly intimate relations with a new class of American friends belonging to the Democratic party; and I have entertained here, or have received long and spontaneous letters from, old friends and acquaintances of the Republican party who did not support you at the last election. Three distinguished Democrats, two of them public men, and the other of exceptional literary and educational note . . . talked with me freely of your immense administrative power and success—as evinced in such questions as the Panama Canal, the Russian and Japanese war, the Labour troubles, and other like matters—and they all spoke of, and seemed to sympathize with, the widespread affection which your countrymen feel for you. The Republicans, men of the highest eminence, held the same [opinion]. They seemed in this respect to share the sentiment of a great mass of their party. . . .
>
> The deduction I draw from these conversations and letters is a conviction that it is of untold importance that you should have a leading part at this conjuncture. . . . Your mode of thought on international policy, and your deep and wide interest in the history of the past, would be of immeasurable service now and hereafter. I may be biased in this matter by my own regard for you, and my earnest desire to see you at the center of the world's affairs; but, after all, that is on my part no ignoble motive.

Trevelyan had never quite recovered from being the recipient of the Colonel's gigantic epistle describing his "royal" tour of Europe in the spring of

1910. It and dozens more in their long correspondence demonstrated a mastery of foreign affairs that made the old historian dream of having Roosevelt back in the White House. Other representatives, official and unofficial, of the belligerent nations exhibited a similar desire, as the war on all sides lost momentum and gained in ferocity. Each believed they had his sympathy. Count Albert Apponyi and Baron Hengelmüller, the retired Austrian ambassador to Washington, wrote pleading the causes respectively of Budapest and Vienna. Sir Edward Grey asked him to receive J. M. Barrie and A. E. W. Mason, two English writers touring America as propagandists for His Majesty's Government. Rudyard Kipling reported that female Belgian refugees in Britain were thankful to have been only raped by German soldiers, not executed as well. "Frankly we are aghast at there being no protest from the U.S." The antisemitic Cecil Spring Rice complained that Oscar Straus and other wealthy Jews were preaching pacifism at the White House, so that Wall Street would continue to profit from war-related exports. "It is no good arguing with these financiers—appealing to their sense of honor is like shooting them in the foreskin."

Roosevelt reminded his correspondents that the only influence he retained was that of his pen. And he still wanted to be fair to Wilson. "An ex-President," he reminded Kipling, "must be exceedingly careful in a crisis like this how he hampers his successor in office who actually has to deal with the situation." Trevelyan's salute, however, inspired him to publish a major essay, "The World War: Its Tragedies and Its Lessons," in *The Outlook* on 23 September. For the first time he gave the full range of his views on the war, writing with strong feeling but also with objectivity and erudition.

"THERE CAN BE NO HIGHER international duty," he declared, "than to safeguard the existence and independence of industrious, orderly states, with a high personal and national standard of conduct, but without the military force of the great powers." Examples of these were Belgium, Holland, Switzerland, the Scandinavian countries, and Uruguay. The first had just been trampled underfoot—was still being trampled—while the United States, the world's most righteous republic, raised no objection.

Roosevelt did not blame any of the belligerents for taking up arms, allowing that each had reasonable grievances. Austria-Hungary was right to punish Serbia for the murder of Franz Ferdinand, yet Serbia was right to oppose Austrian expansionism in the Balkans. Tsar Nicholas, as the protector of all Slavs, could not have remained passive after Hötzendorf attacked Belgrade; Kaiser Wilhelm felt a similar ethnic compulsion to defend Vienna; and Germany had been wise to strike France before that nation, unreconciled to the loss of Alsace-Lorraine, struck *her*. The British had acted nobly in honoring their ancient pledge to uphold Belgian neutrality, and they were wise to oppose Prussian militarism. Even in the Far East, where the war had spread, Japan was justified in besieging Germany's naval base at Kiaochow,* China, thus ending a nineteen-year provocation. The fall of that garrison looked imminent, and in Roosevelt's opinion would greatly improve the local balance of power.

He took no side except that of Belgium. "It seems to me impossible that any man can fail to feel the deepest sympathy with a nation which is absolutely guiltless of any wrongdoing." That was, any man whose ethics were not perverted by the amorality of war. Roosevelt noted that Britain had ignored the neutrality of Denmark when fighting France in 1807, "and with less excuse the same is true of our conduct toward Spain in Florida nearly a century ago." The only principle that applied in major conflicts, those that wrought fundamental change, was "the supreme law of national self-preservation," a deterministic force that had no scruples.

"But Germany's need to struggle for her life," he went on, "does not make it any easier for the Belgians to suffer death." He had read German military textbooks, and the tactician in him accepted the logic of Friedrich von Bernhardi's "necessary terror" in attack. However, as a human being, he was revolted at its injustice. King Albert's subjects had fought with wonderful courage against a force they could not withstand. As a result, they were suffering, "somewhat as my own German ancestors suffered when Turenne ravaged the Palatinate, somewhat as my Irish ancestors suffered in the struggles that attended the conquests and reconquests of Ireland in the days of Cromwell and William." The agony of the Belgians might not yet compare with that of the Germans themselves at French hands in 1674 and 1689. Even so, the sack of Louvain was "altogether too nearly akin to what occurred in the seventeenth century for us of the twentieth century to feel overmuch pleased at the amount of advance that has been made."

He remarked with a touch of disdain that it was probably impossible for most Americans, "living softly and at ease," to feel what it was like to be crushed by a conquering power. If they did not read European history, they could not understand how complicated a policy neutrality was, and how morally compromising. This brought on his *idée fixe* about peace and arbitration treaties.

> I suppose that few of them now hold that there was value in the "peace" which was obtained by the concert of European powers when they prevented interference with Turkey [in 1894–1896] while the Turks butchered some hundreds of thousands of Armenian men, women and children. In the same way I do not suppose that even the ultrapacifists really feel that "peace" is triumphant in Belgium at the

---

* Now Tsingtao.

present moment. President Wilson has been much applauded by all the professional pacifists because he has announced that our desire for peace must make us secure it for ourselves by a neutrality so strict as to forbid our even whispering a protest against wrong-doing, lest such whispers might cause disturbance to our ease and well-being. We pay the penalty of this action—or rather, supine inaction—by forfeiting the right to do anything on behalf of peace for the Belgians at present.

The last two sentences were too provocative for Lawrence Abbott, who cut the one about Wilson, and deleted the sarcastic clause in the other. Roosevelt was not the only eminent person to speak out against the administration's apathy on the Belgian issue—William Dean Howells and Senator John Sharp Williams of Mississippi were just as disapproving—but he was, after all, the President's most visible political opponent, and might deter Wilson from coming around slowly to Belgium's side.

Roosevelt emphasized that he was not advocating military intervention. Americans, he wrote, had no quarrel with any of the belligerents, although the Japanese (perpetually resentful of "yellow peril" prejudice in California) needed watching. The United States was therefore in a position to try to bring about peace. Whoever represented it in negotiations (he was careful not to ascribe that privilege exclusively to Wilson) should make clear that Congress would not tolerate any accord that compromised the national security.

The only possible good he saw coming out of the current conflict was a spread of democracy in Europe, or "at least a partial substitution of the rule of the people for the rule of those who esteem it their God-given right to govern the people." He noted approvingly that socialist parties in the belligerent countries had all backed the decisions of their governments to fight. Having watched old Franz Joseph rinse and spit, and marveled at the Kaiser's ignorance, and marched among all the monarchs now bridling at one another, he felt it would be a good thing if most of their crowns toppled.

Probably, after the war, there would be an increase in the number of international disputes submitted to justice, because justice was what democracy aspired to. But what court should administer it? Roosevelt, coming to the end of his long essay, echoed what he had said to the Nobel Prize committee about the impotence of the Hague tribunal. Work must begin at once to replace it with "an efficient world league" for peacekeeping. "Surely the time ought to be ripe for the nations to consider a great world agreement among all the civilized military powers *to back righteousness by force.*"

◈

RUMORS BEGAN TO CIRCULATE that private citizens lobbying for an American peace committee thought that Theodore Roosevelt would be the ideal person to press for a diplomatic settlement of the war. *The New York Times* reported that Oscar Straus was spending many hours with the Colonel, both in New York and Oyster Bay, and that both men were cagey about their discussions. Sources in Washington were quoted as acknowledging that Roosevelt had "a thorough knowledge of the conditions in Europe," and enjoyed cordial friendships with many of the belligerent leaders, particularly Wilhelm II.

These qualifications also occurred to the editor of the mass-market New York *World*. He sent a representative, John N. Wheeler, to Oyster Bay to ask if the Colonel would be willing to go abroad as a war correspondent, at the staggering salary of three thousand dollars a week. Roosevelt hesitated, then declined.

"It would reflect on the dignity of this country and the position I have held."

John Wheeler, who had just formed a popular-press syndicate, had another idea. "How about doing a series on the lessons this country should learn from the war?"

Roosevelt thought he had written plenty about that already in *The Outlook,* but the opportunity to broadcast his views to the largest possible audience was irresistible. "You will hear from me," he said.

⁂

HE WROTE FOUR PIECES at once, because he had to spend most of October on the road. Deliberately adopting a journalistic style, he compared what had happened to prosperous, pleasure-loving Europe to the fate that had befallen the *Titanic*. "One moment the great ship was speeding across the ocean, equipped with every device for comfort, safety, and luxury. . . . Suddenly, in one awful and shattering moment, death smote the floating host, so busy with work and play." The "lesson" for Americans in Europe's catastrophe was to see how quickly even the most civilized nations reverted to barbarism, and how vulnerable great powers were to sudden attack. The United States was no exception, now that the Panama Canal was open. Its army was as small as Persia's. Its navy was by some counts third in the world, but a single lethal blow to its battleship fleet, and San Francisco or New York would be as open to destruction as Louvain. "Under such circumstances, outside powers would undoubtedly remain neutral exactly as we have remained neutral as regards Belgium."

Although he did not refer to Wilson or Bryan by name, his evident contempt for them caused the pro-Democratic New York *World* to pass on the series. So did the Hearst news organization. *The New York Times,* however, ran the first article prominently in its Sunday edition on 27 September. It increased the paper's circulation by several thousand copies. Other periodicals rushed to reprint Roosevelt's series, and by mid-October he was reaching a readership of fifteen million. Wheeler urged him to continue with as many more war articles as he pleased.

He obliged with another five, dashed off between whistle-stops, for weekly publication through the end of November. By the time he was through, he had thoroughly unburdened himself on the responsibilities of the United States to the Hague Conventions of 1899 and 1907; on the causes of the war (chiefly "fear . . . and the anger born of that fear"); on the development of an "international conscience" to chasten national self-interest; on the dangers inherent in disarmament; on the necessity for active, rather than passive neutrality; on preparedness ("the one certain way to invite disaster is to be opulent, offensive, and unarmed"); and on the current dereliction of the American military.

In his public appearances, Roosevelt stuck to Progressive domestic boilerplate, drummed out with more energy than enthusiasm. It was clear to him that the electorate had lost interest in political reform. So had he, although he insisted he was as radical as ever. His mind was elsewhere. When he encountered old friends on the road, he wanted to talk only about the war, and about the burning of Louvain in particular. Word that German troops had virtually destroyed the great cathedral at Reims caused him further anguish.

EDITH ROOSEVELT WORRIED about her husband's gloom whenever he climbed onto another train. To cheer him up after an especially onerous trip to Philadelphia, where the Pinchots had pushed him for speech after speech, she went into New York to meet his train and spent the night of 29 October with him. He had no time to come home: he was needed the following day in Princeton, New Jersey.

She brought with her a long letter from Ethel in Paris. "You cannot imagine the conditions here— If we knew them at home our country would not be able to be neutral— It's appalling." The American Hospital was full of Belgian soldiers, hideously mutilated by shrapnel and shell, "—hardly any from bullets." Every day, more civilian refugees arrived, including many unattached children, "—alone, not knowing even their own names—put on the train by the mayors of the towns just to get them out of the way, and after all had been ruined, some of them wounded, very few boys, & many of the boys with their right hands cut off."

Roosevelt had received similar reports, and worse, from Kipling and other witnesses better informed than his credulous daughter. All wanted to convince him that German soldiers on the warpath were Neanderthal in their savagery. The Colonel reserved judgment on most of their stories. Mutilated soldiers were what a nurse should be expected to see, thirty miles from the front in wartime. But Ethel had plainly only heard about handless little boys, as Kipling had only heard about rapes and mass executions. "My experience in the Spanish war has taught me that there is a tendency to exaggerate such outrages," Roosevelt wrote him.

He granted that when millions were at war, "some thousands of unspeakable creatures will commit unspeakable acts," but did not see that nationality was any constraint. He reminded Kipling that even so patriotic a historian as William Lecky had found that "frightful atrocities" were committed by English soldiers in the Irish uprising of 1798, and that in 1900, Britain's current allies, the French and the Russians, had behaved abominably on the march to Peking. In an admission he would never have made before he met Natalie Curtis, he added: "I have known Americans do unspeakable acts against Indians."

Ethel's letter, all the same, brought the war home in a personal way that made him forget, at Princeton, his promise not to make it a campaign issue. The fact that the university's former president was now President of the United States may also have prompted him to launch into an impassioned speech on preparedness that had his audience, mainly students, cheering vociferously.

❧

ON 3 NOVEMBER, the Progressive Party lost all its state contests except in California, where Hiram Johnson was reelected. Only one Progressive kept his seat in the House of Representatives. Nationwide, the Party registered just two million votes—half its strength in 1912—to six million apiece for the two major parties. This was good news to the GOP, an effectively leaderless force that regained many of its defectors from 1912. But it was not good news to Woodrow Wilson, who had hoped those defectors would vote Democratic, as a show of confidence in him. He was still far from popular. A prolonged recession had disillusioned the electorate with New Freedom, and by extension, New Nationalism. In a post-election poll of nine thousand "leading men of the country" by *The Lawyer and Banker,* Wilson came second to Secretary of the Interior Franklin K. Lane as their preferred Democratic candidate for the presidency in 1916. And Lane was far behind their favorite Republican, Charles Evans Hughes.

Of the twelve names polled, Theodore Roosevelt came in last, with only 11 votes to Hughes's 1,584. Having made a career out of attacking precisely the combination embodied in the phrase *Lawyer and Banker,* he could not expect readers of such a magazine to rank him much higher, even if he was a declared candidate. Still, he had just participated in his third failed campaign in five years—confessedly an "utter and hopeless one" as far as Progressivism was concerned. His words from a past moment of triumph resounded hollowly: *We, here in America, hold in our hands the hope of the world, the fate of the coming years; and shame and disgrace will be ours if in our eyes the light of high resolve is dimmed, if we trail in the dust the golden hopes of men.*

Once again the Colonel returned to a Sagamore Hill deserted by politicians and reporters. Little Richard was pining for Ethel. So was he. She gave off and attracted more love than any other of his children. "I wish I could stroke your neck and hair," he wrote her. Happily, both Derbys would be back home in time for Christmas. Alice was likely to be less difficult, this festive season, now that Nick had been reelected to Congress. And Edith too should be happier, once she heard that Kermit and Belle were safely settled in Buenos Aires.

Roosevelt persuaded himself that he looked forward to private life, although Wilson's cool refusal to speak out about Belgium tormented him. For the moment, he did not have a big book to write, nor was any publisher asking for one. *An Autobiography* had been a disappointment for Macmillan, and *Life-Histories of African Game Animals* was so technical that Scribners had printed it almost as an act of charity. *Through the Brazilian Wilderness,* just out, was earning excellent reviews, and in narrative quality was probably the best thing he had ever done. But its early sales did not compare to those of *African Game Trails.*

For as long as the European war lasted, Roosevelt felt inclined to focus on journalism. Next February he would have a new editorial platform, as guest columnist for *Metropolitan* magazine. Pacifism, preparedness, and moral cowardice were to be his themes; he was bored with partisan argument. Let those intellectuals who were more policy-minded than he was—brilliant young men such as Herbert Croly and Walter Lippmann—adapt what survived of Progressivism to suit a magazine they had just founded, *The New Republic.*

"It is perfectly obvious that the bulk of our people are heartily tired of me," Roosevelt wrote William Allen White, in a posterity letter tinged with regret.

> I shall fight in the ranks as long as I live for the cause and the platform for which we fought in 1912. But at present any attempt at action on my part which could be construed . . . into the belief that I was still aspiring to some leadership in the movement would, I am convinced, do real harm. It has been wisely said that while martyrdom is often right for the individual, what society needs is victory. It was eminently proper that Leonidas should die at Thermopylae, but the usefulness of Thermopylae depended upon its being followed by the victory of Themistocles at Salamis. . . . When it is evident that a leader's day is past, the one service he can render is to step aside and leave the ground clear for the development of a successor. It seems to me that such is now the case as regards myself. "Heartily know that the half-gods go when the Gods arise."

CHAPTER 20

Two Melancholy Men

The coming on of his old monster Time
Has made him a still man; and he has dreams
Were fair to think on once, and all found hollow.

THE WINTER OF 1914–1915 found the Allies and Central Powers entrenched opposite each other in two freezing fissures that divided Western Europe like a fault line, all the way north from Switzerland to Ypres and the Belgian ports. Another fissure ran alongside the Bzura-Ravka riverline west of Warsaw and cracked down the map into Galicia, holding eight ill-supplied Russian armies at bay. Gone was the mobility that had characterized the early months of the war: the Schlieffen Plan's rotation, the cavalry sweeps, the cuts and thrusts of maneuvers at Tannenberg and in the Marne. Abandoned, too, was the delusion of the soldiers dug in that a trench was a temporary thing that would last only as long as it took for politicians to settle the misunderstandings of last summer. The war was going to be long, and mortal beyond calculation: a continuum of attrition, to be won by whichever power had the largest reserves of blood, bread, industrial plant, and patience. Germany had by now lost well over a million men, France almost that number. On the Eastern Front, 750,000 Russian, German, and Austrian soldiers had fallen in just six weeks.

Across the Atlantic, Woodrow Wilson and Theodore Roosevelt hunkered down in their own psychological ditches. They were two melancholy men counterposed on either side of a foreign issue that most Americans chose to ignore—in Wilson's words, "a war with which we have nothing to do." White House aides were alarmed at the President's inability to recover from the death of Ellen Wilson, five months before. He was not the type to share deep emotion with anybody except Colonel House and the few women closest to him: his two daughters, his sister and cousins, and a clutch of married confidantes. None could console him. From time to time grief forced Wilson to reveal that he felt "wiped out," unable to think straight. The unremarkable Democratic vote in the recent elections made him feel that his domestic reform program had failed. He frightened Colonel House by saying he would not mind being assassinated.

Roosevelt appeared on the surface to be content. He insisted, as he had in late 1910 and 1912, that his politicking days were over ("I *never* wish to leave Sagamore again!") and that his heart and mind were at ease. Family and friends used to such protestations saw that he was, on the contrary, unhappier than at any time they could remember. He had regained the seventy pounds of flesh he lost to malaria, and it was not the firm musculature of earlier years, but a fatness around the waist and neck that disgusted him. "I am now pretty nearly done out," he confided to his former White House physician, Dr. Presley Rixey. "The trouble is that I have rheumatism or gout and things of that kind to a degree that make it impossible for me to take very much exercise; and then in turn the fact that I cannot take exercise prevents my keeping in good condition." Like many another ovoid person, he did not relate his weight gain to compulsive eating.

Ted was concerned enough about him to call old Rough Riders and ask them to rally round. "Father is in very bad shape. Won't you come out and see if you can cheer him up." Those who did tried the dubious therapy of encouraging Roosevelt to think of raising a volunteer division to fight in Mexico or, if need be one day, overseas. Edith lost patience with these fantasies. "Both you men," she said to her husband and Frank Knox, "are exactly like small boys playing at soldiers."

She sat in glowing firelight, with needlework on her lap.

"It's a lovely game. But as far as the Mexican trouble is concerned, Theodore, you know quite as well as I do that Mr. Wilson will never let you, *or* your division, get into it at all."

William Allen White correctly diagnosed that the Colonel was suffering from power deprivation. As the ambivalent leader of a dying party, he no longer looked or sounded presidential. It was inconceivable, given what was happening in Europe, that he could ever again call upon straw-hatted idealists to stand and fight at Armageddon. In his despair that nothing was being done for the Belgians (or was it frustration at not being in control?), he was resorting increasingly to ugly language against Wilson and Bryan. His series of articles on the war had become near-libelous after the election. That infallible sign of Rooseveltian frustration, the tendency to castrate political opponents, had resurged: "Weaklings who raise their shrill piping for a peace that shall consecrate successful wrong occupy a position quite as immoral as and infinitely more contemptible than the position of the wrong-doers themselves. . . . It comes dangerously near flattery to call the foreign policy of the

United States under President Wilson and Secretary Bryan one of milk and water."

White tried to tease him back into the kind of civilized essay-writing that suited him best. "Your cistern is dry on politics. . . . I understand that you have a contract with the *Metropolitan*. If I were you I would go strong on the discussion of modern tendencies in architecture with here and there a few remarks on Sir Oliver Lodge's views on abnormal psychology, and I might take a swipe at the national moving picture censorship, but I would not have anything to do with friend Bryan or friend Wilson."

Roosevelt did not rise to White's humor. "I am more like a corpse than like the cistern of which you spoke." He laboriously explained that *Metropolitan* magazine was interested only in his views on "international, social and economic questions," and would not permit him to write literary essays—much as he might want to. "Like you I make my living largely by my pen. I don't care to go into work that will take me beyond the time when Quentin, my youngest son, is launched into the world, but that won't be for three years yet. . . ."

He did not mention a financial threat that loomed ahead of him: the $50,000 libel suit he had brought on himself, last July, by accusing William Barnes, Jr., of aiding and abetting the "rotten" state government of New York. The case had been expensively delayed and relocated from Albany to Syracuse, on the ground that Boss Barnes's dominance of the former city would preclude a fair jury. It was now due to be tried in April. Roosevelt knew from his libel suit against George Newett that even if he successfully defended himself, the costs he would incur were likely to be enormous. If he lost—and Barnes was a wealthy and formidable adversary—Quentin might have to be "launched" much sooner than 1918.

Metropolitan was a large, lavishly illustrated monthly owned by Harry Payne Whitney, a racehorse breeder so blinkered with wealth that he did not seem to notice that its editor, Henry J. Whigham, had a radical bias that veered close to socialism. Roosevelt was willing to live with that as long as Whigham let him preach his own, more paternalistic brand of politics. The magazine, in addition, was a strong supporter of preparedness.

"After this January," he told White, "I shall do my best to avoid mentioning Wilson's and Bryan's names."

❧

AS THE NEW YEAR progressed, however, he managed to mention them often, and harshly. Always his anger was directed at their interpretation of neutrality. They seemed to think it was a right that could be proclaimed, he wrote, whereas in fact it was only a privilege conceded by belligerent nations—for as long as those nations felt so disposed. Nor was it necessarily virtuous: "To be neutral between right and wrong is to serve wrong." Roosevelt felt that American apathy about the war was solidifying, and decided to move quickly before it became a cement resistant to chipping. Taking advantage of the New York publishing industry's extraordinary ability to print and distribute a bound book in little more than two weeks, he edited his ten war articles of the previous fall for publication before the end of January. He supplemented them with two newer pieces on military training and "utopian" peace plans.

"A LARGE, LAVISHLY ILLUSTRATED MONTHLY."
Metropolitan *magazine, TR's main journalistic outlet from 1915 to 1918.*

The resultant twelve-chapter volume, entitled *America and the World War,* was issued by Scribners. It made permanent the breach between him and the administration, and established him as Wilson's doctrinal foil. Critical reaction, when not dismissive, was divided. To Roosevelt's chagrin, reviewers sympathetic to Britain, Belgium, and France accused him of favoring Germany. The reverse obtained with those who described themselves as "German-American," a locution he detested.

In a letter to a woman asking him to announce that he was an "Anglo-

American," he disclaimed all hyphenated allegiances. "England is not my motherland any more than Germany is my fatherland. My motherland and fatherland and my own land are all three of them the United States."

His new book, hortatory by purpose, lacked such plain eloquence. Its few statesmanlike passages were obscured by a surf of words so repetitive and overstated as to numb any reader. Roosevelt had always excused his habit of saying everything three, or thirty-three times with the rationale that it was the only way to drum certain basic truths into the public mind. But *America and the World War* took repetition to the point of pugilism, as if he wanted to knock out everyone who did not feel as strongly as he did.

Many bookstore browsers glancing through its table of contents felt that they had already gotten the Colonel's message, and would gain little by reading further:

1. THE DUTY OF SELF-DEFENSE AND OF GOOD CONDUCT TOWARD OTHERS
2. THE BELGIAN TRAGEDY
3. UNWISE TREATIES A MENACE TO RIGHTEOUSNESS
4. THE CAUSES OF THE WAR
5. HOW TO STRIVE FOR WORLD PEACE
6. THE PEACE OF RIGHTEOUSNESS
7. AN INTERNATIONAL *POSSE COMITATUS*
8. SELF-DEFENSE WITHOUT MILITARISM
9. OUR PEACEMAKER, THE NAVY
10. PREPAREDNESS AGAINST WAR
11. UTOPIA OR HELL?
12. SUMMING UP

It was unfortunate that Roosevelt, in his haste to cram together articles originally published separately, had not blended them into a more sequential argument. *America and the World War* had some passages of real power, especially in pieces written after the election, when all gloves were off. His call for a *posse comitatus,* or central police force of neutral nations, sounded all the more urgent now that the Hague tribunal had adjourned for the duration of the war. It was unfortunate, though, that he used the word *posse,* which invited jokes about his youth in the Wild West even though he construed it as Latin. He insisted that he was not advocating unilateral armed action by the United States, only its commitment (perhaps as the founding member) to a postwar peacekeeping league. "I ask those individuals who think of me as a firebrand to remember that during the seven and a half years I was President not a shot was fired at any soldier of a hostile nation by any American soldier or sailor, and there was not so much as a threat of war. . . . The blood recently shed at Vera Cruz . . . had no parallel during my administration."

He poured scorn on Wilson and Taft for allegedly neglecting the navy since he left office. As a result, the Great White Fleet of 1909 was now underfunded and demoralized. The condition of the army was even worse: it numbered only 80,804 officers and men, half of whom were deployed overseas. Yet Wilson, in his latest message to Congress, had scorned preparedness and declared that the United States was secure. This enabled Roosevelt to demolish some of the approving comments that had followed:

> Mr. Bryan came to his support with hearty enthusiasm and said: "The President knows that if this country needed a million men, and needed them in a day, the call would go out at sunrise and the sun would go down on a million men in arms." . . . I once heard a Bryanite senator put Mr. Bryan's position a little more strongly. [He] announced that we needed no regular army, because in the event of war "ten million freemen would spring to arms, the equals of any regular soldiers in the world." I do not question the emotional or oratorical sincerity either of Mr. Bryan or of the senator. Mr. Bryan is accustomed to performing *in vacuo;* and both he and President Wilson, as regards foreign affairs, apparently believe they are living in a world of two dimensions, and not in the actual workaday world, which has three dimensions. . . .
>
> If the senator's ten million men sprang to arms at this moment, they would have at the outside some four hundred thousand modern rifles at which to spring. Perhaps six hundred thousand more could spring to squirrel pieces and fairly good shotguns. The remaining nine million men would have to spring to axes, scythes, hand-saws, gimlets, and similar arms.

In his summary chapter, looking back at the events of late July 1914, Roosevelt wrote, "I feel in the strongest way that we should have interfered, at least to the extent of the most emphatic diplomatic protest at the very outset [of the war] *and then by whatever further action was necessary,* in regard to the violation of the neutrality of Belgium." He thus made it plain that had he been in the White House, he would have been willing to resort to force, on the same grounds that Britain had cited. Wilson would argue that the United States had no treaty obligation to do anything of the kind, but Roosevelt considered its endorsement of The Hague conventions of 1897 and 1907 to be binding. "As President," he boasted, "I ordered the signature of the United States to these conventions."

Elihu Root was no longer at his elbow to remind him, with a sarcastic smile, that his enthusiasm for both documents had been slight. But as Roosevelt pointed out in his peroration, there had been epic changes since then.

> In the terrible whirlwind of the war all the great nations of the world, save the United States and Italy, are facing the supreme test of their history.*. . . Yet, in the face of all this, the President of the United States sends in a message dealing with national defense, which is filled with prettily phrased platitudes of the kind applauded at the less important types of peace congress, and with sentences cleverly turned to conceal from the average man the fact that the President has no real advice to give, no real policy to propose. . . .
>
> For us to assume superior virtues in the face of the war-worn nations of the Old World will not make us more acceptable as mediators among them. . . . The storm that is raging in Europe is terrible and evil; but it is also grand and noble. Untried men who live at ease will do well to remember that there is a certain sublimity even in Milton's defeated archangel, but none whatever in the spirits who kept neutral, who remained at peace, and dared side neither with hell nor with heaven.

WISTER WAS ONE of several friends who saw, with varying degrees of alarm, that Roosevelt's obsession with the war had darkened his personality. David Goodrich, a fellow veteran of the Santiago campaign, went riding with him, and noticed that he kept swinging his half-blind head as he scoped out the icy countryside. He was playing the German game of *Kriegsspiel*—imagining battlefields and figuring out how to deploy troops across them. Hamlin Garland visited him in his new office at *Metropolitan* magazine and found him distinctly older in looks and demeanor. His eyes were dull, and his manner subdued. "He will never run for President again," the novelist lamented. "That he may never lose his sense of humor is my prayer."

Finley Peter Dunne, a fellow contributor to *Metropolitan,* caught the Colonel on a more spirited day, dictating an article to a stenographer. Dunne was put off by the hectoring tone of his sentences, so at odds with the literary grace he was capable of. At a pause in the dictation, Dunne told Roosevelt he felt his recent pieces were unworthy of him.

TR   (*laughing*) They read all right to me.
DUNNE   But you're no judge. You are damaging your reputation as a

---

* Italy entered the war on the Allied side on 23 May 1915.

	writer. Look at those wonderful things you wrote about your experiences in South America.
TR	Oh well (*laughing*), you must suit your implement to your subject. A pen is all right for a naturalist, with a poetic strain in him.
DUNNE	A what?
TR	A poetic strain. You didn't know I had it, but I have and I can use it at times. But when you are dealing with politics you feel that you have your enemy in front of you and you must shake your fist at him and roar the Gospel of Righteousness in his deaf ear.

Shortly afterward, Dunne left *Metropolitan* to write for *Collier's*. He took with him the memory of Roosevelt marching up and down, "striking his palm with a clenched fist and shouting an article that no one but himself ever read."

⇛

WOODROW WILSON MAY HAVE been isolated by grief that February, but he was not immobilized by it. He fully understood that he had to do something soon to revise his definition of neutrality, in the view of growing tensions between the United States, Germany, and Great Britain. "We cannot remain isolated in this war," he said to Joseph Tumulty, "for soon the contagion of it will spread until it reaches our own shores. On the one side Mr. Bryan will censure the administration for being too militaristic, and on the other we will find Mr. Roosevelt criticizing us because we are too pacifist in our tendencies."

On 4 February, the German government issued a shipping advisory so menacing that Wilson had to reply in a similar tone. The issue was America's protectionist policy toward England, under which it exported prodigious quantities of munitions there for war use. Technically, such cargo was contraband and subject to seizure by German warships. But since the Royal Navy controlled the Atlantic, the arms flow might have been on a conveyor belt. Britain had begun to take further advantage of her naval superiority to seize American vessels carrying non-contraband goods to Germany. Sir Edward Grey insisted with a straight face that because the Reich had placed flour, wheat, and corn in official distribution, those items were *de facto* militarized. Cotton, too, was declared contraband, since it was used to clean German rifles. Britain proposed to apply these restrictions even to shipments to Germany's neutral neighbors—countries as harmless as Sweden and Holland—on the grounds that landed goods could be relabeled and reshipped to the Reich.

To that end, it had for the last three months unilaterally blockaded both entrances to the North Sea and sown the water with mines. Desperate for food and humiliated at the impotence of its dreadnoughts, which were jammed in Wilhelmshaven like toys in a drawer, Germany now announced that it had no choice but to use the only marine weapon it could still deploy: the *Untersee-boot,* or U-boat. "The waters surrounding Great Britain, including the whole English Channel, are hereby declared to be a war zone," the advisory ran. "On or after the 18th of February, 1915, every enemy merchant ship found in the said war zone will be destroyed. . . . Even neutral ships are exposed to danger [and] neutral powers are accordingly forewarned not to continue entrusting their crews, passengers, or merchandise to such vehicles."

As Sir Cecil Spring Rice advised the State Department, "This is in effect a claim to torpedo at sight . . . any merchant vessel under any flag."

Wilson hesitated only six days before sending Berlin a note that used the kind of specific language he usually avoided.

> If the commanders of German vessels of war . . . should destroy on the high seas an American vessel or the lives of American citizens, it would be difficult for the Government of the United States to view the act in any other light than as an indefensible violation of neutral rights, which it would be very hard, indeed, to reconcile with the friendly relations now happily subsisting between the two governments.
>
> If such a deplorable situation should arise, the Imperial German Government can readily appreciate that the Government of the United States would be constrained to hold the Imperial Government of Germany to a strict accountability for such acts of their naval authorities, and to take any steps it might be necessary to take to safeguard American lives and property and to secure to American citizens the full enjoyment of their acknowledged rights on the high seas.

ROOSEVELT WAS NOT impressed by the phrase *strict accountability,* because he doubted (against the evidence of Vera Cruz) that Wilson was capable of military action. The President did not seem to hold Britain equally accountable for mining the North Sea. That was the trouble with pacifists: when they tried to assert themselves, they often behaved without logic. It could be argued that a torpedo aimed at a merchantman known to be carrying contraband was less despicable than floating bombs that blew up any ship indiscriminately— an American freighter, say, laden with nothing more lethal than seeds. Wilson's threat to Germany did not insure against an upsurge of anti-British feeling in the United States, should either kind of accident occur. It was bad enough that the Royal Navy had taken to stopping and searching American ships, with scant respect for their flag or passengers. "I hope that at all costs your people will avoid a clash with us, *where we are right*," Roosevelt wrote Spring Rice. "Your government evidently feels a great contempt for the Wilson-Bryan administration; and I don't wonder. . . . But it is just weak and timid but shifty creatures of the Wilson-Bryan type who are most apt to be responsible for a country drifting into war."

In a censuring tone such as he had never directed at his old friend before, he added the hope "that you will under no circumstances yourselves do something wrong, something evil, as regards which I and the men like me will have to clearly take the stand on the other side."

Spring Rice took no offense, believing that Theodore had still not recovered, emotionally or physically, from his near-death experience in Brazil. Sir Edward Grey reacted with similar mildness to a long and almost treasonous letter from the Colonel, saying that Wilson was quite capable of reversing any foreign-policy initiative to win reelection, and reproaching Britain for "assuming" that its naval power gave it the "right" to harass American exporters. He merely replied, "People here will not stand letting goods go past our doors to Germany."

For as long as the winter lasted, Roosevelt picked or sought quarrels with friends whose war views did not agree with his. He clashed so furiously with the pro-German editor George Sylvester Viereck over "divided allegiance" to the American flag that they returned each other's letters. He told St. Loe Strachey that Britain's desire for an Allied monopoly of American trade was indistinguishable from German *Weltmacht;* he accused Count Apponyi of being a latter-day Austrian patriot, and when, in late March, Lord Bryce asked him to endorse a World League for Peace, he wrote back declining to be associated with sentimentalists "who seemingly are willing to see the triumph of wrong if only all physical danger to their own worthless bodies can thereby be averted."

Everyone, except perhaps Apponyi, understood that "T. Vesuvius Roosevelt" had to release lava periodically. But such eruptions were usually short. This one lasted through 13 April, when he checked Edith in to hospital for a hysterectomy. He then had to hurry to Yale to serve as honorary pallbearer at the funeral of the literary scholar Thomas R. Lounsbury.

Upon arrival in the anteroom of Battell Chapel, he found that one of his fellow bearers was William Howard Taft. They had not met face-to-face in almost four years.

Taft made the first move. "How are you, Theodore?"

Roosevelt shook hands, but remained silent and unsmiling.

Barnes v. Roosevelt

> *My tomb is this unending sea*
> *And I lie far below.*
> *My fate, O stranger, was to drown;*
> *And where it was the ship went down*
> *Is what the sea-birds know.*

BY 16 APRIL 1915, two of New York's most patrician law firms had completed their briefs for what promised to be the most entertaining libel suit since *Roosevelt v. Newett:* case 164 A.D. 540 on the Onondaga County court calendar, *William Barnes, plaintiff-appellant, against Theodore Roosevelt, defendant-respondent.* Both sides agreed there was plenty of evidence to show that Barnes had been defamed by Roosevelt nine months before. The only question was whether the latter had been telling the truth or not. If so, there was no libel.

Barnes's counsel, William M. Ivins of Ivins, Wolff & Hoguet, told Elihu Root that he was going to Syracuse "to nail Colonel Roosevelt's hide" to the courthouse wall.

"I know Colonel Roosevelt," Root said. "Be very careful whose hide you nail to that courthouse."

John M. Bowers of Bowers & Sands had already secured a coup for the defendant by getting the trial moved away from Albany, Barnes's power base, to Syracuse, a former Progressive stronghold. To make sure his client got the right jurors, he retained an attorney, Oliver D. Burden, on terms billable to the Colonel. All told, there were four lawyers acting for either party in the case, and a roster of nearly a hundred witnesses. The proceedings seemed likely to last a month.

Barnes and Roosevelt were not only looking at heavy potential costs, but at dire political consequences for whichever of them lost. Defeat for Roosevelt would tarnish his reputation as a square dealer. Defeat for Barnes would probably destroy his dream of running in 1916 for the U.S. Senate. Since they were both Harvard men of distinguished families (Barnes was the grandson of Thurlow Weed, a co-founder of the GOP), they were equally encouraged to hear that Justice William S. Andrews, assigned by the New York Supreme Court to hear their case, boasted the same background. He was in fact Roosevelt's classmate.

Much, therefore, hinged on his reaction to Bowers's motion, when proceedings began on Monday, 19 April: "Your Honor, I move to dismiss the complaint on the ground that the article [Exhibit No. 1, Roosevelt's widely published anti-Barnes press release of 22 July 1914] is not libelous *per se,* and that the complaint contains no innuendo, and therefore, there is nothing to go to the jury." Bowers argued that in a pre-election season, the Colonel had just been asking voters to back a non-machine candidate for governor of New York State. Obviously, he had been unsuccessful. But as a free-speaking citizen, he was "privileged" under the Constitution to draw attention to suspicious dealings in Albany.

Andrews rejected the motion, and ordered testimony to begin the following morning.

⸺

SYRACUSE MAY HAVE VOTED for Roosevelt in 1912, but if the jurors taking their seats at ten o'clock on Tuesday represented its current political mood, the local GOP had reclaimed many lost sheep. Nine were Republicans, two Progressives, and one Democrat. They worked, in exactly equal proportion, as small businessmen, farmers, and artisans. Roosevelt had once been able to call such people his own—except perhaps the Democrat, a coal dealer who might not have approved his interceding in the anthracite strike of 1902. But now he could not be sure what any might think of him.

The rain-spattered crowd that awaited his arrival at the courthouse was sparse, more curious than welcoming. Only one woman tried to raise a "Hurrah for Teddy!" It was not taken up by other spectators. From their point of view, and from that of newsmen clustering around, the Colonel was a disappointing sight—stout, unsmiling, yielding at every turn to the direction of his lawyers. He wore a shapeless suit of brown and a black hat pulled low, as if to discourage stares. As soon as he sat down in the courtroom, facing the jury across the Bowers table, he put on a pair of bowed spectacles. Their lenses were so thick that they obscured the power of his gaze. A roll of fat unflatteringly rested on his collar.

Barnes came in a few minutes later and sat ten feet away and slightly behind him. Big and well-tailored in dark blue, with silver wings of hair framing his center part, he looked what he was, and had never denied being: a political businessman, at home in boardrooms and the cigar-fragrant hideaways of state legislators. He swung in his chair and shot a glance at Roosevelt, who declined to return it. From then on they ignored each other, often swiveling back to back.

If anybody looked likely to dominate the trial, it was William M. Ivins. Sixty-four years old and meticulously overdressed, with gray spats, ribbon pince-nez, and an emerald pin securing his ascot, he arrived escorting a pretty secretary, the only woman admitted to the floor. His appearance might have

"A LAWYER OF INTERNATIONAL REPUTE,
FLUENT IN SIX LANGUAGES."
William M. Ivins.

prompted titters (especially when he donned a popish skullcap), were he not known to be one of the sharpest cross-examiners in the New York bar. Ivins was a lawyer of international repute, fluent in six languages, widely read in philosophy, finance, and diplomatic history, a collector in his spare time of Shakespearean folios and Napoleonic medals.

He was also mortally ill. Few, if any in the courtroom realized it, so quiet and genial was his manner.

At five after the hour everybody rose for Justice Andrews, who entered carrying two bowls of carnations. Plonked down on either side of him, they merely emphasized his austere severity. He directed counsel for the plaintiff to lay out the "merits of the controversy" before any witness was called. Ivins began by describing Theodore Roosevelt as a political giant who happened to be a gifted writer as well—"probably the greatest arbiter of opinion in this country who has been known in its history." The jury, he said, should bear in mind that the libel complained of had not been an impromptu remark, but the deliberate work of the Colonel's "very eloquent pen." Every word of it would therefore have to be documented and proved.

Ivins turned to William Barnes, Jr., as a person substantial in his own right, being the owner-operator of an important newspaper, the *Albany Evening Journal*, and for many years the most powerful figure in New York politics. The jury would learn that Governor Roosevelt had depended on Barnes's services as long ago as 1899, and that President Roosevelt had twice reappointed him to state office. The two men had met and corresponded regularly, exchanging mutual compliments, until their political ways had diverged in 1910. Ever since then, for reasons best known to the defendant, Barnes had become *persona non grata* at Sagamore Hill. Counsel for the plaintiff would attempt to show in cross-examination just what it was that Roosevelt had against him.

Before doing so, however, Ivins wanted jurors to hear the Colonel's exact words of July 1914—words addressed to more than two and a half million newspaper readers, and written "with the same care and the same skill that he had shown in preparing *The Winning of the West* and *African Game Trails*."

It was evident that Ivins's strategy was to appeal to the anti-intellectualism ingrained in the average American juror. He was subtly portraying Roosevelt as a littérateur, an elitist, a poison-pen scribe who visited his political prejudices upon those less "privileged" than himself. Reading with dramatic incisiveness, Ivins gave life to the words complained of by Barnes:

> *In New York State we see at its worst the development of the system of bipartisan boss rule.*
>
> *In New York State the two political machines are completely dominated, the one by Mr. Barnes, the other by Mr. Murphy.*
>
> *The state government is rotten throughout in almost all its departments, and this is directly due to the dominance in politics of Mr. Murphy and his sub-bosses . . . aided and abetted where necessary by Mr. Barnes and the sub-bosses of Mr. Barnes.*
>
> *Mr. Murphy and Mr. Barnes are of exactly the same political type.*

Roosevelt sat mutely listening, his elbow on the defense table, his head wedged against one fist. He seemed unaware of the stares of fifty reporters ranged near him. Each had a small silk American flag to raise whenever a dispatch was ready to be picked up by court attendants.

It occurred to Louis Siebold, Washington correspondent of the New York *World,* that the Colonel was more than just tired, or worried about his ill wife. He was depressed.

After lunch, Ivins called Roosevelt as his first witness.

IVINS	Have you read the statement complained of in the complaint?
TR	I wrote it. . . . (*laughter*)
IVINS	Did you write it of and concerning the plaintiff William Barnes, Jr.?
TR	I did.

"That is all," Ivins said, returning to his table. Roosevelt sat dumbfounded while the silk flags fluttered, releasing the news that the plaintiff had already rested its case.

Bowers, courtly and trim-bearded, came to the Colonel's rescue with some questions about the highlights of his career. Inevitably these led to the Battle of San Juan. Had Bowers consulted Elihu Root beforehand, as Ivins had, he might have learned that the quickest way to get his client to make a fool of himself was to mention Cuba.

TR	My regiment was in the Santiago fight and lost in killed and wounded, over a third—
IVINS	I object to the number lost in killed and wounded as immaterial in this case.
COURT	We all know what the result of that battle was.

Roosevelt recited his later résumé. Since coming back from Brazil, he said, he had worked as a writer, with some side activity in politics.

Bowers asked him to describe his early relations with Senator Thomas Platt, the "Easy Boss" of New York State and Barnes's political mentor. It was an adroit defense move, because it forestalled what was sure to be the prosecution's main line of questioning. Ivins jumped up. "Why all this 1899? Case is *in praesenti,* if your Honor please." Andrews overruled him.

Roosevelt said that he had worked with Platt throughout his two years as governor, and thus gotten to know Barnes as their mutual go-between. Bowers asked if he remembered any meetings in which Platt or Barnes had tried to stop him calling for a franchise tax on big businesses. Roosevelt said he did, but to the attorney's frustration, he could not recall how many, or what either man had specifically asked him to do. "Mr. Barnes spoke of our duty to protect corporations. . . . I cannot give you the language, the exact language."

The spectacle of Theodore Roosevelt straining both to hear and think clearly was a shock to many observers. He had always been famous for the perfection of his memory, but here he was unable to drum up facts in his own defense. When he did think of something, it was too late:

TR   Mr. Bowers and your Honor, may I be allowed to state the
            conversation that I had with Mr. Barnes on the propriety
            and nature of the boss and the domination of the machine?
COURT   That is not important. . . .
TR   (*incredulous*) May I not be permitted to show that there was
            this boss system, that there was a system of complete control
            by bosses of politics?
COURT   That is entirely immaterial so far as this libel is concerned.

Roosevelt was not used to being silenced. Clearly, Andrews was a different breed of judge from the one who had treated him so well in Marquette. Whether out of anger or annoyance, he sharpened up, and Bowers was able to elicit germane evidence by a different line of questioning. On one occasion, the defendant now recalled, Barnes had cynically said, "The people are not fit to govern themselves. They have got to be governed by the party organization, and you cannot run an organization, you cannot have leaders, unless you have money." Barnes and Platt had often lobbied him in this fashion, insisting that reform legislation, or failure to reappoint conservatives to office, would result in corporate campaign funds being withdrawn from the GOP. As for his allegations of bipartisan corruption, he remembered Barnes pleading the case of a Democratic legislator named Kelly, who protested against the franchise tax bill in behalf of two wealthy businessmen, Robert Pruyn and Anthony N. Brady.

This sounded more like the old Roosevelt, with precise citation of names and growing animation on the stand. The rest of the afternoon went well for him, although he played into Ivins's hands by describing Barnes as "a very able man," and saying that they had cooperated amicably for ten years.

❧

THROUGHOUT THE FOLLOWING DAY, Roosevelt made the most of Bowers's gentle interrogation. He became comfortable with court procedure, learning not to be upset by Ivins's objections, and conversationally drawing the judge as well as the jury into his accounts of private lobbying by Barnes in the New York State Capitol, Senator Platt's "Amen Corner" in Manhattan, and even Sagamore Hill and the White House. Some anecdotes sounded prosy, as if he had gotten them by heart. Ivins was seen staring at him quizzically whenever he became orotund. But there was no denying that the Colonel was back on form, and the silk flags shook often as he scored point after evidentiary point against Barnes.

The most telling was his introduction of a letter from the boss, begging him not to propose a state printing house in his 1900 gubernatorial message. For years, Barnes's own printing company had been the contractor of choice for the Albany legislature. *It is not my desire to intrude my personal matters upon you,* Barnes had written, *but I wish merely to state that the establishment of a state printing house here would be a serious, if not a fatal, blow to me financially.* Andrews permitted Bowers to read the governor's curt rebuff: *There is a perfect consensus of opinion that there should be a state printing office.*

In other testimony, Roosevelt exposed Barnes's animus against the progressive administration of Governor Hughes, admitting that he did not care for Hughes himself. He tellingly dropped the name of "my cousin, Franklin D. Roosevelt," who, as a Democratic state senator, had had to fight Barnes and Murphy in combination to get an electoral reform bill passed. Young Franklin was now in Washington, and, if the tense state of affairs there permitted, would come north to confirm this collusion.

Partnership between bosses was not illegal, but the Colonel made it sound like the pact between Wilhelm II and Franz Ferdinand. He quoted Barnes as saying before the Saratoga convention in 1910 that direct nominations, "if ever adopted by the state, will lead to untold evils in public life and place therein the cheapest citizens." Such prejudice was liable to impress members of the jury, none of whom looked as if he could afford Barnes's standard of living.

Bowers asked when he had last seen the plaintiff. Roosevelt said it had been at the annual Lincoln Day banquet in New York in 1911. Effectively and dramatically, he described how Barnes had boasted that conservatives were now in control of the state GOP, jeering that progressives and their ilk "were out."

The Colonel looked a happier man when the court adjourned at 5 P.M.

BY NOW THE TRIAL was being treated as a major story in New York newspapers, shouldering aside headlines bearing the words YPRES and DARDENELLES. Court artists rejoiced in the contrasting physical presences of Roosevelt and

Barnes (ignoring each other in court) and Ivins, with his skullcap and spats, looking like an illustration from a Dickens novel.

Thursday was the day the old lawyer had been waiting for, and he lit into Roosevelt with relish.

IVINS	Has your occupation in life, apart from your public service, been that of an author?
TR	An author and a ranchman and an explorer.
IVINS	Then you have had three professions?
TR	I have followed all three vocations, or avocations.
IVINS	And more or less simultaneously?
TR	More or less simultaneously. (*Laughter*)

"I have also been an officeholder," he tried to add, but Ivins had already managed to imply that, by spreading himself too thin, he could be seen as a dilettante.

Roosevelt smelled danger, and was uncharacteristically terse as Ivins pressed him to talk more about himself. A series of easy autobiographical questions soothed him. He began to answer at greater length. Ivins congratulated him on his memory. "It is pretty good," Roosevelt admitted.

Ivins switched to a much more detailed interrogation. He focused on one of the low points of Roosevelt's career: the tax-avoidance controversy that had nearly disqualified him from the gubernatorial nomination in 1898, until Elihu Root rescued him with an argument just short of fraud. Campaign finance was one of Ivins's specialties—he had published a little book on the subject—and it was emphatically not one of the defendant's. Roosevelt soon had cause to regret that he had been tricked into praising his own memory. After drawing a few more blanks, he fell back on vehement protestations that he stood for "righteousness" in politics.

IVINS	Now, does that rule apply to other people, in their judgment with regard to righteousness and the opportunities for its expression, as well as it does for you?
TR	Of course it does.
IVINS	Does that apply to Mr. Barnes just as much as it does to you?
TR	It does apply to Mr. Barnes just as much as it does to me.
IVINS	. . . Has not every man an equal right to determine his own rule of righteousness and his time of applying it?
TR	He has if he has the root of righteousness in him. If he is a wrongdoer, he has not.

IVINS   Who is the judge, you or he?

TR   It may be that I am the judge, of him. If I had to be the judge—

Justice Andrews sat expressionless between his two bowls of carnations. Roosevelt began to flounder, punching the air as he had in the courthouse in Marquette, Michigan.

TR   I will give you an exact example. Senator Burton—

IVINS   You need not gesticulate.

BOWERS   (*for the defense*) Why not?

IVINS   I do not object to his answering. I object to his manner.

BOWERS   Oh, is that it?

IVINS   I do not want to be eaten up right here now. (*Laughter*)

Pleased to have exposed the defendant as both complacent and excitable, Ivins went on to taunt him about his infallibility ("You did not at that time have an attack of righteousness?") and reprimand him for making speeches ("You need not treat me as a mass meeting, because I am not."). Roosevelt managed to control his temper through the rest of the day, arguing that he could not be blamed for using the services of political bosses when they saw their way clear to supporting his policies.

Ivins kept harping on his literary productivity. One exchange between them caused gasps around the courtroom:

IVINS   Since [1898] you have probably written more than any other man in the United States, haven't you?

TR   I don't know, but I have written from 100,000 to 150,000 letters.

When he returned to the witness chair on Friday, Ivins asked why, after more than ten years of working with Barnes, he had excluded the boss from his autobiography.

"I particularly wished not to make any wanton or malicious attack on him."

Ivins tried to disconcert him by revealing that many of the things he had said about the plaintiff in court were taken, word for word, from his general remarks on corruption in that Barnes-free book. "It is because of your excellent memory, is it not?"

Roosevelt let the sarcasm go. He had noticed that he had an avid audience in the jury. They leaned forward every time he spoke, as if activated by a jolt of electric current. He began to address them directly, and Ivins scolded him.

COURT	Mr. Ivins, this witness will be treated as any other ordinary witness. I cannot have any discussion of that kind in this court room.
IVINS	I apologize to your Honor.

Returning to Roosevelt's autobiography, Ivins quoted a line about Senator Platt, *Some of his strongest and most efficient lieutenants were disinterested men of high character,* and asked if Barnes was included. The Colonel hedged. "Mr. Ivins, that is not a question that I could answer by a yes or no. Do you wish me to answer how I feel about it?"

"If you cannot answer it, I do not care for your feelings. I want to know whether you can answer yes or no."

Andrews ruled that Roosevelt must respond accordingly. The stenographer repeated Ivins's question.

TR	Now—
IVINS	No, one moment—I ask for a categorical answer. Yes or no?
TR	Then I must answer you, no. . . . That I did not so include him.
IVINS	Then I will ask you this. If you did not so regard him as a man of high character, why did you invite him to the executive mansion? Why did you consult him in the Capitol? Why did you associate with him? Why did you advise with him?
TR	Because I thought he was above the average of the ordinary political leaders. . . . I believed that he had it in him . . . to become a most useful servant of the state, and I believed that there was a good chance of him so becoming.
BOWERS	(*hinting*) Have you finished, Mr. Roosevelt?
TR	I have.

For the first time, the defendant was beginning to sound like a small boy trying to fib his way out of a situation. By using the phrase *some of* to qualify his praise of Platt's aides in 1899–1900—a group effectively consisting only of Barnes—Roosevelt the autobiographer had adopted a technique he affected to despise in other writers: the employment of "weasel words" that sucked the specificity out of statements. *Some of* enabled him to plead that he had not, in fact, ever thought of Barnes as a "disinterested man of high character." He now cast about desperately for another literary device to save himself, and thought of Robert Louis Stevenson's novel about a man both good and evil. That was it: Barnes was "Doctor Jekyll and Mr. Hyde." He said he had known only the former during his time as governor.

Ivins noted that he had, nevertheless, retained Barnes in a position of high Republican responsibility long after becoming President in 1901. Roosevelt said he had done so as a consequence of his vow to honor President McKinley's legacy. Ivins asked if that had still been the case on 29 January 1907, when he wrote to Barnes on White House stationery: *It was a pleasure to send your reappointment* [as surveyor of the port of Albany] *to the Senate today. Sincerely, Theodore Roosevelt.*

TR   Yes, sir.

IVINS   Then which Mr. Barnes—Mr. Jekyll Barnes or Mr. Hyde Barnes, did you appoint to office and express your pleasure in appointing?

TR   I appointed Mr. Barnes to office and until 1910 I hoped that we were going to get his Dr. Jekyll side uppermost, and I did not abandon hope until 1911.

Ivins let this protestation speak for itself. But he submitted for the jury's further consideration a long series of cordial notes from Roosevelt to Barnes, indicating that Mr. Hyde had not begun to prowl the streets of Albany in his full monstrosity until the Progressive/Republican split of 1912.

THE DEFENDANT REMAINED in the witness stand for four more court days. He suffered further lapses of memory, principally on questions of campaign financing. Ivins tried to represent them as selective amnesia, but they looked to impartial observers like the forgetfulness of a man with larger things on his mind. The trial so far amounted to an entertaining exposé of unremarkable political facts. Both parties to Barnes's lawsuit were—always had been—pragmatic politicians, the one looking for votes and reliable appointees, the other able to supply them, but at a price. As a young governor, Roosevelt had understood that reform legislation was impossible unless he could rely on a Party majority that was boss-controlled and lubricated with corporate contributions. As a power broker, Barnes knew that cooperation with the minority machine was sometimes necessary; the will of the people might even demand it.

Ivins's evidence showed only that early on, Roosevelt had been naïvely eager to believe that Platt's machine men were altruistic. He was certainly so himself (even the most wheedling letters Ivins obtained from the archives showed him to have been active in the public interest). But he had often kept his long-distance glasses on, rather than focus too closely on what the Easy Boss was doing.

Under hard interrogation by William L. Barnum, one of Ivins's associates,

Roosevelt admitted that he had once appointed a Democrat to office because Platt needed to do Tammany Hall a favor. Barnum said that in exchange, the man's sponsor, a state senator, had asked them both to cooperate on a $12 million appropriation for one of his real estate interests. Had such a bill been passed? The Colonel could not remember.

"A little matter of twelve million wouldn't make any impression on you?"

"After sixteen years," Roosevelt snapped, "during which I have had to do with billions of expenditures, the item does not remain in my mind."

It irked him that day after day of cross-examination was being devoted to *his* operations in Albany, long ago, rather than to Barnes's later behavior as the successor of Boss Platt. Justice Andrews seemed to be in no hurry to summon witnesses like Cousin Franklin, who could testify to the venality of

"'WHAT RELATION ARE YOU TO THE DEFENDANT?'"

Assistant Secretary of the Navy Franklin D. Roosevelt.

the plaintiff in recent years. The trial threatened to drag on indefinitely. Barnes quit attending on 26 April, saying that he would return only when called for.

Roosevelt finally stepped down as a witness at noon on the twenty-ninth, with his reputation for total recall much damaged. Nevertheless, Bowers succeeded in introducing some damning evidence against Barnes, including ledger-book proof that the boss had enriched himself on state printing contracts. Whether that made him corrupt or not, the jury would have to decide.

Assistant Secretary of the Navy Franklin Roosevelt's appearance in court on Tuesday, 4 May, created a stir.

"What relation are you to the defendant?" Bowers wanted to know.

"Fifth cousin by blood and nephew by law," Franklin replied, grinning. The line was obviously well rehearsed.

He confirmed that Barnes and Boss Murphy had been partners in legislative shenanigans to which he had been privy. But the lift he gave to the Colonel's case was mainly psychological. As a senior official of the Wilson administration, he was manifestly an important man. His department was on high alert over attacks on transatlantic shipping by German submarines. No fewer than twenty-three merchantmen had been torpedoed since the beginning of May—among them an American oil freighter, the *Gulflight,* with three lives lost—and persistent rumors were circulating that a major liner was being targeted for destruction soon.

Franklin did not comment on the *Gulflight* incident to reporters, but his cousin was under no such compunction. It had been "an act of piracy, pure and simple," the Colonel declared out of court.

DURING THE NEXT TWO days Roosevelt returned to the stand again and again, clarifying and amplifying his testimony for Bowers. When not being questioned, he looked bored. He flinched as Ivins, given the chance to cross-examine, said with mock exhaustion, "I don't know that I care to have anything more to do with Mr. Roosevelt."

The old lawyer was trying for a laugh, but what sounded like a collective groan ran through the courtroom. His witness was, after all, a former head of state.

That night, Thursday, 6 May, an ominous letter reached Roosevelt in the house of his local host, Horace S. Wilkinson. It came from Cal O'Laughlin, who was always ahead of the news, and transmitted the written warning of a "high German official" that the administration's shipping policy was putting

American national unity "to a dangerous test." Citizens of German or Irish ancestry had the right to protest, even sabotage, a neutrality so obviously favoring Great Britain. Their target might be the Cunard flagship *Lusitania,* currently en route from New York to Liverpool.

She had sailed on the first day of the month, amid a strange flurry of other threats—some wired pseudonymously to passengers as they checked in to their cabins—that she might be struck by a U-boat. An advisory signed and paid for by the German Embassy in Washington had appeared alongside her final sailing notice in several newspapers, reminding travelers "intending to embark on the Atlantic voyage" that a state of war existed between the Reich and Great Britain. Any vessel flying the Union Jack in "waters adjacent to the British Isles," was therefore "liable to destruction."

Roosevelt was infuriated by the arrogant tone of the document O'Laughlin enclosed. "It makes my blood boil to see how we are regarded," he wrote back. "Lord, how I would like to be President in view of what he says about the huge German-Irish element and the possible sinking of the *Lusitania.*" Personally, he would hang any such scaremonger, "and I would warn him that if any of our people were sunk on the *Lusitania,* I would confiscate all the German interned ships, beginning with the *Prinz Eitel.*"

Perhaps it was just as well that Roosevelt was out of office in his current mood. He confessed to O'Laughlin that "if I didn't keep a grip on myself," a provocation of this kind "would make me favor instant war with Germany."

He was back in court the following day, Friday, to hear Bowers begin to wind up the case for the defense. For hours, legal arguments droned back and forth between floor and bench, and Roosevelt looked, if possible, even more bored than he had the day before. Ivins took pity on him and walked over with a little green-covered edition of the plays of Aristophanes. "I came across this yesterday, Colonel, and it struck me that it was a first-class translation, and that if you cared to amuse yourself with anything of this sort while this uninteresting testimony is going on, you might enjoy it."

Roosevelt was profoundly touched. "Thank you, thank you. I certainly am de-light-ed, Mr. Ivins."

He remained buried in the book until late in the afternoon, when a messenger brought him a telegram. Reading it, his face changed. At five o'clock the court adjourned, with Andrews warning Bowers that unless more conclusive evidence was offered regarding Barnes's state printing contracts, he would strike out all testimony heard so far on the subject. This was gloomy news for Roosevelt to ponder over the weekend, but it did not compare with the front-page story in the Syracuse evening newspaper, just then going on sale:

THE SYRACUSE HERALD. EXTRA

PRICE TWO CENTS VOL. 29, NO. 11,984. SYRACUSE, N.Y., FRIDAY EVENING, MAY 7, 1915.

THE LUSITANIA SINKS

GREAT WASTE IN PRINTING, SAYS WITNESS IN LIBEL TRIAL

Home, Testifying for Roosevelt, Charges Extravagance.

PROTEST BY IVINS

Barnes Counsel Tries to Bar Testimony—May Be Stricken Out, But It Will Leave Bad Effect on Jury

The Lusitania, British Liner Torpedoed To-day by German Submarine.

First Class Passengers Aboard

Big Cunard Liner Goes Down After Submarine Attack.

HAS 1,400 PASSENGERS

Fate of Those Aboard Liner Unknown, But It Is Believed Most of Them Were Saved by the Ship's Boats.

London, May 7.—The Cunard line steamer Lusitania from New York May 1st for Liverpool, with 1,253 passengers on board, was torpedoed about 2 o'clock this morning at a point about ten miles off Old Head, Kinsale, Ireland, and later went down. It is believed that her passengers are safe. No details of how they may have been rescued, however, are at hand. The message received here says: "It is not known how many of the Lusitania's passengers were saved."

Fate of Passengers Unknown

"'LORD, HOW I WOULD LIKE TO BE PRESIDENT.'"

The evening newspaper that greeted TR as he emerged from the courthouse, 7 May 1915.

On an inside page, it was reported that President Wilson had no comment. This was not surprising, since the story was so fresh, terrible, and incomplete. If the fate of those aboard was "unknown," how could it be that most were "believed" to be safe?

It was clear, all the same, that a German torpedo had sunk the biggest ship in the Cunard fleet, with a mostly American manifest, just offshore of County Cork in Ireland. Many of the first-class passengers listed were known to Roosevelt, including Alfred G. Vanderbilt and Miss Theodate Pope, a young architect and member of the Progressive Party. He went to his lodgings and paced up and down in front of Horace Wilkinson, debating what to say about the catastrophe. On Monday, the twelve Syracusans who would pass judgment on him were due to start hearing from William Barnes, Jr. Two or three had German-sounding names. What verdict were they likely to render, if he criticized Germany's action against an enemy vessel?

"I've got be right in this matter," he said, and went to bed early.

The inevitable telephone call from an Associated Press reporter came around midnight. Wilkinson took it and went to wake Roosevelt.

"All right, I'll speak to him."

The reporter gave him the full story that would appear in tomorrow's papers. There had been 1,918 souls aboard the *Lusitania,* and only 520 had so far been rescued. The ship had sunk in fifteen minutes, going down so fast that at least a thousand passengers were presumed dead, many of them mothers with children.

"That's murder," Wilkinson heard the Colonel saying. "Will I make a statement? Yes, yes. I'll make it now. Just take this."

It appeared as dictated on Saturday, 8 May, in newspapers across the country.

I can only repeat what I said a week ago [sic], when in similar fashion the American vessel the *Gulflight* was destroyed off the English coast and its captain drowned. . . .

This represents not merely piracy, but piracy on a vaster scale of murder than any old-time pirate ever practiced. This is the warfare which destroyed Louvain and Dinant, and hundreds of men, women and children in Belgium. It is warfare against innocent[s] traveling on the ocean, and to our fellow countrywomen, who are among the sufferers.

It seems inconceivable that we can refrain from taking action in this matter, for we owe it not only to humanity but to our own national self-respect.

⟝⟞

WOODROW WILSON'S FIRST reaction to the sinking of the *Lusitania* had been to flee the White House. Evading his secret service detail, he walked the drizzly streets of Washington unrecognized, while newsboys shrieked the story he already knew. When he came back he retired to his study and refused to see any advisers through the weekend. The White House issued a statement saying that the President was pondering "very earnestly, but very calmly, the right course of action to pursue."

Colonel House, who was in London, tried to point him in the direction of an ultimatum. "America has come to the parting of the ways," he cabled, "when she must determine whether she stands for civilized or uncivilized warfare. We can no longer remain neutral."

It seemed to Wilson that all warfare was uncivilized. After going to church on Sunday he spent most of the afternoon being chauffeured around the countryside. It was dark before he got home. Sitting down at his typewriter, he began to tap out a formal note to the German foreign minister, pursuant to the one he had issued in February holding the Reich responsible for any act of violence against American citizens. He called no special session of his cabinet for the following morning. Late in the afternoon he traveled to Philadelphia to speak at a gathering of recently naturalized immigrants. By the time he stepped onstage in Convention Hall, three and a half days had elapsed since the tragedy in the Celtic Sea, and expectation around the world was intense as to what he would say. William Howard Taft had no doubt that if the President called for revenge, Congress would oblige him with a declaration of war.

To general amazement, Wilson did not mention the *Lusitania,* or Germany, or the war. He talked about "ideals" and "visions" and "dreams," and "touching hearts with all the nations of mankind." But one declaration, expressing his personal attitude toward conflict, rang out with particular impact: "The example of America must be the example not merely of peace because it will not fight, but of peace because peace is the healing and elevating influence of the world and strife is not. There is such a thing as a man being too proud to fight."

☙

ONE CONSEQUENCE OF the sinking of the *Lusitania* was that *Barnes v. Roosevelt* was swept off the front pages of newspapers everywhere, even in New York. Suddenly the squabbles of libel lawyers in a salt town upstate sounded petty and irrelevant, in contrast to cable stories of five-ton lifeboats skidding down the decks of the tilted liner, crushing passengers by the dozen, and dead blue babies being fished from the sea like mackerel.

Roosevelt was not sorry for the distraction. He felt that his case was going badly, and disliked having millions of people read Justice Andrews's rulings against him. He was, besides, angered to the point of frenzy by Wilson's Philadelphia speech. According to *The New York Times,* some four thousand people, many of them German-born, had roared support when the President talked about being "too proud to fight." Stocks had surged next day, and editorials nationwide rejoiced that the administration was keeping a cool head in the crisis. William Randolph Hearst blustered that Germany had every right to sink a ship flying an enemy flag. Taft expressed relief and support of Wilson, in a rebuff to Roosevelt that was lavishly praised by *The New York Times.*

The Colonel raged against them all in a letter to his most militant son:

Dear Archie:
      There is a chance of our going to war; but I don't think it is much of a chance. Wilson and Bryan are cordially supported by all the hyphenated Americans, by the solid flubdub and pacifist vote. Every soft creature, every coward and weakling, every man who can't look more than six inches ahead, every man whose god is money, or pleasure, or ease . . . is enthusiastically in favor of Wilson; and at present the good

citizens, as a whole, are puzzled and don't understand the situation, and so a majority of them also tend to be with him. This is not pardonable; but it is natural. As a nation, we have thought very little about foreign affairs; we don't realize that the murder of the thousand men, women and children in the *Lusitania* is due, solely, to Wilson's cowardice and weakness in failing to take energetic action when the *Gulflight* was sunk but a few days previously. He and Bryan are morally responsible for the loss of the lives of those American women and children—and for the lives lost in Mexico, no less than for the lives lost on the high seas. They are both of them abject creatures, and they won't go to war unless they are kicked into it.

He was overwrought, but this kind of language appealed to Archie. The youth was already asking permission to quit Harvard and serve in an American expeditionary force to Europe, should Wilson decide to send one. Roosevelt did not see that happening soon. He was sure, nonetheless, that America would eventually enter the war.

Like most Northeasterners, he sympathized with the Allied cause, and admired Britain's decision to stand by Belgium and France. Nevertheless, there was much that disturbed him about the blockade policy of the Royal Navy, which Winston Churchill, first lord of the Admiralty, frankly described as a tactic to "starve the whole [German] population—men, women and children, old and young, wounded and sound—into submission."

Dr. Bernhard Dernburg, the Kaiser's personal spokesman in the United States, complained in a public statement that Britain had made the North Sea a war zone long before Germany, "in retaliation," applied a similar designation to the other waters around England and Ireland. American travelers had been repeatedly warned that any vessel suspected of transporting contraband in that theater would be destroyed, whether large or small or belligerent or neutral. The master of the *Gulflight* had been delivering oil to France. As for the *Lusitania*, New York's own collector of customs had certified that she carried "for Liverpool, 260,000 pounds of brass; 60,000 pounds of copper; 180 cases of military goods; 1,271 cases of ammunition, and for London, 4,200 cases of cartridges." Cunard might claim that these items were technically non-contraband, yet Dernburg was correct in saying that the *Lusitania* was registered as "a British auxiliary cruiser." She had gun mounts to prove it. Germany's official notice published on her day of departure could not have more clearly hinted that she was doomed.

Roosevelt knew Dernburg, and five months before had agreed with him that a great nation "fighting for its life" must do what was essential to defend itself and feed itself. But he scoffed at Dernburg's insistence that the rape of Belgium had been "an absolute necessity." Nor did he see that any civilized power had the right to sink ships, whatever their cargo, by means of submarines unable to rescue innocent passengers.

Now that the inevitable calamity had occurred, Roosevelt felt that he had no alternative but to support English democracy against Prussian autocracy. It was not a palatable choice, given Britain's own arrogance at sea. But at last report, Allied forces had not yet drowned any babies or torched any universities.

He decided that he and his sons would show publicly that they had a different idea of pride than Woodrow Wilson. A monthlong "preparedness" camp to train civilians for military duty was scheduled to take place in Plattsburg, New York, in August. Leaving Ted to sign up for himself, Roosevelt put down the names of Archie and Quentin. He promised that he would visit the camp personally and advertise it to the world in his journalism.

Meanwhile, *Barnes v. Roosevelt* dragged on into its fourth week.

⤙◎⤚

THE PRESIDENT REGRETTED his gaffe in Philadelphia, and tried to get it deleted from the official transcript of his speech. He claimed that he been expressing "a personal attitude." But to some ears, *There is such a thing as a man being too proud to fight* had the same smug sound as his confession over the bodies of the marines who died at Vera Cruz: *There are some things just as hard to do as to go under fire.*

On 13 May, his note responding to the *Lusitania* disaster was cabled to James W. Gerard, the American ambassador in Berlin. Gerard had been expecting to be recalled, preparatory to a complete severance of diplomatic relations. Instead, he found himself charged with the delivery of a polite document appealing to the peaceable emotions of the Kaiser's war cabinet.

Wilson stated that the situation was "grave." He reported that several recent German attacks upon his countrymen at sea, traveling freely as was their privilege, had caused "concern, distress, and amazement" in the United States. Over a hundred Americans had died aboard the *Lusitania;* his administration was "loath to believe" that the U-boat commander responsible could have been obeying orders. The man must have been "under a misapprehension" of "the high principles of equity" for which Prussian war planners were famed. Making no mention of Belgium, the President praised Germany's long-standing "humane and enlightened attitude . . . in matters of international right." Surely Germans must agree that underwater attacks upon any merchantman, neutral or belligerent, were going "much beyond the ordinary methods of warfare at sea."

He granted that the action of certain adversaries who sought "to cut Germany off from all commerce" had forced the Reich to resort to extraordinary countermeasures. But the United States was not responsible for either policy. It declined to surrender its travel and trading rights as a neutral nation. Wilson felt obliged to repeat that he held Germany "to a strict accountability for any infringement of those rights, intentional or incidental." He was confident that the Imperial Government would "disavow" the attacks he complained of, make appropriate reparations, and promise that no such outrages would happen again.

The note won general approval, especially in Britain, when its text was released. Wilson's elaborate courtesies fell within the norms of diplomatic style, and did not hide his determination to get satisfaction from the Wilhelmstrasse. At best, that would be an apology and a promise not to attack any more passenger vessels. More likely, there would be an apology and a countermove, designed to draw him into protracted negotiations.

Only the most cynical readers of the President's text (and Americans were not good at cynicism) might wonder if he hoped to be so drawn. In little over a year, he was almost certain to win renomination for another term in the White House. But he could not dream of being reelected, unless he acted now as a man of peace: the mood of the country was overwhelmingly antiwar. It was remotely possible that Wilson might agree with Roosevelt that the nation would, sooner or later, have to fight for the survival of democracy. If so, his pose of unctuous expectation of a humane response from Germany now was just a tactic to gain him five more years of power—and his note a masterpiece of deceptive rhetoric, designed to ensure that when all the belligerents had spent their wrath, they would turn to him as their savior.

ROOSEVELT FACED HIS FIFTH frustrating week in Syracuse, chafing under the mockery of William Ivins and jotting furious rebuttals with a green and gold fountain pen. Barnes, summoned from Albany, made a dignified witness, testifying coolly and precisely. It was noticed, however, that the jurors did not stare at him with the undisguised fascination they accorded the defendant. He was honest in his self-portrayal as a professional politician who understood that lawmakers needed the counsel and financial backing of corporate interests. Posturing ideologues and ill-informed common voters (Barnes denied ever calling them "riff-raff") only impeded the legislative process.

On Thursday, 20 May, Ivins summed up his case by accusing Roosevelt of a lifetime habit of turning on former associates. He quoted Shakespeare's famous directive *I charge thee, fling away ambition; by that sin fell the angels.* The last words members of the jury heard were those of Justice Andrews, who instructed them to forget that the defendant had ever been President of the United States, and concentrate only on whether one man's libelous charges against another were true. If not, malice could be established by circumstantial evidence, and punitive damages imposed.

At 3:45 P.M. the jurors withdrew. Three hours later they sent out for dinner, and at 11:30 P.M., reported that they were unable to agree. Andrews escorted them across the street to the city jail and locked them up for the night. They remained at loggerheads all day Friday and through to 10:15 on Saturday morning, by which time Roosevelt was red-faced with tension. The court clerk asked if they had reached a verdict, and the foreman said yes.

"How do you find?"

"For the defendant."

Roosevelt had never been one to display deep emotion in public, and he kept himself in check now, merely grinning as spectators roared applause. But he fought tears afterward as he took the jury aside and thanked each member personally. "I will try all my life," he said, his voice shaking, "to act in private and public affairs so that no one of you will have cause to regret the verdict you have given this morning."

William Ivins returned to New York an exhausted man, with few weeks left to live. Legal analysts concluded that his performance had been impeccable and his cross-examinations brilliant, but that he had been defeated by a defendant beyond the reach of ordinary justice. Behind him in Syracuse he left, securely tacked to the courthouse wall, the hide of William Barnes, Jr.

CHAPTER 22

Waging Peace

What was a man before him, or ten of them,
While he was here alive who could answer them,
And in their teeth fling confirmations,
Harder than agates against an egg-shell?

THE PRESIDENT'S OFFICIAL DEMEANOR, as he waited for Germany's reply to his note, was no different than it had been since the death of Ellen Wilson nine months before: calm, controlled, apparently affable but reserved beyond reach. He smiled brilliantly, if rather too often. When the grin disappeared, he was not always able to prevent his long jaw from clamping his lips shut, as if to discourage the person smiled upon from asking a favor. Or worse still, from presuming to advise him. Wilson had such a horror of being instructed he would walk away from anyone who waxed too confidential. The thinness of his skin was as real as it was metaphorical: he could not even touch boiled eggs, which had to be cracked open for him.

He felt, not without reason, that he was stronger and smarter than anyone else in the administration. His acuity showed in the speed with which he grasped and cut short any argument, often rejecting a conclusion before it had been fully stated. Lobbyists and petitioners retired feeling that they had not been heard. To that extent Wilson was, or seemed, cold. A Calvinist restraint hindered his attempts to charm the public. He longed to be called "Woody" by the sort of people who called Roosevelt "Teddy," and reacted with joy when they did. But that rarely happened, to the puzzlement of his three daughters and small circle of adoring friends. They remembered him before his bereavement as a delightfully warm man, a lover of dinner-table repartee, limericks, and the patter songs of Gilbert and Sullivan, which he would sing in a pleasant tenor voice. The younger Wilson had always had a healthy libido and made no effort to conceal it. While remaining faithful to his wife (as far as anyone knew: there had been rumors), he confessed that he never went to New York alone without feeling certain temptations.

Now, secretly, as Washington burst into full spring flower, he felt them again, without having to stray farther than four blocks from home. It transpired that the President had not been altogether alone the weekend after the *Lusitania* went down. The weather had been beautiful, and so, in his opinion, was Mrs. Edith Bolling Galt, the big dark Southern widow who went driving with him. He blamed her for his rhetorical gaffe the following Monday: "I do not know just what I said in Philadelphia . . . my heart was in such a whirl."

Wilson had in fact already proposed marriage. Mrs. Galt had said no, but in a way that implied she would not mind if he raised the subject again.

ON 30 MAY, Count Johann von Bernstorff, the German ambassador in Washington, handed over a qualified apology for the destruction of the *Lusitania*. His minister, Count von Jagow, argued that the liner "undoubtedly had guns on board" when she sailed, "mounted under decks and masked." Germany therefore had the right to sink her "in just self-defense." The real responsibility for the disaster must lie with the Cunard company, for not informing American passengers that they were being used "as protection for the ammunition carried." Jagow would have more to say on the subject, but in the meantime, the government of the United States might like to reflect on these complaints, and consider whether it should not visit its wrath on Great Britain instead.

The note said nothing about reparations, and its testy, provisional tone suggested dissension within the Wilhelmstrasse. Wilson began to draft a reply that conveyed his willingness to hear more, but (over Bryan's protests), reiterated in stronger language the outrage he had expressed already.

FOR ROOSEVELT, TOO, the new season brought release from what he admitted had been "the very nadir" of his life. He set such store by his victories in *Roosevelt v. Newett* and *Barnes v. Roosevelt* that when he updated his biography in *Who's Who*, the two trials totaled almost a fourth of the available space, dwarfing such achievements as the Panama Canal, the Treaty of Portsmouth, and the Conservation Conference of 1908. "I have never seen Theodore in finer form," Edith Roosevelt wrote her sister Emily. "He bubbles over with good spirits, and I do my best to pant and puff after him."

Once more his hasty step and high-pitched laughter were heard down the corridors of *Metropolitan* magazine. He cheerfully tolerated the left-wing views of his younger colleagues, including Israel Zangwill, Sonya Levien,

George Bellows, and John Reed, who professed admiration for the Mexican revolutionary Pancho Villa.

"Villa," Roosevelt said, "is a murderer and a rapist."

Reed tried to provoke him. "What's wrong with that? I believe in rape."

But Roosevelt only grinned. "I'm glad to find a young man who believes in something."

Not even an invoice from Bowers & Sands for $31,159.64 affected his good humor. Court costs and the expenses of scores of witnesses were sure to raise this total above $40,000. Coincidentally, Congress owed him a nearly identical sum: it had never gotten around to spending the Nobel Prize money he rolled over in 1906, to establish "a foundation for industrial peace." That cause seemed almost quaint now, in view of the war.

Friends offered to help him with his legal bill, but he declined. George Meyer visited him at Sagamore Hill and asked how the trial had gone.

"Why, I won it."

"Oh, I know that, but I can't remember how much damages you got."

"Would you mind saying that again, George?"

Meyer did, and Roosevelt, twinkling, placed a fatherly hand on his head. "My dear fel-low, *I* was the de-*fend*-ant."

⸺

IN THE SECOND WEEK of June, he treated himself to a short vacation in an environment so airy and unpopulated as to purge all memory of the stuffy courtroom in Syracuse. His trip to the barrier islands of Louisiana was a pilgrimage of a sort, because in 1904 he had designated part of the sandy, crescent-shaped archipelago just east of New Orleans as Breton National Wildlife Refuge. He sailed there aboard a yacht belonging to the state Conservation Commission, accompanied by three local friends and a photographer. Two members of the Louisiana Audubon Society trailed behind in an underpowered motorboat.

Roosevelt might have been unaccompanied for all the attention he paid to anyone else, as skein after skein of birds rose to protest his invasion of the sanctuary he had given them. Each island gave off its alarmed guard, flashing and fluttering, croaking and bleating, until the sky seemed alive with graceful long-winged things. No doubt they reacted in the same way to visitors less disposed to exult in their clamor: the eggers and poachers and plume-hunters looking for feathers, or even whole birds, to ornament the hats of fashionable ladies (such as Mrs. Edith Bolling Galt of Washington, D.C.).

The waters of the Gulf were calm, but they too were full of movement. Silver shrimp undulated back and forth. Schools of mullets and sardines drifted darkly, like cloud shadows. Always, it occurred to him, the animal world was in flight from death, or was pursuing other life with deathly intent. "Nature is ruthless, and where her sway is uncontested there is no peace save the peace of death; and the fecund stream of life, especially of life on the lower levels, flows like an immense torrent out of non-existence for but the briefest moment before the enormous majority of beings composing it are engulfed in the jaws of death, and again go out into the shadow."

Having only one good eye did not prevent him observing, with the accuracy of the field naturalist he had once hoped to be, a big humming hornet pursue a greenhead horsefly and light on it from behind. Poor little Belgium! The greenhead managed to turn before it was stung, and sink its lancet into the marauder's body. Fly and hornet grappled frantically for a few minutes, and then the sting found its target. The fly fell dead. But it had given a good account of itself before yielding to superior power. Roosevelt watched the hornet rubbing its sore spot with a spare pair of legs, and stagger off hunchbacked, evidently "a very sick creature."

He saw the same aerial warfare operate on a thousandfold larger scale, as three man-of-war birds pursued a royal tern with a fish in its claws. The tern was a strong flier, and ascended almost out of view, but its pursuers were even stronger, their enormous wings beating and finally engulfing it. Out of the mêlée, the fish fell. But before it could hit the water, one of the giant birds snatched it up.

A swim was proposed one day, as the yacht drifted between two islands under the burning midday sun. Captain Sprinkle of the motorboat effectively cautioned that there was a large shark in the water. The critters tended to operate like U-boats, off landfalls.

Early the following evening, 10 June, a commission mail boat hove to alongside Roosevelt's yacht, moored off Battledore Island, and the pilot shouted hot news from the Associated Press office in New Orleans: William Jennings Bryan had resigned as secretary of state. The President, apparently, had rejected his urgent pleas for a peaceable compromise with Germany over its submarine policy.

Roosevelt went into an instant frenzy. "This means war." He demanded to be returned to the mainland, so that he could take the next train north and sign up for military service. But night had come on, and his companions had islands they still wanted him to see. The pilot came aboard and offered to relay any comment he cared to make back to the AP. Under the dim light of a lamp swinging in the cabin, Roosevelt scribbled a statement on coarse yellow paper: *Of course I heartily applaud the decision of the President, and in common with all other Americans who are loyal to the traditions handed down by the men who served under Washington, and by the others who followed Grant and Lee in the days of Lincoln, I pledge him my heartiest support in all the steps he takes to uphold the honor and the interests of this great Republic which are bound up with the maintenance of democratic liberty and of a wise spirit of humanity among all the nations of mankind. Theodore Roosevelt.*

He could have given second thought to a change in political attitude that was sure to be received with incredulity in Washington. But he allowed the pilot to go off with it next morning. Within twenty-four hours, his praise of Woodrow Wilson was a front-page story as far away as Fairbanks, Alaska.

⬠

WILLIAM JENNINGS BRYAN was replaced by Robert Lansing, a rigidly correct bureaucrat who could not have been more of a contrast to the departing Commoner. Bryan had been agonizing since early February over the President's haughty policy toward Germany. He knew, as few people did, that Lansing—formerly counselor at the State Department—was the original author of the phrase *strict accountability*, in a note draft that Wilson had approved. Those two words, Bryan felt, were seeds of war for the United States. They would eventually crack and grow. How, he asked, could Germany not feel discriminated against, in the face of the administration's callow capitulation to the British naval blockade? What did a neutral power expect, if its citizens insisted on traveling aboard vessels as vulnerable as the *Lusitania*? As he put it, in a bitter reproach to the President, "Why be shocked at the drowning of a few people if there is to be no objection to starving a nation?"

Wilson was not used to that kind of bluntness, and Bryan had probably sealed his fate there and then. He was not a partisan of Germany. For all his much-mocked "grape juice diplomacy," he had been the only high official in Washington who sincerely believed that Americans should be (in Wilson's glib formula) "impartial in thought as well as in action . . . neutral in fact as well as in name." The truth was that the administration's anglophilia stopped just short of alliance. When Wilson pictured Europe, he saw Oxford's dreaming spires. He could no more have sat on a charger at Döberitz, discussing field tactics with the Kaiser, than he could have held his own in the Hungarian parliament. "England is fighting our fight," he told Joseph Tumulty. Lansing was strongly pro-Ally. Ambassador Walter Hines Page sucked up to Sir Edward Grey with the obsequiousness of an Andrew Carnegie. Colonel House took Texan satisfaction in being invited to stay on English country estates, and regularly advised Wilson that Germany was a menace to Anglo-American relations.

A hail of vituperation beat on Bryan's bald head as he tried to justify his resignation as something other than a betrayal of the President in a time of crisis. "Mr. Bryan has done the one thing in his power most likely to bring about war between the United States and Germany," the New York *World* declared, in one of its rare agreements with Theodore Roosevelt. *The Washington Post* was thankful that the Peerless One would no longer be "making mischief" as secretary of state, and the *Lowell* (Mass.) *Sun* looked back in disgust at his long career of "peace piffle." Only a minority of commentators—and they wrote mainly for America's German-language newspapers—gave Bryan credit for dissociating himself from a foreign policy he passionately believed to be inhumane.

Remarkably, Wilson displayed no animus against the old idealist, and wrote him a farewell letter full of respect. The White House let it be known that when the two men took their leave of each other, they had both said, "God bless you."

Next morning, Bryan stated that for the first time in months he had been able to sleep through the night.

"GOOD MORNING, LITTLE Miss Anarchist, I understand you are cutting my copy."

Somehow, Roosevelt had found out that Sonya Levien, his junior colleague at *Metropolitan* magazine, was of radical Russian background. It bothered him no more than the short work she made of some of his essays. The Colonel remained, as ever, a delight for editors to work with. No matter how sick he might be (since Brazil, his fever attacks had multiplied), or how distracted by other responsibilities, his copy was always ready when due, revised down to the last semicolon. The same went for galleys, which he checked the moment he received them. If passages he had labored over fell victim to Miss Levien's scissors, his good humor never failed. "I always regard with stoical calm the mutilation of my bantlings."

Although he now regretted his AP statement in support of the President, and was once again violently abusing the administration, Miss Levien was struck by the contrasting mildness of his personality. "There was an air of suppressed amiability about him which made one realize what fun his children must have had with him." He was unable to resist any boy or girl of romping age: their company made him revert to childhood himself. One morning when the anteroom to the Colonel's office was crowded, as usual, with politicians, newspapermen, foreigners, and favor-seekers, Miss Levien was alarmed to hear roars and shrieks emanating from his sanctum. She went to investigate and found Roosevelt "on his knees playing bear with the adorable, red-headed freckle-nosed son of Mr. Dunne."

For all the Colonel's charm, she found him unsentimental about her personal experience of growing up among the working poor. When she said that the sordid privations and deadly monotony of those days had made her a socialist, he scoffed that "radicals laid too much stress upon the drudgery of the day laborer's work." So much for his own claim to be a radical, a few years back. Much of the work of artists, directors, and writers, he told Miss Levien, was drudgery of the most monotonous kind. But he saw nothing sordid in it, only enjoyment and satisfaction if the end product—a painting, a play, a T-girder—benefited civilization. Of course, "There are people who enjoy nothing, who have not the capacity for fun and contentment—no matter in what status of life they happen to be."

She saw that Roosevelt could not understand the difference between the kind of boredom he complained of on the campaign trail, and the spiritual despair of miners and factory workers who saw nothing ahead of them but brute labor and an unpaid old age. His response to her attempts to enlighten him on that score was invariable: that the life of the working poor could be improved by social legislation, but that ultimately every man's success or failure depended upon "character."

What he meant by *character* was as vague as his concept of *righteousness*. But there was no doubt in Miss Levien's heart that Roosevelt—child of privilege as he was—embodied both words. He was radiant, original, irresistible. "I wonder how a man so thick-set, of rather abdominal contour, with eyes heavily spectacled, could have had such an air of magic and wild romance about him, could give one so stirring an impression of adventure and chivalry." Like so many others who tried to describe him, she turned to images of electricity: his smile was "an arc-light" coming down the corridor toward her, and the "magnetic sparkle" that animated his face was duplicated by "the sparkle of his mind." No matter who came to see him (on one occasion, an African dignitary festooned with rings and beads), she observed that they reacted the same way when the Colonel, genially shaking hands, propelled them toward the elevator. "Their faces had that trance-like expression, as if living over again within themselves some dramatic moment just passed; some, smiling at nothing in particular; others, excited and muttering to themselves, all showing some sign of having passed through a tidal moment in their lives."

Whatever Roosevelt had lost of actual power to shape events, he was obviously still capable of inspiring all those who did not feel threatened by him. Aside from ever-wistful Progressives, and a few furtive Republicans wondering whether he would consider returning to the GOP, with a view to running for president in 1916, there was now a growing body of military men who wished to serve under him if (as he kept predicting) the United States was compelled to abandon its policy of neutrality. He had not forgotten his dream of leading a force of super-Rough Riders into battle, and took it for granted that the War Department would allow him to do so as a major-general. The plan sounded old, even antiquated, when he spelled it out to General Frank Ross McCoy on 10 July. "My hope is, if we are to be drawn into this European war, to get Congress to authorize me to raise a Cavalry Division, which would consist of four cavalry brigades each of two regiments, and a brigade of Horse Artillery of two regiments, with a pioneer battalion or better still, two

pioneer battalions, and a field battalion of signal troops in addition to a supply train and a sanitary train."

Roosevelt vaguely explained that he meant motor trains, "and I would also
like a regiment or battalion of machine guns." But it was obvious he still
thought the quickest path to military glory was the cavalry charge—ignoring
the fact that modern Maxim-gun fire had proved it to be an amazingly effective form of group suicide. And he also chose to forget that the last time he
had tried to haul his heavy body onto a horse, at Sagamore Hill in May, he had
ended up on the ground with two broken ribs.

He knew nonetheless that he would prefer to die heroically in Europe
rather than in Mexico. Ted could fight Pancho Villa if he liked, but none of his
other sons were free to volunteer. "Whereas I should expect all four to go in if
there were a serious war, and would of course go in myself."

THE COLONEL SPENT the second half of July on the West Coast, attending a
series of events connected with the Panama-Pacific International Exposition
in San Francisco. A belated celebration of the opening of the Panama Canal,
it was the biggest such show ever held, and he was saluted with a special "Roosevelt Day" on the twenty-first. His speech in response was a harsh contrast to
the exuberant hymn to expansionism he had indulged in at Mechanics' Pavil-
ion twelve years before. Then, he had called upon Californians to look to the
Orient instead of the Occident for their commercial future, and had welcomed an emergent Japan as one of the "great, civilized powers." Now, he lectured them to look again across the Pacific, to see the consequences of China's
failure to arm against foreign predators. As a result, that opulent nation had
been dismembered, province after province, "until one-half of her territory is
now under Japanese, Russian, English, and French control." If the United
States was going to continue to "Chinafy" its foreign policy, at cost of preparing itself militarily against threats that might come at it any moment, from either warring hemisphere, then it might as well announce that the Panama
Canal Zone was an asset it could no longer hold or defend.

If, on the other hand, it was resolved to tolerate no more *Lusitania*s, it
should begin at once to build an army that did not take second place to that
of Argentina, and embark on a program of universal military service like
Switzerland's. Preparedness was all. "No nation ever amounted to anything if
its population was composed of pacifists and poltroons, if its sons did not
have the fighting edge."

He was listened to with respect by twenty thousand people, but they were
unconvinced by his alarmism. It was the same when he repeated himself in
San Diego.

"Colonel," somebody asked him, "are you not inciting us to war?"

Eyes and teeth flashing, Roosevelt talked about going to Döberitz with the Kaiser. "If you had heard and seen what I saw when I was in Germany, you would feel just as I do."

He headed home at the beginning of August with a clearer idea of the breadth and depth of American apathy about Europe. Then, in mid-month, the New York *World* published the first of a series of reports of secret German activities within the United States.

The article described plans to buy up all American plants exporting chlorine, so as to prevent France from matching the Reich's poison-gas capability; sedition and sabotage in munitions factories; a vast secret propaganda campaign; and, most chillingly, the construction of time bombs programmed to blow up American ships. Several of the plotters were men known to Roosevelt, including Count Franz von Papen, the emissary who had brought him greetings from Wilhelm II the year before. The government at once moved to have Papen recalled to Germany. On the nineteenth, another British liner, the *Arabic,* was torpedoed as it sailed from Liverpool to New York. Two Americans died as it went down.

"The time for words on the part of this nation has long passed," Roosevelt said in a public statement. "The time for deeds has come."

A few days later he went upstate to visit the Plattsburg preparedness camp, where Ted, Dick Derby, Willard Straight, and a large number of friends were in their third week of military training. In egalitarian fashion, they called themselves "citizen soldiers," but the tone of the gathering was distinctly Ivy League.

Ted noted with approval that more than half of his 1,400 fellow trainees were Harvard graduates. "I suppose some Yale men would fight if there was a war, but it is more clear than ever that Yale is the great middle class college, and the middle classes are not naturally gallant."

Roosevelt was amused to see that his eldest son had only the rookie rank of "sergeant," whereas Archie and Quentin, who had attended an earlier, five-week course for students, were graded as officer material. Ted's clubby, pipe-puffing smugness was a running family joke. But there was no denying his will to succeed. Having entered business in a carpet mill, Theodore Roosevelt, Jr., was now earning six figures as the coming young man at Bertron, Griscom & Co.

Sixteen rows of tents stretched for half a mile on the grounds of an army base that beautifully overlooked Lake Champlain. Roosevelt gazed with a historian's eye at an ancient embankment at the eastern end of the reservation, and across the water to the Green Mountains of Vermont. He had minutely described the Battle of Plattsburg in his first book, *The Naval War of 1812.*

Then, as now, he had been an apostle of preparedness: *A miserly economy in preparation may in the end involve a lavish outlay of men and money which after all comes too late to do more than partially offset the evils.*

The camp was run by Major General Leonard Wood, his fellow veteran of the Santiago campaign, and now commander of the U.S. Army's Eastern Department. Wood, too, was a passionate preparedness man. He believed that young men of eighteen and over should be subjected to "universal, compulsory, military training . . . for two months a year for four years." President Wilson did not, but had no objection if patriotic businessmen wanted to spend the hottest part of the year suffering, at their own expense, in the hands of army instructors. It was an excellent way for them to lose weight and persuade themselves that they might one day save Manhattan from the wrath of Wilhelm II.

Roosevelt spent Wednesday, 25 August, touring the encampment and watching exercises along the lakeshore. The training program as laid out by Wood was intense, compressing four years of regular army education into four weeks of dawn-to-dusk discipline. Men of all ages were learning how to drill, shoot, and run with forty-pound bags on their shoulders, until the oldest and plumpest were half dead from fatigue. Among them were "Lieutenant" John P. Mitchel, playing hookey from his peacetime job as mayor of New York. He was flanked by his police commissioner and a platoon of the city's finest. "Corporal" Robert Bacon, the former ambassador to France (and since Louvain, one of the most urgent interventionists in the country), marched with "Private" James D. Perry, bishop of Rhode Island; "Corporal" Dick Little, the Chicago humorist; "Sergeant" Alfred R. Allen of the University of Pennsylvania medical facility; "Private" Frank Crowninshield, editor of *Vanity Fair;* and "Private" Richard Harding Davis, the only man present who knew what it was like to be held prisoner by German soldiers. The rest of the regiment, divided into two battalions of eight companies apiece, consisted largely of bankers, lawyers, retailers, and former college jocks.

Wood was an astute political operator, mindful that the Republican presidential nomination in 1916 was wide open, and that further submarine attacks on Americans abroad might well change popular attitudes to the war. As a Harvard man himself, as well as a Medal of Honor winner, Rough Rider, colonial governor, and former chief of staff, he did not lack qualifications. He knew that cartoonists around the country were mocking his trainees as "TBMs"—tired businessmen playing at being soldiers. For those reasons he had gone out of his way to make the course so rigorous that they could not think of quitting, for fear of disgrace. In time, Wood hoped, these recruits would form the core of a highly professional military reserve.

Only the older ones could remember the days when he and Roosevelt had been among the most glamorous heroes of the Spanish-American War. Now, posing for an official photograph, they were both graying and portly, their tunics straining at every button. But they remained as physically contrasted as ever—Wood personifying his own name with a stance that might have been carved out of hickory, Roosevelt talking, smiling, and swiveling in small shoes and cavalry chaps.

"BOTH GRAYING AND PORTLY, THEIR TUNICS STRAINING AT EVERY BUTTON."
TR and General Leonard Wood at Plattsburg, 25 August 1915.

The Colonel was in a jovial mood. He chowed with the regiment at sunset, eating as heartily as if he had been a rookie himself. Expectations were high that he would deliver a rambunctious after-dinner speech. He did not disappoint, firing off salvos of his new favorite word, *poltroon,* and abusing "college sissies" and "hyphenated Americans" with tooth-snapping vigor. To general hilarity, an Airedale terrier interrupted him by rolling on the grass and displaying.

"I like him," Roosevelt said. "His present attitude is strictly one of neutrality."

It was tempting to segue to an attack on Woodrow Wilson, but he avoided any personal references, not wanting to make things difficult for Wood. The administration was in a state of high tension over the *Arabic* incident, and Wilson was not likely to react kindly to criticism emanating from an army-sponsored program.

Reporters following him were not discouraged. They waited until the Colonel was just about to board his train home, and asked him directly if he supported the President. While still declining to name names, he said that any peace-loving prose stylist living in a house once inhabited by Abraham Lincoln should emigrate to China. "Let him get out of the country as quickly as possible. To treat elocution as a substitute for action, to rely upon high-sounding words unbacked by deeds, is proof of a mind that dwells only in the realm of shadow and of shame."

⁂

JULIAN STREET, A YOUNG journalist assigned to write a profile of Roosevelt for *Collier's,* had an appointment to interview him in his Manhattan office the following morning. Expecting to encounter a fierce militarist, Street was pleasantly disappointed. "As the Colonel advanced to meet me he showed his hard, white teeth, wrinkled his red, weather-beaten face, and squinted his eyes half shut behind the heavy lenses of his spectacles, in suggestion, as it seemed to me, of a large, amiable lion which comes up purring gently as though to say, 'You needn't be afraid. I've just had luncheon.'"

Before they could talk, a clutch of newsmen arrived to announce that the secretary of war, Lindley M. Garrison, had telegraphed a reprimand to General Wood for allowing Roosevelt to cast aspersions on President Wilson at an army base. Street looked, fascinated, as the Colonel dictated a statement absolving Wood of responsibility.

At first Roosevelt spoke gravely, and the faces of the reporters mirrored his sober expression. "It was not until he lapsed briefly into irony, turning on, as he did so, that highly specialized smile, that I perceived how truly those young men reflected him. . . . To watch their faces was like watching the faces of an audience at a play: when the hero was indignant they became indignant; when he sneered they sneered; and when he was amused they seemed to quiver with rapturous merriment."

Street visited with Roosevelt several more times over the course of the next few days, trying to get as much out of him as possible before he left for a three-week hunting trip to Quebec. In the event, he got a major scoop: Roosevelt flatly declared that he would not accept any party's nomination in 1916. Then, with sublime appropriateness, he packed his guns and went north in search of a bull moose.

During his absence, Street wrote the profile. The young man was convinced that Roosevelt was the greatest man alive. For journalistic purposes, however, he decided to go no further than to call him "the most interesting American." The phrase leaped out as the title of his magazine piece, and also of the book that might grow out of it: a portrait of the Colonel as the prophet of preparedness and, not inconceivably, President of the United States again someday.

That fantasy made Street worry about the consequences of publishing his "scoop." Some momentary political situation could arise in which Roosevelt might regret disqualifying himself as a candidate in 1916. With a deadline from *Collier's* looming, Street took his manuscript to Sagamore Hill to show to Edith.

She sighed heavily at the thought of her husband being dragged into another presidential run. "It almost killed us last time!" But she said he would be home soon, and promised to ask him about withdrawing his statement.

On 27 September she wrote Street, "The Master of the house is home, & entirely approves of the omission."

⁓

ROOSEVELT GOT HIS BULL MOOSE, in addition to another that caused him considerable embarrassment, because the province of Quebec had licensed him to shoot only one specimen. He had to explain, in a bizarre deposition endorsed by both of his guides, that the second moose had pursued him both in water and on land, uttering strange cries and banging its antlers against trees. It was evidently as insane as Amos Pinchot, and as unwilling to let him go. He had had to kill it before it killed him.

Shaken by the experience, he told Charles Washburn early in October that his hunting days were over. He did not want to risk his deteriorating body on any more strenuous chases. It would be a humiliation, he said, to end up being "taken care of."

Washburn observed that the Colonel had aged much over the last year and a half. "This mighty human dynamo," he noted in his diary, "is working with a somewhat diminished energy." But so, to a greater or lesser extent, were all the Roosevelt Familiars. Their time was passing. The death on 28 September of the beautiful Mrs. Henry Cabot Lodge, once the presiding grace of Henry Adams's old salon in Washington, had poleaxed the senator and caused Adams to relive the nightmare of his own wife's suicide. "Jusserand is deeply depressed," Sir Cecil Spring Rice wrote Roosevelt, almost incoherent with grief himself. "She is [*sic*] the last of . . . the most delightful circle of friends we have ever known—How the world changes. Poor Cabot!"

Springy and Jules regretted more than the loss of their beloved "Nannie." They were mourning an era when their respective countries had been proud and inviolate and not hemorrhaging youth. Now all was disorder and death. Golden Rule diplomacy had given way to a new, scientific barbarism that burned libraries, dropped bombs out of the sky, cast babies into the sea, poisoned the very air that troops breathed, and—in its latest nihilistic advance—invented a flamethrower that vaporized men on the spot. War, once movement, had become stasis. Emperors had little sway. The world's richest and most resourceful country would do nothing to stop its rivals from damaging one another to the point that they all had to be saved. Was that what Wilson was waiting for? Or was he just, as Roosevelt complained to Edith Wharton, a "shifty, adroit, and selfish logothete," interested only in being reelected next year?

The man was unreachable to all of them, unreadable. In the first months of his presidency, Wilson had impressed the world at large as an inspiring new American voice, less preachy than Roosevelt, more self-confident than Taft. As James Bryce had remarked then, "Terse, clear and vigorous diction is extremely rare in this country. . . . When it is heard, and especially when it is accompanied by a certain imaginative or emotional color it produces an effect great in its proportion to its rarity." The language was still terse, and clear when Wilson wanted it to be, but his preference for prose rather than speech, for stately notes laced with subtle qualifications and dispatched while he himself remained unseen, had vitiated his once full-bodied image. The President sounded, in short, not quite human.

"All these letters to Germany!" Roosevelt snorted to Julian Street. "Of late I have come almost to the point of *loathing* a bee-*you*-ti-ful, *pol*-ished *dic*-tion!"

Actually, the President's most recent note to Count Jagow was more blunt than polished, going to the limit of diplomatic courtesy in stating that Germany's failure, so far, to apologize and pay reparations for the *Lusitania* tragedy was "very unsatisfactory," and that any further "illegal and inhuman" attack upon Americans traveling freely on the high seas would be regarded as "deliberately unfriendly."

On 5 October, Wilson was rewarded with a partial capitulation by Germany. Ambassador Bernstorff stated that his government was prepared to pay indemnity for the American lives "which, to its deep regret, have been lost on the *Arabic*," and announced that German submarines would in future operate under orders "so stringent that the recurrence of [such] incidents . . . is considered out of the question."

Representatives of all shades of opinion hailed the news as a triumph for the President. The chorus of praise drowned out a few cautionary voices pointing out that Germany had still not atoned for the sinking of the *Lusitania,* nor had it abandoned its submarine strategy. Even so, Wilson had been successful in his negotiations so far—what Roosevelt scornfully called "waging peace"—and clearly deserved the support of the American people as he continued to demand guarantees of their neutrality and safety.

In addition to which, he now had a claim to their personal good wishes. On the day after the German concession, Wilson announced that he was engaged to Mrs. Edith Bolling Galt.

—∽—

"I AM GIVING CERTAIN finishing touches to a book which Scribners will publish next spring," Roosevelt wrote Quentin on 18 October. Outside his study window, the trees of Sagamore Hill were at their peak of fall brilliancy. "I shall dedicate it to you and Archie," he went on, "as the opening chapters are those I wrote about our Arizona trip."

Quentin had joined his brother at Harvard, and the diaspora of the Roosevelt children was now complete. Dispersed, too, were any present hopes that the Colonel may have entertained of prevailing in his campaign to warn Americans of their folly in supporting a President too proud to fight. It was obvious to all political observers that Wilson would run for, and probably win, reelection next year on the merits of a foreign policy that seemed to gratify 90 percent of the country—"waging peace." Once again Roosevelt found himself shouting into a wind that bore his words back at him, mostly unheard.

And once again he turned to writing for solace. Quentin (who had already stocked his bookcase in Cambridge with copies of George Canning's *Poetry of the Anti-Jacobin,* Austen Layard's *Nineveh and Its Remains,* and a life of Genghis Khan) was to be his literary correspondent, just as Kermit had once been the recipient of his presidential posterity letters. Roosevelt had been pleased to discover, during Quentin's last year at Groton, that the boy was something of a scribe himself, the author of some imaginative prose pieces in the school magazine. "He is maturing rapidly, and is really a very successful person."

As a token of their camaraderie as men of the pen, Roosevelt confided that Charles Scribner had declined first serial rights on two chapters of the new book "which *I* thought were the best." He now had eleven chapters nearly ready. Many were pieces he had published as periodical articles, and since they all dealt with nature or literature in varying degrees, he decided to group them under the ungainly title, *A Book-Lover's Holidays in the Open.* He lavished particular care on an account of his visit to the Breton bird sanctuary last June. The result was the most eloquent of all his writings on conservation.

The extermination of the passenger-pigeon meant that mankind was just so much poorer; exactly as in the case of the destruction of the cathedral at Reims. And to lose the chance to see frigate-birds soaring in circles above the storm, or a flight of pelicans winging their way homeward across the crimson afterglow of the sunset; or a myriad terns flashing in the bright light of midday as they hover in a shifting maze above the beach—why, the loss is like the loss of a gallery of the masterpieces of the artists of old time.

"A FLIGHT OF PELICANS WINGING THEIR WAY HOMEWARD."
Bird life on Breton Island, Louisiana, photographed during TR's visit.

CHAPTER 23

The Man Against the Sky

The shadow fades, the light arrives,
And ills that were concealed are seen.

IN THE NEW YEAR of 1916 the one journalist in America who knew Theodore
Roosevelt and Woodrow Wilson equally well tried to sum up their essential
differences. "With T.R.," Ray Stannard Baker wrote, "the executive spirit
comes first. The temptation for Wilson is to think and express too much—
that of T.R. to act too much. Wilson works with ideas, T.R. directly with
men."

Expanding his comparison, Baker observed that whereas Wilson the ratio-
nalist sought to persuade by argument, Roosevelt "like an angry boy" wanted
to shout down all those who disagreed with him. "In the present crisis T.R. is
appealing to every kind of emotion . . . anything to stampede the nation into
terror of war and great armaments."

Baker worried that Germany's continuing reluctance to atone for the *Lusitania* incident, combined with the arrogance of the British in searching and
seizing American freighters destined for any ports but their own, had brought
the freedom-of-the-seas issue to a head—and with it, such divisive questions
as preparedness and military intervention, sure to be debated in the coming
presidential campaign. Like most of his countrymen, Baker was opposed to
any thought of going to war overseas, and hoped that Wilson was too. Offensive strategy was not the President's forte: his disastrous overreaction against
Mexico in 1914 had demonstrated that. It would be fatal if he yielded now to
Roosevelt's constant taunts of cowardice.

"I can understand how a man like T.R. might hate and despise a man like
Wilson," Baker wrote, "thinking him a mere academic theorist with no 'red
blood,' but, in my judgment, the future lies with the Wilsons."

Roosevelt was regretfully of the same opinion. He believed that during his own presidency, he could have aroused Americans to whatever degree of righteous anger a foreign provocation might justify. But they seemed to have lost their moral fiber under the administrations of Taft and Wilson—so much so, they were prepared to forget about Belgium and the *Lusitania*. He confessed to Kermit that during the last year he had begun to feel like a locomotive in a snowstorm. "I have accumulated so much snow on the cow catcher that it has brought me to a halt. . . . The majority of our people are bound now that I shall not come back into public life."

He would not mind that, if only they would listen to him and not insult him by thinking he cared only for war. "I'm a domestic man," he told Julian Street. "I have always wanted to be with Mrs. Roosevelt and my children, and now with my grandchildren. I'm not a brawler. I detest war. But if war came I'd have to go, and my four boys would go, too, because we have ideals in this family."

It was quite natural, he said, that men whose patriotism had atrophied would allow a soothsayer like Wilson to furnish them an excuse to stay home. But he still believed that his own, much more direct appeals to the national sense of honor would prevail in the end—even if he shouted away the last remnants of his former presidential dignity.

Street, an unabashed hero-worshipper, asked him if he thought he had genius.

"Most certainly not. I'm no orator, and in writing I'm afraid I'm not gifted at all. . . ." Roosevelt pondered the question further, then said with a smile, "If I have anything at all resembling genius, it is the gift for leadership."

TRUE TO HIS VOW to keep crusading, he wrote another war volume while still checking the proofs of *A Book-Lover's Holidays in the Open*. It consisted largely of diatribes against the administration that he had already published in *Metropolitan* magazine, updated and notched several tones higher on the shrillness scale. The opening chapter was new, and carried criticism of Woodrow Wilson to the verge of personal insult. He entitled it "Fear God and Take Your Own Part" (a quote from George Borrow), and tried some hot passages out at a conference of the National Americanization Committee in Philadelphia on 20 January. The choice of location was deliberate: Wilson had made his infamous "too proud to fight" address in that city, before another immigration-minded audience. Roosevelt was evidently setting himself as the President's ideological foil, just as Republicans and Progressives were negotiating the possibility of uniting behind a fusion candidate in the spring.

If by doing so he meant to signal his own availability, he could not have more effectively encouraged isolationists, pacifists, hyphenated Americans, and other interest groups to unite behind someone else. Even those of his hearers who did fear God might have wondered if the Colonel's personal deity was not Mars. He advocated military training in the nation's high schools, followed by compulsory field service; a chain of new, federally financed munitions plants, located inland so as to be safe from seaboard attack; an accelerated naval construction program; and enlargement of the current seventy-four-thousand-man army to a force of a quarter of a million. As always when reading from a typescript, he improvised freely, hurling regular insults at all persons lacking manly qualities.

The Washington Post awarded him four of its seven front-page lead columns the next morning (the other stories being a declaration by the King of Greece that nobody could win in Europe, a report of hand-to-hand fighting between Russians and Austrians on the Bessarabian front, and a rumor that vigilantes employed by William Randolph Hearst had captured Pancho Villa). Some of Roosevelt's latest thunderings were featured in a special box, along with the text of a letter that he had sent to the National Security League, currently meeting in Washington. This document, read to the League by his sister Corinne Roosevelt Robinson, was even more contemptuous of administration policies than his speech had been. The *Post* reported that it had been applauded by an audience of manufacturers, merchants, lawyers, and not a few fire-breathing women.

Wilson remained impassive. "The way to treat an adversary like Roosevelt," he said, "is to gaze at the stars over his head."

THE COLONEL LIKED his rabble-rousing chapter title so much that he decided to apply it to his whole war book. *Fear God and Take Your Own Part* was rushed to press in advance of *A Book-Lover's Holidays*. Its main theme, preparedness, had become the issue of the hour.

For as long as Britain and France had seemed to be holding their own in Europe, the great majority of Americans who were pro-Allies had winked at Wilson's policy of being "neutral in fact as well as in name." They realized that, with Bryan gone, the word *neutral* implied a prejudice toward Germany on the part of the administration that stopped just short of provocation. Ominously, though, the winter so far had been a season of triumph for the Central Powers, now buttressed by Turkey. British forces were routed at Gallipoli, besieged in Mesopotamia, and outmaneuvered in East Africa. The Western Front was impregnably defended by Germany, and Serbia and Bosnia lay helpless in the grip of Austria-Hungary. At latest count, France had lost two and a half million men. Eight Russian armies were beaten back in the East, while Bolshevism smoldered like an underground fire beneath the palaces of St. Petersburg—or Petrograd, as that city now called itself. The Japanese were allies—of sorts—to Britain and France in the Far East, but since seizing Kiaochow had shown themselves to be rapacious for territory and natural resources. Roosevelt warned that their sophisticated new battleships posed a long-term threat to the U.S. Navy.

Almost to his disbelief, he found that an appreciable minority of Americans were beginning to listen to him. With the phrase *world war* replacing *European war* in everyday speech, he no longer sounded like the lonely saber-rattler of last May. Even pacifists had to agree that the globe was smaller and more dangerous, now that two oceans were mixing at Panama, and Zeppelins floating across the English Channel to bomb Londoners. Day by day, paper by paper, America's editorial writers acknowledged the wisdom of taking at least some of the defense precautions shouted for by the Colonel.

And not only him: over the past half-year, several of Roosevelt's literary friends had issued alarums as urgent as his own. Frederic Louis Huidekoper's scholarly history, *Military Unpreparedness,* was the bible of the Plattsburg movement. Owen Wister's bestselling *The Pentecost of Calamity,* an anguished dirge to the death of German liberalism, compared the obliteration of the University of Louvain to the fate awaiting democracy itself, if Prussians in jackboots were to despoil the rest of Europe. Edith Wharton's *Fighting France* testified to the willingness of millions of *poilus* to die for the culture enshrined at Reims and Chartres.

Hearing these voices, Woodrow Wilson became a reluctant convert to the cause of preparedness. His enthusiasm for men in uniform remained slight, but he acknowledged the need for increased defense spending, if only to reassure Americans that he would keep the country secure. The moment had come, he announced at a dinner of railroad executives in New York on 27 January, for decisive action. "Does anybody understand the time?"

Wilson paused for effect. A gigantic Stars and Stripes hung tentlike over his head, covering the entire ceiling of the Waldorf ballroom. His new wife watched adoringly from an upper gallery. "Perhaps when you learned," the President said, "that I was expecting to address you on the subject of preparedness, you recalled the address which I made to Congress something more than a year ago, in which I said that this question of military preparedness was not a pressing question. But more than a year has gone by since then, and I would be ashamed if I had not learned something in fourteen months."

He was applauded for his willingness to admit fault. Fourteen months was about the length of Roosevelt's campaign to make him a more interventionist figure in world affairs. Wilson did not indicate who, or what, had taught him his new defense philosophy. But he said he was for the immediate recruitment of a five-hundred-thousand-man "Continental" army, which would be voluntary, federally controlled, and supplementary to the National Guard. He also wanted "a proper and reasonable program for the increase of the navy."

Wilson proceeded westward in his first campaign swing since 1912. He ventured with considerable courage into the heartland of isolationism, via pro-German Milwaukee to Kansas City and St. Louis, Missouri, the two most antiwar cities in the country. Graceful, smiling, elegant, and humorous, he demonstrated over and again a mastery of persuasive oratory. His sentences seemed to flow as if unpremeditated, but journalists transcribing them noticed his wizardry in qualifying every phrase likely to thrill interventionists with another that reaffirmed his love of peace. "You have laid upon me," he would tell a crowd, "this double obligation: 'We are relying on you, Mr. President, to keep us out of this war, but we are relying on you, Mr. President, to keep the honor of the nation unstained.' " In St. Louis, he said, "I don't want to command a great army," before vowing to build up "incomparably the greatest navy in the world."

Roosevelt marveled at Wilson's Bach-like ability to combine every theme with its own inversion. He was an equivocator himself, but this kind of skill mocked his clumsy habit of balancing one thing against the other. Half in awe, he analyzed fifteen presidential policy statements through 10 February, and found that Wilson had taken forty-one different positions on preparedness. "Each of these 41 positions contradicted from 1 to 6 of the others. In many of the speeches, the weasel words of one portion took all the meaning out of the words used in another portion, and those latter words themselves had a weasel significance as regards yet other words."

Hitherto, Roosevelt had made free with epithets like "skunk" and "prize jackass" in his private references to Wilson. But he had avoided calling him names in public. The temptation became overwhelming to do so now, with an insult that sounded slanderous, but which no lawyer with a large dictionary could find actionable. He chose the splendid noun *logothete*, which he had recently tried out on Edith Wharton. It had vague connotations of word-spinning, but in fact meant little more than a bureaucrat, or petty accountant in ancient Constantinople. That gave him an ideal qualifier. When *Fear God and Take Your Own Part* came out in the second week of February, it contained Roosevelt's latest and funniest contribution to political invective. He wrote that the President's self-justifications in alternately trying to cow and cuddle up to bandits south of the border were "worthy of a Byzantine logothete."

The publication of *Fear God* coincided with the first anniversary of Wilson's demand for "strict accountability" from Germany for any armed action hurtful to the United States. Roosevelt did not fail to mention this in his opening pages. He added the names of seven ships, other than the *Lusitania,* that had been sunk in the interim, with some two hundred Americans aboard. "If any individual finds satisfaction in saying that nevertheless this was 'peace' and not 'war,' it is hardly worth while arguing with him."

⌒

ON 11 FEBRUARY, he and Edith sailed for the West Indies on a little steamer, the *Guiana*. Caribbean waters were not immune to U-boat attacks, but Roosevelt was in need of sunshine and rest. The ideological temper he had worked himself up into in recent months, combined with several sharp attacks of "jungle fever," had jaded him. Besides, he wanted to get away from a biennial pest he could not seem to shake: swarms of importuners begging him to reenter party politics, either as a candidate or a campaigner.

The difference this time was that some of the supplicants were coming from conservative quarters. It had been observed on Wall Street that Roosevelt the *Metropolitan* columnist was no longer the progressive ideologue he had been in his early days at *The Outlook*. His attitudes toward corporatism and inherited wealth had definitely inched rightward since he became aware, around the time of Plattsburg, that many bankers and industrialists (above all arms manufacturers, raking in mountains of Allied money) were as keen on intervention as he was.

Roosevelt still talked about federal control of competition, sounding like one of his shellac discs from 1912. But the kind of restraints he now spelled out in print were so pro-business they could have been—and possibly were—dictated by George W. Perkins. Government commissions, he now held, would ensure "ample profit" for industrial investors and greater efficiency "along German lines." If certain corporations engaged in foreign trade were "Americanized" (a euphemism for *nationalized*), their earnings would increase, and they would be more responsive when their resources were urgently called for.

Another sign of Rooseveltian recidivism was the Colonel's new willingness to treat the new-money crowd with respect. Through *Metropolitan* magazine, he had made friends with Harry Payne Whitney, the kind of sporty millionaire he once despised. He allowed Judge Elbert H. Gary of U.S. Steel and seventeen fellow plutocrats to fete him privately in New York, and was also guest of honor at a secretive luncheon at the Harvard Club, hosted by the publishing magnate Robert Collier. Downtown rumors alleged that "Teddy" was being groomed for another presidential run, this time as a Republican.

Roosevelt told the truth about the meetings to his latest confidant, John J. Leary, Jr., of the New York *Tribune*, on the understanding that he not be named as a source. "Behind it all, I believe, was a desire of these men—all Americans, men who have done things and are doing big things, men who have a stake in the country—to take counsel together on the big problem of national preparedness." Far from asking or accepting their political support, he had told them that if the GOP in 1916 adopted a "hyphenated" platform, or nominated a candidate on the strength of "mongrel" promises, he, Theodore Roosevelt, would campaign for the reelection of President Wilson. "And, by Godfrey, I mean it!"

Leary understood the Colonel's adjectives to refer to anything or anyone that compromised America's duty to defend democracy around the world. Wilson at least half-recognized that duty now. "I dislike his policies almost to the point of hate," Roosevelt said, "but I am too good an American to stand by and see him beaten by a mongrel American."

⌁

IF EDITH HOPED that a seven-week cruise would take her husband's mind off Europe, she forgot that most of the islands of the Lesser Antilles belonged to Britain or France, and were therefore as obsessed with the war as he was. As the *Guiana* steamed south, it frequently encountered armored cruisers of the Royal and French navies. A constant guard was being maintained against reincarnations of the German raider *Karlsruhe,* which had terrorized the entire Caribbean in 1914, before blowing up mysteriously off Barbados.

When Roosevelt stepped ashore on Martinique on 22 February, he found himself on French soil. The island was a *département* of the Republic and, in local opinion, indistinguishable from it. Fort-de-France had just been advised, by cable, of a German attack on the city of Verdun that was going beyond all previous extremes of military violence. The governor of Martinique welcomed Roosevelt with commensurate solemnity, and thanked him for his long crusade for the Allied cause. Not to be outdone, the mayor of Fort-de-France recalled that President Roosevelt had been the first head of state to rush aid to Martinique in 1902, after the catastrophic eruption of Mont Pelée.

Roaring cheers and cannon fire shook the air as the distinguished visitors rode through town in an open automobile. House façades displayed the tricolors of France and the United States. At every stop, Roosevelt received full honors, as he had six years before in Paris. He asked to see something of the island, and was taken to the ridge of Vert-Pré, with its double view of the Atlantic and the Mer des Antilles. Northward, the ocean stretched blue and white-capped all the way to Brittany. To the west, the calm shallows of the New World lolled.

At 5 P.M. the Roosevelts returned to Fort-de-France for a military review. Bugles sounded in the city square, and a double file of troops presented arms. Roosevelt inspected both ranks with the governor at his side. Then he joined Edith on the reviewing stand while the whole company saluted them *en défilé.*

Most of the marchers were youths of Quentin's age, conscripted for service in Europe and only a month or two in uniform. But the effect of France's preparedness program—even more intense, apparently, than that administered by General Wood at Plattsburg—was evident in their machine-like drill. A cavalry charge ensued. Then the entire island company, officers and youths, stamped to a halt in front of the Roosevelts and inclined the French flag at their feet.

Edith, who had always considered herself partly French, began to weep. So did another woman on the stand. Roosevelt turned to the governor and, courteously abandoning his own language, said, "Je vois que Madame Guy pleure. Madame Roosevelt pleure aussi, et moi, je sens les larmes me monter aux yeux: c'est impressionnant."*

Later he was asked to present the Croix de Guerre to a wounded corporal, and said companionably, "Moi aussi j'ai une balle allemande au dos. L'assassin qui me l'a tiré était un Allemand."†

Edith excused herself from a grand banquet in the Chamber of Commerce garden that night. She thus missed a unique opportunity to hear her husband compared to Cyrano de Bergerac. Speaking with considerable emotion, the governor recalled being present at the Sorbonne in April 1910, when Roosevelt had delivered his famous address exhorting Frenchmen to gird themselves for moral battle. Now the hour of blood and dust had come, and the students he had inspired were fighting for their country.

In youth, "l'ardent colonel des Rough-Riders" had fought likewise. More recently, as everybody in Martinique knew, he had been a lonely American oracle, shouting that democracy must be protected against barbarism—unlike certain of his countrymen who took refuge in "une neutralité prudente." Turning to Roosevelt, the governor accorded him one of the most moving tributes he had ever heard:

> Vous nous donnez l'exemple rare, presque unique, d'un homme politique qui n'est pas un politicien, d'un homme d'action qui est en même temps un homme de pensée; d'un parlementaire qui ne parle que s'il a quelque chose à dire; d'un écrivain qui sait se battre et d'un soldat qui sait écrire. Et tout cela avec une gaîté franche, une absence de morgue qui séduit les plus humbles et qui en impose aux plus puissants. Il y a en vous quelque chose de notre Cyrano de Bergerac qui risque sa vie pour une idée; qui lutte sans souci des dangers pour son idéal, mais qui

---

* "I see that Madame Guy is crying. So is Madame Roosevelt, and I feel tears coming myself. This is impressive."
† "I too have a German bullet in my back [sic]. The assassin who shot me was a German."

entre deux combats dépose sa cuirasse et son épée pour lire Lucrèce et commenter Platon.*

⟋⟍

AFTER VISITING THE New York Zoological Society's tropical research station in British Guiana, maintained by Charles William Beebe, Roosevelt proceeded to Trinidad. He arrived there on 3 March, and received a disquieting batch of cablegrams from New York. They informed him that prospective delegates to the Republican and Progressive conventions (scheduled to run simultaneously in Chicago, in early June) were already pledging themselves to him, as an expected bipartisan candidate for president. John McGrath had announced that the Colonel had no political ambitions, but the pledges would not stop. No less a GOP stalwart than Augustus Peabody Gardner of Massachusetts was now calling himself a "Roosevelt Republican."

Roosevelt remained silent while he went birding in the Trinidadian interior with an entomologist and mycologist, two of the inexhaustible list of friends he seemed able to call on wherever he traveled. They spent an afternoon in a cave stranger than anything dreamed by Hieronymus Bosch. It concealed itself high in the mountains, behind a gush of clear water. Scrabbling through into pitch darkness, Roosevelt heard all around him a weird flapping and fluttering, combined with metallic clacks, growls, pipes, and wails. As torches lit up the gloom, he saw slabs and ledges slathered two feet deep with guano. Obese, naked *guacharo* chicks sat in this nitrous clay, peering blindly out of cup-shaped hollows, while overhead their parent birds sat guard like nighthawks. Bats furred the ceiling. Roosevelt was amazed to see slender fungi growing out of the guano, although there was no light to feed them.

That night he slept with his companions in the humid hut of a black coconut farmer. His clothes from the cave were still wet the next morning when he rode back to Port of Spain.

From there, on 9 March, he cabled a long statement to New York, for immediate release to all newspapers:

I MUST REQUEST AND I NOW DO REQUEST AND INSIST THAT
MY NAME BE NOT BROUGHT INTO THE MASSACHUSETTS

---

* "You offer us a rare, almost unique, example of a political person who is not a politician, of a man of action who is at the same time a man of thought; of a public speaker who does not speak unless he has something to say; of a writer who knows how to fight and a warrior who knows how to write. And all this with a frank gaiety, a lack of pomposity that seduces the humblest and impresses the most powerful. There is in you something of our Cyrano de Bergerac, who risked his life for an idea; who fought without fear of danger for his belief, but between battles set aside his armor and his sword to read Lucretius and expound Plato."

PRIMARIES AND I EMPHATICALLY DECLINE TO BE A CANDIDATE
IN THE PRIMARIES OF THAT OR ANY OTHER STATE. . . .

    I DO NOT WISH THE NOMINATION. I AM NOT IN THE LEAST
INTERESTED IN THE POLITICAL FORTUNES EITHER OF MYSELF
OR ANY OTHER MAN. I AM INTERESTED IN AWAKENING MY
FELLOW COUNTRYMEN TO THE NEED OF FACING UNPLEASANT
FACTS. . . .

    I WILL NOT ENTER ANY FIGHT FOR THE NOMINA-
TION. . . . INDEED, I WILL GO FURTHER AND SAY IT WOULD BE
A MISTAKE TO NOMINATE ME UNLESS THE COUNTRY HAD IN
ITS MOOD SOMETHING OF THE HEROIC.

He did not say what the "facts" were that Americans had to face. Nor did
he directly mention the war. But he did refer to "tremendous national and international problems" confronting Woodrow Wilson's "unmanly" administration, and cited Washington and Lincoln as two presidents who had not
sought to escape action "behind clouds of fine words." He went on at tremendous length, trying the patience of Trinidad's wartime censor, who was required to check every word transmitted out of the island. Late that evening the
cable went off. On 10 March, *The New York Times* published it under the
headline ROOSEVELT'S HAT AGAIN IN THE RING.

⟞⟠⟝

WHEN HE RETURNED home a fortnight later, he found two booms for the
Republican presidential nomination under way. One—perhaps more of a discreet, offstage rumble than a boom—was in behalf of Justice Charles Evans
Hughes, and represented the wishes of Party stalwarts who had supported
Taft for reelection in 1912. Few of them were enthusiastic about their choice,
but Hughes had the supreme virtue of being so colorless and closemouthed as
to be virtually attack-proof. A joke went around that "no one wanted Hughes,
but everyone was for him."

    The other boom was for the author of *Fear God and Take Your Own Part.*
Roosevelt's book had become a surprise bestseller. Two biographical sketches
of him were out, both frankly adoring: Julian Street's *The Most Interesting
American,* and a memoir by Charles G. Washburn, *Theodore Roosevelt: The
Logic of His Career.* Quite apart from his literary celebrity, he appeared to
have inspired scores of Progressive and Republican campaign planners with a
desire for "something of the heroic."

    They thought he was talking about political heroism. He meant the sol-
dierly kind. Whatever desire for power still burned in Roosevelt related solely
to the war—manifesting itself in fantasies of how *he*, last spring, would have
handed the German ambassador his passports and made him sail home on the

Lusitania. He did not see his boom lasting through the convention. Recriminations over the great bolt of 1912 were still too fierce to admit any real possibility that he could reunite both wings of the GOP. Nor was he deceived by the sales of his book into thinking that a majority of Americans believed in preparedness—much less overseas military action. As Robert Bacon wrote to a friend in France, "In America there are fifty thousand people who understand the necessity of the United States entering the war immediately on your side. But there are a hundred million Americans who have not even thought of it. Our task is to see that the figures are reversed."

Roosevelt had seen Hughes's candidacy coming for a long time. Typically, the justice would neither confirm nor deny a desire to be nominated. But he had much to recommend him. Hughes was progressive without being Progressive, a man of icy brilliance, enrobed now with all the majesty of a seat on the Supreme Court. The only virtue he lacked, in abundance, was charm. But Grover Cleveland had managed to do without it and serve two distinguished terms in the White House, to say nothing of George Washington.

What, though, would a President Hughes do about such recent provocations as Britain's rejection of Secretary Lansing's proposal to classify armed merchantmen as warships? And Pancho Villa's cross-border raid on Columbus, New Mexico, killing eight civilians and seven U.S. troopers? And Germany's torpedoing of the Channel ferry *Sussex*, with four Americans aboard? Roosevelt had no evidence to go on, but suspected that the justice would prove to be "another Wilson with whiskers."

JOVIAL AND RED-BROWN from the Caribbean sun, Roosevelt returned to Sagamore Hill and found a book of poems in the mass of mail awaiting his attention. It was entitled *The Man Against the Sky*, and had been sent to him by Edwin Arlington Robinson, strangest of all the literary figures he had patronized. Robinson had done little over the past twenty-seven years but write austere, elliptical poetry and try to keep from starving. When inspiration failed, he would try without success to drink himself to death. There was too much blood in his sunsets and aching regret in his love lyrics for most magazine editors to read, let alone print anything by him. What books he had managed to publish were either self-financed or commercial failures. In 1905, Roosevelt had had to exercise the power of the presidency to persuade Scribners to reissue *The Children of the Night*, simultaneously awarding Robinson a no-show government job. As the poet, forever grateful, wrote Kermit: "I don't know where I would be without your astonishing father. He fished me out of hell by the hair of the head, and so enabled me to get my last book together and in all probability to get it published."

That had been *The Town Down the River*, which came out in 1910 and ended in an enigmatic ode entitled "The Revealer—Roosevelt." Except for some haunting verses here and there, it showed an attrition of his gifts, indicating that Robinson would have been better off left in hell. He seemed to write best when he was nearest to suicide.

The Roosevelts had seen him only once or twice since then: a mousy, half-deaf little man who had come to Sagamore Hill in 1913 and remained almost mute—not that any of the Colonel's guests ever had much opportunity to speak. Now Robinson repaid their hospitality with a book of such original power as to justify the belief, among a few cognoscenti, that he was the finest poet in America. He confessed in an accompanying note that he had recently emerged from one of his depressive slumps.

"Your letter deeply touches me," Roosevelt wrote on 27 March. "There is not one among us in whom a devil does not dwell; at some time, on some point, that devil masters each of us. . . . It is not having been in the Dark House, but having left it, that counts."

He was referring to a terrifying poem in the book, describing Robinson's *Döppelganger*-like experience of having witnessed his own death in a house full of demonic shadows. Roosevelt responded more to the poet's feeling of rebirth—*After that, from everywhere, / Singing life will find him*—than to whatever agonies Robinson may have suffered before a door mysteriously opened and let him out.

He did not elaborate on his own periods of melancholy, or say if he had ever felt overmastered by them. Robinson had long ago, with sly word play in "The Revealer," implied that Roosevelt was too happily constituted to suffer real despair. *Theodoros* in Greek connoted a man gifted by the gods with equal quantities of positivity and personal courage—someone who was, in a later simile, sweeter than honey and stronger than a lion. Had he not killed his share of lions in Africa, and come home purged and purified, to shout out his message that a life of total engagement was the only one worth living? Then and now, Robinson perceived him to be much more than "biceps and sunshine."

The title poem in *The Man Against the Sky* was not, as some might think, another portrait of Roosevelt. It did celebrate his anti-materialistic philosophy. Robinson's extraordinary imagery, at once elusive and allusive, was pitched to fly right past the Colonel's ears. But the central metaphor of a giant figure reaching the top of a black hill, gazing with inscrutable emotion at a world on fire beyond, then descending by slow stages out of sight (whether to Elysian fields or some unseen doom), was there for any Roosevelt-watcher to ponder.

⌒

ON THE LAST DAY of March, Roosevelt made his first overt move toward a return to the GOP by lunching with Elihu Root. Four years had passed since their estrangement at the last Republican National Convention—years in which Root had felt no annoyance at Roosevelt calling him a "thief," only regret that someone he loved could be so unable to accept that his rulings as chairman might have been fair.

They met in New York, at Robert Bacon's town house on Park Avenue. Henry Cabot Lodge and Leonard Wood attended. All five men found themselves linked by their dislike of the President. To Roosevelt's sardonic amusement, Root and Lodge also had bitter things to say about Taft. But it was no time to upbraid them for supporting an un-reelectable President. The prime purpose of the lunch was to let the press and Progressive Party know that Athos and D'Artagnan had reconciled. Wood wrote with satisfaction in his diary, "Roosevelt and Root seemed to be glad to be together again, really so."

The New York Times and *The Washington Post* treated the lunch as front-page news, on a par with dispatches describing "the greatest of conflicts" ongoing at Verdun. Political commentators were agreed that Roosevelt was making himself available as a candidate for nomination by both the Progressive and Republican parties. Supporters of the President felt qualms. Wilson did not look strong. Pancho Villa's raid had been a severe embarrassment to him, and a four-thousand-man punitive American expedition, headed by Brigadier General John J. "Black Jack" Pershing, had so far failed to raise much more than a cloud of alkali dust. Lindley Garrison had resigned as secretary of war, in protest against the President's feeling that an enlarged, all-white National Guard was preferable to a segregated Continental Army. The first anniversary of the sinking of the *Lusitania* loomed in six weeks' time, and Germany had still not yet acknowledged her "strict accountability" for that outrage.

A mild irony of the lunch at Bacon's house was that, despite its appearance of solidarity, every guest felt ambivalent about the Roosevelt boom. Root and Wood aspired to the presidency themselves, and Lodge was secretly for Hughes. Roosevelt himself wished he was not still the last hope of die-hard Progressives. Having re-embraced the party of William Howard Taft and Boies Penrose (not to mention William Barnes, Jr.), he felt he could not in good faith allow his Bull Moose followers to nominate him again. That would signal a belief that the Progressive movement was still viable, whereas he had long ago told Kermit that it had "vanished into the *Ewigkeit*."*

But his boom would not stop. George von Lengerke Meyer created a Roosevelt Republican Committee, and funds flowed in. To the fury of the brothers Pinchot, George Perkins discreetly aided this organization. A Theodore Roosevelt Non-Partisan League worked hand in hand with a Women's Roosevelt League. Catholic bishops and Detroit auto executives pondered convention strategy. The old cry, "We want Teddy!" was heard in Maine and

* Eternity.

454 • COLONEL ROOSEVELT

Minnesota. Advertisements ran in newspapers and magazines. "Campaign" headquarters opened in New York, Boston, and Chicago, even though the Colonel insisted he would not contest a single primary. "What I am really trying to do," he wrote Hiram Johnson (another presidential hopeful), "is . . . get the Republicans and Progressives together for someone whom we can elect and whom it will be worth while electing." Although his head told him that person was Justice Hughes, his heart could not help beginning to throb with seasonal ambition. By 5 April he was ready to take seriously the teasing threat of a delegate-elect to the Republican convention, "You know, Colonel, I may make up my mind that we will have to nominate you."

"Don't you do it if you expect me to pussy-foot on any single issue I have raised," Roosevelt said, adding yet another phrase to the dictionary of American political slang.

⁂

AT THIS JUNCTURE, Woodrow Wilson demonstrated once more that he was a political operator without peer.

The attack on the *Sussex* had typically caused him to go into seclusion, while he deliberated how to respond and waited for an authoritative statement that it had indeed been torpedoed by a U-boat. Meanwhile there had been such a surge of national anger at the loss of American lives aboard, combined with frustration over General Pershing's inability to track down Pancho Villa, that Wilson saw he must address it, or risk having the anger translate into a general conviction that his foreign policy had failed. On 18 April, he ordered Joseph Tumulty to go to Capitol Hill at 4:30 P.M. sharp, and inform the leaders of Congress that the President had "important affairs" to communicate to both Houses at 1 P.M. the following afternoon. The White House simultaneously announced that Wilson had written a new note to Germany, unprecedented in its harshness, which was ready for dispatch the moment he finished his address.

These drumrolls, so precisely timed for effect, created such suspense that Roosevelt sounded peevish when he complained that Wilson wanted to hold a "town meeting" rather than act like a commander in chief.

When the hour came for the President to appear, Congress was more excited than at any time since it had awaited William McKinley's request for war against Spain in 1898. Wilson entered looking like a man with his mind made up, and the applause that greeted him as he made his way to the lectern was subdued but prolonged. All he said by way of preamble was, "Gentlemen of the Congress, a situation has arisen in the foreign relations of the country of which it is my plain duty to inform you very frankly."

He reviewed his diplomatic communications with the Wilhelmstrasse since February 1915, stressing the good faith of the United States in consistently believing Germany's protestations that it would moderate its submarine offensive against the Allies. Despite a strong warning by the State Department at the beginning of this offensive, and much patience on his own part, "the commanders of German undersea vessels have attacked merchant ships with greater and greater activity, not only upon the high seas surrounding Great Britain and Ireland but wherever they could encounter them, in a way that has grown more and more ruthless, more and more indiscriminate as the months have gone by."

Greater and greater, more and more. Throughout his fifteen-minute address, the President kept pounding out repetitive qualifiers, stressing the incremental nature of the tests Germany had put on America's patience. "Tragedy has followed tragedy. . . . Great liners like the *Lusitania* and the *Arabic,* and mere ferryboats like the *Sussex,* have been attacked without a moment's warning . . . and the roll of Americans who have lost their lives on ships thus attacked and destroyed has grown month by month, until the ominous toll has mounted into the hundreds." Nevertheless, he had been willing to wait until evidence of Germany's deliberate intent to keep the United States at bay with false promises could be tolerated no longer.

That time had now come, Wilson said. "The government of the United States is at last forced to the conclusion that there is but one course it can pursue, and that unless the Imperial German government should immediately declare and effect an abandonment of its present methods of warfare against passenger and freight-carrying vessels, this government can have no choice but to sever diplomatic relations with the government of the German Empire altogether."

He made clear that he was not asking, but expecting all legislators present to approve a decision which could well lead to war. He managed to do this with a winning combination of self-confidence and chagrin. As he folded up his script he caught the grave expression of William J. Stone, chairman of the Senate Foreign Relations Committee, and said, "I hope you do not feel as sad as I feel."

The applause that accompanied his exit from the chamber was noticeably louder than that which had greeted him.

⨾

ROOSEVELT WAS ONE of the minority of Americans who did not admire the President's masterly address. Even if Germany backed down, he said, it would only prove that Wilson should have forced the issue fourteen months before, thus saving the lives of many women and children, and making imperative a national preparedness program.

He seemed to realize that however the Wilhelmstrasse reacted, he had lost a lot of his rhetorical ground as a proponent of forceful policymaking. Which meant, he wrote his sister Bamie, "there is in my judgment hardly any chance that the Republican convention will turn to me." He was not going to declare himself a candidate: his only message now was preparedness. There was a danger that even that theme had been co-opted by the wily President. "Mere outside preaching and prophecy tend after a while to degenerate into a scream . . . and I am within measurable distance of that point."

On 4 May, just three days before the *Lusitania* anniversary, Count Jagow replied to the President's ultimatum with a promise that German submarine commanders would henceforth honor the rights of all noncombatants at sea. In return, he expected America to insist that Great Britain show an equal respect for international maritime law. Secretary Lansing replied that the United States "could not for a moment entertain" such a presumption on its relations with another country. Helpless, Jagow lapsed into silence. Wilson's triumph was complete. An early move among isolationist Democrats to oppose his renomination with Champ Clark faded.

And so, much more slowly, did the Progressive/Republican boom for Roosevelt. He took a flying trip to Detroit to assail Henry Ford's pacifism, and at the end of May traveled to Kansas City to deliver a Memorial Day address apparently designed to antagonize every hyphenated citizen in the country. "I have been enthusiastically received," he wrote Fanny Parsons, "—save for one playful Latin-American gentleman who threw a knife at me."

Ray Stannard Baker visited Wilson in the White House and asked him directly whom he would prefer to campaign against in the fall—Roosevelt or Hughes.

"It matters very little," said the President, serene as ever. "Roosevelt deals in personalities and does not argue upon facts and conditions. One does not need to meet him at all. Hughes is of a different type. If he is nominated he will have to be met."

Wilson's major address of the month, before the League to Enforce Peace, took up the theme Sir Henry Campbell-Bannerman, Andrew Carnegie, Roosevelt, Taft, and many other oracles had sounded in their differing ways over the past six years: that of a new international organization with power to prevent all future wars. Such a body, he said, should respect the right of all members, small and large, to determine their own destiny, while remaining inviolate for one another. "So sincerely do we believe these things that I am sure that I speak the mind and wish of the people of America when I say that the United States is willing to become a partner in any feasible association of nations formed in order to realize these objections."

If it was the mind and wish of Americans to reelect Woodrow Wilson in November, he was doubtless hinting at the long-term goal of his presidency.

⟝⟞

ON THE NIGHT of Thursday, 8 June, ten leaders of the Progressive and Republican parties, convening in Chicago, met to explore the possibility of uniting behind a fusion candidate. Roosevelt was neither present nor near at hand: his non-candidacy required him to be at home in Sagamore Hill, pretending not to be interested in incoming long-distance telephone calls.

It was soon obvious that George Perkins's delegation was willing to trade away almost every plank of the old Bull Moose platform, on condition that Theodore Roosevelt was nominated by the GOP. Members of the Republican delegation, including Winthrop Murray Crane and Nicholas Murray Butler, the antiwar president of Columbia University, made it equally clear that they would as soon vote for Senator Charles W. Fairbanks of Indiana, the most uncharismatic politician in America.

Sir Cecil Spring Rice, observing both conventions on behalf of Sir Edward Grey, was struck by the ambivalence of the Republican delegates who had traveled with him from Washington. "All were united in asseverating that they hated Teddy like hell and wanted to get back at him," he wrote his wife, "but [felt] that he was the only man who could save the country."

From what, the ambassador did not say. Possibly from international contempt: the United States was a pariah at the moment, with Mexico resentful of Pershing's mission, Britain and France furious at a suggestion by Wilson that no parties to the world war were free of responsibility for its outbreak, and Germany seething at the haughty tone of his last note. The European situation was desperate. Ten thousand shells a day were falling on Verdun, and still troops were horded in from east and west to die, with no resolution in sight after three and a half months: *Stellungskrieg,* standing war, motionless mortality. General Falkenhayn's announced intention was to bleed France white. The Battle of Jutland had been not so much a victory for Britain as a strategic retreat by the German navy. Russia was resurgent against Austria on the southwestern front. The British minister of war, Lord Kitchener—he whom Roosevelt had once taunted with a reference to Shakespeare's "vasty deep"—had gone down at sea with all his aides, victims of a German-laid mine. Meanwhile, petty politicians in Chicago were still squabbling over Roosevelt's bolt in 1912.

"They believed," Spring Rice said of his travel companions, "that if he turned up at Chicago [today] he would carry the whole place with him. On the other hand Cabot thought if he only kept away he might have a dog's chance, but that if he came he would spoil everything."

Long ago, Henry Adams had observed that the only rock on Roosevelt's coast was the senator from Massachusetts. "We all look for inevitable shipwreck there." None of their friends had ever been able to understand the mu-

"THE ONLY ROCK ON ROOSEVELT'S COAST."
Senator Henry Cabot Lodge.

tual attraction of two such contrary souls. Lodge was overtly for Roosevelt, covertly for Hughes, but in the suspicion of many delegates, not averse to being nominated himself.

The bipartisan conference adjourned without result and on the following day, Friday, the Republican convention took its first ballot. Hughes led with $253^1/_2$ votes; five other candidates, including Lodge, scored ahead of Roosevelt, who got only 65. A second ballot increased his total to 81, but Hughes's mushroomed to $328^1/_2$.

By nine o'clock that evening it was clear that the justice was going to be nominated—without enthusiasm—unless the Progressive convention could suggest another candidate acceptable to both parties. A second conference began just before midnight, with constant calls going back to Sagamore Hill. Roosevelt, aghast at the prospect of a campaign pitting Charles the Baptist against the Byzantine Logothete, got on the line and asked Nicholas Murray Butler if he had any chance to win on a future ballot. Butler said no. The Republican leadership would prefer to choose between Elihu Root, Philander Chase Knox, and Senator Fairbanks. Roosevelt said none were congenial to his Progressive supporters. Instead of himself, he suggested Leonard Wood or Henry Cabot Lodge.

At the mention of the last name, Butler showed some interest. When the two parties reassembled on Saturday morning, 10 June, a telegram from the Colonel urged both of them to support Lodge as a man of "the broadest national spirit." Perkins's communication of this news to the Progressives provoked anguished cries of "No." The protests swelled and transformed into such passion for Roosevelt that at 12:37 P.M., Perkins was unable to delay his nomination. That was three minutes too late to influence Republicans voting a few blocks away in Convention Hall. They had already decided on Hughes.

It remained only for Roosevelt to make his final break with the Progressive rank and file. He did so with another telegram declining their nomination "at this time." Its brusque tone was no more shocking than his demand that his "conditional refusal" be referred to George Perkins's National Committee to accept as absolute. "If they are not satisfied they can . . . confer with me and then determine on whatever action we may severally deem appropriate to meet the needs of the country."

Oswald Garrison Villard, editor of the *New York Evening Post,* watched as the import of these words sank in on the delegates. Roosevelt was not only rejecting them (in the very hall where he had once vowed to battle for the Lord) but, with the silky-smooth collusion of George Perkins, making it impossible for them to nominate anybody else who might damage the Republican Party's choice. "Around me," Villard reported, "men of the frontier type could not keep back their tears at this self-revelation of their idol's selfishness, the smashing of their illusions about their peerless leader."

ROOSEVELT'S BRUSQUENESS masked considerable hurt. Against all his instincts, he had allowed himself to believe that the miracle might happen, that the Republican nomination he had always wanted (in preference to that of 1912) was coming to him just as Americans realized that he, of all the men in the world, was probably the best equipped to arrest the general breakdown of civilization. *If I have anything at all resembling genius, it is the gift for leadership.* But leadership once again, and probably forever now, was denied him. The future of America was in the hands of two aloof and cagey deliberators. Wilson and Hughes were men who waited for events to happen and then reacted. They lacked his ability to see events coming and act accordingly, faster than anyone else on the political scene. Since Belgium, he had known in his bones that the United States must go to war, as he had known the same after the *Maine* blew up in '98. Now he could only wait until whichever nominee faced up to telling the American people this disagreeable fact.

"Theodore," Corinne Robinson said, bursting in on him as he sat brooding in his library, "the people wanted you." She had attended both conventions in Chicago.

He smiled at her. "If they had wanted me *hard* enough, they could have had me."

With other family and friends he affected his usual good humor, and joked that the country obviously "wasn't in a heroic mood." Wheezing with a sudden attack of dry pleurisy (which he blamed on the bullet in his chest), he admitted, in an off-the-record interview with John J. Leary, that he was deeply disappointed. To the newspaperman's surprise, he quoted the prophet Micah— *What doth the Lord require of thee, but to do justly, and to love mercy, and to walk humbly with thy God*—taking apparent comfort in the kind of biblical text William Jennings Bryan was always spouting.

His secretary interrupted to ask if he wanted to comment on a news flash that the President had called out the National Guard to help secure the Mexican border.

"No," Roosevelt said. Then, with a click of teeth: "Let Hughes talk—it's his fight."

There were spasms of anger in subsequent days, along with coughing fits so violent he pulled some tendons. Pride in Kermit, who had come north from Argentina with Belle to present Kermit Roosevelt, Jr., age five months, for inspection, and in Ted, Archie, and Quentin, re-registered at Plattsburg, prompted him to rage at the offspring of some of his friends. "If they were mine I'd want to choke them—pretty boys who know all the latest tango steps and the small talk, and the latest things in socks and ties—tame cats, mollycoddles."

At such times, only Edith Roosevelt could hush him. "Now, Theodore. That is just one of those remarks that make it so difficult sometimes for your friends to defend you."

"Why, *Edie*!"

CHAPTER 24

Shadows of Lofty Words

Far journeys and hard wandering
Await him in whose crude surmise
Peace, like a mask, hides everything
That is and has been from his eyes.

AS A BOY, ROOSEVELT USED TO PLAY a running game with his siblings and friends, called "stagecoach." It involved bursts of motion, interrupted by imaginary collisions that caused all passengers aboard to fly off in various directions.

In recent years, he had suffered similar feelings of acceleration and ejection, often enough to wonder if the game had not been a forecast of his future. He lay now amid the dust of yet another political crash, feeling no particular desire to get back on the road. Reading *The Man Against the Sky* had revived his interest in poets and poetry. "A poet," he liked to say, "can do much more for his country than the proprietor of a nail factory." He devoured *Spoon River Anthology* and invited Edgar Lee Masters to visit him at Sagamore Hill. Hearing that the nature bards Bliss Carman and Madison Cawein were in financial straits, he quietly raised funds for them.

His taste in verse was unpredictable. One of Robert Frost's bitterest poems, "A Servant to Servants," with its central image of a caged, naked psychotic, spoke to him more than the popular lyrics in *North of Boston*. He astonished the poet by reciting some lines from it at a meeting of the Poetry Society of America. What may have appealed to him was the dogged voice of the first-person narrator, a caretaker resigned to unending, thankless responsibilities: *By good rights I ought not to have so much / Put on me, but there seems no other way.*

In that spirit, Roosevelt heard himself promising once again to take part in an election campaign, although this time he so disliked the ticket (vitiated by

Senator Fairbanks in the number two spot) that he resented being asked. It was bad enough having to endorse Charles Evans Hughes, who had never shown any gratitude for his help in 1910, and who had developed a severe attack of amnesia when asked to testify for the defense in *Barnes v. Roosevelt*.

However, the prospect of four more years of Woodrow Wilson was so unthinkable that Roosevelt felt he should do whatever was necessary to put Hughes in the White House. On 26 June 1916, he announced his support for Hughes, and dined with the candidate a couple of days later. He agreed to kick off the Republican campaign with a major address in Lewiston, Maine, at the end of August, and to follow up with four or five shorter speeches at spaced intervals, on the understanding that Hughes would back him up on preparedness and a strong policy toward Mexico. More than that Roosevelt declined to do, on the unarguable ground that his forceful personality would make the candidate seem weak. Privately, he referred to Hughes as "the Bearded Lady."

Strength would appear to be required in Mexico, since General Carranza, the *de facto* ruler of that country, was objecting to Pershing's pursuit of Pancho Villa, and as a sign of displeasure, had just killed fourteen American soldiers. He had also taken twenty-three prisoners. Clearly Pershing was going to need massive reinforcements. Roosevelt donned the imaginary uniform of a major general and cast about for recruiters. "I don't believe this administration can be kicked into war, for Wilson seems about as much a milksop as Bryan," he wrote Seth Bullock. "But there is, of course, the chance that he may be forced to fight. If so, are you too old to raise a squadron of cavalry in South Dakota?"

He was concerned that Kermit, who was in New York pending reassignment to another foreign branch of National City Bank, was the only one of his sons who had not had the benefit of military training at Plattsburg in 1915. General Wood was running a similar camp this summer, and the other boys were already registered for it. Kermit could try to catch up with them by joining the "TBM" program in July.

Roosevelt underestimated the President's willingness to go to war in Mexico. "The break seems to have come," Wilson privately concluded. But before he and his new secretary of war, Newton D. Baker, could agree on a plan of action, Carranza released the prisoners and offered to negotiate terms that would permit Pershing to continue operations.

❧

COINCIDENTALLY, AN ENGLISH infantryman going into battle on the Somme on the first day of July used Wilson's phrase, *the break,* to describe his feeling, as twenty-one thousand men fell dead around him, that what was left of the pre-war world and its values had finally split and fallen apart. Memory was not erased so much as made irrelevant, in the face of Maxim-gun fire that drilled efficiently through line after line of uniforms. Even at Verdun (where French and German soldiers were now reduced to hand-to-hand combat in caves) there had never been such butchery as this.

⌒

CARRANZA'S PEACE GESTURE did not slow Roosevelt's drive to raise a volunteer division. When the War Department heard about it, Secretary Baker was more amused than angry. On 6 July, having received an encouraging flood of applications, the Colonel formally requested authority to proceed with recruitment. His letter to Baker was less boastful and more detailed than the one he had sent President Taft at the time of the first Mexican troubles, and he dropped none of the distinguished names, military and civilian, he had already settled on for command posts. The influence of his younger son was detectable in a proposal to create "one motor-cycle regiment with machine guns . . . an engineering regiment, [and] an aviation squadron."

Baker referred his letter to the adjutant general of the army, who replied, much as Taft had done, that "in the event of war with Mexico," the administration would consider his offer.

Roosevelt, fretful and still coughing with dry pleurisy, had said nothing about wanting to fight anywhere else in the world. But his current reading included the military memoirs of Baron Grivel in French. He also wrote an article for *Collier's Weekly* entitled "Lafayettes of the Air: Young Americans Who Are Flying for France."

⌒

ON 4 AUGUST, Miss Flora Whitney, the nineteen-year-old daughter of the owner of *Metropolitan* magazine, came out in Newport. In local parlance, she was the "first bud" of the debutante season. Five hundred guests danced fox-trots in the blue-and-gold ballroom of the Whitney mansion on Bellevue Avenue, and Flora, slender as a calla lily in a white dress with silver trim, twirled in the arms of her dinner partner, Mr. Quentin Roosevelt of Oyster Bay. They danced all night, then took a sunrise dip in the sea.

Quentin was on a pass from Plattsburg, and in no hurry to return. He admitted, even to his father, that he did not enjoy himself there. Ted loved it. So did Archie, who had just graduated from Harvard. Kermit was at least no gloomier there than anywhere else. Quentin found camp life a bore. He was not lazy, nor did he lack courage. But parade-ground drill bothered his back, agonizingly sometimes. His ironic sense of humor, unshared by any of his siblings except Alice, made it difficult for him to take military life seriously.

He was the same age as Flora—or would be in the fall—and he shared her eager appetite for fun. There was plenty of that available at Newport, and on the other Whitney estates in upstate New York, South Carolina, and Old Westbury, Long Island. Slick-haired, fast-driving boys like himself zoomed in on these places, their autos crammed with girls daringly dressed in the latest modes from Paris—none more daring than Flora, who was *arty*, if not a

"FLORA DREAMED OF BEING A DESIGNER ONE DAY."

Flora Payne Whitney.

teensy bit affected, in her love of "modern" jewelry and fabrics that only she could mix and carry off. She smoked straw-tipped Benson & Hedges cigarettes, which she kept in a red-beaded case. Her spiffy Scripps-Booth torpedo roadster had wire wheels and a silver radiator shell. Since her mother was the famous sculptor Gertrude Vanderbilt Whitney, a hint of *la bohème* was to be expected of her. Flora dreamed of being a designer one day. Her small chiseled face was more unusual than pretty, with long-lashed hazel eyes and gull's-wing brows that made her look fiercer than she was.

Quentin had been friendly with her for almost a year. Before going up to Harvard, he had gotten into the habit of driving out to Westbury and enjoying the society of people more entertaining than the dour Brahmins forever visiting his parents. He was not the only Roosevelt attracted to Flora. Archie had briefly paid court, and although he was a handsome youth, blond and skinny as a whippet, she had made clear her preference for his younger brother. So far, Quentin had no stronger feelings for her than affection and a mutual interest in poetry. This was just as well, from the point of view of Flora's parents: he was just the sort of name-but-no-money college boy they wanted to protect her from. Now that she was "introduced to society," there would be many scions of the Four Hundred seeking to add a Whitney to their portfolios.

Nevertheless, Quentin's claims on her—should he choose to exercise them—could not be discounted. He was the son of a former President of the United States. He had his father's charm, but none of the obsessive need to cajole and convert that was making the Colonel so difficult to take these days. Growing up in the White House had given Quentin a sense of self-worth that had little in it of vanity. He did not need to work at impressing people, being used to their deference. At Harvard he had fitted right in with the best sort. "You get a speaking acquaintance with a lot of others," he reported to Kermit, "but you don't know them any more than the little Yids I sit next to in class."

Flora could have found someone better looking to squire her on the night she "came out." With his lofty forehead, Rooseveltian teeth, and furrowed brows, Quentin was not likely to improve with age. But he was tall and powerfully built and to her, adorable.

⸺✢⸺

ROOSEVELT'S ARTICLE ABOUT American volunteer pilots in France ("We are all of us indebted to these young men of generous soul . . . proudly willing to die for their convictions") reflected a growing popular awareness that war was no longer constrained by gravity. One "aeroplane" dispatched across no-man's-land with a camera could survey more battleground in half an hour than a reconnaissance patrol in a month. For days before the German attack on Verdun, the French had been alerted to its imminence by a steady droning east of the Meuse.

Secretary Baker was pleased to confirm in mid-August that Congress had voted $13 million toward the reorganization and equipping of an army air arm. Aspiring fliers thrilled to the size of this appropriation, building as it did on passage of an ambitious National Defense Act. Now patriotic young men unattracted to ground or naval warfare could, if they wanted in any future emergency, serve their country in the skies. *Quelle gloire!*

Quentin dutifully completed his course at Plattsburg, then spent as many late-summer days as he could with Flora. He had to cram for his next semester at Harvard, having determined to pass through university in three years and then add two more at the Massachusetts Institute of Technology. He told Kermit he would like to be a mechanical engineer.

ON 31 AUGUST, ROOSEVELT inaugurated the Republican fall campaign as promised, with a major policy statement in Lewiston, Maine. Absentmindedly, he referred to it as "my *Lusitania* speech." The verbal slip was telling. Instead of musing how he could best help Hughes as a candidate, he was still brooding over an act of war that had found Woodrow Wilson wanting fifteen months before. His speech—an unfavorable comparison of the President to Pontius Pilate—was roaringly received, and reached millions of newspaper readers in transcript. It buttressed his new image as an elder statesman of the GOP, but disturbed many undecided voters who felt that he was too pugnacious a campaigner for Hughes's good. "Roosevelt would be a really great man," the naturalist John Burroughs wrote in his journal, "if he could be shorn of that lock of his hair in which that strong dash of the bully resides."

Two days later, the President effortlessly reclaimed national attention by appearing on the porch of "Shadow Lawn," his summer cottage at Long Branch, New Jersey, and thanking a delegation of Democratic officials for renominating him to another term. Slim and laughing, natty in white slacks and a dark blazer, he looked almost young, the happiness of his remarriage radiating from him. It was difficult for reporters who had covered the Colonel in recent months to believe that Wilson, soon to be sixty, was the older man.

There was much for him to be happy about. He had just negotiated an end to a threatened railroad strike that would have paralyzed the country and damaged his candidacy. In doing so he had openly sided with labor against capital, and persuaded Congress to reduce the daily hours worked by rail union members from ten to six, with no loss of pay. The public rejoiced, and Roosevelt fumed. He wanted to boast about the time *he* had settled the great anthracite strike of 1902, *without* partiality, but thought it would hurt Hughes if he carped against a piece of progressive legislation.

The United States was prospering, with exporters reaping huge profits from war-related sales. Americans dismissed the President's unpopularity abroad, seeing him as a patient but firm negotiator who—as his propagandists were forever trumpeting—"kept us out of war." It even redounded to Wilson's advantage that he no longer showed any partiality toward Great Britain. That country's cruel crackdown on Irish unrest, and its continuing harassment of Europe-bound merchant ships, had created widespread voter anger.

Canadian air signaled the end of summer. Yachts returned to their docks. Maids stripped the linen covers from parlor furniture. Department stores stocked up with black velvet caps and the new zebra boa. Charlie Chaplin's new movie *The Count* opened on Broadway. Quentin Roosevelt returned to college, beset by memories of Flora in an orange bathing suit, and realized that he had fallen in love with her.

⌒

THE CAMPAIGNS OF THE two parties cranked up. Roosevelt fretted over Hughes's dryasdust speaking style, and in a letter to the candidate, repeated the advice he had given Henry Stimson in 1910: "What the average voter wants is not an etching, but a poster, a statement so broad and clear and in such simple language that he can thoroughly understand it." Hughes took the advice of an old pro with good grace. In return, he politely asked Roosevelt to stay off the subject of hyphenated minorities through the election, and the Colonel just as politely agreed. Then they went their separate rhetorical ways.

Wilson chose to follow the tradition that a sitting president should not stump for himself. He remained at Shadow Lawn while Democratic orators itemized his record of progressivism, preparedness, and peace. Hughes was uncertain how to attack him on these issues without seeming reactionary in one direction and warlike in the other. Party wags suggested that the former justice had moved "from the bench to the fence."

For the sake of solidarity, Roosevelt agreed to do the RNC a favor on 3 October, and shake hands with William Howard Taft at a reception for Hughes in the Union League Club. "It was one of those friendly affairs," he said afterward, "where each side, before entering the meeting place, made sure its hardware was in good working order." The clasp between the two former presidents was brief and virtually wordless. For the rest of the evening, GOP stalwarts kept them apart, as if afraid that Roosevelt might use his right fist for some other purpose. Hughes complained in mock chagrin, "I was only the side show."

Four days later, the Woodrow Wilson College Men's League, consisting of 2,500 bright young progressives and independents, paid court to the President at Shadow Lawn. Wilson saw an opportunity to mock the Republican Party for fielding a surrogate candidate. Without naming Roosevelt directly, he won cheers when he observed that there was only one oracle in the GOP—"a very articulate voice [that] professes opinions and purposes at which the rest in private shiver and demur." It was a voice for war not peace, "shot through with

every form of bitterness, every ugly form of hate, every debased purpose of revenge . . . discontented and insurgent."

⤥

AS HE SPOKE, residents of Newport boggled at the insurgence offshore of
a sea-green, 213-foot German submarine. It cruised into the inner harbor,
where thirty-seven warships of the U.S. North Atlantic squadron lay at anchor, and docked as coolly as if it had been a yacht putting in for tea at the
Casino. The captain emerged, a neat bearded figure with an Iron Cross on his
breast, and said something to the crowd clustering the waterfront. Miss Margaret Fahnestock, a fellow debutante of Flora's, translated for him. He identified himself as Lieutenant Hans Rose, and produced a letter for the German
ambassador in Washington, Count Bernstorff. An Associated Press reporter,
hardly able to believe the dimensions of his scoop, undertook to mail it.
Somebody asked if the submarine was in need of supplies.

"We require nothing, thank you," Rose said. He added, smiling, that he
and his crew of thirty-three had been at sea for seventeen days. They had more
than enough food and fuel to get home to Wilhelmshaven. "Maybe soon,
maybe never!" Anyone who wanted was welcome to tour his vessel, the U-53.

Men, women, and children took turns clambering down its stairwell and
found the interior spotless and comfortable. Six torpedoes were clearly visible. "A constant comment of those permitted on board," the AP man noted,

"RESIDENTS OF NEWPORT BOGGLED AT . . .
A SEA-GREEN, 213-FOOT GERMAN SUBMARINE."
The U-53 pays a visit to America, 7 October 1916.

"was on the thorough preparedness which the vessel seemed to exhibit despite her many days at sea." One of Newport's hyphenated citizens presented an officer with an Irish Republican flag. This elicited some more Prussian humor.

"The first British ship we sink," the officer promised; "we will hoist this flag in honor of Ireland."

People ashore observed that the new banner was already flying when, at 5:17 P.M., the U-53 set off again. A flotilla of pleasure craft followed it out of the harbor, but as it approached Fort Adams it settled low as an alligator and began to accelerate. The small boats hove to, rocking in its wash. It remained in sight until darkness fell, then its lights doused and it slid underwater, leaving behind nothing but a trail of moonlit foam.

Early the next morning, Sunday, SOS signals from the sea lane off Nantucket began to bombard radio receivers at Newport Naval Station. Six eastbound ships loaded with contraband had been sunk by the U-53, including a British liner carrying a large number of American citizens. All had been permitted to lower lifeboats before they were struck. Eighteen children were among the many in need of rescue.

Rear Admiral Albert Greaves, commander of the U.S. Atlantic fleet, dispatched all his available warships. Throughout the day, a crescendo of crackling in the radio office heralded the approach of Royal Navy destroyers looking for the U-53. But it was nowhere to be found. By nightfall, two hundred refugees had been brought to Newport, and were being luxuriously comforted by Beeckmans and Vanderbilts.

President Wilson remained noncommittal at Shadow Lawn, saying that he had no "official" knowledge of the sinkings. On Monday afternoon he issued a statement: "The country may rest assured that the German government will be held to the complete fulfillment of its promises to the government of the United States."

Roosevelt followed up with a statement of his own. He sounded more sick at heart than outraged in affirming, "Now the war has been carried to our very shores." The administration's dismissive attitude to seaborne terrorism, going back to the *Lusitania,* had made it inevitable that something like this would happen. "President Wilson's ignoble shirking of responsibility has been clothed in an utterly misleading phrase, the phrase of a coward, *He kept us out of war.* In actual reality, war has been creeping nearer and nearer, until it stares at us from just beyond our three-mile limit, and we face it without policy, plan, purpose or preparation."

⏤

THE COLONEL'S PROMISED "swing" for Hughes—a high-speed tour of the West and Southwest—was marked by tumultuous, sometimes hysterical receptions. They left him unmoved. On his way back through Indiana, he turned fifty-eight. George Perkins and Henry L. Stoddard drove him back to Oyster Bay, raw-voiced and spent, in the small hours of 29 October.

"Old trumps," he said as the car wound its way through Long Island fog, "let me tell you. . . . I've done my bit for Hughes. . . . I am positively through campaigning forever."

"LET ME TELL YOU. . . . I'VE DONE MY BIT FOR HUGHES."
TR on the campaign trail, fall 1916.

Yet he stayed at home only long enough to hear, two days later, that a pair of British steamers, the *Marina* and the *Rowanmore,* had been torpedoed in the Atlantic, with eight American travelers lost between them. The administration could argue—in fact, was arguing—that the U-53 had previously not broken international law in its sinkings off Nantucket. This double attack, however, proved that Germany had decided to ignore Wilson's *Sussex* ultimatum of five months before.

The first of November found Roosevelt on a flying trip through Ohio. He felt he had to compensate for Hughes, who kept maundering about the tariff in order to avoid saying anything that might alienate antiwar voters. John Leary became concerned at Roosevelt's red-faced fervor and told him that some reporters were saying he had arteriosclerosis.

"Just what is that?"

Leary explained.

"Well, they are right."

His blood pressure was not reduced by an announcement that eleven of the nineteen Progressives who had helped him formulate his policies in 1912 were going to vote Democratic. On 2 November, Amos Pinchot publicly taunted him with an assertion that the Bull Moose platform had been "out-and-out pacifist."

The Colonel contained himself for twenty-four hours, then wrote Pinchot, "Sir, when I spoke of the Progressive Party as having a lunatic fringe, I specifically had you in mind."

That night he appeared at Cooper Union in New York. He was greeted with a whistling, stomping chorus of "We want Teddy!" that went on for ten minutes. There was not a single cry for Hughes.

A sense spread through the audience that Roosevelt was going to let rip, as he had when he jumped onto a table in Atlanta in 1912. But nothing he had said then, or since, compared with the attack on Woodrow Wilson that now rasped into every corner of the hall.

> During the last three years and a half, hundreds of American men, women, and children have been murdered on the high seas and in Mexico. Mr. Wilson has not dared to stand up for them. . . . He wrote Germany that he would hold her to "strict accountability" if an American lost his life on an American or neutral ship by her submarine warfare. Forthwith the *Arabic* and the *Gulflight* were sunk. But Mr. Wilson dared not take any action. . . . Germany despised him; and the *Lusitania* was sunk in consequence. Thirteen hundred and ninety-four people were drowned, one hundred and three of them babies under two years of age. Two days later, when the dead mothers with their dead babies in their arms lay by the scores in the Queenstown morgue, Mr. Wilson selected the moment as opportune to utter his famous sentence about being "too proud to fight."

Roosevelt threw his speech script to the floor and continued in near-absolute silence.

> Mr. Wilson now dwells at Shadow Lawn. There should be shadows enough at Shadow Lawn: the shadows of men, women, and children

who have risen from the ooze of the ocean bottom and from graves in foreign lands; the shadows of the helpless whom Mr. Wilson did not dare protect lest he might have to face danger; the shadows of babies gasping pitifully as they sank under the waves; the shadows of women outraged and slain by bandits; the shadows of . . . troopers who lay in the Mexican desert, the black blood crusted round their mouths, and their dim eyes looking upward, because President Wilson had sent them to do a task, and then shamefully abandoned them to the mercy of foes who knew no mercy.

Those are the shadows proper for Shadow Lawn: the shadows of deeds that were never done; the shadows of lofty words that were followed by no action; the shadows of the tortured dead.

❧

ON THE FOLLOWING NIGHT, with thirty-six hours to go before the election, Roosevelt slumped in the back of Regis Post's car, humming to himself. They were returning from a Republican rally in Connecticut.

"The old man's working out something," Post said to John Leary, who sat up front. "He always thinks hardest when he makes that queer noise. I wonder what's up?"

What was up was a drift of voter sympathy toward Wilson that Roosevelt feared would erode the last of Charles Evans Hughes's support. Leary had already, with a young man's optimism, predicted that a defeat for Hughes would bode well for Roosevelt in 1920.

"You are wrong there," the Colonel said. "This was my year—1916 was my high twelve. In four years I will be out of it."

❧

HUGHES MANAGED, all the same, to attract enough votes on 7 November that *The New York Times* called the election for him. Wilson took the news with a grace that said much for his inner equilibrium. But then returns from late-counting states showed that Republicans and former Progressives had deserted Hughes in the Midwest, canceling out his early gains elsewhere. The great bulk of those desertions could be ascribed to Roosevelt's warlike rhetoric, which had made Hughes's candidacy seem more pro-intervention than it actually was. In the end, after two days of statistical swings, the normally Republican state of California reelected Wilson by a margin of only 3,773 votes. Hughes was so angry in defeat that he did not concede until 22 November.

"I hope you are ashamed of Mr. Roosevelt," Alice Hooper wrote Frederick Jackson Turner. "If one man was responsible for Mr. Wilson he was the man—thus perhaps Mr. Roosevelt ought to see the Shadows of Shadow Lawn and the dead babies in the ooze of the Sea!"

At Sagamore Hill, Roosevelt began to pack up his papers for deposit in the Library of Congress. Hamlin Garland came to visit and found him cheerful, clomping around in spurred boots, but grayer and more slowly spoken than before.

"I am of no use, Garland. I feel my years."

⌘

IN A SERIES OF quick coincidences that seemed like coordination, Wilson's election was followed by leadership changes in four of the belligerent powers. All portended a protraction of the war and a worsening of the fighting. Emperor Franz Joseph died, and was succeeded by his great-nephew Karl, an impulsive young man convinced that the Habsburg monarchy was eternal. Two new, aggressive prime ministers came to power: Alexander Trepov in Russia and David Lloyd George in Britain. At the Wilhelmstrasse, an even more aggressive commoner, Arthur Zimmermann, replaced Count Jagow as secretary of state for foreign affairs.

On 12 December, Count Bernstorff visited the White House with a surprise proposal from Chancellor Bethmann-Hollweg. The German ambassador had never revealed what was in the letter Captain Rose had handed over in Newport, except to dismiss it as "unimportant." It had certainly not advised him that Germany was about to moderate its war at sea. Since then, Britain and France had been losing shipments at the rate of sixty thousand tons a month. Sir Edward Grey wrote a panicky envoi to Arthur Balfour, his successor as foreign minister: "The submarine danger seems to me to be increasing so rapidly that unless in the next two months or so we abate it, the Germans will see their way to victory."

The document Bernstorff now gave to the President, copied to all the Allied powers, expressed Germany's "willingness to enter henceforth into peace negotiations." But its language—probably Zimmermann's—was so truculent, warning of "further bloodshed" if it was rejected, that Wilson read it in disbelief.

He was put out because the proposal, already making headlines around the world, preempted one he had been secretly working on himself. Cecil Spring Rice had suspected for some time that Wilson was up to something. "The President's great ambition," the ambassador informed Balfour on 15 December, "is to play a high and moral part on a great stage."

Four days later, Wilson cabled his own peace note to the belligerents, calling on them to make "an avowal of their respective views as to the terms upon which the war might be concluded." He pointed out that none of the fourteen powers now variously at war had ever said, in precise words, what they wanted of one another. Precision was necessary, because to him their general objectives seemed to be "virtually the same." He offered to serve as the facilitator of a conference that would result in "a league of nations to ensure peace and justice throughout the world."

Wilson had touched on this idea before, in his address to the League to Enforce Peace, but now he zealously promulgated it to the world. "If the contest must continue to proceed toward undefined ends by slow attrition until the one group of belligerents or the other is exhausted; if million after million of human lives must continue to be offered up . . . hopes of peace and of the willing concert of free peoples will be rendered vain and idle."

Secretary Lansing felt obliged to offer an extraordinary public qualification: "The sending of this note will indicate the possibility of our being forced into the war." He was reprimanded by Wilson and tried to withdraw his words, but the effect of them remained.

Roosevelt, massively attired as Santa Claus for the Cove School Christmas party at Oyster Bay, guffawed. "The antics of the last few days have restored what self-respect I lost in supporting Hughes."

<hr />

PLAYING ALONG WITH WILSON, Germany replied more favorably than Britain or France to the notion of a peace conference. The Allies published a joint note on 11 January 1917 that took exception to the President's remark about the similarity of the aims of the warring powers. They declined to specify all their settlement demands in advance of any negotiations, but provided a sample list so unacceptable to Germany (including liberation of the Slavs, and expulsion of the Turks from Europe) that Wilson saw that the time had come for him to exert rhetorical force, rather than mere argument, in separating nations bent on self-destruction.

Sneer as Roosevelt might about his preference for "elocution" over acts, a close reading of the President's policy statements to date indicated a steadily increasing willingness to go to war in defense of democracy. Amid the camouflage of elegant circumlocutions, certain phrases glinted like gunmetal: *thrust out into the great game of mankind. . . . America will unite her force and spill her blood. . . . The business of neutrality is over. . . .* Even his campaign slogan, *He kept us out of war,* had always been carefully phrased in the past tense.

Wilson saw, now, the paradox that every belligerent was desperate for peace, yet determined to win without concession. The apocalyptic battles of Verdun and the Somme had only just come to an end, with no clear victor. Germany was malnourished by the blockade, yet energized industrially by its conquest of oil-rich Romania (the Kaiser's new chief of staff, Field Marshal Paul von Hindenburg, had tripled artillery and machine-gun production). Britain had lost ninety-six thousand men in the Somme alone, while developing a formidable new weapon, the tank. France was nearly prostrate, although triumphant that Verdun had not fallen. Russia was crippled by strikes and impoverished by the influx of three and a half million refugees, while the Tsar looked for protection to an army almost stripped of arms.

On 22 January, Wilson made one of his sudden appearances before Congress. He said he was speaking "for the great silent mass of mankind" in calling for "a peace without victory" in Europe. Victory achieved at the cost of more Verduns, and worse, "would mean peace forced upon the loser . . . at an intolerable sacrifice, and would leave a sting, a resentment, a bitter memory upon which terms of peace would rest, not permanently, but only as upon quicksand."

It was inconceivable, he said, that the United States should not try to bring about some concord stronger and more liberal than this. He spelled out the essentials of the agreement he had in mind—freedom of the seas; general disarmament; self-determination for all nations (including "a united and autonomous Poland"); and common membership, after the war's end, in a league of nations "which will make it virtually impossible that any such catastrophe would ever overwhelm us again."

Congress heard the word *us,* and gave him only moderate applause.

⌒

GERMANY'S RESPONSE, on the last day of the month, was to announce an immediate resumption of all-out submarine warfare.

Count Bernstorff wept after he delivered this advisory to Lansing. The President's first reaction, as he read it, was incredulity. If he could believe his eyes, the German foreign minister was offering him a special concession. One American passenger liner a week would be permitted to sail to Falmouth, England, provided it was painted with vertical white-and-red stripes, followed a specific course via the Scilly Isles, arrived on Sunday, and departed on Wednesday. With Prussian exactitude, Herr Zimmermann begged to state that the stripes were to be "one meter wide." Any deviation from these requirements would result in the liner being sunk on sight.

Colonel House visited the White House the next morning and found Wilson in near despair, saying he felt "as if the world had suddenly reversed itself."

House knew what Roosevelt was psychologically barred from believing: that Wilson *the man* had wanted to go to war with Germany for almost a year and a half. However, Wilson the politician was constrained by the enormity of such a step, involving as it would a regearing of the entire economy of the United States—and requiring a degree of popular support unimaginable even now. Germany's insolent note was not just a provocation. It was a *casus belli,* like the list of demands Austria-Hungary had sent Serbia after the assassination of Franz Ferdinand. Both instruments were phrased in such a way as to be unacceptable. Unless he was truly the "coward" Roosevelt kept calling him, Wilson had no choice now but to sever diplomatic relations with Germany, and then, if the Reich sent one more torpedo into any American ship, ask Congress for a declaration of war.

Captain Rose of the U-53 obliged on 3 February by sinking the USS *Housatonic* off the Scillies. At 2 P.M. Count Bernstorff was handed his passports. Wilson went back to Capitol Hill to announce that he had instructed Secretary Lansing to recall Ambassador Gerard from Berlin. He did not mention the attack on the *Housatonic,* details of which were still coming through to the State Department. But he did significantly say: "If American ships and American lives should in fact be sacrificed . . . I shall take the liberty of coming again before the Congress to ask that authority be given to me to use *any means that may be necessary* for the protection of our seamen and our people . . . on the high seas."

Even as Wilson's threat was being released to the press, an awareness that war was coming provoked various acts of vandalism along the Eastern seaboard. The water cocks of an American submarine in Philadelphia were opened in an effort to scuttle her. The crew of an Austrian freighter interned in New York harbor wrecked their own engine room. The *Kronzprinzessin Cecilie* was disabled in Boston by direct order of the German government.

Overnight, the youngest and least prepossessing member of Wilson's cabinet became the second most powerful man in Washington. Secretary of War Newton Diehl Baker was short, pale, bookish, and bespectacled, a lawyer whose only previous distinction was a spell as mayor of Cleveland. He was also—ludicrously, in view of his title—a pacifist who had spoken out against militarism within days of the attack on the *Lusitania*.

Here he was now, deciding as one of his first emergency responsibilities what to do about a letter from a former President of the United States. Roosevelt had not bothered to wait for Wilson's speech before sending it:

Sir:

I have already on file in your Department, my application to be permitted to raise a Division of Infantry, with a divisional brigade of cavalry in the event of war. . . . In view of the recent German note, and of the fact that my wife and I are booked to sail next week for a month in Jamaica, I respectfully write as follows.

If you believe that there will be war, and a call for volunteers to go to war, immediately, I respectfully and earnestly request that you notify me at once, so that I may not sail.

Baker's reply was dismissive. "No situation has arisen which would justify my suggesting a postponement of the trip you propose." He wrote too late to block another letter from the Colonel, scribbled in extreme haste: "In view of the breaking of relations with Germany I shall of course not go to Jamaica, and will hold myself in readiness for any message from you as to the division. I and my four sons will of course go if volunteers are called for against Germany."

"SHORT, PALE, BOOKISH, AND BESPECTACLED."

Secretary of War Newton D. Baker.

The secretary could see further correspondence looming. In peacetime, his job was one of the laziest sinecures in Washington, involving little more than supervision of a small army spread out thin as pepper grains across the table-cloth of the country. But he had never doubted that should the United States ever mobilize, he would be transformed into a converter of energies sweeping back and forth between Congress and the armed services, the press and secret agencies, commission seekers and their backers, contractors and quartermasters, and dozens of other conduits that were bound to multiply for as long as the war lasted. Over the past eleven months, Baker had prepared himself for such an emergency in ways slightly comic—practicing, for example, a one-stroke zigzag signature. But his main asset was a brain that saw most clearly under stress.

Among his urgent priorities was the securing of all foreign ships held in

American harbors from further acts of sabotage, and rapid action to prevent the Panama Canal from being blocked at either end. He had also to prepare for a possible order from Congress to raise, train, and equip a million-man army, by whatever means Wilson thought best. That order might never come: a group of isolationists in the Senate, led by Robert La Follette, was already ganging up in opposition to it. But whatever happened, Baker was determined not to send Theodore Roosevelt into battle.

Ironically, on 5 February he had to slash his zigzag beneath the commission of Theodore Roosevelt, Jr., as a major of infantry in the Officers' Reserve Corps. The President countersigned.

⌐⊂⊃⌐

SIR CECIL SPRING RICE sent Arthur Balfour a cogent explanation as to why Wilson would have to resort to a draft to get a million men into uniform. "It is not immediately evident to an American citizen of German descent resident in Omaha, Nebraska, that he should shed his German blood because an American negro from New Orleans has been drowned on a British ship, carrying munitions to France."

The ambassador did, all the same, see signs of domestic bellicosity spreading as U-boats continued to destroy neutral ships. A majority of the President's cabinet now favored intervention. Wilson went back before Congress on the twenty-seventh to ask for authority to arm American merchantmen. He emphasized that he was not "proposing or contemplating war." However, a great nation had a right and a duty to defend itself. The House Democratic leadership introduced a bill appropriating $1,000,000,000 for the purpose. As a result, the word *billion* began to creep into everyday speech, along with a new Wilsonism, *armed neutrality*.

Nothing in the President's stately demeanor that day betrayed the fact that he was in possession of intelligence so explosive as to remove all doubt that he would soon be forced to ask for a declaration of war. British cryptographers had provided him with the decoded text of an incendiary telegram from Arthur Zimmermann to the German minister in Mexico. Wilson was waiting for a State Department retranslation of the decode, but some of the original, operative words leaped out bold and clear:

U BOOT KRIEG ZU BEGINNEN . . . AMERIKA . . . NEUTRAL . . .
SCHLAGEN WIR MEXICO. . . . KRIEGFÜHRUNG . . .
FINANZIELLE . . . MEXICO IN TEXAS . . . NEU-MEXICO . . .
ARIZONA . . . JAPAN . . .

U-boat warfare had begun. Germany would try to keep America neutral. Contract an alliance with Mexico if unsuccessful. Declare joint war against the United States. Provide finances. Mexico could recover Texas, New Mexico, and Arizona. Japan might join in. . . .

On the face of it, the Zimmermann telegram looked delusional. Carranza was currently well-disposed toward the Wilson administration, and Japan was allied with Britain. However, if Britain collapsed (German submarines had sunk 536,000 deadweight tons of her shipping this month alone), who doubted that the Japanese would realign themselves?

Certainly not Theodore Roosevelt. He had never felt easy about "that polite, silent and inscrutable race of selfish and efficient fighting men." Zimmermann's plot jibed with the scenario he had tried to impress on President Taft in 1910 ("a war in which Mexico was backed by Japan or some other big powers"), and also with one he had sketched out in 1914, of Germany defeating Britain, then forming an alliance with Japan against the United States.

Wilson released the verified text of the telegram to the press overnight on 28 February. The sun rose next morning, Thursday, 1 March, on a nation shocked from its complacency. Everything the Colonel had been saying for two and a half years, at the cost of becoming a screechy-voiced scold, now sounded prophetic—as did the supporting chorus of his fellow interventionists. A new degree of neurosis attached to Texan memories of the Alamo, and to Californian dread of the Yellow Peril. Irish and German hyphenates clung to their sentimental notions of "home," but no longer flaunted them.

With only four days to go before the end of the Sixty-fourth Congress, events accelerated toward decisive action, if not—yet—a declaration of war. The House at once passed the Armed Ships bill. It would have cleared the Senate, but for a last-minute filibuster by Robert La Follette. Wilson issued a statement blaming him and ten other isolationist senators for thwarting popular desire: "A little group of willful men, representing no opinion but their own, have rendered the great government of the United States helpless and contemptible."

There was now as much of a sense of emergency on Capitol Hill as in the White House. Republicans and Democrats alike appealed to the President to summon a premature session of the Sixty-fifth Congress, which otherwise would not assemble until December.

On Monday, 5 March, the President drove in gusty rain to the Capitol to deliver his second inaugural address. He had been sworn in privately the day before. Thirty-two secret service agents guarded his carriage, and more than twice as many swordsmen of the Second Cavalry framed them in a nervously jiggling square. Pennsylvania Avenue was lined on both sides with National Guardsmen in olive drab, rifles at the ready. Many of them were bronzed from recent service in Mexico. The roofs of neighboring buildings bristled with sharpshooters. Machine gunners covered the crowd waiting in East Capitol Park.

"I beg your tolerance, your countenance, and your united aid," Wilson shouted into the wind. He gave no hint of when, or even whether, he would ask Americans to take up arms, but talked of "the shadows that now lie dark across our path," and prayed to God to give him "wisdom and prudence" in the days that lay ahead. Few spectators could hear what he was saying, but they were visually reassured by the long jaw jutting over the balustrade, the confident poise, and the statuesque proximity of Edith Wilson. Rolling cheers followed the presidential car all the way back downtown, along with impromptu choruses of "America."

⁂

ROOSEVELT, WHOSE FIRST reaction to the Zimmermann telegram had been to crumple his newspaper in rage, exulted to Kermit that "the lily-livered skunk in the White House" had at last begun to act like a man. He restrained himself from public commentary, not wanting to appear disloyal to the President at a time of crisis, or to jeopardize his dream of raising a volunteer division (or two, or three, or four) with Secretary Baker's approval.

Even now, Wilson seemed to hope that "armed neutrality" would be enough to keep the United States at peace. On 9 March, professedly bedridden with a cold, he summoned the new Congress. However, he postponed the date of its assembly to 16 April, six weeks off. That rendered Senator La Follette powerless in the interim to stop an executive order requiring all American freighters to arm themselves. For the next ten days the President remained out of sight, while his wife fronted for him.

In Russia, meanwhile, half-starved workers revolted against an imperial ban on organized demonstrations. The first news of food riots in Petrograd and Moscow reached Washington via Stockholm on 12 March. Vast crowds were reported to be on the rampage, roaring "Down with autocracy!" The Russian army, weakened by the loss of three and a half million men, was either unable or unwilling to restore order. Leon Trotsky, a Bolshevik exile living in New York, rejoiced that after twelve years of seismic buildup, the revolution of the proletariat was at last happening. Five days later *The Washington Post* confirmed that the Tsar had abdicated. A socialistic "provisional government" headed by Prince Lvov and dominated by the social democrat Aleksandr Kerensky was announced. "Unless improbable events occur," *The New York Times* reported, "Russia has today become a republic."

The news caused more satisfaction in the United States than in Britain and France. Both were in terror that Russia would now withdraw from the war and enable the Central Powers to turn all their firepower on the Western Front. This, plus the deaths of fifteen Americans in yet another "submarining" (the word had become a verb) put pressure on Wilson to summon Congress sooner.

On 20 March the President met with his cabinet and asked each member for advice. All were in favor of a prompt declaration of war against Germany, although Josephus Daniels, the secretary of the navy, cried as he committed himself. Newton D. Baker, all vestiges of past pacifism shed, argued for rapid rearmament with an earnestness that impressed Robert Lansing.

After the meeting, which Wilson closed without indicating his own feelings, Baker returned to the War Department to be confronted by a telegram from Roosevelt: IN VIEW OF THE FACT THAT GERMANY IS NOW ACTUALLY ENGAGED IN WAR WITH US I AGAIN EARNESTLY ASK PERMISSION TO BE ALLOWED TO RAISE A DIVISION FOR IMMEDIATE SERVICE AT THE FRONT.

Baker wrote back to say that no additional forces could be raised except by an act of the new Congress. When that body reassembled, the administration would present a plan "for a very much larger army than the force suggested in your telegram." He let Roosevelt know that there was unlikely to be a commission for him. "General officers for all the volunteer forces are to be drawn from the regular army."

The result was an impatient speech by the Colonel that night in the Union League Club of New York City. Entirely at home again among Republicans who, four years before, had shunned him, he joined Elihu Root, Charles Evans Hughes, and Joseph Choate in endorsing a resolution, "War now exists by act of Germany." He noted that more than two years had passed since the administration had demanded strict accountability for all U-boat attacks on American citizens. Germany was now killing more of them than ever, "and she has proposed to Japan and Mexico an alliance for our dismemberment as a nation."

It was irresponsible, he said, to wait another year for revenge, while the administration raised its million-man army. "We can perfectly well send an expeditionary force abroad to fight in the trenches now—" He corrected himself. "Within four or five months."

Closeted afterward with Root, Hughes, and Robert Bacon, he begged them to do everything they could to persuade the President to let him fight in Europe. Hughes was struck by Roosevelt's emotion as he said, "I shall not come back, my boys may not come back, my grandchildren may be left alone, but they will carry forward the family name. I must go."

WILSON RESPONDED TO his cabinet's consensus for war only by announcing that he would advance the forthcoming session of Congress by two weeks. He said he would then present lawmakers with "a communication concerning grave matters of national policy." In an almost perverse display of calm, he let state papers pile up while he relaxed with his wife, socialized, and shot pool.

Roosevelt, too, took time off before what he knew would be one of the most momentous addresses in American history. He told reporters that he was heading for Punta Gorda, Florida, to hunt shark and devilfish for the rest of the month. "I shall be back by April 2, when Congress assembles."

When he passed through Washington on his way south, the city was already flaming with flags.

Dust in a Windy Street

He may have stumbled up there from the past,
And with an aching strangeness viewed the last
Abysmal conflagration of his dreams,—
A flame where nothing seems
To burn but flame itself, by nothing fed;
And while it all went out
Not even the faint anodyne of doubt
May then have eased a painful going down
From pictured heights of power and lost renown.

HENRY ADAMS WAS JUST ABOUT to have dinner in Washington on the rainy evening of 2 April 1917 when he heard the hoofbeats of Woodrow Wilson's cavalcade departing the White House and heading for Capitol Hill. By the time the old historian had finished eating, newsboys in Lafayette Square were already yelling out the story of their "extry" editions: the President had asked Congress to declare war on Germany.

Theodore Roosevelt's slow train from Florida did not get into Union Station until noon the following day. By then he had read the full text of Wilson's address. Surrounded by a huge crowd outside the platform gates, he dictated a statement to reporters: "The President's message is a great state paper which will rank in history among the great state papers of which Americans in future years will be proud."

His tribute was awkwardly worded but heartfelt. All the rage he had nurtured against Wilson gave way to something like admiration. Yesterday's timid, selfish, cold-blooded sophist, the narrow and bitter partisan and debaucher of brains, had at last come to see things *his* way. Here, streaming across the front page of *The Washington Post* in double-width columns (juxtaposed with a dispatch that another U.S.-flagged steamer had been torpe-

doed, with eleven dead), was the oratory, impassioned yet rational, of a statesman whose mind was made up:

> With a profound sense of the solemn and even tragical nature of
> the step I am now taking and of the grave responsibilities which it in-
> volves, but in unhesitating obedience to what I deem my constitutional
> duty, I advise that the Congress declare the recent course of the imper-
> ial German government to be in fact nothing less than war against the
> government and people of the United States; that it formally accept the
> status of belligerency which has been thus thrust upon it, and that it
> take immediate steps not only to put the country in a more thorough
> state of defense, but also to exert all its power and employ all its re-
> sources to bring the government of the German Empire to terms and
> end the war.

Wilson noted that among the steps he was requesting Congress to authorize were the extension of liberal financial credit to the Allies, a powering-up
of American industrial resources, and an addition of at least half a million
men to the army by means of a universal draft, with equally large increments
to follow. "We have seen the last of neutrality," he said. The United States had
"no quarrel with the German people"—only with the autocratic oligarchy
that had sent them to war without consulting them. Autocracy could not be
allowed to pervert any postwar partnership of free nations. "The world must
be made safe for democracy."

Reportedly, this last line had not kindled the immediate ovation the President expected. But Senator John Sharp Williams, a Missouri Democrat who
had served in Congress since the days of Grover Cleveland, had recognized it
as the keynote of Wilson's future foreign policy: an active, and if necessary
forcible, imposition of American values upon "the world." Williams had
stood and applauded until his perception spread through both legislative bodies (the judiciary too, as represented by all nine members of the Supreme
Court) and an enormous roar had built and built.

If Roosevelt had not delayed his departure from Punta Gorda, in order to
harpoon the second largest devilfish ever measured, he could have gotten to
Washington in time to witness this triumph—so much greater than any he
had experienced as president. But he found himself, on the morning after, an
out-of-towner with no business to do in a city electric with urgency. The newsmen who greeted him vanished after taking his statement. They had other
leads to pursue. Congress was about to debate a war resolution, over Senator
La Follette's filibuster. Antiwar lobbyists were besieging the Capitol. Senator
Lodge, of all people, was reported to have knocked one pacifist down.

Alice Longworth was on hand to take her father to lunch. He had a few hours to kill between trains, so they went to congratulate Lodge on his pugilism. The "Brahmin Bruiser" was away from his office. Roosevelt decided to pay a call on Woodrow Wilson.

The White House was closed to visitors without appointment, as it had been since the spring of 1913. But when the guard at the northwest gate saw who was sitting with Alice in her big car, he automatically waved it through. The driveway that had been theirs for seven and a half years uncurled; the familiar portico loomed up; the glass doors to the vestibule swung open. Ike Hoover emerged from the usher's office. The time was a few minutes before three.

Roosevelt asked if he could see Wilson. Hoover regretted that the President was not at home: he had just gone to the West Wing for a cabinet meeting. Could the Colonel return later in the day? Roosevelt explained that he had no time, and left his card. He asked that Wilson be informed that he had come to congratulate him on "that remarkable state paper."

Alice drove him back to the station. Starved as ever for his company, she volunteered to ride with him as far as Baltimore. Before he climbed into the train after her, Roosevelt admitted to a stray reporter, "I don't know just what I'm going to do when I reach New York." He said the next few days in Congress were crucial to his plans. "I can't say anything more about organizing a division to go to the firing line until I find out something more about the policy of this government. I am sorry not to have seen the President."

TED AND KERMIT MET him in New York and drove him out to Oyster Bay, where Edith was brooding over a telephone call from Harvard. Quentin, her youngest and least martial son, was "coming down to get into the war." She had been unable to dissuade him on the grounds of his bad back and his poor eyesight. He said he intended to train as a fighter pilot.

Archie had an announcement too. He was engaged to Miss Grace Lockwood of Back Bay, Boston, and wanted to marry her as soon as possible, in order to be available for service the moment Congress answered Wilson's recruitment call.

Over the next few days, Sagamore Hill became something of a military personnel center as the Colonel prepared his four sons for postings. Frontline service in the new army was what they all wanted: none would sit behind a steel desk. Ted and Archie, with two terms at Plattsburg apiece, were sure of being commissioned as infantry officers. Quentin might have trouble passing the aviation section physical, but if so, he was willing to go north and see if the less fussy Canadians would take him.

Kermit remained—as ever—a man difficult to place. Aside from being only half trained, he was temperamentally unsuited to the static warfare in

Europe. His father understood that. They had the bond that came of killing lions and elephants together, and of enduring months of green hell in Brazil. The same fever lurked in their respective systems, and something of the same wanderlust. Kermit's war, Roosevelt felt, should be far-ranging, profiting from his restlessness and flair for languages. Perhaps the British could use him in Mesopotamia, where Sir Frederick Maude had just brilliantly captured Baghdad.

In the small hours of Good Friday, 6 April, the House of Representatives declared war on Germany, 373 to 50 (Miss Jeannette Rankin, the first woman in Congress, sobbing as she called "no"). Even Wilson was surprised at how rapidly the majority mood on Capitol Hill had changed from isolationism to intervention. At 1:11 P.M., he interrupted his lunch to sign the resolution, proclaiming: "A state of war between the United States and the Imperial German government, which has been thrust upon the United States, is hereby formally declared." Mobilization telegrams flashed to every army post in the country, and cables to all American ships at sea.

Roosevelt stayed home that Easter weekend, composing an editorial for *Metropolitan* magazine in praise of Wilson's change of heart. He did not apologize for the insults he had showered on the President in the past, saying only, "Of course, when war is on, all minor considerations, including all partisan considerations, vanish at once."

On Monday, 9 April, he decided to go south and call again at the White House. He did not telephone ahead and ask Wilson to receive him. "I'll take chances on his trying to snub me. He can't do it! I'd like to see him try it!"

Joseph Tumulty heard he was coming nevertheless. When, at eleven the following morning, Alice dropped her father off, the secretary was waiting, wreathed in smiles. Roosevelt disappeared into the Red Room and emerged forty-five minutes later, looking pleased but not triumphant. A couple of dozen reporters waited to hear what he had to say. Beyond, in Pennsylvania Avenue, sightseers pressed against the railings. A little group of suffragettes jiggled yellow pickets.

"The President received me with the utmost courtesy and consideration," Roosevelt told the newsmen. But when it came to repeating the substance of their conversation, he became uncharacteristically cagey. Turning to Tumulty, who remained at his elbow, he joked, "If I say anything I shouldn't, be sure to censor it."

Uninhibited, he might have announced that he and Wilson had chatted easily, swapped anecdotes, and in short, gotten on as well as they had in May 1914. And he could have repeated his tension-relieving remark: "Mr. President, what I have said and thought, and what others have said and thought, is all dust in a windy street if we can make your message good." Instead, he dictated a terse statement to the effect that he had asked for authority to raise a division of volunteer soldiers, many of them already trained and available— "such a division to be sent as part of any expeditionary force to France at an early moment." The President, he said, had neither accepted nor rejected his request, and would come to a decision "in his own good time."

Meanwhile, Roosevelt wanted it understood that his proposed division would not conflict with Wilson's call for a universal, obligatory draft. The volunteers he sought would either be over twenty-five or excluded from regular conscription by the War Department. "I have been in communication with Secretary Baker, but do not intend to call on him."

Baker took the hint—or rather, yielded to an even heavier one from Franklin D. Roosevelt—that the Colonel would be receiving visitors that evening in Representative Longworth's townhouse on M Street. When he arrived he found the place mobbed. Roosevelt had been holding court all afternoon. The British, French, and Japanese ambassadors and a long list of legislators and policymakers, including the chairmen of the House and Senate military committees and officers of the National Defense Council, were being briefed on the Roosevelt Division in such detail that it might already be en route to Brest. Its chief recruiter came out in high spirits, thrust an arm through Baker's, and led him upstairs to a private room.

"I am aware," Roosevelt said with winning frankness, "that I have not had enough experience to lead a division myself." He had sensed that was one of Wilson's doubts about his request. "But I have selected the most experienced officers from the regular army for my staff." He was willing to serve under whatever commander the President might appoint, as well as the commander of the entire expeditionary force.

Baker felt himself being strongarmed, and would only say, as he had in their correspondence, that he was taking the proposal under advisement. The Colonel must appreciate that mobilization was a hugely complex process that could not be swayed by personal considerations.

Roosevelt returned to New York unencouraged. He tried to make the best of his interviews, saying to John Leary, "I had a good talk with Baker—I could twist him about my finger, could I have him about for a while." As for the President, "He seemed to take it well, but—remember, I was talking to Mr. Wilson."

⊱⊰

ON 12 APRIL, having heard nothing from the administration, Roosevelt decided to appeal directly to Congress for legislation permitting volunteer soldiers to serve on the Western Front. He understood that a general deployment of Baker's draft army was unlikely until the spring of 1918. But it was plain that the Allies were desperate for reinforcements. Britain had already announced that it was sending a high-level mission to Washington, headed by Arthur Balfour, in an effort to speed up the dispatch of American war aid.

In an urgent letter to George Chamberlain (D., Oregon), chairman of the Senate Military Affairs Committee, Roosevelt wrote:

> Let us use volunteer forces, in connection with a portion of the regular army, in order at the earliest possible moment, within a few months, to put our flag on the firing line. We owe this to humanity. We owe it to the small nations who have suffered such dreadful wrong from Germany. Most of all we owe it to ourselves, to our national honor and self-respect. For the sake of our own souls, for the sake of the memories of the great Americans of the past, we must show that we do not intend to make this merely a dollar war. Let us pay with our bodies for our soul's desire.

With, that he left for Boston, and Archie's rushed-up wedding in Emmanuel Episcopal Church.

THE ROOSEVELTS KNEW that this was probably the last time they would assemble as a complete family before war tore them apart. Their celebration on Saturday, 14 April, was muted. Quentin, serving as best man, waited with Archie in the chancel, which was draped with the national and state flags. Ted, Kermit, and Dick Derby served as ushers. Theodore and Edith sat with Alice and Nick, Ethel and Belle, and several Roosevelt cousins. Saltonstalls, Aspinwalls, Websters, and Peabodys sprinkled both sides of the aisle. At noon, Grace Lockwood—sharp-featured and skinny in white satin—came down the aisle on the arm of her father. She was a graduate of the Navy League's "female Plattsburg" in Chevy Chase, Maryland, so the patriotic bunting was quite to her taste, as were the glittering uniforms of many attendees from the Harvard Officers' Reserve Corps.

Grace understood the necessity of a postponed honeymoon. For the next few weeks, Archie would have to remain close to home, pending assignment to active duty.

A DISPATCH TO *The New York Times* on the day after the wedding reported that a long-exiled Russian Communist leader, "Nikolai" Lenin, was en route to Petrograd from Switzerland. He had been given safe conduct across German railroads. Lenin and his fellow *Bolsheviki* were for universal peace, so they could accomplish their design to co-opt the Russian revolution.

This news (and the hasty departure from New York City of Leon Trotsky) complicated the efforts of Count Ilya Tolstoy to drum up American support for Prince Lvov's provisional government. The son of the famous novelist was in the United States on a propaganda tour. He hoped that Theodore Roosevelt might be named head of an advisory commission that President Wilson planned to send to his country. The Colonel was otherwise preoccupied, but dictated a message for Tolstoy to take home: "Through you I send my most hearty congratulations and good wishes to the men who have led the Russian people in this great movement for democratic freedom."

Describing himself as "a fellow radical," he cautioned the Duma majority against the danger of "unbalanced extremists" who sought to go beyond democracy. "See that the light of the torch is not dimmed by any unwise and extreme action, and above all not by any of those sinister and dreadful deeds which a century and a quarter ago in France produced the Red Terror, and then by reaction the White Terror."

Privately, he told John Leary that Russia's flimsy new republic might soon fall apart. If the Bolsheviks managed to win or steal power in Petrograd, they would probably negotiate a peace treaty with Germany, so as to be able to consolidate themselves at home. That would leave the Reich, in turn, free to deploy all its Eastern armor along the Western Front.

"If we do not wake up," Roosevelt fretted, "Germany will have won this war, and then *we will* be in it."

❧

ON 15 APRIL HE heard from Secretary Baker that his request to serve as a volunteer commander in the war was denied for "purely military" reasons. The War College Division of the General Staff had recommended that no American troops be sent to Europe until they were sufficiently numerous, equipped, and trained. "This policy," Baker wrote, ". . . does not undertake to estimate what, if any, sentimental value would attach to a representation of the United States in France by a former President of the United States." It was possible that pressure from the Allies might prompt the early dispatch of an American expeditionary force, but in that case, command positions would be given to regular officers "who have devoted their lives exclusively to the study and pursuit of military matters, and have made a professional study of the recent changes in the art of war."

Baker could not have made it clearer that he and Wilson considered Roosevelt to be an amateur soldier from the last century. The shock was enough to reduce the hero of San Juan Heights to temporary silence. He brooded for a week, then replied with an eighteen-page letter, rejecting Baker's rejection. "My dear sir, you forget that I have commanded troops in action in the most important battle fought by the United States army during the last half century." He noted that field assignments were being showered on division and brigade commanders who did not have "one tenth" of his experience. Moving on to direct criticism, he ascribed the War Department's current need for an emergency training program to its failure to initiate preparedness two and a half years before. If back then the Springfield munitions factory had been cranked into instant high gear, "we would now be a million rifles to the good." Baker's current advisers in formulating mobilization policy were "well-meaning men, of the red-tape and pipe-clay school . . . hidebound in the pedantry of that kind of wooden militarism which is only one degree worse than its extreme opposite, the folly which believes that an army can be improvised between sunrise and sunset."

Baker mercifully did not reply, in words he already shared with a friend, that he wished to avoid "a repetition of the San Juan Hill affair, with the commander rushing his men into a situation from which only luck extricated them." As gently as he could, he wrote, "For obvious reasons, I cannot allow myself to be drawn into a discussion of your personal experience and qualifications." Nor would he discuss those of his consultants, except to say that they were patriotic and high-minded officers. "The war in Europe is confessedly stern, steady, and relentless. It is a contest between the morale of two great contending forces." Should the United States jump into the struggle with a division of "hastily summoned and unprofessional" volunteers, the Allies would be depressed and disillusioned, "deeming it an evidence of our lack of seriousness about the nature of the enterprise."

Senator Chamberlain had similar doubts about sponsoring the Colonel's amendment to the draft bill. Pressed by Henry Cabot Lodge, he allowed it to go forward under the name of Senator Warren Harding of Ohio. This move surprised political observers who remembered Harding as chairman of the 1916 Republican convention, disdainfully (with eagle profile) maneuvering to block Roosevelt's nomination. But the eagle was far-sighted, and looking ahead, saw no other likely nominee on the GOP's horizon for 1920—unless it be himself. He was happy to do whatever was necessary to keep Party seniors happy.

On 24 April, Harding expanded the amendment to empower the President of the United States to appoint as many as four volunteer divisions of men not subject to conscription. The measure was optimistic in assuming that Wilson would override the policy of his own War Department. It did not name Roosevelt as a potential commander, but the ensuing agitated debate was as much about him as about the incompatibility of voluntary and drafted service. Lodge threw all his own prestige, as ranking minority member of the Foreign Relations Committee, into the fray on behalf of the Colonel.

"He is known in Europe as is no other American. His presence there would be a help and an encouragement to the soldiers of the allied nations. . . . For

Heaven's sake, is there any reason why he should not be given an opportunity, if he desires, to give his life for what he regards as the most sacred of all causes?"

While the debate continued—postponing, to the relief of many congressmen, a proposal to prohibit liquor consumption in the Capitol—Roosevelt worked to ensure the fastest possible dispatch of his sons to the war. He asked Spring Rice to find out if British army regulations would permit Kermit to enlist without compromising his American citizenship. And he fattened Newton D. Baker's already bulky "Roosevelt" file with a request to help Quentin get into the army flying school at Fort Monroe, Virginia.

"It will give me pleasure," Baker replied, "to think that your boy is there and a part of our establishment."

The secretary's pleasure was sincere. He had not enjoyed hurting a great man who was, palpably, aging but still full of ardor. Nor did he discount the power of the Roosevelt lobby on Capitol Hill. The passions unleashed in the Senate over the Harding amendment indicated that a vengeful Lodge could hinder the administration in its attempt to get the draft bill passed. Balfour's British mission had arrived in Washington on 22 April, and a French one dominated by Marshal Joseph Joffre was due any day. Both statesmen were known to admire Roosevelt profoundly. It would be an embarrassment for Baker if a quarrel with him slowed the pace of American mobilization.

Quentin was summoned to Washington for examination as a candidate for flight training in the signal corps. Doctors at Walter Reed Army Hospital poured hot and cold water into his ears, dropped belladonna into his eyes, made him hop along blindfolded, and then, conveniently ignoring his shortsightedness, declared him fit for service. He was billeted, not to Fort Monroe, but to Hazelhurst Field, Mineola, Long Island, an easy motorcycle spin from Sagamore Hill.

⌥

BY THE FIRST WEEK of May, Roosevelt was receiving two thousand volunteer applications a day. Meanwhile, the administration's draft bill passed both houses of Congress, but the Harding amendment was still so hot an issue it had to be settled by a House-Senate conference. The principal argument against letting Roosevelt have his division was that crackpot militiamen across the country might organize and demand that Wilson send them abroad too.

The leaders of the Allied missions were not encouraged by this discordance, judging from their looks and demeanor. Ellen Maury Slayden, the wife of an antiwar congressman from Texas, wrote a description of Arthur Balfour in her journal: "All the lines of him were drooping except his mouth, where there lingered a shadow of the usual British sneer at all things American, although somewhat chastened by their present desperate need for our help. His trousers drooped because they didn't fit, each corner of his long-tailed coat seemed to have a weight in it, his arrow string tie was limp, and his turned-down collar so low that he might have worn a locket."

The foreign secretary certainly was desperate, more so than Mrs. Slayden knew. His government was on the verge of bankruptcy, and would soon have

"THE FOREIGN SECRETARY CERTAINLY WAS DESPERATE."
Arthur Balfour (right) with René Viviani in Washington, April 1917.

to beg Washington for relief. Over the last six months its American debt, swollen by borrowing on Wall Street to keep the sterling-dollar exchange rate stable, had become an overdraft of $358 million. So much of what the Allies had bought in the way of food was being sent to the bottom by U-boats that a famine in Great Britain was no more than six weeks away. What London needed, even more than extra men, was extra credit. Touched as Balfour was to see Roosevelt rounding up volunteers willing to fight and die alongside Field Marshal Sir Douglas Haig's troops in Flanders, he had to accept the verdict of his chief military adviser, Lieutenant General George Bridges, that conditions there were "too serious . . . for untrained men or amateurs of any sort." They agreed, in other words, with Baker, and Bridges telegraphed London to warn of the inadvisability of "any form of volunteer group from America." Britain would have to wait—and bleed—until the U.S. Army was ready to send over an expeditionary force of regular soldiers.

Baker accordingly resisted Marshal Joffre's pleadings for a Roosevelt division to be attached to *his* troops further south. Last month's disastrous French offensive in the Soissons-Reims sector had cost 120,000 casualties and caused dozens of divisions to mutiny. Although this shameful news was being kept secret, Joffre had replaced his commander in chief, General Robert Nivelle, with General Henri-Philippe Pétain.

Roosevelt and Joffre were able to take stock of each other at a private dinner in Henry Frick's mansion in New York on 9 May. Earlier in the day, the Colonel had been excluded from a city reception for the French mission, by order of the State Department. His rapprochement with the administration would appear to be over. Joffre—a big, beaming, pink-and-white man—was overjoyed to be seated next to an American who could speak his language. Afterward it was noticed that he had learned, in return, at least one word of English: *"Bul-lee."*

"He did not tell me anything I did not know, or suspect," Roosevelt told Leary. "France does want our men. She wants them badly, more than she wants supplies."

There was another dinner for the missions at the Waldorf two nights later. It was hosted by Governor Charles S. Whitman of New York, with Roosevelt seated well away from the guests of honor. But Balfour quietly arranged to come out to Sagamore Hill for "high tea" on Sunday the fifteenth. The State Department, alerted by a sudden deployment of secret service agents, was powerless to stop him.

For four hours, he and Roosevelt renewed their acquaintance: grayer and sadder statesmen than they had been when they were respectively prime minister and president. The war they had long seen coming both joined them and separated them now. Balfour confided that he found Woodrow Wilson's White House to be lacking in urgency. Roosevelt talked of his frustrated desire to serve. Their only auditors, as they talked far into the night, were Balfour's parliamentary assistant Sir Ian Malcolm, and a rookie pilot from Mineola, Private Quentin Roosevelt.

THAT SAME WEEKEND, Roosevelt received another letter from Secretary Baker. The House-Senate conference was moving toward approval of the draft bill with the Harding amendment intact, but Baker did not want Roosevelt to think this presaged well for his division. "Since the responsibility for action and decision in this matter rests upon me, you will have to regard the determination I have already indicated as final, unless changing circumstances require a re-study of the whole question."

The only "changing circumstance" Roosevelt could see ahead was Woodrow Wilson's empowerment, under the pending act, to summon up five hundred thousand volunteer soldiers. Roosevelt believed he could supply almost half that number out of the pool of applications he already had in hand—but what chance was there of the President turning to *him*, if it was so obviously Baker's desire to do without volunteers altogether?

Almost none, according to a message from Cal O'Laughlin in Washington. "Tumulty tells me confidentially that the President will approve the army conscription bill, but that he will not exercise his authority for the acceptance of your division."

On 18 May, Wilson signed the bill into law, inflicting compulsory registration for military service upon ten million men between the ages of twenty-one and thirty-one. The stroke of his pen made him the most powerful commander in chief in American history. In an extraordinary accompanying statement, he acknowledged that a clause in the Draft Act permitted him to give an independent command to Theodore Roosevelt. "It would be very agreeable for me to pay Mr. Roosevelt this compliment, and the Allies the compliment, of sending to their aid one of our most distinguished public men, an ex-President who has rendered many conspicuous public services and proved his gallantry in many striking ways. Politically, too, it would no doubt have a very fine effect and make a profound impression. But this is not the time . . . for any action not calculated to contribute to the immediate success of the war. The business now at hand is undramatic, practical, and of scientific definiteness and precision."

The statement was Wilsonian in sounding like a tribute but parsing as dismissal. Roosevelt, by implication, was an old military showman who would only strut the French stage in the manner of Debussy's "Général Lavine—excentric."

James Amos was with the Colonel when he received a follow-up telegram from Wilson explaining that the statement had been based on "imperative considerations of public policy and not upon personal or private choice." Amos had never seen his boss so cast down. "He was truly in a black mood."

For a day or two more, Roosevelt hoped that some intervention, such as an appeal from the French government, would make Wilson grant him his desperate desire. That was nothing less than death in battle: he knew he would not come back. Denied the consummation, he would have to cede it to one or more of his sons. "I don't care a continental whether they fight in Yankee uniforms or British uniforms or in their undershirts, so long as they're fighting."

Kermit was at Plattsburg, doing some last-minute training to qualify for a commission in the British army. Ted and Archie were there too, awaiting orders as major and second lieutenant respectively in the U.S. Officers' Reserve Corps. Their father was not so downcast that he did not press for their transfer overseas, the moment Wilson announced that John J. Pershing was to be the commander of the American Expeditionary Force in Europe.

"My dear General Pershing," Roosevelt wrote, "I very heartily congratulate you, and especially the people of the United States, upon your selection." There was no need to add that he had made Pershing's present glory possible, having promoted him in 1905 over the heads of 835 senior officers. "I write you now to request that my two sons, Theodore Roosevelt, Jr., aged 27,* and Archibald B. Roosevelt, aged 23, both of Harvard, be allowed to enlist as privates under you, to go over with the first troops."

Pershing replied that it would be "a waste" for two such promising young officers to enlist, and undertook to find them places on his staff at no loss of rank.

With Quentin almost certain to be assigned to the general's force as well (Baker talked grandly of an "army of the air" leading the American attack), Roosevelt's next, painful duty was to dismiss all his volunteers. Those eligible for the draft might yet be lucky, and serve; but those ineligible needed to hear from him, rather than the President, that they were not wanted.

Before issuing a notice of general release, he discussed its wording with about twenty of his "ghost" commanders, including Seth Bullock, Jack Greenaway, a former Rough Rider, and John M. Parker, a still-passionate Progressive. Parker was the only man, apart from Roosevelt, who had actually lobbied Woodrow Wilson in behalf of the division. He was able to quote the President's exact words: "Colonel Roosevelt is a splendid man and patriotic citizen, as you say, but he is not a military leader. His experience in military life has been extremely short. He and many of the men with him are too old to render efficient service, and in addition to that fact, he as well as others have shown intolerance of discipline."

John Leary attended the meeting. "Never, except in a house of death, have I noticed a greater air of depression. All except the Colonel showed it plainly. He, it was apparent to those who knew him best, felt worse than any other."

The notice went out on 21 May. It was a somber summary of the division's aims, but stated that "as good American citizens we loyally obey the decision of the Commander in Chief of the American army and navy."

A WEEK LATER, Georges Clemenceau published an open letter to Wilson, appealing to him to change his mind about the volunteer division. "It is possible that your own mind, enclosed in its austere legal frontiers . . . has failed to be

---

* Ted was in fact twenty-nine.

impressed by the vital hold which personalities like Roosevelt have on popular imagination," Clemenceau wrote, in language unlikely to have been approved by the Quai d'Orsay. "The name of Roosevelt has this legendary force in our country at this time." *Poilus* were asking why the Colonel had not been sent over. "Send them Roosevelt. I tell you, because I know it—it will gladden their hearts."

Wilson did not reply. Roosevelt complained to fellow members of the Harvard Club that he had been cashiered by a jealous rival determined to deny him the right *pro patria mori.* "I told Wilson that I would die on the field of battle, that I would never return if only he would let me go!"

"If you could really convince the President of that," Elihu Root said, "I'm quite sure he would send you at once."

QUENTIN ROOSEVELT'S POSTING to Long Island filled Flora Whitney with joy. She and Quentin were besotted with each other, to the extent that they had secretly become engaged. The Whitney estate at Old Westbury was near enough to Mineola for them to spoon whenever Quentin got an evening pass from Hazelhurst Field, and Sagamore Hill was available for weekend trysts. Edith Roosevelt had taken to Flora (as she had not to Grace). Knowing how little time the two nineteen-year-olds were likely to have together, she encouraged their closeness.

"Ah, Fouf," Quentin wrote from camp, using Flora's family nickname, "I don't yet see how you can love me,—still I feel as tho' it were all a dream from which some time I will wake . . . with nothing left to me but the memory of beauty and the wonder of it all."

He was a year and a half younger than the youngest men who flocked to register on "Draft Day," 5 June, and just as unready as she to face the horrifying fact that after six or seven more weeks of rapture, he might never see her again. It was difficult for Quentin to imagine himself flying solo before the end of the month. But that was the speed at which he was being flung into the air, in a lumbering, hard-to-control Curtiss Jenny that cruelly taxed his back. France was hopelessly calling for five thousand American pilots and fifty thousand aviation "mechanicians." The U.S. Army (seventeenth in the world, packing only one and a half days' worth of ammunition) had fewer than a hundred trained pilots. A story in *The New York Times* reported seventy-five British planes had been shot down in a single dogfight. Apparently, service aloft was more dangerous than life in the trenches.

The war had so long been regarded by Americans as something they were "kept out of" that its sudden, here-and-now reality was shocking, even to the Colonel's children. On 17 June, just as Ethel was giving birth to a little girl, Ted and Archie came to Sagamore Hill to announce, in great secrecy, under the new Espionage Act, that they would be leaving for France in three days' time. Quentin and Flora felt impelled to reveal *their* own secret at the family's final gathering before the two regulars sailed. They were so barely grown up that Edith might have reacted in horror, except that all over the country, the

"HE WAS ASSIGNED TO THE NINETY-FIFTH
AERO SQUADRON."

Lieutenant Quentin Roosevelt.

accelerating pace of "mobilization" had made short order of maternal scruples. She gave them her blessing.

Flora was as sure as Quentin that their engagement was a commitment for life. Outside of that, and the flamboyant "freshness" with which she dressed, bobbed her hair, and rode horses, she was an insecure girl, tongue-tied when

the Roosevelts quoted poetry to one another, and in awe of the public figures
who constantly visited the Colonel. She adored her father, but Harry Whitney
had the globetrotting restlessness of the wealthy, and she saw little of him.
Her famous mother was interested only in art and artists. Roosevelt, in contrast, embraced Flora as he did anyone who passed Edith's muster, radiating
such affection that she understood Sagamore Hill would remain "home" to
her, however long Quentin stayed away.

Ted and Archie sailed on the twentieth, with orders attaching them to General Pershing's advance headquarters in Paris. Roosevelt was overjoyed to be
able to boast that they were among the first in line for the Front. He pushed to
have Kermit similarly placed in Mesopotamia, writing to Lloyd George, "I
pledge my honor that he will serve you honorably and efficiently." Early in July,
an acceptance call came through from Balfour's roving ambassador in New
York, Lord Northcliffe. Kermit was tracked down in Boston, where he was sitting for a portrait by John Singer Sargent, and by mid-month he was gone too.

Quentin simultaneously graduated as a first lieutenant in the Flying
Corps. He was assigned to the Ninety-fifth Aero Squadron, with orders to
proceed overseas at once. Fanny Parsons watched him emerging khaki-clad
from Christ Church after communion with his mother, and got a sick feeling
they might never share the sacrament again. His departure was set for Monday, 23 July. He told Edith that he wanted to spend his last night with Flora,
on the Whitney yacht. Helpless against the rush of events, she could hold him
at Sagamore Hill only through Saturday.

Before going to bed that evening, she went to his bedroom and tucked
him in.

⌒

FLORA WROTE QUENTIN a farewell letter to take with him.

> *Dearest . . .*
>
> *With every breath I draw there will be a thought of you and a wish for
> your safety, success and good luck. . . .*
>
> *All I do from now will be for you. . . . There is nothing in me that
> could make you care for me as much as I care for you—and you
> couldn't anyway, because it's absolute worship on my part.*
>
> *And be careful and don't take any unnecessary risks—or do any-
> thing solely for bravado—please, please, dear?*

On Monday morning, Theodore and Edith went into Manhattan to see
their youngest son off on the SS *Olympia*. Alice joined them at the Cunard
dock. The Whitney family was there en masse. None of them knew Flora was

engaged, but they were showing rare support for her and her soldier boyfriend.

The liner, war-painted troopship gray, was in no hurry to leave. Humid heat built up along the waterfront. Quentin seemed to want to do nothing but sit on a bale of hides holding hands with Flora. By lunchtime, his parents and sister could stand it no longer and said goodbye. They left the young couple in care of the Whitneys and drove home to Sagamore Hill. Alice sensed Roosevelt's utter desolation.

She murmured to herself, *The old Lion perisheth for lack of prey and the stout Lion's whelps are scattered abroad.*

CHAPTER 26

The House on the Hill

They are all gone away,
The House is shut and still,
There is nothing more to say.

HAVING LITTLE RELIGION, Roosevelt was confessedly fatalistic. "I have always believed in the truth of the statement that 'He who seeks his life shall lose it.' " Perhaps the same applied to seeking a soldier's death. He was being punished for the fatal insolence of wanting to go gloriously.

Sagamore Hill had been a lonely place before, after his various political defeats and the marriages and resettlements of his children. But he had always been able to count on the politicians returning, and even when Ted and Kermit had tried to seek *their* lives, on the West Coast and in South America, somehow or other the same flame kept bringing them back. Alice, too. Although she was now a fixture of the Washington establishment, she was never happier than when she could leave Nick to his violin and his mistresses and revisit the home of her childhood.

But the diaspora of four sons to the war—not to mention Eleanor and Belle, hurrying to beat an imminent law against the wives of servicemen going overseas—plus an almost total transferal of press attention to what was happening "over there," filled the old house with an emptiness that only extreme youth could assuage. Ethel brought her little boy and baby girl often, but not often enough for a wistful grandfather. And there was Flora Whitney, with a gulf of her own inside her. She visited the Roosevelts again and again, as if she were already their daughter-in-law.

Quentin had done what he could to create interdependence between her and them, leaving a farewell note to Flora in his father's hands: "I love you, dearest, and always shall, far, far, more than you will ever know or believe. . . . Ah, sweetheart, war is a cruel master to us all."

"FLORA CAME OVER for dinner with Mother and me," Roosevelt wrote Quentin on 28 July. "So darling and so pretty. . . . I cannot overstate how fond I have grown of her, and how much I respect and admire her—so pretty and young and yet so good and really wise."

His praise might have signified more, were he not in the habit of applying the same adjectives to all the women in his family. It was too early for him to adjust to Flora as a species different from those others, so avant-garde in her affectations ("I am perfectly mad about amber"), mercurial, hungry for new experiences that she could not quite specify, except to be certain that Quentin would provide them. She found a sympathetic friend in Ethel, to whom she poured out emotions the Roosevelts would have recoiled from: "If the fates can be as cruel as to take him from me, I need all the courage I can get from him and his influence now, while he is concretely mine, so that my life has to be lived *for* him and not *with* him. . . . It was hard during that last day but toward evening I got to a point where I couldn't cry. I felt as if the tears of the centuries had amassed themselves somewhere between my throat and my stomach and intended to remain there."

In the midst of her anguish, Flora could tell that Edith was also pining for Quentin—the most vulnerable of the Roosevelt children, with his bad back and unmilitary nature. If that aloof woman had more particular reasons for loving him, Flora was too shy to ask. The Colonel was more approachable, yet again, there was a uniformity about the way he talked about his sons, except in occasional references to Kermit. They were equally brave and fine and determined to do their duty. Dick Derby was also brave and fine, in arranging to be sent back to France as a military doctor—and Nick Longworth would be brave and fine too, except that members of Congress were barred from enlisting. In his all-embracing pride, Roosevelt was actually harder than Edith for Flora to reach. She begged Ethel to tell her what she could do to help the family. "I am so sorry for your Mother that when I am with her . . . I almost forget my own troubles."

The secrecy and slowness of troopship movements was such that the Roosevelts had to wait for weeks to hear if their last son had crossed over safely. On 9 August, a letter came from Major Theodore Roosevelt, Jr. He had not yet seen anything of Quentin in Paris, or of Kermit, who was due to pass through en route to Mesopotamia. But Ted had tremendous news of his own: he was appointed commander of the First Battalion, Twenty-sixth Infantry, AEF First Division—so far, the only war-ready unit Pershing had been able to establish in France. Archie expected to be assigned a place in the same division soon.

Roosevelt was overjoyed. "I had no idea," he wrote back, "that you could make a *regular* regiment in a line position." Evidently Pershing had felt Ted's bulldog drive and decided to make use of it as soon as the AEF started fighting. Nobody knew when that might be.

"I am busy writing and occasionally speaking," Roosevelt reported. "I have had various offers which are good from the financial side; but my interest of course now lies entirely in the work of you four boys, for my work is of no real consequence—what I did was in the Spanish War and in the decade following. . . ."

His habit of referring back to his days as Rough Rider and commander in chief had become compulsive as he adjusted to the fact that he was not wanted by the War Department. In a snub the Colonel's friends could not see as anything but cruel, Secretary Baker announced that William Howard Taft had been appointed a major general. On close inspection of the official order, it became clear that Taft's title was only a "certificate of identity," awarded to him as a high officer of the American Red Cross. But the thought of the peace-loving former president lumbering around in khaki was grotesque. Roosevelt tried to make a joke of it. "Major General Taft! How the Kaiser must have trembled when he heard the news!"

As August dragged on with no further word from France, he showed symptoms of extreme stress. For the first time in his life, he had difficulty sleeping. He agonized about possibly having to tell Edith that one of her sons had been killed. An attack of Cuban fever laid him low in mid-month. It did not lapse as quickly as usual, and inflamed the leg he had hurt in Brazil. He sat around the house with his head and back throbbing and his thigh done up in a moistened clay poultice.

His tendency to rant returned. Once more Woodrow Wilson was "an absolutely selfish, cold-blooded, and unpatriotic rhetorician." Seven months after the start of Germany's submarine offensive, Wilson and the "well-meaning little humanitarian" in the War Department were still struggling to create and supply a fighting force. "With our enormous wealth and resources," Roosevelt wrote Arthur Lee, "I still believe that we shall become a ponderable element in the war next spring; but until that time I doubt if we will count for as much as Belgium or Romania."

He was diverted by the arrival of some more army-stamped letters, although Quentin had yet to be heard from. Kermit and Belle were at last in Paris, and stopping at the Ritz. Ted and Archie had been transferred near the Front—where, the censor would not let them say. Archie had been put in Ted's regiment. Roosevelt did not like the sound of that. Having one brother under the other was prejudicial to discipline. *He* would not have allowed it, back when *he* was in command of a regiment!

Another thing that disturbed him was the way Belle and Kermit were sticking together. They had eighteen-month-old "Kim" with them, and Belle was pregnant again. Eleanor at least had gone over with the independent purpose of working for the American YMCA in Paris. She had the use of a large house on Rue de Villejust, in the sixteenth arrondissement. Belle talked of joining her parents in Madrid after Kermit moved on to Mesopotamia. But she was a clingy woman, and Kermit was capable of yielding to pressure from her to seek a staff assignment with the British army in France. He had never had a sense of career direction. "This is war," his father cajoled him. "It needs the sternest, most exclusive, and most business-like attention; and no officer (especially an officer of a foreign nationality who has been approved by favor) must try to get his wife near him on the campaign. . . . He must devote himself solely to his grim work."

As ever, Roosevelt sought comfort in books. He was not always successful. "One of the most ominously instructive things in history," he wrote a correspondent, "is the difference between Hannibal's career when, although in an incredibly difficult position, he had behind him the war party of Carthage and an army . . . and the last unhappy decade of his life when he was in Asia Minor, continually asked by Asiatic kings to help them do something against Rome, and yet absolutely powerless to accomplish anything in positions in which they had put him."

⟨⟩

SAGAMORE HILL

SEPT 1ST 1917

Dearest Quentin,

We were immensely pleased to get a note from Miss Emily Tuckerman saying that you, and the blessed Harrahs, were all in Paris together. I hope you saw Eleanor.

Miss Given Wilson* is just leaving for six months in France with the Red Cross; she is immensely pleased. The other evening she and darling Flora came over to dinner. Really, we are inexpressibly touched by Flora's attitude towards [us]; she is the dearest girl; and the way that pretty, charming pleasure-loving young girl has risen to the heights as soon as the need came is one of the finest things I have ever seen. By George, you are fortunate.

I suppose you are now hard at work learning the new type of air-

---

* Irene M. Given-Wilson, a Red Cross official close to Quentin Roosevelt. The Harrahs are unidentified.

game. My disappointment at not going myself was down at bottom chiefly reluctance to see you four, in whom my heart was wrapped, exposed to danger while I stayed at home in do-nothing ease and safety. But the feeling has now been completely swallowed in my immense pride in all of you. I feel that Mother, and all of you children, have by your deed justified my words!!

I hope to continue earning a good salary until all of you are home, so that I can start Archie and you all right. Then I intend to retire. An elderly male Cassandra has-been can do a little, a very little, toward waking the people now and then; but undue persistence in issuing Jeremiads does no real good and makes the Jeremiah an awful nuisance.

I am just publishing a book, for which Mother gave me the title: "The Foes of our own Household;" I dedicate it on behalf of both of us to our sons and daughters—the latter to include daughters in law, and Flora shall have her copy with a special inscription to show that she is included among those of whom I am most proud.

I make a few speeches; I loathe making them; among other reasons because I always fear to back up the administration too strongly lest it turn another somersault. At the moment New York City, having seen the National Guard, fresh from gathering at the Armories, parade, believes that Germany is already conquered!

Your loving
Father

QUENTIN DID NOT remain in Paris more than forty-eight hours. He was dispatched to Issoudun, in central France, where a huge American aviation instruction center was being built in a quagmire of Auvergnois mud. To his chagrin, it was far from the *zone des armées* where Ted and Archie were girding for battle.

"I confess I'm sorry," he wrote Flora, "for I wanted to get started flying and have it over with, I know my back wouldn't last for very long."

He doubted that he would get into the air for another two months, so preliminary and bureaucratic was all the organization of the base. It was possible he might not be assigned to the Front until next spring. Remote as Issoudun was, he had already seen enough of the war's effects in Paris (streets and cafés strangely quiet and lacking in laughter, haunted-looking women in black, a gas-blinded boy his age being helped along) to understand its "appalling reality," and how serious was the challenge of "driving the Boche back." He could feel the wall of German expansionism pressing on France like a tectonic plate. Until the Allies were reinforced by America's draft army, "no amount of talk, of airplane fleets that loom large only in the minds of newspapermen," would relieve the pressure.

Quentin felt changed by his translocation from a life of promise to a life of threat. "The thing that it brings home the most is the greatness of the responsibility," he told Flora, "—and the fact that it has got to be fought to a decision. For if there is no decision, we will go through it all again in fifteen years. That would be about the time we had settled down."

In more cheerful letters he reported being absorbed in mechanical work, as supply officer in charge of a fleet of fifty-two trucks. Since he had an easy command of French, he was also constantly called on to interpret between American and local officials, and mediate when quarrels broke out—a task that suited his genial personality. He had taken to smoking a pipe, and made friends with a wealthy French family, the Normants, who had a riverside château nearby at Romorantin.

Flora registered the presence of a daughter about her own age *chez* Normant. But the tone of Quentin's last August letter, written under a full moon, was reassuring: "Ah, dearest, if I have to pay the price of war, yet I am happy, in that earth has no higher blessing than the knowledge of a love that fills one's heart and soul."

❧

AMONG THE LUCRATIVE speaking and writing opportunities that the Colonel had mentioned to Ted was an invitation to write war commentary for the *Kansas City Star*, one of the most admired newspapers in the country. It paid $25,000 a year. He accepted, liking both the quickness of newspaper publication and the chance to address himself, once again, to a Midwestern readership. War spirit was lacking in many areas of the breadbasket states. At the same time, Harry Whitney (aware, at last, of Flora's engagement to Quentin) offered a new, nonexclusive contract at the *Metropolitan*. It would pay him $5,000 for a "short monthly editorial" in the magazine, on whatever subject caught his attention. Roosevelt accepted that too, and in the third week of September, set off with Edith to meet with the *Star*'s editorial team in Missouri.

It was therapeutic for them both to get away. Edith found herself constantly imagining the sound of Quentin's step on the piazza at Sagamore Hill, as if he were about to show up for dinner. Then she would hear the real sound of Flora's. Every appearance of the girl, however welcome, was a reminder that Quentin and she might never have what Roosevelt delicately called "their white hour." To that end, he had suggested to Flora that he should try to use his influence to get her over to France, so she could marry Quentin before the Air Corps was ready for frontline deployment. The Whitneys were resignedly agreeable, and Flora had written to see what Quentin thought about the idea. Everybody awaited his reaction.

No less a bandmaster than Lieutenant Commander John Philip Sousa, USN, conducting a two-hundred-piece ensemble, welcomed the Roosevelts to Kansas City with a performance of "The Stars and Stripes Forever." The

"IT WAS THERAPEUTIC FOR THEM BOTH TO GET AWAY."

Theodore and Edith Roosevelt, 1917.

lovely town rippled with flags and ghastly portraits of the Colonel. Ten thousand citizens cheered his way to the newspaper office, a magnificent Italianate brick pile by Jarvis Hunt. Although Roosevelt was not required to contribute any articles before October, he wrote a couple before lunch. They observed only the third of the *Star*'s famous style rules ("Use short sentences. Use short first paragraphs. Use vigorous English"), and they were penned on manuscript paper, front and back, to the distress of the production department. His copy editor was tolerant, but the rules were applied to good effect on the prose of the paper's next recruit, the cub reporter Ernest Hemingway.

The Roosevelts moved on to Chicago, where on 26 September the Colonel gave a speech for the National Security League, assailing Senator La Follette and other pacifists as "old women of both sexes." He noticed soldiers among his segregated audience and said he would give anything to go to war with them. "I greet you as comrades, you with the white faces and you with the black faces." In a separate address at Camp Grant, he sarcastically complimented the troops in training on having one rifle for every three men, saying that he had seen camps on Long Island where recruits were still drilling with broomsticks. A spokesman for the War Department promised that there would be guns aplenty when America's new army was ready to go overseas.

Edith became concerned about her husband's psychological and physical condition as she accompanied him to several more speaking engagements in Illinois, Wisconsin, and Minnesota. "He is in good spirits with his head up," she wrote Corinne Roosevelt Robinson, "but at times the horrid futility of beating the air comes upon him in a great wave." On occasion he publicly allowed his gloom to show, and said that he felt "blackballed" by the Wilson administration. He was graying faster now, his mustache almost white, his belly and buttocks massive. Energy still animated his speeches, but it came in sporadic bursts, as from a fading battery.

Other women besides Edith—the novelist Mary Roberts Rinehart, Ida Tarbell, and Josephine Stricker, his new secretary—noticed how quickly the Colonel had deteriorated. He was prone to irrational rages. Back in New York at the beginning of October, he showed such fatigue in an appearance at Madison Square Garden that Edith sentenced him to two weeks at Jack Cooper's Health Farm, outside Stamford, Connecticut.

He reported there on the tenth, and found himself the camp's only patient. Arrangements had been made to keep his treatment private. "The household enthralls me," he wrote Eleanor. "The men are professional athletes, touching the underworld on one side, and gilded youth and frayed gilded age on the other." Jack Cooper was "an old-time skin-glove fighter [and] intimate friend of noted criminals and millionaires." His partner was another retired pugilist, whose only reading seemed to be *YMCA Weekly*. An Irish domestic and a dismayingly fat Hungarian cook made up the rest of the establishment.

Cooper examined Roosevelt and told him that he was hypertense and thirty-five pounds overweight. "What's the matter, Colonel?"

"Well, I feel myself slipping a bit both mentally and physically. I'm an abnormal eater and I can't see how you're going to do much good . . . but I'm told you can."

Cooper said that he could continue to eat as much as he liked, providing he consented to a daily routine of long hikes, gym exercise, massage, and sessions on something called "the Reducycle." Roosevelt was agreeable. For the next ten days, until he could stand the monotony no longer, he obeyed every house rule—even breaking his lifetime habit of dressing for dinner.

The Reducycle, a machine of Cooper's own invention, was designed to cause prodigious sweating. Roosevelt had to pump its pedals for twenty-five minutes every morning, while steam nozzles enveloped him in a miasma of humid heat. He lost up to two pounds per session. Cooper monitored his heart and lungs, which performed satisfactorily.

On 22 October, the Colonel returned to Sagamore Hill, looking much thinner but exhausted. "Cooper's not a success," Edith wrote in her diary.

⟠

FLORA RECEIVED A chilling rejection from Quentin. He wrote that he dreaded "temporarily" marrying her, only to be killed a month later, or becoming one of the war's many paraplegics, "a useless chain to which you were tied." In a follow-up letter, he changed his mind and asked what she thought of a wedding in Paris next summer, when he should have completed his term of duty at the Front and would be eligible, with luck, for some leave.

He wrote that he was back to flying practice and enjoying it, although cramped hours in the cockpit of a little French Nieuport, at freezing high altitudes, badly bothered his back. "I don't see how the angels stand it." He also liked the male comradeship of camp, but referred often to a dull longing for Flora that would not go away.

She felt the same. "Oh, Quentin . . . I want you so desperately & the hollow, blank feeling that is a living nightmare almost kills me at times." His letters came irregularly, sometimes one a day, sometimes none for a week. Their datelines indicated that the fault was not always due to shipping delays. Like Flora, Quentin was easily cast down. He confessed to her that all he saw ahead was "endless gray vistas of war." His engineer's nature, loving coordination, was outraged by the reshufflings and reversals that kept the Aviation Service in a perpetual state of organizational flux. At any given moment he was truck officer, groundskeeper, pilot, purchasing agent in Paris, or recalled to Issoudun to fly again. About his only certainty was that he would, eventually, be put into service as a "fighter up in the ceiling," not as "a bomb dropper." His commander had promised him that, but warned that he would not be sent forward to the line for at least three months.

Ted and Archie were already there, but they were not seeing any action. The Allies, concerned at the AEF's greenness, had persuaded Pershing to dig his First Division into a relatively quiet sector of the Front, near Nancy. Ironically, it was Kermit, the last brother to be commissioned, who looked likely to taste battle first. Belle had allowed him to proceed to Mesopotamia, where he was now on duty with the British army, and ranked as an "honorary" captain.

For Theodore Roosevelt, as his fifty-ninth birthday approached, the mere fact that all his sons were trained and ready for war was thrilling. He hung a huge service flag, with four stars on it, from the upper story of Sagamore Hill. In a letter to Ted, who had just turned thirty, he wrote, "You and your brothers are playing your parts in the greatest of the world's great days, and what man of spirit does not envy you? You are having your crowded hours of glorious life; you have seized the great chance, as was seized by those who fought at Gettysburg, and Waterloo, and Agincourt, and Arbela and Marathon."

AT THE BEGINNING OF November, Russian troops defending imperial outposts in the Baltic yielded to Bolshevik calls that they lay down their arms and fraternize with the enemy. Kerensky's provisional government, weakened by transport and railroad strikes, desperately ordered the Petrograd garrison to reinforce the Eastern Front. There was no response. Nor would troops outside the capital move to prevent Vladimir Ilyich Lenin's revolutionary detachments from seizing control of key communications, banking, and transport infrastructures. On the morning of the sixth, Lenin published a proclamation of "Soviet" government in Russia, undertaking to give all citizens communal ownership of land, control over industrial production, and freedom from war. Kerensky's government took refuge in what used to be Nicholas II's Winter Palace.

For forty hours, civilian, military, and naval forces besieged the gilded redoubt, threatening to destroy it if power was not transferred to the proletariat. By daybreak on 8 November, Lenin was the presumptive ruler of Russia. He was elected chairman of the Council of People's Commissars later in the day, and Trotsky became his commissar for foreign affairs. Their first joint action was to issue a decree of peace with Germany, pending negotiation of a formal armistice.

Coincidentally, Roosevelt had just finished writing a foreword to Herman Bernstein's edition of *The Willy-Nicky Correspondence: Being the Secret and Intimate Telegrams Exchanged Between the Kaiser and the Tsar.* He said the telegrams not only illuminated the dark relationships of despots just before the war, but that they were prophetic in showing "the folly of the men who would have us believe that any permanent escape from anarchy in Russia can come from the re-establishment of the autocracy, which was itself the prime cause of that anarchy."

⤙⤚

IN THE MIDDLE of the month, he suffered the most devastating review of his literary career. Stuart P. Sherman, chief book critic of *The Nation*, took advantage of the publication of *The Foes of Our Own Household* to speak out on behalf of all the antiwar mollycoddles Roosevelt had sought to emasculate over the years. He argued that the Colonel had become a split personality because of his tendency to be "impressed with the two-sidedness of things." *Foes*, consisting of twelve reprinted articles on domestic and foreign policy, was really two books, Sherman observed. "Just as one of them was written by a judicious, progressive, and patriotic Aristotelean, exactly in the same way the other was written by a willful, angry, and furiously inequitable extremist." Roosevelt's musings on social and political questions were "judicious, progressive . . . timely and weighty," the thought of an eminently skilled polemicist. But when dealing with matters of defense and warfare, he perverted the words of past statesmen to suit his rhetorical purpose. "Any man who desires to believe that Washington and Lincoln saw eye to eye with Mr. Roosevelt," Sherman remarked, "should give his days and nights to the study of *The Foes of Our Own Household;* but any man who desires to know what [they] actually thought and said had better go to the original documents."

The critic was less effective in comparing Roosevelt's executive philosophy to that of Wilhelm II, if only because Woodrow Wilson had also come to believe in strong central control, compulsory military service, national self-assertion, patriotism, and preparedness. But Sherman drew attention to the "pervasive and sustained ugliness" of the Colonel's personal campaign against Wilson, and to his love of war for war's sake. "Apparently he cannot contemplate with equanimity a future in which our children shall be deprived of the 'glory' of battle with their peers."

For once, Roosevelt elected to let a pacifist berate him without reply. His silence implied, more than an attempt at self-defense would have, that he was beginning to doubt himself. He had entered his sixtieth year. An impotent old age was being forced on him, while Georges Clemenceau had been made prime minister of France at seventy-six. "I have never regretted anything so much as the absence of the Roosevelt army, nor understood the reason for it," his fellow Cassandra wrote him.

A bitter winter was settling in, with a national coal famine threatening, and obligatory fasts imposed upon all citizens by the President's new food czar, Herbert Hoover. Flora no longer offered youthful cheer. Quentin had inexplicably stopped writing to her, and she exuded misery. Her visits became fewer, and in early December stopped altogether. Just before Christmas, sub-zero temperatures gripped Oyster Bay. Theodore and Edith found themselves so alone and cold that they closed off most of Sagamore Hill and tried to keep warm in just two or three west-facing rooms with wood-burning fireplaces. In blustery weather, the flag with four stars flapped loudly enough to disturb their sleep. Often they repeated to each other the lines of Edwin Arlington Robinson that most addressed their situation: *There is ruin and decay / In the House on the Hill: / They are all gone away, / There is nothing more to say.*

CHAPTER 27

The Dead Are Whirling
with the Dead

The beauty, shattered by the laws
That have creation in their keeping,
No longer trembles at applause,
Or over children that are sleeping;
And we who delve in beauty's lore
Know all that we have known before
Of what inexorable cause
Makes Time so vicious in his reaping.

ALICE ROOSEVELT LONGWORTH, who could be relied upon to be *au centre* of the gayest, most fashionable crowd on New Year's Eve, was partying with the Ned McLeans at their annual dance in Washington when the lights doused, signaling the approach of midnight. As the hour struck, a huge electric sign at the end of the ballroom blazed out in red, white, and blue: GOOD LUCK TO THE ALLIES IN 1918.

Her parents, at the same time, were trying to keep warm in one of the last big houses on Long Island that still relied on gaslight after dark. The northeastern weather that January was so arctic—colder than any ever recorded—that they decided to make their third great concession to modern times, after buying an automobile and paving the driveway. The Colonel agreed to pay an electrical contractor something over $1,500 to wire his mansion. Unfortunately, the system promised only light, not warmth. But he would no longer have to strain his one good eye when he read, and the freezing hallways and bathrooms would at least look more welcoming.

Comforts, real or imagined, had to be seized upon in a season that offered little in the way of good news. Quentin's long silence was disturbing. Even allowing for the irregularity of military mail (with as much as four or five weeks needed for an exchange of letters), something had to be wrong with him. It was likely not serious, or his commanding officer—or Ted, or Archie, or Eleanor—would have cabled. Edith was so exasperated at his failure to reply to her letters that she refused to write any more until he became ashamed of himself.

Roosevelt felt Flora's desolation enough to have sent Quentin a stern reproof: "If you wish to lose her, continue to be an infrequent correspondent. If however you wish to keep her, write her letters—interesting letters, and love letters—at least three times a week. Write no matter how tired you are . . . write if you're smashed up in a hospital; write when you are doing your most dangerous stunts; write when your work is most irksome and disheartening; write all the time!" He signed himself, "Affectionately, a hardened and wary old father."

The strange thing was that Quentin was the most epistolary of his children, quick to pour out jokes, stray observations, confessions, even poems on paper. Not that the others were slack correspondents. Ted and Dick Derby sent long letters through Eleanor, whose house in Paris functioned as a Rooseveltian hostel and information center. Kermit's mail from Mesopotamia took many weeks to come, but could otherwise be relied on. Even taciturn Archie (due to become a father in six or seven weeks' time) kept Grace fully briefed in Boston. His latest proud news was that he had been promoted to captain. Neither he nor Ted had much to say about Quentin, but being at the Front, that was not surprising. Or were they holding something back?

IF SO, THEY WERE AMATEURS compared to Woodrow Wilson, preparing with fanatical secrecy to make yet another surprise appearance before Congress. He had sensed a misalignment among the war's strategic blocks since the Bolshevik coup of last November, and especially after Russia's negotiation of a provisional peace with Germany. Now, thanks to the transferal of 77 German divisions from the Eastern Front to the Western, the Central Powers were at last ascendant over the Anglo-French Entente, at 177 divisions to 173. And they could draw on a further 30 divisions in consequence of Austria's epic defeat of the Italian army at Caporetto. This imbalance would prevail until General Pershing's army (still only four divisions strong, and untested in any major engagement) began to swell with a steady influx of stateside troops in the summer.

By then the war might be over—or so Lloyd George and Clemenceau, two deeply worried ministers, kept warning Wilson. Their messages combined impatience at the slowness of American mobilization with a craven dependence on the administration's goodwill. Britain had lost an estimated four hundred thousand men in its last six-month offensive, with a blindly determined General Haig sending his last reserves to die in the mud and *Scheisse* of Passchendaele. Wilson could not help being sympathetic, although he had lost much of his earlier sentimental attachment to Great Britain. He saw that its protectiveness toward France was really motivated by fear that a victorious Reich might threaten its overseas empire, and prevent the British Petroleum Company from acquiring significant real estate in Mesopotamia.

Logistically and psychologically, the Allies would seem to need all the good luck that Ned and Evalyn McLean wished them. But Wilson's sharp-pencil mind, never clearer than when plotting dynamic curves against a time-line, saw that the Central Powers were not *yet* as strong as they needed to be, to win the war. Their principal weapon—the U-boat—had been made much less lethal by new detection techniques and American-built patrol craft and destroyers. The German navy was still landlocked. Perhaps most to the point, Marxist discontent was surging powerfully among Europe's labor and peasant classes. The Bolsheviks had called upon Western workers to throw over their governments. Trotsky sounded not unlike the Pope in urging a peace conference, before the belligerents became so degenerate as to keep fighting for the sake of fighting.

Wilson's phenomenal instinct for the right moment prompted him to move toward a sudden announcement of settlement terms that he believed the whole world would ascribe to. On Saturday, 5 January, he huddled with Colonel House, who at his behest had spent several months soliciting and collating the recommendations of experts on the European situation. Even as the two men met, Lenin was moving murderously to overturn the results of an election that had, to Bolshevik rage, placed a liberal majority in control of Russia's constituent assembly. By late Sunday night, totalitarianism reigned again in the land of the tsars, and Wilson had a typed "Statement of the War Aims and Peace Terms of the United States," for democratic governments to consider, negotiate, and adopt—he hoped, at a conference to end all wars.

The statement listed a series of talking points. They were bound, at first, to antagonize the parties that Wilson most wanted to bring together: Germany, France, and Britain. All three nations still claimed they were at war for defensive reasons. So, less plausibly, did America. But it was the only belligerent sure to gain strength, no matter how long it fought. Wilson was gambling on the exhaustion, not to say internal rebellion, of the others. Sooner rather than later, a *pax Americana* should prevail.

Wilson presented his "Fourteen Points" to Congress on Tuesday afternoon, carefully speaking in plain language that ordinary people could understand. Not for him, this time, the fine style and sly syntax that so irritated Roosevelt. His propaganda chief, George Creel of the Committee on Public Information, had arranged for the address to be broadcast around the world via a Marconi station in New Jersey, equipped with a one-hundred-thousand-cycle alternator. Wilson was not bothered by the sight of empty seats in the House chamber, including a few in the row reserved for cabinet members. He was addressing the larger audience he liked to refer to, with a sense of suzerainty, as "mankind."

It was an audience largely ignorant of American foreign policy, and therefore unaware that not one of the Fourteen Points was new. Lansing had presented each of them in various diplomatic communications. But they gained in impact now by being presented all together, just when their relevance was broadest. Wilson said he wanted to see open peace negotiations; absolute freedom of the seas; radical disarmament; impartial settlement of colonial disputes; recognition of Russia's right to shape its own future "unhampered and unembarrassed" by outside constraints; the evacuation by Germany of Belgium, Alsace, and Lorraine, and by Austria-Hungary of the Balkans; Serbian access to the Mediterranean; an ethnic redrawing of Italy's northern frontier; national liberation of Ottoman provinces from Turkish rule; free passage through the Dardenelles; an independent Polish state with seaboard facilities; and—closest to his heart—"A general association of nations [with] specific covenants for the purpose of affording mutual guarantees of political independence and territorial integrity to great and small states alike."

The last point was yet another bang on the peace-league gong that Roosevelt and others had sounded over the years. This time, however, its reverberations refused to die. Creel printed the President's speech for translation and distribution as far away as China and Lapland (and projection over German territory in scattershot "leaflet shells"), achieving a saturation of international opinion that made Woodrow Wilson, the former girls'-school teacher and parochial Presbyterian, look like the only visionary statesman in the world.

THE FOURTEEN POINTS registered seriously, if not favorably, on both sides of the Western Front. "Le bon Dieu n'avait que dix," Clemenceau grumbled.* Britain balked at Wilson's freedom-of-the-seas demand, which would compromise its blockade capability. France wanted stronger language to guarantee war reparations. Vague conciliatory noises came from Germany and Austria. But on the whole, the President seemed to have succeeded brilliantly in drafting a text negotiable by all the governments concerned. No immediate move could be expected toward the great peace conference he envisaged. If and when it happened, the United States had earned a coequal place at the table. Not a few political prophets saw Wilson himself sitting there as chief negotiant.

---

* "The good Lord only had ten."

"I am sorry from the bottom of my heart for Colonel Roosevelt," William Howard Taft said to a dinner companion. "Here he is, the one man in the country most capable of doing things, of handling the big things in Washington, denied the opportunity. . . . My heart goes out to him."

Roosevelt emerged from his doldrums, as he had so often before, by launching into a period of manic public activity. Pausing only to write his January quota of articles for *Metropolitan* magazine and the *Kansas City Star,* plus an introduction to Henry Fairfield Osborn's *The Origin and Evolution of Life,* he delivered ten speeches in nine days in New York, to audiences as diverse as the National Security League and the Boy Food Scouts of P.S. 40. Ray Stannard Baker caught up with him at a memorial service for Joseph Choate, and noted how his personality galvanized the somber proceedings. Witty and graceful, able both to conjure up the ghost of Sir Horace Walpole in the same breath as a Latin epigram (*suaviter in modo, fortiter in re*),* he seemed almost the Bull Moose of old. Jack Cooper's Reducycle had trimmed his waistline by several inches. "Roosevelt remains a virile and significant figure in American life," Baker wrote.

Republican strategists in Washington were of similar opinion. Already thinking ahead to November's congressional elections and the presidential campaign of 1920, they lured Roosevelt down late in the month for four days of policy talk. He took Edith with him, and Alice again made her town house available as a place where the Colonel could hold court, in the manner of a deposed king plotting a return to the throne. Father and daughter enjoyed the comings and goings of Party stalwarts who believed that Wilson's current pride preceded a fall from public esteem. But for Edith, who had not seen the capital since she left it in 1909, the visit was painful. M Street was noisy and dirty now with automobile traffic. There were uniforms everywhere, and ugly wooden army buildings. She could not sit in Henry Adams's parlor without seeing, across Lafayette Square, the radiant mansion where she had brought up Archie and Quentin, married Alice off, and entertained so many of the world's best people. Its gates were shut to her, its servants obeyed another Edith. Adams was clearly dying, a little gray dormouse of a man. Henry Cabot Lodge had lost his wife's reflected charm. Springy was gone from the British Embassy, a failed envoy, maligning his replacement, Lord Reading, with the single word *Jew.* Boozy Nick and brittle Alice went their separate ways.

"Mother found much sadness," Roosevelt reported to Kermit after returning home. "Our old friends are for the most part dead or else of hoary age." A quotation from Oscar Wilde occurred to him: *The dust is dancing with the dust, the dead are whirling with the dead.*

---

* Courtly in manner, courageous in action.

TWO MONTHS' WORTH of snow lay thick around Sagamore Hill in early February, and still the iron cold persisted. On the morning of Tuesday the fifth, when the Colonel motored to Manhattan to work in his *Metropolitan* office, the thermometer dropped to seven degrees below zero.

For obvious reasons, he did not inform Josephine Stricker, his secretary, that he had a severe pain in the rectum. An abscess had formed there, brought on by an attack of fever. Since returning from Brazil, Roosevelt had noticed a correlation between these proclivities of his system. The abscess had been lanced less than twenty-four hours before in Oyster Bay, but he did not feel much relief. His habit was to ignore body signals, so he kept his morning appointments, lunched at the Harvard Club, and dictated through the afternoon to Miss Stricker.

Around four o'clock he felt his trousers filling with blood and fled to the Langdon Hotel, where he kept a suite of rooms. Miss Stricker followed, unsuspecting, and continued to take dictation until she noticed his face was white. She gave him a glass of whiskey that seemed to revive him, but then he staggered to the sofa and fainted, leaving a trail of blood across the carpet. By the time his city physician, Dr. Walton Martin, arrived to treat him, his temperature was 103°F and he sat in a red puddle. He had to be forced to go to bed. Edith found him there later, in care of three implacable nurses. "What a jack I am," he said. "Did you ever see such a performance?"

His pain increased during the night, aggravated by an ominous throbbing in both ears. On Wednesday morning Dr. Martin and an otologist, Arthur B. Duel, agreed that he had to be taken to the Roosevelt Hospital on West Fifty-ninth Street, for examination and surgery under general anesthesia.

The name of the facility, deriving from a great-uncle who had founded it in 1871, was coincidental: it was known for its modern technology, and was rated as one of the finest hospitals in New York. Roosevelt declined an ambulance, and asked to be chauffeured in his own car. A distraught Ethel Derby visited him before he was wheeled to the operating theater. "Father looks terribly white and seems so sick," she wrote her husband. "I can't bear to have him suffering so."

Roosevelt's only complaint was to say that he was weary of malaria relapses, and would like "to be fixed up once and for all." At 4:10 P.M. he was anesthetized. The rectal abscess proved not to have leached into his intestines, as Dr. Martin had feared. But a contributory fistula was found and had to be removed. Two more, potentially lethal abscesses were discovered in his left and right aural canals. Dr. Duel punctured both ears. Knowing his patient's tendency to bleed heavily, he had to work at risky speed to avoid another hemorrhage. As it was, the operation took almost an hour and a half. An exhausted Martin told Edith and Ethel afterward that the Colonel "should have no further trouble."

On the contrary, Roosevelt was so ill the following morning that newspapermen posted a death watch in the hospital lobby. His fever resurged. He was racked by labyrinthine dizziness, vomited repeatedly, and complained of being deaf in the left ear. His eyes kept oscillating from side to side. Duel and Martin could not hide their pessimism.

A fall in his temperature to 99°F proved only temporarily encouraging. That evening his condition became desperate. He was given morphine to ease the agony that pulsed from all three of his wounds. Shortly before dawn next morning, Friday, 8 February, it was announced that Theodore Roosevelt was fighting for life. At 9 A.M. a rumor hit the wires that he had died.

The hospital denied this, but conceded that his surgeons were on emergency call. Another operation, however, was as likely to kill the Colonel as blood poisoning. His left ear was still suppurating, and now the mastoid process appeared to be involved, threatening the base of the brain. Probing that deep might have terrible consequences. Ethel found her father so mummified in bandages that she could see little of his face, and his voice—whispering something about her fighting brothers—was almost inaudible. The infection advanced to the limit of his tolerance, then stopped and began to subside. By the end of the day he was asking for food.

"He's a peach," one of the nurses said.

ROOSEVELT REMAINED HOSPITALIZED for a month. His recovery from sepsis was rapid, but extreme vertigo afflicted him through the middle weeks of February. The slightest movement of his head brought on waves of nausea. That made it doubly difficult for him to reorient himself to his surroundings, because of his blind left eye. He was told that the deafness in his left ear would probably be permanent.

Edith and Ethel alternated in sitting with him. They read him newspaper articles soothing to his blood pressure, and get-well letters from the sackfuls delivered daily by Miss Stricker. The first he answered came from William Howard Taft, who mentioned that he had been through a similar rectal experience. Roosevelt dictated a sympathetic reply, and said of himself, "Am rather rocky, but worth several men."

The President wrote. Cables came from King George V and Clemenceau. Edwin Arlington Robinson penned a few touching words. There was no message from Cecil Spring Rice: Edith suppressed the news that he had just died of a heart attack, en route home to England.

A letter arrived from Quentin. It had been mailed before he had heard of his father's illness, and did not explain his mysterious silence earlier that winter. But visits from Flora, looking pretty and more in love than ever, reassured Roosevelt that all was now well. Quentin's only complaint was that he was still being held back from the Front. His commanding major had "called him down" for demanding to be transferred to the lines, saying that he was needed at Issoudun as an instructor for draftees. Roosevelt advised him to keep trying nevertheless. He should remember for the moment that he had been one of the first volunteers of the war. "You stand as no other men of your generation can stand. You have won the great prize."

When, at last, Quentin confessed what had been wrong with him for so long, he wrote not to his parents but Ethel. Horrified, she shared the truth with them on 27 February. He had succumbed to pneumonia a few weeks before Christmas, as a result of high-altitude training, and had been sent to the Riviera to recuperate. Archie, in a sharp letter endorsed by Ted, had accused him of "slacking" behind the lines. Quentin had consequently sunk into a depression, compounded by his longing for Flora and guilt over the fact that he had a taste for what doughboys in the trenches called *la guerre de luxe*— shopping and theatergoing with Eleanor on visits to Paris, and hopping his Nieuport over to Romorantin for weekends with the hospitable Normants. His Plattsburg buddy Hamilton Coolidge often accompanied him in convoy. They had their own rooms on the château's second floor, overlooking the river Sauldre, and liked to laze up there on Sunday mornings, wearing white robes and breakfasting on croissants and *café au lait*.

Edith Roosevelt was furious at Archie's insensitivity, and more than a little protective. Of all of her children, Quentin was the one most like her in Gallic tastes and temperament. The others spoke French, but Quentin did so with instinctive rapidity, gesturing as he talked. He identified with the *gaîté,* the elegance and subtle snobbery of French culture, as opposed to the Nordic, Slavic, and even Mongol militarism his father admired. Archie and Ted were warriors, cut from coarser cloth. In her own hand, Edith wrote a cable of support, and signed it simply, "Roosevelt."

> YOUR LETTER TO ETHEL CAME. AM SHOCKED BY ATTITUDE OF
> TED AND ARCHIE. IF YOU HAVE ERRED AT ALL IT IS IN TRYING
> TOO HARD IN GETTING TO THE FRONT. YOU MUST TAKE CARE
> OF YOUR HEALTH. WE ARE EXCEEDINGLY PROUD OF YOU.

The Colonel was released from hospital on 4 March, the same day that news came from Brest-Litovsk that Russia had capitulated to Germany in a peace treaty of alarming import. Whether out of desperation or long-term design, the Bolsheviks had sacrificed vast areas of formerly Tsarist territory to the Central Powers, including the Ukraine, Georgia, Poland, Finland, and the

Baltic provinces. Germany could henceforth count on nearly all of Russia's oil production, most of its iron ore, and a cornucopia of its food products. Instead of retreating behind its own borders, as Wilson had demanded in the sixth of his Fourteen Points, the Reich had effectively occupied a large swath of Russia west of Moscow. With relief forces daily amplifying those entrenched along the Hindenburg Line, a major offensive against Paris looked inevitable—most likely in the early spring, before Pershing's army achieved its full fighting mass.

Enraged, Woodrow Wilson began to sound like Clemenceau. The Prussians, he publicly declared, had shown what they thought of his formula for world peace. "There is therefore but one answer open to us. Force, force to the utmost, force without stint or limit."

⤶⤷

THE APPROACH OF SPRING had cracked most of Oyster Bay's ice by the time Roosevelt, still unsteady on his feet, returned to Sagamore Hill. Cove Neck exuded its ancient reek of salt marsh, clam flats, tangled rigging, and seawater. The first crocuses were out. It would be a long time before the enfeebled squire could walk around his property, much less ride a horse. "The destruction of my left inner ear," he wrote Quentin, "has made me lose my equilibrium . . . but in two or three months I should be all right."

Looking over the letter after Miss Stricker had typed it, he scrawled an impulsive postscript: "I wish you could get darling Flora to cross the ocean and marry you! I would escort her over."

On 13 March, Edith came down to breakfast and found her husband already up, pondering a telephone call from United Press. Captain Archibald Roosevelt of Company B, Twenty-sixth Infantry, AEF, had reportedly won France's Croix de Guerre "under dramatic circumstances." A War Department telegram later in the morning advised that Archie had been "slightly wounded." Then a cable from Ted came to say that he had been hit in an arm and leg by shrapnel. Ted's terseness implied there could be worse medical news to come. As soon as Archie was transferable, Eleanor would look after him in Paris.

The Roosevelts were especially moved because Grace, staying with her parents in Boston, had just given birth to Archibald Roosevelt, Jr.—their eighth grandchild. That evening a proud Colonel wrote to tell Archie, Sr., how they had celebrated his blooding in battle: "At lunch Mother ordered in some madeira; all four of us filled the glasses* and drank them off to you; then Mother, her eyes shining, her cheeks flushed, as pretty as a picture, and as spirited as any heroine of romance, dashed her glass on the floor, shivering it

---

* A family friend was visiting.

in pieces, saying 'that glass shall never be drunk out of again'; and the rest of us followed suit and broke our glasses too." He did not add that his own eyes had been wet at that moment.

A few days later he read in an upstate newspaper the prediction of an AEF official in France that Quentin was a young officer worth watching, "as game as they make 'em in aviation." Roosevelt did not hesitate to rebroadcast this quote, along with reports that Ted had nearly been killed in the same battle that wounded Archie, and that Kermit, having acquitted himself bravely in Mesopotamia (learning Persian as he did so), now wished to fight under General Pershing.

Roosevelt's paternal pride swelled steadily. So did his stomach, as every day of improved health turned him back into the trencherman of yore. He argued that the government's food restrictions did not apply to comestibles produced by the Sagamore Hill farm. Ethel was amazed at the amount of lunch he could put away. After one feast she wrote Dick Derby, "Father had 2 plates (cereal plates) of tomatoes, 2 plates of applesauce, 1 plate of potato, grouped around the *pièce de résistance* which was spare ribs of pork. I counted 18 which he ate, & then he refused to let me count further!! He certainly 'eat hearty.' "

Although Roosevelt still chafed over his inability to fight in France, he had become resigned to it enough to accept whatever political or journalistic assignments gave him a feeling of being useful. One of these was a request from Will H. Hays, the new chairman of the RNC, to deliver a formal statement of Party war policy at Portland, Maine, on 28 March. It was intended to be the keynote of the fall Congressional campaign, for which Hays had high hopes.

The Colonel's consultations and correspondence on the speech—he sent a draft to William Howard Taft for suggestions—helped distract him from headlines confirming that the German offensive in northeastern France had begun promptly, on the first day of spring. A bombardment of unbelievable intensity battered Allied artillery emplacements around Arras, while poisonous phosgene fumes spilled like fog into every bunker. The phosgene was mixed with lacrimators, which so stung the eyes of gunners that they pulled off their gas masks, weeping, only to inhale the fog and die. Then concentrated units of storm troopers moved in and drove the British Fifth Army westward, effectively wiping it out.

Under the circumstances, Roosevelt's prediction, in Maine, of three more years of war, necessitating a five-million-man American army, did not sound alarmist. He returned home to hear that the Germans had recaptured all the territory they had lost in the Battle of the Somme. A terrified Jules Jusserand told President Wilson that the Arras salient was now no farther from Paris than Baltimore was from Washington. Clemenceau's government was considering a retreat to Bordeaux.

Wilson remained outwardly impassive, but the emergency was so acute that Jusserand and Lord Reading begged him to allow units of the AEF to be "brigaded" among the French and British armies. General Pershing was adamant against such dissipation of American strength. The President's growing number of critics in Washington suggested that he look to Oyster Bay for guidance. "Wilson always follows T.R., eventually," one of them sneered at a dinner party attended by the secretary of the treasury, William G. McAdoo. "I suppose soon we will hear that he's deaf in one ear."

"Many think he's already deaf in both," McAdoo replied.

Wilson reluctantly agreed to a temporary transfer of ninety thousand U.S. troops. The Allied line held from Reims in the south to Amiens in the north, and the war of attrition resumed. Pershing went back to building up his army and found a place for Kermit as a captain of artillery in the armored car service.

QUENTIN HAPPENED TO have been in Paris just after the first German shells landed. He calculated his chance of being hit at one hundred thousand to one, and with a boy's bravado found the slight danger thrilling. It was enough, however, to remind him of the tenuousness of life, and his father's obsession about getting Flora over to marry him. Letters to that effect kept arriving, written in the Colonel's forceful hand, and not mincing words:

> As for your getting killed, or ordinarily crippled, afterwards, why she would a thousand times rather have married you than not have married you under those conditions; and as for the extraordinary kinds of crippling, they are rare, and anyway we have to take certain chances in life. You and she have now

Quentin foresaw trouble with Flora's parents, and with the passport authorities who were making it difficult for American civilians to cross the Atlantic unless they had war duties in Europe. Perhaps, he wrote her, she could work with Eleanor in the Parisian YWCA, or as a military secretary. She was fluent in French. He was sure he would be flying at the Front by the time she arrived, but wedding leave was permitted. After that he would be able to join her "every six months for a couple of days."

When Quentin next heard from his father, in a letter dated 8 April, Sagamore Hill's maple buds were red and its willow tips green. Robins and sparrows and redwing blackbirds had begun to sing, and frogs were noisy in the lawn ponds. "The Hon. Pa," as Quentin affectionately called him, was still capable of an ecstatic response to the sights and sounds of nature—all the more, this season, because he had come so close to death.

A second German offensive in the Lys sector, recapturing Passchendaele and driving another twelve miles toward Paris, hampered communications between the Roosevelts and their sons for the rest of the month. What information reached them was mostly disturbing. A medical report indicated that Archie's wounds were more serious than they had thought. His left arm had

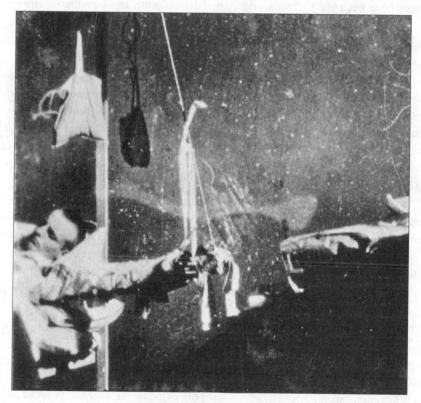

"ARCHIE'S WOUNDS WERE MORE SERIOUS THAN THEY HAD THOUGHT."

Captain Archibald Roosevelt, Croix de Guerre, in traction.

been so severely fractured that the main nerve was cut, and his left kneecap smashed by a shrapnel fragment deeply embedded in lower bone. Medics wanted to amputate the leg, but Eleanor and Ted had managed to dissuade them. There was a photograph of him lying in traction, with his medal pinned to his pillow.

Quentin was lucky not to be in the same hospital. Flying to Paris to see Archie, he had snapped a connecting rod in low clouds, and crash-landed in a pine grove. He had broken his right arm and hurt his always-vulnerable back. The accident had led to a "ghastly" week of depression when "everything looked black." He shared this information with Flora but not his father, who thought soldiers should be positive. (Archie, scarcely able to move, was already swearing to report back for duty.)

Roosevelt chafed at Quentin's renewed silence. "I simply have no idea what you are doing—whether you are fighting, or raging because you can't get into the fighting line." Nor could he guess that Ted was in Flanders, helping to hold back the Lys offensive at Saint-Mihiel. All he knew was that the imbalance there between German and Allied forces, and the passing of the first anniversary of America's entry into the war, had revived his contempt for unpreparedness. He wrote two articles for the *Kansas City Star* so savagely critical of the administration that his editor, Ralph Stout, rejected them.

For some time now the Colonel and his youngest son had been unconsciously moving in tandem, with alternate or parallel fluctuations of mood, and physical ups and downs. Through the middle of May, they both showed signs of rising tension—Quentin over intimations from his commanding officer that he and Ham Coolidge would soon be in action, and Roosevelt over two arduous tours he had agreed to undertake on behalf of the National Security League's "Committee on Patriotism."

Ethel wrote Dick on the seventeenth that she was sitting on the piazza at Sagamore Hill with her parents. "Just across from me is Father, rocking violently to & fro—and ever so busy talking to himself. Poor lamb—he is having a horrid time, for he has too much to do, and it frets him terribly, this looking ahead [and] feeling driven."

Two days later, at Romorantin, Edith Normant took photographs of Quentin and Ham swimming in the Sauldre, then posing in the cockpits of their freshly painted Nieuports, ready to take off for the Front.

⌒

ROOSEVELT HAD THE NOVEL experience of being pelted with peonies at his first speaking stop in Springfield, Ohio, on 25 May. He was the guest of Wittenberg College, a Lutheran school so saturated with Teuton *Kultur* it could well have been an adjunct of its namesake university in Saxony. There to hear him was an audience crammed with German-speaking farmers. They carried great bouquets of the fragrant flowers, which a local nursery had given away free as part of a war chest drive.

John Leary, reporting for the New York *Tribune,* was alarmed when Roosevelt walked onstage and the first soft bombs were tossed at him. Any one could have contained something dangerous. The Colonel's appearance was not calculated to please these *Volk,* because they already knew that he disapproved of their preference for the German liturgy in church. (He felt it was sure to alienate younger worshippers, and turn them away from the faith, as had happened in his own Dutch Reformed Church.)

Roosevelt took his time walking to the podium, as if to emphasize his lack of hostility. The rain of petals continued, until he stood grinning on a perfumed carpet of pink and white.

Moving on to Chicago, he checked in to the Blackstone Hotel. The first person he saw on entering its restaurant was William Howard Taft. Fellow diners applauded as Taft stood up and called, "Theodore!" The two former presidents shook hands with obvious pleasure, straining to hear each other over cheers around the room. They took a small window table and plunged into conversation.

Afterward, a happy Roosevelt told Leary, "He feels exactly as I do about those creatures in Washington and the way they're carrying on."

QUENTIN AND HAM may have wanted to give Edith Normant the impression that they were headed straight into action, but their orders were to fly first to Orly. It was a ferry-pilot field just east of Paris, at any rate closer to glory than the mudflats of Issoudun. If present trends continued, the Front might well come to them: the Germans had launched another offensive, driving the Allies back from the Aisne to the Marne. Wilhelm II, delighted to pretend that he, and not General Erich Ludendorff, was the strategist of this new *Kaiserschlacht,* posed for photographs on the lookout at Craonne, where Napoleon had faced the powers that eventually overwhelmed him.

Quentin went to see Eleanor in her house on the Avenue du Bois de Boulogne. From its east-facing windows, the flashing of guns could be seen like summer lightning. Just as disturbing was the sight of Ted, crimson-eyed and racked with such spasms of coughing that he had to sleep sitting up. He had been gassed and temporarily blinded at Cantigny, in the first American group action of the war. Two hundred of his comrades had been killed around him. But he had refused to give up command of his battalion, or to be evacuated until the three-day assault was over. His superiors were saying they had never seen such heroism.

With this and Archie's example to ponder, not to mention the news that Kermit had been awarded the British Military Cross for bravery in Mesopotamia, Quentin felt compelled to prove himself as the last whelp of "the old Lion." But his only assignment was to test the airworthiness of new planes shipped through Orly. He fell into another of his depressions, worsened by a report from Oyster Bay that Flora had almost no chance of getting a passport to France. Given that, it was small consolation that her parents had agreed to let them marry. "It seems to me now," he wrote her, "as tho' nothing could ever fill that void that the last year has left in my heart."

It was a year that had taken him from Newport to Nieuport, and Quentin could not see how the experience had bettered him. If French soldiers retreating from the Front were right in shouting "La guerre est finie" at Americans going the other way, he might at least survive, and unite with Flora after all; but what sort of world would they have to adjust to?

General Pershing tried to persuade a despairing Clemenceau that the war was not over. The United States was ready to announce that it had a million troops in France, and a million—or more—on the way. The Allies simply needed to hold the Germans off, at this moment of the Reich's maximum advancement west and east. Overextension always preceded collapse, in Pershing's view. The strategic situation was poised. "It may not look encouraging just now," he said, "but we are certain to win in the end."

On 7 June, the day Quentin hoped he might be sent into action, Roosevelt was hit by an attack of erysipelas, a streptococcal inflammation of the leg that had bothered him so often since his traffic accident in 1902. He was in Chicago en route to Omaha, still traveling as a spokesman for the National Security League. "Jack, I'm pretty sick," he confided to John Leary. It was his way of saying that he was running a temperature of 104°F. Fortunately Edith was at hand to nurse him on the train, along with a doctor to control his fever. Roosevelt insisted on keeping every engagement the League had mapped out for him, distracting himself from pain by reading Polybius and what his wife described as "hundreds of thousands" of ten-cent magazines.

When they got back home in the middle of the month, a cable from Quentin was waiting. He and Ham Coolidge had been ordered forward at last.

"My joy for you and pride in you drown my anxiety," Roosevelt wrote. "Of course I don't know whether you are to go in the pursuit planes—or battle planes or whatever you call them."

In fact, as Quentin reported to Flora, he had already ridden to the Front on his motorcycle, after detaching himself from an emotional, one-armed embrace by Archie. "He evidently felt that he was saying a last fond farewell to me."

That lugubrious soul was convinced that no Roosevelt in uniform would return to America alive. Quentin thought this funny, as well as the fact that the anti-aircraft shells he would be dodging in the future were known among pilots as "Archies." He had already, he boasted, experienced flak on his maiden patrol along the lines as a member of the First (U.S.) Pursuit Group. "It is really exciting when you see the stuff bursting in great black puffs around you, but you get used to it in about fifteen minutes."

WITH KERMIT NOW attached to the Seventh Field Artillery Regiment of the First Division in France, Roosevelt could congratulate himself on the "first-ness" of all his sons. News that Ted had been cited for both a Croix de Guerre and American Silver Star turned him into something of a paterfamilial bore. Finley Peter Dunne heard him out and said, "Colonel, one of these days those boys of yours are going to put the name of Roosevelt on the map."

As his erysipelas ebbed, he spent the latter part of June at Sagamore Hill, lazing on the piazza with a pile of books and listening to birds. "I have finished my last tour of speechmaking," he wrote Quentin, in words that his family had long learned to ignore. Immediately came the disclaimer: "From now on I shall speak . . . only just enough to put whatever power I have back of the war, and to insist that we carry it through until we win such a peace as will ensure against danger from Germany for at least a generation to come."

For at least a generation to come. Before Quentin left Romorantin, a son had been born to one of the Normants, and he had found a macabre souvenir on his pillow. It was a baby doll and box of chocolates labeled, "From the *poilu* of 1938."

In the place he was now—the censor would not allow him to say where—men had no interest in times beyond the present. The average life of a chase pilot on the Front in the summer of 1918 was eleven days. Quentin was clear-eyed about his own vulnerability, having lost a Mineola comrade earlier in the year. In an attempt to condition Flora to the prospect of him being shot down, he assured her that death came quickly to aviators, as opposed to gassed doughboys or drowning sailors. "There's no better way,—if one has got to die. . . . 30 seconds of horror and it's all over,—for they say that it's all in that length of time, after the plane's been hit."

To his mother, he was determinedly upbeat. "The real thing is that I'm on the Front—cheers, oh cheers—and I'm very happy." Then he learned that he was being transferred to a "hot" sector on one of the salients threatening Paris.

On the Fourth of July, Roosevelt dined with Fanny Parsons in Manhattan. She too had a son in uniform abroad. They both felt, and shared, a lift in the national morale. After the terror of March and April and the good news in June of U.S. troops repelling Ludenorff's last offensive at Château-Thierry and Belleau Wood, the war finally looked winnable. For however many more months it continued, American power, burgeoning with the force of lava long suppressed, was evidently going to shape the outcome.

Little tricolors decorated the Colonel's table. He was in the same high spirits that had enchanted Fanny forty years before. Then the headwaiter brought over an evening paper, pointing to a cable report that Quentin had just made his first sortie over the German line. Roosevelt read it without comment and set the paper aside, but Fanny noticed that his face had darkened. For the rest of the meal they talked with less animation.

❧

SIX DAYS LATER, Quentin shot down his first "Boche." He was in command of a small squadron of Nieuports, and was flying as top man on a high patrol when he got blown off course at 5,200 meters. Descending out of the sun, he came upon a trio of Pfalz monoplanes. "Great excitement!" he wrote Flora. "They had white tails with black crosses. . . . I was scared perfectly green, but then I thought to myself that I was so near I might as well take a crack at one of them." He fired, then hustled for home, fifteen kilometers away beyond Château-Thierry. In his rearview mirror was the pleasing sight of his victim tumbling into lower clouds, and two outraged pursuers unable to catch up with him. There was no confirmation yet that he had scored a kill, but he had tasted what passed for blood in the air, and that evening tooled in to Paris to celebrate. He and Eleanor had dined at Ciro's and gone on to Grand Guignol.

Now (Quentin was writing on 11 July) his squadron had relocated yet again. He was billeted in a little French town not far from Reims, where he had first seen airplanes flying, nine summers before. Flora would want to know about his quarters: a ground-floor room in a white plaster house with a weathercock on the roof and a blooming garden behind. "O ruin! There goes an *alerte* & I must run, or rather fly, so I'll just finish this off. Goodbye, dear sweetheart, & a kiss from your QR."

❧

ROOSEVELT HEARD ABOUT Quentin's score that same day, in a cable dispatch that thrilled him. He wrote to tell Ethel, who had taken her children to Islesboro, Maine, for the hot months. "Whatever now befalls Quentin, he has had his crowded hour, and his day of honor and triumph."

On the afternoon of Tuesday, 16 July, a cryptic advisory from Paris alerted reporters: WATCH SAGAMORE HILL IN EVENT OF [DELETED BY CENSOR]. The Colonel was dictating to Miss Stricker when Philip Thompson, a reporter from the Associated Press, showed the cable to him. "Something has happened to one of the boys," Roosevelt said, closing the door in case Edith was within earshot.

Rapid deduction (Archie and Ted incapacitated, Kermit not yet at the Front) made it plain that the news concerned Quentin. But what news? He had no choice but to ask Thompson not to alarm Edith, and continue to dictate as if nothing had happened. One of his letters of the day was to Kermit. He made no mention of the AP advisory, but could not resist saying, "It seems dreadful that I, sitting at home in ease and safety, should try to get the men I love dearest into the zone of fearful danger and hardship. . . . Mother, who has the heroic spirit if ever a woman had, would not for anything in the world have you four behave otherwise than you have done, although her heartstrings are torn with terrible anxiety."

Then a cable from Pershing arrived:

REGRET VERY MUCH THAT YOUR SON LT. QUENTIN ROOSEVELT
REPORTED AS MISSING. ON JULY 14 WITH A PATROL OF TWELVE
PLANES HE LEFT ON A MISSION OF PROTECTING PHOTOGRAPHIC
SECTION. SEVEN ENEMY PLANES WERE SIGHTED & ATTACKED,
AFTER WHICH ENEMY PLANES RETURNED AND OUR PLANES
BROKE OFF COMBAT RETURNING TO THEIR BASE. LT. ROOSEVELT
DID NOT RETURN. A MEMBER OF THE SQUADRON REPORTS
SEEING ONE OF OUR PLANES FALL OUT OF THE COMBAT AND
INTO THE CLOUDS AND THE FRENCH REPORT AN AMERICAN
PLANE WAS SEEN DESCENDING. I HOPE HE MAY HAVE LANDED
SAFELY. WILL ADVISE YOU IMMEDIATELY ON RECEIPT OF
FURTHER INFORMATION.

At sunset Roosevelt changed out of his knickerbocker suit, bathed, and dressed for dinner as usual. With Ethel and the grandchildren away, the house was as quiet as it had ever been. For whatever reason, Edith left her daily diary blank when they went to bed.

Before breakfast the next day, Thompson returned to say that further dispatches from Europe indicated that Quentin had been killed. The reports, already printed in the morning papers, were unconfirmed but ominously definite. The Colonel paced up and down the piazza. "But—Mrs. Roosevelt? How am I going to break it to her?"

He disappeared into the house. Thompson was left alone as early morning breezes swept up the hillside from the bay.

Thirty minutes later Roosevelt emerged with a one-line statement. "Quentin's mother and I are very glad that he got to the Front and had a chance to render some service to his country, and to show the stuff there was in him before his fate befell him."

He was due in town around noon, preparatory to leaving early Thursday for Saratoga Springs, where he had promised to address the New York State Republican convention. An organizer of the event called to ask, sympathetically, if he wanted to cancel. Roosevelt replied that on the contrary, he would honor his engagement. Taft was going to be there. Together, they had to set the Party on a course that would humiliate Woodrow Wilson in the fall Congressional elections. "I must go; it is my duty."

Telegrams of condolence began to arrive by the hundreds. Roosevelt spent a couple of hours dictating acknowledgments to them. At times he choked and cried, but would not stop until his chauffeur came to take him and Miss Stricker into Manhattan. Edith emerged from the house to see them off, then turned red-eyed to Philip Thompson.

"We must do everything we can to help him," she said, as if her own feelings did not matter.

Roosevelt had no sooner reached his office than Hermann Hagedorn, a thirtyish writer at work on a biography of him, came to pick him up for lunch. They walked through streets emblazoned with press posters announcing Quentin's death. Albert Shaw, editor of *American Review of Reviews,* awaited them at the Harvard Club.

"Now, Colonel, you know it may not be true," Shaw said. "I would not make up my mind until I hear from General Pershing direct."

"No, it is true," Roosevelt said. "Quentin is dead."

With that he changed the subject, and talked lucidly throughout the meal, giving Hagedorn his take on the events of 1912. But there was a dim look behind his spectacles. Afterward Hagedorn noted, "The old side of him is gone, the old exuberance, the boy in him has died."

Edith came later by train to stay with her husband overnight. Alice telegrammed to remind them that the newspaper reports were still unconfirmed. She was coming up from Washington anyway.

Roosevelt went upstate the following morning, Thursday, 18 July, not knowing that during the night, the Allies had launched the Second Battle of the Marne. It was a devastatingly powerful counterattack, driving German forces back from Château-Thierry toward the country west of Reims where Quentin had disappeared.

At 3:20 that afternoon the chairman of the convention in Saratoga Town Hall announced that the next speaker would be Theodore Roosevelt. "Before the Colonel begins, I wish to voice on behalf of this audience our common sorrow and our common pride in what has come to afflict him in these fateful days of the war."

There was a tumultuous standing ovation when Roosevelt walked onstage in a gray suit with black cravat. But it subsided the moment he laid his speech on the lectern and held up his hand. Isaac Hunt, an upstate delegate who had been his first ally in the New York Assembly, thirty-six years before, was chilled by the anguish on his face.

Roosevelt looked around the room, noticed a number of women on the floor for the first time in state party history, and hailed them as "My fellow voters, my fellow citizens, with equal rights of citizenship here in New York." For the next hour, whenever he spoke off the cuff, he addressed himself to them. His typed text was a standard appeal for an end to hyphenated Americanism, a speeded-up war effort under Republican governance, and postwar preparedness. He wanted to see the current army extended so as to be able to completely overwhelm the Central Powers. "Belgium must be reinstated and reimbursed [*applause*]. France must receive back Alsace and Lorraine [*applause*]. Turkey must be driven from Europe [*applause*]; Armenia must be made free and the Syrian Christians protected and the Jews given Palestine [*applause*]."

He made no reference whatever to Quentin, except obliquely toward the end of his script, when he looked again at the female delegates and said, "Surely in this great crisis, where we are making sacrifices on a scale never before known, surely when we are demanding such fealty and idealism on the part of the young men sent abroad to die, surely we have the right to ask and to expect an equal idealism in life from the men and women who stay home."

The words said little, but his listeners were transfixed by what he left unsaid. Before he got back to New York the following morning, Friday, an urgent effort was under way to draft him for governor. Taft, Elihu Root, Charles Evans Hughes, and even William Barnes, Jr., subscribed to it. Roosevelt declared that he was not available. "I have only one fight left in me," he told his sister Corinne, "and I think I should reserve my strength in case I am needed in 1920."

She was alarmed. "Theodore, you don't really feel ill, do you?"

"No, but I am not what I was."

Later in the day he motored to Oyster Bay with Edith, Alice, and Ethel, who had come down from Maine. When they got home, a cable from Eleanor in Paris was waiting for them: QUENTIN'S PLANE WAS SEEN TO DIVE 800 METERS, NOT IN FLAMES. SEEN TO STRIKE GROUND. COULD HAVE BEEN UNDER CONTROL AS DID NOT SPIN. CHANCE EXISTS HE IS A PRISONER.

Flora Whitney was nowhere to be seen.

⁓

IT TURNED OUT that Flora had also received a cable from Eleanor—EVERY REASON BELIEVE REPORT QUENTIN ABSOLUTELY UNTRUE—and was clutching to it like an oar in a storm. Newspapers got hold of the story, and a new uncertainty built up through Saturday morning.

The Colonel, clutching himself at every "duty" that would keep him from breaking down, went ahead with a prearranged reception for some Japanese Red Cross officials. They were brought to Sagamore Hill by Henry P. Davison, chairman of the American Red Cross war council, and his son Trubee. The young man watched fascinated as Roosevelt took his guests on a trophy tour of the North Room, then delivered a speech of welcome, which he had evidently composed earlier in the week.

After the Japanese bowed their way out, bearing copies of the speech exquisitely calligraphed on rice paper, Trubee Davison took Roosevelt aside and asked, "What hope have you for Quentin?"

Roosevelt reached into his pocket. "Trubee, just twenty minutes before you arrived, I received this telegram from President Wilson."

The telegram confirmed that Quentin had been killed in action. His death had been certified by German military authorities and broadcast by the Wolfe press agency in Berlin. A handwritten translation of the dispatch was brought to the Roosevelts later in the day:

> *On Saturday July 14th an American squadron comprising of 12 planes tried to break the German defense over the Marne. In a violent combat one American aviator stubbornly made repeated attacks. This culminated in a duel between him and a German non Commissioned officer who after a short fight succeeded in getting a good aim at his brave but inexperienced opponent whose machine fell after a few shots near the village of Chamery 10 kilometers north of the Marne.*
>
> *His pocket case showed him to be Lieut. Quentin Roosevelt of the Aviation section of the U.S.A. The personal belongings of the fallen airman are being carefully kept with a view of sending them later to his relatives.*
>
> *The earthly remains of the brave young airman were buried with military honors by the German airmen near where he fell.*

CHAPTER 28

Sixty

Ye gods that have a home beyond the world,
Ye that have eyes for all man's agony,
Ye that have seen this woe that we have seen, —
Look with a just regard,
And with an even grace,
Here on the shattered corpse of a shattered king,
Here on a suffering world where men grow old,
And wander like sad shadows till, at last,
Out of the flare of life,
Out of the whirl of years,
Into the mist they go,
Into the mist of death.

WHEN AMERICAN FORCES ADVANCED through the tiny village of Chamery, in the Marne province of France, they came upon a cross-shaped fragment of a Nieuport fighter sticking out of a field just east of the road to Coulonges. Some German soldier had taken a knife and scratched on it the word ROO-SEVELT. It marked Quentin's grave, and a few yards away the rest of his plane lay wrecked. By the time the last troops passed on toward Reims, nothing was left except the cross. All other bits of the Nieuport had been reverently stolen.

The autopsy performed by the Germans before Quentin's burial indicated that he had been killed before he crashed. Two bullets had passed through his brain. He had been thrown out on impact, and photographed where he fell.

❧

WOODROW WILSON'S TELEGRAM of Saturday, 20 July 1918 ("Am greatly distressed that your son's death is confirmed. I had hoped for other news"), was not the last blow to strike the Roosevelts that weekend. It was followed within hours by a cable from Eleanor stating that Ted had been hurt in action. She said his wound was not serious. But she had also been reassuring about Quentin.

Ted was a casualty of the counteroffensive headlined in forty-two-point type across the top of Sunday morning's front page of *The New York Times:* ALL GERMANS PUSHED BACK OVER THE MARNE; ALLIES GAIN THREE MILES SOUTH OF SOISSONS; NOW HOLD 20,000 PRISONERS AND 400 GUNS. Under such a banner, the story about him ("Oldest Roosevelt Son Is Wounded: News of Theodore's Injury Comes on Heels of Confirmation of Quentin's Death") drew the eye much more than another given exactly the same columnar weight: "Ex-Tsar of Russia Killed by Order of Ural Soviet."

Theodore and Edith therefore had an added reason to attend early mass and adjust, or try to adjust, to the enormity of the void that had opened so suddenly in their landscape. But they had to brace for a special order of service. That Sunday happened to be the third of the month, when the names of all parish members serving the country were read out. Quentin's was not included. He was the first citizen of Oyster Bay to be killed in the war.

They returned home in luxurious sunshine to receive what promised to be an unendurable number of condolence calls. One, late in the afternoon, was from Flora. She was, in Ethel's words, "perfectly wonderful . . . calm and controlled." A less sentimental person might have perceived that the girl was in a state of near catatonia, so stiff with shock that she could neither think nor feel. Flora wanted to be alone, but irrationally wanted to share her solitude with those equally bereft—the Colonel above all. As he received mourners and endured their attempts at comfort, he gave no sign of desolation, emanating only what Corinne called an "ineffable gentleness."

Quentin had died so young, without building an adult life away from home, that Sagamore Hill was still infused with his personality. Edith, better equipped to handle the catastrophe than her husband, saw that what was needed for them all was to get away from the house. She said to Ethel, "Why not come to Islesboro to see you?" Theodore had never visited that part of Maine, where the Derby family had summered for decades. Its strangeness alone would be a distraction. Little Richard and tiny "Edie" would be there to administer innocent therapy, and Flora could come too, if she felt like it.

Ethel went north at once to prepare to receive them. Behind her she left details of the itinerary they were to follow on Thursday. They must take an overnight Pullman from New York to Rockland, then transfer to a small steamer that would deposit them on the south end of Islesboro, at a place called Dark Harbor.

❧

THE LANDING DID NOT at first sight justify its depressing name, being an inlet full of morning light. But the gray and brown-shingled "cottages" of

New England patriarchs looming through stands of pine, hump-roofed and dormered above their rubblestone terraces, did their best to uglify the shoreline and camouflage the fortunes that secluded Dark Harbor from poorer parts of Islesboro. If Ethel had hesitated to marry, she had at least married well. This year she was staying not in the big Derby house, with its black timbers and prisonlike Norman tower, but in a smaller cottage owned by a Wall Street accountant. It surveyed Penobscot Bay from the top of a knoll and had the virtue of a breezy piazza sheltered from the afternoon sun. Importantly for Roosevelt, who liked to keep mobile even when reading, there was a rocking chair on the porch, and a rowboat at the foot of some granite steps cut down to the sea.

He and Edith arrived on Friday unannounced, but an islander at the dock recognized them and called out, "Three cheers for the man who ought to be in France." Ethel was waiting to greet her parents. As they rode off in a buggy—Islesboro permitted no automobiles—the Colonel was seen to be already deep in conversation with Richard and Edie.

"In time of trouble, the unconsciousness of children is often a great comfort," he wrote Belle later.

That was even more so for Edith than for himself. Although she had to be, in her own expression, the central card upon which the rest of the Roosevelt pack leaned, her pain was unassuageable. She could not indulge, as Theodore did, in conventional pieties about Quentin dying "as the heroes of old died, as brave and fearless men must die when a great cause calls"—words that betrayed his inability, so far, to grasp his own responsibility in the matter. For Archie, born to fight and be wounded and fight again, Edith was capable of smashing a triumphal glass to the floor; for Quentin, constituted differently, she made a gesture more womanly than melodramatic. She said she would not wear black for him. White summer linen better expressed his obliteration.

There was blackness enough, in and around Dark Harbor, to reflect her husband's grief and guilt over the next two weeks. He often rowed out alone, past coal-black rocks and pebble beaches blackening as the tide washed in. Great piles of blue-black clamshells along the shore memorialized the island's vanished Indians. Black-headed loons yodeled. He wrote Kermit that from out in the bay, "I can see the moose, caribou and black bear in the glades or by the pools—ghosts all!"

Nevertheless, the place was purifying, with its salt- and balsam-scented breezes and lack of mainland noise. Pious Ethel conducted household prayers every night. Except for a patriotic address that Roosevelt felt he had to give one Sunday at the Islesboro Inn, he and Edith were left undisturbed. An almost mute Flora came north on 6 August to be with them for their last four days. She confided to Ethel that she seemed incapable of feeling anything "except occasionally a great overpowering hurt."

"It is no use pretending that Quentin's death is not very terrible," Roosevelt wrote Belle on the eve of their departure from the island. "There is nothing to comfort Flora at the moment; but she is young. . . . As for Mother, her heart will ache for Quentin until she dies."

❧

THEY WERE ALL BRACING for the delivery of a trunk of personal effects that Ham Coolidge had promised Quentin he would send to Sagamore Hill, in the event of it becoming surplus equipment.

It arrived, packed by Ham but also reflecting, in the orderliness of its contents (such as a sheaf of Flora's letters, neatly numbered and tied) Quentin's integrated personality. The mechanic in him had enjoyed fitting things together, in sequences that made for power or taut structure. Even his poems were balanced, their meter meticulous, their rhyme schemes sometimes complex—*abcccb, adcccd*—but logical.

As Edith and Flora undertook the task of going through these leavings of a life, Roosevelt and Miss Stricker tried to extract, from an inpouring of condolence letters and newspaper tributes, some sense of the man Quentin had become during the year he had spent in France. The most informative testimony came from fellow aviators, who wrote that he was a reincarnation of his father—specifically, the young "Teedie" who had so enlivened the Harvard class of 1880. Emerging from their reminiscences was a jovial, toothy, myopic, often wildly exuberant youth, garrulous and gregarious, courtly toward women, with a habit of bursting into rooms and attracting instant attention.

There was little evidence, however, of the personal momentum that had always characterized the Colonel. Quentin's energy had been explosive rather than propulsive. And often he had suffered the drag of depression—a "black gloom" that he could not hide from Ham Coolidge, and freely confessed to Flora. It was more chronic than the rare attacks of melancholy that Roosevelt had no trouble surmounting. As Edith had long ago remarked, Quentin was "a complex sort of person," with a tendency to "smoulder."

Only in two respects had he ever approached fulfillment: as a boy born to fly, and as Flora's lover. Test-piloting a French Spad, he wrote that he had felt "part of the machine," as if it were an extension of his own body. "It asks you for what it wants. . . . If it gets a puff under a wing and wants an aileron to take care of it, you can feel it in the pressure of the stick. . . . Same with the flippers." His last 120 h.p. Nieuport had been just as responsive: "You can climb at the most astonishing rate,—& do perfectly wicked *chandelles*."[*]

So Quentin had written Flora, confident she would share his delight, even

---

[*] Tight, smooth, climbing turns that reverse direction by 180 degrees.

if she wondered what candles had to do with it. As he was part of his plane, she was part of him. "The months that have gone, instead of blurring, have etched you deeper and deeper into my heart."

The most consolation she could give herself was to say, numbly, "His back will never hurt him now."

—⁂—

IN HIS OXFORD LECTURE on biological analogies in history, Roosevelt had spoken of the tertiary period, wherein "form succeeds form, type succeeds type, in obedience to laws of evolution, of progress and retrogression, of development and death." He was now in his own such transition, moving into a precipitous decline that was as much disillusionment as grief. Only twice before had he suffered as much—at nineteen, when his father died, and at twenty-four, when the loss of his first wife and mother, in the same house on the same night, had almost unhinged him. But then he had been young and full of growth. Neither catastrophe had taught him anything about himself except that he was strong enough to survive.

The death of Quentin, in contrast, hit him after a spring in which he had himself nearly died, and toward the end of a decade that he had always said would be his last. Archie's narrow escape and Ted's gassing had prepared him for worse news from the Front, but the tension inherent in such anticipation had, paradoxically, weakened him, the longer he braced himself. Roosevelt had little physical resilience any more. Cuban and Amazonian pathogens were rampant in his system, which had been further battered by erysipelas and a recent attack of ptomaine poisoning.

But what made this loss so devastating to him was the truth it conveyed: that death in battle was no more glamorous than death in an abattoir. Under some much-trodden turf in France, Quentin lay as cold as a steer fallen off a hook. *Look now, in your ignorance, on the face of death,* the boy had written in one of his attempts at fiction. The words seemed to admonish a father who had always romanticized war.

"There is no use writing about Quentin," Roosevelt told Edith Wharton, "for I should break down if I tried." But by the end of August he had steeled himself enough to write a generalized eulogy for all the Quentins fallen and still falling in Europe:

> Only those are fit to live who do not fear to die; and none are fit to die who have shrunk from the joy of life and the duty of life. Both life and death are parts of the same Great Adventure. . . . Never yet was a country worth dying for unless its sons and daughters thought of life as something concerned only with the selfish evanescence of the indi-

vidual, but as a link in the great chain of creation and causation, so
that each person is seen in his true relations as an essential part of the
whole, whose life must be made to serve the larger and continuing life
of the whole.

After this magnificent beginning, his tribute degenerated into an embarrassing argument that the bed and battleground were equal fields of honor.
Prowess on each was necessary to militate against race suicide. Straining for

"Look now, in your ignorance, on the face of death."
Quentin photographed by the Germans in front of his crashed plane.

eloquence, Roosevelt sank to a level of bathos more suited to the death of Little Nell. He went on at length about dark drinks proffered by the Death
Angel, and girls whose boy-lovers were struck down in their golden mornings.
But the hackneyed images did not work. Theodore Roosevelt was just another
bereaved father unable to say what he felt. Much more expressive were the
words he was heard sobbing in the stable at Sagamore Hill, with his face
buried in the mane of his son's pony: "Poor Quentyquee!"

⤙⤚

WHEN THE ARMY offered to exhume and repatriate Quentin's body, the Roosevelts declined. "We greatly prefer that Quentin shall continue to lie on the
spot where he fell in battle, and where the foemen buried him," the Colonel
wrote. He had heard from Pershing that the crash site had become a shrine for

passing troops. "After the war is over, Mrs. Roosevelt and I intend to visit the grave, and then to have a small stone put up . . . not disturbing what has already been erected in his memory by his French and American comrades in arms."

In another gesture of sympathy, a Congressional commission released the Nobel Peace Prize money—$45,483 in cash and liquidated securities—that Roosevelt had been trying to get back for years. He was perversely pleased that the fund's trustees had never been able to agree how to spend it, because he now had his own ideas for its disbursal. Every cent would go to war-related charities, or individuals and organizations planning to improve social conditions in the postwar world. His list of major recipients included the American, Japanese, and Italian Red Cross, the Salvation Army, the Jewish Welfare Board, "Mrs. Theodore Roosevelt, Jr., now working in the Y.M.C.A. in France," Herbert Hoover, for use in Belgian war relief, a hospitality council for "colored troops [and] colored women and girls in and about the camps and cantonments," and Maria Bochkareva of the Women's Death Battalion, "as a token of my respect for those Russians who have refused to follow the Bolshevists in their betrayal to Germany of Russia, of the Allies, and of the cause of liberty through the world." He allocated small, but attention-getting amounts to ethnic groups persecuted or fighting for freedom against autocracies—Czechs, Serbs, Armenians, and Assyrian Christians. In something of a first for a former president, he promised to allocate "further sums of money from my royalties on certain scenarios of motion pictures."

One of the movies he had in mind was to be a McClure Productions six-reeler entitled *The Fighting Roosevelts,* starring three different actors as himself in boyhood, youth, and maturity. The draft script called for a dramatic final climax, with one of his sons dying on the Western Front—an ending that could obviously be reshot, should any more of them fall.

On 4 September, Archie, transferred back to the United States for advanced therapy on his paralyzed left arm, returned limping to Sagamore Hill. The splendor of his blue and gold sleeve stripes, denoting a year's service at the Front, in no way impressed Archibald Roosevelt, Jr., whom Grace had rushed down from Boston to show to him. Little Archie was only five months old, so both father and son were strangers. They eyed each other with a mutual lack of interest, while the rest of the family party tried to adjust to "Big" Archie's worryingly limp arm. Two operations in Paris had failed to reconnect the severed main nerve well enough to restore full mobility.

Archie had become skeletal during his long convalescence. His hollow cheeks drew back from protruding teeth, and he wore a new, habitual frown. He admitted to be suffering from a "bad case of nerves." Even if doctors at the Columbia Base Hospital in the Bronx—who had granted him only temporary home leave—were successful in fixing his arm and digging the shrapnel out of his leg, they had warned him he might not be able to rejoin Ted's regiment for another eight months. Which was all Archie wanted to do. Like many soldiers who had seen the worst of the war, he had become addicted to it.

&

"FALL HAS COME," Roosevelt wrote Kermit on 13 September. "The dogwood berries are reddening, the maple leaves blush, the goldenrod and asters flaunt their beauty; and log fires burn and crumble in the north room in the evenings."

Very slowly, he was recovering his joy in the natural world, after a summer of finding himself unable to think of much but mortality. Hearing that Ted had been nearly blinded and killed, Dick Derby thrown into the air by a shell, and seeing how "crippled" Archie was had compounded his grief over Quentin's fate. However, all were safe for the moment, as well as Kermit, detached to an artillery school in Saumur. General Pershing had written to say that Ted was about to be promoted to a colonelcy. Two Colonel Roosevelts in one family, plus two decorated captains and one dead hero, added up to plenty of honor.

That did not help him feel any less sidelined, or any less beaten down physically and emotionally. The "gentleness" Corinne discerned in her brother struck others as exhaustion, if not desuetude: the Rooseveltian *vigor di vita* was gone. One day his literary colleague Mary Roberts Rinehart drove from New York out to Oyster Bay with him and Edith. "The Colonel sat with his chauffeur, saying nothing. Most of the time his head was bent on his breast, and I can still see his sturdy broad-shouldered figure, stooped and tired. For the first time he seemed old to me, old and weary."

Roosevelt was loath to divide what was left of his energy between politics and war work, saying that he would tour in the fall only on behalf of Secretary McAdoo's fourth "Liberty Loan" appeal. Extra military funds were urgently needed: the number of soldiers, sailors, and marines in service was now approaching three million, and the latest registration had increased the pool of potential draftees to an almost incredible twenty-four million—one and a half times as much as the total manpower of Britain and France. Roosevelt's still-smoldering anger toward Woodrow Wilson was fueled by this evidence of how the nation could have armed itself after the sinking of the *Lusitania*, shortening the war and saving countless lives. Quentin's included, perhaps.

The most he would do to help the GOP in its campaign to win back the Senate in November was volunteer a major address at Carnegie Hall, one week before the election, and write supportive letters and articles. On the twenty-eighth he set off on his fund-raising tour, regretfully leaving behind the sight of beach rosemary in pale, late bloom along Lloyd's Neck.

AS HE TRAVELED WEST via Ohio to Missouri and Nebraska, he edited a selection of his recent journalism for book publication by Scribners. Charles
Scribner was emboldened to invest in him yet again, on the strength of widespread sympathy engendered by newspaper syndication of "The Great Adventure." Inevitably, that phrase became the title of the hardback release.

"It's pretty poor business to be writing little books in these times of terrible action," Roosevelt apologized in a letter to Belle, "but it's all I can do, or
at least all I am allowed to do by the people in power in Washington."

Scribbling on dutifully, he used up the last of the triple-carbon notebooks
that had served him so well in Africa and Brazil.

His speeches attracted large, affectionate crowds, but after nearly forty
years of shouting at people he was no longer capable of saying anything new.
It was enough for these tens of thousands of regular folks to say that they had
"seen" the great Teddy. He still felt a kinship with them: it was they and their
kind who had helped him become, in his own words, "at heart, as much a
Westerner as an Easterner." On his way home in early October, he spent the
night in Billings, Montana, where once, as a dude ranchman from New York,
he had knocked out a barroom bully. George Myers, his old cattleman, was on
hand to visit with him at his hotel.

"Have you got a room, George?"

Myers shook his head.

"Share mine with me," Roosevelt said, "and we'll talk about old times."

HE ARRIVED BACK EAST complaining of acute inflammatory pain in his
left leg and both feet. Rheumatism was a disease he had long been afraid of,
since it had racked his sister Bamie for most of her life, and made a hopeless
invalid of his favorite presidential appointee, William Henry Moody. He had
himself been bothered by it, on and off, since his last years in the White
House, but never as sharply as now. If the two physicians he consulted—
Drs. Walton Martin in Manhattan and George W. Faller in Oyster Bay—
detected symptoms of rheumatic fever, a life-threatening pathology that
often struck patients in October, they kept their concern from him. He was
given conventional anti-inflammatory medicine and told to rest as much as
possible.

Returning to Oyster Bay, he put himself in Dr. Faller's care, and adjusted
to the irony that he was once again prostrated, just when the presidency of
Woodrow Wilson was nearing the zenith of its achievement. On the night he
and George Myers had sat talking "about old times" in a hick town in Montana, the new Chancellor of Germany, Prince Maximilian of Baden, had

asked the President ot begin negotiations for a "restoration of peace," along the lines of his "Fourteen Points" agenda of last January.

Roosevelt's tour had coincided, moreover, with the greatest combined offensive of the war: nine armies, including Pershing's, assailing the Central Powers from Flanders all the way south to Palestine. The giant operation was still continuing, and Pershing was making a bloody mess of it in the Argonne, but an armistice on the Western Front was obviously imminent.

Britain and France did not want the President to negotiate anything less triumphant than unconditional surrender by each enemy in turn. Wilson declined to do what any belligerent wanted. Sure that he, alone and at last, held the fate of the world in his hands, he had responded with a "note of inquiry" asking Prince Maximilian to confirm whether Germany accepted all of the Fourteen Points—thereby endorsing the idea of a League of Nations—and to attest that a prince had constitutional authority to end a war waged by generals.

This sounded to Roosevelt like the prelude to another drawn-out period of "elocution" while more and more *poilus,* tommies, and doughboys died. "I regret greatly," he said in a dictated statement, "that President Wilson has entered into these negotiations, and I trust that they will be stopped." The Fourteen Points were "couched in such vague language that many of them may mean anything or nothing . . . while others are absolutely mischievous." *Freedom of the seas,* for example, could be construed as permission to go on deploying U-boats. *Disarmament* could force America to give up the defense system it had so belatedly and expensively created. Giving *autonomy* instead of *independence* to oppressed subject races would be "a base betrayal of the Czechoslovaks, the Armenians, and our other smaller allies, and the cynical repudiation of the idea that we meant what we said when we spoke of making the world safe for democracy."

He earnestly hoped, he said, that Wilson would "refuse to compound a felony by discussing terms with felons."

These words showed that, ailing or not, the Colonel still packed a rhetorical punch. Similar statements by Henry Cabot Lodge and a nearly insubordinate General Pershing enraged the administration. Political strategists fantasizing another run by Roosevelt for the presidency in 1920 had a fair idea who he would choose as his secretary of state and secretary of war. Following up, Roosevelt sent an open telegram to Lodge, and carbon-copied it to Senators Poindexter and Hiram Johnson for promulgation "from one ocean to the other." It expressed his fervent hope that the Senate would disavow the Fourteen Points "in their entirety," and take independent action to ensure Germany's unconditional surrender.

"Let us dictate peace by the hammering of guns," he wrote, "and not chat about peace to the accompaniment of the clicking of typewriters."

The President, goaded, issued a personal appeal to the nation the next day,

25 October. It was egotistical enough to make Roosevelt seem bashful: "My fellow countrymen, the congressional elections are at hand. . . . If you have approved of my leadership and wish me to continue to be your unembarrassed spokesman in affairs at home and abroad, I earnestly beg that you express yourselves unmistakably to that effect by returning a Democratic majority to both the Senate and the House of Representatives."

Wilson made things worse by saying it was "imperatively necessary," with peace negotiations impending, that the Senate remain loyal to him. A loss by his party of either house would "certainly be interpreted on the other side of the water as a repudiation of my leadership." The respect that America's allies entertained for him would be seriously undermined if they saw voters in the United States electing a legislature that was "not in fact in sympathy with the attitude and action of the administration."

The folly of this statement, implying that Republicans put party above patriotism, and that only Democrats were idealistic enough to impose *pax Americana* on the world, admitted of no rational explanation. Wilson was neither tired nor sick nor inclined to be bothered by anything Roosevelt said about him. But he was bothered, to a degree that made him lose his famous calm, by the addressee of Roosevelt's telegram. He had hated Henry Cabot Lodge ever since he heard that the senator had accused him of turning white and "womanish" after Vera Cruz. The prospect of Lodge, an outspoken opponent of Wilson's League of Nations idea, becoming chairman of the Senate Foreign Relations Committee was more than the President could bear. He had had to be dissuaded from directly naming Lodge in his appeal.

Roosevelt sniffed a vote-getting issue and threw away the political address he had promised to give at Carnegie Hall. He composed a new one, passing the sheets to Alice Longworth as he wrote them.

TWO DAYS LATER the Colonel turned sixty. Archie and Ethel and their three children joined Alice and Edith in a celebration tinged with worry about his condition. He looked well, and somewhat thinner than he had been a year before, but his joints were burning with rheumatism. Ethel noticed that he still became dizzy if he moved too fast. He told her that ever since his abscess operation he had had "queer feelings" in his head.

She was encouraged to find him optimistic for a victorious end to the war, and philosophical about his birthday. Jokingly, he referred to himself as "Methuselah's understudy" and "an elderly literary gentleman of quiet tastes and an interesting group of grandchildren."

He pretended to have recovered from Quentin's death, but Edith knew better. "I can see how constantly he thinks of him," she wrote Kermit, ". . . sad thoughts of what Quentin would have counted for in the future."

A well-wisher the following afternoon made sure Roosevelt kept brooding, by delivering part of the seat of Quentin's crashed plane.

Carnegie Hall was crammed beyond its legal capacity when he arrived there that night. Women composed at least half of the audience, and practically every prominent Republican in New York State sat on the podium. No sooner had the Colonel walked onstage than a voice yelled, "Unconditional surrender." He grinned and waved his speech script in reply. As he prepared to speak, another shout came, "Rub it in, Teddy!"

He spoke for more than two hours, excoriating Wilson for turning the war from a moral to a partisan issue. "If the President of the United States is right in the appeal he has just made to the voters, then you and I, my hearers, have no right to vote in this election or to discuss public questions while the war lasts."

Over the next few days, his condition deteriorated sharply, to the point that on the evening of 2 November, when he returned home after attending a Negro War Relief benefit with Archie, he found it difficult to walk for the pain in his legs. Next morning he tried to get up for breakfast, and found that he could not get one shoe on. At various times he was told he was suffering from multiple rheumatism, lumbago, sciatica, or gout. All he knew for certain was that he felt steadily worse. He remained bedridden, learning from newspapers that Turkey and Austria-Hungary were both out of the war. Moreover, Pershing had launched an offensive across the Meuse so ferocious that the First American Army was now recognized to be a force equal to any in the world. The papers did not report that Black Jack was encouraging the German Third and Fifth armies to retreat with liberal quantities of mustard gas. The British had simultaneously swept clear through to Ghent, and Marshal Ferdinand Foch's forces were elsewhere engaged in driving every last "Boche" off French soil. In a magnanimous gesture, Wilhelm II had offered sixty of his personal palaces as treatment centers for victims of the Allied onslaught. Nevertheless, the German war cabinet was insisting that he abdicate.

On election day, 5 November, Roosevelt hobbled into the blacksmith's shop that served as Oyster Bay's polling place and cast his ballot. Edith accompanied him. For all his support of universal suffrage, she was still not able to vote. They had the satisfaction of hearing next morning that the Democrats had lost both houses of Congress, in a Republican triumph devastating to Wilson's hope of dominating the postwar international scene. Speaker Champ Clark was dethroned. Political analysts put most of the blame on the President for demanding a vote of confidence. Roosevelt congratulated himself as "probably the chief factor" in preventing Wilson from doing "what he fully intended to do, namely, double-cross the Allies, appear as an umpire between them and the Central Powers and get a negotiated peace which would put him personally on a pinnacle of glory in the sight of every sinister pro-

German and every vapid and fatuous doctrinaire sentimentalist throughout the world."

He was equally contemptuous of the Kaiser, after reading on 10 November that Wilhelm II had resigned in the face of mass desertions and mutinies in all German services. The Red Flag was now flying in eleven German cities— even over the imperial harbor at Kiel—and the Reichstag was in danger of being taken over by a combination of socialist soviets. An armistice delegation representing its centrist majority was suing for peace in the Forest of Compiègne.

"If I had been the Kaiser," Roosevelt snorted, "when my generals told me that the war was lost, I would have surrounded myself with my six healthy and unharmed sons, and would have charged up the strongest part of the Allied lines in the hope that God in his infinite goodness and mercy would give me a speedy and painless death."

Flat on his back that same day, he heard that Lieutenant Colonel Theodore Roosevelt, Jr., had gone AWOL from military convalescence and reassumed command of the Twenty-sixth Infantry Regiment, just in time to participate in Pershing's final offensive. Kermit had gotten to the Front too, and fought in the same division. Quentin was avenged. Family honor was satisfied.

⟢

AROUND THREE O'CLOCK the following morning, floodlights illuminated the Statue of Liberty in New York Harbor. Newspaper presses throughout the city thumped out an announcement by the State Department: "The Armistice has been signed." At 6 A.M., local time, hostilities would cease on the Western Front.

Steam whistles began to blow long before dawn, in a continuous wail punctuated by motor horns and church chimes. By seven all Manhattan was throbbing, as fire crackers, cap pistols, brass bands, air-raid sirens, and even cow bells added to the cacophony. Impromptu parades joined together and marched up Fifth Avenue. Soldiers and sailors grabbed girls off the sidewalks and kissed them with a promiscuity unimaginable in prewar days. Airplanes roared overhead at dangerously low altitudes. There was a crescendo of noise through the day, approaching its climax in the late afternoon, just as Roosevelt was driven into town and returned to the hospital room he had occupied in February. It had windows facing toward Broadway, only one block distant. For as long as he remained awake, he could hear roaring and music in Columbus Circle.

Dr. John H. Richards announced overnight that the Colonel was back in Roosevelt Hospital because he needed to be "near his physician." His ailment, diagnosed as "lumbago," was not considered serious. "His blood pressure and heart action are those of a man of forty years."

Subsequent bulletins, issued every few days by Richards and others, were equally positive, but vague enough to confuse reporters as to what, exactly, was wrong with Roosevelt. If he was in no danger, why had his wife moved into an adjoining room? And why was his treatment taking so long? On 21 November, a rumor that he was facing an operation impelled his old literary friend Hamlin Garland to come and see him.

"I found him in bed propped up against a mound of pillows," Garland wrote in a diary entry. "He looked heavier than was natural to him and his mustache was almost white. There was something ominous in the immobility of his body."

After some chat about their youthful experiences out West, Garland said that he and a few friends would like permission to buy the field in France where Quentin was buried and turn it into a memorial park, "so that when you and Mrs. Roosevelt go there next summer, you will find it cared for and secure."

Roosevelt's eyes misted over. "That's perfectly lovely of you, Garland." But he needed to consult Edith before coming to a decision.

Corinne Roosevelt came in with a cake, and Garland rose to go. The Colonel would not let him. "Sit down!"

For half an hour the three of them talked about books and poetry. Roosevelt mentioned politics only once. "I wanted to see this war put through and I wanted to beat Wilson. Wilson is beaten and the war is ended. I can now say *Nunc dimittis*, without regret."

Garland came back four days later to ask again about the memorial. Roosevelt seemed stronger: his operation had been merely a dental procedure, to remove two formerly abscessed teeth. Yet he emanated sadness, and his voice had a moribund sound. The stillness of his body, mummified in thick blankets, again struck Garland. It contrasted strangely with the movement of his arm as he reached out to shake hands. He was evidently in worse condition than the hospital would admit.

Edith, Roosevelt said, was opposed to the idea of a park around Quentin's grave. She felt that her son had been "only an ordinary airman," doing his duty. Many others had fallen: "Quentin was no more hero than they, and should not be honored above his merits because he was our son."

Other visitors came. All paid affectionate respects. Some sought the Colonel's counsel, as if they feared they might soon be deprived of it. William Howard Taft, Henry Cabot Lodge, Elihu Root, and Henry White wanted to discuss the League of Nations issue, which Wilson was determined to press. Messianic as ever, the President had announced that he would personally represent the United States at a postwar peace conference scheduled to begin in Paris in the new year of 1919. White was the single Republican on his negotiating team—and a weak choice, in Lodge's opinion, altogether too obsequious to men of power. Wilson had not chosen a senator of either party to accompany him. He appeared to think that his foreign prestige would be enough to enshrine the Fourteen Points in a treaty so perfect, it could not fail to be endorsed.

Roosevelt was mostly silent as he listened to these senior statesmen of the GOP debating peace policy. White got the impression that he was not averse to the League, leaning more to Root's cautious approval than to Lodge's harsh opposition. But in letters and articles dictated to Miss Stricker and a new personal assistant, Miss Flora Whitney, the Colonel made clear that he liked best Sir Edward Grey's old idea of a League that would not require great powers to scale down their defenses. He scoffed at the hypocrisy of Wilson's grand-sounding phrase *self-determination for all peoples,* noting that the President was in no hurry to grant liberty to Haiti or Santo Domingo.

Two of his future biographers stopped by with honey on their lips, looking for last-chapter material. Lawrence Abbott told him that his speeches at the Sorbonne and London's Guildhall in 1910 had "contributed directly" to the success of France and Britain in winning the war. Joseph Bucklin Bishop showed him the typescript of an epistolary volume that Scribners wanted to put out, under the title *Theodore Roosevelt's Letters to His Children.* The Colonel read it entranced. "I would rather have that book published than anything that has ever been written about me."

November gave way to December. By now Roosevelt was walking again, but only for short painful periods. Even sitting in a chair hurt. He was in his fourth week of hospitalization, on top of the week he had spent bedridden at Sagamore Hill. Unable to write anything but brief notes, he allowed Flora to think she was helping him with her laborious stenography. She was learning shorthand as part of her recovery process. Their relationship was quasi-familial, tender and sorrowful on both sides.

He did what he could to hinder Wilson's diplomacy, after the President set sail for France in a confiscated German liner renamed the *George Washington.* In letters addressed to Clemenceau, Lloyd George, and Balfour, as well as such other foreign opinion-makers as Lord Bryce and Rudyard Kipling, Roosevelt argued that the Democratic Party's defeat in the recent Congressional election amounted to a vote of no confidence in the administration. In any other free political system, he told Balfour, the chief executive would have had to resign. Speaking for the Republican Party, he declared that a majority of American opinion stood for "absolute loyalty to France and England in the peace negotiations." That meant a retreat from the Fourteen Points, which he thought were susceptible to interpretation in Germany's favor, and an abandonment of any presumption by the United States to act "as an umpire between our allies and our enemies."

Except for describing himself as "one of the leaders" of this new majority,

Roosevelt did not say what was now acknowledged by political strategists: the 1920 GOP presidential nomination would be his if he wanted it. A number of Republicans and former Progressives called to sound him out about running. He declined to encourage them.

"I am indifferent to the subject," he said, lying back on his pillows. "Since Quentin's death, the world seems to have shut down upon me." But when William Allen White reported that Leonard Wood was a candidate, he said with studied casualness, "Well, probably I shall have to get in this thing in June." Then he produced an article he had dictated that amounted to an advance campaign platform.

"I tell you no secret when I say that the cards are arranged for the nomination of T.R.," Hiram Johnson wrote a journalist on 14 December. "He has gained immeasurably in public esteem, I think."

If so, the gain was registered at home, not abroad. That evening's newspapers broadcast the story that Woodrow Wilson was being received in Paris with a hysteria that far eclipsed the welcome given Roosevelt in 1910. A crowd of two million had greeted the President as the savior of Western civilization, showering him with roses as he rode up the Champs-Élysées to the Arc de Triomphe.

⤙

ROOSEVELT WOKE THE following day with his left wrist in such agony it had to be splinted. Much more alarmingly, he showed symptoms of a pulmonary embolism. The hospital kept this secret from the press. His temperature shot up to 104°F, then subsided. Dr. Richards had been talking of sending him home, but it was obvious now that he should be watched day and night. Edith could do nothing but sit at his bedside while he slept, reading Shakespeare in an effort to stay calm. "Poor dear, I wish I could take the pain. . . . There are so many things which he wants to do and cannot."

He was buoyed by the appearance of Eleanor, back from France, except that she brought news that her husband had been left with a permanent limp. Roosevelt wished Ted could have been sent home on sick leave, like Archie. But he and Kermit were stuck in Europe, pending discharge from service.

Stuck too, the Colonel resigned himself to the prospect of Christmas in hospital. He would have to forgo his thirty-year ritual of playing Santa Claus at the Cove School in Oyster Bay. Archie was appointed to substitute for him.

Margaret Chanler paid a visit, and was disconcerted by her old friend's listlessness. "I am pretty low now," he admitted, taking her by the hand, "but I shall get better. I cannot go without having done something to that old gray skunk in the White House."

He did get better, enough that Edith got permission to take him home for Christmas. They agreed that it would be best to leave early on the holiday itself, when no press photographers would be around. Corinne came in on Christmas Eve and found Roosevelt in his bathrobe, bandaged but bright-eyed. He told her that there seemed to be "a strong desire" among Republicans to nominate him for the presidency in 1920. His health, however, might prevent him ever again entering public life.

"Well, anyway, no matter what comes, I have kept the promise that I made to myself when I was twenty-one."

"What promise, Theodore?"

"I promised myself that I would work *up to the hilt* until I was sixty, and I have done it."

Vertigo assailed him on Christmas morning as the hospital elevator dropped to the ground floor. Dr. Richards reached to steady him, but he flinched.

"Don't do that, doctor. I am not sick and it will give the wrong impression."

Bracing himself when the door opened, he walked firmly down the corridor to his waiting car.

⸻

ALICE, ETHEL, ARCHIE, AND GRACE were waiting at Sagamore Hill when Edith brought him home. Lunch was going to be late, and the grandchildren were napping upstairs. Roosevelt looked white and battered, but clearly happy, after seven weeks away, to be back among his books and trophies. He gazed with rapture at the snow-whitened landscape around the house.

There was a great turkey on the table, and mince pie and plum pudding and ice cream. The Colonel's frailty, however, cast a pall upon the feast. He reveled in the excitement of the boys and girls as they opened their presents, heaped around the tree in the North Room. Before going to bed early, he noticed sympathetically that little Richard Derby had asthma, like himself as a child.

⸻

ROOSEVELT LAY NOT in the bedroom he and his wife customarily shared, but in an adjacent chamber with corner windows facing south and west. It had been Ethel's bedroom prior to her marriage, and back in days that Alice could scarcely remember, a gated nursery. It was said to be "the warmest room in the house" (so far as the phrase had any meaning at Sagamore Hill), because of its high, sunny exposure on winter afternoons. Edith wanted him there for that reason, and also because she could have quick access to him during the night.

A coal fire burned in the corner hearth. Servants kept it going around the clock. Propped up in a mahogany sleigh bed, Roosevelt saw faded blue curtains, a blue plush armchair, a tufted sofa, a chest of drawers with swing mirror, a lift-top desk, and an Italian walnut nightstand, a souvenir of his second honeymoon. No bearskin rugs snarled on the carpeted floor, but there were carved heads and masks on the wall to comfort him.

Every morning he breakfasted in bed, then got up and painfully dressed himself. Shaving, however, was impossible, so a barber came daily to freshen him up. Later he would limp downstairs to his study, where there was a log fire and a chaise longue. He could recline there, reading or dictating. Anemia enfeebled him. His inflammation traveled mysteriously from joint to joint, ending up on the last day of the month in just one finger. At the same time his temperature shot up to 103°F. It may have been precipitated by a surge of mixed emotions: an envelope from France had come, enclosing Marshal Pétain's posthumous citation of Lieutenant Quentin Roosevelt for a Croix de Guerre.

Compared to such news, foreign dispatches reporting that Woodrow Wilson had been welcomed in London as rapturously as in Paris, and was now en route to Rome by royal train, were but the rattling of distant drums.

ON NEW YEAR'S DAY, 1919, rheumatism flared afresh in Roosevelt's right wrist. He gave up dressing and kept to the sofa in his bedroom, weakly trying to acknowledge at least some of the letters that still came up the hill in sacks, six days a week. Looking back over the past two years, he calculated that he had answered twenty-five thousand of them, and rejected well over two thousand speaking invitations. Now there was talk of him being president again, the sacks were sure to bulk larger.

Despite worsening pain, he dictated a *Kansas City Star* editorial on Friday, 3 January. The article—his thirteenth for that paper since the Armistice—was a final statement of his views on the League of Nations issue, before the Paris Peace Conference opened in the middle of the month.

"We all of us desire such a league," Roosevelt said, "only we wish to be sure that it will help and not hinder the cause of world peace and justice." Speaking as "an old man who has seen those dear to him fight," he said that Americans did not wish to send any more of their sons to die in wars provoked by obscure foreign quarrels.

He also dictated a new article for the *Metropolitan,* putting himself on record in favor of a constitutional amendment awarding equal voting rights to women. In a letter sent that same day to Senator George H. Moses of New Hampshire, he said it was "a misfortune" that his old friend Henry Cabot Lodge and some other New England senators were "so very bitter about woman suffrage." He begged Moses not to oppose the amendment. "It is coming anyhow, and it ought to come."

The effort of this literary work exhausted him, and he told Edith that he felt as miserable as at any time during his hospitalization. Alarmed, she summoned Dr. Faller, who could do little but prescribe a course of arsenic injections to reduce the swelling in his patient's wrist.

Roosevelt suffered so much general pain overnight that on Saturday morning Edith engaged a full-time nurse. Since none of their children were around for extra help (Alice, Ethel, and Archie had gone their various ways after the holidays), she placed a desperate call to James Amos. The Colonel's former valet was now working for the William J. Burns International Detective Agency in New York, but he agreed to come back temporarily into the family service.

When Amos arrived that afternoon, he was shocked to see how ravaged Roosevelt looked. He bathed him with extreme care and coaxed him into a fresh pair of pajamas. "By George," Roosevelt said gratefully, "you never hurt me a bit." Amos turned his armchair so he could sit looking out over Oyster Bay, then put him to bed and monitored him through the night.

Roosevelt was in too much discomfort to sleep well, but when Dr. Faller stopped by on Sunday morning, he seemed somewhat better. He stayed in his room all day, dictating two or three letters to Edith, and correcting the typescript of his *Metropolitan* article. She was touched by his exceptionally gentle mood, and whenever she passed the sofa she could not help kissing him and stroking his short, little-boy's hair. "As it got dusk," she wrote Ted later, "he watched the dancing flames and spoke of the happiness of being home, and made little plans for me. I think he had made up his mind he would have to suffer for some time & with his high courage had adjusted himself to bear it."

They were still together when, at around ten o'clock, he asked her to help him sit up. He said he felt as if his lungs or heart were about to give in. "I know it is not going to happen, but it is such a strange feeling." She gave him a sniff of sal volatile and sent at once for Dr. Faller, who found Roosevelt's bronchi clear and his pulse beating steadily and calmly.

Leaving the nurse in charge, Edith accompanied Faller downstairs for a discreet conversation in the library. She said that her husband was insomniac, and asked permission to give him morphine. Faller assented, saying that he himself would rest easier if he knew the Colonel was comfortable.

Edith watched while the nurse administered the shot shortly before midnight. James Amos took over, and the two women retired to their bedrooms. Roosevelt lay on the sofa for a while, saying little. Amos noticed a look of great weariness on his face.

"James, don't you think I might go to bed now?" He had to be half-lifted onto the mattress, then asked to be turned on his side. For a while he lay staring at the fire.

Then he said, "James, will you please put out the light?"

A SMALL LAMP on the dresser filled the room with a dim yellow glow. Amos switched it off and sat where he could see Roosevelt, or at least hear him breathing in the darkness. It was a calm, moonless night, and the big house was still. Edith came in at twelve-thirty to check on her husband. She found him sleeping peacefully, and did not kiss him for fear of waking him. When she visited again at two o'clock, he was still asleep. Amos had moved closer to what was left of the fire.

About an hour later the valet was startled by a new note in Roosevelt's respiration—"roughling" was the only word he could think of. He touched his master's forehead. It felt dry and warm. Then Roosevelt began to breathe irregularly, with intermittent periods of silence. Each time he started again, his respiration sounded weaker. Eventually Amos had to lean close to hear any sound at all.

AT FOUR O'CLOCK, Edith woke to find the nurse standing over her. She hurried through and called, "Theodore, darling!" But there was no response from the sleigh bed.

In Memoriam T.R.

THEODORE ROOSEVELT'S DEATH CERTIFICATE, signed by Dr. Faller, declared that he had succumbed at 4:15 A.M. on Monday, 6 January 1919, to an embolism of the lung, with multiple arthritis as a contributory factor. In a simultaneous press statement, Faller and two consulting physicians hedged slightly, saying that the blood clot might have gone to the brain. They revealed for the first time that their patient had been struck by a near-fatal pulmonary embolism some three weeks earlier. Neither of these detachments, they felt, necessarily related to the inflammatory rheumatism that had troubled him for some twenty years. They did not seem to know that in early childhood Roosevelt had shown many symptoms of rheumatic heart disease—an affliction notoriously capable of recurring in later life, often in winter weather. It was left to other observers to note that he had never entirely recovered from his prostration in the Brazilian jungle, or from the bullet John Schrank had fired into his chest. Not to be discounted, either, was the fact that he had recently suffered a devastating bereavement. In a more sophisticated era of professional diagnosis, a review of his medical history would indicate that "the cause of death was myocardial infarction, secondary to chronic atherosclerosis with possible acute coronary occlusion."

If so, he could be said in more ways than one to have died of a broken heart.

THE NEWS OF THE COLONEL'S death came too late for the morning papers that Monday, but it spread around the world with extraordinary swiftness by telephone, telegraph, and cable.

A common reaction among the millions of Americans who had imagined him to be indestructible, and headed again for the presidency, was a sense of shock so violent they took refuge in metaphor. For Henry A. Beers, "a wind had fallen, a light had gone out, a military band had stopped playing." For John Burroughs, a pall seemed to cover the sky. For William Dudley Foulke, as well as the editors of the *New York Evening Post,* there had been an eclipse of the sun. For General Fred C. Ainsworth, a storm center was swept away. For Hamlin Garland, a mountain had slid from the horizon. For Kermit Roosevelt, who heard the news with Ted at the U.S. Army headquarters in Coblenz, the earth had lost one of its dimensions.

"You will know how the bottom has dropped out for me," he wrote his mother.

Archibald Roosevelt announced that a funeral of stark simplicity would take place in two days' time at Christ Episcopal Church in Oyster Bay. The burial would follow in Youngs Memorial Cemetery, nearby on a hillside overlooking the cove. President Wilson issued a proclamation from Paris, appointing Vice President Thomas R. Marshall to represent him at both ceremonies, and directing government offices to fly their flags at half-mast for a month. Both houses of Congress adjourned, as did the Supreme Court, closing without any proceedings for the first time in its history. Secretaries Newton D. Baker and Josephus Daniels ordered army, marine, and naval posts around the world to fire salutes to the former commander in chief at sunrise on the day of his obsequies, Wednesday, 8 January, and to continue firing at half-hourly intervals until sunset.

Baker offered to send a full guard of honor to Oyster Bay. Archie politely declined to be obligated to the bureaucrat who had prevented Roosevelt from serving his country. "It was my father's wish that he would be buried among the people of Oyster Bay, and that the funeral service would be conducted entirely by those friends among whom he had lived so long and happily."

In a further effort to keep the exercises private, Archie let it be known that there were only 350 pew seats available, with standing room for perhaps 150 extra invited guests. He agreed to accommodate forty-five members of Congress, as representatives of the people, but said he could not invite any members of the Wilson administration other than Marshall, two naval aides, and Assistant Secretary of State William Phillips, deputizing for the absent Robert Lansing.

The discipline Archie had acquired as a soldier enabled him to handle the anguished telegrams that inundated Sagamore Hill, as bales of afternoon newspapers blackened with the headline ROOSEVELT DEAD thumped onto sidewalks across the country. Even so, he had difficulty controlling himself when some children from the Cove School delivered an arrangement of pink and white carnations that they had personally chosen and bought.

Alice Longworth and Ethel Derby called from Washington and South Carolina to say they were hurrying north to help Edith—although "Mother, the adamantine," as Roosevelt used to call her, was more likely to comfort them in their mutual desolation. She also had to handle the anguish of her husband's humbler mourners, from James Amos (inconsolable in the library, sobbing "Gone . . . gone" into cupped brown hands) to Charlie Lee the coachman and thrifty pilgrims walking from the railroad depot. "You did not expect to visit us for this reason," she said to George Syran, a New York porter who had sent coffee every morning to the Colonel's hospital room. "He's gone now, so you must take good care of me."

In a letter recounting his visit, the porter wrote: "She had a crying smile on her, I'm sorry I haven't the power to describe that devine face. . . . Her heart was torn out of her roots."

A perpetual drone in the sky over Cove Neck puzzled residents on neighboring parts of the North Shore. It came from military airplanes, ordered by the army aviation directorate to patrol the house where Quentin Roosevelt's father lay dead. Pilots dropped wreaths of laurel on the lawn, buzzing so low that the wind from their propellers shook the bare trees around. The aerial watch continued through Monday night and all the next day, with alternate flights of five planes operating out of Mineola. For most of the time they kept high and circled far, but their noise became steadily more oppressive, like the throb of an organ pedal beneath a fugue that needed to resolve. Only in the predawn hours of Wednesday, as snow began to fall, did silence return to Sagamore Hill.

"The wind from their propellers shook the bare trees."
The Air Corps maintains a vigil over Sagamore Hill after TR's death.

THE SNOW TAPERED OFF around noon, when Edith and Archie, wearing his captain's dress uniform and French war medal, received relatives and close friends at home for a valedictory service in the North Room. The Colonel's silver-handled oak coffin was set up in front of the fireplace. Before its lid was screwed down, Ethel went through for a last glimpse of her father. "He looked as if he were asleep—and weary," she recorded. "But not stern."

She had become used to the grimness that had settled increasingly upon him during the last ten months. The coffin rested on one of his lion skins, and was covered with the Stars and Stripes, with a pair of Rough Rider flags crossed at the foot. Edith had requested no floral decorations, but raised no objection to a wreath of soft yellow mimosa blossoms, contributed at great expense by some veterans of the First U.S. Volunteer Cavalry. Yellow was the regimental color, and Roosevelt had grown to love the scent of mimosa in Brazil.

At 12:30, six undertakers wearing black skullcaps transferred the coffin to a motor hearse waiting under the *porte cochère*. Edith did not venture outside. In the austere tradition of Puritan widows, she retired to her bedroom alone while the rest of the house party climbed into automobiles and followed the hearse down the hill. There was no military escort. A squad of mounted policemen had ridden all the way from New York to march ahead of their former commissioner. But Archie, citing Roosevelt's disdain for *pompe funèbre,* had asked them to wait at the church.

The cortege made slow going, carving tracks in the snowy shore road. As it approached Oyster Bay village, the cloud cover broke. A shaft of sunshine irradiated Christ Church and several thousand bystanders cordoned off by the police. Shortly before one o'clock, the hearse reached the church door.

Already a silence unrelated to the weather prevailed in most cities and large towns in the northeastern, central, and western states. Not just New York's federal buildings, but schools, courts, firehouses, exchanges, and movie palaces closed in a show of reverence for the dead Colonel. Streetcars and subway trains ground to a halt. Factory wheels stopped spinning. The downtown financial district, so long a target of his righteous wrath, was deserted. Bell ringers in Trinity Church, St. Paul's, and City Hall waited for 2 P.M., the presumed hour of internment of the only president born in Manhattan.

The hush was even more profound inside his parish church. Melted snow could be heard dripping from the roof. Roosevelt had requested no music of any kind. Five hundred congregants watched the coffin come down the nave, through lozenges of stained-glass light. It was still carried by the six men in skullcaps. There were no official pallbearers. Archie followed with the family party, prominently including Flora Whitney. He noticed a distraught William

Howard Taft sitting in a rear pew, settled his companions up front, then made Taft come and join them.

Thomas Marshall sat in aloof eminence, the official bearer of a floral arrangement from the President of the United States. (It consisted of the same economical carnations that had appealed to the students of Cove School.) Charles Evans Hughes showed up, impassive behind his whiskers. Warren Harding and General Wood looked prepresidential, now that they no longer had to worry about a front-runner for next year's Republican nomination. Henry Cabot Lodge, the senior senator present, was flanked by Hiram Johnson and Philander Chase Knox. The House was represented by the outgoing Speaker, Champ Clark, and his aged predecessor, "Uncle Joe" Cannon. Governor Al Smith of New York attended as an unwelcome envoy from Tammany Hall, and Elihu Root and Joe Murray as Roosevelt's oldest political patrons. A democratic variety of attendees crowded the other rows, most so strange to one another that only the Colonel could have embraced them all in his vast bear hug of acquaintance.

The service was almost cruelly short and spartan. Roosevelt's favorite hymn, "How Firm a Foundation, Ye Saints of the Lord," was recited, rather than sung, by the Reverend George F. Talmage:

When through fiery trials Thy pathway shall lie,
My grace, all sufficient, shall be Thy supply.

At no time until the benediction did Father Talmage mention the name of the deceased. When he did, it evoked tears. "Theodore," he said, "the Lord bless thee and keep thee. The Lord make his face to shine upon thee, and be gracious to thee."

A single pull of the church's bell alerted Edith, across the bay, that her husband was beginning his final journey. Outside, the mounted police waited in formation. They were no longer to be dissuaded from forming an honor guard. Spectators sobbed as the cortege, now lengthened enormously with other automobiles, wound back toward the bend of Cove Neck.

There was no room in the tiny parking lot of Youngs Cemetery for any vehicle except the hearse. Roosevelt's grave awaited him at the top of a steep knoll. He had always enjoyed the birdsong in that fir-forested corner, and had long ago decided he wanted to be buried there. Typically, his chosen site involved a long hard climb. Slippery snow made it even harder for the six undertakers. They bent forward at an angle of nearly forty-five degrees as they labored under their burden. Father Talmage led the way in his surplice. He had as much difficulty in avoiding a soaked front hemline as Alice, Ethel, and Flora. Big men like Taft and Wood puffed in the rear. Only a party of fifty children from Cove School trotted up the path with ease.

The graveside view made the ascent worthwhile. There was a cutting breeze, bringing with it stray whiffs of wood smoke, but the sun was now fully out, and the bay glistened half white and half bright blue. Small spirals of mist rose from the frozen reeds. Already the snow between the surrounding trees was dotted with the spoor of rabbits and squirrels.

"THEY BENT FORWARD . . . AS THEY LABORED UNDER THEIR BURDEN."

TR's coffin is carried to his grave overlooking Oyster Bay, 8 January 1919.

A laurel lining and berm of flowers camouflaged the fresh hole in the ground. Standing over it, a police bugler blew taps. Then the flag was unfolded from the coffin, revealing a rectangle of silver that read:

THEODORE ROOSEVELT

OCTOBER 27, 1858–JANUARY 6, 1919

As the engraved words sank out of sight, Father Talmage read the litany of committal. Lieutenant Otto Raphael, Roosevelt's favorite Jewish policeman, muttered his own burial prayer in Hebrew. A flight of white geese wheeled and settled in the cove.

One of the last mourners to remain behind, while the rest of the company straggled downhill, was Taft. He stood by the grave for a long time, crying.

⟨⁓⟩

IN SUBSEQUENT DAYS and weeks, commentators and orators made up for the lack of a eulogy at the Colonel's funeral. He had died so suddenly, and the glory of America's late but decisive role in ending the world war had so plainly been earned at his urging, that he was at once invested with a godlike glow. The acolytes who had venerated him for so long—the Lawrence Abbotts, the Gifford Pinchots, the Julian Streets—resorted to levels of hyperbole not heard since the assassination of Lincoln. Given the poignancy of his sufferings over the last year, a considerable minority of Roosevelt-haters elected to keep their opinions private for the time being. Even H. L. Mencken reserved fire. "The man was a liar, a braggart, a bully, and a fraud," he wrote a friend. "But let us not speak evil of the dead."

Among the superlatives granted Roosevelt by those who belonged to neither extreme camp, simple words came nearest to sincerity. "He was the most encouraging person that ever breathed," Edna Ferber declared, on behalf of all the writers and artists he had befriended. "The strongest character in the world has died," Will H. Hays said to a reporter. "I have never known another person so vital," wrote William Allen White, "nor another man so dear."

Woodrow Wilson's sentiments, conveyed in his proclamation of national mourning and a cable to Edith Roosevelt, were *pro forma*. This was to be expected from a head of state engaged in complex negotiations abroad. But two of his closest aides, Edward M. House and William G. McAdoo, verged on indiscretion in proclaiming Theodore Roosevelt one of the greatest of presidents. Newspapers that had savaged Roosevelt consistently throughout his career ran eloquent editorials. The New York *Sun* predicted that he would endure as a colossus in American history. "There are personalities so vivid, there is vitality so intense, so magnetically alert, as Motley said of Henry of Navarre, that 'at the very mention of the name, the figure seems to leap from the mists of the past, instinct with ruddy, vigorous life.' " The *New York Evening Post* agreed:

> Something like a superman in the political sphere has passed away. He saw the nation steadily and he saw it whole. Where other politicians dealt with individuals, Mr. Roosevelt reached out for vast groups. . . . He boldly thrust out his hand and captured the hearts and the suffrages of a whole race, an entire church, a block of states. Never have we had a politician who, with such an appearance of effortless ease, drew after him great masses and moulded them to his will.

From flag-bedecked platforms and pulpits in London (where for the first time in history a memorial service displaced evensong at Westminster Abbey),

Paris, Rome, and throughout the Allied zone of occupancy in Germany, foreign speakers vied with American ones in celebrating the man who was commonly seen as instrumental in awakening his country to its social and strategic responsibilities. He was hailed as a liberator by Cubans and Serbs. Representatives of a nation only three months old announced that "Theodore Roosevelt was always a great friend of the Czechoslovaks." In Tokyo, he was remembered as the peacemaker of the Russo-Japanese War and "perhaps the only great American who understood us." Long biographies and appreciations were published in the major European newspapers. Jules Jusserand, who of all diplomats knew the Colonel best, had to be discreet in praising him at President Wilson's elbow in Paris, but in private he was panegyrical. "I met in him a man of such extraordinary power that to find a second at the same time on this globe would have been an impossibility; a man whom to associate with was a liberal education, and who could be in every way likened to radium, for warmth, force and light emanated from him and no spending of it could ever diminish his store."

The tribute most awaited in Washington was that of Senator Henry Cabot Lodge. He addressed a joint memorial session of Congress on 9 February in the presence of two thousand rapt listeners, including Taft, members of the Supreme Court, and officers of the cabinet, armed services, and diplomatic corps. His survey of the life and accomplishments of his oldest friend lasted almost two hours. With characteristic erudition, he began with an Arab lament, *A tower is fallen, a star is set! Alas! Alas!*, and ended with a quotation from John Bunyan, describing the passage of Mr. Valiant-for-Truth across the river of death: "So he passed over, and all the trumpets sounded for him on the other side." By then Lodge was so overcome he half-fell back into his seat, and silence filled the House chamber.

THE EULOGIES AND POEMS and memorial proceedings had hardly been printed and bound before the worshipful biographies began to appear. William Draper Lewis's *The Life of Theodore Roosevelt* and William Roscoe Thayer's *Theodore Roosevelt: An Intimate Biography* were substantial studies, reflecting some personal acquaintance with the great man, but their incense content was only a few degrees less fragrant than that of Lawrence Abbott's *Impressions of Theodore Roosevelt*, Niel MacIntyre's *Great-heart*, and William Hard's *Theodore Roosevelt: A Tribute*.

Expectations were high that the authorized biography by Joseph Bucklin Bishop would be a scholarly and unbiased corrective. But Bishop was not yet ready to publish. Then in November 1919 Stuart Sherman, who had savaged Roosevelt in *The Nation* two years before, published a review of the hagiographies. Entitled "Roosevelt and the National Psychology," it amounted to the first effective attack on the Colonel's posthumous reputation.

"Mr. Roosevelt's great and fascinating personality," he began, "is part of the national wealth, and should, so far as possible, be preserved undiminished." But those who insisted in canonizing a man so lustily, imperfectly, and on occasion tragically human offered posterity nothing more than "a whitewashed plaster bust." Noting that the Colonel was always clear-eyed about himself, Sherman quoted his negative response in 1918 to a friend who told him he would be President again: "No, not I. . . . I made too many enemies, and the people are tired of my candidacy." Roosevelt had understood then what his worshippers refused to allow—that both he and the American people had changed since his glory days at the turn of the century. And in changing, it was the people, not he, who had moved ahead.

Sherman looked back at the life of Theodore Roosevelt and found it to be a three-act drama, ultimately tragic because the protagonist had been brought down by his own gifts. First there was the young reformer, alone among the money-grubbing or inheritance-squandering materialists who dominated American society in the eighties and nineties, preaching and personifying his famous gospel of the Strenuous Life. "Under the influence of this masterful force, the unimaginative plutocratic psychology was steadily metamorphosed into the psychology of efficient, militant, imperialistic nationalism." So long as the United States had no army to speak of, and no empire to fatten on, the energies Roosevelt had inspired had pushed toward a more perfect Union. But then, with amazing swiftness, both he and the nation had been elevated to supreme power.

As president, Roosevelt had been even more strenuous, establishing an ideal in the popular mind of a federal government as virile, incorruptible, and morally driven as himself. Panama should have been a warning to his supporters that the reformer at home was an imperialist abroad, but then and now, the American people had little understanding of foreign affairs.

It was not until Roosevelt visited Germany in 1910 that the imperial strain had begun to overmaster him. His address to the University of Berlin had shown the degenerative process at work, even as he spoke. Sherman quoted a "beautiful" passage from that speech, *It is only by working along the lines laid down by philanthropists, by lovers of mankind, that we can be more sure of lifting our civilization to a higher and more permanent plane of well-being,* and asked if any reader, nine years later, heard in them the authentic note of the Colonel's voice. He then quoted the sentences immediately following: *But woe to the nation that does not make ready to hold its own in time of need against all who would harm it. And woe thrice over to the nation in which the average man loses his fighting edge.* Time and again thereafter, and compulsively during the war years, Roosevelt had indulged this rhetorical tic: always, first, the salute to men of benign instinct, then the harsh warning that if they did not fight and breed, they were doomed. In doing so, the former straight talker had become "the greatest concocter of 'weasel' paragraphs on record." His misfortune was that when Americans found out that he was less interested in fighting for social justice than fighting for fighting's sake, they had shown themselves unwilling to be either patronized or cajoled.

Summarizing, Sherman felt that Roosevelt had been more of an autocrat than a democrat, a warrior, not a peacemaker, a man of action who scoffed at philosophical scruples. His end had been tragic, Yet there was something undeniably epic about him:

> Mr. Roosevelt has attained satisfactions which he thought should console fallen empires: he has left heirs and a glorious memory. How much more glorious it might have been if in his great personality there had been planted a spark of magnanimity. If, after he had drunk of personal glory like a Scandinavian giant, he had lent his giant strength to a cause of the plain people not of his contriving nor under his leadership. If in addition to helping win the war he had identified himself with the attainment of its one grand popular object. From performing this supreme service he was prevented by defects of temper which he condemned in Cromwell, a hero who he admired and in some respects strikingly resembled.

THESE EXCHANGES BETWEEN the wholeheartedly adoring and the ambivalently disparaging set the tone for seventy years of retrospective controversy. But for the postwar decade and beyond, it was Roosevelt the hero, "Theodore Rex" the masterful president, "Teddy" the lovable who loomed in popular perception. A powerful stimulant to nostalgia for him was the publication in late 1919 of *Theodore Roosevelt's Letters to His Children,* the book of all his books he had most wanted to see in print. An instant bestseller, it revealed the Colonel to have been, behind his often grim public face, the most delightful of private correspondents, able to express adult feelings in language (and hilarious pictograms) that enchanted the young.

By the end of that year, as Roosevelt's historical stock surged, that of Woodrow Wilson—outmaneuvered by Clemenceau and Lloyd George at the Paris Peace Conference, thwarted by Henry Cabot Lodge and other senatorial opponents of his cherished League of Nations treaty—fell precipitously. He collapsed of a stroke and became a peevish recluse for the rest of his presidency. Scholars wondered whether any head of state since Napoleon had ever suffered such a loss of power. The concurrent rise of Warren Gamaliel Harding as the Republican Party's challenge to everything Wilson had ever stood for led to a rout of Democratic candidates in the presidential election of 1920.

Most of the sixteen million men and women who voted for Harding, in a landslide victory, did so to honor the memory of the candidate they would unquestionably have preferred, had Roosevelt lived to run again.

Joseph Bucklin Bishop's official life of the Colonel came out that fall: two dignified volumes entitled *Theodore Roosevelt and His Time: Shown in His Own Letters.* There were the requisite iconic frontispieces, protected with flaps of tissue paper. The scholarship was dogged, the coverage ample (if selective), and the index beyond reproach. But the overall tone was so reverential that only the occasional "scoop" document, such as Roosevelt's mammoth 1911 letter describing his European tour, infused the dryasdust pages with the breath of life.

Even more monumental, in its clothbound, gold-stamped breadth and bulk, was Hermann Hagedorn's Memorial Edition of *The Works of Theodore Roosevelt,* issued between 1923 and 1926 in twenty-four volumes. Merely to divide that number into the years of Roosevelt's adult life, allowing for the fact that he had spent nearly eight years as president, was to be persuaded by William Allen White's remark: "The man was gigantic."

A Women's Roosevelt Memorial Association was formed to reconstruct the Colonel's vanished birthplace, at 28 East Twentieth Street in Manhattan, as a museum and educational center. Designed by a *Lusitania* survivor, Theodate Pope Riddle, in consultation with the two surviving Roosevelt sisters, it was dedicated to the public as "Roosevelt House" in 1923. Four female trumpeters in Grecian robes blew a voluntary over the entryway where Teedie Roosevelt and Edie Carow had sat reading over half a century before.

Simultaneously, a rival, masculine Roosevelt Memorial Association launched a campaign to create shrines in Washington, D.C., and downtown Oyster Bay, Long Island. (Sagamore Hill was obviously destined to become another such site one day, but for as long as Edith survived, it would remain her private property.) The group, dominated by Hermann Hagedorn as executive director and backed by such dignitaries as Elihu Root and Leonard Wood, took advantage of Roosevelt's posthumous reputation to accumulate an impressive fund for the Washington memorial. In 1925, Hagedorn unveiled a design for it, by John Russell Pope, which was so grandiloquent—a two-hundred-foot ejaculation of Potomac water from a white granite island in Tidal Bay, triangulated between the Lincoln and Washington monuments— that even President Coolidge wondered if more time should not pass before Theodore Roosevelt was accorded his proper place in history. Southern lobbyists planning a Jefferson memorial for the site successfully held the RMA off.

Meanwhile the sculptor Gutzon Borglum, who had been among the Progressive delegates nominating Roosevelt for president in 1912, conceived of a bas-relief in the Black Hills of South Dakota that would proclaim the Rough Rider unequivocally, and for all time, as the co-equal of Washington, Jefferson, and Lincoln. Not for him Pope's fragile fountain, subject to winds, ice, and drought. He meant to carve his quartet out of imperishable rock, each face sixty feet high. Coolidge agreed to write an appropriate entablature, identifying them in English, Latin, and Sanskrit. In October 1927, the first contours of Washington's face began to emerge from Mount Rushmore. The other three colossi would have to wait their turn.

By the end of the decade, Theodore Roosevelt was commonly regarded as the third greatest American president, after Washington and Lincoln. Then, in 1931, Henry F. Pringle, a political journalist whose only previous book was a study of the government of Al Smith, published *Theodore Roosevelt: A Biography*. Soundly researched and brilliantly written, it coincided not only with the onset of the Great Depression—that apparent proof of the vanity of American ideals—but with a postwar revulsion against military values, and a consensus among those making policy never again to attempt the kind of democratic imperialism that Roosevelt (and for that matter Woodrow Wilson) had wished upon the world.

Even more damaging was the fact that Pringle was the first major biographer who declined to take Roosevelt seriously. He mocked the Rough Rider's fake humility and, with documentary evidence and authoritative anecdote, demolished many legends that Hagedorn and others had so long taken as gospel. He made full use of the Roosevelt presidential papers on deposit in the Library of Congress, and was clever enough to conceal the fact that he knew little about the final decade of his subject's life. If he was often unfair, his prejudice was excusable as a reaction against too much myth. When the time came to award that year's Pulitzer Prize for biography, Pringle was the obvious recipient.

Undeterred in 1931, the Roosevelt Memorial Association purchased Analostan Island in the Potomac as a new site for their shrine. But by then, the Colonel had already become such a caricature in some circles that cynics predicted the island would never be more than a base for a bridge.

THE FOLLOWING NOVEMBER, Roosevelt's self-proclaimed "fifth cousin by blood and nephew by law" was elected President of the United States. For most of Franklin's life, he had had to contend with the fact that his surname famously denoted someone else. Now the reverse began to apply.

Franklin was generous enough, and sincere, in insisting that Cousin Theodore was "the greatest man I ever knew." He had managed, despite the crippling misfortune of polio, to get where he was by emulating the Colonel's career path: from Harvard via the New York legislature to the Navy Department, and then on to Albany as governor of New York. He had even run unsuccessfully for vice president. But it was clear from the moment of his inauguration in 1933 that the new "Roosevelt" would henceforth make his own imperious way.

Theodore Roosevelt, Jr., had less luck in trying to emulate the late Colonel. Retiring from the army with a chestful of decorations—the Distinguished Service Cross, the Silver Star, the Purple Heart, and the Croix de Guerre—he entered politics and successively became a New York State assemblyman, assistant secretary of the navy, and Republican nominee for the governorship of New York in 1924. But innocent involvement in the Harding administration's "Teapot Dome" oil-field-leasing scandal compromised his campaign against the incumbent governor, Al Smith. Ted's diminutive stature, face-dividing grin, and harsh cries of "Bully" did not evoke enough memories of his father to beguile the electorate, and Cousin Eleanor made things worse by barnstorming the state in an automobile reconfigured as a teapot. He was badly defeated, in a presidential election year that otherwise went well for the GOP.

President Hoover appointed Ted governor of Puerto Rico, and then of the Philippines. He was a popular and able administrator, but Franklin's election ended his political career, and he became an executive of the publishing house of Doubleday, Doran & Co. In further imitation of his father, he built a mansion on the grounds of Sagamore Hill, and became notoriously bookish, given to loud recitations of Kipling and Omar Khayyám. It was a question whether Ted or Alice—the sibling he felt closest to—was the more vituperative in criticizing the New Deal as a perversion of the Square.

Brother and sister were both "American Firsters" in the early days of World War II. But Ted's Plattsburg conscience soon prompted him to switch from isolationism to principled support of the administration's preparedness program. A week after Pearl Harbor, he was appointed a brigadier general on active duty, and from June 1942 through 1943 fought with wild courage in North Africa and Italy. Although he was fifty-six on the countdown to D-Day, and wizened and lame with arthritis, he persuaded General Omar Bradley that his presence in Normandy would be inspirational to the assaulting forces. On 6 June 1944, Ted hobbled ashore from the first boat to hit Utah beach, and at once took command of a landing operation that threatened to degenerate into bloody chaos. His all-day heroism under constant fire won him the Medal of Honor. General Roosevelt was chosen to lead the Ninetieth Division into further battle, but on the eve of his appointment on 12 July, he died of a heart attack. He was buried in Normandy two days later, on the twenty-sixth anniversary of Quentin's death. General George Patton, an honorary pallbearer at the funeral, described Ted as "one of the bravest men I have ever known."

Kermit Roosevelt never recovered from the sensation, on hearing of the death of his father, that he had nothing left to stand on. A proficient but not a natural soldier, he wrote a book about his service in Mesopotamia, *War in the Garden of Eden,* and spent the immediate postwar years building up a mercantile business, the Roosevelt Steamship Company. He remained a shipping executive with various lines throughout the 1930s. Commerce satisfied Kermit no more than banking. His nomadic nature and marvelous talent for languages fought against the confinements of marriage and work. Depression steadily claimed him. He became a philanderer and insatiable drinker and, as his body thickened, developed a startling resemblance to his father. Dour and bloated, he rejoined the British army as soon as Hitler invaded Poland in 1939. He drove himself to fight well at the Battle of Narvik, but the condition of his heart—that vulnerable organ of so many Roosevelts—alarmed regimental medics, and he was declared unfit for further service. Returning stateside in 1941, he drank himself to the point of collapse and had to be institutionalized. The President, who had a soft spot for Kermit as a Democrat *malgré lui,* heard about his dereliction and appointed him a major in the U.S. Army in Alaska, far from the fleshpots of New York. There, on 4 June 1943, Kermit killed himself with a bullet to his head.

Archie went to work in 1920 for the oil company that was to embarrass his eldest brother. He resigned with belated outrage when the Teapot Dome scandal broke. Never one to dissemble his moral opinions, Archie testified against Sinclair Oil before a Senate investigative committee in 1924. After that he went into investment banking and spent the rest of his civilian career as a municipal bond salesman. He prospered enough to survive the Great Depression, living a quiet family life with his beloved "Gracie." Like Ted, Archie was an isolationist at the beginning of World War II. But the waters of Pearl Harbor had hardly resettled in December 1941 before he was back in uniform as a lieutenant colonel. Fighting on Biak Island, New Guinea, in May 1944 he was wounded in the same arm and leg that had been so severely shattered a quarter-century before. In a further replay of the events of 1918, he was awarded another Purple Heart and Silver Star and sent home to convalesce. On VJ-Day, he was the last of Theodore Roosevelt's sons still alive.

He did not age well, turning to Scotch and Communist-bashing as antidotes to the constant pain of his war wounds. During the McCarthy era, his conservatism deteriorated into political paranoia. His only attempt at a book, apart from an unfinished, conspiracist memoir, was a selection of some of his father's worst speeches, published in 1968 as *Theodore Roosevelt on Race, Riots, Reds, Crime.* According to Archie, President Roosevelt had railed in 1903 against the civic threat posed by "Beatniks." Family members hurriedly bought up as much of the print run as could be found in bookstores and let the old warrior go into retirement. As he lay dying in 1979, a confused recluse in Florida, he kept repeating, "I'm going to Sagamore Hill."

Each of Theodore Roosevelt's sons except Quentin fathered four children.

Ethel and Richard Derby also contributed four, although little Richard died prematurely at age eight. Ethel survived until 1977, outliving Dr. Derby by fourteen years. In most respects private and shy, a Republican supporter of the civil rights movement, she retained in old age a startling ability to bellow the word "Americanism" at dinner parties.

Flora Whitney died in 1986, inevitably wikipeded as "a wealthy socialite." Having become, at age twenty-one, almost a widow and almost a daughter to Quentin's parents, she spent a year trying to recover from his death—not to mention the Colonel's. A statue of Flora carved by her mother early in 1919 shows her hollow-eyed beneath a bandeau, trying to force herself into the depths of a small armchair. In 1920 she married one of Quentin's Harvard friends, but found him an inadequate substitute. Her second marriage, to the artist George Macculloch Miller III, was successful. Flora fulfilled herself further by becoming the rescuer, dominant executive, and lifetime patron of the Whitney Museum of American Art.

The last person anyone would have expected to add to the number of Roosevelt grandchildren was Alice, who in 1925 scandalized *le tout* Georgetown by producing an unmistakable, female miniature of Senator Borah. Alice was then forty-one years old, and delighted at her achievement. "Hell, yes, isn't it wonderful?" She never confirmed or denied Paulina Longworth's paternity. Nick loved Paulina on sight and never treated her as anything other than his legitimate daughter. He became Speaker of the House of Representatives that same year, and remained in that office until a few weeks before his death in 1931.

Alice, first of Theodore Roosevelt's children to be born, was the final one to die, in 1980. By then she had been for at least six decades the acidulous, eccentric doyenne of Washington society, fawned over by presidents of every political stamp. Invitations to her famous dinners, at which she would convulse guests with imitations of Cousin Eleanor, were as prized as passes to the White House. Her attempts at writing—a family memoir and an aborted newspaper column—had nothing of the charm of her talk, which made something like poetry out of the *non sequitur*. Some of it was captured and distilled by an Englishman, Michael Teague, whose *Mrs. L: Conversations with Alice Roosevelt Longworth* was published in 1981. It amounted to a transcribed recording of the kind of erudite wit that used to be prized in the days when the well-born were also, by definition, the well-read.

Edith Kermit Roosevelt died in 1948 at the age of eighty-seven, still living in Sagamore Hill and surrounded with the Colonel's books, guns, hides, horns, and glittering prizes, as if he were still liable to burst through the door with reporters in tow. By then she had adjusted, if not to bereavement of *him,* to the deaths in war of Quentin, Kermit, and Ted, comforting herself with grandchildren and her lifelong passion for reading. Her memories in her final, bedridden days extended back from the present, disagreeably dominated by Harry Truman, through seventeen administrations to that of Abraham Lincoln. Perhaps the earliest of these impressions (confirmed to her amazement by a visitor with a photograph) was of standing with six-year-old "Teedie" Roosevelt in a window overlooking Broadway, on the day that the Emancipator's funeral procession came uptown, to a thump of drums.

☙

AFTER THE OLD WOMAN had been buried beside her husband in Youngs Cemetery, the Roosevelt Memorial Association moved to execute its long-postponed plan to buy and restore Sagamore Hill as a museum. The purchase was announced in 1949, with a certain amount of weariness on the part of Hermann Hagedorn, who had yet to see his idol's image recover from the desecration inflicted on it by Henry Pringle. Indeed, the RMA would soon have to rename itself the Theodore Roosevelt Association, to make clear to donors which president it wished to celebrate.

The enduring influence of Pringle's book, however, was salutary, in that it compelled scholars to assess the Colonel as a man, and not a god or monster. Between 1951 and 1954, Harvard University published *The Letters of Theodore Roosevelt* in eight massive volumes. Edited and annotated with impeccable scholarship by Elting E. Morison, John M. Blum, and others, the series effectively filled a lacuna left by the Memorial Edition of *The Works of Theodore Roosevelt* thirty years before. It was perhaps even more impressive in its totality than the Hagedorn set—and not just because Morison admitted that his team had eliminated ten letters for every one of the fifteen thousand he printed. Excepting those frankly addressed to "posterity," most were written only to be read by the recipients, and revealed a more personal Roosevelt than books and speeches he had meant for print. And the Colonel in his revelation proved to be, in Julian Street's updatable phrase, arguably "the most interesting American" who ever lived.

In 1958, the year of the centennial of his birth, Carleton Putnam published *Theodore Roosevelt: The Formative Years,* a superb piece of scholarship that was intended to be the first part of a four-volume biography. Only one small, significant omission marred the book's narrative flow: the fact that the young Roosevelt, attending his first Republican convention in 1884, had sought to put a black man in the chair. Putnam proved to be a retired airline executive living in Virginia, whose racial views distracted him to such an extent that his book was not followed by any sequel.

Edward Wagenknecht's *The Seven Worlds of Theodore Roosevelt* also came out in 1958. It was a revelatory character study that avoided psychobiography and presented only facts, culled from what seemed to be a reading of every book and manuscript in the Theodore Roosevelt Collection at Harvard.

Viewing "T.R." as a sort of solar system of linked but separate worlds (those of Action, Thought, Human Relations, Family, Spiritual Values, Public Affairs, and War and Peace), it compressed in fewer than three hundred pages the fundamentals of a polygonal personality.

Three years later, a major one-volume biography appeared. It was William Henry Harbaugh's *The Life and Times of Theodore Roosevelt,* a determinedly objective book that exposed the work of Henry Pringle as superficial. The ponderousness of Harbaugh's prose lent weight to his concluding observation:

> Whatever the Colonel's ultimate place in the hearts of his countrymen—and it yearly grows warmer and warmer—there is no discounting those incisive perceptions and momentous actions that made him such a dynamic historical force. . . . Long after the rationalizations, the compromises, the infights, the intolerance and the rest have been forgotten, Theodore Roosevelt will be remembered as the first great President-reformer of the modern industrial era.

Signs of the warming trend that Harbaugh spoke of proliferated after Sagamore Hill was declared a National Historic Site in 1962. President Kennedy signed the act of acquisition. On 22 November 1963 he flew to Texas with a speech he intended to deliver at the Dallas Trade Mart, extensively quoting Theodore Roosevelt on foreign policy. The speech was not given, but subsequent presidents showed an increasing willingness to admire, and even identify with, the Republican Roosevelt.

Richard Nixon invoked the image of "the man in the arena" so often, and with such relish in its details of dust and sweat and blood, as to suggest that he found them masochistically agreeable. After resigning his office on 9 August 1974 he bade farewell to White House staffers with a moving, if irrelevant, quotation from *In Memory of My Darling Wife,* the eulogy Roosevelt had written for Alice Hathaway Lee ninety years before. Weeping, Nixon observed, "That was TR in his twenties. He thought the light had gone out of his life forever—but he went on."

The Vietnam War era climaxing with Nixon's debasement saw the rise of a presentist subculture among historians who, rejecting Harbaugh, continued to see Theodore Roosevelt as a bully, warmonger, and racist. He was castigated for being unaware of the civil rights movement, free sex, meditation, and mutually assured destruction. This revisionism nevertheless drew useful parallels, such as that between the massacres of My Lai in 1968 and Moro Crater in 1906—the latter inflicted on Filipino rebels by General Leonard Wood with no dissenting word from his commander in chief.

Although doubts on the New Left about Roosevelt's imperialistic "Americanism" persisted through the decade, two biographies at the end of it marked the beginning of a more objective reassessment that steadily gathered force. This writer's *The Rise of Theodore Roosevelt* (1979) and David McCullough's *Mornings on Horseback* (1981) won literary prizes, and reassured post-Watergate readers that whatever Roosevelt "went on" to, after his twenties, had not been an abuse of presidential power. They coincided with the appearance of Sylvia Jukes Morris's *Edith Kermit Roosevelt: Portrait of a First Lady* (1980), which documented one of the great marriages in American history.

Three decades later, the shifting sands of historiography seem to have allowed the monolith of Theodore Roosevelt to settle. Sand being sand, nothing of his future reputation can be predicted. He is still buffeted by revisionist storms, some emanating from academe and obsessing on the latest *idée fixe* in that quarter, "masculinity." But the prevailing breeze of popular opinion is favorable. A C-SPAN survey in 2009, rating the leadership of American presidents, placed "T. Roosevelt" at number four, after Washington, Lincoln, and Franklin Roosevelt. Substantial books on him continue to appear and are eagerly read. Three recent examples, by Kathleen Dalton, Candice Millard, and Patricia O'Toole, demonstrate that for all the Rough Rider's machismo, fair-minded women feel no need to condescend to him. Douglas Brinkley's study of the Rooseveltian conservation record, *The Wilderness Warrior: Theodore Roosevelt and the Crusade for America* (2009) became a national bestseller even though it was over nine hundred pages long.

THE EMPLACEMENT of Theodore Roosevelt Bridge across the Potomac River in Washington gives many commuters the impression that it, and not the forested island beneath, is the twenty-sixth President's official memorial. Somewhere among those trees, however, he stands eighteen feet tall, one bronze fist upraised, eternally lecturing the doves and mockingbirds.

Solemn words are carved on granite tablets nearby. But they, and all the millions of others that have been published about him, come no closer to the truth than those of a small boy in Cove School, Oyster Bay, on June 16, 1922. As part of a class exercise paying tribute to the late Colonel, Thomas Maher wrote: "He was a fulfiller of good intentions."

ACKNOWLEDGMENTS

THE AUTHOR IS VARIOUSLY and often profoundly indebted to the following kind people: Terry C. Anderson; Kay Auchincloss; Lowell E. Baier; John M. Bell; Laurence Bergreen; Douglas Brinkley; Matthew J. Bruccoli; Robert B. Charles; Gleise Cruz; Wallace F. Dailey; Michelle Daniel; Judy Davidowitz; Jack Fisher; Josette Frank; John Allen Gable; Megan Gavin; David Gerstner; Matthew James Glover; Lewis L. Gould; Nan Graham; Francine du Plessis Gray; Susan Hannah; Ruth Hartley; George and Nanette Herrick; John Hutton; Gordon Hyatt; Joseph Kanon; Dodie Kazanjian; Patrick Kerwin; Simon Keynes; Elmer R. Koppelmann; Jennifer Kramer; Gary Lavergne; Mary LeCroy; Richard Lindsey; Alice Low; Andrew Marks; Paul Marks; Curt Meine; Timothy Mennel; Marc Miller; Sylvia Jukes Morris; Thomas R. Mountain; John Novogrod; Martin Obrentz; Joseph A. O'Brien; Allen Packwood; John Gray Peatman; Richard Pennington; Jacqueline Philomeno; Christina Rae; Frederick Roberts Rinehart II; Theodore and Connie Roosevelt IV; Tweed Roosevelt; Benjamin and Donna Rosen; Benjamin Steinberg; Joanna Sturm; Michael and Marcia Thomas; Keith Topley; John Frederick Walker; John D. Weaver; Sara Wheeler; Richard Derby Williams.

ARCHIVES

Papers denoted with an asterisk are located in the Theodore Roosevelt Collection, Houghton Library, Harvard University (TRC). It and the Theodore Roosevelt Papers at the Library of Congress (TRP) are the two main repositories of documents relating to the twenty-sixth President. Both collections are in the process of being electronically copied by the Theodore Roosevelt Center at Dickinson State University, North Dakota. The aim of this institution is to create a unified digital archive of Roosevelt's papers, freely accessible to researchers worldwide via the Internet.

ABB	Lawrence Abbott Papers*
ABRP	Archibald B. Roosevelt Papers*
AC	Author's Collection
AJB	Arthur J. Balfour Papers, British Library, London
AL	Arthur Lee Papers, Cortauld Institute, London
AMNH	American Museum of Natural History, New York
ARC	Anna Roosevelt Cowles Papers*
ASP	Albert Shaw Papers, New York Public Library
BEV	Albert J. Beveridge Papers, Library of Congress
CSR	Cecil Spring Rice Papers, Churchill College, Cambridge, UK
DUN	Finley Peter Dunne Papers, Library of Congress
EAR	Edwin Arlington Robinson Collection, New York Public Library
EMH	Edwin M. Hood Papers, Library of Congress
ERDP	Ethel Roosevelt Derby Papers*
EW	Edith Wharton Papers, Beinecke Library, Yale University
FWM	Flora Whitney Miller Papers*
HCLP	Henry Cabot Lodge Papers, Massachusetts Historical Society, Cambridge
HH	Hermann Hagedorn Papers*
HKB	Howard K. Beale Papers, Princeton University[†]
HP	Henry Pringle Papers*
HW	Henry White Papers, Library of Congress
JHMD	James Herbert Morse Diaries, New-York Historical Society
JJJ	Jean Jules Jusserand Papers, Quai d'Orsay, Paris
JJL	John J. Leary Papers*
JRGP	James R. Garfield Papers, Library of Congress
JS	Julian Street Papers, Princeton University Library
KRP	Kermit Roosevelt Papers, Library of Congress
LBS	Lucius Burrie Swift Papers, Indiana Historical Society
MLM	Morgan Library and Museum, New York
OL	John Callan O'Laughlin Papers*

[†] This valuable collection of notes and interview transcripts relating to TR, made by Beale over the course of several decades, has been destroyed by its curators.

OW	Owen Wister Papers, Library of Congress
PAR	Frances Theodora Smith Parsons Papers*
PCK	Philander Chase Knox Papers, Library of Congress
RSB	Ray Stannard Baker Papers, Library of Congress
SCR	Charles Scribner's Sons Papers, Princeton University Library
SHA	Albert Shaw Papers, New York Public Library
STR	Willard Straight Papers, Cornell University Library
SUL	Mark Sullivan Papers, Library of Congress
SULH	Mark Sullivan Papers, Hoover Institution, Stanford University
TRB	Theodore Roosevelt Birthplace National Historic Site Collection, New York
TRBU	Theodore Roosevelt Collection, Gotlieb Center, Boston University
TRC	Theodore Roosevelt Collection, Harvard
TRJP	Theodore Roosevelt, Jr., Papers, Library of Congress
TRP	Theodore Roosevelt Papers, Library of Congress
WB	Willard Bartlett Papers, Columbia University
WCF	Walt Kuhn Family and Armory Show Records, Smithsonian Archives of American Art
WFP	Williams Family Papers, privately held
WHTP	William Howard Taft Papers, Library of Congress
WR	Whitelaw Reid Papers, Library of Congress
WWP	Woodrow Wilson Papers, Library of Congress

SELECT BIBLIOGRAPHY

Only those sources that have multiple citations in the Notes are listed here. All others are cited where they relate to the text.

The most comprehensive bibliography of Theodore Roosevelt is the online catalogue of the Theodore Roosevelt Collection, compiled by Wallace F. Dailey, curator of the Theodore Roosevelt Collection, Houghton Library, Harvard University. It includes manuscripts and photographs, and expands on an earlier print version, Gregory C. Wilson, comp., *Theodore Roosevelt Collection: Dictionary Catalogue and Shelflist,* 5 vols., plus one-volume *Supplement,* Wallace F. Dailey, comp. (Cambridge, Mass., 1970, 1986).

BOOKS

Abbott, Lawrence F. *Impressions of Theodore Roosevelt.* New York, 1919.

Adams, Henry. *The Letters of Henry Adams.* J. C. Levenson, Ernest Samuels, Charles Vandersee, Viola Hopkins Winner, eds. 6 vols. Cambridge, Mass., 1988.

Amos, James E. *Theodore Roosevelt: Hero to His Valet.* New York, 1927.

Asquith, Margot. *The Autobiography of Margot Asquith.* Boston, 1963.

Bailey, Thomas A. *A Diplomatic History of the American People.* 8th ed. New York, 1969.

Baker, Ray Stannard. *American Chronicle.* New York, 1945.

Balfour, Michael. *The Kaiser and His Time.* New York, 1964, 1972.

[Begbie, Harold]. *The Mirrors of Downing Street: Some Political Reflections by a Gentleman with a Duster.* New York, 1921.

Bishop, Joseph Bucklin. *Theodore Roosevelt and His Time: Shown in His Own Letters.* 2 vols. New York, 1920.

Bourne, Kenneth, ed. *British Documents on Foreign Affairs: Reports and Papers from the Foreign Office Confidential Print, Part One, From the Mid-Nineteenth Century to the First World War.* Multiple vols. Frederick, Md.; 1990.

Bull, Bartle. *Safari: A Chronicle of Adventure.* New York, 1988.

Butt, Archibald W. *The Letters of Archie Butt: Personal Aide to President Roosevelt.* Lawrence F. Abbott, ed. New York, 1924.*

———. *Taft and Roosevelt: The Intimate Letters of Archie Butt, Military Aide.* 2 vols. New York, 1930.

Cherrie, George K. *Dark Trails: Adventures of a Naturalist.* New York, 1930.

Clemenceau, Georges. *Discours de guerre.* Paris, 1934, 1968.

Cooper, John Milton. *Woodrow Wilson: A Biography.* New York, 2009.

Cordery, Stacy A. *Alice: Alice Roosevelt Longworth, from White House Princess to Washington Power Broker.* New York, 2007.

---

* Quotations from this book have been checked against transcripts of Butt's original letters, preserved in the Marble Library of Emory University, Atlanta, Ga.

Cowley, Robert, ed. *The Great War: Perspectives on the First World War.* New York, 2004.

Davis, Oscar King. *Released for Publication: Some Inside Political History of Theodore Roosevelt and His Times, 1898–1918.* Boston, 1925.

Dugdale, Edgar T., ed. *German Diplomatic Documents 1871–1914.* Vol. 3. London, 1930.

Dunne, Finley Peter. *Mr. Dooley Remembers: The Informal Memoirs of Finley Peter Dunne* [1936]. Philip Dunne, ed. Boston, 1963.

Dyer, Thomas G. *Theodore Roosevelt and the Idea of Race.* Baton Rouge, La., 1980.

Ecksteins, Modris. *Rites of Spring: The Great War and the Birth of the Modern Age.* Boston, 1989.

Gable, John Allen. *The Bull Moose Years: Theodore Roosevelt and the Progressive Party.* Port Washington, N.Y., 1978.

Garland, Hamlin. *Companions on the Trail: A Literary Chronicle.* New York, 1931.

———. *My Friendly Contemporaries: A Literary Log.* New York, 1932.

———. *Roadside Meetings.* New York, 1930.

Gerard, James W. *Face to Face with Kaiserism.* New York, 1918.

———. *My Four Years in Germany.* New York, 1917.

[Gilbert, Clinton W.]. *The Mirrors of Washington: With Fourteen Cartoons by Cesare.* New York, 1922.

Gilbert, Martin. *A History of the Twentieth Century.* Vol. 1, 1900–1933. Toronto, 1997.

Goetsch, Charles C. *Essays on Simeon Baldwin.* West Hartford, Conn., 1981.

Gould, Lewis L., ed. *Bull Moose on the Stump: The 1912 Campaign Speeches of Theodore Roosevelt.* Lawrence, Kan., 2008.

———, ed. *Four Hats in the Ring: The 1912 Election and the Birth of Modern American Politics.* Lawrence, Kan., 2008.

Grey, Edward, Viscount. *Twenty-five Years: 1892–1916.* Vol. 2. New York, 1925.

Hagedorn, Hermann. *Edwin Arlington Robinson: A Biography.* New York, 1938.

———. *The Roosevelt Family of Sagamore Hill.* New York, 1954.

Harbaugh, William H. *The Life and Times of Theodore Roosevelt.* Rev. ed. New York, 1975.

Hechler, Kenneth W. *Insurgency: Personalities and Politics of the Taft Era.* New York, 1964.

Heckscher, August. *Woodrow Wilson: A Biography.* New York, 1991.

House, Edward M. *The Intimate Papers of Colonel House.* 4 vols. Charles Seymour, ed. Cambridge, Mass., 1926.

Karp, Walter. *The Politics of War: The Story of Two Wars Which Altered Forever the Political Life of the American Republic.* New York, 1979.

La Follette, Belle and Fola. *Robert M. La Follette.* 2 vols. New York, 1953.

La Follette, Robert M. *La Follette's Autobiography: A Personal Narrative of Political Experiences.* Madison, Wis., 1913.

Leary, John J., Jr. *Talks with T.R.: From the Diaries of John J. Leary, Jr.* Boston, 1920.

Lee, Dwight E., ed. *The Outbreak of the First World War: Causes and Responsibilities.* Lexington, Mass., 1970, 1975.

Lee of Fareham, Viscount. *A Good Innings.* Vol. 1. Privately printed, London, 1939.

———. *"A Good Innings": The Private Papers of Viscount Lee of Fareham, P.C., G.C.B., G.C.S.I., G.B.E.* Alan Clark, ed. London, 1974.

Link, Arthur S., ed. *The Papers of Woodrow Wilson.* Princeton, N.J., 1966–1990.

———. *Wilson: The Road to the White House.* Princeton, N.J., 1947.

Longworth, Alice Roosevelt. *Crowded Hours: Reminiscences of Alice Roosevelt Longworth.* New York, 1933.

Looker, Earle. *Colonel Roosevelt, Private Citizen.* New York, 1932.

Lorant, Stefan. *The Life and Times of Theodore Roosevelt.* Garden City, N.Y., 1959.

MacDonogh, Giles. *The Last Kaiser: The Life of Wilhelm II.* New York, 2000.

McGerr, Michael. *A Fierce Discontent: The Rise and Fall of the Progressive Movement in America, 1870–1920.* New York, 2003.

Marks, Frederick J., III. *Velvet on Iron: The Diplomacy of Theodore Roosevelt.* Lincoln, Neb., 1979.

Millard, Candice. *The River of Doubt: Theodore Roosevelt's Darkest Journey.* New York, 2005.

Miller, Char. *Gifford Pinchot and the Making of Modern Environmentalism.* Washington, D.C., 2001.

Miller, Leo E. *In the Wilds of South America.* New York, 1918.

Morris, Edmund. *The Rise of Theodore Roosevelt.* Rev. ed. New York, 1979, 2001.

———. *Theodore Rex.* New York, 2001.

Morris, Sylvia Jukes. *Edith Kermit Roosevelt: Portrait of a First Lady.* New York, 1980.

Mowry, George E. *Theodore Roosevelt and the Progressive Movement.* New York, 1946, 1960.

Naylor, Natalie, et al., eds. *Theodore Roosevelt: Many-Sided American.* Interlaken, N.Y., 1992.

Nevins, Allan. *Henry White: Thirty Years of American Diplomacy.* New York, 1930.

New York (State) Supreme Court. *William Barnes, Plaintiff-Appellant, Against Theodore Roosevelt, Defendant-Respondent.* Walton, N.Y., 1917.

O'Laughlin, John C. *From the Jungle Through Europe with Roosevelt.* Boston, 1910.

O'Toole, Patricia. *When Trumpets Call: Theodore Roosevelt After the White House.* New York, 2005.

Papen, Franz von. *Memoirs.* Brian Connell, trans. London, 1952.

Parsons, Frances Theodora. *Perchance Some Day.* Privately printed memoir, 1951 (copy in TRC).

Pringle, Henry F. *The Life and Times of William Howard Taft.* 2 vols. New York, 1939.

———. *Theodore Roosevelt, A Biography.* New York, 1931.

Putnam, Carleton. *Theodore Roosevelt: The Formative Years, 1858–1886.* New York, 1958.

Remey, Oliver, et al. *The Attempted Assassination of Ex-President Theodore Roosevelt.* Milwaukee, Wis., 1912.

Republican National Committee. *Official Report of the Proceedings of the National Republican Convention, 1912.* The Internet Archive, http://www.archive.org/.

Robinson, Corinne R. *My Brother Theodore Roosevelt.* New York, 1921.

Robinson, Edwin Arlington. *Collected Poems.* New York, 1922.

———. *The Town Down the River.* New York, 1910.

Rondon, Cândido M. *Lectures Delivered by Colonel Cândido Mariana da Silva Rondon . . . On the 5th, 7th and 9th of October 1915 at the Phenix Theatre of Rio de Janeiro, on the Roosevelt-Rondon Scientific Expedition.* R. G. Reidy and Ed. Murray, trans. Rio de Janeiro, 1916; New York, 1969.

Roosevelt, Eleanor Butler. *Day Before Yesterday: The Reminiscences of Mrs. Theodore Roosevelt, Jr.* Garden City, N.Y, 1959.

Roosevelt, Emlen, ed. *Roosevelt vs. Newett: A Transcript of the Testimony Taken and Depositions Read at Marquette, Michigan (May 26–31, 1913).* Privately printed, 1913.

Roosevelt, Kermit. *The Happy Hunting-Grounds.* New York, 1920.

———. *The Long Trail.* New York, 1921.

———, ed. *Quentin Roosevelt: A Sketch with Letters.* New York, 1921.

Roosevelt, Theodore. *African and European Addresses.* Lawrence F. Abbott, ed. New York, 1910.

———. *An Autobiography.* New York, 1913; Library of America, 2004.

————. *The Letters of Theodore Roosevelt.* 8 vols. Cambridge, Mass., 1951–54.

————. *The Works of Theodore Roosevelt.* Memorial Edition. 24 vols. New York, 1923–1926.*

Rosewater, Victor. *Back Stage in 1912: The Inside Story of the Split Republican Convention.* Philadelphia, 1932.

Slayden, Ellen Maury. *Washington Wife: Journal of Ellen Maury Slayden from 1897–1919.* New York, 1963.

Stoddard Henry L. *As I Knew Them: Presidents and Politics from Grant to Coolidge.* New York, 1927.

Strachan, Hew. *The First World War.* New York, 2004.

Straus, Oscar. *Under Four Administrations.* Boston, 1922.

Street, Julian. *The Most Interesting American.* New York, 1915.

Stürmer, Michael. *The German Empire, 1870–1918.* New York, 2000.

Sullivan, Mark. *Our Times: The United States, 1900–1925.* Vols. 3–5. New York, 1930.

Teague, Michael. *Mrs. L: Conversations with Alice Roosevelt Longworth.* London, 1981.

Thayer, William Roscoe. *Theodore Roosevelt: An Intimate Biography.* Boston, 1919.

Thompson, Charles Willis. *Presidents I've Known and Two Near Presidents.* Indianapolis, 1929.

Tuchman, Barbara W. *The Proud Tower: A Portrait of the World Before the War, 1890–1914.* New York, 1966.

Turner, Frederick J. *Dear Lady: The Letters of Frederick J. Turner and Alice Forbes Perkins Hooper, 1910–1932.* San Marino, Calif., 1970.

Vivieros, Esther de. *Rondon conta sua vida.* Rio de Janeiro, 1958.

Wagenknecht, Edward. *The Seven Worlds of Theodore Roosevelt.* New York, 1958; Guilford, Conn., 2008.

Wall, Joseph Frazier. *Andrew Carnegie.* Pittsburgh, Pa., 1970, 1989.

Wallace, David H. *Sagamore Hill National Historic Site: Historic Furnishings Report.* Vol. 1, *Historical Data.* Harpers Ferry, Va., 1989.

Washburn, Charles G. *Theodore Roosevelt: The Logic of His Career.* Boston, 1916.

Wharton, Edith. *A Backward Glance.* New York, 1933, 1985.

White, William Allen. *The Autobiography of William Allen White.* New York, 1946.

————. *Masks in a Pageant.* New York, 1928.

Wister, Owen. *The Pentecost of Calamity.* New York, 1917.

————. *Roosevelt: The Story of a Friendship, 1880–1919.* New York, 1930.

Wood, Frederick S., ed. *Roosevelt As We Knew Him: The Personal Recollections of One Hundred and Fifty of His Friends and Associates.* Philadelphia, 1927.

Zahm, John Augustine. *Through South America's Southland: With an Account of the Roosevelt Scientific Expedition to South America.* New York, 1916.

ARTICLES

Alves de Lima, José C. "Reminiscences of Roosevelt in Brazil," *Brazilian American,* Feb. 1927.

Babir, Karl. "Alfred Thayer Mahan, Theodore Roosevelt, the Middle East, and the Twentieth Century." *Journal of Middle Eastern and North African Intellectual and Cultural Studies,* 2.1 (Spring 2004).

* There is an alternative collection, *The Works of Theodore Roosevelt,* National Edition, 20 vols. (New York, 1926). It is almost identical in content with the Memorial Edition but is arranged differently. For a brief survey of the Memorial Edition, see Wagenknecht, *The Seven Worlds of Theodore Roosevelt,* 345.

Blakey, George T. "Calling a Boss a Boss: Did Roosevelt Libel Barnes in 1915?" *New York History*, 60.2 (Apr. 1979).

Burton, David H. "Theodore Roosevelt and His English Correspondents: A Special Relationship of Friends." *Transactions of the America Philosophical Society*, n.s., 63, pt. 2, 1973.

Enders, Armelle. "Theodore Roosevelt explorateur: Positivisme et mythe de la frontière dans l'*expediçào cientifica Roosevelt-Rondon* au Mato Grosso et en Amazonie." Nuevo Mundo Mundo Nuevos, 2 Feb. 2005, http://nuevomundo.revues.org/.

German, James C., Jr. "Roosevelt, Taft, and United States Steel." *The Historian*, 34.4 (1972).

Greene, John Robert. "Theodore Roosevelt and the Barnes Libel Case: A Reappraisal." *Presidential Studies Quarterly*, 19.1 (Winter 1989).

Holli, Melvin, and C. David Tompkins. "Roosevelt *vs.* Newett: The Politics of Libel." *Michigan History*, 47.4 (Dec. 1963).

Holmes, James R. "Theodore Roosevelt and Elihu Root: International Lawmen." *World Affairs*, 169.4 (Spring 2007).

Levien, Sonya. "The Great Friend: A Personal Story of Theodore Roosevelt as He Revealed Himself to One of His Associates in Magazine Work." *Woman's Home Companion*, Oct. 1919.

Margulies, Herbert F. "La Follette, Roosevelt and the Republican Presidential Nomination of 1912." *Mid-America*, 58.1 (1976).

Masheck, Joseph. "Teddy's Taste: Theodore Roosevelt and the Armory Show." *Art Forum*, 9.2 (1970).

Murakata, Akiko. "Theodore Roosevelt and William Sturgis Bigelow: The Story of a Friendship." *Harvard Library Bulletin*, 23.1 (1975).

Murphy, Gary. "Mr. Roosevelt Is Guilty: Theodore Roosevelt and the Crusade for Constitutionalism, 1910–1912." *Journal of American Studies*, 36.3 (Dec. 2002).

Osborn, Henry Fairfield. "Theodore Roosevelt, Naturalist." *Natural History*, 19.1 (Jan. 1919).

Pavord, Andrew C. "The Gamble for Power: Theodore Roosevelt's Decision to Run for the Presidency in 1912." *Presidential Studies Quarterly*, 26.3 (Summer 1996).

Potts, E. Daniel. "Theodore Roosevelt and the Progressive Party, 1912–1916: A Reinterpretation." *Pacific Circle: Proceedings of the Second Biennial Conference of the Australian and New Zealand American Studies Association*. St. Lucia, Queensland, 1968.

Rice, Gary. "Trailing a Celebrity: Press Coverage of Theodore Roosevelt's African Safari, 1909–1910." *Theodore Roosevelt Association Journal*, 21.3 (Fall 1996).

Sá, Dominichi M. de, et al. "Telegraphs and an Inventory of the Territory of Brazil: The Scientific Work of the Rondon Commission (1907–1915)." *História, Ciêncas, Saúde-Manguinhos*, 15.3 (July–Sept., 2008), http://www.scielo.br/.

Sherman, Stuart P. "Roosevelt and the National Psychology," *The Nation*, 109.2836 (8 Nov. 1919).

Stagner, Stephen. "The Recall of Judicial Decisions and the Due Process Debate." *American Journal of Legal History*, 24.3 (July 1980).

Unpublished Works and Interviews

Cherrie, George K. Diary of the Roosevelt-Rondon Expedition, 1913–1914 (AMNH).

Dawson, F. Warrington. "Opportunity and Theodore Roosevelt." Pre-publication ts., 1924 (KRP).

Gable, John Allen. "The Bull Moose Years: Theodore Roosevelt and the Progressive Party, 1912–1916." Ph.D. diss. Kenyon College, 1965.

Hagedorn, Hermann. "Some Notes on Colonel Roosevelt from Henry L. Stimson." Ts., 12 Dec. 1923 (TRB).

O'Laughlin, John Callan. Diary of the Republican National Convention, June 1912 (OL).

Pratt, Walter Merriam. "Theodore Roosevelt: His Cabinet, Family, Funeral Notices." Bound scrapbook (TRB).

Roosevelt, Nicholas. "Account of the Republican National Convention at Chicago, June 12, 1912." Bound volume (TRC).

Roosevelt, Philip J. "Politics of the Year 1912: An Intimate Progressive View." Ts. (TRC).

Roosevelt, Theodore. Diary, 1909 (TRC).

———. Diary, 1910 (TRB).

Roosevelt Memorial Association. "The Story of the Roosevelt Medals." Ts., ca. 1940 (TRB).

Wertheim, Stephen A. "The League That Wasn't: Theodore Roosevelt, Elihu Root, William Howard Taft and a Legalist League of Nations." AB diss. Harvard, 2007.

WEBSITES

GHDI: German History in Documents and Images, http:germanhistorydocs.ghi-dc.org/.

The Internet Archive, http://www.archive.org/.

Measuring Worth, http://www.measuringworth.com/.

NOTES

The names of Roosevelt family members are abbreviated thus in the Notes:

TR	Theodore Roosevelt
EKR	Edith Kermit Roosevelt
ARL	Alice Roosevelt Longworth
TR.Jr.	Theodore Roosevelt, Jr. ("Ted")
EBR	Eleanor Butler Roosevelt (Mrs. Theodore Roosevelt, Jr.)
KR	Kermit Roosevelt
ERD	Ethel Roosevelt Derby
ABR	Archibald Bulloch Roosevelt ("Archie")
QR	Quentin Roosevelt

Two other monograms are used: WHT for William Howard Taft, and WW for Woodrow Wilson. Abbreviations denoting collections and repositories are listed above in Archives.

Contemporary (2010) dollar equivalents occasionally appear in parentheses after figures cited for TR's lifetime. Unless otherwise indicated, these equivalents are taken from the annual CPI/GDP deflator indices posted on Measuring Worth (http://www.measuringworth.com/).

PROLOGUE

Chronological Note: On 23 Mar. 1909, twelve days after handing over the presidency to WHT, TR sailed from Hoboken, N.J., on the SS *Hamburg*. He used his hat to wigwag, in expert semaphore, "Goodbye and good luck." Arriving in Naples on 4 Apr., he changed to another German steamship and sailed the following day via the Suez Canal to Mombasa. Disembarking there on 21 Apr., he boarded a special upland train at 2.30 P.M. on Thursday, 22 Apr.

3 **Sitting above the cowcatcher** This account of TR's journey to the interior of British East Africa (later Kenya) is based on "Through the Pleistocene," the first chapter of his book *African Game Trails* (1910), cited hereafter as vol. 5 of *The Works of Theodore Roosevelt,* Memorial Edition (New York, 1923–26). Other documentary details come from reports in the *East African Standard,* 24 Apr. 1909; *The Leader of British East Africa,* 7 Aug. 1909; and *Uganda Railway, British East Africa,* a glossy booklet sent by TR to his publisher in 1909 (SCR). Minor descriptive touches derive from the author's own native background in Kenya.

3 **a "Royal" grade** *East African Standard,* 24 Apr. 1909. TR's great rifle, now privately owned, is illustrated and described in R. L. Wilson, *Theodore Roosevelt Hunter-Conservationist,* Boone and Crockett Club special edition, Missoula, Mont., 2009, 174–77. This book is an excellent pictorial record of TR's expeditions.

3 **It contrasts with** See TR's essay "The Pigskin Library," TR, *Works,* 14.463ff. Forty-six surviving volumes are preserved in TRC, along with the aluminum valise. Matched against "the original list" of titles compiled by TR himself, they project a total of 73 volumes. For the genesis of the library, see Corinne Roosevelt Robinson, *My Brother Theodore Roosevelt* (New York, 1921), 252–53. For TR's current range of reading, see Biographical Note below, 590.

3 **Less disconcerting** TR, *Works,* 5.15–18.

4 **"this great fragment"** Ibid., 5.5, xxvi.

4 **finding again the Dark Continent** See Edmund Morris, *The Rise of Theodore Roosevelt* (rev. ed., New York, 2001), 15.

4 **"Doctor," he had said** Ibid., 129.

4 **Hustling for votes** This distaste for electoral politics, owing much to the corruption of the Gilded Age, was a comparatively recent phenomenon in TR's immediate family. Several of his ancestors in revolutionary and federal times had been public men. See Carlton Putnam, *Theodore Roosevelt: The Formative Years, 1858–1886* (New York, 1958), 3–6.

> *Biographical Note:* Claes Martenszen van Rosenvelt, whose surname probably derived from a farm, Rosevelt ("Rose Field" on the island of Tholen in Zeeland, Holland), is established as the first American Roosevelt in Timothy Field Beard and Henry B. Hoff, "The Roosevelt Family," *The New York Genealogical and Biological Record,* 118.4 (Oct. 1987), 1–2.

5 **Not surprisingly** Morris, *Theodore Rex,* 98–99, 180–81; Carl Cavanaugh Hodge, "Theodore Roosevelt and the Transoceanic Naval Arms Race, 1897–1909," *Theodore Roosevelt Association Journal,* 30.1–2 (Winter–Spring, 2009); Peter Larsen, "Theodore Roosevelt and the Moroccan Crisis, 1904–1906" (Ph.D. diss., Princeton University, 1984), 307–8. For a compact study of TR's personal style in foreign affairs, see Frederick W. Marks III, *Velvet on Iron: The Diplomacy of Theodore Roosevelt* (Lincoln, Neb., 1979).

5 **His Nobel** In the opinion of a modern expert on foreign policy, TR "approached the global balance of power with a sophistication matched by no other American president." Henry Kissinger, *Diplomacy* (New York, 1994), 41.

5 **That does not stop him** Theodore Roosevelt, *The Letters of Theodore Roosevelt,* Elting E. Morison, John Blum, et al., eds., 8 vols. (Cambridge, Mass., 1951–1954), 1.324. Henceforth TR, *Letters.*

6 **Such are the intellectual** TR quoted in memorandum, "Curtis at the Conference," 20 Aug. 1887 (HKB). TR to Henry Cabot Lodge, 15 Feb. 1887; TR, *Letters,* 1.509; TR, *Works,* 5.4. For a typical statement of TR's philosophy of activism, see TR, "Latitude and Longitude Among Reformers," *Works,* 15.379.

6 **Having spent much** See David H. Burton, "Theodore Roosevelt and His English Correspondents: A Special Relationship of Friends," *Transactions of the America Philosophical Society,* n.s., 63, pt. 2 (1973). Great Britain and Germany had agreed in 1890 to partition inland East Africa, while allowing the sultanate of Zanzibar to continue in control of the coastal strip. Relations between the two protectorates were testy. Britain scored a strategic coup in 1903, when its 584-mile Mombasa–Kisumu railroad opened for business, with the intent of connecting British East Africa to Lake Victoria and the Nile. But the venture was hugely expensive, and looked unlikely ever to pay for itself unless enough white farmers could be coaxed to develop the countryside it traversed. Hence the eagerness of British imperialists to assist TR's safari, in the hope he would encourage settlement of the Protectorate in his book—seen as a certain international bestseller.

6 **"I am the only"** TR en route to Africa, ca. 28 Mar. 1909, quoted in E. Alexander Powell, *Yonder Lies Adventure* (New York, 1932), 319.

6 **Fifty-six eminent** TR, *Works*, 5.24–25. The list of gun donors included the Duke and Duchess of Bedford; the Earls of Lonsdale and Warwick; Lord Curzon, former viceroy of India; Sir Edward Grey, British foreign minister; Sir George Otto Trevelyan, historian; and Col. J. H. Patterson, author of *The Man-Eaters of Tsavo.*

6 **Germany's current arms buildup** Just before TR arrived in Mombasa, Austria-Hungary announced that it, too, would be laying down three new dreadnoughts. (*The Leader of British East Africa,* 10 Apr. 1909.) For a compact account of the British-German "Navy Scare of 1909," see chap. 33 of Robert Massie, *Dreadnought: Britain, Germany, and the Coming of the Great War* (New York, 1991).

6 **His safari has generated** TR's financial arrangement with the Smithsonian was that he would pay all safari expenses incurred by himself and KR (about two-fifths of a total estimated cost of $50,000), leaving museum fund-raisers to cover the rest. This presupposed $20,000 from him ($385,000 in today's [2010] dollars) and $30,000 ($533,000) from his sponsors, but early on it became clear that the safari was going to cost twice as much as he had planned. He was therefore obliged to solicit further funds, including $27,000 ($480,000) from Carnegie. All monetary equivalents are from Measuring Worth (http://www.measuringworth.com/).

7 **He wants to show** Morris, *The Rise of TR,* 27; Sylvia Jukes Morris, *Edith Kermit Roosevelt: Portrait of a First Lady* (New York, 1980), 23–26; TR to EKR, n.d., ca. 7 Aug. 1909 (KRP).

8 **"Jambo Bwana King ya Amerik!"** "Greetings, Lord King of America!" Quoted in Bartle Bull, *Safari: A Chronicle of Adventure* (New York, 1988), 169.

8 **the largest safari yet mounted** For detailed accounts of the expedition, supplementary to TR's own, see Bull, *Safari,* chap. 5, Wilson, *TR Hunter-Conservationist,* chap. 9, and Tweed Roosevelt, "Theodore Roosevelt's African Safari," in Natalie Naylor et al., eds., *Theodore Roosevelt: Many-Sided American* (Interlaken, N.Y., 1992), 413–32. The size and scope of TR's safari remains a record in Kenya history.

8 **a third term in 1908** TR's *first* term must be understood to have been the three and a half executive years he inherited from William McKinley, and his *second* the four years he won in the election of 1904. In his lifetime, there was no constitutional limit to the number of terms a president could serve.

8 **Mount Kenya** In 1909, Kenya was spelled *Kenia,* and denoted only the highlands of British East Africa. Ten years later, the entire region down to the coast was renamed "Kenya Colony and Protectorate."

8 **"If I am where"** Robinson, *My Brother TR,* 251.

8 **He has, besides** Bull, *Safari,* 160–63; Paul Russell Cutright, *Theodore Roosevelt: The Making of a Conservationist* (Urbana, Ill., 1985), 26–37, 169–82. TR's youthful 622-item "Roosevelt Museum of Natural History," featuring an impressive collection of Nile bird skins, was accepted by the Smithsonian in 1882. For TR's conservation record as President, see Douglas Brinkley, *The Wilderness Warrior: Theodore Roosevelt and the Crusade for America* (New York, 2009). The classic work on the hunter-conservationist paradox is John F. Reiger, *American Sportsmen and the Origins of Conservation,* 3rd ed. (Corvallis, Ore., 2001).

8 **this highly professional expedition** TR, *Works,* 5.5–6; Kermit Roosevelt, *The Long Trail* (New York, 1921), 44–45.

9 **His son may not qualify** KR to EKR, 10 Aug. 1909 (KRP); Sylvia Morris, *Edith Kermit Roosevelt,* 298. In the early days of the expedition, KR's title of *Bwana Mdogo* became *Bwana Maridadi* ("Master Dandy"), a change not entirely to TR's liking. However, the mandolin-strumming youth soon won general respect.

9 **How Edith Roosevelt feels** Sylvia Morris, *Edith Kermit Roosevelt,* 347–49; EKR to Mrs. William D. Foulke, 7 Apr. 1909, Foulke Papers, Library of Congress.

9 **By now she should** Sylvia Morris, *Edith Kermit Roosevelt,* 348; Archibald W.

Butt, *Taft and Roosevelt: The Intimate Letters of Archie Butt, Military Aide,* 2 vols. (New York, 1930), 25.

9 **My dear Theodore** TR, *Letters,* 7.3–4.

11 **"I am no hanger-on"** Ibid., 6.1230.

11 **there is one title** TR to J. Alden Loring et al. on board SS *Hamburg,* quoted in Frederick S. Wood, *Roosevelt As We Knew Him: The Personal Recollections of One Hundred and Fifty of His Friends and Associates* (Philadelphia, 1927), 221–22. See also Henry F. Pringle, *Theodore Roosevelt, A Biography* (New York, 1931), 510. On the very day TR quit the White House, he had pleasedly patted the shoulder of a reporter addressing him as "Colonel." "This man knows how to flatter me." *The New York Times,* 6 Mar. 1909.

11 **If war ever comes** TR's safari luggage contained a military greatcoat with gold braid round the sleeves. When preparing for his trip, he had to be dissuaded from ordering the elaborate dress uniform of a colonel of cavalry, to wear at formal events on his emergence from the jungle. EKR clinched the matter by threatening to match his outfit with that of a camp follower. (Sylvia Morris, *Edith Kermit Roosevelt,* 333.) See Whitelaw Reid to TR ("My earnest advice would be not to wear it, since it would certainly attract enormous attention"), 23 Sept. 1908 (WR); Archibald Butt, *The Letters of Archie Butt: Personal Aide to President Roosevelt,* Lawrence F. Abbott, ed. (New York, 1924); Wood, *Roosevelt As We Knew Him,* 419.

11 **"an outrage and an indecency"** TR to Roy W. Howard of United Press, 16 Mar. 1909 (TRP). See also TR, *Letters,* 6.1403–5; Gary Rice, "Trailing a Celebrity: Press Coverage of Theodore Roosevelt's African Safari, 1909–1910," *Theodore Roosevelt Association Journal,* 22.3 (Fall 1996).

11 **A touch** *bon marché* EKR to KR, 19 Oct. 1917 (KRP). TR's $50,000 contract in 1909 would be worth $888,000 in 2010. (Measuring Worth) "I think there is such a thing as making too much money out of a given feat," TR rather embarrassedly wrote Henry Cabot Lodge. (Lodge, *Selections,* 2.305.) He was also earning $12,000 ($213,000) a year as contributing editor of *The Outlook.*

11 **He rides out to hunt** This excursion (24 Apr. 1909) is misdated in TR, *Works,* 5.27.

Chronological Note: In order to correct some confusion in earlier accounts, the following chronology gives the main dates, major kills, and general itinerary of the Smithsonian–Theodore Roosevelt Expedition. It is based on a compilation of TR's safari diaries for 1909 and 1910 (TRC and TRB), supplemented by those of KR and F. Warrington Dawson, and articles in the East African newspapers. Capitalized place-names denote bases of operations.

1909

Apr. 21: TR arrives Mombasa; 22: overnight train inland; 23: arrives KAPITI depot.

FIRST SAFARI (5 WEEKS)

Apr. 24: begins to hunt and camp in KITANGA RANCH region; 29: 1st 2 lions. May 2: 2 lions, 1 lioness; 3: Bondini; 5: Kilima Kiu camp; 6: cow eland, rhino near Juja; 9: bull giraffe; 11: Potha camp; 12: visits U.S. Machakos mission; 13: JUJA FARM for 1 week; 16: cow rhino; 16: 1st hippo, Rewero River; 19: Nairobi Falls; 20: Kamiti camp; 21: 1st buffalo; 24: TR charged by buffalo; 25: breaks Kamiti camp; 26: NAIROBI for 8 days; stays at Government House; 27: governor's reception, dance; 28: moves to McMillan townhouse; 31: dinner Norfolk Hotel.

SECOND SAFARI (7 WEEKS)

June 3: leaves NAIROBI, via U.S. Kijabe mission, en route SOTIK; 5: begins moonlight marches across "the Thirst"; 10: camps on southern Guaso Nyero (5 days); 14: kills lioness; welcomed by Masai; 15: limestone springs camp (9 days); 16: 3 giraffes; 18: rhino, topi, wildebeest; 20: rhino cow, calf; 23: lion; 24: Masai pool camp (3 days); 25: big maned lion; 27: plains camp (6 days); 29: 7 kills, including 1 rhino; 30:

First overseas mail. July 3: breaks camp; begins northward trek to Naivasha; 4: cow rhino; 6: rejoins naturalists at Guaso Nyero; 7: writing day; 11: reaches NAIVASHA; 12: camps on Attenborough Farm (12 days); 13: begins hippo hunting; 16: fever; 20: mass hippo kill; 23: employs Dawson as press secretary; 24: train to NAIROBI for 11-day stay in McMillan townhouse; 25ff: works on correspondence, chapters for Scribners. Aug. 3: dinner in his honor; speech, "Education in Africa."

Third Safari (3 weeks)
Aug. 4: train via Kijabe mission (stone-laying ceremony) to NAIVASHA for 4 days; 8: leaves for Aberdare range; 11: arrives NYERI; Kikuyu dance welcome; 14: fever; ascends foothills of Mount Kenya; 18: begins elephant hunting; 19: 1st bull elephant; 22: returns NYERI to write.

Fourth Safari (2 weeks)
Aug. 25: begins solo, 2-week hunt on the plains; 27: camps on headwater of northern GUASO NYERO; 29: trophy eland. Sept. 3: rejoined by main safari; 4: treks back north to Mount Kenya foothills; arrives MERU BOMA; 5: marching along equator; 7: begins 2-week hunt in and around Boma; 11: elephant bull; 13: elephant cow; 15: N'gouga Crater Lake; 16: rhino; 17: buffalo hunt; 21: safari divides; TR heads for 3-week hunt in GUASO NYERO valley. Oct. 15: arrives back in NYERI; receives mail; 17: crossing Aberdares; 20: returns NAIVASHA; 21: NAIROBI for 4-day stay.

Sixth Safari (5 weeks)
Oct. 25: leaves NAIROBI for Londiani; 27: begins March to Mount Elgon highlands; 27: turns 51; 31: arrives UASIN GISHU plateau. Nov. 1: begins 4-week hunt for Victoria Nyanza fauna; giraffe camp; 9: moves to River 'Nzoi; 9: follows honey-bird; 12: love letter to EKR; 14: meets up with American Museum of Natural History expedition; 15: 3 elephant cows; 18: arrives Lake Sergoi; 20: witnesses Nandi lion hunt; 26: returning to Londiani; 30: arrives Londiani; pays off, dismisses East African safari personnel; to Njoro for 10 days in and around Delamere ranch. Dec. 11: returns NAIROBI to prepare for Uganda safari (1 week).

Seventh Safari (9 weeks)
Dec. 17: farewell dinner; 18: departs NAIROBI by train via Nakuru for Kisumu; 19: arrives Kisumu; overnight steamer voyage across Lake Victoria to Entebbe, Uganda; 20: arrives Entebbe; reception by governor; dedicates mission; 21: in KAMPALA, prepares new safari team for northward trek; 23: begins 13-day march through sleeping sickness country; 28: kills charging elephant.

1910
Jan. 2: crosses Kafu into Unyoro kingdom; 5: arrives Butiaba, on Lake Albert; 7: embarks down White Nile; 8: stops at Wadelai; 9: arrives "Rhino Camp," Lado Enclave; 10: begins 3-week hunt for white rhino. Feb. 1: hunts hippo; 3: sails on downriver; 4: arrives Nimule; 7: begins 10-day march past White Nile Rapids; 17: arrives GONDOKORO.

EIGHTH SAFARI (8 DAYS)

Feb. 18: upriver to Rajaf; 19: arrives Rajaf; begins to hunt eland, bongo; 23: 5 bull eland; 26: returns Rajaf, on to GONDOKORO. Mar. 1: down the Nile on *Dal* for next fortnight; 14: arrives KHARTOUM, pays off remaining safari personnel; returns to public life.

12 **his own Dutch surname**   See Biographical Note above, 582.

12 **After two years of drought**   *The Leader of British East Africa*, 29 May 1909; TR, *Works*, 5.27, 23.

12 **What he really wants**   TR, *Works*, 5.28, 45–46; Alexander Nemerov, "Vanishing Americans: Abbott Thayer, Theodore Roosevelt, and the Attractions of Camouflage," *American Art*, Summer 1997.

12 **Trippa, troppa**   TR, *Works*, 5.41 [sic]; Theodore Roosevelt, *An Autobiography* (New York, 1913; Library of America, 2004), 251–52. TR quoted entirely from phonetic memory, not sure if his Dutch was correct or not (it wasn't). A printed words-and-music version of this song in TRB begins, *Trippel trippel toontjes, / Kippen in de boontjes*. ("Wiggle, wiggle, little toes, / Snug inside their booties.")

13 **By "veldt law"**   Morris, *The Rise of TR*, 202–12; TR, *Works*, 5.29. TR's 1909 diary from this day on is filled with diagrammatic sketches that meticulously show the order and point of entry of all the bullets that brought down his specimens (TRC). See 20.

13 **He follows**   TR, *Works*, 5.70–71; TR in *The Leader of British East Africa*, 7 Aug. 1909.

13 **Right in front**   TR, *Works*, 5.72–73.

13 **He tries to notate**   Another of TR's phonetic transcriptions on safari was of the following rendition, by African missionary-school students, of the U.S. national anthem: *O se ka nyu si bai di mo nseli laiti / Wati so pulauli wi eli adi twayi laiti silasi gilemi*. TR, *Works*, 5.365.

13 **They cluster around**   TR, *Works*, 5.76–80; Kermit Roosevelt, *The Long Trail*, 68. For connoisseurs of hunting chants, TR's was as follows: *Whack! fal, lal, fal, lal, tal, ladeddy; / Whack! hurroo! for Lanigan's ball*. He probably learned the song as a child in 1863, when it was popularized by Bryant's Minstrels in New York.

13 **The firelight glows**   TR, *Works*, 5.80.

14 **Like a python**   The general procedure of TR's safari was to travel (camping frequently en route) for a month or more, before looping back to Kapiti or Nairobi to restock, ship specimens, and communicate with the outside world. Each foray focused on a particular group of museum-desired fauna.

14 **As leader**   TR, *Works*, 5.459–68. After TR's death, Charles William Beebe wrote that "he was one of the best field naturalists we have ever had in Africa." TR, *Works*, 4.xiii.

14 **But his main**   TR, *Letters*, 7.8–9, TR; *Works*, 5.62.

15 **He is aware**   One admittedly "wrought up" description of a tropical storm pleased TR so much that he begged his editor not to delete it. TR, *Letters*, 7.33–34.

Biographical Note: TR took with him to Africa two custom-made, watertight, antproof steel-frame writing boxes, covered with black bridle leather and sling-strapped for portage. The boxes contained 30 thick manuscript pads, enough for 1,500 pages of copy, with commensurate numbers of carbon sheets and two dozen indelible pencils.

By June 1, he had completed six "chapters" of about 7,000 to 8,000 words each, and had decided on a title for his book: *African Game Trails* (TR, *Letters*, 7.16). Robert Bridges, TR's editor at Scribners, was amazed at the steadiness, promptness, and copiousness of his dispatches. "I have always said that you are the best contributor we had" (Bridges to TR, 24 June 1909 [SCR]).

The Bridges/Roosevelt correspondence in SCR reveals TR's professionalism as an author. For example, on 17 July 1909, he sends instructions as to how his text may be split or shortened for serialization ("In the book, of course, I want the chapters to appear just as I have written them"), suggests chapter titles and illustrations, indicates the probable subject matter of future installments, and urges early publication in hardcover ("I am told that no less than eight books on hunting and travelling in British East Africa have been or are now being written. . . . The object of course is to forestall our book.") He requests a $20,000 contractual payment, suggests a negotiant (F. Warrington Dawson) for French serial and book rights, and repeatedly presses the value of his son's photographs. "I regard this book as a serious thing," he wrote in another letter. "I have put my very best into it and I cannot consent to have it appear in any but first class form." TR to Bridges, 26 Mar. 1910 (SCR).

15 **He is an honest writer**   See, e.g., TR, *Works,* 5.55: "Generally each head of game cost me a goodly number of bullets; but only twice did I wound animals which I failed to get. . . . Some of my successful shots at Grant's gazelle and kongoni were made at three hundred, three hundred and fifty, or four hundred yards, but at such distances my proportion of misses was very large indeed—and there were altogether too many even at short ranges."

Biographical Note: Asked if he considered himself a good shot, he joked, "No, but I shoot often." Lord Cranworth, Sir Frederick Jackson, and Bartle Bull have harshly criticized TR for this profligacy. Before losing the sight of his left eye, he had been a good marksman, managing once to put five bullets through the same target hole. But lack of target practice caused him to grow rusty as President—so much so that in 1908, he called in Admiral W. S. Sims, the navy's ranking gunnery expert, to prepare him for Africa. Sims set up "a little apparatus" on the upper floor of the White House, consisting of a clamped gun firing at a revolving needle at 60-foot range. "We put the President on the machine," he told a dinner audience long afterward, "and from the point of view of a rhinoceros, he did not shoot for sour apples." TR's half-blindness caused him problems in the early stages of his safari, but he shot better with practice, getting about half of his trophies at ranges of 200+ yards. After his death, the professional hunter Stewart Edward White pointed out that target shooting and game shooting are two very different skills. "So far from being a poor shot, [TR] was an exceedingly good game-shot, a much better game-shot than the majority of riflemen." Sims to Roosevelt Memorial Association, 1926, quoted in "The Story of the Roosevelt Medals," ts. (TRB); Wood, *Roosevelt As We Knew Him,* 223; Bull, *Safari,* 173, 180–81; TR, *Works,* 2.xxiii–xxiv.

15 **his indelible pencil**   A holograph chapter of *African Game Trails,* still in the original pad, is preserved in TRBU, and an almost complete copy of the original (topsheet) ms. is in TRC.

15 **One copy of each**   Bibliographical note by R. W. G. Vail enclosed in TRC ms. of *African Game Trails;* Lawrence F. Abbott, *Impressions of Theodore Roosevelt* (New York, 1919), 173–74; Wood, *Roosevelt As We Knew Him,* 364ff.; TR, *Letters,* 7.19–21. It took about a month for one of TR's envelopes to reach New York. By early July, Scribners already had six chapters in hand. "You can't imagine how pleased we are to have so much good material in so early," Robert Bridges wrote him (9 July 1909 [SCR]).

15 **As he falls** TR, *Works,* 5.90–91, 187–88, 132–34, 155–56, 163–67. TR's account of his hunt after buffalo, arguably the most dangerous game in Africa, is modest. "We walked toward them, rather expecting a charge; but when we were still over two hundred yards away they started back for the swamp, and we began firing." The African hunters with him admitted afterward to feelings of panic as the buffalo massed to charge them on the open plain. TR took command, shouting an order that kept them standing still until the buffalo swerved into the papyrus. "We lost our heads, but the Colonel kept his, and saved us all from certain death." F. Warrington Dawson, quoting his own diary, 31 May 1909, in "Opportunity and Theodore Roosevelt," prepublication ts., 35–36 (KRP).

16 **In a sudden** TR, *Works,* 5.205–6.

16 **But he is looking** Ibid., 5.280.

16 **Then, curling up** Ibid., 5.450; KR diary, 15 July 1909 (KRP). KR photographed this incident.

16 **zero at the bone** The phrase is Emily Dickinson's. TR sweated out this and other attacks of chronic fever with the aid of whiskey from Dr. Mearns's medicine chest— the only alcohol he was seen to take on safari. With quaint precision, he calculated his consumption at "just six ounces in eleven months." Wood, *Roosevelt As We Knew Him,* 333; TR, *Works,* 5.450. By May 1915, this had changed in his memory to "seven tablespoons of brandy." See 278.

16 **Although he assures himself** TR, *Letters,* 7.22. Dawson, "Opportunity and TR," 38, puts TR's total as of 20 May 1909 at "some 60 specimens of big game, including about 20 species." Nine days later, *The Leader of British East Africa* reported his big-game bag had risen to 86 specimens. TR and KR together shot, by mid-July 1909, 12 lion, 7 rhino, 6 giraffes, 6 topi, 5 buffalo, 4 eland, and 3 hippos, plus numerous other lesser species and an indeterminate quantity of game for food.

16 **The trouble with such luck** *The New York Times* commented on a report that TR had shot 18 antelope and 2 wildebeest on his first major hunt: "It really does seem to be a good deal of killing for a faunal naturalist." William J. Long wrote in the San Francisco *Examiner,* "The worst thing about the whole bloody business . . . is not the killing of a few hundred wild animals . . . but the brutalizing influence which [such] reports have upon thousands of American boys." Rice, "Trailing a Celebrity."

17 **scrawled trophy tally** For a sample such press release, see TR, 18 June 1909, quoted in Rice, "Trailing a Celebrity."

17 **their avid interest** In the case of local reporters, the interest was by no means friendly. Both *The Leader of British East Africa* (Nairobi) and the *East African Standard* (Nairobi) were enraged by TR's press ban. The former felt that it "bode[d] a lack of consideration . . . not far short of contempt" (24 Apr. 1909).

17 **The fact is** George Juergens, *News from the White House: The Presidential Press Relationship in the Progressive Era* (Chicago, 1981), 14–21 and *passim.* See also TR, *Letters,* 3.252–53, and Oswald Garrison Villard, *Fighting Years* (New York, 1939), 151.

17 **American editors** TR noticed an unusual number of "vacationing" journalists aboard the SS *Hamburg* when he crossed the Atlantic eastbound in April. TR, *Letters,* 6.1403. For WHT's unhappy relationship with the press, see Juergens, *News from the White* House, 91ff.

17 **Hence the presence** Dawson had met TR at Messina with a letter of recommendation from Henry White, the American ambassador in Paris. He had volunteered his services as TR's safari press secretary, only to be rebuffed: "You may come with me as far as the African coast, if you promise not to follow me afterward and not to ask for any interviews." But TR raised no objections when Dawson set him-

self up as a correspondent covering the safari out of Nairobi: "You see, you happen to be a gentleman." (Dawson, "Opportunity and TR," 11–26.) TR also developed a soft spot for W. Robert Foran of the New York *Sun,* to whom he extended similar privileges. (TR to Foran, 17 July 1909 [TRP].) Although Foran never became as intimate with the Colonel as Dawson, he followed him for much longer, even chartering a "ghost" safari at the end of 1909 to report on TR's final expedition down the White Nile. See Bull, *Safari,* 176.

17 **That hippo "bull"** TR, *Works,* 5.214–16; Dawson, "Opportunity and TR," 43. Another "joke" image that caused TR some irritation was that of *Bwana Tumbu* ("Boss with Big Belly"), his supposed nickname among the porters on safari. It appears to have been coined by reporters in the United States.

17 **The lake lies almost still** TR, *Works,* 5.216–17.

17 **Darkness falls** Ibid.; Dawson, "Opportunity and TR," 45–48. Dawson describes TR as "in a state of such depression as I have never witnessed in that hardy and optimistic nature . . . positively haggard." (Ibid., 48.) See also Dale B. Randall, *Joseph Conrad and Warrington Dawson: The Record of a Friendship* (Durham, N.C., 1968), 25.

18 **He need not worry** *The New York Times,* 22 July 1909; F. Warrington Dawson diary, 23 July 9, Dawson Papers, Duke University.

18 **The letters, dictated** Lodge, *Selections,* 2.330–35; John C. O'Laughlin to TR, 30 July 1909 (OL); Dawson, "Opportunity and TR," 37.

18 **"Remember that I never"** Henry Cabot Lodge, *Selections from the Correspondence of Theodore Roosevelt and Henry Cabot Lodge, 1884–1918* (New York, 1925), 2.344–45. In this same letter, TR writes in response to a forwarded article reviewing his presidency, "It almost frightened me to realize how completely the past was past as far as I was concerned."

18 **He admits** Dawson, "Opportunity and TR," 58, 63. According to TR, his safari received no periodicals except for occasional ancient issues of the *Owego Gazette* addressed to Dr. Loring.

18 **one startling remark** TR, *Letters,* 7.21 (italics added). See also Allan Nevins, *Henry White: Thirty Years of American Diplomacy* (New York, 1930), 297–99. Dawson may be excused for inattention if this was the day, cited by him afterward, when TR kept him "taking dictation . . . from 9 in the morning until 2:20 at night, our only pause being meals." (Randall, *Joseph Conrad and Warrington Dawson,* 25.) However, Dawson, in his memoir, exaggerates the extent of his secretarial services to TR. He does not appear to have seen the Colonel again before a family emergency called him home in the early fall of 1909.

18 **He is nearer death** TR, *Works,* 5.245. The packthread simile is TR's.

19 **There are no bullets** Lodge, *Selections,* 2.333; TR, *Works,* 5.414, 244–45. In 1919, Cuninghame was still marveling at TR's "complete coolness" in a situation of extreme danger (they were surrounded by a rampaging herd of cows and young bulls), not to mention his eccentric behavior afterward. "I never saw a man so boyishly jubilant, waving his hat and dancing about. . . . Half an hour later, when we were back in camp . . . he sat down in a chair and began to read Balzac." R. J. Cuninghame interview, *The New York Times,* 8 Jan. 1919.

19 **Hunters' etiquette** TR, *Works,* 5.246.

19 **Soon they were all splashed** Ibid., 5.247.

19 **Blood, nakedness** Perhaps the most powerful indictment of TR the hunter was penned in 1907 by Rev. William J. Long, whom TR had himself pilloried as a "nature faker" in love with sentimental theories of animal behavior. Replying to the President's attacks, Long wrote in an open letter, "Who is he to write, 'I don't believe that some of these nature-writers know the heart of wild things'? As to that,

I find after carefully reading two of his big books, that every time Mr. Roosevelt gets near the heart of a wild thing he invariably puts a bullet through it." Mark Sullivan, *Our Times* (New York, 1930), 3.155.

20 **"Life is hard and cruel"** TR, *Works,* 5.196. As with ugliness, so with beauty. Warrington Dawson noticed that TR admired even the most peaceful sunset as "action," a conflict of colors as night vanquished day. Big-game hunting had sharpened the Colonel's aesthetic awareness, given him "a faculty beyond ordinary faculties, a state of mind distinctly creative and in many ways similar to . . . the artistic." Dawson, "Opportunity and TR," 68.

20 **he has already read** TR to ERD, 24 June 1909 (ERDP); TR, *Works,* 14.465, 5.158. TR knew Khayyam's *Rubaiyat* in several versions, and complained that the Edward Fitzgerald edition was more realization than translation. He constantly quoted Lewis Carroll, remarking on safari, for example, that he felt "the way Alice did in Looking-Glass country, when the elephants 'did bother so.' " TR, *Works,* 5.295.

Biographical Note: At the end of his safari TR wrote an essay about his compulsion to read in the wilderness. He cited, from memory, a classical canon including the Bible and Apocrypha, Homer's *Iliad* and *Odyssey,* the works of Aeschylus, Sophocles, Aristotle, Theocritus, Euripides, Polybius, Arrian, and Dante's *Divine Comedy* (all in translation). In German, he read the *Nibelungenlied,* plus the poetry of Schiller, Koerner, and Heine. In French, he read the essays of Montaigne, Voltaire's *Siècle de Louis XIV,* Saint-Simon's *Mémoires,* Barbey d'Aurevilly's *Le chevalier des Touches,* the elder Dumas's *Les louves de Machecoul* and *Tartarin de Tarascon,* Flaubert's *Salammbô,* and Arthur de Gobineau's *Essai sur l'inégalité des races humaines.* It is unclear whether he read Manzoni's *I Promessi Sposi* in Italian, although as President, he did manage Michaelis's *L'Origine degli Indo-Europei.* (TR, *Letters,* 4.795.) He listed the poems of Keats, Shelley, Tennyson, Kipling, Browning, Longfellow, Emerson, Poe, and George Cabot Lodge. He did not detail his academic reading, apart from Alexander Sutherland's *The Origin and the Growth of the Moral Instinct,* "because as yet scientific books rarely have literary value." He confessed to an enjoyment of popular fiction, ranging from Harris's *Tales of Uncle Remus* to Owen Wister's *The Virginian* and Emily Eden's *The Semi-Attached Couple,* but also cited the Finnish historical novels of Zacharias Topelius, Tolstoy's *Anna Karenina,* and Gogol's *Taras Bulba,* reread "because I wished to get the Cossack view of what was described by Sienkiewicz from the Polish side." See TR, "The Pigskin Library," *Works,* 14.463–74. See also the much longer reading list, compiled for Nicholas Murray Butler in 1903. (TR, *Letters,* 3.641–44.) For an extensive survey of TR the reader, see chap. 2, "The World of Thought," in Edward Wagenknecht, *The Seven Worlds of Theodore Roosevelt* (New York, 1958, Guilford, Conn., 2008).

20 **His ear for sounds** TR, *Works,* 5.37, 387, 353, 96, 121. TR was amused to hear some Kenyan settlers referring to tree hyraxes as "Teddy bears." Ibid., 352.

21 **One sound falls** TR to ERD, 24 June 1919; TR to ABR, 21 Jan. 1910, privately held.

21 **He is proud** TR to Corinne Roosevelt Robinson, 21 June 1909 (TRC); TR, *Letters,* 7.30. See also TR's admiring portrait of KR on safari in TR, *Works,* 4.120–21.

21 **Possibly the image** See Putnam, *TR,* 157ff., or Morris, *The Rise of TR,* 75–77.

21 **He has grown used** TR's desire to escape public attention while on safari was periodically frustrated by social invitations, which he felt he had to accept, from

government authorities in Nairobi and from prominent settlers in the "White Highlands." On 3 Aug., for example, he was guest of honor at a banquet in Nairobi's Railway Institute, attended by the Protectorate's elite, in various stages of inebriation. He was presented with a rhinoceros foot, and sat through a flattering address printed on silk and read by the public recorder. An extract from his speech in response, "Education in Africa," is quoted on page 22. (*The Leader of British East Africa,* 7 Aug. 1909.) As a result of his stays on local ranches, he formed lasting friendships with such colonial notables as Governor Sir Percy Girouard, Lord Delamere, Lord Cranworth, Sir Alfred Pease, and Sir William Northrup McMillan—into whose family his granddaughter Grace would one day marry.

21 **He has to laugh**   TR, *Works,* 5.161–62.

21 **Snug in his tent**   Ibid., 5.262.

21 **He has to drive**   Ibid.

21 **It is plain to him**   Ibid., 5.37; *The Leader of British East Africa,* 7 Aug. 1909. The only blanket order J. Alden Loring could recall TR issuing on safari was a ban on the whipping of porters, although it was a punishment sanctioned by the British East Africa administration. Wood, *Roosevelt As We Knew Him,* 216.

22 **the Song of Solomon**   TR to Lawrence F. Abbott, 21 Oct. 1909 (ABB). TR, who had not read the Bible through before he went to Africa, boggled at some of its racier parts. "I must say that it contains matter that I should not care to have my children read until they had reached the years of discretion." To J. Alden Loring, quoted in Wood, *Roosevelt As We Knew Him,* 220.

22 **Oh, sweetest of all**   For more of the text of this letter, see Sylvia Morris, *Edith Kermit Roosevelt,* 351–52. It was one of the very few *billets-doux* from TR that EKR, after his death, did not destroy. Had their daughter Ethel not saved a handful, one of the great loves in American history would be undocumented.

22 **Moving on to Londiani**   KR diary, 30 Nov. 1909 (KRP); *The Leader of British East Africa,* 7 Aug. 1909; TR, *Letters,* 7.39–40.

23 **From now on**   TR, *Works,* 5.357.

23 **He is generous**   Lawrence F. Abbott wrote, after a few months of handling TR's finances, "He had less interest in money, as mere money, than almost any man that I have ever known." *Impressions of TR,* 210.

23 **totaling almost $40,000**   In contemporary (2010) dollars, this sacrifice amounted to $711,000 (Measuring Worth). As President, TR earned $50,000 ($888,000) a year. He felt that his prize money, totaling almost $37,000 ($696,000) in 1906, had been earned while he was a public servant, and therefore was not his personal property. He directed that it be used to endow a foundation dealing with what he then considered to be the largest problem of the age—labor/capital strife. See Morris, *Theodore Rex,* 473, 723. For the later history of this bequest, see 539.

23 **He is therefore relieved**   TR, *Letters,* 7.13–15, 24–25, 36–37. For an extended account of Carnegie's infatuation with TR as a potential "Great Peace Maker," see Joseph F. Wall, *Andrew Carnegie* (Pittsburgh, Pa., 1970, 1989), 924–35.

24 **"The very large edition"**   Robert Bridges to TR, 21 Oct. 1909, 10 Feb. 1910 (SCR). In this letter, Bridges tried to interest TR in a follow-up travel series focusing on the American Southwest. "We should of course be willing to pay a very large sum for it." When TR showed no enthusiasm, Bridges offered a staggering $5,000 per article. TR declined, but, as will be seen, eventually did write some Southwestern pieces for *Scribner's Magazine.*

24 **In Nairobi's little bookstore**   TR, *Letters,* 7.44; Randall, *Joseph Conrad and Warrington Dawson,* 28; TR, *Works,* 5.357, 14.463–64.

24 **It is elephant country**   TR, *Works,* 5.373–75, 423.

24 **He is in superb health**   The sentence in *African Game Trails,* "An elderly man with

a varied past which includes rheumatism does not vault lightly into the saddle, as his sons, for instance, can" is an example of TR's self-mocking humor. In a letter to Henry Cabot Lodge dated 5 Feb. 1910, he reports that while he and Kermit remained healthy, all the other members of his party "have been down with fever of dysentery; one gun bearer has died of fever, four porters of dysentery and two have been mauled by beasts." During their visit to one Ugandan village, "eight natives died of sleeping sickness." TR, *Letters*, 7.47.

24 **His stride is tireless**   E. M. Newman in Wood, *Roosevelt As We Knew Him*, 223; TR, *Works*, 5.417. According to Newman, TR's pace when marching "compelled the average man to maintain a dog trot to keep up with him."

24 **He looks better**   TR boasted on 21 Jan. 1910, "I have not for years passed nine months of such good health." (TR to Anna Roosevelt Cowles [ARC].) See also TR, *Works*, 5.298, 375–76; John C. O'Laughlin in the *Chicago Tribune*, 13 Mar. 1910.

25 **Yet on the seventh day**   TR, *Letters*, 7.348–49.

25 **a three-week halt**   TR states in a letter to Henry Cabot Lodge that he is encamped "about two degrees north of the equator." His actual position was nearer three degrees north, in the vicinity of the spot now known as Rhino Camp.

> *Biographical Note:* Bartle Bull notes that TR's bag of nine white rhinos, including four cows and a calf, exceeded his licensed quota by three. The species was then, as now, one of the most endangered in Africa. His excessive kill offended even the sensibilities of the time. "Do those nine white rhino ever cause ex-President Roosevelt a pang of conscience?" Lord Cranworth wrote in a 1912 memoir. " . . . I venture to hope so." (Bull, *Safari*, 179–80.) TR admits in *African Game Trails* that the white rhino was already virtually extinct in Africa outside of the Lado Enclave. It was, however, the only major game animal he had not yet collected for his sponsors. "We deemed it really important to get good groups for the National Museum in Washington and the American Museum in New York, and a head for National Collection of Heads and Horns [in] the Bronx Zoological Park." Kermit killed at least one charging cow in self-defense. "He was sorry . . . but I was not, for it was a very fine specimen, with the front horn thirty-one inches long." (TR, *Works*, 5.389, 399, 408.) The kills, plus five found skulls, enabled Edmund Heller to write a definitive Smithsonian study, "The White Rhinoceros." See TR, *Letters*, 7.46. For the role unwittingly played by Winston Churchill in this hunt, see below, 604–605.

25 **he feels that he has advanced**   TR, *Letters*, 7.348–49.

25 **A letter from Henry Cabot Lodge**   Lodge, *Selections*, 2.357. "The country is crazy-mad about Father," ERD wrote KR. Sylvia Morris, *Edith Kermit Roosevelt*, 352.

25 **"At present it does not"**   Lodge, *Selections*, 2.362. After reaching Gondokoro on 17 Feb., TR and KR took a final eight-day hunt for eland on the Belgian Congo side of the river. (TR, *Works*, 5.430–37.) At the end of the month he paid off his Uganda porters and sent them back to Kampala. On 28 Feb., he set sail from Gondokoro with KR and the naturalists aboard the *Dal*.

25 **Three members**   *Chicago Tribune*, 12 Mar. 1910. Another correspondent described the barge as "a crowded cemetery for animals, with the lid off." *St. Louis Post-Dispatch*, 12 Mar. 1910.

25 **They listen frustrated**   John C. O'Laughlin in the *Chicago Tribune*, 12 Mar. 1910. See also John C. O'Laughlin, *From the Jungle Through Europe with Roosevelt* (Boston, 1910), 28–36. In letters home to his wife, 15, 20 Mar. 1910 (OL),

O'Laughlin confidentially reported that "Mr. Roosevelt will run again in 1912." There is no other evidence to suggest that TR admitted such an ambition so early.

26 **the Nile birds he pursued** TR, *Works*, 5.448. Three of TR's youthful specimens, mounted by himself, are preserved in the American Museum of Natural History: an Egyptian spur-winged lapwing, a white-tailed lapwing, and a crocodile bird. For an account of his ornithological researches in Egypt and the Levant in 1872–1873, see Cutright, *TR*, 39–69.

26 **"whirls and wakes"** TR, *Works*, 5.448.

26 **All that remains** Ibid., 5.450–52; KR diary, 17 Feb. 1910 (KRP). The total bag of the Smithsonian–Theodore Roosevelt African Expedition, as it is now officially known, was 4,900 mammals, 4,000 birds, 500 fish, and 2,000 reptiles—approximately 11,400 items, plus 10,000 plant specimens and a small collection of ethnological objects.

26 **"Kermit and I"** TR, *Works*, 5.453. TR told John C. O'Laughlin at Gordon's Tree, four miles south of Khartoum, that he had just finished the last chapter of his book. *Chicago Tribune*, 15 Mar. 1910.

26 **"the twentieth century"** TR, *Letters*, 7.149. The *Dal* can be seen approaching civilization in "TR's Return from Africa," a newsreel in *Theodore Roosevelt on Film*, Library of Congress, http://memory.loc.gov/.

CHAPTER 1: LOSS OF IMPERIAL WILL

29 **Epigraph** Edwin Arlington Robinson, *Collected Poems* (New York, 1922), 359.

29 **He was informed** *Chicago Tribune* and AP dispatch, 14 Apr. 1910. The governor of Khartoum was away at the time of TR's visit.

29 **On its boards** Alan Moorehead, *The White Nile* (New York, 1971), 339–41.

29 **Rebuilt by Kitchener** *Encyclopaedia Britannica*, 11th ed. (1911), 15.773; ERD to Edwin Arlington Robinson, 21 Mar. 1910 (ERDP); TR, *Letters*, 7.349–51.

30 **the blood of General Gordon** TR to EKR, quoted in Earle Looker, *Colonel Roosevelt, Private Citizen* (New York, 1932), 106.

30 **Khartoum's North Station** AP report, *Chicago Tribune*, 15 Mar. 1910.

31 **That evening, Roosevelt** Ibid.; Walter Wellman, "The Homecoming of Roosevelt," in *American Review of Reviews*, 41.5 (10 May 1910).

31 **He was not unwilling** O'Laughlin, *From the Jungle Through Europe*, 41–42.

31 **However, another contender** Abbott, *Impressions of TR*, 214–16. TR's contract with *The Outlook* had been negotiated while he was still President. According to Abbott, he had "half a dozen editorial articles . . . ready for publication" within five days of quitting the White House. The first, an attack on socialism, ran in the magazine on 20 Mar. 1909. Another, on Tolstoy (15 May 1909), criticized the novelist for "foolish and fantastic" pacifism, not to mention "a dark streak . . . of moral perversion." (TR, *Works*, 14.417.) It was reprinted in Russia, and came to the attention of its subject. "An article on me by Roosevelt," Tolstoy noted on 20 May 1909. "The article is silly, but I was pleased. It aroused my vanity." (R. F. Christian, trans., *Tolstoy's Diaries* [London, 1985], 2.614.) For more of TR's views on Tolstoy, see Abbott, *Impressions of TR*, 188–91.

31 **Edith Kermit Roosevelt** See Sylvia Morris, *Edith Kermit Roosevelt*, 9–10.

31 **In the event** *Chicago Tribune*, 16 Mar. 1910.

32 **They dismounted** *Chicago Tribune*, 16 Mar. 1910; AP dispatch, 15 Mar., in ibid.; Morris, *The Rise of TR*, 685. Winston Churchill's classic account of the Battle of Omdurman in his *The River War: An Historical Account of the Reconquest of the Soudan*, 2 vols. (London, 1899).

32 **Slatin certainly** In a transcendent moment of tit for tat, years later, Slatin per-

mitted the Mahdi's skull to be handed over to Kitchener, who had to be persuaded not to use it as a drinking cup. Gordon Bank-Shepherd, *Between Two Flags: The Life of Baron Sir Rudolf von Slatin Pasha, GCVO, KCMG, CB* (New York, 1973); *Chicago Tribune*, 16 Mar. 1910.

32 **His soul revolted** TR, *Works*, 5.438; TR, *Letters*, 8.946. To TR's sardonic amusement, the Marquis de Mores, his youthful rival from Badlands days and a supporter of Arab independence, had been killed in 1896, while attempting to enlist in the Mahdi's service. A band of Tuaregs had not been "able to appreciate the fine frenzy of his altruism." Ibid.

32 **If that was what** The importation of large quantities of terrorist arms into Egypt, beginning in Dec. 1909, was publicized by S. Verdad in *The New Age*, 5 May 1910.

32 **Omdurman fascinated** *Chicago Tribune*, 17 Mar. 1910.

32 **One long, anguished letter** Pinchot to TR, 31 Dec. 1909 (TRP); TR, *Letters*, 7.45–46; TR to Anna Roosevelt Cowles, 21 Jan. 1910 (ARC).

33 **"We have fallen"** Pinchot to TR, 31 Dec. 1909 (TRP). See also William H. Harbaugh, *The Life and Times of Theodore Roosevelt* (rev. ed., New York, 1975), 361–62, 78. Having already successfully hosted national and North American conservation conferences in May 1908 and Feb. 1909, TR suggested on the eve of his departure from office "that all nations should be invited to join together in conference on the subject of world resources . . . their inventory, conservation and wise utilization." His idea was that the forty-five participant powers in the Hague Peace Conference should form the nucleus of a world conservation movement. In the event, he sent out invitations to fifty-eight nations, calling upon them to meet in the fall of 1909. Taft withdrew the invitations, and the world conference was aborted. Michael J. Lacey, "The Mysteries of Earth-Making Dissolve: A Study of Washington's Intellectual Community and the Origins of American Environmentalism in the Late Nineteenth Century" (Ph.D. diss., George Washington University, 1979), 401–3.

33 **illegal coal claims** Alaska's Chugach National Forest had been expanded by TR on his last day in office. According to Pinchot, J. P. Morgan and the Guggenheim mining syndicate were involved in these fraudulent claims. (Char Miller, *Gifford Pinchot and the Making of Modern Environmentalism* [Washington, D.C., 2001], 209.) But as Pinchot himself made clear in testimony to Congress, the "central item" in his quarrel with Taft and Ballinger was their "reversals of water power policy" nationwide.

33 **Taft, consequently, had had no choice** For WHT's own feeling, early in 1910, that "a complete break within the Republican party" was coming, see Butt, *Taft and Roosevelt*, 272. For detailed accounts of the rivalry between Ballinger and Pinchot, 1909–1910, see Harold T. Pinkett, *Gifford Pinchot: Private and Public Forester* (Urbana, Ill., 1970), 116–29, and Miller, *Gifford Pinchot*, 209–17.

33 **Taft had endorsed** George E. Mowry, *Theodore Roosevelt and the Progressive Movement* (New York, 1946, 1960), 52, 63–64. For a detailed account of the 1909 tariff battle in Congress, see Kenneth W. Hechler, *Insurgency: Personalities and Politics of the Taft Era* (New York, 1964), 92–145.

33 **"Honored Sir"** J. Corry Baker to TR, 6 Jan. 1910 (TRP).

33 **"I flatter myself"** Butt, *Taft and Roosevelt*, 179.

33 **"My political career"** Abbott, *Impressions of TR*, 53. "*Don't lay down*," one GOP politician begged TR. "The people will fall over one another in due time to follow your leadership." William Bradford Jones to TR, 7 Jan. 1910 (TRP).

34 **one delicate encounter** *The Washington Post*, 18 Mar. 1910. See also *The Times*, 18 Mar. 1910, and TR, *Letters*, 7.350–51.

34 **He had not hesitated** Morris, *Theodore Rex*, 323–38, 347–51, 440–42; Michael

B. Oren, *Power, Faith and Fantasy: America in the Middle East, 1776 to the Present* (New York, 2007), 309–16. Oren notes (316) that TR's affirmation at the 1906 Algericas Conference of three key principles—minority rights, free U.S. trade, and support for the Anglo-French alliance—"would remain cornerstones of American diplomacy in the region for the next fifty years."

34 **On the morning** KR diary, 18 Feb. 1910 (KRP); Abbott, *Impressions of TR,* 206–7. Frank Harper joined Abbott in Rome.

34 **an ever-expanding grand tour** See Wallace Irwin's Homeric parody, *The Teddysee* (New York, 1910). This poem appeared first as a serial in *The Saturday Evening Post.*

34 **Even the Calvinist Academy** TR, *Letters,* 7.364–65.

35 **I searched** Abbott, *Impressions of TR,* 185. The work cited is W. E. H. Lecky, *History of the Rise and Influence of the Spirit of Rationalism in Europe,* 2 vols. (New York, 1879). During this 22-hour journey, TR was also seen reading an account of Britain's campaign against the Sudanese caliphate, and working on the text of his address to the University of Berlin. According to O'Laughlin, he toyed with the idea of delivering it in German. *Chicago Tribune,* 19 Mar. 1910.

35 **Roosevelt was not new** TR to Henry Cabot Lodge, 24 Aug. 1884, in Lodge, *Selections,* 1.9. "It was Lecky's history of the Eighteenth Century that made me a Home Ruler," he wrote John Morley in 1908. (TR, *Letters,* 7.) Lecky was an Irish Protestant, M.P. for Trinity College, Dublin, and one of the most distinguished scholars of the Victorian age. He merits rereading as the last great practitioner in English of history as literature. His *Rationalism in Europe* is available at Positive Atheism (http://www.positiveatheism.org).

35 **two clerical provocations** TR, *Letters,* 7.57; Abbott, *Impressions of TR,* 213–14.

35 **"Moi-même, je suis libre-penseur"** TR to Jules Cambon, quoted in Geneviève Tabouis, *Jules Cambon par l'un des siens* (Paris, 1938), 105.

36 **He scoffed at theories** For an extensive discussion of TR's religious beliefs, see chap. 5, "The World of Spiritual Values" in Wagenknecht, *The Seven Worlds of TR.*

36 **As President, he** TR, *Letters,* 5.842–43. TR's two main objections to "In God We Trust," neither of which convinced Congress, were that "no legal warrant" justified engraving the pietism on American coins, and that doing so "cheapened" it by associating religion with commerce. For a detailed account, see Willard B. Gatewood, Jr., *Theodore Roosevelt and the Art of Controversy: Episodes of the White House Years* (Baton Rouge, La., 1970), 213–35.

36 **the gospel he preached** Owen Wister, *Roosevelt: The Story of a Friendship* (New York, 1930), 230; Marks, *Velvet on Iron,* chap. 3, "The Moral Quotient."

36 **Public works, for example** Garstin and TR "exhaustively" discussed irrigation and Aswán on the last leg of the journey to Wadi Halfa. (*Chicago Tribune,* 19 Mar. 1910.) TR's remark about the strategic value of Kitchener's railroad is quoted in the same article.

36 **There, on 21 March** O'Laughlin, *From the Jungle Through Europe,* 55–56. It is not clear how this warning was transmitted to TR. The Egyptian nationalists may have heard of a remark he had made about Boutros Pasha's assassin, at a dinner in Khartoum attended by hundreds of tarbooshed servants: "I would sentence him to be taken out and shot." Abbott, *Impressions of TR,* 155.

36 **"Theodore, what"** Cleveland Dodge in Wood, *Roosevelt As We Knew Him,* 223.

36 **One thing he had** TR, *Letters,* 7.359; *The New York Times,* 23 Mar. 1910. If TR had not quite "summoned" Pinchot, he had certainly written, in response to the latter's *cri de coeur* of 31 Jan. 1909, "I do wish I could see you. Is there any chance of you meeting me in Europe?" TR, *Letters,* 7.51.

37 **Roosevelt remained mute** TR, *Letters,* 7.63–64.

37 **Remembering the squalor** Ibid., 7.63, 351–52. See Karl K. Barbir, "Alfred Thayer Mahan, Theodore Roosevelt, the Middle East, and the Twentieth Century," *The Journal of Middle Eastern and North African Intellectual and Cultural Studies*, 2.1 (Spring 2004). This useful article is marred by the inclusion of an alleged boast by TR that is so uncharacteristic in language and attitude that it cannot be credited without corroboration.

37 **Roosevelt detected** Lodge, *Selections*, 2.364. "I must say," TR wrote Whitelaw Reid on 24 Mar., "I should greatly like to handle Egypt and India for a few months. At the end of that time I doubtless would be impeached by the House of Commons but I should have things moving in fine order first." TR, *Letters*, 7.63.

37 **But he saw** TR, *Letters*, 7.351. In *Power, Faith, and Fantasy*, 258ff., Michael B. Oren makes clear the ambivalent attitude of most Americans toward Britain's occupancy of Egypt in the last decades of the 19th century. TR's contrasting sharp certainty in 1910 is seen as the consequence of his might-makes-right Middle Eastern policies as President. His Cairo speech, however, should also be related to his lifelong horror of terrorism, reawakened by his stay in General Gordon's palace, and his tour of Omdurman in company with Slatin Pasha. See also TR's 31 May 1910 Guildhall address, 72–74.

37 **The real danger** TR, *Letters*, 7.351.

37 **Sir Eldon Gorst** Ibid., 7.353.

38 **Islamic fundamentalists** Sheik Ali Youssuf in *North American Review*, June 1910; Abbott, *Impressions of TR*, 186–87.

38 **Small and struggling** Cairo University's enrollment in 1910 was only 123 students, down disastrously from 403 in 1909. Egyptian State Information Service, winter 1998.

38 **He tried not** The word *contempt* was TR's own. TR, *Letters*, 7.65.

38 **Swinging into** Theodore Roosevelt, *African and European Addresses*, Lawrence F. Abbott, ed. (New York, 1910), 26.

38 **The tarboosh-wearers** Sheik Ali Youssuf in *North American Review*, June 1910; O'Laughlin, *From the Jungle Through Europe*, 69. Abbott, a white Christian American in TR's thrall, contradicts Youssuf's account of derision among the Muslims.

38 **All good men** Abbott, *Impressions of TR*, 156–57.

39 **Next day, comments** *The Times* and *The Washington Post*, 30 Mar. 1910. Oren, *Power, Faith, and Fantasy* (318) calls this "the first major anti-American demonstration ever in the Middle East." Among the many outraged telegrams protesting TR's speech was one reading (in French): "We see with sorrow that you have no accurate idea of the capacity of the Egyptians whom you have wounded in their feelings and their pride." (Unsigned fragment, 29 Mar. 1910 [TRP].) Also preserved in TRP is a letter, 30 Mar. 1910, from the sirdar of the Sudan, Sir Reginald Wingate: "You have assisted us more than you can possibly imagine, and I am proportionally grateful." For a presentist critique of TR's performance in Egypt, see Barbir, "Alfred Thayer Mahan, Theodore Roosevelt, the Middle East, and the Twentieth Century."

39 **When he embarked** Sheik Ali Youssuf in *North American Review*, June 1910. About a year later, TR recalled that his "good advice" to the Egyptians had been received "with well-dissembled gratitude." TR, *Works*, 6.455.

CHAPTER 2: THE MOST FAMOUS MAN IN THE WORLD

40 **Epigraph** Robinson, *Collected Poems*, 75.

40 **as if he were still** Wellman, "The Homecoming of Roosevelt."

40 **He saw less** TR, *Letters*, 7.354.

40 **Moving on**   Ibid., 7.354–59; John C. O'Laughlin memo, ca. Apr. 1910 (OL). In an open letter to *The Outlook,* TR made sure that Catholics and Protestants back home understood his scruples. "The more an American sees of other countries the more profound must be his feelings of gratitude that in his own land there is not merely complete toleration but the heartiest goodwill and sympathy between sincere and honest men of different faith." TR, *Letters,* 7.358.

41 **He rejoiced**   TR, *Letters,* 7.359–60; KR diary, 4 Apr. 1910 (KRP); *The New York Times,* 5 Apr. 1910. Citations for the rest of this chapter frequently refer to TR's two epistolary accounts of his European experiences, to Sir George Otto Trevelyan, 1 Oct. 1911, and to David Gray, 5 Oct. 1911. (TR, *Letters,* 7.348–99, 401–15.) Enormously long and often very funny, these letters have been separately published in *Cowboys and Kings: Three Great Letters by Theodore Roosevelt,* Elting E. Morison, ed. (Cambridge, Mass., 1954). More than any of TR's other writings, they convey the full charm of his personality.

41 **Roosevelt was unfazed**   TR, *Letters,* 7.362–63. Before leaving Rome on 7 Apr., TR lunched with the Italian historian Guglielmo Ferrero, whose works he had read, and learned from, as President. (Morris, *Theodore Rex,* 495–96; and Ferrero, "Theodore Roosevelt: A Characterization," *South Atlantic Quarterly,* 9 [1910].) TR was determined to make his trip through Europe an intellectual as well as a political odyssey. "Cannot you arrange," he typically wrote to the American ambassador in Sweden, "to have me see Sven Hedin, Nathorst, Colthorp, Nordenskiöld and Montelius? Cannot I see with the last-named the collection of Swedish antiquities, and I would also like to see the battle flags of Gustavus and Charles XII, and the tombs of the kings. Cannot I meet Professor and Mrs. Retzius?" TR to Charles H. Graves, 22 Apr. 1910 (TRP).

41 **Edith's unmarried younger sister**   See Sylvia Morris, *Edith Kermit Roosevelt,* 350–51 and *passim.* There is a vignette of Emily Carow in O'Laughlin, *From the Jungle Through Europe,* 98: "She reminded me of a little humming bird as she flitted from side to side . . . pointing out the beauties of the landscape."

41 **Lanky, passionate**   Miller, *Gifford Pinchot,* prologue *passim;* Sullivan, *Our Times,* 4.386.

41 **Roosevelt, in contrast**   Sullivan, *Our Times,* 4.486, describes Pinchot as one "whose eyes, as they pass through the world, instinctively look about for a hero, and for martyrdom in the hero's service." For a concise analysis of the relationship between Pinchot and TR, see Miller, *Gifford Pinchot,* 147–76.

41 **"One of the best"**   Ibid., 233. A long political letter from TR to Henry Cabot Lodge, written this day, avoids any mention of Pinchot. TR, *Letters,* 7.69–74.

41 **All warned**   Mowry, *TR,* 108, 125.

42 **He was more**   Lodge, *Selections,* 2.367; TR, *Letters,* 7.336. See also Morris, *Theodore Rex,* 486–87.

42 **Four days later**   EKR diary, 13 Apr. 1910 (TRC).

42 **A familiar, courtly figure**   TR, *Letters,* 7.368; Henry White to Mrs. White, 15 Apr. 1910 (HW).

43 **the great comet**   Halley's Comet was just beginning its 1910 passage past the sun. It was observed in perihelion at 5° Aquarius over Curaçao on 19 Apr.

43 **After a reunion**   Henry White to Mrs. White, 15 Apr. 1910 (HW); TR, *Letters,* 7.369.

43 **He spoke in French**   Ibid.

43 **Roosevelt had detected**   TR, *Letters,* 7.360–61. *Tempora mutantur:* "The times are changing."

43 **The best that could**   TR, *Letters,* 7.369, 409. TR was both right and wrong about Franz Ferdinand. The archduke was reactionary in the sense that he wanted to strengthen and centralize Austria-Hungary's power over its restive Balkan neigh-

bors. But he was liberal in believing that the only way to do this was to allow Slavs more representation in the imperial government.

43 **Meeting later**   TR, *Letters*, 7.366.

43 **At the same time**   Martin Gilbert, *A History of the Twentieth Century: Volume 1: 1900–1933* (Toronto, 1997), 188. Germany's former chancellor, Bernhard von Bülow, used the phrase "Nibelungen loyalty" to describe this compulsion. Michael Stürmer, *The German Empire, 1870–1918* (New York, 2000), xxviii.

44 **Roosevelt repeated**   TR, *Letters*, 7.377–78.

44 **For the next thirty-six**   O'Laughlin, *From the Jungle Through Europe*, 105; Henry White to Henry Cabot Lodge, 23 Apr. 1910 (HCLP). "They [Europeans] look on him as the greatest man in the world, and think it strange that with his youth and energy he should be in private life." (Wellman, "The Homecoming of Roosevelt.") For TR's half-puzzled, half-tickled reaction to his celebrity, see TR, *Letters*, 7.81.

44 **He did not see**   Carl E. Schorske, *Fin-de-Siècle Vienna: Politics and Culture* (New York, 1981), xxvi–xxvii, 344; Barbara Tuchman, *The Proud Tower: A Portrait of the World Before the War, 1890–1914* (New York, 1966), 329. The rising suicide rate by Austro-Hungarian youth had become such a problem, just as TR arrived in Vienna, that Sigmund Freud's Psychoanalytic Society called a meeting to discuss its subconscious causes. For an intellectual history describing the comet-haunted year of 1910 as "the year when all [Europe's] scaffolds began to crack," see Thomas Harrison, *1910: The Emancipation of Dissonance* (Berkeley, Calif., 1996).

44 **All he knew**   On the same day that TR was entertained at Schönbrunn, a member of Serbia's Black Hand terrorist group was arrested in Chiasso, Switzerland, on a charge of plotting to kill him. *The New York Times*, 17, 19 Mar. 1910.

44 **Halfway through the banquet**   TR, *Letters*, 7.370.

44 **Roosevelt was met**   TR, *Letters*, 7.372–73. Apponyi, surrounded by an official delegation, hailed TR as "one of the leading efficient forces for the moral improvement of the world." (O'Laughlin, *From the Jungle Through Europe*, 111.) For the imperial-versus-royal paradox in the union of Austria and Hungary, see Andrew Wheatcroft, *The Habsburgs: Embodying Empire* (New York, 1995), 278–81.

44 **He noticed**   TR, *Letters*, 7.372–73; KR diary (KRP); *The Times*, 19 Apr. 1910.

45 **Multicultural himself**   Nicholas Roosevelt, *Theodore Roosevelt: The Man As I Knew Him* (New York, 1967), 56; Wellman, "The Homecoming of Roosevelt"; TR, *Letters*, 7.374.

45 **an extempore address**   TR, *Letters*, 7.374. TR, speaking from memory, wrongly attached the name of King Béla III, rather than Andrew II, to the Golden Bull. A sarcastic British correspondent, filing from Vienna, was thus able to report on the "fervor and inaccuracy" of his speech, as well as Apponyi's "stage management" of the occasion. *The Times*, 20 Apr. 1910.

45 **His carriage had to force**   *The New York Times*, 19 Apr. 1910; O'Laughlin, *From the Jungle Through Europe*, 114–15.

45 **the most famous man in the world**   Wellman, "The Homecoming of Roosevelt." As late as the early years of World War I, a friend of TR's found that he could travel "all over Europe" with no other credential than a letter from the Colonel. Wood, *Roosevelt As We Knew Him*, 400.

45 **"When he appears"**   *The Times*, 16 Apr. 1910.

45 **"Like the elder"**   TR to Robert Bacon, TR, *Letters*, 7.65. For TR's previous relationship with Bacon, his Harvard classmate and former secretary of state, see James Brown Scott, *Robert Bacon: Life and Letters* (New York, 1923), *passim*, and Morris, *Theodore Rex*, 167–68, 456–57.

45 **Both ambassadors**   Scott, *Bacon*, 136–43. The last-named Frenchmen were fa-

vorites of TR's. He had been corresponding with them for years, and admired their mix of mind and action. Estournelles de Constant, author of *La conciliation internationale,* had just become a fellow winner of the Nobel Peace Prize. Coubertin, author of many books on education, was the founder of the modern Olympic Games.

46 **"Quand on parle"** TR quoted in *Journal des Débats Politiques et Littéraires,* 24 Apr. 1910. Jusserand compared TR's way of searching for the *mot juste* in French to that of someone grasping at "a slippery piece of soap" in the bath. Wister, *Roosevelt,* 166.

46 **Shortly before three** *Journal des Débats,* 24 Apr., and *The Times,* 25 Apr. 1910.

46 **he proceeded to read** The following quotations from TR's Sorbonne address are taken from the version in TR, *Works,* 15, 349–76.

47 **This touched on** "To them [the French] the German menace is like a constant nightmare, which may perhaps be explained by the fact that most of the older men know what an invasion means." British naval attaché report, 22 Jan. 1910, quoted in Kenneth Bourne, ed., *British Documents on Foreign Affairs: Reports and Papers from the Foreign Office Confidential Print,* pt. 1, ser. F, 13.100. (Hereafter Bourne, *British Documents.*)

47 **Roosevelt bit off** *The Times,* 25 Apr. 1910; *Le Gaulois,* quoted in *Literary Digest,* 21 May 1910.

47 **It is not the critic** TR, *Works,* 15.354. According to *The Times,* 25 Apr. 1910, TR won further ovations when he repeated one of his own paragraphs, a declaration that "property belongs to man and not man to property" in French. He resorted to antique French for a closing quote from Froissart: *Le royaume de la France ne fut onques se déconfit qu'on n'y trouvât bien toujours á qui combattre* ("The realm of France was never so stricken that there were not left men who would valiantly fight for it.") For a modern reprint of his speech, see John Allen Gable, ed., *The Man in the Arena: Speeches and Essays by Theodore Roosevelt* (Oyster Bay, N.Y., 1991). It is available on many Internet websites, and remains one of TR's most-quoted orations.

47 **one of his greatest rhetorical triumphs** *Journal des Débats,* 24 Apr. 1910; Jules Jusserand to TR, 10 May 1910 (TRP); TR, *Letters,* 7.379–80; *The New York Times,* 25 Apr. 1910. After TR's departure, an American military officer in Paris reported that the Briand government had suppressed a "monster" May Day demonstration by socialist and revolutionary groups. For the first time in fifteen years, policemen were allowed to use firearms in their own self-defense. This policy was "freely attributed in intelligent quarters" to TR's morale-boosting speech. Abbott, *Impressions of TR,* 166.

47 **Only two** *Literary Digest,* 18 June 1910; TR, *Works,* 15.645; Jules Jusserand to TR, 10 May 1910 (TRP); TR, *Letters,* 7.77. "Never since Napoleon dawned on Europe, has such an impression been produced there as has been made by Theodore Roosevelt," *Le Temps* commented.

48 **He wanted to** TR, *Letters,* 7.381. For an account of the Dreyfus case and its effect on French morale after 1906, see Tuchman, *The Proud Tower,* 171–226.

48 **For two and a quarter hours** *The Times* and *The New York Times,* 28 Apr. 1910. "The maneuver was necessarily too rapid," TR told the military governor of Paris afterward. "You have made your men do in half an hour what should in reality take four hours." *The Times,* 28 Apr. 1910.

48 **two aides** O'Laughlin continued to act as the semi-official chronicler of TR's travels, in charge of a press contingent that grew to six by the time his tour reached Paris. Harper to Arthur Beaupré, 25 Apr. 1910 (TRP).

48 **They traveled east** ERD to Edwin Arlington Robinson, 28 Apr. 1910; TR, *Letters,* 7.382–83.

48 **A sobering display** TR could see from the bridge of his own ship the German imperial yacht *Meteor,* and a small launch named *Alice Roosevelt* in honor of his daughter. ARL had launched the *Meteor* from a New Jersey shipyard in 1902. There was some speculation that TR had been snubbed at Kiel by the no-show of a local resident, Prince Heinrich of Prussia. But a letter of profound apology from the prince (Wilhelm II's brother), indicates that it was caused by a staff failure. *Chicago Tribune,* 3 May 1910; Sylvia Morris, *Edith Kermit Roosevelt,* 234–35; Heinrich ("Henry") to TR, May 1910 (TRP).

48 **signs of ominous enlargement** The work of widening the Kaiser Wilhelm (now Kiel) Canal was completed by 1914.

49 **King Frederick VIII** TR, *African and European Addresses,* 138. Crown Princess Alexandra of Denmark was the daughter of Edward VII.

49 **"as funny a kingdom"** TR, *Letters,* 7.385–86. For an account of TR's visit, and a discussion of the publicity his Nobel Prize brought to newly independent Norway, see Wayne Cole, *Norway and the United States, 1905–1955: Two Democracies in Peace and War* (Ames, Iowa, 1989).

49 **The pesky little millionaire** Wall, *Andrew Carnegie,* 931; TR, *Letters,* 7.47–49. For TR's initial efforts to make the appeal seem to come from Elihu Root, see TR, *Letters,* 7.42, 55. For the presidential involvement with arms control (at the time of the Second Hague Peace Conference) that TR refers to, see Frederick C. Leiner, "The Unknown Effort: Theodore Roosevelt's Battleship Plan and International Arms Limitation Talks, 1906–1907," *Military Affairs,* 48.3 (1984), and Morris, *Theodore Rex,* 485, 726. For an amusing, recently discovered letter in which TR dismisses Carnegie as "a perfect goose" in public affairs, see *Theodore Roosevelt Association Journal,* 30.3 (Summer 2009), 20–23.

49 **Christiana was** Wall, *Andrew Carnegie,* 934; Tuchman, *The Proud Tower,* 278.

49 **Roosevelt's oration** *Chicago Tribune,* 6 May 1910; TR, *Works,* 18.410.

50 **He gave conditional** TR, *Works,* 18.414.

50 **"international police power"** Ibid., 18.415.

50 **"There's a trace of the savage"** Wall, *Andrew Carnegie,* 935, 980. For the unexpectedly favorable reaction of an influential Norwegian commentator to TR's speech, see *American Review of Reviews,* 42.3 (Aug. 1910).

50 **Coughing and feverish** EKR to TR.Jr., 8 May 1910 (TRJP); *The New York Times,* 9 May 1910. "I don't like living in these palaces because you can't ring your bell and complain of your room!" TR quoted in Abbott, *Impressions of TR,* 296.

50 **He sent a telegram** TR, *Letters,* 7.390; New York *Tribune,* 8 May 1910.

51 **It had shone** Margot Asquith, *The Autobiography of Margot Asquith* (Boston, 1963), 269.

51 **The first thing** TR, *Letters,* 7.390; Wellman, "The Homecoming of Roosevelt."

51 **the foremost nation** Tuchman, *The Proud Tower,* 291; Edward Grey, *Twenty-five Years: 1892–1916* (New York, 1925), 2.22; TR, *Letters,* 7.391. Between 1900 and 1910, Germany's steel production increased 1,355 percent to Britain's 154 percent. For other statistics, see Giles MacDonogh, *The Last Kaiser: The Life of Wilhelm II* (New York, 2000), 321.

51 **Germany's fields and forests** For a vivid picture of pre-war Germany, see Owen Wister, *The Pentecost of Calamity* (New York, 1917), 18–23. See also Modris Eck-steins, *Rites of Spring: The Great War and the Birth of the Modern Age* (Boston, 1989), 77–82.

51 **There was a frenzied scurrying** O'Laughlin, *From the Jungle Through Europe,* 148; EKR diary, 10 May 1910 (TRP).

51 **Wilhelm II in 1910** TR, *Letters,* 7.393; John C. G. Röhl, ed., *Kaiser Wilhelm II: New Interpretations—The Corfu Papers* (Cambridge, UK, 1982), 3–10, 14–19; Ragnhild Fiebig von Hase, "The Uses of 'Friendship': The 'Personal Regime' of

Wilhelm II and Theodore Roosevelt, 1901–1909," in Annika Mombauer and Wilhelm Deist, eds., *The Kaiser: New Research on Wilhelm II's Role in Imperial Germany* (Cambridge, UK, 2004), 143–94.

51 **Two years earlier** MacDonogh, *The Last Kaiser*, chap. 12; John C. G. Röhl, *The Kaiser and His Court: Wilhelm II and the Government of Germany* (Cambridge, UK, 1996).

52 **a fantasist of Münchausian dimensions** Ecksteins, *Rites of Spring*, 87–88. TR had sensed the Kaiser's reincarnation fantasy as long before as 1902. "He writes to me pretending that he is a [direct] descendant of Frederick the Great! I know better and feel inclined to tell him so." See Morris, *Theodore Rex*, 185–86, and Michael Balfour, *The Kaiser and His Time* (New York, 1964, 1972), 85.

52 **Were it not** O'Laughlin, *From the Jungle Through Europe*, 148; *Manchester Guardian*, 20, 21 May 1910; James W. Gerard, *Face to Face with Kaiserism* (New York, 1918), 20.

53 **They stood face-to-face** Abbott, *Impressions of TR*, 252–53. Accounts vary as to how long this conversation lasted. TR remembered it as three hours, the New York *Tribune* reported "more than an hour," and Stanley Shaw, in his *William of Germany* (London, 1913), wrote that "the shades of evening began to fall before it ended." Abbott is precise in recalling that the party managed to catch its 4 P.M. train back to Berlin, but forgets that the Kaiser also escorted the Roosevelts on a tour of Sans Souci. Whatever the case, TR (who saw the Kaiser twice again) had plenty of time to take his measure, and write a perceptive portrait of him. TR, *Letters*, 7.394–99.

54 **Reporting afterward** TR, *Letters*, 7.395. For the epistolary relationship of TR and Trevelyan, see Burton, "Theodore Roosevelt and His English Correspondents."

54 **At least we agreed** TR, *Letters*, 7.396.

54 **Roosevelt asked** Ibid., 7.398. At a meeting of the Navy League in Berlin on 22 May 1910, Admiral Hans von Köster noted that every naval power was currently trying "to reach the highest possible degree of readiness for war." Bourne, *British Documents*, pt. 1, ser. F, 21.77–78.

54 **This sounded reasonable** TR, *Letters*, 7.399.

54 **By the time** EKR diary, 10 May 1910 (TRC); *Chicago Tribune*, 12 May 1910.

55 **He cabled** *Chicago Tribune*, 12 May 1910; Henry F. Pringle, *The Life and Times of William Howard Taft* (New York, 1939), 542.

55 **More vocal wear** KR diary, 11 May 1910 (KRP); *Chicago Tribune*, 12 May 1910; O'Laughlin, *From the Jungle Through Europe*, 150–51. TR's "suite" was also accredited with naval and military aides-de-camp. *Foreign Relations of the United States, 1910*, 528.

55 **"Roosevelt, *mein Freund*"** There are various versions of the Kaiser's words, overheard by many listeners. This version was repeated by Henry White to Lawrence Abbott on the evening after the ceremony. The phrase *mein Freund* struck White as unusually intimate for Wilhelm II, on such a military occasion. Nevins, *Henry White*, 302.

55 **Roosevelt knew this** Morris, *Theodore Rex*, 186; New York *Tribune*, 12 May 1910; O'Laughlin, *From the Jungle Through Europe*, 150.

55 **Lifting his hat** *Chicago Tribune*, 12 May 1910; Looker, *Colonel Roosevelt*, 122–23.

> *Biographical Note:* This paragraph represents the author's interpretation of a curious passage that Looker wrote after interviewing EKR many years later. Since Looker had known all the Roosevelts intimately from his days as a member of the "White House Gang," and since EKR endorsed his book with a per-

sonal letter (facsimile, 116), the passage deserves attention. In its entirety, it reads as follows: "In talks with his family he [TR] indicated that 'the Kaiser most evidently showed, in company with some lesser sovereigns, a sort of double-barreled perspective as he went through this show. He was sitting on his horse seeing two different divisions of things happening about himself. One included his own observations of my own impressions of the pageant, the Staff's impressions and his own as the various battle units passed by us all. The other was as if his mental ghost had spurred away from us, halted, faced about, and was now scrutinizing himself and all of us through foreign eyes in order to understand what the rest of the world would think. As if the rest of the world at this particular moment was the slightest bit interested or even amused! It was just the same dual thought that made it possible for him to look upon his own human acts in one way and upon such Imperial acts, as he selected from the point of view of his "divine right," in another. He was actually, as far as I could discover, one of the last of those curious creatures who sincerely believed himself to be a demi-god.' "

56 **When Edith saw**   Looker, *Colonel Roosevelt,* 129–30. In 1912, TR told a reporter, "I tried him with everything I knew, but the only subject on which I could strike fire was war. He knows military history and technique. He knows armies, and that is all. I couldn't get a spark from him on anything else." Oscar King Davis, *Released for Publication: Some Inside Political History of Theodore Roosevelt and His Times, 1898–1918* (Boston, 1925), 92.

56 **He recovered**   *Chicago Tribune,* 13 May 1910. The text of TR's Berlin University address is in TR, *Works,* 14.258–83.

56 **Wilhelm had never**   *Chicago Tribune,* 13 May 1910.

57 **"the great house of Hohenzollern"**   TR, *Works,* 14.259. TR was privately tickled to discover, in conversations with Wilhelm II, that "his own knowledge of Hohenzollern history was more detailed and accurate than that of the Emperor." Albert Shaw, "Reminiscences of Theodore Roosevelt," ts. in SHA.

57 **The case of the Jew**   TR, *Works,* 14.264.

57 **He listed the main**   "Practically all the theories of world-development and so forth which Mr. Roosevelt was expounding had been based on the works of the very men he was addressing." An eyewitness, quoted in *The New Age,* 26 May 1910.

57 ***genus Americanus egotisticus***   This phrase was applied to TR by the Kaiser's good friend Poultney Bigelow in *Seventy Summers* (London, 1925), 273–74.

58 **But it was a warm afternoon**   *Chicago Tribune,* 13 May 1910.

58 **newspapers gave it scant attention**   Admiral Köster stated on 22 May 1910 that representatives of the German Navy League had listened "with the greatest interest" to TR's speech. A few words in particular ("Woe to the nation . . . whose citizens have lost their courage for battle and their martial spirit") had "deeply implanted themselves in German hearts." Bourne, *British Documents,* pt. 1, ser. F, 21.78.

58 **substantive interviews**   O'Laughlin, *From the Jungle Through Europe,* 151–52.

58 **a set of photographs**   For facsimiles, see Stefan Lorant, *The Life and Times of Theodore Roosevelt* (Garden City, N.Y., 1959), 526–27. The original photographs are still on display at Sagamore Hill National Historic Site.

59 **"Oh, no"**   TR, *Letters,* 7.83; John J. Leary, *Talks with T.R.* (Boston 1920), 41.

CHAPTER 3: *HONORABILEM THEODORUM*

60 **Epigraph**   Robinson, *Collected Poems,* 3.

60 **Roosevelt emerged**   *The New York Times,* 17 May 1910.

60 **Reid had won**   TR, *Letters,* 7.401–2; Viscount Lee of Fareham, *A Good Innings* (privately printed, London, 1939), 1.415–16. The relationship of TR and Arthur Lee is fully detailed in this two-volume work. For an abridged version, see *"A Good Innings": The Private Papers of Viscount Lee of Fareham, P.C., G.C.B., G.C.S.I., G.B.E.,* Alan Clark, ed. (London, 1974). See also the section on Lee in Burton, "Theodore Roosevelt and His English Correspondents." For TR and Reid, see David R. Contosa and Jessica R. Hawthorne, "Rise to World Power: Selected Letters of Whitelaw Reid, 1895–1912," *Transactions of the American Philosophical Society,* 76.2 (1986).

61 **His Majesty turned**   TR, *Letters,* 7.402; *The New York Times* and New York *Tribune,* 17 May 1910.

61 **Edward VII's personal throat doctor**   *The New York Times,* 17 May 1910. One of Edward's last acts had been to summon Ambassador Reid to Buckingham Palace, and, between spasms of coughing, plan the details of Roosevelt's visit. Royal Cortissoz, *The Life of Whitelaw Reid* (New York, 1921), 2.411–12.

61 **he was hard-pressed**   TR also found time to view, with EKR, Edward VII's coffin lying in state at Buckingham Palace. The next day it was transferred to Westminster Hall.

61 **"Confound these kings"**   Abbott, *Impressions of TR,* 294. Abbott left the king's name blank, but he was identified in the press as Haakon of Norway.

61 **She floated into**   KR diary, 16 May 1910 (KRP); Alice Roosevelt Longworth, *Crowded Hours* (New York, 1933), 177. ARL's butterfly brilliance is communicated in Michael Teague, *Mrs. L: Conversations with Alice Roosevelt Longworth* (London, 1981). The standard biography is Stacy Cordery, *Alice: Alice Roosevelt Longworth, From White House Princess to Washington Power Broker* (New York, 2007).

62 **"a voodoo"**   Teague, *Mrs. L.,* 140.

63 **"one of the finest fellows"**   Henry White to Mrs. White, 18 May 1910 (HW); TR, *Letters,* 7.402.

63 **Emerging one morning**   *The New York Times,* 20 May 1910; Henry White to EKR, 27 Nov. 1922 (correcting the account in Robinson, *My Brother TR,* 261–62). TRC.

63 **inside information**   Wilhelm II to Theobald von Bethmann-Hollweg, misdated "5 May 1910," in Edgar T. Dugdale, ed., *German Diplomatic Documents 1871–1914* (London, 1930), 3.414.

63 **It did not seem to cross his mind**   Nor, apparently, did the Kaiser notice that Roosevelt, criticizing two out-of-power Tories, had said nothing about his interview with Grey, the key figure in British foreign relations.

63 **"I'm going to a Wake"**   Alice Hooper reporting to Frederick Jackson Turner in *Dear Lady: The Letters of Frederick Jackson Turner and Alice Forbes Perkins Hooper, 1910–1932* (San Marino, Calif., 1970), 303. The very proper Mrs. Hooper remained "quite honestly shocked" nine years later.

63 **"I hardly know"**   Unless otherwise identified, the following quotations by TR are taken from his narrative letter to David Gray ("For nobody's eyes but yours") in TR, *Letters,* 7.409–12. See also below, 625.

63 **In contrast to**   *The New York Times,* 20 May 1910; Abbott, *Impressions of TR,* 296–97. According to Alice Hooper, Reid remained afraid until the final hour that TR would insist on wearing the uniform of an American colonel of cavalry. See above, 584, and Turner, *Dear Lady,* 303.

63 **denying Achduke Franz**   TR got this story direct from the Kaiser. Abbott, *Impressions of TR,* 298–99.

65 **Monarch vied with monarch**   TR's stories were apparently well circulated in the

royal courts of Europe. Wilhelm II's favorite was the one of Ben Daniels, marshal of Dodge City, who got his ear "bit off" in the pursuit of frontier justice. Sullivan, *Our Times*, 4.435; TR, *Letters*, 7.367.

65 **three more kings** Nevins, *Henry White*, 304.

65 **They knew** TR, *Letters*, 7.366–67.

65 **"glass coaches"** Unless otherwise identified, the following quotations are taken from TR, *Letters*, 7.412–13.

66 **Band music blared** The following account of Edward VII's funeral is based on the reporting of *The Times*, *Pall Mall Gazette*, and *Manchester Guardian*, supplemented by *The New York Times* and New York *Tribune*, 20, 21 May 1910. Indented quotations by TR continue to derive from his letter to David Gray, cited above.

66 **the strange reticence** For TR's similar behavior in Buffalo after the death of President McKinley, see Morris, *Theodore Rex*, 11.

66 **Pichon's feelings overcame him** TR told Mark Sullivan afterward that at the climax of Pichon's rage, his hair "stood out like a head of lettuce." Sullivan, *Our Times*, 4.436.

67 **"One remembers"** *The New York Times*, 21 May 1910. Pichon complained afterward that TR "did not exchange half a dozen words within him during the journey." *The New Age*, 2 June 1910.

67 **"destined to make history"** New York *Tribune*, 21 May 1910.

67 **The Tsar whom everybody** Later Nicholas II regretted not attending, and in the spring of 1911 pressingly invited TR to visit Russia. But by then TR had had his fill of star-encrusted monarchs. TR, *Letters*, 7.302.

68 **The midday heat** *Manchester Guardian*, 21 May 1910.

68 **Roosevelt suffered** *The New York Times*, 20 May 1910.

68 **The cloister of St. George's** Asquith, *Autobiography*, 271; *Chicago Tribune* and *Manchester Guardian*, 21 May 1910.

68 **Not until** *Chicago Tribune* and *The New York Times*, 20 May 1910; TR, *Letters*, 7.413.

69 **"Dear old Springy"** For the relationship of TR and Spring Rice, see Morris, *The Rise of TR*, 357–59; Stephen Gwynn, ed., *The Letters and Friendships of Cecil Spring Rice: A Record* (Boston, 1929), *passim;* and Burton, "Theodore Roosevelt and His English Correspondents." On 24 May, TR and EKR visited the scene of their wedding, St. George's Church in Hanover Square, incognito. They asked to see the register for 1886. The verger, indicating a marked page, informed them that it bore the signature of "Mr. Roosevelt, the former President of the United States, who was married here 23 years ago." He remained unaware of the identity of his visitors until after they left. *The New York Times*, 25 May 1910.

69 **Winston Churchill, whom he considered** Lodge, *Selections*, 2.385.

> *Biographical Note:* While in British East Africa, TR had drawn a sharp distinction between Churchill and an American novelist of the same name—"Winston Churchill the gentleman." (Lodge, *Selections*, 2.349.) His strange dislike for the Englishman is easier to document than explain. Before listing some instances, their many similarities should be considered. They were both politicians of privileged background who swung leftward in mid-career, soldiers of heroic courage, men of letters celebrating the life of action. Hyperactive, garrulous, egotistical, and family-minded, they worshiped their respective early dying fathers and needed enemies to function at maximum efficiency. Power did not corrupt them.
> Their first recorded meeting took place in Dec. 1900. Churchill, just elected to Parliament at age 26, was then on a speaking tour of America, and TR, at 41,

was governor of New York and vice president–elect. He had read the younger man's memoirs of military service in India and the Sudan, and regretted that he could not attend his Manhattan lecture. "I am really sorry as I am a great admirer of Mr. Churchill's books, and should very much like to have a chance to meet him socially." (TR, *Letters,* 2.1454.) The chance materialized later in the month, when Churchill dined with the Roosevelts in Albany and "incensed his hosts by slumping in his chair, puffing on a cigar, and refusing to get up when women came into the room." (Sylvia Morris, *Edith Kermit Roosevelt,* 539; for another abrasive encounter, see Robinson, *My Brother TR,* 189.) TR thought Churchill was interesting, but "not an attractive fellow." (TR, *Letters,* 3.116–17.) His disapproval deepened in 1904, when Churchill, in what looked to TR like opportunism, bolted Britain's foundering Conservative Party and joined the new Liberal government. In 1906, TR read Churchill's biography of Lord Randolph Churchill, found it "vulgar," and concluded that the author had inherited "levity, lack of sobriety, lack of permanent principle, and inordinate thirst for that cheap form of admiration which is given to notoriety." (Lodge, *Selections,* 2.231–32.) Exactly the same accusations would one day be leveled against TR himself. In 1908, when TR was planning his safari, he read a first-serial account by Churchill of killing a white rhinoceros in the Lado Enclave, and was overcome by competitive bloodlust. "I should consider my entire African trip a success if I could get to that country and find the game as Mr. Churchill describes it. . . . The white rhino is the animal I care most to get— even more than the elephant." (TR, *Letters,* 6.1383.) Churchill subsequently sent him a presentation copy of *My African Journey,* which TR acknowledged with ill grace: "I do not like Winston Churchill but I suppose ought to write him." (TR, *Letters,* 6.1465, 1467.) As recorded above (592), he went on to kill nine white rhinos to Churchill's one.

Churchill's booziness and lack of consideration for other people were bound to irritate TR, who set great store by probity and good manners. Subconsciously, however, he may have been more disturbed by the many parallels between them. In 1898, for example, both men almost simultaneously participated in historic cavalry charges. Of the two engagements, that at Omdurman was much more bloody, and of their respective published accounts, Churchill's was incomparably superior. It might be added that Churchill was capable of empathy with, even admiration for, his enemies, whereas TR always demonized them.

70 **The foreign secretary approved** Grey, *Twenty-five Years,* 2.92. EKR and ARL worried about TR overplaying his role as an outsider. "Don't try and talk through your nose and say '*Amurika,*' " they begged—in vain. Teague, *Mrs. L,* 137.

70 **By then, Roosevelt** Lee, *A Good Innings,* 1.416; TR quoted in Joseph Bucklin Bishop, *Theodore Roosevelt and His Time: Shown in His Own Letters* (New York, 1920), 2.260. Seth Bullock, asked why TR had no patience for kings, said he thought the Colonel "preferred aces." Kenneth C. Kellar, *Seth Bullock: Frontier Marshal* (Aberdeen, S.D., 1972), 165.

70 **On 26 May** *The New York Times,* 27 May 1910; Lorant, *Life and Times of TR,* 532–33; TR, *Letters,* 7.407. For TR's improvised speech at the Cambridge Union, see TR, *African and European Addresses,* 143ff. It was a humorous response to a poem about his penchant for preaching, published in *The Gownsman* in advance of his arrival: *Oh! We're ready for you, Teddy, our sins are all reviewed, / We've put away our novels and our statues in the nude. / We've read your precious homilies, and hope to hear some more / At the coming visitation of the moral Theodore.*

70 **Coincidentally, he** EKR diary, 28 May 1910 (TRC); Lee, *A Good Innings,*

1.423–24; TR, *Letters*, 7.405. See also [Harold Begbie], *The Mirrors of Downing Street: Some Political Reflections by a Gentleman with a Duster* (New York, 1921), 77–80.

70 **"All I would do"** TR, *Letters*, 7.405. See *King Henry IV, Part I*, act 3, scene 1.

70 **The most distinguished of them** [Begbie], *Mirrors of Downing Street*, 61–69; Kenneth Young, *Arthur J. Balfour: The Happy Life of the Politician, Prime Minister, Statesman, and Philosopher, 1848–1930* (London, 1962).

71 **"predestined to succumb"** Dugdale, *German Diplomatic Documents*, 2.54. In a letter written shortly before Balfour's speech, Cecil Spring Rice cited Denmark, Holland, Belgium, and Italy as being especially nervous, along with Austria. "These small states . . . are useful indicators, like the birds which stir and fuss when the tiger is on the move." Gwynn, *Cecil Spring Rice*, 2.145.

71 **Was the Tory** Shortly before leaving Germany, TR had told the German Chancellor that "The mood of the British was such that an unforeseen event might lead to war. He criticized very sharply in this connection Mr. Balfour's famous election speech." Bethmann-Hollweg memo, 14 May 1910, quoted in Dugdale, *German Diplomatic Documents*, 3.413.

71 **"So it is"** TR, *Letters*, 6.962–63.

71 **"It would be a fitting"** Young, *Balfour*, 283.

71 **For some reason** Although the Balfour memorandum was marked "Not sent to Roosevelt," Young surmises that the proposal itself did reach TR. There is, however, no copy in TRP, and no sign of a reply from TR in either TRP or AJB. The copy seen by Young is cited only as being in a set of "Royal papers," which supports the supposition that it was intended for Edward VII's eyes. Its wording and topical references further suggest that it was prepared later in 1909 than Young assumes—possibly even in early 1910. Balfour may have intended discussing his plan orally with TR, when they met at Chequers. Unfortunately neither man, nor Arthur Lee (who was responsible for sending Balfour's book to TR in 1908), left a record of what they actually did discuss that weekend.

71 **Arthur Lee was delighted** Lee, *A Good Innings*, 1.422; Gwynn, *Cecil Spring Rice*, 2.115; TR, *Letters*, 6.1241, 7.403. The ambassador's other nightmares included Slavs advancing west and Huns advancing north. See Burton, "Theodore Roosevelt and His English Correspondents."

72 **"I never heard a man"** J. S. Sandars to "E," 29 May 1910 (AJB).

72 **felt it his duty** TR, *Letters*, 7.402–3.

72 **He said he had just** All quotations from TR's Guildhall speech are taken from TR, *African and European Addresses*, 157ff. Extra details, including audience reaction, are from *Manchester Guardian*, 1 June 1910.

72 **"This will cause"** Lee, *A Good Innings*, 1.425. At one point in TR's address, Balfour emitted "an audible 'Haw haw!' "—presumably his Etonian way of enunciating "Hear, hear!" Otherwise, he and Grey presented stiff faces during the speech—Grey so much so that an American reporter was convinced that he disapproved. The foreign minister, however, later wrote: "I listened to it with a glow of satisfaction." *The New York Times*, 1, 4 June 1910; Grey, *Twenty-five Years*, 2.91.

73 **"I just *love* that man"** Lee, *A Good Innings*, 1.425. See also Whitelaw Reid to Philander Knox, 31 May 1910 (WR): "Arthur Balfour and Lord Cromer made no secret of their delight. . . . Edward Grey was equally pleased (although under more necessity to conceal it)." TR was even franker to a group of Irish nationalist M.P.s, who met with him the following day and were disappointed to hear that he by no means favored Home Rule. "I think they were too lenient with you," he genially informed Arthur Alfred Lynch, who had deserted the British army in South Africa but been forgiven by the British government. "If I had been in their place I would certainly have had you hanged." Lee, *A Good Innings*, 1.426.

73 **"Well, the attitude"** TR to ABR, 3 June 1910 (ABRP).

73 **Liberal newspapers** *The New York Times,* 1, 3, 4 June 1910; *Manchester Guardian,* 1 June 1910. See also *Literary Digest,* 11 June 1910.

73 **Conservative reactions** TR, *African and European Addresses,* vii; *The Times,* 1 June 1910; Abbott, *Impressions of TR,* 160. For John St. Loe Strachey's White House visit in 1902, see Morris, *Theodore Rex,* 181, 188.

73 **George Bernard Shaw** Shaw quoted in *Chicago Tribune,* 3 June 1910; Stead in *Manchester Guardian,* 2 June 1910. TR reciprocally considered Shaw to be "a blue-rumped ape." Wagenknecht, *Seven Worlds,* 137.

74 **"I was an auditor"** TR, *Letters,* 7.403.

74 **"I should have thought"** Ibid., 7.404.

74 **lunching with a grateful King** For an account of this *haut-bourgeois* luncheon, see ibid., 7.414–15. TR also dined with Robert Scott on the eve of the latter's last voyage to the Antarctic.

74 **"He has enjoyed himself"** Gwynn, *Cecil Spring Rice,* 2.151.

74 **STATEMENT INCORRECT** TR, *Letters,* 7.87.

74 **One last public appearance** The following account of TR's honorary degree ceremony at Oxford is based on reports in *The New York Times,* 8 June, and *The Times,* 9 June 1910. See also TR, *Letters,* 7.406–7 and Sullivan, *Our Times,* 4.431. Quotations from the proceedings are taken from TR, *African and European Addresses,* 175–249.

74 **For once, Roosevelt was** Among the scholars whom TR consulted in preparing his lecture were Henry Fairfield Osborn, president of the American Museum of Natural History, and James Bryce, the former regius professor of modern law at Oxford, and current British ambassador to the United States. After a blue-pencil review of the draft manuscript, which contained specific comparisons of two moribund European monarchies to the *megatherium* and *glyptodon,* Osborn wrote: "I have left out certain passages that are likely to bring on war between the United States and the governments referred to." (Pringle, *TR,* 519.) For the long and eventually strained relationship of TR and Bryce, see Burton, "Theodore Roosevelt and His English Correspondents."

75 *Behold, Vice-Chancellor* This translation seems to have been written by Curzon himself.

75 **More than ever** TR, *Works,* 14.66. For the complete text of TR's Romanes Lecture, see ibid., 65–106.

77 **Roosevelt was using** According to Douglas Harper's *Online Etymology Dictionary,* the word *ethnic* acquired racial overtones only in American English, ca. 1945.

77 **"It would appear"** Nicholas Murray Butler, *Across the Busy Years: Recollections and Reflections* (New York, 1939), 1.321. The "longitude" of TR's text, running to almost 12,000 words, was apparent even to the speaker. According to one report, his voice began to fail, and he dropped whole chunks of text toward the end. Even so, TR spoke for an hour and a quarter. *The New York Times,* 8 June 1910.

77 **attended by the heads** Prime Minister Herbert Asquith; Chief Justice Lord Alverstone; Randall Davidson, Archbishop of Canterbury.

77 **"at the time of the singing"** Grey, *Twenty-five Years,* 2.90.

78 **the two men took a preliminary hike** This account of TR's expedition with Grey is based on his own narrative in TR, *Works,* 22.364–69, and a detailed map of the expedition route in *The New Forest Commemorative Walk* (Nature Conservancy of Britain, 1979). See also Paul Russell Cutright, "TR Listens to the Music of British Birds," *Theodore Roosevelt Association Journal,* Spring 1987. In the summer of 2006, the author retraced TR's steps with a British ornithologist, Mr.

Richard Pennington, who identified twenty-eight of the species seen and heard in 1910.

78 **Roosevelt listened and watched** TR, *Works*, 22.365–67.

78 **the unstoppable mockingbird** See TR's rapturous description in *Works*, 2.61–62. Grey wrote years later that he "had one of the most perfectly trained ears for bird songs that I have ever known." Cutright, "TR Listens to the Music."

78 **"the woods and fields"** TR, *Works*, 22.369. The Forest Park Hotel, where TR and Grey stayed, still operates in Brockenhurst, Hampshire.

78 **"Take care of him"** Kipling to Brander Matthews, 10 June 1910, quoted in Bishop, *TR*, 2.259.

78 **Similar imagery** *The New York Times*, 9 June 1910; *The New Age*, 16 May 1910; *Literary Digest*, 18 June 1910.

79 **eight thousand letters** *Chicago Tribune*, 10 June 1910. Most of these letters were mailed after TR's Guildhall speech.

79 **a spokesman for** *The New York Times*, 5 June 1910.

79 **"I have had"** WHT to TR, 26 May 1910 (WHTP). TR replied evasively to WHT, in a letter unlikely to reach America before he did. "As to your more than kind invitation that I should visit the White House, I shall ask you about this to let me defer my answer until I reach Oyster Bay, and to find out what work is in store for me." TR, *Letters*, 7.88–89.

79 **passengers saw little of him** The phrase, and all other details in this paragraph, come from *The New York Times*, 19 June 1910.

80 **But she knew him well enough** In Mar. 1898, TR had been ready to go to war in Cuba, even as EKR lay at the point of death with an abdominal abscess. "I shall chafe my heart out if I am kept [*sic*] here instead of being at the front," he wrote. Sylvia Morris, *Edith Kermit Roosevelt*, 170–71.

80 **"I love Father"** ERD to Edith Gregori, 8 Aug. 1910 (ERDP).

80 **He agreed to speak** William Bayard Hale, "The Colonel and John Bull," *World's Work*, Aug. 1910.

81 **Later in the day** Ibid.

CHAPTER 4: A NATIVE OYSTER

82 **Epigraph** Robinson, *Collected Poems*, 359.

82 **Joseph Youngwitz** Youngwitz identified himself and described his purchase to a reporter during the course of the day. (*The New York Times*, 18 June 1910.) His name appears in the U.S. Census for 1910.

82 **Straw boaters undulated** Some of the boaters, sold by street vendors, were banded with the word "DEE-LIGHTED." New York *World*, 19 June 1910; Eleanor Butler Roosevelt, *Day Before Yesterday: The Reminiscences of Mrs. Theodore Roosevelt, Jr.* (Garden City, N.Y., 1959), 49.

82 **At 7:30 A.M.** The following description of TR's return to New York is based on accounts in *The New York Times*, New York *World*, and *New York Evening Post*, 18, 19 June 1910; "TR's Return to New York," newsreel in *Theodore Roosevelt on Film*, Library of Congress; and photographs in Lorant, *Life and Times of TR*, 538–39. The *World* estimated the total crowd at one and a half million. By all accounts, it was the greatest individual welcome ever accorded by New York City, until the parade for Charles Lindbergh in 1927.

83 **"He was smiling"** EKR quoted in Looker, *Colonel Roosevelt*, 143.

83 **"Will you kindly"** Butt, *Taft and Roosevelt*, 396.

83 **"Think—for the first"** Ibid., 399.

83 **Roosevelt embraced his sisters** Anna "Bamie" Roosevelt Cowles (1855–1931); Corinne Roosevelt Robinson (1861–1933).

83 **Ted presented**   Sylvia Morris, *Edith Kermit Roosevelt,* 339–40; Eleanor B. Roosevelt, *Day Before Yesterday,* 13–14.

84 **Franklin Delano Roosevelt**   "Franklin ought to go into politics," TR wrote, after FDR's campaign as a Democrat for the New York State Senate was announced. ". . . He is a fine fellow." (To Anna Roosevelt Cowles, 10 Aug. 1910 [ARC].) For the intertwined history of the Oyster Bay (Republican) and Hyde Park (Democratic) branches of the Roosevelt family, see Stephen Hess, *America's Political Dynasties* (New York, 1966, 1996), 167ff.

85 **"my original discoverer!"**   *The New York Times,* 19 June 1910. See Morris, *The Rise of TR,* 131–33.

85 **latest issue of *The Outlook***   TR, "Our Colonial Policy," *The Outlook,* June 1910.

85 **He had to turn**   New York *World,* 19 June 1910.

85 **"I am ready"**   *The New York Times,* 19 June 1910.

86 **[We] figured it**   Butt, *Taft and Roosevelt,* 396.

86 **Just above Franklin**   *The New York Times,* 19 June 1910.

86 **"about five years ago"**   Ibid.

87 **That evening**   The wording of this paragraph closely follows that of TR's own account in TR, *Works,* 22.369.

87 **He and his first wife**   For TR's marriage (1880–1884) to Alice Hathaway Lee, see Putnam, *TR;* Morris, *The Rise of TR;* and Michael Teague, "Theodore Roosevelt and Alice Hathaway Lee: A New Perspective," *Harvard Library Bulletin,* 32.3 (Summer 1985).

87 **Being a young widower**   For a short account of TR's tenure as squire of Sagamore Hill, 1880–1919, see Natalie Naylor, "Understanding the Place: Theodore Roosevelt's Hometown of Oyster Bay and His Sagamore Hill Home," *Theodore Roosevelt Association Journal,* 30.1–2 (Winter–Spring 2009). The most extended study is Hermann Hagedorn, *The Roosevelt Family of Sagamore Hill* (New York, 1954).

87 **"One thing"**   *The New York Times,* 19 June 1910.

87 **a vow of political silence**   TR's vow was transmitted to WHT twice on 18 June, verbally by Secretary of Agriculture James Wilson and in a note delivered by Archie Butt. (Butt, *Taft and Roosevelt,* 404; Pringle, *TR,* 534.) For TR's literary ambitions at this time, see Henry L. Stoddard, *As I Knew Them: Presidents and Politics from Grant to Coolidge* (New York, 1927), 327.

87 **During the next**   TR, *Works,* 22.370–71.

88 ***Birds of Oyster Bay***   A copy of this extremely rare paper, printed in Mar. 1879, is in TRC.

88 **Over the weekend**   New York *World,* 19 June 1910; *New York Evening Post* and *Literary Digest,* 18 June 1910. A veteran journalist rated TR's current candle-power as higher than that of Jack Johnson. Charles Willis Thompson, *Presidents I've Known and Two Near Presidents* (Indianapolis, 1929), 27.

88 **the right to doze**   For Taft's somnolence, see Butt, *Taft and Roosevelt,* 18, 504 ("I have never seen a man with such capacity for sleep"), and Irwin H. Hoover, *Forty-two Years in the White House* (Boston, 1934), 269.

88 **were convinced**   Morris, *Theodore Rex,* 508.

88 **The letters Archie Butt**   For the diplomatic role played by Archibald Butt in the writing of these letters, see Butt, *Taft and Roosevelt,* 388–92. WHT made a show of reluctance over them ("I do not want to say anything at first which might mislead Roosevelt into thinking that I expect of desire advice"), but the querulous tone of the first letter speaks for itself. WHT declined to address TR as "Colonel" in his second communication, saying that plain "Mr." was good enough.

89 **"I do not know"**   WHT to TR, 26 May 1910 (TRP).

89 **Taft took credit for**   Ibid.

89 **"[They] have done"**   Ibid. Henry Cabot Lodge was of the same angry opinion. Lodge to TR, 30 Apr. 1910 (TRP).

89 **He mentioned**   WHT to TR, 14 June 1910 (WHTP).

89 **Now, my dear**   TR, *Letters*, 7.89.

90 **Two days later**   Joseph H. Choate (eyewitness) to Carrie Choate, ca. 1910 (HKB); Robinson, *My Brother TR*, 262–63.

90 **"I am like Peary"**   Charles G. Washburn, *Theodore Roosevelt: The Logic of His Career* (Boston, 1916), 166. A copy of the exquisite dinner program is preserved in SUL.

90 **"I am very much pleased"**   Thomas Dreier, *Heroes of Insurgency* (Boston, 1910), 30. Quoted in Pringle, *TR*, 535. Actually, La Follette was far from being pleased. Ambitious to run for the presidency on a progressive platform, he got the feeling, during this visit, that TR had similar designs. For the political *pas de deux* now embarked on by both men—full of courtly gestures, solo variations, and teetering *levées* (with La Follette constantly afraid that he would be dropped), see Herbert F. Margulies, "La Follette, Roosevelt and the Republican Presidential Nomination of 1912," *Mid-America*, 58.1 (1976).

90 **Most of the pilgrims**   In private, the progressives were not so circumspect. "Glorious to have him back and ready to lead the great fight against special interest and for the common weal," Garfield wrote in his diary. TR was reportedly "in absolute agreement" with the aims of Garfield and Pinchot, and asked them to work out for him a declaration of principles that he could publicly espouse. This would appear to be the nucleus of TR's "New Nationalism" speech. James Garfield diary, 23 June 1910 (JRGP).

91 **"He says he will"**   Butt, *Taft and Roosevelt*, 416.

91 **Colonel Roosevelt is now**   New York *World*, 20 June 1910.

91 **"democracy of the heart"**   Mowry, *TR*, 52.

91 **a fifth of the general populace**   The population of the United States in 1910 was 91,972,266, or 93,402,000 if Alaska, Hawaii, and Puerto Rico were included (*Encyclopaedia Britannica*, 11th ed. [1911]).

91 **Roosevelt had been wary**   Morris, *Theodore Rex*, 144–45 and *passim;* Sullivan, *Our Times*, 4.351.

92 **"hideous human swine"**   TR, *Letters*, 5.264. TR complained to Owen Wister, who as a young writer showed Zolaesque inclinations, "I think that *conscientious descriptions of the unspeakable* do not constitute an interpretation of life. . . . There's nothing masculine in being revolting." Wister, *Roosevelt*, 34.

92 **From infancy, he had**   Leary, *Talks with T.R.*, 208–9. "I have never known that wonderful experience of being 'flat broke,' " TR told his old Rough Rider friend Jack Greenaway. Wood, *Roosevelt As We Knew Him*, 341.

92 **His radicalism**   In June 1910, TR was offered the presidency of the National Trades and Workers Association at the enormous salary of $100,000. He turned the job down.

93 **Booker T. Washington**   Ten years after their famous dinner, TR concluded that Washington was "the highest type of all-round man I have ever met." Louis R. Harlan, ed., *The Booker T. Washington Papers* (Urbana, Ill., 1972–1989), 1.439.

93 **If he was less motivated**   "Roosevelt," WW sagely remarked, "never works the heart out of himself." Arthur S. Link, ed., *The Papers of Woodrow Wilson* (Princeton, N.J., 1966–1990), 56.

93 **During Roosevelt's absence**   Herbert Croly, *The Promise of American Life* (New York, 1909). TR had ordered a copy of the English edition to be held for him in London. (TR, *Letters*, 7.76.) Gary Murphy, "Mr. Roosevelt Is Guilty: Theodore Roosevelt and the Crusade for Constitutionalism, 1910–1912," *Journal of Amer-*

ican Studies, 36.3 (Dec. 2002) notes, "There is scarcely a theme or a recommendation of the New Nationalism which Roosevelt had not already enunciated before Croly's work."

93 **"An individuality such"** Croly, *The Promise of American Life,* 174. An odd feature of this book, published nine months after TR's departure from the White House, was that it consistently spoke of him as if he were still in power. On 4 Oct. 1910, Ray Stannard Baker noticed the book lying on TR's desk at Sagamore Hill, "with passages heavily scored and pages on the fly-leaf with references." Notebook K, 153 (RSB).

93 **Roosevelt's Special Message** Morris, *Theodore Rex,* 506–8. Mowry, *TR,* 34, dates the "rebirth" of progressive reform (after its earlier trial run as populism) to 1902, the *annus mirabilis* of TR's first term. Except for Robert M. La Follette, then in his own first term as governor of Wisconsin, "Roosevelt stood virtually alone as a nationally known progressive Republican."

93 **The issues he raised then** The complete text of TR's Special Message of 31 Jan. 1908 is reprinted in TR, *Letters,* 6.1572–91.

93 **The opponents** TR, *Letters,* 6.1587.

94 **converging at state and local levels** The phrase is taken from John Allen Gable, *The Bull Moose Years: Theodore Roosevelt and the Progressive Party* (Port Washington, N.Y., 1978), 9.

Historical Note: The summer of 1910 also marked the convergence, within the Republican Party, of insurgency and progressivism, hitherto two separate movements. As Kenneth W. Hechler differentiates them, insurgency was agrarian in its values, and nonetheless narrow for being fought out primarily in Washington's corridors of power. Progressivism's typical battleground had been the state capitol or city hall, where "social reformers, champions of the rights of labor, and scions of the business world advocat[ed] a greater sense of responsibility to the public." (Hechler, *Insurgency,* 24.) Although the two movements became one for campaign purposes through 1912 and beyond, their Jeffersonian-versus-Hamiltonian differences prevented them from achieving true unity.

94 **"Is this not"** *Literary Digest,* 25 June 1910, quoted in Gable, *The Bull Moose Years,* 9. This was a commentary on a widely publicized prediction, by the chairman of the Roosevelt Club of St. Paul, Minn., that TR, Gifford Pinchot, and James Garfield were destined to lead a new party with a progressive agenda.

94 **The fact that** Hechler, *Insurgency,* 217; Butt, *Taft and Roosevelt,* 300–301. For a full account of this purge, and WHT's role in it, see Mowry, *TR,* chap. 4.

94 **"I might be able"** TR, *Letters,* 7.74.

94 **On 29 June** Sullivan, *Our Times,* 4.447. Sullivan was an eyewitness to this encounter.

94 **Cannily, he emphasized** Davis, *Released for Publication,* 192.

94 **Many times** See, e.g., Morris, *The Rise of TR,* 756.

95 **He did not like** The satirist Finley Peter Dunne stated flatly, "Nobody liked Hughes—nobody at all." Philip Dunne, ed., *Mr. Dooley Remembers: The Informal Memoirs of Finley Peter Dunne* (Boston, 1963), 142.

95 **Even Taft supported** Pringle, *Taft,* 560.

96 **"Our governor"** *The New York Times,* 30 June 1910.

96 **After coffee** William N. Chadbourne interview, Apr.–May 1955 (TRB). A modern historian points out that TR had spent so many years in Washington that he had few close contacts in the state GOP. John Allen Gable, "The Bull Moose Years: Theodore Roosevelt and the Progressive Party, 1912–1916" (Ph.D. diss., Kenyon College, 1965), 16.

96 **"What shall I do?"** Chadbourne interview, Apr.–May 1955 (TRB).

96 **"I believe"** TR, *Letters*, 7.97. The wording of TR's telegram allowed for the fact that he did not personally attach much value to the direct primary. He told Lawrence Lowell, the president of Harvard, that same day that the machine would soon manage to manipulate it. (Lowell to Owen Wister, 8 Aug. 1930 [OW].) Wister writes of TR's commitment to help Hughes: "In all his life, I see no decision more crucial than this one." Trifling in itself, it largely determined the future course of his life. Wister, *Roosevelt*, 280–82.

96 **He was bursting** Margaret Terry Chanler, *Roman Spring* (Boston, 1934), 199–201.

97 **"I know this man"** Butt, *Taft and Roosevelt*, 418.

97 **"Jimmy, I may"** Ibid., 261.

97 **He came out of the house** The following account of TR's reunion with WHT is taken from the only primary record available, in Butt, *Taft and Roosevelt*, 393–431.

98 **Before leaving** *New York Evening Post*, 1 July 1910; Lodge, *Selections*, 2.351; Paul T. Heffron, "William Moody: Profile of a Public Man," *Yearbook of the Supreme Court Historical Society*, 1980. TR's other Supreme Court appointments were Oliver Wendell Holmes and William Rufus Day.

98 **He had looked to Moody** As early as 26 Sept. 1907, Moody, just appointed to the Supreme Court, had written sarcastically to TR about "those who regard [the Constitution] as a benign gift from the Fathers, designed to protect those of sufficient wealth from the consequences of their misdoing." He went on: "Above all I dread a reactionary in your place. It is not so much for what he would do within the four years, but for what he could perpetuate . . . by the power of appointment, which for the next six years is of vital importance to our future development" (TRP).

CHAPTER 5: THE NEW NATIONALISM

100 **Epigraph** Robinson, *Collected Poems*, 26.

100 **Roosevelt returned home** The *New York Times* headline on 1 July 1910 was DEFY ROOSEVELT IN BOTH HOUSES. TR was denounced in the assembly for interfering in the legislative process.

100 **"And the 'Hundred' "** *Literary Digest*, 9 July 1910; New York *Sun*, 1 July 1910.

100 **chairman of the convention** In the confusing terminology of 1910, this office (both at the state and national level) was qualified by the adjective *temporary* before and through most of the convention. It changed to *permanent* only when the party elected its chairman for the next two or four years. The distinction may now be conveniently ignored.

101 **"Archie, I am"** Butt, *Taft and Roosevelt*, 434.

101 **"I could cry"** Lucius Burrie Swift to Mrs. Swift, 8 July 1910 (LBS).

101 **"Are you aware"** Victor Murdock interviewed by Hermann Hagedorn, 10 Nov. 1940 (TRB).

102 **Roosevelt was struggling** The fairest analysis of TR's complex political situation in the summer of 1910 remains that of Sullivan, *Our Times*, 4.443–45.

102 **"The greatest service"** TR, *Letters*, 7.102.

102 **That meant** Ibid., 7.102–3.

102 **"Of course you must"** Ibid., 7.101, 7.95.

103 **"He is evidently"** Ibid., 7.96. For some sample vacillations by WHT, see Mowry, *TR*, 56.

103 **A poll conducted** *World's Work*, July 1910. Even fewer respondents expressed any concerns about TR breaking the two-term tradition of U.S. presidents.

103 **He was in receipt** Lodge, *Selections*, 2.386–87.

103 **"My proper task"** TR to Fremont Older, 18 Aug. 1910 (TRP).

103 **the *Outlook* offices** At 287 Fourth Avenue, Manhattan.

104 **a Haynes-Apperson** EKR to KR, 7 Aug. 1910 (KRP); W. C. Madden, *Haynes-Apperson and America's First Practical Automobile: A History* (Jefferson, N.C., 2003), 92.

104 **On a visit** TR, *Letters*, 7.115–16. Griscom went to Sagamore Hill to confide that while he was still a Taft man, he thought TR had behaved more honorably as leader of the Republican Party.

104 **Then Barnes announced** *The New York Times*, 17 Aug. 1910; Butt, *Taft and Roosevelt*, 483.

104 **But he kept** TR had made his vow of "two months' " silence on 18 June, which projected freedom to speak around 18 Aug.

104 **"Have you seen?"** Butt, *Taft and Roosevelt*, 481.

104 **"It makes me ill"** Ibid., 482.

104 **A news flash** Butt, *Taft and Roosevelt*, 483. TR made his vow to "close up like a native oyster" on 18 June 1910. Sullivan, *Our Times*, 4.442.

105 **"So they want"** *Literary Digest*, 3 Sept. 1910.

105 **"Teddysee"** The word is a coinage of the humorous poet Wallace Irwin (1876–1959), who later in the year published a Homeric account of TR's post-presidential wanderings in 1909–1910 entitled *The Teddysee*. This book-length parody, forgotten now, is a classic of American satire, rising occasionally to heights of surreal imagination. See. e.g., 38–43 for an account of TR's Western tour.

105 **"Ugh! I do dread"** TR, *Letters*, 7.80.

105 **The truth was** Ibid., 7.111–13; James Garfield diary, 10 Aug. 1910 (JRGP). TR's left shinbone had been severely damaged in a trolley accident in Lenox, Mass., on 3 Sept. 1902. For an account of this near-fatal accident and its immediate effects, see Morris, *Theodore Rex*, 141–43, 146–49, 150. As will be seen, TR continued to be plagued by bone and malaria problems for the rest of his life.

106 **"It is incredible"** Sullivan, *Our Times*, 4.449; *Literary Digest*, 10 Sept. 1910.

106 **"I don't care *that*"** Davis, *Released for Publication*, 200–201.

106 **insurgent candidates were registering** The Iowa state convention earlier in the month dramatized the President's unpopularity in the Midwest. Boos and catcalls drowned out a resolution to endorse WHT for reelection. A giant portrait of TR was then winched down over the platform, to a roar of applause. (Mowry, *TR*, 128.) See ibid., 129–30 for other progressive triumphs through Sept.

106 **his "credo"** The word is that of James Garfield, who worked with Gifford Pinchot on TR's Osawatomie address. Garfield diary, 11 Aug. 1910 (JRGP). See Davis, *Released for Publication*, 209–11 for TR's elaborate, and unsuccessful, effort to keep the controversial paragraphs of his address at Denver from reporters.

106 **Riding across the prairie** Quoted by Carey in Wood, *Roosevelt As We Knew Him*, 236.

107 **Yet it had been there** TR to Cal O'Laughlin in *Chicago Tribune*, 16 Mar. 1910. TR's dream of leading cavalry volunteers into battle actually predated the Spanish-American War. EKR and Cecil Spring Rice used to call him in the 1890s "Theodore the Chilean volunteer" and "teaze [*sic*] him about his dream of leading a cavalry charge." EKR to Spring Rice, 25 Mar. 1899 (CSR).

107 **"against popular rights"** Bishop, *TR*, 2.301. See also TR, "Criticism of the Courts," *The Outlook*, 24 Sept. 1910, and Murphy, "Mr. Roosevelt Is Guilty." TR also attacked the Court's decision in *U.S. v. E. C. Knight Co.* (1895). The Lochner case remains one of the most controversial in Supreme Court history. See David E. Bernstein, "*Lochner v. New York*: A Centennial Retrospective," *Washington University Law Review Quarterly*, 85.5 (2005).

107 **At 2:15 P.M.** *Nebraska State Journal,* 1 Sep. 1910; Robert S. LaForte, "Theodore Roosevelt's Osawatomie Speech," *Kansas Historical Quarterly,* Summer 1996.

107 **Addressing himself** The following extracts from TR's "New Nationalism" address are taken from TR, *Works,* 19.10–30.

108 **"The essence of any struggle"** William Harbaugh was the first to note the Marxian nature of these words in his *TR,* 367. He emphasizes, however, that TR's speech overall was Jacksonian in invoking "equality of opportunity within a propertied framework. . . . Roosevelt preached no proletarian uprising and envisioned no broad destruction of private property. Nor, significantly, did he call for the upbuilding of labor as a countervailing force."

108 **Gifford Pinchot sat** LaForte, "Theodore Roosevelt's Osawatomie Speech." The original draft of the speech appears to have been written by Herbert Croly, author of *The Promise of American Life,* and the final version by Gifford Pinchot. (Miller, *Gifford Pinchot,* 234–35.) TR's textual contributions were minor, but the ideology of all those who worked on the speech derived so much from the progressive agenda he had himself initiated as President that he may still be considered the *fons et origo* of New Nationalism.

109 **Throughout his address** *Nebraska State Journal,* 1 Sept. 1910.

109 **Roosevelt's "New Nationalism"** *New York Evening Post,* 31 Aug., *Fort Wayne Sentinel,* 1 Sept., *The New York Times,* 3 Sept. 1910; Harbaugh, *TR,* 369; *Harper's Weekly,* 10 Sept., *Literary Digest,* 10 Sept., New York *Tribune,* 1 Sept. 1910.

110 **He never once** *New York Evening Post,* 1 Sept. 1910.

110 **Roosevelt himself granted** TR, *Letters,* 7.797; Bishop, *TR,* 2.303; Mowry, *TR,* 132.

110 **He tried to sound** *Proceedings of the Second National Conservation Congress* (Washington, D.C., 1911), 12–34, 82–93; WHT to Charles P. Taft, 10 Sept. 1910 (WHTP). On 24 Sept. 1910, TR published a defensive essay, "Criticism of the Courts," in *The Outlook,* attempting to show that what he had said in Denver and Osawatomie was less sensational than newspaper reports implied.

110 **"when a majority"** James Bryce to Sir Edward Grey, Bourne, *British Documents,* pt. 1, ser. C, 13.381. Bryce was an old friend of TR's. They first met in 1887, when Bryce was researching his classic *The American Commonwealth.* "He has immense go and quickness—alertness—of mind." Bryce to Cecil Spring Rice, 19 May 1887 (CSR).

111 **"A break between"** *Harper's Weekly,* 10 Sept. 1910.

111 **"When I see you"** Lodge, *Selections,* 2.389–90.

111 **Roosevelt answered that** TR, *Letters,* 7.123. In "Criticism of the Courts," TR noted that Stephen A. Douglas, in debate, had attacked Abraham Lincoln for "making war" on the Supreme Court. "If for Abraham Lincoln's name mine were substituted," he wrote, "this para [of invective] would stand with hardly an alteration." Throughout the campaign of 1910, TR did not hesitate to compare himself to the Emancipator.

111 **To Edith** EKR to Jules Jusserand, 6 Oct. 1910 (JJJ); Abbott, *Impressions of TR,* 88–89; WHT to Charles P. Taft, 10 Sept. 1910 (WHTP).

112 **There was one** By the end of Sept., *African Game Trails,* published on 24 Aug., had sold 25,000 copies. (Robert Bridges to TR, 4 Oct. 1910.) It went through five printings in 1910 alone. See, however, chap. 13 for its subsequent publishing history.

112 **"rather like the diary"** Cecil to Florence Spring Rice, 1 Nov. 1910 (CSR).

112 **the author's movie-camera memory** See, e.g., TR, *Works,* 5.148ff.

> *Biographical Note:* Anecdotes about TR's memory are so numerous that it is difficult to select the best examples. He himself described it as "photographic"

to Albert Shaw, editor of the *American Review of Reviews,* while his doctor, Alexander Lambert, noted that "his ear memory was as accurate as his eye memory." Oscar Straus told James Morse that TR "read books not by lines but by pages, [and] could quote the exact words *and imitate the tones* of all who conversed with him." Champ Clark once visited him in the White House to plead the case of a cadet who had been court-martialed, along with six others, at the Naval Academy in Annapolis. On this minor matter, TR amazed the congressman by repeating "substantially the entire transcript[s]" of all seven cases, totaling some 49 pages of closely typed legal cap. George Smalley, foreign correspondent of *The Times,* watched the President receiving a series of senators, and was reminded of the omniscience that had made Léon Gambetta a master of French politics. "He knew as much as they did about their districts and candidates and local affairs." On another occasion, TR learnedly lectured some Chinese diplomats on their society and its problems. He explained afterward that he was remembering a book he had read about China some time before, "And as I talked the pages of the book came before my eyes." (He said the same in 1910, after treating members of the Hungarian parliament to a surprise flood of rhetoric on the Mongol invasions of the Danube Valley.) His memory for people was contextual as well as visual. In 1912, he recognized a train engineer he had seen ten years before in Lenox, Mass. "Do you wear overalls? . . . There's steam around you. Somewhere in New England." When a high school graduate said shyly that he would not remember her, TR put his hand in front of his eyes and said, "Yes, you were in a rodeo in Denver two years ago and you were riding on a calico pony." To an elderly correspondent that same year, he wrote: "I remember you very well, and to show it I will tell you that you were wounded at a battle in the Civil War, and stayed to look on at the fight, and then found your wounds so stiff that you could hardly move."

TR frequently flattered authors by quoting their work at length—in the case of the essayist Edward S. Martin, "word for word a bit of dialogue . . . that I suppose was ten lines long." He astonished the humorist George Ade by recalling in detail a short story Ade himself had forgotten. When he met the poet Edgar Lee Masters, "he talked of [my] *Spoon River Anthology,* and seemed to know it all . . . some of it by heart." TR's memory in later life, however, was not infallible, and throughout his career he suffered from the selective amnesia characteristic of politicians. Albert Shaw, "Reminiscences of Theodore Roosevelt," ts. (SHA); TR, *Works,* 3.xvi; James H. Morse diary (italics added), 9 Nov. 1911 (JHMD); Champ Clark, *My Quarter Century of American Politics* (New York, 1912), 1.437–38; George W. Smalley, *Anglo-American Memories: Second Series* (New York, 1912), 378; *Theodore Roosevelt Association Journal,* 5.3 (Summer 1979); Stanley M. Isaacs interviewed by Hermann Hagedorn, ca. 1920s (TRB); TR, *Letters,* 7.477; Wood, *Roosevelt As We Knew Him,* 381, 382, 375, 389, and *passim.* See also Biographical Note below, 661.

112 **"So, with the lion-skin"** TR, *Works,* 5.184.

112 ***The Nation* noted** 22 Sept. 1910.

112 **he intended to** Theodore Roosevelt and Edmund Heller, *Life-Histories of African Game Animals,* 2 vols. (New York, 1914).

112 **Lloyd Griscom arranged** TR, *Letters,* 7.135; Butt, *Taft and Roosevelt,* 516–21.

113 **Covers were laid** Butt, *Taft and Roosevelt,* 517, 522–25; Patricia O'Toole, *When Trumpets Call: Theodore Roosevelt After the White House* (New York, 2005), 107–8. TR wrote Henry Cabot Lodge afterward, confirming that WHT had raised the subject of the convention. He quoted the President as saying that "Barnes and Company were crooks, and that he hoped we would beat them." TR, *Letters,* 7.135.

113 **To Roosevelt's annoyance**   TR told Ray Stannard Baker that he felt that WHT and his aides had entrapped him. "It happened once: but *never again!*" Baker, notebook K, 155 (RSB).

113 **"If you were"**   Butt, *Taft and Roosevelt*, 524.

113 **"Twenty years ago"**   Bishop, *TR*, 2.304.

113 **Now here he was**   *The New York Times*, 27 Sept. 1910; Abbott, *Impressions of TR*, 35ff.

114 **He did it by exuding**   *New York Evening Post*, 27 Sept., *The New York Times*, 28 Sept. 1910.

114 **He soothed it**   Ibid.; TR, *Letters*, 7.176.

114 **"We are against"**   *The New York Times*, 28 Sept. 1910.

114 **He paced the stage**   Davis, *Released for Publication*, 224–25. Writing about fourteen years after the event, Davis claimed that his editors in New York, unaffected by TR's onstage personality, had found the speech itself too "dull and prosaic" to print. Davis remembered wrongly: it was published in full by *The New York Times* on 28 Sept. 1910.

115 **"Theodore," said Elihu Root**   Overheard by William N. Chadbourne. Chadbourne interview, Apr.–May 1955 (TRB).

115 **"If it means"**   Elihu Root to Willard Bartlett, 1 Oct. 1910 (WB).

115 **"It shows an utter"**   *The New York Times*, 29 Sept. 1910. Two days earlier, the *New York Evening Post* described TR as "the big, overshadowing, indisputable 'it' of this gathering."

115 **"I do not think"**   Davis, *Released for Publication*, 225–26.

116 **"We have got"**   *Literary Digest*, 8 Oct. 1910.

116 **Home at Sagamore Hill**   Baker, notebook K, 153–57, 4 Oct. 1910 (RSB). Elihu Root's response when Stimson reported that TR meant to take no future part in politics was "Bet you a dollar." Elting E. Morison, *Turmoil and Tradition: A Study of the Life and Times of Henry L. Stimson* (Boston, 1960), 136–38.

116 **"The time to beat"**   Mowry, *TR*, 154.

116 **Roosevelt spent**   Davis, *Released for Publication*, 263; Baker, notebook K, 173, 8 Oct. 1910 (RSB).

117 **On 22 October**   Charles C. Goetsch, *Essays on Simeon Baldwin* (West Hartford, Conn., 1981), 83–86, 142.

117 **"So far as I am aware"**   Goetsch, *Simeon Baldwin*, 85, 151–52.

117 **"When I'm mad at a man"**   Sullivan, *Our Times*, 3.232. In a letter to Corinne Roosevelt Robinson, 4 June 1930, Sullivan quotes TR as saying something almost identical to him (SULH).

117 **In an open letter**   *The New York Times*, 25 Oct. 1910.

117 **fellow-servant defense**   This argument, in tort suits prior to the establishment of workers' compensation law, was based on the assumed liability of fellow employees, not their employer, for on-the-job accidents.

117 **In a return**   Goetsch, *Simeon Baldwin*, 153–56.

118 **"the felt necessities"**   Oliver Wendell Holmes, Jr., *The Common Law* (Cambridge, Mass., 1963), 5.

118 **"One thing always"**   TR, *Letters*, 7.162.

118 **"stewards for the public good"**   Goetsch, *Simeon Baldwin*, 99.

118 **two thousand words long**   TR's letter to Baldwin is printed in TR, *Letters*, 7.149–52.

119 **Even in 1881**   Morris, *The Rise of TR*, 118–19.

Biographical Note: An essay by Robert B. Charles corrects the received idea, in the above and other Roosevelt biographies, that TR's youthful legal studies were perfunctory. Charles discovered seven volumes of manuscript notes in the

Columbia Law School Library that, in his words, "indicate that TR studied law with vigor." Painstakingly organized and lucidly written over a period of two years, the notes total 1,189 pages and "lay a foundation for the belief that TR's study . . . was broad, systematic, regular, [and] intended to prepare him for private practice." Charles quotes a classmate's description of TR: "He was very quick in comprehension, very articulate in examination, and the most rapid and voluminous reader of references in the school." (Robert B. Charles, "Theodore Roosevelt, the Lawyer," in Naylor et al., *TR*, 121–39.) See also Charles's more extensive survey, "Theodore Roosevelt's Study of Law: A Formative Venture." (Unpublished ts. [TRC].) For an appreciation of TR's judicial philosophy by Justice Benjamin N. Cardozo, see Morris, *Theodore Rex*, 542, 737–38.

119 **"I shall waste"** Goetsch, *Simeon Baldwin,* 159. With that, Baldwin privately retained as his counsel Alton B. Parker of New York. Parker could be relied on to go after Roosevelt with vigor, having been defeated by him in 1904 for the presidency of the United States. See also TR's pre-election summary of his anti-constructionist views on the Constitution in *The Outlook*, 5 Nov. 1910.

119 **"Darn it, Henry"** TR quoted in Stimson's obituary, *The New York Times,* 21 Oct. 1950. TR's spiritual and physical weariness in early Nov. 1910 is documented by Hamlin Garland in *Companions on the Trail: A Literary Chronicle* (New York, 1931), 451–53.

120 **The first Socialist** Victor L. Berger.

120 **For the Republican** Hechler, *Insurgency,* 187; Butt, *Taft and Roosevelt,* 556.

120 **Roosevelt, in contrast** TR, *Letters,* 7.156n. A cartoon by Jay Darling in the Des Moines *Register* showed Roosevelt attempting to drag the camel of New York politics through the eye of the needle of reform, while representatives of Wall Street, Tammany Hall, and the Old Guard hung heavily on its tail. *Literary Digest,* 19 Nov. 1910.

120 **Less than five months** John Langdon Heaton, *The Story of a Page: Thirty Years of Public Service and Public Discussion in the Editorial Pages of the New York World* (New York, 1913), 336; *Literary Digest,* 19 Nov. 1910.

120 **"I am glad"** EKR to KR, 31 Oct. 1910 (KRP).

120 **Only one journalist** Sullivan, *Our Times,* 4.447.

121 **He suggested** Ibid., 4.453–54.

121 **One piece of good news** Goetsch, *Simeon Baldwin,* 163–64.

122 **The governor-elect felt** TR, *Letters,* 7.177.

122 **Gradually Roosevelt** TR in *The Outlook,* 19 Nov. 1910; TR, *Letters,* 7.148, 163.

122 **And he was pleased** On 24 Sept. 1910, *Harper's Weekly* appropriated one of TR's most cherished slogans in praising Wilson's economic policy as "a square deal to both labor and capital." Six days later, WW abandoned his lifetime opposition to state regulation of corporations.

122 **On 19 November** *The New York Times,* 20 Nov. 1910; Butt, *Taft and Roosevelt,* 562.

123 **"I think you are a trump"** TR, *Letters,* 7.176–77.

123 **That did not stop** Amassa Thornton to WHT, 25 Nov. 1910 (WHTP); TR, *Letters,* 7.128, 135. Hughes had been sworn in as an associate justice on 10 Oct. 1910. TR's admiration for White derived from the justice's dissent in *Lochner v. New York.*

123 **Taft was happy** TR, *Letters,* 7.180, 179; WHT to TR, 30 Nov. 1910 (WHTP). In a further gesture of goodwill, WHT sent EKR a mahogany settee that she had bought for the White House and regretted having to leave behind her. He personally paid for a duplicate settee to be installed in its place. Sylvia Morris, *Edith Kermit Roosevelt,* 337–38.

123 **Notwithstanding their politesse** Butt, *Taft and Roosevelt*, 185, 504–73 *passim*. Apparently, even the President's tongue was overweight, causing severe obstructive sleep apnea. For more on the alarming state of WHT's health in the fall of 1910, see O'Toole, *When Trumpets Call*, 143–14.

123 **What I now** TR to Eleanor B. Roosevelt, 27 Nov. 1910 (TRJP).

CHAPTER 6: NOT A WORD, GENTLEMEN

124 **Epigraph** Robinson, *Collected Poems*, 59.

124 **his first attempt at autobiographical writing** TR's 1880 manuscript article, "Sou'-sou'westerly," was finally published in *Gray's Sporting Journal*, 13.3 (Fall 1988).

124 **But to older ears** TR, *Letters*, 7.182, 196; Thompson, *Presidents I've Known*, 164.

124 **Henry Stimson, a close** Hermann Hagedorn, "Some Notes on Colonel Roosevelt from Henry L. Stimson," 12 Dec. 1923 (TRB); EKR diary, 23 Jan. 1911 (TRC).

124 **"You are now"** George H. Haynes, *The Life of Charles G. Washburn* (Boston, 1931), 147.

124 **It had the used** The word *used* is Washburn's. Details in this paragraph not taken from his eyewitness description are from Baker, notebook K, 153–60 (RSB) and David A. Wallace, *Sagamore Hill National Historic Site: Historic Furnishings Report*, Vol. 1, *Historical Data* (Harpers Ferry, Va., 1989), 96ff.

126 **Their breeding showed** According to ARL, TR thought that addressing servants by their first names, without an honorific, was demeaning.

126 **"I adhere to"** Haynes, *Washburn*, 147.

126 **Because Roosevelt was** TR, *Works*, 14.ix. *Literary Digest* referred to TR on 27 Nov. 1915 as "our nineteen-sided citizen." TR himself remarked that "most men seem to live in a space of two dimensions," implying that he did not. Harbaugh, *TR*, 384.

126 **"a changed man"** Butt, *Taft and Roosevelt*, 579.

126 **"I don't see"** Ibid., 580–81.

> *Historiographical Note:* The year 1911 marks a climacteric in the life of Theodore Roosevelt. As Taft discerned, he needed philosophy to get through it, and rebuild his political personality while he adjusted to grandfatherhood and the closing-in of middle age. The Roosevelt that emerged from this period was, if not ambivalent about his future course in life, ambiguous enough politically that biographers have never achieved consensus as to whether that course was vainglorious or self-sacrificing. The philosophical historian David H. Burton suggests that this disagreement may be explained in terms of the Heisenberg principle of uncertainty. ("History, Hubris, and the Heisenberg Principle," *Thought*, Mar. 1975.) Normally applied to physics, the principle also applies to the tension inherent in any biographical narrative between action and character. Heisenberg held (in Burton's paraphrase) to "the practical impossibility of simultaneously stating the exact position and momentum of [any] object in question." When a usually fast-moving man decelerates to near-stasis, as TR did after the election of 1910, it is easy to agree on where and what he is, as a sum of his experiences so far. But "a perfect measurement of position entails less than a perfect assessment of momentum." Hence, Burton writes, "the perennial problem of historical subjectivity" in chronicling the later life of Theodore Roosevelt. Narrative biographers, preoccupied with "a past which is more or less fixed," are confused by the *non sequiturs* of his post-1911 career,

which ideological biographers twist into theory, at cost to general understanding. Whether the aging TR indeed brought "hubris" on himself, this biography will attempt to show.

126 **now published in book form**   TR, *The New Nationalism* (New York, 1910).

126 **Many progressives**   Walter Johnson, *William Allen White's America* (New York, 1947), 190; TR to KR, 27 Jan. 1915 (TRC).

127 **He knew that they**   TR, *Letters*, 7.208, 199; Hechler, *Insurgency*, 202. La Follette had indeed engineered the League's creation as a vehicle for himself. Margulies, "La Follette."

127 **La Follette begged**   La Follette to TR, 19 Jan. 1911, quoted in Pringle, *TR*, 549; TR, *Letters*, 7.163, 181. For an eloquent summary of TR's political quandary at the end of 1911, see Harbaugh, *TR*, 372–73.

127 **La Follette wanted**   Robert M. La Follette, *La Follette's Autobiography: A Personal Narrative of Political Experiences* (Madison, Wis., 1913), 495–96.

127 **the insurgents' tendency to overreach**   "To put it baldly and briefly," Owen Wister remarked of the referendum and the recall, "they express American impatience." Wister, *Roosevelt*, 291.

127 **"I think"**   TR, *Letters*, 7.201–2.

128 **Roosevelt praised it**   Ibid., 7.206.

128 **"a virtual adjunct"**   WHT quoted in Pringle, *Taft*, 588.

128 **"to see radicalism"**   TR to the National Civic Foundation, 13 Jan. 1911, transcript in TRB; Morris, *The Rise of TR*, 123, 181–82; Hechler, *Insurgency*, 179–80.

129 **He is a sort**   Baker, notebook K, 165–66 (RSB).

129 **"If I go down"**   Davis, *Released for Publication*, 206.

129 **other progressive writers**   See, e.g., TR to Benjamin B. Lindsay, in TR, *Letters*, 7.298. TR openly used the pages of *The Outlook* to help Lindsay fight for child labor law reform in Colorado.

129 **"There is no fake"**   Hamilton W. Mabie, quoted in Garland, *Companions on the Trail*, 481.

129 **They knew that**   TR, *Letters*, 7.311.

129 **In January alone**   *The Outlook*, 11, 21, 28 Jan. 1910.

129 **Roosevelt was pleased**   Bull, *Safari*, 166; Charles Scribner to TR, 21 Feb. 1911 (SCR). $28,620 in 1911 equals about $498,000 in contemporary (2010) dollars (Measuring Worth).

129 **"It is a great"**   TR, *Works*, 6.458, 460.

130 **It styled itself**   John Hays Hammond, *The Autobiography of John Hays Hammond* (New York, 1935), 615.

130 **The word *judicial***   Ibid., 613. Root had just been appointed a member of the Hague court of arbitration by WHT. He was also president of the Carnegie Endowment. For Root's moderating influence on TR's forceful foreign policy inclinations, see James R. Holmes, "Theodore Roosevelt and Elihu Root: International Lawmen," *World Affairs*, 169.4 (Spring 2007).

130 **"If we do not"**   Pringle, *Taft*, 2.39.

130 **a word that the dictionary**   The 1910 edition of *Webster's Practical Dictionary* helpfully defined *righteous* as "According with, or performing, that which is right."

130 **A case in point**   TR, *Letters*, 7.243.

131 **"I most earnestly hope"**   Ibid., 7.243–44.

Chronological Note: TR's mention of Japan as a possible belligerent was prompted by a current severe strain in U.S.-Japanese relations. The divisive issue was the perennial one of repressive measures directed against Orientals living, or seeking to live, in California, Oregon, and Washington. TR considered this exclusionary policy "necessary and proper," at least in regard to immigration. He admired the Japanese for their martial qualities, but "they are utterly cold-blooded where their own interest is concerned." They were more likely, he felt, to attack the Asian mainland before they ever took on the United States. But, as he had prophetically remarked two years before, the U.S. Navy must never allow its Pacific fleet to become vulnerable. "If the Japanese could sink it, as they did the Russian fleet at Port Arthur, they could land a quarter of a million men on our [west] coast and it would take us several years and cost us an enormous sum in men and money to dislodge them." TR, *Letters,* 7.239; TR to E. Alexander Powell, ca. 28 Mar. 1909, quoted in Powell, *Yonder Lies Adventure,* 318.

132 **"My brigade commanders"** TR, *Letters,* 7.244.
132 **Edith saw no prospect** EKR (writing en route) to Cecil Spring Rice, 5 Apr. 1910 (CSR). She added, however, "I wish I could tell you of all the men who beg to follow him to fight Japan or Mexico or anyone!"
132 **Roosevelt rolled on** TR, *Letters,* 7.245; Butt, *Taft and Roosevelt,* 605–6.
133 **He pressed** *The New York Times,* 19 Mar. 1911.
134 **"The Panama Canal I naturally"** Stenographic transcript of TR's speech, from his own typescript, reproduced in University of California *Chronicle,* Apr. 1911, and quoted in James F. Vivian, "The 'Taking' of the Panama Canal Zone: Myth and Reality," *Diplomatic History,* 4 (Winter 1980).
134 **He had come to Berkeley** EKR to Cecil Spring Rice, 5 Apr. 1910 (CSR); Horace M. Albright (eyewitness), "Memories of Theodore Roosevelt," *Theodore Roosevelt Association Journal,* Winter 1987. TR's five Earl Lectures at the Pacific Theological Seminary were published as *Realizable Ideals* (San Francisco, 1912), and reprinted in TR, *Works,* 15.575ff.
134 **Roosevelt was referring** Morris, *Theodore Rex,* 84–85, 112–14.
134 **The revolution, he joked** Vivian, "The 'Taking' of the Panama Canal Zone."
134 **What his script said** See the survey of reportage in ibid.
134 **If I had followed** TR quoted in *The New York Times,* 24 Mar. 1911.
135 **cheated of its expectations** See Morris, *Theodore Rex,* 271–97.
135 **agreed with Senator Root** Undated speech draft ts., ca. May 1914 (PCK). Knox inserted the adverb *practically* by hand. He also altered the second sentence, deleting a direct reference to TR. As originally drafted, it read, "We did not take it from Colombia, we took it from the Panamans [*sic*], and it may be this was the sense in which Colonel Roosevelt made the statement that he took Panama." Knox accepted that Colombia had suffered "serious damage" in the revolution of 1903, while "corresponding benefits accrued to us." Quite apart from financial gains, the United States got "sovereignty and jurisdiction over a 10-mile zone in a dependent country," hitherto tied to Bogotá. The United States therefore had a "moral" right to compensate Colombia "not for what she lost but what we gained."
135 **the fuss his "boast" had caused** A bitterly critical 1911 pamphlet, "I Took the Isthmus," is preserved in the Pratt Collection at TRB. TR remained unapologetic about his speech at Berkeley. Vivian, in the essay cited above, strives to absolve him of indiscretion. But TR was always quick to correct misreports of his remarks, and his silence during the ensuing controversy seems significant. It is possible, as Vivian says, that "I took the Canal Zone" may have been a verbal slip (TR's script is marked "read"). But a year later, TR firmly wrote, "In 1903 I took Panama" on the proof of an article submitted to him by Lawrence F. Abbott. See the facsimile in Abbott, *Impressions of TR,* 62. His handwriting speaks for itself, as does a sen-

tence in his autobiography, "I took Panama without consulting the Cabinet." See also TR, *Works,* 22.623, and TR to Albert Cross, 4 June 1912 ("I know plenty of people who . . . opposed the taking of the Panama Canal"), TR, *Letters,* 7.554. There is a further reference to "our taking . . . the Panama zone" in TR, *Letters,* 7.854.

135 **He had other priorities** For TR's appearance in Madison on behalf of La Follette, during which he privately expressed his disillusionment with WHT, see Belle and Fola La Follette, *Robert M. La Follette,* 2 vols. (New York, 1953), 1.327–29.

135 *Qui plantavit curabit* "He who has planted will preserve," TR's family motto. In a long, ruminative letter to Lady Delamere, written before starting west, TR noted that he had enjoyed more years of power than either Hamilton or Lincoln. "For the last century none of the men who reached the summit had careers that lasted longer—I mean careers in the maturity of their success." The letter is reproduced in Lord Charnwood, *Theodore Roosevelt* (Boston, 1923), 251ff.

135 **Old friends were not** Bryce to Sir Edward Grey, 5 Apr. 1911, in Bourne, *British Documents,* pt. 1, ser. C, 14.284; EKR to Cecil Spring Rice, 5 Apr. 1911 (CSR). Bryce compared TR's political position, *"mutatis mutandis,* to that held in England by Mr. Gladstone from 1875 to 1880." A suspicious Robert La Follette reached even further back in Victorian imagery to describe TR's intentions regarding himself: "He is willing to have someone do the Light Brigade, stop Taft, and get shot." Margulies, "La Follette."

135 **He sought to please** Stimson would not accept his appointment until he had talked it over with TR. (Butt, *Taft and Roosevelt,* 655.) Many years later, he confirmed that he and Fisher had been appointed as "a sop to the progressives." Hermann Hagedorn, "Some Notes on Colonel Roosevelt from Henry L. Stimson," 12 Dec. 1923 (TRB).

136 **But Roosevelt felt** James Garfield diary, 17 Feb. 1911 (JRGP).

136 **"up to the North Pole"** *The Washington Post,* 15 Feb. 1911; Pringle, *Taft,* 592. For TR's increasing doubts about Canadian reciprocity, see TR, *Letters,* 7.241, 297.

136 **On Capitol Hill** *The New York Times,* 9, 23 Apr. 1911.

136 **"Not a word, gentlemen"** *The New York Times,* 17 Apr. 1911.

136 **If anyone was** James Garfield diary, 22–23 May 1911 (JRGP). At this time, WW was in the midst of his first, highly successful national speaking tour, espousing a progressive agenda that (apart from some unapologetic Bible-thumping) could have been written by TR. See August Heckscher, *Woodrow Wilson: A Biography* (New York, 1991), 231–35. TR himself had been impressed with WW as a presidential possibility since early in the year. Johnson, *William Allen White's America,* 192.

136 **a signed editorial** TR, "The Arbitration Treaty with Great Britain," *The Outlook,* 20 May 1911.

137 **a series of arbitration treaties** Pringle, *Taft,* 738–41; TR, *Letters,* 7.296.

137 **"Personally, I don't see"** Pringle, *Taft,* 738–39.

137 **Roosevelt's hottest language** E.g., "Sentimentality is as much the antithesis and bane of healthy sentiment as bathos is of pathos." TR, *Works,* 4.224.

137 **"The United States ought"** TR, "The Arbitration Treaty with Great Britain," *The Outlook,* 20 May 1911.

137 **a jubilee in Baltimore** Butt, *Taft and Roosevelt,* 672–74; William Manners, *T.R. and Will: A Friendship That Split the Republican Party* (New York, 1969), 210. "They can investigate me until they are black in the face," TR told John C. O'Laughlin on 2 June (OL).

137 **Taft advised him** TR, *Letters,* 7.290; *The New York Times,* 7 June 1911.

137 **Roosevelt denied** *The New York Times,* 7 June 1911; Harbaugh, *TR,* 374.

138 **"this huge big storm cloud"**   *The Letters of Henry Adams,* ed. J. C. Levenson, Ernest Samuels, et al. (Cambridge, Mass., 1988), 6.444–45.

138 **escape the cataclysm**   In 1911, General Friedrich von Bernhardi's book *Deutschland und der Nächtse Krieg (Germany and the Next War)* was published to enormous acclaim in Germany. This influential book persuaded citizens of the Reich that war was a "biological necessity," creative as well and destructive, and therefore "an indispensable factor of culture."

138 **Roosevelt believed**   TR to Baron Hermann von Eckardstein, quoted in Tyler Dennett, *Roosevelt and the Russo-Japanese War* (New York, 1925), 1.

138 **it reawakened moral fervor**   See, e.g., TR's reaction to a speech by WHT in praise of pacifism. "Taft . . . committed himself without any qualification to the proposition that in any internecine or international war, the sorrow and the harm caused far outweighed any possible good that was ever accomplished." (TR, *Letters,* 7.289.) See also TR's address to the Sorbonne, 47.

138 **friends felt their gorges rise**   See, e.g., Elmer Ellis, *Mr. Dooley's America: A Life of Finley Peter Dunne* (New York, 1941), 171.

138 **He used the strongest**   TR, *Letters,* 1.509; New York *World,* 31 May 1911; TR to Hiram P. Collier, *Letters,* 7.281.

139 **Taft remarked**   WHT to Philander Knox, 9 Sept. 1911, quoted in Pringle, *Taft,* 748.

139 **There is nothing**   TR, *Works,* 5.227–28.

CHAPTER 7: SHOWING THE WHITE FEATHER

140 **Epigraph**   Robinson, *Collected Poems,* 55.

140 **He had flabbergasted his parents**   *The New York Times,* 5 June 1911. QR's surviving school reports for 1910–1914, preserved at Sagamore Hill, show that he regularly stood first in his class.

140 **Always precocious**   Earle Looker, *The White House Gang* (New York, 1929), *passim;* TR, *Letters,* 7.235, 468.

140 **Archie, Quentin's former**   TR to E. Alexander Powell ("My son Archie, a boy with a wooden head"); Powell, *Yonder Lies Adventure,* 310; TR, *Letters,* 7.261; Sylvia Morris, *Edith Kermit Roosevelt,* 321, 367. TR tutored ABR in history and civics, EKR in French. TR, *Letters,* 7.315.

141 **"a young girl entitled"**   TR, *Letters,* 7.315.

141 **The Roosevelt retinue**   Wallace, *Sagamore Hill,* 1.22–27; TR, *Letters,* 7.316. Scholars of race nomenclature might note that in the latter, TR refers to his male servants alternately as "black," "colored," and "native Americans."

141 **"I am really thinking"**   TR, *Letters,* 7.295; *Bulletin of the American Museum of Natural History,* 23 Aug. 1911. See also TR, *Letters,* 7.219–22, 303–4. "I wish I could devote myself exclusively to work as a naturalist," he wrote Henry Fairfield Osborn on 5 July 1911 (AMNH). TR's monograph was an expansion of his critical appendix on protective coloration theory in *African Game Trails* (reprinted in TR, *Works,* 6.375–405). The main proponent of the theory, the artist Abbott H. Thayer, replied to TR's criticisms in the July issue of *Popular Science Monthly* and in the America Museum *Bulletin* on 14 Sept. 1912. TR's final word on the subject was published in *American Museum Journal,* Mar. 1918. For a beautifully illustrated discussion of the whole confrontation, see Alexander Nemerov, "Vanishing Americans: Abbott Thayer, Theodore Roosevelt, and the Attraction of Camouflage," *American Art,* Summer 1997.

141 **Roosevelt followed it**   See TR, *Works,* 14.439–47, 195–203, 52–57; TR, *Letters,* 7.302. TR's reviews of the Chamberlain and Weigall books are in TR, *Works,* 14.52–57, 195–203.

141 **Somehow, he could not** TR, *Letters,* 7.311.

141 **"As you know"** Ibid., 7.310; TR, Last Will and Testament, 13 Dec. 1912, copy in AC. TR was disappointed to hear from Charles Scribner on 21 Aug. that *African Game Trails* had not proved to be the bestseller he had expected, after its promising launch in the fall of 1910. "While it did not do all we had hoped for, the sale falling off rather suddenly at the last," Scribner wrote, "we are by no means through with it and we are thoroughly contented." He enclosed a check for $4,178, representing a half-year of royalties on all Roosevelt rights held by his house (SCR). TR's income from his many books issued by various publishers is summarized below, 657.

143 **"The kaleidoscope changes"** TR, *Letters,* 7.311.

143 **Not only he** Ibid., 7.164–65; Mowry, *TR,* 166.

143 **"I very earnestly"** TR, *Letters,* 7.334.

143 **"The word *panic*"** Ibid. TR's phrase, "fear, unreasoning fear" may have implanted itself in the memory of his young cousin Franklin Roosevelt, who had not yet left town on vacation.

> *Historical Note:* TR was accused of approving (or, technically, promising not to prosecute), a deal transferring ownership of the world's richest known tract of iron ore from the Tennessee Coal Company to U.S. Steel for only $30 million. By 1911, the tract was valued at $2 billion. In doing so, the Stanley Committee alleged, he had made himself a puppet of the steel magnates Henry Clay Frick and Judge Elbert H. Gary. TR read to Stanley one of his self-exonerating "posterity letters," dictated immediately after meeting with the two men on 4 Nov. 1907, and delivered within the hour to his attorney general, Charles Joseph Bonaparte. It reported that Frick and Gary had informed him, with Secretary of State Elihu Root standing by as a witness, that "a certain business firm" (Moore & Schley) owning a majority of the shares of TCC would fail and cause a "general industrial smashup" unless it was bought at once by U.S. Steel. They had argued convincingly that they were performing a public service in acquiring an asset they really did not want. In return, they asked for a guarantee of antitrust protection. "I answered," Roosevelt wrote, "that while of course I could not advise them to take the action proposed, I felt it no public duty of mine to interpose any objection." Congressman Stanley, intimidated as much by TR's extraordinary record-keeping as by the forcefulness of his reading, failed to follow up with an interrogation that could have shown how manipulated the President had in fact been, at the hands of two adroit businessmen congenial to Elihu Root. (*The New York Times,* 6 Aug. 1911; TR, *Letters,* 5.830–31.)
>
> For a detailed account of the Wall Street panic of 1907, centering on the USS/TCC "deal" and upholding TR's testimony, see Jean Strouse, *Morgan: American Financier* (New York, 1999), chap. 28. But see also James C. German, Jr., "Roosevelt, Taft, and United States Steel," *The Historian,* 34.4 (1972). This article lists at least half a dozen examples of deception practiced by Gary and Frick during their interview with TR on 4 Nov. 1907, including a false statement that Moore & Schley held a majority of TC&I stocks; no mention of the fact that TC&I was U.S. Steel's principal competitor in iron ore holdings; and concealment of TC&I's true profitability at the time of the purchase. TR was led to believe that the company's stock was worthless.

143 **Even *The New York Times*** On 6 Aug. 1911. The *New York Evening Post* agreed, albeit with editorial tongue in cheek. "The Colonel enthusiastically approves everything the President did in 1907 . . . [as being] the source of unqualified satis-

faction and pride to the man best able to judge the whole matter, namely, the principal actor in it" (7 Aug. 1911).

144 **"very young looking"** TR, *Letters,* 7.322.

144 **News came from San Francisco** EKR diary, 17 Aug. 1911 (TRC); TR to TR.Jr., 17 Aug. 1911, private collection. TR probably read Michelet's famous diatribe against Jesuit misogyny at Harvard, in preparation for his senior thesis, "Practicability of Giving Men and Women Equal Rights" (1880). As translated into English by Charles Cocks (London, 1845), the preface to the book reads, "Whether we be philosophers, physiologists, political economists, or statesmen, we all know that the excellency of the race, the strength of the people, come especially from the women. Does not the nine months' support of the mother establish this? . . . We all are, and ever shall be, the debtors of women" (viii). TR quoted the last phrase, and held to the precept, continually through his life.

144 **Grimly determined** Eleanor B. Roosevelt, *Day Before Yesterday,* 44–45, 58; TR, quoting Ted, to Cecil Spring Rice, 10 Aug. 1912 (CSR).

144 **"Do remember"** TR, *Letters,* 7.344.

144 **he was expressing** See, e.g., TR's articles on progressive justice in *The Outlook,* 24 June and 22 July, and on Alaska land policy in ibid., 22 July, 5, 12 Aug. 1911. See also TR, *Letters,* 7.323–24.

144 **gambled his whole government** See Pringle, *Taft,* 586, for a gaming slogan, coined by Laurier in Aug. 1911, that may have hastened the prime minister's retirement.

145 **About the only** Hechler, *Insurgency,* 185; Mowry, *TR,* 173–74. La Follette announced for the presidency on 17 June 1911.

145 **La Follette imagined** *The Outlook,* 27 May 1911; Mowry, *TR,* 177–78. In Apr., La Follette, reacting to expressions of Rooseveltian goodwill relayed by an intermediary, Gilson Gardner, had convinced himself that TR wanted him to run against Taft as the official candidate of Republican progressives. Gardner later denied he had transmitted any such message. (La Follette, *Autobiography,* 512–16.) It is possible that La Follette, like many presidential aspirants before and since, mistook flattery for endorsement.

145 **"My present intention"** TR, *Letters,* 7.336. WW then was the strongest candidate, period. A midsummer presidential preference poll of 2,414 primary-state subscribers to *World's Work* magazine returned 1,505 ballots, awarding 519 votes to WW, 402 to WHT, and 274 to TR, with all other candidates scoring only double figures. Arthur S. Link, ed., *The Papers of Woodrow Wilson* (Princeton, 1966–1990), 23.234.

145 **a second "Morocco crisis"** Hew Strachan, *The First World War* (New York, 2004), 39–40; Gwynn, *Cecil Spring Rice,* 2.163; TR, *Letters,* 7.343.

146 **Roosevelt raged** Lodge, *Selections,* 2.409. TR added that the Kaiser's strategists "are under solemn treaty to respect the territories of both countries, and they have not the slightest thought of paying the least attention to these treaties unless they are threatened with war as the result of their violation." It is difficult to guess from whom TR may have gotten his "personal" information about German war plans, but he did spend many hours with Wilhelm II at Döberitz.

146 **Taft and Governor Wilson chose** *The New York Times,* 3 Sept. 1911.

146 **Wilson's statement** Ibid. TR's political enemy, Governor Simeon Baldwin of Connecticut, also contributed to this peace manifesto.

146 **As an example** TR, *Letters,* 7.448. See also Lodge, *Selections,* 2.404–5.

146 **"The fact of"** Butt, *Taft and Roosevelt,* 753. TR's article was prominently quoted and summarized in *The New York Times,* 9 Sept. 1911, under the headline ROOSEVELT ASSAILS THE TAFT TREATIES. See also his even more emphatic year-end statement in TR, *Letters,* 7.447–50.

147 **"This is the only"** The following conversation is taken from Stoddard, *As I Knew Them*, 315–17. Stoddard was the editor of the New York *Mail* at the time.

147 **On 15 September** In preparation for the President's arrival, the City Club in St. Louis installed new elevator cables. *The New York Times*, 14 Sept. 1911.

147 **Canadians had voted** *The New York Times*, 6 Sept. 1911; Pringle, *Taft*, 750. For a full discussion of the reciprocity issue, see Pringle, *Taft*, 582ff.

147 **He had supported** TR, *Letters*, 7.345. George Dangerfield links the cession of power from the Lords to the Commons on 10 Aug. 1911 to the subsequent decline of reform Liberalism in Britain. Unionist Toryism, too, was doomed to disappear with the rise of militant labor and the onset of World War I. George Dangerfield, *The Strange Death of Liberal England* (London, 1935; Stanford, Calif., 1997), 63–69.

147 *I found I was* TR, *Letters*, 7.362. The full text of this letter, completed 1 Oct. 1911, is in ibid., 7.348–99. Five days later, TR wrote a sequel, describing his visit to Great Britain as special ambassador to Edward VII's funeral, but with the extreme circumspection that always characterized his discussion of diplomatic matters, he addressed it to an American friend, David Gray, on the ground that it might be too frank for English eyes. See TR, *Letters*, 7.401–15. Later he changed his mind, and allowed Gray to send a copy to Sir George Otto Trevelyan.

> *Historiographical Note:* In 2009 a third "posterity" letter written in this same period by TR to Trevelyan, and carbon-copied to Gray, came to light. Obviously intended to supplement TR's tour reminiscences with an equally primary account of some of his earlier dealings with Wilhelm II and other statesmen, the letter, dated 9 Nov. 1911, has been published in facsimile, with an accompanying article and appendices. See Gregory A. Wynn, " 'Under Your Own Roof': An Important TR Letter Discovered," *Theodore Roosevelt Association Journal*, 30.3 (Summer 2009).

148 **She was knocked** The accident dislocated the top three vertebrae in EKR's neck. EKR diary, 30 Sept. 1911 (TRC); TR to KR, 2, 5 Oct. and to Fanny Parsons, 6 Oct. 1911 (TRC); TR, *Letters*, 7.432; Sylvia Morris, *Edith Kermit Roosevelt*, 373–74. EKR's diary remains blank through 10 Nov. 1911.

148 **The family doctor** TR, *Letters*, 7.429–36; New York *Tribune*, 21 Oct. 1911; TR, *Works*, 18.262. TR's speech, entitled "The Conservation of Womanhood and Childhood," was an early formulation of his views on welfare and the judiciary, which became central elements of the Progressive Party platform in 1912. It appears in TR, *Works*, 18.244–75.

148 **Germany being "compensated"** MacDonogh, *The Last Kaiser*, 325.

148 **Meanwhile Taft** Mowry, *TR*, 184; La Follette, *Autobiography*, 532. According to Mowry, the receptions accorded WHT in the Midwest were so chilly, he was jokingly said to have added some Southern states to his itinerary, "so that he might thaw out." For an account of the Progressive convention's rather ambivalent feelings regarding La Follette, see Margulies, "La Follette."

149 **Roosevelt was stunned** TR, *Letters*, 7.430. The claim in Mowry, *TR*, 191, that "Roosevelt's reaction was as instantaneous as it was violent" is not supported by TR's behavior during the next two months, nor by the tone of his public references to the Taft administration. Mowry's pioneer researches in the Roosevelt papers were sometimes hampered by his tendency to take TR's political temperature and find it feverish. This misperception, shared by many historians, can be ascribed to TR's own tendency (noticeable also in affectionate letters) to overexpress himself. For a corrective view, see Andrew C. Pavord, "The Gamble for Power: Theodore Roosevelt's Decision to Run for the Presidency in 1912," *Presidential Studies Quarterly*, 26.3 (Summer 1996).

149 **For two and a half** Margulies, "La Follette"; Mowry, *TR*, 183, 293–94.

149 **As James Bryce noted** Bryce to Sir Edward Grey, 24 Oct. 1911, Bourne, *British Documents*, pt. 1, ser. C, 15.48; Moody quoted in German, "Roosevelt, Taft, and United States Steel." The latter concludes that TR was indeed misled. He was falsely told, among other things, that Moore & Schley held a majority of TC&I stocks; TC&I's potential wealth and competitive threat to U.S. Steel were underplayed; he did not know that TC&I was paying dividends, and investing heavily in itself, at the time of purchase. In 1920, however, the Supreme Court found the steel company innocent of antitrust activity.

150 **I know you"** TR, *Letters*, 7.430–31.

150 **He told two** Ibid., 7.417, 422. According to La Follette, *Autobiography*, 535–37, TR had by this time been informed by two roving correspondents, Gilson Gardner and John C. O'Laughlin, as to the impressive extent of progressive opposition to WHT across the country. But the senator's suggestion that this information caused TR at once to lust for the nomination is contradicted by the repeated testimony of TR's letters for the rest of 1911. Harbaugh, *TR*, 384, comments: "Whatever his subconscious desires, his rational self opposed a bid for the nomination."

150 **At Carnegie Hall** TR, *Letters*, 7.424, 421. This letter is a good example of TR's need to imagine enemies. On 20 Oct. 1911, *The New York Times*, to cite just one newspaper generally critical of him, gave his Carnegie Hall speech long, respectful, and positive coverage, with copious quotations of the text. It reported that the hall was "crowded to the doors," that he was greeted with a universal standing ovation, and that he expressed his "highest respect for the judiciary." TR noticed only that the *Times* did not print his speech in full.

150 **worked with extreme care** TR, *Letters*, 7.435. "Nobody knows how much time I put into my articles for *The Outlook*," TR told Charles Washburn one day, pulling a manuscript out of his pocket. Washburn, *TR*, 151.

150 **The article, headlined** TR, *Letters*, 7.454; *Boston Globe*, 17 Nov. 1911; Mowry, *TR*, 192. Although the issue of *The Outlook* containing TR's editorial was datelined 18 Nov., his words were effectively published two days earlier.

150 **Roosevelt tersely reaffirmed** The following quotations are taken from *The Outlook*, 18 Nov. 1911.

151 **Admitting that he** The Northern Securities Company was dissolved by order of the Supreme Court in Mar. 1904, Standard Oil and American Tobacco in the spring of 1911. Although TR authorized all three successful prosecutions, he was not satisfied with the last two, feeling that the essential dominance of either trust in its industry was unaffected by the Court's vague application of a "rule of reason" to antitrust law. This dissatisfaction fueled his demand for "continuous and comprehensive government regulation" of combinations. TR, *Letters*, 7.277–78; Harbaugh, *TR*, 379–81.

151 **as long as they did not monopolize** A contemporary historian waxes poetical in his sample listing of Progressive Era trusts: "Continental Cotton and U.S. Glue; National Biscuit and National Glass; American Bicycle and American Brass." Michael McGerr, *A Fierce Discontent: The Rise and Fall of the Progressive Movement in America, 1870–1920* (New York, 2003), 151.

151 **But those who thought** Harbaugh, *TR*, 380, remarks on the irony that TR here echoed the very reservations about piecemeal prosecutions that had enraged him when Justice Oliver Wendell Holmes expressed them in dissenting from the *U.S. v. Northern Securities* decision of 1904.

151 **it was regarded** *Boston Globe*, 17 Nov., *The New York Times*, 18 Nov., *The Washington Post*, 17 Nov., New York *World*, 18 Nov. 1911. Andrew Carnegie, Grenville M. Dodge, and other industrial magnates also praised TR's editorial.

"To some extent," George E. Mowry comments, "the *Outlook* article regained for Roosevelt the support of the business interests he had lost at Osawatomie." Mowry, *TR*, 192.

152 **"He presents"** New York *World*, 18 Nov. 1911.

152 **As so often** TR, *Letters*, 7.455; Harbaugh, *TR*, 381–83, analyzes the "inconsistencies" in TR's basically moralistic economic thinking.

152 **Or so he** TR, *Letters*, 7.441–42; Sullivan, *Our Times*, 4.461–62.

152 **"since Mr. Roosevelt"** *Boston Globe*, 28 Nov. 1911.

152 **La Follette was** Margulies, "La Follette"; Stoddard, *As I Knew Them*, 388; *Wall Street Journal*, 9 Nov. 1910.

153 **On 11 December** Pavord, "The Gamble for Power"; Stoddard, *As I Knew Them*, 388ff. For political gossip emanating from the RNC meeting, see Butt, *Taft and Roosevelt*, 784ff.

153 **A group of three** Stoddard, *As I Knew Them*, 390–91; TR, *Letters*, 7.261–62.

153 **Colonel, I never knew** Stoddard, *As I Knew Them*, 391–92. See also TR, *Letters*, 7.469.

> *Historiographical Note:* A letter from John C. O'Laughlin to a fellow journalist, James Keeley (16 Dec. 1911 [OL]), contains the following indiscretion about a conversation he had just held with TR: "Probably the sensational aspect of our talk related to a proposition which was made to him by Taft through a mutual friend. He told me this in dead confidence, but I can repeat it to you because I know he would not object. The President said he would withdraw and support Mr. Roosevelt provided the latter would agree to appoint him on the Supreme bench. I cannot conceive of a President of the United States making such a proposal. Mr. Roosevelt, of course, refused to listen to anything of the kind. He will enter into no deal for the presidency." The story is unsupported by other evidence. An expert on the partisan politics of this period points out WHT was in too strong a position to risk the disgrace of such a ploy being made public. WHT in any case had turned down an offer of an associate seat on the Supreme Court during TR's presidency, saying that he was interested only in becoming chief justice. That office was unlikely to become vacant for some years, since Edward Douglass White had assumed it only recently. Lewis L. Gould to author, 3 Aug. 2009 (AC).

153 **There was no arguing** Knox, however, was convinced that "if he [TR] is drafted for service by the people not the politicians he will not refuse." La Follette got similar intimations from other attendants at the meeting. Pavord, "The Gamble for Power"; La Follette, *Autobiography*, 551–52.

153 **"The Search for Truth"** *The Outlook*, 2 Dec. 1911, reprinted in TR, *Works*, 14.418–38. All quotations below are from this source.

154 **Arthur Balfour alone excepted** Although Balfour was a bona fide published philosopher and a politician at least as skilled and successful as TR, it could be argued that the latter's empirical understanding of the world—the basis, rather than the goal, of philosophy—was larger and more sympathetic. Balfour remained to the end of his life an intellectual elitist comfortable only in his own aristocratic class, and even within that class he held himself aloof. See John David Root, "The Philosophy and Religious Thought of Arthur J. Balfour (1848–1930)," *Journal of British Studies*, 19.2 (Spring 1980).

154 **Reyles's dying swan** Originally *La Muerte del Cisne*. TR read this text in a French translation (Paris, 1911). Bibliographical details of all the books cited in his essay appear in TR, *Works*, 14.52–93.

155 **"Subject to bursts"** Henry Osborn Taylor, *The Classical Heritage of the Middle Ages* (1910), quoted in TR, *Works*, 14.420.

155 **He took up** In the year preceding TR's essay, the issue of *fides versus ratio* had become fraught in Roman Catholicism. Sparked by Pope Pius X's reactionary encyclical *Pascendi Dominici Gregis* (1907), attacking the validity of intuition, scientism, and mystical aspirations as bases for belief as opposed to scriptural orthodoxy, it had burst into doctrinal flame in 1910, when the pontiff ordered all Catholic clerics to swear an oath repudiating modernism. The resultant ideological schism tormented the Church for the rest of the century, and was moderated only by John Paul II in his great encyclical *Fides et Ratio* (1998).

157 **The year ended** TR, *Letters*, 7.450. "If I should run and be defeated," TR told one of the "fool friends" urging him to commit himself, "I should be covered with obloquy." He had had enough of that the winter before. Regis H. Post, "How Roosevelt Made the Government Efficient," *World's Work*, Apr. 1921.

157 **Theodore Roosevelt had** See, e.g., TR, *Letters*, 7.451–52.

157 **His best interest** Some biographers, e.g. Mowry, *TR*, 192ff., attempt to show that TR had become ambitious for the presidency in the fall of 1911, and that the steel suit was a jump-start to his campaign to defeat Taft. Their arguments, due to a common inability to conceive of TR as anything other than a politician, do not hold up in the light of his countless, and laboriously emphatic, denials of any such ambition. See the representative selection of apologia in TR, *Letters*, 7.446–69.

158 **"Alice, when you"** Butt, *Taft and Roosevelt*, 776. Butt had been promoted to major. According to ibid., 811–12, several other TR associates in the administration received similar storm warnings.

CHAPTER 8: HAT IN THE RING

159 **Epigraph** Robinson, *Collected Poems*, 21.

159 **"They say that"** TR speech in Manhattan, 7 Nov. 1910, transcript in TRB.

159 **"You can put it"** Sylvia Morris, *Edith Kermit Roosevelt*, 371. Meanwhile Helen Taft was telling her own husband with equal accuracy, "I think you will be renominated, but I don't see any chance for the election." Butt, *Taft and Roosevelt*, 68.

159 **His response to** TR, *Letters*, 7.466; Margulies, "La Follette"; Mowry, *TR*, 203.

159 **"It now looks"** Link, *Papers of Woodrow Wilson*, 23.596.

160 **the *hajj* that converged** Mark Sullivan uses the simile of "strewn iron filings mobilizing to the pull of a revitalized magnet." (*Our Times*, 4.469–71.) See also Mowry, *TR*, 199–202; TR, *Letters*, 7.470–493, 8.1474.

160 **In cabs and carriages** TR, *Letters*, 7.315.

160 **Midwesterners loyal** La Follette, *Autobiography*, 581–82; Pringle, *TR*, 554; Mowry, *TR*, 200–202.

160 **"He is not"** Butt, *Taft and Roosevelt*, 834–35. "What struck me as significant," Butt wrote the next day, "was the fact that never once [in a visit lasting from three to four hours] did the Colonel mention the President." Ibid., 833.

160 **"I would much"** Post, "How Roosevelt."

160 **"I am not"** TR, *Letters*, 7.470–71. Norris was a La Follette supporter.

161 **Nothing less** Ibid., 7.474. Andrew C. Pavord, "The Gamble for Power," argues that TR, in Jan. 1912, was not looking for personal glory. Profoundly idealistic, he felt that the radical reform program he had tried to launch in his second term had been thwarted by Congress, then under the control of Speaker Joseph Cannon and Senator Nelson Aldrich, and thereafter by the Taft administration. He now saw an opportunity to transform the desire of some progressives that he reenter politics into a "mass demand of the people" for completion of his presidential legacy. Through the rest of this month and into February, "Roosevelt was presented with a huge amount of evidence that such a demand truly existed."

161 **He was attractive**   Harbaugh, *TR*, 385–86.
161 **his latest article**   TR, "Judges and Progress," *The Outlook*, 6 Jan. 1912. James
    Bryce reported to his government that this article "has thrilled with horror minds
    of a conservative bent, and especially the higher ranks of the legal profession."
    (Bourne, *British Documents*, pt. 1, ser. C, 15.66.) Elihu Root, an eloquent repre-
    sentative of both groups, argued before the New York State Bar Association on 19
    Jan. that the philosophy of popular recall "abandons absolutely the conception of
    a justice which is above majorities. . . . It denies the vital truth taught by religion
    and realized by the hard experience of mankind, and which has inspired . . . every
    declaration for human freedom since Magna Charta [*sic*]—the truth that human
    nature needs to distrust its own impulses and passions, and to establish for its own
    control the restraining and guiding influence of declared principles of action."
    The New York Times, 20 Jan. 1912.
161 **"Theodore Roosevelt is"**   *Baltimore American*, 24 Jan. 1912.
161 **"It was the President"**   Adams, *Letters*, 6.490.
161 **"What can you do?"**   La Follette, *Autobiography*, 547.
161 **Taft had executive control**   Mowry, *TR*, 226–27. In anticipation of a run by TR,
    WHT had pressured state Republican committees to hold their conventions as
    early as possible, before his campaign took hold. Ibid., 209.
162 **He now began**   TR, *Letters*, 7.451.
162 **"In making any"**   Ibid., 7.481.
162 **The only major papers**   Mowry, *TR*, 225.
162 **Again citing Lincoln**   TR, *Letters*, 7.483–84.
163 **On 16 January**   Mowry, *TR*, 205.
163 **"Roosevelt obsession"**   Sullivan, *Our Times*, 4.472.
163 **"I fear things"**   Butt, *Taft and Roosevelt*, 814.
163 **"as hard as nails"**   Hermann Hagedorn, "Some Notes on Colonel Roosevelt
    from Henry L. Stimson," 12 Dec. 1923 (TRB). Corinne Roosevelt Robinson told
    Archie Butt that her brother "could never forgive" Taft's insult. The breach be-
    tween him and the President was "irrevocable." Butt, *Taft and Roosevelt*, 811–13.
163 **"It is hard"**   Butt, *Taft and Roosevelt*, 804.
163 **Major Butt noticed**   Ibid., 839.
163 **La Follette, too**   Gable, "The Bull Moose Years" (diss.), 30–31; La Follette, *Au-
    tobiography*, 541–45, 586ff.; Sullivan, *Our Times*, 4.473; Margulies, "La Follette";
    The New York Times, 4 Jan. 1912.
163 **He had hoped to**   *The New York Times*, 6 Jan. 1912. La Follette was an obses-
    sive, but not self-obsessed candidate for the presidency. His primary interest was
    to advance the cause of progressivism, and his initial reaction to the Roosevelt
    presidential boom at the end of 1911 had been to offer to withdraw in TR's favor.
    But the latter's indecision made him soldier on. See Harbaugh, *TR*, 392–94.
163 **Within two days**   Mowry, *TR*, 210; TR, *Letters*, 7.485. Since TR had been so in-
    scrutable on the question of his possible candidacy through Dec. 1911 and the
    first half of Jan. 1912, and since the governor's letter was subject to several sub-
    missions, withdrawals, and revisions through 10 Feb. 1912, historians have long
    debated as to when, exactly, he decided to run against Taft and La Follette. The
    most exhaustive analysis of the available evidence is that of John Allen Gable,
    who concludes that TR "made up his mind sometime between the Norris letter of
    Jan. 2 and Jan. 16." By 18 Jan., TR's availability was a matter of record. Gable,
    "The Bull Moose Years" (diss.), 31–32, 66–69. See also La Follette, *Robert M. La
    Follette*, 1.385–86.
164 **All this coordination**   Margulies, "La Follette"; TR, *Letters*, 7.487–93.
164 **Pandemonium ensued**   *The New York Times*, 24 Jan. 1912. The convention also
    endorsed James Harris for the Republican National Committee.

165 **"Do not for one"**   TR, *Letters*, 7.493. TR's continuing reluctance to run in Feb. 1912 was proclaimed not only by himself in countless letters, but by friends and intimates who could sense both his doubts and his almost deterministic acceptance of fate. Albert Bushnell Hart remembers being invited to Sagamore Hill on 26 Jan. to listen, with others, to TR reading a proposed statement of candidacy. They felt it was too self-explanatory, and TR withdrew it, as if he was glad to postpone the moment of reckoning. Hart notes that by delaying almost another month before making a very different announcement, TR lost delegates in Colorado and elsewhere whose numbers might have clinched his nomination in June. (Wood, *Roosevelt As We Knew Him*, 254–56.) As late as mid-February, when TR was working on his Columbus speech in Manhattan, a young progressive named John A. Kingsbury took an evening stroll with him. "I remember that I was very genuinely impressed that night that the Colonel meant what he said when he told me that he would much prefer to retire to his home in Oyster Bay to lead the life of a private citizen . . . but that he could see the drift of events and he felt certain that he was going to be drafted." (Kingsbury to Hermann Hagedorn, 31 Oct. 1921 [TRB].) See also Nicholas Roosevelt, *TR*, 79–82.

165 **By 2 February**   The petition was drafted by John C. O'Laughlin of the *Chicago Tribune*, operating, as he often did, on both sides of the media/governmental divide.

165 **Woodrow Wilson preceded**   La Follette, *Robert M. La Follette*, 1.400; Ray Stannard Baker, "Notes and Memoranda," 21 (RSB).

165 **La Follette, in contrast**   La Follette, *Autobiography*, 605–7, 609; Wister, *Roosevelt*, 299–301; William Allen White, *The Autobiography of William Allen White* (New York, 1946), 449. All three authors were eyewitnesses. See also La Follette, *Robert M. La Follette*, 1.399–403, and Margulies, "La Follette." The various accounts differ only slightly in details.

165 **"That was"**   TR, *Letters*, 7.499; *The New York Times*, 4 Feb. 1912; La Follette, *Robert M. La Follette*, 1.399; White, *Autobiography*, 448; Benjamin P. De Witt, *The Progressive Movement* (New York, 1915), 39–40. "In my judgment," Gifford Pinchot wired the Minnesota Progressive Republican League, "La Follette's condition is so serious that further candidacy is impossible." *The New York Times*, 12 Feb. 1912.

166 **"Politics are hateful"**   Sylvia Morris, *Edith Kermit Roosevelt*, 376.

166 **He brushed aside**   Margulies, "La Follette."

166 **Roosevelt supporters bolted**   *The New York Times*, 7 Feb. 1912. There was a similar bolt by progressives in Nebraska on 14 Feb. Ibid., 15 Feb. 1912.

166 **On the ninth**   For the text of the governors' petition, see TR, *Letters*,, 7.511.

166 **A principle is**   *The New York Times*, 11 Feb. 1912. With the implicit endorsement of Hiram Johnson of California, the total of governors appealing to TR was actually nine.

166 **Taft, seriously disturbed**   *The New York Times*, 13 Feb. 1912.

166 **Actually, he meant**   This was revealed by Mark Sullivan, writing with some discretion when Taft was still alive. Sullivan, *Our Times*, 4.480.

167 **"If I were any"**   TR, *Letters*, 7.503.

167 **He admitted**   Ibid., 7.498; Mowry, *TR*, 226.

167 **"It seems to me"**   Root to TR, 12 Feb. 1912 (TRP).

167 **"The time has come"**   TR, *Letters*, 7.504.

167 **Little more than two**   Ibid., 7.495; TR, "Judges and Progress," *The Outlook*, 6 Jan. 1912. In his letter of reply to Stimson, TR's professed scruples about the recall of the judiciary, extending all the way up from the state to Supreme Court level, were so hedged with conditionals and veiled threats as to leave little doubt that he would move to implement it if reelected President. (TR, *Letters*, 7.494–95.)

Eleven years later, Stimson was still puzzled as to what made TR change his mind about running for the nomination after his disclaimer of 7 Jan. 1912. Hermann Hagedorn, "Some Notes on Colonel Roosevelt from Henry L. Stimson," 12 Dec. 1923 (TRB).

168 **Roosevelt set**   The following quotations from TR's speech, entitled "A Charter of Democracy," are taken from *The New York Times*, 22 Feb. 1912. The version printed in TR, *Works*, 19.163–97 is almost identical with the newspaper transcript, except that "I" is usually rendered as "we" (i.e., the Progressive Party), and a few extra passages, apparently written much later, have been interpolated.

> *Historical Note:* TR has been much criticized by biographers for the alleged impulsiveness and political indiscretion of his Ohio address. But it was one of his most deliberate and long-prepared orations. A sequential line of judicial criticism can be traced back to his article, "Judges and Progress" in *The Outlook*, 6 Jan. 1912, itself essentially a repetition of complaints he had made about the social insensitivity of the New York Court of Appeals at Carnegie Hall on 20 Oct. 1911. That speech in turn harked back through his attacks on Judge Baldwin to his address to the Colorado state legislature on 29 Aug. 1910—inspired, as he admitted, by his conversation with former justice William H. Moody the preceding spring. Whether or not George Mowry and John Allen Gable are correct in calling TR's Ohio address an "egregious mistake" and "serious blunder," it was hardly impulsive. He extensively discussed its draft contents with Herbert Croly, James Garfield, Frank Munsey, William L. Ward, Oscar Straus, and other advisers, including a disapproving Gifford Pinchot. Straus was surprised at his inflexible determination to include the recall proposal. (See above, 614; Stoddard, *As I Knew Them*, 395–96; Straus, *Under Four Administrations*, 310–11; Mowry, *TR*, 212–13; Gable, "The Bull Moose Years" [diss.], 35; Wood, *Roosevelt As We Knew Him*, 258–61.) For modern revisionist views, see Pavord, "The Gamble for Power," and Murphy, "Mr. Roosevelt Is Guilty." In 1927, Henry L. Stoddard wrote: "No public man ever prepared his speeches so long in advance of delivery as Roosevelt; none ever gave them more careful revision. Those 'impulsive' phrases which his opponents by their denunciation made popular, were the most deliberately thought out phrases of all, and usually got the reaction he deserved." *As I Knew Them*, 311–12.

168 **"Shape your constitutional"**   *The New York Times*, 22 Feb. 1912.
169 **"I know of no"**   Ibid.
169 **The reaction to**   Ibid., 5 Mar. 1912; Sullivan, *Our Times*, 4.477; *Current Literature*, Apr. 1912. Such comments, however, were all initial, and often reflective of shock. A modern legal historian has shown, in an important corrective article, that as the summer and fall of 1912 wore on, many liberal judicial thinkers inclined to TR's point of view—Felix Frankfurter, for one, remarking, "Thanks to T.R. there is live thought on the subject." See Stephen Stagner, "The Recall of Judicial Decisions and the Due Process Debate," *American Journal of Legal History*, 24.3 (July 1980).
169 **It was to be**   Heaton, *The Story of a Page*, 299; *Wall Street Journal*, quoted in Sullivan, *Our Times*, 4.537, 490–91; *The New York Times*, 23 Feb. 1912.
169 **Doubts about**   *The New York Times*, 28 Feb., 24 Mar. 1912; Sullivan, *Our Times*, 4.480–81; William Roscoe Thayer, *Theodore Roosevelt: An Intimate Biography* (Boston, 1919), 353–54; Adams, *Letters*, 6.518.
169 **An appalled Henry**   *The New York Times*, 22 Feb. 1912. As early as 5 May 1910, TR had written Lodge from Christiania, Norway, to say there was a need for "very radical change" in the American judiciary. Lodge, *Selections*, 2.380.

170 **"My hat"**   Sullivan, *Our Times*, 4.477. The earliest version of this famous quote, consisting of the first sentence only, appears in a no-headline special dispatch out of Cleveland to *The New York Times* on 22 Feb. 1912, printed in the following day's paper. TR appears to have said it on board his train to a local county commissioner, William F. Eirick, who leaked their conversation as follows. Q: "Colonel, I have a question I want to ask." A: "I know what it is. I'll make a statement on Monday. My hat is in the ring." A separate article in the same issue reports that TR seemed surprised when his remark was repeated to him by newsmen on his return journey, but did not deny making it. He used it again in a letter to Governor Hadley on 29 Feb. (TR, *Letters*, 7.513.) Where Mark Sullivan got the second sentence from is unclear.

170 **"I will accept"**   TR, *Letters*, 7.511. "The Colonel made a mistake when he said he would 'accept' the nomination," George Harvey remarked in *Harper's Weekly*, 20 Apr. 1912. "What he meant to say was that he would 'intercept' it."

170 **Grant thought**   Robert Grant's letter to James Ford Rhodes, 22 Mar. 1911, on which the rest of this chapter is based, is printed as an appendix in TR, *Letters*, 8.1456–61. See also White, *Autobiography*, 451–52.

170 **William Roscoe Thayer**   See his account of this evening in Thayer, *TR*, 351–55.

170 **Dante's phrase**   *"Vidi e conobbi l'ombra di colui / Che fece per viltade il gran rifiuto"* (I saw and recognized the shade of him / Who through cowardice made the great refusal), Dante, *The Inferno*, canto 3, line 60. In TR's time, this was believed to refer to Pietro da Morrone, later Pope Celestine V.

171 **feeling saddened**   Thayer, *TR*, 354.

CHAPTER 9: THE TALL TIMBER OF DARKENING EVENTS

172 **Epigraph**   Robinson, *Collected Poems*, 62.

172 **The contrary forces**   Alexander Lambert address to the Roosevelt Memorial Association, 20 Sept. 1923, transcript in HP; *Boston Globe*, 29 Feb. 1912. See also Dr. Lambert's account in TR, *Works*, 3.xix. Either he or TR misidentified Hallowell as "General."

172 **"I am alone"**   Quoted in TR, *Works*, 3.xix. Notwithstanding his assertion to Robert Grant that he felt "as fine as silk," TR was evidently under considerable stress during his Boston visit. Twice, he turned and snapped at reporters and photographers badgering him. (*Boston Globe*, 29 Feb. 1912.) This was in such contrast to his normal bonhomie as to suggest deep doubt about the course he had chosen.

172 **In a cultural essay**   TR, "Productive Scholarship," *The Outlook*, 13 Jan. 1912, reprinted in TR, *Works*, 14.340–48. TR was proud of this essay, and sent a copy to Edith Wharton. The novelist had visited Sagamore Hill in the fall of 1911 and been charmed. "The house was like one big library, and the whole tranquil place breathed of the love of books and of the country. . . . I felt immediately at home there." TR to Edith Wharton, 5 Jan. 1912, EW; Edith Wharton, *A Backward Glance* (New York, 1933, 1985), 316–17.

172 **"We made"**   White, *Autobiography*, 458.

173 **"Gentlemen, the first"**   Ibid., 453.

173 **Bourne had been**   "I am keenly aware," TR wrote Henry L. Stimson on 2 Feb. 1912, "that there are not a few among the men who claim to be leaders in the progressive movement who bear an unpleasant resemblance to the lamented Robespierre and his fellow progressives of 1791 and '92." TR, *Letters*, 7.494.

173 **"I move that"**   White, *Autobiography*, 453.

173 **"This rebellion"**   Ibid., 452.

174 **"He aims"** James H. Morse diary, 29–30 Mar., 27 Apr. 1912 (JHMD); Elihu Root quoted in Adams, *Letters*, 6.515.

174 **"I never thought"** Lodge, *Selections*, 2.423–24; Putnam, *TR*, chap. 25. As senior senator from the Bay State, Henry Cabot Lodge had been embarrassed by TR's aggressive defense of judicial recall, in a speech before the Massachusetts legislature on 26 February: "All I ask is that the people themselves . . . shall be given a chance to declare whether they will stand by the Supreme Court of the nation when it stands for human rights, or by the chief court of their own state when it stands against human rights. If that be revolution, make the most of it." *Boston Globe*, 27 Feb. 1912.

174 **I am opposed** Ibid., 2.423.

174 **"My dear fellow"** TR, *Letters*, 7.515.

174 **"He will either"** Butt, *Taft and Roosevelt*, 846–47.

174 **Butt listened** Ibid., 844.

174 **"If the old"** Ibid., 848.

174 **By early March,** *The New York Times*, 27 Feb., 2 Mar. 1912.

175 **a $50,000 startup budget** See Stoddard, *As I Knew Them*, 399.

176 **Roosevelt, in contrast** *The Washington Post*, 1 Mar. 1912. It must be understood that opinion polls, in 1912, were local rather than national. They were conducted mainly by newspapers soliciting readers.

176 **"You understand"** TR, *Letters*, 7.506.

176 **One day he allowed** The following paragraphs derive from the account, dated 2 Mar. 1912, in Baker, notebook N, 16 (RSB).

177 **men like Ward and Flinn** Flinn, like many of Roosevelt Republican insiders in 1912, was less interested in "social and industrial justice" than in self-advancement.

178 **charms of Ormsby McHarg** Mowry, *TR*, 200, 238. TR was not initially aware that McHarg, an energetic turncoat who had worked for and against him in the past, had gone south in his aid. But he heard enough about McHarg's methods to send him a "posterity letter" on 4 Mar. 1912, stating that he would appreciate "your personal assurance that you never endeavored by promises of patronage or by use of money . . . to try to influence any man to support me." (TR, *Letters*, 7.516.) McHarg was glad to supply the assurance, and glad to continue supplying delegates.

178 **seven Harvard men** TR, *Letters*, 7.517.

178 **It followed that** *The New York Times*, 21 Mar. 1912; Mowry, *TR*, 230–32.

178 **a progressive enthusiast** Mowry, *TR*, 232.

179 **On 19 March,** Morris, *The Rise of TR*, 200; *The New York Times*, 20 Mar. 1912; TR, *Letters*, 7.525; Stoddard, *As I Knew Them*, 402. The truth, as so often in the grassroots squabbles of 1912, was almost comically petty, with overtones of the great battle of Tweedledum and Tweedledee. TR was in fact the preference of conservatives in the North Dakota GOP, if only because their leader, whose name was Hanna, was opposed to a progressive rival, whose name was Gronna. After Hanna and Gronna, egged on by La Follette, had flailed each other to exhaustion, the forces of reform prevailed. See Mowry, *TR*, 231.

179 **"The prairies"** Bourne, *British Documents*, pt. 1, ser. C, 15.81.

179 **"I tend to get"** TR, *Letters*, 7.526–29, 532.

179 **A childhood friend** Frances Theodora Parsons, *Perchance Some Day* (privately printed, 1951), 238. For the teenage relationship of Fanny Parsons and TR, see Morris, *The Rise of TR*, 50–52.

179 **Carnegie Hall was crammed** *The New York Times*, 21 Mar. 1912; TR, *Letters*, 7.529.

180 **"It will be"** *The New York Times*, 21 Mar. 1912.

180 **"The courts should"** Ibid.; TR, *Works*, 19.206–8. William Draper Lewis of the University of Pennsylvania Law School suggested in a scholarly article that TR was clearly talking about judicial *opinions* on the constitutionality of acts, rather than *decisions* on practical points of law. (Stagner, "The Recall of Judicial Decisions.") See also William Draper Lewis, *The Life of Theodore Roosevelt* (Philadelphia, 1919), 340–42.

180 **sheet after sheet** *The New York Times*, 21 Mar. 1912.

180 **The leader for** TR, *Works*, 19.222–23. See also Abbott, *Impressions of TR*, 80–83, and for an affecting account of how this speech was written, Lewis, *TR*, 444–46. The latter source makes plain that Corinne Roosevelt Robinson erred in assuming that TR improvised his peroration. (*My Brother TR*, 267.) It was in fact carefully written out in pencil on "several soiled sheets of gray tissue manuscript," which TR kept separate from the text he intended to give out to the press. Evidently he did not want to blunt the drama of *viva voce* delivery of one of his most eloquent utterances.

180 **"Roosevelt, confound him"** Abbott, *Impressions of TR*, 82–83. The political oratory of TR and WW in 1912 has been collected in two complementary anthologies: Lewis L. Gould, ed., *Bull Moose on the Stump: The 1912 Campaign Speeches of Theodore Roosevelt* (Lawrence, Kan., 2008) and John W. Davidson, ed., *A Crossroads of Freedom: The 1912 Campaign Speeches of Woodrow Wilson* (New Haven, Conn., 1956).

> *Historiographical Note:* Since few stenographic records of what TR actually said on the campaign trail in 1912 are available in TRC or TRP, Gould's anthology relies much on contemporary newspaper reports. So does this biography. Journalistic transcripts, however, often vary considerably one from another. They may simply reproduce TR's own typed speech scripts, handed out in the form of press releases (but he was inclined to reshuffle or even toss aside such scripts on the podium, talking off the cuff when the mood struck him). Throughout his public career, he could be cavalier, even with the scripts of his major addresses printed as urtext in TR, *Works*. The improvisational humor he used to temper his seriousness can only be imagined—along with the radiance of the personality that infused these frequently dull texts with life. For a rare example of TR interacting with his audience, see Gould, *Bull Moose*, 18–30.

180 **Republicans amenable** *The New York Times*, 27 Mar. 1912.

180 **It turned out that** Ibid., 27, 28 Mar. 1912.

181 **The net results** Ibid., 27, 31 Mar. 1912.

181 **He received the news** TR took a three-day swing to Portland, Maine, after his Carnegie Hall speech, then campaigned in the Midwest from 26 to 30 Mar.

181 **"They are stealing"** *The New York Times*, 28 Mar. 1912; Pringle, *Taft*, 771.

181 **Roosevelt roared** *Chicago Tribune* and *The New York Times*, 28 Mar. 1912.

181 **He was back** On 2 Apr., Republicans in Wisconsin, a progressive primary state that TR had ceded to its favorite son, awarded 133,354 votes to La Follette and 47,514 to Taft. TR netted 628.

181 **At the top** Owen Wister, who had not seen TR for several years, briefly traveled with him during this campaign swing. "The energy, the action, the hammered words, the blaze of genial, jocund power, the prompt and marvelous application of some special sentence to some special place—I can call it nothing but gigantic." Wister, *Roosevelt*, 307.

182 **a major address** In this uncompromising speech, TR castigated the august

Joseph Choate and other Wall Street lawyers who had united in opposition to the referendum and recall, and compared their conservatism to that of New Yorkers defending the Dred Scott decision of 1857. See TR, "The Recall of Judicial Decisions" in TR, *Works,* 19.255ff., and, for a rare expression of contemporary legal support, Peter S. Grosscup, "Recall of Judicial Decisions Approved," *Ohio Law Bulletin,* 22 Apr. 1912.

182 **"No one can explain"** Adams, *Letters,* 6.532. Under intense pressure from TR and Medill McCormick's *Chicago Tribune,* Governor Charles Deneen had followed the example of Governor Hughes of New York in 1910, and called a special session of the Illinois legislature to authorize a direct, preferential presidential primary. It did so on 30 Mar., undeterred by William B. McKinley's ban on "changes in the rules of the game while the game is in progress." Other legislatures were encouraged to move just as fast, and do the same. Matthew James Glover, "Theodore Roosevelt Wins Illinois' First Presidential Primary," unpublished ms. (AC).

182 **"The *Titanic* is wrecked"** Adams, *Letters,* 6.534. For the next few days Adams obsessedly drew comparisons between the great shipwreck and the blow that TR, iceberg-like, had inflicted on the GOP. The former called into question the efficiency of modern mechanics; the latter, the smooth workings of the American political system. "We are drifting at sea in the ice, and can't get ashore. . . . Our Theodore is not a bird of happy omen. He loves to destroy." Adams, *Letters,* 6.534–38.

182 **The President, nearly frantic** *The New York Times,* 16 Apr. 1912.

182 **"Major Butt was"** Ibid., 20 Apr. 1912. According to local survivors, Butt had handled the catastrophe as if on army duty, controlling crowd hysteria and helping women and children aboard lifeboats. Marie Young, who had taught music to Archie and Quentin Roosevelt in the White House, was reportedly the last woman to catch a glimpse of him, waving to her from an upper deck as her boat pulled away. (Ibid.) Walter Lord, in *A Night to Remember* (1955), doubts the legend of Butt's heroism on the ground that the accounts of it by Ms. Young and another Washington woman sound over-embellished. As quoted in the *Times,* they certainly sound so. But the two women nevertheless corroborated each other, and the behavior they describe is consistent with the punctilio and physical forcefulness self-evident in Butt's three volumes of correspondence. A memorial fountain to him and his traveling companion, the Washington artist Frank Millett, survives on the Ellipse south of the White House.

182 **"Theodosus the Great"** Alice Hooper to Frederick Jackson Turner in Turner, *Dear Lady,* 123.

182 **I am the will** See Lorant, *Life and Times of TR,* 560–61 and 571.

183 **They did what they could** TR, *Letters,* 7.542–43; *The New York Times,* 21 May 1912.

183 **"Since I have been"** TR, *Letters,* 7.507–8.

183 **"I think Taft"** Ibid., 7.537.

183 **"I am in"** Thompson, *Presidents I've Known,* 220. The following account is based on reports in the *Boston Globe* and *The New York Times,* 26 Apr. 1912. All quotations are taken from the former source.

184 **Moreover, Taft was** Mowry, *TR,* 226–27.

184 **Mr. Roosevelt ought not** *Boston Globe,* 26 Apr. 1912.

185 **After returning** Pringle, *Taft,* 781–82. *The New York Times,* annoyed that Taft should stoop to the level of a personal attack, called his Boston appearance "one of the most deplorable occasions in the history of our politics." Sullivan, *Our Times,* 4.482.

185 **a momentary shiver** The image of the shiver comes from the *Boston Globe*'s re-

port of this meeting (27 Apr. 1912), as do the words of TR's speech quoted here. See also Sullivan, *Our Times,* 4.482–85.

185 **Roosevelt said that** TR's criticism was well founded. One of WHT's self-quotations was to the effect that reciprocity would make Canada "only an adjunct of the United States." These words caused an explosion of outrage both in Canada and Britain, where on 4 May the *Pall Mall Gazette* remarked that the President's "blazing indiscretion" might cause embarrassed Americans "to turn to Roosevelt after all for political sobriety."

185 **Later he spoke** *The New York Times,* 28 Apr. 1912.

186 **"Now you have me"** Ibid.

186 **"He is essentially"** Harbaugh, *TR,* 402.

186 **"VOTE OF BAY STATE"** *The New York Times,* 27, 30 Apr., 2 May 1912. In TR's own wry summing-up of the vote, "Apparently there were about eighty thousand people who preferred Taft, about eighty thousand who preferred me, and from three to five thousand who, in an involved way, thought they would vote for both Taft and me." TR, *Letters,* 7.539–40.

186 **"In this fight"** *The New York Times,* 2 May 1912; TR, *Letters,* 7.539–40.

186 **By early May** *The New York Times,* 4 May 1912.

187 **Over the next week** The Michigan state convention in April managed to elect two delegations simultaneously from the same platform, after reaching such a pitch of violence that Governor Osborn was compelled to deploy the state militia against Taft goons supplied by the sugar beet industry. Louise Overacker, *The Presidential Primary* (New York, 1926, 1974), 205.

187 **"If I am defeated"** Pringle, *Taft,* 757.

187 **"I am a man"** *The New York Times,* 5 May 1912. In another speech, WHT compared himself to "a man of straw."

187 **Their vocabulary** *The Washington Post,* 15 May 1912.

187 **"honeyfugler"** A now extinct word, meaning one who seduces or cheats by sweet talk.

187 **their Pullmans parked** *The New York Times,* 15 May 1912.

187 **"the hypocrisy, the insincerity"** Pringle, *Taft,* 787.

188 **a compromise candidate** The first politician to suggest Hughes was William Barnes, Jr., citing the "grave" condition of the Republican Party. Barnes bitterly blamed progressivism for the plague of preferential primaries spreading across the nation. "This so-called reform has done more to confuse and corrupt legislators than anything in politics for fifty years." *The New York Times,* 17 May 1912.

188 **"I will name"** *The New York Times,* 21 May 1912. The satirical magazine *Life* remarked, "The popular demand for Colonel Roosevelt is steadily increasing, but however great the demand may become, it can never be as great as the supply." Sullivan, *Our Times,* 4.491.

188 **"TRnadoes"** Alice Hooper to Frederick Jackson Turner in Turner, *Dear Lady,* 123. For a documentary account of how hard TR worked (and was worked) on the campaign trail, see William H. Richardson, *Theodore Roosevelt: One Day of His Life* (Jersey City, 1921). The day in question was 23 May 1912.

188 **"Your judgment"** Link, *Papers of Woodrow Wilson,* 24.446.

188 **more popular votes** The precise size of this vote is difficult to calculate, because authorities are divided on how many, and which, states contributed to it. Mowry, e.g., cites "thirteen," without naming them, and gives the candidate totals as TR, 1,157,397; WHT, 761,716; and La Follette, 351,043. Bishop lists 13 states, including Georgia but not New York. Lewis L. Gould lists 12 states, excluding both Georgia and New York. His resultant figures are TR, 1,164,765; WHT, 768,202; and La Follette 327,357. (Mowry, *TR,* 236; Bishop, *TR,* 2.322; Lewis M. Gould,

ed., *Four Hats in the Ring: The 1912 Election and the Birth of Modern American Politics* [Lawrence, Kan., 2008], appendix B.) In a letter to the author (1 Aug. 2008), Gould disqualifies New York as a primary state in 1912 because of heavy-handed manipulation of the vote by Boss Barnes, and because delegates were elected locally rather than apportioned on the basis of a statewide vote, which mysteriously was never recorded. But these criteria might also disqualify, say, Boss Flinn's Pennsylvania or Boss Walter F. Brown's Ohio, or Washington State, whose mix of local primaries and district mini-conventions became a vexed issue at the national convention. New York's election, which netted WHT 83 delegates to TR's 7, was widely referred to as a "primary" at the time, despite the lack of a statewide total. See Overacker, *The Presidential Primary,* 13, 135. On 4 June 1912, *The New York Times* did at least compute the popular vote in New York County at 33,492 for WHT and 16,933 for TR, or a 2-for-1 majority for the President. If the total GOP state vote in 1912 was about the same as it was in 1916, i.e., 147,038, and if WHT and TR divided it much as they did the New York County vote, we may estimate their respective primary vote shares at 97,633 and 49,404. These figures, added to Gould's for the other twelve primary states, project the grand totals given here. Whichever set is preferred, TR's absolute popular majority among GOP voters is clear. See below, 638–39.

CHAPTER 10: ARMAGEDDON

189 **Epigraph** Robinson, *Collected Poems,* 66.

189 **a baby parade** *The New York Times,* 30 May 1912.

189 **Next morning** Heaton, *The Story of a Page,* 343.

189 **A further similarity** TR was about 20 percent behind WHT in delegates in the first week of June, and Wilson about 37 percent behind Clark.

191 **his own claimants** Gould, *Four Hats in the Ring,* 67. The *Atlanta Constitution,* 18 June 1912, cited affidavits by three Taft members of the Georgia delegation stating that they had been offered cash bribes of up to $400 apiece to switch their votes to TR. McHarg does not appear to have been directly involved.

191 **Still, he had** Bishop, *TR,* 2.322–23; *The New York Times,* 9 June 1912.

191 **chairman of the convention** Technically in 1912, *temporary chairman.* See above, 612.

191 **"Elihu," Roosevelt** TR quoted by Finley Peter Dunne in *The American Magazine,* 24 Sept. 1912.

191 **On 3 June** TR, *Letters,* 7.555.

191 EXCEPTION OF A VERY FEW Barnes was alluding to New York's imbalance of 7 delegates for TR and 83 for Taft. The phrase *temporary chairman* in this telegram has been shortened to *chairman,* for reasons explained above (612).

192 **"Root," he complained** Mowry, *TR,* 242; TR, *Letters,* 7.548–49, 555.

192 **Unfortunately, most** Gould, *Four Hats in the Ring,* 66. Owen Wister describes delegates to the Republican convention in 1912 as coins pre-stamped with image and value. Notwithstanding their marks, the coins did not achieve currency until they had passed through a machine carefully calibrated by the National Committee. "A coin might be full weight, but if it were stamped with Roosevelt's image, it might be rejected in favor of a short weight coin bearing Taft's image." Wister, *Roosevelt,* 310.

192 **not a professional** Rosewater (1871–1940), editor of the *Omaha Bee,* is generally portrayed as a conservative, but he had been comfortable with some of the reforms of TR's second administration. In June 1912, Rosewater was acting chairman of the RNC, substituting for Harry S. New. He left a record of his convention experi-

ences in a memoir, *Back Stage in 1912: The Inside Story of the Split Republican Convention* (Philadelphia, 1932).

193 **The rest of the Committee** Gould, *Four Hats in the Ring,* 66–67. At the beginning of June, TR's forces in Chicago launched an attempt to stack the committee by having at least five newly elected members take seats at the hearings at once, rather than waiting for the convention to authorize them. Among these were William Allen White of Kansas and R. D. Howell of Nebraska, who had displaced Rosewater as a delegate and now hoped to displace him as acting chairman. (*The New York Times,* 3 June 1912.) But since current members of the committee were entitled to keep serving until 18 June, the Roosevelt *putsch* never went anywhere.

193 **"theft, cold-blooded"** *The New York Times,* 8 June 1912.

193 **For a while** Davis, *Released for Publication,* 292; Nicholas Roosevelt, *TR,* 86.

193 **"If circumstances demand"** Sullivan, *Our Times,* 4.497. The version of this quote given in Pringle, *Taft,* 796, comes with acquired dental effects.

193 **proceeded to throw out** For accounts of the hearings disputing TR's accusations of delegate-stealing, see Rosewater, *Back Stage in 1912,* 80–120, and Pringle, *Taft,* 799ff.

193 **Perhaps thirty** Lewis Gould states that TR, on the basis of a modern impartial analysis, deserved "another twelve or fourteen" delegates from Texas, plus "probably . . . another twenty or so" from other states. With his 19 awardees, that would have given him an extra complement of 53, still far short of the number he needed to clinch the nomination. Earlier authorities, notably John Allen Gable in 1965, George E. Mowry in 1946, and Senator Borah, Governor Hadley, and Gilbert E. Roe (a La Follette supporter) back in 1912, differ in their assessments of TR's chances of winning the nomination, but all agree that he was entitled to about 50 more delegates. See Gould, *Four Hats in the Ring,* 67, and Gable, "The Bull Moose Years" [diss.], 39.

193 **An impartial observer** This sentence quotes De Witt, *The Progressive Movement,* 82. See also Mowry, *TR,* 239–40; Gould, *Four Hats in the Ring,* 67. The former notes that TR, arranging the nomination of WHT in 1908, used many of the strong-arm tactics he accused the White House of using in 1912.

193 **All the same, Roosevelt** The clearest analysis of the bias of the Republican National Committee in 1912 remains that in Bishop, *TR,* 2.324–26.

Historiographical Note: The exact number of delegates won in primary elections by TR and WHT in 1912 has been the subject of much dispute among historians and biographers. (See above, 637, for the similar elusiveness of the total primary vote.) Mowry, e.g., allows WHT only 48 delegates, whereas Bishop gives him 68, and Sullivan and Pringle 71. There is even disagreement on how many primaries were held. In their general tendency to emphasize TR's popularity among rank-and-file GOP voters, these historians mystifyingly exclude New York. Technically, it is true that the Barnes machine exerted an undue influence on the voting in that state, but the canvass held on 26 March was very definitely a primary, and treated as such by all participants.

The 83 delegates pledged to WHT from New York, plus the 7 pledged to TR, should be therefore included in the overall tally, making the President's unpopularity less marked, while a recalculation of TR's performance hardly affects the decisiveness of the outcome. The following table, compiled in calendar order, includes delegates-at-large who remained loyal to their candidate despite contrary instructions (as in Massachusetts) or who were added on by state conventions (as in Ohio). It does not, however, include 28 Taft delegates from the primary in Georgia, a state where the GOP was effectively disenfranchised.

STATE	TAFT	TR
North Dakota	o	o
(La Follette)		
New York	83	7
Wisconsin	o	o
(La Follette)		
Illinois	2	56
Pennsylvania	9	65
Nebraska	o	16
Oregon	o	10
Massachusetts	18	26
Maryland	o	16
California	o	26
Ohio	14	34
New Jersey	o	28
South Dakota	o	10
TOTALS	126	294

When these numbers are subtracted from the aggregates brought by each candidate to the convention, it will be seen that the real conflict in the spring of 1912 was not between WHT and TR, but between two delegate-producing systems: the modern primary one, confined to northern states tolerant of progressivism, and the old caucus-convention method, supreme in the South and other regions where authority mattered more than popularity. If the primary states had not so suddenly doubled in number, they would have posed less of a challenge to what Taft called "the principles of the party . . . the retention of conservative government and conservative institutions." (Gable, "The Bull Moose Years" [diss.], 40.) They gave TR a more than two-to-one advantage, whereas a reverse imbalance in favor of the President applied in the other 35 states, contributing to his overall majority. Until one or other of the systems won out (TR himself was not persuaded that the primary should be adopted everywhere), it would always be foolhardy for a popular candidate to take on a party-sanctioned one.

194 **"The Taft leaders"** *The New York Times,* 9 June 1912.
194 **There was nothing** For TR's post-campaign sabbatical at Oyster Bay, see Sullivan, *Our Times,* 4.496–504.
194 **"confusion and comparative"** *The New York Times,* 16 June 1912.
194 **He found Roosevelt** Nicholas Roosevelt, "Account of the Republican National Convention at Chicago, June 12, 1912, compiled from notes taken on the spot," bound vol., 1 (TRC). See also Nicholas Roosevelt, *TR,* 86ff.
194 **"Well, Nick"** Nicholas Roosevelt, "Account of the RNC," 1.
194 **The New York party** Harper, a stenographer dispatched by *The Outlook* to assist TR on his tour of Europe in 1910, had stayed with him ever since. The following account of TR's journey to Chicago is based on Nicholas Roosevelt, "Account of the RNC." Extra details from *The New York Times* and *Syracuse Herald,* 15, 16 June 1912, and Sullivan, *Our Times,* 4.505–6.
195 **"the great effort"** Nicholas Roosevelt, "Account of the RNC," 1, 20.
195 **In mid-afternoon** John C. O'Laughlin, "Diary of the National Republican Convention," 14–15 June 1912 (OL). It had been O'Laughlin who first conceived the idea of TR making a dramatic pilgrimage to the Chicago convention. (O'Laugh-

lin to TR, 7 June 1912 [OL].) Mowry, *TR*, 244–45 cites the Taft campaign's nervousness about the fickle loyalty of 66 Negro delegates, whom Roosevelt agents in Chicago were courting "by one means or another."

195 **a new, tan campaign hat**   Sullivan, *Our Times*, 4.505–6 and 510 (illustration).

195 **People packed**   Nicholas Roosevelt, "Account of the RNC," 7.

196 **"Chicago is"**   *Syracuse Herald* and *The New York Times*, 16 June 1912.

196 **"It is a fight"**   *The New York Times*, 16 June 1912. Meanwhile, Chicago bookies were betting 2 to 1 that TR would not be nominated. Decatur *Sunday Review*, 16 June 1912.

196 **The crowd in**   Nicholas Roosevelt, "Account of the RNC," 12, 16; *The New York Times*, 16, 17 June 1912.

196 **The fervor of**   William Jennings Bryan, *A Tale of Two Conventions* (New York, 1912), 10; White, *Autobiography*, 464; Nicholas Roosevelt, "Account of the RNC," 20; *The New York Times*, 17–18 June 1912.

197 **cries of "Shame"**   *The New York Times*, 18 June 1912. The following extracts from TR's Auditorium address, entitled "The Case Against the Reactionaries," are taken from TR, *Works*, 19.285–317.

197 **William Jennings Bryan**   "The Arabs are said to have seven hundred words which mean *camel*," Bryan wrote in his report of the speech. "Mr. Roosevelt has nearly as many synonyms for *theft*, and he used them all tonight." Bryan, *A Tale of Two Conventions*, 16.

198 **"I am never surprised"**   O'Laughlin, "Diary of the National Republican Convention," 17 June 1912 (OL).

198 **the fanaticism of his followers**   "I can liken it only to a belief in God," one Taft delegate recalled. "They thought Roosevelt was infallible—I have never known such intensity of feeling before or since." (Ezra P. Prentice interviewed by Mary Hagedorn, 28 June 1955 [TRB].) William Allen White wrote that he was "thrilled to my heart" by the speech, yet at the same time, "I was disturbed, I suppose a little frightened, at the churning which he gave to the crowd." *Autobiography*, 464–45.

198 *At Three o'Clock*   Sullivan, *Our Times*, 4.511. Sullivan was unsure whether this flyer was circulated during the GOP or Progressive Party conventions of June and August, 1912, respectively. But two accounts by participants confirm the earlier date. Prentice interview, op. cit.; Henry J. Allen in Wood, *Roosevelt As We Knew Him*, 273.

199 **"I am for Teddy"**   Marshall Stimson, "Colonel Roosevelt and the Presidential campaign of 1912," n.d., memorandum in TRB.

199 **By the time**   Except where otherwise indicated, the following account is based on the reportage of *The New York Times, Syracuse Herald, Emporia Gazette,* and *Atlanta Constitution,* 18–23 June 1912, and *Official Report of the Proceedings of the National Republican Convention* (1912, Internet Archive [http://www.archive.org/]), hereafter *Proceedings of the 15th RNC*. Mark Sullivan's account reproduces some brilliant sketches of the conventioneers in action. Sullivan, *Our Times*, 4.512–30.

199 **"the mere monstrous embodiment"**   Morris, *The Rise of TR*, 481. For discussion of the relationship between James and TR, see Philip Horne, "Henry James and 'the Forces of Violence': On the Track of 'Big Game' in 'The Jolly Corner,'" *The Henry James Review*, 27 (2006).

199 **The bands that had**   White, *Autobiography*, 463. According to Gould, *Four Hats in the Ring*, 70, the Roosevelt campaign spent $10,000 on bands during the course of the convention.

199 **Victor Rosewater's gavel**   Since the convention had not yet elected its chairman, Rosewater presided over its initial business in his capacity as acting chairman of the Republican National Committee. See Rosewater, *Back Stage in 1912*, 160–64.

199 **But first** *Emporia Gazette*, 18 June, *The New York Times*, 19 June 1912.

199 **Contrary to rumors** Nicholas Roosevelt, "Account of the RNC," 24; Lewis, *TR*, 441.

199 **Hadley, a calm** Harlan Hahn, "The Republican National Convention of 1912 and the Role of Herbert S. Hadley in National Politics," *Missouri Historical Review*, 59.4 (1965).

200 **"Mr. Chairman," he said** *Proceedings of the 15th RNC*, 32. Except where otherwise indicated, all convention quotations are taken from this source.

200 **William Barnes, Jr.** *The New York Times*, 20 June 1912; *Proceedings of the 15th RNC*, 32.

200 **Hadley said** For the negotiations that permitted Hadley to make his move, see Rosewater, *Back Stage in 1912*, 153–59.

200 **The latest** *New York Times* **estimate** 16 June 1912.

201 **"Elihu Root is the ablest"** *Proceedings of the 15th RNC*, 43. TR's original tribute, abbreviated by Hedges, was even more fulsome: "He is the greatest man who has appeared in the public life of any country in any position, on either side of the ocean in my time." Quoted by Walter Wellman in *American Review of Reviews*, Jan. 1904. For another cadenza of superlatives about Root, written when TR was on the Nile in 1910, see TR, *Letters*, 7.48.

201 **"Cousin Theodore"** Nicholas Roosevelt, "Account of the RNC," 26.

201 **for the first time** Gould, *Four Hats in the Ring*, 72.

201 **rows of emptying benches** *Atlanta Constitution*, 19 June 1912.

202 **Hadley, elegant in** White, *Autobiography*, 471; *Proceedings of the 15th RNC*, 108.

202 **"Are you going to abide"** *The New York Times*, 20 June 1912.

202 **"I will support"** Ibid.

202 **Instantly every Roosevelt delegate** Nicholas Roosevelt, "Account of the RNC," 26, 40–41. For a verbal portrait of Root as chairman, see White, *Autobiography*, 470–71.

203 **The demonstration was** *The New York Times*, 20 June 1912. See also Sullivan, *Our Times*, 4.528–30, and Bryan, *A Tale of Two Conventions*, 45–47, 55–56.

204 **"That question is not"** *Proceedings of the 15th RNC*, 144–46.

204 **"No man can be"** Ibid., 160. "In other words," Owen Wister wrote, "the counterfeit Taft coins were allowed to decide that they were genuine, and the genuine Roosevelt coins were counterfeit." Wister, *Roosevelt*, 312.

205 **That night the woman** *Lowell* (Mass.) *Sun*, 20 June 1912. Suspicions among Taft leaders that the demonstration was not entirely spontaneous were confirmed when it transpired that Mrs. Davis had tried out her portrait-waving stunt two nights earlier, jumping onto a table in the Congress Hotel and stimulating great enthusiasm among Roosevelt supporters. Later in the week she was seen visiting with Alice Roosevelt Longworth. *The New York Times*, 22 June 1912.

205 **But throughout the day** Nicholas Roosevelt, "Account of the RNC," 31–33; W. Franklin Knox in Wood, *Roosevelt As We Knew Him*, 267–79; Travers Carman in Abbott, *Impressions of TR*, 84–85; Davis, *Released for Publication*, 302–10; Gould, *Four Hats in the Ring*, 72–73; TR, *Letters*, 7.570. According to Carman, an eyewitness, the representative of 38 Southern delegates offered him all their nominating votes if he would agree to an organization-controlled platform. These votes, added to the most recent assessment of TR's core strength, would assure him of victory. Two aides urged him to accept. He put his hands on their shoulders and said, "I have grown to regard you both as brothers. Let no act or word of yours make that relationship impossible." This is, however, but one of many conflicting stories in the above sources as to what transpired between TR and Hadley (who came to see him with a group of supporters seek-

ing permission to make the governor a compromise candidate), and between TR and other negotiants whose names he chose not to reveal. After the convention, Hadley said that TR was promised "Washington and Texas" for cooperating with the Taft forces; Knox said TR wanted "at least four states" as his price; and TR himself stated that he was offered "Washington (not California or Texas)," but insisted on all or nothing. The truth is probably impossible to ascertain. But as Mowry remarks, "The facts clearly indicate that the Colonel would have tolerated no nomination but his own." (Mowry, *TR*, 251–52.) See also Rosewater, *Back Stage in 1912*, 180–81.

205 **"receiver of stolen goods"** This phrase, commonly attributed to TR, was first hurled at Root by William Flinn, in the aftermath of the chairmanship vote. *Proceedings of the 15th RNC*, 88.

205 **unconvicted felons** The epithet was TR's. He was still applying it to Root in 1916. Thompson, *Presidents I've Known*, 204, 209.

205 **He knew what venality** See TR's subsequent essay, "Thou Shalt Not Steal," in TR, *Works*, 19.318ff. For an analysis of the rage that gripped TR in Chicago, by a friend who was worried by it, see White, *Autobiography*, 464. "Ambition, I am satisfied, was not the governing passion."

205 **"I never saw"** Stoddard, *As I Knew Them*, 305. Stoddard was active in the campaign and conferred frequently with TR and the Executive Committee.

206 **"Theodore, remember"** Sylvia Morris, *Edith Kermit Roosevelt*, 381.

206 **The last of his visitors** [Clinton W. Gilbert], *The Mirrors of Washington: With Fourteen Cartoons by Cesare* (New York, 1922), 250. See also Claudius O. Johnson, *Borah of Idaho* (New York, 1936), 137–40. Borah at this time was under pressure from William Barnes, Jr., to run for vice president with Charles Evans Hughes, should the latter emerge as a compromise candidate. Ibid., 139.

206 **Their cheers and oratory** Stoddard, *As I Knew Them*, 305. Possibly TR heard William Flinn bellowing from a tabletop: "I am going to follow Theodore Roosevelt, the greatest leader of men of this day, and we are going to carry Pennsylvania for him." *The New York Times*, 20 June 1912.

206 **"My fortune"** Stoddard, *As I Knew Them*, 306. See also Amos Pinchot, *History of the Progressive Party, 1912–1916* (New York, 1958), 164–65. Some authorities, notably Gable, "The Bull Moose Years" (diss.), 43–44, believe that this incident took place the following evening, Thursday 20 June. The sequence of events, however, suggests Wednesday evening—or more precisely, the small hours of Thursday morning.

206 **"You see"** [Gilbert], *The Mirrors of Washington*, 250. According to another insider account, the final straw that broke TR's back was the news that the GOP Credentials Committee had voted to severely reduce the time its protesting members needed to present their cases. George Henry Payne, *The Birth of the New Party, or, Progressive Democracy* (New York, 1912), 25–26.

206 **When he arrived** The committee bolt, reportedly ordered by TR, occurred at 11:45 P.M. *The New York Times*, 20 June 1912.

206 **"As far as I"** Pringle, *Taft*, 808–9.

206 **After he left** *The New York Times*, 20 June 1912; Nicholas Roosevelt, "Account of the RNC," 34–35.

207 **a period of uneasy calm** Bryan, *A Tale of Two Conventions*, 61.

207 **After that he was** *The New York Times*, 21 June 1912; Longworth, *Crowded Hours*, 200.

207 **It is no pleasant** Bryan, *A Tale of Two Conventions*, 64–65.

207 **This could not have been achieved** The "crisis" moment that Bryan had anticipated occurred when two Californian delegates for Taft were seated in defiance of that state's primary rules by a vote of 542 to 529. "Had this vote gone the other

way, there would unquestionably have been a general break for Roosevelt." Lewis, *TR*, 359, 363–64.

208 **"If you don't look out"** *The New York Times,* 22 June 1912.

208 **During the umpteenth** Ibid., 22 June 1912.

208 **The atmosphere on Saturday** Nicholas Roosevelt, "Account of the RNC," 41–43. Instead of "Amen" at the end of the opening prayer, one delegate called out, "Toot toot." During the course of the day, as Root tried to move things along, a delegate from Mississippi arose in mock complaint. "Mr. Chairman, I make the point of order that the steam roller is exceeding the speed limit." *Lowell* (Mass.) *Sun,* 22 June 1912.

208 **The Roosevelt family** *Lowell* (Mass.) *Sun, The New York Times,* 22 June 1912; Longworth, *Crowded Hours,* 202.

208 **She joined in** Nicholas Roosevelt, "Account of the RNC," 42; *The New York Times,* 22 June 1912. "They are all *white hot,*" ERD wrote that day to her friend Dorothy Straight. 22 June 1912 (ERDP).

208 **racked with tuberculosis** White, *Autobiography,* 470.

208 **But the pertinent** The full text of TR's message is in TR, *Letters,* 7.562–63.

209 **Sirs, I have heard** *Proceedings of the 15th RNC,* 378–79.

209 **a howl of rage** Lewis, *TR,* 361. It was this act, more than any other by Root, that caused TR to break from him, saying that the Massachusetts delegation had been "publicly raped," and contemptuously comparing the senator to Autolycus, Shakespeare's "snapper-up of unconsidered trifles." Nicholas Roosevelt, *Theodore Roosevelt,* 13.

209 **They headed** *The New York Times,* 22 June 1912.

210 **"Why weren't you"** White, *Autobiography,* 473. The original ts. of TR's speech to the bolting delegates is preserved in TRC. For a photograph of him presiding at the Orchestra Hall meeting, see Lorant, *Life and Times of TR,* 569.

210 **He felt as he had** White, *Autobiography,* 452, 473.

210 **The fight promised** Ibid., 474.

210 **"He was not downcast"** Ibid., 474–75.

210 **"I care more"** Philip C. Jessup, *Elihu Root,* 2 vols. (New York, 1938), 2.202. In 1919, still brooding, Root told Finley Peter Dunne that "it was on his [TR's] advice that I declared myself for Taft before he himself determined to throw his hat into the ring." Dunne, "Remembrances" (DUN).

CHAPTER 11: ONWARD, CHRISTIAN SOLDIERS

211 **Epigraph** Robinson, *Collected Poems,* 324.

211 **"My public career"** TR quoted in E. A. Van Valkenburg, "Roosevelt the Man," *Philadelphia North American,* 9 Jan. 1919. TR indicated on 10 July that he would have withdrawn from the race had WW been nominated before Taft. TR, *Letters,* 7.575.

211 **For about a week** "Pop is praying for the nomination of Champ Clark," KR told Franklin Roosevelt before the Democratic convention. A TR lieutenant, Francis J. Heney, was dispatched to Baltimore to negotiate a progressive defection in the event of a win by the conservative Clark. TR's mail during this period contained proposals that WW, or even William Jennings Bryan, be tapped to run with him on a third-party ticket. According to O. K. Davis, Bryan strongly hinted to TR and other GOP progressives in Chicago that he would lead a bolt of his own supporters from the Democratic Party if Clark was nominated in Baltimore. The two splinter movements would then unite under TR in a new, potentially irresistible Progressive Party. Arthur S. Link, *Wilson: The Road to the White House* (Princeton, N.J., 1947), 422; Davis, *Released for Publication,* 316–17.

211 **the Socialist Eugene V. Debs**   Gould, *Four Hats in the Ring,* compensates for the neglect historians and biographers have shown to Debs's candidacy in 1912. Although Debs, in his third presidential race, scored well over 900,000 votes (a record for the American Socialist Party), his 6 percent share of the national total hardly compared with those of the three major candidates.

211 **anti-Negro prejudice**   See McGerr, *A Fierce Discontent,* chap. 6.

212 **Word had gotten out**   TR, *Letters,* 7.561; Morris, *The Rise of TR,* 254–55. WW had little discernible race hatred, but felt that Southern blacks, having no educational or social qualifications for suffrage, compounded the evil of Reconstruction. In the fifth volume of his *History of the American People* (1900–1903), he imputed the rise of the "great" Ku Klux Klan to "the intolerable burden of governments sustained by the votes of ignorant negroes," and described its nocturnal vigilantism with obvious relish (58–60). See also his article, "The Reconstruction of the Southern States," *The Atlantic Monthly,* 87 (1901). As president of Princeton, WW opposed the admission of black students, and was not above joking about "coons." (Morris, *Theodore Rex,* 207.) For a sober analysis of the racial aspects of WW's campaign, see Link, *Wilson: The Road to the White House,* 501–5.

212 **Four of the seven governors**   *The New York Times,* 8 July 1912; TR, *Letters,* 7.569. Osborn eventually changed his mind about WW, and—too late—campaigned for TR. See Gable, *The Bull Moose Years,* 24–25.

212 **as the head**   Hadley to TR, 5 July 1912 (TRP). Hadley eventually supported WHT, not to Osborn's surprise. "Hadley is a politician." Osborn to TR, 5 July 1912 (TRP).

212 **As for veterans**   Mowry, *TR,* 256–57; Link, *Wilson: The Road to the White House,* 468; E. Daniel Potts, "Theodore Roosevelt and the Progressive Party, 1912–1916: A Re-Interpretation," *Pacific Circle: Proceedings of the Second Biennial Conference of the Australian and New Zealand American Studies Association* (St. Lucia, Queensland, 1968), 186.

212 **the nascent Progressive Party**   When the Party celebrated its first birthday in 1913, it chose to on 2 July, the anniversary of WW's nomination. According to Henry Stoddard, TR had to fight to prevent it being called the Progressive Republican Party. "He insisted that [would be] a hopeless name down South; with a party having some other title, he would gain thousands of votes there." Stoddard, *As I Knew Them,* 406.

212 **Had Wilson not**   TR, *Letters,* 7.598; Gable, *The Bull Moose Years,* 20–21.

212 **"She was quite radiant"**   E. A. Van Valkenburg, "Roosevelt the Man." Albert J. Beveridge wrote many years later that TR in 1912 was possessed of "a kind of exaltation," equally composed of fervor, unselfishness, and "an august dignity." TR, *Works,* 8.xxi.

> *Biographical Note:* In Wood, *Roosevelt As We Knew Him,* 252–53, the banker Otto Kahn gave this account of a conversation with TR in the winter of 1916:
>
> Q. What did induce you to make the run on the Progressive ticket?
> A. (*head shoving forward*) If a man does a thing which he discerns clearly to be against his interest, if he accepts the burden, strain and bitterness of a fight, at the end of which he sees discomfiture, defeat and lasting disability, if he leads a forlorn hope . . . how would you diagnose his motives?
> Q. It seems to me the answer is—
> A. (*interrupting*) The answer is that his motives disregard his personal interests, that he is actuated by a compelling sense of what his duty, his conscience and his station require him to do.

Potts, "Theodore Roosevelt and the Progressive Party," dissents from the received view that TR left the GOP in order to revenge himself on corporate conservatives and WHT in particular. He argues that TR's moral conscience always dictated his decisions in moments of crisis. When the Party was threatened with a similar split in 1884, for example, the young TR cited three moral reasons to stay *with* it: the cause (resentment against the nomination of James G. Blaine) was not overwhelming, the time was not right, and the effect of his leaving would not be demonstrably "proper." See Putnam, *TR*, chap. 25; Lewis, *TR*, 368–70; and TR, "How I Became a Progressive," TR, *Works*, 19.435–40.

213 **"weaving the inevitable"**   White, *Autobiography*, 468. On the eve of the convention, EKR told John C. O'Laughlin that "she did not want her husband nominated, [and] looked forward with dread to returning to the White House." O'Laughlin, "Diary of the National Republican Convention," 16 June 1912 (OL).

213 **other visitors as well**   e.g., Elizabeth Cameron in Adams, *Letters*, 6.550.

213 **The Roosevelt children**   According to the manager of the Progressive Party, TR held a family conference after WW's nomination and warned that the consequences of his proceeding with a third-party campaign would be dire. "Some of the finest minds in the country, some of the men I most admire and love are going to stop coming here." David Hinshaw, interviewed by Hermann Hagedorn, n.d. (TRB).

213 **To the puzzlement**   Morris, *Theodore Rex*, 400; Longworth, *Crowded Hours*, 228–29; Cordery, *Alice*, 221–22. Longworth's talent was recognized by no less an authority than the conductor Leopold Stokowski, who said that music was his "natural element." His fellow quartet players were all professionals. He was also an excellent pianist and dabbled in composition. Later in life he became president of the Washington Chamber Music Society.

213 **"first, last and always"**   This slogan was repeatedly chanted at the Chicago convention by supporters of TR.

213 **Representative Longworth's position**   Longworth, *Crowded Hours*, 192–94; Cordery, *Alice*, 223–28. In old age Alice told Michael Teague that she had briefly considered divorcing Nicholas Longworth in 1912, but was dissuaded by TR and EKR. Teague, *Mrs. L*, 158.

213 **Ted was an ardent**   Longworth, *Crowded Hours*, 197; Eleanor B. Roosevelt, *Day Before Yesterday*, 58–59.

214 **the Land of Beyond**   Robert W. Service's imagery had a powerful effect on thousands of young romantically inclined Americans in the early 20th century. Kermit Roosevelt, *The Happy Hunting Grounds* (New York, 1920) makes plain its author's lifelong wanderlust.

214 **He was due to sail**   KR left for Brazil on 27 July 1912.

214 **a thirtyish surgeon**   She had met him in Berlin in May 1909. KR to ERD, 19 May 1913 (ERDP).

214 **"How is my sweet"**   Butt, *Taft and Roosevelt*, 829. In a conversation with her piano teacher, ERD said of her shyness, "I wonder if it could be Papa I get it from? Can it be that he seems so terribly the opposite of shy because at heart he really is so?" Emma Knorr in Washington *Herald*, 27 July 1931.

214 **"Oh Dorothy"**   ERD to Dorothy Straight, ca. 22 June 1912 (ERDP).

214 **Archie had little patience**   ABR to QR, 12–27 Sept. 1917 (ABRP); TR to Cecil Spring Rice, 10 Aug. 1912 (CSR). Archie Roosevelt's personal characteristics of truculent terseness, intense focus (from a slightly obtuse angle) on one matter at a time, and unconcern about offending people, are consistent with a modern diagnosis of Asperger's syndrome.

214 "tranquil, efficient"   TR to ERD, 21 Aug. 1912 (ERDP).

215 "I'm feeling like"   Sullivan, *Our Times*, 4.506. There is some uncertainty as to when TR said this, but it was definitely part of the American political vernacular by the weekend of 22–23 June, when WHT received a telegram congratulating him on "having lassoed the bull moose." (*The New York Times*, 24 June 1912.) Before the end of the month the moose had traveled as far as Germany, where it was the subject of a mocking editorial in the *Berliner Tagblatt* (29 June 1912). TR described himself as feeling "as rugged as a bull moose" as early as 30 Sept. 1894, in a letter to Henry Cabot Lodge. TR, *Letters*, 1.399.

215 **Governor Osborn wrote**   Chase Osborn to TR, 1 July 1912 (TRP); TR, *Letters*, 7.569.

215 **"I suppose that"**   TR, *Letters*, 7.567–68.

215 **On 7 July**   *The New York Times*, 8 July 1912. For a detailed account of the pre-convention work of organizing the Progressive Party, see Gable, *The Bull Moose Years*, chap. 2.

217 **the Party's biggest bankroller**   Mowry, *TR*, 222. By the end of the 1912 campaign, however, Frank Munsey's contributions slightly exceeded Perkins's.

217 **"Roosevelt has the right"**   Frederick Jackson Turner in Turner, *Dear Lady*, 124.

217 **his palatial estate overlooking the Hudson**   Now Wave Hill, a public park in New York City. Coincidentally, but no doubt pleasingly to both men, TR had summered there as a boy.

217 **He had come**   John A. Garraty, *Right-Hand Man: The Life of George W. Perkins* (New York, 1960), *passim*. See also William J. Boies, "George W. Perkins," *World's Work*, Dec. 1901; White, *Autobiography*, 459–561, 519. In 1912, Perkins told Henry L. Stoddard that he had "all the money a man should possess" and intended to devote the rest of his life to "public affairs." Stoddard, *As I Knew Them*, 423.

217 **Exquisitely undertailored**   The phrase is William Allen White's. See White, *Autobiography*, 459–561, 519. Since at least the turn of the century, when they had worked together to create the Palisades Intersate Park, Roosevelt had held Perkins to be "one of the most delightful men I have ever met." TR, *Letters*, 3.53.

217 **White always a surname**   At least until 1917, when he became "W.A."

217 **To White, that sounded**   White, *Autobiography*, 459.

218 **One of the reasons**   Mowry, *TR*, 225; Hagedorn, *The Roosevelt Family*, 310; TR, *Letters*, 7.567. "I'd much rather discuss ornithology than politics," TR told a Columbia University professor in between platform discussions. (Wood, *Roosevelt As We Knew Him*, 263.) For a detailed account of these discussions, see Gable, "The Bull Moose Years" (diss.), 133–40.

218 **Excepted only were**   Gould, *Four Hats in the Ring*, 129; TR, *Letters*, 7.564.

218 **"I regard"**   TR, *Letters*, 7.577.

218 **all hailed from Southern states**   Specifically, Georgia, Florida, Alabama, and Mississippi.

218 **his racial views**   See Morris, *Theodore Rex*, chaps. 2 and 27.

219 **Taft's deliberate score**   Butt, *Taft and Roosevelt*, 511.

219 **"inhuman cruelty and barbarity"**   See Morris, *Theodore Rex*, 49–50, 110–11, 246, 258–62.

219 **Yet stray observations**   TR, *Letters*, 5.226; M. A. DeWolfe Howe, *James Ford Rhodes: American Historian* (New York, 1929), 119–20; Bull, *Safari*, 179. Rhodes's account of a conversation on race with TR (16 Nov. 1905) should be considered in the light of his own opinion that the Negroes of the Yazoo delta were a million years behind their fellow whites. According to Grogan, TR remarked that, fantasies of button-pushing aside, "integration [was] the only answer" to the color problem in the United States.

219 "We have made" TR, *Letters,* 7.585–86.
219 He noted that Ibid., 7.587–89. According to TR, 7 out of every 8 black delegates at the Republican convention voted for WHT. Gable, *The Bull Moose Years,* 63.
220 The machinery does not TR, *Letters,* 7.590.

> *Biographical Note:* Even allowing for "the pastness of the past," and the fact that TR never shared the virulent racism of, e.g., Owen Wister, Henry Adams, and Augustus Saint-Gaudens, it is difficult not to see him now as anything other than paternalistic in his attitude to blacks. His genuine admiration, approaching reverence, for Dr. Washington was shared by many liberal white Republicans in the early years of the 20th century. However, the very uniqueness they ascribed to the author of *Up from Slavery* emphasized their consensus that Negroes generally languished at the opposite end of the scale of achievement. The best that can be said for TR's paternalism is that it was good-natured and devoid of fear. His descriptions of his black safari employees in *African Game Trails* are affectionate, but almost always dismissive, e.g.: "Most of them were like children, with a grasshopper inability for continuity of thought and realization for the future." (TR, *Works,* 4.120.) For a detailed analysis of the reasoning behind his letter to Joel Harris, see Gable, "The Bull Moose Years" (diss.), 167ff. For the agonized subsequent discussions of race policy in the provisional National Progressive Committee, ending in the decision to endorse TR's attitude, see "Proceedings of the Provisional National Progressive Committee, 3–5 August 1912," bound ts. (TRC).
>
> TR had no patience with blanket or "scientific" theories of race, describing Houston Stewart Chamberlain, xenophobic author of *The Foundations of the Nineteenth Century* (1899), as "an able man whose mind is not quite sound," and remarking of Joseph de Gobineau's famous *Essai sur l'inégalité des races humaines* (1855) that "to approach it for serious information would be much as if an albatross should apply to a dodo for a lesson in flight." (TR, *Works,* 14.201, 464–65.) Racial extremism on the liberal side also irritated him, especially in regard to foreign policy: "I have some worthy friends in Boston appeal to me to give self-government to a number of individuals who regard themselves as overdressed when they wear breech-clouts." (TR, *Works,* 15.548.)
>
> The only extended study of TR's racial attitudes is Thomas G. Dyer's *Theodore Roosevelt and the Idea of Race* (Baton Rouge, La., 1980). It is flawed by presentism, and a failure to examine TR's long and close relationship with Booker T. Washington—a subject worthy of a book in itself. For a more balanced analysis relevant to the politico-racial situation in 1912, see Gable, *The Bull Moose Years,* chap. 3, "Lily White Progressivism." See also McGerr, *A Fierce Discontent,* chap. 6., and David W. Southern, *The Progressive Era and Race: Reform and Reaction, 1900–1917* (Wheeling, W.V., 2005). Two contemporary essays on race by TR are self-revelatory: "The Negro in America," and "The Foundations of the Nineteenth Century" in TR, *Works,* 14.185–202 and 412–18.

220 Many of the Progressive Except where otherwise indicated, the following account is based on "First National Convention of the Progressive Party," typed minutes (TRC), and daily reports in *The New York Times, The Washington Post, Chicago Tribune, Boston Globe,* and *Atlanta Constitution,* 5–8 Aug. 1912.
220 Barbed wire no longer White, *Autobiography,* 483.
220 The semi-religious glow *The New York Times,* 23 June 1912; Stoddard, *As I Knew Them,* 410. For TR's appointment of Straus to his cabinet ("I want to show Russia and some other countries what we think of Jews in this country"), see Straus, *Under Four Administrations,* chap. 9.

221 **The record size** Many states sent double or triple the number of their allotted delegates, dividing votes between them.

221 **They were scrubbed** Nicholas Roosevelt, "Account of the RNC," 40–41; White, *Autobiography*, 483–84.

221 **White was struck** White, *Autobiography*, 483. A photograph reproduced in *The New York Times*, 7 Aug. 1912, dramatically shows how many women attended the convention. Woman suffrage was still considered a states' rights issue in the early months of 1912. Only six states (Colorado, Utah, Wyoming, Idaho, California, and Washington) allowed women to vote. For TR's belated, but unqualified conversion to the cause, see TR, *Letters*, 7.595–96.

221 **too fond of battleships** TR, *Letters*, 7.594. TR, in turn, regretfully wrote of Miss Addams, "She is a disciple of Tolstoy." Ibid., 7.833.

222 **She had agreed** *The Washington Post*, 6 Aug. 1912; *Chicago Tribune*, 6 Aug. 1912. Jane Addams (1860–1935) won the Nobel Peace Prize in 1931. She first became famous in the 1890s as the founder of Hull House, a pioneer social settlement in Chicago, and later as a writer and lecturer on social problems. For TR's courtship of Miss Addams, and her subsequent role in the formation of the Progressive Party, see Katherine Joslin, *Jane Addams* (Urbana, Ill., 2004), 133ff.

222 **an opening prayer** The devout quality of the convention was established by this prayer, which occupies seven full pages of the typed "Proceedings."

222 **The former senator** *Atlanta Constitution* and *Boston Globe*, 6 Aug. 1912; Stoddard, *As I Knew Them*, 408–9. O. K. Davis amusingly reports that TR had to be dissuaded from delivering his acceptance speech from the balcony of the Congress Hotel. Davis, *Released for Publication*, 320–26.

222 **in the days of McKinley** This phrase forms the title of one of the great presidential biographies, by Margaret Leech (New York, 1959).

222 **His ego** In his unpublished "Autobiography of an American Boy," Beveridge wrote, "This miracle of the invisible powers in my behalf has strengthened the sureness of achievement which is so vital a part of me" (BEV). For a contemporary sketch (1910), see Dreier, *Heroes of Insurgency*, 103–22.

222 **"We stand for"** *"Pass Prosperity Around": Speech of Albert J. Beveridge* (Progressive Party pamphlet [AC]). Nervous at first, Beveridge seemed to be in competition with Warren Harding for alliterative mastery: "Parties exist for the people, not the people for the parties. Yet for years the politicians have made the people do the work of the parties instead of the parties doing the work for the people." Speech scholars contemplating a monograph on the extraordinary fondness of politicians for the letter *p* should note TR's own attraction to it. See Morris, *The Rise of TR*, 224–25.

223 **"It was not a convention"** *The New York Times*, 6 Aug. 1912.

223 **Enthusiasm became ecstasy** Except where otherwise indicated, this account of the second day of the Progressive convention is based on *The New York Times*, *Chicago Tribune*, and *Atlanta Constitution*, 7 Aug., and *The Washington Post*, 8 Aug. 1912. The survey of attendees derives mainly from Gable, *The Bull Moose Years*, 34–59. Black delegates attended on the second day of the convention not only from the Northern states TR had mentioned in his letter to Joel Harris, but also from Virginia, West Virginia, Kentucky, Tennessee, and Arkansas. By the peculiar political standards of the time, these Southern states were considered to be "border" territory, with their electoral votes not yet wholly lost either to the Republican or Progressive parties. Lewis L. Gould to author, 2 Dec. 2008, AC.

223 **Two black Northern** These same delegates had conspicuously boycotted the previous day's proceedings, in a show of sympathy for their excluded Southern brothers. *Atlanta Constitution*, 6 Aug. 1912.

223 **Roosevelt led the singing** *Atlanta Constitution*, 7 Aug. 1912.

223 **"I have been"** *The New York Times,* 7 Aug. 1912.

223 **Senator Root's mocking prophecy** Quoted in Adams, *Letters,* 6.515.

223 **His smile betrayed** A reporter sitting just below TR in the press box noted, "It was evident that the fanaticism had got past him, and that he himself had no realization of the intense Christian feeling in that crowd all over the hall." (*The New York Times,* 7 Aug. 1912.) Richard Harding Davis wrote of the demonstration, "There was in it something inspired, spiritual, almost uncanny. It caught one by the throat." Davis, "The Men at Armageddon," *Collier's,* 24 Aug. 1912.

224 **It said something** Morris, *The Rise of TR,* 54–56; Hermann Hagedorn, *Roosevelt in the Bad Lands* (Boston, 1921), 473; Sullivan, *Our Times,* 4.509. For TR's relationships with all these men, see Morris, *The Rise of TR, passim.*

224 **not even Alice** Cordery, *Alice,* 229.

225 **The explosion somehow** *Atlanta Constitution,* 7 Aug. 1912.

225 **Roosevelt's address** TR to KR, 12 Aug. 1912 (TRC); TR, *Works,* 19.376, 386. TR's entire speech is reprinted in *Works,* 19.358–411.

225 **He dismissed** TR, *Works,* 19.358. TR's complaint about press bias was to become a leitmotif of his campaign from now on. In mid-August a researcher armed with a foot rule measured the coverage he and the Progressive agenda had in fact received, since the start of the month, in *The New York Times* and *Sun.* The total just for ten days was 2,148½ column inches, or something over 200,000 words, most of it front-page reportage under banner headlines. WHT or even WW would have been glad of half as much. *The New York Times* editorial, 18 Aug. 1912.

225 **The dead weight** TR, *Works,* 19.372.

226 **new or revived federal agencies** The genesis of the future Federal Trade and Securities Exchange Commissions, as well as the Social Security and Occupational Safety and Health administrations, may be traced back to these 1912 proposals by TR. He did not, however, suggest that the federal government should itself provide medical insurance. That was the responsibility of employers, and, on occasion, state governments.

226 **"I say in closing"** TR, *Works,* 19.411.

227 **voices singing his name** *The Washington Post,* 8 Aug. 1912.

227 **"Colonel," Robins said** Raymond Robins interview, n.d. (TRB).

227 **In another room** Gable, *The Bull Moose Years,* 98–99.

227 **"Each one of those"** Raymond Robins interview, n.d. (TRB). One of these planks, written by Amos Pinchot, tied the high cost of living to business, a view that TR rejected as "utter folly." (Gable, "The Bull Moose Years" [diss.], 245.) The others were for prohibition, a single tax, and constitutional amendment by referendum.

227 **"Each one of those"** Raymond Robins interview, n.d. (TRB).

227 **a compromise platform** A sheaf of Perkins's draft paragraphs, preserved in the Pforzheimer Collection subsection of TRC, shows that he and TR initially conceived of their platform as a Republican document, in the hope of victory at the GOP convention in June. Gable, *The Bull Moose Years,* 98–106, is an exhaustive account of the platform deliberations. See also Davis, *Released for Publication,* 328–36.

227 **"much the most important"** TR, *Letters,* 8.1068. For the last-minute, behind-the-scenes story of how this document was assembled, only to have a confused Dean Lewis misrepresent it to the convention (nearly costing TR the support of George Perkins), see Gable, *The Bull Moose Years,* 98–106 and Davis, *Released for Publication,* 328–36.

Historical Note: The Progressive Party platform for 1912 amounted to a redrafting, for practical campaign purposes, of TR's 1910 New Nationalism program. Not until the Democratic platform of 1964 did any major party demand so many and such specific reforms. These were, in partial summary: direct primaries to nominate state, national, and presidential candidates, plus direct elections to the U.S. Senate; federal jurisdiction over national problems formerly treated as state problems; a universal minimum wage, and broader laws to protect, insure, and compensate abused or injured industrial workers; an eight-hour day work limit for women and juvenile employees, plus welfare benefits; facilitated organization of labor unions, and limitation of injunctions in labor disputes; farm relief; a more elastic currency; a downwardly revised, but still protective tariff; at least four nonpartisan regulatory commissions, with power over corporate pricing and all interstate business; further application of the initiative, referendum, and recall (but severely limited in application to judicial decisions); accelerated conservation and protection of natural resources, including a vast flood control program for the Mississippi River and its tributaries; development of Alaskan coal fields; woman suffrage; a national health service; federal income and graduated inheritance taxes; a two-battleships-per-year rearmament schedule; national highways; and a parcel post system.

228 **"There is no"** *The New York Times,* 8 Aug. 1912.
228 **When Judge Lindsey** Ogden (Utah) *Examiner,* 8 Aug. 1912.
228 **singing the Doxology** Mansfield (Ohio) *News,* 8 Aug. 1912.

CHAPTER 12: THERE WAS NO OTHER PLACE ON HIS BODY

229 **Epigraph** Robinson, *Collected Poems,* 31
229 **"In form, two thousand"** *Proceedings of the 15th RNC,* 436.
229 **The more measured** *The New York Times,* 7 Aug. 1912.
230 **Ray Stannard Baker** Baker, notebook M, 17–20 (RSB).
230 **And at the lowest** Robert Donovan, *The Assassins* (New York, 1955), 135, 137.
230 **"Of course I do not"** TR to KR, 13 July 1912 (TRC). See also Gould, *Four Hats in the Ring,* 155.
230 **Wilson was the 2-to-1** *The Washington Post,* 7 Aug. 1912.
230 **he hopped across the court** The last words of this sentence are taken from Nicholas Roosevelt's diary of 10 Aug. 1912. See Nicholas Roosevelt, *TR,* 98–99.
230 **"He is a real"** Link, *Papers of Woodrow Wilson,* 25.26. For TR's embrace of (and self-identification with) Bergson's currently popular theory of *élan vital,* see TR, *Works,* 14.435 and *passim.*
231 **He had not been impressed** William Starr Myers, ed., *Woodrow Wilson: Some Princeton Memories* (Princeton, N.J., 1946), 42–43.
231 **Wilson is a good man** TR, *Letters,* 7.592.
232 **"I know it"** *The New York Times,* 13 Aug. 1912.
232 **After his desperate** Pringle, *Taft,* 818; *The New York Times,* 13 Aug. 1912. For WHT's decision not to campaign actively, see Gould, *Four Hats in the Ring,* 126ff.
232 **Taft knew that** Butt, *Taft and Roosevelt,* 694 and *passim;* Pringle, *Taft,* 82. "Ike" Hoover, the veteran White House usher, considered WHT to be, after Calvin Coolidge, the most self-centered of the nine presidents he had known. TR rated third. Hoover, *Forty-Two Years,* 232.
232 **"I have no"** WHT quoted in Pringle, *Taft,* 823.
232 **What with Ted** Eleanor B. Roosevelt, *Day Before Yesterday,* 60–61.
233 **By the time everybody** Ibid., 62.
233 **After a few weeks** Ibid., 61.
233 **One night after dinner** Nicholas Roosevelt, *TR,* 99.
233 **"Yes, yes!"** Ibid.

233 **A more agitated** EKR to ERD, n.d., ca. Aug. 1912 (ERDP); Cordery, *Alice*, 231–32.

234 **"I wish to goodness"** EKR to ERD, n.d., ca. Aug. 1912 (ERDP).

234 **By the end of the month** For Debs's double challenge to TR and WW in the summer of 1912, see Gould, *Four Hats in the Ring*, chap. 5. TR made two brief campaign trips into New England during the second half of Aug., attracting large, enthusiastic crowds. In Providence, R.I., on the 16th he spoke on tariff and currency reform, and made what appears to have been the first use of a phrase that reentered the American political vocabulary 70 years later: "The Republican proposal is only to give prosperity to [wealthy industrialists] and then to let it trickle down." *The New York Times*, 17 Aug. 1912.

234 **Wilson chose** Dunkirk (N.Y.) *Evening Observer* and *The New York Times*, 16 Aug. 1912.

234 **340 pounds** WHT admitted to this weight at the end of his presidential term. *New York Times*, 12 Dec. 1913.

234 **"As the campaign"** WHT on 26 Aug. 1912, quoted in Pringle, *Taft*, 815.

235 **All of them stood** *The New York Times*, 27 Aug. 1912.

235 **Woman suffrage was an issue** The cover illustration of the pro-Wilson *Harper's Weekly*, 17 Aug. 1912, showed TR shouting "Woman Suffrage Forever" through a megaphone, with a billboard proclaiming, "Great Vaudeville Act—The Call of the Wild."

236 **small silver bull mooses** Thompson, *Presidents I've Known*, 184. TR had previously (28–31 Aug.) undertaken a short campaign swing through New England. See Gould, *Bull Moose*, 41–51, for an important address in Vermont on the social-industrial aspects of Progressive policy.

236 **He intended to barnstorm** TR's itinerary is detailed day by day in the trip journal of George E. Roosevelt (TRC). The Colonel traveled with George and four other aides in a private car hitched to various public trains. Another private car, chartered by the press, was in turn hitched to his.

236 **"He looked, as usual"** Baker, notebook M, 34–35 (RSB). TR's speech is in Gould, *Bull Moose*, 51–56.

236 **A citizen of** TR, *Letters*, 7.570–71; *The New York Times*, 13 July, 1 Aug. 1912; Wood, *Roosevelt As We Knew Him*, 273ff.; Thompson, *Presidents I've Known*, 190.

236 **a convenient code** Thompson, *Presidents I've Known*, 141.

236 **"Friends," he yelled** Ibid., 175.

237 **"My fellow citizens"** *The New York Times*, 10 Sept. 1912.

237 **gloved hands clapping** Ibid.

237 **Two nights later** Donovan, *The Assassins*, 136. According to the self-styled "written proclamation" of John Schrank, quoted in the *New York Press*, 15 Sept. 1912, the time of this vision was 1:30 A.M. on the 12th. For his earlier vision of McKinley and TR at the same hour on 15 Sept. 1901, see Morris, *Theodore Rex*, 17.

238 **his oratory became impersonal** Exhorted by a Progressive official to "come out stronger" against WW, TR said, "No, that would be entirely wrong. Give Wilson a chance to make good. Don't handicap him before he has had an opportunity to do anything." David S. Hinshaw interviewed by J. F. French, 1922 (TRB).

238 **Only California** When TR arrived in Los Angeles on the 16th, 200,000 people lined the streets and shouted his name. Mowry, *TR*, 276.

238 **"a quiet, steady"** *The New York Times*, 23 Sept. 1912.

238 **"There was no applause"** David S. Hinshaw interviewed by J. F. French, 1922 (TRB). White wrote a charming account of TR's visit to Emporia in his *Autobiography*, 493–96.

238 **five 78 rpm shellac discs**   Victor C-12406 through 12410, all recorded on 22 Sept. 1912. These recordings and four cylinders recorded the previous month for the Edison Company can be heard on numerous Internet sites. The most representative is "The Right of the People to Rule," downloadable from the Library of Congress's American Memory archive (http://lcweb2.loc.gov/ammem). It contains TR's famous exhortation to "Spend and be spent." Another, "The Progressive Covenant with the People," ends with him declaiming his Armageddon line with enormous relish. The pleasant voices of Wilson and Taft can be heard on the Vincent Voice Library website at http://vvl.lib.msu.edu/.

239 **"I am hoarse"**   TR to KR, 27 Sept. 1912 (TRC).

239 **Arkansas. Tennessee.**   At Memphis, on 26 Sept., TR gave a far-seeing, nonpartisan address to the Levee Convention. In language clearly written for the most part by Gifford Pinchot, he called for wholesale federal development and protection of the Mississippi drainage basin, using the plant and technology that would soon become available to the United States upon completion of the Panama Canal. See Gould, *Bull Moose*, 126–36.

239 **"Theodore Roosevelt has"**   *African Methodist Episcopal Church Review,* 29.2 (Oct. 1912).

239 **"It is impossible"**   *The New York Times,* 29 Sept. 1912. See Gould, *Bull Moose,* 136–42, for an account of TR's successful appeal for support in New Orleans, and Arthur S. Link, "Theodore Roosevelt and the South in 1912," in *North Carolina Historical Review,* 23 (July 1946) for TR's popularity elsewhere in Dixie: "Roosevelt found . . . that it was his misfortune that people often shout one way and vote another."

240 **He practically called**   *The New York Times,* 29 Sept. 1912.

240 **He blustered on**   George Roosevelt trip journal, 29 Sept. 1912; Thompson, *Presidents I've Known,* 187; *The New York Times,* 30 Sept. 1912; Wood, *Roosevelt As We Knew Him,* 276. The *Atlanta Constitution* report quoted in Gould, *Bull Moose,* 143–48, downplays the hostility TR provoked.

240 **He got the impression**   Willard Straight to Henry P. Fletcher, 3 Oct. 1912 (STR).

Chronological Note: The investigation had been triggered by an article in the August issue of *Hearst's Magazine,* showing that the payment had originally been made by John D. Archbold of Standard Oil to Senator Boies Penrose of Pennsylvania. The latter, an archenemy of Progressivism, claimed in 1912 that he had accepted it in behalf of TR's reelection campaign. The President, he said, not only knew about the $25,000, but had demanded a larger contribution if Standard Oil was not to be prosecuted under the Sherman Act. Although Penrose could not offer any proof of his allegation, he and the ever-vengeful Robert La Follette jointly called for a Senate examination of all contributions to the 1904, 1908, and 1912 campaigns. A subcommittee for the purpose, chaired by Moses E. Clapp of Minnesota, grilled TR on 4 Oct. 1912. He preempted his appearance by publishing a long letter to Clapp. In it, he denied Penrose's allegation, and attached documents from his presidential papers to prove that in 1904 he had directed that no contributions from John D. Rockefeller's highly unpopular trust should be accepted by the Republican National Committee. See TR, *Letters,* 7.602–5, and *Campaign Contributions: Testimony Before a Subcommittee of the Committee on Privileges and Elections,* U.S. Senate, 2 vols. (Washington, D.C., 1913).

240 **a conference of**   *The New York Times,* 7 Oct. 1912.

241 **Wilson had come up**   Link, *Wilson: The Road to the White House,* 476–77; Heckscher, *Woodrow Wilson,* 260–61; Gould, *Four Hats in the Ring,* 164–65. For

an analysis of the contrasting yet often complementary platforms of TR and WW in the campaign of 1912, see John Milton Cooper, Jr., *Woodrow Wilson: A Biography* (New York, 2009), 173–80.

241 **Johnson had a twenty-two-state** Gable, *The Bull Moose Years,* 111.

241 **In Indiana, Albert Beveridge** Gable, "The Bull Moose Years" (diss.), 273–84; TR, *Letters,* 7.595; TR to KR, 1 Nov. 1912, ts. (TRC). For a detailed account of the organization of the Progressive Party, see Gable, *The Bull Moose Years,* 22–57.

241 **"Children, don't crowd"** Thompson, *Presidents I've Known,* 144.

241 **The Colonel was back** Davis, *Released for Publication,* 355–56.

241 **Roosevelt seemed a new** *The Outlook,* 12 Oct. 1912; Philip J. Roosevelt, "Politics of the Year 1912: An Intimate Progressive View," ts. (TRC), 28, 40; Gould, *Bull Moose,* 151–54.

242 **"I'm fur Teddy"** Mrs. Rudolph Schori to TR, 21 Jan. 1913, pasted into the manuscript of TR's autobiography (MLM). Later, in Duluth and Chicago, TR used his briefing book to further effect, quoting some highly xenophobic remarks made by WW about European immigrants "of the lowest classes" in a magazine article in 1899. Gould, *Bull Moose,* 158–59.

242 **Munsey, a strict dieter** Munsey's advice fell on deaf ears. Stoddard, *As I Knew Them,* 407–8.

242 **Rumors persisted** Davis, *Released for Publication,* 362.

242 **His speech** Gould, *Bull Moose,* 161–62.

242 **After dinner** Philip Roosevelt, "Politics of the Year 1912," 49. TR's voice loss in the Coliseum was unfortunate, because his speech was an effective attack on WW as governor of the most corporate-friendly state in the Union. "He did precisely and exactly nothing [in New Jersey]. It is as simple to describe what [he] accomplished against the trusts as it is to write a volume on the natural history of the snakes in Ireland. There are no snakes in Ireland." Gould, *Bull Moose,* 166.

242 **He returned to Chicago** Davis, *Released for Publication,* 369.

243 **Roosevelt lies and curses** Ishpeming (Mich.) *Iron Ore,* 12 Oct. 1912, copy in TRC.

243 **"Let's go at him."** Davis, *Released for Publication,* 369.

243 **Later that afternoon** The following account of the events of 14 Oct. 1912 is based on the eyewitness reportage of Philip Roosevelt in "Politics of the Year 1912"; O. K. Davis to George Perkins, 15 Oct. 1912, ts. copy (AC); Davis, *Released for Publication,* 370–90; Oliver Remey, Henry F. Cochems, and Joseph C. Bloodgood, *The Attempted Assassination of Ex-President Theodore Roosevelt* (Milwaukee, Wis., 1912); Thompson, *Presidents I've Known,* 147–50; and "Incidents in the Political Life of Theodore Roosevelt as Related by Owen Crozier," ts. copy (TRB).

243 **"I want to be"** Davis, *Released for Publication,* 372.

244 **"He'll never get up"** Philip Roosevelt, "Politics of the Year 1912," 54.

244 **Looking down, he** Ibid.

244 **"Don't hurt him"** TR, *Letters,* 7.705; Philip Roosevelt, "Politics of the Year 1912," 54.

244 **What he saw** Full-length photograph of Schrank, 14 Oct. 1912, Library of Congress.

244 **"What did you"** Davis, *Released for Publication,* 149.

244 **"He pinked me"** Remey et al., *The Attempted Assassination,* 16.

244 **Terrell had heard** Davis, *Released for Publication,* 378; Philip Roosevelt, "Politics of the Year 1912," 55. TR later remembered saying, "I am ahead of the game and can afford to take the chances." TR, *Works,* 6.xiii.

244 **"No, Colonel"** Davis, *Released for Publication,* 378; Leary, *Talks with T.R.,* 30; Emlen Roosevelt, ed., *Roosevelt v. Newett: A Transcript of the Testimony Taken*

and Depositions Read at Marquette, Michigan (privately printed, 1913), 71, cited hereafter as *Roosevelt v. Newett.*

245 **"It's all right"** Davis, *Released for Publication*, 380. Afterward TR wrote KR, "As I did not cough blood, I was pretty sure that the wound was not a fatal one." (19 Oct. 1912 [TRC].) The auditorium where TR spoke is now the Milwaukee Theater.

245 **Cochems preceded him** *New York Press*, 15 Oct. 1912; Stan Gores, "The Attempted Assassination of Teddy Roosevelt," *Wisconsin Magazine of History*, 53 (Summer 1970).

245 **Roosevelt stepped forward** O. K. Davis to George Perkins, 15 Oct. 1912 (AC); E. W. Leach (eyewitness) in *Racine Journal*, 13 Aug. 1921. A surviving photograph of the shirt still evokes an emotional reaction. See Lorant, *Life and Times of TR*, 573.

245 **"I'm going to ask you"** *Chicago Tribune*, 15 Oct. 1912.

245 **Waiting for the noise** Philip Roosevelt, "Politics of the Year 1912," 57; Davis, *Released for Publication*, 381.

245 **His heart was racing** TR, *Letters*, 7.705. A stenographic text of TR's speech, varying considerably from the original script, is reproduced in Gable, *The Man in the Arena*, 102ff. It appears to have been much abridged before its first publication in Elmer H. Youngman's *Progressive Principles* (New York, 1913), 102–14.

245 **Roosevelt swung his head** The image of the steel-gray stare is Philip Roosevelt's. ("Politics of the Year 1912," 58.) O. K. Davis was similarly rebuffed when he, too, tried to stop TR from going on. "He paused in his speech, and swung around on me with an expression on his face that can be described accurately only by the word 'ferocity.' " Davis, *Released for Publication*, 383.

245 **After about forty-five minutes** Philip Roosevelt, "Politics of the Year 1912," 58; Leach in *Racine Journal*, 13 Aug. 1921; Crozier, "Incidents in the Political Life of Theodore Roosevelt"; Davis, *Released for Publication*, 385.

246 **Incredibly, members** Philip Roosevelt, "Politics of the Year 1912," 58; *New York Press*, 15 Oct. 1912; Thompson, *Presidents I've Known*, 149–50.

247 **Before being stripped** TR, *Letters*, 8.1449; TR to KR, 19 Oct. 1912, ts. (TRC). This was an inside joke. Many years before, Bullock had been convulsed by one of TR's favorite stories, about the Rough Rider who shot someone and who, in response to his question, "How did it happen?" answered, "With a .38 on a .45 frame, Colonel." TR, *An Autobiography*, 380.

247 **Meanwhile, at** *New York Press*, 15 Oct. 1912.

247 **Never let** Remey et al., *The Attempted Assassination*, 60 (facsimile).

247 **News of the drama** *New York Press* and *The New York Times*, 15 Oct. 1912. See also Nicholas Roosevelt, *TR*, 67, and Sylvia Morris, *Edith Kermit Roosevelt*, 385–86. A medical soap opera commenced while TR was being examined in Milwaukee. The eminent surgeon Dr. Joseph C. Bloodgood of the Johns Hopkins Hospital in Baltimore happened to be in the Auditorium to witness TR's speech, and followed him to the Emergency Hospital to offer assistance if needed. He was unimpressed with the quality of the local care, and said urgently to O. K. Davis, "Get him out of here just as quickly as you can. This is no place for him." Both Bloodgood and Terrell recommended Mercy Hospital's John B. Murphy as the best specialist for his case. TR assented and was checked out of the Emergency Hospital at 11:25 P.M. (Davis, *Released for Publication*, 389; TR to J. Keeley, 30 Dec. 1912 copy (AC); Loyal Davis, *J. B. Murphy: Stormy Petrel of Surgery* [New York, 1938], 262–63; *New York Press*, 15 Oct. 1912.) For subsequent episodes of the soap opera, involving the rivalry of four Chicago surgeons, see Davis, *Murphy*, 263–72.

247 **It lay embedded** Davis, *Murphy*, 267; EKR to Emily Carow, 17 Oct. 1912 (TRC);

Philip Roosevelt, "Politics of the Year 1912," 57. TR's personal doctor, Alexander Lambert, pointed out that the spectacle case deflected the bullet upward. "[Had] the bullet gone through the arch of the aorta or auricles of the heart, Colonel Roosevelt would not have lived 60 seconds." Bishop, *TR*, 2.339.

248 **"There was no other place"**   Crozier, "Incidents in the Political Life of Theodore Roosevelt."

248 **His breathing hurt**   TR, *Letters*, 7.705; Philip Roosevelt, "Politics of the Year 1912," 58–59.

248 **He was asleep**   Davis, *Released for Publication*, 390, 393; Davis to George Perkins, 15 Oct. 1912 (AC); Gores, "The Attempted Assassination."

249 **Even at that**   *Chicago Tribune*, 16 Oct. 1912; Remey et al., *The Attempted Assassination*, 71; photograph in Milwaukee County Historical Society collection.

249 **At 10:30**   Remey et al., *The Attempted Assassination*, 66–67.

249 **X-ray reproductions**   One of these can be seen in ibid., 32.

249 **The surgeon was closemouthed**   Davis, *Murphy*, 267. Murphy privately told TR that a few splinters of rib bone had penetrated his pleura, and that his speech after the attack had aggravated the laceration. The surgeons were afraid that if they extracted the bullet immediately, "there might be either a collapse of the pleura or an infection of the pleural cavity." Bishop, *TR*, 2.345.

249 **The records show**   Davis, *Murphy*, 268. One of the examining doctors remarked that TR's musculature had much to do with the stopping of Schrank's bullet. "Colonel Roosevelt has a phenomenal development of the chest. . . . He is one of the most powerful men I have ever seen laid on an operating table." (Bishop, *TR*, 2.338–39.) A score for the 12-year-old Teedie Roosevelt in 1870–1871, "widening his chest by regular, monotonous motion." Robinson, *My Brother TR*, 50.

249 **Perhaps the best**   Sylvia Morris, *Edith Kermit Roosevelt*, 387ff.

249 **Dr. Murphy's pointed reference**   Davis, *Murphy*, 273, notes that the reference was "out of place" in a medical bulletin. "But in the light of the Colonel's [libel] suit it grows evident that the patient had asked that some such allusion to liquor should be made."

249 **It was from**   Davis, *Released for Publication*, 395.

250 **Among the other**   *The New York Times*, 15, 16 Oct. 1912; Link, *Papers of Woodrow Wilson*, 25.421–22, 425. WW privately joked about the effect his courteous gesture would have on TR. "Teddy will have apoplexy when he hears of this." Cooper, *Woodrow Wilson*, 170.

250 **Similar messages**   Davis, *Released for Publication*, 396; *The New York Times*, 16–18 Oct. 1912; *Chicago Tribune*, 21 Oct. 1912. The crowned heads included George V of England, Wilhelm II of Germany, Franz Joseph of Austria, Tsar Nicholas II of Russia, and the Emperor of Japan. For editorial reactions, domestic and international, to the attack on TR, see *The Outlook* and *Literary Digest*, 26 Oct. 1912.

250 **He informed the judge**   Remey et al., *The Attempted Assassination*, 94–96; Gores, "The Attempted Assassination."

250 **After a week**   TR, *Letters*, 7.632; *The New York Times*, 27, 28 Oct. 1912.

251 **"I am in fine"**   TR, *Letters*, 7.631–32.

251 **Hiram Johnson was**   The following description of TR's appearance in the Garden is based on illustrated articles in *The New York Times* and *Syracuse Herald*, 31 Oct. 1912.

251 **"Quiet, down there!"**   Hagedorn, *The Roosevelt Family*, 325.

251 **"—Perhaps not so"**   The complete text of TR's speech, entitled "The Purpose of the Progressive Party," is in Gould, *Bull Moose*, 187–92.

251 **This was**   Gable, "The Bull Moose Years" (diss.), 270; Gould, *Bull Moose*, 188. TR's appearance, at the Garden—stigmatized, suffering, elevated high above the

faithful—marked the climax of the quasi-Christian symbolism of his campaign. See, e.g., Robinson, *My Brother TR*, 275.

> *Chronological Note:* WW addressed a Democratic rally the following night, 31 Oct., and Tammany Hall timekeepers made sure that the ovation for him lasted half an hour longer than the one for TR. Ignoring medical advice, TR returned to the Garden on 2 Nov., still manifestly in pain, to speak on behalf of Oscar Straus's gubernatorial candidacy. He then made a couple of election-eve appearances on Long Island. The last speech he made, at the Oyster Bay Opera House, was a furious reply to some minor criticisms leveled against him by Elihu Root. Heckscher, *Woodrow Wilson*, 262; *The New York Times*, 2, 5 Nov. 1912.

252 **At seven the Colonel**   EKR to KR, 6 Nov. 1912 (KRP); Cordery, *Alice*, 234.
252 **The phone call**   TR actually knew as early as 7:30 P.M. that a landslide for WW impended, but the Democratic National Committee did not claim victory until 10:30. WW acknowledged his triumph at 10:45. *Atlanta Constitution* and *The New York Times*, 6 Nov. 1912.
252 **THE AMERICAN PEOPLE**   *The New York Times*, 6 Nov. 1912.
252 **"Like all other"**   *New York Evening Post*, 6 Nov. 1912.

CHAPTER 13: A POSSIBLE AUTOBIOGRAPHY

253 **Epigraph**   Robinson, *Collected Poems*, 16.
253 **"Well, we have"**   TR to KR, 5 Nov. 1912, ts. (TRC).
253 **In his still-fragile**   Ibid. After the last line, TR characteristically added, "I am absolutely happy and contented." See also his posterity letter sent on the same date to Arthur Lee, in TR, *Letters*, 7.634–35.
254 **"You know him"**   EKR to KR, 6 Nov. 1912 (KRP).
254 **Gradually, Roosevelt realized**   In further analysis, TR ran second in 23 states, seven of them in the South, where his "lily-white" Party policy proved effective in weakening WHT's machine support. He swept Pennsylvania with a 50,000-vote margin over WW, plus California with 11 out of 13 electoral votes, and Michigan, Minnesota, South Dakota, and Washington besides. He was only 1,000 votes behind WHT in Vermont, and 3,000 behind WW in Maine. The governor's winning margins in North Dakota and Montana were not much greater, at 4,000 and 6,000. New York City rejected its native son by a plurality of 122,777 votes, but TR racked up convincing wins in Pittsburgh, Detroit, Chicago, and Los Angeles. He performed strongly in the Midwest and West, and secured a majority of the nation's normal GOP vote by a margin of more than half a million. (Gould, *Bull Moose*, 176–77; *Literary Digest*, 16 Nov. 1912; Gable, *The Bull Moose Years*, 131–32.) Gould points out that TR did not technically defeat WHT in either California or South Dakota, since the President was not on the ballot in those states.
254 **stomped and burned**   *The New York Times*, 10 Nov. 1912.
254 **Even if he**   A progressive Republican candidate for governor in Minnesota received almost four times as many votes as the Progressive Party candidate. TR himself did best in states where the GOP vote was traditionally high. Potts, "Theodore Roosevelt and the Progressive Party"; Gable, *The Bull Moose Years*, 132.
254 **He would now**   John Milton Cooper, in Naylor et al., *TR*, 505, expresses a contrary view, suggesting that WW would have been nominated as the only possible foil to TR, and during the campaign would have attracted away from him much of WHT's conservative/corporate support.

254 **There remained**   James E. Amos, *Theodore Roosevelt: Hero to His Valet* (New York, 1927), 147–48. "To me and to some of the others who were near him it always seemed that after the shooting things began to break against him. Up to that moment his life had been a rising scale of successes. People talked about his star and his destiny. Things broke for him. After that they broke the other way."

254 **poor Nick**   Representative Longworth was defeated by only 97 votes—which ARL guiltily blamed on herself, for attending a Progressive rally in Columbus earlier in the year. He took solace in alcohol, breaking down completely on 13 Nov., to her "infinite sorrow and pity." Cordery, *Alice,* 235–36.

255 **Roosevelt admitted**   TR to KR, 24 May 1913, ts. (TRC); Willard Straight to Henry P. Fletcher, 3 Oct. 1912 (STR). Apparently TR did not know that *The Outlook* had taken out a $25,000 accident insurance policy on him, and made a claim after he was incapacitated in Milwaukee. The insurance company argued that only TR could have claimed, and tried to have the policy voided. TR then mystifyingly announced that TR would not file any claim himself. *The New York Times,* 8, 9 Nov. 1912.

255 **And he suspected**   Encouraged by timid signals from Ethel, Dr. Derby had begun to press his suit again in October. Their ultimately fruitful, two-and-a-half-year romance is touchingly documented in WFP.

255 **Roosevelt was willing**   TR to KR, 11 Nov. 1912, ts. (TRC).

255 **"I get from"**   Ibid. TR's *Outlook* salary was $12,000.

255 **There remained**   *African Game Trails* sold 36,127 copies in 1910, about 4,700 copies in 1911, and about 1,019 copies in the first half of 1912. (Charles Scribner to TR, 7 Feb. 1911, 21 Feb. and 22 Aug. 1912 [SCR].) Author's estimates based on payments to TR, where no sales figures are available.

256 **Looking back**   Charles Scribner to TR, 1 Feb. and 22 Aug. 1912 (TRP). TR had, all the same, an impressive total of 15 titles in print at the end of 1912, many of them in multiple editions, and all still earning royalties. This total did not include the "Elkhorn Edition" of his complete works to date (26 vols.), nor any of his foreign editions and translations.

> *Biographical Note:* The information in these paragraphs is based on scattered royalty statements and "stock accounts" sent to TR by his various publishers in 1912, and preserved in TRC. From 1913 through 1919 he appears to have earned a further $58,125 in advance payments and royalties. (TR file, SCR.) Posthumously, he once again became a bestselling author, thanks to the publication of *Theodore Roosevelt's Letters to His Children.* (See Epilogue.) It is impossible to calculate how many copies of TR's books were bought during his lifetime and in the decade or so after his death. A memo prepared by his main publisher, Scribners, in 1933, lists 876,375 copies sold by that house to date. Scribners to William H. Bell, 25 Nov 1933 (SCR).

256 **The Century Company**   *Hero Tales from American History* (New York, 1895), addressed to young readers, was co-authored by Henry Cabot Lodge. *Stories of the Great West* (New York, 1909), was a selection of chapters and articles previously published by TR.

256 **He was not sure**   TR to KR, 21 Jan. 1913, ts. (TRC); Charles Scribner to William B. Howland, 2 Dec. 1912 (SCR).

256 **not that *they***   John Adams's autobiography was abandoned in mid-sentence, and John Quincy Adams's was a scissors-and-paste job compiled by his son Charles Francis.

256 **"This is the first"**   Charles Scribner to TR, 2 Dec. 1912 (SCR).

256 **"another proposition"**   Howland to Scribner, 3 Dec. 1912 (SCR).

257 **The proposition had come** Macmillan statement, 30 Apr. 1914 (TRP). TR's advance was not payable until publication day, 19 Nov. 1913. There is no of record what, if anything, he was paid by *The Outlook* for first serial rights.

257 **reputation for promptness** See Abbott, *Impressions of TR,* 173–74.

257 **His third book project** Charles Scribner to TR, 17 June and 16 Sept. 1913 (SCR).

257 **John F. Schrank, meanwhile** Remey et al., *The Attempted Assassination,* 98, 101–2.

257 **he insisted that** TR was inclined to agree with Schrank. "I very gravely question if he has a more unsound mind than Eugene Debs." Bishop, *TR,* 2.344.

257 **He bequeathed** Gores, "The Attempted Assassination"; *Chicago Tribune,* 15 Oct. 1912; *The New York Times,* 19 Nov. 1912; Oshkosh *Daily Northwestern,* 15 Oct. 1912.

257 **incarceration for life** The lunacy commission's euphemism, "until cured" was understood in 1912 to mean a life sentence. *The New York Times,* 23 Nov. 1912.

257 **"Only Bull Moose"** *Chicago Tribune,* 23 Nov. 1912. TR told St. Loe Strachey on 16 Dec. that he did not consider Schrank to be any more insane than Senator La Follette or Eugene Debs. He blamed his own journalistic enemies for having excited the little man to action. "I have not the slightest feeling against him." (TR, *Letters,* 7.676–77.) Schrank was shortly transferred to Wisconsin's Central State Hospital for the Criminally Insane, and remained there until his death on 15 Sept. 1943—the anniversary of his first vision of the ghost of McKinley. He was a model prisoner and exhibited no further evidence of aberrant behavior until Franklin D. Roosevelt sought a third term as President in 1940. Schrank then became agitated, and was heard to say that "if he was free he would take a hand in the matter." During his 31-year incarceration, he was visited by no one and received no letters. (Gores, "The Attempted Assassination.") See also Remey et al., *The Attempted Assassination,* 117ff. for Schrank's complete testimony in 1912.

258 **Much as Roosevelt** Gable, *The Bull Moose Years* 149–55. For TR's years as a self-described "literary feller," see Morris, *The Rise of TR,* chap. 15.

258 **George Perkins, seeking** Garland, *Companions on the Trail,* 505–6.

258 **an excellent life** *Ulysses S. Grant: His Life and Character* (1898). Garland (1860–1940) was to achieve fame in 1917 with his autobiographical *Son of the Middle Border.* He was awarded the Pulitzer Prize for a sequel, *Daughter of the Middle Border,* in 1921. His three volumes of literary reminiscences, *Roadside Meetings* (1930), *Companions on the Trail* (1931), and *My Friendly Contemporaries* (1932), are richly anecdotal.

258 **"I'll begin it immediately"** Garland, *Companions on the Trail,* 507.

258 **Abbott's idea** Abbott, *Impressions of TR,* 176–78.

259 **On October 27, 1858** TR, *An Autobiography,* 256.

259 **Ever since the election** "Minutes of the National Committee of the Progressive Party, 1912–1916," bound ts., 5–20 (TRC); Mowry, *TR,* 289. In an editorial dated 8 Jan. 1913, Munsey proposed a merger between the Progressive and Republican parties. For a detailed account of the intraparty battle against Perkins, see Mowry, *TR,* chap. 11.

259 **Showing as much** *Chicago Tribune,* 9 Dec. 1912; Mowry, TR, 285.

260 **convinced by his support** TR, *Letters,* 7.665.

260 **"The doctrine of"** Gable, *The Bull Moose Years,* 154. A case in point soon materialized in Idaho, where the state supreme court, on 2 Jan. 1913, jailed and fined the editor and publisher of the Boise *Capital News* on contempt charges for criticizing its decision to deny local candidates the right to run as Progressives on the national ballot. The result was outrage in all sections of the American press, and wide circulation of TR's triumphant reaction: "There could be

no better proof that we need in many states at least the power to recall judges from the bench when they act badly." TR, *Letters*, 7.687.

260 **"I have had"** TR to KR, 27 Dec. 1912 and 21 Jan. 1913. The manuscript of TR's autobiography, bound in two vols., is in MLM. Except for chap. 1, which seems to be a copy of Lawrence Abbott's redaction of his first "interview" session with TR, and a few late pages on conservation written by Gifford Pinchot at the author's request, all the other chapters are original typescripts dictated and heavily edited by TR. Some pages are so dense with handwritten "inserts" that the four margins are filled to capacity. It is clear that he regarded the book as an important document.

260 **a lock of honey-colored hair** This memento of Alice Hathaway Lee Roosevelt is preserved at Sagamore Hill National Historic Site.

261 **The company of** TR, *Letters*, 7.688.

261 **He was intrigued** TR to KR, 11 Nov. 1912, ts. (TRC); TR, *Letters*, 8.829; Endicott Peabody in *Boston Transcript*, 22 July 1918. TR was particularly impressed with QR's story, "From a Train Window," *Grotonian*, Oct. 1914.

261 **Kermit claimed** KR to ERD, 12, 26 Nov. 1913 (ERDP); EKR to Anna Roosevelt Cowles, 15 Oct. 1913 (ARC); KR to ERD, 12 May 1913 (ERDP).

261 **"As president of"** TR, *Letters*, 7.660.

261 **More excitingly** Ibid.

261 **At Symphony Hall** *Lowell* (Mass.) *Sun, The New York Times*, 28 Dec. 1912.

262 **And the great Parkman** Morris, *The Rise of TR*, 120, 393, 412.

262 **None of the members** Pringle, *TR*, 572.

262 **He proceeded to say** TR's lecture, "History as Literature," has been widely reprinted. The version cited here, taken from the *American Historical Review*, Apr. 1913, appears in TR, *Works*, 14.3–28. It is the source of the following quotations.

262 **Literature may** TR, *Works*, 14.7.

263 **"the preacher militant"** Wister, *Roosevelt*, 232.

263 **He must ever remember** TR, *Works*, 14.23.

263 **"He is so"** Turner, *Dear Lady*, 139.

264 **"T.R. came and went"** Akiko Murakata, "Theodore Roosevelt and William Sturgis Bigelow: The Story of a Friendship," *Harvard Library Bulletin*, 23.1 (1975).

265 **With some awkwardness** Lodge, *Selections*, 2.426–34. Lodge's *Early Memories*, published in the fall of 1913, stopped short of his political career and said nothing about his relationship with TR.

265 **A much frostier** *The New York Times*, 5 Jan. 1913.

265 **"No, dear, no"** Eleanor B. Roosevelt, *Day Before Yesterday*, 65.

265 **His wisecrack** *The New York Times*, 5 Jan. 1913.

265 **In a bizarre speech** Logansport (Ind.) *Journal-Tribune*, 5 Jan. 1913.

265 **For the rest** The first chapter of TR's autobiography, "Boyhood and Youth," appeared in *The Outlook* on 22 Feb. 1913. Eleven further chapters followed fortnightly. The McClure Newspaper Syndicate began reprinting them on 13 April.

266 **"It is very difficult"** TR, *Letters*, 7.689.

266 **He was shy** TR, *An Autobiography*, 258, 263–64. TR did permit himself one reference to "my son Kermit" in describing a lion hunt in Africa, presumably because KR had been mentioned often in *African Game Trails*. Elsewhere in his manuscript, he deleted some accidental references to Ted before sending it to the printer. See chap. 9, 24 (MLM).

266 **Adult traumas** Morris, *The Rise of TR, passim*.

266 **"an optimist"** Wister, *Roosevelt*, 331–32.

267 **That land of the West** TR, *An Autobiography*, 346. His quotation "gone with

lost Atlantis" is from Rudyard Kipling's poem "Philadelphia" in *Rewards and Fairies* (1910).

267 **On Tuesday**   *The New York Times,* 5 Mar. 1913.

267 **the Colonel went that morning**   Ibid. To New Yorkers in 1913, the term *Futurism* was not necessarily associated with the movement of that name in Italy.

267 **a bedlam of aesthetic debate**   See Milton W. Brown, *The Story of the Armory Show* (New York, 1988), chap. 9.

267 **some Valhallan landscapes**   Pinckney Marcius-Simons (1867–1909) is often misnamed in TR studies as "Marcus Symonds" or "Bruseius Simons." A skilled, New York–born genre painter in the 1880s, he later developed a vaguer, more mystical style, apparently influenced by Wagner's *Ring of the Nibelungen* and *Parsifal*. He died in Bayreuth. For TR's emotional reaction to three Simons works (which still hang in Sagamore Hill), see TR, *Letters,* 4.757–78. "I wish 'the light that never was on land or sea' in the pictures I am to live with—and this light your paintings have." See also TR, *An Autobiography,* 586.

267 **As for sculpture**   Longworth, *Crowded Hours,* 65.

267 **"Art," Roosevelt admitted**   TR quoted in Butt, *Letters,* 355–56.

268 **His executive dining room**   Morris, *Theodore Rex, passim;* Albert Bigelow Paine, *Thomas Nast: His Period and His Pictures* (New York, 1904), 556ff.; Garland in *Roosevelt House Bulletin,* 2.2 (Fall 1923).

> *Historiographical Note:* A comprehensive study of TR's patronage of artists and the arts as President remains to be written. His activism included the classical restoration and renaming of the White House; dynamic backing for the McMillan Commission's 1902 plan to de-clutter and beautify Washington, along the lines of Pierre L'Enfant's original design; relocating the proposed Lincoln Memorial on Capitol Hill to its present site; ordering the removal of the former Pennsylvania Railroad Station on the Mall at Sixth Street, N.W.; campaigning for a National Art Gallery; and pressuring his fellow regents on the Smithsonian Institution board to acquire major collections of Oriental, British, and contemporary American art. Shortly before leaving the White House he appointed and empowered a Fine Arts Council, under the advisement of the American Institute of Architects. But the gesture was quixotic, since neither Congress nor President Taft showed any interest in continuing the cultural policies of the Roosevelt administration. See TR, *Letters,* 4.817; Glenn Brown, "Roosevelt and the Fine Arts," *American Architect,* 116 (1919); "Roosevelt and Our Coin Designs: The Letters Between Theodore Roosevelt and Augustus Saint Gaudens," *The Century Magazine,* Apr. 1920; reminiscences of Christopher LaFarge and Glenn Brown in Wood, *Roosevelt As We Knew Him,* 169–72; Willard B. Gatewood, Jr., "Theodore Roosevelt, Champion of Governmental Aesthetics," *Georgia Review,* 67.21 (Summer 1967); Richard H. Collin, *Theodore Roosevelt, Culture, Diplomacy, and Expansion* (Baton Rouge, La., 1985); Steven L. Levine, "Race, Culture, and Art: Theodore Roosevelt and the Nationalist Aesthetic" (Ph.D. thesis, Kent State University, 2001). Aviva F. Taubenfeld's *Rough Writing: Ethnic Authorship in Theodore Roosevelt's America* (New York, 2008) is an important study of TR's literary patronage related to the immigrant experience.

268 **Unlike most**   The British novelist Arnold Bennett visited New York 15 months before the Armory Show and was dismayed at the low esteem in which Europhile Americans held their own culture. "They associate art with Florentine frames, matinée hats, distant museums, and clever talk full of allusions to the dead." Bennett, *Your United States* (New York, 1912), 163–64.

268 **He felt that** TR, "A Layman's View of an Art Exhibition," TR, *Works*, 14.405ff. Originally published in *The Outlook*, 29 Mar. 1913.

268 **Roosevelt was in** Journalistic glimpses of TR at the Armory Show describe his pace as leisurely and his mood one of calm enjoyment. He was escorted by Arthur B. Davies, president of the exhibition, Walt Kuhn, and Robert W. Chanler. The following account of what he saw is based on TR's above-cited article, and on a virtual, though partial, tour of the exhibition compiled by Shelley Staples for the University of Virginia at http://xroads.virginia.edu/. Extra visual details, and identification of the artworks that caught TR's eye, come from the scrapbooks, photographs, and clippings collected by Walt Kuhn in WCF. The Kuhn archive also includes a complete typed list of all the exhibits.

268 **He was predisposed** TR, *Works*, 14.410. Chanler (1872–1930) was a French-trained muralist whose intricately woven style was inspired by the polyphony of J. S. Bach. (Chanler, *Roman Spring*, 188–89.) For TR's "American ideal" in the creative arts, see Taubenfeld, *Rough Writers*, 2–12, and Wagenknecht, *The Seven Worlds of TR*, 65–79.

269 **It was clear that** Davies (1862–1928) was, despite his romantic style, a member of "The Eight." Considered by many in his day to be the greatest living American artist, he was an enthusiastic promoter of the European avant-garde. It was largely due to him that the Armory Show, originally intended as a survey of American art, became international. Davies selected most of the foreign works on display, leaving the American galleries to his colleague William Glackens.

269 **Roosevelt was taken** TR, *Works*, 14.410. Ms. Myers's satiric sculpture is illustrated in *The Century Magazine*, 85.4 (Aug. 1913).

> *Biographical Note:* TR's casual evocation of the fifteenth idyll of Theocritus in reference to a piece of contemporary American sculpture might have struck some readers of his review as "showing off." But nobody viewing the carved figures and reading the poem—both invoking nervous, chatterboxy, overdressed women, recoiling from yet half-excited by the press of flesh in a crowded street—could dispute the brilliance of the analogy. Such *aperçus* were so much a feature of his private conversation and correspondence that he could have published more of them if he chose.
>
> TR's memory was as comprehensive as it was photographic. It went far beyond the normal politician's knack of remembering names and faces, although his ability in that regard was phenomenal. What he saw or heard, and in particular what he read, registered with an almost mechanistic clarity. A few days after the Armory Show, he received a letter from KR, asking if he could remember the words of a poem by Edith Thomas (1854–1925) about exile south of the border.
>
> "[It] runs as follows, I think," TR replied, and wrote in his clear hand: *Beside the lake whose wave is hushed to hear, / The surf beat of a sea on either hand, / Far from Castile, / Afar in Toltec land, / Fearless I died who living knew not fear. / Dark faces frowned between me and the sky; / The Gordian knife drove deep; life grew a dream / Far from Castile! / Who heard my cry extreme / That held the sum of partings? / World, goodbye!* (TR to KR, 26 Mar. 1913, ts. [TRC].)
>
> He was not copying. His punctuation differed in several particulars from Thomas's, although he correctly reproduced the exclamation mark that inflected her repetition of "Castile." He erred on one image, writing "Gordian knife" instead of "Indian blade," and divided four lines that should have been couplets. Otherwise, he got the poem as right as if he had memorized it hours before. In fact, he was remembering its first printing in 1894, in an issue of *The*

Atlantic Monthly that had coincidentally carried an article by himself. The poem must have registered there and then, because he had quoted a phrase from it, probably without thinking, two years later in the fourth volume of his book *The Winning of the West:* "Dark faces frowned through the haze, the war-axes gleamed, and on the frozen ground the soldiers fell." Edith M. Thomas, "A Good-By" and TR, "The College Graduate and Public Life," *The Atlantic Monthly,* Aug. 1894; TR, *The Winning of the West* (New York, 1896), 4.60.

269 **What pleased Roosevelt**   Other American works TR singled out for especial praise were Kate T. Cory's "Arizona Desert," Mahonri Young's studies for the Sea Gull Monument in Salt Lake City, Leon Dabo's "Canadian Night," Amos Chew's plaster, "Pelf," and Émile Bourdelle's "Heracles." TR, *Works,* 14.410.

270 **European moderns**   The Armory Show grouped artists geographically according to their current domicile. Hence Whistler was hung in the British galleries, and Kandinsky in the German.

270 **Then came the slap**   See Brown, *Story of the Armory Show,* 168ff.

270 **obviously mammalian**   The phraseology here is TR's, in *Works,* 14.408.

270 **A phrase he**   TR, *Letters,* 7.710.

270 **Nakedness seemed**   Henri's "Figure in Motion," clearly influenced by the photography of Eadweard Muybridge, was described by William Zorach as "the "nudest nude I ever saw." It and Pascin's "Three Girls" may be seen on the above-cited website of Shelley Staples.

270 **As James Bryce**   Wagenknecht, *The Seven Worlds of TR,* 22.

270 **his subsequent review**   TR, *Works,* 14.405. The tone of TR's review may be contrasted with that of, e.g., Kenyon Cox in *Harper's Weekly,* 15 Mar. 1913: "This thing [modernism/Cubism] is not amusing: it is heartrending and sickening . . . nothing less than the total destruction of the art of painting . . . revolting and defiling . . . pathological. . . . As to Matisse . . . it is not madness that stares at you from his canvasses, but leering effrontery."

271 **What disturbed him**   "Something is wrong with the world," the financier James D. Stillman wrote after touring the Armory Exhibition. "These men know." McGerr, *A Fierce Discontent,* 241.

271 **In this recent**   TR, *Works,* 14.407.

Biographical Note: Joseph Mascheck, "Teddy's Taste: Theodore Roosevelt and the Armory Show," *Art Forum,* 9.2. (1970), challenges the received opinion of TR's review as unsubtle and uninformed. He points out that TR's personal collection of art and *objets d'art,* much of which can still be seen at Sagamore Hill, contains some "very fine items," including Oriental bronzes and screens, a signed drawing by the Roman Baroque master Pietro Testa, a few "sublime landscapes," including those of Marcius-Simons, plus French porcelains, a large corpus of statues by Frederic Remington, and "a number of truly superb Indian rugs and blankets." As for TR's seeing eye, Mascheck notes that he already had demonstrated, in his criticism of the Thayer theory of protective coloration (see above, 141, 623), "a grasp of the total visual field . . . quite out of Thayer's reach," plus an "extremely Post-Impressionistic" ability to identify with both observer and observed. Mascheck agrees with several Rooseveltian assessments of individual items on display in the Armory, especially the "very remarkable works" of Chanler. He traces and authenticates all TR's quotes of pretentious art-writing, and remarks that even a humorous reference to "colored puzzle-pictures" in the Sunday papers was well-chosen, since John Sloan had long earned money doing just that. As for the Navajo rug, "Roosevelt needs no utilitarian apology for formal beauty: in fact, what he seems to be *after* is pure decorative value." As a postscript, it might be noted that when Walter Pach visited wartime France in 1914 to buy modern art for New York galleries, he went armed with a "To Whom It May Concern" letter from TR. "As a result," Bennard B. Perlman writes, "Pach was successful in acquiring and transporting back to the United States art by Picasso, Derain, Redon, Rouault, Dufy, and Matisse." *American Artists, Authors, and Collectors: The Walter Pach Letters, 1906–1958,* Bernard B. Perlman, ed. (New York, 2003), 7.

272 **A cartoon by Kemble** *Baltimore Evening Sun,* 5 Mar. 1913. The image, preserved by Walt Kuhn in WCF, shows a gift note attached to the portrait of TR, reading: "Dear Woodrow, I leave this to your tender care. I have no use for it. Yours, William."

272 **the "Square Deal"** New York *World* editorial, ca. Mar. 1913 (WCF).

272 **drew a caricature** Preserved in WCF.

272 **It turned out** *Baltimore Evening Sun,* 3, 5 Mar. 1913; *Atlanta Constitution,* 6 Mar. 1913. WHT's chair, if left behind at all, was presumably too large for WW.

272 **"Don't you suppose"** Thompson, *Presidents I've Known,* 274.

272 **The great government** *The New York Times,* 5 Mar. 1913.

273 **an armed attack** *The Washington Post,* 5 Mar. 1913. Wilson had been more or less forced to appoint Bryan, who had swung the Baltimore convention for him the year before, and who still commanded the loyalty of the Democratic Party's populist majority. Heckscher, *Woodrow Wilson,* 269.

273 **found themselves barred** *The New York Times,* 6 Mar. 1913.

273 **On Friday, 4 April** The following account of ERD's wedding is based on newspaper reports, chiefly *The New York Times,* 6 Apr. 1913, and Wister, *Roosevelt,* 319–20.

273 **"I feel very strongly"** TR, *Letters,* 7.718.

274 **This had been** EKR to Emily Carow, 10 Feb. 1913 (TRC). A conspicuous Harvard no-show at the wedding, to ARL's considerable anger, was Nick Longworth. He remained depressed over the loss of his Congressional seat through most of 1913. Sylvia Morris, *Edith Kermit Roosevelt,* 394–95.

274 **He seemed near** *Syracuse Herald,* 6 Apr. 1913.

274 **such a concourse** Wister, *Roosevelt,* 319. For an extended survey of TR's "familiars," see ibid., 45ff.

275 **"I am working"** TR to ERD, 1 Apr. 1913 (ERDP).

275 **heroism at San Juan** *An Autobiography,* 512–24.

276 **write more "picturesquely"** Abbott's adverb is barely legible in a note penciled on a page of chap. 3 of TR's manuscript in MLM. It may be "pictorially," but phrases in the note that can be read ("I wish Mr. T. R. could and would [illegible]") convey his editorial unhappiness. EKR, too, expressed misgivings about the quality of the ms., which she blamed on the pressure of having to publish serially. "I hope he will get the opportunity to polish it up." EKR to ERD, ca. June 1913 (ERDP).

276 **Roosevelt revised some** TR manuscript of *An Autobiography* (MLM).

276 **asking Gifford Pinchot** See TR, *Letters,* 7.716–17. TR actually pasted Pinchot's draft into his text, with minimal alterations. *An Autobiography* ms., chap. 11 (MLM).

CHAPTER 14: A VANISHED ELDER WORLD

277 **Epigraph** Robinson, *Collected Poems,* 99. TR chose a stanza from this poem ("The Wilderness") as an epigraph to his book of travel essays, *A Book-Lover's Holidays in the Open* (New York, 1916).

277 **The county courthouse** See *Roosevelt v. Newett* for the full cast of characters participating in TR's libel suit. The following account of the proceedings is based on this source, and newspaper reports, mainly those of *The New York Times*, 28 May–1 June 1913. *Roosevelt v. Newett,* privately published by TR's cousin Emlen Roosevelt, is marred by the exclusion of depositions for the defense. For a summary of these, see Charles A. Palmer, "Teddy Roosevelt's Libel Trial," *Litigation,* 19.3 (Spring 1993).

277 **A jury of** *Sheboygan Press,* 27 May 1913.

278 **Newett was due** Ibid.; *Atlanta Constitution,* 1 June 1913.

278 **"All that Roosevelt"** *Roosevelt v. Newett,* 12.

278 **Newett was a stalwart** Melvin Holli and C. David Tompkins, "Roosevelt v. Newett: The Politics of Libel," *Michigan History,* 47.4 (Dec. 1963); *Roosevelt v. Newett,* 12. TR's other attorneys were W. S. Hill of Marquette and William Van Benschoten of New York. Newett was represented by William Belden, a prominent local corporate lawyer, and Horace Andrews, head counsel for the Cleveland Cliffs Iron Company of Ohio.

278 **I have never** *Roosevelt v. Newett,* 13–14.

278 **"about seven tablespoons"** "Brandy" *sic.* See above, 588.

279 **"Because of my"** TR quoted by Jay G. Hayden, correspondent for the *Detroit News,* in an interview with Hermann Hagedorn, 10 Dec. 1948 (TRB).

279 **Doctors Lambert** *Roosevelt v. Newett,* 45–70.

279 **"He is about"** Ibid., 58–61.

280 **He sat tilted** *Cedar Rapids Republican,* 29 May 1913.

280 **By mid-morning** *Roosevelt v. Newett,* 109. In pretrial depositions, the defense had relied on the testimony of distant witnesses who had found TR's behavior strange on four occasions: during campaign appearances in Ohio and Michigan on 17 May and 8–9 Oct. 1912; at an air show in St. Louis on 11 Oct. 1910; and at a dinner for Speaker Joseph Cannon in Washington on 7 May 1906. The first three of these allegations were easily rebuffed with primary evidence, and just before the trial began, a former reporter prepared to swear to the fourth skipped across the Canadian border to escape an unrelated charge of grand larceny. Palmer, "Teddy Roosevelt's Libel Trial."

280 **James Pound said** *Roosevelt v. Newett,* 111–12.

280 **Pound returned triumphant** Ibid., 325, 92, 178. There were no trial proceedings on Friday, Decoration Day.

280 **By Saturday morning** *Roosevelt v. Newett,* 355–56.

281 **"a tool of the steel trust"** During TR's speech on 9 Oct. 1912, a man in the audience had objected to this characterization of Young, calling TR a "liar." The exchange prompted Newett's editorial. TR subsequently carried Marquette County. Holli, "Roosevelt v. Newett."

281 **The trial was won** *Roosevelt v. Newett,* 358.

281 **Throughout, Roosevelt had** *Atlanta Constitution,* 1 June 1913; *Roosevelt v. Newett,* 358.

281 **After it was all over** The jury foreman significantly forgot to use the word *plaintiff* in announcing, "We find for Theodore Roosevelt." *The New York Times,* 1 June 1913.

281 **"Are you and Newett"** The wording of this anecdote closely follows that of Thompson, *Presidents I've Known,* 125. See also ibid., 194–95.

281 *Roosevelt v. Newett* **was** *The New York Times,* 2 and 3 June, *Fort Wayne News,* 28 May 1913.

282 **"I am very glad"** TR to KR, 2 June 1913, ts. (TRC). According to Abbott, *Impressions of TR,* 284–85, Bowers & Sands, TR's New York law firm, waived its fee on the ground that he had been unjustly libeled.

282 **It occurred to him**   EKR to ERD and Richard Derby, 11, 28 May 1913 (ERDP); TR to KR, 1 May and 2 June 1913, ts. (TRC). KR's new employer was the Anglo-Brazilian Forging, Steel Structural & Importing Company, a start-up venture promising high future rewards. KR to ERD, 30 Apr. 1913 (ERDP).

282 **"Sometime I must"**   Kermit Roosevelt, *The Long Trail*, 65.

282 **Roosevelt had in fact**   TR to ERD, 1 June 1913 (ERDP); TR, *Letters*, 7.731; *Chicago Tribune*, 8 Dec. 1912.

282 **"Great risks and hazards"**   *The Outlook*, 1 Mar. 1913.

282 **For a variety of reasons**   EKR ascribed TR's need for physical adventure in the spring of 1913 to political frustration. "Father needs more scope," she wrote ERD, "and since he can't be President must go away from home to have it." Sylvia Morris, *Edith Kermit Roosevelt*, 397.

283 **In Paris, on the**   See Ecksteins, *Rites of Spring*, chap. 1, for the famous premiere of *Le Sacre du Printemps* at the Théâtre des Champs-Élysées on 29 May 1913, and the portents it held for a world about to slip into war.

283 **He found his**   TR to KR, 24 May 1913. ts. (TRC). TR's current reading included Vladimir Simkhovitch's *Marxism versus Socialism*. (TR, *Letters*, 7.742.) Although the book confirmed his prejudices about the equalization of wealth, he was hardly less approving of free-market capitalism.

283 **"It is rather"**   TR, *Letters*, 7.741.

283 **"I shall be glad"**   TR, *Works*, 6.4; TR, *Letters*, 7.741.

284 **The pious doctrines**   *The New York Times*, 23 Apr. 1913. The Hobson-Sheppard Resolution of 1913, calling for a prohibition amendment to the Constitution, was the seed of the Eighteenth Amendment of 1919. It passed the House in 1914, but failed to achieve a two-thirds vote in the Senate. For Bryan's role as a prohibitionist, see Mark Edward Lerner, *Dictionary of American Temperance Biography* (Westport, Conn. 1984), 69–70, 442.

284 **"Thou Shalt Not"**   TR, *Letters*, 7.739.

284 **He was sufficiently alarmed**   EKR to ERD, 11 May 1913 (ERDP); TR, *Letters*, 7.729. "For the first time," Edith wrote TR's sister Bamie, "He begins to wish his hand was on the helm." (12 May 1913 [TRC].) TR's attitude to the California-Japan crisis of 1913 is spelled out in TR, *Letters*, 7.720–22 and 727–31. The Wilson administration was itself sufficiently concerned about the Pacific threat to devote a cabinet debate to it on 16 May. Heckscher, *Woodrow Wilson*, 301.

284 **Like David Livingstone**   The Victorian era's saintly missionary converted only one African, who subsequently reverted to paganism. Tim Jeal, *Livingstone* (New York, 1973), 80–81.

284 **"go up the Paraguay"**   TR, *Works*, 6.3; TR, *Letters*, 7.741.

284 **his essay on faith**   See above, 154–57.

284 **There was a certain**   TR, *Letters*, 7.741; See also John Augustine Zahm, *Through South America's Southland: With an Account of the Roosevelt Scientific Expedition to South America* (New York, 1916), 4–9; TR, *Works*, 6.4.

285 **Chapman suggested**   Frank Chapman to Henry Fairfield Osborn, 24 June 1913 (AMNH); *National Cyclopaedia of American Biography*, 37.387–98, 40.320.

285 **Roosevelt reviewed**   TR to Frank Chapman, 30 July 1913 (AMNH); TR, *Works*, 6.ix–x, 5–6. Cherrie had given help to opponents of the Venezuelan dictator Cipriano Castro, immortalized by TR as "that unspeakably villainous little monkey."

285 **he was recruited**   TR, *Works*, 6.5. Miller was twenty-six. TR offered to pay the traveling expenses of both naturalists, on condition that they would publish nothing competitive with his own memoir of the expedition. The museum agreed to provide scientific equipment and take care of the transportation of specimens. TR to Henry Fairfield Osborn, 20 July 1913 (AMNH).

285 **Anthony Fiala, a** Zahm, *Through South America's Southland,* 11; Candice Millard, *The River of Doubt: Theodore Roosevelt's Darkest Journey* (New York, 2005), 33–34; TR to Lauro Müller, 14 Oct. 1913 (TRP); Sylvia Morris, *Edith Kermit Roosevelt,* 296–97; TR to KR, 30 June 1913, ts. (TRC).

285 **graduated at last** TR had attended ABR's commencement in Andover on 13 June 1913.

286 **Two days later** The chronology of TR's movements from 12 July–22 Aug. 1913 in TR, *Letters,* 8.1481 is inaccurate. The correct sequence of night stops is July 12–14: El Tovar; 15: Phantom Ranch; 16–31: Kaibab Plateau; Aug. 1: House Rock Valley; 2–3: Lees Ferry; 4: Painted Desert; 5–6: Tuba; 7: camp; 8: Marsh Pass; 9: Kayenta; 10: Bubbling Spring Valley; 11: Navajo Mountain; 12: Rainbow Bridge, Utah; 13–14: camp; 15–16: Kayenta; 17–18: camp; 19–20: Walpi; 21: Ganado; 22: Gallup, N.M.

286 **Moonlit and mysterious** The following account of TR's vacation in Arizona is based on his articles "A Cougar Hunt on the Rim of the Grand Canyon," "Across the Navajo Desert," and "The Hopi Snake Dance," *The Outlook,* 4, 11, and 18 Oct. 1913. They are cited as reprinted in TR, *Works,* 4. Supplementary details and chronology from Nicholas Roosevelt, *TR,* 110ff.

286 *Leave it as* See Morris, *Theodore Rex,* 225–26.

286 **"He still has"** Nicholas Roosevelt, *TR,* 117.

287 **Roosevelt indulged in** TR, *Works,* 4.22. A lookout southeast of Vista Encantada was dedicated by the National Park Service in 1990 as "Roosevelt Point."

287 **The soil was so arid** It is a conjecture that the future author of "The Waste Land" may have read TR's article "Across the Navajo Desert" in *The Outlook* that fall, before moving to England in the spring of 1914.

287 **Roosevelt was reminded** TR, *Works,* 4.26, quoting Joaquin Miller, *Song of the Sierras* (Boston, 1871), xii.

287 **Kayenta was** TR, *Works,* 4.31, 36. See Elizabeth Compton Hegemann, *Navaho Trading Days* (Albuquerque, 1963), 224ff., for a photographic memoir of the Wetherills and the entire region TR traversed in 1913.

287 **On 10 August** Nicholas Roosevelt, *TR,* 120; TR, *Works,* 4.37.

288 **He noted the next** TR, *Works,* 4.38.

288 **proposals to cut up and sell** Dana and Mary R. Coolidge, *The Navajo Indians* (Boston, 1930), 268.

288 **Although he held no brief** TR, *Works,* 4.28.

288 **Roosevelt's attitude** Hagedorn, *Roosevelt in the Bad Lands,* 355; Morris, *The Rise of TR,* 304–5, 466–67. The most comprehensive survey of TR's prepresidential Indian policies is that of Dyer, *TR and the Idea of Race,* 70–83.

288 **As President** See Lewis L. Gould, *The Presidency of Theodore Roosevelt* (Lawrence, Kan., 1991), 207–9. But see also McGerr, *A Fierce Discontent,* 205–9.

289 **He had protected** Natalie Curtis, *The Indians' Book* (New York, 1907), 476. Natalie Curtis, later Burlin (1875–1921), was related to the great Western photographer Edward S. Curtis, a family friend of the Roosevelts. This connection helped smooth her introduction to TR in 1903. See Natalie Curtis, "Mr. Roosevelt and Indian Music: A Personal Reminiscence," *The Outlook,* 5 Mar. 1919, and TR, *Letters,* 3.523. Her pioneering musicology, using cylinder recordings, was taken seriously in Europe, where composers such as Béla Bartók were conducting similar researches. Ferruccio Busoni's *Red Indian Fantasy* for piano and orchestra (1915) was based on themes from *The Indians' Book.* A biographical website devoted to Miss Curtis is available at http://www.nataliecurtis.org/.

289 **"These songs cast"** Reproduced in facsimile in Curtis, *The Indians' Book.*

289 **He talked to her** TR, *Works,* 4.41.

289 *Dawn, beautiful dawn* Ibid., 4.44.

289 **Roosevelt decided**   Ibid., 4.42. TR also wrote that Kayenta "would be an excellent place for a summer school of archeology and ethnology." Ibid., 38–39.

289 **At mid-morning**   TR, *Works*, 4.47; Natalie Curtis, "Theodore Roosevelt in Hopi-Land," *The Outlook*, 17 Sept. 1919. The following anecdote, with quotations, is taken entirely from this source.

290 **It was Natalie Curtis**   Miss Curtis's embarrassment was compounded when she found that the good-looking young "cowboy" who had helped her milk the gasoline from a parked car was none other than Archie. Curtis, "Theodore Roosevelt in Hopi-Land."

291 **Roosevelt then gave himself**   Except where otherwise indicated, the following account of TR's stay in Walpi is based on his essay "The Hopi Snake-Dance," in TR, *Works*, 4.48–72.

292 **On Wednesday morning**   Curtis, "Theodore Roosevelt in Hopi-Land."

292 **Roosevelt listened and memorized**   In her memoir of TR's visit, Miss Curtis remarked on the "impersonality" with which he absorbed what she had to tell him. This, plus the "electric snap" of his comprehension and the accuracy of his memory, gave him "an astonishing command of data in subjects that no one would imagine he could know . . . without years of study."

292 **At dawn the following day**   Curtis, "Theodore Roosevelt in Hopi-Land"; TR, *Works*, 4.63–64.

292 **privately wishing**   TR, *Works*, 4.64.

293 **When each priest**   Ibid., 4.65–68.

293 **At five o'clock**   "Hopi Indians Dance for TR [at Walpi, Ariz.] 1913," a film available online from the Library of Congress at http://memory.loc.gov/, shows TR watching this event with a woman who may be Natalie Curtis.

294 **"If I don't write"**   Curtis, "Theodore Roosevelt in Hopi-Land."

294 **"I can never afford"**   Ibid. Miss Curtis, writing in 1919, misremembered her own and TR's schedule, but she was specific in describing the editorial session she had with him before he left Walpi. Even for a writer of his promptitude, completing such a lengthy manuscript so soon was a remarkable feat. He may have already written the parts of it that covered the events of 19 and 20 Aug.

294 **The Colonel returned**   TR arrived back in New York on 26 Aug. 1913. His three Arizona articles were published in *The Outlook* on 4, 11, and 18 Oct. 1913.

294 **He was overjoyed**   EKR was slightly piqued not to have been consulted about TR's proposed expedition until it was a fait accompli. She wrote KR from Europe to complain, "In his letters to me he preserves a sphinx like silence and except for the fact that he sails on October 4th I know nothing of his plans." 15 July 1913 (KRP).

294 **One of her favorite quotations**   Sylvia Morris, *Edith Kermit Roosevelt*, 397. EKR was probably thinking of the passage in Boccaccio's version of the story, "Therefore let us flee hence in secret and go there together, thou and I; and what span of life we have left in the world, heart of my body, let us spend it together in delight." R. K. Gordon, ed., *The Story of Troilus* (London, 1934), 88.

294 **"I am having"**   TR to QR, 29 Sept. 1913 (TRC).

294 **On 27 September**   *The New York Times*, 28 Sept. 1913. TR also forced the nomination of Samuel Seabury, a Democrat, as associate justice running on the Progressive ticket.

295 **Finally he allowed**   *The New York Times*, 4 Oct. 1913. The official text of TR's speech, entitled "The United States and the South American Republics," is in TR, *Works*, 18.391–405. TR was embarrassed when some paragraphs he decided not to read, being overly critical of Woodrow Wilson's foreign policy, were accidentally released to newspapers.

295 **he sold *The Outlook***   EKR to ERD, 4 July 1913 (ERDP). TR's income from writ-

ing and speaking in 1913, based on his wife's figures and royalty statements in SCR, was approximately $46,000, or $764,000 in contemporary (2010) dollars. This total does not include whatever he may have earned from his inheritance and investments. His and EKR's frequent protestations of poverty in later life were those of old-money aristocrats, as reflexive as middle-class complaints about the weather. Before returning home from South America, EKR informed ERD that in order to get through the winter alone at Sagamore Hill, she would require the in-house services of a cook, a kitchen maid, a waitress, a chambermaid, and a par-lormaid (20 Oct. 1913 [ERDP]).

295 **Quentin and Archie** Having qualified for Harvard, ABR congratulated himself on at last being able to associate with men "of my own class." Apparently Andover had not come up to his social standards. ABR note, n.d., enclosed in EKR to KR, 9 Mar. 1913 (KRP).

295 **Alice was more** EKR to KR, 24, 27 May 1913 (KRP); EKR to ERD, 15 July 1913 (ERDP). According to ARL in later life, TR and EKR showed more concern for the social consequences of a loud public divorce than for her or Nick's personal distress. "Although they didn't quite lock me up, they exercised considerable pres-sure . . . told me to think it over very carefully indeed. . . . Not done, they said. Emphatically." Teague, *Mrs. L,* 158. See also Cordery, *Alice,* 238.

295 **"Naturally," he wrote** TR, *An Autobiography,* 243 (foreword, dated 1 Oct. 1913).

INTERLUDE: GERMANY, OCTOBER—DECEMBER, 1913

296 **Inevitably, they dwarfed** Illustration in *The Outlook,* 18 Oct. 1913. There is a full account of the dedication in *The Times,* 20 Oct. 1913.

296 **The Battle of Leipzig** Also known in various languages as the Battle of Nations, because of the multiplicity of armies that took part. Germans usually refer to the monument as *der Volkerschlachtdenkmal.*

297 **in tomorrow's European papers** See, e.g., page 8 of *The Times,* 20 Oct. 1913.

297 *His* **particular phobia** Bismarck's constant, typically Prussian refrain had been, "The Reich is in danger." (Ecksteins, *Rites of Spring,* 66.) For a discussion of the anthropological significance of the Battle of Nations monument, see Rudy Koshar, *From Monuments to Traces: Artifacts of German Memory, 1890–1990* (Berkeley, Calif., 2000) 43–47.

297 *"Ich gehe mi Euch"* Lawrence Sondhaus, *Franz Conrad von Hötzendorf* (Boston, 2000), 133. In an alternate translation of this remark, the Kaiser sounds more peremptory: "you would be at Belgrade" becomes "you must be in Bel-grade." (H. W. Koch, ed., *The Origins of the First World War: Great Power Ri-valry and German War Aims* [London, 1972], 136.) Conrad himself was the source of the quotation.

297 **Franz Ferdinand jealously** Sondhaus, *Conrad,* 133.

297 **French comments had** *The New York Times,* 19 Nov. 1913; Koshar, *From Mon-uments to Traces,* 47.

298 **An eruptive bigness** Ecksteins, *Rites of Spring,* 69; Tuchman, *The Proud Tower,* 344; Schorske, *Fin-de-Siècle Vienna,* 345. Tuchman misdates the premiere of Strauss's *Festliches Präludium,* Op. 61, which marked the opening of the Vienna Konzerthaus on 19 Oct. 1913.

298 **"It is only by"** Tuchman, *The Proud Tower,* 344.

298 **In last year's** Ecksteins, *Rites of Spring,* 73.

299 **Chancellor ever more** Franz von Papen, *Memoirs,* trans. Brian Connell (London, 1952), 13.

299 **"fureur d'hégémonie"** Georges Clemenceau, *Discours de guerre* (1934, 1968), 12.

299 **Early in November** Except where otherwise indicated, the following account of the Zabern affair is based on David Schoenbaum, *Zabern 1913: Consensus Politics in Imperial Germany* (London, 1982), and on Sebastian Compagnon, "Novembre 1913: Saverne la tranquille se rebelle," online study published by the University of Strasbourg at http://mcsinfo.u-strasbg.fr/.

299 **"Should you kill"** Schoenbaum, *Zabern 1913*, 98. The author has retranslated the words in Schoenbaum's source, Arnold Heydt, *Der Fall Zabern* (Strasbourg, 1934), 7–8.

299 **"And me, I'll"** *Zaberner Anzeiger*, 6 Nov. 1913, quoted in Compagnon, "Novembre 1913." The local report inflated the shooting-range scuffle into an actual sword attack on an Alsatian.

299 **"For every one"** Ibid.

300 **"*Tête de macchabée!*"** Ibid.

300 **"As far as I"** Schoenbaum, *Zabern 1913*, 103.

300 **shouts of "*Bettscheisser*"** Ibid., 111–12.

301 **The Chancellor, sounding** Transcript of Bethmann-Hollweg's remarks at World War I Document archive (http://wwi.lib.byu.edu/); James W. Gerard (eyewitness), *My Four Years in Germany* (New York, 1917), 67. Gerard, the American ambassador to Germany, gives a personal account of the Zabern affair and its effect on the German people in ibid., 59ff.

301 **During the debate** Schoenbaum, *Zabern 1913*, 125.

301 **rage and shame** The British peer Lord Milner was in Germany at the time of the Zabern crisis and reported that "the people were so incensed that a revolt against the brutality of the system was with difficulty controlled." (Robert T. Loreburn, *How the War Came* [New York, 1920], 283.) Meanwhile, Alsatians began to refer to themselves bitterly as *Muss-Pruessen*, compulsory Prussians. Tuchman, *The Proud Tower*, 344.

301 **One day, at** Clemenceau, *Discours de guerre*, 18 (trans. author).

> *Historical Note:* On 5 Jan. 1914, Reuter and Forstner appeared before a military tribunal in Strasbourg on charges of overriding the civil authority in Zabern. They were acquitted after defense lawyers argued that they had been doing their duty in a situation threatening riot. The Crown Prince personally congratulated Reuter and decorated him. Nevertheless, the German and Reichsland parliaments pressed the issue of abuse of military power so forcefully that on 19 Mar., Wilhelm II issued a new regulation that compelled the army to seek civil clearance for acts of social discipline.
>
> In 1916, the "hurricane" that Clemenceau had so long predicted mowed down Günter von Forstner. The lieutenant's offenses remained largely forgotten until 1931, when Sergeant Willy Höflich published a memoir, *Affaire Zabern*. In retrospect, the incident can be seen as having been doubly divisive, driving a wedge not only between German democratic opinion and royal authority, but between the citizens of Alsace-Lorraine and their temporary overlords ("perhaps the final factor which decided the advocates of the old military system of Germany in favor of a European war"). Gerard, *My Four Years in Germany*, 91.

CHAPTER 15: *EXPEDIÇÃO CÍENTIFICA ROOSEVELT-RONDON*

305 **Epigraph** Robinson, *Collected Poems*, 67.

305 **On the first day** TR, *Works*, 6.110.

> *Chronological Note:* Upon arrival at Barbados on 10 Oct. 1913, TR and his expedition colleagues were joined by Leo Miller. They steamed on south without

visiting Panama, where President Wilson had just triggered, via electric signal, the fall of the last canal dike separating the Atlantic and Pacific oceans. If TR was wistful at not seeing this consummation of what he considered the greatest initiative of his presidency, he gave no sign. Earlier in the year, he had joked about keeping clear of Colombia, to avoid being jailed there for enabling the Panama Revolution of 1903. (James T. Addison to Hermann Hagedorn, 26 Apr. 1921 [AC].) He was happy now simply to be away from all things political. "I think he feels like Christian in *Pilgrim's Progress* when the bundle fell from his back," EKR wrote on 15 Oct. 1913 to Anna Roosevelt Cowles, "—in this case it was not made of sins but of the Progressive Party." She watched her husband laughing at deck sports, "as I have not heard him laugh for years" (TRC). KR was at dockside when the Roosevelts arrived in Bahia, Brazil, on 18 Oct. Three days later in Rio de Janeiro, TR began his official tour of the "ABC nations," Argentina, Brazil, and Chile. In all three countries, and also in transit through Uruguay, he received elaborate welcomes and hospitality from the governing, intellectual, and social elite. There were numerous formal sightseeing excursions, and he sent regular travel articles home to *The Outlook*. Three compilations of these are printed in TR, *Works*, 4.73–110.

His formal lectures at the universities of Rio and São Paulo (24, 27 Oct.), the Museo Sociale Argentino in Buenos Aires (7, 10, 12 Nov.), and the university in Santiago (22 Nov.) amounted to repetitions of the political and moral points he had been making for the past several years. They were reprinted in *The Outlook*.

After TR's momentous change of plan in Rio for his Amazon expedition, described in this chapter, and his visit to that city's Theatro Municipal on 22 Oct. to see the Ballets Russes in *Swan Lake,* his travels were without important incident. He left Cherrie and the rest of his scientific team behind to prepare for the expedition, and continued south with EKR and KR to São Paulo on 26 Oct. The family party proceeded via Montevideo (4 Nov.) to Buenos Aires (5–14 Nov.), before crossing the Andes by rail, via Tucumán and Mendoza to Santiago (21–25 Nov.). EKR sailed home from Valparaiso on 26 Nov. TR and KR recrossed the Andes from Puerto Varas via Lakes Esmeralda and Fria into the plains of northern Patagonia on 29–30 Nov., riding some of the way on horseback and also traveling by steamboat, ox railway, and automobile. On the shore of Nahuel Huapi, one of the world's remotest bodies of water, TR was accosted by an English peer who said, "You won't remember me; when I last saw you, you were romping with little Prince [Olaf of Norway] in Buckingham Palace." (TR, *Works*, 4.100.)

He returned to Buenos Aires on 4 Dec., and left next day for Asunción, Paraguay, whence, on 9 Dec., he sailed up the River Paraguay, heading back into Brazil. For TR's serialized account of these travels, see *The Outlook,* 24 Jan.–6 June 1914.

305 **For a week**   Unless otherwise indicated, the narrative, scenic, and atmospheric details in this and the following chapter come from TR's and Father Zahm's respective travel books, *Through the Brazilian Wilderness* (TR, *Works,* 6) and *Through South America's Southland.* The chronology is based on two expedition diaries: those of George K. Cherrie, 1913–1914 (AMNH), and Kermit Roosevelt, 1914 (KRP). Other firsthand accounts (cited when used) are those of Cândido M. Rondon, *Lectures Delivered by Colonel Cândido Mariana da Silva Rondon . . . On the 5th, 7th and 9th of October 1915 at the Phenix Theatre of Rio de Janeiro, on the Roosevelt-Rondon Scientific Expedition,* trans. R. G. Reidy and Ed. Murray (Rio de Janeiro, 1916; New York, 1969); Esther de Vivieros, *Ron-*

don conta sua vida (Rio de Janeiro, 1958), an "as told to" biography largely dictated by Rondon; Leo E. Miller, *In the Wilds of South America* (New York, 1918), chaps. 13–16; George K. Cherrie, *Dark Trails: Adventures of a Naturalist* (New York, 1930), Part Six; and Kermit Roosevelt, *Happy Hunting Grounds*, chap. 1. The fullest account of the expedition, apart from TR's, is Millard, *The River of Doubt*.

305 **Roosevelt stoked himself**   TR, *Works*, 6.110; Sylvia Morris, *Edith Kermit Roosevelt*, 416; TR to ERD, 8 Oct. 1913 (ERDP). Nicholas Roosevelt had noticed in Arizona that "his waist was larger than his chest." *TR*, 13.

306 **He had come north**   TR's social and hunting activities between 12 and 31 Dec. 1913 are fully described in TR, *Works*, 6.47–110. See also Zahm, *Through South America's Southland*, 419–41; Miller, *In the Wilds*, 214–29; and Rondon, *Lectures*, 16–30.

306 **He had already**   Zahm, *Through South America's Southland*, 438. For a detailed account of this hunt, see TR, *Works*, 6.63–92.

306 **He had not found**   TR, *Works*, 6.77. Cruising up the Paraguay, TR became agitated when he heard some sailors shooting at birds from the bow of the *Riquelme*. "By George, this thing must stop." And so it did, on his order. Zahm, *Through South America's Southland*, 424.

306 **a tiny man**   Rondon was five foot three. Millard, *The River of Doubt*, 73.

306 **Roosevelt had met up**   Rondon, *Lectures*, 15ff.; TR, *Works*, 6.50. In 1927, José Alves de Lima, a minor diplomat and memorialist, claimed to have "selected" Rondon as TR's guide long before Müller did. (Alves de Lima, "Reminiscences of Roosevelt in Brazil.") The boast is implausible. However, TR was certainly aware of Rondon's existence, and value as a consultant, before arriving in Rio. TR to Lauro Müller, 14 Oct. 1914 (TRC).

307 **It had been he**   TR, *Works*, 6.xiii–xvi, 10; Rondon, *Lectures*, 10–12. Several alternative expeditions, all plotted by Rondon, were offered to TR, in case he declined to explore the Dúvida.

307 **Cândido Rondon was**   TR, *Works*, 6.xiv, 73.

307 **a mysterious river**   Ibid., 6.xiv. Rondon discovered the Dúvida in 1909.

307 **Roosevelt would advertise**   Ibid., 6.10.

307 **Müller could not have**   Even before meeting Müller, TR praised him, on the basis of information supplied by Elihu Root, as "one of the men to whom this entire western hemisphere must look up." Alves de Lima, "Reminiscences of Roosevelt in Brazil."

307 **Müller dreamed of building**   Armelle Enders, "Theodore Roosevelt explorateur: Positivisme et mythe de la frontière dans l'*expediçào cientifica Roosevelt-Rondon* au Mato Grosso et en Amazonie," Nuevo Mundo Mundo Nuevos (http://nuevomundo.revues.org/), 2 Feb. 2005, 3–5. Müller's dream of an inland capital was realized in 1960 with the building of Brasília. For TR's two major South American addresses on the Monroe Doctrine, see *The Outlook*, 14, 21 Mar. 1914.

308 **"I want to be the first"**   Rondon interviewed by Douglas O. Naylor in *The New York Times*, 6 Jan. 1929.

308 **"I have already"**   Osborn, "Theodore Roosevelt, Naturalist," *Natural History*, 19.1 (Jan. 1919). See also Osborn to TR, 26 Dec. 1913 ("I shall hear with the greatest relief of your arrival in Manaos"), AMNH.

308 **his six colleagues**   TR may be seen posing with his colleagues en route to Rio in a contemporary documentary, *Theodore Roosevelt—The River of Doubt*, available online at http://www.loc.gov/. The movie, titled with extracts from *Through the Brazilian Wilderness*, includes footage of many of the episodes described in this and the following chapter.

308 **Cherrie and Miller, in** TR, *Letters*, 7.754. Their official employer, Henry Fairfield Osborn of the American Museum, was considerably less enthusiastic. Millard, *The River of Doubt*, 60.

308 **Roosevelt had told** TR, *Works*, 6.xiv–xv.

308 **Kermit, of course** TR, *Letters*, 7.756; KR to Belle Willard, n.d. (KRP); Millard, *The River of Doubt*, 276–77. EKR, worried about her husband's safety in the jungle, had been instrumental in persuading TR to take KR with him. KR to ERD, Nov. 1913 (ERDP).

308 **At daybreak** The following account of TR's New Year hunt is based on TR, *Works*, 6.110–14.

309 **Rondon was used** For an excellent short biography of Rondon in English, see Todd A. Diacon, *Stringing Together a Nation: Cândido Mariano da Silva Rondon and the Construction of a Modern Brazil, 1906–1930* (Durham, N.C., 2004).

309 **He was about** TR, *Works*, 6.50–51.

309 **not entirely believable** Miller, *In the Wilds*, 196–97.

310 **Roosevelt tried to** Cherrie, *Dark Trails*, 282; TR, *Works*, 6.112.

310 **He relaxed** Zahm, *Through South America's Southland*, 450.

310 **The great river** Rondon, *Lectures*, 33–34; TR, *Works*, 6.70.

311 **Now that he saw** TR, *Works*, 6 passim.

311 **One evening this** Rondon, *Lectures*, 33–44; Zahm, *Through South America's Southland*, 449–50. Rondon and Zahm both mention TR's rapturous reaction to this sunset, and agree that he observed it from the deck of the *Nioac*, a day or two after his São Lourenço hunt. Yet he, puzzlingly, dates it back to 14 Dec. 1913, when he was still aboard the *Riquelme*. (TR, *Works*, 6.58–59.) Possibly there were two such "evenings of extraordinary splendor and beauty."

311 **As far as Kermit** KR to EKR, 12 Jan., 8 Feb. 1914; Zahm, *Through South America's Southland, passim;* John Cavanaugh, "Father Zahm," *Catholic World*, Feb. 1922. Zahm's gushy prose style is unreadable now, but his breadth of scholarship continues to impress. He is venerated at his alma mater for enriching its theological curriculum with scientific studies (symbolically, he made Notre Dame the nation's first electrically lit college campus), and for endowing it with his personal Dante collection, one of the top such archives in the United States.

312 **Kermit did not know** Zahm, *Through South America's Southland*, 428; TR estate tabulation file, 7 Mar. 1920 (SCR).

312 **Father Zahm was sorry** KR diary, 6–7 Jan. 1914 (KRP); Zahm, *Through South America's Southland*, 460; TR, *Works*, 6.xv; Millard, *The River of Doubt*, 34.

312 **Roosevelt spent his last** This paragraph paraphrases TR's own account in *Works*, 6.123–24.

313 **A gasoline launch** George Cherrie diary, 6–7 Jan. 1914.

313 **The two commanders** TR, *Works*, 6.128; Diacon, *Stringing Together a Nation*, 43. The military-propaganda aspects of the expedition are noted by Armelle Enders in "Theodore Roosevelt explorateur," 1.

313 **Rondon's "commission"** See Dominichi M. de Sá, Magali Romero Sá, and Nísia Trindade Lima, "Telegraphs and an Inventory of the Territory of Brazil: The Scientific Work of the Rondon Commission (1907–1915)," *História, Ciêncas, Saúde-Manguinhos*, 15.3 (July–Sept. 2008), http://www.scielo.br/. Commission members not named were Dr. Euzébio de Oliveira (geologist), Henrique Reinisch (zoologist), Dr. Fernando Soledade (entomologist), Arnaldo Blake de Sant'anna (taxidermist), Frederico Hoehne (a botanist of international repute), Lieutenants Alcides Lauriodó and Joaquin Mello Finho (general duty), and Thomaz Reis (cinematographer).

313 **Roosevelt's team** For Fiala's disastrous record as an Arctic explorer, see Millard, *The River of Doubt*, 31–32. KR, a natural linguist, had found himself thinking in Portuguese for at least six months. KR to ERD, 2 June 1913 (ERDP).

313 **his Swiss servant** For more on the mysterious Sigg, see Zahm, *Through South America's Southland,* 463, 498–500, and Millard, *The River of Doubt,* 46–47.

313 **an opportunity to hunt** KR diary, 8–10 Jan. 1914 (KRP); TR, *Works,* 6.129, 132–45; Zahm, *Through South America's Southland,* 462.

314 **After dinner** TR, *Works,* 6.136.

315 **At first sight** Ibid., 6.155ff.; Zahm, *Through South America's Southland,* 474; Miller, *In the Wilds,* 225.

315 **It did not look** TR, *Works,* 6.156; Cherrie diary, 18 Jan. 1914 (AMNH); TR, *Works,* 6.151.

315 **Roosevelt had begun** TR, *Letters,* 8.905; TR, *Works,* 6.160. TR's tent came complete with a floor rug.

315 **Rondon and Lyra** Diacon, *Stringing Together a Nation,* 36; Millard, *The River of Doubt,* 34.

316 **This was too much** Diacon, *Stringing Together a Nation,* 43; Cherrie, *Dark Trails,* 247; TR, *Works,* 6.224. The resignations of Hoehne, Soledade, Blake de Sant'anna, and Reis became formal on 23 Jan. 1914. Reinisch stayed with the expedition. De Sá et al., "Telegraphs."

316 **On 19 January** TR, *Works,* 6.160. TR mentions only one Canadian canoe here. There were in fact two, as he confirms on page 300.

316 **Sixty-four other** TR, *Works,* 6.160, 163; Vivieros, *Rondon,* 388; Rondon, *Lectures,* 37.

316 **If the Dúvida** Miller, *In the Wilds,* 240.

317 **We were now** TR, *Works,* 6.161.

317 **He left Robert Bridges to cut** Bridges did not do so.

317 **Next morning** TR, *Works,* 6.168.

317 **The command detachment** Rondon, *Lectures,* 38; Miller, *In the Wilds,* 226; KR diary, 29 Jan. 1914 (KRP).

317 **A daily camp rhythm** Miller, *In the Wilds,* 230; Zahm, *Through South America's Southland,* 378; TR, *Works,* 6.169–70; Rondon-Naylor interview, *The New York Times,* 6 Jan. 1929.

319 **"one felt"** Zahm, *Through South America's Southland,* 479.

319 **By now Kermit** KR to EKR, 12 Jan., 8 Feb. 1914 (KRP); Miller, *In the Wilds,* 225. It is possible that Lizzie was the "giant land turtle" mentioned in TR, *Works,* 6.

319 **Zahm was alarmed** Zahm, *Through South America's Southland,* 479–80; Vivieros, *Rondon,* 389.

319 **Relief for him** Miller, *In the Wilds,* 227; TR, *Works,* 6.173–74. Despite Zahm's eagerness to travel ahead in a *caminhão,* he objected bitterly to having to sit next to its black driver. Vivieros, *Rondon,* 389.

319 **Kermit was not** KR diary, 26 Jan. 1914 (KRP); TR, *Works,* 6.49; Vivieros, *Rondon,* 389–90. Zahm's attitude toward South American Indians may be intimated from his description of the Guarani as "noble redmen" who had been "gathered by the Jesuits into the most interesting theocratic community of which there is any record." He praised "the childlike docility with which they submitted to the guidance of their father-priests." Zahm, *Through South America's Southland,* 393, 397.

319 **he had himself founded** Enders, "Theodore Roosevelt explorateur," 6–8, analyzes Rondon's complex philosophy as the patron and protector of Brazilian Indians. For an exhaustive discussion of his education in the teachings of Comte, see Fernando Correia da Silva, "Cândido Rondon: Explorer, Geographer, Peacemaker, 1865–1958," http://www.vidaslusofonas.pt/. Positivism is still a strong religious force in Brazil.

319 **When Roosevelt first** TR, *Works,* 6.183–84.

320 **The great cascade** Zahm, *Through South America's Southland,* 496; TR, *Works,* 6.181–88; Vivieros, *Rondon,* 393.

320 **compared to Niagara** Morris, *The Rise of TR,* xxiv.

320 **Father Zahm had** Vivieros, *Rondon,* 394.

320 **The Serviço de Proteção's** Ibid.

320 **When the two colonels** Ibid., 394–95 (trans. author). See also Rondon, *Lectures,* 46–49.

321 *Every ~~American~~ member* Memo, 1 Feb. 1914, preserved in KRP. "Dr. Zahm had gotten much on TR's 'nerves.' " (Cherrie diary, 3 Feb. 1914 [AMNH].) KR rejoiced in Zahm's dismissal, on the grounds that he was "thoroly [*sic*] incompetent and selfish." (KR diary, 30 Jan. 1914 [KRP].)

321 **"Cat very sad"** KR diary, 1, 2 Feb. 1914 (KRP); KR to Belle Willard, 31 Jan. 1914 (KRP). KR's proposal and Belle's acceptance letters are quoted in Millard, *The River of Doubt,* 51–52 and 67–68.

321 **He took what consolation** In his diary, KR uses the Portuguese word *moribundia* (dying) to describe his spells of depression.

321 **The rain thinned** TR, *Works,* 6.192, 94; Rondon, *Lectures,* 77; Rondon-Naylor interview, *The New York Times,* 6 Jan. 1929.

322 **Meanwhile the Papagaio** The language of this sentence is mostly TR's in *Works,* 6.188–89.

322 **Father Zahm salvaged** Rondon, *Lectures,* 49–50; TR, *Works,* 6.195.

322 **There followed** KR diary, 3–6 Feb. 1914 (KRP); TR, *Works,* 6.198; Frank Chapman in TR, *Works,* 6.xviii.

322 **Kermit, Cherrie, and Miller** Cherrie diary, 6 Feb. 1914 (AMNH); TR, *Works,* 6.195; Miller, *In the Wilds,* 231–32. The Canadian canoes were left behind because they became heavy in the rain. Diacon, *Stringing Together a Nation,* 41.

322 **The carts were** TR, *Works,* 200–201; KR to EKR, 8 Feb. 1914 (KRP).

322 **Groups of Nhambiquaras** Cherrie diary, 23 Feb. 1914 (AMNH); Miller, *In the Wilds,* 232; TR, *Works,* 6.209.

323 **Hard rain** This paragraph summarizes KR diary, 3–23 Feb. 1914 (KRP); Miller, *In the Wilds,* 234–37; TR, *Works,* 6.196–228; Vivieros, *Rondon,* 393–99.

323 **Fiala nearly drowned** Cherrie diary, 8 Feb. 1914 (AMNH). See also Millard, *The River of Doubt,* 114–15.

323 **Books were classified** TR, *Works,* 6.231; Vivieros, *Rondon,* 400.

323 **The three Brazilian** Miller, *In the Wilds,* 231; TR, *Works,* 6.231.

324 **sketched out a title page** Bishop, *TR,* 2.363.

325 **their Gi-Paraná colleagues** Amílcar, Miller, Oliveira, and Mello.

325 **Seven shovel-nosed** TR, *Works,* 6.231–33 ; KR diary, 25 Feb. 1914 (KRP).

325 **The inscrutable river** Cherrie diary, 26 Feb. 1914 (AMNH); Miller, *In the Wilds,* 23. See Millard, *The River of Doubt,* 172 on the coloration of Amazonian tributaries—the milky, the black, and the clear.

325 **Goodbyes were exchanged** Cherrie diary, 27 Feb. 1914 (AMNH); TR, *Works,* 6.233–34. Aside from the 6 principals, the expedition force consisted of 2 solders, 8 "regional volunteers," and 6 laborers. All were highly paid for their dangerous work.

326 **Then with a parting** Miller, *In the Wilds,* 241–42.

CHAPTER 16: ALPH, THE SACRED RIVER

327 **Epigraph** Robinson, *Collected Poems,* 16.

327 **"We were quite"** TR, *Works,* 6.233.

327 **He noted the date** Ibid.

328 **There were so** Miller, *In the Wilds,* 206.

328 **Roosevelt found himself** Vivieros, *Rondon,* 407 ("corrente escura, volumosa, porque era plena estação das águas").

328 **"Kermit landed"** TR, *Works*, 6.234–35.

328 **The jungle was lovely** Descriptive passages in this chapter adhere closely to those of TR in *Through the Brazilian Wilderness*. (TR, *Works*, 6.233ff.) Details supplied by Rondon, Cherrie, and Kermit Roosevelt are attributed when important.

328 **Roosevelt had the** TR, *Works*, 6.236; KR diary, 27 Feb. 1914 (KRP); Vivieros, *Rondon*, 408.

329 **He studied** TR, *Works*, 6.237.

329 **a big affluent** KR diary, 28 Feb. 1914 (KRP); TR, *Works*, 6.237.

329 **"very good eating"** TR, *Works*, 6.239.

329 **After twenty kilometers** Rondon, *Lectures*, 72–73.

329 **Curls, falls, ponds** TR, *Works*, 6.241. Rondon named these rapids Navaitê, after a tribe of Indians thought to be living in the area.

329 **There was nothing** Rondon, *Lectures*, 74; TR, *Works*, 6.242–43; KR diary, 3 Mar. 1914 (KRP).

330 **The next one** TR, *Works*, 6.243–44. The *camaradas* were classified as "regional volunteers" by the Brazilian Telegraphic Commission, and highly paid for their trouble.

331 **On the morning** Cherrie diary, 11 Mar. 1914 (AMNH); Rondon, *Lectures*, 79.

331 **There were spells** Rondon, *Lectures*, 77; TR, *Works*, 6 *passim*.

332 **When he floated** Rondon-Naylor interview, *The New York Times*, 6 Jan. 1929. Rondon added: "He was what we Brazilians call a *pandego* (man of constant good humor)."

332 **"I never saw"** Ibid.

332 **descent into the** TR, *Works*, 6.245; Rondon, *Lectures*, 79. Rondon listed 114 survey stations along the Dúvida.

332 **By midday** The following account synthesizes the sometimes conflicting testimonies of TR in his *Works*, 6.257–59, and Rondon in his *Lectures*, 80–83, supplemented by Vivieros, *Rondon*, 409–10.

332 **Rondon ordered** Rondon, *Lectures*, 80.

332 **Kermit and Simplício clambered** TR's account, based on what KR told him, makes no mention of Simplício's presence on the upturned boat.

333 **All of this** Cherrie, *Dark Trails*, 289.

333 **"Well, you have"** Rondon, *Lectures*, 81.

333 **He no longer made** Ibid.

333 **It was clear** Diacon, *Stringing Together a Nation*, 43, notes that Rondon suppressed his rage against KR in later published accounts of the expedition, no doubt to avoid distressing TR.

333 AQUI PERECEU Rondon, *Lectures*, 83; Vivieros, *Rondon*, 410.

333 **To him, it said** Rondon, *Lectures*, 83; Vivieros, *Rondon*, 410; TR, *Works*, 6.259.

333 **The portage began** Rondon, *Lectures*, 86; TR, *Works*, 6.260–61.

334 **Rondon examined** Candice Millard has revealed that the Indians living alongside the Dúvida in 1914 were the cannibalistic Cinta Larga. Millard, *The River of Doubt*, 223–31.

334 **Later that** TR, *Works*, 6.260.

334 **Every dispensable possession** Ibid., 6.262–63.

334 **"Our position"** Ibid., 6.264; Rondon, *Lectures*, 87–88; Cherrie diary, 16 Mar. 1914 (AMNH); TR, *Works*, 6.264.

335 **Rondon decided** Millard, *The River of Doubt*, 154–62 and *passim*; Rondon-Naylor interview, *The New York Times*, 6 Jan. 1929.

335 **On behalf** Cherrie diary, 18 Mar. 1914 (AMNH); Rondon, *Lectures*, 87–89; TR, *Works*, 6.267. According to Armelle Enders, it was actually Lauro Müller's idea to honor TR in this way. Enders, "Theodore Roosevelt explorateur," 9.

335 **Roosevelt was taken** TR, *Works*, 6.268.

335 **There was little** Cherrie diary, 19 Mar. 1914 (AMNH); Cherrie, *Dark Trails*, 297.

335 **One morning** Rondon, *Lectures*, 92. Millard, *The River of Doubt*, 245 misdates this conversation.

335 **"First of all"** The following dialogue is quoted in Vivieros, *Rondon*, 411 (trans. author). See also Rondon, *Lectures*, 91–92, and Diacon, *Stringing Together a Nation*, 44–45.

336 **Clearing skies** Cherrie, *Dark Trails*, 298; TR, *Works*, 6.278 and *passim*.

336 **On 27 March** Cherrie diary, 27 Mar. 1914 (AMNH); TR, *Works*, 6.xx, 281–82, 296.

336 **Twelve years before** Morris, *Theodore Rex*, 141–49. In September 1908, TR told KR that his shin had never really healed. Kermit Roosevelt, *The Long Trail*, 37–38.

336 **in the summer of 1910** See 610.

337 **three black vultures** Cherrie diary, 27 Mar. 1914 (AMNH); Cherrie, *Dark Trails*, 308.

337 **There was a** KR diary, 28 Mar. 1914 (KRP); Cherrie, *Dark Trails*, 308; TR, *Works*, 6.282–83.

337 **The Americans overruled** Rondon, *Lectures*, 99–100; KR diary, 28 Mar. 1914 (KRP).

337 **Roosevelt kept** TR, *Works*, 6.283. TR gave his spare pair of shoes to KR, whose own fell apart because of constant immersion in the river.

337 **Cherrie accompanied** Cherrie, *Dark Trails*, 305–6. According to Cherrie, TR "had been ill intermittently" since about the middle of Mar., when he began to suffer from fever and dysentery. KR's diary makes no mention of these earlier ailments, but he too began to worry about the condition of TR's heart. It was characteristic of TR himself to say nothing of his 27 Mar. bruise except that "the resulting inflammation was somewhat bothersome." (TR, *Works*, 6.296.) He was equally reticent about his later sufferings.

337 **Together at** TR, *Works*, 6.284; Cherrie diary, 29 Mar. 1914 (AMNH). The phrase "arrow of light" is Cherrie's.

337 **When they descended** Cherrie diary, 2 Apr. 1914 (AMNH); Cherrie, *Dark Trails*, 301.

337 **As if in** TR, *Works*, 6.283–86; KR diary, 30–31 Mar. 1914 (KRP).

338 **By the time** Rondon, *Lectures*, 101; TR, *Works*, 6.263.

338 **The following day's** Rondon, *Lectures*, 104; TR, *Works*, 6.287–88.

338 **"Worried a lot"** KR diary, 2 Apr. 1914 (KRP).

Biographical Note: Archibald Roosevelt, Jr., in conversation with the author in 1988, speculated that TR "probably had—was born with—a bicuspid aortic valve like Cousin Kim's [Kermit Roosevelt, Jr.], instead of the normal tricuspid. People with that problem often overcompensate for it in early life, but they get a telltale heart murmur—which is probably what TR's doctor at Harvard heard when he warned him to lead a sedentary life. They also are susceptible to oral bacteria, which can lead to very high fevers and even endocarditis if the bloodstream is infected." Both ABR, Jr., and KR, Jr., began to suffer from calcium buildup close to the aortic valve at approximately the same age as TR developed heart trouble on the Dúvida. ABR, Jr., interview, Apr. 1988 (AC).

338 **The next morning** Rondon, *Lectures*, 104; TR, *Works*, 6.290.

338 **Rondon took some men** The following incident is reported by TR in *Works*, 6.290–93, and Rondon in *Lectures*, 105–6, as well as Vivieros, *Rondon*, 416–17. Supplemental details come from Cherrie diary, 3 Apr. 1914 (AMNH).

338 **He was a known** For an earlier knife-wielding incident involving Julio, see Millard, *The River of Doubt,* 91–92.

339 **"We must go after"** Vivieros, *Rondon,* 416 (trans. author).

339 **"Paixão is following"** TR, *Works,* 6.293. TR spelled Paixão phonetically as "Paishon."

339 **The murdered man** TR, *Works,* 6.295–96.

339 **Late the following** Cherrie's memoir of the expedition has caused some confusion among later writers as to when this attack took place. He dates it just after Rondon's 28 Mar. announcement that the canoes were going to have to be abandoned. However, Cherrie's diary makes no reference to TR becoming ill before the heart problems that afflicted him on 2 Apr. Millard cites an official report by Dr. Cajazeira stating that TR's fever struck him around 2:30 P.M. on 4 Apr. (*The River of Doubt,* 295–96). Rondon and KR confirm that the fever mounted that evening, and that TR lapsed overnight into delirium. (Rondon-Naylor interview, *The New York Times,* 6 Jan. 1929; Rondon, *Lectures,* 108; KR diary, 4 Apr. 1914 [KRP].) See also TR, *Works,* 6.296.

339 **He had to endure** Cherrie diary, 3, 4 Apr. 1914 (AMNH); Rondon, *Lectures,* 108; TR, *Works,* 6.296. Cherrie gives TR's temperature this night as "39.8° (Centigrade)."

339 **He became delirious** KR diary, 4 Apr. 1914 (KRP); Kermit Roosevelt, *Happy Hunting Grounds,* 47; Samuel Taylor Coleridge, "Kubla Khan, or a Vision in a Dream" (1797).

340 **The doctor laced him** Millard, *The River of Doubt,* 295–96.

340 **In terror** Kermit Roosevelt, *Happy Hunting Grounds,* 47. The pathetic fallacy implicit in KR's reference to the "rushing river" and overnight deluge may owe something to his reading of Edgar Allan Poe's fable "Silence."

340 **"The expedition cannot"** Vivieros, *Rondon,* 418 (trans. author). See also Cherrie, *Dark Trails,* 253–54 and Rondon-Naylor interview, *The New York Times,* 6 Jan. 1929. TR told Charles Washburn in Jan. 1915 that he would have shot himself if he felt completely unable to go on. Wood, *Roosevelt As We Knew Him,* 261.

340 **the sunless gorge** The adjective, borrowed from "Kubla Khan," is TR's.

340 **"Bôa Esperança"** Rondon, *Lectures,* 109.

340 **Dr. Cajazeira noted** Millard, *The River of Doubt,* 323; KR diary, 5 Apr. 1914 (KRP).

340 **"Am in a"** KR diary, 4 Apr. 1914 (KRP).

341 **"*Tenente!*"** Rondon, *Lectures,* 114. Reminiscing in old age to Esther Vivieros, Rondon gave Julio's cry as "*Senhor Coronel!*" ("Mr. Colonel!"). His early recall is more likely to be accurate.

341 **The sound of** Rondon, *Lectures,* 114; Vivieros, *Rondon,* 417; see also TR, *Works,* 6.294–95.

341 **After a record** Rondon, *Lectures,* 110–11.

341 **"The expedition is"** Vivieros, *Rondon,* 417–18 (trans. author). See also Rondon, *Lectures,* 114–15. The earlier account is much more discreet.

341 **"Shut up!"** Vivieros, *Rondon,* 417. TR's explosion is quoted in English.

342 **"the duty of"** Rondon, *Lectures,* 114. An ailing Kermit, in his diary entry for this day, states that Rondon and Lyra had been "in a blind rage to kill" Julio three days before. If so, Rondon may have imputed some of his own excitement to TR when relating the incident to Vivieros. But all sources agree that after discovering Julio's dropped rifle, Rondon declined to pursue him.

342 **"Let the law"** Vivieros, *Rondon,* 418. See also TR, *Works,* 6.294–95.

342 **Julio did not show** Rondon, *Lectures,* 115.

342 **It was pleasant** TR, *Works,* 6.298–99; Vivieros, *Rondon,* 418. The phrase "gleam like tossing silver" is TR's.

342 **Roosevelt ate little** Cherrie diary, 8 Apr. 1914 (AMNH); Cherrie, *Dark Trails*, 305–6.

342 **Rondon doubted** Rondon, *Lectures*, 110, 113; Millard, *The River of Doubt*, 322; Cherrie diary, 8, 10 Apr. 1914 (AMNH); TR, *Works*, 6.307. "There were a good many days," Cherrie remarked afterward, " . . . when I looked at Colonel Roosevelt and said to myself, he won't be with us tonight: and I would say the same thing in the evening, he can't possibly live until morning." Cherrie in TR, *Works*, 6.xix.

343 **Maple buds** TR, *Works*, 6.301–2, 307.

343 **"How I longed"** Ibid., 6.300.

343 **On 14 April** Rondon, *Lectures*, 118; TR, *Works*, 6.303.

343 **he had a violent** Rondon, *Lectures*, 117; Millard, *The River of Doubt*, 332–33; KR diary, 14, 15 Apr. 1914 (KRP).

343 **an old black fisherman** Rondon, *Lectures*, 119; Cherrie diary, 15 Apr. 1914 (AMNH).

343 **"But is he truly"** Rondon, *Lectures*, 119. (Retranslated from the Portugese original, 100.)

343 **When Roosevelt** Rondon, *Lectures*, 119.

344 **Dr. Cajazeira was** Millard, *The River of Doubt*, 322–23; KR diary, 16 Apr. 1914 (KRP); Kermit Roosevelt, *Happy Hunting Grounds*, 48; TR, *Works*, 6.306; Cherrie diary, 21 Apr. 1914 (AMNH).

344 **It took another** Cherrie diary, 26 Apr. 1914 (AMNH).

344 **Early in the** Rondon, *Lectures*, 67–68.

344 **The lieutenant had** Rondon, *Lectures*, 167; Cherrie diary, 26 Apr. 1914 (AMNH); TR, *Works*, 6.318–19. Pirineus was the officer who lost part of his tongue to a piranha, in the anecdote told by TR on 309.

344 **It was agreed** Despite Rondon's efforts, the Rio Roosevelt quickly became known as the "Rio Téodoro," which was easier for Brazilians to pronounce. TR himself preferred the more informal name, and allowed it to be engraved in the map of South America prepared for his book *Through the Brazilian Wilderness*. See the frontispiece to TR, *Works*, 6. The river's official name remains Rio Roosevelt.

345 **The dedicatee seemed less moved** KR diary, 26 Apr. 1914 (KRP).

345 **When the American** Vivieros, *Rondon*, 421; Cherrie diary, 28 Apr. 1914 (AMNH). He added, "Col. Roosevelt does not improve nor gain strength as rapidly as we had hoped."

345 **Roosevelt's estimate** TR, *Works*, 6.320; TR to Anthony Fiala, 8 July 1915 (AMNH).

346 **"some small achievement of worth"** See 346.

346 **At 2:30 P.M.** Cherrie diary, 29, 21 Apr. 1914 (AMNH); KR diary, 28 Apr. 1914 (KRP). According to Rondon, TR was in such pain during this voyage that he spent most of it lying facedown—"not a position in which he could write his notes." Vivieros, *Rondon*, 421.

346 **Each man to his** TR, *Works*, 6.308.

346 **Roosevelt did not** Vivieros, *Rondon*, 421–22; KR diary, 29 (actually, 30) Apr. 1914 (KRP).

346 **"Father about"** KR diary, 30 Apr. 1914 (KRP).

346 **Arrangements were made** Ibid., 1, 5 May 1914 (KRP); *The New York Times*, 6 May 1914.

346 **Before leaving** Cherrie diary, 1 May 1914 (AMNH); *The New York Times*, 19 May 1914.

346 **Dear Arthur** TR, *Letters*, 7.761.

346 **two abscesses** TR tended to belittle his ailments. KR speaks of "a veritable

plague of deep abscesses," and Rondon describes them as "numerous." He was also suffering from malnutrition, and the lingering aftereffects of malaria.

347 **We have put on the map** TR, *Letters,* 7.761. See ibid., 7.759–60, for TR's telegram from Manáos to Lauro Müller, tersely summarizing the trials and triumphs of the *Expediçào Scientifica Roosevelt-Rondon.* KR did not accompany his father back to New York, but remained in Belém preparatory to departure for Madrid.

347 **He was profoundly** Rondon appears to have chartered, or commandeered, the *Cidade de Manáos* to get him to Belém ahead of TR. Cherrie diary, 2–3 May 1914 (AMNH).

347 **"I hope and pray"** Vivieros, *Rondon,* 422 (trans. author).

CHAPTER 17: A WRONG TURN OFF APPEL QUAY

348 **Epigraph** Robinson, *Collected Poems,* 231.

348 **The first published** Middletown (N.Y.) *Times-Press,* 20 May 1914; *The New York Times,* 20–21 May 1914. *The Times* printed side-by-side photographs to show how dramatically TR had aged since leaving the United States six months before.

348 **He claimed that** *The New York Times* and *The Washington Post,* 20 May 1914. George Cherrie reported TR's fever attack.

348 **The President had** WW to TR, 23 May 1914 (WWP); TR to WW, 23 May 1914 (TRC).

348 **At three o'clock** *The Washington Post,* 27 May 1914.

349 **Wilson had been** Morris, *Theodore Rex,* 18.

349 **Roosevelt had always** "Woodrow Wilson is a perfect trump." TR, *Letters,* 3.275.

349 **"What is"** D. H. Elletson, *Roosevelt and Wilson: A Comparative Study* (London, 1965), 61; Link, *Papers of Woodrow Wilson,* 12.262.

349 **When Wilson became** Link, *Papers of Woodrow Wilson,* 12.454; Heckscher, *Woodrow Wilson,* 76–77; "Dr. Woodrow Wilson Defines Material Issues," *The New York Times,* 24 Nov. 1907.

349 **Roosevelt's reciprocal** TR, *Letters,* 8.836; Sullivan, *Our Times,* 4.137. "No American ever knew where he was during the many months I have been on this coast," Sir Christopher Cradock, the local British naval commander, wrote Cecil Spring Rice from Vera Cruz on 30 May 1914. "They stand fools to the world" (CSR).

349 **"morality and not expediency"** WW at Mobile, Ala., on 27 Oct. 1913, quoted in *The New York Times,* 28 Oct. 1913. See also Cooper, *Woodrow Wilson,* 140–41.

350 **So he had lifted** Cooper, *Woodrow Wilson,* 242.

350 **Wilson had gone before** *The New York Times,* 21 Apr. 1914.

350 **Chronic wrongdoing** Fourth Annual Message (Dec. 1904), TR, *Works,* 17.295, 299.

350 **In a development** Thomas A. Bailey, *A Diplomatic History of the American People,* 8th ed. (New York, 1969), 558–59.

350 **Roosevelt had thrilled** According to Rondon, the ailing TR had been avid to get home in case of war, exclaiming, "Oh, Mexico! Oh, Mexico!" Rondon-Naylor interview, *The New York Times,* 6 Jan. 1929.

350 **For a while** Henry J. Forman oral history, "So Brief a Time" (1959–1960), conducted by Doyce B. Nunis, Young Research Library, UCLA, 228. In 1914, Forman was a reporter for the New York *Sun,* covering the White House. See also Cooper, *Woodrow Wilson,* 243–45.

350 **"I never went"** Speech at the Brooklyn Navy Yard, 11 May 1914, *The New York Times,* 12 May 1914.

351 **Booth Tarkington's** *Penrod*   Tarkington had once been a student of WW's at Princeton. *Penrod* was a bestseller in 1914, and gave rise to many sequels and cinema adaptations. TR was seen absorbed in it, one foot tucked under him, on his train journey south, while hovering Progressives competed for his attention. (*The New York Times*, 27 May 1914.) There is also an amusing photograph in TRC of him reading the book with an intensity that threatens to scorch the pages.

351 **the Colonel's latest**   *Life-Histories of African Game Animals* (New York, 1914), is not included in any of the editions of TR's collected works. Advertised as the first categorical survey of the large fauna of any continent outside the United States, it was praised for its readability in *The New York Times Book Review*, 24 May 1914. "Latin binomials do not clutter the book with italics. . . . The treatment [of zoological data] is especially direct and lucid, and the vast amount of information which he [TR] has gathered at first hand [is] of inestimable service to our all too small fund of knowledge of animal psychology." The book received scientific sanction in a major review by C. Hart Merriam in *American Museum Journal*, 16.3 (Mar. 1916). It proved to be a disappointment to Scribners, slowly selling only 2,000 copies. Publisher's memo to William H. Bell, 1933 (SCR).

352 **When Roosevelt rose**   *The Washington Post* and *The New York Times*, 27 May 1914.

352 **"He is a great"**   Joseph P. Tumulty, *Woodrow Wilson As I Know Him* (New York, 1921), 287–88.

> *Historiographical Note:* This first meeting of TR and WW in the White House has escaped the attention of historians. Consequently, the President's famous remark, quoted by Tumulty, has always been ascribed to TR's second call upon him, in the spring of 1917. Tumulty was present at both meetings, but when writing his memoir in 1921, remembered only the later, which he called the "one and only." He said, further, that it took place entirely in the Red Room. The author believes that Tumulty simply forgot about the first, and conflated his memories. The secretary was wrong, e.g., in stating that in 1917, TR and WW "had not met since they were political opponents in 1912." That could only be true of their encounter in the spring of 1914. Tumulty was far more likely to have asked the President *then* what he thought of his visitor, and WW more inclined to have found TR irresistible *then* than three years later, when their relations were strained. It is a matter of record that TR, on the earlier occasion, was in a boyish mood (*vide* the hat-bopping incident, and the copy of *Penrod* in his pocket). Tumulty was, however, correct in recalling that the substance of the 1917 visit was TR's desire to command a division of volunteer troops in World War I. See 486–87.

352 **It was still hot**   *The Washington Post* and Middletown (N.Y.) *Times-Press*, 27 May 1914; *The New York Times*, 7 May 1914. See also Millard, *The River of Doubt*, 337–39.

353 **Veteran observers**   Trenton (N.J.) *Evening Times*, 27 May 1914.

353 **"I'm almost regretful"**   A stenographic transcript of TR's address was printed in *The Washington Post* and other major newspapers on 27 May 1914.

354 **Again and again**   *The Washington Post*, 27 May 1914.

354 **a *pium*-like swarm**   Gus Karger of the *Cincinnati Times-Star* attended TR's meeting with the Progressives and got the feeling that "in cold blood . . . he was contemplating the best method of 'dumping them' if their canine loyalty should become uncomfortable to himself." Quoted in O'Toole, *When Trumpets Call*, 258.

354 **Edith Roosevelt, who**   Sylvia Morris, *Edith Kermit Roosevelt*, 403: "The reason

for her not going is obscure. Analysis of the evidence available, from thyroid pills and frequent depressions, indicates that [EKR] was undergoing menopause." Another factor may have been the fact that Belle was the daughter of a prominent Democrat, EKR being politically much more partisan than her husband. Belle, in addition, like countless brides before and since, had to compete with a mother's passion for a favorite son.

354 **Their initial meetings** For an awkward hour the previous day, TR and Alfonso had breakfasted back-to-back on the same train from Paris to Madrid. There had been no qualified intermediary to reintroduce them, so they pretended to be unaware of each other. *The New York Times,* 9 June 1914.

354 **Roosevelt treated** TR to EKR, 11 June 1914 (KRP).

354 **Plainclothes detectives** *The New York Times,* 9, 10 June 1914.

355 **To Roosevelt's mild irritation** TR to EKR, 11 June 1914 (KRP); *The New York Times,* 9 June 1914.

355 **A guest list drawn** KR to ERD, 1 June 1914 (ERDP); *The New York Times,* 16 July 1914; KR to ERD, 4, 30 Apr. 1913 (ERDP). EKR did not record the wedding in her otherwise conscientiously kept diary.

355 **"I believe"** TR to EKR, 11 June 1914 (KRP).

355 **He stopped in Paris** *The New York Times,* 7 June 1914; Straus, *Under Four Administrations,* 360. Herrick, who had known TR since the early days of the McKinley administration, was impressed with the balance of his political views and the ease with which he held his own in conversation with members of the French Academy. Herrick wrote afterward to his son, "I believe it to be an undeniable fact—that Roosevelt is one of the greatest, if not the greatest man of the time." T. Bentley Mott, *Myron T. Herrick: Friend of France* (New York, 1929), 103–4.

355 **Paris that June** Owen Wister visited Paris at the same time, and was struck by its air of dilapidation and self-doubt ("The French face . . . too often a face of worried sadness, or revolt") in contrast with Germany's clicking efficiency and "contentment." (Wister, *The Pentecost of Calamity,* 54.) See also Ecksteins, *Rites of Spring,* 46.

355 **Georges Clemenceau's passionate** Clemenceau, *Discours de guerre,* 17; Strachan, *The First World War,* 46; François Lesure and Roger Nichols, eds., *Debussy Letters* (Cambridge, Mass., 1987), 292. Debussy, writing to Robert Godet, was looking back to the Franco-Prussian War, which he regarded as a catastrophe for French culture.

356 **"suffrage bomb"** *The Washington Post,* 15 June 1914.

356 **The old church** See above, 604. The British prime minister H. H. Asquith had also been married there.

356 **Obscurely basking** Wood, *Roosevelt As We Knew Him,* 307–8.

356 **Afterward the Lees** Lee, *A Good Innings,* 1.523ff. Chequers was deeded to the nation in 1921.

356 **country palace near Prague** Gilbert, *A History of the Twentieth Century,* 305.

356 **Wilhelm neither** Ibid.

357 **While Roosevelt** Nevins, *Henry White,* 326; *The Washington Post,* 18 June 1914; *The New York Times,* 17 June 1914.

357 **Roosevelt more or less** TR's address, "A Journey in Central Brazil," is printed in *Geographical Journal,* 45.2 (Feb. 1915), with a magnificent foldout map based on the observations of Lyra and Rondon.

357 **The nearest he got** *Geographical Journal,* 45.2 (Feb. 1915); *Daily Express,* 17 June 1914.

357 **"This is my"** *The New York Times,* 18 June 1914. See also TR, *Letters,* 7.779–80.

357 **He used virtually** *The New York Times,* 18 June 1914; Lee, *A Good Innings,*
1.524. TR was well acquainted with Balfour's views on this subject, having already devoured abstracts of the former Tory leader's Gifford Lectures, given at the
University of Glasgow the previous winter. (Balfour to TR, 29 Sept. 1915 [AJB].)
The lectures were published in 1915 under the title *Theism and Humanism.*

357 **He called on** *The New York Times,* 16 June 1914.

357 **other members of the government** Robert Massie, *Castles of Steel: Britain, Germany, and the Winning of the Great War at Sea* (New York, 2003), 166–72. The
following supplementary list of other persons seen by TR during his short visit to
England is given simply to indicate the breadth of his British acquaintance on the
eve of World War I: Lloyd George, chancellor of the exchequer, and Lord Lewis
Harcourt, colonial secretary; Sir Edward Carson, Austen Chamberlain, Henry
Chaplin, George Cave, and Viscount Walter Hume Long, leaders of the Tory Opposition; Lord Northcliffe, the press baron; Geoffrey Robinson Dawson and J. L.
Garvin, editors respectively of *The Times* and *The Observer;* Sir Bertrand Daw-
son, physician to the King; Fred S. Oliver, the department store magnate; Edward
Lyttelton, headmaster of Eton; George Otto Trevelyan, the historian; Sir Leander
Starr Jameson, the Boer War raider; and Lord Roberts, the apostle of war pre-
paredness.

358 **"Excuse me sir"** Lee, *A Good Innings,* 1.526. Alice Longworth, who had crossed
over with her father at the end of May, did not accompany him on his return voyage.

358 **Five minutes after** TR, *Letters,* 7.769; TR interviewed by *The New York Times,*
19, 25 June 1914.

358 **"When Roosevelt"** Walter Hines Page to WW, 12 July 1914 (WWP).

358 **Roosevelt had rejected** See Morris, *Theodore Rex,* chaps. 18 and 19.

359 **Roosevelt angrily insisted** Abbott, *Impressions of TR,* 140. Abbott was a fellow
passenger on the *Imperator,* and witnessed TR's "thoroughly lively" interview
with the Colombian diplomat.

359 **"If anybody"** *The New York Times,* 26 June 1914. Du Bois had been minister to
Colombia during the Taft administration. For a more extended statement of his
views, politely but damagingly critical of TR, see ibid., 2 July 1914.

359 **The handling of** Ibid.

360 **He went on** *The New York Times,* 25 June 1914.

360 **In doing so** The casualties in the Panamanian Revolution, both victims of
Colombian artillery fire, were one donkey and a Chinese immigrant. Morris,
Theodore Rex, 290.

360 **"We have gone"** *The New York Times,* 12 May 1914.

360 **a run for the U.S. Senate** Pinchot failed to unseat Boies Penrose.

361 **"You may expect"** *The New York Times,* 28 June 1914; Wood, *Roosevelt As We
Knew Him,* 396. For the similar warning of a Harvard doctor who examined TR
on the eve of his graduation, see Morris, *The Rise of TR,* 108–9.

361 **"Oh! I guess"** *The New York Times,* 29 June 1914.

361 **"Es ist nichts"** Stürmer, *The German Empire,* 100.

361 **His assassination** Strachan, *The First World War,* 10.

362 **Apparently, Franz Ferdinand** The archduke was warned to stay away by Bosnian
authorities, but he did not take their alarmism seriously.

362 **After a journey** EKR diary, 30 June 1914 (TRC); *Titusville* (Pa.) *Herald* and *The
New York Times,* 1 July 1914; *Greenville* (Pa.) *Evening Record,* 1 July 1914.

362 **"It is such"** *The New York Times,* 1 July 1914.

363 **"thoroughly exhausted"** Lewis, *TR,* 415–16. The *Titusville* (Pa.) *Herald,* 1 July
1914, also noted TR's husky voice and lack of gestural force.

363 **"What on earth"** Lewis, *TR,* 453.

363 **Roosevelt was back** *The New York Times,* 2 July 1914.
363 **"It was not"** EKR to Anna Roosevelt Cowles, 15 Oct. 1913 (ARC); TR, *Letters,* 7.772.
363 **He would still** Lawrence Abbott to his father, 13 May 1914 (ABB). John Mc-Grath, 23, had replaced Frank Harper as TR's secretary.
363 **"If I had been"** TR, *Letters,* 7.768.
364 **In Berlin, Wilhelm** Count Szögyéni to Count Berchtold, 5 July 1914, in GHDI: German History in Documents and Images (http://germanhistorydocs.ghi-dc.org/).
364 **"a serious complication"** Ibid.
364 **"The future lies"** Gilbert, *A History of the Twentieth Century,* 313.
364 **While Washington waited** *Oakland Tribune,* Ludington (Mich.) *Daily News,* Anaconda (Mont.) *Standard, Nevada State Journal,* Titusville (Pa.) *Herald, Orange County* (N.Y.) *Times,* and Brownwood (Tex.) *Daily Bulletin,* 29–30 June 1914.

CHAPTER 18: THE GREAT ACCIDENT

365 **Epigraph** Robinson, *Collected Poems,* 12.
365 **When the *Imperator*** *The New York Times,* 16, 17 July 1914.
365 **little Richard** This ill-fated boy was the eighth Richard to be born in eight generations of the Derby family in the United States. TR, *Letters,* 8.1015.
365 **So would Ted** EKR diary, 16–31 July 1914 (TRC).
365 **That young lady** Belle Willard Roosevelt had just turned 22.
366 **the slender graduate** John C. O'Laughlin to wife, 15 Sept. 1914 (OL).
366 **A delegation** *The New York Times,* 19 July 1914.
366 **In New York State** Ibid., 23 July 1914.
366 **On the same** Gilbert, *A History of the Twentieth Century,* 318.
367 **The terms of this ultimatum** On 8 July, the German ambassador in Vienna delivered a virtual command from the Kaiser, stating "most emphatically that Berlin expected the [Dual] Monarchy to act against Serbia, and that Germany would not understand it if . . . the present opportunity were allowed to go by . . . without a blow struck." Lee, *Outbreak of the First World War,* 62.
367 **In mid-Atlantic** *The New York Times,* 1 Aug. 1914. The Kaiser himself had suggested, as early as 20 July, that German liners in foreign waters be put on war alert. Lee, *Outbreak of the First World War,* 69.
367 **he allowed Theodore Roosevelt** See Morris, *Theodore Rex,* 388–91.
367 **"Then I must"** Lee, *Outbreak of the First World War,* 87.
367 **At 11:10 A.M.** Gilbert, *A History of the Twentieth Century,* 320; Lee, *Outbreak of the First World War,* 143; Strachan, *The First World War,* 10; Mark Mitchell and Allan Evans, citing the Austrian imperial archives in *Moriz Rosenthal in Word and Music* (Bloomington, Ind., 2006), 173.
367 **Wilhelm II, however** Gilbert, *A History of the Twentieth Century,* 322; Lee, *Outbreak of the First World War,* 58.
368 **To Edith Wharton** Wharton, *A Backward Glance,* 338, specifically describing the atmosphere in Paris on 31 July 1914.
368 **On 29 July** Strachan, *The First World War,* 11.
368 **The idea of a world war** The first potential belligerent to invoke it seriously appears to have been the Hungarian prime minister István Tisza, who warned on 8 July that an Austrian attack on Serbia would lead to "intervention by Russia and consequently world war." Lee, *Outbreak of the First World War,* 61.
368 RUSSIA READY *The Washington Post,* 30 July 1914.
369 **"It's the Slav"** Gilbert, *A History of the Twentieth Century,* 326.

369 **"An ignoble war"**   These exchanges between "Willy" and "Nicky" are taken from Michael S. Neiberg, ed., *The World War I Reader: Primary and Secondary Sources* (New York, 2007), 46–47.

369 **more than one ally**   Strictly speaking, Britain was not allied to France under the Triple Entente, as France was to Russia. Strategically, however, neither Britain nor France could stand for German mobilization in the summer of 1914.

369 **When Goschen**   G. P. Gooch and Harold Temperley, *British Documents on the Origins of the War, 1898–1914* (London, 1926), vol. 11, doc. 293.

370 **The combined vagueness**   Lee, *Outbreak of the First World War*, 82. The double assurance of Wilhelm II and Bethmann-Hollweg on 5 July that Germany would stand by Austria in its Serbian quarrel is known to historians as "the blank check" that precipitated World War I.

370 **The last forty-eight**   Ibid., 118.

370 **"those peace people"**   Nevins, *Henry White*, 502.

370 **"Germany does not"**   Moltke to Bethmann-Hollweg, 30 July 1914, in GHDI.

370 *Forces for good*   TR, *Works*, 14.274–75.

371 **the new autocrats**   The phrase is that of Martin Gilbert in *A History of the Twentieth Century*, 329.

371 **"the French Socialist Republic"**   Superscript by the Kaiser on St. Petersburg dispatch, 25 July 1914, GHDI, no. 160.

371 **"That is the match"**   Wister, *The Pentecost of Calamity*, 10–11. See also Wister, *Roosevelt*, 321.

372 **for the first time in history**   Gerard, *My Four Years in Germany*, 70.

372 **That insult**   Since the Reichstag elections of 1912, and especially since the Zabern affair of 1913, when the German crown prince had actually proposed a military *coup d'état* to Bethmann-Hollweg, Prussian conservatives "had come to regard war as a 'tempering of the nation.' " Lee, *Outbreak of the First World War*, 55–56.

372 **Ordinary Berliners**   The following description of Berlin on the eve of World War I owes much to the vivid account of Modris Ecksteins in *Rites of Spring*, chap. 2. See also Lee, *Outbreak of the First World War*, 121.

372 *Holy flame*   Author's translation.

372 **"a dance of death"**   Gilbert, *A History of the Twentieth Century*, 326. There were similar demonstrations of war fever in other German cities, including Munich. Sullivan, *Our Times*, 5.5.

CHAPTER 19: A HURRICANE OF STEEL

373 **Epigraph**   Robinson, *Collected Poems*, 74.

373 **"The situation"**   TR to QR, 2 Aug. 1914 (ERDP).

373 **A packhorse**   QR to KR, 2 Feb. 1916 (KRP).

373 **As a little girl**   Longworth, *Crowded Hours*, 235.

375 **Balfour's dream**   See 71.

375 **he also had his Saxon side**   The Kaiser, flattering TR during his presidency, had come up with a triple adjective: "Let us rejoice that, thank Heaven, the Anglo-Saxon-Germanic Race is still able to produce such a specimen." (Wilhelm II to TR, 14 Jan. 1904 [TRP].) For TR's German days, see Putnam, *TR*, 102–13, or Morris, *The Rise of TR*, 43–47.

375 **"From that time"**   TR, *An Autobiography*, 274.

375 **"I wish I had"**   TR to Finley Peter Dunne, quoted in Ellis, *Mr. Dooley's America*, 154.

375 **"the battle forced"**   Quote in Ecksteins, *Rites of Spring*, 93.

375 **"If they refuse"** Barbara Tuchman, *The Guns of August* (New York, 1962, 1979), 141.

376 **"The lamps are going out"** Grey, *Twenty-five Years*, 2.20. There was a personal poignancy to Grey's metaphor. He was afflicted with dimming vision, and had been told by oculists that he would become functionally blind in a few years. Ibid., 61–62.

376 **"You've got to"** Felix Frankfurter, eyewitness.

376 **Booth would only say** Charles Booth (1840–1916) was a stellar example of the high Victorian ideal of a businessman devoting himself to the making of money and enlightened philanthropy. He was author of a 17-volume social study, *Life and Labor of the People in London* (1891–1903). The steamer *Aidan,* which had altered its itinerary to bring the ailing TR home from Brazil in May 1914, belonged to Booth's fleet. His brother, Alfred Booth, was chairman of the Cunard Line, which on this same day delayed the departure from New York of its flagship *Lusitania.*

376 **"would result in"** TR, *Letters*, 8.826.

376 **"The European world"** *The New York Times,* 4 Aug. 1914. WW reckoned without the strong inherited patriotism of German-Americans. When the Reich declared war on Russia, the *New York Herald* ran a banner headline, ALLE DEUTSCHEN HERZEN SCHLAGEN HEUTE HOHER ("All German hearts beat faster today"). Sullivan, *Our Times,* 5.8.

377 **When other powers** Japan declared war against Germany on 23 Aug. and Turkey against the Allies on 11 Nov. 1914. Italy hesitated until 24 May 1915 before turning against its former Triple Entente partner, Austria-Hungary.

377 **Theodore Roosevelt's gift** *The Washington Post* reported on this date, 5 Aug. 1914, that strategists in the nation's capital regarded the Canal as "the biggest war menace that hangs over America and the western hemisphere."

377 **"God has stricken me"** Heckscher, *Woodrow Wilson,* 334.

378 **"Let us be"** *The New York Times,* 6 Aug. 1914.

378 **"I simply do not"** TR to George S. Viereck, 8 Aug. 1914 (TRC).

378 **Having lost** See Morris, *The Rise of TR,* 229–31. TR sent WW a supportive telegram even before Ellen Wilson died. "Very deep sympathy. Earnestly hope reports of Mrs. Wilson's condition are exaggerated." TR to WW, 5 Aug. 1914 (TRP).

378 **"It is not"** TR, *Letters,* 7.790.

378 **"The melancholy thing"** TR, *Letters,* 7.794. Münsterberg (1863–1916) was one of the most eloquent of TR's German-American friends attempting to recruit him as a spokesman for their cause. A pioneer industrial psychologist, antifeminist, and protégé of William James, he died suddenly in 1916 after publishing *The Photoplay,* the first major work of film theory.

378 **The message he** Papen, *Memoirs,* 14; TR, *Letters,* 8.1165.

379 **Roosevelt bowed back** TR, describing this visit later, dated it as occurring "within a week of the outbreak of the war," and identified his caller only as "a young member of the German Embassy staff in Washington," and "I think a Count." (TR, *Letters,* 8.1165; Leary, *Talks with T.R.,* 41.) But the evidence that it was Papen is, on top of these qualifications, compelling. In his memoirs, Papen mentions being entrusted with Wilhelm II's goodwill message before being posted to the United States in the new year of 1914. He also states that he came to New York at this time, straight from an espionage visit to Mexico, in order to set up a base for further spying and propaganda work at the Manhattan headquarters of "a German firm in Hanover Street." (Papen, *Memoirs,* 21, 31.) Papen left Galveston, Tex., at midnight on 4 Aug. 1914, and probably saw TR in New York on 7 Aug. TR was back in Oyster Bay the following day.

379 **"In common with"** TR, "The Foreign Policy of the United States," *The Outlook*, 22 Aug. 1914.

379 **daily in black headlines** "The dispatches were as if black flocks of birds, frightened from their familiar rookeries, came darting across the ocean, their excited cries a tiding of stirring events." (Sullivan, *Our Times*, 5.2.) See ibid., 1–46, and *American Review of Reviews*, Oct. 1914, for the impact of the war on American newspapers.

379 **swamping even, on 15 August** *The Washington Post*, e.g., put the canal opening on page 10. The *Syracuse Herald* gave it a slender column on page 2, beneath a banner headline: STUPENDOUS BATTLE BETWEEN GERMANS AND THE ALLIED FORCES IS NEAR AT HAND.

379 **Diaghilev's dancers** At the Theatro Municipale in Rio on 22 Oct. 1913.

379 **"It must indeed be"** Baker, notebook III.74 (14 Aug. 1914 [RSB]).

380 **On 19 August** *The New York Times*, 28 Oct. 1913; Sullivan, *Our Times*, 5.43–44. WW's phrase "impartial in thought" is often misquoted as "neutral in thought."

380 **Boredom gave way** Richard Harding Davis, "The Germans in Brussels," *Scribner's Magazine*, Nov. 1914. Davis's first version of this account, which is less rich in detail, appeared in the New York *Tribune* on 24 Aug. 1914. The final version was published in his book *With the Allies* (New York, 1914), 21–28.

381 **onslaught on the** Sullivan, *Our Times*, 5.26.

381 **the Italian word *fasci*** From the Latin *fasces*, evoking a bundle of rods, unbreakable because bound, irresistible when rammed. Fascism did not attain the status of a national political party until after World War I. But in Aug. 1914, Mussolini was rapidly converting his personal ideology from pacific socialism to aggressive, interventionist activism, in favor of an all-powerful nation-state. Three months later, he founded a revolutionary newspaper, *Il Popolo d'Italia,* which bore banner quotes from Louis Blanqui and Napoleon: "He who has steel, has bread," and "Revolution is an idea that has found bayonets." On 24 Nov. he formed a pro-war *fasci di azione rivoluzionaria* (power group for revolutionary action) that quickly grew and claimed 5,000 members by the year's end.

381 **Roosevelt had been confidentially** See 146.

381 **"If the Franco-British"** TR, *Letters*, 7.810–11. In his long-term scenario, TR included a prophecy that came true after World War II: "If Germany is smashed, it is perfectly possible that later she will have to be supported as a bulwark against the Slav by the nations of Western Europe." Ibid., 812.

382 **The same prospect** Gilbert, *A History of the Twentieth Century*, 345–46; Alan Kramer, *Dynamic of Destruction: Culture and Mass Killing in the First World War* (New York, 2007), 7–11.

382 **"The Prussian"** Gerard, *Face to Face with Kaiserism*, 131.

382 **It was all** Davis, *With the Allies*, 90–95. See also Brand Whitlock, *Belgium: A Personal Narrative* (New York, 1919), chap. 26.

382 **The imperial embassy** Sullivan, *Our Times*, 5.58.

382 **"I am an ex-President"** TR, *Letters*, 7.812.

382 **"If you have"** TR to Frederick H. Allen, 31 Aug. 1914 (TRC).

383 **Belle had fallen** EKR diary, 16 July 1914 and *passim* (TRC).

383 **"Ted and Eleanor"** TR, *Letters*, 7.816.

383 **In a crescendo of carnage** The ecstasy affected even Calvinist intellectuals. "This war is great and wonderful beyond all expectations," Max Weber wrote a friend. *The New York Review of Books*, 18 Feb. 1988.

383 **"The fire-ants"** TR, *Works*, 6.113–14.

383 **Elsewhere in Brazil** TR, *Works*, 6.142; Strachan, *The First World War*, 55.

384 *Masses, slaves, arise*   Eugène Pottier (1816–1887). Author's translation of French original. The text varies in later Russian, British, and American versions.

384 **The government of**   Gerard, *My Four Years in Germany,* 91; Tuchman, *The Proud Tower,* 419. On the eve of Germany's declaration of war against Russia, Sir Edward Grey had passionately burst out, "It is the greatest step toward Socialism that could possibly have been made. We shall have Labour Governments in every country after this." Grey, *Twenty-five Years,* 2.239–40.

384 **When Wilson thought**   "I find the President singularly lacking in appreciation of the importance of this European crisis," Colonel House wrote on 28 Sept. 1914. "I find it difficult to get his attention centered upon the one big question." Sullivan, *Our Times,* 5.35.

384 **"I gather"**   Cecil Spring Rice to TR, 18 Sept. 1914 (CSR).

385 **Before Roosevelt**   TR, *Letters,* 8.862.

> *Biographical Note:* Earlier in the year, TR had resisted a suggestion that he should encourage Progressives to support Wilson, rather than allow them to drift back into a Republican Party dominated by the likes of Boies Penrose. He agreed, however, that "permanently, there is only room for two national parties in this country, and one of these must be the opposition." (TR to Alex Moore, 10 July 1914 [TRC].) Interviewing TR on 14 Aug. 1914, Ray Stannard Baker heard him "express doubt as to whether the American people really know what they [were] doing" in voting for his philosophy of government. "I do not believe," Baker concluded, "that T. R. has ever really believed in people. He has led people, he has advertised popular measures, but he has never really believed that the people must rule. His idea of leadership has been domination rather than education & service. He has done great good as a publicist, as a political revivalist, but by George, I can't help feeling that his time has passed." Notebook III.73 (RSB).

385 **"He is most"**   O'Laughlin to his wife, 6 Sept. 1914 (OL).

385 **"there should be"**   Ibid. See 47.

385 **hurricane of steel**   See 301.

386 **The war had wrought**   *The New York Times,* 26 Sept. 1914; EKR diary, 27 Sept. 1914, misdated 14 Sept. (TRC). As things transpired, a security scare diverted the ship to Glasgow.

386 **Edith said goodbye**   EKR to ERD, 5 Oct. 1914 (ERDP); TR to KR, 17 Jan. 1915 (TRC).

386 **I have something special**   Trevelyan to TR, 1 Sept. 1914 (TRP).

386 **Your mode of thought**   For recent analyses of TR's foreign policy toward Britain and Europe, see William N. Tilchin, *Theodore Roosevelt and the British Empire: A Study in Presidential Statecraft* (New York, 1997), and Serge Ricard, *Théodore Roosevelt: principes et pratique d'une politique étrangère* (Aix-en-Provence, 1991). Howard K. Beale's massive *Theodore Roosevelt and the Rise of America to World Power* (Baltimore, 1956) remains the most comprehensive overall survey, and Frederick W. Marks's elegant *Velvet on Iron* (op. cit.) the most concise. An excellent specialized study is Henry J. Hendrix, *Theodore Roosevelt's Naval Diplomacy: The U.S. Navy and the Birth of the American Century* (Annapolis, Md., 2009). See also Raymond A. Esthus, *Theodore Roosevelt and Japan* (Seattle, 1966), and A. Gregory Moore, "Dilemma of Stereotypes: Theodore Roosevelt and China, 1901–1909," (Ph.D. diss., Kent State University, 1978).

387 **Other representatives**   TR, *Letters,* 8.819–20; Hengelmüller to TR, 24 Sept. 1914, reprinted at TR's request in *The New York Times,* 8 Nov. 1914.

387 **Sir Edward Grey asked** In his letter, dated 10 Sept. 1914, the foreign minister included a fair amount of anti-German propaganda of his own. See Grey, *Twenty-five Years*, 2.143–44. The author of *Peter Pan* lunched with the Roosevelts on 3 Oct. He did not like TR, whom he found oppressively talkative, and EKR did not like him. "A mousy, moody little man." EKR to ERD, 5 Oct. 1914 (ERDP).

387 **Rudyard Kipling reported** Kipling to TR, 15 Sept. 1914 (TRP).

387 **"It is no good"** Cecil Spring Rice to TR, 10 Sept. 1914 (CSR). The ambassador's conspiracists, "toiling in a solid phalanx to compass our destruction," also included Adolph Ochs and "the arch-Jew," Jacob Schiff of Kuhn, Loeb & Co. (Spring Rice to Valentine Chirol, 13 Nov. 1914 [CSR].) For a brief account of Straus's negotiations, which were concerned not with commerce but with his plan to launch a new mediatory effort by the Wilson administration, see Straus, *Under Four Administrations*, 378–85, and Grey, *Twenty-five Years*, 2.119–21. The plan was rejected by both Germany and Great Britain.

387 **"An ex-President"** TR to Rudyard Kipling, 3 Oct. 1914 (TRC).

387 **Roosevelt did not blame** See also TR, *Letters*, 7.794.

388 **Even in the Far East** Kiaochow surrendered on 7 Nov. 1914. For a modern endorsement of the view that all the belligerents in World War I were right as well as wrong, see Joachim Remak in Lee, *Outbreak of the First World War*, 147–49.

388 **"It seems to me"** TR in *The Outlook*, 23 Sept. 1914.

388 **He had read** Friedrich von Bernhardi, *Germany and the Next War* (U.S. edition, New York, 1914).

388 **"somewhat as my own"** TR in *The Outlook*, 23 Sept. 1914.

388 **"living softly"** Ibid.

388 **butchered some hundreds of thousands** Not to be confused with the Turkish-Armenian massacre of 1915.

389 **The last two** "For this error of judgment . . . I am afraid Roosevelt never forgave me." (Abbott, *Impressions of TR*, 250–51.) TR restored the deleted language when he republished the essay in Jan. 1915.

389 **"Surely the time"** TR in *The Outlook*, 23 Sept. 1914. TR's essay is reprinted in TR, *Works*, 20.14–35.

Historiographical Note: TR herewith revived his earlier call for "a League of Peace" at Christiania, Norway, in May 1910. Just eight days after the beginning of the war, he had tried the idea out privately on Hugo Münsterberg, envisaging "the kind of caprice among the great powers which will minimize the armaments of all and will solemnly bind all the rest to take joint action against any offender." (TR, *Letters*, 7.795–96.) He spelled out this vision in more detail on 18 Oct. in *The New York Times*, by which time it had become "a great World League for the Peace of Righteousness." Six weeks later in *The Atlantic Monthly*, the Cambridge classicist Goldsworthy Lowes Dickinson published the first of two influential articles advocating the organization of a "League of Nations." TR rejected his concept as excessively theoretical and lacking in the vital dimension of "international force." (TR, *Letters*, 852–55.) Nevertheless, Lowes Dickinson later helped frame the official League of Nations Covenant of 1919. For a detailed history of TR's proposal, 1910–1917, see Stephen A. Wertheim, "The League That Wasn't: Theodore Roosevelt, Elihu Root, William Howard Taft and a Legalist League of Nations" (AB diss., Harvard, 2007).

389 **Rumors began** *The New York Times*, 14 Sept. 1914.

390 **"It would reflect"** John N. Wheeler, *I've Got News for You* (New York, 1961), 43–44. TR nursed ancient grudges against the *World*, going back to its opposition

to his candidacy in the presidential election of 1904. For his subsequent persecution of the paper and its publisher, see James McGrath Morris, *Joseph Pulitzer: A
Life in Politics, Print, and Power* (New York, 2010), chaps. 29, 30. By 1914, Pulitzer
was dead.

390 **"One moment"** *The New York Times,* 27 Sept. 1914.

390 **"Under such circumstances"** Ibid.

390 **Although he did not** Wheeler, *I've Got News,* 44–45; John N. Wheeler to TR,
14 Oct. 1914 (TRP).

391 **He obliged with** *The New York Times,* 4, 11, 18 Oct., and 1, 8, 15, 22, 29 Nov.
1914. Reprinted with variations in TR, *Works,* 20.36–216.

391 **"the one certain way"** TR, *Works,* 20.107.

391 **When he encountered** Parsons, *Perchance to Dream,* 253.

391 **Word that Germany** TR, *Works,* 20.4.227. For an eloquent private statement of
TR's war views in the early fall of 1914, see his letter to Hugo Münsterberg, 3 Oct.
1914, TR, *Letters,* 8.822–25.

391 **"You cannot imagine"** ERD to EKR, 6 Oct. 1914 (ERDP).

391 **Roosevelt had received** Rudyard Kipling to TR, 15 Sept. and 20 Oct. 1914
(TRP).

392 **"My experience in"** TR to Kipling, 3 Oct. 1914 (TRC). Kipling had complained
that the tone of TR's war articles was too mild.

392 **He granted that** Ibid. Five days before a campaigning TR wrote this letter, he
was waylaid in Cleveland by members of a Belgian government commission
charged with alerting key American figures to the suffering inflicted on their
country. They found the Colonel sympathetic but unwilling to criticize WW's silence on the issue. "If you were President, what would you do?" "Exactly what
Mr. Wilson is doing." The commissioners said they were going on to meet with
former President Taft. "You'll like him awfully," TR replied, "he'll agree with
everything you say." Lalla Vandervelde, relief lobbyist, in *Monarchs and Millionaires* (New York, 1925), 71–73.

392 **an impassioned speech** Parsons, *Perchance Some Day,* 255. See also Robinson,
My Brother TR, 282–83: "Unless I am very much mistaken, [that was] the first
speech on that subject in the United States during the Great War." Both women
were eyewitnesses to the occasion. For an example of TR's formidable aggression
on this issue, see his letter to the pacifist Andrew Dickson White in TR, *Letters,*
8.827–28.

392 **In a post-election poll** *The New York Times,* 20 Dec. 1914.

392 **"utter and hopeless"** TR, *Letters,* 8.831.

392 *We, here in America* See 180. In a letter to Lyman Abbott, forecasting the death
of the Progressive Party, TR made plain that he felt progressivism as a "movement" would go on. "I honestly feel that none of us have any cause to be ashamed
of what we did in 1912." 7 Nov. 1914 (TRP).

> *Historical Note:* The narrative of this book will not deal with the Progressive
> Party's prolonged death throes through the spring of 1916. TR dutifully ful-
> filled his duties as Party chief until then, but his heart was elsewhere. For a de-
> tailed account, see Gable, *The Bull Moose Years,* chaps. 9 and 10, and the
> relevant correspondence in TR, *Letters,* 8.843–1085.

393 **"I wish I could stroke"** TR, *Letters,* 8.832.

393 **And Edith too** Kipling reported that he had seen KR and Belle just before they
sailed from Liverpool. "Happiness wasn't the word to describe 'em!" To TR, 15
Sept. 1915 (TRP).

393 **Roosevelt persuaded himself** TR to KR, 11 Nov. 14 (TRC).

Biographical Note: With TR's approval, John C. O'Laughlin, who had once served as assistant secretary of state and was a capable private envoy, went to London in Nov. 1914 to ask if Sir Edward Grey would be interested in TR as a peace broker between the Powers. The foreign minister, reluctant to go behind WW's back, was courteously discouraging. He praised TR's recent war articles, but said that he did not agree with him about the apathy of the Wilson administration. "The President has been strictly correct, as has Ambassador Page." O'Laughlin to TR, 29 Nov. 1914 (OL).

393 **Through the Brazilian** See. e.g., *The New York Times,* 15 Nov. 1914 ("Colonel Roosevelt . . . is blessed with a power for minute and careful observation. . . . One more excellent volume [added] to a list which is already a praiseworthy record"); *The Spectator,* 19 Dec. 1914 ("The art of the narrator is invariably swift and keen. A better record of adventure . . . it would be difficult to find"); *Geographical Journal,* Feb. 1915. On 6 Nov., TR sent a copy of *Through the Brazilian Wilderness* to Cândido Rondon, with apologies for it being in English. "Malheureusement, cette terrible guerre européene a empeché toute traduction allemande et française, aussi ne puis-je vous en envoyer qu'un exception en anglais." For the full text of his letter, see Vivieros, *Rondon,* 424–25.

393 **For as long as** Sullivan, *Our Times,* 5.199.

393 **Next February** H. J. Whigham, editor of *Metropolitan* magazine, recalled in old age that TR at first rebuffed his approaches because he felt that the salary offered ($25,000) was too much for the work required: "I would not feel that if I were writing an article once a month that I was really earning the money properly." He would prefer, he said, to write many more articles for the Wheeler syndicate for the same sum. It took the combined efforts of Whigham and Harry Whitney, the magazine's owner, to persuade him to sign on. Whigham interiewed by Hermann Hagedorn, 12 May 1949 (TRB).

393 **brilliant young men** Soon after the election, TR invited Croly, Lippmann, and another co-founder of *The New Republic,* Walter Weyl, to dine with him—"just you three and I." He clearly wanted to pass on his Progressive-ideological torch. Lippmann, who impressed TR as "on the whole, the most brilliant young man of his age in all the United States," had just brought out a new book of political essays. Entitled *Drift and Mastery,* it won Lippmann early fame as an astute analyst of American domestic unrest. TR reviewed it favorably, along with Croly's *Progressive Democracy,* in *The Outlook.* Although he later split with *The New Republic* on its attitude to the war, Lippmann continued to revere him. TR to Croly et al., 11 Nov. 1914; TR, *Letters,* 8.872; TR *Works,* 14, 214–22.

393 **"It is perfectly obvious"** TR, *Letters,* 8.835–39.

393 **"Heartily know"** Ibid. TR appears to be slightly misquoting an unidentified verse he had read in Charles Henry Parkhurst's *Portraits and Principles of the World's Great Men and Women* (Springfield, Mass., 1898), 177.

CHAPTER 20: TWO MELANCHOLY MEN

394 **Epigraph** Robinson, *Collected Poems,* 27.

394 **The winter of 1914** Ecksteins, *Rites of Spring,* 100; Robert Cowley, ed., *The Great War: Perspectives on the First World War* (New York, 2004), 37.

394 **"a war with which"** Sullivan, *Our Times,* 5.88.

394 **White House aides** Heckscher, *Woodrow Wilson,* 340–42.

395 **Roosevelt appeared** TR, *Letters,* 8.849; TR to KR, 11 Nov. 1914 (TRC); TR, *Letters,* 8.903.

395 **"Father is"** Gordon Johnston interviewed by Ethel Armes, ca. 1920 (TRB).

Johnston was shocked by TR's appearance. "I had never seen him so low." For other depictions of TR at this time, see Charles Washburn in Wood, *Roosevelt As We Knew Him,* 394; Nicholas Roosevelt, *TR,* 155; Looker, *Colonel Roosevelt,* 11, 56.

> *Biographical Note:* A contributing cause to TR's depression may have been his reading at this time of Adolf Fischer's *Menschen und Tiere in Deutsch-Südwest Afrika.* Reviewing it for *The Outlook* on 20 Jan. 1915, he noted that responsible conservationists had only recently saved the big-game fauna of Southwest Africa (now Namibia) from "almost complete annihilation" by trophy hunters, white and black. "This is one of the many, many reasons why the present dreadful war fills me with sadness. The men, many of whom I have known—Germans, Englishmen, Frenchmen, Belgians—who have been opening the Dark Continent to civilization, are now destroying one another and ruining the work that has been done." (TR, *Works,* 14.574.) For a brief account of the war in Africa, see Strachan, *The First World War,* 80–95.

395 **"Both you men"**   Quoted by Knox in Looker, *Colonel Roosevelt,* 164.
395 **"Weaklings who raise"**   TR, *Works,* 20.77–78 (not included in the original *New York Times* article of 1 Nov. 1914, but added for republication in Jan. 1915).
396 **"Your cistern"**   William Allen White to TR, 28 Dec. 1914 (TRP).
396 **"I am more like"**   TR, *Letters,* 8.870–71. TR's new contract, dated 5 Dec. 1914, required him to "use the *Metropolitan Magazine* exclusively for three years as your medium for articles on the great social, political, and international questions." He would receive $25,000 annually for a minimum contribution of 50,000 words. Extra articles would be paid for at the same rate, and he could write on other subjects for other periodicals. Copy in AC.
396 ***Metropolitan* was a large**   Ellis, *Mr. Dooley's America,* 240, describes *Metropolitan* as "a right-wing socialist periodical." This paradox is endorsed by Antony C. Sutton in *Wall Street and the Bolshevik Revolution* (Studies in Reformed Theology, 2001, chap. 11, http://www.reformed-theology.org/). Sutton notes *Metropolitan*'s connection, via Whitney, with the House of Morgan and the liberal financier Eugene Boissevain. He argues that many American plutocrats in the early Bolshevik era, eager to bring down foreign imperialism, aided revolutionary forces in Russia either directly, through cash contributions, or indirectly, by patronizing anti-Tsarist propaganda at home. Editor Whigham's brand of politics allowed him to employ such relative conservatives as TR and Finley Peter Dunne as well as the outspoken Communist John Reed.
396 **"After this January"**   TR, *Letters,* 8.871.
396 **"To be neutral"**   Ibid., 8.903.
397 **The resultant twelve-chapter volume**   *America and the World War* is reprinted in TR, *Works,* 20.1–216.
397 **Critical reaction**   "In our hour of need," St. Loe Strachey complained in *The Spectator* (6 Feb. 1915), "we should have expected a better understanding."
398 **England is not**   TR, *Letters,* 8.867.
398 **"I ask those"**   Ibid., 20.105–6. TR's oft-repeated claim that no shot was fired at a "foreign" foe during his presidency depended on the classification of Filipinos as territorial wards of the United States.
399 **He poured scorn**   TR, *Works,* 20.94; Sullivan, *Our Times,* 5.207. Of the stateside army, most troops were required to man coastal defenses, leaving a mobile land force of fewer than 25,000. Ibid.
399 **Mr. Bryan came**   TR, *Works,* 20.212–13.
399 **"I feel in the"**   Ibid., 20.194 (italics added).

Historical Note: One of the great what-ifs of American history is the course World War I might have taken had TR been returned to the White House in 1912. He speculated often on the subject himself. "If I had been President," he wrote Cecil Spring Rice late in 1914, "I should have acted on the thirtieth or thirty-first of July, as head of a signatory power of the Hague [conventions] . . . saying that I accepted [them] as imposing a serious obligation which I expected not only the United States but all other neutral nations to join us in enforcing. Of course I would not have made such a statement without backing it up." (TR, *Letters,* 8.821.) In *Diplomacy* (New York, 1994), 29–50, Henry Kissinger argues that TR would have taken the U.S. into the war for strategic reasons, on the ground that a victory for the Central Powers, and the consequent weakening of Britain's hold on the North Atlantic, would have threatened the world balance of power in general, and America's hemispheric security in particular. WW, in contrast, advocated neutrality only for as long as it would take him to impose upon the belligerents his "messianic" vision of a negotiated peace based on American moral principles. While Kissinger regrets that WW's and not TR's foreign policy prevailed (fostering the myth of American exceptionalism for the rest of the century), he does not consider the possibility that TR, re-elected with all the prestige of his proven success as an international mediator (not to mention his personal *knowledge* of most of the European potentates prosecuting the war), could have brought about a diplomatic solution before the end of 1914.

Determinists might counter that a certain cosmic inevitability caused Franz Ferdinand's automobile, on 28 June, to take the wrong turning that proved so right for Gavrilo Princip—leading over the course of the next four years to societal changes that had been generating since the end of the nineteenth century. In such a view, TR might as well have tried to mediate the eruption of Mont Pelée.

399 **"As President"** TR, *Letters,* 8.87.

400 **In the terrible** Ibid., 8.214–16.

400 **He was playing** Looker, *Colonel Roosevelt,* 57.

400 **"He will never"** Hamlin Garland, *My Friendly Contemporaries: A Literary Log* (New York, 1932), 45. The phrase *distinctly older* is Garland's.

400 **TR (*laughing*)** Dunne, *Mr. Dooley Remembers,* 184–85.

401 **"striking his palm"** Ibid.

401 **"We cannot remain"** Tumulty, *Woodrow Wilson,* 228.

401 **Britain proposed** This policy was announced on 1 Mar. 1915. For the Wilson administration's complicity with it, see Walter Karp, *The Politics of War: The Story of Two Wars Which Altered Forever the Political Life of the American Republic* (New York, 1979), 176–82.

402 **"The waters surrounding"** *The New York Times,* 7 Feb. 1915.

402 **"This is in effect"** Spring Rice to William Jennings Bryan, 1 Mar. 1915, *The American Journal of International Law,* 12 (1918), 866.

402 **If the commanders** *Foreign Relations of the United States Supplement,* 1915, 98–100.

402 **"I hope that"** TR, *Letters,* 8.879, 888–89.

403 **In a censuring tone** Ibid., 8.889.

403 **almost treasonous letter** Ibid., 8.876–81; Grey, *Twenty-five Years,* 2.154.

403 **For as long as** TR, *Letters,* 8.910, 899, 906–7, 918.

403 **"T. Vesuvius Roosevelt"** Title of a poem by W. Irwin in *Collier's Weekly,* 12 Jan. 1907.

403 **he checked Edith** Sylvia Morris, *Edith Kermit Roosevelt,* 406. The operation,

performed on 14 Apr., was a success, and restored EKR's health, which had been troubled for several years.

403 **Upon arrival** William Lyon Phelps, *Autobiography with Letters* (New York, 1939), 618. Throughout the winter, WHT had been outspoken in his praise of WW's war policy. It is hard to believe that TR did not say something to him, but Phelps was a close witness to the encounter, and TR's account of the incident avoids any mention of a verbal response. (TR, *Letters*, 8.1118.) According to secondary newspaper reports, the two men exchanged the briefest of greetings.

CHAPTER 21: *BARNES V. ROOSEVELT*

404 **Epigraph** Robinson, *Collected Poems*, 230.

404 **the most entertaining libel suit** See George T. Blakey, "Calling a Boss a Boss: Did Roosevelt Libel Barnes in 1915?" *New York History*, 60.2 (Apr. 1979).

404 **Barnes's counsel** TR.Jr. to KR, 29 May 1915 (KRP). A later version of this anecdote is in Bishop, *TR*, 2.366.

405 **Roosevelt's classmate** Andrews (1858–1936) was a respected judge of the legal-realist school. Elected later to a seat on the New York Court of Appeals, he famously dissented against the majority opinion of Justice Benjamin N. Cardozo in *Palsgraf v. Long Island Railroad Co.* (1928).

405 **"Your Honor, I move"** New York (State) Supreme Court, *William Barnes, plaintiff-appellant, against Theodore Roosevelt, defendant-respondent*, 4 vols. (Walton, N.Y., 1917), 1.129. Except where otherwise indicated, all testimony in the Syracuse trial is quoted from this source (hereafter cited as *Barnes v. Roosevelt*). Narrative and descriptive details derive from the observant reporting (with illustrations) of the New York *World*, 19 Apr.–23 May 1915, supplemented by accounts in *The New York Times, New York Evening Post*, and *Syracuse Herald*.

405 **A roll of fat** Visible in a photograph in the New York *World*, 21 May 1915.

406 **William M. Ivins** *The New York Times*, 22 Oct. 1905; New York State Bar Association, *Proceedings of the Thirty-Ninth Annual Meeting* (New York, 1916), 505; Julius Henry Cohen, *They Builded Better Than They Knew* (New York, 1946), chap. 10.

407 **"probably the greatest"** *Barnes v. Roosevelt*, 1.142–43.

407 **"with the same care"** *Syracuse Herald*, 20 Apr. 1915.

407 **In New York State** Ibid. See 366.

408 **Roosevelt sat mutely** *New York Evening Post*, 19 Apr., New York *World*, 21 Apr. 1915. Siebold wrote that TR "seemed to be laboring under a degree of depression in striking contrast to the usual volatility of spirit characteristic of him." The reporter for *The New York Times* thought TR cheerful enough, but noted his lapses of memory. A careful reading of the transcript supports Siebold's view, as does a chilling photograph in the same issue of the *World*.

408 **Have you read** *Barnes v. Roosevelt*, 1.193.

408 **My regiment was** Ibid., 1.199.

408 **"Why all this"** Ibid., 1.206–7.

409 **"Mr. Barnes spoke"** Ibid., 1.226.

409 **Mr. Bowers and** Ibid., 1.236–37.

409 **"The people are not"** Ibid., 1.242.

409 **precise citation of names** TR's pronunciation of the word "Barnes" reminded one reporter of the plop of a pebble dropped in water. *The New York Times*, 21 Apr. 1915.

409 **"a very able man"** *Barnes v. Roosevelt*, 1.243.

410 *It is not my desire* Ibid., 1.335–38.

410 **In other testimony** Ibid., 1.272–73, 307–8; *The New York Times*, 23 Apr. 1915.

410 **Bowers asked** Ibid., 1.322.

410 **The Colonel looked a happier** New York *World*, 22 Apr. 1915.

410 **Court artists** For an excellent rendering of the trial's *dramatis personae*, including a melancholy-looking TR, see the *Syracuse Herald*, 20 Apr. 1915.

411 **Has your occupation** *Barnes v. Roosevelt*, 1.357; *New York Evening Post*, 22 Apr. 1915.

411 **"It is pretty good"** *Barnes v. Roosevelt*, 1.363.

411 **the tax-avoidance controversy** John M. Corry, *Rough Ride to Albany: Teddy Runs for Governor* (New York, 2000), 142–65.

411 **a little book on the subject** William M. Ivins, *Machine Politics and Money in Elections in New York City* (New York, 1887).

411 **Now, does that** *Barnes v. Roosevelt*, 1.394–95.

412 **"You did not"** Ibid., 1.401–2.

412 **Since [1898]** Ibid., 1.407. TR was not exaggerating, although the lower figure was probably the more accurate in 1915. Of his lifetime total of letters, approximately 150,000 survive today.

412 **"I particularly wished"** Ibid., 1.422.

412 **"It is because"** Ibid., 1.424.

412 **as if activated by a jolt** The electrical metaphor comes from the court reporter of *The New York Times*, 22 Apr. 1915. He applied it also to the audience. See also Blakey, "Calling a Boss a Boss" for TR's effect on the jury.

413 **Mr. Ivins, this witness** *Barnes v. Roosevelt*, 1.438.

413 **"Mr. Ivins, that is not"** Ibid., 1.439–40.

413 **"Doctor Jekyll"** Ibid., 1.441.

414 **Ivins noted that** Ibid., 1.442.

414 **Yes, sir** Ibid.

414 **even the most wheedling** *The New York Times*, 27 Apr. 1915.

415 **"A little matter"** Ibid.

416 **Barnes quit attending** Ibid.

416 **"What relation"** *The New York Times*, 5 May 1915.

416 **"I don't know"** Ibid., 7 May 1915.

416 **That night, Thursday** TR, *Letters*, 8.921–22.

417 **a strange flurry** A. A. and Mary Hoehling, *The Last Voyage of the Lusitania* (New York, 1956), 39–40. One of the telegram recipients was Alfred G. Vanderbilt.

417 **An advisory signed** Ibid. See ibid., 96, for a facsimile reproduction of the German Embassy warning.

417 **"It makes my blood"** TR, *Letters*, 8.922.

417 **"I came across this"** *The New York Times*, 8 May 1915. Ivins had probably seen a recent article by TR (*Ladies' Home Journal*, Apr. 1915) complaining about having to wade through "a German edition of Aristophanes, with erudite explanations of the jokes." TR, *Works*, 4.91.

417 **Reading it, his face** Bishop, *TR*, 2.375.

418 **Many of the first** *Syracuse Herald*, 7 May 1915. Vanderbilt drowned, but Miss Pope survived after being nearly given up for dead. Later in life, as Theodate Pope Riddle, she designed the Theodore Roosevelt Birthplace memorial in New York City.

418 **Two or three** Bishop, *TR*, 2.375–76.

419 **1,918 souls aboard** *The New York Times*, 8 May 1915. The commonly accepted statistics of the *Lusitania* disaster are 1,959 passengers and crew, with 1,195 dead and 885 bodies unrecovered. Of the 139 Americans aboard, only 11 survived.

419 **"That's murder"** Bishop, *TR*, 2.376.

419 **I can only repeat** *Oshkosh Daily Northwestern,* 8 May 1915, e.g. (AP dispatch).

419 **Woodrow Wilson's first** Heckscher, *Woodrow Wilson,* 364. See also *The New York Times,* 10 May 1915.

419 **"America has come"** Edward M. House, *The Intimate Papers of Colonel House,* 4 vols., Charles Seymour, ed. (Cambridge, Mass., 1926), 1.434.

419 **After going to church** *The New York Times,* 10 May 1915.

419 **Sitting down** Heckscher, *Woodrow Wilson,* 364.

420 **Late in the afternoon** Ibid., 364–65.

420 **He talked about** Albert Bushnell Hart, ed., *Selected Addresses and Public Papers of Woodrow Wilson* (New York, 1918), 88.

420 **Roosevelt was not sorry** TR to Fanny Parsons, 6 May 1915 (TRC); TR to ERD, 12 May 1915 (ERDP); *The New York Times,* 11–13 May 1915; TR, *Letters,* 8.1328.

420 *Dear Archie* TR, *Letters,* 8.922. The *Gulflight,* though destroyed, was not actually sunk.

421 **"starve the whole"** Horace C. Peterson, *Propaganda for War: The Campaign Against American Neutrality, 1914–1917* (Norman, Okla., 1939), 83.

421 **Dr. Bernhard Dernburg** *The New York Times,* 9 May 1915.

421 **New York's own collector** The cargo manifest also included an enormous quantity of boxes and barrels labeled "cheese," "beef," and "oysters," whose contents may have been less nutritious than indicated. Dernburg was aware of more munitions aboard the *Lusitania* than he revealed, perhaps because he did not want to betray the presence in the New York port collector's office of a spy reporting on arms exports. On 3 May 1915 the detective reported to Franz von Papen, the German intelligence officer who had visited with TR after the outbreak of the war (see above, 378–79), that the ship carried 12 crates of detonators, 6,026 crates of bullets, 492 cases of "military equipment," and 223 auto wheels. (Papen, *Memoirs,* 42.) In the 1950s, the Royal Navy surreptitiously targeted the submerged hull of the *Lusitania* in a series of depth-charge "exercises" that shattered it almost beyond recognition. Nevertheless, in 2008 divers found the wreck bestrewn with 4 million rounds of .303 ammunition. *Daily Mail,* 20 Dec. 2008.

421 **Roosevelt knew Dernburg** TR, *Letters,* 8.857–61.

422 **"a personal attitude"** *The New York Times,* 12 May 1915.

422 **his note responding** The note, which was almost entirely the work of WW, was signed by Bryan as secretary of state.

422 **Wilson stated that** *The New York Times,* 14 May 1915.

423 **Only the most cynical** This is the thesis that Walter Karp argues at book length in *The Politics of War.* Most historians disagree, seeing WW as genuinely peace-minded in 1915–1916, if indeed (in Karp's word) vainglorious later on. But the President's flag-waving bellicosity toward Mexican provocateurs in the Tampico and Vera Cruz incidents of 1914 speaks volumes, as does his confession to Colonel House in Sept. 1915 that he had long wanted the United States to join the world war. (*Intimate Papers,* 2.84.) There is no doubt that the eventual entry of the United States into World War I was the logical, if attenuated, consequence of WW's demand in Feb. 1915 for a "strict accountability" from Germany for violations of neutrality by its warships.

423 **a green and gold fountain pen** For the provenance of this instrument, see Ambrose Flack's enchanting reminiscence, "Theodore Roosevelt and My Green-Gold Fountain Pen," *The New Yorker,* 22 May 1948.

423 **made a dignified witness** Blakey, "Calling a Boss a Boss." See also Stewart F. Hancock, Jr., "*Barnes v. Roosevelt:* Theater in the Courtroom," *New York State Bar Journal,* 63.8 (Dec. 1991).

423 **On Thursday, 20 May** Shakespeare, *Henry VIII,* act 3, scene 2; *The New York Times,* 21 May 1915.

423 **At 3:45 P.M.** *The New York Times,* 23 May 1915.

424 **"I will try"** Ibid. It turned out that the jury had been unanimously in favor of TR all along, dividing 11 to 1 only on the minor issue of whether or not to split costs. Stewart F. Hancock, Jr., himself an appellate court judge and the son of one of TR's lawyers, concludes that both plaintiff and defendant scored damaging points against each other, TR being shown to have selective amnesia about his acceptance of "boss" help and corporate contributions as governor and president, and Barnes being exposed as a pig at the public trough. Although the proof "fell far short of portraying Barnes as an evil man," TR's 1914 libel had clearly been defamatory. He was saved from conviction by virtue of his role as a "star performer" who "held his audience" for eight full days of arm-waving testimony. (Hancock, *"Barnes v. Roosevelt."*) Even EKR, commenting to Cecil Spring Rice on 30 May, wryly described the verdict as "illegal" (CSR).

424 **William Ivins returned** Ivins died on 23 July 1915. His career is affectionately recounted in Cohen, *They Builded Better Than They Knew.* Barnes's fortunes never recovered from the verdict against him. He was passed over for nomination to the U.S. Senate in 1916, and quickly lost force in New York State politics. When he died in 1930 he was remembered only as a figure in "one of the most extraordinary libel suits in the history of the country." Boston *Herald,* 1 July 1930.

CHAPTER 22: WAGING PEACE

425 **Epigraph** Robinson, *Collected Poems,* 526.

425 **The President's official** These two paragraphs owe much to the observations of Margaret Axson Elliott ("Madge," sister of WW's first wife) in *My Aunt Louisa and Woodrow Wilson* (Chapel Hill, N.C., 1944). See also Asquith, *Autobiography,* 330; Thompson, *Presidents I've Known,* 253ff.; and for WW's sexuality, Heckscher, *Woodrow Wilson,* 108–9, 185–88. The evidence of an affair with Mary Allen Peck in 1908 is inconclusive, but certainly suggests that in his sixth decade, WW was not short of testosterone.

426 **Now, secretly** Heckscher, *Woodrow Wilson,* 365; Link, *Papers of Woodrow Wilson,* 33.133ff.

426 **Wilson had in fact** Ishbel Ross, *Power with Grace: The Life Story of Mrs. Woodrow Wilson* (New York, 1975), 36.

426 **On 30 May** *The New York Times,* 1 June 1915.

426 **"the very nadir"** Robinson, *My Brother TR,* 290.

426 **"I have never"** Sylvia Morris, *Edith Kermit Roosevelt,* 406.

426 **He cheerfully tolerated** Sonya Levien, "The Great Friend: A Personal Story of Theodore Roosevelt as He Revealed Himself to One of His Associates in Magazine Work," *Woman's Home Companion,* Oct. 1919.

427 **"Villa," Roosevelt said** Barbara Gelb, *So Short a Time: A Biography of John Reed and Lousie Bryant* (New York, 1973), 48.

427 **Not even an invoice** Financial file, 16 June 1915 (TRP). Sylvia Morris, *Edith Kermit Roosevelt,* 406, estimates TR's total costs at $42,000; Thayer, *TR,* 400, at $52,000. Only $1,443 was recoverable from Barnes. *Barnes v. Roosevelt,* 1.125–26.

427 **Congress owed him** TR, *Letters,* 6.1539.

427 **"Why, I won it"** Thompson, *Presidents I've Known,* 114–15. Thompson was an eyewitness to this exchange.

427 **Each island gave off** Most of the language, and all of the natural observations in the next five paragraphs are TR's. See "Bird Reserves," in TR, *Works,* 4.197–227.

427 **fashionable ladies** Ross, *Power with Grace,* 18.

428 **"Nature is ruthless"** TR, *Works,* 4.206–7.

428 **a big humming hornet** Ibid., 20.210–11.

428 **like U-boats** Ibid., 20.213–14. "British Admiralty Confidential Daily Voyage Notice 15th April 1915, issued under Government War Risks Scheme: German Submarines Appear to Be Operating Chiefly Off Prominent Headlands and Landfalls," *American Journal of International Law* (New York, 1918), 12.867.

428 **Early the following** *The Washington Post,* 12 June 1915; Dudley Haddock to Charter Heslep, 14 May 1963 (EMH); *The New York Times,* 10 June 1915.

428 **"This means war"** Haddock to Heslep, 14 May 1963 (EMH).

429 **He could have** Ibid. The statement did not reach New Orleans until late the following day, 11 June, and Haddock put it out on the wires that night. By the following morning it was front-page news. See, e.g., *The Washington Post,* 12 June 1915, and *Fairbanks Daily News-Miner,* 12 June 1915.

429 **"Why be shocked"** Karp, *The Politics of War,* 200. For Bryan's frantic efforts to keep the administration neutral in the first half of 1915, see ibid., chap. 9.

429 **the only high official** Ibid., 171.

429 **"England is fighting"** Ibid.; Joseph P. Tumulty, *Woodrow Wilson As I Know Him* (New York, 1921), 231.

429 **A hail of vituperation** See, e.g., New York *World,* 9 June 1915; *The Washington Post,* Trenton (N.J.) *Evening Times,* and *Lowell* (Mass.) *Sun,* 10 June 1915.

430 **"God bless you"** *Atlanta Constitution,* 10 May 1915.

430 **Next morning** Ibid.

430 **"Good morning"** Levien, "The Great Friend."

430 **Somehow, Roosevelt had** Ibid.; TR, *Letters,* 1.229.

430 **"There was"** Ibid. The boy in the office was Philip Dunne, later a distinguished screenwriter.

430 **"radicals laid"** Levien, "The Great Friend." TR jokingly wrote at the end of a letter to one of *Metropolitan*'s left-wing contributors, "Your rational-individualist and rational-Socialist friend, Theodore Roosevelt." TR, *Letters,* 8.962.

430 **Much of the work** Levien, "The Great Friend."

431 **"I wonder how"** Ibid. One dignified old gentleman was heard breaking into song as he sank to street level.

431 **Whatever Roosevelt had lost** "How I wish I were President at this moment!" TR to Roman Romanovich von Rosen, 7 Aug. 1915 (TRP).

431 **"My hope is"** TR, *Letters,* 8.947.

432 **Roosevelt vaguely explained** Ibid.; TR to KR, 27 May 1915 (TRC).

432 **He knew nonetheless** TR, *Letters,* 8.948.

432 **Then, he had called** Morris, *Theodore Rex,* 228–29.

432 **Now, he lectured** *The New York Times,* 22 July 1915.

432 **"No nation ever"** Ibid.

433 **"Colonel," somebody asked** Marshall Stimson memorandum, n.d. (TRB).

433 **The article described** *The Washington Post,* 15–20 Aug. 1915; Sullivan, *Our Times,* 5.184–96. Another victim of U.S. wrath was Karl Bünz, Germany's consul general in New York, arrested on charges of financial conspiracy. Bünz had once performed a useful service to TR during the Venezuela crisis of 1902–1903. TR now sought to repay that old favor by trying, unsuccessfully, to keep him out of prison. (Morris, *Theodore Rex,* 189; Leary, *Talks with T.R.,* 43–44.) In December, Papen was expelled for complicity in acts of sabotage. He later (1932) served as Chancellor of Germany before stepping aside in favor of Adolf Hitler.

433 **"The time for"** *The New York Times,* 22 Aug. 1915.

433 **A few days later** For the background and subsequent history of the civilian preparedness program centering on Plattsburg, see John G. Clifford, *Citizen Soldiers: The Plattsburg Training Camp Movement, 1913–1920* (Lexington, Ky., 1972).

433 **"I suppose"** TR.Jr. to KR, 21 July 1915 (KRP).

433 **Roosevelt was amused** TR, *Letters,* 8.962–63; Eleanor B. Roosevelt, *Day Before Yesterday,* 66. By the time TR.Jr. went to war in 1917, he had accumulated a fortune conservatively estimated at $425,000. (EBR to "mother," 8 Jan. 1919 [TRJP].) For a compact portrait of TR.Jr., see Charles W. Snyder, "An American Original: Theodore Roosevelt, Junior," *Theodore Roosevelt Association Journal,* 17.2 (Spring 1991). See also H. Paul Jeffers, *Theodore Roosevelt, Jr.: The Life of a War Hero* (Novato, Calif., 2002).

434 **A *miserly economy*** TR copied this extract out by hand, along with similar pronouncements at other stages of his career, for Julian Street to quote in *The Most Interesting American.* Ms. preserved in JS.

434 **The camp was run** Clifford, *Citizen Soldiers,* 48–49, 82–83; Sullivan, *Our Times,* 5.226. TR.Jr. was a founder-member of a preparedness-advocacy group, formed early in 1915, which at first called itself the American Legion (not to be confused with the permanent organization founded after World War I), then gradually took on more substantial shape and power as the Military Training Camps Association (MTCA). Eleanor B. Roosevelt, *Day Before Yesterday,* 71; Clifford, *Citizen Soldiers,* 60–69.

Historical Note: TR was no stranger to the fantasy of a surprise invasion of the United States. Earlier in the summer of 1915, he had acted as a consultant to a film entitled *The Battle Cry of Peace,* produced and directed by his movie-mogul neighbor, J. Stuart Blackton of Vitagraph Pictures. (See 283.) *Battle Cry,* based on Hudson Maxim's alarmist *Defenseless America* (New York, 1915), opened at the same time as the Plattsburg camp, and was a box-office smash, despite negative reviews mocking its deliberate sensationalism.

All that exists of the movie today is a 400-foot fragment, eerily showing choked and blinded New Yorkers trying to escape from a lower Manhattan dense with the smoke and rubble of firebombed buildings. For a full account of the production and phenomenal success of *Battle Cry,* and the ideological quarrel it caused between TR and Hugo Münsterberg, see chap. 2 of David A. Gerstner, *Manly Arts: Masculinity and Nation in Early American Cinema* (Durham, N.C., 2006). See also TR, *Letters,* 8.989–91.

434 **It was an excellent** For the sample sufferings of one trainee, see Arthur Lubow, *The Reporter Who Would Be King: A Biography of Richard Harding Davis* (New York, 1992), 315–16.

434 **Davis, the only man present** Lubow, *The Reporter Who Would Be King,* 309–12, 315–16.

435 **"I like him"** Clifford, *Citizen Soldiers,* 85.

435 **It was tempting** TR had shown an advance copy of his remarks to Wood and allowed the general to edit them. Charles McGrath clumsily gave the unedited version to the press. *The New York Times,* commenting on this release, allowed that TR "could use more moderation in his expression," but nevertheless praised him for performing "a service to his country" in drawing attention to the need for national preparedness. TR, *Letters,* 8.965; *The New York Times,* 26 Aug. 1915.

435 **"Let him get out"** *The New York Times,* 26 Aug. 1915.

435 **"As the Colonel"** Street, *The Most Interesting American,* 5.

435 **a reprimand to General Wood** Garrison's furious telegram, which left Wood apologetic but secretly unrepentant, is quoted in Clifford, *Citizen Soldiers,* 86–87. Dudley F. Malone, a WW appointee who attended Plattsburg as an observer for the administration, denounced TR's speech as "both novel and treasonable." *The New York Times,* 27 Aug. 1915.

436 **the Colonel dictated** "I am, of course, solely responsible for the whole speech,"

TR declared, avoiding comment on his unscripted remarks at Plattsburg station. "General Wood had no more idea than Secretary Garrison what I was going to say." *The New York Times,* 27 Aug. 1915.

436 **"It was not"** Street, *The Most Interesting American,* 9–10.

437 **The young man was convinced** Street in TR, *Works,* 9.203.

437 **"The Master of the house"** Julian Street, "Mrs. Roosevelt Edits a Statement of Her Husband's," ts. (JS).

437 **He had to explain** TR's deposition, dated 24 Sept. 1915, is printed as an appendix in TR, *Works,* 4.604–6.

437 **Shaken by the** Wood, *Roosevelt As We Knew Him,* 395.

437 **Washburn observed** Ibid.; Adams, *Letters,* 6.702; Spring Rice to TR, 10 Oct. 1915 (TRP).

438 **a "shifty, adroit"** TR to Edith Wharton, 1 Oct. 1915 (EW).

438 **"Terse, clear"** Bourne, *British Documents,* pt. 1, ser. C, 15.149.

438 **"All these letters"** Street, *The Most Interesting American,* 15.

438 **the President's most recent** *The New York Times,* 22 July 1915.

438 **On 5 October** Bailey, *A Diplomatic History,* 580–81.

439 **Representatives of all** Ibid., 581; New York *World,* 6 Oct. 1915.

439 **On the day after** Cooper, *Woodrow Wilson,* 302–3. WW married Mrs. Galt on 18 Dec. 1915.

439 **"I am giving"** TR to QR, 18 Oct. 1915 (TRC).

439 **It was obvious** TR quoted in Street, *The Most Interesting American,* 31–32; TR to KR, 15 Oct. 1915 (TRC).

Chronological Note: An important chapter in TR's life came to an end on 14 Nov. 1915, when Booker T. Washington died. TR spoke at the memorial service in Tuskegee, Ala., on 12 Dec., and lobbied successfully for the appointment of Robert R. Moton to succeed Washington as principal of the Tuskegee Institute. In private correspondence he showed no resentment against Washington for supporting WW in 1912, calling the black educator "a genius such as does not arise in a generation." Wood, *Roosevelt As We Knew Him,* 345–46; TR, *Letters,* 8.996–97.

439 **Roosevelt had been pleased** TR, *Letters,* 8.1455, 829; TR to KR, 8 Apr. 1915 (TRC).

439 **As a token** TR to QR, 18 Oct. 1915 (TRC).

440 **The extermination of** TR, *Works,* 4.226–27.

CHAPTER 23: THE MAN AGAINST THE SKY

441 **Epigraph** Robinson, "The Revealer (Roosevelt)," *The Town Down the River,* 127.

441 **"With T.R."** Baker, notebook VIII.63, 11 Jan. 1916 (RSB).

441 **"In the present crisis"** Ibid. Contributing to the "crisis" atmosphere was the recent sinking, by an Austrian-flagged submarine, of the Italian liner *Ancona,* with 25 American citizens aboard. The submarine was actually German, but this inflammatory fact was kept secret for years.

441 **"I can understand"** Baker, notebook VIII.63–64, 11 Jan. 1916 (RSB).

442 **Roosevelt was regretfully** Street, *The Most Interesting American,* 32–33; TR to KR, 27 May 1915 (TRC).

442 **"I'm a domestic"** Street, *The Most Interesting American,* 33.

442 **"Most certainly"** Ibid., 53.

442 **the possibility of uniting** On 11 Jan. 1915, the Progressive National Committee,

strong-armed by George W. Perkins, had publicly indicated a willingness to unite with the GOP under "a common leadership," if Republicans would adopt a sufficiently Rooseveltian (i.e., patriotic, pro-preparedness, and socially fair) platform for the coming campaign. See TR, *Letters*, 8.1000, and Mowry, *TR*, 331.

443 **persons lacking manly qualities** For the effeminacy imputed to pacifists by TR and his fellow interventionists in World War I, see Gerstner, *Manly Arts*, 53ff.

443 **"The way to treat"** Sullivan, *Our Times*, 5.202.

443 **the winter so far** Gilbert, *A History of the Twentieth Century*, 391–93; *The New York Times*, 28, 21 Jan. 1916.

444 **an appreciable minority** The phrase is TR's, in *Letters*, 8.1013.

444 **Owen Wister's bestselling** Wister, *The Pentecost of Calamity*, chap. 14. For TR's influence on the draft of this elegant little book, see Wister, *Roosevelt*, 349ff.

444 **millions of *poilus*** Edith Wharton, *Fighting France: From Dunkerque to Belfort* (New York, 1915), 238. Mrs. Wharton begged TR in the fall of 1915 to visit the Western Front and publicize the plight of the French. He declined, saying he would do so only when allowed to fight there. "But I won't have the chance to try. The shifty, adroit and selfish logothete in the White House cannot be kicked into war." (1 Oct. 1915 [EW].) She replied that she felt the same way about WW. "I think it was the saddest moment of my life when I realized that my country *wanted* him to be what he is." (19 Oct. 1915 [ERDP].) Later TR wrote the introduction to Wharton's *The Book of the Homeless* (New York, 1916), an anthology raising funds for war refugees.

444 **"Does anybody understand"** *The New York Times*, 28 Jan. 1916.

445 **"a proper and reasonable"** Ibid. At another dinner at the Biltmore later that evening, WW, speaking extemporaneously, made an obtuse reference to certain "humbugs" who had "been at large a long time," and could be silenced only by allowing them to expose themselves to public ridicule. His audience of movie producers listened mystified as the President rambled on about watching himself on film, in tones that implied he had drunk one toast too many.

445 **Wilson proceeded** Heckscher, *Woodrow Wilson*, 376–79; Sullivan, *Our Times*, 5.228–30, 277–78; *The New York Times*, 30 Jan., 4 Feb. 1916. Actually WW had asked Congress to double the size of the standing army to 140,000, and to increase the size of the fleet to 27 battleships, plus ancillary vessels—the largest defense appropriations yet requested in American history.

445 **"Each of these"** Sullivan, *Our Times*, 5.230.

445 **epithets like "skunk"** TR, *Letters*, 7.809.

445 **"a Byzantine logothete"** TR, *Works*, 20.243.

446 **"If any individual"** Ibid., 20.245–46.

446 **"jungle fever"** TR.Jr. to KR, 8 Mar. 1916 (KRP).

446 **mountains of Allied money** Mowry, *TR*, 333, notes that the earnings of the Dupont Company of Delaware increased from $5.6 million in 1914 to $57.8 million in 1915. For a detailed account of TR's swing to the right, 1915–1916, see ibid., chap. 13.

446 **Roosevelt still talked** Ibid., 334–35.

446 **He allowed Judge Elbert** *The New York Times*, 19, 21 (editorial), and 22 Dec. 1915.

446 **"Behind it all"** Leary, *Talks with T.R.*, 49–50.

447 **"I dislike"** Ibid., 51.

447 **When Roosevelt stepped** The following account is based on Louis Achille, *Visite de M. et de Mme. Roosevelt à la Martinique, 22 février 1916* (Fort-de-France, 1916), 1–14. Previously the Roosevelts had toured the islands of St. Thomas, St. Croix, St. Kitts, Antigua, Guadeloupe, and Dominica, where TR was hailed (as he

had been in British East Africa) as the "King of America." *The New York Times,* 8, 4 Mar. 1915.

447 **Roosevelt had been the first** Achille, *Visite,* 1–3. For the happy effect of the Mont Pelée eruption on TR's plans for a Panama Canal, see Morris, *Theodore Rex,* 113.

448 **"Je vois que"** Achille, *Visite,* 6.

448 **the governor recalled** Ibid., 8–9.

448 **Vous nous donnez** Ibid., 9. In reply, TR, speaking in French, said again how profoundly touched he had been to see Martinique's young men preparing to fight for the rights of small as well as great nations. He raised his glass in salute: "Mesdames, Messieurs, je bois à la santé de la France toujours glorieuse et bientôt victorieuse." Ibid., 13–14.

449 **After visiting** For an account of this episode, see TR's essay "A Naturalist's Tropical Laboratory," in TR, *Works,* 4.255–72. Beebe's tribute to TR, "The Naturalist and Book-Lover: An Appreciation," is printed as an introduction to this volume.

449 **No less a GOP** *The New York Times,* 2 Mar. 1916. Gardner was also an outspoken advocate of preparedness. For more on his current political maneuverings, which greatly annoyed TR, see TR, *Letters,* 8.1034–35.

449 **They spent an afternoon** TR, *Works,* 4.278–82.

449 **I MUST REQUEST** Stoddard, *As I Knew Them,* 429–31; *The New York Times,* 10 Mar. 1916. The full text of TR's cable is reprinted in TR, *Letters,* 8.1024–26.

450 **A joke went around** Mowry, *TR,* 346.

450 **a surprise bestseller** George H. Doran, *Chronicles of Barabbas, 1884–1934* (New York, 1935), 217. Doran's royalty statement to TR, 16 Oct. 1916, shows 12,128 copies of the original edition sold in North America (TRP). In mid-1916, according to Doran, the retail magnate Walter Scott underwrote a mass-market edition of *Fear God* at 50 cents a copy. The entire 100,000-copy print run sold out. The book was also published in Great Britain.

451 **"In America"** Karp, *The Politics of War,* 222.

451 **Pancho Villa's cross-border raid** The raid occurred on 9 Mar. 1916, the same day TR issued his "Trinidad statement." Mexican bandits had earlier, on 10 Jan., massacred 16 Texan businessmen en route to San Ysabel. WW declined military revenge, arguing that the Texans traveled at their own risk.

451 **"another Wilson"** TR, *Letters,* 8.1026.

451 **mass of mail** TR's boom in the spring of 1916 increased his mail receipt to 1,000 letters a day. TR, *Letters,* 8.1039.

451 **"I don't know"** Edwin Arlington Robinson to KR, 23 Feb. 1913 (KRP).

452 **The Roosevelts had** EKR to KR, 20 Jan. 1913 (KRP); Scott Donaldson, *Edwin Arlington Robinson: A Poet's Life* (New York, 2007), 313–14. For a recent sampling of Robinson's work, perceptively introduced, see Robert Mezey, ed., *The Poetry of Edwin Arlington Robinson* (New York, 1999).

452 **He confessed** The note has been lost, but its content may be extrapolated from TR's reply, and the known circumstances of Robinson's life.

452 **"Your letter"** TR, *Letters,* 8.1024. TR added that he had used some lines of Robinson as the epigraph to *A Book-Lover's Holidays in the Open.* See TR, *Works,* 20.3.

452 *After that, from everywhere* Edwin Arlington Robinson, *The Man Against the Sky* (New York, 1916), 97.

452 **Robinson had long ago** Edwin Arlington Robinson, *The Town Down the River* (New York, 1910), 125–29; Wood, *Roosevelt As We Knew Him,* 392.

452 **The title poem** Robinson, who was habitually self-mocking when commenting

on his own work, joked that the purpose of this apocalyptic 300-line poem, one of the most difficult in the American canon, was "to cheer people up." He added more seriously that he meant also "to indicate the futility of materialism as a thing to live by—even assuming the possible monstrous negation of having to die by it." (To Albert R. Ledoux, 2 Mar. 1916 [EAR].) An earlier letter to Lewis Isaacs, written at the time of the poem's composition (30 Aug. 1915), refers to the German threat to civilization, and another (6 Jan. 1916) makes plain his continuing awareness of TR as a force *redux* in American life: "Tell Marian [MacDowell] that if she keeps on hating me hard enough she will probably get over it in time—just as others are getting over hating the Colonel" (EAR).

Images of the antithesis between mindless materialism at home and a distant *Gotterdämmerung* threatening the whole world, along with multiple references to "gods" and "gifts," recur throughout *The Man Against the Sky,* arguably Robinson's greatest cycle of poems. TR praised it highly in a letter to KR, 31 Mar. 1916 (KRP). For critical studies of the book, see R. Meredith Bedell, "Perception, Action, and Life in *The Man Against the Sky,*" *Colby Library Quarterly,* 11 (Mar. 1976), and Robert S. Fish, "A Dramatic and Rhetorical Analysis of 'The Man Against the Sky' and Other Selected Poems of Edwin Arlington Robinson" (Ph.D. thesis, University of Oklahoma, 1970).

453 **They met in New York** TR, *Letters,* 8.1029; Sullivan, *Our Times,* 5.200–201. For a detailed account of the lunch, see Jessup, *Elihu Root,* 2.344–47.

453 *The New York Times* See Gable, *The Bull Moose Years,* 232–45, for the intraparty TR boom in 1916.

453 **Pancho Villa's raid** *The New York Times,* 16 Mar. 1916. Fortunately for his future career, Pershing had by this time managed to euphemize his original nickname of "Nigger Jack," awarded to him when he commanded a regiment of black cavalry in the Indian Wars. Cowley, *The Great War,* 415.

453 **"into the *Ewigkeit*"** TR to KR, 16 Jan. 1915 (TRC). A cartoon in the New York *Sun* on 22 Apr. 1916 showed TR, big stick in hand, contemplating the skeleton of a moose. The caption read "Alas poor Yorick."

453 **But his boom** Mowry, *TR,* 342–43; Gable, *The Bull Moose Years,* 244–45; *The New York Times,* 1–10 Apr. 1916; TR, *Letters,* 8.1028.

454 **"You know, Colonel"** *The New York Times,* 6 Apr. 1916.

Biographical Note: A comic anecdote by Clara Barrus conveys TR's tempestuous vigor at this time. On 4 Apr., "fairly bursting with energy and good cheer," he attended a reception at the salon of the society painter Princess Elisabeth Lwoff-Parlaghy (a world-class eccentric in her own right, and something of a German appeaser). Having "talk[ed] his way through other people's talk like a snow-plow going through a snow-bank," TR bade adieu to the princess and began to descend to street level. "He halted abruptly on the steps, his eye arrested by the portrait of Andrew Carnegie which hung above the stairway. Shaking his fist close to the painted face, he exclaimed through his teeth, 'You look just like what you are—you damned old pacifist!' And down the stairs he bolted—the solemn, foreign-looking liveried flunkeys standing aghast at the explosion. . . . The perturbed princess almost screamed her query, 'Wh—what was that he said?' And when somebody repeated the remark without any elision, [she], speaking no word, said much in her quickened breath and dilating nostrils." (Clara Barrus, *The Life and Letters of John Burroughs,* 2 vols. [New York, 1925, 1968], 2.230–31.)

In the fall of 1918, Princess Lwoff asked TR to pose for what was to be his last portrait. Privately owned and held by the American Museum of Natural History, it is reproduced on the cover of this biography.

454 **The attack on** Heckscher, *Woodrow Wilson*, 385

454 **On 18 April** *The New York Times*, 19 Apr. 1916.

454 **a "town meeting"** Ibid.

454 **Wilson entered** *Atlanta Constitution*, 20 Apr. 1916; speech transcript in *The New York Times*, 20 Apr. 1916.

455 **ferryboats like the *Sussex*** The sinking of the *Sussex* impoverished the world by more than the loss of a few American lives. Among many others drowned was the great Spanish composer Enrique Granados, whose opera *Goyescas* had just been produced at the Metropolitan Opera.

455 **"I hope you"** *Atlanta Constitution*, 20 Apr. 1916.

455 **Roosevelt was one** *The New York Times*, 20 Apr. 1916.

456 **he had lost** "He has become, in my judgment, almost wholly an evil influence in public affairs," Ray Stannard Baker noted on 27 Apr. 1916, "an aggrieved and bitter man [who] belongs in the nineteenth, and not the twentieth century." Notebook IX.118 (RSB).

456 **"there is in my"** TR to Anna Roosevelt Cowles, 24 Apr. 1916 (ARC); *The New York Times*, 20 Apr. 1916.

456 **Secretary Lansing replied** Sullivan, *Our Times*, 5.132.

456 **"I have been"** TR to Fanny Parsons, 30 May 1916 (PAR). For a letter from TR to Ford, considerably gentler than his speech, explaining why he found pacifism "the enemy of morality," see TR, *Letters*, 8.1022.

456 **"It matters"** Ray Stannard Baker, *American Chronicle* (New York, 1945), 287.

456 **"So sincerely"** Heckscher, *Woodrow Wilson*, 392.

457 **was willing to trade** As a lollipop, TR let it be known that if elected in November, he would reappoint Elihu Root as his secretary of state. Albert Shaw, "Reminiscences of Theodore Roosevelt," ms. (ASP).

457 **"All were united"** Cecil to Florence Spring Rice, 8 June 1916 (CSR). For an eyewitness account of the Progressive proceedings, see Julian Street, "The Convention and the Colonel," *Collier's Weekly*, 57.5 (1 July 1916). TR characteristically cited this article as "The Colonel and the Convention." TR, *Letters*, 8.1085.

457 **The European situation** Ecksteins, *Rites of Spring*, 144; Gilbert, *A History of the Twentieth Century*, 397.

457 **Roosevelt had once taunted** See 70.

457 **"They believed"** Cecil to Florence Spring Rice, 8 June 1916 (CSR).

457 **"We all look"** Adams, *Letters*, 5.323.

458 **By nine o'clock** Mowry, *TR*, 351–52. TR's preference was for Wood, as a preparedness man as committed as himself. He had already privately ascertained that Wood was willing to run. (Nicholas Roosevelt, *TR*, 108.) Lodge he regarded merely as "a stopgap" who could not be nominated, but who would block the boom for Hughes, and then transfer his support back to TR. Thomas Robins interview, n.d. (TRB).

459 **another telegram declining** TR, *Letters*, 8.1062–63.

459 **"Around me"** Villard, *Fighting Years*, 316. See TR, *Letters*, 8.1074 for the devastated reactions of two Progressives, Thomas Robins and William Allen White.

460 **"Theodore"** Robinson, *My Brother TR*, 303.

460 **With other family** TR to Anna Roosevelt Cowles, 16 June 1916 (ARC); Leary, *Talks with T.R.*, 31; Micah 6:8.

460 **His secretary interrupted** Leary, notebook 3, 18 June 1916 (JJL). A slightly different version of this conversation appears in Leary, *Talks with T.R.*, 65–69.

460 **"If they were mine"** Leary, notebook 3, 18 June 1916 (JJL).

460 **"Now, Theodore"** Hermann Hagedorn (eyewitness) in *Roosevelt House Bulletin*, 6.10 (Fall 1948).

CHAPTER 24: SHADOWS OF LOFTY WORDS

461 **Epigraph**   Robinson, *Collected Poems*, 17.

461 **As a boy**   Kermit Roosevelt, *Happy Hunting Grounds*, 15–16.

461 **In recent years**   Morris, *Theodore Rex*, 424; TR, *Letters*, 8.1064–65; Wood, *Roosevelt As We Knew Him*, 388ff.; TR, *Letters*, 8.887. See Edgar Lee Masters, "At Sagamore Hill" in *Starved Rock* (New York, 1919), 95ff., for an unforgettable account in verse of being received by TR.

461 *By good rights*   Robinson, *My Brother TR*, 324; Robert Frost, *North of Boston* (New York, 1915), 72. Corinne Roosevelt Robinson, herself a published poet (*The Call of Brotherhood and Other Poems* [New York, 1913]) and officer of the Poetry Society, maintained a salon at her Madison Avenue home for bards visiting New York. TR's encounter with Frost appears to have taken place in late 1916. For more on TR's poetic tastes, see TR, *Letters*, 8.1228, and chap. 2, "The World of Thought," in Wagenknecht, *The Seven Worlds of TR*.

462 **a severe attack of amnesia**   Leary, *Talks with T.R.*, 62.

462 **On 26 June**   *The New York Times*, 27, 29 June 1916; TR, *Letters*, 8.1082–23; Leary, *Talks with T.R.*, 52. It was a matter of some concern to the designers of Republican campaign buttons in 1916 that both Hughes and Fairbanks wore old-fashioned beards, as opposed to the smooth, contemporary-looking jawlines of Wilson and his running mate, Thomas R. Marshall. As a cabbie in Chicago remarked at the time of the GOP convention, "Americans had a right to see a man's chin before being asked to vote for him." Julian Street, "The Convention and the Colonel," *Collier's Weekly*, 57.5 (1 July 1916).

462 **"I don't believe"**   Kenneth C. Kellar, *Seth Bullock: Frontier Marshal* (Aberdeen, S.D., 1872), 177.

462 **Kermit could try**   KR did so on 5 July, serving in the Sixth Business Man's Regiment through 8 Aug.

462 **"The break seems"**   Heckscher, *Woodrow Wilson*, 404–5.

462 **Coincidentally**   David Jones, *In Parenthesis* (London, 1982), ix, cited in Ecksteins, *Rites of Spring*, 211; Gilbert, *A History of the Twentieth Century*, 397–98, 408. The death toll on 1 July 1916 was the highest of World War I. Quite apart from ground fire, the heavy-artillery rate was 60 shells a second.

463 **Roosevelt's drive to raise**   *The New York Times*, 19, 20 June 1916. Bullock informed TR that South Dakota was good for a whole regiment. Kellar, *Seth Bullock*, 177.

463 **His letter to Baker**   TR, *Letters*, 8.1087–88.

463 **"in the event of"**   Ibid., 8.1091.

463 **memoirs of Baron Grivel**   Georges Lacour-Gayet, *Mémoires du vice-amiral Baron Grivel* (Paris, 1914).

463 **"Lafayettes of the Air"**   *Collier's Weekly*, 29 July 1916.

463 **On 4 August**   *The New York Times*, 5 Aug., *The Washington Post*, 6 Aug. 1916; Whitney Museum of American Art, *Flora Whitney Miller: Her Life, Her World* (New York, 1987), 17. Hereafter *Flora*.

463 **He admitted**   TR, *Letters*, 8.1094; QR to ABR, 28 Dec. 1917 (ABRP). At Plattsburg, QR had been found unfit for rifle service because of defective vision, plus a tendency, when drilling, to toss rather than shoulder arms. John T. McGovern, *Diogenes Discovers Us* (Freeport, N.Y., 1933, 1967), 233.

463 **His ironic sense**   ABR found KR annoyingly sassy at Harvard. "Perhaps the main trouble is that he is generally funny and knows it, hence, when he cannot think of anything funny to say, he becomes fresh." ABR to TR, 14 Nov. 1915 (KRP).

464 **fast-driving boys**   Three weeks after Flora's ball, QR was ticketed for speeding by a policeman in Hicksville, Long Island. *The New York Times*, 25 Aug. 1916.

464 **Flora, who was** *Flora, passim*. See also Flora Miller Biddle, *The Whitney Women and the Museum They Made* (New York, 1999).

465 **Archie had briefly paid court** QR to Flora Whitney, ca. 25 Oct. 1915 (FWM).

465 **"You get a"** QR to KR, 2 Feb. 1916 (KRP).

465 **"We are all"** *Collier's Weekly*, 29 July 1916.

465 **Secretary Baker was pleased** Frederick Palmer, *Newton D. Baker: America at War* (New York, 1931), 1.283–84.

466 **He told Kermit** QR to KR, 2 Feb. 1916 (KRP). A period of hard study was especially desirable for QR, who for reasons best known to himself had devoted his entire Mathematics "A" examination sheet to a poem. (McGovern, *Diogenes Discovers Us*, 232.) It is reproduced in Kermit Roosevelt, *Quentin Roosevelt*, 28ff.

466 **"Roosevelt would be"** TR, *Letters*, 8.1110; *The New York Times*, 1 Sept. 1916; Barrus, *John Burroughs*, 2.238.

467 **Quentin Roosevelt returned** QR to Flora Whitney, 31 July, 24 Sept. 1917 (FWM).

467 **Roosevelt fretted** TR, *Letters*, 8.1099, 1199, 1101.

467 **"from the bench"** Congressional Quarterly, *The CQ Guide to American Government* (Washington, D.C. 1969), 93. Ironically, WW's reputation as a "cold" politician was moderated by Hughes's own icy public persona. When the latter lost his voice in transit across Illinois, Will H. Hays, a member of the RNC, remarked, "Thank God. We have a chance to carry Indiana." (Thomas Robins interview, n.d. [TRB].) For an account of Hughes's boxed-in campaign, See S. D. Lovell, *The Presidential Election of 1916* (Carbondale, Ill., 1980).

467 **For the sake of** Leary, *Talks with T.R.*, 198; *The New York Times*, 4 Oct. 1917; Irwin, *A History of the Union League Club*, 184–85.

467 **Four days later** *The New York Times*, 8 Oct. 1916.

468 **It cruised into** *Syracuse Herald*, 8 Oct. 1916; *The New York Times*, 8 Oct. 1916.

468 **He added, smiling** Ibid.; *Logansport* (Ind.) *Tribune* (AP dispatch), 8 Oct. 1916.

469 **"The first British ship"** *The New York Times*, 8 Oct. 1916.

469 **Throughout the day** *Newport Mercury*, 14 Oct. 1916; *The New York Times* and *Trenton* (N.J.) *Evening Times*, 9 Oct. 1916.

469 **President Wilson remained** *Trenton* (N.J.) *Evening Times*, 9 Oct. 1916.

469 **"Now the war"** *The New York Times*, 11 Oct. 1916.

470 **"Old trumps"** Stoddard, *As I Knew Them*, 319. TR had been speaking earlier this night at the Academy of Music in Brooklyn, not, as Stoddard remembers, at the Academy of Music in Philadelphia.

Biographical Note: Around this time, TR was asked by Henry Fairfield Osborn, president of the American Museum of Natural History, to endorse Madison Grant's *The Passing of the Great Race* (New York, 1916), a pro-Nordic racist diatribe with little foundation in science. "I hope . . . you may find an opportunity of saying something about it," Osborn wrote on 16 Oct., "for at this time when the melting pot theory is so popular we cannot dwell too strongly on the value to this country of the finer elements." TR received and read the book, with his usual speed, on the last day of the month, and responded to Osborn with some uncertainty. "It is suggestive and stimulating, as is true of Gobineau's and Chamberlain's books [see above, 647]; it shares their faults, and absolutely lacks the very qualities which Huxley and Darwin so eminently showed." He said he needed to discuss the question of an endorsement over lunch. Osborn (to whom TR owed many Brazil-related favors) appears to have been a persuasive advocate. TR then allowed his name to be used in publicizing *The Passing of the Great Race*, doing lasting damage to his reputation.

He immediately regretted what he had done. On 15 Nov., Worral F. Mountain, the mayor of East Orange, N.J., visited TR and listened while "he tore paragraph after paragraph of Grant's book to pieces of pure facts, and quoted not only American, but German and French historians as his authority. . . . He pathetically regretted that the book had been dedicated to him." Osborn / TR correspondence (AMNH); Worrall Mountain diary, 15 Nov. 1916, photocopy provided to author by Thomas R. Mountain (AC). See also Dyer, *TR and the Idea of Race*, 17, and John P. Jackson, Jr., and Nadine M. Weidman, *Race, Racism and Science* (Santa Barbara, Calif., 2004), 110ff.

470 **a pair of British steamers** *The New York Times*, 31 Oct. 1916.

471 **"Just what"** Leary, notebook 3, 3 Nov. 1916 (JJL).

471 **eleven of the nineteen** *The New York Times*, 1, 2 Nov. 1916. Five more Progressives, including William Allen White, publicly approved the pro-Democrat statement, but declined to endorse WW.

471 **"Sir, when I"** TR, *Letters*, 8.1122.

471 **During the last** Speech transcript from *The New York Times*, 4 Nov. 1916.

471 **Roosevelt threw** Leary, *Talks with T.R.*, 332–33.

471 **Mr. Wilson now dwells** *The New York Times*, 4 Nov. 1916. Leary makes clear that these last two paragraphs were delivered extempore. At TR's final, disgusted gesture, "the house was on its feet . . . storming the platform." Leary, notebook 3, 3 Nov. 1916 (JJL).

472 **"The old man's"** Leary, notebook 5, 5 Nov. 1916 (JJL); see also Leary, *Talks with T.R.*, 3.

472 **Wilson took the news** Tumulty, *Woodrow Wilson*, 218.

472 **"I hope you are"** Alice Hooper to Frederick Jackson Turner in Turner, *Dear Lady*, 221.

473 **Roosevelt began to pack** TR, *Letters*, 8.1133. By executive order in 1903, TR had transferred to the Library of Congress the papers of Presidents Washington, Madison, Jefferson, and Monroe as well as those of Alexander Hamilton and Benjamin Franklin. He now offered his own, asking only that they be held confidential until his death. The papers, forming the nucleus of TRP, arrived at the library in the new year of 1917 in six enormous locked trunks. "The Lord only knows where the key is," TR advised. "Break the cases open, and start to work on them!" Today, TRP consists of approximately a quarter of a million items. For the full story of its acquisition, see the introduction by Paul T. Heffron to the TRP Index at http://lcweb2.loc.gov/ammem.heffron.

473 **"I am of no use"** Garland, *My Friendly Contemporaries*, 128–29.

473 **leadership changes** Gilbert, *A History of the Twentieth Century*, 423. Zimmermann was the political ally of Field Marshal Paul von Hindenburg and General Erich Ludendorff, who by late 1916 had replaced Falkenhayn as the virtual dictators of Reich war policy.

473 **The German ambassador** *Fort Wayne News*, 9 Oct. 1916; Grey to Balfour, pencil draft inscribed "about end of Nov / 16" (AJB).

473 **The document Bernstorff** Sullivan, *Our Times*, 5.245–46.

473 **"The President's"** Spring Rice to Balfour, 15 Dec. 1916 (AJB).

473 **Four days later** *The New York Times*, 21 Dec. 1916.

474 **"If the contest"** Ibid., 21 Dec. 1916.

474 **Secretary Lansing felt** Heckscher, *Woodrow Wilson*, 422.

474 **Roosevelt, massively attired** Leary, notebook 5 (JJL).

474 **a sample list** *The New York Times*, 11 Jan. 1917.

474 **certain phrases glinted** Edgar E. Robinson and Victor J. West, *The Foreign Policy of Woodrow Wilson, 1913–1917* (New York, 1918), 126–28.

475 **On 22 January** Heckscher, *Woodrow Wilson*, 424–25.

475 **It was inconceivable** Sullivan, *Our Times*, 5.250–52.

475 **only moderate applause** Florence Spring Rice (eyewitness) to unnamed aunt, 9 Feb. 1917 (CSR).

475 **the German foreign minister was** Sullivan, *Our Times*, 5.256–58.

475 **"as if the world"** House, *Intimate Papers*, 1.439.

475 **House knew what** Ibid., 2.84.

476 **Captain Rose of the U-53** *Trenton* (N.J.) *Evening Times*, 3 Feb. 1917.

476 **"If American ships"** *The Washington Post*, 4 Feb. 1917 (italics added). The *Housatonic*, a freighter loaded with wheat, was sunk at noon GMT, i.e., 7 A.M. Washington time, so WW undoubtedly knew about the disaster when he went before Congress at 2 P.M. However, there was no confirmation that any of the 26 Americans aboard had been killed, and whether Rose had broken international law. In fact he had not.

476 **The water cocks** *Trenton* (N.J.) *Evening Times*, 3 Feb., *The Washington Post*, 4 Feb., *Mansfield* (Ohio) *News*, 17 Feb. 1917.

476 **Sir: I have** TR, *Letters*, 8.1149–50.

477 **"No situation"** Ibid.

477 **"In view of"** TR to Baker (facsimile), 3 Feb. 1917; Palmer, *Newton D. Baker*, 1.194.

477 **Over the past** Palmer, *Newton D. Baker*, 1.116–17. See Baker's reminiscence of the transformative effect of World War I, quoted in ibid., for the lucidity of expression that used to be the norm among American public figures.

477 **Among his urgent** Ibid., 1.85–86.

478 **Ironically, on** *The New York Times*, 6 Feb. 1917.

478 **"It is not"** Spring Rice to Balfour, 9 Feb. 1917 (AJB).

478 **He emphasized that** Sullivan, *Our Times*, 5.264–65.

478 **U BOOT KRIEG** Thomas Boghardt, "The Zimmermann Telegram: Diplomacy, Intelligence and the American Entry into World War I" (Working Paper No. 6–04, BMW Center for German and European Studies, 2003), 35, http://cges.georgetown.edu/.

479 **"that polite, silent"** TR, *Letters*, 8.957–58.

479 **"a war in which"** See 479.

479 **one he had sketched** TR to E. A. Van Valkenburg and William Draper Lewis on 5 Sept. 1914. See Bishop, *TR*, 2.370–71.

479 **A new degree of neurosis** One theory that did not occur to newspaper readers unschooled in *Realpolitik* was that Zimmermann might have disbelieved his own telegram—seeking only to curry the favor of his superiors in the Prussian military. A more plausible speculation is British intelligence officials used their intercept to alarm Wilson, in order to goad him and Congress into a declaration of war on their side. At the time, Britain's role in deciphering and handing over the telegram was kept secret. Boghardt, "The Zimmermann Telegram," 10–14, 19.

479 **"A little group"** *The New York Times*, 5 Mar. 1917.

479 **Republicans and Democrats alike** Richard Lowitt, "The Armed-Ship Controversy: A Legislative View," *Mid-America*, 46 (Jan. 1964).

479 **On Monday, 5 March** *Newark* (Ohio) *Advocate*, 5 Mar., *The New York Times*, *The Washington Post*, 6 Mar. 1917.

480 **"I beg your tolerance"** *Syracuse Herald*, 5 Mar., *The New York Times*, *The Washington Post*, *Galveston* (Tex.) *Daily News*, 6 Mar. 1917.

480 **"the lily-livered skunk"** Leary, *Talks with T.R.*, 327–28; TR to KR, 1 Mar. 1917 (TRC). The newspaper-crumpling incident was one of the few occasions anyone ever heard TR swear. Leary chose not to record the epithet.

480 **On 9 March** Heckscher, *Woodrow Wilson*, 434–35. The USS *Algonquin* was sunk by a U-boat on 12 Mar. 1917.

480 **The first news** *The New York Times*, 12 Mar., *Mansfield* (Ohio) *News*, 12 Mar. 1917.

480 **The Russian army** Gilbert, *A History of the Twentieth Century*, 439, 442; *The Washington Post* and *The New York Times*, 17 Mar. 1917.

481 **On 20 March** Heckscher, *Woodrow Wilson*, 437.

481 **After the meeting** Cooper, *Woodrow Wilson*, 383; TR, *Letters*, 8.1164.

481 **Baker wrote back** TR, *Letters*, 8.1164.

481 **"and she has"** *The New York Times*, 21 Mar. 1917.

481 **"We can perfectly"** Ibid.

481 **"I shall not come"** Wood, *Roosevelt As We Knew Him*, 421.

481 **"a communication"** Heckscher, *Woodrow Wilson*, 437.

482 **"I shall be"** *The New York Times*, 24 Mar. 1917. For an account of TR's expedition—unusual for him, because he had no interest in fishing—see TR, *Works*, 4.314ff.

482 **flaming with flags** This phrase, written on 25 Mar. 1917, is taken from *Washington Wife: Journal of Ellen Maury Slayden from 1897–1919* (New York, 1963), 296.

CHAPTER 25: DUST IN A WINDY STREET

483 **Epigraph** Robinson, *Collected Poems*, 63.

483 **Henry Adams was just** Adams, *Letters*, 6.749.

483 **Theodore Roosevelt's slow train** *Oshkosh Daily Northwestern*, 3 Apr. 1917. The following account of TR's brief visit to Washington is taken from this source, plus the *Oakland Tribune*, same date, *The Washington Post*, *Trenton Evening Times*, and *The New York Times*, 4 Apr. 1917. See also Looker, *Colonel Roosevelt*, 179.

483 **another U.S.-flagged steamer** The *Aztec*.

484 **With a profound** *The Washington Post*, 3 Apr. 1917. WW began his address with "Gentlemen of the Congress," ignoring the presence before him of Jeannette Rankin (R, Mont.), the first woman ever to sit in the House of Representatives.

484 **Williams had stood** *The New York Times*, 4 Apr. 1917.

484 **second largest devilfish** TR's host in Florida, Russell J. Coles, announced that the wingspan of the Colonel's specimen was 16 feet 8 inches. The only larger devilfish, or manta ray, then known was in the American Museum of Natural History, and spanned 18 feet 2 inches. *The New York Times*, 4 Apr. 1917.

484 **Senator Lodge, of all people** *San Antonio Light*, 2 Apr. 1917. The pacifist, a young man, had called Lodge a "coward" for announcing that he would vote for a war resolution. Accounts vary as to who threw the first punch.

485 **The White House was** *The New York Times*, 4 Apr. 1917.

485 **Roosevelt asked** *Oakland Tribune*, 3 Apr. 1917.

485 **"I don't know"** *Lowell* (Mass.) *Sun*, 4. Apr. 1917.

485 **Edith was brooding** EKR to Flora Whitney, 11 Mar. 1918 (FWM). QR came down from Harvard two days later. EKR diary, 5 Apr. 1917 (TRC).

485 **Quentin might have** On 14 Apr., a Royal Flying Corps spokesman announced in Montreal that "if no American troops go to France, young Roosevelt will serve with the Canadian air forces." *The New York Times*, 15 Apr. 1917.

486 **"A state of war"** *The New York Times* and *Decatur Daily Review*, 6 Apr. 1917.

486 **"Of course, when"** *Metropolitan*, Apr. 1917.

486 **"I'll take chances"** Leary, *Talks with T.R.*, 93.

486 **When, at eleven** *The New York Times*, 11 Apr. 1917. This visit has been frequently misdated by biographers, and as frequently misrepresented as the first encounter between TR and WW in the White House. See above, 348–52.

486 **"The President received"** Ibid. There is a photograph of TR holding this impromptu press conference in Lorant, *Life and Times of TR*, 610.

486 **"If I say"** Ibid.

486 **Uninhibited, he** *Titusville* (Pa.) *Herald,* 11 Apr. 1917; TR, *Letters,* 8.1173; *The New York Times,* 11 Apr. 1917.

487 **"I have been"** *The New York Times,* 11 Apr. 1917.

487 **receiving visitors that evening** Pringle, *TR,* 594–95 (misdated).

487 **"I am aware"** Newton D. Baker to Henry Pringle, 6 Nov. 1930, quoted in Pringle, *TR,* 595; *The New York Times,* 6, 11 Apr. 1917.

487 **"I had a good"** Leary, *Talks with T.R.,* 96, 99. Remarks like these betrayed one of TR's weaknesses—an inability to understand his opponents. WW had obviously not been briefed on his proposed division, and wanted to know where TR thought its equipment might come from. The regular army itself was woefully short of rifles and ammunition, and conscription would make it shorter still. TR replied that the French might help. "They have the equipment. They need men." He added that he and his volunteers, many of them men of wealth, would initially fund the division themselves. The President seemed interested, but kept asking questions. Looker, *Colonel Roosevelt,* 181; Leary, *Talks with T.R.,* 97–98.

488 **Let us use** TR, *Letters,* 8.1171.

488 **The Roosevelts knew** Longworth, *Crowded Hours,* 254; *The New York Times,* 15 Apr., *La Crosse Tribune,* 22 Apr. 1917.

488 **waited with Archie** Since graduating from Harvard, ABR (who had a tendency to follow in the footsteps of his eldest brother) had been working for a carpet company in Thompsonville, Conn. ABR, "Lest We Forget," *Everybody's Magazine,* May 1919.

489 **the hasty departure** On 27 Mar., Trotsky had sailed from New York to join his radical colleagues in Petrograd. He was secretly arrested in Halifax, Canada, by British military authorities fearful that he would work against the Allied cause in Russia. *The New York Times,* 11 Apr. 1917.

489 **Count Ilya Tolstoy** *The New York Times,* 21 Apr. 1917; TR, *Letters,* 8.1186. The commission was eventually headed by Elihu Root.

489 **Describing himself** TR, *Letters,* 8.1186.

489 **Privately, he told** Leary, *Talks with T.R.,* 98.

489 **"If we do not"** Ibid., 99.

489 **"This policy"** TR, *Letters,* 8.1174–75.

489 **"My dear sir"** Ibid., 8.1176–84, 1177, 1178, 1180.

490 **"a repetition of"** Alvin Johnson, *Pioneer's Progress: An Autobiography* (New York, 1952), 253.

490 **"For obvious reasons"** TR, *Letters,* 8.1183–84.

490 **and looking ahead** Harding was also uneasy about having a flagrantly pro-German mistress. See James D. Robenalt, *The Harding Affair: Love and Espionage During the Great War* (New York, 2009). Nobody in 1917 was so cynical as to suggest that Harding might have an interest in making it possible for Roosevelt to die gloriously in battle, but nine decades later, the thought does arise.

490 **assuming that Wilson** While remaining cagey about TR's chances of being accepted for a command, WW had personally encouraged him to push for the volunteer amendment. TR, *Letters,* 8.1170.

490 **"He is known"** *The New York Times,* 29 Apr. 1917.

491 **While the debate** Ibid.; Spring Rice to TR, 19 Apr. 1917 (CSR).

491 **"It will give me"** Palmer, *Newton D. Baker,* 1.206.

491 **Quentin was summoned** Longworth, *Crowded Hours,* 254–55; Kermit Roosevelt, *Quentin Roosevelt,* 32.

491 **By the first week** Bishop, *TR,* 2.424.

491 **"All the lines of him"** Slayden, *Washington Wife,* 308. Balfour's depressed look can clearly be seen in a photograph opposite p. 148 of Palmer, *Newton D. Baker,* 1.

492 **His government was** Strachan, *The First World War,* 228.

493 **They agreed, in other**   Palmer, *Newton D. Baker,* 1.202.

493 **Marshal Joffre's pleadings**   Strachan, *The First World War,* 248. Joffre's current army rank was ambiguous, because he himself had been replaced by Nivelle. But as the hero of the Marne, and leader of a crucially important mission, he was still perceived in America as the embodiment of France's war effort.

493 **Roosevelt and Joffre**   Leary, *Talks with T.R.,* 222; TR to Anna Roosevelt Cowles, 17 May 1917 (ARC); Leary, notebook 5 (JJL).

493 **"He did not tell"**   Leary, *Talks with T.R.,* 223.

493 **There was another**   Charles Hanson Towne, *The Balfour Visit* (New York, 1917) 59ff.; Leary, *Talks with T.R.,* 223–24; Leary, notebook 5 (JJL). To avoid upsetting the State Department, TR announced afterward that he and Balfour had been discussing the latter's Gifford lectures on "Theism and Humanism." See 673.

493 **"Since the responsibility"**   Palmer, *Newton D. Baker,* 1.202.

494 **Roosevelt believed**   Bishop, *TR,* 2.424.

494 **"Tumulty tells me"**   O'Leary to TR, 17 May 1917, OL.

494 **"It would be very agreeable"**   Ibid., 2.425.

494 **an old military showman**   Claude Debussy, *Préludes,* bk. 2.6 (Paris, 1913).

494 **James Amos**   Amos, *TR: Hero to His Valet,* 67; TR, *Letters,* 8.1195.

494 **"I don't care a continental"**   Leary, *Talks with T.R.,* 239.

494 **Kermit was at Plattsburg**   TR, *Letters,* 8.1194.

495 **"My dear General"**   Ibid., 8.1193.

495 **Pershing replied**   TR, *Letters,* 8.1193. The general did not add that he agreed with Baker and Wilson about the unwisdom of sending a TR-headed division to Europe. Cowley, *The Great War,* 417.

495 **"army of the air"**   Cowley, *The Great War,* 294.

495 **"Colonel Roosevelt is"**   Quoted in a memo by Parker, ca. 1928, transcribed and edited by Gary L. Lavergne in "John M. Parker's Confrontation with Woodrow Wilson," *Theodore Roosevelt Association Journal,* 10.2. During his interview with WW on the afternoon of 18 May 1917, Parker enraged the President by calling him an "autocrat" and "hired man of the people."

495 **"Never, except"**   Leary, *Talks with T.R.,* 115. TR's only ally in the Wilson administration wrote years later, "The only fault I ever had to find in him was that he took defeat too hard." Anne W. Lane and Louise H. Wall, eds., *The Letters of Franklin K. Lane* (New York, 1922), 306.

495 **"as good American"**   TR, *Letters,* 8.1195–97.

495 **"It is possible"**   *The New York Times,* 28 May 1917.

496 **"I told Wilson"**   Pringle, *TR,* 599.

496 **secretly become engaged**   QR recalls their betrothal this month in a letter to Flora Whitney, ca. Nov. 1917 (FWM).

496 **Edith Roosevelt had taken**   QR to Flora Whitney, 15 Nov. 1917 (FWM); EKR to QR, quoted in QR to Flora Whitney, 18 May 1918 (FWM). EKR was a woman whose affection had to be earned by prospective daughters-in-law. Eleanor qualified by virtue of shared Mayflower ancestors. Belle, regrettably, was a Democrat. Grace was too independent and pushy. Flora was a touch *nouveau,* but she had been received by British royalty, and there was much to be said for her expectations. Moreover, the girl spoke French as well as QR, and might pass for a Parisienne with her darkness and smallness and balletic way of posing for photographs.

496 **"Ah, Fouf"**   QR to Flora Whitney, 28 May 1917 (FWM).

496 **He was a year**   Palmer, *Newton D. Baker,* 1.287; McGerr, *A Fierce Discontent,* 289; Palmer, *Newton D. Baker,* 1.287; *The New York Times,* 9 Apr. 1917.

496 **The war had so**   QR to KR, 19 June 1917.

497 **Flora was as sure**   For a full account by Thomas Fleming of the love affair of QR and Flora Whitney, see Cowley, *The Great War,* 286–303.

498 **Ted and Archie** EKR diary, 20 June 1917 (TRC); TR to Lloyd George, 20 June 1917 (TRC). See also TR, *Letters,* 8.1201–3; Longworth, *Crowded Hours,* 256–57; EKR diary, 14 July 1917 (TRC).

498 **Quentin simultaneously** *The New York Times,* 15 July 1917; Parsons, *Perchance Some Day,* 265.

498 **He told Edith** EKR diary, 21 July 1917 (TRC); TR, *Letters,* 8.1356.

498 *Dearest . . .* Flora to QR, 19 July 1917 (FWM).

498 **On Monday morning** EKR diary, 23 July 1917 (TRC); EKR to ERD, 23 July 1917 (TRC).

499 **She murmured** Flora to ERD, 24 July 1917 (FWM); Longworth, *Crowded Hours,* 257–58.

CHAPTER 26: THE HOUSE ON THE HILL

500 **Epigraph** Robinson, *Collected Poems,* 81.

500 **"I have always believed"** TR to H. C. Stokes, 5 Aug. 1914 (TRC).

> *Biographical Note:* TR's last major statement on religion, an essay entitled "Shall We Do Away with the Church?" appeared in *Ladies' Home Journal,* Oct. 1917. It confirmed that faith, for him, was a social rather than spiritual force. Decrying clerical formalism as "the enemy of religion" from the days of the Pharisees to those of modern "ultra-sabbatarians," he argued that nevertheless, "a churchless community . . . is a community on the rapid downgrade." Conversely, communities already depressed by economic or other misfortune, such as the "abandoned-farm" regions of New York and the poor-white South, became revitalized when church activities resumed. The church was a sort of moral gymnasium: to attend Sunday services was to "tone up" one's system for the rest of the week. Communal worship gave the individual a sense of belonging to a larger whole. It helped resolve the opposing tensions of "envy and arrogance." There was much to be said, too, for the aesthetic beauty of the litany and religious music. TR acknowledged that charismatic evangelists could arouse "that flame of the spirit which mystics have long known to be real and which scientist now admit to be real," but he noted that such ardor subsides quickly. He was contemptuous of Calvinism because of its "tendency to confuse pleasure and vice." The ideal faith was democratic rather than domineering, and valued good works over dogma.

500 **He was being punished** In an impotent gesture, TR published his entire correspondence with Newton D. Baker in the Aug. 1917 issue of *Metropolitan* magazine.

500 **"I love you, dearest"** QR to Flora Whitney, 23 July 1917 (FWM).

501 **"Flora came over"** TR to QR, 28 July 1917 (FWM).

501 **It was too early** Flora to QR, 18 Dec. 1917; Flora to ERD, 24 July 1917 (FWM).

501 **"I am so sorry"** Flora to ERD, 24 July 1917 (FWM).

501 **On 9 August** TR, *Letters,* 8.1221–22. ABR was transferred to the Twenty-sixth Infantry in late July 1917. ABR, "Lest We Forget."

501 **"I had no idea"** TR, *Letters,* 8.1221–22.

502 **In a snub** *The New York Times,* 8 Aug. 1917; TR to Julian Street, ca. 8 Aug. 1917 (JS). Taft had his own joke during this period of delay-plagued mobilization. "When I see the way things are going in Washington, it makes my blood fairly boil," he told Albert Beveridge. "But when I think how much madder they must make T.R., I feel a whole lot better." Leary, *Talks with T.R.,* 200.

502 **symptoms of extreme stress** Carleton B. Case, *Good Stories About Roosevelt* (Chicago, 1920), 115; TR, *Letters*, 8.1207; EKR to KR, 19 Aug. 1917 (KRP).

502 **"an absolutely selfish"** TR, *Letters*, 8.1224. For an example of TR's paranoia about WW at this time, see his reprimand to William Allen White for a making a complimentary reference to the President in ibid., 8.1197–99.

502 **Seven months after** TR to KR, 10 Dec. 1917 (TRC); TR, *Letters*, 8.1225.

502 **He was diverted** KR to TR, 12 Aug. 1917 (KRP); TR, *Letters*, 8.1226–27.

502 **Another thing** Eleanor B. Roosevelt, *Day Before Yesterday*, 77–78; TR, *Letters*, 8.1207.

503 **"One of the"** TR, *Letters*, 8.1229.

503 **Dearest Quentin** Original in TRC.

504 **"I confess"** QR to Flora Whitney, 19 Aug. 1917 (FWM).

504 **"appalling reality"** Ibid.

505 **"The thing that"** Ibid.

505 **called on to interpret** QR to Flora Whitney, 20 Aug. 1917 (FWM).

505 **Flora registered** QR to EBR, 20 Jan. 1918 (TRJP). Flora's later feelings about Edith Normant are suggested by a large cross drawn over the girl's image in a photograph QR sent her. Scrapbook, 17 Feb. 1918 (FWM).

505 **"Ah, dearest"** QR to Flora Whitney, 31 Aug. 1917 (FWM).

505 **Among the lucrative** Sylvia Morris, *Edith Kermit Roosevelt*, 415; H. J. Whigham interviewed by Hermann Hagedorn, 12 May 1949 (TRB).

505 **It was therapeutic** EKR to KR, 19 Aug. 1917 (KRP); TR, *Letters*, 8.1347.

506 **No less a bandmaster** EKR to KR, 22 Sept. 1917 (KRP); *Oakland Tribune*, 23 Sept. 1917; Kenneth S. Lynn, *Hemingway* (New York, 1987), 68. TR's contributions to the paper were posthumously collected and published as *Roosevelt in the Kansas City Star: War-time Editorials* (Boston, 1921).

507 **The Roosevelts moved** *The New York Times*, 27 Sept. 1917; TR, *Letters*, 8.1243.

507 **Edith became concerned** EKR to Corinne Roosevelt Robinson, 26 Sept. 1917 (TRC); Sylvia Morris, *Edith Kermit Roosevelt*, 553; unidentified news photographs, Sept. 1917, Pratt Collection scrapbook (TRB).

507 **Other women** EKR to Ruth Lee, 26 Sept. 1917 (AL); Mary Roberts Rinehart, *My Story* (New York, 1931), 241; Ida Tarbell in Baker, notebook XIV.74–75 (RSB); EKR to ERD, mid-Oct. 1917 (ERDP).

507 **"The household enthralls"** TR, *Letters*, 8.1246.

507 **"What's the matter"** Jack Cooper interviewed by J. F. French, ca. 1922 (TRB).

508 **Cooper said that** Ibid.

508 **The Reducycle, a machine** Ibid.

508 **"Cooper's not"** EKR diary, 22 Oct. 1917 (TRC). TR had, nevertheless, reduced his waist measurement by "three or four inches," according to EKR's count, "and he is just *hard* muscle." EKR to KR, 27 Oct. 1917 (KRP).

508 **Flora received** QR to Flora Whitney, 9, 13 Sept. 1917 (FWM).

508 **"I don't see"** QR to Flora Whitney, 15, 25 Sept. 5 Dec., Oct. 1917 (FWM).

508 **She felt the same** Flora Whitney to QR, 1 Nov. 1917 (EDRP).

508 **He confessed to her** QR to Flora Whitney, 15 Nov., 11 Oct. 1917 (FWM).

509 **Belle had allowed** *The New York Times*, 27 Sept. 1917.

509 **For Theodore Roosevelt** *Boston Evening Transcript* photograph, ca. 4 Oct. 1917 (KRP); TR, *Letters*, 8.1245.

509 **At the beginning of November** Gilbert, *A History of the Twentieth Century*, 474–77.

509 *The Willy-Nicky Correspondence* New York, 1918.

509 **"the folly of"** Ibid., iii.

510 *The Foes of Our Own Household* New York, 1917. Reprinted in TR, *Works*, 21.

510 **He argued that** *The Nation*, 15 Nov. 1917.

510 **The critic was** Ibid.

510 **"I have never"** To TR, 8 Oct. 1917, Georges Clemenceau, *Correspondance, 1858–1928* (Paris, 2008), 523.

510 **Flora no longer** In an effort to cheer Flora (and himself) up, TR took her with him on a short speaking trip to Toronto at the end of November. His rapturous reception in that city, where he spoke in favor of Canada's Victory Loan, served only to intimidate Flora. *The New York Times*, 27 Nov. 1917.

511 *There is ruin* Robinson, *Collected Poems*, 82.

CHAPTER 27: THE DEAD ARE WHIRLING WITH THE DEAD

512 **Epigraph** Robinson, *Collected Poems*, 355.

512 **partying with the Ned McLeans** Longworth, *Crowded Hours*, 266.

512 **The Colonel agreed** Wallace, *Sagamore Hill*, 1.30.

513 **"If you wish to"** TR, *Letters*, 8.1266–67.

513 **Ted and Dick Derby** Eleanor B. Roosevelt, *Day Before Yesterday*, 77–78; TR, *Letters*, 8.1266–67.

513 **This imbalance** The United States had declared war on Austria-Hungary on 7 Dec. 1917.

514 **mud and *Scheisse*** The latter was real. Torrential rains, combined with British bombardment of the clay fields around Passchendaele, destroyed the area's intricate sewage system and turned the mud into a slough of human and animal waste.

514 **On Saturday, 5 January** Cooper, *Woodrow Wilson*, 321; Sullivan, *Our Times*, 5.446; Gilbert, *A History of the Twentieth Century*, 482–83; Heckscher, *Woodrow Wilson*, 470–71.

514 **Wilson presented** Lloyd Morris, *Not So Long Ago* (New York, 1949), 414; Heckscher, *Woodrow Wilson*, 471. For a newsman's take on the hyperactive Creel, who may have been an inspiration to Joseph Goebbels, see Sullivan, *Our Times*, 5, chap. 21.

515 **"A general association"** WW's original typescript text quoted in Daniel Boorstin, ed., *An American Primer* (Chicago, 1966), 2.772ff.

515 **The last point** Lloyd George had proposed many of the same ideas as WW, only three days before in London. Strachan, *The First World War*, 303–4.

515 **"Le bon Dieu"** Charles à Court Repington, *The First World War: 1914–1918* (Boston, 1920), 472.

516 **"I am sorry"** Leary, notebook 8 (JJL).

516 **ten speeches in nine days** TR, *Letters*, 8.1493. For a charming account of TR's tour of city child-welfare facilities on 16 and 17 Jan. 1918, see Sara J. Baker, *Fighting for Life* (New York, 1939), 176–82.

516 **Witty and graceful** Baker, notebook XV.42 (RSB). Offstage, Carl Akeley found TR to be consumed that night with a sense of doom threatening one or more of his sons.

516 **Republican strategists** A front-page story in the *The New York Times*, 24 Jan. 1918, reported that TR had again become "leader of the Republican Party."

Biographical Note: The immediate reason for TR's visit to Washington in Jan. 1917 was a crisis in confidence in the administration's management of the war effort. He and Senator George F. Chamberlain, a respected Democrat and chairman of the Senate Committee on Military Affairs, had attacked Newton D. Baker's War Department at a meeting of the National Security League in New York, Chamberlain sensationally announcing, "The military establishment of America had broken down." The result was a short-lived bipartisan campaign, involving TR, to create a coalition war cabinet like that of Lloyd

George's government in Britain. However, Roosevelt Republicans—the old term could now be revived—had been trying since Nov. 1917 to get the Colonel to come to town and help them plot ways to break the Democratic monopoly of the government. "They were all of them anxious to have me take some position of leadership," TR reported to William Allen White, "and equally anxious that . . . I should not think it committed them to making me the candidate in 1920." He was being coy when he wrote this, because Senators Smoot and Bourne had already made clear that they wanted him to run for another term as president. Alice exulted in the prospect of a resurgent GOP. "My father president again and my husband speaker. . . ." Sullivan, *Our Times,* 5.74–75; TR, *Letters,* 8.1274, 1307; ERD to Richard Derby, 6 Dec. 1917 (ERDP); Cordery, *Alice,* 264.

516 **He took Edith**   TR, *Letters,* 8.1276–77; Longworth, *Crowded Hours,* 264ff.; *The Washington Post,* 22–25 Jan. 1917 *passim;* Adams, *Letters,* 2.782; Cecil Spring Rice to Florence Spring Rice, 13 Sept. 1917 (CSR). Spring Rice, never popular with the Wilson administration, had been effectively sidelined as British ambassador since Balfour's visit to Washington in the spring of 1917. He was succeeded by Rufus Daniel Isaacs, 1st Lord of Reading, in the new year of 1918, allegedly on the grounds of ill health.

516 **"Mother found"**   TR to KR, 29 Jan. 1918 (TRC). TR unconsciously inverted Wilde's original lines, from *The Harlot's House* (1885): *The dead are dancing with the dead, / The dust is whirling with the dust.*

517 **severe pain in the rectum**   The following narrative of TR's near-death experience in Feb. 1917 is largely based on information collected by John J. Leary in notebook 7 (JJL), and on daily letters sent by ERD to her husband in France (TRC). Specific medical details come from the report of Dr. Walton Martin to Richard Derby, 16 Feb. 1918 (ERDP). Quotations are cited separately.

517 **An abscess had formed**   The abscess, inflaming his right buttock, appeared near the site of the one lanced by Dr. Cajazeira in Brazil. EKR to KR, 10 Feb. 1918 (KRP); Walton Martin to Richard Derby, 16 Feb. 1918 (ERDP).

517 **Around four**   Josephine Stricker, "Roosevelt a Hero to His Private Secretary," New York *Tribune,* 5 Oct. 1919; Leary, notebook 7 (JJL). Apparently, TR felt he had to keep an engagement back at his club, where a gathering of artists and writers expected to have dinner with him. They were informed that the Colonel was "ill with jungle fever." Baker, notebook XV.73, 5 Feb. 1917 (RSB).

517 **His pain**   Walton Martin to Richard Derby, 16 Feb. 1918 (ERDP).

517 **The name of the**   James R. Lathrop, *History and Description of the Roosevelt Hospital, New York City* (New York, 1893). The hospital was endowed by James Henry Roosevelt (1800–1863).

517 **"Father looks terribly"**   ERD to Richard Derby, 6 Feb. 1917 (ERDP). ERD inadvertently transposed the last two words.

517 **Roosevelt's only complaint**   Leary, notebook 7 (JJL).

517 **At 4:10 P.M.**   The details of this operation, in which four surgeons participated, are in the report of Walton Martin to Richard Derby, 16 Feb. 1918 (ERDP).

518 **"should have no"**   Leary, notebook 7 (JJL).

518 **On the contrary**   Walton Martin to Richard Derby, 16 Feb. 1918 (ERDP). Duel told Julian Street that he had operated on four cases similar to TR's, and all the patients had died. Memo, "In the Roosevelt Hospital, February 1918" (JS).

518 **"He's a peach"**   Leary, notebook 7 (JJL).

518 **He was told**   Walton Martin to Richard Derby, 16 Feb. 1918 (ERDP).

518 **The first he**   WHT to TR, 8 Feb. 1918 (TRP); TR to WHT, 12 Feb. 1918

(WHTP). In 1902, as governor of the Philippines, WHT reported his alimentary problems to the War Department in more detail than seemed necessary for national security. See Taft file #164, Elihu Root Papers, Library of Congress.

519 **Edwin Arlington Robinson penned** To TR, 5 Mar. 1919 (TRP); TR, *Letters,* 8.1298.

519 **"You stand"** TR to QR, 16 Feb. 1918 (TRC).

519 **When, at last** ERD to Richard Derby, 27 Feb. 1918 (ERDP); QR to Flora Whitney, 16 Feb. 1918 (FWM); QR to EBR, 20 Jan., 4 Feb. 1918 (TRJP) ("How can I write 'interesting' letters like Arch's when, aside from my epistolary talents, he is at the Front & I'm *embuscé?*"); Edith Normant scrapbook (FWM).

519 **in Gallic tastes** Hamilton Coolidge to Flora Whitney, 18 Sept. 1918 (FWM). In another letter Ham spoke enviously of QR's "complete mastery of the language." (To "Mother," 10 Mar. 1918 [TRC].) "[The Normants] say I must be half French." QR to Flora Whitney, 13 Feb. 1918 (FWM).

519 YOUR LETTER Original, ca. 28 Feb. 1918, in TRC. There is no record of TR reprimanding ABR for demoralizing QR. In late Apr., the latter heard from Eleanor that ABR was saying "I had more brains than any of the rest of the family, but he didn't think I'd get as far as the rest of the family. . . . I lacked push." QR to Flora Whitney, ca. May 1918 (FWM).

520 **"There is therefore"** Heckscher, *Woodrow Wilson,* 474. On 8 Mar. 1918, Clemenceau reminded the French Chamber of Deputies "that we are at war, that it is necessary to wage war, to think only of war. . . . So let us wage war." Strachan, *The First World War,* 259–60.

520 **still unsteady** John Leary compared TR's gait at this time to that of "a landlubber on a pitching deck at sea—with his legs wide apart as though to brace himself." Leary, notebook 8 (JJL).

520 **Cove Neck exuded** ERD to Richard Derby, 24 Feb. 1918 (ERDP); TR to QR, 5 Mar. 1918 (TRC). QR had not known about his father's near-death experience until he picked up a French newspaper and read, five days after the event, "La condition de M. Roosevelt est sérieuse, et les médicins ont conseillés une nouvelle opération." He had had to wait three more days for a reassuring telegram from Flora. QR to Flora Whitney, 13 Feb. 1918 (FWM).

520 **"I wish you"** TR to QR, 5 Mar. 1918 (TRC).

520 **On 13 March** EKR to KR, 17 Mar. 1918 (KRP); TR, *Letters,* 8.1300–301. ABR, fighting in the Twenty-sixth Infantry's first line engagement of the war, had been wounded in the Toul sector. ABR, "Lest We Forget."

520 **just given birth** On 18 Feb. 1918. In the author's opinion, "Archie Junior" was, of all TR's direct descendants, the one who inherited the most of the Colonel's personal and intellectual characteristics. See Archibald Roosevelt, Jr., *For Lust of Knowing: Memoirs of an Intelligence Officer* (Boston, 1988).

520 **"At lunch Mother"** TR, *Letters,* 8.1301; ERD to Richard Derby, 12 Mar. 1918 (ERDP). TR wrote Clemenceau to say that ABR had won a French medal, and added, "I am prouder of his having received it than of my having been President!" TR, *Letters,* 8.1303.

521 **A few days** TR, *Letters,* 8.1301; Richard Derby to TR, 13 Mar. 1918 (ERDP).

521 **now wished to fight** TR, *Letters,* 8.1310.

521 **"Father had 2"** ERD to Richard Derby n.d., ca. Mar. 1918 (ERDP). The Sagamore Hill farm raised cows, hogs, and chickens, and was therefore self-supporting in milk and eggs. Crops included standard vegetables and fruits, plus hay, corn, and apples for sale. TR, *Letters,* 8.1352.

521 **It was intended** TR, *Letters,* 8.1299.

521 **poisonous phosgene fumes** Strachan, *The First World War,* 295.

521 **Under the circumstances** *The New York Times,* 28 Mar. 1918.

521 **He returned home** On his way back, TR stopped in Boston to admire Archie, Jr. TR, *Letters,* 8.1494.

> *Biographical Note:* TR flattered himself that his mammoth Portland speech, which took three hours to deliver, "amounted to the acceptance, by the Republicans of Maine, of the Progressive platform of 1912 developed and brought up to date." (TR, *Letters,* 8.1307.) But its title ("Speed Up the War and Take Thought for After the War") made clear what his current priorities were. He berated the administration for its unpreparedness and consequent slow pace of mobilization, recommended the creation of a five-million-man army (on the assumption the war would last another three years), demanded that Congress revoke the charter of the German-American Alliance, and called for a declaration of war against Turkey. Although he did, in fact, lay out a domestic policy plan far more detailed and progressive than that of the Democrats in 1918, his bellicose rhetoric naturally got most coverage in the national press. The speech was printed and widely circulated. See *The New York Times,* 29 Mar. 1918.

521 **A terrified Jules Jusserand** Heckscher, *Woodrow Wilson,* 474.

522 **"Wilson always follows"** ERD to Richard Derby, quoting an attendee at the dinner, 27 Mar. 1918 (ERDP); Heckscher, *Woodrow Wilson,* 475. McAdoo's remark was particularly striking because he happened to be WW's son-in-law.

522 **a place for Kermit** TR, *Letters,* 8.1316.

522 **He calculated** QR to Flora Whitney, 24 Mar. 1918 (FWM).

522 **As for your getting killed** *(handwritten)* TR to QR, 17 Mar. 1918 (TRC).

522 **Quentin foresaw** QR to Flora Whitney, 27 Mar. 1918 (FWM).

522 **When Quentin next heard** TR, *Letters,* 8.1311.

523 **What information reached** Richard Derby to TR, 13 Mar. 1918 (ERDP); medical report, 12 Mar. 1918 (ERDP); Eleanor B. Roosevelt, *Day Before Yesterday,* 95; QR to Flora Whitney, 30 Apr. 1918 (FWM).

523 **Quentin was lucky** QR to Flora Whitney, 30 Apr., 2 May 1918 (FWM); Eleanor Roosevelt to mother, 19 Apr. 1918 (TRJP); Richard Derby to TR, 13 Mar. 1918 (ERDP).

524 **Roosevelt chafed** TR, *Letters,* 8.1311; ERD to Richard Derby, 22 Apr. 1918 (ERDP); TR, *Letters,* 8.1312. Shipments of men and matériel, Stout wrote, were in fact accelerating at a compound rate. By June, the flood should be overwhelming. "Neither a newspaper or a public man," he cautioned TR, "can afford to be too far ahead of the people." Quoted in ERD to Richard Derby, 22 Apr. 1918 (ERDP).

524 **Ethel wrote Dick,** 17 May 1918 (ERDP).

524 **Two days later** Edith Normant scrapbook (ERDP).

524 **Roosevelt had the** Leary, notebook 8 (JJL).

525 **Roosevelt took his** Ibid.

525 **"Theodore!"** Ibid.; Wood, *Roosevelt As We Knew Him,* 435 (eyewitness account).

525 **"He feels"** Leary, notebook 8 (JJL). See also TR's follow-up letter to WHT: "What a dreadful creature he [WW] is! . . . In this really very evil crisis, we need a leader and not a weathercock." (TR, *Letters,* 8.1336–37.) WHT, evidently no longer a pacifist, believed that WW was more interested in talking than fighting, and was a Bolshevik sympathizer to boot.

525 **If present trends** Gilbert, *A History of the Twentieth Century,* 496.

525 **like summer lightning** The image is Eleanor's, in *Day Before Yesterday,* 97.

525 **Just as disturbing** EBR to mother, 4 June 1918 (TRJP); Eleanor B. Roosevelt,

Day Before Yesterday, 97; official citation for "conspicuous gallantry" published in *Harvard Club Bulletin,* Aug. 1918 (KRP).

525 **With this and** TR, *Letters,* 8.1338; QR to Flora Whitney, 2 June 1918 (FWM). QR to Flora Whitney, 2 June 1918 (FWM).

526 **"La guerre est finie"** Cowley, *The Great War,* 424.

526 **General Pershing tried** Strachan, *The First World War,* 298; Gilbert, *A History of the Twentieth Century,* 499.

526 **On 7 June** EKR to KR, 9 June 1918 (KRP); Leary, notebook 9 (JJL); EKR to Corinne Roosevelt Robinson, 16 June 1918 (CRR).

526 **When they got back** EKR to Corinne Roosevelt Robinson, 16 June 1918 (CRR).

526 **"My joy for you"** TR to QR, 19 June 1918.

526 **"He evidently felt"** QR to Flora Whitney, 17 June 1918 (FWM).

526 **"It is really"** QR to ERD, 17 June 1918 (FWM); QR to Flora Whitney, 17 June 1918 (FWM).

527 **"Colonel, one of"** TR to KR, 25 June 1918 (KRP).

527 **a pile of books** One item on TR's reading pile reflected his understandable new interest in combat flying. It was Henry Bordeaux's *Le Chevalier de l'air: Vie héroïque de Guynemer* (Paris, 1918). TR appears to have read it in French, but he wrote an introduction to the American edition, translated by Louise M. Sill and published as *Georges Guynemer, Knight of the Air* (New Haven, Conn., 1918). With palpable concern for Quentin, he wrote that "the air service in particular is one of such peril that membership in it is of itself a high distinction."

527 **"I have finished"** TR to QR, 19 June 1918 (TRC).

527 **a macabre souvenir** QR to Flora Whitney, 20 June 1918 (FWM).

527 **"There's no better"** QR to Flora Whitney, 23 Feb. 1918 (FWM).

527 **"The real thing"** QR to EKR, 25 June 1918 (TRC); QR to Flora Whitney, 29 June 1918 (FWM). This posting was to Touquin, a patrol center for the area between Château-Thierry and Reims. QR was billeted in the adjacent village of Mauperthuis.

527 **On the Fourth** Parsons, *Perchance to Dream,* 274.

527 **Little tricolors** Ibid.

528 **Six days later** QR to Flora Whitney, 11 July 1918 (FWM). A later letter from Hamilton Coolidge to Flora revealed that inexperience had something to do with this encounter: at first QR had "joined [the] Boche formation by mistake," thinking it was his own. 16 July 1918 (FWM).

528 **He and Eleanor** Eleanor B. Roosevelt, *Day Before Yesterday,* 100. During this visit, QR told EBR that if any of his family were to die in the war, he hoped it would be himself, because his other brothers and Dick all had children. "I think he had a very distinct feeling that he might never get home again," EBR wrote her mother. 28 July 1918 (TRJP).

528 **a little French town** Mauperthuis, adjacent to Saints and Touquin.

528 **"O ruin!"** QR to Flora Whitney, 11 July 1918 (FWM).

528 **"Whatever now befalls"** TR, *Letters,* 8.1351.

528 **On the afternoon** TR to KR, 21 July 1918 (KRP); *The New York Times,* 18 July 1918; Philip Thompson, "Roosevelt and His Boys," *McClure's Magazine,* Nov. 1918; Hagedorn, *The Roosevelt Family,* 412.

528 **"It seems dreadful"** TR to KR, 16 July 1918 (KRP).

529 **Then a cable** John J. Pershing to TR, 17 July 1918 (ERDP). The chronology of events affecting TR and EKR over the next few days is somewhat confused, due to conflicting newspaper reports. It is reconstructed here on the basis of primary accounts. Pershing's cable was not released to the press until late on 18 July.

529 **At sunset** Sylvia Morris, *Edith Kermit Roosevelt,* 423.

529 **"But—Mrs. Roosevelt?"** Thompson, "Roosevelt and His Boys." By now (7:30

A.M.), TR had at least informed EKR that QR was missing. Her telegram transmitting this news to ERD in Maine was received "early" on the 17th. ERD to Richard Derby, 17 July 1918 (ERDP).

529 **He disappeared** Thompson, "Roosevelt and His Boys."

529 **"Quentin's mother"** *The New York Times*, 18 July 1918.

529 **"I must go"** Bishop, *TR*, 2.452.

530 **Telegrams of condolence** Josephine Stricker, "Roosevelt a Hero to His Private Secretary," New York *Tribune*, 5 Oct. 1919.

530 **"We must do"** Sylvia Morris, *Edith Kermit Roosevelt*, 423.

530 **Roosevelt had no sooner** Hermann Hagedorn memo, 20 Sept. 1923 (HP).

Biographical Note: The Harvard-educated Hagedorn (1882–1964) had attracted TR's attention in 1912 by publishing a poem and contributing the fee ($10) to the Progressive Party. A friend and patron of Edwin Arlington Robinson, he began accumulating biographical materials on TR in 1917. His research materialized in three valuable if saccharine books, *The Boys' Life of Theodore Roosevelt* (New York, 1918), *Roosevelt in the Bad Lands* (Boston, 1921), and *The Roosevelt Family of Sagamore Hill* (New York, 1954). From 1918 on he dedicated most of his career to memorializing TR, editing the National and Memorial editions of TR's collected works and serving as director of three successive Theodore Roosevelt associations. A letter TR wrote introducing Hagedorn to William W. Sewell in 1917 should serve as a model to public figures entrusting their lives to a responsible biographer: "I want you to tell him everything, good, bad and indifferent. Don't spare me the least bit. Give him the very worst side of me you can think of, and the very best side of me that is truthful. . . . Tell him about our snowshoe trips. . . . Tell him about the ranch. Tell him how we got Red Finnegan and the two other cattle thieves. Tell him everything." TR, *Letters*, 8.1244–45.

530 **"Now, Colonel"** Hermann Hagedorn memo, 20 Sept. 1923 (HP).

530 **Afterward Hagedorn noted** Pringle, *TR*, 601. See also Wood, *Roosevelt As We Knew Him*, 429–30.

530 **Edith came** ERD to Richard Derby, 17 July 1918 (ERDP).

530 **"Before the Colonel"** *The New York Times*, 19 July 1918.

530 **"My fellow voters"** Lafayette Gleason, verbatim transcript of TR's remarks at Saratoga on 17 July 1918, preserved by Elmer R. Koppelmann. Copy in AC.

531 **"Surely in this great crisis"** Sullivan, *Our Times*, 5.500.

531 **Before he got** TR, *Letters*, 8.1341; WHT to TR, 19 July 1918 (WHTP); Bishop, *TR*, 2.453–54.

531 **"I have only one"** Robinson, *My Brother TR*, 346.

531 QUENTIN'S PLANE *The New York Times*, 20 July 1918.

531 EVERY REASON 12:50 P.M., 19 July 1918 (FWM).

531 **Newspapers got** *The New York Times*, 20 July 1918.

531 **The Colonel, clutching** F. Trubee Davison interviewed by Mary Hagedorn, 30 Mar. 1955 (HH).

531 **speech exquisitely calligraphed** One of these copies is preserved in the Pratt Collection (TRB). Included is an introduction by J. B. Millet, who collaborated on the speech, noting that after the first report of QR's disappearance, he had suggested to TR that they postpone their work (presumably on the afternoon of 16 July). TR insisted on finishing it. "I saw by his manner, and by his kindly words to me, that it was a relief to have a subject before him to which he could give his whole heart." Ibid.

532 **"What hope"** Ibid. "It was one of the most extraordinary demonstrations of control and courage that I have ever seen."

532 **The telegram confirmed** WW to TR, 20 July 1918 (TRP).

532 **On Saturday** Original in ERDP. Chamery is misspelled "Chambry." According to an American POW who witnessed the ceremony on 15 July 1918, QR was buried in the presence of a detachment of approximately 1,000 German soldiers, with officers standing at attention before the ranks. "I was told afterward . . . that they paid Lieut. Roosevelt such honor not only because he was a gallant aviator, who died fighting bravely against odds, but because he was the son of Colonel Roosevelt, whom they esteemed as one of the great Americans." Kermit Roosevelt, *Quentin Roosevelt*, 175–76.

CHAPTER 28: SIXTY

533 **Epigraph** Robinson, *Collected Poems*, 97.

533 **When American forces** A friend ["Bill"] to Flora Whitney, 10 Aug. 1918 (FWM). This description, reporting a personal visit to QR's grave shortly after his burial, is cited as more primary than that given in Kermit Roosevelt, *Quentin Roosevelt*, 176.

533 **The autopsy** Official German press announcement, relayed to the Roosevelts from the Spanish Embassy in Berlin, quoted in ERD to Flora Whitney, "Thursday," July 1918 (FWM). See also Kermit Roosevelt, *Quentin Roosevelt*, 172–74.

533 **Woodrow Wilson's telegram** *The New York Times*, 21 July 1918. See also EBR to mother, 19 July 1918 (TJRP).

534 **"Ex-Tsar of Russia"** The official Russian wireless announcement quoted by *The Times* reported only Nicholas's death on 16 July. His wife and son were said to be "in a place of security." No mention was made of the four Romanov daughters.

534 **That Sunday happened** ERD to Richard Derby, 21 July 1918 (ERDP).

534 **They returned home** Ibid.; Robinson, *My Brother TR*, 346.

534 **"Why not come"** ERD to Richard Derby, 22 July 1918 (ERDP).

534 **brown-shingled "cottages"** Earle G. Shettleworth, Jr., *The Summer Cottages of Islesboro, 1890–1930* (Islesboro, Maine, 1989), 28 and *passim*; Belfast (Maine) *Republican Journal*, 1 Aug. 1918. Ethel's summer home is now known as the Edward Adams Cottage. Other visual and atmospheric details in this section derive from a tour arranged for the author by the Islesboro Historical Society in Sept. 2006.

535 **He and Edith arrived** EKR to KR, 28 July 1918 (KRP); Belfast (Maine) *Republican Journal*, 1 Aug. 1918.

535 **"In time"** TR, *Letters*, 8.1360.

535 **That was even** ERD to KR, 28 July 1918 (KRP); TR to ABR, 21 July 1918 (ABRP); ERD to Richard Derby, 21 July 1918 (ERDP).

535 **"I can see"** TR to KR, 28 July 1918 (KRP).

535 **Nevertheless, the place** TR, *Letters*, 8.1358; Belfast (Maine) *Republican Journal*, 1 Aug. 1918; Flora Whitney to ERD, 28 Aug. 1918 (ERDP).

536 **"It is no use"** TR, *Letters*, 8.1360.

536 **Even his poems** QR, untitled poem about star-gazing, 1915, preserved in FWM.

536 **explosive rather than propulsive** "I *do* lack push, and I haven't any idea why." QR to Flora Whitney, ca. early May 1918 (FWM).

536 **"black gloom"** Hamilton Coolidge memorial to QR, unfinished ms., copied in ERD to Flora Whitney, 4 June 1919 (FWM); Coolidge to Flora, 16 July 1918 (FWM).

536 **As Edith had** Sylvia Morris, *Edith Kermit Roosevelt*, 397; EKR to Anna Roosevelt Cowles, 5 May 1912 (ARC).

536 **Only in two**   As far as one can tell, QR's affair with Flora was unconsummated. His letters to her are devoid of any hint of sexual intimacy. One (6 Oct. 1917 [FWM]) loftily invokes the virtue of coming to marriage "clean and pure." As such, it reads like an outtake from his father's college diary of 38 years before. See Morris, *The Rise of TR*, 63.

536 **Test-piloting**   QR to ERD, 22 Dec. 1917 (ERDP); QR to Flora Whitney, 27 Jan. 1918 (FWM).

537 **"The months that"**   QR to Flora Whitney, 21 Feb. 1918 (FWM).

537 **"His back will"**   Quoted in ERD to KR, 25 Aug. 1918 (KRP).

537 **"form succeeds form"**   TR, *Works*, 14.70.

537 **ptomaine poisoning**   TR injudiciously ate lobster salad at an inland restaurant on 1 May, and the following evening, addressing a Liberty Loan rally in Boston, was overcome with violent abdominal pain and nausea. "He came near to having to leave the platform," his host for the night recalled, "and only finished by one of those incredible acts of will, recalling the Hatha Yoga of India, by which he habitually . . . ignored physical pain and disability." Before going to bed, TR dosed himself with one of his favorite medicines, ammonia. William Sturgis Bigelow to Hermann Hagedorn, 23 May 1919 (HH).

537 *Look now*   QR, "The Greatest Gift," ms., ca. 1918 (TRC).

537 **"There is no"**   TR to Edith Wharton, 15 Aug. 1918 (EW); TR, *Letters*, 8.1403.

537 **Only those are fit**   TR, "The Great Adventure," *Metropolitan* magazine, Oct. 1918. The article was prepublished in newspapers on 17 Sept. 1918, and is reprinted in TR, *Works*, 21.263ff.

538 **His tribute degenerated**   TR, *Works*, 21.266–67.

538 **Much more expressive**   Charles Lee interviewed by Hermann Hagedorn, c. 1919, TRB.

538 **the Roosevelts declined**   TR, *Letters*, 8.1381; Kermit Roosevelt, *Quentin Roosevelt*, 203. The grave, which was elaborately rebuilt by the French after Chamery was retaken, no longer exists, since QR's remains were transferred after World War II to the American Cemetery at Colleville-sur-Mer. However, a roadside fountain in the village, installed by his mother, perpetuates QR's memory, and the field where he died speaks for itself. Chamery is located on the modern D14 north of Jaulgonne-sur-Marne, between Cierges and Coulonges.

539 **Every cent would go**   TR, *Letters*, 8.1363–66.

539 **One of the movies**   *The Fighting Roosevelts*, directed by William Nigh, was released in 1919.

539 **On 4 September**   *The New York Times*, 5 Sept. 1918; TR, *Letters*, 8.1368.

539 **Archie had become**   EKR to ERD, "Wed." [4 Sept.] 1918, photograph enclosed (ERDP); *The New York Times*, 3 Sept. 1918. ABR was still undergoing therapy at this institution four months later. *The New York Times*, 6 Jan. 1919.

540 **he had become addicted**   For an analysis of this phenomenon, see Ecksteins, *Rites of Spring*, 232.

540 **"Fall has come"**   TR to KR, 13 Sept. 1918 (WFM).

540 **plenty of honor**   Richard Derby was also awarded a Croix de Guerre in 1918.

540 **"The Colonel sat"**   Rinehart, *My Story*, 260. This was on 16 Sept. 1918.

540 **he would tour**   The Liberty Loan campaign used hundreds of traveling celebrities (including Charlie Chaplin, Douglas Fairbanks, and Mary Pickford) to publicize and sell low-yield bonds for the prosecution of the war.

540 **On the twenty-eighth**   Leary, notebook 9 (JJL); TR to KR, 13 Sept. 1918 (KRP).

541 **As he traveled**   EKR to KR, 22 Sept. 1918 (KRP). The date of syndication was 17 Sept. 1918. (Bishop, *TR*, 2.458.) TR's most recent royalty statement from Scribners totaled only $365. Charles Scribner to TR, 19 Sept. 1918 (SCR).

541 **"It's pretty poor"**   TR to Belle Roosevelt, 27 Oct. 1918 (ABRP).

541 On his way home   Hagedorn, *Roosevelt in the Bad Lands*, 410.

541 "Have you got"   Ibid., 473.

541 He arrived back   ERD to Richard Derby, 30 Oct. 1918 (ERDP).

541 If the two physicians   See below, 725.

542 "restoration of peace"   Heckscher, *Woodrow Wilson*, 481.

542 a bloody mess   The American army took "three weeks and 100,000 casualties to achieve what Pershing . . . had thought they could do in a single day." Cowley, *The Great War*, 427–29.

542 "I regret greatly"   *The New York Times*, 13 Oct. 1918.

542 Similar statements   Cowley, *The Great War*, 430; Heckscher, *Woodrow Wilson*, 483; Strachan, *The First World War*, 324.

542 Following up, Roosevelt   TR, *Letters*, 8.1380–81.

542 The President, goaded   *Warren (Pa.) Evening Times*, 26 Oct. 1918.

543 He had hated   [Gilbert], *The Mirrors of Washington*, 34–38.

543 Roosevelt sniffed   Longworth, *Crowded Hours*, 274.

543 "queer feelings"   ERD to KR, 27 Oct. 1918 (KRP).

543 Jokingly, he   TR, *Letters*, 8.1383; Leary, *Talks with T.R.*, 76.

543 "I can see"   Sylvia Morris, *Edith Kermit Roosevelt*, 428.

544 A well-wisher   *The New York Times*, 29 Oct. 1918. TR later learned that on his birthday, Hamilton Coolidge had been killed in action, leaving behind an unfinished memoir of QR. See Kermit Roosevelt, *Quentin Roosevelt*, 213ff.

544 Carnegie Hall was crammed   *The New York Times*, 29 Oct. 1918.

544 He spoke for more   Ibid. This was not, as some accounts have claimed, TR's last speech. He spoke again (with ABR) to a Boys' Victory Mobilization meeting in Manhattan on 1 Nov., and returned to Carnegie Hall the next night to address the benefit for Negro War Relief.

544 Over the next   EKR to KR, 2 Nov. 1918 (KRP); Hagedorn, *The Roosevelt Family*, 422.

544 learning from newspapers   Cowley, *The Great War*, 430; Gilbert, *A History of the Twentieth Century*, 520; *Syracuse Herald*, 5 Nov. 1918.

544 On election day   *The New York Times*, 6 Nov. 1918; TR, *Letters*, 8.1397.

545 "If I had been"   Quoted in John H. Richards interview (HP). See also TR, *Letters*, 8.1396.

545 Flat on his back   TR, *Letters*, 8.1390; Eleanor B. Roosevelt, *Day Before Yesterday*, 111–13.

545 Around three o'clock   *The New York Times*, 12 Nov. 1918.

545 Steam whistles   Garland, *My Friendly Contemporaries*, 200; Sullivan, *Our Times*, 5.520–25; *The New York Times* and New York *Tribune*, 12 Nov. 1918.

545 Dr. John H. Richards   *The New York Times*, 12, 14 Nov. 1918.

546 On 21 November   Garland, *My Friendly Contemporaries*, 202.

546 After some chat   Ibid., 202–3.

546 Garland came back   EKR to KR, 24 Nov. 1918 (KRP); Garland, *My Friendly Contemporaries*, 204.

546 Edith, Roosevelt said   Ibid. The idea of doing something about QR's grave nevertheless continued to haunt TR. On 3 Dec. he wrote Ted to ask if French authorities would let him buy the field himself, and perhaps inter there the bodies of "two or three others like Ham Coolidge." (TR, *Letters*, 8.1411.) Nothing came of this plan.

546 and a weak choice   Hammond, *Autobiography*, 640. Even Colonel House, who was a delegation member along with White, Robert Lansing, and General Tasker H. Bliss, thought that WW should have sent a team consisting of three Democrats plus Root and WHT. Ibid., 639.

547 Roosevelt was mostly   Nevins, *Henry White*, 350ff.; Biddle, *The Whitney Women*,

49; TR, *Letters,* 8.1400. During his three-month spell of illness beginning in early Oct. 1918, TR dictated 22 articles for the *Kansas City Star,* plus others for *Metropolitan* magazine and a review for *American Museum Journal* of Leo G. Miller's *In the Wilds of South America.* ("A Faunal Naturalist in South America," TR, *Works,* 24.525–29.) The period also saw the publication, by Scribners, of the book version of *The Great Adventure.*

547 **He scoffed** TR, *Letters,* 8.1400. The phrase *self-determination* was actually borrowed by WW from Lloyd George. Cooper, *Woodrow Wilson,* 421. After the last League advocate left, a perplexed-looking TR remarked, "I want to get along with those fellows and especially Will Taft. . . . [But] if the League of Nations means that we will have to go to war every time a Jugo Slav wishes to slap a Czecho Slav in the face, then I won't follow them." Dr. John H. Richards interview, ts. (HP).

547 **Two of his future** Abbott, *Impressions of TR,* 167; Joseph Bucklin Bishop, *Notes and Anecdotes of Many Years* (New York, 1925), 149–50.

547 **She was learning** QR to ERD, 12 Feb. 1918 (ERDP).

547 **He did what** TR, *Letters,* 8.1415. See also ibid., 8.1396–1411, and TR, "President Wilson and the Peace Conference," *Roosevelt in the Kansas City Star,* 272–77.

> *Biographical Note:* TR's vision of the postwar world included (along with harshly punitive containment of Germany), "a Zionist state around Jerusalem." But he insisted to an American rabbi that the latter state should have "full religious freedom," and that American Jews who felt a "kinship" for it, rather than for the United States, should immigrate there and "become emphatically . . . foreigners." He also favored an independent Armenia and Ukraine, although he saw the latter joining Russia. He doubtfully agreed with James Bryce that there was "just a chance" that Arab lands freed from Ottoman oppression might develop a religious toleration to emulate that of Moorish civilization "in the golden days of Baghdad and Cordova." Germany's former colonies in Africa should become protectorates of strong powers experienced in colonial administration (Britain, France, Belgium, and Portugal), rather than the kind of weak neutrals WW preferred, such as Holland and Sweden. The United States should remain disinterested in this reapportionment: the prime purpose of its defense and foreign policy must be to maintain a republican independence from Old World empires. (TR, *Letters,* 8.1372–97, 1400.) See also *Roosevelt in the Kansas City Star,* 241–95.

547 **Except for** TR, *Letters,* 8.1415; John Milton Cooper, "If TR Had Gone Down with the Titanic: A Look at His Last Decade," in Naylor et al., *TR,* 500, 511.

548 **"Since Quentin's death"** Bishop, *TR,* 2.468; White, *Autobiography,* 548–49. According to White, TR's "rather radical" article draft called for an eight-hour day, old age pensions, and social insurance. It does not appear to have survived.

548 **"I tell you"** Stanley Washburn Papers, Library of Congress.

548 **Roosevelt woke** *The New York Times,* 7 Jan. 1919. Reviewing TR's final illness, this article refers to him suffering "from [a] pulmonary embolism at the Roosevelt Hospital three weeks ago," i.e., mid-Dec. 1918. Other newspaper reports suggested it occurred around 4 Dec., but all concur that he was "in a critical condition" for some time.

548 **His temperature shot up** Straus, *Under Four Administrations,* 391. This may have been during "a brief thirty-six hours" attack of "pneumonia" mentioned in Robinson, *My Brother TR,* 361.

548 **"Poor dear"** *The New York Times,* 6 Dec. 1918 and 7 Jan. 1919; EKR to KR, 15 Dec. 1918 (KRP).

548 **He was buoyed** TR, *Letters*, 8.1416–17.

548 **He would have to** Ibid.

548 **"I am pretty low"** Chanler, *Roman Spring*, 202.

548 **He did get better** EKR to KR, 24 Dec. 1918 (KRP).

549 **Corinne came in** Robinson, *My Brother TR*, 362.

549 **"Well, anyway"** Ibid.

549 **"Don't do that"** Dr. John H. Richards interview, ts. (HP). According to the Roosevelt Hospital's cautious discharge statement, the Colonel was expected to make a full recovery "in the time ordinarily taken for such cases" of inflammatory rheumatism, and should "be able to take up his usual duties in six weeks or two months." *The New York Times*, 25 Dec. 1918.

549 **Alice, Ethel, Archie** ERD to Richard Derby, 25 Dec. 1918 (ERDP); TR to KR, 27 Dec. 1918 (TRC).

549 **There was a** ERD to Richard Derby, 25 Dec. 1918 (ERDP); ERD to KR, 25 Dec. 1918 (KRP); TR to KR, 27 Dec. 1918 (KRP).

549 **It had been Ethel's** Wallace, *Sagamore Hill*, 1.62–63.

549 **Propped up in** 1918 furniture inventory in Wallace, *Sagamore Hill*, 1.71 and 335.

550 **Every morning** *The New York Times*, 7 Jan. 1919; EKR to KR, ca. 30 Dec. 1918 (KRP).

550 **It may have been** ERD to Richard Derby, 31 Dec. 1918 (ERDP). See also Kermit Roosevelt, *Quentin Roosevelt*, 208–9.

550 **On New Year's Day** Josephine Stricker to AP, Steubenville (Ohio) *Herald-Star*, 6 Jan. 1919; Ferdinand C. Iglehart, *Theodore Roosevelt: The Man As I Knew Him* (New York, 1919), 281.

550 **"We all of us"** *Roosevelt in the Kansas City Star*, 292–95.

> *Biographical Note:* In his final comment on the world situation, TR observed that the concert of powers envisioned by WW was so vague that Germany, Russia, Turkey, and Mexico might believe they were welcome to join it, on equal terms with the United States, Britain, and France. But equality was not a right or a reward. Governments responsible for the recent war would have to earn full membership of the League of Nations, in part by paying "the sternest reparation . . . for such horrors as those committed in Belgium, Northern France, Armenia, and the sinking of the *Lusitania*." Weak or neutral nations should not expect to have a "guiding voice" in the League's strategic decisions. That was the prerogative of the strong nations who had fought for peace. As perhaps the strongest of the strong in 1919, the United States should henceforth police only its own hemisphere. The "civilized" powers of Europe and Asia would have to control their own forces of disorder. TR was confident that if WW made these strictures clear at the peace table, Clemenceau and Lloyd George would agree. "I believe that such an effort made moderately and sanely, but sincerely and with utter scorn for words that are not made good by deeds, will be productive of real and lasting international good." (Ibid.)

550 **In a letter** TR to George H. Moses, 3 Jan. 1919 (TRP).

550 **The effort of** ERD to Richard Derby, 8 Jan. 1919 (ERDP). The following narrative of the events of 4–6 Jan. 1919 is based mainly on primary accounts by EKR and James Amos. These are: EKR to ERD, 3, 4, 5 Jan. 1919 (ERDP); EKR to KR, 6 Jan. 1919 and 25 Mar. 1923 (KRP); EKR to TR.Jr., 12 Jan. 1919 (TRJP); James Amos, "The Beloved Boss," *Collier's Weekly*, 7 Aug. 1926; Amos, *Theodore Roosevelt: Hero to His Valet* (New York, 1927), 154–58. There are two other near-primary accounts: ERD to Richard Derby, 8 Jan. 1919 (ERDP), and George Syran to Mr. and Mrs. Osbourne, 11 Jan. 1919, privately owned. Minor conflicts of

chronology are resolved in favor of EKR's recall. Individual sources are cited again below only for quotations. For Dr. Fuller's report to the press, see *The New York Times,* 7 Jan. 1919.

551 **Since none of their** James Amos, "The Beloved Boss"; Amos, *TR: Hero to His Valet.* Amos had left the Roosevelts amicably in the fall of 1913, after more than ten years in their service. He continued, however, to serve them off and on, since TR often hired him as a valet-cum-bodyguard on long railroad trips.

551 **When Amos arrived** Amos, "The Beloved Boss."

551 **two or three letters** See, e.g., TR to Edward N. Buxton, 5 Jan. 1919 [in EKR's handwriting] (ERDP); Cutright, *TR,* 265; TR, *Letters,* 8.1422.

551 **correcting the typescript** Henry J. Whigham interviewed by Hermann Hagedorn, 12 Jan. 1949 (HH). This may have been the last manuscript TR actually touched. After his death a scribbled memo of uncertain date was found on his bedside table: *Hays—see him; he must go to Washington for 10 days; see Senate & House; prevent split on domestic policies.* (Reproduced in Lorant, *Life and Times of TR,* 624.) By publishing the memo at the end of TR, *Letters,* 8, the editors infuse it with a valedictory quality it may not deserve. It is unlikely TR wrote it any time in 1919, in view of the acute rheumatism that attacked his right hand on New Year's Day.

551 **could not help kissing him** ERD to Richard Derby, 8 Jan. 1919 (ERDP).

551 **"As it got dusk"** EKR to TR.Jr., 12 Jan. 1919 (TRJP).

551 **They were still together** EKR to KR, 6 Jan. 1919 (KRP); ERD to Richard Derby, 8 Jan. 1919 (ERDP).

551 **Leaving the nurse** EKR to KR, 25 Mar. 1923 (KRP); ERD to Richard Derby, 8 Jan. 1919 (ERDP). The Orientalist William Sturgis Bigelow, a licensed physician, had recommended morphine to EKR after witnessing TR's agonies with ptomaine poisoning earlier in the year. See above, 720. "I want you particularly to tell Dr. Bigelow," she wrote Henry Cabot Lodge, "that I did not forget the talk he and I had about the use of morphine, and after he [TR] had had 2 or 3 sleepless nights in succession, we gave him morphine the night before he died so that he was able to go to sleep and forget his pain." Murakata, "TR and William Sturgis Bigelow."

551 **Faller assented** ERD to Richard Derby, 8 Jan. 1919 (ERDP).

551 **"James, don't you"** Amos, *TR: Hero to His Valet,* 156.

551 **He had to be** George Syran to Mr. and Mrs. Osbourne, 11 Jan. 1919, privately owned. This letter, written only five days after TR's death and reflecting conversations between Syran, Amos, and "downstairs" staff at Sagamore Hill, preconfirms almost all the details that Amos published eight years later in *TR: Hero to His Valet.*

551 **"James, will you"** Amos, *TR: Hero to His Valet,* 156.

552 **A small lamp** Ibid., 156; EKR to KR, 6 Jan. 1919 (KRP).

552 **"roughling"** The word is so spelled by Syran, quoting Amos later that morning.

552 **Each time he started** Interviewed later that day, Amos said he counted five seconds between each of TR's breaths. *New York Evening Post,* 6 Jan. 1919.

552 **At four o'clock** Amos, *TR: Hero to His Valet,* 157; EKR to KR, 6 Jan. 1919 (KRP).

EPILOGUE: IN MEMORIAM T.R.

553 **Theodore Roosevelt's death certificate** Copy in TRC.

553 **two consulting physicians** John H. Richards and John A. Hartwell, of the Roosevelt Hospital in New York.

553 **They revealed** *New York Evening Post,* 6 Jan., *The New York Times,* 7 Jan. 1919.

553 **other observers** *New York Evening Post,* 6 Jan. 1919, e.g. Altogether, TR had five narrow escapes from death: his streetcar accident in Sept. 1902, the assassination attempt of Oct. 1912, the septicemia crises of Apr. 1914 and Feb. 1918, and his first embolism attack in Dec. 1918.

553 **"the cause of death"** Speculative report on TR's final illness, compiled by Drs. Paul and Andrew Marks, 19 Jan. 2010 (AC). The authors of this document are, respectively, president emeritus of Memorial Sloan-Kettering Cancer Center and cardiologist/professor at Columbia University College of Physicians and Surgeons.

553 **a broken heart** John H. Richards quoted in *New York Evening Post,* 6 Jan. 1919; ERD to KR, 6 Jan. 1919 (ERDP). "Mother and I felt that part of his illness was due to his grief for Quentin— It took the fight from him . . . must have been his heart."

> *Biographical Note:* Drs. Marks and Marks comment further, in a review of the medical narrative provided them by the author, as follows: "One can speculate that in the 1870s, when [TR] was 'advised by Harvard doctors on graduation to lead sedentary scholarly life because of heart weakness,' that the examining physician may have heard a heart murmur. The heart murmur could have been secondary to early childhood rheumatic heart disease or a congenital heart valve abnormality." However, "his rigorous [subsequent] life suggests that if he did have a heart murmur it did not significantly impair cardiac function." TR's recurrent attacks of "Cuban fever" after 1898 were consistent with malaria. "The parasite can reside in the liver for years—with bouts of septicemia recurring and causing these symptoms." His frequent "acute joint pains" probably were attacks of gout. Given his increasing weight, after his 50th birthday, joint symptoms could also reflect degenerative osteoarthritis, particularly of the hip, knee, and ankle joints." Returning to the question of TR's coronary vulnerability, the doctors concede some likelihood of endocarditis. "But if he had endocarditis, possibly related to his leg infection seeding a damaged heart, his terminal course would have been marked by high fevers and evidence of infectious, embolic showers which would have been noticed by his physicians, i.e. hemorrhages, speech or motor deficiencies etc. . . . Further, embolism is unlikely since Faller recorded [six hours before TR's death] 'normal heart and pulse'—and this is very unlikely associated with a pulmonary embolus." Allowing that the undisclosed amount of morphine administered to the patient four hours before his death may have caused the respiratory depression noticed by James Amos, the doctors nevertheless conclude that TR's "recurrent chest pain/discomfort, obesity, and high blood pressure all make coronary artery disease likely," leading to their speculative diagnosis of "myocardial infarction" as the prime cause of death.
>
> For a conflicting opinion, stating that TR's final illness was "most compatible with polyarticular gout," but also with "reactive arthritis [and/or] rheumatic fever," see Robert S. Pinals, "Theodore Roosevelt's Inflammatory Rheumatism" *Journal of Clinical Rheumatology,* 14.1 (Feb. 2008).
>
> The author has deposited a copy of his narrative of TR's recorded medical problems in TRC.

553 **it spread around the world** Arthur Krock of *The New York Times* told Henry Pringle that he had watched President Wilson receiving cabled news of TR's death

en route to Modena, Italy. According to Krock, who was looking through a window of the presidential car, WW's face registered "transcendent triumph." Pringle treated this anecdote, which Krock retailed to him eleven years later, seriously in his 1931 biography of TR (602). It is true that WW received the news while traveling, but his reaction (so far as Krock could discern it through plate glass) can only be guessed at.

553 **headed again for the presidency** "Among party leaders today it was conceded that if Colonel Roosevelt had lived, he undoubtedly would have had the nomination for the presidency." *The New York Times,* 7 Jan. 1919.

553 **took refuge in metaphor** Henry A. Beers, *Four Americans: Roosevelt, Hawthorne, Emerson, Whitman* (New Haven, Conn., 1919), 8; "Theodore Roosevelt in Memoriam," *Natural History,* Jan. 1919; William Dudley Foulke, *A Hoosier Autobiography* (New York, 1922), 221; *New York Evening Post,* 6 Jan. 1919; Slayden, *Washington Wife,* 354; Garland, *My Friendly Contemporaries,* 214; Sylvia Morris, *Edith Kermit Roosevelt,* 435.

554 **Archibald Roosevelt announced** *The New York Times,* 7, 8 Jan. 1919.

554 **"It was my father's"** Ibid.

554 **In a further** Ibid.

554 ROOSEVELT DEAD A large fragile scrapbook album in TRC contains a collection of these headlines.

554 **Even so, he** Undated news clip in "Theodore Roosevelt" scrapbook, Pratt Collection (TRB).

554 **"Mother, the adamantine"** TR, *Letters,* 8.1266.

555 **"Gone . . . gone"** George Syran to Mr. and Mrs. Osbourne, 11 Jan. 1919.

555 **"You did not"** Ibid.

555 **"She had a"** Ibid. [*sic*]. During the afternoon of 6 Jan., the sculptor James Earle Fraser took a plaster cast of TR's face. The macabre result may be seen in Lorant, *Life and Times of TR,* 627. According to Hamlin Garland, some books TR had been reading were still resting on the counterpane. *Roosevelt House Memorial Bulletin,* 2.2 (Fall 1923).

555 **A perpetual drone** *The New York Times,* 7 Jan. 1919; Sylvia Morris, *Edith Kermit Roosevelt,* 434; undated news clip in "Theodore Roosevelt" scrapbook, Pratt Collection (TRB). The air vigil was ordered by General William L. Kenly, director of military aeronautics.

555 **The aerial watch** *The New York Times,* 9 Jan. 1919.

556 **The snow tapered off** Except where otherwise indicated, the following account of TR's funeral is based on ERD to Richard Derby, 8 Jan. 1919 (ERDP), and EBR to "mother," 8 Jan. 1919 (TRJP), supplemented by reports in *The New York Times, New York Evening Post,* New York *World, Oakland Tribune, Waterloo* (Iowa) *Evening Courier* (AP), *Greenville* (Pa.) *Evening Record* (UP), 8 and 9 Jan. 1919, and clippings and photographs in the "Theodore Roosevelt" scrapbook, Pratt Collection (TRB).

556 **"He looked"** ERD to Richard Derby, 8 Jan. 1919 (ERDP).

556 **Roosevelt's disdain for *pompe*** See 67.

556 **He noticed a distraught** EBR to "mother," 8 Jan. 1919 (TRJP).

557 ***When through fiery trials*** Copied by John J. Leary (JJL).

557 **"Theodore," he said** Abbott, *Impressions of TR,* 313; New York *World,* 9 Jan. 1919.

557 **A single pull** John J. Leary funeral notes (JJL).

558 **As the engraved words** TR's coffin was lowered into the ground by a compressed-air device at 1:47 P.M. New York *World,* 9 Jan. 1919.

558 **Lieutenant Otto Raphael** "Roosevelt Night," Middlesex Club proceedings,

Boston, 27 Oct. 1921, 4–5 (TRB). For TR's relationship with Raphael, see TR, *An Autobiography*, chap. 6.

558 **One of the last** Albert Cheney interview, 1920, TRB. Youngs Cemetery still functions. TR's grave is maintained by the town of Oyster Bay.

559 **"The man was"** Carl Bode, ed., *The New Mencken Letters* (New York, 1997), 96.

559 **Among the superlatives** Wood, *Roosevelt As We Knew Him*, 380; *The New York Times*, 7 Jan. 1919; White, *Autobiography*, 552.

559 **Woodrow Wilson's sentiments** *The New York Times*, 8 Jan. 1919.

559 **Something like a superman** *New York Evening Post*, 6 Jan. 1919.

560 **He was hailed** "Theodore Roosevelt" scrapbook, Pratt Collection (TRB); *The New York Times*, 8 Jan. 1919; Aimaro Sato, former Japanese ambassador to the United States and delegate to the Russo-Japanese peace conference at Portsmouth, N.H., in 1905, quoted in *The New York Times*, 10 Jan. 1919; Jules Jusserand address at Waldorf-Astoria, New York, 27 Oct. 1919, in *Journal of American History*, 13.3 (Fall 1919). Edith Wharton, recalling her meetings with TR in 1933, used the same simile as Jusserand: "Each of these encounters glows in me like a tiny morsel of radium." Wharton, *A Backward Glance*, 317.

560 **His survey of** New York *Tribune* and *The New York Times*, 10 Feb. 1919. The quotation is from part 2 of Bunyan's *Pilgrim's Progress*.

561 **"Mr. Roosevelt's great"** *The Nation*, 109.2836 (8 Nov. 1919).

562 **Mr. Roosevelt has attained** Ibid.

562 **"Teddy" the lovable** When Walter Lippmann was the senior statesman of American political journalism, he looked back on the many presidents he had known, and wrote that TR was the only one who could be described as "lovable." Ronald Steel, *Walter Lippmann and the American Century* (Boston, 1980, New Brunswick, N.J. 1999), 64.

562 **the book of all his books** Joseph Bucklin Bishop, ed., *Theodore Roosevelt's Letters to His Children* (New York, 1919). Largely as a result of this book, TR's royalties increased from $3,150 in 1919 to $31,930. A modern reissue, illustrated and edited by Joan Paterson Kerr, is *A Bully Father* (New York, 1995).

563 **Roosevelt's mammoth 1911 letter** Bishop, TR, 2.184–259; TR, *Letters*, 7.348–99. Even Stuart Sherman allowed, in a review of Bishop's biography, that the Trevelyan letter was "a masterpiece . . . probably one of the longest epistles in the world." *The Nation*, 112.2896 (5 Jan. 1921).

563 **"The man was"** William Allen White, *Masks in a Pageant* (New York, 1928), 326. The luxury Memorial Edition of TR's *Works* was limited to 1,500 copies, 500 "for presentation" and 1,000 for sale. Hagedorn also published, in 1926, a cheaper National Edition, differently distributed among 20 volumes. For a summary of the contents of the Memorial Edition, see Wagenknecht, *The Seven Worlds of TR*, 345.

> *Personal Note:* The author of this biography hereby expresses gratitude to the memory of John Gray Peatman, who in 1980 offered him a set of the Memorial Edition, "at the same price I paid for it in 1924—ten dollars a volume."

563 **Four female trumpeters** John R. Lancos, "Theodore Roosevelt Birthplace: Study in Americanism," in Naylor et al., *TR*, 26ff.; Sylvia Morris, *Edith Kermit Roosevelt*, 18. "Roosevelt House" is now Theodore Roosevelt Birthplace National Historic Site.

563 **In 1925, Hagedorn** Nan Netherton, "Delicate Beauty and Burly Majesty: The Story of Theodore Roosevelt Island," National Park Service draft ts., 1980, 76–77. Copy in AC. Pope's column of spray was intended to evoke TR's geyser-like en-

ergy. Roosevelt Memorial Association, *Plan and Design for the Roosevelt Memorial in the City of Washington* (New York, 1925).

564 **"fifth cousin by blood"** See 416.

564 **"greatest man I ever knew"** James L. Golden, "FDR's Use of the Symbol of TR in the Formation of His Political Persona and Philosophy," in Naylor et al., *TR*, 577.

565 **Theodore Roosevelt, Jr.** The principal source for the following paragraphs is Charles W. Snyder, "An American Original: Theodore Roosevelt, Jr." in Naylor et al., *TR*, 95–106. The most comprehensive family history of the Roosevelts after TR's death is Sylvia Morris, *Edith Kermit Roosevelt*, 441–516.

565 **Cousin Eleanor made things** Eleanor Roosevelt's campaign behavior sparked decades of hatred between the Oyster Bay (Republican) and Hyde Park (Democratic) branches of the Roosevelt family.

565 **It was a question** TR.Jr. could never bring himself to acknowledge that TR, reelected in 1912, would have been as centralized an authoritarian as FDR.

565 **"one of the bravest"** Patton quoted in Naylor et al., *TR*, 103. After World War II, a sentimental desire for juxtaposition led the Roosevelt family to override TR's and EKR's wishes (see 546) and transfer QR's remains to the same cemetery. The bones of the two brothers now lie side by side.

565 **nothing left to stand on** See 554.

566 *War in the Garden of Eden* New York, 1919.

566 **His nomadic nature** Sylvia Morris, *Edith Kermit Roosevelt*, 492–507.

566 **Archie went to work** See David M. Esposito, "Archibald Bulloch Roosevelt, 1894–1979," in Naylor et al., *TR*, 107ff.

566 **a selection of** Archibald Roosevelt, ed., *Theodore Roosevelt on Race, Riots, Reds, Crime* (Metairie, La., 1968).

566 **"Beatniks"** Esposito in Naylor et al., *TR*, 115.

566 **"I'm going to"** Quoted by Archibald Roosevelt, Jr., interview with author, 3 Oct. 1981.

567 **bellow the word "Americanism"** Author's personal recollection.

567 **Flora Whitney died** Biddle, *The Whitney Women*, 45–68 and *passim*. Gertude Vanderbilt Whitney's statue of Flora is reproduced in *Flora*, 17.

567 **"Hell, yes"** Cordery, *Alice*, 314. For full details of this episode in ARL's life, see ibid., chap. 15.

567 **lifelong passion for reading** See New York Society Library, *The President's Wife and the Librarian: Letters at an Exhibition* (New York, 2009).

568 **Perhaps the earliest** Sylvia Morris, *Edith Kermit Roosevelt*, 1–2; Stefan Lorant, "The Boy in the Window," *American Heritage*, 6.4 (June 1955).

568 **filled a lacuna** For other lacunae in TR, *Works*, see Wagenknecht, *The Seven Worlds of TR*, 345.

568 **Theodore Roosevelt Collection** This archive, which the RMA began to amass in New York immediately after TR's death, temporarily transformed his birthplace into the nation's first presidential library. Removed to Harvard University's Widener and Houghton libraries and endowed with a curator in 1953, it now (2010) totals 56,000 manuscript, print, and visual items.

569 **Whatever the Colonel's** Harbaugh, *TR* (1961), 521–22.

569 **On 22 November 1963** John Robert Greene, "Presidential Co-option of the image of TR," in Naylor et al., *TR*, 601–2.

569 **Richard Nixon invoked** Ibid., 603.

570 **Three decades later** Notable post-centennial books about TR unmentioned in this Epilogue are George Mowry, *The Era of Theodore Roosevelt, 1900–1912* (New York, 1958); Raymond A. Esthus, *Theodore Roosevelt and Japan* (Seattle, 1966); Willard B. Gatewood, Jr., *Theodore Roosevelt and the Art of Controversy:*

Episodes of the White House Years (Baton Rouge, La., 1970); John Allen Gable, *The Bull Moose Years: Theodore Roosevelt and the Progressive Party* (Port Washington, N.Y., 1978); Frederick W. Marks III, *Velvet on Iron: The Diplomacy of Theodore Roosevelt* (Lincoln, Neb., 1979); Thomas G. Dyer, *Theodore Roosevelt and the Idea of Race* (Baton Rouge, La., 1980); John Milton Cooper, *The Warrior and the Priest: Woodrow Wilson and Theodore Roosevelt* (Cambridge, Mass., 1983); Paul Russell Cutright, *Theodore Roosevelt: The Making of a Conservationist* (Urbana, Ill., 1985); Lewis L. Gould, *The Presidency of Theodore Roosevelt* (Lawrence, Kan., 1991); John D. Weaver, *The Brownsville Raid* (College Station, Tex., 1992); Natalie Naylor et al., *Theodore Roosevelt: Many-Sided American* (Interlaken, N.Y., 1992); Edmund Morris, *Theodore Rex* (New York, 2001); Henry J. Hendrix, *Theodore Roosevelt's Naval Diplomacy: The U.S. Navy and the Birth of the American Century* (Annapolis, Md., 2009).

570 **Three recent** Kathleen Dalton, *Theodore Roosevelt: A Strenuous Life* (New York, 2002); Millard, *The River of Doubt* (2005); O'Toole, *When Trumpets Call* (2005).

570 **"He was a fulfiller"** Manuscript in TRC.

ILLUSTRATION CREDITS

Unless otherwise credited, all images are from the Theodore Roosevelt Collection, Houghton Library, Harvard University, Cambridge, Mass.

Frontispiece Theodore Roosevelt by George Moffett, 1914.

INDEX

Page numbers in *italics* refer to illustrations.

Abbott, Lawrence F., 113, 129, 241, 258,
    259, 260, 275, 276, 279, 280, 295, 363,
    389, 547, 560
  as TR's travel secretary, 31, 32, 33, 34,
    35, 39, 48, 50
Abbott, Lyman, 129, 183, 275, 295, 363
Abercrombie & Fitch, 21
Abernathy, Jack, 164
Abruzzi, Duke of, 44
Académie de Sciences Morales et
    Politiques, 46
Adams, Brooks, 169
Adams, Henry, 138, 161, 169, 182, 268,
    437, 457, 483, 516
Addams, Jane, 221–22, 223, 228,
    237, 260
Aehrenthal, Alois von, 43
Africa:
  British territories in, 29–30, 32, 34,
    36, 72
  European imperialism in, 34, 37, 145,
    147, 148
  U.S. involvement in, 34
  see also British East Africa; *specific
    countries*
*African Game Trails: An Account of the
    African Wanderings of an American
    Hunter-Naturalist* (Roosevelt), 112,
    129, 255, 256, 276, 279, 295, 307,
    317, 393
*African Methodist Episcopal Church
    Review*, 239
Agnus, Felix, 161
Ahmad, Muhammad, 32
Aidan, 346, 348
Ainsworth, Fred C., 554
Albania, 297
Albany Evening Journal, 407
Albert, King of Belgium, 34, 48, 67, 369
Aldrich, Chester H., 120, 164
Alfonso XIII, King of Spain, 64, 354
Algeria, 34
Allen, Alfred R., 434

Allen, Henry J., 202, 208
Amazon River, 307, 308, 346
America and the World War (Roosevelt),
    397, 398–400
American Bar Association, 169
American Historical Association, 257,
    261–64
American Historical Review, 266
American Ideals (Roosevelt), 256
American Museum of Natural History,
    283, 284, 306, 315
American Society for Judicial Settlement
    of International Disputes, 130,
    137, 138
Amílcar de Magalhães, Captain, 313, 316,
    323, 344
Amos, James, 219, 277, 280, 494, 551,
    552, 554
Andrews, William S., 405, 407, 408,
    409, 410, 412, 413, 415, 417, 420,
    423, 424
Androscoggin, 84, 85
Antiquities Act (1906), 286
Antônio, Joaquim, 343
Apponyi, Albert, 44, 45, 387, 403
Arabic, 433, 436, 438
Arab nationalism:
  in Egypt, 31, 32, 36, 37, 38, 39, 72
  in Sudan, 30, 32, 34
arbitration:
  Taft's preference for, 130, 137, 138, 139,
    146, 147
  TR's opposition to, 130, 138–39, 145,
    146, 147, 388, 389
  Wilson's attempt at, 378
  see also pacifism
Arizona, TR's vacation in, 285–88, 289–94
arms control movement, Carnegie as
    leader in, 24, 49
Army, U.S.:
  preparedness of, 399
  TR as reservist in, 11
  TR's reorganization of, 5

EDMUND MORRIS was born in Nairobi, Kenya, in 1940. He was schooled there, and studied music, history, and literature at Rhodes University, Grahamstown, South Africa. After leaving Africa at the age of twenty-four, he worked for six years as an advertising copywriter in London and New York. He became a full-time writer in 1972. His first book, *The Rise of Theodore Roosevelt,* began life as a screenplay. It was published in 1979 and won the Pulitzer Prize and the National Book Award. In 1985, Morris was appointed the official biographer of President Ronald Reagan. The resultant work, *Dutch: A Memoir of Ronald Reagan* (1999), was and remains controversial because of its unusual narrative technique. *Theodore Rex* (2001), the second volume of Morris's Roosevelt trilogy, won the *Los Angeles Times* Book Prize for Biography. Before completing his trilogy with *Colonel Roosevelt,* Morris published a short life of Beethoven.

He lives in New York and Kent, Connecticut, with his wife and fellow biographer, Sylvia Jukes Morris.

ABOUT THE TYPE

This book was set in Sabon, a typeface designed by the well-known German typographer Jan Tschichold (1902–1974). Sabon's design is based upon the original letter forms of Claude Garamond and was created specifically to be used for three sources: foundry type for hand composition, Linotype, and Monotype. Tschichold named his typeface for the famous Frankfurt typefounder Jacques Sabon, who died in 1580.